CODE OF ALABAMA

1975

With Provision for Subsequent Pocket Parts

Prepared Under the Supervision of

The Code Revision Subcommittee of
The Legislative Council

Robert H. Harris, Chairman

by

The Editorial Staff of the Publishers

Under the Direction of

A. D. Kowalsky, S. C. Willard, W. L. Jackson,
M. A. Sancilio, and T. R. Troxell

VOLUME 15

1992 REPLACEMENT VOLUME

*Including Acts through the 1992 Regular and First Special Sessions
and annotations taken through Southern Reporter,
Second Series, Volume 595, page 856*

THE MICHIE COMPANY
Law Publishers
Charlottesville, Virginia
1992

Table of Titles

In Addition, This Publication Contains

Table of Contents

VOLUME 15

User's Guide

In order to assist both the legal profession and the layman in obtaining the maximum benefit from the Code of Alabama, a User's Guide has been included in Volume 1. This guide contains comments and information on the many features found within the Code of Alabama intended to increase the usefulness of this set of laws to the user. See Volume 1 of this set for the complete User's Guide.

Scope of Annotations

The annotations contained in this volume are derived from the following sources:

Southern Reporter, Second Series, through volume 580, p. 566.
Federal Reporter, Second Series, through volume 934, p. 1266.
Federal Supplement, through volume 764, p. 193.
Federal Rules Decisions, through volume 136, p. 231.
Bankruptcy Reporter, through volume 127, p. 500.
Supreme Court Reporter, through volume 111, p. 2280.
Opinions of the Clerk of the Supreme Court of Alabama.

CODE OF ALABAMA

TITLE 23.

HIGHWAYS, ROADS, BRIDGES AND FERRIES.

TABLE OF CONTENTS

CHAPTER 1.

ALABAMA HIGHWAYS.

Article 1.

General Provisions.

Article 2.

Highway Department.

2

Article 1.

General Provisions.

Cross references. — As to taking up and disposition of animals running at large on state and federal aid highways, see § 3-2-20 et seq. As to prohibition against staking, pasturing, etc., animals upon highway rights-of-way, see § 3-3-1 et seq. As to regulation, construction, maintenance, etc., of streets, highways, ferries, etc., in and by municipalities, see § 11-49-1 et seq. As to criminal damage to property, see § 13A-7-20 et seq. As to motor vehicles and traffic generally, see § 32-1-1.1 et seq. As to state highway patrol, see § 32-2-20 et seq.

§ 23-1-1. Contracts and regulations relative to federal assistance.

The State Highway Department, by and through the director, is hereby authorized to enter into all necessary contracts and agreements with the United States government or any agency or officer thereof in accordance with any act of Congress relating to the construction, maintenance and beautification of highways, bridges, tunnels or ferries, or other matters relating thereto, to establish, promulgate and enforce all reasonable rules and regulations which may be necessary for the effective implementation and cooperation with the provisions of such acts and to do all other things necessary to secure to the state and its counties and municipalities the full benefits provided by such acts. (Acts 1977, No. 20, p. 28.)

Collateral references. — Highway contractor's liability to highway user for highway surface defects. 62 ALR4th 1067.

§ 23-1-2. Bid guaranty.

Any other provisions of the law to the contrary notwithstanding, bidders for contract projects which contracts are with the State of Alabama, in behalf of the State Highway Department, to be paid, in whole or in part, from funds allocated to the highway department from any source whatsoever, or where contracts are with any of the several counties of the state for a highway, road, street or bridge project, to be paid for, in whole or in part, from funds allocated to the county from any source whatsoever, shall be required to file with the bid, as a bid guaranty, a certified check or bid bond payable to the awarding authority as follows:

(1) A certified check payable to the awarding authority for an amount not less than five percent of the contractor's bid, but in no event more than $10,000.00; or

(2) A bid bond payable to the awarding authority in an amount not less than five percent of the bid, but in no event more than $10,000.00. (Acts 1967, No. 306, p. 849.)

Collateral references. — Highway contractor's liability to highway user for highway surface defects. 62 ALR4th 1067.

§ 23-1-3. Closing of public roads to traffic; acquisition of materials.

The state, acting through the highway department and its duly authorized employees, and the various counties of the state, acting through the county commissions and their duly authorized employees, in the doing of public roads work shall have and exercise the right, power and authority, when deemed necessary or advisable to do so, to close public roads to traffic and, when possible so to do, to make detour roads and to contract for such land as may be necessary for such detour roads; also to acquire, by purchase or by condemnation, land necessary for drainage ditches and borrow pits, lime and stone quarries, clay and clay pits, sand and sand pits and gravel and gravel pits, together with any and all other material of every character that may be necessary or essential or desired in the construction and maintenance of highways and bridges, and to tap and draw materials from the same to such extent as may be desired, and the highway department shall also have the right to acquire by purchase or condemnation rights-of-way necessary for ingress and egress to such material pits as above named. (Code 1923, § 1332; Acts 1927, No. 347, p. 348; Code 1940, T. 23, § 26.)

Section includes construction of all highways of state. — This section does not put a limitation on the sort of highways to be constructed, that is to say, whether they shall be those which have been delegated to the counties for construction or those which have been delegated to and remain under the jurisdiction of other state agencies. Not being limited, this section includes the construction of all the highways of the state. Blanton v. Fagerstrom, 249 Ala. 485, 31 So. 2d 330 (1947).

And materials may be taken in one county for highway in another. — It is of no consequence that materials condemned or taken in one county are used in the construction or maintenance of highways in another county. Blanton v. Fagerstrom, 249 Ala. 485, 31 So. 2d 330 (1947).

Since taking is not limited to lands or materials contiguous to highway. — There is nothing in this section that limits the taking of materials deemed to be necessary or essential or desired in the construction and maintenance of highways to lands or materials contiguous to the highway upon which it is to be used. Blanton v. Fagerstrom, 249 Ala. 485, 31 So. 2d 330 (1947).

Construction company not liable to persons using road lawfully withdrawn. — Company constructing highway owed no special duty to persons, who found their way around barricades, erected in pursuance of this section, and used highway with knowledge that it was lawfully withdrawn from public use, to safeguard them from injuries due to conditions attending construction work. Carter v. Franklin, 234 Ala. 116, 173 So. 861 (1937).

Collateral references. — Condemnation of materials for highways. 172 ALR 131.

§ 23-1-4. Permit required to dig up, etc., roads for utilities, railroads, etc.; restoration of road required upon completion of work; bond, etc., to guarantee restoration.

No state-controlled road shall be dug up or used for laying pipelines, pole lines, sewers, railways or for other similar purposes without the written permit of the highway department, and such work shall be done only in accordance with the regulations prescribed by the department, and the cost of replacing the road in as good condition as it was before such work was done shall be paid by the person, firm or corporation to whom or in whose behalf such permit was given. Such person, firm or corporation so desiring such work shall furnish the state with a cash deposit or certified check upon a solvent bank or surety bond in guaranty company qualified to do business in Alabama, in the amount required by the highway department, conditioned that the sum is to be forfeited to the state in the event that said road is not placed in as good condition as it was prior to said work being done, within 15 days from the time said work is completed. (Code 1923, § 1334; Acts 1927, No. 347, p. 348; Code 1940, T. 23, § 28.)

Collateral references. — Highway contractor's liability to highway user for highway surface defects. 62 ALR4th 1067.

§ 23-1-5. Payment of costs of relocation of utility facilities necessitated by construction of highways.

(a) Whenever the State Highway Director shall determine and order that the relocation of any utility facility is necessitated by the construction of any project on the national system of interstate and defense highways, including the extensions thereof within urban areas, the utility owning or operating such utility facility shall relocate the same in accordance with the order of the State Highway Director; provided, however, that if the cost of such utility facility relocation is eligible and approved for reimbursement by the federal government, the cost of the relocation of such utility facility shall be paid by the state as a part of the cost of the construction of such project out of the funds then or thereafter available for such highway construction after the utility has furnished the State Highway Director with all papers, records or other supporting documents required by said director. After the final federal bureau of public roads audit, the utility shall repay to the state the difference, if any, between the total amount paid by the state to the utility for said relocation and the total amount collected by the state from federal participation on such utility relocation, plus the state's matching share of said federal participation.

(b) Whenever the State Highway Director shall determine and order that the relocation of any utility facility is necessitated by the construction of any highway, road or street, other than the highways that are a part of the national system of interstate and defense highways referred to in subsection

(a) of this section, the utility owning or operating such facility shall relocate the same in accordance with the order of the State Highway Director at its own expense; provided, however, that if the facilities so to be relocated are owned by any utility which had a gross income of $50,000,000.00 or less for the calendar year immediately preceding said relocation or in the case of utilities which may be hereafter organized and created which have a gross income of $50,000,000.00 or less in their first complete year of operation or in the calendar year immediately preceding said relocation, the cost of such relocation of such utility facility shall be paid by the state as a part of the cost of the construction of such project out of the funds then or thereafter available for such highway construction after the utility has furnished the State Highway Director with all papers, records or other supporting documents required by said director. After the final Federal Bureau of Public Roads audit, the utility shall repay to the state the difference, if any, between the total amount paid by the state to the utility for said relocation and the total amount collected by the state from federal participation on such utility relocation, plus the state's matching share of said federal participation.

(c) The State Highway Director is authorized to enter into contracts or agreements and to conform any existing contracts or agreements with utilities in order to effectuate the purposes of this section.

(d) The word "utility" shall include publicly, privately and cooperatively owned utilities. The words "cost of relocation" shall include the entire amount paid by such utility properly attributable to such relocation after deducting therefrom any increase in the value of the new facility and any salvage value derived from the old facility. The words "national system of interstate and defense highways" mean the national system of interstate and defense highways or interstate system described in subsection (d) of Section 103 of Title 23, United States Code. (Acts 1961, No. 474, p. 529; Acts 1982, No. 82-275, p. 346, § 1.)

Collateral references. — Relocation: constitutionality of state legislation to reimburse public utilities for cost of relocating their facilities because of highway construction, conditioned upon federal reimbursement of state under terms of Federal-Aid Highway Act. 75 ALR2d 419.

§ 23-1-6. Signs, markers and advertising — On rights-of-way.

Signs, markers and advertising on the rights-of-way of state controlled highways are prohibited except those official signs or markers placed thereon by the State Highway Department or under its authority. (Code 1923, § 1344; Acts 1927, No. 347, p. 348; Code 1940, T. 23, § 36.)

Cross references. — As to outdoor advertising along highways generally, see § 23-1-270 et seq.

Collateral references. — 40 C.J.S., Highways, § 254. 60 C.J.S., Motor Vehicles, § 17. Construction and application of restrictive covenants to the use of signs. 61 ALR4th 1028.

§ 23-1-7. Signs, markers and advertising — Tourist attractions.

(a) Upon the request of the director of publicity and information, the Director of the State Highway Department may cause to be constructed and erected along state highways appropriate directional markers designating major tourist attractions of Alabama.

(b) The Director of the Bureau of Publicity and Information shall determine the attractions to be so designated and shall upon the recommendation of the Director of the State Highway Department determine the number of markers needed and the location of such markers.

(c) Expenses incurred in carrying out the provisions of this section shall be paid from that portion of the proceeds of the privilege license tax levied on lodgings by Chapter 26 of Title 40, earmarked for state travel advertising and travel promotion by the Bureau of Publicity and Information for tourist advertising and shall be paid upon warrants drawn by the State Comptroller, upon the approval of the Director of the Bureau of Publicity and Information, not to exceed $10,000.00 per fiscal biennium.

(d) This section shall not be construed as repealing the provisions of Chapter 7 of Title 41 which prohibit the purchase of advertising in newspapers, magazines, programs or other periodicals published in the state with funds appropriated for tourist advertising. (Acts 1967, No. 217, p. 583.)

§ 23-1-8. Numbers and names of highways.

All highways built or maintained by and through federal or state aid shall be designated by numbers and by names, where such highways are known by names, on the directional signs erected along said highways and upon the maps authorized and published by the state. Memorial or other distinctive highways built or maintained by federal or state aid, such as the Bankhead Highway, Craft Highway, Bee Line Highway, Spanish Trail Highway, Brandon Highway, Jefferson Davis Highway, Dixie Highway, Jackson Highway, Lee Highway and such other memorial roads as may hereafter be designated, shall be designated on such markers, signs and maps by names as well as by numbers. (Acts 1931, No. 703, p. 827; Code 1940, T. 23, § 39.)

Cross references. — As to prohibition on the expenditure of state funds for the purpose of erecting and maintaining road, bridge or building signs in the memory of any individual, see § 23-1-8.1.

§ 23-1-8.1. Expenditure of state funds for erection and maintenance of signs designating roads, bridges, etc., in honor or memory of individuals.

After September 1, 1979, no state funds shall be expended in this state for purposes of erecting and maintaining signs designating roads, bridges or buildings in honor or in memory of any individual; provided, however, that the state highway department may continue to prepare and erect such signs so long as the actual cost of such preparation and maintenance is paid for by private funds or city or county government funds. (Acts 1979, No. 79-707, p. 1259.)

Cross references. — As to the numbers and names of highways, see § 23-1-8.

§ 23-1-9. Elimination of railroad grade crossings.

Whenever the funds of the state are being expended for the construction, maintenance or repair of a public highway, the highway department shall have the power and authority to compel all railways operating in this state to construct viaducts, tunnels, underpasses or bridges to the full extent of the width of the right-of-way and over the tracks as owned or operated by any railway when, in the judgment of the highway department, such viaducts, tunnels, underpasses or bridges are necessary for the safety of the general public and whereby a dangerous grade crossing is eliminated. The highway department may appropriate out of the funds credited to the highway department for the construction and maintenance of highways an amount not to exceed 50 percent of the cost to construct said viaducts, tunnels, underpasses or bridges to the full extent of the width of the right-of-way and over the tracks as owned or operated by any railway in this state. If after due notice to a railroad that such a viaduct, tunnel, underpass or bridge, in the judgment of the highway department, is necessary to be built or constructed across the width of the right-of-way and over the tracks of the railway and such railway fails or refuses to comply with the order of the highway department as provided in this section, the highway department is empowered and authorized to forthwith build or construct such viaducts, tunnels, underpasses or bridges, and the amounts so expended for such construction as provided in this section, shall constitute a charge against such railway and the highway department shall render a bill to such railway stating the amounts expended and for what purpose; and upon the failure or refusal of such railway to make payment of the amount due the state, the highway department shall forward all data and information to the Attorney General of this state, who shall immediately institute an action in the name of the State of Alabama, as provided by law, for the recovery of the amount as reported by the highway department as due by the railway for the funds to be expended in the construction of viaducts, tunnels, underpasses or bridges across the width of the right-of-way and over the tracks of such railway. Upon the recovery of such funds, the amount shall be paid into the state treasury and credited to the account of the highway department from which such funds were withdrawn; but said railway shall not be required to pay exceeding 50 percent of the cost thereof. (Code 1923, § 1343; Acts 1927, No. 347, p. 348; Code 1940, T. 23, § 35; Acts 1959, No. 653, p. 1578, § 2; Acts 1961, Ex. Sess., No. 213, p. 2208.)

§ 23-1-10. "Blue reflective markers" and "fire/water hydrant" defined; purpose and installation of blue reflective markers.

(a) For purposes of this section, the following words and phrases shall have the respective meanings ascribed to them, except where the context clearly indicates otherwise:

(1) BLUE REFLECTIVE MARKERS. — Nonlighted, but reflective devices which are blue in color of the reflected light and conform to the most recent edition of the Manual on Uniform Traffic Control Devices for Streets and Highways and/or other standards issued or endorsed by the highway director and the federal highway administrator.

(2) FIRE/WATER HYDRANT. — All standpipe hydrants installed on public and private water delivery systems which are installed along public roads within the state, and which are of a size and style to allow adequate water supply to fill fire suppression vehicles of municipal and/or certified volunteer fire departments or furnish a supply of water to trucks at a fire scene.

(b) Blue reflective markers shall be used exclusively for the purpose of indicating the location of fire/water hydrants which are located on public roadways within the state, or on private property with the owner's permission. Markers which are installed so as to be adhered to paved road surfaces or which are placed anywhere within the highway right-of-way shall be placed in conformance with the most recent edition of the manual on uniform traffic control devices for streets and highways and/or other standards issued or endorsed by the highway director and the federal highway administrator.

(c) Blue reflective markers may be installed by any municipality, county, fire district, fire or water authority, or any certified volunteer fire department within their primary coverage areas and shall be recognized by all fire departments and firefighters for the purpose stated. (Acts 1983, 3rd Ex. Sess., No. 83-806, p. 19.)

ARTICLE 2.

HIGHWAY DEPARTMENT.

§ 23-1-20. Creation.

There shall be a State Highway Department. (Acts 1939, No. 13, p. 9; Code 1940, T. 23, § 1.)

Cited in Pruett v. Las Vegas, Inc., 261 Ala. 557, 74 So. 2d 807 (1954).

Collateral references. — 39 C.J.S., Highways, § 155.

§ 23-1-21. Highway Director.

The chief executive officer of the highway department shall be known as the Highway Director, who shall be appointed by the Governor and shall hold office at the pleasure of the Governor. All the powers, authority and duties vested in the highway department shall be exercised by the Highway Director.

Before entering upon the duties of his office, the Highway Director shall execute to the State of Alabama a bond, to be approved by the Governor, in an amount to be fixed by the Governor, for the faithful performance of his duties. (Code 1923, § 1302; Acts 1927, No. 347, p. 348; Acts 1931, No. 10, p. 7; Acts 1939, No. 13, p. 9; Code 1940, T. 23, § 2; Acts 1943, No. 122, p. 123; Acts 1961, Ex. Sess., No. 208, p. 2190.)

Effect of delegation of powers and duties. — It was not the purpose of the statutes to provide that by making a contract or setting up stipulations delegating to another the power and duty to represent the director in the discharge of his duties under the law in respect to such contract, that the director thereby deprived himself of that power when exercised with the consent of the other party to the contract, and with the approval of the governor. McFarland v. McKee, 252 Ala. 434, 41 So. 2d 574 (1949).

This section neither requires the highway director to make every decision and approve every transaction in a 5,000 employee department nor prevents him from delegating some of those decisions. United States Fid. & Guar. Co. v. Bass, 619 F.2d 1057 (5th Cir. 1980).

Governor has direct fiscal responsibility over road construction payments. — The legislature has fixed the approval by the governor as a condition precedent to the validity of monetary payments arising out of contracts for road construction entered into by the highway department through its director. In other words, the governor, as chief executive officer of the state, has a direct fiscal responsibility over the payment of state funds under road contracts made by his appointed subordinates. Rainer v. Tillett Bros. Constr. Co., 381 So. 2d 36 (Ala. 1980).

Cited in Pruett v. Las Vegas, Inc., 261 Ala. 557, 74 So. 2d 807 (1954); Engelhardt v. United States Civil Serv. Comm'n, 197 F. Supp. 806 (M.D. Ala. 1961).

Collateral references. — 39 C.J.S., Highways, §§ 161-163.

§ 23-1-21.1. Definitions.

The following terms, whenever used or referred to in this section and Sections 23-1-21.2 and 23-1-21.3, shall have the following meanings, except in those instances where the context clearly indicates a different meaning:

(1) DIRECTOR. The Director of the State of Alabama Highway Department.

(2) PUBLIC TRANSPORTATION. Transportation which is appropriate to transport people by bus, rail or other conveyance, serving the general public. The terms "mass transportation," "mass transit," "public transit," "ridesharing," "carpooling," "vanpooling," and "buspooling" are included within this definition and shall be considered synonymous with "public transportation."

(3) MUNICIPALITY. Any city, town, or like governing body.

(4) COUNTY. Any county in the State of Alabama.

(5) TRANSIT AUTHORITY. Any transit authority organized within the state or authority organized to serve a metropolitan or urbanized area which borders on the state boundary.

(6) LOCAL ENTITIES. Municipalities, cities, towns, counties, business and nonprofit corporations, transit authorities, planning bodies, or similar organizations or consolidations thereof, including those bordering on the state boundary.

(7) PLANNING BODY. Any planning organization duly constituted under state law, whether a city, county, or regional planning commission, or a metropolitan planning organization.

(8) COMPREHENSIVE TRANSPORTATION PLANNING PROCESS. A continuing planning process carried on cooperatively between the state and local entities for the purpose of transportation planning. (Acts 1982, No. 82-456, p. 709, § 1; Acts 1985, No. 85-753, p. 1252, § 1.)

§ 23-1-21.2. Authority of director with regard to public transportation.

The director, acting alone or through, and in cooperation with local entities, is hereby delegated the authority to:

(1) Enter into agreements with local entities to provide public transportation and to administer any program or programs, whether rural or urban, relative to public transportation resulting from federal transportation legislation. This shall include but not be limited to applying for, accepting, and expending federal public transportation funds in accordance with applicable federal laws and regulations.

(2) Enter into agreements with the United States for federal assistance for public transportation.

(3) Enter into agreements with local entities to perform and/or cooperate in the performance of transportation planning for public transportation improvements. However, the director shall not perform such planning until such time as the local entities affected enter into agreement with the director to carry out a planning process.

(4) Provide any available technical assistance to local entities for formulating a program of public transportation projects to assure that said projects are in accordance with the comprehensive transportation planning process where such process is established and is a prerequisite for federal assistance.

(5) Administer any state funds authorized from time to time by the legislature for the purpose of public transportation.

(6) Develop and promulgate such rules and regulations as are determined necessary to insure compliance with federal laws and regulations. (Acts 1982, No. 82-456, p. 709, § 2; Acts 1985, No. 85-753, p. 1252, § 1.)

§ 23-1-21.3. Cooperation with federal, state and local entities in administration of public transportation programs.

The director is authorized to administer any public transportation program with such flexibility as to permit full cooperation between federal, state, and local entities, so as to result in effective and economical programs which are responsive to needs and found to be in the public interest. (Acts 1982, No. 82-456, p. 709, § 3.)

§ 23-1-22. Chief engineer — Office created; appointment, salary, expenses and bond; applicability of merit system.

(a) There is hereby created within the State Highway Department the position of chief engineer, which shall be filled by appointment by the Highway Director, with the approval of the Governor. Such appointment shall also be subject to approval by the State Board of Registration for Engineers and Land Surveyors. The salary of the chief engineer shall be as determined pursuant to Chapter 6 of Title 36, and he shall be allowed traveling expenses when traveling on business of the state pursuant to Article 2 of Chapter 7 of Title 36, all to be paid from funds of the State Highway Department as salaries and expenses of other State Highway Department employees are paid. The chief engineer shall give bond for the faithful performance of his duties in an amount to be approved by the Governor.

(b) The chief engineer shall serve under the direction of the Highway Director and otherwise be entitled to all the privileges and responsibilities as other merit system employees, and his service and removal shall be subject to the state merit system regulations. (Acts 1959, No. 497, p. 1231, § 1; Acts 1969, No. 506, p. 963.)

Cited in United States Fid. & Guar. Co. v. Bass, 619 F.2d 1057 (5th Cir. 1980).

Collateral references. — 39 C.J.S., Highways, § 162.

§ 23-1-23. Chief engineer — Qualifications.

The chief engineer shall be a registered professional engineer in the State of Alabama with a minimum of 15 years' progressive professional engineering experience pertaining to the planning, development, construction, maintenance and repair of highways and bridges. He shall hold a degree in civil engineering from an engineering school of recognized standing. The chief engineer shall have a detail knowledge of engineering principles and their application pertaining to highways and bridges. He shall maintain citizenship in the State of Alabama and shall continuously be a registered engineer in the State of Alabama as a condition while serving in this office. (Acts 1959, No. 497, p. 1231, § 2; Acts 1969, No. 506, p. 963.)

§ 23-1-24. Chief engineer — Duties.

The duties of the chief engineer in the State Highway Department shall include the administration of technical phases of the organization, and direction and coordination of the engineering activities of the highway department. The chief engineer shall affix his signature to the title sheets of all plans let to contract by the State Highway Department. The duties of the chief engineer shall be subject to and under the control and supervision of the

Highway Director. (Acts 1959, No. 497, p. 1231, § 3; Acts 1969, No. 506, p. 963.)

§ 23-1-25. Legal division — Creation; appointment of chief counsel.

There is hereby established and created in the State Highway Department a legal division, which shall be headed by and be under the direction, supervision and control of an officer who shall be designated as chief counsel for the State Highway Department, to be appointed by the Highway Director with the approval of the Attorney General, subject to provisions of the state merit system laws. (Acts 1963, No. 581, p. 1267, § 1.)

§ 23-1-26. Legal division — Appointment of assistant counsel; chief and assistant counsel to be commissioned and take oath as assistant attorneys general.

The Highway Director, with the approval of the Attorney General, shall be authorized, subject to the provisions of the State Merit System Law, to appoint not more than five assistant counsel as may be necessary to transact the legal business of the State Highway Department. The chief counsel and the assistant counsel shall each be commissioned as assistant attorneys general and take the oath required of other assistants of the Attorney General. The chief counsel and the assistant counsel and their stenographic and clerical assistants shall constitute the legal division of the State Highway Department. (Acts 1963, No. 581, p. 1267, § 2.)

§ 23-1-27. Legal division — Salaries.

The salaries of the chief counsel and assistant counsel shall be fixed in accordance with the merit system pay plan for assistant attorneys general and shall be paid as the salaries of other state officials and employees are paid from funds appropriated or otherwise available to the State Highway Department. (Acts 1963, No. 581, p. 1267, § 3.)

Cross references. — As to merit system, see § 36-26-1 et seq.

§ 23-1-28. Legal division — Offices, etc.; expenses.

The chief counsel and the assistant counsel shall be furnished with offices, necessary stenographic and clerical help, subject to the provisions of the State Merit System Law, and office equipment, stationery and postage and shall be allowed traveling expenses when traveling on business of the state pursuant to Article 2 of Chapter 7 of Title 36, all to be paid by the State Highway Department from funds appropriated or otherwise available therefor. (Acts 1963, No. 581, p. 1267, § 4.)

§ 23-1-29. Legal division — Charging of salaries and expenses.

The salaries of the chief counsel, assistant counsel, stenographic and clerical help and other expenses of the legal division shall be charged, so far as practicable, to the division or function of the State Highway Department for which the expense was incurred. (Acts 1963, No. 581, p. 1267, § 5.)

§ 23-1-30. Legal division — Functions and duties.

The functions and duties of the legal division of the State Highway Department shall, as all other assistant attorneys general, include the following:

(1) To advise the State Highway Director and other personnel of the State Highway Department on the legal aspects of all highway department business;

(2) To examine and advise as to the legality of all contracts and agreements entered into by the State Highway Department or the Highway Director;

(3) To take all legal action necessary or desirable in the acquisition of rights-of-way for state and interstate highways;

(4) To appear in court as attorney for the State of Alabama and the State Highway Department in the acquisition of rights-of-way for state and interstate highways; and

(5) To represent the State Highway Department and the State Highway Director in all legal proceedings to which the State Highway Department or the State Highway Director is a party. (Acts 1963, No. 581, p. 1267, § 6.)

Collateral references. — 39 C.J.S., Highways, § 158(a).

§ 23-1-31. Legal division — Private practice prohibited.

The chief counsel and assistant counsel shall devote their full time to the State Highway Department and shall not, during their incumbency in office, engage in the private practice of law. (Acts 1963, No. 581, p. 1267, § 7.)

§ 23-1-32. Offices; highway director full-time position.

The highway department shall be provided with suitable offices at the State Capitol or such other places as the needs of the department may require, but no office in any other place than the Capitol shall be established as an office of said department without the consent and approval of the Governor in writing. All offices shall be kept open at such times as the business of the department and the convenience and interest of the public may require. The offices shall be conveniently and properly furnished at the expense of the state and shall be the depository for all records of the highway department. The State Highway Director shall give his entire time to the duties of his office. (Code

1923, § 1306; Acts 1927, No. 347, p. 348; Acts 1931, No. 10, p. 7; Code 1940, T. 23, § 7.)

§ 23-1-33. Official records of department; appointment of assistants and personnel.

The highway department shall keep an official record of all its acts and doings. The State Highway Director shall, under provisions of the merit system, appoint such assistants and personnel as may be necessary for the proper carrying on of the work of the highway department. The compensation of such assistants and personnel shall be paid out of the state highway funds. (Code 1923, § 1311; Acts 1927, No. 347, p. 348; Acts 1931, No. 10, p. 7; Code 1940, T. 23, § 9.)

Cross references. — As to merit system, see § 36-26-1 et seq.

Cited in United States Fid. & Guar. Co. v. Bass, 619 F.2d 1057 (5th Cir. 1980).

Collateral references. — 39 C.J.S., Highways, § 156.

§ 23-1-34. Copies of plans and specifications to be kept; files and records open to public inspection; records as evidence.

The highway department shall keep on file in its office copies of all plans and specifications prepared by the highway department, and the files and records of such department shall, under reasonable regulations, be kept open for inspection of the public at all reasonable hours. Certified copies of records shall be received in evidence in all the courts of this state. (Code 1923, § 1315; Acts 1927, No. 347, p. 348; Code 1940, T. 23, § 12.)

Collateral references. — Highway contractor's liability to highway user for highway surface defects. 62 ALR4th 1067.

§ 23-1-35. Annual report to Governor.

On or before April 1 in each year, the highway department shall submit a printed report to the Governor, stating as nearly as possible the number of miles of road built or improved and also the culverts and bridges constructed during the preceding fiscal year, showing the cost and general character of same, and the location of material suitable for road construction, showing where such roads, culverts and bridges have been constructed. The department shall also recommend to the Governor and legislature such legislation as it deems advisable and furnish any other information concerning road and bridge improvements as may be deemed expedient by the Governor and the legislature. (Code 1923, § 1304; Acts 1927, No. 347, p. 348; Acts 1931, No. 10, p. 7; Code 1940, T. 23, § 5.)

§ 23-1-36. Employees used on transferred county roads and bridges.

Whenever responsibility for the construction, maintenance and repair of county roads and bridges is transferred by law from any county commission to the State Highway Department, the employees used by the State Highway Department in any such county in connection with the construction, maintenance and repair of the county's roads and bridges shall be drawn insofar as possible from residents of the county. In the event of a vacancy in any such position of employment in the classified service of the state, the personnel director, upon request of the State Highway Director that the personnel director certify to him the names of persons eligible for appointment to the position, shall establish a county register of eligibles who are residents of the county in which the vacancy occurs, and the personnel director shall certify the names of persons appearing on the county register for appointment to the position. If, however, no appointment is made from the county register or if there is no county register, appointment shall be made from the statewide register. (Acts 1956, 1st Ex. Sess., No. 4, p. 11.)

Cross references. — As to divestment of functions of state highway department with respect to construction, repair and maintenance of roads and bridges in certain counties, see § 23-1-100 et seq.

§ 23-1-37. Use of convict labor.

The highway department may work convicts in the construction or maintenance of public roads and bridges of Alabama, as may now or may hereafter be provided by law, or may work convicts in the construction, repairing or maintaining public roads or bridges by contract or agreement with the Department of Corrections as to the number of convicts required to do such work; provided, that the charge for labor of such convicts shall be in accordance with the terms of the contract which shall be negotiated by and between the Director of the State Highway Department and the Department of Corrections, with the approval of the Governor, and no other expense incurred by the use of such convicts shall be chargeable to the highway department, except such necessary tools and implements used in the construction, repairing or maintaining of the public roads and bridges upon which the convicts are employed. (Code 1923, § 1337; Acts 1927, No. 347, p. 348; Code 1940, T. 23, § 31; Acts 1965, No. 652, p. 1176.)

Cross references. — As to hiring or leasing of convicts to state agencies, see § 14-5-10.

Collateral references. — 60 Am. Jur. 2d, Penal & Correctional Institutions, §§ 34-40.

§ 23-1-38. Paying expenses of nonemployees prohibited.

Any officer or employee of the State Highway Department who pays or authorizes to be paid the expense account of any person not employed by the State Highway Department shall be guilty of a misdemeanor. (Acts 1951, No. 713, p. 1251.)

§ 23-1-39. Seal; power to administer oaths, etc.

The highway department shall have a seal and shall have the power to administer oaths, take affidavits and make certificates. (Code 1923, § 1305; Acts 1927, No. 347, p. 348; Acts 1931, No. 10, p. 7; Code 1940, T. 23, § 6.)

§ 23-1-40. Duties and powers generally.

(a) It shall be the duty of the highway department to designate the roads to be constructed, repaired and maintained and to construct, standardize, repair and maintain roads and bridges of this state; and it shall have authority to make contracts or agreements to construct or pave the roadway only of the street or streets which will serve to connect the state highway constructed or repaired by the highway department within any municipality in the State of Alabama.

(b) In such municipalities in which the highway department has not designated the street or streets which are a part of the state highways constructed or repaired by the highway department, it shall be the duty of the highway department to designate such street or streets. The highway department may also cooperate or contract with any municipality or county in the paving or improving of any street or streets, highway or highways or walkway or walkways upon which a state educational or eleemosynary institution, or the property thereof, may front or abut; provided, that where said state educational or eleemosynary institution or the property thereof fronts or abuts on both sides of such street or streets, highway or highways or walkway or walkways, the highway department is hereby authorized to and shall expend an amount of money sufficient to cover the entire cost thereof; provided further, that where such institution or the property thereof fronts or abuts on only one side of such street or streets, highway or highways or walkway or walkways, the said department shall expend an amount of money sufficient to cover only one half of the cost thereof; provided, that in such case, with the special approval of the Governor, said department shall be authorized to expend a sum of money sufficient for the entire cost and, provided further, the said department may also, with the special approval of the Governor, improve or pave any street or streets, driveway or driveways, including curb and gutter, and walkway or walkways on, by or through the grounds upon which a state educational or eleemosynary institution is located and to pay the entire cost thereof.

(c) The highway department shall cause to be made and kept in its office a general highway map of the state which shall show all state roads.

(d) The highway department shall collect information and prepare statistics relative to the mileage, character and condition of the roads and bridges in all counties of the state.

(e) The highway department shall investigate and determine the methods of road construction best adapted to the various sections of the state and shall establish standards for the maintenance of roads and bridges which have been constructed with state aid.

(f) The highway department may, at all reasonable times, be consulted by county and municipal officials relative to any matter relating to the construction of roads and bridges or culverts, and the department may also call on all county and municipal officials for any information or assistance it may require and it shall be their duty to supply the same.

(g) The highway department shall determine the character and have the general supervision over the construction and maintenance of all the public roads, bridges and culverts in the state where the funds of the state are used and shall have a general supervision over the expenditure of any funds apportioned to any county of the state for the construction and maintenance of all public roads, bridges and culverts in each county. (Code 1923, §§ 1303, 1316; Acts 1927, No. 347, p. 348; Acts 1935, No. 339, p. 773; Acts 1939, No. 13, p. 9; Code 1940, T. 23, §§ 3, 13; Acts 1951, No. 887, p. 1530.)

Cross references. — As to authority of department to construct, maintain, etc., roads leading from a state highway to lands included in the state park system, see § 9-14-4. As to divestment of functions of state highway department with respect to construction, repair and maintenance of roads and bridges in certain counties, see § 23-1-100 et seq. As to duty of highway department relative to establishment and supervision of a state plan for safe, effective and efficient rail transportation services, planning pursuant to the Federal Rail Revitalization and Regulatory Reform Act, etc., see § 37-10-1 et seq.

Highway department cannot be sued. — State highway commission (now department) and its members in official capacity were agencies of state and declaratory judgment action against them was without equity on ground it was essentially a prohibited action against the state under Constitution 1901, § 14. Barlowe v. Employers Ins. Co., 237 Ala. 665, 188 So. 896 (1939).

Contract obligation is not subject to doctrine of sovereign immunity. — Once the highway department has legally contracted under state law for goods or services and accepts such goods or services, the highway department also becomes legally obligated to pay for the goods or services accepted in accordance with the terms of the contract; it follows that this obligation is not subject to the doctrine of sovereign immunity and is enforceable in the courts. State Hwy. Dep't v. Milton Constr. Co., 586 So. 2d 872 (Ala. 1991).

Fixing time on contractor's bond. — Final settlement with highway contractor is not made, so as to fix time for an action on surety bond, until approval of amount due him by governor and examiner of accounts. United States Fid. & Guar. Co. v. Yeilding Bros. Co. Dep't Stores, 225 Ala. 307, 143 So. 176 (1932).

Final settlement with highway contractor does not depend on his consent, nor require settlement of amount in fact due him; that being question of which he is entitled to judicial determination. United States Fid. & Guar. Co. v. Yeilding Bros. Co. Dep't Stores, 225 Ala. 307, 143 So. 176 (1932).

Court cannot hold that necessary administrative officers have determined amount due highway contractor when all have not done so pursuant to departmental practice prescribed by executive. United States Fid. & Guar. Co. v. Yeilding Bros. Co. Dep't Stores, 225 Ala. 307, 143 So. 176 (1932).

Record and date of proper administrative officers' determination of amount due highway contractor fixed right of laborers and materialmen to commence an action on contractor's bond. United States Fid. & Guar. Co. v. Yeilding Bros. Co. Dep't Stores, 225 Ala. 307, 143 So. 176 (1932).

Cited in Scott v. Lee, 236 Ala. 420, 183 So. 344 (1938); McFarland v. McKee, 252 Ala. 434, 41 So. 2d 574 (1949); Pruett v. Las Vegas, Inc.,

261 Ala. 557, 74 So. 2d 807 (1954); Davis v. State, 346 So. 2d 936 (Ala. 1977); Rainer v. Tillett Bros. Constr. Co., 381 So. 2d 36 (Ala. 1980).

Collateral references. — 39 C.J.S., Highways, § 157.

Liability, in negligence action, of state highway, or turnpike authorities. 62 ALR2d 1222.

Design: liability of governmental entity or public officer for personal injury or damages arising out of vehicular accident due to negligent or defective design of highway. 45 ALR3d 875.

Liability, in motor vehicle-related cases, of governmental entity for injury or death resulting from design, construction, or failure to warn of narrow bridge. 2 ALR4th 635.

Highway construction contractor's liability for injuries to third persons by materials or debris on highway during course of construction or repair. 3 ALR4th 770.

Highways: Governmental duty to provide curve warnings or markings. 57 ALR4th 342.

Governmental tort liability as to highway median barriers. 58 ALR4th 559.

Highway contractor's liability to highway user for highway surface defects. 62 ALR4th 1067.

§ 23-1-41. Self-insurance program for department employees.

(a) The highway department is authorized and empowered and may, with the approval of the Governor provide for a self-insurance program covering a certain amount to be paid to the employees of the highway department who may be killed or injured in the line and scope of their employment; provided, that the amount paid to any such party on account of death or injury shall not exceed the amount or amounts as provided by the Workers' Compensation Act of this state. The director of the highway department may, with the approval of the Governor, enter into an agreement with an agency, company or corporation qualified to administer a self-insured Workers' Compensation program to administer the program or, in the alternative, the director may elect to administer the program with highway department personnel. The cost of this program shall be paid out of the funds of the highway department as provided by law, and to that end and for that purpose, the department may, with the consent and approval of the Governor, disburse any moneys appropriated or set apart for the construction, repair or maintenance of the public roads, bridges and highways of this state.

(b) The provisions of the 1981 amendments to this section shall be retroactive to February 1, 1980.

(c) Notwithstanding the provisions of subsection (b) of this section, any reinsurance policies which are in effect as of May 17, 1981, shall continue in force until September 30, 1981. (Code 1923, § 1303; Acts 1927, No. 347, p. 348; Acts 1935, No. 339, p. 773; Acts 1939, No. 13, p. 9; Code 1940, T. 23, § 3; Acts 1951, No. 887, p. 1530; Acts 1981, No. 81-625, p. 1040.)

Cross references. — As to workers' compensation, see § 25-5-1 et seq.

When section considered part of insurance policy. — When this section is endorsed on face of a policy, it must be read into contract to determine its nature, character and the obligations which it assumes, disregarding the superfluous provisions dealing generally and relating to liability under the Workmen's Compensation Act. Employers Ins. Co. v. Harrison, 250 Ala. 116, 33 So. 2d 264 (1947).

Where in procuring a policy of insurance, state officials act under authority of this section, the provisions of this section must be considered as much a part of the policy as if they were formally embodied therein. United States Fid. & Guar. Co. v. Dunlap, 276 Ala. 616, 165 So. 2d 404 (1963).

This section places a limit as to the amount of insurance the highway department can contract and pay for. Hale v. United

States Fid. & Guar. Co., 45 Ala. App. 379, 231 So. 2d 156 (1970).

Provisions of Workmen's Compensation Act are not incorporated into section. — The sole effect of this section was to limit the amount of insurance the highway department was authorized to pay for and in nowise incorporated the terms of the Workmen's Compensation Act into the section. Employers Ins. Co. v. Harrison, 33 Ala. App. 199, 33 So. 2d 260, rev'd on other grounds, Employers Ins. Co. v. Harrison, 250 Ala. 116, 33 So. 2d 264 (1947).

The sole effect of the reference to the "Workmen's Compensation Act" in this section was to place a limit on the amount of insurance the highway department could contract and pay for. United States Fid. & Guar. Co. v. Dunlap, 276 Ala. 616, 165 So. 2d 404 (1963).

The 1951 amendment to this section clearly answers the contention that the legislature intends for the insurance coverage thereby obtained for state highway department employees to be limited to that afforded under the workmen's compensation law. United States Fid. & Guar. Co. v. Dunlap, 276 Ala. 616, 165 So. 2d 404 (1963).

Injury or death covered under this section need not be accidental. — For an injury or death to be compensable under the workmen's compensation law, it must result from an accident which arises out of and in the course of the employment, whereas the injury or death covered under this section need not be accidental. United States Fid. & Guar. Co. v. Dunlap, 276 Ala. 616, 165 So. 2d 404 (1963).

And is covered if it occurs "in line and scope" of employment. — Death or injury is covered if it occurs "in the line and scope" of employment. United States Fid. & Guar. Co. v. Dunlap, 276 Ala. 616, 165 So. 2d 404 (1963).

Employee's action under insurance policy issued to state highway department. — See Employers Ins. Co. v. Rhodes, 240 Ala. 226, 198 So. 616 (1940); Glens Falls Ins. Co. v. Anderson, 280 Ala. 626, 197 So. 2d 276 (1967).

§ 23-1-42. Roads, etc., located on state institutions.

(a) The roads and streets, drives and parking areas located on the campus of any state institution of higher learning, the Alabama state hospitals, the Partlow State School and Hospital and the Alabama Agricultural Center in the City of Montgomery shall be deemed a part of the state highway system and may be constructed, maintained and repaired by the State Highway Department in the same manner as other highways and roads in the state highway system.

(b) The State Highway Department or the director thereof is hereby authorized and empowered to expend any funds in the public road and bridge fund to effectuate the purpose of this section, provided such expenditure is first approved by the Governor. (Acts 1959, No. 500, p. 1235.)

Collateral references. — Legal aspects of speed bumps. 60 ALR4th 1249.

Highway contractor's liability to highway user for highway surface defects. 62 ALR4th 1067.

§ 23-1-43. State agricultural experiment station roads.

The State Highway Department shall construct, repair and maintain all roads on land owned by the state which is located within the boundaries of any state agricultural experiment station or of any branch or substation, and such roads shall be considered a part of the state highway system. (Acts 1956, 1st Ex. Sess., No. 129, p. 191.)

§ 23-1-44. Right of entry for purpose of making surveys and taking soil samples.

(a) All officers and employees of the highway department are hereby authorized and empowered to enter upon and go across the lands of any individual or corporation in the State of Alabama for the purpose of making any and all surveys necessary for the construction of any highways, roads and bridges to be constructed by it or under its supervision and to enter upon the property of individuals or corporations for the purpose of securing samples of the land to determine if same can be used as a source of material for the construction, maintenance and improvement of public highways, roads and bridges.

(b) Such officers or employees are not relieved of civil liability for any damages caused by any acts authorized in subsection (a) of this section.

(c) Such officers or employees may erect or place such stobs, stakes, monuments or other markers as may be required in carrying out such survey. (Acts 1939, No. 210, p. 363; Code 1940, T. 23, §§ 40-42.)

§ 23-1-45. Acquisition of rights-of-way.

Any other provision of law to the contrary notwithstanding, the state director of the highway department shall have authority to acquire the rights-of-way deemed necessary by the highway department for the construction of a state road, either by purchase or by the exercise of the right of eminent domain in condemnation proceedings as provided under the laws of this state, or the county or municipality in which such road deemed necessary by the state director of the highway department is located shall acquire such rights-of-way deemed necessary by the state director of the highway department, when requested to do so by said State Highway Director. Should the county or municipality fail or refuse to acquire said rights-of-way, the state director of the highway department shall have authority to acquire such rights-of-way as first above authorized. Rights-of-way acquired under the provision of this section shall be paid for in the manner prescribed by law. (Acts 1955, No. 566, p. 1230.)

Cross references. — As to eminent domain generally, see § 18-1A-1 et seq.

Legislature has plenary power over streets of city except as limited by the Constitution. King v. City of Mobile, 273 Ala. 109, 134 So. 2d 746 (1961).

And this rule applies to a tunnel which is an extension of a state highway system. King v. City of Mobile, 273 Ala. 109, 134 So. 2d 746 (1961).

Tunnels are and can be part of the state highway system, and are included under the statutes giving the proper state authorities the power to purchase rights-of-way for highways. King v. City of Mobile, 273 Ala. 109, 134 So. 2d 746 (1961).

Cited in City of Tuskegee v. Sharpe, 292 Ala. 14, 288 So. 2d 122 (1973); Hill v. State, 394 So. 2d 106 (Ala. Crim. App. 1981).

§ 23-1-46. Changes or additions to state road system.

The highway department shall have full authority to make such changes or additions to the system of state roads to conform to the requirements of the federal aid law as it may deem proper and construct or maintain the same with state aid under the provisions of this title. (Code 1923, § 1336; Acts 1927, No. 347, p. 348; Code 1940, T. 23, § 30.)

Cited in Mobile County v. Barnes-Creary Supply Co., 224 Ala. 168, 139 So. 270 (1932).

Collateral references. — 40 C.J.S., Highways, §§ 175, 179.

§ 23-1-47. Authority to maintain, etc., city and town streets and roads.

(a) It is hereby declared by the Legislature of Alabama that all city and town streets and roads in the State of Alabama, including viaducts, bridges and culverts, do now, and will in the future, serve a state purpose and are of benefit to the people of the state, that said streets and roads, including viaducts, bridges and culverts, are public highways and bridges and that it is a proper and legitimate function for the state to provide for the cost of maintaining, improving, constructing and reconstructing such streets and roads in cooperation with the city or town involved.

(b) The State Highway Department, hereinafter referred to as the department, in cooperation with the city or town involved, is hereby authorized and empowered to make expenditures from its funds for all, or any part of, the costs of maintaining, improving, repairing, constructing and reconstructing all or any portion of the streets and roads, including viaducts, bridges and culverts, in every city and town in the State of Alabama; provided, however, that nothing contained in this section shall require the department to maintain, improve, repair, construct or reconstruct the streets and roads or portions thereof in any city or town in the state; and provided further, that nothing contained in this section shall affect the duties and obligations of the department to maintain and repair the streets and roads or any portion thereof in any city or town which are or may hereafter be designated as connecting link roads under the provisions of Article 4 of this chapter. (Acts 1963, 1st Ex. Sess., No. 34, p. 110.)

Cited in Rainer v. Tillett Bros. Constr. Co., 381 So. 2d 36 (Ala. 1980).

Collateral references. — Liability, in motor vehicle-related cases, of governmental entity for injury or death resulting from failure to repair pothole in surface of highway or street. 98 ALR3d 101.

Liability, in motor vehicle-related cases, of governmental entity for injury or death result-ing from design, construction, or failure to warn of narrow bridge. 2 ALR4th 635.

Highway construction contractor's liability for injuries to third persons by materials or debris on highway during course of construction or repair. 3 ALR4th 770.

Governmental tort liability as to highway median barriers. 58 ALR4th 559.

§ 23-1-48. Application by counties for construction or maintenance of state road or bridge.

Whenever a county commission shall desire that a state road or bridge on a state road in said county be constructed or maintained with state aid, written application shall be made by the county to the highway department under such rules and regulations as the department may prescribe. Such application, when made, shall be considered by the department and, if approved by it, the commissioners shall direct an engineer to view said road or bridge and cause to be made surveys, plans, specifications and estimates of the cost of construction or maintenance, and the highway department may thereupon appropriate out of the state highway fund such part of the estimated cost of such work as it may deem proper, and the highway department shall proceed to do such work by contract or with its own force. If it deems best, the department may accept appropriations from the county for said work, which shall be paid into the State Treasury to the credit of the state highway fund, before the work begins. Whenever a county fails to make application for the construction or maintenance of a road or bridge or the department deems it best for such work to be done, it may proceed to construct or maintain any part of the state road or bridge upon a state road and pay part or all of the cost of such work out of the state highway fund. (Code 1923, § 1323; Acts 1927, No. 347, p. 348; Code 1940, T. 23, § 20.)

Cited in Rainer v. Tillett Bros. Constr. Co., 381 So. 2d 36 (Ala. 1980).

Collateral references. — Liability, in motor vehicle-related cases, of governmental entity for injury or death resulting from design, construction, or failure to warn of narrow bridge. 2 ALR4th 635.

Governmental tort liability as to highway median barriers. 58 ALR4th 559.

Highway contractor's liability to highway user for highway surface defects. 62 ALR4th 1067.

§ 23-1-49. Furnishing of competent engineers.

The highway department shall furnish a competent engineer, when needed, during the progress of road or bridge construction, repair or maintenance in any county under the provisions of this title, who shall supervise said work and see that the plans and specifications are complied with. (Code 1923, § 1324; Acts 1927, No. 347, p. 348; Code 1940, T. 48, § 21.)

Collateral references. — Highway contractor's liability to highway user for highway surface defects. 62 ALR4th 1067.

§ 23-1-50. Authority to procure equipment; payment of expenses.

Subject to the provisions of Chapter 4, Title 41, the highway department is authorized to rent, construct, or purchase such buildings, stock, machinery, tools, materials and other equipment as it may find necessary for use in carrying out the provisions of this chapter and pay for the same out of the state highway fund. It shall also, subject to the provisions of Chapter 4 of Title 41, pay out of said fund the necessary expenses of the department of every description, including traveling expenses of the officials and engineers, superintendents, foremen and clerks, etc., while in the actual performance of their duties authorized or imposed by this chapter and also the cost of all supplies or materials furnished for said department and for the maintenance of all machinery used by the department or its agent. (Code 1923, § 1335; Acts 1927, No. 347, p. 348; Code 1940, T. 23, § 29.)

Cited in Rainer v. Tillett Bros. Constr. Co., 381 So. 2d 36 (Ala. 1980).

§ 23-1-50.1. Road machinery and equipment management program; equipment management surplus reserve account.

(a) It is the intent of the legislature to give the State of Alabama Highway Department authority to accumulate depreciation, equipment replacement allowances and salvage value on road machinery and equipment sufficient to upgrade, replace or make extraordinary repairs to the highway department's road machinery and equipment as determined by a road machinery and equipment management program to be developed by the highway department.

(b) Unless the context clearly indicates otherwise, the following words and phrases will have the following meanings:

(1) ROAD MACHINERY AND EQUIPMENT. — Self-propelled equipment or other equipment commonly referred to in the State Highway Department as rental equipment.

(2) DEPRECIATION. — That process of allocating the original cost per fixed asset over the productive life of the asset using some generally accepted method of depreciation.

(3) EQUIPMENT REPLACEMENT ALLOWANCE. — An amount, when added to the depreciation and salvage value of a unit of road machinery and equipment and accumulated in a special account, that will provide the funds to upgrade, replace or make extraordinary repairs to that unit of road machinery and equipment.

(4) EQUIPMENT MANAGEMENT SURPLUS RESERVE ACCOUNT. — A special revolving account or fund to be established in the public road and bridge fund of the State of Alabama Highway Department to accumulate depreciation, equipment replacement allowances and salvage value to be used to upgrade, replace or make extraordinary repairs to road machinery and equipment.

(5) HIGHWAY DEPARTMENT DIVISIONS. — Those divisions of the highway department responsible for road construction and maintenance over a specified geographic area of the state.

(6) EXTRAORDINARY REPAIRS. — Repairs made to extend an asset's useful life beyond that which was originally estimated.

(7) SALVAGE VALUE. — That portion of a unit of road machinery and equipment's cost that is recovered at the end of its productive life.

(8) GENERAL OFFICE. — Those general and administrative offices of the highway department located in Montgomery, Alabama.

(c) There is hereby created in the public road and bridge fund of the State of Alabama Highway Department an equipment management surplus reserve account. The Highway Director is hereby directed to establish a road machinery and equipment management program which will determine the type, number and distribution between the general office and highway department divisions of the road machinery and equipment necessary to carry out the mission of the highway department in an efficient manner. This system must also determine the productive life of all of the road machinery and equipment and establish depreciation rates, equipment replacement allowance and salvage value which, when accumulated in the equipment management surplus reserve account, will provide the necessary funds to upgrade, replace or make extraordinary repairs to road machinery and equipment.

(d) The equipment management surplus reserve account must be subdivided into subaccounts; one for the general office and one each for each of the highway department divisions. Depreciation, equipment replacement allowance and salvage value will be credited to the account of the general office or highway department division to which the unit of road machinery and equipment is assigned and will not be commingled or transferred between the highway department division and the general office. The funds in each of these subaccounts of the general office and highway department divisions will be available to them to upgrade, replace or to make extraordinary repairs to road machinery and equipment.

(e) There is hereby appropriated all of the funds created to the equipment management surplus reserve accounts, due to the depreciation, equipment replacement allowance and salvage value of road machinery and equipment, for upgrading, replacement or extraordinary repairs to road machinery and equipment; these funds to not revert at the end of each fiscal year, but carry over to each succeeding year. It is the intent of the legislature that funds appropriated from the equipment management surplus reserve account be used only to upgrade, replace or make extraordinary repairs to road machinery and equipment, and that they not be used to increase the number of units of equipment of the highway department. It is the further intent of the legislature to use these funds to maintain the present level of road maintenance, as opposed to using said funds to place the state in a competitive position with private enterprise. Specific funds must be appropriated by the

27

state legislature to increase the number of units of road machinery and equipment.

(f) Any other provision of law to the contrary notwithstanding, at the end of the productive life of a unit of road machinery or equipment covered by the equipment management surplus reserve account established as provided for in this section, such unit of road machinery or equipment shall be sold at the discretion of the Highway Director, either at public auction as provided for by the laws of the State of Alabama, or by a negotiated sale between the highway department and any other state department or agency, and the proceeds from any such sale, whether at public auction or by such negotiation, shall be paid into the equipment management surplus reserve account and credited to the subaccount to which the unit of road machinery or equipment is credited. (Acts 1981, No. 81-316, p. 450.)

Collateral references. — 39A C.J.S., Highways, § 157.   39 Am. Jur. 2d, Highways, Streets, and Bridges, §§ 64, 73, 122.

§ 23-1-51. Purchase of motor fuels, oils, greases and lubricants.

(a) All motor fuels, oils, greases and lubricants bought by or for the State Highway Department for use in each county in which the construction, maintenance and repair of the county roads and bridges have been transferred to the State Highway Department shall be purchased from vendors and suppliers residing in the county where such motor fuels, oils, greases and lubricants are to be used. All such purchases shall be made on the basis of competitive bids, and contracts and purchase orders shall be awarded to the lowest responsible bidder as provided by law.

(b) The Division of Purchases and Stores of the State Finance Department, with the approval of the State Highway Department, shall make rules and regulations relating to the manner of advertising for bids, receiving bids and executing contracts for such items as are enumerated in subsection (a) of this section.

(c) Any contract entered into or any purchase order issued prior to August 26, 1965, shall remain in full force and effect until the terms thereof have been complied with. (Acts 1965, No. 580, p. 1077.)

Cited in Rainer v. Tillett Bros. Constr. Co., 381 So. 2d 36 (Ala. 1980).

§ 23-1-52. License exemption for vehicles of department.

Motor vehicles used by the highway department, its officials or engineers, shall not be subject to any state, county or municipal license. (Code 1923, § 1313; Acts 1927, No. 347, p. 348; Code 1940, T. 23, § 10.)

§ 23-1-53. Contracts to do work — Authority.

The highway department may enter into contracts with any of the counties of the state or with any of the municipalities of this state, as it may with individuals, firms or private corporations, to do any work in the construction, repair or maintenance of the roads, bridges or highways in this state. (Code 1923, § 1327; Acts 1927, No. 347, p. 348; Code 1940, T. 23, § 22.)

Cited in Wynn v. First Nat'l Bank, 229 Ala. 639, 159 So. 58 (1934); Rainer v. Tillett Bros. Constr. Co., 381 So. 2d 36 (Ala. 1980).

Collateral references. — Highway construction contractor's liability for injuries to third persons by materials or debris on highway during course of construction or repair. 3 ALR4th 770.

§ 23-1-54. Contracts to do work — How drawn and approved.

Every contract for road or bridge construction, repair or maintenance under the provisions of this chapter shall be made in the name of the State of Alabama, approved by the highway department and the Governor. (Code 1923, § 1330; Acts 1927, No. 347, p. 348; Code 1940, T. 23, § 24.)

Governor has direct fiscal responsibility over road construction payments. — The legislature has fixed the approval by the governor as a condition precedent to the validity of monetary payments arising out of contracts for road construction entered into by the highway department through its director. In other words, the governor, as chief executive officer of the state, has a direct fiscal responsibility over the payment of state funds under road contracts made by his appointed subordinates. Rainer v. Tillett Bros. Constr. Co., 381 So. 2d 36 (Ala. 1980).

And he must approve even supplemental highway construction agreements. — Where a supplemental agreement deals with highway construction, and in words and in effect supplements the original contract, it is one which requires approval by the governor. To construe the requirements of the statutes otherwise would allow an incongruous result; viz., the governor's approval would be required for highway construction contracts but for "claims" for money arising out of those contracts, which might even exceed the sum of money originally agreed upon, only the signature of his subordinate would be necessary. Rainer v. Tillett Bros. Constr. Co., 381 So. 2d 36 (Ala. 1980).

Cited in McFarland v. McKee, 252 Ala. 434, 41 So. 2d 574 (1949).

§ 23-1-55. Contracts to do work — Preconditions.

No contracts for construction, repair or renewals of highways, bridges or culverts shall be let without the approval of the Governor and until after all necessary right-of-way for such highways and right for material for construction and right-of-way for ingress and egress to said material have been legally procured and all documents covering such procurement have been placed on file with the Highway Director of the department. (Code 1923, § 1333; Acts 1927, No. 347, p. 348; Code 1940, T. 23, § 27.)

Cross references. — As to eminent domain generally, see § 18-1A-1 et seq.

Governor has direct fiscal responsibility over road construction payments. — The legislature has fixed the approval by the governor as a condition precedent to the validity of monetary payments arising out of contracts for road construction entered into by the highway department through its director. In other words, the governor, as chief executive officer of the state, has a direct fiscal responsibility over the payment of state funds under road contracts made by his appointed subordinates. Rainer v. Tillett Bros. Constr. Co., 381 So. 2d 36 (Ala. 1980).

And he must approve even supplemental highway construction agreements. — Where a supplemental agreement deals with highway construction, and in words and in effect supplements the original contract, it is one which requires approval by the governor. To construe the requirements of the statutes otherwise would allow an incongruous result; viz., the governor's approval would be required for highway construction contracts but for "claims" for money arising out of those contracts, which might even exceed the sum of money originally agreed upon, only the signature of his subordinate would be necessary. Rainer v. Tillett Bros. Constr. Co., 381 So. 2d 36 (Ala. 1980).

Collateral references. — 40 C.J.S., Highways, § 208.

§ 23-1-56. Contracts to do work — Qualification of bidders.

(a) *Prequalifications of contractors.* — The Highway Director shall require all bidders to furnish a statement under oath, on such forms as the highway department may prescribe, of detailed information with respect to their financial resources, equipment, past record and experience of both the firm and personnel of the organization, together with such other information as the highway department may deem necessary for carrying out the provisions of this chapter. Such forms shall include a financial statement actually prepared by a certified public accountant (C.P.A.) or any independent licensed public accountant approved by the Alabama State Highway Department, an inventory of equipment listing its location and book value, a listing of material and equipment houses with whom a line of credit is established as well as those firms from whom principal materials and equipment have been purchased during the past three years, a listing of completed construction projects and bonding companies with whom business has been done for the past three years and a combined statement of the applicant that includes other wholly owned or substantially owned interest, as well as any other pertinent information required by the highway department. Should the applicant's financial statement fail to substantiate the limits required, further consideration may be given to the present market value in lieu of book value of listed assets when properly supported with substantiating evidence. A statement of an independent licensed public accountant shall not be required for the issuance of certificates under $50,000.00.

(b) *Furnishing forms; certificate of qualification.* — Any bidder desiring to submit a bid for the performance of any contract or contracts which the highway department proposes to let shall apply to the highway department for qualifications and shall use for that purpose the form prescribed and furnished by the highway department. The highway department shall be required to act promptly upon the application for qualification and must act thereon within 30 days after the same is presented to them. Upon the receipt of any application for qualification, the highway department shall cause the same to be examined and the statements therein to be verified and shall, thereupon, determine whether the applicant is competent, responsible and possesses the financial resources which satisfy the terms of this chapter. If the applicant is found to possess the qualifications prescribed by this chapter and by the rules and regulations promulgated by the highway department, the highway department shall issue to him a certificate of qualification, which shall be valid for a period of one year or such shorter period of time as the highway department may prescribe, unless thereafter revoked by the highway department for cause as provided in subsection (c) of this section. The certificate of qualification shall contain a statement fixing the actual amount of work in terms of estimated cost which the applicant will be permitted to have on contract with the highway department and not completed at any one time. Such certificate of qualification shall authorize the holder to bid on all work on which bids are taken by the highway department during the period of time therein specified.

(c) *Revocation of certificate.* — A certificate of qualification may be revoked by the highway department only after notice to the qualified bidder and an opportunity to be heard. The notice shall be in writing and shall state the grounds of the proposed revocation and may be served by any sheriff of the State of Alabama or by registered or certified mail, as the highway department shall direct. Any qualified bidder aggrieved by the decision of the highway department upon the matter revoking his certificate may appeal from such decision to the circuit court of Montgomery County, Alabama, in the manner provided in subsection (f) of this section.

(d) *Prerequisites to award of certificate.* — No bidder shall be given a certificate of qualification unless his financial statement and the investigation made by the highway department shall show that he possesses net worth sufficient in the judgment of the highway department to render it probable that he can satisfactorily execute his contracts and meet his obligations therein incurred. The maximum amount of work that an applicant will be permitted to have on contract with the highway department and not completed at any one time shall be not more than 10 times the net worth as shown by the applicant's latest financial statement. In the discretion of the highway department, the certificate may contain a statement limiting such bidder to the submission of bids upon a certain class or classes of work. All applicants for qualifications shall expressly authorize the highway department to obtain all the information which they may deem pertinent with respect to the financial worth and assets and liabilities of the applicant from banks or other financial institutions, surety companies, dealers in materials, equipment or supplies or other persons having business transactions with any applicant and shall expressly authorize all such financial institutions or other persons to furnish any such information requested from them by the highway department. All information filed with, or furnished to, the highway department by applicants or other persons in connection with the administration of this chapter shall be kept in confidence by the highway department and shall not be revealed to any person except upon the proper subpoena or order of a court of competent jurisdiction. All applications shall be accompanied by satisfactory evidence that the applicant has complied with the workers' compensation law and is not in default in the payment of any sum due from him under the provisions of such law. Where the applicant is a foreign corporation, the application shall be accompanied by a certificate of the Secretary of State that such corporation is authorized to do business in this state. The highway department may require all qualified bidders to file financial statements from time to time, at such intervals as it may prescribe. This chapter shall be administered without reference to the residence of applicants, and its provisions and the rules and regulations of the highway department, adopted pursuant thereto, shall apply equally to residents and nonresidents of the State of Alabama. This chapter shall not apply to the purchase of material, equipment or supplies.

(e) *Rules and regulations.* — For the purpose of carrying into effect the terms of this chapter and insuring to the state and public the award of all contracts to competent and responsible bidders, the highway department shall be empowered to prepare and promulgate such rules and regulations, not inconsistent with the terms of this chapter, as it may deem proper. Such rules and regulations may cover the requirements of the highway department with respect to equipment, past record and experience of applicant, personnel or organization and such other matters as the highway department may deem necessary to enable it to pass upon the qualifications of applicants. The highway department may, in its discretion, make public from time to time a list of qualified bidders, but such list shall be general in character and shall not indicate the size of contract or character of work with respect to which such bidders have been qualified.

(f) *Appeal from final action of awarding authority.* — All applicants for qualifications shall be promptly notified by the highway department of its final action upon their applications. Any applicant aggrieved by the decision of the highway department may, within 10 days after receiving notice of such decision, request in writing a reconsideration of his application by the highway department and may submit additional evidence bearing upon his qualifications. The highway department shall, thereupon, again consider the matter and may either adhere to or modify its previous decisions. The highway department shall act upon any request for reconsideration within 15 days after the filing thereof and shall forthwith notify the applicant of the action taken. Upon being notified of the final action of the highway department upon such reconsideration, the applicant who is still aggrieved by the decision of the highway department may, within 10 days after receiving notification of such decision, take an appeal therefrom to the circuit court of Montgomery County, Alabama. Such appeal shall be perfected by the filing of a bond with the clerk of said court in such amount as the clerk may fix, conditioned upon the payment by the appellant of the cost of the appeal in case the decision of the highway department shall be sustained. An issue shall be made up under the direction of the court between the applicant and the highway department. The court shall hear the evidence offered by the appellant and the highway department and decide the case without the intervention of a jury. If the court finds that there is no ground for the correction, modification or reversal of the decision of the highway department, it shall dismiss the appeal; otherwise, it shall make the order with respect to the qualification which it finds should have been made by the highway department, which order shall be binding upon the highway department. An appeal from such decision may be prosecuted to the Court of Civil Appeals or Supreme Court of Alabama in the same way and manner that appeals in civil cases are provided for by law and by the Alabama Rules of Appellate Procedure. Any applicant who has been refused qualification or who is dissatisfied with the highway department's decision as to the actual amount of work that he will be permitted to have under contract at any one time or any limitation as to the class or classes of work on which he is authorized to bid may, at any time, file a new application for qualification. Such new application shall be promptly considered and acted upon by the highway department.

(g) *Unqualified bidders.* — The highway department shall not be authorized to consider any bid filed with it by any person who has not been qualified under the terms of this chapter. Bids from unqualified bidders discovered by the highway department prior to the reading thereof to be from such person shall be returned without being read. If the highway department finds, subsequent to the opening of the bids, that facts exist which would disqualify the lowest bidder or that such bidder is not competent and responsible, the highway department shall reject such bid despite the fact of prior qualification of such bidder. It shall be unlawful to award any contract to any bidder not qualified to bid thereon at the time fixed for receiving bids.

(h) *False representations as to financial position.* — It shall be unlawful for any applicant for qualification to knowingly make a false statement with respect to his financial worth in any application for qualification, financial statement or other written instrument filed by him with the highway department under the terms of this chapter, or the rules and regulations adopted pursuant thereto. Any person violating the provisions of this subsection shall, upon conviction, be fined not less than $100.00 nor more than $500.00, and shall be disqualified from submitting bids on contracts advertised for letting by the highway department for a period of two years following the date of his conviction.

(i) *Persons not qualified not to receive proposals.* — It shall be unlawful for the highway department or any servant, agent or employee or any other person to furnish or deliver any proposal relating to a highway, road or bridge job to any person other than a duly qualified bidder or his authorized representative. The name of the proposed bidder shall be inserted in the face of the proposal, and such proposal shall not be transferable. No proposal shall be issued later than 24 hours before the hour set for the opening of bids. Any violation of the provisions of this subsection shall constitute a misdemeanor, and the person adjudged guilty shall be fined not more than $500.00 and imprisoned for not more than six months, one or both, at the discretion of the court. (Code 1923, § 1343; Acts 1927, No. 347, p. 348; Code 1940, T. 23, § 35; Acts 1959, No. 653, p. 1578, § 2; Acts 1961, Ex. Sess., No. 213, p. 2208.)

Cited in Rainer v. Tillett Bros. Constr. Co., 381 So. 2d 36 (Ala. 1980).

Collateral references. — Highway contrac- tor's liability to highway user for highway surface defects. 62 ALR4th 1067.

§ 23-1-57. Agreements and contracts with adjoining states and federal government relative to bridges.

The highway department may enter into agreements and contracts with adjoining states and the federal government relative to the acquisition, construction, maintenance and repair of bridges across any river or stream forming the boundary between this state and an adjoining state upon the following terms and conditions:

(1) Any bridge, the subject of such agreement or contract, shall be open to the public and no toll or other charge shall be levied for the privilege of crossing it.

(2) Any bridge, the subject of such agreement or contract, shall connect a highway in this state designated as a "state highway" or a "United States highway" with a highway in the adjoining state designated as a "state highway" or a "United States highway."

(3) The agreement or contract may fix the amount the State of Alabama will pay, but the amount so agreed upon shall not be governed by the distance of the boundary from the bank of the stream, and the amount agreed upon shall be paid solely from funds made available to the highway department for the construction of roads and bridges.

(4) Any contract made pursuant to this section shall also conform to all federal laws, rules and regulations governing agreements or contracts between states relative to the acquisition, construction, maintenance and repair of interstate bridges and shall contain such terms and stipulations as are requisite to securing the maximum amount of aid from the federal government, subject only to the limitations contained in this section. (Code 1923, § 1320; Acts 1927, No. 347, p. 348; Code 1940, T. 23, § 17; Acts 1949, No. 410, p. 582.)

Cross references. — As to exemption of bonds of public corporations from laws govern- ing usury or limiting interest rates, see § 8-8-7.

Collateral references. — 11 C.J.S., Bridges, §§ 11, 35, 48.

§ 23-1-58. Interest of employees, etc., in construction, etc., of roads and bridges prohibited.

Neither the director nor any other person in the employ of the highway department shall be, either directly or indirectly, interested in any contract or agreement for the construction or maintenance of any road or bridge in this state or in the sale of any machinery, material or anything whatever entering into the construction, repair or maintenance of the roads and bridges of this state. (Code 1923, § 1321; Acts 1927, No. 347, p. 348; Code 1940, T. 23, § 18.)

Collateral references. — Highway contractor's liability to highway user for highway surface defects. 62 ALR4th 1067.

Products liability: sufficiency of evidence to support product misuse defense in actions concerning commercial or industrial equipment and machinery. 64 ALR4th 10.

§ 23-1-59. Rules and regulations of department.

(a) The highway department shall have the right and power to adopt all reasonable and necessary rules and regulations for the better construction, repair and maintenance of the public roads and bridges in Alabama under the jurisdiction of the department which the department shall deem proper. The department shall have the power to enter into contracts and agreements with the owners or operators of telegraph or telephone lines, community antenna television systems, power transmission lines, gas districts, gas, water, sewer or other pipelines which are constructed, to be constructed or operated along or across the right-of-way of public roads, bridges and highways of this state and to prescribe all reasonable rules and regulations as to the construction, repair or maintenance of the poles, wires and lines of such telegraph, telephone, community antenna television systems or power companies and pipelines of gas districts, gas, water, sewer or other pipeline companies so as to insure the safety of the travelling public in using the roads, bridges and highways in this state.

(b) The highway department may prescribe any reasonable rules and regulations so as to prevent unnecessary trespassing upon or injury to any of the public roads, bridges or highways of the state upon which state money may be expended or appropriated or upon any part of the right-of-way of any of the public roads or highways in the state upon which state money may be expended or appropriated.

(c) The highway department may prescribe rules and regulations as to the weight or tonnage of vehicles to be used upon any of the public roads, bridges or highways of the state upon which state money may be expended or appropriated, except as may be otherwise provided by law.

(d) The highway department, in addition to the right, authority and powers conferred upon it by this title, is authorized to make all such reasonable rules and regulations as the department may deem necessary to carry out the provisions of this title. (Code 1923, § 1319; Acts 1927, No. 347, p. 348; Code 1940, T. 23, §§ 16, 35; Acts 1969, No. 419, p. 820; Acts 1969, No. 475, p. 931.)

Cited in McFarland v. McKee, 252 Ala. 434, 41 So. 2d 574 (1949); Rainer v. Tillett Bros. Constr. Co., 381 So. 2d 36 (Ala. 1980).

Collateral references. — 39 C.J.S., Highways, § 158.

Governmental tort liability as to highway median barriers. 58 ALR4th 559.

Governmental liability for failure to post highway deer crossing warning signs. 59 ALR4th 1217.

Products liability: sufficiency of evidence to support product misuse defense in actions concerning commercial or industrial equipment and machinery. 64 ALR4th 10.

Radio or television aerials, antennas, towers, or satellite dishes or discs as within terms of covenant restricting use, erection, or maintenance of such structures upon residential property. 76 ALR4th 498.

§ 23-1-60. Authority of Highway Director to alter plans or character of work, determine need for extra work, make supplemental agreements, etc.

The following implementation of the provisions of the Alabama State Highway Department standard specifications for highways and bridges is hereby adopted as a statutory provision, any and all other laws in conflict notwithstanding:

(1) ALTERATION OF PLANS OR CHARACTER OF WORK. — The Highway Director shall have the authority to make, at any time during the progress of any construction on any highway project under his jurisdiction, such changes or alterations of construction details, including alterations in grade or alignment of roadway or bridges, or both, as may be necessary or desirable for the successful completion of the project. The aforementioned changes or alterations may or may not increase or decrease the original planned quantities; however, under no circumstances shall changes or alterations involve any work beyond the termini of the original construction project, except as may be necessary to satisfactorily complete the project in the most feasible and economical manner, in the judgment of the Highway Director.

(2) EXTRA WORK. — The Highway Director shall have the authority to determine the need for new or additional work not contemplated or included in the original construction contract. This new or additional work shall not extend beyond the termini of the original construction project, except as may be necessary to satisfactorily complete the project in the most feasible and economical manner, in the judgment of the Highway Director.

(3) SUPPLEMENTAL AGREEMENT OR FORCE ACCOUNT ORDER. — The highway director shall have the authority to enter into a supplemental contract with the prime contractor, setting forth the estimated quantities of extra work and specifying the unit prices or lump sum agreed upon by the parties involved; provided, that such supplemental contract shall not be subject to any competitive bid laws of this state. If a satisfactory unit price or lump sum cannot be agreed upon, the highway director shall have the authority to direct that extra work be performed on a force account basis, as defined by the Alabama State Highway Department standard specifications for highways and bridges. (Acts 1969, No. 228, p. 553.)

Every contract for road construction shall be made in the name of the state of Alabama, approved by the highway department and the governor. Rainer v. Tillett Bros. Constr. Co., 381 So. 2d 36 (Ala. 1980).

No contracts for construction of highways shall be let without approval of the governor. Rainer v. Tillett Bros. Constr. Co., 381 So. 2d 36 (Ala. 1980).

Governor has direct fiscal responsibility over highway construction payments. — The legislature has fixed the approval by the governor as a condition precedent to the valid-ity of monetary payments arising out of contracts for road construction entered into by the highway department through its director. In other words, the governor, as chief executive officer of the state, has a direct fiscal responsibility over the payment of state funds under road contracts made by his appointed subordinates. Rainer v. Tillett Bros. Constr. Co., 381 So. 2d 36 (Ala. 1980).

The authority of the highway director to make supplemental contracts is statutory. Rainer v. Tillett Bros. Constr. Co., 381 So. 2d 36 (Ala. 1980).

Director may bind state by entering into supplemental contract. — This section allows the director to make changes in construction as may be necessary, to determine the need for new or additional work not contemplated in the original contract, and to enter into a supplemental contract with the prime contractor reflecting those changes. In other words, after the original highway contract has been executed, the director may determine that previously uncontemplated work must be done to complete a project, he may amend the "construction details," and he may make the changes binding on the state by entering into a supplemental contract. Rainer v. Tillett Bros. Constr. Co., 381 So. 2d 36 (Ala. 1980).

But highway construction supplemental agreement still requires governor's approval. — Where a supplemental agreement deals with highway construction, and in words and in effect supplements the original contract, it is one which requires approval by the governor. To construe the requirements of the statutes otherwise would allow an incongruous result; viz., the governor's approval would be required for highway construction contracts but for "claims" for money arising out of those contracts, which might even exceed the sum of money originally agreed upon, only the signature of his subordinate would be necessary. Rainer v. Tillett Bros. Constr. Co., 381 So. 2d 36 (Ala. 1980).

§ 23-1-61. State highway fund — Appropriations; vehicle license fees deposited in fund; manner of making payments from fund.

There is hereby appropriated to the highway department for its use the entire net revenue derived by the state from the sale of motor vehicle, trailer and tractor licenses, and such other appropriations or funds received by the highway department shall be expended and accounted for as provided in this article. Said state highway fund shall be paid out of the treasury on the comptroller's warrant drawn upon presentation to him of the certificate of the highway department approved by the Governor. (Code 1923, § 1317; Acts 1927, No. 347, p. 348; Code 1940, T. 23, § 14.)

Collateral references. — 60 C.J.S., Motor Vehicles, §§ 136(1), 143.

§ 23-1-62. State highway fund — Purposes for which used.

(a) All proceeds arising from the sale of state highway bonds and the revenue appropriated to the highway department, when received by the state treasurer, shall be set aside in a special fund known as the state highway fund and be used for no other purpose than in the carrying out of the provisions of this chapter. The revenue derived by the state from the sale of motor vehicle, trailer and tractor licenses and all other appropriations shall be used for the following purposes:

(1) To provide a sinking fund sufficient for the retirement of the said road bonds as they shall mature;

(2) For the expense of the highway department and for the maintenance of roads and bridges constructed under the provisions of this chapter; and

(3) For the purchase of supplies and material, livestock and machinery, and any balance for the construction of roads and bridges.

(b) Annually, at such times as it may deem most convenient or suitable, the highway department shall, out of said revenues, set apart a sum sufficient for the providing of said sinking fund and for the further expenses of the highway department and the maintenance of roads and bridges, and the sum so set apart shall be used for no other purposes whatever. The proceeds of the sale of state road bonds and the moneys appropriated by congress under the act known as the federal aid law shall be used exclusively for the purpose of constructing highways and bridges and the acquisition of bridges and of material. (Code 1923, § 1318; Acts 1927, No. 347, p. 348; Code 1940, T. 23, § 15.)

Contract obligation is not subject to doctrine of sovereign immunity. — Once the highway department has legally contracted under state law for goods or services and accepts such goods or services, the highway department also becomes legally obligated to pay for the goods or services accepted in accordance with the terms of the contract; it follows that this obligation is not subject to the doctrine of sovereign immunity and is enforceable in the courts. State Hwy. Dep't v. Milton Constr. Co., 586 So. 2d 872 (Ala. 1991).

Collateral references. — 40 C.J.S., Highways, § 176.

§ 23-1-63. Limitation of obligations, etc., outstanding or authorized on inauguration date of incoming Governor.

The Director of the State Highway Department shall not, on the inauguration date of an incoming Governor, have outstanding obligations, encumbrances or commitments or shall have authorized the obligating, encumbering or committing of, except for debt service, any more than seven twenty-fourths of the total estimated revenue available to the State Highway Department for the first fiscal year of an incoming state administration. (Acts 1951, No. 609, p. 1053.)

ARTICLE 3.

PUBLIC ROADS, BRIDGES AND FERRIES.

§ 23-1-80. County commissions — Powers and duties generally.

The county commissions of the several counties of this state have general superintendence of the public roads, bridges and ferries within their respective counties so as to render travel over the same as safe and convenient as practicable. To this end, they have legislative and executive powers, except as limited in this chapter. They may establish, promulgate and enforce rules and regulations, make and enter into such contracts as may be necessary or as may be deemed necessary or advisable by such commissions to build, construct, make, improve and maintain a good system of public roads, bridges and ferries in their respective counties, and regulate the use thereof; but no contract for the construction or repair of any public roads, bridge or bridges shall be made where the payment of the contract price for such work shall extend over a period of more than 20 years. (Code 1923, § 1347; Acts 1927, No. 347, p. 348; Code 1940, T. 23, § 43; Acts 1953, No. 729, p. 984.)

I. General Consideration.
II. Powers.

I. GENERAL CONSIDERATION.

Grant of legislative powers under this section is valid. Floyd v. State, 15 Ala. App. 654, 74 So. 752 (1917); Windham v. State, 16 Ala. App. 383, 77 So. 963 (1918), and authorities cited.

"Public roads" defined. — "Public roads," over which the commissions are hereby given general superintendence, are not confined to public county roads, and it is proper for the county commission to appropriate county funds not otherwise set apart towards the partial payment of improvements of a town of the streets and sidewalks around a block occupied by county buildings. Town of Eutaw v. Coleman, 189 Ala. 164, 66 So. 464 (1914).

Determination of whether road is public or private. — A trial court's determination of whether a road is public or private might affect not only the rights of the individual litigants but also the but also the rights of members of the public to use the road, the duty of the county to maintain it, and the liability of the county for failure to maintain it; therefore, the county must be joined as a party, since if not joined, neither it nor other members of the public are bound by the trial court's ruling. Boles v. Autery, 554 So. 2d 959 (Ala. 1989).

Powers of county commissions with regard to public roads are prescribed in this section. Wright v. Pickens County, 268 Ala. 50, 104 So. 2d 907 (1958).

Standard of care in maintaining roadways. — Since a county can be sued for its negligence, and is exclusively responsible for the maintenance and control of its roadways, its standard of care is to keep its streets in a reasonably safe condition for travel, and to remedy defects in the roadway upon receipt of notice. Jefferson County v. Sulzby, 468 So. 2d 112 (Ala. 1985).

The correct standard is that a county keep a road in a reasonably safe condition for travel and that it remedy defects on receipt of notice of those defects. This standard applies to a public dirt road as well as to a paved metropolitan highway, and the customary absence of signs on dirt roads and the poor maintenance of dirt roads do not provide conclusive evidence of a lack of negligence in the present case. The standard to be applied is what reasonably should have been done, not what customarily is done. Macon County Comm'n v. Sanders, 555 So. 2d 1054 (Ala. 1990).

Section 11-8-10 does not prohibit warrants. — A county's governing body, under the provisions of this section, can contract for payment of the cost of constructing, improving and maintaining roads and bridges by issuing interest-bearing warrants payable solely out of the county's distributive part of the state gasoline tax, and such warrants are not prohibited by the County Financial Control Act, § 11-8-10. Taxpayers & Citizens v. Lawrence County, 273 Ala. 638, 143 So. 2d 813 (1962).

Interest on warrants. — This section does not define the limits in amount, or in the rate of interest of funding warrants. Bullock County v. Sherlock, 242 Ala. 262, 5 So. 2d 800 (1942).

Period for payment of contract for road improvement. — Where contract between the state and a county for improvement of highways, the cost of which was to be shared by county, stipulated for no payments by county on contract price over a period of more than 10 years, and no period was stipulated for completion of entire project, the law would define the contract to mean that project was to be completed within a reasonable time and this section placed a limit on such reasonable time and wrote into the contract an obligation of the state to complete the project so that stipulated payments by county would not extend over more than 10 (now 20) years and such contract was not prohibited by this section. Bullock County v. Sherlock, 242 Ala. 262, 5 So. 2d 800 (1942).

County commission's exercise of powers not subject to review by mandamus. — Absent an allegation of fraud, corruption, or unfair dealing on the part of the commission, the commission's exercise of the discretionary powers vested in it is not subject to judicial review by mandamus. Furthermore, mandamus is not proper where another adequate remedy exists. Barber v. Covington County Comm'n, 466 So. 2d 945 (Ala. 1985).

Where proceedings collaterally attacked. — The grant of powers under this section is general and plenary, and on collateral attack it is presumed that the proceedings of the county commission are regular. Floyd v. State, 15 Ala. App. 654, 74 So. 752 (1917).

Evidence upon collateral attack. — Upon a collateral attack on the action of the county commission, the minutes of the regular session of the county commission, in due form, are admissible in evidence. Floyd v. State, 15 Ala. App. 654, 74 So. 752 (1917).

Section 35-2-51(b) not repealed. — Section 11-3-10 and this section provide general authority of county commissions over roads and do not repeal the specific provision of § 35-2-51(b) by virtue of which recordation of a plat constitutes a dedication of the roads therein with no requirement of acceptance by any county governing authority. Blair v. Fullmer, 583 So. 2d 1307 (Ala. 1991).

Cited in Holifield v. Robinson, 79 Ala. 419 (1885); Kirby v. Court of Comm'rs, 186 Ala. 611, 65 So. 163 (1914); Rudolph v. City of Birmingham, 188 Ala. 620, 65 So. 1006 (1914); Craven v. State, 18 Ala. App. 48, 88 So. 457 (1921); State v. Kirkpatrick, 19 Ala. App. 50, 95 So. 490 (1922); Stone v. State ex rel. J.S. Walton & Co., 260 Ala. 363, 71 So. 2d 23 (1954); Opinion of the Justices, 263 Ala. 653, 83 So. 2d 714 (1955); Clark v. Marengo County, 469 F. Supp. 1150 (S.D. Ala. 1979); Cook v. County of St. Clair, 384 So. 2d 1 (Ala. 1980).

Collateral references. — 11 C.J.S., Bridges, §§ 12, 48.

II. POWERS.

Nature of power conferred. — This section does not confer authority to make a law, but only to provide rules under which the existing law can be efficiently and effectively administered. Terry v. State, 18 Ala. App. 333, 92 So. 85 (1921).

Extent of power. — A county's power to make contract for maintenance and construction of public roads and bridges within county is unlimited except such contract must not exceed period of time fixed by this section. Herbert v. Perry, 235 Ala. 71, 177 So. 561 (1937).

Act giving each county commissioner supervision of construction and maintenance of roads and bridges in his district did not transfer governmental powers of entire commission to levy and allocate road taxes, establish, change and discontinue roads, make contracts, adopt rules and regulations, etc., to each commissioner. Court of Comm'rs v. Johnson, 229 Ala. 417, 157 So. 481 (1934).

Statutory duties and powers of each county commissioner to supervise construction and maintenance of roads and bridges in his district held administrative and subordinate to and in aid of entire commission. Court of Comm'rs v. Johnson, 229 Ala. 417, 157 So. 481 (1934).

Orders of county commission, dividing one commissioner's district into two sections, employing foremen and workmen thereof, directing foremen to take charge of county's equipment and implements, declaring them responsible for road conditions in their sections and subject to court's orders and prohibiting commissioner from hiring extra help without commission's order, held within such commission's power and discretion. Court of Comm'rs v. Johnson, 229 Ala. 417, 157 So. 481 (1934).

The county commission has jurisdiction to order a road closed by railroad reopened and repaired. Alabama Great S.R.R. v. Denton, 239 Ala. 301, 195 So. 218 (1940).

County, acting through official board, had right to improve county highway for purpose of eliminating railroad grade crossing and to acquire necessary right-of-way by exercise of the power of eminent domain, and also had authority to enter into arrangement with state highway department to have such improvement work done by state. Sherlock v. Mobile County, 241 Ala. 247, 2 So. 2d 405 (1941).

It is well established that a large discretion is vested in the county governing bodies concerning the matter of public roads and bridges. Bentley v. County Comm'n, 264 Ala. 106, 84 So. 2d 490 (1955).

County commissioners have general superintendence over public roads. — This section confers upon county commissions of this state general superintendence of public roads within their respective jurisdictions so as to render travel over the same safe and convenient. To this end, they have certain discretionary powers as enumerated in this section. Barber v. Covington County Comm'n, 466 So. 2d 945 (Ala. 1985).

And counties are under duty to keep streets in safe condition. — Governmental entities, by virtue of their exclusive authority to maintain and control the roadways, are under a common-law duty to keep the streets in repair and in a reasonably safe condition for their intended use. Jefferson County v. Sulzby, 468 So. 2d 112 (Ala. 1985).

When exercise of power may be restrained or reviewed. — The exercise of the discretionary power of the commissions cannot be restrained or reviewed unless it has been in a fraudulent, corrupt or unfair conduct of the business of the county. Ensley Motor Co. v. O'Rear, 196 Ala. 481, 71 So. 704 (1916); Bentley v. County Comm'n, 264 Ala. 106, 84 So. 2d 490 (1955); Wright v. Pickens County, 268 Ala. 50, 104 So. 2d 907 (1958).

The action of a county governing body, in the exercise of discretionary powers vested in it, is not subject to judicial review except for fraud, corruption or unfair dealings. Taxpayers & Citizens v. Lawrence County, 273 Ala. 638, 143 So. 2d 813 (1962).

Duties of commission under fourteenth amendment. — Where there has been a city and county cooperative funding for city paving and the county commission has contributed with the understanding that its funds would be utilized for street paving in predominantly black areas within the city, relief of lack of paving in such areas does not discharge the county commissioners from their duties in the county under the equal protection clause of the fourteenth amendment. Selmont Imp. Ass'n v. Dallas County Comm'n, 339 F. Supp. 477 (S.D. Ala. 1972).

Prima facie case of racial discrimination in street paving shown. — See Selmont Imp. Ass'n v. Dallas County Comm'n, 339 F. Supp. 477 (S.D. Ala. 1972).

Purchase of automobile. — It is within the authority of the county commission to purchase and maintain an automobile for the purpose of inspecting the roads and bridges of a county. Ensley Motor Co. v. O'Rear, 196 Ala. 481, 71 So. 704 (1916).

Counties may issue interest-bearing bonds to road contractor for construction of public roads and bridges within county, which bonds mature within period prescribed by this section. Herbert v. Perry, 235 Ala. 71, 177 So. 561 (1937).

Such warrants may be sold at either a public or private sale. Burleson v. Court of County Comm'rs, 235 Ala. 576, 180 So. 572 (1938).

Such right not prohibited by the Constitution. — Proposed interest-bearing county warrants payable out of gasoline fund derived monthly from state issued for construction of public highway do not fall within inhibitions of Constitution. Herbert v. Perry, 235 Ala. 71, 177 So. 561 (1937). See also Bentley v. County Comm'n, 264 Ala. 106, 84 So. 2d 490 (1955).

May finance road construction by issuing interest-bearing revenue warrants. — This section confers on counties generally the power to finance road construction by the issuance of interest-bearing revenue warrants to be secured by and payable out of the revenue from a license tax without special legislation. Rollings v. Marshall County, 263 Ala. 317, 82 So. 2d 428 (1955).

Erection of bridge between counties. — The expense of erecting a bridge on the line of two counties cannot be forced on one county without the consent of its county commission. The bridge in such case becomes necessary only when declared to be so by the judgment of both counties. Pickens County v. Greene County, 171 Ala. 377, 54 So. 998 (1911).

Acts not within powers granted by this section. — This section does not authorize a county to employ assistant counsel in a criminal prosecution, although the validity of a road law is involved therein. Walker v. Bridgforth, 9 Ala. App. 257, 62 So. 323 (1913).

§ 23-1-81. County commissions — Authority to purchase or establish bridges, ferries and causeways.

The county commission of each county is invested with authority to purchase or establish toll bridges, free bridges, causeways and ferries or free ferries within their respective jurisdictions as provided in this article and may levy a special tax to purchase or build such bridges and causeways when, in the opinion of such county commission, the public good requires it. (Code 1852, § 1189; Code 1867, § 1381; Code 1876, § 1678; Code 1886, § 1442; Code 1896, § 2498; Code 1907, § 3023; Code 1923, § 6442; Code 1940, T. 23, § 45.)

May erect bridges on private roads. — This section does not restrict the power of the commissioners to erect bridges. They may erect bridges on private ways, and the county is liable for injuries caused by defects in such bridges. Barks v. Jefferson County, 119 Ala. 600, 24 So. 505 (1898).

Liability of operator of ferry for injuries. — The operator of a public ferry, owned by a county, is not liable for injuries arising because of failure of the county to provide a barrier for the sides of the ferry. The operator is liable only for his own negligence. Hilburn v. McKinney, 204 Ala. 158, 85 So. 496 (1920).

Cited in Hill v. Averett, 27 Ala. 484 (1855); Barbour County v. Horn, 48 Ala. 566 (1872); Barbour County v. Horn, 48 Ala. 649 (1872); Collins v. Ewing, 51 Ala. 101 (1874); Meriwether v. Lowndes County, 89 Ala. 362, 7 So. 198 (1890).

Collateral references. — 39 C.J.S., Highways, § 39.

§ 23-1-82. County commissions — Eminent domain.

The county commissions of the several counties of the state are given the right of eminent domain for the purpose of establishing and changing public roads, bridges and ferries in their respective counties, except in cases where the highway department has jurisdiction over such highways. When an appeal is taken from any assessment in a condemnation proceeding brought by a county, such appeal shall not deprive the county obtaining the judgment of condemnation of a right of entry for any and all purposes named in the condemnation proceeding provided the amount of damages assessed shall have been paid into court in money and a bond shall have been given in not less than double the amount of damages assessed, with good and sufficient sureties, to be approved by the clerk of the court to which the appeal is taken, conditioned to pay such damages as the owner of the property may sustain. Said amount of damages may be paid into court and said bond in double the amount of such damages, with good and sufficient sureties, may be given at the time of taking the appeal or at any time thereafter that the applicant may desire the right of entry pending the appeal; provided, however, that in condemnation proceedings in which any county having a population of 400,000 inhabitants or more, according to the last or any subsequent federal census, is a party and where an appeal is taken, such county shall have the immediate right of entry pending said appeal as if a good and sufficient right of entry bond had been filed. (Code 1907, §§ 5773-5776; Code 1923, § 1352; Acts 1927, No. 347, p. 348; Code 1940, T. 23, § 44; Acts 1953, No. 595, p. 847.)

Cross references. — As to eminent domain generally, see § 18-1A-1 et seq.

Section satisfies requirement of Constitution 1901, section 235. — By the terms of this section the condemnor need not make an election at the time he or the landowner appeals from the judgment of condemnation entered by the probate court. The condemnor may appeal, and at a later date elect to enter the property and at that time, the time of entry, pay the amount of damages into court and file his bond in double the amount of damages. Constitution 1901, § 235 is satisfied by such a provision because that section merely requires payment and bond before entry. Opinion of the Justices, 259 Ala. 524, 67 So. 2d 417 (1953). See note to Constitution, § 235.

Section applies to pending litigation. — A statute granting the condemnor the right of entry for the first time pending an appeal is remedial only, and the Constitution does not prohibit such statutes from applying to pending litigation. Opinion of the Justices, 259 Ala. 524, 67 So. 2d 417 (1953).

And does not impair obligation of contracts. — The object of the 1953 amendment was to provide means equitable and just to all parties, whereby a person or corporation entitled to exercise the rights of eminent domain could enter into possession of the property condemned and without being compelled to await the delay resulting from litigation in cases of appeal from such award. The statute affects the mode of putting the award into effect, and, therefor, only affects the remedy. The courts generally hold that remedies are subject to legislative control, and so long as an ample remedy is furnished, the obligation of contracts is not impaired by any change of the remedy. So long as there remains a right to condemn private property, the substantive rights remain the same and changes in matters of procedure, whether by amendment or new acts, do not affect the substantive right, or perhaps more properly speaking, the right given by a substantive law. Opinion of the Justices, 259 Ala. 524, 67 So. 2d 417 (1953).

Nor deprive condemnee of any vested right. — When the legislature authorized the condemnor to enter at any time pending an appeal, upon the payment of damages and the execution of bond, the defendant in pending condemnation proceedings was not deprived of any vested right or of any cause of action or defense within the meaning of Constitution

1901, § 95. Opinion of the Justices, 259 Ala. 524, 67 So. 2d 417 (1953).

Statutes providing for the right of entry pending appeal upon the payment of damages or the execution of bond are upheld by the courts upon the theory that when the government or other entity having the right of eminent domain has the damages assessed in a preliminary manner either by viewers or a jury that the only remaining right which is vested in the landowner is the right to receive just compensation and damages. The very essence of the power of eminent domain is the right of the sovereign or its agents to divest the landowner of his property and to take away from the landowner his vested rights to possess the property. On the other hand, the vested right of the landowner is to demand the payment of adequate compensation and damages. It is readily concluded that this section does not deprive the landowner of his substantial vested right, his right to receive just compensation and damages prior to entry. Opinion of the Justices, 259 Ala. 524, 67 So. 2d 417 (1953).

Cited in Thompson v. State, 21 Ala. 48 (1852); Ex parte Keenan, 21 Ala. 558 (1852); Sultzner v. State, 43 Ala. 24 (1869); Goodwin v. McConnell, 187 Ala. 431, 65 So. 788 (1914); Calhoun County v. Logan, 262 Ala. 586, 80 So. 2d 529 (1955).

Collateral references. — Eminent domain: deduction of benefits in determining compensation or damages in proceedings involving opening, widening, or otherwise altering highway. 13 ALR3d 1149.

§ 23-1-83. Transfer of general fund surplus to road fund by county.

The county commission of any county in this state may transfer to the road fund of the county any surplus of the general funds of the county in the county treasury or any part of such surplus whenever, in the judgment of such commission, it will promote the interest of the county to make such transfer. Any surplus of the general fund so transferred shall be used only for the working of the public roads or the building of bridges or otherwise improving the roads of such counties. (Code 1907, § 5766; Code 1923, § 1351; Acts 1927, No. 347, p. 348; Code 1940, T. 23, § 47.)

When transfer not justified. — A transfer of a portion of the general fund to the road fund cannot be justified under this section where the county is much indebted, and there are warrants having priority unpaid. Rhodes v. Marengo County Bank, 205 Ala. 667, 88 So. 850 (1921).

Cited in County of Montgomery v. City of Montgomery, 190 Ala. 366, 67 So. 311 (1914).

§ 23-1-84. Authority of county to expend funds derived from fees, etc., levied on vehicles and fuels.

(a) The several counties of the state are hereby authorized to expend the funds derived from fees, excises or license taxes levied by the state relating to the registration, operation or use of motor vehicles upon the public highways, and also the money derived from any fees, excises or license taxes levied by the state relating to fuels used for propelling such vehicles, for the cost of constructing, reconstructing, maintaining and repairing of public roads and bridges.

(b) It is the intention of the legislature by the passage of this section to implement the provisions of Amendment 93 to the Constitution of Alabama 1901.

(c) The provisions of this section are retroactive. (Acts 1959, 1st Ex. Sess., No. 50, p. 95.)

§ 23-1-85. Construction of electric transmission, telegraph or telephone lines in right-of-way of county highways.

The right-of-way is granted to any person or corporation having the right to construct electric transmission, telegraph or telephone lines within this state to construct them along the margin of the right-of-way of public highways, subject to the removal or change by the county commission of the county, except in cases where the highway department has jurisdiction over such highway. (Code 1907, § 5817; Code 1923, § 1357; Acts 1927, No. 347, p. 348; Code 1940, T. 23, § 48.)

Streets of a city are "highways" within the meaning of this section and a telephone company may construct its lines along such highways. Southern Bell Tel. & Tel. Co. v. City of Mobile, 162 F. 523 (S.D. Ala. 1907).

And such right-of-way constitutes an easement and as such cannot be deprived except by due process of law. Southern Bell Tel. & Tel. Co. v. City of Mobile, 162 F. 523 (S.D. Ala. 1907).

But right herein given does not give the right to intrude poles into that part of the road set apart and dedicated to the use of the traveling public. Gilbert v. Southern Bell Tel. & Tel. Co., 200 Ala. 3, 75 So. 315 (1917). But see Town of New Decatur v. American Tel. & Tel. Co., 176 Ala. 492, 58 So. 613 (1912), to the effect that this section was not intended to include streets of city.

"Along the margin of the right-of-way" refers to the space between the traveled part of the roadway and edge of the right-of-way, not to the fixed outer line delimiting the right-of-way. Studdard v. South Cent. Bell Tel., 356 So. 2d 139 (Ala. 1978).

Not applicable to railroad property. — This section does not give an easement along the right-of-way of a railroad, since it is apparent that "public highways" is meant to embrace only public roads. Louisville & N.R.R. v. Western Union Tel. Co., 195 Ala. 124, 71 So. 118 (1915), expressly overruling Western Union Tel. Co. v. South & N.A.R.R., 184 Ala. 66, 62 So. 788 (1913).

Collateral references. — 39 C.J.S., Highways, § 139.

§ 23-1-86. Establishment, etc., within municipalities.

The county commission of any county, with the consent or permission of the city council or governing body of any municipality, may establish, construct and maintain any road, street or bridge within the corporate limits of such municipality except in cases where the highway department has jurisdiction over such road, street or bridge. (Code 1923, § 1367; Acts 1927, No. 347, p. 348; Code 1940, T. 23, § 49.)

§ 23-1-87. Expense of building county line bridges, ferries or causeways.

Whenever a bridge, ferry or causeway is necessary on the line between two counties, the same must be built at the joint expense of such counties, in proportion to the amount of taxable property in each. When the cost of building any county line bridges is so great that it cannot be paid by the counties which such stream divides, which fact may be determined by the county commission of either county, such counties, or either of them, may make such contracts and incur such debt as may be necessary, within constitutional limits, to procure for the use of such counties, or either of them, or the inhabitants thereof, the free use of a thoroughfare for vehicles and foot passengers over or across any bridge that may be built by any person, firm or corporation over any stream forming the dividing line between such counties; and to pay any debt that may be thereby incurred, any county may issue its bonds when such issue is authorized by vote as required by law. A county line bridge or ferry, in the meaning of this section, shall be construed to be a bridge or ferry across a stream or slough between two counties whether the actual dividing line between said counties runs on either bank or in the center of said stream or slough. If a toll bridge, ferry or causeway is in operation on any such line, the same may be purchased by either county alone or at the joint expense of the counties connected thereby, in proportion to the taxable property in each. (Code 1852, § 1190; Code 1867, § 1382; Code 1876, § 1679; Code 1886, § 1443; Code 1896, § 2499; Code 1907, § 3025; Acts 1915, No. 677, p. 736; Code 1923, § 6444; Code 1940, T. 23, § 50.)

Both counties must concur. — When read in connection with statutes in pari materia, and in the light of the general scheme for local government through county organizations, it seems to be entirely clear that this section contemplates the concurrence of the judgments of the county commissions of the two counties interested, and that neither can act independently of the other. Therefore, a bridge over a stream dividing two counties becomes necessary within the meaning of this section only when it has been declared by the concurring judgment of the commissions of both counties to be necessary, after which the effect of the statute is to fix the proportions in which the expenses involved shall be borne. Pickens County v. Greene County, 171 Ala. 377, 54 So. 998 (1911).

Collateral references. — 11 C.J.S., Bridges, § 36.

§ 23-1-88. Facilities between adjoining counties — Authority of counties to build, establish, etc.

Adjoining counties may purchase, establish, build, maintain and operate bridges and ferries or public highways across streams, swamps, waters or marshes which form the boundary between two counties upon such terms as may be agreed upon by the county commissions of the adjoining counties. (Acts 1920, No. 98, p. 146; Code 1923, § 6461; Code 1940, T. 23, § 51.)

§ 23-1-89. Facilities between adjoining counties — Extension of aid by other counties.

The county commission of any county in the state that will be benefited by the establishment of such means of communication as are set forth in Section 23-1-88 may also extend aid in the purchase, establishment, construction and maintenance of such means of communication, although no part of such bridges, highways or ferries may be located in such county. The county commission of any county is made the sole judge as to whether the county would be benefited by the bridge, ferry or other improvement as is provided for in this article. (Acts 1920, No. 98, p. 146; Code 1923, § 6462; Code 1940, T. 23, § 52.)

§ 23-1-90. Extension of aid by municipalities.

The governing authority of any municipality that would be benefited by the purchase, establishment, construction or maintenance of the bridges, causeways, highways or ferries, or combination of same, mentioned in this article may extend aid to the establishment, construction or maintenance of the same. (Acts 1920, No. 98, p. 146; Code 1923, § 6463; Code 1940, T. 23, § 53.)

§ 23-1-91. Aid for development of access roads or bridges to certain facilities by contiguous counties or municipalities.

The county commission of any county or governing body of any municipality in this state is hereby authorized, upon the adoption by a majority vote of a resolution duly recorded in its minutes, to aid and participate in the development of any access roads or bridges to any project undertaken by any public athletic or recreational board for the promotion of athletics, recreation, race tracks and related facilities in any other contiguous county or in aid of the development in any other contiguous county or any industrial site or access roads and bridges of any project undertaken pursuant to the provisions of Sections 11-54-80 through 11-54-101 or pursuant to Sections 11-54-20 through 11-54-32. In any county, including the county in which said project is located, the county commission may appropriate county funds or authorize the use of equipment and employees of the county to aid in the promotion of any project which comes within the purview of this section, and any municipal governing body may likewise appropriate municipal funds or authorize the use of equipment and employees of the municipality to aid in the promotion of any such project. (Acts 1967, Ex. Sess., No. 120, p. 173.)

§ 23-1-92. Advertisement for contract bids — Requirement.

No contract where the estimated cost of the work will exceed $250.00 shall be made except after advertisement for 30 days in some newspaper published in the county, describing the character of the work to be done and the time and place of letting, and then only to the lowest reasonable and responsible bidder for such work, who shall enter into bond in double the amount of such bid, conditioned for the proper performance of such contract according to the plans and specifications and within the time prescribed by the order of the county commission of such work, which bond shall be approved by the judge of probate of said county. Where the estimated cost of the work exceeds $2,500.00, advertisement as above must also be made in a daily paper published in this state of at least 5,000 daily circulation once a week for 30 days. The county commission shall have the right to reject any or all bids. (Code 1923, § 1361; Acts 1927, No. 347, p. 348; Code 1940, T. 23, § 54.)

Section operative where not in conflict with special or local law. — The provisions of this section are operative in all cases within their purview where they are not in conflict with an existing special or local law applicable to the county concerned. State v. Fourth Nat'l Bank, 270 Ala. 135, 117 So. 2d 145 (1959).

Enforcement of noncomplying contract

may be enjoined. — The enforcement of a contract for the construction of roads entered into without a compliance with the provisions of this section may be enjoined. State v. Fourth Nat'l Bank, 270 Ala. 135, 117 So. 2d 145 (1959).

But contractor may recover on contract or quantum meruit despite irregularity. — Where a contract is not within the corporate power, expressly prohibited by law or violative of public policy, no recovery may be had by a contractor or a furnisher of supplies or materials to a public agency either on express contract or quantum meruit, but where the power to contract lies within the competence of the city or county, and there has been an irregular exercise of that power, recovery may be had although the express contract is void. State v. Fourth Nat'l Bank, 270 Ala. 135, 117 So. 2d 145 (1959).

Cited in Kimbrell v. State, 272 Ala. 419, 132 So. 2d 132 (1961).

Collateral references. — 11 C.J.S., Bridges, § 20. 40 C.J.S., Highways, § 208.

65 Am. Jur. 2d, Public Works & Contracts, §§ 53-62.

Liability of municipality to contractor for mistake in estimates prepared by municipal officers or employees. 16 ALR 1131.

Conspiracy or combination to prevent actual competition in bids for public works as affecting contract for the work or recovery therefor. 62 ALR 224.

Variation by bidder from specifications on bid for public works. 65 ALR 835.

Evasion of law requiring contract for public work to be let to lowest responsible bidder by subsequent changes in contract after it has been awarded pursuant to that law. 69 ALR 697.

Right to require bid on unit basis, with reservation to public authorities of right to determine amount or extent of work. 79 ALR 225.

Mandamus to compel consideration, acceptance or rejection of bids. 80 ALR 1382.

Fact that bidder furnishes bond, as affecting right to award contract to one other than lowest financial bidder. 86 ALR 131.

What is covered by term "work," in statute relating to bids for public contracts. 92 ALR 835.

Alternation of plans or materials as necessary or proper factor in proposal for or acceptance of bids. 96 ALR 712.

Change in proposals for public contract after submission of bids as justification for withdrawal of bid or refusal to enter into contract. 104 ALR 1149.

Labor conditions or relations as factor in determining whether public contract should be let to lowest bidder. 110 ALR 1406.

Right or duty of public authorities to require single bid or to let single contract for entire improvement or for two or more separate improvements. 123 ALR 577.

Statute requiring competitive bidding for public contract as affecting validity of agreement, subsequent to the award of a contract, to allow the contractor additional compensation for extras or additional labor and material not included in the written contract. 135 ALR 1265.

Differences in character or quality of materials, articles, or works as affecting acceptance of bids for public contracts. 27 ALR2d 917.

Determination of amount involved in contract within statutory provision requiring public contracts involving sums exceeding specified amount to be let to lowest bidder. 53 ALR2d 498.

Revocation, prior to execution of formal written contract, of vote or decision of public body awarding contract to bidder. 3 ALR3d 864.

Liability of municipality on quasi contract for value of property or work furnished without compliance with bidding requirements. 33 ALR3d 1164.

Right of bidder for state or municipal contract to rescind bid on ground that bid was based upon his own mistake or that of his employee. 2 ALR4th 991.

Public contracts: Authority of State or its subdivision to reject all bids. 52 ALR4th 186.

§ 23-1-93. Advertisement for contract bids — Exceptions.

In the event of the destruction of a bridge, or damage thereto, rendering the same impassable, or in any other emergency, the county commission may contract for the repair or rebuilding of such bridge without advertisement if the public good requires it, except in cases where the highway department has jurisdiction over such bridges. (Code 1923, § 1362; Acts 1927, No. 347, p. 348; Code 1940, T. 23, § 55.)

Collateral references. — 11 C.J.S., Bridges, § 40.

65 Am. Jur. 2d, Public Works & Contracts, § 39.

What is emergency, within statutory provision accepting emergency contract or work from requirement of bidding on public contracts. 71 ALR 173.

§ 23-1-94. Construction of article not to conflict with local or special laws.

Nothing in this article shall be construed to authorize the county commissions of the several counties to establish, promulgate or enforce any rules, regulations or laws which may be in conflict with a local or special law providing for the working, maintenance, change, discontinuance or improvement of the public roads, bridges or ferries of such county now in force or which may hereafter be enacted, except in cases where the highway department has jurisdiction over such highways. (Code 1923, § 1348; Acts 1927, No. 347, p. 348; Code 1940, T. 23, § 64.)

§ 23-1-95. Violation of rules, etc., enacted by county commissions.

No person shall violate any rule, regulation or law which may be adopted or promulgated by the county commission of any county under the authority conferred by this article relating to the use, control, care, operation or maintenance of any such public road, bridge or ferry, except in cases where the highway department has jurisdiction over such highways. (Code 1923, § 1349; Acts 1927, No. 347, p. 348; Code 1940, T. 23, § 61.)

ARTICLE 3A.

ROADS AND BRIDGES IN CAPTIVE COUNTIES.

§ 23-1-100. "Captive county" defined.

Unless different meanings are expressly specified in subsequent provisions of this article the term "captive county" means a county where the state highway department by local law or general law with local application is responsible for the construction, repair and maintenance of the roads and bridges of the respective county. (Acts 1979, No. 79-688, p. 1217, § 1.)

§ 23-1-101. Powers and duties of county commissions of captive counties as to construction, repair and maintenance of county roads and bridges generally.

The county commission of each of the captive counties shall be solely responsible for the construction, repair and maintenance of the county roads and bridges in its respective county in accordance with the laws of the State of Alabama. Each county governing body shall have all the powers and jurisdiction with respect to county roads and bridges which are or which hereafter may be vested in or required of county governing bodies by the general laws of this state, or vested in or required of the governing body of each of the captive counties by local law and, except as may be otherwise provided herein, members of the county governing bodies of the captive counties shall perform all the duties and services and shall exercise all the powers and authority with respect to construction, repair or maintenance of county roads and bridges which are or hereafter may be provided by law for members of county governing bodies. (Acts 1979, No. 79-688, p. 1217, § 2.)

Collateral references. — Liability, in motor vehicle-related cases, of governmental entity for injury or death resulting from design, construction, or failure to warn of narrow bridge. 2 ALR4th 635.

§ 23-1-102. Transfer to counties of unexpended funds maintained by State Highway Department; payment to counties of tax proceeds, federal aid accruals, etc.

Any unexpended moneys remaining in the fund required by law to be maintained by the State Highway Department for use in the construction, repair and maintenance of county roads and bridges in each of the captive counties shall be paid over to the respective governing body of each of the captive counties except as otherwise provided by this article. Thereafter, all funds and moneys designated by law for use in the construction, repair and maintenance of county roads and bridges in each of the captive counties and to which each of said counties may be entitled, whether from the proceeds of the state gasoline tax, the motor vehicle tax or other state tax, federal aid accruals or from any other source whatsoever shall be paid to the county governing body of the respective captive county by the appropriate county or state official. (Acts 1979, No. 79-688, p. 1217, § 3.)

§ 23-1-103. Transfer to counties by highway department of facilities and properties for construction, repair and maintenance of roads; resolution of disputes as to transfers.

The State Highway Department shall transfer and turn over to the governing body of each of the captive counties adequate facilities and properties to build, maintain and repair roads in said county from equipment presently being used by the State Highway Department in carrying out the functions and duties in relation to roads and bridges in each of said captive counties respective and/or from surplus equipment returned to the state from other counties also, but not limited to road equipment, machinery and supplies of like kind, amount, nature and present value as of 1979 to the respective road equipment, machinery and supplies which each of the captive counties was required to transfer and turn over to the State Highway Department in accordance with the legislation enacted prior to the adoption of this article, which legislation required the State Highway Department to construct, repair and maintain roads and bridges in each of the captive counties.

Any dispute which may arise as a result of this section shall be resolved by the majority of the members of a committee consisting of the Highway

Director or his agent, the chairman of the county governing body of the respective county or his agent and one member from the legislative delegation of the respective county to be selected by the legislative delegation. (Acts 1979, No. 79-688, p. 1217, § 4.)

§ 23-1-104. **Furnishing of counties with lists of persons employed by highway department therein; employment by counties of persons on lists; employment status of other persons employed by department in counties; liability for accumulated obligations due and payable to present employees of department; payment by department of accumulated sick leave of transferred employee.**

The State Highway Department shall furnish a list to each captive county with the name, position, rate of pay and length of service of all persons who are presently employed by the State Highway Department in the respective captive county. The respective counties may employ personnel not to exceed 75 percent of the employees on the list furnished by the State Highway Department for the construction, repair and maintenance of county roads and bridges in accordance with personnel policy as adopted by the respective counties. The remaining employees now employed by the State Highway Department in each said county shall remain an employee of the State Highway Department subject to the regular employment practices of said department. All persons employed by each respective county shall be paid at the same rate of pay as was paid by the State Highway Department. All present and accumulated obligations due and payable to the present employees as a result of their employment with the State Highway Department shall be the obligation of the State of Alabama, including but not limited to, accumulated sick leave, vacation time and retirement and any other accumulated benefits earned by the said employees. Payment shall be made to the employees on or before the effective date of this article. Provided, however, that the State Highway Department shall pay to the respective county governing body an amount equal to 100 percent of the value of the accumulated sick leave for the account of each employee who transfers to the captive county. Such funds shall be held in trust for the employee and shall be used to pay such employee for approved sick leave. In lieu of the funds being held in trust for future approved sick leave, the employee may elect to accept an amount equal to 50 percent of the value of the then accumulated sick leave in full settlement and payment of his accrued sick leave account. Approved sick leave shall be that leave so designated by any county merit system to which the employee may transfer, or such leave as approved by the county governing body, or the county engineer at the direction of the county governing body. (Acts 1979, No. 79-688, p. 1217, § 5; Acts 1980, No. 80-724, p. 1466.)

1980 amendment constitutional. — Where the new substantive rights created by the amendment have any prospective field of operation, the amendment is constitutionally sound. By the same token, Ala. Const., §§ 22 and 95 prohibit retroactive application of the amendment. Kemp v. Britt, 410 So. 2d 31 (Ala. 1982).

"Obligations" include sick leave benefits. — Such benefits, are "due and payable" upon an employee's transfer; such benefits are not a continuing obligation of the state, payable for such leave taken by an employee or upon his retirement pursuant to § 36-26-36. Kemp v. Britt, 410 So. 2d 31 (Ala. 1982).

Effect of this section is to create substantive rights not mere remedial effects in employees who choose to transfer to the new highway departments of the various, heretofore "captive," counties. Kemp v. Britt, 410 So. 2d 31 (Ala. 1982).

1980 amendment created option regarding payment of accumulated benefits. —

Under the terms of the 1979 "pre-amendment" legislation, payment for accumulated employee benefits was to be made to the employees. The 1980 Act, however, provided for an option to be exercised by each transferring employee: the payment of 100 percent of the employee's accrued sick leave benefits to the county to which he or she transferred, or payment of 50 percent of "the value of the then accumulated sick leave in full settlement and payment of his accrued sick leave account." This right of option was a creation of the 1980 amendment and is a substantive right in the affected employees — a right which is materially less than the right created by the 1979 Act. Kemp v. Britt, 410 So. 2d 31 (Ala. 1982).

Accumulated sick leave obligation of state. — Accumulated sick leave benefits due and payable to employees of the state highway department shall be the obligation of the state of Alabama. Kemp v. Britt, 410 So. 2d 31 (Ala. 1982).

§ 23-1-105. Effect of article upon contracts for construction, repair and maintenance of county roads and bridges entered into by highway department.

Any contract for the construction, repair and maintenance of county roads and bridges in each of the captive counties entered into by the State Highway Department prior to the adoption of this article shall remain in full force and effect until the terms thereof shall have been complied with. (Acts 1979, No. 79-688, p. 1217, § 6.)

§ 23-1-106. Effect of article upon outstanding financial obligations incurred by counties; disposition of funds received by state from counties for road and bridge work therein.

All outstanding financial obligations which were incurred prior to the adoption of this article for the construction, repair or maintenance of county roads and bridges in each of the captive counties shall, upon adoption of this article, become outstanding financial obligations of the respective captive county and shall be retired or paid in accordance with the terms under which such indebtedness was incurred.

All funds, including escrow funds, received by the state from the respective captive counties to be used for road and bridge work in the respective counties, after payment of current obligations of said counties, respectively, shall be returned to each of said counties, respectively. (Acts 1979, No. 79-688, p. 1217, § 7.)

§ 23-1-107. Effective date.

This article after its passage and approval by the governor, or upon its otherwise becoming state law shall become effective October 1, 1979, or October 1, 1980, at the discretion of the individual county commissions. (Acts 1979, No. 79-688, p. 1217, § 10.)

ARTICLE 4.

MUNICIPAL CONNECTING LINK ROADS.

§ 23-1-110. Purpose of article.

It is hereby declared by the Legislature of Alabama that city and town streets and roads or portions thereof, including viaducts and bridges, which constitute the route of connection between or extension of state roads in the Alabama state highway system, hereby designated as municipal connecting link roads, have in the past, do now and will in the future serve a state purpose and are for the general benefit of the state; and that it is a proper and legitimate function of the state to designate such municipal connecting link roads and to provide for the cost and manner and extent of maintenance, repair, construction and reconstruction of the same by the state independently or in cooperation with the city or town involved. (Acts 1949, No. 284, p. 408, § 1.)

Cited in Johnson v. City of Opelika, 260 Ala. 551, 71 So. 2d 793 (1954).

§ 23-1-111. Designation.

The State Highway Department, hereinafter referred to as the department, shall, as early as practicable after July 26, 1949, designate such streets or roads, including viaducts and bridges, as are municipal connecting link roads in each city or town of this state under the then existing state highway system and, thereafter, shall designate such municipal connecting link roads for additional state roads in the state highway system at the time such roads are opened for travel. Such designation shall also be made promptly of any street or road in any city or town not constituting a part or portion of the state highway system wherever necessary to care for arterial or main highway traffic, and the provisions of this article shall apply to such streets or roads so designated. The department shall keep a record of such municipal connecting link roads so designated and shall promptly, after designation in each case, furnish to the city or town involved a statement of the municipal connecting link roads so designated therein. (Acts 1949, No. 284, p. 408, § 2.)

§ 23-1-112. Maintenance and repair — Responsibility.

The department is hereby authorized, empowered, directed and required to maintain and repair, under its control and supervision, such designated municipal connecting link roads, to make appropriations and expenditures out of its funds for such program and is authorized to enter into any and all contracts, inclusive of agreements with cities and towns, and with any federal agency of the United States of America authorized to do so, for such purpose; provided, that nothing contained in this section shall require the department to sweep, sprinkle or light said municipal link roads. (Acts 1949, No. 284, p. 408, § 3.)

Cited in Johnson v. City of Opelika, 260 Ala. 551, 71 So. 2d 793 (1954).

Collateral references. — 63 C.J.S., Municipal Corporations, § 1044.

Governmental tort liability for injury to roller skater allegedly caused by sidewalk or street defects. 58 ALR4th 1197.

§ 23-1-113. Maintenance and repair — Stipulations and conditions.

The following stipulations and conditions shall obtain as to state maintenance of municipal connecting link roads:

(1) State maintenance of a city or town street traversed by a state maintained highway route shall not extend beyond the back of the curb where a curb and gutter section exists and not beyond the back or roadway ditch or the toe of fill slope where no curb and gutter is in place except as necessary in the placing and maintaining of highway markers, etc.

(2) The city or town shall prepare a drawing, from which prints can be made, showing width of right-of-way of street traversed by a highway route maintained by the state and it shall indicate thereon the width of right-of-way on intersecting streets for a distance of 200 feet each way from the center of the highway.

(3) City or town to perform routine clean-up operations such as removal of leaves, trash, soil from gutters, soil from drop inlets and catch basins, etc., and shall be responsible for the trimming and maintenance of all trees and shrubbery within the right-of-way of the street or that affects traffic using the highway.

(4) The state will place and maintain center stripes and lane stripes. The city or town will mark parking spaces, bus stop areas and other markings outside the travel lanes.

(5) The city or town will be responsible for all drainage that enters the city's or town's storm sewer system, including all catch basins, sand traps, drop inlets and such. The state shall perform normal routine maintenance on roadway drainage structures not a part of the city or town storm sewer system, but the state shall assume no responsibility for a general drainage problem. In the correction of a drainage problem where the roadway structure is affected, the state will assume its fair share of the cost of any correction of opening needed in the roadway structure.

(6) Traffic control on a city or town street maintained in part by the state shall be under the joint control of the city and the state.

(7) The establishing of speed zones and the placing of traffic lights shall be subject to joint approval of the city or town and the state officials. After city or town and state representatives have decided on the speed to apply and the extent of speed zones, they shall be set out in city or town ordinances and the state will furnish, erect and maintain speed zone markers. After city or town and state representatives have agreed on the need for a traffic light and the type of light has been agreed on, the city will furnish, erect and maintain the light. The time interval of the light shall favor traffic along the highway route or traffic along the intersecting city or town street according to relative volume and importance, and when necessary or desirable, the point shall be settled by the taking of a traffic count. Should the city or town or the state question the need for an existing or proposed speed zone or traffic light, the question shall be settled in conference as provided.

(8) The city or town shall have authority to make any repairs to city or town facilities underground or overhead without asking permission of the state, but they shall notify the state immediately should that work affect the free flow of traffic. The city or town shall repair, in a manner satisfactory to the state, any pavement disturbed in any work they do. Any addition to city or town facilities, where the work of installation and maintenance would affect that part of the city street maintained by the state, shall be planned after conference with state officials, and the details of the plans shall be worked out in that conference. Any work that affects that part of a city street maintained by the state and to be performed by other than city forces shall be done only after a permit has been issued by the state. Such permits shall be subject to approval by the city or town.

(9) No permit shall be issued by the city or town or the state for any advertising sign to be suspended over the street and highway. The city or town shall have the right to permit the placing of any sign or marker, with or without written permit, so long as the sign does not interfere with highway markers or other traffic-control devices and provided they do not overhang the curb, in a curb and gutter section, or the shoulder line of the roadway where no curb and gutter exists. The only exceptions shall be signs to be erected by the city or town or civic organizations, with the approval of the city or town, that are temporary in nature and are intended to give information to the general public. In such cases, a formal permit, approved by both the state and the city, shall be issued for erection by other than city or town forces or forces employed by the city or town, and those signs shall not interfere with traffic or confuse or obscure traffic-control devices or markings.

(10) Where maintenance operations require it or make it desirable, the city or town police will provide protection for state forces and equipment and will cooperate in the handling of traffic should it be necessary to close all or part of the highway route.

(11) The state shall have no responsibility for the maintenance of "truck routes" where such routes are separate from regularly established highway routes. (Acts 1949, No. 284, p. 408, § 4.)

State exempt from maintenance beyond the curb. — Subdivision (1) clearly stipulates that street maintenance of a city or town street traversed by a state-maintained highway route shall not extend beyond the back of the curb where a curb and gutter section exists. The state, therefore, is expressly exempt from the duty of maintenance beyond the curb and this notwithstanding the fact that the street, according to the official map of the city, is 50 feet wide and this figure from the measurements offered in evidence would include the sidewalks on both sides of the street. Johnson v. City of Opelika, 260 Ala. 551, 71 So. 2d 793 (1954).

ARTICLE 5.

PRIVATE ROADS.

§ 23-1-130. Establishment.

Private roads may be established by the county commission on the application of any person, such roads not to exceed 15 feet in width and to be opened and kept in repair by the person on whose application they are established without exemption on public roads. (Code 1907, § 5841; Code 1923, § 1370; Acts 1927, No. 347, p. 348; Code 1940, T. 23, § 65.)

Cited in Clark v. Marengo County, 469 F. Supp. 1150 (S.D. Ala. 1979).

Collateral references. — 39 C.J.S., Highways, §§ 1, 2.

§ 23-1-131. Proceedings; limitations as to location; damages.

In establishing a private road, the same rules must be observed and the same proceedings had as in the case of public roads; but no road must be opened through any person's yard, garden, orchard, garage, stable, lot, ginhouse or curtilage without his consent, and the applicant must pay the owner of the land over which such road passes all damages resulting thereto from the establishment of such road, to be assessed as in case of public roads. (Code 1907, §§ 5842, 5843; Code 1923, § 1371; Acts 1927, No. 347, p. 348; Code 1940, T. 23, § 66.)

Purpose. — This section and its predecessors were enacted to ensure that the rights of private landowners were protected in the establishment of private roads across their land. Thompson v. Champion Int'l Corp., 500 So. 2d 1048 (Ala. 1986).

Requirements as to signs, etc., need not be complied with where road built across own land. — This section, when read in conjunction with the case law, does not require a landowner to comply with all statutes governing markings, signs, and barriers on public roads when merely constructing a roadway across its own land. Thompson v. Champion Int'l Corp., 500 So. 2d 1048 (Ala. 1986).

Payment of cost of appeal from assessment of damages is not a condition precedent to the jurisdiction to establish and direct the opening of a private road. Commissioners' Court v. Ballard, 185 Ala. 501, 64 So. 311 (1913).

As to time of exercising power, see note of Commissioners' Court v. Ballard, 185 Ala. 501, 64 So. 311 (1913), under § 23-1-80.

Collateral references. — Exercise of eminent domain for purpose of logging road. 86 ALR 552.

ARTICLE 6.

ALABAMA HIGHWAY AUTHORITY.

Cited in Rainer v. Tillett Bros. Constr. Co.,
381 So. 2d 36 (Ala. 1980).

§ 23-1-150. Purpose and construction of article.

It is the intention of the legislature by the passage of this article to authorize the incorporation of the Director of Finance, the Highway Director, the Attorney General, the State Treasurer and the executive secretary to the Governor of Alabama for the purpose of constructing public roads and bridges, together with work incidental and related thereto, through a corporation to be composed of said officials whose incorporation is hereby authorized, to vest such corporation with all powers, authorities, rights, privileges and titles that may be necessary to enable it to accomplish such purpose and to appropriate and pledge funds for the use of such corporation. This article shall be liberally construed in conformity with the said purpose. (Acts 1955, 1st Ex. Sess., No. 43, p. 66, § 1.)

Collateral references. — 40 Am. Jur. 2d,
Highways, Streets & Bridges, § 616.

§ 23-1-151. Incorporation — Authorization.

The Director of Finance, the Highway Director, the Attorney General, the State Treasurer and the executive secretary to the Governor may become a corporation, with the powers and authorities provided in this article, by proceeding according to the provisions of this article. (Acts 1955, 1st Ex. Sess., No. 43, p. 66, § 2.)

§ 23-1-152. Incorporation — Application.

To become a corporation, the Director of Finance, the Highway Director, the Attorney General, the State Treasurer and the executive secretary to the Governor shall present to the Secretary of State of Alabama an application signed by them which will set forth:

(1) The name, official designation and official residence of each of the applicants, together with a certified copy of the commission evidencing each applicant's right to office;

(2) The date on which each applicant was inducted into office and the term of office of each of the applicants;

(3) The name of the proposed corporation, which shall be Alabama highway authority;

(4) The location of the principal office of the proposed corporation; and

(5) Any other matter relating to the incorporation which the applicants may choose to insert and which is not inconsistent with this article or the laws of the State of Alabama.

The application shall be subscribed and sworn to by each of the applicants before an officer authorized by the laws of the State of Alabama to take acknowledgments to deeds. The Secretary of State shall examine the application, and if he finds that it substantially complies with the requirements of this section, he shall receive and file it and record it in an appropriate book of records in his office. (Acts 1955, 1st Ex. Sess., No. 43, p. 66, § 3.)

§ 23-1-153. Incorporation — Certificate.

When the application has been made, filed and recorded as provided in Section 23-1-152, the applicants shall constitute a corporation under the name proposed in the application and the Secretary of State shall make and issue to the applicants a certificate of incorporation, pursuant to this article, under the great seal of the state and shall record the same with the application. There shall be no fees paid to the Secretary of State for any work in connection with the incorporation or dissolution of the corporation so organized, which, for convenience, is referred to in this article as "the corporation." (Acts 1955, 1st Ex. Sess., No. 43, p. 66, § 4.)

§ 23-1-154. Members, officers and directors; quorum; vacancies; compensation; record of proceedings.

The applicants named in the application, and their respective successors in office, shall constitute the members of the corporation. The Director of Finance shall be the president of the corporation, the executive secretary to the Governor shall be the vice-president of the corporation, the Highway Director shall be the secretary of the corporation and the State Treasurer shall be the treasurer of the corporation and shall act as custodian of its funds. The members of the corporation shall constitute all the members of the board of directors of the corporation, and any three members of the said board of directors shall constitute a quorum for the transaction of business. Should any of said officials of the state die or should his term of office as Director of Finance, Highway Director, Attorney General, State Treasurer or executive secretary to the Governor, as the case may be, expire, or should he resign therefrom, his successor in office shall take his place as a member, officer and director of the corporation. No member, officer or director of the corporation shall draw any salary, in addition to that now authorized by law, for any service he may render or any duty he may perform in connection with the corporation. All proceedings had and done by the board of directors shall be reduced to writing by the secretary of the corporation and recorded in a substantially bound book. Copies of such proceedings, when certified by the secretary of the corporation under the seal of the corporation, shall be received in all courts as prima facie evidence of the matters and things therein certified. (Acts 1955, 1st Ex. Sess., No. 43, p. 66, § 5.)

§ 23-1-155. Powers.

The corporation shall have the following powers:

(1) To have perpetual succession by its corporate name unless sooner dissolved pursuant to Section 23-1-160;

(2) To maintain actions and have actions maintained against it and to prosecute and defend in any court having jurisdiction of the subject matter and of the parties;

(3) To have and to use a corporate seal and to alter the same at pleasure;

(4) To construct, reconstruct and relocate, or to cause to be constructed, reconstructed and relocated, public roads and bridges, including work incidental or related thereto, in the State of Alabama;

(5) To acquire by purchase, gift or condemnation or any other lawful means and to convey, or cause to be conveyed, to the State of Alabama any real, personal or mixed property necessary or convenient in connection with the construction of public roads and bridges and approaches thereto in the State of Alabama or the reconstruction or relocation of public roads and bridges in said state;

(6) To exercise the right of eminent domain as freely and completely as, and in the same manner that, the State of Alabama is empowered to exercise such right;

(7) To borrow money for its corporate purposes and, in evidence of such borrowing, to sell and issue its bonds and to refund any thereof by the issuance of refunding bonds (any such bonds, including refunding bonds, being collectively referred to in this article as "bonds");

(8) As security for payment of the principal of and the interest on its bonds, to pledge the proceeds of the appropriations and pledges provided for in this article; and

(9) To appoint and employ such officers, attorneys and agents as the business of the corporation may require. (Acts 1955, 1st Ex. Sess., No. 43, p. 66, § 6; Acts 1963, 1st Ex. Sess., No. 25, p. 90; Acts 1967, No. 226, p. 595; Acts 1969, No. 785, p. 1414, § 1.)

§ 23-1-156. Contracts; conveyance of property to state.

All contracts of the corporation for the construction, reconstruction and relocation of roads and bridges, and work incidental or related thereto and the acquisition of property necessary therefor, shall be in writing, shall be subject to the rules and regulations and shall be let under the supervision of the State Highway Department and shall be subject to approval by the governor and by the State Highway Department. All work provided for in any such contract shall be supervised by the State Highway Department. All persons engaged in the supervision or performance of any such work of construction, reconstruction or relocation that may be done by the corporation without the award of a contract therefor shall be employees of the State Highway Department. The corporation shall make and enforce all reasonable rules and regulations not inconsistent with the terms of this article or the laws of the State of Alabama

as may in its opinion be proper and suitable for the protection of said roads, bridges, approaches and appurtenances and for the safety of the traveling public. Any property acquired by the corporation by purchase, condemnation or otherwise shall be forthwith conveyed to the State of Alabama. All roads and bridges constructed by the corporation shall constitute part of the public highway system in the state. (Acts 1955, 1st Ex. Sess., No. 43, p. 66, § 8.)

§ 23-1-157. Bonds — Generally.

(a) The bonds of the corporation shall be signed by its president and attested by its secretary, and all interest coupons applicable to such bonds shall be signed by the president; provided, that a facsimile of the signature of one, but not of both, of said officers may be imprinted or otherwise reproduced on any such bonds in lieu of their being manually signed and a facsimile of the president's signature may be imprinted or otherwise reproduced on any such interest coupons in lieu of their being manually signed. The seal of the corporation shall be affixed to such bonds; provided, that a facsimile of said seal may be imprinted or otherwise reproduced on any such bonds in lieu of being manually affixed thereon.

(b) Any bonds of the corporation may be executed and delivered at any time and from time to time, shall be in such form and denominations and of such tenor and maturities, shall bear such rate or rates of interest payable and evidenced in such manner, may contain provisions for redemption prior to maturity and may contain other provisions not inconsistent with this article, all as may be provided by the resolution of the board of directors whereunder such bonds are authorized to be issued; provided, that no bond of the corporation shall have a specified maturity date later than 20 years after its date. Any bond of the corporation having a specified maturity date more than five years after its date shall be made subject to redemption at the option of the corporation at the end of the fifth year after its date and on any interest payment date thereafter under such terms and conditions as may be provided in the resolution under which such bond is authorized to be issued.

(c) Bonds of the corporation may be sold from time to time as the board of directors may deem advantageous; provided, that the aggregate principal amount of bonds of the corporation which may be issued under this article shall be limited to $50,000,000.00, but the said limitation shall not apply to refunding bonds which may be issued under this article and also shall not apply to bonds of the corporation which may be issued under any other act which may at any time be enacted; provided further, that no bonds shall be issued under this article by the corporation in any instance where the aggregate of the principal thereof and interest thereon maturing during any fiscal year of the State of Alabama, when added to the total principal and interest maturing during the same fiscal year with respect to all bonds of the corporation then outstanding, if any there be, including bonds issued under this article and any other bonds of the corporation, exceeds 50 percent of the sum of, in the case of bonds issued during either of the fiscal years ending

September 30, 1955, and September 30, 1956, one ninth of the proceeds of the gasoline excise tax levied under Section 40-17-31, collected by the State of Alabama during the fiscal year ending September 30, 1954, or, in the case of bonds issued during any fiscal year ending subsequent to September 30, 1956, two twenty-firsts of the proceeds of the gasoline excise tax levied under Section 40-17-31, collected by the State of Alabama during the fiscal year next preceding the fiscal year during which such bonds shall be issued.

(d) Bonds of the corporation must be sold only at public sale, either on sealed bids or at public auction, to the bidder whose bid reflects the lowest net interest cost to the corporation for the bonds being sold, computed to their respective maturities; provided, that if no bid acceptable to the corporation is received, it may reject all bids. Notice of each such sale shall be given by publication in either a financial journal or a financial newspaper published in the City of New York, New York, and also by publication in a newspaper published in the State of Alabama which is customarily published not less than six days during each calendar week, each of which notices must be published at least one time not less than 10 days prior to the date fixed for the sale. The board of directors may fix the terms and conditions under which each such sale may be held; provided, that none of the bonds may be sold for a price less than the face value thereof and provided, further, that such terms and conditions shall not conflict with any of the requirements of this article.

(e) Subject to the provisions and limitations contained in this article, the corporation may, from time to time, sell and issue refunding bonds for the purpose of refunding any matured or unmatured bonds of the corporation issued under this article and then outstanding.

(f) Approval by the Governor of Alabama of the terms and conditions under which any bonds of the corporation may be issued shall be requisite to their validity. Such approval shall be entered on the minutes of the respective meetings of the board of directors at which the bonds are authorized and shall be signed by the Governor. Such approval by the Governor may be shown on any such bonds by his facsimile signature when authorization thereof is contained in the said approval signed by him.

(g) The corporation may pay out of the proceeds from the sale of its bonds all expenses, including fees of fiscal agents and attorneys and other charges, which said board of directors may deem necessary and advantageous in connection with the issuance of such bonds. Bonds issued by the corporation under this article shall not be general obligations of the corporation, but shall be payable solely out of the funds appropriated and pledged therefor.

(h) As security for the payment of the principal of and interest on any bonds issued by it under this article the corporation is hereby authorized and empowered to pledge for payment of said principal and interest the funds that are appropriated and pledged for payment of said principal and interest. All such pledges made by the corporation shall take precedence in the order of the adoption of the resolutions containing such pledges. All contracts made and all bonds issued by the corporation pursuant to the provisions of this article shall be solely and exclusively obligations of the corporation and shall not be

an obligation or debt of the State of Alabama. Bonds issued by the corporation under this article shall be construed to be negotiable instruments although payable solely from a specified source as provided in this article.

(i) All bonds issued by the corporation and the income therefrom shall be exempt from all taxation in the State of Alabama. Any bonds issued by the corporation may be used by the holder thereof as security for any funds belonging to the state or to any instrumentality or agency of the state in any instance where security for such deposits may be required by law.

(j) Unless otherwise directed by the court having jurisdiction thereof or by the document that is the source of authority, a trustee, executor, administrator, guardian or one acting in any other fiduciary capacity may, in addition to any other investment powers conferred by law and with the exercise of reasonable business prudence, invest trust funds in bonds of the corporation.

(k) Neither a public hearing nor consent by the State Department of Finance or any other department or agency shall be a prerequisite to the issuance of bonds of the corporation. (Acts 1955, 1st Ex. Sess., No. 43, p. 66, § 7; Acts 1959, 1st Ex. Sess., No. 44, p. 82, § 1.)

§ 23-1-158. Bonds — Disposition of proceeds.

The proceeds of all bonds, other than refunding bonds, issued by the corporation, remaining after paying the expenses of their issuance, shall be turned in to the treasury, shall be carried in the public road and bridge account and shall be subject to be drawn on by the corporation, upon the approval of the State Highway Department and the Governor, but solely for the purpose of constructing, reconstructing and relocating public roads and bridges, or work incidental or related thereto, in the State of Alabama, including the acquisition of property necessary for such construction and incidental and related work; provided, that if such action shall be necessary in order to comply with any federal legislation relating to federal aid in construction of roads, the corporation may authorize the State Highway Department to expend directly any portion of such proceeds for constructing, reconstructing and relocating such roads and bridges or work incidental or related thereto. The proceeds from the sale of any refunding bonds of the corporation remaining after paying the expenses of their issuance shall be used only for the purpose of refunding the principal of outstanding bonds of the corporation and of paying any premium that may be necessary to be paid in order to redeem or retire the bonds to be refunded. (Acts 1955, 1st Ex. Sess., No. 43, p. 66, § 8.)

§ 23-1-159. Bond — Payments by State Treasurer.

Out of the revenues appropriated and pledged for such purpose, the State Treasurer is authorized and directed to pay the principal of and interest on the bonds issued by the corporation under the provisions of this article, as such principal and interest shall respectively mature, and he is further authorized and directed to set up and maintain appropriate records pertaining thereto. (Acts 1955, 1st Ex. Sess., No. 43, p. 66, § 10.)

§ 23-1-160. Dissolution.

At any time when no securities of any kind of the corporation, whether issued under this article or under authorization contained in any other statutes, are outstanding, the corporation may be dissolved upon the filing with the Secretary of State of an application for dissolution, which shall be subscribed by each of the members of the corporation and which shall be sworn to by each such member before an officer authorized to take acknowledgments to deeds. Upon the filing of said application for dissolution, the corporation shall cease and any property owned by it at the time of its dissolution shall pass to the State of Alabama. The Secretary of State shall file and record the application for dissolution, in an appropriate book of record in his office, and shall make and issue, under the great seal of the state, a certificate that the corporation is dissolved and shall record the said certificate with the application for dissolution. (Acts 1955, 1st Ex. Sess., No. 43, p. 66, § 11; Acts 1969, No. 785, p. 1414, § 2.)

ARTICLE 7.

ALABAMA HIGHWAY FINANCE CORPORATION.

§ 23-1-170. Purpose and construction of article.

It is the intention of the legislature by the passage of this article to authorize the incorporation of a public corporation for the following purposes:

(1) To issue bonds to assure the availability of funds for payment of the state's share of the cost of constructing roads and bridges as shall from time to time be constructed with funds supplied jointly by the state and federal government; and

(2) To construct and maintain, or participate in the construction and maintenance, or lend its aid in construction and maintenance or contract for construction and maintenance of roads and bridges in the State of Alabama, as well as the approaches thereto, including the reconstruction and relocating of approaches, causeways and like or other highway facilities which may, from time to time, be constructed and maintained with funds to be supplied jointly by the state and federal government, together with work incidental and related thereto, through a corporation to be composed of said officials whose incorporation is hereby authorized to vest such corporation with all powers, authorities, rights, privileges and titles that may be necessary to enable it to accomplish such purpose, and to appropriate and pledge funds for the use of such corporation.

All construction and maintenance referred to in this section shall be done under the direction and supervision of the State Highway Department. The State Highway Department may assign, contract or delegate the work of construction and maintenance under its general powers, subject to approval by the Governor. This article shall be liberally construed in conformity with the said purposes. (Acts 1965, No. 228, p. 327, § 1.)

Cited in Rainer v. Tillett Bros. Constr. Co., 381 So. 2d 36 (Ala. 1980).

§ 23-1-171. Incorporation — Authorization.

The Highway Director, the Attorney General and the Director of Finance may become a corporation, with the powers and authorities provided in this article, by proceeding according to the provisions of this article. (Acts 1965, No. 228, p. 327, § 2.)

§ 23-1-172. Incorporation — Application.

To become a corporation, the Highway Director, the Attorney General and the Director of Finance shall present to the Secretary of State of Alabama an application signed by them which shall set forth:

(1) The name, official designation and official residence of each of the applicants, together with a certified copy of the commission evidencing each applicant's right to office;

(2) The date on which each applicant was inducted into office and the term of office of each of the applicants;

(3) The name of the proposed corporation, which shall be Alabama highway finance corporation;

(4) The location of the principal office of the proposed corporation, which shall be Montgomery, Alabama; and

(5) Any other matter relating to the incorporation which the applicants may choose to insert and which is not inconsistent with this article or the laws of the State of Alabama.

The application shall be subscribed and sworn to by each of the applicants before an officer authorized by the laws of the State of Alabama to take acknowledgments to deeds. The Secretary of State shall examine the application, and if he finds that it substantially complies with the requirements of this section, he shall receive and file it and record it in an appropriate book of records in his office. (Acts 1965, No. 228, p. 327, § 3.)

§ 23-1-173. Incorporation — Certificate.

When the application has been made, filed and recorded, as provided in Section 23-1-172, the applicants shall constitute a public corporation under the name proposed in the application and the Secretary of State shall make and issue to the applicants a certificate of incorporation pursuant to this article, under the great seal of the state, and shall record the same with the application. There shall be no fees paid to the Secretary of State for any work in connection with the incorporation or dissolution of the corporation so organized, which, for convenience, is referred to in this article as "the corporation." (Acts 1965, No. 228, p. 327, § 4.)

§ 23-1-174. Members, officers and directors; quorum; vacancies; compensation; record of proceedings.

The applicants named in the application and their respective successors in office shall constitute the members of the corporation. The Highway Director shall be the president of the corporation, the Attorney General shall be its vice-president, the Director of Finance shall be the secretary of the corporation and the State Treasurer shall be the treasurer of the corporation and shall act as custodian of its funds. The members of the corporation shall constitute all the members of the board of directors of the corporation, and any two members of the said board of directors shall constitute a quorum for the transaction of business. Should any of said officials of the state die or should his term of office as Highway Director, Attorney General or Director of Finance, as the case may be, expire or should he resign therefrom, his successor in office shall take his place as a member, officer and director of the corporation. No member, officer or director of the corporation shall draw any salary, in addition to that now authorized by law, for any service he may render or any duty he may perform in connection with the corporation. All proceedings had and done by the board of directors shall be reduced to writing by the secretary of the corporation and recorded in a substantially bound book. Copies of such proceedings, when certified by the secretary of the corporation under the seal of the corporation, shall be received in all courts as prima facie evidence of the matters and things therein certified. (Acts 1965, No. 228, p. 327, § 5.)

§ 23-1-175. Powers.

The corporation shall have the following powers:

(1) To have succession by its corporate name without time limit;

(2) To maintain actions and have actions maintained against it and to prosecute and defend in any court having jurisdiction of the subject matter and of the parties;

(3) To have and to use a corporate seal and to alter the same at pleasure;

(4) To construct, reconstruct and relocate, or to cause to be constructed, reconstructed and relocated, public roads and bridges, including work incidental or related thereto in the State of Alabama;

(5) To receive, take and hold by sale, gift, lease, devise or otherwise real and personal estate of every description and to manage the same;

(6) To acquire by purchase, gift or the exercise of the power of eminent domain or any other lawful means and to convey, or cause to be conveyed, to the State of Alabama any real, personal or mixed property necessary or convenient in connection with the construction of public roads and bridges and approaches thereto in the State of Alabama or the reconstruction or relocation of public roads and bridges in said state;

(7) To exercise the right of eminent domain as freely and completely as, and in the same manner that, the State of Alabama is empowered to exercise such right;

(8) To borrow money and issue its bonds in evidence thereof subject to the provisions of Section 23-1-177;

(9) As security for payment of the principal of and the interest on its bonds, to pledge the proceeds of the appropriations and pledges provided for in this article;

(10) To appoint and employ such attorneys as the business of the corporation may require;

(11) To receive from the several counties of the State of Alabama interest-bearing warrants of such counties secured by a pledge of the proceeds of gasoline tax appropriated from time to time to the counties by the state, or any part or percentage thereof, or any other fund or security in payment of, or to secure the payment of the county's portion of the cost of any roads or bridges built in such county and to sell such county warrants, or borrow money on the security thereof; provided, that any funds received from the sale of the warrants of any county or the proceeds of any loan made on the security of the warrants of any county shall be expended in such county;

(12) To enter into contracts with counties, the Highway Department of Alabama or other agency performing any of the functions thereof, road district authorities, persons, firms or corporations, federal emergency administrator of public works and any other branch of the federal government in furtherance of its public purposes and objects either relative to the work done or to be done; and

(13) To turn over to the Highway Department any and all funds of the corporation as from time to time may be necessary or proper for the most economical construction of such roads and to comply with all federal or other legislation relating to federal aid roads or other federal moneys. (Acts 1965, No. 228, p. 327, § 6.)

Cross references. — As to eminent domain generally, see § 18-1A-1 et seq.

§ 23-1-176. Contracts; conveyance of property to state.

All contracts of the corporation for the construction, reconstruction and relocation of roads and bridges, and work incidental or related thereto and the acquisition of property necessary therefor, shall be in writing, shall be subject to the rules and regulations and shall be let under the supervision of the State Highway Department and shall be subject to approval by the Governor and by the State Highway Department. All work provided for in any such contract shall be supervised by the State Highway Department. All persons engaged in the supervision or performance of any such work of construction, reconstruction or relocation that may be done by the corporation without the award of a contract therefor shall be employees of the State Highway Department. Any property acquired by the corporation by purchase, condemnation or otherwise shall be forthwith conveyed to the State of Alabama. All roads and bridges constructed by the corporation shall constitute part of the public highway system in the state. (Acts 1965, No. 228, p. 327, § 8.)

§ 23-1-177. Bonds — Generally.

(a) The bonds of the corporation shall be signed by its president and attested by its secretary, and the seal of the corporation shall be affixed thereto or printed or otherwise reproduced thereon, and any interest coupons applicable to such bonds shall be signed by the president; provided, that a facsimile of the signature of one, but not both, of said officers may be printed or otherwise reproduced on any such bonds in lieu of his signing the same and a facsimile of the president's signature may be printed or otherwise reproduced on any such interest coupons in lieu of his signing the same.

(b) Any bonds of the corporation may be executed and delivered by it at any time and from time to time, shall be in such form and denominations and of such tenor and maturities, shall bear such rate or rates of interest payable and evidenced in such manner, may contain provisions for redemption prior to maturity and may contain such other provisions not inconsistent with this article, all as may be provided by the resolution of the board of directors under which such bonds are authorized to be issued; provided, that no bond of the corporation shall have a specified maturity date later than 20 years after its date.

(c) Bonds of the corporation may be sold from time to time as the board of directors may deem advantageous; provided, that the aggregate principal amount of bonds of the corporation, other than refunding bonds, which may be issued under this article after February 1, 1978, shall be limited to $25,000,000.00; and provided, further, that no bonds, other than refunding bonds, may be sold or issued by the corporation unless the Governor shall have first determined that the issuance of the bonds proposed to be issued will be necessary to assure the availability of funds for payment of the state's share of the cost of roads and bridges that shall from time to time be constructed with funds supplied jointly by the state and the federal government.

(d) Bonds of the corporation must be sold only at public sale, either on sealed bids or at public auction, to the bidder whose bid reflects the lowest net interest cost to the corporation for the bonds being sold, computed to their relative maturities; provided, that if no bid acceptable to the corporation is received it may reject all bids. Notice of each such sale shall be given by publication in either a financial journal or a financial newspaper published in the City of New York, New York and also by publication in a newspaper published in the State of Alabama that is customarily published not less often than five days during each calendar week, each of which notices must be published at least one time not less than 10 days prior to the date fixed for the sale. The board of directors may fix the terms and conditions under which each such sale may be held; provided, that none of the bonds may be sold for a price less than the face value thereof; and provided, further, that such terms and conditions shall not conflict with any of the requirements of this article.

(e) Subject to the provisions and limitations contained in this article, the corporation may from time to time sell and issue refunding bonds for the purpose of refunding any matured or unmatured bonds of the corporation then outstanding. Approval by the Governor of Alabama of the terms and conditions under which any bonds of the corporation may be issued shall be requisite to their validity. Such approval shall be entered on the minutes of the meetings of the board of directors at which the bonds are authorized and shall be signed by the Governor. Such approval by the governor may be shown on any such bonds by a facsimile of his signature printed or otherwise reproduced thereon when authorization thereof is contained in the said approval signed by him.

(f) The corporation may pay out of the proceeds from the sale of its bonds all expenses, including fees of attorneys and other charges, which said board of directors may deem necessary and advantageous in connection with the issuance of such bonds. Bonds issued by the corporation shall not be general obligations of the corporation but shall be payable solely out of the funds appropriated and pledged therefor by act of the legislature. As security for the payment of the principal of, and interest on, any bonds issued by it, the corporation is hereby authorized and empowered to pledge for payment of such principal and interest the funds that are appropriated and pledged by act of the legislature for payment of said principal and interest.

(g) All contracts made and all bonds issued by the corporation pursuant to the provisions of this article shall be solely and exclusively obligations of the corporation and shall not be an obligation or debt of any kind of the State of Alabama. Bonds issued by the corporation when not registered shall be construed to be negotiable instruments although payable solely from a specified source as provided in this article. All bonds issued by the corporation and the income therefrom shall be exempt from all taxation in the State of Alabama. Any bonds issued by the corporation may be used by the holder thereof as security for any funds belonging to the state or to any instrumentality or agency of the state in any instance where security for such deposits may be required by law.

(h) Unless otherwise directed by the court having jurisdiction thereof or by the document that is the source of authority, a trustee, executor, administrator, guardian or one acting in any other fiduciary capacity may, in addition to any other investment powers conferred by law and with the exercise of reasonable business prudence, invest trust and other fiduciary funds in bonds of the corporation.

(i) Neither a public hearing nor consent by the State Department of Finance or any other department or agency shall be a prerequisite to the issuance of bonds by the corporation. All obligations issued by the corporation shall be exempt from the laws of the state governing usury or prescribing or limiting interest rates including but without limitation to the provisions of

Chapter 8 of Title 8, as it now exists and as it may at any time be amended. (Acts 1965, No. 228, p. 327, § 7; Acts 1978, No. 580, p. 652, § 1; Acts 1981, No. 81-379, p. 561.)

Cross references. — As to exemption of bonds of public corporations from laws governing usury or limiting interest rates, see § 8-8-7.

Cited in Rainer v. Tillett Bros. Constr. Co., 381 So. 2d 36 (Ala. 1980).

§ 23-1-178. Bonds — Disposition of proceeds.

The proceeds of all bonds, other than refunding bonds, issued by the corporation remaining after paying the expenses of their issuance shall be turned in to the treasury, shall be carried in the public road and bridge account and shall be subject to be drawn on by the corporation, upon the approval of the State Highway Department and the Governor, but solely for the purpose of constructing, reconstructing and relocating public roads and bridges, or work incidental or related thereto, including the acquisition of property necessary therefor, in the State of Alabama; provided, that such funds may be used only for payment of the state's share of the cost of constructing, reconstructing and relocating public roads and bridges, or work incidental or related thereto, which have been or will be constructed, reconstructed or relocated under programs financed jointly by the state and the federal government; and provided further, that if such action shall be necessary in order to comply with any federal legislation relating to federal aid in construction of roads, the corporation may authorize the State Highway Department to expend directly any portion of such proceeds for constructing, reconstructing and relocating such roads and bridges, or work incidental or related thereto. The proceeds from the sale of any refunding bonds of the corporation remaining after paying the expenses of their issuance shall be used only for the purpose of refunding the principal of outstanding bonds of the corporation and of paying any premium that may be necessary to be paid in order to redeem or retire the bonds to be refunded. (Acts 1965, No. 228, p. 327, § 8.)

§ 23-1-179. Bonds — Payments by State Treasurer.

Out of the revenues appropriated and pledged for such purpose, the State Treasurer is authorized and directed to pay the principal of and interest on the bonds issued by the corporation under the provisions of this article, as such principal and interest shall respectively mature, and he is further authorized and directed to set up and maintain appropriate records pertaining thereto. (Acts 1965, No. 228, p. 327, § 10.)

§ 23-1-180. Dissolution.

At any time when no bonds of the corporation are outstanding, the corporation may be dissolved upon the filing with the Secretary of State of an application for dissolution, which shall be subscribed by each of the members of the corporation and which shall be sworn to by each such member before an officer authorized to take acknowledgments to deeds. Upon the filing of said application for dissolution, the corporation shall cease and any property owned by it at the time of its dissolution shall pass to the State of Alabama. The Secretary of State shall file and record the application for dissolution, in an appropriate book of record in his office, and shall make and issue, under the great seal of the state, a certificate that the corporation is dissolved and shall record the said certificate with the application for dissolution. (Acts 1965, No. 228, p. 327, § 1.)

§ 23-1-181. Appropriations and pledges of revenue for payment of principal and interest on bonds generally; sinking fund.

(a) Where used in this section the following words and terms shall be given the following respective meanings:

(1) BONDS. Such term, without qualifying words or phrases, means bonds of the corporation issued under this article.

(2) CODE. The Code of Alabama, 1975.

(3) CORPORATION. Alabama Highway Finance Corporation, a public corporation and instrumentality of the State of Alabama that was organized and is existing under this article.

(4) GASOLINE TAX APPROPRIATION STATUTE. Division 2 of Article 2 of Chapter 17 of Title 40.

(5) HIGHWAY GASOLINE TAX.

a. The excise tax levied in Section 40-17-31, as amended, exclusive of those portions of said tax in respect of aviation fuel and marine gasoline, as those terms are used in said section; and

b. The excise tax levied by Article 3 of Chapter 17 of Title 40, exclusive of that portion of the said tax in respect of diesel fuel.

(6) NET GASOLINE TAX PROCEEDS. The entire proceeds from the highway gasoline tax less the cost of collection and less any refunds of the said proceeds pursuant to the provisions of Article 3 of Chapter 17 of Title 40, or pursuant to the provisions of either of Divisions 3 and 4 of Article 2 of said Chapter 17.

(7) STATE'S SHARE OF THE NET GASOLINE TAX PROCEEDS. The 45 percentum of the net gasoline tax proceeds allocated and appropriated for state highway purposes in Section 40-17-72.

(b) For the purpose of providing funds to enable the corporation to pay at their respective maturities the principal of and interest on any bonds that may be issued by it under the provisions of this article and to accomplish the purposes and objects of its creation, there hereby is irrevocably pledged to said purpose and appropriated so much as may be necessary for said purpose of the following, subject, however, to the provisions, hereinafter set forth in this subsection, as to the rank of the pledges herein made:

(1) So much as may be necessary for such purpose of those portions of the motor vehicle license taxes and registration fees that are provided to be distributed to the state pursuant to the provisions of Division 1 of Article 5 of Chapter 12 of Title 40 as amended, remaining after the costs of collection thereof;

(2) To such extent and to such extent only as the revenues appropriated under subdivision (1) of this subsection may not be sufficient to pay at their respective maturities the principal of and interest on the bonds, so much as may be necessary for such purpose, when added to the amounts appropriated in subdivision (1) of this subsection, of the state's share of the net gasoline tax proceeds;

(3) To such extent and to such extent only as the revenues appropriated under subdivisions (1) and (2) of this subsection may not be sufficient to pay at their respective maturities the principal of and interest on the bonds, so much as may be necessary for such purpose, when added to the amounts appropriated in subdivisions (1) and (2) of this subsection, of the entire proceeds of the following excise taxes remaining after payment of the costs of collection thereof:

a. the excise tax levied by Article 1 of Chapter 17 of Title 40 on distributors and storers of motor fuel, as therein defined; and

b. the excise tax levied by Article 3 of Chapter 17 of Title 40, exclusive of that portion of the said tax in respect of gasoline.

The term "costs of collection," as used in this subdivision, shall mean that portion of the excise taxes referred to in this subdivision that may be appropriated by the legislature to the Department of Revenue for its operating expenses;

(4) To such extent and to such extent only as the revenues appropriated under subdivisions (1), (2) and (3) of this subsection may not be sufficient to pay at their respective maturities the principal of and interest on the bonds, so much as may be necessary for such purpose, when added to the amounts appropriated in subdivisions (1), (2) and (3), of all that portion of the receipts from the inspection fee on certain petroleum products imposed by Division 1 of Article 5 of Chapter 17 of Title 8 that is required by the division to be deposited to the credit of the public road and bridge fund; and

(5) To such extent and to such extent only as the revenues appropriated under subdivisions (1), (2), (3) and (4) of this subsection may not be sufficient to pay at their respective maturities the principal of and interest on the bonds, so much as may be necessary for such purpose, when added to the amounts appropriated in subdivisions (1), (2), (3) and (4), of the receipts from the fee in respect of identification markers on motor vehicles that is provided for in Section 40-17-150.

(c) All moneys hereby appropriated and pledged shall constitute a sinking fund for the purpose of paying the principal of and interest on the bonds. All pledges made by the corporation shall take precedence among themselves in the order of the adoption of the resolutions making such pledges, except as may be otherwise provided in such resolutions; provided, that any such pledges made for the benefit of any refunding bonds that may be issued under the provisions of this article shall be subordinate to any pledge made, either before or after the issuance of such refunding bonds, under the provisions of this article for the benefit of bonds, other than refunding bonds, issued under the provisions of this article.

(d) The appropriations and pledges herein made, for the benefit of any bonds, including refunding bonds, issued under this article, of the taxes and fees referred to in subdivisions (1) through (5), inclusive, of subsection (b), shall be subject and subordinate to all pledges of the said taxes and fees lawfully made as security for (1) any bonds issued by Alabama Highway Authority prior to December 1, 1977, or (2) any refunding bonds that may be issued by Alabama Highway Authority after December 1, 1977, for the purpose of refunding any of the bonds referred to in clause (1) of this sentence if, and only if, the aggregate amount of principal and interest that will mature with respect to such refunding bonds during any fiscal year of the State of Alabama does not exceed the amount of principal and interest, with respect to the bonds refunded by such refunding bonds, that have a stated maturity during the same fiscal year, or that would have had a stated maturity during the same fiscal year if such bonds had not been refunded.

(e) Any pledge for the benefit of any refunding bonds issued under this article shall also be subject and subordinate to the following: (1) Any pledge or pledges of the tax proceeds and fees referred to in subdivisions (1) through (5), inclusive, of subsection (b) that may have been made prior to the issuance of such refunding bonds pursuant to authorization in any statute effective at the time of such issuance, and (2) any pledge or pledges authorized, by any statute in effect at the time of the issuance of such refunding bonds, to be made for the benefit of any then-unissued bonds, other than refunding bonds, provided for in any such statute; and provided, further, that the priorities of any such refunding bonds over each other as to any such pledge shall be as may be provided in the resolutions of the board of directors authorizing any such refunding bonds.

(f) The appropriations and pledges herein made for the benefit of any bonds, other than refunding bonds, issued under this article shall be prior and superior to any appropriations and pledges for the benefit of any obligations that may at any time be issued under the provisions of Article 10 of this chapter. (Acts 1978, No. 580, p. 652, § 2.)

Cross references. — As to appropriations and pledges of revenue for payment of principal and interest on bonds of federal aid highway finance authority, see § 23-1-314.

Collateral references. — 39A C.J.S., Highways, § 158.

Article 8.

Relocation Assistance.

§§ 23-1-200 through 23-1-209. Repealed by Acts 1989, No. 89-522, p. 1070, § 5, effective May 4, 1989.

Article 8A.

Relocation Assistance.

§ 23-1-210. Authorization to provide relocation assistance.

When any department, agency or instrumentality of the state, or any county, municipality or other political subdivision or any other public or private entity subject to the provisions of the federal Uniform Relocation Assistance and Real Property Acquisition Policies Act of 1970, as amended, Public Law 91-646 and 100-17, hereinafter referred to as the federal Uniform Relocation Act, undertakes any project which results in the acquisition of real property or in any person or persons being displaced from their homes, businesses or farms such state department, agency or instrumentality, county, municipality or other political subdivision, or other public or private entity is hereby authorized to provide relocation assistance, and to make relocation payments to such displaced person and to do such other acts and follow such procedures and practices as may be necessary to comply with the provisions of the federal Uniform Relocation Act. (Acts 1989, No. 89-522, p. 1070, § 1.)

U.S. Code. — The federal Uniform Relocation Act is codified as 42 U.S.C.A. § 4601.

§ 23-1-211. Payments.

Any payment made or to be made under the authority granted by this article shall be for compensating or reimbursing the displaced person or owner of real property in accordance with the requirements of the federal Uniform Relocation Act and such payments shall not for any purpose be deemed or considered compensation for real property acquired or compensation for damages to remaining property. (Acts 1989, No. 89-522, p. 1070, § 2.)

U.S. Code. — The federal Uniform Relocation Act is codified as 42 U.S.C.A. § 4601.

Lessees who are compelled to vacate their leasehold by reason of the taking are "owners" within the terms and purposes of this article, and there is no error in the court's instructing the jury about the payment made to the tenants of the property. Ritchey v. State, 293 Ala. 265, 302 So. 2d 83 (1974) (decided under former § 23-1-207).

§ 23-1-212. Authority of Highway Director.

The Director of the Alabama Highway Department is hereby authorized to issue such regulations and procedures determined to be necessary or appropriate to carry out this article and the federal Uniform Relocation Act being subject to change at any time, such regulations and procedures will not be subject to the Alabama Administrative Procedure Act. (Acts 1989, No. 89-522, p. 1070, § 3.)

U.S. Code. — The federal Uniform Relocation Act is codified as 42 U.S.C.A. § 4601.
Cross references. — For Alabama Administrative Procedure Act, see Title 41, chapter 22.

ARTICLE 9.

HIGHWAY BEAUTIFICATION.

Cross references. — As to deposit of trash, litter, etc., on public thoroughfares, see §§ 23-5-6 through 23-5-9.

Division 1.

Scenic Enhancement.

§ 23-1-220. Short title.

This division may be cited as the "Highway Beautification Act — Scenic Enhancement." (Acts 1967, No. 432, p. 1101, § 1.)

§ 23-1-221. Purpose of division.

The purpose of this division is to promote the safety, convenience and enjoyment of travel on, and protection of, the public investment in highways of this state and for the restoration, preservation and enhancement of scenic beauty within and adjacent to the state and federal-aid highways. (Acts 1967, No. 432, p. 1101, § 2.)

§ 23-1-222. Authority of State Highway Director to acquire land.

The State Highway Director is hereby authorized to acquire land necessary for the restoration, preservation and enhancement of scenic beauty and the establishment of rest areas within, and adjacent to, state and federal-aid highways of this state, including acquisition of publicly owned and controlled rest and recreation areas and sanitary and other facilities within, or adjacent to, the highway right-of-way necessary to accommodate the traveling public. (Acts 1967, No. 432, p. 1101, § 3.)

§ 23-1-223. Interest in acquired land; manner of acquisition.

The interest in any land authorized to be acquired and maintained under this division may be the fee simple or any lesser interest, as determined by the State Highway Director to be necessary to accomplish the purpose of this division. Such acquisition may be by gift, purchase, exchange or condemnation. (Acts 1967, No. 432, p. 1101, § 4.)

Cross references. — As to eminent domain generally, see § 18-1A-1 et seq.

Division 2.

Junkyard Control.

§ 23-1-240. Short title.

This division may be cited as the "Highway Beautification Act — Junkyard Control." (Acts 1967, No. 643, p. 1455, § 1.)

§ 23-1-241. Definitions.

For the purposes of this division, the following terms shall have the meanings respectively ascribed to them by this section:

(1) JUNK. Old or scrap copper, brass, rope, rags, batteries, paper trash, rubber debris, waste or junked, dismantled or wrecked automobiles, or parts thereof, iron, steel and other old or scrap ferrous or nonferrous material.

(2) JUNKYARD. Any establishment or place of business which is maintained, operated or used for storing, keeping, buying or selling junk or for the maintenance or operation of an automobile graveyard. The term shall include garbage dumps and sanitary fills.

(3) AUTOMOBILE GRAVEYARD. Any establishment or place of business which is maintained, used or operated for storing, keeping, buying or selling wrecked, scrapped, ruined or dismantled motor vehicles or motor vehicle parts.

(4) INTERSTATE SYSTEM. That portion of the national system of interstate and defense highways located within this state or officially designated, or as may hereafter be so designated, by the director and approved by the United States Department of Transportation pursuant to the provisions of Title 23, United States Code, "Highways."

(5) PRIMARY SYSTEM. That portion of connected main highways as officially designated, or as may hereafter be so officially designated, by the state highway director and approved by the United States Department of Transportation pursuant to Title 23, United States Code, "Highways."

(6) DIRECTOR. The State of Alabama Highway Department.

(7) SCRAP PROCESSOR. Any person, firm or corporation engaged only in the business of buying scrap iron and metals, including, but not limited to, old automobiles, for the specific purpose of processing into raw material for

74

remelting purposes only and whose principal product is ferrous and nonferrous scrap for shipment to steel mills, foundries, smelters and refineries and maintaining an established place of business in this state and having facilities and machinery designed for such processing. (Acts 1967, No. 643, § 1455, § 3.)

§ 23-1-242. Declaration of policy.

The regulation of junkyards in areas adjacent to any state highway included in the national system of interstate and primary highways is hereby declared to be in the public interest and necessary to promote the public safety, health, welfare, convenience and enjoyment of public travel, to protect the public investment in public highways, to preserve and enhance the scenic beauty of lands bordering on such highways and to promote the conservation of our natural mineral resources by encouraging the recycling of the reusable scrap iron and metals. The legislature hereby finds and declares that junkyards which do not conform to the requirements of this division are a public nuisance. (Acts 1967, No. 643, p. 1455, § 2.)

Collateral references. — Automobile wrecking yard or place of business as nuisance. 84 ALR2d 653.

§ 23-1-243. License — Required.

No person shall establish, operate or maintain a junkyard, any portion of which is within 1,000 feet of the nearest edge of the right-of-way of any interstate or primary highway, without obtaining a license to do so from the director. (Acts 1967, No. 643, p. 1455, § 4.)

§ 23-1-244. License — Issuance, revocation and renewal; fees.

The director shall have the sole authority to issue licenses for the establishment, maintenance and operation of junkyards within the limits defined in this division, and may revoke said licenses at any time a junkyard fails to conform to the requirements of this division, and shall charge therefor a fee of $25.00, payable annually in advance. All licenses issued under this section shall expire on January 1 following the date of issue. Licenses may be renewed from year to year upon payment of the requisite fee. Proceeds from such fees shall be deposited with the State Treasurer for credit to the State Highway Department public road and bridge fund. (Acts 1967, No. 643, p. 1455, § 5.)

§ 23-1-245. License — Conditions.

No license shall be granted for the establishment, maintenance or operation of a junkyard within 1,000 feet of the nearest edge of right-of-way of any highway on the interstate or primary system, except:

(1) Those which are screened by natural objects, plantings, fences or other appropriate means so as not to be visible from the main-traveled way of the system or otherwise removed from sight;

(2) Those located within areas which are zoned for industrial use under authority of law;

(3) Those located within unzoned industrial areas, which areas shall be determined by actual land uses and defined by regulations promulgated by the director; or

(4) Those which are not visible from the main-traveled way of the system. (Acts 1967, No. 643, p. 1455, § 6.)

§ 23-1-246. Screening — Existing junkyards.

Any junkyard lawfully in existence on September 8, 1971, which is located within 1,000 feet of the nearest edge of the right-of-way and visible from the main-traveled way of any highway on the interstate or primary system, shall be screened, if considered feasible by the director. The screening shall be at locations on the right-of-way or in areas outside the right-of-way acquired for such purposes, so as not to be visible from the main-traveled way of the interstate or primary system. (Acts 1967, No. 643, p. 1455, § 7.)

§ 23-1-247. Screening — Rules and regulations.

The director shall have the authority to promulgate rules and regulations governing the location, planting, construction and maintenance, including the materials used, in screening junkyards as required under provisions of this division. (Acts 1967, No. 643, p. 1455, § 8.)

§ 23-1-248. Authority of director — Acquisition of land.

(a) When the director determines that the topography of the land adjoining the interstate or primary systems will not permit adequate screening of such junkyards or that screening would not be economically feasible, the director shall have the authority to acquire by gift, purchase, exchange or eminent domain such interests in lands as may be necessary, including fee simple title, to secure the relocation, removal or disposal thereof.

(b) When the director determines that it is in the best interest of the state, he may acquire such lands upon payment of just compensation to the owners, or interest in said lands as may be necessary to provide adequate screening of such junkyards.

(c) Damages resulting from any taking of property in eminent domain shall be ascertained in the manner provided by law. (Acts 1967, No. 643, p. 1455, § 9.)

§ 23-1-249. Authority of director — Regulations; agreements with United States department of transportation.

The director may:

(1) Promulgate regulations he deems necessary to implement and enforce provisions of this division; and

(2) Enter into agreements with the United States Department of Transportation pursuant to Title 23, United States Code, and any amendments thereto, relating to the control of junkyards in areas adjacent to the interstate and primary systems and to take action in the name of the state to comply with the terms of this agreement. (Acts 1967, No. 643, p. 1455, § 11.)

§ 23-1-250. Penalty for violation of division; abatement of nuisances.

The establishment, operation or maintenance of any junkyard contrary to the provisions of this division shall be a public nuisance. Any person, partnership or corporation that establishes, maintains or operates any junkyard contrary to the provisions of this division shall be deemed guilty of a misdemeanor and, upon conviction thereof, shall be penalized by a fine of not less than $100.00 nor more than $1,000.00, said fine to be applicable only after receipt by said person, partnership or corporation of written notification that said person, partnership or corporation is violating any provision of this division and their failure to comply with the requirements contained in this division within 30 days from the date of the receipt of said notice, and in addition thereto, the director may apply to the circuit court of the county in which said junkyard may be, for an injunction to abate such nuisance. (Acts 1967, No. 643, p. 1455, § 10.)

§ 23-1-251. Construction of division.

Nothing in this division shall be construed to abrogate or affect the provisions of any lawful ordinance, regulation or resolution which are more restrictive than the provisions of this division. (Acts 1967, No. 643, p. 1455, § 12.)

Division 3.

Outdoor Advertising.

Cited in State v. Waller, 395 So. 2d 37 (Ala. 1981).

§ 23-1-270. Short title.

This division shall be known as and may be cited as the "Highway Beautification Act — Outdoor Advertising." (Acts 1971, 3rd Ex. Sess., No. 276, p. 4544, § 1.)

§ 23-1-271. Definitions.

For the purposes of this division, unless otherwise indicated, the following terms shall have the meanings respectively ascribed to them by this section:

(1) BUSINESS AREA. Any part of an adjacent area which is at any time zoned for business, industrial or commercial activities under the authority of any law of this state or not zoned, but which constitutes an unzoned commercial or industrial area as defined in this section.

(2) CENTERLINE OF THE HIGHWAY. A line equidistant from the edges of the median separating the main-traveled ways of a divided highway or the centerline of the main-traveled way of a nondivided highway.

(3) DIRECTOR. The State of Alabama Highway Department.

(4) ADJACENT AREA. An area which is adjacent to and within 660 feet of the nearest edge of the right-of-way of any interstate or primary highway, which 660 feet distance shall be measured horizontally along a line normal or perpendicular to the centerline of the highway.

(5) ERECT. To construct, build, raise, assemble, place, affix, attach, create, paint, draw or in any other way bring into being or establish, but it shall not include any of the foregoing activities when performed as an incident to the change of advertising message or customary maintenance of the sign structure.

(6) INTERSTATE HIGHWAY. Any highway at any time officially designated as a part of the national system of interstate and defense highways by the director and approved by the appropriate authority of the federal government.

(7) MAINTAIN. To allow to exist.

(8) PRIMARY HIGHWAY. Any highway, other than an interstate highway, at any time officially designated as a part of the federal-aid primary system by the director and approved by the appropriate authority of the federal government.

(9) SIGN. Any outdoor advertising sign, display, device, notice, figure, painting, drawing, message, placard, poster, billboard or other thing which is designed, intended or used to advertise or inform, any part of the advertising or informative contents of which is visible from any place on the main-traveled way of any portion of an interstate highway or primary highway.

(10) AN UNZONED COMMERCIAL, BUSINESS OR INDUSTRIAL AREA. The land occupied by the regularly used building, parking lot, storage or processing area of a commercial, business or industrial activity, and the land within 600 feet thereof on each side of the highway. The unzoned area shall not include:

a. Land on the opposite side of an interstate or primary freeway highway from an unzoned commercial, business or industrial area, as defined above;

b. Land predominantly used for residential purposes;

c. Land zoned by state or local law, regulation or ordinance;

d. Land on the opposite side of a nonfreeway primary highway which is determined scenic by the Department of Highways.

All measurements shall be from the outer edges of the regularly used buildings, parking lots, storage or processing areas of the commercial or industrial activities, not from the property lines of the activities, unless said property lines coincide with the limits of the regularly used buildings, parking lots, storage or processing areas and shall be along or parallel to the edge or pavement of the highway.

(11) COMMERCIAL OR INDUSTRIAL ACTIVITIES FOR PURPOSES OF UNZONED INDUSTRIAL AND COMMERCIAL AREAS. Those activities generally recognized as commercial or industrial by local zoning authorities in this state, except that none of the following activities shall be considered commercial or industrial.

a. Outdoor advertising structures;

b. Agricultural, forestry, ranching, grazing, farming and similar activities, including but not limited to, wayside fresh produce stands;

c. Activities normally or regularly in operation less than three months of the year;

d. Transient or temporary activities;

e. Activities not visible from the main-traveled way;

f. Activities more than 660 feet from the nearest edge of the right-of-way;

g. Activities conducted in a building principally used as a residence;

h. Railroad tracks and minor sidings; or

i. Areas which are predominantly used for residential purposes.

(12) SAFETY REST AREAS. An area or site established or maintained within or adjacent to the right-of-way by or under public supervision or control for the convenience of the traveling public.

(13) INFORMATION CENTER. An area or site established or maintained at safety rest areas for the purpose of informing the public of places of interest within the state and providing such other information as the director may consider necessary.

(14) MAIN-TRAVELED WAY. The through traffic lanes exclusive of frontage roads, auxiliary lanes and ramps.

(15) URBAN AREA. An urbanized area so designated by the Bureau of the Census, within boundaries fixed by responsible state and local officials, subject to approval by the Secretary of the United States Department of Transportation, or an urban place as designated by the Bureau of the Census having a population of 5,000 or more and not within any urbanized area, within boundaries fixed by responsible state and local officials, subject

to approval by the Secretary of the United States Department of Transportation.

(16) MOTORIST DIRECTIONAL SIGNS. Any signs, displays or devices giving directional information pertaining to food services, lodging, gasoline and automotive services, resorts, attractions, campgrounds, truck stops, natural wonders, scenic and historical sites and areas suited for outdoor recreation.

(17) REMOVING AUTHORITY. Any governmental entity. (Acts 1971, 3rd Ex. Sess., No. 276, p. 4544, § 3; Acts 1978, No. 383, p. 347; Acts 1979, No. 79-672, p. 1183.)

§ 23-1-272. Declaration of policy.

The legislature hereby finds and declares:

(1) That outdoor advertising is a legitimate commercial use of private property adjacent to roads and highways;

(2) That the erection and maintenance of outdoor advertising signs, displays and devices in areas adjacent to interstate highways and primary highways should be regulated in order to protect the public investment in such highways, to promote the recreational value of public travel, to preserve natural beauty and to promote the reasonable, orderly and effective display of such signs, displays and devices;

(3) That outdoor advertising is an integral part of the business and marketing function and an established segment of the national economy and should be allowed to operate in business areas;

(4) Regulatory standards set forth in Section 23-1-274 are consistent with customary use in this state and will properly and adequately carry out each and all of the purposes of this division; and

(5) Motorist directional signs are essential to the economic interests of the state and the interests of the traveling public; therefore, no motorist directional sign not otherwise permitted under Section 23-1-273 shall be removed on a statewide basis, unless by mutual agreement between the sign owner and the State Highway Department, until all other nonconforming signs are removed. (Acts 1971, 3rd Ex. Sess., No. 276, p. 4544, § 2; Acts 1979, No. 79-672, p. 1183.)

§ 23-1-273. Erection or maintenance of signs — Prohibited in adjacent areas; exceptions.

No sign shall, subject to the provisions of Section 23-1-274, be erected or maintained in an adjacent area after February 10, 1972, nor shall any outdoor advertising sign, display or device with the purpose of its message being read from the main-traveled way of an interstate highway or primary highway be erected after April 11, 1978, outside of an urban area beyond 660 feet of the nearest edge of right-of-way of an interstate or primary highway, except the following:

(1) Directional and official signs, including, but not limited to, signs pertaining to natural wonders, scenic and historical attractions, safety rest

areas and information centers, which are authorized by the director, under promulgated rule, and which comply with regulations promulgated by the director relative to their lighting, size, number, spacing and other such requirements as may be appropriate to implement this division; provided, that such regulations shall not be inconsistent with, nor more restrictive than, such national standards as may be promulgated from time to time by the Secretary of Transportation of the United States pursuant to subsection (c) of Section 131, of Title 23, United States Code.

(2) Signs lawfully in existence on October 22, 1965, determined by the state, subject to the concurrence of the United States Secretary of Transportation, to be landmark signs, including signs on farm structures or natural surfaces of historic or artistic significance, the preservation of which would be consistent with the purposes of this section.

(3) Signs advertising the sale or lease of property upon which they are located.

(4) Signs advertising activities conducted on the property on which they are located. For the purposes of this subdivision, the promotion of activities at other locations or the dissemination of information about activities conducted upon other property shall not be considered activities conducted on the property on which a sign is located.

(5) Signs located in business areas on February 10, 1972, and signs to be erected in business areas subsequent to February 10, 1972, which when erected, will comply with the provisions of Section 23-1-274; provided, that no advertising, sign, display or device with the purpose of its message being read from the main-traveled way shall be erected after April 11, 1978, outside an urban area beyond 660 feet of the edge of the right-of-way of an interstate or primary highway, whether located in a business area or not.

(6) Signs or devices which advertise or designate exclusively the location of the facilities of any public utility located along the interstate or primary highway for the convenience or protection of the using public or the protection of the facilities of the public utility.

(7) Motorist directional signs lawfully erected and in existence on May 5, 1976, which do not conform to requirements of present state laws and whose removal would work a substantial economic hardship in a specific or defined area. The State Highway Department, upon receipt of a petition, declaration or resolution from any state, county or municipal agency, from any industry association or any group of private business persons or their employees, claiming that the removal of such motorist directional signs would work a substantial economic hardship in specific or defined areas, shall forward such petition, declaration or resolution to the United States Secretary of Transportation to approve retention of such motorist directional signs. (Acts 1971, 3rd Ex. Sess., No. 276, p. 4544, § 4; Acts 1978, No. 383, p. 347; Acts 1979, No. 79-672, p. 1183.)

Collateral references. — Construction and application of restrictive covenants to the use of signs. 61 ALR4th 1028.

§ 23-1-274. Erection or maintenance of signs — Controls; criteria.

The director shall effectively control, or cause to be controlled, the erection and maintenance of outdoor advertising signs, displays and devices in all business areas that are erected subsequent to February 10, 1971. Whenever a bona fide state, county or local zoning authority has made a determination of customary use as to size, lighting and spacing, such determination may be accepted in lieu of controls by agreement in the zoned commercial and industrial area within the geographical jurisdiction of such authority. In all other controlled commercial and industrial areas, the criteria set forth below shall apply:

(1) SIZE OF SIGNS.

a. The maximum area for any one sign shall be 1,200 square feet with a maximum height of 30 feet and maximum length of 60 feet, inclusive of any border and trim, but excluding the base or apron, supports and other structural members.

b. The area shall be measured by the smallest square, rectangle, triangle or circle or combination thereof which will encompass the entire sign.

c. A sign structure may contain one or two signs per facing and may be placed double-faced, back-to-back or V-type; provided, that if two signs are used facing the same direction, the aggregate total area shall not exceed 1,200 square feet.

(2) LIGHTING.

a. Signs shall not be erected or maintained which contain, include or are illuminated by any flashing, intermittent or moving lights, except those giving public service information such as, but not limited to, time, date, temperature, weather or news.

b. Signs shall not be erected or maintained which are not effectively shielded so as to prevent beams or rays of light from being directed at any portion of traveled way of any interstate or primary highway and are of such intensity or brilliance as to cause glare or to impair the vision of the driver of any motor vehicle.

c. Signs shall not be erected or maintained which shall be so illuminated that they obscure or interfere with any official traffic sign, device or signal.

(3) SPACING.

a. Signs shall not be erected or maintained in such a manner as to obscure, or otherwise physically interfere with an official traffic sign, signal or device or which obstructs or physically interferes with the driver's view of approaching, merging or intersecting traffic.

b. Signs shall not be erected or maintained which do not comply with all applicable county or municipal codes and ordinances, including, but not limited to, zoning, buildings and sign codes, as locally interpreted, applied and enforced.

c. Signs shall not be erected or maintained closer to another sign other than a sign described in subdivisions (1), (2), (3) and (5) of Section 23-1-273 than the following prescribed distances. These spacing provisions do not apply to signs separated by buildings or other obstructions in such manner that only one sign located within the above spacing distance is visible from the highway at any one time. The minimum distance between signs shall be measured along the nearest edge of the pavement between points directly opposite the signs along each side of the highway.

1. On all interstate highways and freeway primary highways, there must be at least 500 feet between sign structures on the same side of the highway.

2. On interstate highways and freeway primary highways located outside the zoning authority of incorporated cities, no sign structure is permitted adjacent to or within 500 feet of an interchange or intersection at grade or safety roadside rest areas. Such distances shall be measured along the highway to the nearest point of beginning or ending of pavement widening at the exit from or entrance to the main-traveled way.

3. On primary highways located outside the zoning authority of incorporated cities, there must be at least 300 feet between sign structures on the same side of such highway.

4. On primary highways located within the zoning authority of incorporated cities, there must be at least 100 feet between sign structures on the same side of such highway.

(4) GENERAL.

a. Signs shall not be erected or maintained which imitate or resemble any official traffic sign, signal or device.

b. Signs shall not be erected or maintained upon trees, or painted or drawn upon rocks or other natural features.

c. Signs shall not be erected or maintained which are structurally unsafe or in substantial disrepair.

d. Signs which are obsolete shall be removed. (Acts 1971, 3rd Ex. Sess., No. 276, p. 4544, § 5.)

Collateral references. — Validity and construction of state or local regulation prohibiting the erection or maintenance of advertising structures within a specified distance of street or highway. 81 ALR3d 564.

§ 23-1-275. Erection or maintenance of signs — Permits; identification tags or decals.

(a) No sign permitted by the provisions of Section 23-1-274 may be erected without first obtaining a permit therefor from the director. No permit shall be required for signs conforming to the provisions of this division which are in existence upon February 10, 1972, until the end of the fifth calendar year. The application for a permit shall be on a form provided by the director and shall contain such information as the director may require. Upon receipt of an application containing all required information in due form and properly executed, the director shall issue a permit to the applicant for the erection of the sign, provided such sign will not violate any provisions of this division. A charge of $25.00 will be made for each location covered in the permit. The application for a permit shall be accompanied by the required fee.

(b) Permits shall be for the calendar year, and shall be renewed annually upon payment of a fee of $10.00 for the following calendar year without the necessity of filing a new application. The fee shall not be prorated for fractions of the year. Only one permit shall be required for double-faced, back-to-back or V-type signs. Advertising copy may be changed at any time without the payment of an additional fee, and nothing in this division shall be construed to give the director any power of censorship with regard thereto.

(c) Permit fees for signs under this division shall become due and payable on January 1 of each year and delinquent on February 15 thereafter. A 25 percent penalty shall be charged and collected for any delinquent permit issued after February 15.

(d) In addition to the permit, the director shall issue an identification tag or decal to the applicant upon payment of the fee which shall be permanently affixed to the sign, display or device for which the permit was issued. Such tag or decal shall be so affixed in a uniform position on all such signs, displays and devices. The size, location and content, including identification numbers, and the materials from which such tags or decals are to be made shall be determined by the director. All signs, displays and devices which do not have the tag or decal attached thereto as provided in this section, shall be considered as being nonconforming within the terms of this division.

(e) The director shall issue a permit for the sign, display or device described in any application duly made under this section unless it is in violation of this division. Any permit may be revoked after a public hearing upon 30 days written notice if the director finds that any statements made in the application thereof were false or misleading or that the advertising sign, display or device covered thereby is not in good general condition and in reasonable state of repair or is otherwise in violation of this division, provided such false or misleading statement has not been corrected and that the sign, display or device has not been brought into compliance with this division prior to said public hearing. The director for good cause shown at such hearing may extend the time within which such sign, display or device may be brought into conformance or other remedial action taken. (Acts 1971, 3rd Ex. Sess., No. 276, p. 4544, § 11; Acts 1978, No. 383, p. 347.)

Collateral references. — Construction and application of restrictive covenants to the use of signs. 61 ALR4th 1028.

§ 23-1-276. Erection or maintenance of signs — Name and address of owner and date of erection to appear on signs, etc.

Each sign or structure regulated by this division shall have stated thereon the name and address of the owners thereof and the date of its erection; provided, that if the address of the owner is on file with the director, it need not be stated on such sign or structure. (Acts 1971, 3rd Ex. Sess., No. 276, p. 4544, § 10.)

§ 23-1-277. Erection or maintenance of signs — Exceptions to Sections 23-1-275 and 23-1-276.

The provisions of Sections 23-1-275 and 23-1-276 shall not be applicable to signs of less than one square foot in area, excluding the support, erected by a public utility to mark the location of any buried telephone cable, electric power line, gas line, waterline or other underground public utility facility, for the protection of the facilities of the public utility. (Acts 1971, 3rd Ex. Sess., No. 276, p. 4544, § 18.)

§ 23-1-278. Enforcement of division generally.

(a) Any sign erected or maintained in an adjacent area after February 10, 1972, and any outdoor advertising sign, display or device erected with the purpose of its message being read from the main-traveled way of any interstate highway or primary highway outside of an urban area and beyond 660 feet of the right-of-way after April 11, 1978, in violation of the provisions of this division or the rules and regulations promulgated under the provisions of this division may be removed by the director upon 30 days' prior notice by certified or registered mail to the owner thereof and to the owner of the land on which said sign is located or through court proceedings at the option of the director. No notice shall be required to be given to the owner of the sign or to a property owner whose name is not stated on the sign or on the structure on which it is displayed or whose address is not stated thereon and is not on file with the director.

(b) The courts of this state shall have jurisdiction, in accordance with the provisions of Sections 6-6-220 through 6-6-232, over actions for declaratory judgment, initiated by the director, the owners of signs or the owners of property on which signs are located, to determine and adjudicate controversies arising under or out of the enforcement of this division and to set forth the rights, duties and responsibilities of the various parties arising under this division, including decrees of injunction and ordering removal of signs. In addition the courts of this state shall have such injunctive powers as may be necessary to enforce or compel compliance with the provisions of this division in cases filed by the director for injunction in the enforcement of this division, including the power to enjoin the continuing maintenance of any sign erected or maintained in violation of the provisions of this division and the removal of any such signs on complaint filed by the director. Proceedings hereunder being largely equitable in nature, the courts shall set forth the rights, duties and responsibilities of the parties under this division on the facts presented without intervention of a jury except as may be otherwise provided by statute or the Constitution of Alabama. In the event a sign or signs involved in any proceeding hereunder are found to be maintained, permitted to exist or erected in violation of any of the provisions of this division, the court trying the cause, on being petitioned by the director, shall order the removal of the sign or signs, subject to Sections 23-1-280, 23-1-281 and 23-1-282, where applicable, by the sign owner or jointly by the sign owner and property owner if joined in the proceeding or separately by the property owner; provided, that the director, acting through personnel of the State of Alabama Highway Department, may remove such signs at the option of the director as provided herein or as ordered by the court. Court costs shall be taxed against a sign owner or property owner on which a sign is located if a court determines that such parties have erected or maintained a sign in violation of this division. Jurisdiction and procedure of courts are not limited by this division.

(c) In any proceeding hereunder in the courts of this state, an allegation or averment setting forth the owner of the real property or the owner of a sign located thereon to be a particular party or parties shall be deemed to establish prima facie ownership of the real property or the sign to be in such party or parties, respectively, unless within 30 days from the service of process upon them, such party or parties file in the proceeding a sworn denial of ownership and, in addition thereto, set forth any interest in and to such real property or sign to which they claim to be entitled. In any proceeding hereunder in the courts, employees of the State of Alabama Highway Department may testify, from general knowledge, that a particular highway is an interstate or primary highway or as to the location of geographical boundaries of urban areas, incorporated municipalities and other zoned areas. In addition to other official maps, maps prepared by the State of Alabama Highway Department as to the location of geographical boundaries of urban areas hereunder shall be received in evidence in aid of establishment of such boundaries when offered on the general knowledge of employees of the highway department that such map or maps were prepared by the State of Alabama Highway Department for the purpose of establishing the geographical boundaries of an urban area.

(d) In the event a determination is made by the director that a particular sign or signs have been erected or are being maintained or allowed to exist in violation of any of the provisions of this division, upon written notice to the owner of such sign or signs, such owner of the sign or signs shall have a duty to submit to the director all factual and documentary evidence in his possession, under his control or reasonably obtainable by such sign owner relating to the date or dates of the erection of the sign or signs, the names of individuals erecting same and all information relating in any manner to the erection of the sign or signs, the names of individuals erecting same and all information relating in any manner to the location thereof which would tend to have a bearing on whether the sign or signs were erected in violation of or are being maintained or allowed to exist in violation of any of the provisions of this division.

All officers and employees of the State of Alabama Highway Department are hereby authorized and empowered to enter upon and go across any land located within the State of Alabama for the purpose of inspection of any sign determined by the director to be in existence in violation of this division or any amendment thereto. Any officer and employee of the State of Alabama Highway Department who, acting lawfully under this division, enters upon or crosses any lands located within this state for the purpose of inspection or removal of any such sign and in and about the activity of inspection or removal of any such sign is hereby vested with full police power to arrest or prefer charges against any person or persons who interferes with the performance of his duty. (Acts 1971, 3rd Ex. Sess., No. 276, p. 4544, § 12; Acts 1978, No. 383, p. 347.)

Removal of illegal signs without just compensation to owners. — This section gives the director of the Alabama Highway Department the authority to remove illegal signs without just compensation to the owners, provided there is adequate notice. State Hwy. Dep't v. Morgan, 584 So. 2d 499 (Ala. 1991).

Collateral references. — Construction and application of restrictive covenants to the use of signs. 61 ALR4th 1028.

§ 23-1-279. Nonconforming signs — Removal and payment of compensation generally.

(a) Signs outside of business areas which are lawfully in existence on February 10, 1972, but which do not conform to the requirements in this division, are declared nonconforming and, subject to Sections 23-1-280, 23-1-281 and 23-1-282, shall be removed by the sign owner and/or property owner under agreement with the director, or under the authority of the director, upon agreement between the parties as to just compensation. In the event no agreement can be reached as to just compensation, the sign shall be removed and payment made therefor through petition filed in probate court in accordance with Section 23-1-282. Outdoor advertising signs, displays or devices with the purpose of their message being read from the main-traveled way of any interstate highway or primary highway erected prior to April 11, 1978, outside of an urban area and beyond 660 feet of the edge of the right-of-way of such interstate or primary highway and not otherwise lawful under Section 23-1-273, as amended, are declared nonconforming and, subject to Sections 23-1-280, 23-1-281 and 23-1-282, shall be removed by the sign owner and/or property owner under agreement with the director or under the authority of the director, upon agreement between the parties as to just compensation. In the event no agreement can be reached as to just compensation, the sign shall be removed and payment made therefor through petition filed in probate court in accordance with Section 23-1-282.

(b) Signs lawfully erected after February 10, 1972, and which subsequently do not conform to the requirements of this division, shall be removed by the sign owner and/or property owner under agreement with the director or under the authority of the director, upon agreement between the parties as to just compensation. In the event no agreement can be reached as to just compensation, the sign shall be removed and payment made therefor through petition filed in probate court in accordance with Section 23-1-282.

(c) Should any commercial or industrial activity which has been used in defining or delineating an unzoned area cease to operate, the unzoned area shall be redefined or redelineated based on the remaining activities. Any signs located within the former unzoned area, but located outside the unzoned area based on its new dimensions, shall become nonconforming and, subject to Sections 23-1-280, 23-1-281 and 23-1-282, shall be removed by the sign owner and/or property owner under agreement with the director or under the authority of the director, upon agreement between the parties as to just compensation. In the event no agreement can be reached as to just compensation, the sign shall be removed and payment made therefor through petition filed in probate court in accordance with Section 23-1-282. (Acts 1971, 3rd Ex. Sess., No. 276, p. 4544, § 6; Acts 1978, No. 383, p. 347.)

Grandfather provision for signs erected prior to February 10, 1972. — Essentially, this section sets forth a grandfather provision whereby owners of outdoor advertising signs are entitled to compensation for removal of signs, but they must have been lawfully erected prior to February 10, 1972. State Hwy. Dep't v. Morgan, 584 So. 2d 499 (Ala. 1991).

Collateral references. — Nuisance: billboards and other outdoor advertising signs as civil nuisance. 38 ALR3d 647.

Classification and maintenance of advertising structure as nonconforming use. 80 ALR3d 630.

Construction and application of restrictive covenants to the use of signs. 61 ALR4th 1028.

§ 23-1-280. Nonconforming signs — Just compensation — When paid.

Just compensation shall be paid by the removing authority upon the removal of any of the following signs which are not then in conformity with the provisions of this division whether or not removed pursuant to or because of the provisions of this division:

(1) Signs lawfully in existence on February 10, 1972.

(2) Signs lawfully in existence on land adjoining any highway made an interstate or primary highway after February 10, 1972.

(3) Outdoor advertising signs, displays or devices erected with the purpose of their message being read from the main-traveled way of any interstate highway or primary highway erected outside of an urban area and beyond 660 feet of the edge of the right-of-way of such interstate or primary highway erected prior to April 11, 1978, and not otherwise lawful under Section 23-1-273, as amended.

(4) Signs lawfully erected on or after February 10, 1972.

Notwithstanding any provision of law to the contrary, no removing authority shall remove or cause to be removed, or cause the alteration in any manner of, any lawfully erected sign along any public street or highway within the state without paying just compensation. (Acts 1971, 3rd Ex. Sess., No. 276, p. 4544, § 7; Acts 1978, No. 383, p. 347; Acts 1979, No. 79-672, p. 1183; Acts 1988, No. 88-228, p. 360.)

§ 23-1-281. Nonconforming signs — Just compensation — For what paid.

The just compensation required by the provisions of Section 23-1-280 shall be paid for the following:

(1) The taking from the owner of such sign, all right, title and interest in and to such sign, and his leasehold relating thereto, and compensation therefor, including severance damage to the remaining portion of the sign, shall be included in the amounts paid to the respective owner, exclusive of any damage of factories involved in manufacturing, erection, maintenance or servicing of any outdoor advertising signs or displays.

(2) The taking from the owner of the real property on which the sign is located or the right to erect and maintain such signs thereon. (Acts 1971, 3rd Ex. Sess., No. 276, p. 4544, § 8.)

§ 23-1-282. Nonconforming signs — Just compensation — To whom paid; agreements; civil actions.

(a) Compensation required under the provisions of Sections 23-1-280 and 23-1-281 shall be paid to the person or persons entitled thereto. If the director and the owner or owners reach an agreement on the amount of compensation payable to such owner or owners in respect to any removal or relocation, the director may pay such compensation to the owner or owners and thereby acquire or terminate his rights or interest as by purchase; provided, that any sign, display or device lawfully in existence along the interstate system or the federal-aid primary system on February 10, 1971, which is not in conformity with the provisions contained in this division shall not be required to be removed until just compensation has been paid therefor. Notwithstanding any other provision of this division, no sign, display or device otherwise required to be removed under this division, for which just compensation is authorized to be paid by the director, shall be required to be removed if the federal share of at least 75 percent of the just compensation to be paid upon removal of such sign, device or display is not available for such payment.

(b) If the director and the owner do not reach agreement as to such amount of compensation, the director may institute an action to have such compensation determined in a civil action. Such an action shall be instituted by filing a petition in the probate court of the county where the advertising device and land are located. Such action for determination of compensation shall thereupon proceed and be treated in accordance with the provisions of this title and Title 18 of this Code to the extent not inconsistent with the provisions of this division, the same as if such action had been commenced thereunder by a petition by the state for the taking of property under its power of eminent domain. (Acts 1971, 3rd Ex. Sess., No. 276, p. 4544, § 9.)

Collateral references. — Actionable nature of advertising impugning quality or worth of merchandise or products. 42 ALR4th 318.

Construction and application of restrictive covenants to the use of signs. 61 ALR4th 1028.

§ 23-1-283. Nonconforming signs — Just compensation — Sufficient federal funds required.

Despite any contrary provisions in this division, no sign shall be required to be removed unless at the time of removal there are sufficient funds, from whatever source, appropriated and immediately made available to the director with which to pay the just compensation required under Sections 23-1-280 through 23-1-282 and unless, at such time, the federal funds required to be contributed to this state under Section 131, Title 23, United States Code, have been appropriated and are immediately available to the state. (Acts 1971, 3rd Ex. Sess., No. 276, p. 4544, § 17.)

§ 23-1-284. Agreement with United States Secretary of Transportation.

The director, on behalf of the state, is authorized and directed to seek agreement with the Secretary of Transportation of the United States, acting under the provisions of Section 131, Title 23, United States Code, as amended, that the provisions of this division are in conformance with Section 131, Title 23, United States Code, and provide effective control of outdoor advertising signs as set forth therein. (Acts 1971, 3rd Ex. Sess., No. 276, p. 4544, § 14.)

§ 23-1-285. Director authorized to accept federal funds.

The director may accept any allotment of funds by the United States, or any agency thereof, appropriated to carry out the purposes of Section 131, Title 23, United States Code, as amended, from time to time. The director shall take such steps as may be necessary, from time to time, to obtain from the United States, or the appropriate agency thereof, funds allotted and appropriated, pursuant to Section 131, Title 23, United States Code, for the purpose of paying the federal government's 75 percent share of the just compensation to be paid to sign owners and owners of real property under the terms of subsection (g) of Section 131, Title 23, United States Code, and Sections 23-1-280 through 23-1-282. (Acts 1971, 3rd Ex. Sess., No. 276, p. 4544, § 15.)

§ 23-1-286. Rules and regulations.

The Highway Director is hereby authorized to adopt such rules and regulations as are necessary and appropriate to carry out the provisions of this division. (Acts 1971, 3rd Ex. Sess., No. 276, p. 4544, § 16.)

§ 23-1-287. Disposition of fees.

All fees collected for the issuance of permits provided for under this division shall be paid into the state treasury to be credited to the public road and bridge fund. (Acts 1971, 3rd Ex. Sess., No. 276, p. 4544, § 20.)

§ 23-1-288. Penalty for violation of division, etc.

Whoever erects or maintains a sign in violation of the provisions of this division or in violation of rules and regulations promulgated by the director under the provisions of this division shall be guilty of a class C misdemeanor and shall upon conviction be punished as provided in Title 13A. (Acts 1971, 3rd Ex. Sess., No. 276, p. 4544, § 13; Acts 1978, No. 383, p. 347.)

ARTICLE 10.

FEDERAL AID HIGHWAY FINANCE AUTHORITY.

Cross references. — As to Alabama highway authority, see § 23-1-150 et seq. As to Alabama highway finance corporation, see § 23-1-170 et seq.

§ 23-1-300. Purpose and construction of article.

(a) It is the intention of the legislature by the passage of this article to authorize the incorporation of the Director of Finance, the Highway Director, the Attorney General, the State Treasurer and the Executive Secretary to the Governor of Alabama for the purpose of anticipating and providing for the federal share of the cost of constructing federal-aid projects on the state highway system and thus to accelerate the construction of such federal aid projects in the state by the issuance of the obligations of such corporation, which shall not be bonds or debts of the state but shall be payable solely from federal-aid highway funds and the tax proceeds and investment income provided therefor by this article.

(b) This article shall be liberally construed in conformity with the said purpose. (Acts 1976, No. 565, p. 764, § 1; Acts 1981, No. 81-387, p. 574, § 1; Acts 1988, No. 88-652, p. 1041, § 1; Acts 1992, No. 92-204, § 1.)

The 1992 amendment, effective April 16, 1992, in subsection (a) deleted the former clause (i) designation preceding "the federal share," substituted "federal-aid projects on the state highway system" for "federal-aid interstate and defense highways, (ii) the federal share of the cost of constructing federal-aid primary highways, and (iii) replacing bridges on the state highway system together with work incidental and related to the construction of all such highways and bridges," substituted "such federal aid projects" for "such interstate, defense and primary highways and bridge replacement," and deleted "to be received during the federal fiscal years ending 1978 through 1995" following "from federal-aid highway funds."

Collateral references. — 39A C.J.S., Highways, §§ 154-157.

39 Am. Jur. 2d, Highways, Streets & Bridges, § 13.

§ 23-1-301. Definitions.

When used in this article, the following words and phrases shall have the following respective meanings unless the context clearly indicates otherwise:

(1) AUTHORITY. The Alabama Federal Aid Highway Finance Authority, a public corporation and instrumentality of the state authorized to be organized under the provisions of this article.

(2) BOARD OF DIRECTORS. The board of directors of the authority.

(3) BONDS. The bonds (including refunding bonds issued to refund outstanding obligations) that in this article are authorized to be sold and issued by the authority.

(4) CORPORATION. The authority.

(5) GASOLINE TAX APPROPRIATION ACT. Division 2 of Article 2 of Chapter 17 of Title 40.

(6) HIGHWAY GASOLINE TAX.

a. The excise tax levied in Section 40-17-31 exclusive of those portions of said tax in respect of aviation fuel and marine gasoline, as those terms are used in said section; and

b. The excise tax levied by Article 3 of Chapter 17 of Title 40, exclusive of that portion of the said tax in respect of diesel fuel.

(7) LEGISLATURE. The Legislature of Alabama.

(8) NET GASOLINE TAX PROCEEDS. The entire proceeds from the highway gasoline tax less the cost of collection and less any refunds of the said proceeds pursuant to the provisions of Article 3 of Chapter 17 of Title 40 or pursuant to the provisions of either of Divisions 3 and 4 of Article 2 of Chapter 17 of Title 40.

(9) NOTE. The authority's promise to pay solely from the funds provided by this article which has a specified maturity date not later than three years after its date, which recites on its face that it is issued in anticipation of the sale by the authority of bonds and which is payable to the order of a named payee.

(10) OBLIGATIONS. Any bonds, temporary bonds or notes authorized by this article to be issued by the authority.

(11) STATE. The State of Alabama.

(12) STATE SHARE OF THE NET GASOLINE TAX PROCEEDS. The 45 percent of the net gasoline tax proceeds allocated and appropriated for state highway purposes in Section 40-17-72.

(13) TEMPORARY BOND. Any bond issued under this article which has a specified maturity date not later than three years after its date and which recites on its face that it is issued in anticipation of the sale by the authority of bonds.

(14) COST. As applied to any highway construction project, all costs of construction or acquisition of any part of any such highway construction project, including, but without limitation to, the costs of supervising, inspecting and constructing any such highway construction project and all costs and expenses incidental thereto, the costs of locating, surveying and

mapping, resurfacing, restoration and rehabilitation, acquisition of rights-of-way, relocation assistance, elimination of hazards of railway-grade crossings, acquisition of replacement housing sites, acquisition, rehabilitation, relocation and construction of replacement housing and improvements which directly facilitate and control traffic flow, including grade separation of intersections, widening of lanes, channelization of traffic, traffic-control systems and passenger loading and unloading areas, and any other cost of any federal aid projects on the state highway system which is to be repaid or reimbursed to the state by the United States of America pursuant to the written agreement provided for in Section 23-1-313.

(15) FEDERAL SHARE. That portion of the cost of any federal aid projects on the state highway system which is to be repaid or reimbursed to the state by the United States of America pursuant to the written agreement provided for in Section 23-1-313. (Acts 1976, No. 565, p. 764, § 2; Acts 1981, No. 81-387, p. 574, § 2; Acts 1988, No. 88-652, p. 1041, § 2; Acts 1992, No. 92-204, § 1.)

The 1992 amendment, effective April 16, 1992, substituted "federal aid projects on the state highway system" for "interstate, defense, primary highway or bridge replacement" in subdivisions (14) and (15); deleted former subdivision (16) which related to the definition of primary highways; and deleted former subdivision (17) which related to the definition of bridge replacement.

§ 23-1-302. Incorporation — Authorization.

The Director of Finance, the Highway Director, the Attorney General, the State Treasurer and the Executive Secretary to the Governor may become a corporation with the powers and authorities provided in this article by proceeding according to the provisions of this article. (Acts 1976, No. 565, p. 764, § 3.)

§ 23-1-303. Incorporation — Application.

(a) To become a corporation, the Director of Finance, the Highway Director, the Attorney General, the State Treasurer and the Executive Secretary to the Governor shall present to the Secretary of State of Alabama an application signed by them which will set forth:

(1) The name, official designation and official residence of each of the applicants;

(2) The date on which each applicant was inducted in the office and the term of office of each of the applicants;

(3) The name of the proposed corporation, which shall be Alabama Federal Aid Highway Finance Authority;

(4) The location of the principal office of the proposed corporation; and

(5) Any other matter relating to the proposed corporation which the applicants may choose to insert and which is not inconsistent with this article or the laws of the State of Alabama.

(b) The application shall be subscribed and sworn to by each of the applicants before an officer authorized by laws of the State of Alabama to take acknowledgments to deeds.

(c) The Secretary of State shall examine the application and, if he finds that it substantially complies with the requirements of this section, he shall receive and file it and record it in an appropriate book of records in his office. (Acts 1976, No. 565, p. 764, § 4.)

§ 23-1-304. Incorporation — Certificate.

(a) When the application has been made, filed and recorded as provided in Section 23-1-303, the applicants shall constitute a corporation under the name proposed in the application and the Secretary of State shall make and issue to the applicants a certificate of incorporation pursuant to this article under the great seal of the state and shall record the same with the application.

(b) There shall be no fees paid to the Secretary of State for any work in connection with the incorporation or dissolution of the corporation so organized. (Acts 1976, No. 565, p. 764, § 5.)

§ 23-1-305. Members; officers and directors; quorum; filling of vacancies; compensation of members, officers or directors; record of proceedings.

(a) The applicants named in the application and their respective successors in office shall constitute the members of the corporation.

(b) The Director of Finance shall be the president of the corporation, the Executive Secretary to the Governor shall be the vice-president of the corporation, the Highway Director shall be the secretary of the corporation and the State Treasurer shall be the treasurer of the corporation and shall act as custodian of its funds.

(c) The members of the corporation shall constitute all the members of the board of directors of the corporation, and any three members of said board of directors shall constitute a quorum for the transaction of business.

(d) Should any of said officials of the state die or should his term of office (as Director of Finance, Highway Director, Attorney General, State Treasurer or Executive Secretary to the Governor, as the case may be) expire or should he resign therefrom, his successor in office shall take his place as a member, officer and director of the corporation.

(e) No member, officer or director of the corporation shall draw any salary in addition to that now authorized by law for any service he may render or any duty he may perform in connection with the corporation.

(f) All proceedings had and done by the board of directors shall be reduced to writing by the secretary of the corporation and recorded in a substantially bound book. Copies of such proceedings, when certified by the secretary of the corporation under the seal of the corporation, shall be received in all courts as prima facie evidence of the matters and things therein certified. (Acts 1976, No. 565, p. 764, § 6.)

Collateral references. — 39A C.J.S., Highways, §§ 161-174.

§ 23-1-306. Powers generally.

The corporation shall have the following powers:

(1) To have perpetual succession by its corporate name unless sooner dissolved pursuant to Section 23-1-318.

(2) To commence actions and have actions commenced against it and to prosecute and defend in any court having jurisdiction of the subject matter and of the parties.

(3) To have and to use a corporate seal and to alter the same at pleasure.

(4) To construct, reconstruct and relocate or to cause to be constructed, reconstructed and relocated federal aid projects on the state highway system, including work incidental or related thereto, in the State of Alabama.

(5) To acquire by purchase, gift or condemnation or any other lawful means or any combination of such means and to convey or cause to be conveyed to the State of Alabama any real, personal or mixed property necessary or convenient in connection with the construction of federal aid projects on the state highway system and approaches thereto in the State of Alabama or the reconstruction or relocation of federal aid projects on the state highway system in said state.

(6) To exercise the right of eminent domain as freely and completely as, and in the same manner that, the State of Alabama is empowered to exercise such right.

(7) To borrow money for its corporate purposes and in evidence of such borrowing to sell and issue its obligations and to refund such obligations.

(8) To pledge the proceeds of the appropriations and pledges provided for in this article as security for payment of the principal of and the interest on its obligations.

(9) To appoint and employ such officers, attorneys and agents as the business of the corporation may require. (Acts 1976, No. 565, p. 764, § 7; Acts 1981, No. 81-387, p. 574, § 3; Acts 1988, No. 88-652, p. 1041, § 3; Acts 1992, No. 92-204, § 1.)

The 1992 amendment, effective April 16, 1992, substituted "federal aid projects on the state highway system" for "interstate, defense, primary highways and bridge replacements" in subdivision (4), substituted "federal aid projects on the state highway system" for "interstate, defense, primary highways and bridge replacements" in two places in subdivision (5), and deleted "and" at the end of subdivision (8).

§ 23-1-307. Bonds and notes — Authorization for issuance.

The authority shall have the power and is hereby authorized and empowered to sell and issue its bonds not exceeding $212,000,000.00 in aggregate principal amount in order to provide as soon as practicable the federal share of the cost of constructing federal aid projects on the state highway system in anticipation of the receipt by the state of such federal portions as they become available either during, upon or after completion of such construction. The authority shall have the power, in addition to any other powers granted in this article, to borrow money for temporary use for any of the purposes for which it is authorized by this article to issue bonds and, in evidence of such borrowing, to issue from time to time temporary bonds or notes. Any such temporary borrowing may be made in anticipation of the sale and issuance of bonds and in such event the principal proceeds from the sale of such bonds shall, to the extent necessary, be used for payment of the principal of and interest on the temporary bonds or notes issued in anticipation of the sale and issuance of such bonds. Subject to the provisions and limitations contained in this article, the authority may, from time to time, sell and issue refunding bonds for the purpose of refunding any matured or unmatured obligations of the authority issued under this article and then outstanding; provided, that the provisions of this section limiting the aggregate principal amount of bonds authorized to be issued by the authority to $212,000,000.00 shall not apply to refunding bonds. (Acts 1976, No. 565, p. 764, § 8; Acts 1981, No. 81-387, p. 574, § 4; Acts 1988, No. 88-652, p. 1041, § 4; Acts 1992, No. 92-204, § 1.)

The 1992 amendment, effective April 16, 1992, substituted "federal aid projects on the state highway system" for "interstate and defense highways and the federal share of the cost of constructing primary highways and bridge replacements" in the first sentence.

Collateral references. — 39A C.J.S., Highways, § 158.

§ 23-1-308. Bonds and notes — Form, denominations, terms, redemption, etc.

Any obligations authorized by this article shall be in such forms and denominations and of such tenor and maturities, shall bear such rate or rates of interest payable and evidenced in such manner and may contain other provisions not inconsistent with this article as may be provided in the resolution or resolutions of the board of directors in which such obligations are authorized to be issued; provided, that none of the bonds shall have a maturity date later than 15 years after its date and none of the temporary bonds or notes shall have a maturity date later than three years after its date. The authority may at its election retain in the resolution or resolutions under which any obligation is issued an option to redeem all or any thereof at such redemption price or prices and after such notice or notices and on such terms and conditions as may be set forth in the said resolution or resolutions and as may be briefly recited in the face of such obligation with respect to which such option of redemption is retained. (Acts 1976, No. 565, p. 764, § 9; Acts 1981, No. 81-387, p. 574, § 5.)

§ 23-1-309. Bonds and notes — Execution.

The obligations authorized by this article shall be signed by the president or vice-president of the authority, as the board of directors shall designate, and attested by its secretary or an assistant secretary, as the board of directors shall designate; provided, that a facsimile of the signature of one but not of both of the said officers may be printed or otherwise reproduced on any of the obligations authorized by this article in lieu of their being manually signed. All interest coupons applicable to the bonds or temporary bonds shall be signed by the president or vice-president of the authority, as the board of directors shall designate; provided, that a facsimile of the signature of such officer may be printed or otherwise reproduced on any of the interest coupons in lieu of their being manually signed. The seal of the authority shall be impressed on the bonds and temporary bonds authorized by this article; provided, that a facsimile of the said seal may be printed or otherwise reproduced in lieu of being manually impressed thereon. (Acts 1976, No. 565, p. 764, § 10; Acts 1981, No. 81-387, p. 574, § 6.)

§ 23-1-310. Bonds and notes — Issuance and sale generally.

Obligations of the authority may be sold at either public or private sale in such manner and at such price or prices and at such time or times as may be determined by the board of directors to be most advantageous; provided, that none of the obligations may be sold for a price less than 97 percent of par or face value. Approval by the Governor of Alabama of the terms and conditions under which any of the obligations authorized by this article may be issued shall be requisite to their validity, which approval, signed by the Governor, shall be entered on the minutes of the respective meetings of the board of directors at which such obligations proposed to be issued are authorized. Neither a public hearing or consent by the State Department of Finance nor any other department or agency shall be a prerequisite to the issuance of any of the obligations. All obligations issued by the authority shall be exempt from the laws of the state governing usury or prescribing or limiting interest rates, including, but without limitation to, the provisions of Chapter 8 of Title 8 of this Code, as it now exists and as it may at any time be amended. (Acts 1976, No. 565, p. 764, § 11; Acts 1981, No. 81-387, p. 574, § 7.)

§ 23-1-311. Bonds and notes — Payment generally; pledge of funds for payment of principal and interest thereon generally; negotiability.

(a) The obligations authorized by this article shall not be general obligations of the authority, but shall be payable solely out of the funds appropriated and pledged in or permitted to be pledged pursuant to Sections 23-1-314 and 23-1-315.

(b) As security for the payment of the principal of and interest on the obligations issued by it under this article, the authority is hereby authorized and empowered to pledge for payment of the said principal and interest the funds that are appropriated and pledged in or permitted to be pledged pursuant to Sections 23-1-314 and 23-1-315 for payment of said principal and interest.

(c) Any notes or temporary bonds issued under this article shall also be payable from the proceeds of any bonds in the anticipation of which such notes or temporary bonds are issued.

(d) All contracts made and all obligations issued by the authority pursuant to the provisions of this article shall be solely and exclusively the obligation of the authority and shall not be an obligation or debt of the state.

(e) Any obligation issued under this article, except bonds or temporary bonds registered as to principal or as to both principal and interest, and any interest coupons applicable thereto, shall be construed to be negotiable instruments although payable solely from a specified source as provided in this article. (Acts 1976, No. 565, p. 764, § 12; Acts 1981, No. 81-387, p. 574, § 8.)

§ 23-1-312. Bonds and notes — Exemption from taxation; use as security for deposits; eligibility as investment for fiduciary funds.

(a) Any obligations authorized by this article and the income therefrom shall be exempt from all taxation in the state.

(b) Any of the obligations authorized by this article may be used by the holder thereof as security for the deposit of any funds belonging to the state or to any instrumentality or agency of the state in any instance where security for such deposits may be required by law.

(c) Unless otherwise directed by the court having jurisdiction thereof or by the document that is the source of power, a trustee, executor, administrator, guardian or one acting in any other fiduciary capacity may, in addition to any other investment powers conferred by law and with the exercise of reasonable business prudence, invest fiduciary funds in any of the obligations authorized by this article. (Acts 1976, No. 565, p. 764, § 13.)

§ 23-1-313. Bonds and notes — Disposition of proceeds from sale generally.

The authority shall pay out of the proceeds from the sale of the obligations authorized by this article all expenses that the board of directors may deem necessary and advantageous in connection with the sale and issuance thereof. The proceeds from the issue of any obligations authorized by this article, (i) except the proceeds of bonds which were issued to pay principal and interest of temporary bonds or notes and in anticipation of which such temporary bonds or notes shall have been issued, and (ii) except the proceeds of refunding bonds issued to refund any outstanding obligation, remaining after paying the expenses of their sale and issuance, shall be deposited in the State Treasury, shall be credited to the road and bridge fund and shall be subject to be withdrawn by the authority, upon the approval of the State Highway Department and the Governor, but only for the purpose of paying the federal share of the cost of federal aid projects on the state highway system or work incidental or related to any such construction within the state (including the acquisition of property necessary for such construction and related work) to be repaid to the state by the federal government, and such proceeds shall be used for no other purpose. The proceeds from the sale of the obligations shall not be expended for any highway construction project until such time as the United States Secretary of Transportation or his designated representative shall have approved the design and location of the project, shall have formally stated in writing that such project will be eligible for federal aid matching funds when such funds become available and shall have entered into a written agreement providing for the repayment of such funds. Provided, however, in cases where the Federal Highway Administration has delegated the authority to the Highway Department to approve the design, location, and programming of federal funds for certain federal aid projects or classes of projects, then the approval by the Highway Department shall be sufficient. Proceeds of bonds issued to provide funds for payment of the principal of and interest on temporary bonds or notes issued in anticipation of the sale and issuance of such bonds shall be used solely for the purpose of paying the expenses of the sale and issuance of such bonds and the payment of the principal of and interest on such temporary bonds or notes. Proceeds of refunding bonds issued for the purpose of refunding any outstanding obligations of the authority remaining after payment of the expenses of their issuance shall be used solely for payment of the principal of and interest on such outstanding obligations of the authority and for paying any premium that may be necessary to be paid in order to redeem and retire the obligations to be refunded. (Acts 1976, No. 565, p. 764, § 14; Acts 1981, No. 81-387, p. 574, § 9; Acts 1988, No. 88-652, p. 1041, § 5; Acts 1992, No. 92-204, § 1.)

The 1992 amendment, effective April 16, 1992, substituted "federal aid projects on the state highway system" for "interstate, defense, primary highways and bridge replacements" in the second sentence, and added the present fourth sentence.

§ 23-1-314. Bonds and notes — Appropriations and pledges of revenue for payment of principal and interest generally; sinking fund.

(a) For the purpose of providing funds to enable the authority to pay at their respective maturities and due dates the principal of and interest on the obligations that may be issued by it under this article, there hereby is irrevocably pledged and appropriated each year all federal aid funds for federal aid projects on the state highway system to be received by the State

Highway Department from the United States government to the extent that such funds may be required to pay the principal of and interest on such obligations, and the State Highway Department is hereby authorized and directed to set aside the first moneys so received in each such fiscal year and deposit the same in the sinking fund provided for in subsection (c) of this section until there shall have been accumulated therein an amount at least sufficient to pay the principal of and interest on the obligations issued by the authority hereunder which mature, are subject to mandatory redemption or otherwise become due during the 12-month period of such federal fiscal year. All federal aid funds for federal aid projects on the state highway system received by the State Highway Department from the United States government during each such federal fiscal year shall be held in trust by the state and applied to the extent required to the payment of the principal of and interest on the obligations authorized to be issued under this article.

(b) Should said federal aid funds for federal aid projects on the state highway system be insufficient or unavailable to pay the principal of and interest on the obligations issued under the authority of this article, at the respective maturities, mandatory redemption dates or due dates of such principal and interest, there is also irrevocably pledged to said purpose and appropriated so much of the following as may be necessary (subject, however, to the provisions of subsection (d) of this section):

(1) To such extent and to such extent only as the funds appropriated in the first sentence of subsection (a) of this section and at the time available for such purpose (herein called "the available federal aid funds") may not be sufficient to pay at their respective maturities, mandatory redemption dates or due dates the principal of and interest on such obligations, so much as may be necessary for such purpose of those portions of the motor vehicle license taxes and registration fees that are provided to be distributed to the state pursuant to the provisions of Division 1 of Article 5 of Chapter 12 of Title 40 remaining after payment of the costs of collection thereof.

(2) To such extent and to such extent only as the available federal aid funds and the revenues appropriated under subdivision (1) of this subsection may not be sufficient to pay at their respective maturities, mandatory redemption dates or due dates the principal of and interest on such obligations so much as may be necessary for such purpose, when added to the available federal aid funds and the amounts appropriated in subdivision (1) of this subsection, of the state share of the net gasoline tax proceeds.

(3) To such extent and to such extent only as the available federal aid funds and the revenues appropriated under subdivisions (1) and (2) of this subsection may not be sufficient to pay at their respective maturities, mandatory redemption dates or due dates the principal of and interest on such obligations, so much as may be necessary for such purpose, when added to the available federal aid funds and the amounts appropriated in subdivisions (1) and (2) of this subsection, of the entire proceeds of the following excise taxes remaining after payment of the costs of collection thereof:

    a. The excise tax levied by Article 1 of Chapter 17 of Title 40 on distributors and storers of motor fuel as therein defined; and

    b. The excise tax levied by Article 3 of Chapter 17 of Title 40, exclusive of that portion of the said tax in respect of gasoline.

The term "costs of collection," as used in this subdivision, shall mean that portion of the excise taxes referred to in this subdivision that may be appropriated by the legislature to the Department of Revenue for its operating expenses.

(4) To such extent and to such extent only as the available federal aid funds and the revenues appropriated under subdivisions (1), (2) and (3) of this subsection may not be sufficient to pay at their respective maturities, mandatory redemption dates or due dates the principal of and the interest on such obligations, so much as may be necessary for such purpose, when added to the available federal aid funds and the amounts appropriated in subdivisions (1), (2) and (3) of this subsection, of all that portion of the receipts from the inspection fee on certain petroleum products, imposed by Division 1 of Article 5 of Chapter 17 of Title 8, that is required by the division to be deposited to the credit of the public road and bridge fund.

(5) To such extent and to such extent only as the available federal aid funds and the revenues appropriated under subdivisions (1), (2), (3) and (4) of this subsection may not be sufficient to pay at their respective maturities, mandatory redemption dates or due dates the principal of and interest on such obligations, so much as may be necessary for such purpose, when added to the available federal aid funds and to the amounts appropriated in subdivisions (1), (2), (3) and (4) of this subsection, of the receipts from the fee in respect of identification markers on motor vehicles that is provided for in Section 40-17-150.

(c) All moneys hereby appropriated and pledged shall be paid into the State Treasury and shall constitute a sinking fund which shall be held in trust to be used to pay the principal of and interest on the obligations. As security for the payment of the principal of and interest on the obligations issued under this article, the authority is authorized to pledge the proceeds of the appropriation and pledge provided for in this section. All pledges made by the authority shall take precedence among themselves in the order of the adoption of the resolutions making such pledges, except as may be otherwise provided in such resolutions.

(d) The pledges made of the proceeds, or specified portions of the proceeds, from the taxes and fees referred to in subdivisions (1) to (5) of subsection (b), inclusive, of this section, shall, with respect to each obligation issued hereunder, be subject and subordinate to (1) all pledges of the proceeds (or portions thereof) of the said taxes and fees lawfully made as security for any bonds issued prior to September 15, 1990, by the Alabama Highway Authority, and (2) any refunding bonds that may be issued by the Alabama Highway Authority after September 15, 1990, for the purpose of refunding any of the bonds referred to in clause (1) of this sentence if, and only if, the aggregate amount of principal and interest that will mature with respect to such refunding bonds during any fiscal year of the state does not exceed the amount of principal and interest, with respect to the bonds refunded by such refunding bonds, that have a stated maturity during the same fiscal year, or that would have had a stated maturity during the same fiscal year if such bonds had not been refunded. (Acts 1976, No. 565, p. 764, § 15; Acts 1978, No. 583, p. 663; Acts 1981, No. 81-387, p. 574, § 10; Acts 1988, No. 88-652, p. 1041, § 6; Acts 1992, No. 92-204, § 1.)

The 1992 amendment, effective April 16, 1992, in subsection (a), in the first sentence substituted "funds for federal aid projects on the state highway system" for "interstate, defense, primary highway and bridge replacement funds," and deleted "in each of the federal fiscal years ending in 1978 to 1995, inclusive" following "United States government," and substituted "funds for federal aid projects on the state highway system" for "interstate, defense, primary highway and bridge replacement funds" in the second sentence; in subsection (b) substituted "funds for

federal aid projects on the state highway system" for "interstate, defense, primary highway and bridge replacement funds" in the introductory language, and deleted "and" at the end of subdivision (4); and substituted "September 15, 1990" for "December 1, 1986" in two places in subsection (d).

Cross references. — As to appropriations and pledges of revenue for payment of principal and interest on bonds of Alabama highway corporation, see § 23-1-181.

Collateral references. — 39A C.J.S., Highways, § 158; 60 C.J.S., Highways, §§ 176-178.

§ 23-1-315. Investment of proceeds from sale of bonds and notes and funds in sinking fund; pledge of interest from investments.

Any funds held as the proceeds of obligations issued by the authority under this article and any funds held by the State Treasurer in the sinking fund provided for the payment of such obligations shall be invested in obligations of the United States of America or in certificates of deposit secured by a deposit of obligations of the United States of America to the full amount of such certificates of deposit, and the interest to be earned on such investment of funds may be pledged by the authority to the payment of the principal of and interest on the obligations issued by the authority under this article. (Acts 1976, No. 565, p. 764, § 16.)

§ 23-1-316. Payment by State Treasurer of principal and interest on bonds and notes; maintenance of records pertaining thereto.

Out of the revenues appropriated and pledged and the sinking fund provided pursuant to Sections 23-1-314 and 23-1-315, the State Treasurer is authorized and directed to pay the principal of and interest on the obligations issued by the authority under this article at the respective maturities or due dates of said principal or interest, and he is further authorized and directed to set up and maintain appropriate records pertaining thereto. (Acts 1976, No. 565, p. 764, § 18.)

§ 23-1-317. Authorization of expenditure of federal aid directly by State Highway Department; contracts for construction, reconstruction, etc., of highways; performance, etc., of construction, etc., done by authority without award of contract therefor; promulgation and enforcement of rules and regulations; conveyance of property to state; highways constructed deemed part of public highway system.

(a) If such action shall be necessary in order to comply with any federal legislation relating to federal aid in construction of roads and highways, the authority may authorize the State Highway Department to expend directly any portion of proceeds from obligations issued under this article for constructing, reconstructing and relocating federal aid projects on the state highway system or work incidental or related thereto.

(b) All contracts of the authority for the construction, reconstruction and relocation of federal aid projects on the state highway system, and work incidental or related thereto and the acquisition of property necessary therefor, shall be in writing, shall be subject to the rules and regulations and shall be let under the supervision of the State Highway Department and shall be subject to approval by the Governor and by the State Highway Department. All work provided for in any such contract shall be supervised by the State Highway Department.

(c) All persons engaged in the supervision or performance of any such work of construction, reconstruction or relocation that may be done by the authority without the award of a contract therefor shall be employees of the State Highway Department.

(d) The authority shall make and enforce all reasonable rules and regulations not inconsistent with the terms of this article or the laws of the State of Alabama as may, in its opinion, be proper and suitable for the protection of said federal aid projects on the state highway system and approaches and appurtenances thereto and for the safety of the traveling public; provided, however, that the above provisions shall apply only to the extent that they are not in conflict with any federal legislation, regulation or requirement relating to federal aid in federal aid projects on the state highway system construction.

(e) Any property acquired by the authority by purchase, condemnation or otherwise shall be forthwith conveyed to the State of Alabama.

(f) All federal aid projects on the state highway system constructed by the corporation shall constitute part of the public highway system in the state. (Acts 1976, No. 565, p. 764, § 17; Acts 1981, No. 81-387, p. 574, § 11; Acts 1988, No. 88-652, p. 1041, § 7; Acts 1992, No. 92-204, § 1.)

The 1992 amendment, effective April 16, 1992, substituted "federal aid projects on the state highway system" for "interstate, defense, primary highways and bridge replacement" throughout the section.

§ 23-1-318. Dissolution.

At any time when no securities of any kind of the authority, whether issued under this article or under authorization contained in any other act, are outstanding, the authority may be dissolved upon the filing with the Secretary of State of an application for dissolution, which shall be subscribed by each of the members of the authority and which shall be sworn to by each such member before an officer authorized to take acknowledgments to deeds. Upon the filing of said application for dissolution, the authority shall cease and any property owned by it at the time of its dissolution shall pass to the State of Alabama. The Secretary of State shall file and record the application for dissolution in an appropriate book of record in his office and shall make and issue, under the great seal of the state, a certificate that the authority is dissolved and shall record the said certificate with the application for dissolution. (Acts 1976, No. 565, p. 764, § 19.)

CHAPTER 2.

TOLL ROADS, BRIDGES AND FERRIES.

ARTICLE 1.

ALABAMA TURNPIKE AUTHORITY.

§§ 23-2-1 through 23-2-26. Repealed by Acts 1980, No. 80-136, p. 204, § 3, effective October 1, 1980.

ARTICLE 2.

STATE TOLL BRIDGE AUTHORITY.

§§ 23-2-40 through 23-2-64. Repealed by Acts 1980, No. 80-139, p. 209, § 3, effective October 1, 1980.

ARTICLE 3.

DAUPHIN ISLAND BRIDGE AUTHORITY.

§§ 23-2-80 through 23-2-104. Repealed by Acts 1980, No. 80-135, p. 203, § 3, effective October 1, 1980.

ARTICLE 4.

TOLL TUNNELS AND BRIDGES DESIGNATED AS PARTS OF INTERSTATE HIGHWAY SYSTEM.

§ 23-2-120. Maintenance of tolls; prohibition against further bonded indebtedness.

Whenever the Secretary of Commerce of the United States designates any toll tunnel or toll bridge in the State of Alabama as a part of the interstate highway system and the tolls or income from said toll bridge or toll tunnel have been pledged for the payment of bonds or other outstanding debt, then the tolls shall be allowed to remain on said toll facility to provide the necessary income for the payment of necessary costs of operation and maintenance and the payment of the then outstanding indebtedness of said toll facility. No further bonded indebtedness shall be incurred against said toll facility from the date the same is designated a part of the interstate highway system, and all income from said facility shall be utilized for debt payment as rapidly as possible after necessary costs of operation and maintenance are paid. (Acts 1957, No. 450, p. 612, § 1.)

§ 23-2-121. When newly constructed tunnel or bridge deemed part of existing facility.

Should the density of traffic on the interstate highway system require the construction, as a part of the interstate highway system, of another tunnel or bridge parallel with, and in close proximity to, a then existing toll facility which has been incorporated into the interstate system, then the newly constructed tunnel or bridge shall be considered as a part of the original facility, and tolls shall be allowed to be collected on the newly constructed facility to pay the costs of operation and maintenance and for the retirement of the debt existing on the toll facility. (Acts 1957, No. 450, p. 612, § 2.)

State has authority to lease tunnels to a city for the period required to liquidate existing indebtedness. King v. City of Mobile, 273 Ala. 109, 134 So. 2d 746 (1961).

§ 23-2-122. Toll facilities to be operated as free facilities after payment of outstanding indebtedness.

Upon the payment of the outstanding indebtedness for which the income of the toll facility is pledged, then said facility shall immediately become a free facility, and the necessary costs of operation and maintenance shall be paid in the same manner as such costs are paid for the interstate highway system. (Acts 1957, No. 450, p. 612, § 3.)

Cross references. — As to exemption of bonds of public corporations from laws governing usury or limiting interest rates, see § 8-8-7.

ARTICLE 5.

ALABAMA TOLL ROAD, BRIDGE AND TUNNEL AUTHORITY.

§ 23-2-140. Short title.

This article shall be known, and may be cited, as the Toll Road, Bridge and Tunnel Authority Act. (Acts 1980, No. 80-691, p. 1377, § 25.)

§ 23-2-141. Intent and purpose of article.

The purpose of this article is to facilitate vehicular traffic and safety in the state by providing for the construction of modern toll roads, bridges and tunnels in strategic and essential locations, without taxes and without a pledge of the faith and credit of the state. (Acts 1980, No. 80-691, p. 1377, § 1.)

Collateral references. — 39A C.J.S., Highways, §§ 37, 39.   39 Am. Jur. 2d, Highways, Streets, and Bridges, § 72.

§ 23-2-142. Definitions.

As used in this article, the following words and terms shall have the meanings, respectively, unless the context clearly indicates otherwise:

(1) AUTHORITY. The Alabama Toll Road, Bridge and Tunnel Authority created by this article, or any board, body or commission succeeding to the principal functions thereof or to which the powers given by this article to the authority shall be given by law.

(2) BONDS or TOLL ROAD, BRIDGE OR TUNNEL REVENUE BONDS. Bonds of the authority authorized under the provisions of this article.

(3) Cost. As applied to a toll road, bridge or tunnel project, the cost shall embrace:

a. The cost of construction, including bridges over or under existing highways and railroads;

b. The cost of the acquisition of all land, rights-of-way, property, rights, easements and interests acquired by the authority for such construction;

c. The cost of demolishing or removing any buildings or structures on land so acquired, including the cost of acquiring any lands to which such buildings or structures may be moved;

d. The cost of diverting highways, interchange of highways and access roads to private property, including the cost of land for easements therefor;

e. The cost of all machinery and equipment;

f. The cost of financing charges, including interest prior to and during construction and for one year after completion of construction;

g. The cost of traffic estimates and of engineering and legal expenses;

h. Plans, specifications, surveys, estimates of cost and of revenues;

i. The cost of other expenses necessary or incident to determining the feasibility or practicability of constructing any such project;

j. The cost of administrative expense and such other expense as may be necessary or incident to the construction of the project;

k. The cost of the financing of such construction; and

l. The cost of placing of the project in operation.

Any obligation or expense which may be incurred by the State Highway Department for traffic surveys, borings, preparation of plans and specifications and other engineering services in connection with the planning or construction of a project shall be regarded as a part of the cost of such project and shall be reimbursed to the State Highway Department by the authority.

(4) Owner. All individuals, copartnerships, associations, private or municipal corporations and all political subdivisions of the state having any title or interest in any property, rights, easements and interests authorized to be acquired by this article.

(5) Project, Toll road, bridge and tunnel project or Toll road, bridge or tunnel project. Any type of toll road, bridge, causeway or tunnel established and constructed or to be constructed by the authority under the provisions of this article, and shall include, but shall not be limited to, all toll roads, bridges, causeways, tunnels, overpasses, underpasses, interchanges, entrance plazas, approaches, access roads, toll houses, service areas, service stations, service facilities, communication facilities and administration, storage and other buildings which the authority may deem necessary for the operation of such project, together with all property, rights, easements and interests which may be acquired by the authority for the construction, operation and maintenance of such project.

(6) PUBLIC HIGHWAYS. All public highways, roads and streets in the state, whether maintained by the state or by any county or municipality or other political subdivision. (Acts 1980, No. 80-691, p. 1377, § 2.)

§ 23-2-143. Established and incorporated; members; officers; quorum; vacancies; fidelity bonds; compensation.

(a) There is hereby established a body corporate and politic with corporate succession, to be known as the "Alabama Toll Road, Bridge and Tunnel Authority." The authority is hereby constituted an instrumentality exercising public and essential governmental functions and the exercise by the authority of the powers conferred by this article shall be deemed and held to be an essential governmental function of the state.

(b) The authority shall consist of the Governor, the Lieutenant Governor, the Speaker of the House of Representatives, the Highway Director, one member of the Senate to be appointed by the Lieutenant Governor, one member of the House of Representatives to be appointed by the Speaker of the House and one person from the state at large to be appointed by the Governor.

(c) The Governor shall be chairman of the authority. The authority shall elect a secretary and a treasurer who need not be members and may be one and the same person. Four members of the authority shall constitute a quorum and the concurrence of four members shall be necessary for any action taken by the authority. No vacancy in the membership of the authority shall impair the right of a quorum to exercise all the rights and perform all the duties of the authority. Should any of the said officials of the state die or should his term of office, as such official, expire, or should he resign therefrom, his successor in office shall take his place as a member or officer of the authority. Any vacancy in the appointed membership of the authority shall be filled in the same manner as the original appointment was made.

(d) If the secretary and treasurer are not members of the authority, before the issuance of any toll road, bridge or tunnel revenue bonds under the provisions of this article, the secretary shall execute a surety bond in the penal sum of $25,000.00 and the treasurer shall execute a surety bond in the penal sum of $50,000.00, which shall be sufficient if he be secretary also. Each such surety bond shall be conditioned upon the faithful performance of the duties of the office of secretary or treasurer, as the case may be, to be executed by a surety company authorized to transact business in the State of Alabama as surety, and to be approved by the Governor and filed in the office of the Secretary of State. The cost of such bonds shall be borne by the authority.

(e) The members of the authority shall serve without compensation. The appointed members shall receive reimbursement for their expenses when actively engaged on the authority's business, such expenses to be paid in accordance with Article 2 of Chapter 7 of Title 36. (Acts 1980, No. 80-691, p. 1377, § 3.)

§ 23-2-144. Powers generally.

The authority shall have the following powers:

(1) To adopt bylaws for the regulation of its affairs and the conduct of its business;

(2) To adopt an official seal and alter the same at pleasure;

(3) To maintain a principal office and branch offices at such place or places within the state as it may designate;

(4) To sue and be sued in its own name, including suits in tort;

(5) To acquire and construct toll road, bridge or tunnel projects at such locations as the authority may determine to be desirable, practicable and economically feasible and to maintain, repair and operate such projects;

(6) To issue toll road, bridge or tunnel revenue bonds of the authority for any of its corporate purposes, payable solely from its tolls, other revenues and proceeds of such bonds, and to refund its bonds, all as provided in this article. No bonds issued under the provisions of this article shall constitute a debt or liability of the state or of any political subdivision thereof or a pledge of the faith and credit of the state or of any such political subdivision, and neither the state nor any political subdivision thereof shall ever pay or agree to pay any portion of the same, but such bonds shall be payable solely from the funds pledged or available for their payment as authorized in this article. All such toll road, bridge or tunnel revenue bonds shall contain on the face thereof a statement to the effect that the authority is obligated to pay the same or the interest thereon only from its tolls or other revenues and that neither the state nor any political subdivision thereof is obligated to pay the same or the interest thereon and that neither the faith and credit nor the taxing power of the state or of any political subdivision thereof is pledged to the payment of the principal thereof or the interest thereon;

(7) To fix and revise from time to time, charge and collect tolls for transit over or through toll road, bridge and tunnel projects constructed by it;

(8) To establish rules and regulations for the use of any project;

(9) To acquire, hold and dispose of real and personal property;

(10) To acquire in the name of the authority, by purchase or otherwise, on such terms and conditions and in such manner as it may deem proper, or by condemnation in accordance with the provisions of Title 18, and other provisions of law, insofar as the same may be applicable, any land and other property or any easement or interest therein, which it may determine is reasonably necessary for any toll road, bridge or tunnel project or for its protection and preservation, or for the construction, relocation or recon-struction of any access highway, street or road; and to acquire by purchase or by condemnation, land necessary for drainage ditches, clay, sand and gravel pits, and lime and stone quarries, together with any other material of every character that may be necessary in the construction and mainte-nance of toll road, bridge or tunnel projects and access highways and roads;

(11) To designate points of ingress to and egress from each toll road, bridge or tunnel project and to prohibit entrance to and exit from such project at any point or points not so designated;

(12) To make and enter into contracts and agreements necessary for, or incidental to, the performance of its duties and the execution of its powers under this article, including contracts and agreements for professional services deemed necessary for such purposes by the authority;

(13) To appoint managers, superintendents, tolltakers and such other employees and agents as may be necessary, in its judgment, to the efficient accomplishment of the purposes of this article;

(14) To receive and accept from any federal agency, subject to the approval of the governor, grants for, or in aid of, the construction of any project and to receive and accept aid or contributions from any source of either money, property, labor or other things of value, to be held, used and applied only for the purposes for which such grants and contributions may be made;

(15) To provide coverage for its employees under the provisions of Chapter 5 of Title 25, and the federal Social Security Act; and

(16) To do all acts and things necessary or convenient to carry out the powers granted in this article. (Acts 1980, No. 80-691, p. 1377, § 4.)

U.S. Code. — The federal Social Security Act, referred to in subdivision (15), is codified as 42 U.S.C.A. § 301 et seq.

Collateral references. — 39A C.J.S., Highways, §§ 31-35, 39, 40, 158-160. 40 C.J.S., Highways, §§ 175-179.

39 Am. Jur. 2d, Highways, Streets, and Bridges, §§ 13-15, 32, 41, 72, 73, 91. 40 Am. Jur. 2d, Highways, Streets, and Bridges, §§ 613-617.

§ 23-2-145. Advertisement for construction bids; award of contract; work done by force account.

(a) Before construction is started on any project, the authority shall advertise for sealed bids once each week for three consecutive weeks in a newspaper of general circulation in the county in which the project or undertaking, or some part thereof, is to be located; the authority may also advertise in such other publications as it may deem advisable. Such notices shall state that plans and specifications for the project are on file in the office of the authority and the time and place in which bids will be received and opened. All bids shall be opened publicly at the advertised time and place.

(b) The contract shall be awarded to the lowest responsible bidder complying with conditions of the invitation for bids, unless the authority finds that his bid is unreasonable or that it is not to the interest of the authority to accept it. The bidder to whom the award is made shall be notified by telegram or letter at the earliest possible date. Should the successful bidder fail or refuse to sign the contract or make bond, the authority may award the contract to the second lowest responsible bidder. Should the second lowest bidder fail or refuse to sign the contract or make bond, the authority may award the contract to the third lowest responsible bidder.

(c) Should no bids be received at the time stated in the advertisement for bids, the authority may advertise for and seek other competitive bids, or the authority may direct that the work shall be done by force account under its direction and control. If the authority finds that all bids received are unreasonable and that it is not to the interest of the authority to accept any of the bids, the authority may direct that the work shall be done by force account under its direction and control. On any construction project which the authority has determined to do by force account, the authority shall file plans and specifications and an itemized estimate of cost with the department of examiners of public accounts and upon completion of the project by the authority, the final total costs, together with an itemized list of cost of any and all changes made in the original plans and specifications shall be submitted to the department of examiners of public accounts for its permanent record. Upon the approval of the authority, its duly authorized officer or officers may, when proceeding upon the basis of force account, let any subdivision or unit of work by contract on receiving sealed bids in accordance with this section. This section shall not apply to routine maintenance and repair jobs done by maintenance men who are regular employees of the authority. (Acts 1980, No. 80-691, p. 1377, § 5.)

Collateral references. — 40 C.J.S., High-   40 Am. Jur. 2d, Highways, Streets, and
ways, §§ 177, 178, 208-210.   Bridges, §§ 91-96.

§ 23-2-146. Grade separations at intersections; relocation of public highways; authority to enter private lands to drill, survey, etc.; relocation, etc., of public utility facilities; procedures; costs.

(a) The authority shall have power to construct grade separations at intersections of any toll road, bridge or tunnel project with public highways and to change and adjust the lines and grades of such highways so as to accommodate the same to the design of the grade separation. The cost of such grade separations and any damage incurred in changing and adjusting the lines and grades of such highways shall be ascertained and paid by the authority as a part of the cost of such bridge or tunnel project.

(b) If the authority finds it necessary to change the location of any portion of any public highway, it shall cause a highway of substantially the same type as the original highway to be reconstructed at such location as the authority shall deem most favorable. The cost of reconstruction and any damage incurred in changing the location of any such highway shall be ascertained and paid by the authority as a part of the cost of such bridge or tunnel project.

(c) Any change in line or grade, and any relocation of a public highway, shall be made so as best to serve the interests of the public and at the same time carry out the purposes of this article and any change in line or grade and any relocation shall be approved by the governing body or public agency having the responsibility of maintaining such public highway. In the event such body or agency fails or refuses to approve the change or relocation, the matter may be submitted by the authority to the circuit court of the county in which such body or agency has its principal office and the court shall determine what change in line or grade or relocation shall be made. Approval by such body or agency or by the court shall be conclusive as to the public interest.

(d) In addition to the foregoing powers the authority and its authorized agents and employees may enter upon any lands, waters and premises in the state for the purpose of making surveys, soundings, drillings and examinations as it may deem necessary or convenient for the purposes of this article, and such entry shall not be deemed a trespass, nor shall an entry for such purpose be deemed an entry under any condemnation proceedings which may be then pending. The authority shall make reimbursement for any actual damages resulting to such lands, waters and premises as a result of such activities.

(e) The authority shall also have power to make reasonable regulations for the installation, construction, maintenance, repair, renewal, relocation and removal of tracks, pipes, mains, conduits, cables, wires, towers, poles and other equipment and appliances (herein called "public utility facilities") of any public utility in, on, along, over or under any toll road, bridge or tunnel project. Whenever the authority shall determine that it is necessary that any public utility facilities which now are, or hereafter may be, located in, on, along, over or under any toll road, bridge or tunnel project shall be relocated in such toll road, bridge or tunnel project, or should be removed from such toll road, bridge or tunnel project, the public utility owning or operating such facilities shall relocate or remove the same in accordance with the order of the authority. The cost and expenses of such relocation or removal, including the cost of installing such facilities in a new location, or new locations, and the cost of any lands or any rights or interests in lands, and any other rights, acquired to accomplish such relocation or removal shall be ascertained and paid by the authority as a part of the cost of such toll road, bridge or tunnel project. In case of any such relocation or removal of facilities, the public utility owning or operating the facilities, or its successors or assigns, may maintain and operate the facilities with the necessary appurtenances in the new location or new locations for as long a period and upon the same terms and conditions as it had the right to maintain and operate such facilities in their former location or locations. (Acts 1980, No. 80-691, p. 1377, § 6.)

Collateral references. — 39A C.J.S., Highways, §§ 10, 64-68, 96-99, 139, 140, 168-172. 40 C.J.S., Highways, § 191.

39 Am. Jur. 2d, Highways, Streets, and Bridges, §§ 49, 50, 55-59, 88-96, 103-109, 130, 131.

§ 23-2-147. Bonds; issuance; forms; procedures, etc.

(a) The authority is hereby authorized to provide by resolution for the issuance of bonds of the authority for any of its corporate purposes, including the refunding of its bonds. The principal of and the interest on any issue of such bonds shall be payable solely from, and be secured by a pledge of, tolls and other revenues of all or any part of the toll road, bridge or tunnel project financed in whole or in part with the proceeds of such issue or with the proceeds of bonds refunded or to be refunded by such issue. The proceeds of any such bonds may be used or pledged for the payment or security of the principal or of the interest on bonds, and for the establishment of any or all reserves for such payment or security, or for other corporate purposes as the authority may authorize in the resolution authorizing the issuance of bonds or in the trust agreement securing the same.

(b) The bonds of each issue shall be dated; shall mature at such time or times, not exceeding 40 years from their date or dates as may be determined by the authority; and may be made redeemable before maturity, at the option of the authority, at such price or prices and under such terms and conditions as may be fixed by the authority prior to the issuance of the bonds. The amount of premium on any bond shall not cause the yield to be more than six percent per annum from the date of such bonds to the date of their redemption.

(c) The authority shall determine the form of the bonds, including any interest coupons to be attached thereto, and shall fix the denomination or denominations of the bonds and the place or places of payment of principal and interest, which may be at any bank or trust company within or without the state. The bonds shall be signed by the chairman of the authority or shall bear his facsimile signature; and the official seal of the authority or a facsimile thereof shall be impressed, imprinted, engraved or otherwise reproduced thereon. The official seal or a facsimile thereof shall be attested by the secretary of the authority or shall bear his facsimile signature; and any coupons attached thereto shall bear the facsimile signature of the chairman of the authority. In case any officer whose signature or a facsimile of whose signature shall appear on any bonds or coupons shall cease to be such officer before the delivery of such bonds, such signature or such facsimile shall nevertheless be valid and sufficient for all purposes the same as if he had remained in office until such delivery.

(d) All bonds issued under the provisions of this article shall have and are hereby declared to have all the qualities and incidents of negotiable instruments under the negotiable instruments law of the state. The bonds may be issued in coupon or in registered form, or both, as the authority may determine; and provision may be made for the registration of any coupon bonds as to principal alone and also as to both principal and interest and for the reconversion into coupon bonds of any bonds registered as to both principal and interest. The authority may sell such bonds in such manner and for such price as it may determine to be for the best interest of the authority.

(e) The authority shall have power from time to time, in anticipation of the issuance of bonds, to issue notes and from time to time to issue renewal notes maturing not later than three years from their respective dates, in an amount not exceeding the amount of bonds issued under the provisions of this article. The authorization and issuance of such notes, the interest thereon, the rights of the holders thereof, and the rights, duties and obligations of the authority in respect thereto, shall be governed by the provisions of this article with respect to the issuance of bonds, insofar as the same may be applicable.

(f) The authority may, out of any funds available therefor, purchase notes or bonds, which shall thereupon be cancelled, at not more than the redemption price then applicable, or, if not then redeemable, at a premium of not more than one percent of their face amount, plus accrued interest to the date of purchase.

(g) Neither the members of the authority nor any person executing the notes or bonds shall be personally liable on the notes or bonds, or be accountable by reason of the issuance thereof in accordance with the provisions of this article.

(h) The proceeds of the bonds of each issue shall be disbursed in such manner and under such restrictions, if any, as the authority may provide in the resolution authorizing the issuance of the bonds, or in the trust agreement, hereinafter mentioned securing the bonds.

(i) Prior to the preparation of definitive bonds, the authority may, under like restrictions, issue interim receipts or temporary bonds, with or without coupons, exchangeable for definitive bonds when such bonds shall have been executed and are available for delivery. The authority may also provide for the replacement of any bonds which shall become mutilated or shall be destroyed or lost. Bonds may be issued under the provisions of this article without obtaining the consent of any department, division, commission, board, bureau, or agency of the state, and without any other proceedings or the happening of any other conditions or things than those proceedings, conditions, or things which are specifically required by this article. (Acts 1980, No. 80-691, p. 1377, § 7; Acts 1982, No. 82-540, p. 890, § 1.)

Collateral references. — 39A C.J.S., Highways, § 158. 40 C.J.S., Highways, §§ 176, 192, 204.

39 Am. Jur. 2d, Highways, Streets, and Bridges, § 126. 40 Am. Jur. 2d, Highways, Streets and Bridges, §§ 614, 616. 64 Am. Jur. 2d, Public Securities and Obligations, §§ 79, 104, 261-269.

§ 23-2-148. Refunding bonds; purposes.

The authority may provide by resolution for the issuance of refunding bonds for the purpose of refunding any bonds then outstanding which shall have been issued under the provisions of this article, including the payment of any redemption premium thereon and any interest accrued or to accrue to the date of redemption of such bonds, and, if deemed advisable by the authority, for the additional purpose of constructing improvements, extensions or enlargements of the toll road, bridge or tunnel project or projects in connection with which the bonds to be refunded shall have been issued.

The authority is further authorized to provide by resolution for the issuance of its bonds for the combined purpose of:

(1) Refunding any bonds then outstanding which shall have been issued under the provisions of this article, including the payment of any redemption premium thereof and any interest accrued or to accrue to the date of redemption of such bonds; and

(2) Paying all or any part of the cost of any additional project or projects.

The issuance of such bonds, the maturities and other details thereof, the rights of the holders thereof, and the rights, duties and obligations of the authority in respect to the same, shall be governed by the provisions of this article insofar as the same may be applicable. (Acts 1980, No. 80-691, p. 1377, § 8.)

Collateral references. — 39A C.J.S., High-ways, § 158. 40 C.J.S., Highways, § 176.   64 Am. Jur. 2d, Public Securities and Obligations, §§ 261-269.

§ 23-2-149. Trust agreements securing bond issues; authorized provisions protecting holders; pledge of revenues.

In the discretion of the authority, any bonds issued under the provisions of this article may be secured by a trust agreement by and between the authority and a corporate trustee, which may be any trust company, or bank having the powers of a trust company, within or without the state. The trust agreement or the resolution providing for the issuance of such bonds subject to the provisions of Section 23-2-147, may pledge or assign tolls or other revenues to which the authority's right then exists or which may thereafter come into existence, and the moneys derived therefrom, and the proceeds of such bonds; provided, however, that the trust agreement or resolution shall not convey or mortgage any toll road, bridge or tunnel project or any part thereof. Such trust agreement or resolution providing for the issuance of bonds may contain such provisions for protecting and enforcing the rights and remedies of the bondholders as may be reasonable and proper and not in violation of law; including covenants setting forth the duties of the authority in relation to the acquisition of property and the construction, improvement, maintenance, repair, operation and insurance of the toll road, bridge or tunnel project or projects; the rates of tolls and revenues to be charged; the payment, security or redemption of bonds and the custody, safeguarding and application of all moneys; and provisions for the employment of consulting engineers in connection with the construction or operation of such bridge or tunnel project or projects. It shall be lawful for any bank or trust company incorporated under the laws of this state which may act as depository of the proceeds of bonds or of revenues to furnish such indemnifying bonds or to pledge such securities as may be required by the authority. Any trust agreement or resolution may set forth the rights and remedies of the bondholders and of the trustee and may restrict the individual rights of action by bondholders. In addition to the foregoing, any trust agreement or resolution may contain such other provisions as the authority may deem reasonable and proper for the security of the bondholders. All expenses incurred in carrying out the provisions of any trust agreement may be treated as a part of the cost of the operation of the toll road, bridge or tunnel project or projects.

Any pledge of tolls, other revenues or moneys made by the authority shall be valid and binding from the time the pledge is made. The tolls, other revenues or moneys so pledged and thereafter received by the authority, except that part of the tolls, other revenues or moneys which are necessary to maintain the project or projects in good operating conditions, or to pay the reasonable operating expenses of the authority, or any judgment rendered against it, shall immediately be subject to the lien of the pledge without any physical delivery thereof or further act; and the lien of any such pledge shall be valid and binding as against all parties having claims of any kind in tort, contract or otherwise against the authority, irrespective of whether such parties have notice thereof. Neither the resolution nor any trust agreement by which a pledge is created need be filed or recorded except in the records of the authority. If such trust agreement should be offered for record it shall be filed and recorded without the payment of the mortgage tax required by Chapter 22 of Title 40. The authority may, in its discretion, enter into any supplement to such trust agreement, which supplement shall be governed, so far as may be, by the same provisions of this article as are applicable to the trust agreement. (Acts 1980, No. 80-691, p. 1377, § 9.)

Collateral references. — 39A C.J.S., Highways, § 158. 40 C.J.S., Highways, §§ 176, 204. 64 Am. Jur. 2d, Public Securities and Obligations, §§ 193, 199.

§ 23-2-150. Authority to collect tolls, revenues, etc.; to lease to utilities; toll rates adjusted to conform to trust agreement.

The authority is hereby authorized to fix, revise, charge and collect tolls for the use of each toll road, bridge or tunnel project and the different parts or sections thereof, and to contract with, or to lease to or from, any person, partnership, association or corporation desiring the use of any part thereof, including the right-of-way adjoining the paved portion of approaches and access highways, streets or roads for placing thereon telephone, telegraph, electric light or power lines or pipe lines for gas and water or for petroleum products or for any other purpose except for tracks for railroad or railway use and to fix the terms, conditions, rents and rates of charges for such use. Tolls shall be so fixed and adjusted as to carry out and perform the terms and provisions of any contract with or for the benefit of bondholders. Tolls shall not be subject to supervision or regulation by any other commission, board, bureau or agency of the state. The use and disposition of tolls and revenues shall be subject to the provisions of the resolution authorizing the issuance of such bonds or of the trust agreement securing the bond issue. (Acts 1980, No. 80-691, p. 1377, § 10.)

§ 23-2-151. Revenues deemed trust funds; depository deemed trustee.

All moneys received pursuant to the authority of this article, whether as proceeds from the sale of bonds or as revenues, shall be deemed to be trust funds to be held and applied solely as provided in this article. The resolution authorizing the bonds of any issue or the trust agreement securing such bonds shall provide that any officer with whom, or any bank or trust company with which, such moneys shall be deposited shall act as trustee of such moneys and shall hold and apply the same for the purposes hereof, subject to such regulations as this article and the resolution or trust agreement may provide. (Acts 1980, No. 80-691, p. 1377, § 11.)

§ 23-2-152. Bondholder's and trustee's rights of enforcement; scope of rights.

Any holder of bonds issued under the provisions of this article, or of any of the coupons appertaining thereto, and the trustee under any trust agreement, except to the extent that the rights herein given may be restricted by such trust agreement, may, by civil action or proceeding protect and enforce any and all rights under the laws of this state, or granted hereunder, or under the trust agreement or the resolution authorizing the issuance of bonds and may enforce and compel the performance of all duties required by this article or by the trust agreement or resolution to be performed by the authority or by any officer thereof, including the fixing, charging and collecting of tolls. (Acts 1980, No. 80-691, p. 1377, § 12.)

§ 23-2-153. Tax exempt status of authority's property and revenues; rationale.

The exercise of the powers granted by this article will be in all respects for the benefit of the people of the state, for the increase of their commerce and prosperity and for the improvement of their health and living conditions. Since the operation and maintenance of toll road, bridge or tunnel projects by the authority will constitute the performance of essential functions the authority shall not be required to pay any taxes or assessments upon any toll road, bridge or tunnel project or any property acquired or used by the authority under the provisions of this article or upon the income therefrom. Any toll road, bridge or tunnel project, any property acquired or used by the authority under the provisions of this article and the income therefrom and the bonds issued under the provisions of this article, their transfer and the income therefrom (including any profit made on the sale thereof) shall be exempt from taxation. (Acts 1980, No. 80-691, p. 1377, § 13.)

§ 23-2-154. Bonds legal investments for all purposes; entitled to be deposited with state officers or agencies.

Bonds issued by the authority under the provisions of this article are hereby made securities in which the state and all political subdivisions of this state, their officers, boards, commissioners, departments or other agencies; all banks, bankers, savings banks, trust companies, savings and loan associations, investment companies and other persons carrying on a banking business; all insurance companies, insurance associations and other persons carrying on an insurance business; and all administrators, executors, guardians, trustees and other fiduciaries; and all other persons whatsoever who now are or may hereafter be authorized to invest in bonds or other obligations of the state may properly and legally invest any funds, including capital belonging to them or within their control. The bonds or other securities or obligations are hereby made securities which properly and legally may be deposited with and received by any state or municipal officer or agency of the state for any purpose for which the deposit of bonds or other obligations of the state is now or hereafter may be authorized by law. (Acts 1980, No. 80-691, p. 1377, § 14.)

§ 23-2-155. Authority to maintain own toll roads, bridges and tunnels.

Each toll road, bridge and tunnel project when constructed and opened to traffic shall be maintained and kept in good condition and repair by the authority. (Acts 1980, No. 80-691, p. 1377, § 15.)

Collateral references. — 39A C.J.S., Highways, § 39. 40 C.J.S., Highways, §§ 177, 178, 198.   39 Am. Jur. 2d, Highways, Streets, and Bridges, §§ 64-66, 72, 80, 81, 86-90.

§ 23-2-156. Rules and regulations governing use of toll roads, etc.; violations; penalties; police force; jurisdiction.

(a) The authority is hereby authorized to promulgate reasonable rules and regulations with respect to the use of any toll road, bridge or tunnel project. Such rules and regulations shall relate to vehicular speeds, loads, weights and sizes, safety devices, rules of the road and such other matters as may be necessary and proper to regulate traffic in the interest of safety and the maximum convenience of the persons using the project. Such rules and regulations shall apply according to their terms to all sections of any toll road, bridge or tunnel project under the jurisdiction of the authority, and to its structures and other appurtenances. Insofar as such rules and regulations may be inconsistent with the rules and regulations made by the highway department with respect to such matters or with the laws of the state relating to offenses with respect to highways, the rules and regulations promulgated by the authority shall be controlling. The authority may prescribe such reasonable rules and regulations as it may deem advisable for the protection and preservation of and for the maintenance and preservation of good order within the property under its jurisdiction and control and to prevent unnecessary trespassing upon or injury to or upon any part of the right-of-way or other property of any toll road, bridge or tunnel project.

(b) Such rules and regulations shall provide that law enforcement officers shall be afforded ready access, while in the performance of their official duty, to all property under the jurisdiction of the authority without the payment of tolls. Violation of such rules and regulations shall be a misdemeanor punishable by a fine of not less than $1.00 nor more than $500.00, and, at the discretion of the judge trying the case, also by sentence to hard labor for the county for a term not to exceed six months. Such rules and regulations shall not take effect until duly filed in the office of the Secretary of State or as hereafter may be provided by law and published in a newspaper of general circulation in each county in which the toll road, bridge and tunnel project affected is located and in such other manner as the authority shall prescribe.

(c) Each project may be policed by such force of police as the authority considers necessary. The police officers shall have power to prefer charges against and make arrests of any person or persons violating any law of the State of Alabama, or any of the bylaws, rules or regulations of the authority, as authorized herein on property owned or controlled by the authority. The jurisdiction of such police officers shall not be restricted to any one county but shall extend to all the counties in the state in which any toll road, bridge or tunnel project is located. (Acts 1980, No. 80-691, p. 1377, § 16.)

Collateral references. — 39A C.J.S., Highways, §§ 232-247.
39 Am. Jur. 2d, Highways, Streets, and Bridges, §§ 199-212. 40 Am. Jur. 2d, Highways, Streets, and Bridges, §§ 613, 616.

§ 23-2-157. Lease, grant, etc., of county, city, etc., property to authority.

All counties, cities, towns and other political subdivisions and all public departments, agencies and commissions of the State of Alabama, notwithstanding any contrary provision of law, are hereby authorized and empowered to lease, lend, grant or convey to the authority at its request, upon such terms and conditions as the proper authorities of such counties, cities, towns, political subdivisions and departments, agencies or commissions of the state may deem reasonable and fair, and without the necessity for any advertisement, order of court or other action or formality, other than the regular and formal action of the authorities concerned, any real property which may be necessary or convenient to the effectuation of the authorized purposes of the authority, which real property may include public roads and other real property already devoted to public use. (Acts 1980, No. 80-691, p. 1377, § 17.)

Collateral references. — 39A C.J.S., Highways, §§ 25-36.
39 Am. Jur. 2d, Highways, Streets, and Bridges, §§ 32, 34-39, 41, 44-46. 40 Am. Jur. 2d, Highways, Streets, and Bridges, §§ 613, 616.

§ 23-2-158. Annual report to legislature; contents; annual audit; expense.

On or before the tenth legislative day of each regular session of the legislature, the authority shall make a report of its activities for the preceding calendar year to the legislature. Each report shall set forth a complete operating and financial statement covering its operations during the year and shall contain a complete report of the engineers of the authority as to the physical condition of any project and shall include any recommendations made by such engineers. The authority shall cause an audit of its books and accounts to be made at least once in each year by certified public accountants and the cost thereof may be treated as a part of the cost of construction or of operation of the project. (Acts 1980, No. 80-691, p. 1377, § 18.)

§ 23-2-159. Conflict of interest; penalty.

Any member, agent or employee of the authority who is interested, gainfully or pecuniarily, either directly or indirectly, in any contract of the authority, or in the sale of any property, either real or personal, to or by the authority shall be guilty of a misdemeanor, and upon conviction shall be punished by a fine of not more than $1,000.00 or by imprisonment for not more than one year, or both. (Acts 1980, No. 80-691, p. 1377, § 19.)

§ 23-2-160. Transfer of toll road, bridge, etc., to state; when.

When all bonds issued under the provisions of this article to finance any toll road, bridge or tunnel project or projects and the interest thereon shall have been paid, or a sufficient amount for the payment of all such bonds and the interest thereon to the maturity thereof shall have been set aside in trust for the benefit of the bondholders, such project or projects, if then in good condition and repair, as determined by the State Highway Department, shall be transferred by the authority to the State of Alabama and shall become a part of the state highway system and shall thereafter be maintained by the State Highway Department free of tolls. (Acts 1980, No. 80-691, p. 1377, § 20.)

§ 23-2-161. State Highway Department authorized to expend funds to study proposed projects; reimbursement by authority; authority cannot incur indebtedness which makes state liable.

The State Highway Department is hereby authorized, subject to the approval of the Governor, to expend out of any funds available to it such moneys as may be necessary for the study of any proposed toll road, bridge or tunnel project authorized under this article and to use its engineering and other forces, including consulting engineers and traffic engineers, for the purpose of effecting the study. All such expenses incurred by the department prior to the issuance of revenue bonds under the provisions of this article shall be paid by the department and charged to the appropriate project or projects and the department shall keep proper records and accounts showing each amount so charged.

Upon the sale of toll road, bridge or tunnel revenue bonds for a toll road, bridge or tunnel project, the funds so expended by the department in connection with a project shall be reimbursed by the authority to the department from the proceeds of such bonds and thereafter all expenses incurred in carrying out the provisions of this article shall be payable solely from funds provided under the authority of this article.

Nothing in this article shall be construed so as to authorize the authority to incur indebtedness or liability on behalf of or payable by the state or by any of its political subdivisions. (Acts 1980, No. 80-691, p. 1377, § 21.)

CHAPTER 3.

CONTROLLED ACCESS FACILITIES.

§ 23-3-1. Definitions.

For the purposes of this chapter, the following terms shall have the meanings respectively ascribed to them by this section:

(1) INTERSTATE HIGHWAY. Any highway now included or which shall hereafter be included as a part of the national system of interstate highways, selected by joint action of the Alabama State Highway Department and the United States Bureau of Public Roads.

(2) CONTROLLED ACCESS FACILITY. A highway or street included in the national system of interstate highways especially designed for through traffic and over, from or to which owners or occupants of abutting land or other persons have no right of easement or access from abutting properties. Such highways or streets may be parkways from which trucks, buses or other commercial vehicles shall be excluded or they may be freeways open to use by all customary forms of street and highway traffic. (Acts 1956, 1st Ex. Sess., No. 104, p. 148, § 2.)

§ 23-3-2. Declaration of policy.

It is the declared policy of this state to facilitate the flow of traffic and promote public safety by controlling access to highways included in the national system of interstate highways as selected by joint action of the Alabama State Highway Department and the United States Bureau of Public Roads. (Acts 1956, 1st Ex. Sess., No. 104, p. 148, § 1.)

Cited in State v. Young, 275 Ala. 648, 157 So. 2d 680 (1963).

§ 23-3-3. Authority to plan, etc., facilities; regulation, etc., thereof.

The State Highway Director, acting alone or in cooperation with counties, cities, towns or any federal, state or local agency or any other state having authority to participate in the construction and maintenance of highways, is authorized to plan, designate, establish, regulate, vacate, alter, improve, maintain and provide controlled access facilities for public use wherever such authority or authorities are of the opinion that traffic conditions, present or future, will justify such special facilities; provided, that in the case of designation or vacation, such designations or vacations must be approved by the State Highway Director. Said authorities may regulate, restrict or prohibit the use of such controlled access facilities by the various classes of vehicles or traffic in a manner consistent with Section 23-3-1. (Acts 1956, 1st Ex. Sess., No. 104, p. 148, § 3.)

Collateral references. — 90 C.J.S., Turn-pikes & Toll Roads, § 34.
Power of municipal corporation to limit exclusive use of designated lanes or streets to buses and taxicabs. 43 ALR3d 1394.

§ 23-3-4. Design authority; commercial establishments.

(a) The State Highway Director is authorized to so design any controlled access facility and to so regulate, restrict or prohibit access as to best serve the traffic for which such facility is intended. In this connection, such highway authority is authorized to divide and separate any controlled access facility into separate roadways by the construction of raised curbing, central dividing sections or other physical separations or by designating such separate roadways by signs, markers, stripes and the proper lane for such traffic by appropriate signs, markers, stripes and other devices. No person shall have any right of ingress or egress to, from or across controlled access facilities to or from abutting lands, except such designated points at which access may be permitted or service roads provided, upon such terms and conditions as may be specified from time to time.

(b) Except to the extent authorized by law for toll roads, no automotive service station or other commercial establishment for serving motor vehicle users shall be constructed or located within the right-of-way of or on publicly owned or publicly leased land acquired or used for, or in connection with, the controlled access facility; provided, that this shall not limit the powers granted to the department of conservation by Sections 9-2-9, 9-2-10, 9-2-100, 9-2-101, 9-2-103 through 9-2-108, 9-14-1 through 9-14-6 and 9-14-20 through 9-14-29, when those powers are exercised in accordance with the purposes of such provisions. (Acts 1956, 1st Ex. Sess., No. 104, p. 148, § 4; Acts 1961, Ex. Sess., No. 305, p. 2365; Acts 1967, No. 599, p. 1384, § 1.)

Collateral references. — Governmental liability for failure to post highway deer crossing warning signs. 59 ALR4th 1217.

§ 23-3-5. Acquisition of property and property rights.

(a) For the purpose of this chapter, the highway authorities of the state, acting alone or through the counties, cities and towns, may acquire private or public property and property rights for controlled access facilities and service roads, including rights of access, air, view and light, by gift, devise, purchase or condemnation in the same manner as such authorities are now, or hereafter may be, authorized by law to acquire such property or property rights in connection with highways and streets within their respective jurisdiction. In connection with the acquisition of property or property rights for any controlled access facility, or portion thereof or service road in connection therewith, the state, county, city or town highway authority is hereby authorized, in its discretion, to acquire an entire lot, block or tract of land, even though such entire lot, block or tract of land is not immediately needed for the right-of-way proper; provided, that the authority is not granted to acquire property not immediately needed for the right-of-way proper unless the owner of such property shall consent thereto.

(b) In any event, in any case now or hereafter pending, when property is condemned for limited access highways and an appeal is taken by the state from a judgment of a court of competent jurisdiction and if the award of damages is affirmed on appeal by the Court of Civil Appeals or the Supreme Court of Alabama, then, in such event, the property owner shall be entitled to interest at six percent per annum on the amount of damages awarded from the date of the entry of the judgment awarding such damages. (Acts 1956, 1st Ex. Sess., No. 104, p. 148, § 5; Acts 1967, No. 599, p. 1384, § 2.)

Section recognizes that property right of access is subject to condemnation. — This section is a legislative recognition that the abutting landowner has a property right of access which is subject to condemnation. St. Clair County v. Bukacek, 272 Ala. 323, 131 So. 2d 683 (1961).

The owner of land abutting on a street or highway has a private right in such street or highway, distinct from that of the public, which cannot be taken or materially interfered with without just compensation. Access to the highway is one of those private rights. State v. Payton, 273 Ala. 49, 134 So. 2d 198 (1961).

This section did not repeal former § 18-1-6 (see now § 18-1A-72). — This section, by giving the right to acquire private property without expressing any qualifications or exceptions, did not repeal former § 18-1-6 (see now § 18-1A-72), relating to property that has already been subjected or devoted to a public use. Brittain v. Southern Ry., 280 Ala. 650, 197 So. 2d 453 (1967).

And state highway department had no right to take for highway purposes a railroad spur track devoted and subjected to use for common carriage of goods and susceptible to that use. Brittain v. Southern Ry., 280 Ala. 650, 197 So. 2d 453 (1967).

Collateral references. — Abutting owner's right to compensation for loss of access because of limited access highway or street. 43 ALR2d 1072.

Conveyance of land as bounded by road, street, or other way as giving grantee right to compensation upon taking for public highway. 46 ALR2d 490.

Power to directly regulate or prohibit, without making compensation, abutter's access to street or highway. 73 ALR2d 652.

Use or improvement of highway as establishing grade necessary to entitle abutting owner to compensation on subsequent change. 2 ALR3d 985.

Eminent domain: Compensability of loss of view from owner's property — state cases. 25 ALR4th 671.

§ 23-3-6. Elimination of intersections at grade.

The state or any of its subdivisions shall have authority to provide for the elimination of intersections at grade of controlled access facilities with existing state or county roads, and city or town streets by grade separation of service road or by closing off such roads and streets at the right-of-way boundary line of such controlled access facility. After the establishment of any controlled access facility, no highway or street which is not a part of said facility shall intersect the same at grade. No city or town street, county or state highway or other public way shall be opened into or connected with any such controlled access facility without the consent and previous approval of the Highway Director; provided, that the Highway Director may, whenever he determines that traffic is not thereby impaired, authorize the continued intersection at grade of lightly traveled entrances and minor public roads as ways of access to controlled access facilities in sparsely populated areas. (Acts 1956, 1st Ex. Sess., No. 104, p. 148, § 6.)

This section does not refer to railroads.
Brittain v. Southern Ry., 280 Ala. 650, 197 So. 2d 453 (1967).

§ 23-3-7. Local service roads and streets.

In connection with the development of any controlled access facility, the State Highway Director is authorized to plan, designate, establish, use, regulate, alter, improve, maintain and vacate local service roads and streets or to designate as local service roads and streets any existing road or street if, in his opinion, such local service roads and streets are necessary or desirable. Such local service roads or streets shall be of appropriate design and shall be separated from the controlled access facility proper by means of all devices designated as necessary or desirable by the proper authority. (Acts 1956, 1st Ex. Sess., No. 104, p. 148, § 8.)

§ 23-3-8. Agreements with federal or local governments.

The State Highway Director is authorized to enter into agreements with counties, cities and towns or the federal government respecting the financing, planning, establishment, improvement, maintenance, use, regulation or vacation of controlled access facilities or other public ways in their respective jurisdictions to facilitate the purposes of this chapter. (Acts 1956, 1st Ex. Sess., No. 104, p. 148, § 7.)

CHAPTER 4.

CLOSING AND VACATING STREETS, ALLEYS AND HIGHWAYS.

Cited in Terry Properties, Inc. v. City of Roanoke, 401 So. 2d 25 (Ala. 1981).

ARTICLE 1.

COUNTIES OR MUNICIPALITIES.

§ 23-4-1. Application.

Streets, alleys and other highways, or portions thereof, may be closed and vacated upon the application of the municipality in which they are situated and, where not situated in a municipality, upon the application of the county in which they are situated in the manner provided for in this article. (Acts 1931, No. 49, p. 62; Code 1940, T. 56, § 26.)

Cross references. — As to payment of fair market value of land acquired upon vacation of public street, see § 11-49-6.

Strict construction of vacation statutes. — There is a common law prohibition against the vacation of public ways. Therefore, the vacation statutes are in derogation of the common law prohibition against the vacation of public ways and must be strictly construed. Bownes v. Winston County, 481 So. 2d 362 (Ala. 1985).

Public streets, alleys, or highways can be closed and vacated by counties or municipalities in accordance with this section through § 23-4-6, or by "abutting landowners" in accordance with § 23-4-20. However, there is a common-law prohibition against the vacation of public ways. Thus, the vacation statutes are in derogation of the common-law prohibition against the vacation of public ways and must be strictly construed. Fordham v. Cleburne County Comm'n, 580 So. 2d 567 (Ala. 1991).

Determination of whether road is public or private. — A trial court's determination of whether a road is public or private might affect not only the rights of the individual litigants but also the rights of members of the public to use the road, the duty of the county to maintain it, and the liability of the county for failure to maintain it; therefore, the county must be joined as a party, since if not joined, neither it nor other members of the public are bound by the trial court's ruling. Boles v. Autery, 554 So. 2d 959 (Ala. 1989).

A public road may be abandoned and thus lose its public character in one of several ways. Floyd v. Industrial Dev. Bd., 442 So. 2d 927 (Ala. 1983); Walker v. Winston County Comm'n, 474 So. 2d 1116 (Ala. 1985).

Nonuse for a period of 20 years will operate as a discontinuance of a public road. Floyd v. Industrial Dev. Bd., 442 So. 2d 927 (Ala. 1983); Walker v. Winston County Comm'n, 474 So. 2d 1116 (Ala. 1985); Bownes v. Winston County, 481 So. 2d 362 (Ala. 1985).

Abandonment of a public road may be effected by a formal, statutory action. Floyd v. Industrial Dev. Bd., 442 So. 2d 927 (Ala. 1983); Walker v. Winston County Comm'n, 474 So. 2d 1116 (Ala. 1985).

The statutory method of abandonment was inapplicable where county did not apply to close and vacate the road, and the failure of county authorities to keep the road in repair did not work an abandonment. Auerbach v. Parker, 544 So. 2d 943 (Ala. 1989).

Construction of a new highway replacing an old road may, under the right circumstances and after an appropriate length of time, result in an abandonment of the old road. Floyd v. Industrial Dev. Bd., 442 So. 2d 927 (Ala. 1983).

There can be an abandonment by nonuse for a period short of the time of prescription when there has been the construction of a new highway replacing an old road. Bownes v. Winston County, 481 So. 2d 362 (Ala. 1985).

The obstruction of public road, depriving the public of the use of public convenience, is public nuisance, and an action to abate such a nuisance may be maintained by an individual on behalf of the public, if he has a special interest in the road. Barber v. Covington County Comm'n, 466 So. 2d 945 (Ala. 1985).

Cited in Smith v. Gamble, 344 So. 2d 749 (Ala. 1977); Turner v. Hoehn, 494 So. 2d 28 (Ala. 1986).

§ 23-4-2. Procedure.

(a) The governing body of the municipality where the street, alley or highway, or portion thereof, to be closed and vacated is situated in a municipality and, in other cases, the county commission of the county in which the street, alley, highway, or portion thereof, is situated shall, after causing to be published in a newspaper once a week for three consecutive weeks in the county a notice which shall describe the street, alley, highway or portion thereof proposed to be closed and vacated and also give the date of the hearing, first adopt a resolution to the effect that it is in the public interest that such street, alley, highway or portion thereof be closed and vacated; and thereafter, such governing body may file in the office of the judge of probate in the county in which such street, alley or highway, or portion thereof, is located, its petition requesting the closing and vacating of such street, alley or highway, or such portion thereof.

(b) The petition shall describe with accuracy the street, alley or highway, or portion thereof, to be closed and vacated and shall give the names of the owner or owners of the abutting lots or parcels of land and also the owner or owners of such other lots or parcels of land, if any, which will be cut off from access thereby over some other reasonable and convenient way. The petition shall further set forth that it is in the interest of the public that such street, alley or highway, or portion thereof, be closed and vacated, and that a resolution to that effect has been adopted by the governing body of the municipality or county, as hereinbefore set forth.

(c) Thereupon, the probate court shall set the petition for hearing and shall issue notice of the pendency of the petition to the persons named in the petition. Such notice shall be served upon the said abutting owner or owners and also the person or persons, if any, named in the petition whose access will be affected, resident in this state as civil process is now served, not less than 10 days prior to the hearing of the petition. In case of a nonresident owner or owners or parties in interest or unknown defendants, the probate court shall cause to be published in a newspaper published in the county said notice, which shall contain the nature of the petition and in which shall be described the street, alley or highway, or portion thereof, proposed to be closed and vacated, and all such persons shall be required to appear upon the hearing thereof and to either assent to the granting of the petition or contest the same as they may see fit. Such notice shall be published once a week for three consecutive weeks prior to the date set for the hearing of the petition and shall give the date on which the hearing is to be had. (Acts 1931, No. 49, p. 62; Code 1940, T. 56, § 27.)

A public road may be abandoned and thus lose its public character in one of several ways. One example is nonuse for a period of 20 years which will operate as a discontinuance of a public road. Likewise, an abandonment of a public road may be effected by a formal, statutory action. Floyd v. Industrial Dev. Bd., 442 So. 2d 927 (Ala. 1983); Walker v. Winston County Comm'n, 474 So. 2d 1116 (Ala. 1985).

The county planning commission does not have the power to actually vacate a public street. McClendon v. Shelby County, 484 So. 2d 459 (Ala. Civ. App. 1985), cert. denied, 484 So. 2d 465 (Ala.); 479 U.S. 815, 107 S. Ct. 68, 93 L. Ed. 2d 26 (1986).

Construction of a new highway replacing an old road may, under the right circum-stances and after an appropriate length of time, result in an abandonment of the old road. Floyd v. Industrial Dev. Bd., 442 So. 2d 927 (Ala. 1983).

Where the county commission did not adopt a clear and unequivocal resolution closing the road, the commission did not meet the strict standards set out in §§ 23-4-2 and 23-4-20. The trial court's holding that the commission had not vacated the road and its injunction against property owner's interference with the road were based on findings that were well supported by the record. Fordham v. Cleburne County Comm'n, 580 So. 2d 567 (Ala. 1991).

Cited in Smith v. Gamble, 344 So. 2d 749 (Ala. 1977).

§ 23-4-3. Contest by interested persons.

Upon the hearing of the petition, any person or persons owning lands, or any interest therein, which abut on such street, alley or highway, or any portion thereof, and also the owner or owners of such other lots or parcels of land which will, by the proposed closing and vacating, be cut off from access thereby over some other reasonable and convenient way, may appear and assent in writing to the granting of the petition, or contest the same or suffer the same to be taken in default against him or them; but the resolution of the municipality or county that it is to the public interest that such street, alley or highway, or portion thereof, be closed and vacated shall be prima facie to that effect. If upon the hearing the court shall deny the petition, it shall so order and dismiss the petition. If, on the other hand, the court upon the hearing shall grant the petition, it shall so order, and thereupon, it shall appoint three commissioners, who shall be residents of the county or municipality in which the property is located and freeholders, to assess the damages of the owner or owners of the abutting lands which will result from the closing and vacating of the street, alley or highway, or portion thereof, and also the owner or owners, if any, of such other lots or parcels of land which will be cut off from access thereby over some other reasonable and convenient way who fail to assent to the granting of the petition. Such commissioners shall be duly sworn by the probate judge faithfully to discharge their duties and shall view the lands and hear any evidence which the parties may offer bearing on the damages which will result by such closing or vacating. The commissioners shall submit their report in writing within 10 days after qualification, which report shall assess the damages of the respective nonassenting landowners and shall describe the several tracts as to which such damages are assessed. The commissioners shall each receive $3.00 per day for their services, to be taxed as part of the cost of the proceeding. (Acts 1931, No. 49, p. 62; Code 1940, T. 56, § 28.)

Cited in Smith v. Gamble, 344 So. 2d 749 (Ala. 1977); Floyd v. Industrial Dev. Bd., 442 So. 2d 927 (Ala. 1983); Terry Properties, Inc. v. Standard Oil Co., 799 F.2d 1523 (11th Cir. 1986).

§ 23-4-4. Recordation of report by commissioners; payment of costs and damages.

Upon the coming in of the report of the commissioners, the probate court shall cause the same to be recorded among its records and the petitioner may, within 30 days after the making of such report, pay, or cause to be paid, the cost of the proceeding and the damages assessed by the commissioners; and upon such payment, the street, alley or highway, or portion thereof, ordered to be closed and vacated shall be closed and vacated and all interest of the public therein shall cease and determine. (Acts 1931, No. 49, p. 62; Code 1940, T. 56, § 29.)

Cited in Smith v. Gamble, 344 So. 2d 749 (Ala. 1977); Floyd v. Industrial Dev. Bd., 442 So. 2d 927 (Ala. 1983).

§ 23-4-5. Appeals.

Either the petitioner or any contesting landowner may appeal within 30 days from the order of the probate court closing and vacating the street to the circuit court of the county in which the lands are situated, and upon such appeal, the proceeding shall be tried de novo, either party having the right to demand trial by jury when and as such demand is authorized in civil actions in such court. In case the appeal is taken by any landowner, the appeal shall not suspend the effect of the proceeding in the probate court if the petitioner shall pay into the probate court the damages assessed to such landowner, together with the cost of the proceeding, and shall give bond in double the amount of such assessment, with sureties, to be approved by the probate judge, conditioned upon paying such damages as may be assessed to such landowner upon appeal. From the judgment of the circuit court, an appeal may be taken within 42 days by either party to the Court of Civil Appeals or the Supreme Court in accordance with the Alabama Rules of Appellate Procedure. (Acts 1931, No. 49, p. 62; Code 1940, T. 56, § 30.)

Cited in Floyd v. Industrial Dev. Bd., 442 So. 2d 927 (Ala. 1983).

§ 23-4-6. Article deemed cumulative.

The provisions of this article shall not be held to repeal any existing statute relating to the closing, changing or vacating of streets and highways, but shall be cumulative. (Acts 1931, No. 49, p. 62; Code 1940, T. 56, § 31.)

Cited in Floyd v. Industrial Dev. Bd., 442 So. 2d 927 (Ala. 1983).

ARTICLE 2.

ABUTTING LANDOWNERS.

§ 23-4-20. Vacation of street or alley.

(a) Any street or alley may be vacated, in whole or in part, by the owner or owners of the land abutting the street or alley or abutting that portion of the street or alley desired to be vacated joining in a written instrument declaring the same to be vacated, such written instrument to be executed, acknowledged and recorded in like manner as conveyances of land, which declaration being duly recorded shall operate to destroy the force and effect of the dedication of said street or alley or portion vacated and to divest all public rights, including any rights which may have been acquired by prescription, in that part of the street or alley so vacated; provided, that if any such street or alley is within the limits of any municipality, the assent to such vacation of the city council or other governing body of the municipality must be procured, evidenced by a resolution adopted by such governing body, a copy of which, certified by the clerk or ministerial officer in charge of the records of the municipality must be attached to, filed and recorded with the written declaration of vacation; and if any such street or alley has been or is being used as a public road and is not within the limits of any municipality, the assent to such vacation of the county commission of the county in which such street or alley is situated must be procured, evidenced by resolution adopted by such board or court, a copy of which, certified by the head thereof, must be attached to, filed and recorded with the declaration of vacation. Such vacation shall not deprive other property owners of such right as they may have to convenient and reasonable means of ingress and egress to and from their property, and if such right is not afforded by the remaining streets and alleys, another street or alley affording such right must be dedicated.

(b) The provisions of this section shall not be held to repeal any existing statute relating to the vacation of streets or alleys or parts thereof. (Acts 1939, No. 69, p. 110; Code 1940, T. 56, § 32.)

Cross references. — As to payment of fair market value of land acquired upon vacation of public street, see § 11-49-6. As to vacation of right-of-way fee, see § 11-49-6.

Strict construction of vacation statutes. — There is a common law prohibition against the vacation of public ways. Therefore, the vacation statutes are in derogation of the common law prohibition against the vacation of public ways and must be strictly construed. Bownes v. Winston County, 481 So. 2d 362 (Ala. 1985).

Public streets, alleys, or highways can be closed and vacated by counties or municipalities in accordance with §§ 23-4-1 through 23-4-6, or by "abutting landowners" in accordance with this section. However, there is a common-law prohibition against the vacation of public ways. Thus, the vacation statutes are in derogation of the common-law prohibition against the vacation of public ways and must be strictly construed. Fordham v. Cleburne County Comm'n, 580 So. 2d 567 (Ala. 1991).

This section and § 35-2-54 should be strictly construed so that such statutes cannot be instruments of oppression or be misused and abused. Therefore, all procedural requirements under such statutes must be met. Hammond v. Phillips, 516 So. 2d 707 (Ala. Civ. App. 1987).

Statutes interpreted to protect interests of nonconsenting property owners. — Statutes in derogation of the common-law prohibition against the vacation of public ways will be interpreted to protect the property, interests of nonconsenting property owners affected by the proposed closing, subject only to the rule of remoteness; not only is this a rule of reason but it is mandated by the most basic application of constitutional due process. Gwin v. Bristol Steel & Iron Works, Inc., 366 So. 2d 692 (Ala. 1978).

Abandonment by nonuse. — A public way or easement of passage which the public has in respect to a highway may be abandoned and thus lose its public character in one of two ways. Nonuse for a period of 20 years will operate as a discontinuance of a public road. Likewise, there can be an abandonment by nonuse for a period short of the time of prescription when there has been the construction of a new highway replacing an old road. Bownes v. Winston County, 481 So. 2d 362 (Ala. 1985).

Requirement of payment of fair market value of land prior to giving assent to vacation by municipality not authorized. — Even though the section provides that the city council must give its assent to vacate a street or alley, there is no specific or implied authority in the section that permits a city to require payment of the fair market value of the land to be vacated, before giving its assent. Overton v. Scott Co., 356 So. 2d 134 (Ala. 1978).

County must be joined as party where determination of whether road is public or private. — A trial court's determination of whether a road is public or private might affect not only the rights of the individual litigants but also the rights of members of the public to use the road, the duty of the county to maintain it, and the liability of the county for failure to maintain it; therefore, the county must be joined, as a party, since if not joined, neither it nor other members of the public are bound by the trial court's ruling. Boles v. Autery, 554 So. 2d 959 (Ala. 1989).

An individual may bring an action to enjoin the obstruction of a public road if he suffers an injury different in kind and degree from that suffered by the general public. Williams v. Norton, 399 So. 2d 828 (Ala. 1981).

An individual, as an owner of land which abuts a public road, suffers a special injury if an obstruction of that road denies him convenient access to a nearby waterway or forces him to take a more circuitous route to the outside world. Williams v. Norton, 399 So. 2d 828 (Ala. 1981).

Injunction upheld. — Summary judgment enjoining the University of Alabama at Birmingham, as an abutting landowner, and the city of Birmingham from vacating and closing a city public street and including the vacated area in the campus of UAB without resorting to condemnation procedures was proper, where the district court found that the plaintiffs' properties abutted the street in question in the vicinity of the proposed vacation and that the diversion of through traffic from said street would diminish the value of these properties. Henley v. Herring, 779 F.2d 1553 (11th Cir. 1986).

Where the county commission did not adopt a clear and unequivocal resolution closing the road, the commission did not meet the strict standards set out in § 23-4-2 and this section. The trial court's holding that the commission had not vacated the road and its injunction against property owner's interference with the road were based on findings that were well supported by the record. Fordham v. Cleburne County Comm'n, 580 So. 2d 567 (Ala. 1991).

Cited in Smith v. Gamble, 344 So. 2d 749 (Ala. 1977); Holland v. City of Alabaster, 566 So. 2d 224 (Ala. 1990).

CHAPTER 5.

OFFENSES.

Cross references. — As to prohibition against staking, pasturing, etc., of animals upon highway rights-of-way, see § 3-3-1 et seq.

§ 23-5-1. Obstructing and injuring of public roads. Repealed by Acts 1977, No. 607, p. 812, § 9901, as amended, effective January 1, 1980.

Cross references. — As to criminal tampering, see now §§ 13A-7-24 through 13A-7-26.

§ 23-5-2. Driving around, destruction, etc., of detour or warning sign, or barricade or fence.

(a) For the purposes of this section, the following terms shall have the meanings respectively ascribed to them by this subsection:

(1) DETOUR SIGN. Any sign placed across or on a public road of the state by the state, the county or municipal authorities, or by their contractors, indicating that such road is closed or partially closed, which sign also indicates the direction of an alternate route to be followed to give access to certain points.

(2) WARNING SIGN. A sign indicating construction work in area.

(3) BARRICADE. A barrier for obstructing the passage of motor vehicle traffic.

(4) FENCE. A barrier to prevent the intrusion of motor vehicle traffic.

(5) OFFICIALLY CLOSED. A highway or road that has been officially closed by a governmental unit, the Alabama Highway Department, a city or a county.

(b) Any person who wilfully destroys, knocks down, removes, defaces or alters any letters or figures on a detour or warning sign set upon a highway or road of this state, or who wilfully knocks down, removes, rearranges, destroys, defaces or alters any letter or figures on a barricade or fence erected on any highway or road of this state, or who drives around or through any barricade or fence on any officially closed highway or road of this state or drives around such detour sign or barricade or fence or any person who wilfully ignores or disregards a warning sign before such road has been officially opened to the public traffic by the Alabama Highway Department or, in appropriate cases, by the county or municipal officer responsible for constructing or maintaining such roads, shall be guilty of a misdemeanor; provided, that as long as no damage is done to the new work, this section shall have no application to peace officers in the performance of their duties, nor to employees of the Alabama Highway Department, nor of the contractor, nor of the federal authorities when engaged in inspection of surveys, repairs, maintenance or construction on or alongside such highways, within the right-of-way, nor individuals domiciled or making their livelihood within the affected areas, nor to any person or group of persons who shall be authorized by the Highway Director or any appropriate county or municipal officer.

(c) Every person convicted of a violation of this section shall be punished by a fine of not less than $5.00 nor more than $100.00 or by imprisonment for not more than 30 days, or by both such fine and imprisonment. (Acts 1969, No. 1145, p. 2148.)

Collateral references. — 40 C.J.S., Highways, § 255.
Highway contractor's liability to highway user for highway surface defects. 62 ALR4th 1067.

§§ **23-5-3 through 23-5-5.** Repealed by Acts 1977, No. 607, p. 812, § 9901, as amended, effective January 1, 1980.

Cross references. — As to criminal littering, see now § 13A-7-29.

§ 23-5-6. Trash, litter, etc., upon public thoroughfare — Driver presumed offender when items thrown from vehicle.

If a misdemeanor is committed as set forth in Section 13A-7-29 from a motor vehicle, the driver of the vehicle shall be presumed to be the offender. (Acts 1961, Ex. Sess., No. 55, p. 1920, § 2.)

§ 23-5-7. Trash, litter, etc., upon public thoroughfare — Erection of signs.

The State Highway Department, the county commission of each of the several counties and the governing body of each city or town shall cause signs to be erected at suitable intervals on highways and public thoroughfares in their respective areas of authority, including public parks, informing the public that it is unlawful to perform the acts prohibited by Section 13A-7-29. (Acts 1961, Ex. Sess., No. 55, p. 1920, § 3.)

§ 23-5-8. Trash, litter, etc., upon public thoroughfare — Enforcement.

The Alabama Highway Patrol and the law enforcement officers of the counties, cities and towns of this state are charged with the duty of enforcing the provisions of Section 13A-7-29 and Sections 23-5-6 through 23-5-9. (Acts 1961, Ex. Sess., No. 55, p. 1920, § 4.)

§ 23-5-9. Trash, litter, etc., upon public thoroughfare — Provisions deemed cumulative.

The provisions of Section 13A-7-29 and Sections 23-5-6 through 23-5-8 shall be cumulative to existing statutes relating to the throwing, placing or otherwise depositing of debris, rubbish, trash or other items or substances of a prohibited nature upon the public highways of the state and shall in no wise repeal nor affect any of such laws. (Acts 1961, Ex. Sess., No. 55, p. 1920, § 5.)

§§ 23-5-10 through 23-5-12. Repealed by Acts 1977, No. 607, p. 812, § 9901, as amended, effective January 1, 1980.

Cross references. — As to bribery of public servants, see now § 13A-10-61. As to failure to disclose conflict of interest, see now § 13A-10-62.

§ 23-5-13. Violation of highway department rules or regulations.

Any person, firm or corporation who violates any reasonable rule or regulation prescribed by the highway department for the better construction, repair and maintenance, protection and preservation of the public roads, bridges, highways and rights-of-way of roads and highways of this state shall be guilty of a misdemeanor and, on conviction, shall be punished by a fine of not less than $100.00 nor more than $500.00 and, at the discretion of the judge trying the case, may also be sentenced to hard labor for the county for a term not to exceed six months, unless otherwise provided by law. (Code 1923, § 4449; Acts 1927, No. 347, p. 348; Code 1940, T. 23, § 127.)

§ 23-5-14. Violation of rules, etc., enacted by county commission relative to public roads, etc., of county.

It shall be unlawful for any person, firm or corporation to violate any rule, regulation or law which has heretofore been adopted or promulgated or which may hereafter be adopted or promulgated by the county commission of any county, under the authority conferred by law, relating to the use, control, care, operation or maintenance of the public roads, bridges or ferries of said county; and any person, firm or corporation violating the same shall be deemed guilty of a misdemeanor and, upon conviction, shall be fined not more than $500.00 and may also be sentenced to hard labor for the county for not more than six months. Each violation shall constitute a separate offense. (Acts 1927, No. 347, p. 348; Code 1940, T. 23, § 62.)

CHAPTER 6.

INDUSTRIAL ACCESS ROADS AND BRIDGES.

§ 23-6-1. Definitions.

Where used in this chapter the following words and terms shall be given the following respective meanings unless the context hereof clearly indicates otherwise:

(1) CORPORATION. The public corporation authorized to be created by this chapter.

(2) BOARD OF DIRECTORS. The board of directors of the corporation.

(3) CODE. The Code of Alabama 1975, as amended.

(4) GOVERNMENT SECURITIES. Any bonds or other obligations which as to principal and interest constitute direct obligations of, or are unconditionally guaranteed by, the United States of America, including obligations of any federal agency to the extent such obligations are unconditionally guaranteed by the United States of America and any certificates or any other evidences of an ownership interest in such obligations of, or unconditionally guaranteed by, the United States of America or in specified portions thereof (which may consist of the principal thereof or the interest thereon).

(5) INDUSTRIAL ACCESS ROADS AND BRIDGES. The planning, design and construction of those roads and bridges on the public highway and street system providing access to industrial sites to include necessary right-of-way and utility activities provided by state law.

(6) LEGISLATURE. The Legislature of Alabama.

(7) NET INTEREST INCOME. Interest earned from an investment, net of that which represents a return of accrued interest, and the amount required to offset the amortization of any premium, paid in connection with the purchase of such investment.

(8) PERMITTED INVESTMENTS.

a. Government securities;

b. Bonds, debentures, notes or other evidences of indebtedness issued by any of the following agencies, to the extent that such obligations are secured by the full faith and credit of the United States: Bank for Cooperatives; Federal Intermediate Credit Banks; Federal Financing Bank; Federal Home Loan Banks; Federal Farm Credit Bank; Export-Import Bank of the United States; Federal Land Banks; or Farmers Home Administration, or any other agency or corporation which has been or may hereafter be created by or pursuant to an act of the Congress of the United States as an agency or instrumentality thereof, the bonds, debentures, participation certificates or notes of which are unconditionally guaranteed by the United States of America;

c. Bonds, notes, pass through securities or other evidences of indebtedness of GNMA and participation certificates of FHLMC;

d. Full faith and credit obligations of any state, provided that at the time of purchase such obligations are rated at least "AA" by Standard & Poor's Corporation and at least "Aa" by Moody's Investors Service;

e. Public housing bonds issued by public agencies or municipalities and fully secured as to the payment of both principal and interest by contracts with the United States of America, or temporary notes, preliminary notes or project notes issued by public agencies or municipalities, in each case fully secured as to the payment of both principal and interest by a requisition or payment agreement with the United States of America;

f. Time deposits evidenced by certificates of deposit issued by banks or savings and loan associations which are members of the Federal Deposit Insurance Corporation or the Federal Savings and Loan Insurance Corporation, provided that, to the extent such time deposits exceed available federal deposit insurance, such time deposits are fully secured by obligations described in clauses a, b, c and e above, which at all times have a market value (exclusive of accrued interest) at least equal to such bank time deposits so secured, including interest, and which meet the greater of 100 percent collateralization or the "AA" collateral levels established by Standard & Poor's Corporation for structured financings;

g. Repurchase agreements for obligations of the type specified in clauses a, b, c, and e above, provided such repurchase agreements are fully collateralized and secured by such obligations which have a market value (exclusive of accrued interest) at least equal to the purchase price of such repurchase agreements and which are held by a depository satisfactory to the State Treasurer in such manner as may be required to provide a perfected security interest in such obligations, and which meet the greater of 100 percent collateralization or the "AA" collateral levels established by Standard & Poor's Corporation for structured financings; and

h. Uncollateralized investment agreements with, or certificates of deposit issued by, banks or bank holding companies, the senior long-term securities of which are rated at least "AA" by Standard & Poor's Corporation and at least "Aa" by Moody's Investors Service.

(9) STATE. The State of Alabama. (Acts 1985, No. 85-549, p. 833, § 1.)

§ 23-6-2. Legislative intent; State Highway Department to perform or direct construction; power to assign, contract, etc., work; chapter to be liberally construed.

It is the intention of the legislature by the passage of this chapter to authorize the incorporation of a public corporation for the following purposes:

To issue bonds to assure the availability of funds for payment of the cost of constructing industrial access roads and bridges as shall from time to time be constructed;

To construct industrial access roads and bridges through a corporation to be composed of the officials whose incorporation is hereby authorized;

To vest such corporation with all powers, authorities, rights, privileges, and titles that may be necessary to enable it to accomplish such purpose; and

To appropriate and pledge funds for the use of such corporation.

All construction herein referred to shall be performed by or under the direction and supervision of the State Highway Department. The State Highway Department may assign, contract or delegate the work of construction under its general powers, subject to approval by the Governor. This chapter shall be liberally construed in conformity with the said purposes. (Acts 1985, No. 85-549, p. 833, § 2.)

§ 23-6-3. Authority to incorporate.

The Highway Director, the State Treasurer and the Director of Finance may become a corporation, with the powers and authorities hereinafter provided, by proceeding according to the provisions of this chapter. (Acts 1985, No. 85-549, p. 833, § 3.)

§ 23-6-4. Proceeding to incorporate.

To become a corporation, the Highway Director, the State Treasurer and the Director of Finance shall present to the Secretary of State of Alabama an application signed by them which shall set forth:

(1) The name, official designation and official residence of each of the applicants, together with a certified copy of the commission evidencing each applicant's right to office;

(2) The date on which each applicant was inducted into office and the term of office of each of the applicants;

(3) The name of the proposed corporation, which shall be Alabama Industrial Access Road and Bridge Corporation;

(4) The location of the principal office of the proposed corporation, which shall be Montgomery, Alabama; and

(5) Any other matter relating to the incorporation which the applicants may choose to insert and which is not inconsistent with this chapter or the laws of the State of Alabama.

The application shall be subscribed and sworn to by each of the applicants before an officer authorized by the laws of the State of Alabama to take acknowledgments to deeds. The Secretary of State shall examine the application and, if he finds that it substantially complies with the requirements of this section, he shall receive and file it and record it in an appropriate book of records in his office. (Acts 1985, No. 85-549, p. 833, § 4.)

§ 23-6-5. Certificate of incorporation; recording; no fees to be paid to Secretary of State on incorporation or dissolution.

When the application has been made, filed and recorded, as herein provided, the applicants shall constitute a public corporation under the name proposed in the application and the Secretary of State shall make and issue to the applicants a certificate of incorporation pursuant to this chapter, under the great seal of the state, and shall record the same with the application. There shall be no fees paid to the Secretary of State for any work in connection with the incorporation or dissolution of the corporation so organized (which, for convenience, is herein referred to as "the corporation"). (Acts 1985, No. 85-549, p. 833, § 5.)

§ 23-6-6. Members, officers and directors of corporation; vacancies; compensation; record of proceedings; record as evidence.

The applicants named in the application and their respective successors in office shall constitute the members of the corporation. The Highway Director shall be the president of the corporation, the State Treasurer shall be its vice-president, the Director of Finance shall be the secretary of the corporation, and the State Treasurer shall be the treasurer of the corporation and shall act as custodian of its funds. The members of the corporation shall constitute all the members of the board of directors of the corporation, and any two members of the said board of directors shall constitute a quorum for the transaction of business. Should any of said officials of the state die or should his term of office as Highway Director, State Treasurer, or Director of Finance, as the case may be, expire or should he resign therefrom, his successor in office shall take his place as a member, officer and director of the corporation. No member, officer or director of the corporation shall draw any salary, in addition to that now authorized by law, for any service he may render or any duty he may perform in connection with the corporation. All proceedings had and done by the board of directors shall be reduced to writing by the secretary of the corporation and recorded in a substantially bound book. Copies of such proceedings, when certified by the secretary of the corporation under the seal of the corporation, shall be received in all courts as prima facie evidence of the matters and things therein certified. (Acts 1985, No. 85-549, p. 833, § 6.)

§ 23-6-7. Corporate powers.

The corporation shall have the following powers:

(1) To have succession by its corporate name without time limit;

(2) To sue and be sued and to prosecute and defend, at law or in equity, in any court having jurisdiction of the subject matter and of the parties;

(3) To have and to use a corporate seal and to alter the same at pleasure;

(4) To construct, reconstruct, and relocate industrial access roads and bridges within the state or to cause the same to be constructed, reconstructed, and relocated;

(5) To receive, take and hold by sale, gift, lease, devise or otherwise, real and personal estate of every description, and to manage the same;

(6) To acquire by purchase, gift, or the exercise of the power of eminent domain, or any other lawful means, and to transfer, convey or cause to be conveyed to the state, any real, personal or mixed property necessary or convenient in connection with the construction, reconstruction or relocation of industrial access roads and bridges in the state;

(7) To exercise the right of eminent domain as freely and completely as, and in the same manner as, the state is empowered to exercise such right;

(8) To borrow money and issue its bonds in evidence thereof subject to the provisions of Section 23-6-8 of this chapter;

(9) As security for payment of the principal of and the interest on its bonds, to pledge any funds or revenues from which its bonds may be made payable, including the proceeds of the appropriations and pledges herein provided for;

(10) To appoint and employ such attorneys, accountants, financial advisors, underwriters, trustees, depositories, registrars and other advisors, agents and independent contractors as the business of the corporation may require;

(11) To enter into contracts with counties, the State Highway Department or other agency performing any of the functions thereof, road district authorities, private persons, firms, or corporations the federal emergency administrator of public works and any other branch of the federal government, in furtherance of its public purposes and objects, either relative to work done or to be done; and

(12) To turn over to the State Highway Department any and all funds of the corporation as from time to time may be necessary or convenient for the most economical construction of such industrial access roads and bridges or otherwise for carrying out the business of the corporation. (Acts 1985, No. 85-549, p. 833, § 7.)

§ 23-6-8. Bonds of corporation.

The bonds of the corporation shall be signed by its president and attested by its secretary and the seal of the corporation shall be affixed thereto or a facsimile thereof printed or otherwise reproduced thereon. The signatures of both the president and the secretary on any bonds may be facsimile signatures if the board of directors, in its proceedings with respect to issuance of such bonds, provides for manual authentication thereof (or manual execution of certificates of registration thereon) by a trustee, registrar or paying agent or by named individuals who are employees of the state assigned to the finance department or the state treasurer's office. Any bonds of the corporation may be executed and delivered by it at any time and from time to time, shall be in such form and denominations and of such tenor and maturities, shall bear such rate or rates of interest payable and evidenced in such manner, may contain provisions for redemption prior to maturity for refunding at or before maturity with refunding bonds of the corporation or of another governmental entity or public corporation of the state and for defeasance of any unmatured refunded bonds through the use of any such refunding bonds, and may contain such other provisions not inconsistent herewith, all as may be provided by the resolution of the board of directors under which such bonds are authorized to be issued; provided, that no bond of the corporation shall have a specified maturity date later than 10 years after its date. Bonds of the corporation may be sold from time to time in one or several series and pursuant to a single bond resolution or separate bond resolutions, all as the board of directors may deem advantageous; provided, that the aggregate principal amount of bonds of the corporation at any one time outstanding shall not exceed $50,000,000, excluding refunding bonds, which shall not be considered in determining such limit; provided, further, that no bonds (other than refunding bonds) may be sold or issued by the corporation unless the Governor shall have first determined that the issuance of the bonds proposed to be issued will be necessary to assure the availability of funds for payment of the cost of industrial access roads and bridges that shall from time to time be constructed.

Obligations of the corporation may be sold at either public or private sale in such manner and at such price or prices and at such time or times as may be determined by the board of directors to be most advantageous; provided, that none of the obligations may be sold for a price less than 97 percent of par or face value. Subject to the provisions and limitations contained in this chapter, the corporation may from time to time sell and issue refunding bonds for the purpose of refunding any matured or unmatured bonds of the corporation then outstanding. Approval by the Governor of Alabama of the terms and conditions under which any bonds of the corporation may be issued shall be requisite to their validity. Such approval shall be entered on the minutes of the meetings of the board of directors at which the bonds are authorized, and shall be signed by the Governor. Such approval by the Governor may be (but is not required to be) shown on any such bonds by a facsimile of his signature printed or otherwise reproduced thereon when authorization thereof is contained in the said approval signed by him. The corporation may pay out of the proceeds from the sale of its bonds all expenses, including fees of attorneys and other charges, which said board of directors may deem necessary and advantageous in connection with the issuance of such bonds. Bonds issued by the corporation shall not be general obligations of the corporation but shall be payable solely out of the funds appropriated and pledged therefor in Section 23-6-10 hereof. As security for the payment of the principal of and interest on any bonds issued by it, the corporation is hereby authorized and empowered to pledge for payment of such principal and interest the funds that are appropriated and pledged in Section 23-6-10 hereof for payment of said principal and interest. All such pledges made by the corporation shall take precedence in the order of the adoption of the resolution containing such pledges. All contracts made and all bonds issued by the corporation pursuant to the provisions of this chapter shall be solely and exclusively obligations of the corporation and shall not be an obligation or debt of any kind of the State of Alabama. Bonds issued by the corporation shall be construed to have all the qualities and incidents of negotiable instruments subject to the registration provisions pertaining to transfers. All bonds issued by the corporation and the income therefrom shall be exempt from all taxation in the State of Alabama. Any bonds issued by the corporation may be used by the holder thereof as security for any funds belonging to the state or to any instrumentality or agency of the state in any instance where security for such deposits may be required by law. Unless otherwise directed by the court having jurisdiction thereof, or by the document that is the source of authority, a trustee, executor, administrator, guardian, or one acting in any other fiduciary capacity may, in addition to any other investment powers conferred by law and with the exercise of reasonable business prudence, invest trust and other fiduciary funds in bonds of the corporation. Neither a public hearing nor consent by the State Department of Finance or any other department or agency shall be a prerequisite to the issuance of bonds by the corporation. (Acts 1985, No. 85-549, p. 833, § 8; Acts 1991, No. 91-251.)

The **1991 amendment,** effective July 16, 1991, substituted "$50,000,000" for "$25,000,000.00" in the last sentence of the first paragraph.

§ 23-6-9. Disposition of bond proceeds; industrial access road and bridge construction account; refunding bonds; contracts for construction, etc., of roads and bridges; performance of work done without contract; property acquired by corporation; roads and bridges constructed to be part of public highway system; appropriation for road and bridge construction.

The proceeds of all bonds, other than refunding bonds, issued by the corporation, remaining after paying the expenses of their issuance, shall be turned into the treasury, shall be carried in a special industrial access road and bridge construction account, and shall be available to be drawn upon by the corporation, upon the approval of the State Highway Department and the Governor, but solely for the purpose of constructing, reconstructing and relocating industrial access roads and bridges and work incidental or related thereto, including the acquisition of property necessary therefor. Moneys on deposit in the industrial access road and bridge construction account shall be invested by the State Treasurer at the direction of the corporation in permitted investments which mature at such time or times as the corporation shall direct. Net interest income earned from the investment of bond proceeds deposited into the industrial access road and bridge construction account shall be deposited as received by the State Treasurer into the state public road and bridge fund to be used for state highway purposes.

The proceeds from the sale of any refunding bonds of the corporation remaining after paying the expenses of their issuance shall be used only for the purpose of refunding outstanding bonds of the corporation and of paying any premium that may be necessary to be paid in order to redeem or retire the bonds to be refunded. Bonds refunded prior to their maturity with the proceeds of refunding bonds shall be defeased if the corporation, in its proceedings regarding issuance of the refunding bonds provides for and establishes a trust or escrow fund comprised of moneys or government securities, or both, sufficient to pay, when due, the entire principal of, premium, if any, and interest on the refunded bonds; provided, that such government securities shall not be subject to redemption prior to their maturities other than at the option of the holder thereof. Upon the establishment of such a trust or escrow fund, the refunded bonds shall no longer be deemed to be outstanding, shall no longer be secured by the funds pledged therefor in Section 23-6-10 of this chapter, shall no longer be obligations of the corporation and shall be secured solely by and payable from moneys and government securities deposited in such trust or escrow fund. All contracts of the corporation for the construction, reconstruction and relocation of industrial access roads and bridges, work incidental or related thereto, and the acquisition of property necessary therefor, shall be in writing, shall be subject to the rules and regulations and shall be let under the supervision of the State Highway Department, and shall be subject to approval by the Governor and by the State Highway Department. All work provided for in any such contract shall be supervised by the State Highway Department. All persons engaged in the supervision or performance of any such work of construction, reconstruction or relocation that may be done by the corporation without the award of a contract therefor shall be employees of the State Highway Department. Any property acquired by the corporation by purchase, condemnation or otherwise shall be acquired in the name of the state or shall be forthwith conveyed to the state. All roads and bridges constructed by the corporation shall constitute part of the public highway and street system of the state.

There is hereby appropriated so much of the bond proceeds as may be necessary for the construction of industrial access roads and bridges in the state. (Acts 1985, No. 85-549, p. 833, § 9.)

§ 23-6-10. Revenues of corporation.

For the purpose of providing funds to enable the corporation to pay the principal of, premium, if any, and interest on any bonds issued by it under the provisions of this chapter, and to accomplish the purposes and objects of its creation, there hereby are irrevocably pledged to such purpose and appropriated so much as may be necessary for such purpose of the following: The State Highway Department's portion of the four cent per gallon excise tax levied on gasoline, motor fuel and lubricating oil under the provisions of Title 40, Chapter 17, Article 6. All moneys hereby appropriated and pledged shall constitute a sinking fund for the purpose of paying the principal of, premium, if any, and the interest on bonds of the corporation. (Acts 1985, No. 85-549, p. 833, § 10.)

§ 23-6-11. State Treasurer to disburse funds.

Out of the revenues appropriated and pledged in Section 23-6-10, the State Treasurer is authorized and directed to pay the principal of, premium, if any, and interest on the bonds issued by the corporation under the provisions of this chapter, as such principal, premium, if any, and interest shall respectively mature, and he is further authorized and directed to set up and maintain appropriate records pertaining thereto. (Acts 1985, No. 85-549, p. 833, § 11.)

§ 23-6-12. Dissolution of corporation.

At any time when no bonds of the corporation are outstanding the corporation may be dissolved upon the filing with the Secretary of State of an application for dissolution, which shall be subscribed by each of the members of the corporation and which shall be sworn to by each such member before an officer authorized to take acknowledgments to deeds. Upon the filing of said application for dissolution, the corporation shall cease and any property owned by it at the time of its dissolution shall pass to the State of Alabama. The Secretary of State shall file and record the application for dissolution, in an appropriate book of record in his office, and shall make and issue, under the great seal of the state, a certificate that the corporation is dissolved, and shall record the said certificate with the application for dissolution. (Acts 1985, No. 85-549, p. 833, § 12.)

TITLE 24.

HOUSING.

TABLE OF CONTENTS

Cross references. — As to minimum housing standards and regulation of unsafe buildings in municipalities, see § 11-53-1 et seq.

CHAPTER 1.

HOUSING AUTHORITIES.

U.S. Code. — For federal low rent housing act, see 42 U.S.C. § 1401 et seq.

Housing authorities law is constitutional. — The housing authorities law is not invalid as an unauthorized delegation of legislative powers, and it does not violate the constitutional provision that each law shall contain but one subject which shall be clearly expressed in its title. Brammer v. Housing Auth., 239 Ala. 280, 195 So. 256 (1940).

It was enacted to secure federal aid in providing better homes. — The statutes designated as the housing authorities law were enacted for the purpose of enabling the state and its agencies and subdivisions to take advantage of the aid offered by the federal government in providing a better quality of homes for a class of citizens of moderate means and thereby improving living quarters and eradicating what is termed "slum districts" or quarters. Brammer v. Housing Auth., 239 Ala. 280, 195 So. 256 (1940).

Chapters 1, 2, and 3 of Title 24 were enacted for the purpose of enabling Alabama and its subdivisions to take advantage of federal funds available pursuant to federal housing, redevelopment, and urban renewal act. Chapter 1 was enacted to secure federal aid offered pursuant to the United States Housing Act of 1937, 42 U.S.C. § 1401 et seq. Chapter 2 of Title 24, entitled "Redevelopment Projects," was passed in response to the Housing Act of 1949, 42 U.S.C. § 1441 et seq. Chapter 3 of Title 24 was passed in response to the 1954 amendments to the 1949 act providing for urban renewal projects, 42 U.S.C. § 1450 et seq. City of Birmingham v. Tutwiler Drug Co., 475 So. 2d 458 (Ala. 1985).

And the purpose to be accomplished is for a "public use". — Even if "public use," as used in organic law relating to eminent domain, should be given a narrow meaning, the result and purpose to be accomplished under the housing authority law is for a "public use." Brammer v. Housing Auth., 239 Ala. 280, 195 So. 256 (1940); Blankenship v. City of Decatur, 269 Ala. 670, 115 So. 2d 459 (1959).

Public housing projects are a public use. Hamrick Constr. Corp. v. Rainsville Hous. Auth., 447 So. 2d 1295 (Ala. 1984).

The whole tenor of the housing authorities law indicates a legislative finding that the use of property for the purposes set out in such law is public use. Hamrick Constr. Corp. v. Rainsville Hous. Auth., 447 So. 2d 1295 (Ala. 1984).

Public housing projects of the housing authorities are public uses and thus exempt from garnishment. Hamrick Constr. Corp. v. Rainsville Hous. Auth., 447 So. 2d 1295 (Ala. 1984).

ARTICLE 1.

GENERAL PROVISIONS.

Cross references. — As to redevelopment projects by housing authorities or municipalities, see § 24-2-1 et seq. As to urban renewal projects by housing authorities and municipalities, see § 24-3-1 et seq.

§ 24-1-1. Payments to cities, counties, etc., for maintenance of low rent housing projects, etc.

Any housing authority created by or pursuant to this title may agree to make such payments to the city or county, the state or any political subdivision thereof, which payments such bodies are hereby authorized to accept, as such authority finds consistent with the maintenance of the low rent character of housing projects or the achievement of the purposes of this title. (Acts 1949, No. 490, p. 711, § 1.)

§ 24-1-2. Housing research and studies.

In addition to all its other powers, any housing authority created by or pursuant to this title may, within its area of operation, undertake and carry out studies and analyses of the housing needs, and of the meeting of such needs, including data with respect to population and family groups and the distribution thereof according to income groups, the amount and quality of available housing and its distribution according to rentals and sales prices, employment, wages and other factors affecting the local housing needs and the meeting thereof, and make the results of such studies and analyses available to the public and the building, housing and supply industries. Any such housing authority may also engage in research and disseminate information on the subject of housing. (Acts 1949, No. 490, p. 711, § 2.)

§ 24-1-3. Rural housing projects.

(a) Until a purchaser makes full payment for a dwelling which is constructed by a county or regional housing authority in a rural area, such dwellings shall continue to be the property of such authority, regardless of the title to the land on which it is constructed, and such dwelling shall be exempt from taxation in the same manner as other property of such authority. Any document making land available for use by such authority shall be admitted to record, and accordingly constitute notice, in the same manner as a deed or other instrument relating to real estate.

(b) When a county or regional housing authority provides a dwelling in a rural area under this title, the owner of the land living in the dwelling under a lease or purchase agreement shall be entitled to receive the same homestead exemption as if he had title to the dwelling.

(c) No dwelling shall be provided on a farm by a county or regional housing authority unless it has determined that, by reason of the character of the farm with respect to which the dwelling is to be constructed and the manner of its operation, the farmer is likely successfully to carry out the undertakings required of him under his purchase agreement or lease. (Acts 1949, No. 490, p. 711, § 3.)

§ 24-1-4. Agreements of municipal, county or regional housing authorities to secure federal contributions.

In addition to the powers conferred upon a housing authority created for a city or county or a regional housing authority by other provisions of law, such authority, in any contract for annual contributions with the federal government, may obligate itself, which obligation shall be specifically enforceable and shall not constitute a mortgage, notwithstanding any other laws, to convey to the federal government the project to which such contract relates, upon the occurrence of a substantial default with respect to the covenants or conditions to which such authority is subject. Such contract may further provide that in case of such conveyance, the federal government may complete, operate, manage, lease, convey or otherwise deal with the project in accordance with the terms of such contract. Any such contract shall require that, as soon as practicable after the federal government is satisfied that all defaults by reason of which it shall have acquired the project have been cured and that the project will thereafter be operated in accordance with the terms of the contract, the federal government shall reconvey to such authority the project as then constituted. (Acts 1949, No. 490, p. 711, § 4.)

§ 24-1-5. Powers conferred by Sections 24-1-1 through 24-1-4 supplemental.

The powers conferred by Sections 24-1-1 through 24-1-4 shall be in addition and supplemental to the powers conferred by any other law, and nothing contained therein shall be construed as limiting any other powers of a housing authority. (Acts 1949, No. 490, p. 711, § 5.)

§ 24-1-6. Establishment of rentals and tenant selection in low rent housing projects.

(a) It is declared to be the policy of this state that each housing authority shall manage and operate its low rent housing projects in an efficient manner so as to enable it to fix the rentals for dwelling accommodations at the lowest possible rates consistent with its providing decent, safe and sanitary dwelling accommodations for persons of low income, and that no housing authority shall construct or operate any such project for profit, or as a source of revenue of the city or town. To this end a housing authority shall fix the rentals for such dwellings in its low rent housing projects at no higher rates than it shall find to be necessary in order to produce revenues which, together with all other available moneys, revenues, income and receipts of such authority from whatever sources derived, including federal financial assistance necessary to maintain the low rent character of the projects, will be sufficient:

(1) To pay, as the same become due, the principal and interest on the bonds or other obligations of such authority;

(2) To meet the cost of, and to provide for, maintaining and operating the projects, including the cost of any insurance, and the administrative expenses of such authority;

(3) To meet the cost of discharging all lawful obligations assumed by or imposed upon the authority or its property; and

(4) To create, during not less than the six years immediately succeeding its issuance of any bonds or other obligations, a reserve sufficient to meet the largest principal and interest payments which will be due on such bonds or other obligations in any one year thereafter and to maintain such reserve.

(b) Rentals or payments for such dwellings shall be established and the low rent housing projects administered, insofar as possible, so as to assure that any federal financial assistance required shall be strictly limited to amounts and periods necessary to maintain the low rent character of the projects.

(c) In the operation or management of such low rent housing projects, a housing authority shall at all times observe the following duties with respect to rentals and tenant selection:

(1) It may rent or lease the dwelling accommodations therein only to persons who lack the amount of income which is necessary, as determined by the housing authority undertaking the housing project, to enable them, without financial assistance, to live in decent, safe and sanitary dwellings, without overcrowding;

(2) It may rent or lease the dwelling accommodations only at rentals within the financial reach of such persons;

(3) It may rent or lease to a tenant dwelling accommodations consisting of the number of rooms, but no greater number, which it deems necessary to provide safe and sanitary accommodations to the proposed occupants thereof, without overcrowding; and

(4) It shall not accept any person as a tenant in any such low rent housing project if the person or persons who would occupy the dwelling accommodations have, at the time of admission, an aggregate annual net income, less an exemption of $100.00 for each minor member of the family other than the head of the family and his spouse, in excess of five times the annual rental of the quarters to be furnished such person or persons.

In computing the rental for this purpose of selecting tenants, there shall be included in the rental the average annual cost, as determined by the housing authority, to occupants of heat, water, electricity, gas, a cooking range and other necessary services or facilities, whether or not the charge for such services and facilities is in fact included in the rental; provided, that an authority may agree to conditions as to tenant eligibility or preference required by the federal government pursuant to federal law in any contract for financial assistance with the authority.

(d) Nothing contained in this section shall be construed as limiting the power of an authority to vest in an obligee the right, in the event of a default by the housing authority, to take possession of a housing project or cause the appointment of a receiver thereof, free from all the restrictions imposed by this section with respect to rental rates and tenant selection. (Acts 1939, No. 614, p. 981, § 1; Code 1940, T. 25, § 87; Acts 1955, No. 554, p. 1215.)

Cited in Rainsville Hous. Auth. v. Hamrick Constr. Corp., 456 So. 2d 38 (Ala. 1984).

Collateral references. — 52A C.J.S., Landlord & Tenant, § 792.5.

§ 24-1-7. Creation, etc., of certain housing authorities validated.

(a) The creation, establishment and organization of housing authorities that have issued bonds under the provisions of this title, together with all proceedings, acts and things undertaken or done with reference thereto, prior to July 7, 1943, are hereby validated and declared legal in all respects.

(b) The creation and establishment of housing authorities pursuant to, or purporting to be pursuant to, the provisions of this title and laws amendatory thereto, together with all proceedings, acts and things undertaken, performed or done with reference thereto (including the appointment of commissioners, officers and employees), prior to September 9, 1955, are hereby validated, ratified, confirmed, approved and declared legal in all respects, notwithstanding any want of statutory authority or defect or irregularity in such acts or proceedings. Said housing authorities are hereby declared to have been and to be legally constituted and to be bodies corporate and politic with all the powers, rights and duties set forth in the Housing Authorities Law. (Acts 1943, No. 465, p. 428, § 1; Acts 1955, No. 555, p. 1216, § 1.)

§ 24-1-8. Certain agreements and obligations of housing authorities validated.

(a) All agreements and undertakings of housing authorities created or established under this title prior to July 7, 1943, entered into relating to financing, or aiding in the development or operation of any housing projects, including (without limiting the generality of the foregoing) loan and annual contributions, contracts, agency contracts, leases, agreements with municipalities or other public bodies (including those which are pledged or authorized to be pledged for the protection of the holders of any notes or bonds issued by such housing authorities or which are otherwise made a part of the contract with such holders of notes or bonds) relating to cooperation in aid of housing projects, payments to public bodies in the state, furnishing of municipal services and facilities and the elimination of unsafe and unsanitary dwellings, and contracts for the construction of housing projects, together with all proceedings, acts and things heretofore undertaken or done with reference thereto prior to July 7, 1943, are hereby validated and declared legal in all respects.

(b) All contracts, agreements, obligations and undertakings of housing authorities entered into relating to financing or aiding in the planning, surveying, development, construction, maintenance or operation of any housing or redevelopment project or projects or to obtaining aid therefor from the federal government, including (without limiting the generality of the foregoing) loan and annual contributions, contracts and leases with the federal government, agreements with municipalities or other public bodies (including agreements which are pledged or authorized to be pledged for the protection of the holders of any notes or bonds issued by housing authorities or which are otherwise made a part of the contracts with such holders of notes or bonds) relating to cooperation, contributions, grants or other local participation in aid of housing or redevelopment projects, payments (if any) in lieu of taxes, furnishing of municipal services and facilities, the elimination of unsafe and unsanitary dwellings and contracts for the construction or operation of housing projects, together with all proceedings, acts and things undertaken, performed or done with reference thereto, prior to September 9, 1955, are hereby validated, ratified, confirmed, approved and declared legal in all respects, notwithstanding any defect or irregularity therein or any want of statutory authority. (Acts 1943, No. 465, p. 428, § 2; Acts 1955, No. 555, p. 1216, § 2.)

§ 24-1-9. Issuance, etc., of notes and bonds by housing authorities validated.

(a) All proceedings, acts and things undertaken or done prior to July 7, 1943, in or for the authorization, issuance, execution and delivery of notes and bonds by housing authorities for the purpose of financing or aiding in the development or construction of a housing project or projects, and all notes and bonds issued by housing authorities prior to July 7, 1943, are hereby validated and declared legal in all respects.

(b) All proceedings, acts and things undertaken, performed or done prior to September 9, 1955, in or for the authorization, issuance, sale, execution and delivery of notes and bonds by housing authorities for the purpose of financing or aiding in the undertaking of a housing or redevelopment project or projects, and all notes and bonds issued by housing authorities prior to September 9, 1955, are hereby validated, ratified, confirmed, approved and declared legal in all respects, notwithstanding any defect or irregularity therein or any want of statutory authority. (Acts 1943, No. 465, p. 428, § 3; Acts 1955, No. 555, p. 1216, § 3.)

§ 24-1-10. Establishing eligibility for public housing, rent subsidies, etc., by fraudulent means; misdemeanor; penalty; notice requirement.

(a) "Public housing" as used in this section shall mean housing which is constructed, operated or maintained by the state, a county, a municipal corporation, a housing authority or by any other political subdivision or public corporation of the state or its subdivisions.

(b) Any person who obtains or attempts to obtain, or who establishes or attempts to establish, eligibility for and any person who knowingly or intentionally aids or abets such person in obtaining or attempting to obtain, or in establishing or attempting to establish eligibility for, any public housing, or a reduction in public housing rental charges, or any rent subsidy, to which such person would not otherwise be entitled, by means of a false statement, failure to disclose information, impersonation or other fraudulent scheme or device shall be guilty of a misdemeanor and, upon conviction, shall be punished by a fine of not less than $300.00 nor more than $500.00 or be punished at hard labor for the county not to exceed 60 days, or may be both fined and imprisoned, at the discretion of the court.

(c) Notice of this section shall be printed on the application form for public housing and shall be displayed in the office where such application is made. (Acts 1980, No. 80-627, p. 1084.)

ARTICLE 2.

MUNICIPAL HOUSING AUTHORITIES.

Mobile housing board created pursuant to the authority contained in this chapter is a public body and body corporate and politic. State ex rel. Carter v. Harris, 273 Ala. 374, 141 So. 2d 175 (1961).

Acts 1959, No. 631, p. 1535, was obviously intended to supplant this chapter by authorizing the creation of another agency should it be deemed advisable by the governing body of the city of Mobile, to carry out substantially the duties and responsibilities formerly exercised by the Mobile housing board, a public corporation created and established pursuant to the provisions of this chapter. State ex rel.

Carter v. Harris, 273 Ala. 374, 141 So. 2d 175 (1961).

Cited in City of Birmingham v. Moore, 248 Ala. 422, 27 So. 2d 869 (1946); Jones v. Crawford, 258 Ala. 278, 62 So. 2d 221 (1952); Housing Auth. v. Decatur Land Co., 258 Ala. 607, 64 So. 2d 594 (1953); Watts v. Housing Auth., 150 F. Supp. 552 (N.D. Ala. 1956); Mobile Hous. Bd. v. Cross, 285 Ala. 94, 229 So. 2d 485 (1969); United States v. Housing Auth., 504 F. Supp. 716 (S.D. Ala. 1980).

Collateral references. — 62 C.J.S., Municipal Corporations, §§ 672, 699, 988, 1061.

40 Am. Jur. 2d, Housing Laws & Urban Redevelopment, §§ 1-8.

§ 24-1-20. Short title.

This article may be referred to as the Housing Authorities Law. (Acts 1935, No. 56, p. 126.)

§ 24-1-21. Legislative findings and declaration of necessity.

It is hereby declared that unsanitary or unsafe dwelling and public school accommodations exist in various cities of the state and that such unsafe or unsanitary conditions arise from overcrowding and concentration of population, the obsolete and poor condition of the buildings, improper planning, excessive land coverage, lack of proper light, air and space, unsanitary design and arrangement, lack of proper facilities and the existence of conditions which endanger life or property by fire and other causes; that in all such cities persons of low income are forced to reside in unsanitary or unsafe dwelling accommodations; that in various cities of the state there is a lack of safe or sanitary dwelling and public school accommodations available to all the inhabitants thereof and that consequently persons of low income are forced to occupy overcrowded and congested dwelling accommodations; that these conditions cause an increase in and spread of disease and crime and constitute a menace to the health, safety, morals and welfare of the citizens of the state and impair economic values; that the aforesaid conditions also exist in certain areas surrounding such cities; that these conditions cannot be remedied by the ordinary operations of private enterprises; that the clearance, replanning and reconstruction of the areas in which unsanitary or unsafe housing conditions exist and the provision of safe, sanitary and uncongested dwelling accommodations at such rentals that persons who now live in unsafe or unsanitary or congested dwelling accommodations can afford to live in safe, sanitary and uncongested dwelling accommodations, are public uses and purposes for which public money may be spent and private property acquired; and that it is in the public interest that work on such projects be instituted as soon as possible in order to relieve unemployment which constitutes an emergency. The necessity in the public interest for this article is hereby declared as a matter of legislative determination. (Acts 1935, No. 56, p. 126; Code 1940, T. 25, § 5.)

Public housing projects are a public use. Hamrick Constr. Corp. v. Rainsville Hous. Auth., 447 So. 2d 1295 (Ala. 1984).

The whole tenor of the housing authorities law indicates a legislative finding that the use of property for the purposes set out in such law is public use. Hamrick Constr. Corp. v. Rainsville Hous. Auth., 447 So. 2d 1295 (Ala. 1984).

Public housing projects of the housing authorities are public uses and thus exempt from garnishment. Hamrick Constr. Corp. v. Rainsville Hous. Auth., 447 So. 2d 1295 (Ala. 1984).

§ 24-1-22. Definitions.

The following terms, wherever used or referred to in this article, shall have the following respective meanings, unless a different meaning clearly appears from the context:

(1) AUTHORITY or HOUSING AUTHORITY. A public body organized as a body corporate and politic in accordance with the provisions of this article for the purposes, with the powers and subject to the restrictions set forth.

(2) CITY. Any city or incorporated town in the State of Alabama.

(3) COUNCIL. The legislative body, council, board of commissioners or other body charged with governing the city.

(4) CITY CLERK and MAYOR. The clerk, and the mayor or president of the board of commissioners, respectively, of the city or the officers thereof charged with the duties customarily imposed on the clerk and mayor respectively.

(5) COMMISSIONER. One of the members of an authority appointed in accordance with the provisions of this article.

(6) GOVERNMENT. Such term shall include the state and federal governments and any subdivision, agency or instrumentality, corporate or otherwise, of either of them.

(7) STATE. The State of Alabama.

(8) FEDERAL GOVERNMENT. Such term shall include the United States of America, the federal secretary of housing and urban development or any

agency, instrumentality, corporate or otherwise, of the United States of America.

(9) HOUSING PROJECT. Such term shall include all real and personal property, buildings and improvements, stores, offices, public school buildings, lands for farming and gardening and community facilities acquired or constructed or to be acquired or constructed pursuant to a single plan of undertaking to demolish, clear, remove, alter or repair unsanitary or unsafe housing or to provide dwelling accommodations at rentals within the means of persons of low income. This term may also be applied to the planning of the buildings and improvements, the acquisition of property, the demolition of existing structures, the construction, reconstruction, alteration and repair of the improvements and all other work in connection therewith.

(10) COMMUNITY FACILITIES. Such term shall include real and personal property and buildings and equipment for recreational or social assemblies, for educational, health or welfare purposes and necessary utilities, when designed primarily for the benefit and use of the occupants of the dwelling accommodations.

(11) PERSONS OF LOW INCOME. Persons receiving less than the income determined by the authority as the amount persons must receive to enable them to pay the rent necessary to secure safe, sanitary and uncongested dwelling accommodations, other than dwelling accommodations provided by the authority or any cities, within the boundaries of the authority. Such determinations by the authority from time to time shall be binding and conclusive for all purposes of this article.

(12) BONDS. Any bonds, interim certificates, notes, debentures, warrants or other obligations of the authority issued pursuant to this article.

(13) MORTGAGES. Such term shall include deeds of trust, mortgages, building and loan contracts or other instruments conveying real or personal property as security for bonds and conferring a right to foreclose and cause a sale thereof.

(14) TRUST INDENTURE. Such term shall include instruments pledging the revenues of real or personal properties but not conveying such properties conferring a right to foreclose and cause a sale thereof.

(15) CONTRACT. Any agreement of an authority with or for the benefit of an obligee whether contained in a resolution, trust indenture, mortgage, lease, bond or other instrument.

(16) REAL PROPERTY. Such term shall include lands, lands under water, structures and any and all easements, franchises and incorporeal hereditaments and every estate and right therein, legal and equitable, including terms for years and liens by way of judgment, mortgage or otherwise.

(17) OBLIGEE OF THE AUTHORITY or OBLIGEE. Such term shall include any bondholder, trustee or trustees for any bondholders, any lessor demising property to the authority used in connection with a housing project or any assignee or assignees of such lessor's interest, or any part thereof, and the United States of America, when it is a party to any contract with the authority. (Acts 1935, No. 56, p. 126; Code 1940, T. 25, § 6.)

"Mayor". — The legislature did not intend the word "mayor," as used in this chapter to mean the board of commissioners of a city operating under the optional form of commission government (§§ 11-44-70 through 11-44-105). Wilson v. Lowe, 278 Ala. 578, 179 So. 2d 324 (1965).

The legislature intended for "mayor" in this chapter to mean the "mayor-president" under the optional form of commission government (§§ 11-44-70 through 11-44-105), and not the board of commissioners. Wilson v. Lowe, 278 Ala. 578, 179 So. 2d 324 (1965).

Phrase "officers thereof charged with the duties customarily imposed on the clerk and mayor respectively," refers to the individual officer by whatever name called, who is "charged with the duties customarily imposed on the clerk," and to the individual officer, by whatever name called, who is "charged with the duties customarily imposed on the ... mayor." Wilson v. Lowe, 278 Ala. 578, 179 So. 2d 324 (1965).

Housing authority is a governmental entity. — Municipal housing authority incorporated pursuant to § 24-1-20 is a "governmental entity" as defined by § 11-93-1, and is, therefore, subject to the effect of § 11-93-2 which limits the amount of tort damages and the amount of money under settlements of tort claims that can be recovered against "governmental entities." Guntersville Hous. Auth. v. Stephens, 585 So. 2d 887 (Ala. 1991).

Housing authority is not a municipal corporation nor an arm or a subdivision thereof. Rainsville Hous. Auth. v. Hamrick Constr. Corp., 456 So. 2d 38 (Ala. 1984).

Housing authority is administrative agency exempt from taxation. — The "housing authority," which is a corporation to be created by order of a city government, public in nature and charged with a duty of performing an element of city's police power, is an administrative agency, so that its realty and personalty, being that of a municipality for certain purposes, is exempt from ad valorem taxes, under Constitution 1901, § 91. In re Opinions of Justices, 235 Ala. 485, 179 So. 535 (1938).

§ 24-1-23. Procedure for incorporation of authority; boundaries of authority; denial of petition for incorporation; resubmission of petition after denial.

Any 25 residents of a city or of the area within 10 miles from the territorial boundaries thereof may file a petition with the city clerk setting forth that there is a need for an authority to function in the city and the surrounding area. Upon the filing of such a petition the city clerk shall give notice of the time, place and purpose of a public hearing at which the council will determine the need for an authority in the city and surrounding area. Such notice shall be given at the city's expense by publishing a notice, at least 10 days preceding the day on which the hearing is to be held, in a newspaper having a general circulation in the city and said surrounding area or, if there be no such newspaper, by posting such a notice in at least three public places within the city, at least 10 days preceding the day on which the hearing is to be held. Upon the date fixed for said hearing, held upon notice as provided in this section, an opportunity to be heard shall be granted to all residents and taxpayers of the city and surrounding area and to all other interested persons. After such a hearing, the council shall determine whether unsanitary or unsafe inhabited dwelling accommodations exist in the city and said surrounding area or whether there is a lack of safe or sanitary dwelling accommodations in the city and said surrounding area available for the inhabitants thereof. In determining whether dwelling accommodations are unsafe or unsanitary, the council shall take into consideration the following: the physical condition and age of the buildings; the degree of overcrowding; the percentage of land coverage; the light and air available to the inhabitants of such dwelling accommodations; the size and arrangement of the rooms; the sanitary facilities; and the extent to which conditions exist in such buildings which endanger life or property by fire or other causes. If it shall determine that either or both of the above enumerated conditions exist, the council shall adopt a resolution so finding, which need not go into any detail other than the mere finding. Such resolution may be adopted at the meeting at which it is introduced by a vote of a majority of the members of the council present at such meeting. Such resolution shall take effect immediately and shall not be laid over or published or posted. The council shall promptly notify the mayor who shall thereupon appoint, as provided in this article, five commissioners to act as an authority. Said commission shall be a public body and a body corporate and politic upon the completion of the following proceedings: The commissioners shall present to the secretary of the State of Alabama, an application signed by them, which shall set forth, without any detail other than the mere recital, that a notice has been given and public hearing has been held as aforesaid, that the council made the aforesaid determination after such hearing and that the mayor has appointed them as commissioners; the name and official residence of each of the commissioners, together with a certified copy of the appointment evidencing their right to office, the date and place of their induction into and taking of the oath of office and their desire that the housing authority become a public body and a body corporate and politic under this article; the term of office of each of the commissioners and the place where, if any, the official appointment of each of said members is kept of record; the name which is proposed for the corporation; the location of the principal office of the proposed corporation; and any other matter relating to the incorporation which the commissioners might choose to insert not inconsistent with the Constitution and laws of the State of Alabama. The application shall be subscribed and sworn to by each of said commissioners before an officer authorized by the laws of the State of Alabama to take and certify oaths, who shall certify upon the application that he personally knows the commissioners and knows them to be the officers as asserted in the application, and that each subscribed and swore thereto in the officer's presence. The Secretary of State shall examine the application and if he finds that the name proposed for the corporation is not identical with that of a person or of any other corporation of the state or so nearly similar as to lead to confusion and uncertainty, he shall receive and file it and shall record it in an appropriate book of record in his office. When the application has been made, filed and recorded, as provided in this section, the authority shall constitute a public body and a body corporate and politic under the name proposed in the application. The Secretary of State shall make and issue to the said commissioners a certificate of incorporation pursuant to this article, under the seal of the state, and shall record the same with the application. The boundaries of such authority shall include said city and the area within 10 miles from the territorial boundaries of said city, but in no event shall it include the whole or a part of any other city nor any area included within the boundaries of another authority. In case an area lies within 10 miles of the boundaries of more than one city, such area shall be deemed to be within the boundaries of the authority embracing such area which was first established, all priorities to be determined on the basis of the time of the issuance of the aforesaid certificates by the Secretary of State. If the council, after a hearing as provided in this section, shall determine that neither of the above enumerated conditions exist, it shall adopt a resolution denying the petition. After three months shall have expired from the date of the denial of any such petition, subsequent petitions may be filed, as provided in this section, and new hearings and determinations made thereon. In any civil action or proceeding involving the validity or enforcement of, or relating to any contract of the authority, the authority shall be conclusively deemed to have been established in accordance with the provisions of this article upon proof of the issuance of the aforesaid certificate by the Secretary of State. A copy of such certificate, duly certified by the Secretary of State, shall be admissible in evidence in any such civil action or proceeding, and shall be conclusive proof of the filing and contents thereof. Nothing contained in this section shall be construed as affecting the boundaries heretofore established for any housing authority. (Acts 1935, No. 56, p. 126; Acts 1935, No. 445, p. 947; Code 1940, T. 25, § 7.)

One authority for each municipality. — It is clear from a reading of the statute creating municipal housing authorities that there shall be only one such authority for each municipality. Rupert v. State, 45 Ala. App. 84, 224 So. 2d 921 (1969).

Cited in Wilson v. Lowe, 278 Ala. 578, 179 So. 2d 324 (1965).

Collateral references. — 62 C.J.S., Municipal Corporations, § 672.

§ 24-1-24. Composition of authority; qualifications, appointment, term of office and compensation of housing commissioners; vacancies in office; quorum; officers and employees of authority; delegation of powers and duties by authority.

An authority shall consist of five commissioners appointed by the mayor, who shall designate the first chairman. None of the commissioners may be city officials. The commissioners who are first appointed shall be designated by the mayor to serve for terms of one, two, three, four and five years, respectively, from the date of their appointment. Thereafter, the term of office shall be five years. A commissioner shall hold office until his successor has been appointed and has qualified. Vacancies shall be filled for the unexpired term. Three commissioners shall constitute a quorum. The mayor shall file with the city clerk a certificate of the appointment or reappointment of any commissioner and such certificate shall be conclusive evidence of the due and proper appointment of such commissioner. A commissioner shall receive no compensation for his services but he shall be entitled to the necessary expenses including traveling expenses incurred in the discharge of his duties. However, commissioners serving on the authority board located in any Class 7 municipality, as defined in Section 11-40-12, may receive such compensation as set by the council. This compensation is not mandatory and the amount and whether or not such compensation is to be paid is within the discretion of the council. The authority may, in its discretion, refuse to pay any compensation authorized by the council in such Class 7 municipalities. When the office of the first chairman of the authority becomes vacant, the authority shall select a chairman from among its members. An authority shall select from among its members a vice-chairman, and it may employ a secretary, who shall be executive director, technical experts, attorneys and such other officers, agents and employees, permanent and temporary, as it may require and shall determine their qualifications, duties and compensation. An authority may delegate to one or more of its agents or employees such power or duties as it may deem proper. (Acts 1935, No. 56, p. 126; Code 1940, T. 25, § 8; Acts 1981, No. 81-807, p. 1433.)

Power to appoint a "commissioner" of the Mobile housing board rests with the mayor and not with the board of commissioners of the city of Mobile. Wilson v. Lowe, 278 Ala. 578, 179 So. 2d 324 (1965).

Collateral references. — 62 C.J.S., Municipal Corporations, § 673.

§ 24-1-25. Unconstitutional.

Code commissioner's note. — Code 1940, Title 25, § 11, which was substantially similar to § 24-1-25, was held unconstitutional, since it provided for removal of a housing authority commissioner by the mayor. See Roberts v. Frederick, 295 Ala. 28, 328 So. 2d 277 (1976).

§ 24-1-26. Conflicts of interest of commissioners or employees.

No commissioner or employee of an authority shall acquire any interest, direct or indirect, in any housing project or in any property included or planned to be included in any project, nor shall he have any interest, direct or indirect, in any contract or proposed contract for materials or services to be furnished or used in connection with any housing project. If any commissioner or employee of an authority owns or controls an interest, direct or indirect, in any property included or planned to be included in any housing project, he shall immediately disclose the same in writing to the authority, and such disclosure shall be entered upon the minutes of the authority. Failure to so disclose such interest shall constitute misconduct in office. However, no provision of this section shall be deemed to prohibit any bank, otherwise qualified, an officer, stockholder or employee of which is a commissioner of a local housing authority, from serving such housing authority as a depository bank or fiscal agent. Nothing contained in this section shall prevent commissioners of housing authorities of cities or towns of less than 2,500 population, according to the last or any subsequent decennial census of the United States, from entering into contracts to supply materials or services to be furnished or used in connection with said housing project, provided such contract is entered into as the result of a competitive bid submitted on an invitation advertised for not less than three days. (Acts 1935, No. 56, p. 126; Code 1940, T. 25, § 10; Acts 1951, No. 776, p. 1372.)

§ 24-1-27. Powers and duties of authority generally.

(a) An authority shall constitute a public body and a body corporate and politic exercising public powers, and having all the powers necessary or convenient to carry out and effectuate the purposes and provisions of this article, including the following powers in addition to others granted in this article:

(1) To investigate into living, dwelling and housing conditions and into the means and methods of improving such conditions;

(2) To determine where unsafe or unsanitary dwelling, public school or housing conditions exist;

(3) To study and make recommendations concerning the plan of any city located within its boundaries in relation to the problem of clearing, replanning and reconstruction of areas in which unsafe or unsanitary dwelling, public school or housing conditions exist, and the provision of dwelling accommodations for persons of low income, and to cooperate with any city or regional planning agency;

(4) To prepare, carry out and operate housing projects;

(5) To provide for the construction, reconstruction, improvement, alteration or repair of any housing project or any part thereof;

(6) To take over by purchase, lease or otherwise any housing project undertaken by any government or by any city located within its boundaries;

(7) To manage, as agent of any city located within its boundaries, any housing project constructed or owned by such city;

(8) To act as agent for the federal government in connection with the acquisition, construction, operation or management of a housing project, or any part thereof;

(9) To arrange with any city located within its boundaries or with a government for the furnishing, planning, replanning, opening or closing of streets, roads, roadways, alleys or other places or facilities, or for the acquisition by such city, or a government, of property, options or property rights or for the furnishing of property or services in connection with a project;

(10) To lease or rent any of the dwelling or other accommodations or any of the lands, buildings, structures or facilities embraced in any housing project and to establish and revise the rents or charges therefor;

(11) To enter upon any building or property in order to conduct investigations or to make surveys or soundings;

(12) To purchase, lease, obtain options upon, acquire by eminent domain, gift, grant, bequest, devise or otherwise, any property, real or personal, or any interest therein from any person, firm, corporation, city or government;

(13) To sell, exchange, transfer, assign or pledge any property, real or personal, or any interest therein to any person, firm, corporation, city or government;

(14) To own, hold, clear and improve property;

(15) To pay over to the city in which the authority is organized all or any part of the proceeds received from the sale of any real or personal property; provided, however, that an authority may pay over such proceeds to the city in which it is organized only in such manner and to such extent that such payment will not violate the terms of any then existing contract to which the authority is a party; and, provided further, that an authority shall have no power to so pay over any part of the proceeds derived from the sale of any real or personal property acquired in connection with a redevelopment project, as that term is defined in Section 24-1-4;

(16) To insure or provide for the insurance of the property or operations of the authority against such risks as the authority may deem advisable;

(17) To procure insurance or guarantees from the federal government of the payment of any debts, or parts thereof, secured by mortgages made or held by the authority on any property included in any housing project;

(18) To borrow money upon its bonds, notes, warrants, debentures or other evidences of indebtedness, and to secure the same by pledges of its revenues, and, subject to the limitations hereinafter imposed, by mortgages upon property held or to be held by it, or in any other manner;

(19) In connection with any loan, to agree to limitations upon its right to dispose of any housing project, or part thereof, or to undertake additional housing projects;

(20) In connection with any loan by a government, to agree to limitations upon the exercise of any powers conferred upon the authority by this article;

(21) To invest any funds held in reserves or sinking funds, or any funds not required for immediate disbursement, in property or securities in which savings banks may legally invest funds subject to their control;

(22) To sue and be sued;

(23) To have a seal and to alter the same at pleasure;

(24) To have perpetual succession;

(25) To make and execute contracts and other instruments necessary or convenient to the exercise of the powers of the authority;

(26) To make and from time to time amend and repeal bylaws, rules and regulations, not inconsistent with this article, to carry into effect the powers and purposes of the authority;

(27) To conduct examinations and investigations and to hear testimony and take proof under oath, at public or private hearings, on any matter material for its information;

(28) To issue subpoenas requiring the attendance of witnesses or the production of books and papers and to issue commissions for the examination of witnesses who are out of the state or unable to attend before the authority or excused from attendance;

(29) To make available to such agencies, boards or commissions as are charged with the duty of abating nuisances or demolishing unsafe or unsanitary structures within its territorial limits, its findings and recommendations with regard to any building or property where conditions exist which are dangerous to the public health, morals, safety or welfare; and

(30) To do all things necessary or convenient to carry out the powers given in this article.

(b) Any of the investigations or examinations provided for in this article may be conducted by the authority, or by a committee appointed by it, consisting of one or more commissioners, or by counsel or by an officer or employee especially authorized by the authority to conduct it. Any commissioner, counsel for the authority or any person designated by it to conduct an investigation or examination shall have power to administer oaths, take affidavits and issue subpoenas or commissions.

(c) An authority may exercise any or all of the powers conferred upon it in this article either generally, or with respect to any specific housing project or projects, through or by an agent or agents which it may designate, including any corporation or corporations which are or shall be formed under the laws of this state, and for such purposes an authority may cause one or more corporations to be formed under the laws of this state or may acquire the capital stock of any corporation or corporations. Any corporate agent, all of the stock of which shall be owned by the authority or its nominee or nominees, may, to the extent permitted by law, exercise any of the powers conferred upon the authority in this article.

(d) In addition to all of the other powers conferred upon it in this section, an authority may do all things necessary and convenient to carry out the power expressly given in this article. No provisions with respect to the acquisition, operation or disposition of property by other public bodies shall be applicable to an authority, unless the legislature shall specifically so state. (Acts 1935, No. 56, p. 126; Code 1940, T. 25, § 12; Acts 1953, No. 590, p. 835.)

Housing authority is not a municipal corporation nor an arm or a subdivision thereof. Rainsville Hous. Auth. v. Hamrick Constr. Corp., 456 So. 2d 38 (Ala. 1984).

Housing authority is administrative agency exempt from taxation. — The "housing authority," which is a corporation to be created by order of a city government, public in nature and charged with a duty of performing an element of city's police power, is an administrative agency, so that its realty and personalty, being that of a municipality for certain purposes, is exempt from ad valorem taxes, under Constitution 1901, § 91. In re Opinions of Justices, 235 Ala. 485, 179 So. 535 (1938).

Authorized action will not be controlled by injunction. — The action of a governmental agency, such as the housing board or authority, acting within its authority, will not be controlled or revised by injunction. Brammer v. Housing Auth., 239 Ala. 280, 195 So. 256 (1940).

Nor disturbed by supreme court unless arbitrary, capricious or fraudulent. — In absence of a charge that action of the housing board or authority of Birmingham district in City of Birmingham in selecting locus in quo for erecting and maintaining a low-cost housing unit for negroes was arbitrary, capricious or fraudulent, the action of board or authority would not be disturbed by supreme court. Brammer v. Housing Auth., 239 Ala. 280, 195 So. 256 (1940).

Authority liable for negligence. — The provision of this section authorizing authority to be sued generally indicates legislative intent not to exempt authority from liability for negligence and not to authorize authority to provide by contract for such immunity. Housing Auth. v. Morris, 244 Ala. 557, 14 So. 2d 527 (1943).

Mere fact that housing authority is governmental agency does not relieve it from tort liability in view of this section. Housing Auth. v. Morris, 244 Ala. 557, 14 So. 2d 527 (1943).

City housing authority is not immune from suit brought against it by roofing materials supplier for authority's negligence in failing to require roofing contractor to post bond on theory that housing authority is an administrative agency of a city exercising a governmental function; since state law required execution of bond, authority was under statutory duty to require strict compliance with this law and therefore would be liable to suit for failure to exercise this duty. Housing Auth. v. Headley, 360 So. 2d 1025 (Ala. Civ. App. 1978).

And damages. — Action brought by roofing materials supplier against city housing authority to recover for authority's negligence in failing to require roofing contractor to post bond was tort action arising out of breach of statutory duty, and thus supplier was entitled to recover damages in the amount of his loss and was not limited to 50 percent of contract price under statute stating that laborers and materialmen are protected by bond in "amount not less than 50% of contract price." Housing

Auth. v. Headley, 360 So. 2d 1025 (Ala. Civ. App. 1978).

Evidence as to awards made to others not admissible. — In a proceeding by municipal housing authority for condemnation of land for low rent housing project admission of evidence offered by landowner as to specified sums of money awarded by appraisers to other owners of land condemned for the project was reversible error. Housing Auth. v. Harris, 241 Ala. 419, 3 So. 2d 54 (1941).

Cited in Hamrick Contr. Corp. v. Rainsville Hous. Auth., 447 So. 2d 1295 (Ala. 1984).

Collateral references. — 62 C.J.S., Municipal Corporations, §§ 676, 699.

§ 24-1-28. Acquisition of property by eminent domain.

The authority shall have the right to acquire by eminent domain any property, real or personal, which it may deem necessary to carry out the purposes of this article, after the adoption by it of a resolution declaring that the acquisition of the property described therein is in the public interest and necessary for public use. The authority may exercise the power of eminent domain pursuant to the provisions of Title 18. Property already devoted to a public use may be acquired; provided, that no property belonging to any city within the boundaries of the authority, or to any government, may be acquired without its consent, and that no property belonging to a public utility corporation may be acquired without the approval of the public service commission or other body having regulatory power over such corporation. (Acts 1935, No. 56, p. 126; Code 1940, T. 25, § 15.)

Purpose to be accomplished is for a "public use". — Even if "public use," as used in organic law relating to eminent domain, should be given a narrow meaning, the result and purpose to be accomplished under the housing authority law is for a "public use." Brammer v. Housing Auth., 239 Ala. 280, 195 So. 256 (1940).

Legislature may impose conditions on exercise of power of condemnation. — Having conferred the power upon the housing

board to take private property by condemnation, the legislature can validly impose any reasonable condition upon its exercise as the legislature sees fit. Mobile Housing Bd. v. Cross, 285 Ala. 94, 229 So. 2d 485 (1969).

Cited in Housing Auth. v. Decatur Land Co., 258 Ala. 607, 64 So. 2d 594 (1953).

Collateral references. — 29A C.J.S., Eminent Domain, §§ 2, 5, 64(1). 101 C.J.S., Zoning, § 137.

§ 24-1-29. Acquisition, etc., of property for government housing projects.

The authority may acquire by purchase, or by the exercise of its power of eminent domain as provided in Section 24-1-28, any property, real or personal, which it may deem necessary for any housing project being constructed or operated by a government. The authority upon such terms and conditions, and for such consideration as it shall determine, may convey title or deliver possession of such property, so acquired or purchased, to such government for use in connection with such housing project. (Acts 1935, No. 56, p. 126; Code 1940, T. 25, § 16.)

§ 24-1-30. Authority housing projects subject to local zoning, building, etc., laws.

All housing projects of an authority shall be subject to the planning, zoning, sanitary and building laws, ordinances and regulations applicable to the locality in which the housing project is situated. (Acts 1935, No. 56, p. 126; Code 1940, T. 25, § 17.)

Collateral references. — 101 C.J.S., Zoning, §§ 1, 2, 135.

Zoning: occupation of less than all dwelling units as discontinuance or abandonment of multifamily dwelling nonconforming use. 40 ALR4th 1012.

Zoning: what constitutes "incidental" or "accessory" use of property zoned, and primarily used, for business or commercial purposes. 60 ALR4th 907.

§ 24-1-31. Issuance of bonds by authority; types of and security for bonds generally; liability on bonds.

An authority shall have power to issue bonds, from time to time, in its discretion, for any of its corporate purposes. An authority shall also have power to issue or exchange refunding bonds for the purpose of paying, retiring, extending or renewing bonds previously issued by it. An authority may issue such types of bonds as it may determine, including, without limiting the generality of the foregoing, bonds on which the principal and interest are payable from income and revenues of the authority and from grants or contributions from the federal government or some other source. Such income and revenues securing the bonds may be:

(1) Exclusively the income and revenues of the housing project financed in whole or in part with the proceeds of such bonds;

(2) Exclusively the income and revenues of certain designated housing projects, whether or not they are financed in whole or in part with the proceeds of such bonds; or

(3) The income and revenues of the authority generally.

Any such bonds may be additionally secured by a pledge of any income or revenues of the authority, or a mortgage of any housing project, projects or other property of the authority. Neither the commissioners of an authority nor any person executing the bonds shall be liable personally on the bonds by reason of the issuance thereof. The bonds and other obligations of an authority (and such bonds and obligations shall so state on their face) shall not be a debt of the city, the state or any political subdivision thereof, and neither the city, nor the state or any political subdivision thereof, shall be liable thereon, nor in any event shall such bonds or obligations be payable out of any funds or properties other than those of said authority. The bonds shall not constitute an indebtedness within the meaning of any constitutional, statutory or charter debt limitation or restriction. (Acts 1935, No. 56, p. 126; Acts 1939, No. 148, p. 219; Code 1940, T. 25, § 18.)

Collateral references. — 64 C.J.S., Municipal Corporations, §§ 1902, 1908(a), 1912.

§ 24-1-32. Form, denominations, terms, etc., of bonds; procedure for sale of bonds by authority; issuance of interim certificates, etc.

The bonds of the authority shall be authorized by its resolution and shall be issued in one or more series and shall bear such date or dates, mature at such time or times, not exceeding 60 years from their respective dates, bear interest at such rate or rates, per annum payable semiannually, be in such denominations, which may be made interchangeable, be in such form, either coupon or registered, carry such registration privileges, be executed in such manner, be payable in such medium of payment, at such place or places, and be subject to such terms of redemption, with or without premium, as such resolution or its trust indenture or mortgage may provide. The bonds may be sold at public sale held after notice published once, at least 10 days prior to such sale, in a newspaper circulating in the city and in a financial newspaper published in the City of New York, New York, or in the City of New Orleans, Louisiana; provided, however, that such bonds may be sold to the federal government at private sale without any public advertisement. The bonds may be sold at such price or prices as the authority shall determine. Pending the authorization, preparation, execution or delivery of definitive bonds the authority may issue interim certificates, or other temporary obligations to the purchaser of such bonds. Such interim certificates, or other temporary obligations, shall be in such form, contain such terms, conditions and provisions, bear such date or dates and evidence such agreements relating to their discharge or payment or the delivery of definitive bonds as the authority may by resolution, trust indenture or mortgage determine. In case any of the officers whose signatures appear on any bonds or coupons shall cease to be such officers before the delivery of such bonds, such signatures shall, nevertheless, be valid and sufficient for all purposes, the same as if they had remained in office until such delivery. The authority shall have power, out of any funds available therefor, to purchase any bonds issued by it at a price not more than the principal amount thereof and the accrued interest. All bonds so purchased shall be cancelled. This section shall not apply to the redemption of bonds. Any provision of any law to the contrary notwithstanding, any bonds, interim certificates or other obligations issued pursuant to this article are hereby declared to be negotiable instruments. (Acts 1935, No. 56, p. 126; Acts 1939, No. 148, p. 219; Code 1940, T. 25, § 19; Acts 1970, Ex. Sess., No. 2, p. 2602.)

§ 24-1-33. Powers of authority to secure payment of bonds, etc.

In connection with the issuance of bonds or the incurring of any obligation under a lease and in order to secure the payment of such bonds or obligations, the authority shall have power:

(1) To pledge by resolution, trust indenture, mortgage, subject to the limitations hereinafter imposed, or other contract all or any part of its rents, fees or revenues.

(2) To covenant against mortgaging all or any part of its property, real or personal, then owned or thereafter acquired, or against permitting or suffering any lien thereon.

(3) To covenant with respect to limitations on its right to sell, lease or otherwise dispose of any housing project, or any part thereof, or with respect to limitations on its right to undertake additional housing projects.

(4) To covenant against pledging all or any part of its rents, fees and revenues to which its right then exists, or the right to which may thereafter come into existence, or against permitting or suffering any lien thereon.

(5) To provide for the release of property, rents, fees and revenues from any pledge or mortgage, and to reserve rights and powers in, or the right to dispose of, property which is subject to a pledge or mortgage.

(6) To covenant as to the bonds to be issued pursuant to any resolution, trust indenture, mortgage or other instrument and as to the issuance of such bonds in escrow, or otherwise, and as to the use and disposition of the proceeds thereof.

(7) To covenant as to what other, or additional, debt may be incurred by it.

(8) To provide for the terms, form, registration, exchange, execution and authentication of bonds.

(9) To provide for the replacement of lost, destroyed or mutilated bonds.

(10) To covenant that the authority warrants the title to the premises.

(11) To covenant as to the rents and fees to be charged, the amount, calculated as may be determined, to be raised each year or other period of time by rents, fees and other revenues and as to the use and disposition to be made thereof.

(12) To covenant as to the use of any or all of its property, real or personal.

(13) To create or to authorize the creation of special funds in which there shall be segregated the proceeds of any loan or grant; all of the rents, fees and revenues of any housing project or projects or parts thereof; any moneys held for the payment of the costs of operation and maintenance of any such housing projects or as a reserve for the meeting of contingencies in the operation and maintenance thereof; any moneys held for the payment of the principal and interest on its bonds or the sums due under its leases or as a reserve for such payments; and any moneys held for any other reserves or contingencies, and to covenant as to the use and disposal of the moneys held in such funds.

(14) To redeem the bonds, to covenant for their redemption and to provide the terms and conditions thereof.

(15) To covenant against extending the time for the payment of its bonds or interest thereon, directly or indirectly, by any means or in any manner.

(16) To prescribe the procedure, if any, by which the terms of any contract with bondholders may be amended or abrogated, the amount of bonds the holders of which must consent thereto and the manner in which such consent may be given.

(17) To covenant as to the maintenance of its property, the replacement thereof, the insurance to be carried thereon and the use and disposition of insurance moneys.

(18) To vest in an obligee of the authority the right, in the event of the failure of the authority to observe or perform any covenant on its part to be kept or performed, to cure any such default and to advance any moneys necessary for such purpose, and the moneys so advanced may be made an additional obligation of the authority with such interest, security and priority as may be provided in any trust indenture, mortgage, lease or contract of the authority with reference thereto.

(19) To covenant and prescribe as to the events of default and terms and conditions upon which any or all of its bonds shall become or may be declared due before maturity and as to the terms and conditions upon which such declaration and its consequences may be waived.

(20) To covenant as to the rights, liabilities, powers and duties arising upon the breach by it of any covenant, condition or obligation.

(21) To covenant to surrender possession of all or any part of any housing project or projects upon the happening of an event of default, as defined in the contract, and to vest in an obligee the right, without judicial proceedings, to take possession and to use, operate, manage and control such housing projects, or any part thereof, and to collect and receive all rents, fees and revenues arising therefrom in the same manner as the authority itself might do and to dispose of the moneys collected in accordance with the agreement of the authority with such obligee.

(22) To vest in a trustee or trustees the right to enforce any covenant made to secure, to pay or, in relation to the bonds, to provide for the powers and duties of such trustee or trustees, to limit liabilities thereof and to provide the terms and conditions upon which the trustee or trustees or the holders of bonds or any proportion of them may enforce any such covenant.

(23) To make covenants, other than in addition to the covenants expressly authorized in this section of like or different character.

(24) To execute all instruments necessary or convenient in the exercise of the powers granted in this section or in the performance of its covenants or duties, which may contain such covenants and provisions, in addition to those above specified, as the government or any purchaser of the bonds of the authority may reasonably require.

(25) To make such covenants and to do any and all such acts and things as may be necessary or convenient or desirable in order to secure its bonds,

or, in the absolute discretion of the authority, tend to make the bonds more marketable, notwithstanding that such covenants, acts or things may not be enumerated in this section, it being the intent in this section to give the authority power to do all things in the issuance of bonds, in the provisions for their security, that are not inconsistent with the Constitution of the State of Alabama and no consent or approval of any judge or court shall be required thereof; provided, however, that the authority shall have no power to mortgage all or any part of its property, real or personal, except as provided in this article. (Acts 1935, No. 56, p. 126; Code 1940, T. 25, § 20.)

§ 24-1-34. Contracts, etc., with federal government for construction, etc., of housing projects.

In addition to the powers conferred upon the authority by other provisions of this article, the authority is empowered to borrow money or accept grants from the federal government for or in aid of the construction of any housing project which such authority is authorized by this article to undertake, to take over any land acquired by the federal government for the construction of a housing project, to take over or lease or manage any housing project constructed or owned by the federal government and, to this end, to enter into such contracts, mortgages, trust indentures, leases or other agreements as the federal government may require, including agreements that the federal government shall have the right to supervise and approve the construction, maintenance and operation of such housing project. It is the purpose and intent of this article to authorize every authority to do any and all things necessary to secure the financial aid and the cooperation of the federal government in the construction, maintenance and operation of any housing project which the authority is empowered by this article to undertake. (Acts 1935, No. 56, p. 126; Code 1940, T. 25, § 27.)

Cited in Hamrick Constr. Corp. v. Rainsville Hous. Auth., 447 So. 2d 1295 (Ala. 1984).

§ 24-1-35. Mortgages of authority property in connection with government financed projects.

In connection with any project financed in whole or in part by a government, the authority shall also have power to mortgage all or any part of its property, real or personal, then owned or thereafter acquired, and thereby:

(1) To vest in a government the right, upon the happening of an event of default, as defined in such mortgage, to foreclose such mortgage through judicial proceedings or through the exercise of a power of sale without judicial proceedings, so long as a government shall be the holder of any of the bonds secured by such mortgage.

(2) To vest in a trustee or trustees the right, upon the happening of an event of default, as defined in such mortgage, to foreclose such mortgage

through judicial proceedings or through the exercise of a power of sale without judicial proceedings, but only with the consent of the government which aided in financing the housing project involved.

(3) To vest in other obligees the right to foreclose such mortgage by judicial proceedings, but only with the consent of the government which aided in financing the project involved.

(4) To vest in an obligee, including a government, the right, in foreclosing any mortgage as provided in this section, to foreclose such mortgage as to all or such part or parts of the property covered thereby as such obligee, in its absolute discretion, shall elect. The institution, prosecution and conclusion of any such foreclosure proceedings or the sale of any such parts of the mortgaged property shall not affect in any manner or to any extent the lien of the mortgage on the parts of the mortgaged property not included in such proceedings or not sold as provided in this section. (Acts 1935, No. 56, p. 126; Code 1940, T. 25, § 21.)

As to constitutionality of provisions granting exemptions to housing authorities, see Hamrick Constr. Corp. v. Rainsville Hous. Auth., 447 So. 2d 1295 (Ala. 1984).

Rational basis for protecting mortgagees and obligees. — The protection of the mortgagees and obligees listed in this section is rationally related to the purpose of the housing authorities law both because it helps secure financing for housing projects and because it protects the public interest by insuring that public funds used for such projects may constitute a lien against the property. Hamrick Constr. Corp. v. Rainsville Hous. Auth., 447 So. 2d 1295 (Ala. 1984).

This section must be read in conjunction with other sections of the housing authorities law pertaining to financing. Hamrick Constr. Corp. v. Rainsville Hous. Auth., 447 So. 2d 1295 (Ala. 1984).

Section 24-1-41 limits the right granted in this section and is in accordance with the apparent intent of § 24-1-40 to protect the operation of housing projects from termination because of financial liabilities incurred by housing authorities. Hamrick Constr. Corp. v. Rainsville Hous. Auth., 447 So. 2d 1295 (Ala. 1984).

Public housing projects are public uses and thus exempt from garnishment. Hamrick Constr. Corp. v. Rainsville Hous. Auth., 447 So. 2d 1295 (Ala. 1984).

Collateral references. — 63 C.J.S., Municipal Corporations, § 963.

§ 24-1-36. Investment by state, fiduciaries, banks, etc., in bonds, etc., issued by authorities.

Notwithstanding any restrictions on investments contained in any laws of this state, the state and all public officers, municipal corporations, political subdivisions other than county and public bodies, all banks, bankers, trust companies, savings banks and institutions, building and loan associations, savings and loan associations, investment companies and other persons carrying on a banking business, all insurance companies, insurance associations and other persons carrying on an insurance business and all executors, administrators, guardians, trustees and other fiduciaries may legally invest any sinking funds, moneys or other funds belonging to them or within their control in any bonds or other obligations issued by a housing authority pursuant to this article or issued by any public housing authority or agency in the United States, when such bonds or other obligations are secured by a pledge of annual contributions to be paid by the United States government, or any agency thereof, and the amount of such actual contribution contracted to be paid shall be sufficient to assure the payment by such public housing authority or agency, of both principal and interest on such bonds as the same shall mature, and such bonds and other obligations shall be authorized security for all public deposits, it being the purpose of this section to authorize any persons, firms, corporations, associations, political subdivisions, bodies and officers, public or private, to use any funds owned or controlled by them, including, but not limited to, sinking, insurance, investment, retirement, compensation, pension and trust funds, held on deposit, for the purchase of any such bonds and funds or other obligations; provided, however, that nothing contained in this section shall be construed as relieving any person, firm, or corporation from any duty of exercising reasonable care in selecting securities. (Acts 1939, No. 570, p. 900; Code 1940, T. 25, § 30.)

§ 24-1-37. Remedies of obligee of authority generally.

An obligee of the authority shall have the right, in addition to all other rights which may be conferred on such obligee, subject only to any contractual restrictions binding upon such obligee:

(1) By mandamus, or civil action, both of which may be joined in one action, to compel the authority, and the commissioners, officers, agents or employees thereof, to perform each and every term, provision and covenant contained in any contract of the authority, and to require the carrying out of any or all covenants and agreements of the authority and the fulfillment of all duties imposed upon the authority by this article.

(2) By civil action to enjoin any acts or things which may be unlawful or the violation of any of the rights of such obligee of the authority.

(3) By civil action in any court of competent jurisdiction to cause possession of any housing project, or any part thereof, to be surrendered to any obligee having the right to such possession pursuant to any contract of the authority. (Acts 1935, No. 56, p. 126; Code 1940, T. 25, § 22.)

§ 24-1-38. Remedies conferrable upon obligees of authority by trust indenture, mortgage, etc.

Any authority shall have power by its trust indenture, mortgage, lease or other contract to confer upon any obligee holding, or representing, a specified amount in bonds, lease or other obligations, the right upon the happening of an "event of default" as defined in such instrument:

(1) By civil action in any court of competent jurisdiction to obtain the appointment of a receiver of any housing project of the authority, or any part or parts thereof. If such receiver be appointed, he may enter and take possession of such housing project or any part or parts thereof, and operate and maintain same, and collect and receive all fees, rents, revenues or other charges thereafter arising therefrom in the same manner as the authority itself might do and shall keep such moneys in a separate account or

accounts and apply the same in accordance with the obligations of the authority as the court shall direct.

(2) By civil action in any court of competent jurisdiction to require the authority and the commissioners thereof to account as if it and they were the trustees of an express trust. (Acts 1935, No. 56, p. 126; Code 1940, T. 25, § 23.)

§ 24-1-39. Remedies cumulative.

All the rights and remedies conferred by this article shall be cumulative and in addition to all other rights and remedies that may be conferred upon such obligee of the authority by law or by any contract with the authority. (Acts 1935, No. 56, p. 126; Code 1940, T. 25, § 24.)

§ 24-1-40. Exemption of authority property from mortgage foreclosures, levy and execution and judgment liens.

No interest of the authority in any property, real or personal, shall be subject to sale by the foreclosure of a mortgage thereon, either through judicial proceedings or the exercise of a power of sale contained in such mortgage, except in the case of the mortgages provided for in Section 24-1-35. All property of the authority shall be exempt from levy and sale by virtue of an execution, or other process, to the same extent as now enjoyed by the properties of towns, cities and counties of Alabama. No judgment against the authority shall be a charge or lien upon its property, real or personal. The provisions of this section shall not apply to or limit the right of obligees to foreclose any mortgage of the authority provided for in Section 24-1-35 and, in case of a foreclosure sale thereunder, to obtain a judgment for any deficiency due on the indebtedness secured thereby and issued on the full faith and credit of the authority. Such deficiency judgment shall be a lien and charge upon the property of the authority which may be levied on and sold by virtue of an execution or other judicial process for the purpose of satisfying such deficiency judgment. (Acts 1935, No. 56, p. 126; Code 1940, T. 25, § 25.)

Constitutionality. — This section is constitutional. See Hamrick Constr. Corp. v. Rainsville Hous. Auth., 447 So. 2d 1295 (Ala. 1984).

As to the constitutionality of provisions granting exemptions to housing authorities, see Hamrick Constr. Corp. v. Rainsville Hous. Auth., 447 So. 2d 1295 (Ala. 1984).

Housing authority subject to mandamus. — The fact that the legislature protected housing authority property from judgment liens does not bar the issuance of a writ of mandamus in the extraordinary case where housing authority officers refuse to pay validly imposed judgments. Rainsville Hous. Auth. v. Hamrick Constr. Corp., 456 So. 2d 38 (Ala. 1984).

Cited in Housing Auth. v. Mizell, 368 So. 2d 37 (Ala. Civ. App. 1979).

§ 24-1-41. Title acquired by purchasers at sale of authority property subject to agreements with government.

Notwithstanding anything in this article to the contrary, any purchaser or purchasers at a sale of real or personal property of the authority, whether pursuant to any foreclosure of a mortgage, pursuant to judicial process or otherwise, shall obtain title subject to any contract between the authority and a government relating to the supervision by a government of the operation and maintenance of such property and the construction of improvements thereon. (Acts 1935, No. 56, p. 126; Code 1940, T. 25, § 26.)

This section limits right granted in § 24-1-35 and is in accordance with the apparent intent of § 24-1-40 to protect the operation of housing projects from termination because of financial liabilities incurred by housing authorities. Hamrick Constr. Corp. v. Rainsville Hous. Auth., 447 So. 2d 1295 (Ala. 1984).

§ 24-1-42. Security for funds deposited by authorities in banks and trust companies.

The authority may by resolution provide that all moneys deposited by it shall be secured by obligations of the United States or of the State of Alabama of a market value equal at all times to the amount of such deposits, by any securities in which savings banks may legally invest funds within their control or by an undertaking with such sureties as shall be approved by the authority faithfully to keep and pay over upon the order of the authority any such deposits and agreed interest thereon. All banks and trust companies are authorized to give any such security for such deposits. (Acts 1935, No. 56, p. 126; Code 1940, T. 25, § 28.)

§ 24-1-43. Annual report and recommendations of authority.

The authority shall at least once a year file with the mayor of the city a report of its activities for the preceding year, and shall make any recommendations with reference to any additional legislation or other action that may be necessary in order to carry out the purposes of this article. (Acts 1935, No. 56, p. 126; Code 1940, T. 25, § 29.)

Cited in Wilson v. Lowe, 278 Ala. 578, 179 So. 2d 324 (1965); Roberts v. Fredrick, 295 Ala. 281, 328 So. 2d 277 (1976).

§ 24-1-44. Enforcement of article and contracts of authority.

The authority and its commissioners shall be under a statutory duty to comply or to cause compliance strictly with all provisions of this article and the laws of the State of Alabama and, in addition thereto, with each and every term, provision and covenant in any contract of the authority on its part to be kept or performed. (Acts 1935, No. 56, p. 126; Code 1940, T. 25, § 9.)

Authority liable for not requiring contractor to post bond. — City housing authority is not immune from suit brought against it by roofing materials supplier for authority's negligence in failing to require roofing contractor to post bond on theory that housing authority is an administrative agency of a city exercising a governmental function; since state law required execution of bond, authority was under statutory duty to require strict compliance with this law and therefore would be liable to suit for failure to exercise this duty. Housing Auth. v. Headley, 360 So. 2d 1025 (Ala. Civ. App. 1978).

§ 24-1-45. Conflicting provisions.

Insofar as the provisions of this article are inconsistent with the provisions of any other law, the provisions of this article shall be controlling. (Acts 1935, No. 56, p. 126; Code 1940, T. 25, § 29.)

ARTICLE 3.

COUNTY HOUSING AUTHORITIES.

Collateral references. — 40 Am. Jur. 2d, Housing Laws & Urban Redevelopment, §§ 1-8.

Statutes providing for slum-clearance projects. 105 ALR 911, 130 ALR 1069.

Blighted area: what constitutes "blighted area" within urban renewal and redevelopment statutes. 45 ALR3d 1096.

§ 24-1-60. Legislative findings and declaration of necessity.

It is hereby declared that unsanitary or unsafe dwelling and public school accommodations exist in various counties of the state and that such unsafe or unsanitary conditions arise from overcrowding and concentration of population, the obsolete and poor condition of the buildings, improper planning, excessive land coverage, lack of proper light, air and space, unsanitary design and arrangement, lack of proper facilities and the existence of conditions which endanger life or property by fire and other causes; that in all such counties persons of low income are forced to reside in unsanitary or unsafe dwelling accommodations; that in various counties of the state there is a lack of safe or sanitary dwelling and public school accommodations available to all the inhabitants thereof and that consequently persons of low income are forced to occupy overcrowded and congested dwelling accommodations; that these conditions cause an increase in and spread of disease and crime and constitute a menace to the health, safety, morals and welfare of the citizens of the state and impair economic values; that these conditions cannot be remedied by the ordinary operations of private enterprises; that the clearance, replanning and reconstruction of the areas in counties in which unsanitary or unsafe housing conditions exist and the provision of safe, sanitary and uncongested dwelling accommodations at such rentals that persons who now live in unsafe or unsanitary or congested dwelling accommodations can afford to live in safe, sanitary and uncongested dwelling accommodations, are public uses and purposes for which public money may be spent and private property acquired; that it is in the public interest that work on such projects be instituted as soon as possible in order to relieve unemployment which now constitutes an emergency. The necessity in the public interest for this article is hereby declared as a matter of legislative determination. (Code 1940, T. 25, § 31.)

§ 24-1-61. Definitions.

The following terms, wherever used or referred to in this article shall have the following respective meaning, unless a different meaning clearly appears from the context:

(1) AUTHORITY or HOUSING AUTHORITY. A public body organized as a body corporate and politic in accordance with the provisions of this article for the purposes, with the powers and subject to the restrictions set forth in this article.

(2) COUNTY. All of the county except that portion which lies within the territorial boundaries of any city or incorporated town.

(3) COUNTY COMMISSION. The governing body of any county.

(4) HOUSING COMMISSIONER. One of the members of an authority appointed in accordance with the provisions of this article.

(5) GOVERNMENT. Such term shall include the state and federal governments and any subdivision, agency or instrumentality, corporate or otherwise, of either of them.

(6) STATE. The State of Alabama.

(7) FEDERAL GOVERNMENT. Such term shall include the United States of America, the federal Secretary of Housing and Urban Development or any agency, instrumentality, corporate or otherwise, of the United States of America.

(8) HOUSING PROJECT. Such term shall include all real and personal property, buildings and improvements, stores, offices, public school buildings, lands for farming and gardening and community facilities acquired or constructed, or to be acquired or constructed, pursuant to a single plan of undertaking to demolish, clear, remove, alter or repair unsanitary or unsafe housing or to provide urban or rural dwelling accommodations at rentals within the means of persons of low income. The term "housing project" may also be applied to the planning of the buildings and improvements, the acquisition of property, the demolition of existing structures, the construction, reconstruction, alteration and repair of the improvements and all other work in connection therewith.

(9) COMMUNITY FACILITIES. Such term shall include real and personal property and buildings and equipment for recreational or social assemblies, for educational, health or welfare purposes and necessary utilities, when designed primarily for the benefit and use of the occupants of the dwelling accommodations.

(10) PERSONS OF LOW INCOME. Persons receiving less than the incomes determined by the authority as the amount persons must receive to enable them to pay the rent necessary to secure safe, sanitary and uncongested dwelling accommodations, other than dwelling accommodations provided by

a public housing agency or authority of the county, within the boundaries of the authority. Such determinations by the authority from time to time shall be binding and conclusive for all purposes of this article.

(11) BONDS. Any bonds, interim certificates, notes, debentures, warrants or other obligations of the authority issued pursuant to this article.

(12) MORTGAGE. Such term shall include deeds of trust, mortgages, building and loan contracts or other instruments conveying real or personal property as security for bonds and conferring a right to foreclose and cause a sale thereof.

(13) TRUST INDENTURE. Such term shall include instruments pledging the revenues of real or personal properties, but not conveying such properties or conferring a right to foreclose and cause a sale thereof.

(14) CONTRACT. Any agreement of an authority with or for the benefit of an obligee, whether contained in a resolution, trust indenture, mortgage, lease, bond or other instrument.

(15) REAL PROPERTY. Such term shall include lands, lands under water, structures and any and all easements, franchises and incorporeal hereditaments and every estate and right therein, legal and equitable, including terms for years and liens by way of judgment, mortgage or otherwise, but only so far as such may, from time to time, be treated as real property by the laws of Alabama applicable to other persons or corporations.

(16) OBLIGEE OF THE AUTHORITY or OBLIGEE. Such term shall include any bondholder, trustee or trustees for any bondholders, any lessor demising property to the authority used in connection with a housing project or any assignee or assignees of such lessor's interest, or any part thereof, and the United States of America, when it is a party to any contract with the authority. (Code 1940, T. 25, § 32.)

§ 24-1-62. Procedure for incorporation of authority; boundaries of authority; denial of petition for incorporation; resubmission of petition after denial.

Any 25 residents of a county may file a petition with the county commission setting forth that there is a need for an authority to function in the county. Upon the filing of such a petition, the county commission shall give notice of the time, place and purpose of a public hearing at which the county commission will determine the need for an authority in the county. Such notice by the county commission shall be given at the county's expense by publishing a notice, at least 10 days preceding the day on which the hearing is to be held, in a newspaper having a general circulation in the county or, if there be no such newspaper, by posting such a notice in at least three public places within the county at least 10 days preceding the day on which the hearing is to be held. Upon the date fixed for said hearing, held upon notice as provided in this section, an opportunity to be heard shall be granted to all residents and taxpayers of the county, and to all other interested persons. After such a hearing, the county commission shall determine whether unsanitary or unsafe inhabited dwelling accommodations exist in the county or whether there is a lack of safe or sanitary dwelling accommodations in such county available for the inhabitants thereof. In determining whether dwelling accommodations are unsafe or unsanitary, the county commission shall take into consideration the following: the physical condition and age of the buildings; the degree of overcrowding; the percentage of land coverage; the light and air available to the inhabitants of such dwelling accommodations; the size and arrangement of the rooms; the sanitary facilities; and the extent to which conditions exist in such buildings which endanger life or property by fire or other causes. If it shall determine that either or both of the above enumerated conditions exist, the county commission shall adopt a resolution so finding, which need not go into any detail other than the mere finding. Such resolution may be adopted at the meeting at which it is introduced by a vote of a majority of the members of the county commission present at such meeting. Such resolution shall take effect immediately and shall not be laid over or published or posted. After the county commission has adopted such resolution, it shall thereupon appoint, as provided in this article, five housing commissioners to act as an authority. Said county housing commission shall be a public body and a body corporate and politic upon the completion of the following proceedings: The housing commissioners shall present to the secretary of the State of Alabama, an application signed by them, which shall set forth, without any detail other than the mere recital, that a notice has been given and public hearing has been held as aforesaid, that the county commission made the aforesaid determination after such hearing and that the county commission has appointed them as housing commissioners of the authority; the name and official residence of each of the housing commissioners, together with a certified copy of the appointment evidencing their right to office, the date and place of their induction into and taking of the oath of office and their desire that the housing authority become a public body and a body corporate and politic under this article; the term of office of each of the housing commissioners and the place where, if any, the official appointment of each of said members is kept of record; the name which is proposed for the corporation; the location of the principal office of the proposed corporation; and any other matter relating to the incorporation which the housing commissioners might choose to insert not inconsistent with the Constitution and laws of the State of Alabama. The application shall be subscribed and sworn to by each of said housing commissioners before an officer authorized by the laws of the State of Alabama to take and certify oaths, who shall certify upon the application that he personally knows the housing commissioners and knows them to be the officers as asserted in the application, and that each subscribed and swore thereto in the officer's presence. The Secretary of State shall examine the application and if he finds that the name proposed for the corporation is not identical with that of a person or of any other corporation of the state or so nearly similar as to lead to confusion and uncertainty, he shall receive and file it and shall record it in an appropriate book of record in his office. When the application has been made, filed and recorded, as provided in this section, the authority shall constitute a public body and a body corporate and politic under the name proposed in the application. The Secretary of State shall make and issue to the said housing commissioners, a certificate of incorporation pursuant to this article, under the seal of the state, and shall record the same with the application. The boundaries of such authority shall include all of said county, except that portion which lies within the territorial boundaries of any city or incorporated town. If the county commission, after a hearing as provided in this section, shall determine that neither of the above enumerated conditions exist, it shall adopt a resolution denying the petition. After three months shall have expired from the date of the denial of any such petition, subsequent petitions may be filed as provided in this section and new hearings and determinations made thereon. In any civil action or proceeding involving the validity or enforcement of, or relating to any contract of the authority, the authority shall be conclusively deemed to have been established in accordance with the provisions of this article upon proof of the issuance of the aforesaid certificate by the Secretary of State. A copy of such certificate, duly certified by the Secretary of State, shall be admissible in evidence in any such civil action or proceeding, and shall be conclusive proof of the filing and contents thereof. Nothing contained in this article shall be construed as affecting the boundaries previously established for any housing authority of a city or town, nor shall this article affect any provisions of law defining the boundaries of any housing authority of a city or town. (Code 1940, T. 25, § 33.)

§ 24-1-63. Composition of authority; qualifications, appointment, term of office and compensation of housing commissioners; officers and employees of authority; delegation of powers and duties by authority.

An authority shall consist of five housing commissioners appointed by the county commission, and the county commission shall designate the first chairman. None of the housing commissioners may be county officials or county employees. The housing commissioners who are first appointed shall be designated by the county commission to serve for terms of one, two, three, four and five years, respectively, from the date of their appointment. Thereafter, the term of office shall be five years. A housing commissioner shall hold office until his successor has been appointed and has qualified. Vacancies shall be filled for the unexpired term. Three housing commissioners shall constitute a quorum. The county commission shall record a certificate of the appointment or reappointment of any housing commissioner and such certificate shall be conclusive evidence of the due and proper appointment of such housing commissioner. A housing commissioner shall receive no compensation for his services, but he shall be entitled to the necessary expenses including traveling expenses incurred in the discharge of his duties. When the office of the first chairman of the authority becomes vacant, the authority shall select a chairman from among its members. An authority shall select from among its members a vice-chairman, and it may employ a secretary, who shall be executive director, technical experts, attorneys and such other officers, agents and employees, permanent and temporary, as it may require, and shall determine their qualifications, duties and compensation; except, that none of them shall be a county, state or municipal officer or employee, nor a partner of such, and none of them shall be, or have been for three years last past, a housing commissioner, nor the partner of a housing commissioner. An authority may delegate to one or more of its agents or employees such power or duties as it may deem proper. (Code 1940, T. 25, § 34.)

§ 24-1-64. Removal of commissioners.

The county commission may remove a housing commissioner for inefficiency or neglect of duty or misconduct in office, but only after the housing commissioner shall have been given a copy of the charges against him, which may be made by any citizen of the county or by the county commission, at least 10 days previous to the hearing thereon, and shall have had an opportunity to be heard in person or by counsel. Any obligee of the authority may file with the county commission written charges that the authority is violating wilfully any law of the state or any term, provision or covenant in any contract to which the authority is a party. The county commission shall give each of the housing commissioners a copy of such charges, at least 10 days previous to the hearing thereon, and an opportunity to be heard in person or by counsel and shall, within 30 days after receipt of such charges, remove any housing commissioners of the authority who shall have been found to have acquiesced in any such wilful violation. A housing commissioner shall be deemed to have acquiesced in a wilful violation by the authority of a law of this state or of any term, provision or covenant contained in a contract to which the authority is a party, if he shall not have filed a written statement with the authority of his objections to such violation prior to the aforesaid filing or making of such charges. In the event of the removal of any housing commissioners, the county commission shall record the proceedings, together with the charges made against the housing commissioners and the findings thereon. (Code 1940, T. 25, § 37.)

§ 24-1-65. Conflicts of interest of commissioners or employees. Repealed by Acts 1977, No. 607, p. 812, § 9901, as amended, effective January 1, 1980.

§ 24-1-66. Powers and duties of authority generally.

(a) An authority shall constitute a public body and a body corporate and politic exercising public powers, and having all the powers necessary or convenient to carry out and effectuate the purposes and provisions of this article, including the following powers in addition to others granted in this article:

(1) To investigate into living, dwelling and housing conditions and into the means and methods of improving such conditions;

(2) To determine where unsafe or unsanitary dwelling, public school or housing conditions exist;

(3) To study and make recommendations concerning the plan of the county in relation to the problem of clearing, replanning and reconstruction of areas in which unsafe or unsanitary dwelling, public school or housing conditions exist, and the provision of dwelling accommodations for persons of low income, and to cooperate with the county or any regional planning agency;

(4) To prepare, carry out and operate housing projects;

(5) To provide for the construction, reconstruction, improvement, alteration or repair of any housing project or any part thereof;

(6) To take over by purchase, lease or otherwise any housing project undertaken by any government or by the county;

(7) To manage as agent of the county any housing project constructed or owned by the county;

(8) To act as agent for the federal government in connection with the acquisition, construction, operation or management of a housing project or any part thereof;

(9) To arrange with any city or town or the county or with a government for the furnishing, planning, replanning, opening or closing of streets, roads, roadways, alleys or other places or facilities, or for the acquisition by the county or a government, of property, options or property rights or for the furnishing of property or services in connection with a project;

(10) To lease or rent any of the dwelling or other accommodations or any of the lands, buildings, structures or facilities embraced in any housing project and to establish and revise the rents or charges therefor;

(11) To enter upon any building or property in order to conduct investigations or to make surveys or soundings;

(12) To purchase, lease, obtain options upon, acquire by eminent domain, gift, grant, bequest, devise or otherwise, any property, real or personal, or any interest therein from any person, firm, corporation, city, county or government;

(13) To sell, exchange, transfer, assign or pledge any property, real or personal, or any interest therein to any person, firm, corporation, city, county or government;

(14) To own, hold, clear and improve property;

(15) To insure or provide for the insurance of the property or operations of the authority against such risks as the authority may deem advisable;

(16) To procure insurance or guarantees from the federal government of the payment of any debts, or parts thereof, secured by mortgages made or held by the authority on any property included in any housing project;

(17) To borrow money upon its bonds, notes, warrants, debentures or other evidences of indebtedness and to secure the same by pledges of its

revenues, and, subject to the limitations hereinafter imposed, by mortgages upon property held or to be held by it, or in any other manner;

(18) In connection with any loan, to agree to limitations upon its right to dispose of any housing project, or part thereof, or to undertake additional housing projects;

(19) In connection with any loan by a government, to agree to limitations upon the exercise of any powers conferred upon the authority by this article;

(20) To invest any funds held in reserves or sinking funds, or any funds not required for immediate disbursement, in property or securities in which savings banks may legally invest funds subject to their control;

(21) To sue and be sued;

(22) To have a seal and to alter the same at pleasure;

(23) To have perpetual succession;

(24) To make and execute contracts and other instruments necessary or convenient to the exercise of the powers of the authority;

(25) To make and from time to time amend and repeal bylaws, rules and regulations, not inconsistent with this article, to carry into effect the powers and purposes of the authority;

(26) To conduct examinations and investigations and to hear testimony and take proof under oath, at public or private hearings, on any matter material for its information;

(27) To issue subpoenas requiring the attendance of witnesses or the production of books and papers and to issue commissions for the examination of witnesses who are out of the state or unable to attend before the authority, or excused from attendance;

(28) To make available to such agencies, boards or commissions as are charged with the duty of abating nuisances or demolishing unsafe or unsanitary structures within its territorial limits, its findings and recommendations with regard to any building or property where conditions exist which are dangerous to the public health, morals, safety or welfare; and

(29) To do all things necessary or convenient to carry out the powers given in this article.

(b) Any of the investigations or examinations provided for in this article may be conducted by the authority, or by a committee appointed by it, consisting of one or more housing commissioners, or by counsel or by an officer or employee specially authorized by the authority to conduct it. Any housing commissioner, counsel for the authority or any person designated by it to conduct an investigation or examination shall have power to administer oaths, take affidavits and issue subpoenas or commissions.

(c) An authority may exercise any or all of the powers conferred upon it in this article, either generally or with respect to any specific housing project or projects, through or by an agent or agents which it may designate, including any corporation or corporations which are or shall be formed under the laws of this state, and for such purposes an authority may cause one or more corporations to be formed under the laws of this state or may acquire the capital stock of any corporation or corporations. Any corporate agent, all of the stock of which shall be owned by the authority or its nominee or nominees, may, to the extent permitted by law, exercise any of the powers conferred upon the authority in this article.

(d) In addition to all of the other powers conferred upon it in this section, an authority may do all things necessary and convenient to carry out the powers expressly given in this article. No provisions with respect to the acquisition, operation or disposition of property by other public bodies shall be applicable to an authority, unless the legislature shall specifically so state. (Code 1940, T. 25, § 38.)

§ 24-1-67. Acquisition of property by eminent domain.

The authority shall have the right to acquire by eminent domain any property, real or personal, which is necessary to carry out the purposes of this article, after the adoption by it of a resolution declaring that the acquisition of the property described therein is in the public interest and necessary for public use. The authority may exercise the power of eminent domain pursuant to the provisions of Title 18, and any amendments thereto, or pursuant to the provisions of any other applicable eminent domain laws of the state. Property already devoted to a public use may be acquired; provided, that no property belonging to the county or to any government may be acquired without its consent and that no property belonging to a public utility corporation may be acquired without the approval of the public service commission or other body having regulatory power over such corporation. (Code 1940, T. 25, § 41.)

§ 24-1-68. Acquisition, etc., of property for government housing projects.

The authority may acquire by purchase or by the exercise of its power of eminent domain as provided in Section 24-1-67, any property, real or personal, which is necessary for any housing project being constructed or operated by a government. The authority upon such terms and conditions, and for such consideration as it shall determine, may convey title or deliver possession of such property, so acquired or purchased, to such government for use in connection with such housing project. (Code 1940, T. 25, § 42.)

§ 24-1-69. Authority housing projects subject to local zoning, building, etc., laws.

All housing projects of an authority shall be subject to the planning, zoning, sanitary and building laws, ordinances and regulations applicable to the locality in which the housing project is situated. (Code 1940, T. 25, § 43.)

Collateral references. — Zoning: occupation of less than all dwelling units as discontinuance or abandonment of multifamily dwelling nonconforming use. 40 ALR4th 1012.

Zoning: what constitutes "incidental" or "accessory" use of property zoned, and primarily used, for business or commercial purposes. 60 ALR4th 907.

Alteration, extension, reconstruction, or repair of nonconforming structure or structure devoted to nonconforming use as violation of zoning ordinance. 63 ALR4th 275.

Zoning: construction and effect of statute   approved if not acted on within specified period
requiring that zoning application be treated as   of time. 66 ALR4th 1012.

§ 24-1-70. Issuance of bonds by authority; types of and security for bonds generally; liability on bonds.

An authority shall have power to issue bonds from time to time, in its discretion, for any of its corporate purposes. An authority shall also have power to issue or exchange refunding bonds for the purpose of paying, retiring, extending or renewing bonds previously issued by it. An authority may issue such types of bonds as it may determine, including, without limiting the generality of the foregoing, bonds on which the principal and interest are payable from income and revenues of the authority and from grants or contributions from the federal government or some other source. Such income and revenues securing the bonds may be:

(1) Exclusively the income and revenues of the housing project financed in whole or in part with the proceeds of such bonds;

(2) Exclusively the income and revenues of certain designated housing projects, whether or not they are financed in whole or in part with the proceeds of such bonds; or

(3) The income and revenues of the authority generally.

Any such bonds may be additionally secured by a pledge of any income or revenues of the authority, or a mortgage of any housing project, projects or other property of the authority. Neither the housing commissioners of an authority nor any person executing the bonds shall be liable personally on the bonds by reason of the issuance thereof. The bonds and other obligations of an authority (and such bonds and obligations shall so state on their face) shall not be a debt of the state or any political subdivision thereof, and neither the county, nor the state or any political subdivision thereof, shall be liable thereon, nor in any event shall such bonds or obligations be payable out of any funds or properties other than those of said authority. The bonds shall not constitute an indebtedness within the meaning of any constitutional, statutory or charter debt limitation or restriction. (Code 1940, T. 25, § 44.)

Collateral references. — 87 C.J.S., Towns,
§ 113.

§ 24-1-71. Form, denominations, terms, etc., of bonds; procedure for sale of bonds by authority; issuance of interim certificates, etc.

The bonds of the authority shall be authorized by its resolution and shall be issued in one or more series and shall bear such date or dates, mature at such time or times, not exceeding 60 years from their respective dates, bear interest at such rate or rates, payable semiannually, be in such denominations, which may be made interchangeable, be in such form, either coupon or registered, carry such registration privileges, be executed in such manner, be payable in such medium of payment, at such place or places, and be subject to such terms of redemption, with or without premium, as such resolution or its trust indenture or mortgage may provide. The bonds may be sold at public sale held after notice published once, at least 10 days prior to such sale, in a newspaper circulating in the county and in a financial newspaper published in the City of New York, New York, or in the City of New Orleans, Louisiana; provided, however, that such bonds may be sold to the federal government at private sale without any public advertisement. The bonds may be sold at such price or prices as the authority shall determine. Pending the authorization, preparation, execution or delivery of definitive bonds, the authority may issue interim certificates, or other temporary obligations to the purchaser of such bonds. Such interim certificates, or other temporary obligations, shall be in such form, contain such terms, conditions and provisions, bear such date or dates and evidence such agreements relating to their discharge or payment or delivery of definitive bonds as the authority may by resolution, trust indenture or mortgage determine. In case any of the officers whose signatures appear on any bonds or coupons shall cease to be such officers before the delivery of such bonds, such signatures shall, nevertheless, be valid and sufficient for all purposes, the same as if they had remained in office until such delivery. The authority shall have power, out of any funds available therefor, to purchase any bonds issued by it at a price not more than the principal amount thereof and the accrued interest. All bonds so purchased shall be cancelled. This section shall not apply to the redemption of bonds. Any provision of any law to the contrary notwithstanding, any bonds, interim certificates or other obligations issued pursuant to this article are hereby declared to be negotiable instruments. (Code 1940, T. 25, § 45; Acts 1971, No. 2231, p. 3589.)

§ 24-1-72. Powers of authority to secure payment of bonds, etc.

In connection with the issuance of bonds or the incurring of any obligation under a lease and in order to secure the payment of such bonds or obligations, the authority shall have power:

(1) To pledge by resolution, trust indenture, mortgage, subject to the limitations hereinafter imposed, or other contract all or any part of its rents, fees or revenues.

(2) To covenant against mortgaging all or any part of its property, real or personal, then owned or thereafter acquired, or against permitting or suffering any lien thereon.

(3) To covenant with respect to limitations on its right to sell, lease or otherwise dispose of any housing project, or any part thereof, or with respect to limitations on its right to undertake additional housing projects.

(4) To covenant against pledging all or any part of its rents, fees and revenues to which its right then exists, or the right to which may thereafter come into existence, or against permitting or suffering any lien thereon.

(5) To provide for the release of property, rents, fees and revenues from any pledge or mortgage, and to reserve right and powers in, or the right to dispose of, property which is subject to a pledge or mortgage.

(6) To covenant as to the bonds to be issued pursuant to any resolution, trust indenture, mortgage or other instrument and as to the issuance of such bonds in escrow, or otherwise, and as to the use and disposition of the proceeds thereof.

(7) To covenant as to what other, or additional, debt may be incurred by it.

(8) To provide for the terms, form, registration, exchange, execution and authentication of bonds.

(9) To provide for the replacement of lost, destroyed or mutilated bonds.

(10) To covenant that the authority warrants the title to the premises.

(11) To covenant as to the rents and fees to be charged, the amount, calculated as may be determined, to be raised each year or other period of time by rents, fees and other revenues and as to the use and disposition to be made thereof.

(12) To covenant as to the use of any or all of its property, real or personal.

(13) To create, or to authorize the creation of, special funds in which there shall be segregated the proceeds of any loan or grant; all of the rents, fees and revenues of any housing project or projects or parts thereof; any moneys held for the payment of the costs of operation and maintenance of any such housing projects or as a reserve for the meeting of contingencies in the operation and maintenance thereof; any moneys held for the payment of the principal and interest on its bonds or the sum due under its leases or as a reserve for such payments; and any moneys held for any other reserves or contingencies, and to covenant as to the use and disposal of the moneys held in such funds.

(14) To redeem the bonds, to covenant for their redemption and to provide the terms and conditions thereof.

(15) To covenant against extending the time for the payment of its bonds, or interest thereon, directly or indirectly, by any means or in any manner.

(16) To prescribe the procedure, if any, by which the terms of any contract with bondholders may be amended or abrogated, the amount of bonds the holders of which must consent thereto and the manner in which such consent may be given.

(17) To covenant as to the maintenance of its property, the replacement thereof, the insurance to be carried thereon and the use and disposition of insurance moneys.

(18) To vest in an obligee of the authority the right, in the event of the failure of the authority to observe or perform any covenant on its part to be kept or performed, to cure any such default and to advance any moneys necessary for such purpose, and the moneys so advanced may be made an additional obligation of the authority with such interest, security and priority as may be provided in any trust indenture, mortgage, lease or contract of the authority with reference thereto.

(19) To covenant and prescribe as to the events of default and terms and conditions upon which any or all of its bonds shall become or may be

declared due before maturity and as to the terms and conditions upon which such declaration and its consequences may be waived.

(20) To covenant as to the rights, liabilities, powers and duties arising upon the breach by it of any covenant, condition or obligation.

(21) To covenant to surrender possession of all or any part of any housing project or projects upon the happening of an event of default, as defined in the contract, and to vest in an obligee the right, without judicial proceedings, to take possession and to use, operate, manage and control such housing projects, or any part thereof, and to collect and receive all rents, fees and revenues arising therefrom in the same manner as the authority itself might do and to dispose of the moneys collected in accordance with the agreement of the authority with such obligee.

(22) To vest in a trustee or trustees the right to enforce any covenant made to secure, to pay or, in relation to the bonds, to provide for the powers and duties of such trustee or trustees, to limit liabilities thereof and to provide the terms and conditions upon which the trustee or trustees or the holders of bonds or any proportion of them may enforce any such covenant.

(23) To make covenants other than and in addition to the covenants expressly authorized in this section, of like or different character.

(24) To execute all instruments necessary or convenient in the exercise of the powers granted in this section or in the performance of its covenants or duties, which may contain such covenants and provisions, in addition to those above specified, as the government or any purchaser of the bonds of the authority may reasonably require.

(25) To make such covenants and to do any and all such acts and things as may be necessary or convenient or desirable in order to secure its bonds, or, in the absolute discretion of the authority, tend to make the bonds more marketable, notwithstanding that such covenants, acts or things may not be enumerated in this section, it being the intent in this section to give the authority power to do all things in the issuance of bonds, in the provisions for their security, that are not inconsistent with the Constitution of the State of Alabama and no consent or approval of any judge or court shall be required thereof; provided, however, that the authority shall have no power to mortgage all or any part of its property, real or personal, except as provided in Section 24-1-74. (Code 1940, T. 25, § 46.)

§ 24-1-73. Contracts, etc., with federal government for construction, etc., of housing projects.

In addition to the powers conferred upon the authority by other provisions of this article, the authority is empowered to borrow money or accept grants from the federal government for or in aid of the construction of any housing project which such authority is authorized by this article to undertake, to take over any land acquired by the federal government for the construction of a housing project, to take over or lease or manage any housing project constructed or owned by the federal government and, to this end, to enter into such contracts, mortgages, trust indentures, leases or other agreements as the federal government may require, including agreements that the federal government shall have the right to supervise and approve the construction, maintenance and operation of such housing project. It is the purpose and intent of this article to authorize every authority to do any and all things necessary to secure the financial aid and the cooperation of the federal government in the construction, maintenance and operation of any housing project which the authority is empowered by this article to undertake. (Code 1940, T. 25, § 53.)

§ 24-1-74. Mortgages of authority property in connection with government financed projects.

In connection with any project financed in whole or in part by a government, the authority shall also have power to mortgage all or any part of its property, real or personal, then owned or thereafter acquired, and thereby:

(1) To vest in a government the right, upon the happening of an event of default, as defined in such mortgage, to foreclose such mortgage through judicial proceedings or through the exercise of a power of sale without judicial proceedings, so long as a government shall be the holder of any of the bonds secured by such mortgage.

(2) To vest in a trustee or trustees the right, upon the happening of an event of default, as defined in such mortgage, to foreclose such mortgage through judicial proceedings or through the exercise of a power of sale without judicial proceedings, but only with the consent of the government which aided in financing the housing project involved.

(3) To vest in other obligees the right to foreclose such mortgage by judicial proceedings, but only with the consent of the government which aided in financing the project involved.

(4) To vest in an obligee, including a government, the right in foreclosing any mortgage as provided in this section to foreclose such mortgage as to all or such part or parts of the property covered thereby as such obligee, in its absolute discretion, shall elect. The institution, prosecution and conclusion of any such foreclosure proceedings or the sale of any such parts of the mortgaged property shall not affect in any manner or to any extent the lien of the mortgage on the parts of the mortgaged property not included in such proceedings or not sold as provided in this section. (Code 1940, T. 25, § 47.)

§ 24-1-75. Remedies of obligee of authority generally.

An obligee of the authority shall have the right, in addition to all other rights which may be conferred on such obligee, subject only to any contractual restrictions binding upon such obligee:

(1) By mandamus or civil action, both of which may be joined in one action, to compel the authority, and the housing commissioners, officers, agents or employees thereof, to perform each and every term, provision and

covenant contained in any contract of the authority, and to require the carrying out of any or all covenants and agreements of the authority and the fulfillment of all duties imposed upon the authority by this article.

(2) By civil action to enjoin any acts or things which may be unlawful, or the violation of any of the rights of such obligee of the authority.

(3) By civil action in any court of competent jurisdiction to cause possession of any housing project, or any part thereof, to be surrendered to any obligee having the right to such possession pursuant to any contract of the authority. (Code 1940, T. 25, § 48.)

§ 24-1-76. Remedies conferrable upon obligees of authority by trust indenture, mortgage, etc.

Any authority shall have power by its trust indenture, mortgage, lease or other contract to confer upon any obligee holding or representing, a specified amount in bonds, lease or other obligations, the right upon the happening of an "event of default," as defined in such instrument:

(1) By civil action in any court of competent jurisdiction to obtain the appointment of a receiver of any housing project of the authority, or any part or parts thereof. If such receiver be appointed, he may enter and take possession of such housing project, or any part or parts thereof, and operate and maintain same, and collect and receive all fees, rents, revenues or other charges thereafter arising therefrom in the same manner as the authority itself might do and shall keep such moneys in a separate account or accounts and apply the same in accordance with the obligations of the authority as the court shall direct.

(2) By civil action in any court of competent jurisdiction to require the authority and the housing commissioners thereof to account as if it and they were the trustees of an express trust. (Code 1940, T. 25, § 49.)

§ 24-1-77. Remedies cumulative.

All the rights and remedies conferred by this article shall be cumulative and in addition to all other rights and remedies that may be conferred upon such obligee of the authority by law or by any contract with the authority. (Code 1940, T. 25, § 50.)

§ 24-1-78. Exemption of authority property from mortgage foreclosures, levy and execution and judgment liens.

No interest of the authority in any property, real or personal, shall be subject to sale by the foreclosure of a mortgage thereon, either through judicial proceedings or the exercise of a power of sale contained in such mortgage, except in the case of the mortgages provided for in Section 24-1-74. All property of the authority shall be exempt from levy and sale by virtue of an execution, or other process, to the same extent as now enjoyed by the properties of towns, cities and counties of Alabama. No judgment against the authority shall be a charge or lien upon its property, real or personal. The provisions of this section shall not apply to or limit the right of obligees to foreclose any mortgage of the authority provided for in Section 24-1-74 and, in case of a foreclosure sale thereunder, to obtain a judgment for any deficiency due on the indebtedness secured thereby and issued on the full faith and credit of the authority. Such deficiency judgment shall be a lien and charge upon the property of the authority which may be levied on and sold by virtue of an execution or other judicial process for the purpose of satisfying such deficiency judgment. (Code 1940, T. 25, § 51.)

Mechanic's lien cannot be fastened to property of housing authority. — Efforts of complainant to fasten a mechanic's lien, pursuant to § 35-11-210, on the real property of the housing authority were futile for the reason that it is public property. Rayborn v. Housing Auth., 276 Ala. 498, 164 So. 2d 494 (1964).

Cited in Hamrick Constr. Corp. v. Rainsville Hous. Auth., 447 So. 2d 1295 (Ala. 1984).

§ 24-1-79. Title acquired by purchasers at sale of authority property subject to agreements with government.

Notwithstanding anything in this article to the contrary, any purchaser or purchasers at a sale of real or personal property of the authority, whether pursuant to any foreclosure of a mortgage, pursuant to judicial process or otherwise, shall obtain title subject to any contract made prior to the accrual of the purchaser's right between the authority and a government relating to the supervision by a government of the operation and maintenance of such property and the construction of improvements thereon. (Code 1940, T. 25, § 52.)

§ 24-1-80. Security for funds deposited by authorities in banks and trust companies.

The authority may by resolution provide that all moneys deposited by it shall be secured by obligations of the United States or of the State of Alabama of a market value equal at all times to the amount of such deposits, by any securities in which savings banks may legally invest funds within their control or by an undertaking with such sureties, as shall be approved by the authority, faithfully to keep and pay over upon the order of the authority any such deposits and agreed interest thereon, and all banks and trust companies are authorized to give any such security for such deposits. (Code 1940, T. 25, § 54.)

§ 24-1-81. Low income housing in rural areas.

Without limiting the generality of other provisions of this article, a county housing authority is empowered to borrow money, accept grants and exercise its other powers under this article to provide housing for persons of low income in rural areas. The undertaking of the construction of any dwelling or dwellings under this section shall constitute a "housing project" within the meaning of this article. To these ends, the county housing authority is authorized to enter into such long-term leases or purchase agreements or otherwise to rent or sell housing to persons of low income in rural areas as such county authority deems necessary in order to assure the achievement of the objectives of this article. Such leases or agreements may include such covenants as the county authority deems appropriate regarding the dwelling or dwellings, and the tracts contiguous thereto, which covenants, notwithstanding any rule of law to the contrary, may be made to run with the land where the county authority deems it necessary. The owner of any land on which an unsanitary and unsafe dwelling or dwellings are located may file an application with the county authority requesting that it provide for the construction of a safe and sanitary dwelling or dwellings for persons of low income to be located on said land, or that portion thereof, to be conveyed by said owner to the county housing authority. (Code 1940, T. 25, § 55.)

§ 24-1-82. Annual report and recommendations of authority.

The county housing authority shall, at least once a year, file with the county commission a report of its activities for the preceding year, and shall make any recommendations with reference to any additional legislation or other action that may be necessary in order to carry out the purposes of this article. (Code 1940, T. 25, § 56.)

§ 24-1-83. Enforcement of article and contracts of authority; competitive bidding required on certain contracts.

The authority and its housing commissioners shall be under a statutory duty to comply or to cause compliance strictly with all provisions of this article and the laws of the State of Alabama and in addition thereto, with each and every term, provision and covenant in any contract of the authority on its part to be kept or performed, and shall make no contract for the construction of any house or building costing more than $100.00 or the purchase of any material therefor until after three weeks' advertising for bids and a public letting to the lowest responsible bidder. (Code 1940, T. 25, § 35.)

§ 24-1-84. Conflicting provisions.

Insofar as the provisions of this article are inconsistent with other provisions of this Code, the provisions of this article shall be controlling. (Code 1940, T. 25, § 57.)

ARTICLE 4.

REGIONAL AND CONSOLIDATED HOUSING AUTHORITIES.

Determining value in condemnation. — For case on determination of value in condemnation by housing authority, see Housing Auth. v. Title Guarantee Loan & Trust Co., 243 Ala. 157, 8 So. 2d 835 (1942).

§ 24-1-100. Short title.

This article may be referred to as the "Supplemental Housing Authorities Law." (Acts 1943, No. 541, p. 512, § 17.)

§ 24-1-101. Definitions.

The following terms, wherever used in this article, shall have the following respective meanings, unless a different meaning clearly appears from the context:

(1) AUTHORITY or HOUSING AUTHORITY. Any corporate body created pursuant to this article or this chapter.

(2) MUNICIPALITY. Any city or incorporated town in the state.

(3) FEDERAL GOVERNMENT. The United States of America or any agency or instrumentality thereof.

(4) GOVERNING BODY. The legislative body, council, board of commissioners, county commission or other body charged with governing the city, town or county, as the case may be. (Acts 1943, No. 541, p. 512, § 16.)

§ 24-1-102. Procedure for incorporation.

If the governing body of each of two or more contiguous counties by resolution declares that there is a need for one housing authority to be created for all of such counties to exercise in such counties powers and other functions prescribed for a regional housing authority, a public body corporate and politic to be known as a regional housing authority shall, after the commissioners thereof file an application with the Secretary of State as provided in this section, exist for all of such counties and exercise its powers and other functions in such counties; and, thereupon, any county housing authority created for any of such counties shall cease to exist, except for the purpose of winding up its affairs and executing a deed to the regional housing authority as provided in this section; provided, that the governing body of a county shall not adopt a resolution as aforesaid if there is a county housing authority created for such county which has any bonds or notes outstanding unless, first, all holders of such bonds and notes consent in writing to the substitution of such regional housing authority in lieu of such county housing authority on all such bonds and notes and, second, the commissioners of such county housing authority adopt a resolution consenting to the transfer of all the rights, contracts, obligations and property, real and personal, of such county housing authority to such regional housing authority as provided in this section; and provided further, that when the above two conditions are complied with and such regional housing authority is created and authorized to exercise its powers and other functions, all rights, contracts, agreements, obligations and property, real and personal, of such county housing authority shall be in the name of and vest in such regional housing authority, and all obligations of such county housing authority shall be the obligations of such regional housing authority, and all rights and remedies of any person against such county housing authority may be asserted, enforced and prosecuted against such regional housing authority to the same extent as they might have been asserted, enforced and prosecuted against such county housing authority. When any real property of a county housing authority vests in a regional housing authority as provided in this section, the county housing authority shall execute a deed of such property to the regional housing authority, which, thereupon, shall file such deed in the office provided for the filing of deeds; provided, that nothing contained in this sentence shall affect the vesting of property in the regional housing authority as provided in this section. The governing body of each of two or more contiguous counties shall by resolution declare that there is a need for one regional housing authority to be created for all of such counties to exercise in such counties the powers and other functions prescribed for a regional housing authority only if such governing body finds that unsanitary or unsafe inhabited dwelling accommodations exist in such county or there is a shortage of safe or sanitary dwelling accommodations in such county available to persons of low income at rentals they can afford and that a regional housing authority would be a more efficient or economical administrative unit than the housing authority of such county to undertake housing projects for persons of low income in such county. (Acts 1943, No. 541, p. 512, § 1.)

§ 24-1-103. Area of operation.

The area of operation or boundaries of a regional housing authority shall include, except as otherwise provided elsewhere in this article, all of the counties for which such regional housing authority is created and established; provided, that a regional housing authority shall not undertake any housing project or projects within the boundaries of any municipality or housing authority unless a resolution shall have been adopted by the governing body of such municipality and also by any housing authority which shall have been previously established and authorized to exercise its powers in such municipality, declaring that there is a need for the regional housing authority to exercise its powers within such municipality. (Acts 1943, No. 541, p. 512, § 2.)

§ 24-1-104. Procedure for increase of area of operation.

The area of operation or boundaries of a regional housing authority shall be increased from time to time to include one or more additional contiguous counties not already within a regional housing authority, if the governing body of each of the counties then included in the area of operation of such regional housing authority, the commissioners of the regional housing authority and the governing body of each such additional county or counties each adopt a resolution declaring that there is a need for the inclusion of such additional county or counties in the area of operation of such regional housing authority. Upon the adoption of such resolutions, any county housing authority created for any such additional county shall cease to exist, except for the purpose of winding up its affairs and executing a deed to the regional housing authority as provided in this section; provided, however, that such resolution shall not be adopted if there is a county housing authority created for any such additional county which has any bonds or notes outstanding unless, first, all holders of such bonds and notes consent in writing to the substitution of such regional housing authority in lieu of such county housing authority as the obligor thereon and, second, the commissioners of such county housing authority adopt a resolution consenting to the transfer of all the rights, contracts, obligations and property, real and personal, of such county housing authority to such regional housing authority as provided in this section; and provided further, that when the above two conditions are complied with and the area of operation of such regional housing authority is increased to include such additional county, as provided in this section, all rights, contracts, agreements, obligations and property, real and personal, of such county housing authority shall be in the name of and vest in such regional housing authority, all obligations of such county housing authority shall be the obligations of such regional housing authority and all rights and remedies of any person against such county housing authority may be asserted, enforced and prosecuted against such regional housing authority to the same extent as they might have been asserted, enforced and prosecuted against such county housing authority. When any real property of a county housing authority vests in a regional housing authority as provided in this section, the county housing authority shall execute a deed of such property to the regional housing authority, which thereupon shall file such deed in the office provided for the filing of deeds, provided that nothing contained in this sentence shall affect the vesting of property in the regional housing authority as provided in this section. The governing body of each of the counties in the regional housing authority, the commissioners of the regional housing authority and the governing body of each such additional county or counties shall by resolution declare that there is a need for the inclusion of such county or counties in the area of operation of the regional housing authority only if the governing body of each such additional county or counties finds that unsanitary or unsafe inhabited dwelling accommodations exist in such county or there is a shortage of safe or sanitary dwelling accommodations in such county available to persons of low income at rentals they can afford and the governing body of each of the counties then included in the area of operation of the regional housing authority, the commissioners of the regional housing authority and the governing body of each such additional county or counties find that the regional housing authority would be a more efficient or economical administrative unit if the area of operation of the regional housing authority was increased to include such additional county or counties. (Acts 1943, No. 541, p. 512, § 3.)

§ 24-1-105. Procedure for decrease of area of operation.

The area of operation or boundaries of a regional housing authority shall be decreased from time to time to exclude one or more counties from such area if the governing body of each of the counties in such area and the commissioners of the regional housing authority each adopt a resolution declaring that there is a need for excluding such county or counties from such area; provided, that no action may be taken pursuant to this section if the regional housing authority has outstanding any bonds or notes, unless all holders of such bonds and notes consent in writing to such action; and provided further, that if such action decreases the area of operation of the regional housing authority to only one county, such authority shall thereupon constitute and become a housing authority for such county, in the same manner and effect and with the same boundaries, functions, rights, powers, duties, privileges, immunities and limitations as though such authority were created and constituted a public and corporate body for such county pursuant to this chapter, and the commissioners of such authority shall be thereupon appointed as provided in this chapter for the appointment of commissioners of a housing authority created for a county. The governing body of each of the counties in the area of operation of the regional housing authority and the commissioners of the regional housing authority shall adopt a resolution declaring that there is a need for excluding a county or counties from such area only if: Each such governing body of the counties to remain in the area of operation of the regional housing authority and the commissioners of the regional housing authority find that, because of facts arising or determined subsequent to the time when such area first included the county or counties to be excluded, the regional housing authority would be a more efficient or economical administrative unit if such county or counties were excluded from such area; and, the governing body of each such county or counties to be excluded and the commissioners of the regional housing authority each also find that, because of the aforesaid changed facts, another housing authority for such county or counties would be a more efficient or economical administrative unit to function in such county or counties. Nothing contained in this section shall be construed as preventing a county or counties excluded from the area of operation of a regional housing authority, as provided in this section, from thereafter being included within the area of operation or boundaries of any housing authority in accordance with this article or this chapter. Any property held by a regional housing authority within a county or counties excluded from the area of operation of such authority, as provided in this section, shall, as soon as practicable after the exclusion of said county or counties, respectively, be disposed of by such authority in the public interest. (Acts 1943, No. 541, p. 512, § 4.)

§ 24-1-106. Public hearings and application to Secretary of State required for incorporation or change in area of operation.

The governing body of a county shall not adopt any resolution authorized by Sections 24-1-102, 24-1-104 or 24-1-105 unless a public hearing has first been held which shall conform, except as otherwise provided in this article, to the requirements of this chapter for hearings to determine the need for a housing authority of a county; provided, that such hearings may be held by the governing body without a petition therefor. No housing authority shall constitute a body corporate and politic under this article until the commissioners of such authority have filed and recorded an application therefor with the Secretary of State, which shall conform, insofar as may be applicable, to the provisions of this chapter for the making, filing and recording of an application with the Secretary of State by the commissioners of a housing authority created for a county; provided, that any such application filed and recorded under this article shall set forth that the public hearing or hearings, as required by this article, have been held. In connection with the issuance of bonds or the incurring of other obligations, a regional housing authority may covenant as to limitations on its right to adopt resolutions relating to the increase or decrease of its area of operation. (Acts 1943, No. 541, p. 512, § 5.)

§ 24-1-107. Housing commissioners — Appointment, term of office and removal; filling of vacancies; certificate; powers and duties generally; quorum; chairman and other officers.

The governing body of each county included in a regional housing authority shall appoint one person as a commissioner of such authority, and each such commissioner to be first appointed by the governing body of a county may be appointed at or after the time of the adoption of the resolution declaring the need for such regional housing authority or declaring the need for the inclusion of such county in the area of operation of such regional housing authority. When the area of operation of a regional housing authority is increased to include an additional county or counties as provided in this article, the governing body of each such county shall thereupon appoint one additional person as a commissioner of the regional housing authority. The governing body of each county shall appoint the successor of the commissioner appointed by it. If any county is excluded from the area of operation of a regional housing authority, the office of the commissioner of such regional housing authority appointed by the governing body of such county shall be thereupon abolished. If the area of operation of a regional housing authority consists at any time of an even number of counties, the commissioners of the regional housing authority appointed by the governing bodies of such counties shall appoint one additional commissioner whose term of office shall be as provided in this section for a commissioner of a regional housing authority, except that such term shall end at any earlier time that the area of operation of the regional housing authority shall be changed to consist of an odd number of counties. The commissioners of such authority appointed by the governing bodies of such counties shall likewise appoint each person to succeed such additional commissioner; provided, that the term of office of such person begins during the terms of office of the commissioners appointing him. A certificate of the appointment of any commissioner of a regional housing authority shall be signed by the appointing officer or officers and filed with the other records of the regional housing authority and shall be conclusive evidence of the due and proper appointment of such commissioner. The commissioners of a regional housing authority shall be appointed for terms of five years, except that all vacancies shall be filled for the unexpired terms. Each commissioner shall hold office until his successor has been appointed and has qualified, except as otherwise provided in this section. For inefficiency or neglect of duty or misconduct in office, a commissioner of a regional housing authority may be removed by the officer or officers, or their successors, appointing such commissioner, but he shall be removed only after he has been given a copy of the charges at least 10 days prior to the hearing thereon and has had an opportunity to be heard in person or by counsel. In the event of the removal of such commissioner, a record of the proceedings, together with the charges and findings thereon, shall be filed with the other records of the regional housing authority. The commissioners shall constitute the regional housing authority, and the powers of such authority shall be vested in such commissioners in office from time to time. The commissioners of a regional housing authority shall elect a chairman from among the commissioners and shall have power to select or employ such other officers and employees as the regional housing authority may require. A majority of the commissioners of a regional housing authority shall constitute a quorum of such authority for the purpose of conducting its business and exercising its powers and for all other purposes. (Acts 1943, No. 541, p. 512, § 6.)

§ 24-1-108. Housing commissioners — Meetings; residence.

Nothing contained in this article or in other acts shall prevent meetings of the commissioners of a housing authority anywhere within the perimeter boundaries of the area of operation or boundaries of the authority or within any additional area where the housing authority is authorized to undertake a housing project, nor to prevent the appointment of any person as a commissioner of the authority who resides within such boundaries of such additional area and who is otherwise eligible for such appointment under this article or this chapter. (Acts 1943, No. 541, p. 512, § 11.)

§ 24-1-109. Rights, powers, etc., of authority and commissioners generally.

Except as otherwise provided in this article, a regional housing authority and the commissioners thereof shall, within the area of operation of such regional housing authority, have the same functions, rights, powers, duties, privileges, immunities and limitations provided for housing authorities created for counties and the commissioners of such housing authorities, and all the provisions of law applicable to housing authorities created for counties and the commissioners of such authorities shall be applicable to regional housing authorities and the commissioners thereof; provided, that a regional housing authority or a county housing authority shall not be subject to the limitations provided in Section 24-1-6 with respect to housing projects for persons of low income in rural areas. (Acts 1943, No. 541, p. 512, § 7.)

§ 24-1-110. Consolidated housing authorities.

If the governing body of each of two or more municipalities by resolution declares that there is a need for one housing authority for all of such municipalities to exercise in such municipalities the powers and other functions prescribed for a housing authority, a public body corporate and politic, to be known as a consolidated housing authority, with such corporate name as it selects, shall thereupon exist for all of such municipalities and exercise its powers and other functions within its area of operation, as defined in this section, including the power to undertake projects therein; and, thereupon, any housing authority created for any of such municipalities shall cease to exist except for the purpose of winding up its affairs and executing a deed of its real property to the consolidated housing authority. The creation of a consolidated housing authority and the finding of need therefor shall be subject to the same provisions and limitations of this article as are applicable to the creation of a regional housing authority and that all of the provisions of this article applicable to regional housing authorities and the commissioners thereof shall be applicable to consolidated housing authorities and the commissioners thereof. The area of operation or boundaries of a consolidated housing authority shall include all of the territory within the boundaries of each municipality joining in the creation of such authority, together with any additional territory included within the boundaries of a housing authority that has been created for such municipality; except, that such area of operation may be changed to include or exclude any municipality or municipalities, with its aforesaid additional territory, in the same manner and under the same provisions as provided in this article for changing the area of operation of a regional housing authority by including or excluding a contiguous county or counties. For all such purposes, the term "county" shall be construed as meaning "municipality," the term "governing body" in Section 24-1-107 shall be construed as meaning "mayor or other executive head of the municipality," and the terms "county housing authority" and "regional housing authority" shall be construed as meaning "housing authority of the city" and "consolidated housing authority," respectively, unless a different meaning clearly appears from the context. Except as otherwise provided in this article, a consolidated housing authority and the commissioners thereof shall, within the area of operation of such consolidated housing authority, have the same functions, rights, powers, duties, privileges, immunities and limitations as those provided for housing authorities created for municipalities, counties or groups of counties and the commissioners of such housing authorities, in the same manner as though all the provisions of law applicable to housing authorities created for municipalities, counties or groups of counties were applicable to consolidated housing authorities. (Acts 1943, No. 541, p. 512, § 8.)

§ 24-1-111. Operation of housing authorities in municipality outside area of operation.

In addition to its other powers, any housing authority may exercise any or all of its powers within the territorial boundaries of any municipality not included in the area of operation of such housing authority, for the purpose of planning, undertaking, financing, constructing and operating a housing project or projects within such municipality; provided, that a resolution shall have been adopted by the governing body of such municipality in which the authority is to exercise its powers and by any housing authority previously established by such municipality and authorized to exercise its powers therein declaring that there is a need for the aforesaid housing authority to exercise its powers within such municipality. (Acts 1943, No. 541, p. 512, § 9.)

§ 24-1-112. Procedure for adoption of resolution authorizing operation of housing authority in municipality.

No governing body of a municipality shall adopt a resolution as provided in Sections 24-1-103 or 24-1-111 declaring that there is a need for a housing authority, other than a housing authority established by such municipality, to exercise its powers within such municipality, unless a public hearing has first been held by such governing body and unless such governing body shall have found, in substantially the following terms: That unsanitary or unsafe inhabited dwelling accommodations exist in such municipality or that there is a shortage of safe or sanitary dwelling accommodations in such municipality available to persons of low income at rentals they can afford and that these conditions can be best remedied through the exercise of the aforesaid housing authority's powers within the territorial boundaries of such municipality; provided, that such findings shall not have the effect of thereafter preventing such municipality from establishing a housing authority or joining in the creation of a consolidated housing authority or the increase of the area of operation of a consolidated housing authority. The clerk, or the officer with similar duties, of the municipality shall give notice of the public hearing, and such hearing shall be held in the manner provided in Section 24-1-23 for a public hearing by a council to determine the need for a housing authority in the municipality. During the time that, pursuant to these findings, a housing authority has outstanding, or is under contract to issue, any evidences of indebtedness for a project within the municipality, no other housing authority may undertake a project within such municipality without the consent of said housing authority which has such outstanding indebtedness or obligation. (Acts 1943, No. 541, p. 512, § 10.)

§ 24-1-113. Agreements to secure federal contributions and loans.

In any contract or amendatory or superseding contract for a loan and annual contributions heretofore or hereafter entered into between a housing authority and the federal government with respect to any housing project undertaken by said housing authority, any such housing authority is authorized to make such covenants, including covenants with holders of obligations of said authority issued for purposes of the project involved, and to confer upon the federal government such rights and remedies as said housing authority deems necessary to assure the fulfillment of the purposes for which the housing project was undertaken. In any such contract, the housing authority may, notwithstanding any other provisions of law, agree to sell and convey the project, including all lands appertaining thereto, to which such contract relates to the federal government upon the occurrence of such conditions or upon such defaults on obligations for which any of the annual contributions provided in said contract are pledged, as may be prescribed in such contract, and at a price, which may include the assumption by the federal government of the payment, when due, of the principal of and interest on outstanding obligations of the housing authority issued for purposes of the housing project involved, determined as prescribed in such contract and upon such other terms and conditions as are therein provided. Any such housing authority is hereby authorized to enter into such supplementary contracts and to execute such conveyances as may be necessary to carry out the provisions of this section. Notwithstanding any other provisions of law, any contracts or supplementary contracts or conveyances made or executed pursuant to the provisions of this section shall not be or constitute a mortgage within the meaning or for the purposes of any of the laws of this state. (Acts 1943, No. 541, p. 512, § 12.)

§ 24-1-114. Bonds and other obligations of authorities legal investments.

The bonds and other obligations issued by any housing authority pursuant to this article or this chapter shall be security for public deposits and legal investments to the same extent and for the same persons, institutions, associations, corporations, public and private bodies, including all public bodies except counties, and officers as are bonds or other obligations issued pursuant to this chapter. (Acts 1943, No. 541, p. 512, § 13.)

§ 24-1-115. Assistance and cooperation by municipalities, counties, etc.

Any municipality, county or other public body shall have the same rights and powers to aid and cooperate in the development or administration of any housing project pursuant to this article or this chapter as such public body has under any provision of law relating to its aiding or cooperating in the development or administration of housing projects by a housing authority organized pursuant to Article 2 of this chapter or other laws of this state. (Acts 1943, No. 541, p. 512, § 14.)

§ 24-1-116. Cooperation of authorities.

Any two or more authorities may join or cooperate with one another in the exercise, either jointly or otherwise, of any or all of their powers for the purpose of financing (including the issuance of bonds, notes or other obligations and giving security therefor), planning, undertaking, owning, constructing, operating or contracting with respect to a housing project or projects located within the boundaries of any one or more of said authorities. For such purpose an authority may by resolution prescribe and authorize any other housing authority or authorities so joining or cooperating with it to act on its behalf with respect to any or all of such powers. Any authorities joining or cooperating with one another may by resolutions appoint from among the commissioners of such authorities an executive committee with full power to act on behalf of such authorities with respect to any or all of their powers, as prescribed by resolutions of such authorities. (Acts 1943, No. 541, p. 512, § 15.)

§ 24-1-117. Powers conferred by article supplemental.

The powers conferred by this article shall be in addition and supplemental to the powers conferred by any other law, and nothing contained in this article shall be construed as limiting any other powers of a housing authority. (Acts 1943, No. 541, p. 512, § 18.)

ARTICLE 5.

COOPERATION OF CITIES, COUNTIES, ETC., WITH HOUSING AUTHORITIES.

Collateral references. — Slum-clearance projects. 105 ALR 911, 130 ALR 1069. What constitutes "blighted area" within urban renewal and redevelopment statutes. 45 ALR3d 1096.

§ 24-1-130. Legislative findings and declaration of necessity.

It is hereby declared that unsanitary or unsafe dwelling and public school accommodations exist in various cities of the state and in the area surrounding such cities; that consequently persons of low income are forced to reside in and use such dwelling and public school accommodations; that these conditions cause an increase in and spread of disease and crime and constitute a menace to the health, safety, morals and welfare of the citizens of the state and impair economic values; that the clearance, replanning and reconstruction of the areas in which unsanitary or unsafe housing conditions exist and the provision of safe and sanitary dwelling and public school accommodations at such rentals that persons who now live in unsafe or unsanitary or congested dwelling accommodations or in overcrowded and congested dwelling accommodations can afford to live in safe or sanitary or uncongested dwelling accommodations, are public uses and purposes for which private property may be acquired; and that it is in the public interest that work on such projects be instituted as soon as possible in order to relieve unemployment which constitutes an emergency. The necessity in the public interest for this article is hereby declared as a matter of legislative determination. (Acts 1935, No. 41, p. 85; Code 1940, T. 25, § 1.)

§ 24-1-131. Definitions.

The following terms whenever used or referred to in this article, shall have the following respective meanings, unless a different meaning clearly appears from the context:

(1) HOUSING AUTHORITY. Any housing authority organized pursuant to this title.

(2) CITY. Any city or incorporated town in the State of Alabama.

(3) HOUSING PROJECT. Any undertaking to demolish, clear, remove, alter or repair unsafe or unsanitary housing or to provide dwelling or public school accommodations for persons who live in or use unsafe, unsanitary or congested dwelling or public school accommodations. Such term may also include such recreational or social assemblies for educational, health or welfare purposes and such necessary utilities as are designed primarily for the benefit and use of the occupants of such dwelling accommodations. (Acts 1935, No. 41, p. 85; Code 1940, T. 25, § 2.)

Collateral references. — 62 C.J.S., Municipal Corporations, § 699.

§ 24-1-132. Powers of municipalities, counties, public bodies, etc., to aid housing authorities.

(a) For the purpose of aiding and cooperating in the planning, undertaking, construction or operation by housing authorities of housing projects located within the area in which it is authorized to act, any city, county, municipal corporation, district or other subdivision or public body or agency of the state may, upon such terms, with or without consideration, as it may determine:

(1) Dedicate, release, sell, convey or lease any of its interest in any property or grant easements, licenses or any other rights or privileges therein to a housing authority or the United States of America or any agency thereof;

(2) Cause parks, playgrounds, recreational, community, educational, water, sewer, drainage facilities or any other works which it is otherwise empowered to undertake to be furnished adjacent to or in connection with housing projects;

(3) Furnish, dedicate, close, pave, install, grade, regrade, plan or replan streets, roads, roadways, alleys, sidewalks or other places which it is otherwise empowered to undertake;

(4) Plan or replan, zone or rezone;

(5) Cause services to be furnished to the housing authority of the character which it is otherwise empowered to furnish;

(6) Enter into agreements with respect to the exercise by it of its powers relating to the repair, elimination or closing of unsafe, unsanitary or unfit dwellings;

(7) Do any and all things necessary or convenient to aid and cooperate in its planning, undertaking, construction or operation of such housing projects;

(8) Incur the entire expense of any public improvements made by it in exercising the powers granted in this article; and

(9) Enter into agreements, which may extend over any period, notwithstanding any provision or rule of law to the contrary, with a housing authority respecting action to be taken pursuant to any of the powers granted by this article.

(b) Any law or statute to the contrary notwithstanding, any sale, conveyance, lease or agreement provided for in this section may be made by a city, county, municipal corporation, district or other subdivision or public body or agency of the state without appraisal, public notice, advertisement or public bidding. (Acts 1935, No. 41, p. 85; Acts 1939, No. 616, p. 984, § 2; Code 1940, T. 25, § 3.)

§ 24-1-133. Resolution authorizing exercise of powers granted.

The exercise by any city, county, municipal corporation, district or other subdivision or public body or agency of the state of the powers granted in this article may be authorized by resolution of its governing body adopted by a majority of the members of such governing body present at a meeting of such governing body, which resolution may be adopted at the meeting at which such resolution is introduced. Such a resolution or resolutions shall take effect immediately and need not be laid over or published or posted. (Acts 1939, No. 616, p. 984, § 4; Code 1940, T. 25, § 3(1).)

§ 24-1-134. City or town may lend or donate money to housing authority; reimbursement.

Any city or town creating a housing authority shall have the power from time to time to lend or donate money to such authority or to agree to take such action. A housing authority, when it has money available therefor, shall make reimbursements for all such loans made to it. (Acts 1939, No. 617, p. 986, § 1; Code 1940, T. 25, § 4(1).)

CHAPTER 1A.

ALABAMA HOUSING FINANCE AUTHORITY.

§ 24-1A-1. Legislative findings and declaration of purpose of chapter.

(a) It is hereby found and declared that from time to time there has existed and at the present time there exists an inadequate supply of funds at interest rates sufficiently low to enable the financing of safe and sanitary multi-family dwelling units for citizens of this state and single family dwelling units for citizens of this state with low and moderate income; that the inability to finance such single and multi-family dwelling units results in an inability of builders to construct such housing causing unemployment or underemployment in the housing construction and related businesses and causes a lack of safe and sanitary housing to be available to the citizens of this state; that such unemployment or underemployment in the housing construction and related businesses and an inadequate supply of safe and sanitary housing wastes human resources, increases the public assistance burden of the state, impairs the security of family life, impedes the economic and physical development of the state, adversely affects the welfare and prosperity of all of the people of the state and accordingly creates and fosters conditions adverse to the general health and welfare of the citizens of the state, that the making available in the manner provided in this chapter of a more adequate supply of funds at interest rates sufficiently low to enable the financing of safe and sanitary multi-family dwelling units for citizens of this state and single family dwelling units for citizens of low and moderate income will result in the alleviation or reduction of the adverse consequences which have resulted and may result from continued unemployment and underemployment in the housing construction and related businesses and the inadequate supply of such housing for such persons.

(b) It is hereby further found and determined that the conditions adverse to the general health and welfare of the citizens of the state as noted in subsection (a) of this section can best be solved by a cooperative effort as provided in this chapter between the authority acting on behalf of the state and those engaged in the business of making mortgage loans and such is the purpose of this chapter and it is not the intent of the legislature that the authority have the power to make direct loans to individuals or to acquire or construct housing units for lease or sale or that the authority have urban development or slum clearance functions, although its functions under this chapter are expected to be complementary to and supportive of those functions. (Acts 1980, No. 80-585, p. 899, § 1; Acts 1987, No. 87-556, p. 862, § 1.)

§ 24-1A-2. Definitions.

The following words and phrases used in this chapter, and others evidently intended as the equivalent thereof, shall, in the absence of clear implication otherwise, have the following respective meanings:

(1) AUTHORITY. The public corporation and instrumentality of the state organized pursuant to the provisions of this chapter.

(2) AUTHORIZED INVESTMENTS. Bonds or other obligations of, or guaranteed by, the United States of America or the state; interest bearing bank and savings and loan association deposits; obligations of any agency of the United States of America; any obligations in which a state chartered savings and loan association may invest its funds; any agreement to repurchase any of the foregoing; or any combination thereof.

(3) BOARD OF DIRECTORS. The board of directors of the authority.

(4) BONDS. Bonds or other securities representing an obligation to pay money.

(5) ELIGIBLE HOUSING UNIT. Real and personal properties located in the state constituting a single family dwelling unit for occupancy by low and moderate income families or a multi-family dwelling unit for occupancy by any persons and families without restriction as to the income of such persons or families other than any applicable federal restrictions imposed upon multi-family dwelling units financed from the proceeds of bonds the interest on which is exempt from federal income taxes.

(6) LOW AND MODERATE INCOME FAMILIES. Persons and families of one or more persons, irrespective of race, creed, national origin or sex, determined by the authority to require such assistance as is made available by this chapter on account of insufficient personal or family income taking into consideration, without limitation, such factors as follows:

a. The amount of the total income of such persons and families available for housing needs;

b. The size of the family;

c. The cost and condition of housing facilities available;

d. The ability of such persons and families to compete successfully in the normal private housing market and to pay the amounts at which private enterprise is providing sanitary, decent and safe housing; and

e. If appropriate, standards established for various federal programs with respect to housing determining eligibility based on income of such persons and families.

(7) MORTGAGE LENDERS. National banking associations, banks chartered under the laws of the state, savings or building and loan associations chartered under the laws of the state or of the United States of America, Federal National Mortgage Association approved mortgage bankers and federal or state credit unions. The terms shall also include other financial institutions or governmental agencies which customarily originate or service mortgage loans and mortgages.

(8) MORTGAGE LOANS. Notes and other evidences of indebtedness secured by mortgages.

(9) MORTGAGED PROPERTY. All properties, real, personal and mixed, and all interests therein including grants or subsidies with respect thereto, mortgaged, pledged or otherwise provided in any manner as security for (i) mortgage loans or (ii) loans to mortgage lenders.

(10) MORTGAGES. Mortgages, deeds of trust and other instruments granting security interests in real and personal properties constituting eligible housing units.

(11) MULTI-FAMILY MORTGAGE LOANS. Mortgages on eligible housing units constituting residential dwelling units leased to or occupied by more than one family unit.

(12) SINGLE FAMILY MORTGAGE LOANS. Mortgages on eligible housing units constituting residential dwelling units occupied as the principal residence of the owner-mortgagor by a single-family unit, including, without limitation, detached single family houses, attached single family houses or townhouses and condominium units within larger structures.

(13) STATE. The State of Alabama. (Acts 1980, No. 80-585, p. 899, § 2; Acts 1987, No. 87-556, p. 862, § 2.)

§ 24-1A-3. Incorporation of authority authorized; application; filing; fees.

(a) The nine persons initially designated as members of the authority may become a corporation with the power and authority provided in this chapter by proceeding according to the provisions of this chapter. To become a corporation, the persons so designated shall present to the Secretary of State an application signed by them which shall state:

(1) That the applicants propose to incorporate the authority pursuant to this chapter;

(2) The name and official residence of each of the applicants;

(3) The date on which each applicant was appointed as a member by the Governor and the expiration date of the term for which he was appointed;

(4) The name of the proposed corporation, which shall be "Alabama Housing Finance Authority";

(5) The location of the principal office of the proposed corporation, which shall be in the City of Montgomery; and

(6) Any other matter relating to the authority which the applicants may choose to insert and which is not inconsistent with this chapter or the laws of the state.

(b) The application shall be subscribed and sworn to by each of the applicants before an officer authorized by the laws of the state to take acknowledgments to deeds. The Secretary of State shall examine the application, and if the Secretary of State finds that it substantially complies with the requirements of this section, he shall receive, file and record it in an appropriate book of records in his office.

(c) When the application has been made, filed and recorded as provided in subsection (b) of this section, the applicants shall constitute a corporation under the name stated in the application, and the Secretary of State shall make and issue to the applicants a certificate of incorporation pursuant to this chapter, under the great seal of the state, and shall record the certificate with the application. There shall be no fees paid to the Secretary of State for any work done in connection with the incorporation or dissolution of the authority. (Acts 1980, No. 80-585, p. 899, § 4.)

Collateral references. — 62 C.J.S., Municipal Corporations, § 699.   40 Am. Jur. 2d, Housing Laws and Urban Development, §§ 1-3, 9.

§ 24-1A-4. Members, officers and directors; appointment; qualifications; meetings of board and public notice thereof; salaries; record of proceedings; copies of proceedings as evidence; permanent maintenance of official record; members, officers, etc., not personally liable; legislative oversight committee established; composition; appointment; expenses.

(a) The applicants named in the application, being the seven initial appointees of the Governor by congressional districts, the Director of Finance ex officio and the Superintendent of Banks ex officio, and their respective successors in office, together with the State Treasurer ex officio, an appointee of the Governor from the state at large and the appointees of the Speaker of the House and the Lieutenant Governor, and their respective successors in office, shall constitute the members of the authority. The Governor shall, as soon as convenient after the passage of this chapter, appoint one person from each of the now existing seven congressional districts as members of the authority, and at the expiration of the terms for which they are appointed or the existence of a vacancy, their successors. At the time of their appointment, two of such seven members shall be engaged in the business of home building, two shall be licensed real estate brokers, who are not in the business of home building; one shall be engaged in the business of lending money on the security of mortgages on residential property or the officer, director or employee of a mortgage lender; one shall be an elected commissioner of a county in the state; and one shall be an elected mayor of a municipality. The seven such members first appointed shall be appointed for terms of one, two, three, four, five, six, and seven years respectively, and the Governor in the appointment shall designate the expiration date of the term of the member. In addition to the members appointed by the Governor from each of the seven congressional districts, the Governor shall appoint one additional member from the state at large, such appointment to be for a term ending on June 1, 1990. The Speaker of the House shall appoint two members and the Lieutenant Governor shall appoint two members. The members appointed by the Speaker of the House shall be appointed for three- and five-year terms and the members appointed by the Lieutenant Governor shall be for four- and six-year terms, each commencing January 1, 1982. All successor appointees shall be appointed for the remainder of any unexpired term or, if appointed at the expiration of a term, for terms of seven years. Every member of the authority shall be a citizen of the state and a person of good reputation; and shall hold office for the term of his appointment and until his successor shall have been appointed and qualified. A member, director or officer of the authority may be impeached or removed from office in the same manner and on the same grounds as provided in Section 175 of the Constitution of Alabama and the general laws of the state relating to the impeachment and removal of public officers. At least one member shall be a member of the minority race. The Director of Finance, the State Treasurer and the Superintendent of Banks shall serve as ex officio members of the authority.

(b) The members of the authority shall constitute all the members of the board of directors of the authority, in which all powers of the authority shall be vested, and a majority of the members of the board of directors shall constitute a quorum for the transaction of business.

(c) The board of directors shall elect from among its members, a chairman, a vice-chairman, a secretary, a treasurer and such other officers as it may determine. The board of directors may also elect an assistant secretary and an assistant treasurer, who need not be members of the board of directors.

(d) Regular meetings of the board of directors shall be held at such time and place as shall be fixed by resolution of the board of directors and special meetings of the board of directors shall be held at the call of the chairman or whenever three members of the board of directors so request; provided, that no meeting shall be held unless five days' prior written notice of the time, place and purpose of such meeting shall have been given to each member of the oversight committee and five days' public notice has been given in at least three daily newspapers in diverse parts of the state outlining the time, place and purpose of the meeting. Public notice shall not be waived. Any action taken by the authority under the provisions of this chapter may be authorized by resolution approved by a majority of a quorum present and voting at any regular or special meeting. No member, officer or director of the authority shall receive any salary therefor, but he may be reimbursed for necessary travel and the reasonable expenses of performing the duties of office. All proceedings had and done by the board of directors shall be reduced to writing by the secretary or assistant secretary of the authority, shall be signed by at least three directors and shall be recorded in a substantially bound book and filed in the office of the authority. All proceedings of the board shall be open to the public and all records of the board shall be subject to public inspection during business hours. Copies of such proceedings, when certified by the secretary or assistant secretary of the authority under the seal of the authority, shall be received in all courts as prima facie evidence of the matters and things therein certified. The official records of the authority shall be permanently maintained in the office of the finance director.

(e) No member, officer, director or employee shall be personally liable for the obligations or acts of the authority.

(f) There shall be established a legislative oversight committee to provide recommendations to the board concerning efficient operation of the authority. The committee shall consist of seven members of the House of Representatives, one from each congressional district appointed by the Speaker of the House and seven members of the Senate, one from each congressional district appointed by the Lieutenant Governor. The Governor, Lieutenant Governor and Speaker of the House or their designated representative shall serve as ex officio members. The legislative members, after their initial appointment, shall be named at each organizational session and all members shall serve until their successors are properly qualified.

(g) Each appointed member, officer or director of the authority shall be paid actual expenses incurred in the performance of his duties pursuant to the provisions of this chapter, whether incurred within or without the State of Alabama; provided, however, each legislative member of the oversight committee shall be paid his regular legislative compensation for each day's attendance at meetings when not in legislative session plus actual expenses incurred in the performance of his duties pursuant to the provisions of this chapter when traveling outside the State of Alabama; and the Finance Director, State Treasurer and Superintendent of Banks shall serve without pay but shall be entitled to their actual expenses incurred in the performance of their duties pursuant to the provisions of this chapter. Any payment for compensation or reimbursement for expenses shall be made from any funds of the Alabama Housing Finance Authority. (Acts 1980, No. 80-585, p. 899, § 5; Acts 1981, 3rd Ex. Sess., No. 81-1132, p. 397, § 1; Acts 1983, No. 83-499, p. 700, § 1.)

Collateral references. — 62 C.J.S., Municipal Corporations, § 699. 67 C.J.S., Officers, §§ 35-48, 117-126.

40 Am. Jur. 2d, Housing Laws and Urban Redevelopment, §§ 1-15. 63 Am. Jur. 2d, Public Officers and Employees, §§ 91-98, 171-203.

§ 24-1A-5. Powers of authority.

The authority shall have the following powers:

(1) To have succession by its corporate name until the principal of and interest on the bonds shall have been fully paid and until it shall have been dissolved as provided in this chapter;

(2) To sue and be sued and to prosecute and defend in any court having jurisdiction of the subject matter and of the parties thereto;

(3) To adopt and use a corporate seal and to alter the seal at pleasure;

(4) To establish a fiscal year;

(5) To maintain an office in the City of Montgomery;

(6) To adopt, and from time to time amend and repeal, bylaws and rules and regulations, not inconsistent with this chapter, to carry into effect the powers and purposes of the authority in the conduct of its business;

(7) To purchase mortgage loans from mortgage lenders;

(8) To contract with mortgage lenders for the origination of, or the servicing, of mortgage loans to be made by such mortgage lenders and the servicing of the mortgages securing such mortgage loans;

(9) To make loans to mortgage lenders, provided that (i) the proceeds of such loans shall be required to be used by such mortgage lenders for the making of mortgage loans, and (ii) the mortgages in connection with the mortgage loans so made, together with any additional security required by the authority, shall be mortgaged, pledged, assigned or otherwise provided as security for such loans to mortgage lenders;

(10) To exercise any and all rights accorded to the owner and holder of a mortgage under and in accordance with the terms of said instruments and the applicable laws of the state with respect to the mortgaged property, directly or through mortgage lenders or others acting on behalf of the authority or on behalf of the holders of its bonds, including, but without limitation, the power to foreclose, to sell the equity of redemption, to purchase the equity of redemption and otherwise to sell and dispose of the mortgaged property, all as shall seem in the best interests of the authority and the holders of its bonds;

(11) To sell and issue bonds in order to provide funds for any corporate function, use or purpose;

(12) To mortgage, pledge, assign or grant security interests in any or all of its mortgage loans, mortgages and its interests created thereby in the underlying real and personal properties covered by such mortgages as security for the payment of the principal of, and interest on, any bonds issued by the authority, or as security for any agreements made in connection therewith, whether then owned or thereafter acquired, and to pledge the revenues from which said bonds are payable as security for the payment of the principal of, and interest on, said bonds and any agreements made in connection therewith;

(13) To establish such reserves from the proceeds of any issue of bonds or from revenues of the authority as the board of directors shall determine to

be necessary and desirable in connection with the payment and retirement of the bonds of the authority or in connection with any other purpose, power or function of the authority;

(14) To execute and deliver, in accordance with the provisions of this section and of Section 24-1A-6, mortgages and deeds of trust and trust indentures, or either;

(15) To appoint, employ, contract with and provide for the compensation of, such employees, attorneys, fiscal advisers and agents as the business of the authority may require;

(16) To provide for such insurance as the board of directors may deem advisable, including, but without limitation, casualty insurance, mortgage payment guarantee insurance and bond insurance;

(17) To invest in authorized investments any funds of the authority that the board of directors may determine are not presently needed for other uses, purposes or functions of the authority;

(18) To enter into a management agreement or agreements with any person, firm or corporation for the performance by said person, firm or corporation for the authority of any of its functions or powers upon such terms and conditions as may be mutually agreeable;

(19) To sell, exchange and convey any or all of its properties whenever its board of directors shall find any such action to be in furtherance of the purposes for which the authority was organized;

(20) To make, enter into and execute such contracts, agreements, leases and other instruments and to take such other actions as may be necessary or desirable to accomplish any purpose for which the authority is organized or to exercise any power granted by this chapter;

(21) To issue mortgage credit certificates to those persons and families who have received financing from any mortgage lender for the purpose of acquiring, rehabilitating, or improving single-family residential housing in Alabama. The authority shall have the power and the authority to take all steps, make all conditions, and do all things necessary in order to issue the certificates and implement and enforce the mortgage credit certificate program within the parameters and following the procedures specified by federal law and federal regulations governing the mortgage credit certificate program, notwithstanding any contrary provision in this chapter. The authority shall be the sole and exclusive issuer of mortgage credit certificates in and for the state;

(22) To administer other federal programs, present or future, which assist in the provision and financing of housing, including, but not limited to, allocation and issuance of low income housing tax credits under federal law and regulations including Section 42 of the Internal Revenue Code of 1986, as amended, and to take all other actions necessary or convenient to the implementation and administration of such programs; and

(23) To acquire, hold and dispose of real and personal property. (Acts 1980, No. 80-585, p. 899, § 6; Acts 1989, No. 89-694, p. 1367, § 1.)

U.S. Code. — The Internal Revenue Code is codified as U.S.C.A., Title 26.

Collateral references. — 62 C.J.S., Municipal Corporations, § 699.

40 Am. Jur. 2d, Housing Laws and Urban Redevelopment, §§ 15-26.

§ 24-1A-6. Bonds.

(a) *General.* — The authority may from time to time issue its negotiable bonds in such principal amounts as, in the opinion of the authority, shall be necessary to provide sufficient funds for achieving the corporate purposes thereof, the payment of interest on bonds of the authority, establishment of reserves to secure such bonds and all other expenditures of the authority incident to, and necessary or convenient to, carrying out its corporate purposes and powers.

(b) *Sources of Payment.* — Bonds issued by the authority shall be payable solely out of revenues or property of the authority specified in the resolutions authorizing the issuance of such bonds. To the extent permitted by any contracts with the holders of outstanding bonds and any other contractual obligations or requirements, the authority may pledge any, or all, of its revenues or mortgages or assign any, or all, of its assets (whether real or personal and whether tangible or intangible) to secure the payment of any of its bonds.

Revenues and property out of which bonds may be payable shall include, without limitation:

(1) Payments of principal, interest, premiums and penalties in respect to mortgage loans, loans to mortgage lenders, mortgages and mortgaged property;

(2) Proceeds referable to the foreclosure of mortgages or otherwise realized, by any and all means, upon any mortgaged property;

(3) Payments made in redemption of the equity of such mortgages or similar payments with respect to any redemption of mortgaged property;

(4) Proceeds from the leasing or sale of property which was formerly mortgaged property and which was acquired in the process of enforcing mortgage loans or loans to mortgage lenders;

(5) Proceeds from the sale of mortgage loans, loans to mortgage lenders, mortgages and mortgaged property;

(6) Insurance proceeds referable to mortgage loans, loans to mortgage lenders, mortgages and mortgaged property including, but without limitation, proceeds from casualty insurance and mortgage payment guarantee insurance;

(7) Proceeds from bond insurance;

(8) Grants or subsidies available in connection with any of the foregoing;

(9) Any of the foregoing sources of revenues as may be designated in the proceedings of the board pursuant to which the bonds shall be authorized to be issued.

(c) *Pledge of Revenues and Other Security.* — The principal of and interest on any bonds issued by the authority may be secured by a pledge of the revenues out of which the same are payable and may be secured by a trust indenture evidencing such pledge or by a foreclosable mortgage and deed of trust conveying as security for such bonds all, or any part, of the property of the authority from which the revenues so pledged may be derived. The resolution under which the bonds are authorized to be issued or any such trust indenture or mortgage may contain any agreements and provisions respecting the maintenance and insurance of the property covered by such trust indenture or mortgage, the use of the revenues subject to such trust indenture or mortgage, the creation and maintenance of special funds from such revenues, the rights, duties and remedies of the parties to any such instrument and the parties for the benefit of whom such instrument is made and the rights and remedies available in the event of default as the authority shall deem advisable and which are not in conflict with the provisions of this chapter.

(d) *Execution.* — All bonds issued by the authority shall be signed by the chairman or vice-chairman of its board of directors and attested by its secretary or assistant secretary and the seal of the authority shall be affixed thereto, and any interest coupons applicable to the bonds of the authority shall be signed by the chairman or vice-chairman of its board of directors; provided, however, that a facsimile of the signature of either the signing or the attesting officer, but not both, may be printed or otherwise reproduced on any such bonds in lieu of his manually signing the same, a facsimile of the seal of the authority may be printed or otherwise reproduced on any such bonds in lieu of being manually affixed thereto and a facsimile of the signature of the chairman or vice-chairman of the board of directors may be printed or otherwise reproduced on any such interest coupons in lieu of his manually signing the same.

(e) *General Provisions Respecting Form; Interest Rate; Maturities; Sale and Negotiability of Bonds.* — Any such bonds may be executed and delivered by the authority at any time and, from time to time, shall be in such form and denomination or denominations and of such tenor and maturity or maturities, shall contain such provisions not inconsistent with the provisions of this chapter, and shall bear such rate or rates of interest, payable at such place or places, either within or without the state, and evidenced in such manner, as may be provided by resolution of the board of directors. Bonds of the authority may be sold at public sale, including without limitations the rejection of all bids, at such price or prices and at such times as determined by the board of directors to be advantageous. In addition, if bids are rejected or upon a finding by the Director of Finance of the state that a public sale of the authority's bonds is, under the circumstances, either impractical or undesirable, bonds may be sold at private sale in such manner and at such price or prices and at such time or times as may be determined by the board of directors to be most advantageous. The authority may pay all expenses, premiums and commissions in connection with any financing done by it. All bonds of the authority (including refunding bonds), except bonds registered as to principal or as to both principal and interest, and any interest coupons applicable thereto issued by the authority shall be construed to be negotiable instruments although payable solely from a specified source.

(f) *No State Debt or Obligation.* — All obligations created and all bonds issued by the authority shall be solely and exclusively an obligation of the authority and shall not create an obligation or debt of the state. (Acts 1980, No. 80-585, p. 899, § 8.)

Collateral references. — 64 Am. Jur. 2d,
Public Securities and Obligations, §§ 1-33,
94-96.

§ 24-1A-7. Proceeds from sale of bonds; use; issuance procedures; distribution percentages; allocation of proceeds available for single family mortgage loans.

(a) All moneys derived from the sale of any bonds issued by the authority shall be used solely for the purpose or purposes for which the same are authorized, including costs and expenses of issue. Such costs and expenses may include but shall not be limited to:

(1) The fiscal, legal and other expenses incurred in connection with the issuance of the bonds; and

(2) Except in the case of refunding bonds, interest to accrue on such bonds for a period ending not later than two years from their date.

(b) Bonds shall be issued in series, each of which shall be separately designated in the proceedings authorizing their issuance. The board of directors in the proceedings authorizing a series of bonds (other than refunding bonds) shall specify the purposes for which the proceeds of such series shall be used. The proceeds of a series of bonds shall be used either for making, directly or indirectly, single family mortgage loans or for making, directly or indirectly, multi-family mortgage loans or for making, directly or indirectly, home improvement loans for eligible existing single family housing units, and the proceeds of a single series of bonds shall not be used for any combination of single family mortgage loans, multi-family mortgage loans and home improvement loans. Separate series of bonds may be issued at the same time. No series of bonds, the proceeds which are to be used for multi-family mortgage loans, shall be actually issued prior to January 1, 1981, although the authority may enter into agreements or commitments with regard to the issuance of such bonds prior to January 1, 1981.

(c) In the proceedings authorizing any bonds (other than refunding bonds) the proceeds of which are to be applied, directly or indirectly, to the making of single family mortgage loans, the board of directors shall specify the portion of the proceeds thereof which the board of directors has determined are to be used for the purpose of providing funds with respect to the making, directly or indirectly, of such mortgage loans, and of such portion shall allocate (1) a minimum of 70 percent of such proceeds to the making of mortgage loans with respect to new and previously unoccupied eligible housing units, and (2) not exceeding 30 percent of such proceeds to the making of mortgage loans for existing eligible housing units and for the purchase of existing mortgage loans with respect to eligible housing units; provided, however, that if the authority determines, after 60 days from the date of issuance of any series of bonds issued for the purpose of financing single family mortgage loans, that the proceeds of such series have not been expended or committed to be expended for mortgage loans with respect to new and previously unoccupied eligible housing units, then such proceeds may be used to finance any single family mortgage loans.

(d) If, for any series of bonds the proceeds of which are to be used for making, directly or indirectly, single family mortgage loans, the total requests for mortgage funds by mortgage lenders at the interest rate nearest to the mortgage interest rate actually obtained by the bond issue are less than or equal to an amount equal to the maximum principal amount of mortgage revenue bonds which may be issued under federal law during the then-current calendar year, then the authority shall allocate the net proceeds available for mortgage loans in such manner as it shall determine in its sole discretion.

(e) If, for any series of bonds the proceeds of which are to be used for making, directly or indirectly, single family mortgage loans, the total requests for mortgage funds by mortgage lenders at the interest rate nearest to the mortgage interest rate actually obtained by the bond issue exceed an amount equal to the maximum principal amount of mortgage revenue bonds which may be issued under federal law during the then-current calendar year, then 35 percent of the net proceeds available for mortgage loans shall be allocated equally among the 67 counties of the state for a period of 60 days commencing on the date of issuance of such series of bonds. The authority, in its sole discretion, shall have the option to extend such 60-day period for an additional 30 days, and the further option to extend such period for an additional 30 days. At the expiration of such period, including any extension thereof, the authority may reallocate in the manner provided in subsection (d) of this section any portion of any county's original allocation which is not the subject of a written commitment for mortgage loans by mortgage lenders. The remaining 65 percent of such net proceeds shall be allocated by the authority in the manner provided in subsection (d) of this section. (Acts 1980, No. 80-585, p. 899, § 9; Acts 1981, 3rd Ex. Sess., No. 81-1132, p. 397, § 2.)

Collateral references. — 64 Am. Jur. 2d, Public Securities and Obligations, §§ 37-46, 206-229.

§ 24-1A-8. Refunding bonds.

(a) Any bonds issued by the authority may from time to time be refunded by the issuance, by sale or exchange, of refunding bonds payable from the same or different sources for the purpose of paying:

(1) All or any part of the principal of the bonds to be refunded;

(2) Any redemption premium required to be paid as a condition to the redemption prior to maturity of any such bonds that are to be so redeemed in connection with such refunding;

(3) Any accrued and unpaid interest on the bonds to be refunded;

(4) Any interest to accrue on each bond to be refunded to the date on which it is to be paid, whether at maturity or by redemption prior to maturity; and

(5) The expenses incurred in connection with the refunding; provided, however, that unless duly called for redemption pursuant to provisions contained therein, the holders of any such bonds then outstanding and proposed to be refunded shall not be compelled without their consent to surrender their outstanding bonds for such refunding.

(b) Any refunding bonds may be sold by the authority at public or private sale at such price or prices as may be determined by its board of directors to be most advantageous, or may be exchanged for the bonds to be refunded. Any such refunding bonds may be executed and delivered by the authority at any time and, from time to time, shall be in such form and denomination or denominations and of such tenor and maturity or maturities, shall contain such provisions not inconsistent with the provisions of this chapter, and shall bear such rate or rates of interest, payable at such place or places, either within or without the state, and evidenced in such manner, as may be provided by resolution of the board of directors.

(c) Any refunding bonds issued by the authority shall be issued and may be secured in accordance with the provisions of Section 24-1A-6. (Acts 1980, No. 80-585, p. 899, § 10.)

Collateral references. — 64 Am. Jur. 2d, Public Securities and Obligations, §§ 261-269.

§ 24-1A-9. Limitation on issuance of bonds.

Notwithstanding any other provision of this chapter to the contrary, the authority shall not issue any bonds, other than refunding bonds, subsequent to December 31, 1995. (Acts 1980, No. 80-585, p. 899, § 11; Acts 1981, 3rd Ex. Sess., No. 81-1132, p. 397, § 3; Acts 1981, 3rd Ex. Sess., No. 81-1188, p. 522, § 1; Acts 1983, No. 83-499, p. 700, § 2; Acts 1986, No. 86-459, p. 837; Acts 1987, No. 87-556, p. 862, § 3; Acts 1989, No. 89-694, p. 1367, § 2.)

§ 24-1A-10. Bonds eligible for investment by state and local governments and by executors, trustees, etc.

The state treasurer may invest any idle or surplus moneys of the state in bonds of the authority. The governing body of any county or municipality is authorized in its discretion to invest any idle or surplus money held in its treasury in bonds of the authority. Such bonds shall be legal investments for executors, administrators, trustees and other fiduciaries, unless otherwise directed by the court having jurisdiction of the fiduciary relation or by the document that is the source of the fiduciary's authority, and for savings banks and insurance companies organized under the laws of the state. (Acts 1980, No. 80-585, p. 899, § 12.)

§ 24-1A-11. Applicability of certain provisions of Uniform Commercial Code.

The provisions of subsection (1) of Section 7-9-104, to the contrary notwithstanding, the provisions of Article 9 of Title 7 shall apply with full force and effect to any security interest (whether denominated a pledge, assignment or otherwise) in any tangible or intangible personal property of the authority created or made in connection with any issue of bonds of the authority. (Acts 1980, No. 80-585, p. 899, § 13.)

§ 24-1A-12. Exemption from taxation.

The property and income of the authority, all bonds issued by the authority, the interest payable on and the income derived from such bonds, conveyances by or to the authority and leases, mortgages and deeds of trust or trust indentures by or to the authority shall be exempt from all taxation in the state. The authority shall be exempt from all taxes levied by any county, municipality or other political subdivision of the state, including, but without limitation, license and excise taxes imposed in respect of the privilege of engaging in any of the activities in which the authority may engage. Nothing in this section shall be construed to exempt any private person, firm or corporation from payment of any ad valorem, mortgage or deed taxes or recording fees notwithstanding the fact that the authority shall have acquired an interest in the property or instrument subject to such taxes or fees. (Acts 1980, No. 80-585, p. 899, § 14.)

§ 24-1A-13. Liability of state.

The state shall not in any event be liable for the payment of the principal of, or interest on, any bonds of the authority or for the performance of any pledge, mortgage, obligation or agreement of any kind whatsoever which may be undertaken by the authority, and none of the bonds of the authority or any of its agreements or obligations shall be construed to constitute an indebtedness of the state within the meaning of any constitutional or statutory provision whatsoever. (Acts 1980, No. 80-585, p. 899, § 15.)

§ 24-1A-14. Exemption from usury and interest laws.

All securities issued by the authority shall be exempt from the laws of the state governing usury or prescribing or limiting interest rates, including, but without limitation, the provisions of Chapter 8 of Title 8. (Acts 1980, No. 80-585, p. 899, § 16.)

§ 24-1A-15. Freedom of authority from state supervision and control; authority deemed independent instrumentality.

This chapter is intended to aid the state through the furtherance of the purposes of the chapter by providing an appropriate and independent instrumentality of the state with full and adequate powers to fulfill its functions. Except as expressly provided in this chapter, no proceeding, notice or approval shall be required for the incorporation of the authority, the purchase of any mortgage loans or the making of any loan to a mortgage lender, the acquisition of any mortgage, the acquisition of, or any dealing with respect to, any mortgaged property, the issuance of any bonds, the execution of any mortgage and deed of trust or trust indenture or the exercise of any other of its powers by the authority. (Acts 1980, No. 80-585, p. 899, § 17.)

§ 24-1A-16. Earnings of authority; nonprofit; excess paid to state.

The authority shall be a nonprofit corporation and no part of its net earnings remaining after payment of its expenses shall inure to the benefit of any individual, firm or corporation, except that in the event its board of directors shall determine that sufficient provision has been made for the full payment of the expenses, bonds and other obligations of the authority, then any net earnings of the authority thereafter accruing shall be paid to the state. (Acts 1980, No. 80-585, p. 899, § 18.)

§ 24-1A-17. Dissolution of authority; vesting title to property in state.

At any time when an authority has no bonds or other obligations outstanding, its board of directors may by the unanimous vote of all directors present adopt a resolution declaring that the authority shall be dissolved. Upon filing for record of a certified copy of the said resolution in the office of the Secretary of State, the authority shall thereupon stand dissolved and in the event it shall own any property at the time of its dissolution, the title of all its properties shall thereupon pass to the state. (Acts 1980, No. 80-585, p. 899, § 19.)

§ 24-1A-18. Utilization of services provided by Department of Finance.

The authority shall utilize all administrative services which may be provided by the Department of Finance. (Acts 1980, No. 80-585, p. 899, § 20.)

§ 24-1A-19. Conflict of interest; rules governing.

The entire board of directors, the officers and employees of the authority are hereby subject to the provisions of Chapter 25 of Title 36 and to the rules and promulgations of the State Ethics Commission. (Acts 1980, No. 80-585, p. 899, § 21.)

§ 24-1A-20. Chapter not to aid in refinancing.

This chapter shall not be used to assist any present owner for refinancing purposes. (Acts 1980, No. 80-585, p. 899, § 22.)

§ 24-1A-21. Liberal construction.

This chapter being remedial in nature, the provisions of this chapter shall be liberally construed to effect its purpose. (Acts 1980, No. 80-585, p. 899, § 23.)

CHAPTER 2.

REDEVELOPMENT PROJECTS.

This chapter does not violate Constitution 1901, section 22. No special privilege is granted; even if some individual does receive more benefit than others, that is only incidental and does not affect the public nature of the transaction as a whole. Opinion of Justices, 254 Ala. 343, 48 So. 2d 757 (1950).

This chapter does not violate Constitution 1901, section 23. Opinion of Justices, 254 Ala. 343, 48 So. 2d 757 (1950); Blankenship v. City of Decatur, 269 Ala. 670, 115 So. 2d 459 (1959).

Redevelopment project is public use. — The plan contemplated by this chapter, in connection with the rest of this title, shows that character of public benefit resulting from its observance which should be classified as a public use on the same theory which influenced the justices of the supreme court in so declaring with reference to this title before the adoption of this chapter, and the plan does not violate Constitution 1901, § 23. Opinion of Justices, 254 Ala. 343, 48 So. 2d 757 (1950); Blankenship v. City of Decatur, 269 Ala. 670, 115 So. 2d 459 (1959).

There is no delegation of legislative power in violation of Constitution 1901, § 44 in this chapter. Opinion of Justices, 254 Ala. 343, 48 So. 2d 757 (1950).

And chapter does not authorize unconstitutional lending of credit or grant. — The obligations which may be assumed by a city or county and the donation of the necessary money to accomplish the purposes of this chapter are not a lending of credit or a grant in violation of Constitution 1901, § 94. Opinion of Justices, 254 Ala. 343, 48 So. 2d 757 (1950).

Chapter enacted to take advantage of federal funds. — Chapters 1, 2, and 3 of Title 24 were enacted for the purpose of enabling Alabama and its subdivisions to take advantage of federal funds available pursuant to federal housing, redevelopment, and urban renewal act. Chapter 1 was enacted to secure federal aid offered pursuant to the United States Housing Act of 1937, 42 U.S.C. § 1401 et seq. Chapter 2 of Title 24, entitled "Redevelopment Projects," was passed in response to the Housing Act of 1949, 42 U.S.C. § 1441 et seq. Chapter 3 of Title 24 was passed in response to the 1954 amendments to the 1949 act providing for urban renewal projects, 42 U.S.C. § 1450 et seq. City of Birmingham v. Tutwiler Drug Co., 475 So. 2d 458 (Ala. 1985).

This chapter is applicable to commercial and industrial property as well as to residential property. City of Birmingham v. Tutwiler Drug Co., 475 So. 2d 458 (Ala. 1985).

While the primary purpose of urban renewal and redevelopment statutes is the elimination of residential slums and the improvement of living conditions, the conclusion that only residential property can be condemned for redevelopment is unwarranted. There is nothing in the statute specifically limiting its application to residential areas. City of Birmingham v. Tutwiler Drug Co., 475 So. 2d 458 (Ala. 1985).

This chapter does not require a specific mode of enacting the laws by which redevelopment or renewal projects are initiated. Tutwiler Drug Co. v. City of Birmingham, 418 So. 2d 102 (Ala. 1982).

Condition of entire area determines

whether redevelopment is warranted. — It is the condition of the entire redevelopment area as a whole, not the condition of a particular property, which determines whether redevelopment is warranted under the urban renewal and redevelopment laws. City of Birmingham v. Tutwiler Drug Co., 475 So. 2d 458 (Ala. 1985).

The mere fact that some of the buildings in a redevelopment area are substantial and standard does not require their exclusion from the project. City of Birmingham v. Tutwiler Drug Co., 475 So. 2d 458 (Ala. 1985).

Substantial buildings in slum need not be omitted. — The mere fact that some of the buildings in a slum area are standard and substantial does not require that they be omitted from the operation of the project. Blankenship v. City of Decatur, 269 Ala. 670, 115 So. 2d 459 (1959).

Contrast with chapter 3. — Chapter 3 which deals with "urban renewal" contemplates a project that is materially different from the type project contemplated by chapter 2; while chapter 2 is designed to "clear" a slum, chapter 3 is designed to "prevent" a slum by rehabilitation. Housing Auth. v. Nunn, 292 Ala. 60, 288 So. 2d 775 (1974).

Cited in Watts v. Housing Auth., 150 F. Supp. 552 (N.D. Ala. 1956).

Collateral references. — 62 C.J.S., Municipal Corporations, § 699. 82 C.J.S., Statutes, § 14.

40 Am. Jur. 2d, Housing Laws & Urban Redevelopment, §§ 15-26.

Statutes providing for slum-clearance projects. 105 ALR 911, 130 ALR 1069.

Statutes providing for urban redevelopment by private enterprise. 44 ALR2d 1414.

§ 24-2-1. Legislative findings and declaration of necessity.

(a) It is hereby found and declared:

(1) That there exist in many communities within this state blighted areas, as defined herein, or areas in the process of becoming blighted;

(2) That such areas impair economic values and tax revenues, cause an increase in and spread of disease and crime and constitute a menace to the health, safety, morals and welfare of the residents of the state, and that these conditions necessitate excessive and disproportionate expenditures of public funds for crime prevention and punishment, public health and safety, fire and accident protection and other public services and facilities;

(3) That the clearance, replanning and preparation for rebuilding of these areas and the prevention or the reduction of blight and its causes are public uses and purposes for which public money may be spent and private property acquired and are governmental functions of state concern;

(4) That redevelopment activities will stimulate residential construction which is closely correlated with general economic activity and that the undertakings authorized by this chapter will aid the production of better housing and more desirable neighborhood and community development at lower costs and will make possible a more stable and larger volume of residential construction, which will assist materially in achieving and maintaining full employment; and

(5) That it is in the public interest that advance preparation for such projects and activities be made now.

(b) The necessity in the public interest for this chapter is hereby declared as a matter of legislative determination. (Acts 1949, No. 491, p. 713, § 1.)

§ 24-2-2. Powers of housing authorities or municipalities — Acquisition, clearing and disposal of property; installation of utilities.

Any housing authority now or hereafter established pursuant to this title, or any incorporated city or town may carry out any work or undertaking, hereafter called a "redevelopment project":

(1) To acquire blighted areas, which are hereby defined as areas, including slum areas, with buildings or improvements which, by reason of dilapidation, obsolescence, overcrowding, faulty arrangement or design, lack of ventilation, light and sanitary facilities, excessive land coverage, deleterious land use or obsolete layout, or any combination of these or other factors, are detrimental to the safety, health, morals or welfare of the community;

(2) To acquire other real property for the purpose of removing, preventing or reducing blight, blighting factors or the causes of blight;

(3) To clear any areas acquired and install, construct or reconstruct streets, utilities and site improvements essential to the preparation of sites for uses in accordance with the redevelopment plan;

(4) To sell or lease land so acquired for uses in accordance with the redevelopment plan; or

(5) To accomplish a combination of the foregoing to carry out a redevelopment plan. (Acts 1949, No. 491, p. 713, § 2; Acts 1967, No. 416, p. 1070, § 2.)

The underutilization of property in core of downtown area is detrimental to the welfare of the community in the broad sense of the term "welfare." City of Birmingham v. Tutwiler Drug Co., 475 So. 2d 458 (Ala. 1985).

Using the "fairly debatable" standard to test the validity under subdivision (1) of a resolution declaring the redevelopment of a block to be necessary and in the public interest, the resolution was valid if it was fairly debatable that the block either (1) was a slum or (2) exhibited any combination of the blighting factors enumerated in the statute and that, as a result of the presence of those factors, the block was "detrimental to the safety, health, morals or welfare of the community." City of Birmingham v. Tutwiler Drug Co., 475 So. 2d 458 (Ala. 1985).

Redevelopment of area proper although one block not blighted. — Where the downtown area as a whole was blighted, it was proper to include a particular block in the redevelopment of the downtown area if it was reasonably necessary to do so in order to carry out the redevelopment plan, even if that block itself could not properly have been considered blighted. City of Birmingham v. Tutwiler Drug Co., 475 So. 2d 458 (Ala. 1985).

Cited in Housing Auth. v. Nunn, 292 Ala. 60, 288 So. 2d 775 (1974).

Collateral references. — Blighted area: what constitutes "blighted area" within urban renewal and redevelopment statutes. 45 ALR3d 1096.

§ 24-2-3. Powers of housing authorities or municipalities — Powers under other housing laws; contracts; issuance of bonds and other obligations; eminent domain.

In undertaking such redevelopment projects a housing authority, or the governing body of any incorporated city or town, shall have all the rights, powers, privileges and immunities that such authority has under Chapter 1 of this title, and any other provision of law relating to slum clearance and housing projects for persons of low income, including, without limiting the generality of the foregoing, the power to make and execute contracts, to issue bonds and other obligations and give security therefor, to acquire real property by eminent domain or purchase and to do any and all things necessary to carry out projects in the same manner as though all the provisions of law applicable to slum clearance and housing projects were applicable to redevelopment projects undertaken under this chapter; provided, that nothing contained in Section 24-1-6 shall be construed as limiting the power of an authority or the governing body of any incorporated city or town, in the event of a default by a purchaser or lessee of land in a redevelopment plan, to acquire property and operate it free from the restrictions contained in said section. (Acts 1949, No. 491, p. 713, § 3; Acts 1967, No. 416, p. 1070, § 3.)

Cross references. — As to eminent domain, see § 18-1A-1 et seq.

Collateral references. — Eminent domain: industrial park or similar development as public use justifying condemnation of private property. 62 ALR4th 1183.

§ 24-2-4. Approval of redevelopment plan by governing bodies of cities, counties, etc., in which project situated; assistance of redevelopment projects by cities, counties, etc.

An authority or the governing body of any city or town shall not initiate any redevelopment project under this chapter until the governing body, or agency designated by it or empowered by law to so act of each city, town or village, hereinafter called "municipalities," in which any of the area to be covered by said project is situated has approved a plan, herein called the "redevelopment plan," which provides an outline for the development or redevelopment of said area and is sufficiently complete:

(1) To indicate its relationship to definite local objectives as to appropriate land uses and improved traffic, public transportation, public utilities, recreational and community facilities and other public improvements;

(2) To indicate proposed land uses and building requirements in the area; and

(3) To indicate the method for the temporary relocation of persons living in such areas and also the method for providing, unless already available, decent, safe and sanitary dwellings substantially equal in number to the number of substandard dwellings to be cleared from said area, at rents within the financial reach of the income groups displaced from such substandard dwellings.

Such municipalities are hereby authorized to approve redevelopment plans through their governing body or agency designated by it for that purpose. Any city, municipality, county or other public body shall have the same rights and powers to cooperate with and assist housing authorities with respect to redevelopment projects that such public bodies have pursuant to Article 2 of Chapter 1 of this title, or any other provision of law for the purpose of assisting the development or administration of slum clearance and housing projects in the same manner as though the provisions of such laws were applicable to redevelopment projects undertaken under this chapter. (Acts 1949, No. 491, p. 713, § 4; Acts 1967, No. 416, p. 1070, § 4.)

§ 24-2-5. Advisory board.

For the purpose of coordinating its activities and undertakings under this chapter with the needs and undertakings of other local organizations and groups, a housing authority or the governing body of any incorporated city or town may establish an advisory board consisting of the chairman of the authority, who shall be chairman of the advisory board, and of sufficient members to represent so far as practicable: the general public and consumers of housing; general business interests; real estate, building and home financing interests; labor; any official planning body in the locality; and church and welfare groups. The members of the advisory board shall be appointed by the chairman of the authority or, if the board is established by the governing body of any incorporated city or town, then the members of the advisory board shall be appointed by the mayor of such city or town, and, in such event, the mayor shall be the chairman of the advisory board. (Acts 1949, No. 491, p. 713, § 9; Acts 1967, No. 416, p. 1070, § 9.)

§ 24-2-6. Land in project may be made available for use by private enterprise or public agencies in accordance with redevelopment plan.

(a) The authority or the governing body of any city or town may make land in a redevelopment project available for use by private enterprise or public agencies in accordance with the redevelopment plan. Such land may be made available at its use value, which represents the value, whether expressed in terms of rental or capital price, at which the authority or the governing body of any incorporated city or town determines such land should be made available in order that it may be developed or redeveloped for the purposes specified in such plan.

(b) To assure that land acquired in a redevelopment project is used in accordance with the redevelopment plan, an authority or the governing body of any incorporated city or town, upon the sale or lease of such land, shall obligate purchasers or lessees:

(1) To use the land for the purpose designated in the redevelopment plan;

(2) To begin the building of their improvements within a period of time which the authority fixes as reasonable; and

(3) To comply with such other conditions as are necessary to carry out the purposes of this chapter.

Any such obligations by the purchaser shall be covenants and conditions running with the land where the authority so stipulates. (Acts 1949, No. 491, p. 713, § 5; Acts 1967, No. 416, p. 1070, § 5.)

§ 24-2-7. Tax status of land sold or leased to private individuals or corporations for redevelopment.

Any property which the authority or the governing body of any incorporated city or town leases to private individuals or corporations for development under a redevelopment plan shall have the same tax status as if such leased property were owned by such private individuals or corporations. (Acts 1949, No. 491, p. 713, § 6; Acts 1967, No. 416, p. 1070, § 6.)

§ 24-2-8. Federal financial aid.

An authority or the governing body of any incorporated city or town may borrow money or accept contributions from the federal government to assist in its undertaking redevelopment projects. An authority or the governing body of any incorporated city or town may do any and all things necessary or desirable to secure such financial aid, including obligating itself in any contract with the federal government for annual contributions to convey to the federal government the project to which said contract relates, upon the occurrence of a substantial default thereunder, in the same manner as they may do to secure such aid in connection with slum clearance and housing projects under the provisions of this title. (Acts 1949, No. 491, p. 713, § 7; Acts 1967, No. 416, p. 1070, § 7.)

§ 24-2-9. Investment by public bodies, etc., in bonds, etc., issued by housing authorities, etc.

Bonds or other obligations issued by a housing authority or the governing body of any incorporated city or town, in connection with a redevelopment project pursuant to this chapter, shall be security for public deposits and legal investments to the same extent and for the same persons, institutions, associations, corporations and other bodies and officers as bonds or other obligations issued pursuant to this title in connection with the development of slum clearance and housing projects. (Acts 1949, No. 491, p. 713, § 8; Acts 1967, No. 416, p. 1070, § 8.)

§ 24-2-10. Provisions of chapter cumulative; conflicting laws.

The provisions of this chapter shall be cumulative and supplemental to the powers conferred by any other law and shall be construed in pari materia with other laws relative to redevelopment plans and redevelopment projects. No laws shall be deemed repealed by this chapter unless in specific conflict herewith. (Acts 1949, No. 491, p. 713, § 10; Acts 1967, No. 416, p. 1070, § 10.)

CHAPTER 3.

URBAN RENEWAL PROJECTS.

This chapter does not violate Constitution 1901, section 23. Blankenship v. City of Decatur, 269 Ala. 670, 115 So. 2d 459 (1959).

Chapter enacted to take advantage of federal funds. — Chapters 1, 2, and 3 of Title 24 were enacted for the purpose of enabling Alabama and its subdivisions to take advantage of federal funds available pursuant to federal housing, redevelopment, and urban renewal act. Chapter 1 was enacted to secure federal aid offered pursuant to the United States Housing Act of 1937, 42 U.S.C. § 1401 et seq. Chapter 2 of Title 24, entitled "Redevelopment Projects," was passed in response to the Housing Act of 1949, 42 U.S.C. § 1441 et seq. Chapter 3 of Title 24 was passed in response to the 1954 amendments to the 1949 act providing for urban renewal projects, 42 U.S.C. § 1450 et seq. City of Birmingham v. Tutwiler Drug Co., 475 So. 2d 458 (Ala. 1985).

This chapter authorizes rehabilitation of an area to prevent the spread of blight. Housing Auth. v. Nunn, 292 Ala. 60, 288 So. 2d 775 (1974).

Contrast with chapter 2. — Chapter 3 which deals with "urban renewal" contem-

plates a project that is materially different from the type project contemplated by chapter 2; while chapter 2 is designed to "clear" a slum, chapter 3 is designed to "prevent" a slum by rehabilitation. Housing Auth. v. Nunn, 292 Ala. 60, 288 So. 2d 775 (1974).

Injunctive relief. — Where the finding by the trial court that the redevelopment project did not meet the statutory definition under this chapter did not constitute a finding that the actions of the housing authority were arbitrary and capricious and since the complainants did not allege that the housing authority had acted arbitrarily and capriciously, there was no basis for injunctive relief. Housing Auth. v. Nunn, 292 Ala. 60, 288 So. 2d 775 (1974).

Cited in Barnes v. City of Gadsden, 174 F. Supp. 64 (N.D. Ala. 1958).

Collateral references. — 40 Am. Jur. 2d, Housing Laws & Urban Redevelopment, §§ 15-26.

Statutes providing for slum-clearance projects. 105 ALR 911, 130 ALR 1069.

Statutes providing for urban redevelopment by private enterprise. 44 ALR2d 1414.

§ 24-3-1. Legislative findings and declaration of necessity; municipalities to afford opportunities for redevelopment, etc., by private enterprise.

(a) It is hereby found and declared:

(1) That there exist in communities of the state slum, blighted and deteriorated areas which constitute a serious and growing menace, injurious to the public health, safety, morals and welfare of the residents of the

state, and the findings and declarations heretofore made in Section 24-2-1 with respect to blighted areas are hereby affirmed and restated;

(2) That certain slum, blighted or deteriorated areas, or portions thereof, may require acquisition and clearance, since the prevailing condition of decay may make impracticable the reclamation of the area by conservation or rehabilitation, but other areas, or portions thereof, may, through the means provided in this chapter, be susceptible of conservation or rehabilitation in such a manner that the conditions and evils hereinbefore enumerated may be eliminated, remedied or prevented, and, to the extent feasible, salvable slum and blighted areas should be conserved and rehabilitated through voluntary action and the regulatory process; and

(3) That all powers conferred by this chapter are for public uses and purposes for which public money may be expended and such other powers exercised, and the necessity in the public interest for the provisions of this chapter is hereby declared as a matter of legislative determination.

(b) A city or town, hereinafter called "municipality," to the greatest extent it determines to be feasible in carrying out the provisions of this chapter, shall afford maximum opportunity, consistent with the sound needs of the municipality as a whole, to the rehabilitation or redevelopment of areas by private enterprise. (Acts 1955, No. 553, p. 1210, § 1.)

§ 24-3-2. Housing authorities and municipalities authorized to plan and undertake urban renewal projects.

(a) In addition to its authority under this title, any housing authority created under this title is hereby authorized to plan and undertake urban renewal projects.

(b) The governing body of any incorporated city or town is likewise hereby authorized to plan and undertake urban renewal projects and shall have and possess the same powers and authority granted to or conferred on any housing authority.

(c) As used in this chapter, an urban renewal project may include undertakings and activities for the elimination (and for the prevention of the development or spread) of slums or blighted, deteriorated or deteriorating areas and may involve any work or undertaking for such purpose constituting a redevelopment project authorized by Chapter 2 of this title, or any rehabilitation or conservation work or any combination of such undertaking or work. For this purpose, "rehabilitation or conservation work" may include:

(1) Carrying out plans for a program of voluntary or compulsory repair and rehabilitation of buildings or other improvements;

(2) Acquisition of real property and demolition, removal or rehabilitation of buildings and improvements thereon, where necessary to eliminate unhealthful, unsanitary or unsafe conditions, lessen density, reduce traffic hazards, eliminate obsolete or other uses detrimental to the public welfare, or to otherwise remove or prevent the spread of blight or deterioration or to provide land for needed public facilities;

(3) Installation, construction or reconstruction of streets, utilities, parks, playgrounds and other improvements necessary for carrying out the objectives of the urban renewal project; and

(4) The disposition, for uses in accordance with the objectives of the urban renewal project, of any property or part thereof acquired in the area of such projects; provided that such disposition shall be in the manner prescribed in Chapter 2 of this title for the disposition of property in a redevelopment project area. (Acts 1955, No. 553, p. 1210, § 2; Acts 1967, No. 417, p. 1075, § 2.)

Court cannot supervise discretionary choices made by housing authority unless the authority acts in an arbitrary or capricious manner. Housing Auth. v. Nunn, 292 Ala. 60, 288 So. 2d 775 (1974).

§ 24-3-3. Urban renewal plans.

Any urban renewal project undertaken pursuant to Section 24-3-2 shall be undertaken in accordance with an urban renewal plan for the area of the project. As used in this chapter, an "urban renewal plan" means a plan, as it exists from time to time, for an urban renewal project, which plan shall conform to the general plan for the municipality as a whole and shall be sufficiently complete to indicate such land acquisition, demolition and removal of structures, redevelopment, improvements and rehabilitation as may be proposed to be carried out in the area of the urban renewal project, zoning and planning changes, if any, land uses, maximum densities, building requirements and the plan's relationship to definite local objectives respecting appropriate land uses, improved traffic, public transportation, public utilities, recreational and community facilities and other public improvements. An urban renewal plan shall be prepared and approved pursuant to the same procedure as provided in Chapter 2 of this title, with respect to a redevelopment plan. (Acts 1955, No. 553, p. 1210, § 3.)

§ 24-3-4. Powers, rights, etc., of housing authorities, etc., with respect to urban renewal projects generally; surveys and plans.

An authority shall have all the powers necessary or convenient to undertake and carry out urban renewal plans and urban renewal projects, including the authority to acquire and dispose of property, to make payments to persons and businesses displaced by the acquisition and disposal of any property, to issue bonds and other obligations, to borrow and accept grants from the federal government or other source and to exercise the other powers which Chapter 2 of this title confers on an authority with respect to redevelopment projects. In connection with the planning and undertaking of any urban renewal plan or urban renewal project, the authority, the municipality and all public and private officers, agencies and bodies shall have all the rights, powers, privileges and immunities which they have with respect to a redevelopment plan or redevelopment project, in the same manner as though all of the provisions of Chapter 2 of this title applicable to a redevelopment plan or redevelopment project, were applicable to an urban renewal plan or urban renewal project; provided, that for such purpose the word "redevelopment," as used in Chapter 2 of this title, shall mean "urban renewal," and the word "slum" and the word "blighted," as used in Chapter 2 of this title, shall mean "blighted, deteriorated or deteriorating"; and provided further, that this section shall not change the corporate name of the authority or amend any section of Chapter 2 of this title. In addition to the surveys and plans which an authority is otherwise authorized to make, an authority is hereby specifically authorized to make plans for carrying out a program of voluntary repair and rehabilitation of buildings and improvements and plans for the enforcement of laws, codes and regulations relating to the use of land and the use and occupancy of buildings and improvements, and to the compulsory repair, rehabilitation, demolition or removal of buildings and improvements. The authority is authorized to develop, test and report methods and techniques and carry out demonstrations and other activities for the prevention and the elimination of slums and urban blight. This section shall in no way preclude any municipality or housing authority from acquiring planning funds from any agency of the federal government for the purpose of investigating and planning any urban renewal project to be submitted to the electors of the city or town or housing authority affected under this chapter, and the acquisition of said planning funds shall not require a vote of the duly qualified electors of the city or town or housing authority affected under this chapter. (Acts 1955, No. 553, p. 1210, § 4; Acts 1965, 2nd Ex. Sess., No. 25, p. 38; Acts 1966, Ex. Sess., No. 181, p. 214; Acts 1967, No. 417, p. 1075, § 3; Acts 1969, No. 913, p. 1644; Acts 1971, No. 1359, p. 2301.)

§ 24-3-5. Assistance of urban renewal projects by municipalities, etc.; delegation of powers, etc., of authority to municipalities, etc.

Any municipality or other public body is hereby authorized, without limiting any provision in Section 24-3-4, to do any and all things necessary to aid and cooperate in the planning and undertaking of an urban renewal project in the area in which such municipality or public body is authorized to act, including the furnishing of such financial and other assistance as the municipality or public body is authorized by Chapter 2 of this title to furnish for or in connection with a redevelopment plan or redevelopment project. An authority is hereby authorized to delegate to a municipality or other public body any of the powers or functions of the authority with respect to the planning or undertaking of an urban renewal project in the area in which such municipality or public body is authorized to act, and such municipality or public body is hereby authorized to carry out or perform such powers or functions for the authority. Any public body, including the governing body of an incorporated city or town, is hereby authorized to enter into agreements which may extend over any period, notwithstanding any provision or rule of law to the contrary, with any other public body or bodies respecting action to be taken pursuant to any of the powers granted by this chapter, including the furnishing of funds or other assistance in connection with an urban renewal plan or urban renewal project. (Acts 1955, No. 553, p. 1210, § 5; Acts 1967, No. 417, p. 1075, § 4.)

§ 24-3-6. Workable program.

The governing body of the municipality, or such public officer or public body as it may designate, is hereby authorized to prepare a workable program (which may include an official plan of action, as it exists from time to time, for effectively dealing with the problem of slums and blighted, deteriorated or deteriorating areas within the community and for the establishment and preservation of a well-planned community with well organized residential neighborhoods of decent homes and suitable living environment for adequate family life) for utilizing appropriate private and public resources to eliminate and prevent the development or spread of slums and blight and deterioration, to encourage needed rehabilitation, to provide for the redevelopment of blighted, deteriorated or slum areas or to undertake such of the aforesaid activities or other feasible activities as may be suitably employed to achieve the objectives of such a program. (Acts 1955, No. 553, p. 1210, § 6.)

§ 24-3-7. Acquisition, preparation for development or disposal of undeveloped vacant land by housing authorities, etc.

Notwithstanding any other provision of law, the acquisition, preparation for development or disposal of undeveloped vacant land shall constitute a redevelopment project, under this title or any other law, which may be undertaken in the same manner provided in this title, or any amendments or provisions supplemental thereto, by any housing authority now or hereafter established pursuant to this title or by any governing body of any incorporated city or town, if such acquisition of undeveloped vacant land is determined, as provided in this section, to be essential to the proper clearance, redevelopment, rehabilitation or conservation of a slum or blighted area of a community or to its general slum clearance or urban renewal program. Such determination shall be made by the housing authority of such community or the governing body of any incorporated city or town adopting a resolution to that effect, which shall include a finding that the conditions affecting the land to be acquired (by reason of the predominance of defective or inadequate street layout; faulty lot layout in relation to size or adequacy; lack of accessibility or usefulness; diversity of ownership, tax or special assessment delinquency; defective or unusual conditions of title, improper subdivisions or obsolete plattings; or any one or combination of such factors) substantially impair or arrest the sound growth of the community, retard the provision of needed housing accommodations and constitute an economic or social liability, and that the need for housing accommodations has been or will be increased as a result of the clearance, rehabilitation or conservation of slum or blighted areas in the community. (Acts 1955, No. 553, p. 1210, § 7; Acts 1967, No. 417, p. 1075, § 5.)

§ 24-3-8. Powers conferred by chapter supplemental.

The powers conferred by this chapter shall be in addition and supplemental to the powers conferred by any other law, and nothing contained herein shall be construed as limiting any other powers of a housing authority. (Acts 1955, No. 553, p. 1210, § 9.)

§ 24-3-9. Provisions of chapter cumulative; conflicting laws.

The provisions of this chapter shall be cumulative and supplemental and shall be construed in pari materia with other laws relative to urban renewal plans and urban renewal projects. No law shall be deemed repealed by this chapter unless in specific conflict with this chapter. (Acts 1967, No. 417, p. 1075, § 6.)

CHAPTER 4.

FACTORY-BUILT HOUSING.

REPEALED.

§§ 24-4-1 through 24-4-9. Repealed by Acts 1981, No. 81-706, p. 1183, § 3, effective October 1, 1981.

Code commissioner's note. — Acts 1981, No. 81-705 abolished the modular housing division of the Alabama development office and transferred its powers and duties, etc., to the office of the state fire marshal. The powers and duties, etc., of the fire marshal division of the insurance department relating to manufactured housing have been transferred to the Alabama manufactured housing commission. See § 24-6-4.

CHAPTER 4A.

MANUFACTURED BUILDINGS.

§ 24-4A-1. Legislative findings; purpose of chapter.

The legislature hereby finds that in an effort to meet the housing needs within the state, the private housing and construction industry has developed mass production techniques which can substantially reduce a housing and building cost, and that the mass production of housing and buildings consisting primarily of factory manufacture presents unique problems with respect to the establishment of uniform health and safety standards and inspection procedures. The legislature further finds that by minimizing the problems of standards and inspection procedures, it is demonstrating its intention to encourage the reduction of manufactured building construction costs, and to make housing and home ownership more feasible for all residents of the state. (Acts 1981, No. 81-706, p. 1183, § 1.)

Code commissioner's note. — The functions, powers, duties, etc., of the fire marshal division of the insurance department relating to manufactured housing have been transferred to the Alabama manufactured housing commission, pursuant to § 24-6-4. Therefore, "Alabama manufactured housing commission" or "commission" has been substituted for references to the state fire marshal in this chapter.

Collateral references. — 13 Am. Jur. 2d, Buildings, § 13.

What is "temporary" building or structure within meaning of restrictive covenant. 49 ALR4th 1018.

Products liability: sufficiency of evidence to support product misuse defense in actions concerning commercial or industrial equipment and machinery. 64 ALR4th 10.

§ 24-4A-2. Definitions.

As used in this chapter, the following terms shall have the meanings ascribed to them by this section:

(1) COMMISSION. The Alabama Manufactured Housing Commission.

(2) APPROVED. Conforming to the recognized codes and regulatory requirements adopted by the commission.

(3) APPROVED INSPECTION AGENCY. An organization meeting the commission's requirements to provide inspection of manufactured buildings and to insure compliance with national recognized codes, and rules and regulations adopted by the commission pursuant to this chapter.

(4) LOCAL GOVERNMENT. A city or county government.

(5) MANUFACTURE. The process of making, fabricating, constructing, forming or assembling a product from raw, unfinished or semifinished materials.

(6) INSTALL. The assembly of a manufactured building, components of manufactured building on site and the process of affixing a manufactured building to land, a foundation, footings or an existing building and service connections which are a part thereof.

(7) SITE. The entire tract, subdivision or parcel of land on which a manufactured building is installed.

(8) INSIGNIA. A label, seal or data plate issued by the commission to indicate compliance with the codes and requirements established by the commission pursuant to this chapter.

(9) MOBILE HOME or MANUFACTURED HOME. Any residential dwelling unit constructed to standards and codes as promulgated by the United States Department of Housing and Urban Development.

(10) DWELLING UNIT. One or more habitable rooms which are occupied, intended or designed to be occupied by one or more families with facilities for living, sleeping, cooking and eating.

(11) EQUIPMENT. All materials, appliances, devices, fixtures, fittings or accessories installed in or used in the manufacture and assembly of a manufactured building.

(12) SYSTEM. Structural, plumbing, mechanical, heating, electrical or ventilating elements, materials or components combined for use in a manufactured building.

(13) MANUFACTURED BUILDING. A closed structure, building assembly or systems of subassemblies, which may include structural, electrical, plumbing, heating, ventilating, utility service lines, footings, foundations, porches or other service systems manufactured in manufacturing facilities, for installation or erection, with or without other specified components, as a finished building or as a part of a finished building, which shall include, but not be limited to, residential dwelling units, commercial, institutional, storage and industrial structures. "Mobile homes" or "manufactured homes" are excluded. "Manufactured building" may also mean, at the option of the manufacturer, any building of open construction made or assembled in manufacturing facilities away from the building site, for installation, or assembly and installation, on the building site.

(14) CLOSED CONSTRUCTION. That condition when any building, component, assembly, subassembly or system is manufactured in such a manner that all portions cannot be readily inspected at the site without disassembly or destruction thereof.

(15) OPEN CONSTRUCTION. Any building, building component, assembly or systems manufactured in such a manner that all portions can be readily inspected at the site without disassembly, damage to or destruction thereof.

(16) FEES. Moneys to be paid to the commission from any and all persons, firms, companies, corporations and manufacturers engaged in the manufacture or installation of manufactured buildings.

232

(17) COMPONENT. Any assembly, subassembly or combination of parts for use as a part of a building, which may include structural, electrical, mechanical and fire protection systems, and other systems affecting health and safety.

(18) MODEL. A specific design of manufactured building which is based on size, room arrangement, method of construction, location arrangement or size of plumbing, heating or electrical equipment systems.

(19) MODULAR HOME. A manufactured building built and inspected in accordance with a national building code and in compliance with the provisions of this chapter. (Acts 1981, No. 81-706, p. 1183, § 2.)

Code commissioner's note. — The functions, powers, duties, etc., of the fire marshal division of the insurance department relating to manufactured housing have been transferred to the Alabama manufactured housing commission, pursuant to § 24-6-4.

Collateral references. — What is "temporary" building or structure within meaning of restrictive covenant. 49 ALR4th 1018.

§ 24-4A-3. Powers and duties of commission generally; insignia of approval; modification of units prior to or during installation; authority of local government agencies; fee schedule; manufactured buildings approved by other states.

(a) The commission is authorized to promulgate rules, and enter into contracts, and do such things as may be necessary and incidental to the administration of its authority pursuant to this chapter.

(b) After the effective date of the rules adopted pursuant to this chapter, no manufactured building shall be sold, or offered for sale, or installed, in this state unless it is approved and bears the insignia of approval of the commission.

(c) The Factory-Built Housing Act of 1971 and the rules promulgated under that act shall continue until the effective date of subsection (b) of this section, and thereafter shall be repealed. All personnel of the modular housing division of the Alabama development office shall be transferred without impairment of their merit system status to the commission, and all funds, appropriations, papers, documents, files, materials, equipment, supplies and other effects employed and used for the administration and enforcement of the previous act shall become the property of the commission. All approvals issued by the commission under the provisions of the prior act shall be deemed to comply with the requirements of this chapter.

(d) All manufactured buildings issued and bearing insignia of approval pursuant to subsections (b) and (c) of this section shall be deemed to comply with the requirements of all ordinances or regulations enacted by any local government which are applicable to the construction of manufactured buildings. The determination by the commission of the scope of such approval is final.

(e) No manufactured building bearing commission insignia of approval pursuant to subsection (b) of this section shall be in any way modified prior to or during installation unless approval is first obtained from the commission.

(f) Manufactured buildings which have been issued and bear the insignia of approval pursuant to this chapter upon manufacture or first sale shall not require an additional approval or insignia by a local government in which they are subsequently sold or installed, except a residential dwelling unit that is resold, whether by a manufacturer, manufacturer's representative or dealer; these units must bear an additional seal of approval issued by the commission.

(g) The commission by rule shall establish a schedule of fees to give cost relief to the commission for the work related to the administration and enforcement of this chapter. All fees collected under the provisions of this chapter, or otherwise inuring to the credit of the commission, shall be deposited in the state treasury in a fund to be designated as the "state fire marshals fund."

(h) If the commission determines that standards for construction and inspection of manufactured buildings prescribed by statute or rule of another state are at least equal to standards prescribed by the commission under this chapter and such standards are actually enforced by such other state, the commission may provide by rule that a manufactured building, which has been inspected and approved by such other state or its delegated inspection agency, shall be deemed to have been approved by the commission, and shall authorize the affixing of the appropriate insignia of approval.

(i) The use of the word "modular," singular or in combination with any other word to describe a mobile home or manufactured home, is hereby prohibited, and said use shall constitute a violation of the provisions of this chapter.

(j) Any city or county official who violates the provisions of this chapter by refusing to accept a manufactured building approved by the commission shall personally be liable and not be immune from prosecution if suit is brought by a party to said transaction.

(k) This section shall not apply to factory built housing which is inspected and approved by a local government agency at the place of, and during the time of manufacture in accordance with local building requirements if the requirements are reasonably consistent with standards established by the Southern Building Codes Congress, the National Fire Protection Association and the United States Department of Housing and Urban Development. The cost of the inspection shall be borne by the manufacturer.

(l) All factory-built housing bearing an insignia of approval issued by the commission pursuant to this chapter shall be deemed to comply with the requirements of all ordinances or regulations enacted by any local government which are applicable to the manufacturer of such housing. The determination by the commission of the scope of such approval is final.

(m) No factory-built housing bearing a commission insignia of approval pursuant to this chapter shall be in any way modified prior to or during installation unless approval is first obtained from the commission.

(n) Factory-built housing which has been inspected and approved by a local government agency shall not be modified prior to or during installation unless approval for the modification is first obtained from the local government agency.

(o) The commission by rule shall establish a schedule of fees to pay the costs incurred by it for the work related to administration and enforcement of this section. (Acts 1981, No. 81-706, p. 1183, § 3.)

Code commissioner's note. — The functions, powers, duties, etc., of the fire marshal division of the insurance department relating to manufactured housing have been transferred to the Alabama manufactured housing commission, pursuant to § 24-6-4.

The Factory-Built Housing Act of 1971, to which reference is made in subsection (c) of this section, was codified as former Chapter 4 of this title.

Cross references. — As to Alabama manufactured housing commission fund, see § 24-6-4(b).

Collateral references. — 39A C.J.S., Health and Environment, § 28.

13 Am. Jur. 2d, Buildings, §§ 2, 5.

§ 24-4A-4. Enforcement of chapter; delegation of enforcement authority; promulgation of rules and regulations.

(a) The commission shall enforce the provisions of this chapter and the regulations adopted pursuant hereto; except, that the commission may delegate its enforcement authority to a local government agency, an approved inspection agency or an agency of another state, provided the inspection agencies' inspection requirements conform with the requirements of the commission.

(b) The commission shall promulgate rules and regulations to interpret and make specific the provisions of this chapter. These rules shall include provisions imposing requirements reasonably consistent with recognized and accepted standards adopted by the Southern Building Codes Congress, International, the National Fire Protection Association or any other nationally recognized building standards. (Acts 1981, No. 81-706, p. 1183, § 4.)

Collateral references. — 39A C.J.S., Health and Environment, § 28.

13 Am. Jur. 2d, Buildings, § 5.

§ 24-4A-5. Injunctive relief.

The commission may obtain injunctive relief from the proper circuit court to enjoin the sale, delivery or installation of manufactured building upon an affidavit specifying the manner in which the building does not conform to the requirements of this chapter or to rules issued pursuant hereto. (Acts 1981, No. 81-706, p. 1183, § 5.)

Collateral references. — 13 Am. Jur. 2d, Buildings, §§ 34, 40.

§ 24-4A-6. Penalties.

A person who violates any of the provisions of this chapter or any rule adopted pursuant hereto is guilty of a misdemeanor, punishable by a fine of $500.00, or by imprisonment for 30 days, or both. A separate violation shall be deemed to have occurred with respect to each building unit (building component) involved. (Acts 1981, No. 81-706, p. 1183, § 6.)

§ 24-4A-7. Exemption of pre-engineered metal buildings.

The provisions of this chapter omit pre-engineered metal buildings. (Acts 1981, No. 81-706, p. 1183, § 7.)

CHAPTER 5.

MOBILE HOMES.

Collateral references. — 54 Am. Jur. 2d, Mobile Homes, Trailer Parks & Tourist Camps, §§ 5-16.

ARTICLE 1.

UNIFORM STANDARDS CODE.

§ 24-5-1. Short title.

This article shall be known and may be cited as "The Uniform Standards Code for Mobile Homes Act." (Acts 1971, No. 1938, p. 3129, § 1.)

Code commissioner's note. — The functions, powers, duties, etc., of the fire marshal division of the insurance department relating to mobile homes have been transferred to the Alabama manufactured housing commission, pursuant to § 24-6-4. Therefore, "Alabama manufactured housing commission" or "commission" has been substituted for references to the state fire marshal in this article.

§ 24-5-2. Definitions.

Unless clearly indicated otherwise by the context, the following words when used in this article, for purposes of this article, shall have the meanings respectively ascribed to them in this section:

(1) MOBILE HOME. A structure, transportable in one or more sections, which when erected on site measures eight body feet or more in width and thirty-two body feet or more in length, built on a permanent chassis and designed to be used as a dwelling, with or without a permanent foundation, when connected to the required utilities, and includes the plumbing, heating, air-conditioning and electrical systems contained therein. A mobile home can be new. A new mobile home is a mobile home which is still in the possession of the manufacturer, dealer or first purchaser of the mobile home.

(2) UNIFORM STANDARDS CODE. The federal mobile home construction or safety standards promulgated pursuant to Section 604 of the National Mobile Home Construction and Safety Standards Act of 1974 published in Public Law 93-383, 42 U.S.C. § 5401 et seq. as amended from time to time.

(3) MOBILE HOME CONSTRUCTION. All activities relating to the assembly and manufacture of a mobile home including but not limited to those relating to durability, quality and safety.

(4) LABEL. The approved form of certification by the manufacturer under the provisions of the National Mobile Home Construction and Safety Standards Act of 1974 that is permanently affixed to each mobile home or transportable section thereof, and which serves as the certification by the manufacturer of conformance with the applicable federal mobile home construction and safety standards in effect the date of manufacture.

(5) MANUFACTURER. Any person who manufactures mobile homes and shall include the manufacturer, factory branch or factory representative.

(6) DEALER. Any person other than a manufacturer, as defined in this section, who is duly licensed to sell mobile homes in this state.

(7) PERSON. A person, firm, partnership, company, corporation or association engaged in manufacturing or selling mobile homes.

(8) MARSHAL. The Alabama State Fire Marshal.

(9) COMMISSION. The Alabama Manufactured Housing Commission.

(10) STATE FIRE MARSHAL'S FUND. The fund established to provide necessary revenue for the enforcement of this article. (Acts 1971, No. 1938, p. 3129, § 2; Acts 1980, No. 80-599, p. 1014, § 1.)

Cross references. — As to Alabama manufactured housing commission fund, see § 24-6-4(b). As to state fire marshal generally, see § 36-19-1 et seq.

U.S. Code. — Section 604 of the National Mobile Home Construction and Safety Standards Act of 1974 is codified as 42 U.S.C. § 5403.

Cited in Town of Helena v. Country Mobile Homes, Inc., 387 So. 2d 162 (Ala. 1980).

§ 24-5-3. Establishment of uniform standards.

All construction of mobile homes manufactured after May 28, 1980, in this state must meet the standards of the Uniform Standards Code. (Acts 1971, No. 1938, p. 3129, § 3; Acts 1980, No. 80-599, p. 1014, § 2.)

§ 24-5-4. Inspection or approval; label of approval; certification of manufacturer prior to sale or offer for sale of new mobile home.

No person may sell or offer to sell in the state any new mobile home for use in this state manufactured after May 28, 1980, unless:

(1) A label of approval has been permanently affixed to the mobile home; and

(2) It bears a certification by the manufacturer that the new mobile home to which the label is attached meets or exceeds the Uniform Standards Code. (Acts 1971, No. 1938, p. 3129, § 4; Acts 1980, No. 80-599, p. 1014, § 3.)

§ 24-5-5. Manufacture of mobile homes not bearing label and certification.

No person may manufacture in this state any mobile home after May 28, 1980, unless it bears a label and certification, certifying that the mobile home meets or exceeds the Uniform Standards Code. (Acts 1971, No. 1938, p. 3129, § 5; Acts 1980, No. 80-599, p. 1014, § 4.)

§ 24-5-6. Licenses for sale of mobile homes.

(a) Any manufacturer or dealer within or without this state shall apply for a license to sell mobile homes in this state.

(b) Applications will be obtained from and submitted to the commission.

(c) The original license fee shall be $100.00 and the renewal fee shall be $100.00 per annum. Each sales or manufacturing location shall be required to be licensed at the same rate and basis as others. The license shall be valid from January 1 until December 31 of the year in which it was issued or until revoked as provided in this section.

(d) Any such license may be revoked or suspended by the commission for violation of the provisions of this article, or rules and regulations or standards or codes or specifications adopted pursuant hereto. The commission shall notify the licensee in writing of the reasons why it intends to revoke or suspend the license, and the licensee shall be entitled to a hearing before the commission within 10 days after receipt of such notice of intention to revoke or suspend. At such hearing the commission shall consider the circumstances and shall give the licensee reasonable time, but not less than 30 days, to correct the conditions or circumstances that caused the notice of intention to revoke or suspend the license to be given. (Acts 1971, No. 1938, p. 3129, § 6; Acts 1975, No. 1143, p. 2245; Acts 1980, No. 80-599, p. 1014, § 5.)

§ 24-5-7. Sale of new mobile homes without labels.

A new mobile home which does not bear the label required by this article shall not be offered for sale by any manufacturer or dealer anywhere within the geographical limits of this state. (Acts 1971, No. 1938, p. 3129, § 7; Acts 1980, No. 80-599, p. 1014, § 6.)

§ 24-5-8. Reciprocity. Repealed by Acts 1980, No. 80-599, p. 1014, § 7, effective May 28, 1980.

§ 24-5-9. Inspection of manufacturing, sales, etc., establishments; testing of products, etc.; test records.

(a) The commission shall cause to be inspected, at such times as it may deem proper, any place or establishment within this state where mobile homes are manufactured, sold or offered for sale, for the purpose of ascertaining whether the requirements of this article and the regulations of the commission have been met.

(b) The commission or its duly authorized representatives, may cause products or parts or portions thereof to be analyzed or tested by the state agent or its duly authorized agency. Such analysis or test records may be preserved by the commission, and when sworn to by the state testing agent or its duly authorized agency, shall be prima facie evidence of violations of this article or rules and regulations or standards or codes or specifications adopted pursuant to this article. (Acts 1971, No. 1938, p. 3129, § 8.)

§ 24-5-10. Fees for licenses; authorization; state fire marshal's fund.

(a) A license to sell to licensed dealers or to the public of this state shall be issued for a $100.00 original fee and the renewal fee shall be $100.00 per annum renewable by the first day of each calendar year.

(b) All fees shall be paid to the commission to provide necessary revenue for the enforcement of this article. All fees collected under the provisions of this article, or otherwise inuring to the credit of the commission, shall be deposited in the State Treasury in a fund to be designated as the "state fire marshal's fund," which fund is hereby established. All balances in said fund in excess of $50,000.00 at the end of each fiscal year shall be transferred to the state general fund. The expenses incurred by the commission in carrying out the provisions of this article, together with the compensation of employees required to enforce this article, shall be paid from this fund. (Acts 1971, No. 1938, p. 3129, § 9; Acts 1975, No. 1051, p. 2114; Acts 1980, No. 80-599, p. 1014, § 8.)

Code commissioner's note. — Acts 1988, 1st Ex. Sess., No. 88-875, which amended sections 27-4-2, 27-7-7, 27-8-5 and 27-39-6, pertaining to the collection of certain fees and licenses by the Commissioner of Insurance, provided in section 2 of the act: "It is the legislative intent that nothing in this act shall be construed to affect the Special Examination Revolving Fund, as provided for in Section 27-2-25, Code of Alabama 1975, or the State Fire Marshal's Fund, as provided for in Section 24-5-10, Code of Alabama 1975."

Cross references. — As to Alabama manufactured housing commission fund, see § 24-6-4(b).

§ 24-5-11. Records and statistics as to manufacture, sale, etc., of mobile homes.

(a) The commission shall maintain a system by which accurate statistics regarding the disposition of all mobile homes by licensees may be obtained.

(b) The commission shall require that each licensee in this state maintain adequate records so as to ascertain:

(1) The total number of mobile homes manufactured;

(2) The total number of mobile homes delivered to dealers within and without the state;

(3) The total number of mobile homes sold to individuals within and without the state, including name, address and county; and

(4) Specific information about each mobile home, including serial number, manufacturer's name, model name and/or number and size unit. (Acts 1971, No. 1938, p. 3129, § 10.)

§ 24-5-12. Administration of article.

The commission is hereby charged with the administration of this article. It shall make and amend, alter or repeal general rules and regulations of procedure for carrying into effect all provisions of this article and prescribe means, methods and practices to make effective such provisions. (Acts 1971, No. 1938, p. 3129, § 11.)

§ 24-5-13. Enforcement of article; local ordinances providing for inspection of mobile homes.

(a) No person may interfere, obstruct or hinder an authorized representative of the commission who displays proper commission credentials in the performance of his duties as set forth in the provisions of this article.

(b) In the performance of its duties, the commission or any of its duly authorized representatives is hereby authorized to enter and inspect, at any reasonable time, any place or establishment where mobile homes are manufactured, sold or offered for sale, for the purpose of ascertaining whether the requirements of this article and the regulations of the commission have been met.

(c) Nothing in this article shall prevent the governing authority of any county or municipal corporation from adopting ordinances or resolutions providing for the inspection of mobile homes sold or placed within its limits and to provide penalties for violations thereof, but no such ordinance or resolution shall conflict with any power or authority of the commission or its duly authorized representatives. Any mobile home which has been inspected and approved in accordance with the provisions of this article shall not be required to comply with any local ordinances in conflict with this article. (Acts 1971, No. 1938, p. 3129, § 12.)

§ 24-5-13.1. Commission authorized to enter into contracts with agencies dealing with federal Department of Housing and Urban Development; purpose.

The commission shall be authorized to enter into contracts with any private or public agency which is under contract with the United States Department of Housing and Urban Development to provide services in the enforcement of the Uniform Standards Code. (Acts 1980, No. 80-599, p. 1014, § 10.)

§ 24-5-14. Penalties; disposition of funds.

(a) Whoever violates any provision of this article or any regulation or order issued under the provisions of this article shall be liable for a civil penalty of not to exceed $1,000 for each such violation. Each violation of any section of this article or regulation or order shall constitute a separate violation with respect to each mobile home or with respect to each failure or refusal to allow or perform an act required thereby, except that the maximum civil penalty may not exceed $1,000,000.00 for any related series of violations occurring within one year from the date of the first violation. Before the commission shall impose a civil penalty it shall first advise the violator of its intention to do so and hold a hearing on said violation no sooner than two weeks after notification to the person of the commission's intent to impose civil penalties and the indicated violations.

(b) Any individual or a director, officer or agent of a corporation who knowingly and willfully violates any of the provisions set out in subsection (a) of this section, in a manner which threatens the health or safety of any purchaser, shall be fined not more than $1,000.00 or sentenced to the county jail for not more than one year or both.

(c) Any fines collected under the provisions of subsections (a) and (b) of this section shall be paid into the fire marshal's fund set up by the provisions of this article. (Acts 1971, No. 1938, p. 3129, § 13; Acts 1980, No. 80-599, p. 1014, § 9.)

Cross references. — As to Alabama manufactured housing commission fund, see § 24-6-4(b).

ARTICLE 2.

ANCHORING.

§ 24-5-30. Short title.

This article shall be known and may be cited as the "Uniform Code for the Anchoring of Mobile Homes Act." (Acts 1975, No. 1144, p. 2247, § 1.)

Code commissioner's note. — The functions, powers, duties, etc., of the fire marshal division of the insurance department relating to mobile homes have been transferred to the Alabama manufactured housing commission, pursuant to § 24-6-4. Therefore, "Alabama manufactured housing commission" or "commission" has been substituted for references to the state fire marshal in this article.

§ 24-5-31. Definitions.

When used in this article, unless the context plainly indicates otherwise, the following words and phrases shall have the meanings respectively ascribed to them in this section:

(1) ANSI. The American National Standards Institute or its successor.

(2) GROUND ANCHOR. Any device at the mobile home stand designed for the purpose of securing a mobile home to the ground.

(3) MARSHAL. The Alabama State Fire Marshal.

(4) NFPA. The National Fire Protection Association or its successor.

(5) TIEDOWN. Any device designed to anchor a mobile home to ground anchors.

(6) COMMISSION. The Alabama Manufactured Housing Commission.

(7) INSTALL or INSTALLATION. Siting, placing or anchoring a manufactured home or manufactured building, either one or more units, to land, upon footings, piers or foundations, or connecting the home or building to public or private utilities. Public or private utilities shall not be classified as installers under this section.

(8) INSTALLER. Any person who sites, anchors, places, connects, sets up or installs a manufactured home or manufactured building upon land, footings, piers or foundations.

(9) MANUFACTURED BUILDING. A closed structure, building assembly or systems of subassemblies which may include structural, electrical, plumbing, heating, ventilating, utility service lines, footings, foundations, porches or other service systems manufactured in manufacturing facilities, for installation or erection, with or without other specified components, as a finished building or as a part of a finished building, which shall include, but not be limited to, residential dwelling units, commercial, institutional, storage and industrial structures. "Mobile homes" or "manufactured homes" are excluded. "Manufactured building" may also mean, at the option of the manufacturer, any building of open construction made or assembled in manufacturing facilities away from the building site, for installation, or assembly and installation on the building site.

(10) MANUFACTURED HOME. As defined by the United States Department of Housing and Urban Development. (Acts 1975, No. 1144, p. 2247, § 2; Acts 1991, No. 91-642, p. 1213, § 1.)

The 1991 amendment, effective August 8, 1991, added subdivisions (7) through (10).

§ 24-5-32. Anchorage requirements.

(a) After January 1, 1976, it shall be unlawful for any person to install, allow to be installed, occupy or allow to be occupied any new or used manufactured home or manufactured building unless the home or building is tied down to properly installed ground anchors so as to be able to resist wind loads as specified in the rules and regulations adopted by the commission. The Counties of Mobile and Baldwin are designated as hurricane wind zones. All installers of manufactured homes and manufactured buildings must be certified by the commission to install such structures.

(b) Any manufactured home or manufactured building sold after January 1, 1976, shall comply with the requirements of subsection (a) immediately upon location on the new site. Any existing manufactured home or manufactured building relocated to a new site after January 1, 1976, shall comply with the code requirements of subsection (a) immediately upon location on the new site.

(c) The commission shall promulgate rules and regulations setting forth uniform standards for the manufacture and installation of ground anchors and blocking to be compatible with ANSI A 119.1/NFPA 501B, in order to accomplish the intent of this section. Local building inspectors shall, when required by local jurisdiction, enforce rules and regulations promulgated by the commission to accomplish the intent of this section.

(d) Prior to adoption of the initial rules and regulations and in the event it becomes necessary to make changes in or additions to the rules and regulations adopted in subsection (a), the commission, at least 30 days prior to adopting or promulgating any such rules and regulations or changes or additions, shall mail to all manufacturers and service organizations doing business in Alabama and to the Alabama Manufactured Housing Institute a notice which shall include a copy of the rules and regulations or additions and changes thereto, and a designation of the time and place that the commission will hear and consider any objections to the proposed rules and regulations or additions and changes thereto. The commission shall afford any interested party an opportunity to be heard orally or in writing with respect to the proposed rules and regulations or additions and changes thereto. Sixty days after date of notice and hearing, any rules and regulations or changes and additions thereto shall become effective.

(e) This section shall not apply to any mobile home which is in transit between sites.

(f) The commission shall establish by rule a schedule of fees to pay for the administration of this article. (Acts 1975, No. 1144, p. 2247, § 3; Acts 1991, No. 91-642, p. 1213, § 2.)

The 1991 amendment, effective August 8, 1991, rewrote subsections (a) and (b) and added subsection (f).

§ 24-5-33. Penalties for violations of article; suspension of license tags; additional relief from violations.

(a) It is a misdemeanor for any person to install, allow to be installed, occupy, or allow to be occupied, any manufactured home or manufactured building in this state which is not in accordance with the uniform standards and the rules and regulations adopted and set forth by the commission pursuant to this article.

(b) The commission is authorized to suspend the tag issued under Section 40-12-255 of any person violating either subsection (a) or (b) of Section 24-5-32, and shall be authorized to levy a civil penalty up to $500.00 against any person found in violation of subsection (a) of Section 24-5-32. The commission is moreover authorized to levy a civil penalty up to $500.00 against any installer or installation personnel violating either subsection (a) or (b) of Section 24-5-32 or the rules and regulations adopted and set forth by the commission pursuant to this article. Persons subjected to the operation of this subsection shall be given a hearing by the commission on application therefor, and shall be notified of the availability of a hearing by the commission on imposition of a penalty.

(c) In addition to other penalties provided by law, the commission and district attorneys are authorized to apply to the circuit courts within their respective jurisdictions, and such courts shall have jurisdiction, upon hearing and for cause shown, to grant appropriate additional relief to prevent or restrain violations of this article. (Acts 1975, No. 1144, p. 2247, § 3; Acts 1991, No. 91-642, p. 1213, § 3.)

The 1991 amendment, effective August 8, 1991, rewrote subsection (a) and added the second sentence of subsection (b).

§ 24-5-34. Certain local laws, municipal ordinances, etc., not repealed.

This article shall not repeal any local act, general law of local application or municipal ordinance where provisions thereof have standards, qualifications and requirements for the anchoring of mobile homes equal to or higher than those provided in this article, and such laws, acts or ordinances shall remain entirely in full force and effect. (Acts 1975, No. 1144, p. 2247, § 4.)

CHAPTER 6.

ALABAMA MANUFACTURED HOUSING COMMISSION.

§ 24-6-1. Intent.

It is the express intent of this chapter to give administrative relief to the Fire Marshal Division of the Insurance Department in the supervision of any current or future federal and state statutes and codes relating to manufactured and modular housing and buildings. For such purposes, the Alabama Manufactured Housing Commission is created to perform such administrative functions. (Acts 1985, No. 85-691, p. 1109, § 1.)

§ 24-6-2. Alabama Manufactured Housing Commission created; functions, powers, and duties.

The Alabama Manufactured Housing Commission, hereinafter referred to as "the commission," is hereby created and shall function as the principal executive branch agency with powers to provide for a comprehensive manufactured housing and building program with respect to construction, transportation, site location or manufacturing standards for such structures. The commission shall have such other powers and duties as are hereinafter provided. (Acts 1985, No. 85-691, p. 1109, § 2.)

§ 24-6-3. Appointment of commission members; reappointment; vacancies; secretary; chairman; compensation and expenses; meetings.

The commission shall be composed of six members, five of which shall be appointed by the Governor as follows:

(1) From a list of six nominees submitted by the Alabama Housing Institute, the Governor shall select three members, one of whom shall serve a three-year term of office and two of whom shall serve four-year terms of office each; thereafter all future nominees shall be submitted as herein provided and all successors shall serve terms of office of four years each. Of the three persons selected, one shall be a representative of the modular housing industry, one shall be a representative of the manufactured building industry, and one shall be a representative of the manufactured housing/mobile home industry. No employee of the Alabama Manufactured

Housing Institute shall serve on the Alabama Manufactured Housing Commission as either a nonvoting or voting member and they shall not be responsible for keeping the records of the commission.

(2) The Governor shall appoint from the general public, one member who is a consumer representative whose initial term of office shall be one year and successors shall serve a four-year term of office.

(3) The Governor shall appoint one member who is a representative from any local or state government agency for an initial term of office of two years and successors shall serve a four-year term of office.

Appointed members shall be eligible for reappointment. Any vacancy shall be filled by the Governor for the unexpired term in the same manner as the original appointment was made. The commission shall select a person who shall serve as the sixth member and who shall be a nonvoting member and shall serve permanently as the secretary of the commission, and shall keep all notes and minutes of the meetings. The appointed members shall select from among their number a chairman each three years, who shall preside over the meetings of the commission.

All members, including the secretary, shall be paid $100.00 for each day the commission meets and shall receive the same per diem and allowance as is paid state employees for meetings of the commission. The commission shall meet upon the call of its chairman monthly, or 12 times per year. (Acts 1985, No. 85-691, p. 1109, § 3.)

§ 24-6-4. Functions of commission; transfer of functions, etc., from Fire Marshal's Division within State Department of Insurance; Alabama manufactured housing commission fund; rules and regulations; fees to pay cost of work under this chapter; contracts; employees; effect of chapter on other agencies and departments.

(a) The commission shall be the principal staff agency of the executive branch to provide, with the cooperation of other departments of state governmental units, a comprehensive housing program and procedures which include the relevance for housing programs administered by the state and the governmental structures required to put such programs into effect. The commission shall perform all the duties and exercise all the powers and authority relative to modular housing, manufactured buildings, manufactured housing and mobile homes, heretofore vested in the Fire Marshal's Division within the State Department of Insurance, and other implied powers. All the functions, powers, authority and duties provided by law, specifically, but not limited to: Sections 24-5-1 through 24-5-14; 24-5-30 through 24-5-34; and 24-4A-1 through 24-4A-7, all of the Code of Alabama 1975, all books, records, and supplies, pursuant to and under the authority of the aforesaid code sections through legislative budgetary authority and duties provided by law, specifically, but not limited to: Sections 24-5-1 through 24-5-14; 24-5-30 through 24-5-34; and 24-4A-1 through 24-4A-7, all of the Code of Alabama

1975, and all books, records, supplies, equipment, documents, files, papers, materials, and personnel of the Fire Marshal's Division subject to and authorized by, or under these various code sections and related thereto are also hereby transferred to the commission. Funds in the amount of $110,364.00 appropriated to the Fire Marshal's Division for fiscal year 1985-1986 for those functions and purposes enumerated in the above code sections shall be transferred and appropriated to the commission. Also transferred and appropriated to the commission are all funds received from contracts performed by the commission on or after October 1, 1985, pursuant to Section 24-5-13.1, pertaining to mobile homes, manufactured housing and manufactured buildings. The housing coordinator shall serve as administrator of the commission, and along with all other employees to be transferred, shall be transferred without any impairment to his or their present merit system status. All employees of the said commission shall retain their status as state merit system employees and enjoy the benefit thereof.

(b) There is hereby established a revolving fund in the State Treasury to be known as the "Alabama manufactured housing commission fund." Any proceeds remaining at the end of each fiscal year shall not revert to the state general fund, but shall carry forward to the succeeding fiscal years for the use of the commission. All proceeds from federal grants, loans, funds, fees, and state or federal appropriations received or collected by the commission heretofore or hereafter is so appropriated and to be deposited in this account and is to be used only for and to the enurement of this commission.

(c) The commission is authorized to promulgate such rules and regulations not inconsistent with this chapter as are implied or stated as are necessary to carry out the provisions of this chapter, pertaining specifically to the manufacture, transportation, or site location of said housing and buildings and building programs in the State of Alabama. The commission is further authorized to promulgate such rules and regulations as it may deem necessary to meet the requirements of the Department of Housing and Urban Development, the National Fire Protection Association or any other recognized standards.

(d) The commission, by rules or regulations, shall establish a schedule of fees to pay the cost incurred by the said commission for the work related to the administration and enforcement of this chapter. All fees, funds, and moneys received by the commission are hereby appropriated to the commission and to be used only to the enrichment of the said commission.

(e) The commission may enter into any contracts with public or private agencies.

(f) The commission is authorized to hire or fire an administrator and all other employees under the state merit system law. The commission is authorized to set qualifications for employees and compensation through the merit system, for the necessary employees to carry out the provisions of this chapter.

(g) The commission is authorized to: make comprehensive and detailed plans for combating the shortage of safe and sanitary housing in Alabama;

apply for and accept advances, loans, grants, contributions, and any other forms of assistance from the federal government, state or other public body, or from any other source, public or private; enter into and carry out contracts or agreements in connection with programs funded by the aforesaid sources to serve a public purpose and benefit the citizens of the State of Alabama; and prepare proper legislation to administer the programs.

(h) This chapter shall not prevent an agency or department of state government from administering the program for which they are responsible. (Acts 1985, No. 85-691, p. 1109, § 4.)

CHAPTER 7.

MOWA CHOCTAW HOUSING AUTHORITY.

§ 24-7-1. Definitions.

As used in this chapter, the following words shall have the following meanings ascribed to them:

(1) PROJECT. Any low-rent housing hereafter developed or acquired by the authority with financial assistance of the United States of America acting through the Secretary of Housing and Urban Development.

(2) TRIBE. The Mowa Band of Choctaw Indians.

(3) RESERVATION. Any land, the title to which is held by the Mowa Band of Choctaw Indians. (Acts 1986, No. 86-537, § 5; Acts 1989, No. 89-697, p. 1377, § 1.)

§ 24-7-2. Mowa Choctaw Housing Authority created; membership; terms of office; officers; removal; quorum; proxies; location of meetings.

There is hereby created and established an Indian housing authority for the jurisdictions of Mobile and Washington Counties, to be styled the Mowa Choctaw Housing Authority, whose purpose shall be the provision of safe and decent dwelling places for low-income persons and families in Indian areas.

The Mowa Choctaw Housing Authority shall consist of seven members, and shall be appointed by the Mowa Choctaw tribal council. No person shall be barred from serving as a member of the authority because he is a tenant or home buyer in a tribal housing project.

Members of the Mowa Choctaw Housing Authority, hereinafter styled the authority, shall serve a term of five years from their appointment, and may serve an unlimited number of terms. In the event of a vacancy on the authority, the Mowa Choctaw tribal council shall appoint a successor to fill the unexpired term.

The authority shall select from among its members a chairman, a vice-chairman, a secretary, and a treasurer. No member shall hold two offices upon the authority. The chairman shall preside at meetings of the authority. The vice-chairman shall preside in the absence of the chairman. In the absence of both the chairman and vice-chairman, the secretary shall preside.

The tribal council may remove any member of the authority for neglect of duty, inefficiency, or misconduct in office, but only after a hearing before the authority, and only after such member has been given a written notice of the charges against him at least 10 days prior to the hearing. At such hearing, the member shall have the opportunity to be heard in person or by counsel and to present witnesses on his behalf.

Four members shall constitute a quorum for the conduct of business of the authority. A member who is unable to attend a meeting in person may present, in writing, a dated and signed voting proxy to a designated representative, who shall attend the meeting and act in his place and stead.

The normal domicile of the authority is Mobile and Washington Counties. Meetings of the authority may be held at other locations within the state upon notification of the members by certified mail, at least 10 days prior to the meeting date. (Acts 1986, No. 86-537, § 1; Acts 1989, No. 89-697, p. 1377, § 1; Acts 1991, No. 91-121, p. 142, § 1.)

The 1991 amendment, effective May 16, 1991, substituted the present language of the first paragraph beginning with "decent" for "healthy dwelling places for low-income members of the Mowa Band of Choctaw Indians of Mobile and Washington counties"; and, in the first sentence of the fifth paragraph, substituted "tribal council" for "governor" and deleted "which shall forward findings of fact and their recommendations to the governor" following "before the authority."

§ 24-7-3. Powers and duties; applicable laws; power of appointment.

The authority is hereby authorized:

(1) To undertake research and studies and analyses of housing needs in Mobile and Washington Counties, and means by which such needs may be met, including data with respect to population and family groups and the distribution thereof according to income groups, the amount and quality of available housing and its distribution according to rental and sales prices, and employment, wages and other factors affecting the local housing needs and the meeting thereof, and make the results and analyses available to the public and the building, housing and supply industries;

(2) To enter into contracts with cities, towns, counties, and other housing authorities in the state for the purpose of carrying out the provisions of this chapter;

(3) To establish rentals and select tenants in low income rental housing projects under its jurisdiction;

(4) To issue bonds, notes, and other evidence of indebtedness for the purpose of financing the construction of housing for low-income persons;

(5) To obtain, rent, lease, or otherwise obtain from any county, city, or state, properties of such public bodies as are offered for use to the authority for the purpose of providing housing to low-income persons and families in Indian areas;

(6) To enter into contracts and agreements with agents of the United States government for the purpose of purchasing land, acquiring, constructing, renovating, providing streets, utilities, and landscaping grounds for

rental and other housing for low-income persons and families in designated Indian areas; and

(7) All powers, rights, and functions specified for municipal housing authorities created pursuant to Sections 24-1-20 through 24-1-45.

All provisions of law applicable to housing authorities created pursuant to Title 24 for municipalities and the commissioner of such authorities shall be applicable to the Mowa Choctaw Housing Authority, unless a different meaning clearly appears from the context.

The tribal chairman and the tribal council of the Mowa Band of Choctaw Indians is hereby authorized to exercise all appointing and other powers with respect to an Indian housing authority that are vested in the chief executive officer and governing body of a municipality pursuant to Title 24 with respect to municipal housing authorities. (Acts 1986, No. 86-537, § 2; Acts 1989, No. 89-697, p. 1377, § 1; Acts 1991, No. 91-121, p. 142, § 1.)

The 1991 amendment, effective May 16, 1991, in subdivision (5) substituted "persons and families in Indian areas" for "members of the Mowa Band of Choctaw Indians," and in subdivision (6) inserted "acquiring" and substituted "persons and families in designated Indian areas" for "members of the Mowa Band of Choctaw Indians."

§ 24-7-4. Area of operation.

The area of operation of the authority shall be within Washington and Mobile Counties in areas outside of the corporate boundaries of cities or towns existing at the time of the passage of this amendatory act, and in areas historically considered to be occupied by the Indians of Mobile and Washington Counties; provided, that the authority shall not undertake any housing project or projects within the area of operation of any city, county or regional housing authority unless a resolution shall have been adopted by such city, county or regional housing authority declaring that there is a need for the Mowa Choctaw Housing Authority to exercise its powers within such city, county or regional housing authority's area of operation. (Acts 1986, No. 86-537, § 3; Acts 1989, No. 89-697, p. 1377, § 1.)

§ 24-7-5. Cooperation with municipalities and regional housing authorities.

Consistent with the provisions of any state or federal laws or regulations, the authority shall cooperate with municipalities and regional housing authorities for the purpose of assuring the most economic and efficient use of potential resources available for housing in Mobile and Washington Counties. (Acts 1986, No. 86-537, § 4.)

§ 24-7-6. Contract with government for loans and contributions; state to provide services, accept dedications, etc., on behalf of authority without charge.

(a) The authority shall endeavor to secure a contract with the government for loans and annual contributions covering one or more projects comprising units of low-rent housing and to develop and administer such projects, each of which shall be located within the operating area of the Mowa Choctaw reservation.

(b) During the period commencing with the date of acquisition of any part of the site or sites of any project and continuing so long as either such project is owned by a public body or governmental agency and is used for low-rent housing purposes, or any contract between the authority and the government for loans or annual contributions, or both, in connection with such projects remain unpaid, whichever period is the longest, the state without cost or charge to the authority or the tenants of such project shall:

(1) Furnish or cause to be furnished to the authority and the tenants of such project public services and facilities of the same character and to the same extent as are furnished from time to time without cost or charge by municipalities to their citizens and/or to dwellings located within their jurisdiction;

(2) Accept dedication of all interior streets, roads, alleys, and adjacent sidewalks within the area of such projects, after the authority, at its own expense has completed grading, improving, paving and installation thereof in accordance with specifications acceptable to the state;

(3) Accept necessary dedications of land for, and will grade, improve, pave and provide sidewalks for all streets bounding such project or necessary to provide adequate access thereto;

(4) Without cost or charge to the authority or tenants of such project shall vacate such streets, roads, and alleys within the area of such project as may be necessary in the development thereof, and convey without charge to the authority such interest as the state may have in such vacated areas; and, insofar as it is lawfully able to do so without cost or expense to the authority or to the state, cause to be removed from such vacated areas, insofar as may be necessary, all public or private utility lines and equipment; and

(5) Cooperate with the authority by other lawful action or ways as the state and the authority may find necessary in connection with the development and administration of such project.

(c) The state will, when requested in writing by the authority, assist in the operation and administration of the project by providing or causing to be provided, without cost or expense to the authority, the following additional services:

(1) The services of state employees to assist the authority in developing the necessary site plan for the project; and

(2) The services of state employees in assisting the authority in establishing the necessary administrative capabilities to operate the project. (Acts 1986, No. 86-537, § 6.)

CHAPTER 8.

ALABAMA FAIR HOUSING LAW.

Effective date. — The act which added this chapter became effective August 8, 1991.

§ 24-8-1. Short title.

This chapter shall be known and may be cited as the "Alabama Fair Housing Law." (Acts 1991, No. 91-659, p. 1248, § 1.)

Cross references. — As to the department of economic and community affairs, see § 41-23-1 et seq.

§ 24-8-2. Policy of state.

Within constitutional limitations, it is the policy of this state to provide for fair housing throughout the state. (Acts 1991, No. 91-659, p. 1248, § 2.)

§ 24-8-3. Definitions.

The following words and phrases used in this chapter shall have the following respective meanings unless the context clearly indicates otherwise:

(1) ADECA. The Alabama Department of Economic and Community Affairs.

(2) COVERED MULTIFAMILY DWELLINGS:

a. Buildings consisting of four or more units if the buildings have one or more elevators; and

b. Ground floor units in other buildings consisting of four or more units.

(3) DISCRIMINATORY HOUSING PRACTICE. An act that is unlawful under this chapter.

(4) DWELLING. Any building or structure, or portion of any building or structure, which is occupied as, or designed or intended for occupancy as, a residence by one or more families, and any vacant land which is offered for sale or lease for the construction or location on it of any such building or structure, or portion of it.

(5)a. FAMILIAL STATUS. One or more individuals who have not attained the age of 18 years and are domiciled with:

   1. A parent or another person having legal custody of the individual; or

   2. The designee of the parent or other person having the custody, with the written permission of parent or other person.

b. The protections afforded against discrimination on the basis of familial status apply to any person who is pregnant or is in the process of securing legal custody of any individual who has not attained the age of 18 years.

(6) HANDICAP. With respect to a person:

a. A physical or mental impairment which substantially limits one or more of the person's major life activities;

b. A record of having such an impairment; or

c. Being regarded as having an impairment. The term "handicap" excludes current, illegal use of or addiction to a controlled substance as defined by law.

(7) HOUSING FOR OLDER PERSONS. Housing:

a. Provided under any state or federal program that the attorney general determines is designed specifically and operated to assist elderly persons, as defined in the state or federal program; or

b. Intended for, and solely occupied by persons 62 years of age or older; or

c. Intended and operated for occupancy by at least one person 55 years of age or older for each unit. In determining whether housing qualifies as housing intended and operated for occupancy by at least one person 55 years of age or older, the Alabama Department of Economic and Community Affairs shall develop regulations which require at least the following factors:

   1. The existence of significant facilities and services specifically designed to meet the physical or social needs of older persons, or if the provision of the facilities and services is not practicable, that the housing is necessary to provide important housing opportunities for older persons; and

   2. That at least 80 percent of the dwellings are occupied by at least one person 55 years of age or older for each unit; and

3. The publication of and adherence to policies and procedures which demonstrate an intent by the owner or manager to provide housing for persons 55 years of age or older.

d. Housing does not fail to meet the requirements for housing for older persons by reason of:

1. Persons residing in this housing as of the date of enactment of this chapter who do not meet the requirements of paragraph b or c; or

2. Unoccupied units, provided that these units are reserved for occupancy by persons who meet the new requirements of paragraph b or c.

(8) OFFICE. Office of ADECA.

(9) PERSON. One or more individuals, corporations, partnerships, associations, labor organizations, legal representatives, mutual companies, joint-stock companies, trusts, unincorporated organizations, trustees, trustees in bankruptcy, receivers, and fiduciaries.

(10) To RENT. To lease, to sublease, to let, and otherwise to grant for a consideration the right to occupy premises not owned by the occupant. (Acts 1991, No. 91-659, p. 1248, § 3.)

§ 24-8-4. Unlawful discriminatory housing practices.

It shall be unlawful:

(1) To refuse to sell or rent after the making of a bona fide offer, to refuse to negotiate for the sale or rental of, or otherwise to make unavailable or deny a dwelling to any person because of race, color, religion, sex, familial status, or national origin;

(2) To discriminate against any person in the terms, conditions, or privileges of sale or rental of a dwelling, or in the provision of services or facilities in connection with it, because of race, color, religion, sex, familial status, or national origin;

(3) To make, print or publish, or cause to be made, printed, or published, any notice, statement, or advertisement with respect to the sale or rental of a dwelling that indicates any preference, limitation, or discrimination based on race, color, religion, sex, handicap, familial status, or national origin or an intention to make the preference, limitation, or discrimination;

(4) To represent to any person because of race, color, religion, sex, handicap, familial status, or national origin that any dwelling is not available to inspection, sale or rental when the dwelling is available;

(5) For profit, to induce or attempt to induce any person to sell or rent any dwelling by representations regarding the entry or prospective entry into the neighborhood of a person or persons of a particular race, color, religion, sex, handicap, familial status, or national origin;

(6) To discriminate in the sale or rental, or to otherwise make unavailable or deny, a dwelling to any buyer or renter because of a handicap of:

a. That buyer or renter;

b. A person residing in or intending to reside in that dwelling after it is sold, rented, or made available; or

c. Any person associated with that buyer or renter;

(7) To discriminate against a person in the terms, conditions, or privileges of sale or rental of a dwelling, or in the provision of services or facilities in connection with the dwelling, because of a handicap of:

a. That person;

b. A person residing in or intending to reside in that dwelling after it is sold, rented, or made available; or

c. Any person associated with that person. (Acts 1991, No. 91-659, p. 1248, § 4.)

§ 24-8-5. Discrimination in services, organizations, or facilities relating to business of selling or renting dwellings.

It shall be unlawful to deny any person access to, or membership or participation in, any multiple listing service, real estate brokers' organization, or other service, organization, or facility relating to the business of selling or renting dwellings or to discriminate against him in the terms or conditions of the access, membership, or participation on account of race, color, religion, sex, handicap, familial status, or national origin. (Acts 1991, No. 91-659, p. 1248, § 5.)

§ 24-8-6. Discrimination in residential real estate related transactions.

(a) It shall be unlawful for any person or other entity whose business includes engaging in residential real estate related transactions to discriminate against any person in making available such a transaction, or in the terms or conditions of the transaction, because of race, color, religion, sex, handicap, familial status, or national origin.

(b) As used in this section, "residential real estate related transaction" means any of the following:

(1) The making or purchasing of loans or providing other financial assistance:

a. For purchasing, constructing, improving, repairing, or maintaining a dwelling; or

b. Secured by residential real estate; or

(2) The selling, brokering or appraising of residential real property.

(c) Nothing in this chapter prohibits a person engaged in the business of furnishing appraisals of real property to take into consideration factors other than race, color, religion, national origin, sex, handicap, or familial status. (Acts 1991, No. 91-659, p. 1248, § 6.)

§ 24-8-7. Exemptions.

(a) The provisions of Sections 24-8-4 and 24-8-6 do not apply to rooms or units in dwellings containing living quarters occupied or intended to be occupied by no more than four families living independently of each other, if the owner actually maintains and occupies one of the living quarters as his residence.

(b) The provisions of Sections 24-8-4 and 24-8-6 do not apply to any single-family house sold or rented by an owner when:

(1) The private individual owner does not own more than three single-family houses at any one time; and

(2) In the sale of any single-family house by a private individual owner not residing in the house at the time of the sale or who was not the most recent resident of the house before the sale, the exemption granted by this subsection shall apply only with respect to one sale within a 24-month period; and

(3) A bona fide private individual owner does not own an interest in, nor is there owned or reserved on his behalf, under any express or voluntary agreement, title to or a right to all or a portion of the proceeds from the sale or rental of more than three single-family houses at any one time.

(c) After August 8, 1991, the sale or rental of a single-family house is excepted from the application of this subsection only if the house is sold or rented:

(1) Without the use in any manner of the sales or rental facilities or the sales or rental services of a real estate broker, agent, or salesman, or of the facilities or services of a person in the business of selling or renting dwellings, or of an employee or agent of a broker, agent, salesman, or person; and

(2) Without publication posting or mailing, after notice, of an advertisement or written notice in violation of this chapter. Nothing in this subsection prohibits the use of attorneys, escrow agents, abstractors, title companies, and other professional assistance as necessary to perfect or transfer this title.

(d) For the purposes of this section, a person is considered to be in the business of selling or renting dwellings if he:

(1) Has, within the preceding 12 months, participated as principal in three or more transactions involving the sale or rental of any dwelling or any interest in it;

(2) Has, within the preceding 12 months, participated as agent, other than in the sale of his personal residence, in providing sales or rental facilities or sales or rental services in two or more transactions involving the sale or rental of any dwelling or any interest in it; or

(3) Is the owner of any dwelling designed or intended for occupancy by, or occupied by, five or more families.

(e) The provisions of this chapter shall not prohibit a religious organization, association, or society, or any nonprofit institution or organization operated, supervised, or controlled by or in conjunction with a religious organization, association, or society, from limiting the sale, rental, or occupancy of any dwelling which it owns or operates for other than a commercial purpose to persons of the same religion or from giving preference to those persons, unless membership in the religion is restricted because of race, color, or national origin. The provisions of this chapter shall not prohibit a private club not in fact open to the public, which as an incident to its primary purpose provides lodgings which it owns or operates for other than a commercial purpose, from limiting the rental or occupancy of the lodgings to its members or from giving preference to its members.

(f) It is not unlawful under subdivisions (1) or (2) of Section 24-8-4 for any person to deny or limit the rental of housing to persons who pose a real and present threat of substantial harm to themselves, to others, or to the housing itself.

(g) The provisions of this chapter shall not prohibit conduct against a person because the person has been convicted by any court of competent jurisdiction of the illegal manufacture or distribution of a controlled substance as defined by law.

(h) For purposes of subdivision (6) of Section 24-8-4, the term "discrimination" includes:

(1) A refusal to permit, at the expense of the handicapped person, reasonable modifications of existing premises occupied or to be occupied by the person if the modifications are necessary to afford that person full enjoyment of the premises, except that in the case of a rental, the landlord, where it is reasonable to do so, may condition permission for a modification on the renter agreeing to restore the interior of the premises to the condition that existed before the modification, reasonable wear and tear excepted;

(2) A refusal to make reasonable accommodations in rules, policies, practices, or services when such accommodations may be necessary to afford the person equal opportunity to use and enjoy a dwelling; or

(3) In connection with the design and construction of covered multifamily dwellings for first occupancy after the date that is 30 months after the date of enactment of the Fair Housing Amendments Act of 1988, a failure to design and construct those dwellings in such a manner that:

a. The public use and common use portions of such dwelling are readily accessible to and usable by handicapped persons;

b. All the doors designed to allow passage into and within all premises within such dwellings are sufficiently wide to allow passage by handicapped persons in wheelchairs; and

c. All premises within these dwellings contain the following features of adaptive design:

1. An accessible route into and through the dwelling;

2. Light switches, electrical outlets, thermostats and other environmental controls in accessible locations;

　　　3. Reinforcements in the bathroom walls to allow later installation of grab bars; and

　　　4. Usable kitchens and bathrooms that an individual in a wheelchair can maneuver about the space.

(i) Compliance with the appropriate requirements of the American National Standard for Buildings and Facilities Providing Accessibility and Usability for Physically Handicapped People (commonly cited as "ANSI A117.1") suffices to satisfy the requirements of Section 24-8-7(h)(3)c.

(1) If a unit of local government has incorporated into its laws the requirements in subsection (h)(3), compliance with these laws is considered to satisfy the requirements.

(2) A unit of local government may review and approve newly constructed covered multifamily dwellings for the purpose of making determinations as to whether the design and construction requirements of subsection (h)(3) are met.

(3) The office shall encourage, but may not require, units of local government to include in their existing procedures for the review and approval of newly constructed covered multifamily dwellings, determinations as to whether the design and construction of these dwellings are consistent with subsection (h)(3), and shall provide technical assistance to units of local government and other persons to implement the requirements of subsection (h)(3).

(4) Nothing in this chapter may be construed to require the office to review or approve the plans, designs, or construction of all covered multifamily dwellings, to determine whether the design and construction of these dwellings are consistent with the requirements of subsection (h)(3).

(j)(1) Nothing in subsection (i) may be construed to affect the authority and responsibility of the attorney general to receive and process complaints or otherwise engage in enforcement activities under this chapter.

(2) Determinations by the unit of local government under subsection (i) are not conclusive in enforcement proceedings under this chapter.

(k) Nothing in this chapter may be construed to invalidate or limit any rule, regulation, resolution or ordinance of a political subdivision of the state that requires dwellings to be designed and constructed in a manner that affords handicapped persons greater access than is required by this chapter.

(l) Nothing in this chapter requires that a dwelling be made available to an individual whose occupancy would constitute a direct threat to the health or safety of other individuals or whose occupancy would result in substantial physical damage to the property of others.

(m) Nothing in this chapter limits the applicability of any reasonable local, state, or federal restrictions regarding the maximum number of occupants permitted to occupy a dwelling. Owners and managers of dwellings may develop and implement reasonable occupancy and safety standards based on factors such as the number and size of sleeping areas or bedrooms and the overall size of a dwelling unit so long as the standards do not violate local, state, or federal restrictions. The provisions in this chapter regarding familial status shall not apply to housing for older persons. The provisions of this chapter shall not prohibit the lease application or similar document from requiring information concerning the number, age, sex, and familial relationship of the applicants and the dwellings intended occupants. The owner or manager may consider these factors in determining payment of utilities. The application also may require disclosure by the applicant of the conviction of any intended occupant for violating any laws pertaining to the illegal manufacture or distribution of a controlled substance as defined in Title 22.

(n) The provisions of Section 24-8-4 with respect to discrimination based on sex do not apply to the rental or leasing of dwellings in a single-sex dormitory property. (Acts 1991, No. 91-659, p. 1248, § 7.)

§ 24-8-8. Interference with person in exercise of right granted under chapter.

It shall be unlawful to coerce, intimidate, threaten, or interfere with any person in the exercise of, or on account of his having aided or encouraged any other person in the exercise of any right granted under this chapter. (Acts 1991, No. 91-659, p. 1248, § 8.)

§ 24-8-9. Office to administer provisions and may delegate functions, duties, powers to employees.

(a) The office shall administer the provisions of this chapter.

(b) The office may delegate any of its functions, duties, and powers to its employees including functions, duties, and powers with respect to investigating, conciliating, hearing, determining, ordering, certifying, reporting, or otherwise acting as to any work, business, or matter under this chapter. (Acts 1991, No. 91-659, p. 1248, § 9.)

§ 24-8-10. Powers of office.

The office has the power to:

(1) Promulgate regulations necessary for the enforcement of this chapter which may not exceed the requirements of the 1988 Fair Housing Amendments Act (PL 100-430) and any subsequent amendments to it;

(2) Make studies with respect to the nature and extent of discriminatory housing practices in representative urban, suburban, and rural communities throughout the state;

(3) Publish and disseminate reports, recommendations, and information derived from the studies;

(4) Cooperate with and render technical assistance to public or private agencies, organizations, and institutions within the state which are formulating or carrying on programs to prevent or eliminate discriminatory housing practices;

(5) Cooperate with the United States Department of Housing and Urban Development to achieve the purposes of that department and with other federal, state, and local agencies and departments;

(6) Accept reimbursement pursuant to Title 28, United States Code, Section 817, for services rendered to the United States Department of Housing and Urban Development;

(7) Accept gifts or bequests, grants, or other donations, public or private;

(8) Institute proceedings in a court of competent jurisdiction, for cause shown, to seek appropriate temporary or preliminary injunctive relief pending final administrative disposition of a complaint;

(9) Contract with persons and organizations to perform services as it may consider reasonably necessary to effectuate the purposes of this chapter and to accept reimbursement for services rendered pursuant to the contract. However, the office may not delegate its decision making authority to a nongovernmental agency. This decision making authority includes acceptance of complaints, approval of conciliation agreements, dismissal of complaints, final disposition of complaints, or other enforcement powers granted by this chapter;

(10) Make contractual agreements within the scope and authority of this chapter with any agency of the federal government. An agreement with the Department of Housing and Urban Development may include provisions under which said office shall refrain from processing a charge in this state in any class specified in the agreement;

(11) Administer the programs and activities relating in a manner affirmatively to further the policies of this chapter. (Acts 1991, No. 91-659, p. 1248, § 10.)

§ 24-8-11. Procedures for investigation; subpoenas.

(a) In conducting an investigation, the office shall have access at all reasonable times to premises, records, documents, individuals, and other evidence or possible sources of evidence and may examine, record, and copy the materials and take and record the testimony or statements of persons as are reasonably necessary for the furtherance of the investigation, provided the office first complies with the constitutional provisions relating to unreasonable searches and seizures. The office may issue subpoenas to compel its access to or the production of the materials or the appearance of the persons and may issue interrogatories to a respondent, to the same extent and subject to the same limitations as would apply if the subpoenas or interrogatories were issued or served in aid of a civil action in court. The office may administer oaths. Any examination, recording, copying of materials, and the taking and recording of testimony or statements of persons as reasonably are necessary for the furtherance of the investigation must be solely related to the complaint for which the subpoena was issued.

(b) Upon written application to the office, a respondent is entitled to the issuance of a reasonable number of subpoenas by and in the name of the office to the same extent and subject to the same limitations as subpoenas issued by the office itself. A subpoena issued at the request of a respondent shall show on its face the name and address of the respondent and shall state that it was issued at his request.

(c) Within five days after service of a subpoena upon any person, the person may petition the office to revoke or modify the subpoena. The office shall grant the petition if it finds that the subpoena requires appearance or attendance at an unreasonable time or place, that it requires production of evidence which does not relate to any matter under investigation, that it does not describe with sufficient particularity the evidence to be produced, or that compliance would be unduly onerous or for other good reason.

(d) In case of refusal to obey a subpoena, the office or the person at whose request the subpoena was issued may petition for its enforcement in the circuit court for the county in which the person to whom the subpoena was addressed resides, was served, or transacts business.

(e) Witnesses summoned by a subpoena under this chapter are entitled to the same witness and mileage fees as witnesses in proceedings in court. Fees payable to a witness summoned by a subpoena issued at the request of a party must be paid by that party or, where a party is unable to pay the fees, by the office. (Acts 1991, No. 91-659, p. 1248, § 11.)

§ 24-8-12. Filing of complaint; investigation and notice; resolution by informal methods; filing of answer; local fair housing law; conciliation agreement; completion of investigation; final administrative disposition; burden of proof; termination of efforts to obtain voluntary compliance.

(a) A person who claims to have been injured by a discriminatory housing practice or who believes that he may be injured by a discriminatory housing practice that is about to occur may file a complaint with the office. Complaints must be in writing and shall contain information and be in a form required by the office. Upon receipt of a complaint, the office shall serve notice upon the aggrieved person of the time limits and choices of forums provided under this chapter and shall furnish a copy to the person who allegedly committed the discriminatory housing practice or is about to commit the alleged discriminatory housing practice and advise him of the procedural rights and obligations under the law. Within 30 days after receiving a complaint, or within 30 days after the expiration of any period of reference under subsection (c), the office shall investigate the complaint and give notice in writing to the person aggrieved whether it intends to resolve it. If the office decides to resolve the complaint, it shall proceed to try to eliminate or correct the alleged discriminatory housing practice by informal methods of conference, conciliation, and persuasion. If practicable, conciliation meetings must be held in the cities or other localities where the discriminatory housing practices allegedly occurred. Nothing said or done in the course of the informal endeavors may be made public or used as evidence in a subsequent proceeding under this chapter without the written consent of the persons concerned. An employee of the office who makes public any information in violation of this provision is guilty of a misdemeanor punishable by a fine of not more than $200.00, or imprisoned for not more than 30 days.

(b) A complaint under subsection (a) must be filed within 180 days after the alleged discriminatory housing practice occurred. The complaint must be in writing and shall state the facts upon which the allegations of a discriminatory housing practice are based. A complaint may be reasonably and fairly amended at any time. A respondent may file an answer to the complaint against him, not later than 10 days after receipt of notice, and may be amended reasonably and fairly by the respondent at any time. Both complaint and answer must be verified.

(c) Wherever a local fair housing law provides rights and remedies for alleged discriminatory housing practices which substantially are equivalent to the rights and remedies provided in this chapter, the office shall notify the appropriate local agency of any complaint filed under this chapter which appears to constitute a violation of the local fair housing law, and the office shall take no further action with respect to the complaint if the local law enforcement official, within 30 days from the date the alleged offense was brought to his attention, has commenced proceedings in the matter. In no event may the office take further action unless it certifies that in its judgment, under the circumstances of the particular case, the protection of the rights of the parties or the interest of justice require the action. Complaints referred to the office by the Department of Housing and Urban Development may not be referred by the office to a local agency.

(d) Any conciliation agreement arising out of conciliation efforts by the office must be an agreement between the respondent and the complainant and is subject to the approval of the office. Each conciliation agreement must be made public unless the complainant and respondent otherwise agree and the office determines that disclosure is not required to further the purposes of this chapter.

(e) The investigation must be completed in no more than 100 days after receipt of the complaint. If the office is unable to complete the investigation within 100 days, it shall notify the complainant and respondent in writing of the reasons for not doing so.

(f) The office shall make final administrative disposition of a complaint within one year of the date of receipt of a complaint unless it is impractical to do so. If the office is unable to do so, it shall notify the complainant and respondent, in writing, of the reasons for not doing so.

(g) In any proceeding brought pursuant to this section, the burden of proof is on the complainant.

(h) Whenever an action is filed by an individual in court pursuant to this section or Section 24-8-14 comes to trial, the office shall terminate all efforts to obtain voluntary compliance. (Acts 1991, No. 91-659, p. 1248, § 12.)

§ 24-8-13. Recommendation for hearing by investigator; order for hearing; parties' right to take civil action; amendment of complaint; subpoenas; refusal to allow discovery; hearing; panel opinion and order; review.

(a) If not sooner resolved, the investigator, upon completion of his investigation, shall submit to ADECA a statement of the facts disclosed by his investigation and recommend either that the complaint be dismissed or that a panel of office members be designated to hear the complaint. ADECA, after review of the case file and the statement and recommendation of the investigator, shall issue an order either of dismissal or for a hearing, which is not subject to judicial or other further review.

(b) If the order is for dismissal, ADECA shall mail a copy of the order to the complainant and the respondent at their last known addresses. The complainant may bring an action against the respondent in circuit court within 90 days of the date of the dismissal or within one year from the date of the violation alleged, whichever occurs later, to enforce the rights granted or protected by this chapter and to seek relief as provided for in Section 24-8-14.

(c)(1) If the order is for a hearing, ADECA shall attach to it a notice and a copy of the complaint and require the respondent to answer the complaint at a hearing at a time and place specified in the notice and shall serve upon the respondent a copy of the order, the complaint, and the notice.

(2) Either party may elect to have the claims asserted in the complaint decided in a civil action. ADECA notice must be sent to all parties and inform them of their right to take civil action. An election must be made within 20 days after receipt of the notice. A party making this election shall notify ADECA and all other parties. If an election is made for a civil action, ADECA shall, within 30 days from the date of election, commence and maintain a civil action pursuant to Section 24-8-14 on behalf of the aggrieved person.

(d) At any time before a hearing, a complaint may be amended by ADECA upon the request of the investigator or of the complainant or of the respondent. Complaints may be amended during a hearing only upon a majority vote of the panel of office members for the hearing.

(e) Upon request by any party, ADECA shall issue appropriate subpoenas or subpoenas duces tecum to any witnesses or other custodians of documents desired to be present at the hearing, or at prehearing depositions, unless ADECA determines that issuance of the subpoenas or subpoenas duces tecum would be unreasonably or unduly burdensome.

(f) Upon notification by any party that any party or witness has failed to permit access, failed to comply with a subpoena or subpoena duces tecum, refused to have his deposition taken, refused to answer interrogatories, or otherwise refused to allow discovery, the office, upon notice to the party or witness, shall apply to a court of competent jurisdiction for an order requiring discovery and other good faith compliance unless the office determines that the discovery would be unreasonably or unduly burdensome.

(g) ADECA shall designate a panel of three persons to hear the complaint.

(h) At any hearing held pursuant to this section, the case in support of the complaint must be presented before the panel by one or more of the offices' employees or agents or by legal representatives of the complaining party. Endeavors at conciliation by the investigator may not be received into evidence nor otherwise made known to the members of the panel.

(i) The respondent shall submit a written answer to the complaint and appear at the hearing in person or by counsel and may submit evidence. The respondent may amend his answer reasonably and fairly.

(j) The complainant must be permitted to be present and submit evidence.

(k) Proceedings under this section are subject to the provisions of the Alabama Administrative Procedure Act, and in the case of conflict between the provisions of this chapter and the Alabama Administrative Procedure Act, the provisions of the Alabama Administrative Procedure Act shall govern. A recording of the proceedings must be made, which may be transcribed subsequently upon request and payment of a reasonable fee by the complainant or the respondent. The fee must be set by the office or upon motion of the panel, in which case copies of the transcription must be made available to the complainant or the respondent upon request and payment of a reasonable fee to be set by the office.

(*l*) If, upon all the evidence at the hearing, the panel shall find that the respondent has engaged in any unlawful discriminatory practice, it shall state its findings of fact and serve upon the complainant and the respondent in the name of the office an opinion and order for appropriate relief which may include that the unlawful discriminatory practice be discontinued, actual damages, civil penalties which may not be greater than civil penalties established by the Federal Fair Housing Act in Section 812 and reasonable attorney's fees. The office may retain jurisdiction of the case until it is satisfied of compliance by the respondent of its order.

(m) If, upon all the evidence at the hearing, the panel finds that the respondent has not engaged in any unlawful discriminatory practice, the panel shall state its findings of fact and serve upon the complainant and the respondent an opinion and order dismissing the complaint as to the respondent. A prevailing respondent may apply to the office for an award of reasonable attorney's fees and costs.

(n) A copy of the opinion and order of the office shall be delivered in all cases to such other public officers as the office considers proper. Copies of the opinion and order must be available to the public for inspection upon request, and copies must be made available to any person upon payment of a reasonable fee set by the office.

(o)(1) If an application for review is made to the office within 14 days from the date the order of the office has been given, the office, for good cause shown, shall review the order and evidence, receive further evidence, rehear the parties or their representatives, and if proper, amend the order.

(2) Either party to the dispute, within 30 days after receipt of notice to be sent by registered mail of the order, but not after that time, may appeal

from the decision of the office to the circuit court of the county in which the hearing occurred, or in which the respondent resides or has his principal office. In case of an appeal from the decision of the office, the appeal shall operate as a supersedeas for 30 days only, unless otherwise ordered by the court, and after that the respondent is required to comply with the order involved in the appeal or certification until the questions at issue in it have been determined fully in accordance with the provisions of this chapter.

(3) The office may institute a proceeding for enforcement of its order of subsection (1), or its amended order of subdivision (1) after 30 days from the day of the order, by filing a petition in the circuit court of the county in which the hearing occurred, or where any person against whom the order is entered resides or transacts business.

(4) If no appeal under subdivision (2) is initiated, the office may obtain a decree of the court for enforcement of its order upon a showing that a copy of the petition for enforcement was served upon the party subject to the dictates of the office's order. (Acts 1991, No. 91-659, p. 1248, § 13.)

§ 24-8-14. Civil action; sale, encumbrance, etc. consummated before issuance of order; relief and award.

(a) A civil action must be commenced within one year after the alleged discriminatory housing practice has occurred. However, the court shall continue a civil case brought pursuant to this section, from time to time, before bringing it to trial if the court believes that the conciliation efforts of the office or local agency are likely to result in satisfactory settlement of the discriminatory housing practice complained of in the complaint made to the office or to the local agency and which practice forms the basis for the action in court. Any sale, encumbrance, or rental consummated before the issuance of any court order issued under the authority of this chapter and involving a bona fide purchaser, encumbrances, or tenant without actual notice of the existence of the filing of a complaint or civil action under the provisions of this chapter are not affected. A civil action may be commenced by an aggrieved person whether or not a complaint has been filed with the office.

(b) The court may grant as relief, as it considers appropriate, any permanent or temporary injunction, temporary restraining order, or other order and may award the plaintiff actual damages, and punitive damages, together with court costs and reasonable attorney's fees in the case of a prevailing party, if the prevailing party in the opinion of the court is not financially able to assume the attorney's fees. (Acts 1991, No. 91-659, p. 1248, § 14.)

§ 24-8-15. Similar complaint filed with another agency with authority to investigate violation of chapter.

Before accepting any complaint under this chapter, the office shall determine if the complainant has filed a similar complaint with the Federal Home Loan Bank Board, the Comptroller of the Currency, the Federal Deposit Insurance Corporation of the Federal Reserve System, the United States Department of Housing and Urban Development, or any other agency with authority to investigate and resolve complaints alleging a violation of this chapter. If a complaint has been filed or is filed, subsequently the office shall coordinate efforts to resolve the complaint with that agency in order to avoid multiple investigations of the respondent. (Acts 1991, No. 91-659, p. 1248, § 15.)

TITLE 25.

INDUSTRIAL RELATIONS AND LABOR.

TABLE OF CONTENTS

CHAPTER 1.

GENERAL PROVISIONS.

ARTICLE 1.

IN GENERAL.

§ 25-1-1. Duties of employers, etc., with respect to provision of safe employment.

(a) Every employer shall furnish employment which shall be reasonably safe for the employees engaged therein and shall furnish and use safety devices and safeguards and shall adopt and use methods and processes reasonably adequate to render such employment and the places where the employment is performed reasonably safe for his employees and others who are not trespassers, and he shall do everything reasonably necessary to protect the life, health and safety of his employees and others who are not trespassers.

(b) Every employer and every owner of a place of employment, place of public assembly or public building, now or hereafter constructed, shall so construct, repair and maintain the same as to render it reasonably safe; provided, however, that nothing contained in this section shall be construed or applied so as to impose upon any such owner any duties to his tenant, the

269

members of his family, employees, guests or invitees or others entering upon the premises under the tenant's title, or the public, not now imposed upon him by law.

(c) For the purposes of this section, the following terms shall have the meanings ascribed to them by this subsection:

(1) EMPLOYER. Such term includes every person, firm, corporation, partnership, joint stock association, agent, manager, representative, foreman or other person having control or custody of any employment, place of employment or of any employee, but the terms of this section shall not be construed to cover the employment of agricultural workers or domestic servants.

(2) EMPLOYEE. Such term does not and shall not include agricultural workers or domestic servants.

(3) SAFE and SAFETY. Such terms, applied to any employment or place of employment, place of public assembly or public building, shall mean "reasonably safe" or "reasonable safety" consistent with the lawful purpose of the use and occupancy of the place of employment, place of public assembly or public building and the inherent danger of the employment, the process, operation or situation involved, and, shall include conditions and methods of sanitation and hygiene reasonably necessary for the protection of the life, health and safety of the employees and others who are not trespassers. (Acts 1939, No. 161, p. 232; Code 1940, T. 26, § 12.)

Effect of this section was to enlarge common-law duty of employer, as it formerly obtained under the judge-made law of Alabama, and to impose upon the employer in the operation of mines an absolute personal duty of maintaining the safety of such places of employment. Minyard v. Woodward Iron Co., 81 F. Supp. 414 (N.D. Ala. 1948).

Duty to provide a safe workplace is imposed upon the one who has control or custody of the employment or place of employment. Procter & Gamble Co. v. Staples, 551 So. 2d 949 (Ala. 1989).

Duty to provide safe working environment. — Employers had a statutory, as well as a common law, duty to provide employees with a safe working environment. Bellew v. Sloan, 536 So. 2d 917 (Ala. 1988).

Parties charged with providing a safe workplace are the ones who either have assumed or have been delegated the duty to do so, or who are in such a position that the jobsite functions as they command. Procter & Gamble Co. v. Staples, 551 So. 2d 949 (Ala. 1989).

Duty is generally nondelegable but there is exception. — The duty of providing a safe workplace, then, is generally nondelegable to any party not within the business of the employer; however, there is an exception to the foregoing general rule when an outside party is in control or custody of the worker's employment. Procter & Gamble Co. v. Staples, 551 So. 2d 949 (Ala. 1989).

Defendant could not have assumed or been delegated duty. — Since defendant company was neither a co-employee of the plaintiff's decedent nor in any other way within the business of decedent's employer, defendant company could not have assumed or have been delegated the duty to provide plaintiff's decedent with a safe workplace in the traditional co-employee sense of the tort. Procter & Gamble Co. v. Staples, 551 So. 2d 949 (Ala. 1989).

Defendant had no custody or control over employer's workplace. — Two brief visits by defendant company's safety representatives, coupled with a few telephone calls between defendant company and employer relating to safety and the fact that defendant company provided some safety literature and other suggestions prior to employer's opening, did not amount to "control or custody" of the employer's workplace, as envisioned by subdivision (c)(1); there was a complete absence of evidence that employer had control over the workplace, or, more importantly, that it controlled the manner in which employer's work was done; therefore, defendant company did not undertake to provide plaintiff's decedent a safe place to work. Procter & Gamble Co. v. Staples, 551 So. 2d 949 (Ala. 1989).

Co-employees may be held liable for not providing safe work place. — In accord with this statute, which is merely a codification of earlier common law, under proper facts, supervisory personnel, including corporate officers, may be held liable as co-employees for negligently failing to provide their subordinates with a reasonably safe place in which to work. Such liability may be imposed if it is proved that, as a part of their responsibilities, the defendant supervisory personnel were delegated or assumed their employer's duty to provide a safe work place or a material portion of that duty. Fontenot v. Bramlett, 470 So. 2d 669 (Ala. 1985).

While this section imposes a duty to provide a safe work place upon an employer alone based solely upon his status, the statute in no way prohibits the imposition of liability upon co-employees, including supervisors or corporate officers, where they are delegated or voluntarily assume the duty of maintaining a safe work place. Fontenot v. Bramlett, 470 So. 2d 669 (Ala. 1985).

Summary judgment for defendant executive director of association was improper where defendant had said he would correct potential problems or problem areas and would see that any defect or hazard reported to him was corrected. A reasonable inference from this evidence was that defendant had voluntarily assumed, or had been delegated, the duty to provide the plaintiff with a safe workplace. Ritchie v. Bullock, 529 So. 2d 916 (Ala. 1988).

Summary judgment in favor of shop manager was proper since there could not be drawn from the evidence a reasonable inference that defendant had voluntarily assumed or had been delegated his employer's duty to provide a safe workplace, nor did his general supervisory responsibilities serve to put him in charge of insuring safety in the workplace. Ritchie v. Bullock, 529 So. 2d 916 (Ala. 1988).

Imposition of liability on co-employee is not automatic; it does not arise out of one's job title or even out of the amount of control, in and of itself, which the co-employee exerts at the workplace. Clark v. Floyd, 514 So. 2d 1309 (Ala. 1987).

The liability of a co-employee is not determined solely on the basis of the co-employee's job title or the amount of control he exerts at the workplace. Ritchie v. Bullock, 529 So. 2d 916 (Ala. 1988).

The fact that a co-employee is in an administrative or supervisory position alone does not make that person liable. Neither does the imposition of liability arise out of the amount of control which the co-employee exerts at the workplace, or his overall role with regard to the jobsite. Harris v. Hand, 530 So. 2d 191 (Ala. 1988).

Burden of proving liability of co-employee. — To impose liability on a defendant co-employee, the plaintiff bears the burden of proving the elements of a three-prong test for the co-employee defendant; first, the plaintiff must show that, as part of the defendant co-employee's responsibilities, he voluntarily assumed or was delegated his employer's duty to provide a safe place to work. Second, the plaintiff must show that the co-employee breached that duty by failing, either through omission or commission, to discharge the delegated or assumed obligation with reasonable care. Third, the plaintiff must show that this breach directly or proximately cause the plaintiff's injury. Clark v. Floyd, 514 So. 2d 1309 (Ala. 1987).

This section imposes on employers the duty to provide reasonably safe employment. A co-employee is not liable to another employee unless he (1) voluntarily assumed or (2) was delegated his employer's duty to provide a reasonably safe workplace. A plaintiff must also prove that his co-employee breached the assumed (or delegated) duty by failure to exercise reasonable care and that this breach proximately caused injury to the plaintiff. Harris v. Hand, 530 So. 2d 191 (Ala. 1988).

Evidence required to withstand a summary judgment motion in favor of co-employee defendant. — In action by employee against co-employees for injury occurring before the 1985 amendment requiring a plaintiff to prove willful conduct in order to maintain a co-employee action, summary judgment was properly entered for the defendants except for those co-employees who were responsible for safety conditions and were aware of the safety hazard in existence at the time of the plaintiff's injury. Hawkins v. Miller, 569 So. 2d 335 (Ala. 1990).

Ex officio member does not incur same liability as other members of body. — It may appear that, logically, the converse of the position in Barber Pure Milk Co. v. Alabama State Milk Control Bd., 275 Ala. 489, 156 So. 2d 351 (1963) is that an ex officio member would incur the same liabilities as those incurred by other members of the body. The court sees no logical purpose that would be served by such a blanket holding by this court. The facts of the present litigation are appreciably different from those presented in Barber Pure Milk Co. v. Alabama State Milk Control Bd., 275 Ala. 489, 156 So. 2d 351 (1963). Defendant, as hospital administrator, served as an ex officio member of all the committees at the hospital.

There was no evidence that the defendant took, or was expected to take, an active role in the functions of the safety committee. Absent a showing of active concert with the safety committee, it would be imprudent to hold that defendant assumed personal liability for any inadvertence of hospital wide committees. To do so would expose him and those similarly situated to virtually unlimited personal liability. Jacoups v. Daigle, 521 So. 2d 979 (Ala. 1988).

Sufficient evidence of negligence. — There was sufficient evidence to require submission to the jury and therefore preclude a directed verdict on the negligence of employer, where employer testified that he knew of the dangerous conditions on the roof of new building that required a "toe board" to prevent a fall and that he knew he had a duty to provide a reasonably safe place for plaintiff to work. Bellew v. Sloan, 536 So. 2d 917 (Ala. 1988).

Cited in DuPont v. Yellow Cab Co., 565 So. 2d 190 (Ala. 1990); Weaver v. Frazer, 576 So. 2d 200 (Ala. 1991); Foreman v. Dorsey Trailers, Inc., 256 Ala. 253, 54 So. 2d 499 (1951); Bailey v. Tennessee Coal, Iron & R.R., 261 Ala. 526, 75 So. 2d 117 (1954); McRee v.

Woodward Iron Co., 279 Ala. 88, 182 So. 2d 209 (1966); Kingsberry Homes Corp. v. Ralston, 285 Ala. 600, 235 So. 2d 371 (1970); Southern Ry. v. Kendall, 288 Ala. 430, 261 So. 2d 752 (1972); Kennemer v. McFann, 470 So. 2d 1113 (Ala. 1985).

Collateral references. — 56 C.J.S., Master & Servant, §§ 171-200.

53 Am. Jur. 2d, Master & Servant, §§ 159 et seq., 187 et seq.

Duty of an employer with respect to timbering mine, under common law and general statutes. 15 ALR 1380.

Duty of master providing machine of standard make and in common use to equip same with safety device or guard. 36 ALR 1477.

Duty of master under statutes requiring employers to guard dangerous machinery, as satisfied by providing machine of standard make and in common use. 36 ALR 1485.

Independence of contract considered with relation to statutes imposing on mine owners duties with respect to security of workmen. 43 ALR 353.

Right of employee to injunction preventing employer from exposing employee to tobacco smoke in workplace. 37 ALR4th 480.

§ 25-1-2. Duty of employer to provide sitting accommodations and separate water closets for females.

Any person owning or controlling a store or shop in which any female is employed as a clerk or saleswoman, who fails to provide such female with proper accommodations for sitting or resting when not actively engaged in the work of her employment, or who fails to permit her to do so when not so engaged, or who shall not have in such building, or convenient thereto, separate water closets for the use of such females, shall, on conviction, be fined not less than $50.00 nor more than $500.00. (Code 1896, § 5512; Code 1907, § 6857; Code 1923, § 3991; Code 1940, T. 26, § 337.)

ARTICLE 2.

EQUAL EMPLOYMENT OPPORTUNITY FOR MINORITIES.

§ 25-1-10. Affirmative action programs; definition of minority; American Indians or Alaskan natives included.

Notwithstanding any other provision of law, whenever any employer in this state sponsors or initiates a program of affirmative action designed to cure or eradicate the effects of discrimination in employment, and the intent of the program is to affect the recruitment, selection, appointment, promotion, or other personnel procedures or functions in a manner so as to insure equal employment opportunity for minorities, the term "minority" shall include, in addition to any specifically identified ethnic group or other classification, a person who is a citizen or lawful permanent resident of the United States and who can establish by information contained on his or her birth certificate, by tribal records or by other reliable records, that he or she is an American Indian or Alaskan Native, having origins in any of the original peoples of North America. (Acts 1992, No. 92-626, § 1.)

Effective date. — The act which added this section became effective May 28, 1992.

CHAPTER 2.

DEPARTMENT OF INDUSTRIAL RELATIONS.

§ 25-2-1. Established; seal.

There shall be a Department of Industrial Relations of the State of Alabama, which shall be an executive and administrative department of the state. The Department of Industrial Relations shall have a seal, which shall be affixed by the director to his official acts and deeds and to those of the Department of Industrial Relations. (Acts 1939, No. 161, p. 232; Code 1940, T. 26, § 1.)

Cited in State Farm Mut. Auto. Ins. Co. v. Birmingham Elec. Co., 254 Ala. 256, 48 So. 2d 41 (1950).

§ 25-2-2. Duties generally.

The general functions and duties of the Department of Industrial Relations shall be as follows:

(1) To administer all labor laws and all laws relating to the relationship between employer and employee, including laws relating to hours of work, child labor, female employees and working conditions in places of employment.

(2) To make or cause to be made all necessary inspections to determine whether or not the laws, the administration of which is delegated to the Department of Industrial Relations, and rules and regulations issued pursuant thereto, are being complied with by employers and employees, and to take such action as may be necessary to enforce compliance; provided, however, that there shall be no inspection of boilers which have been inspected, approved and insured by an insurance company authorized to do business in the State of Alabama.

(3) To propose to the board of appeals, provided for in this chapter, such rules and regulations, or amendments thereto and repeals thereof, as may be deemed advisable for the prevention of accidents or the prevention of sickness and diseases in mines. The Director of Industrial Relations may appoint committees composed of employers, employees and experts to suggest and assist in the preparation of rules and regulations or amendments thereof.

(4) To administer, by and under the direction of the Director of Industrial Relations, Chapter 4 of this title.

(5) To cooperate with all authorities of the United States having powers and duties under the Wagner-Peyser Act, approved June 6, 1933 (48 Stat. 113, United States Code, Title 29, Section 49) entitled "An Act to provide for the establishment of a national employment system and for cooperation with the states in the promotion of such system and for other purposes," and to do and perform all things necessary to secure for the State of Alabama the benefits of such act and the promotion and maintenance of a system of public employment offices. The Department of Industrial Relations is hereby designated as the state agency and vested with all powers necessary to cooperate with the United States Employment Service or its successor.

(6) To administer and perform all functions and duties of Chapter 5 of this title, and it shall have power and authority to adopt and enforce all reasonable rules and orders necessary or suitable to that end, and to require any reports, and to take any other action, consistent with the provisions of said Chapter 5 of this title, necessary or suitable to that end.

(7) To make investigations and studies and to collect, collate and compile statistical information and to make and publish reports concerning the conditions of labor generally, including living conditions, hours of work, wages paid and all matters relating to the enforcement and effect of the provisions of this title coming under the jurisdiction of the Department of Industrial Relations and the rules and regulations issued pursuant thereto

and other laws relating to the Department of Industrial Relations. The Director of Industrial Relations shall deliver a copy of each such report to every person making application therefor.

(8) To make an annual report to the Governor covering the activities and accomplishments of the Department of Industrial Relations during the preceding fiscal year, accompanied by the recommendations of the Director of Industrial Relations. The report shall be printed and the Director of Industrial Relations shall deliver a copy to every person making application therefor.

(9) To make recommendations to the legislature for the enactment of laws which, on the basis of information and statistics compiled by the Department of Industrial Relations, appear to be desirable for the protection of laborers and for promoting and fostering amicable relations between employers and employees. (Acts 1939, No. 161, p. 232; Code 1940, T. 26, § 3; Acts 1943, No. 298, p. 252, § 22.)

Cited in Southern Ry. v. Kendall, 288 Ala. 430, 261 So. 2d 752 (1972).

Collateral references. — 81 C.J.S., States, § 58.

§ 25-2-3. Divisions; officers.

The Director of Industrial Relations, with the approval of the Governor, may establish such division or divisions as may, in his discretion, be necessary or desirable for the administration or enforcement of any law or any rule or regulations with which the Department of Industrial Relations is charged or the performance of any of its functions or duties. Each division in the Department of Industrial Relations shall be headed by and be under the direction, supervision and control of an officer who shall be designated as the chief of such division. All chiefs of divisions shall be appointed by the Director of Industrial Relations, subject to the provisions of the merit system. Before entering upon the discharge of their duties, such chiefs of divisions shall take the constitutional oath of office. Each of such officers shall devote his full time to his official duties and shall hold no other lucrative position while serving as such. It is one of the purposes of this chapter to coordinate, in one division of the Department of Industrial Relations, unemployment compensation and employment service. Unemployment compensation and employment service shall be in one division of the Department of Industrial Relations under the direction of the chief of said division. Within said division, but subordinate to the chief thereof, there shall be a full-time salaried director of unemployment compensation and a full-time salaried director of employment service. The salaries of said chief and directors shall be paid solely from federal grants and shall be comparable to those paid similar officers in comparable states, notwithstanding any limitation or maximum in any other law. (Acts 1939, No. 161, p. 232; Code 1940, T. 26, § 25; Acts 1945, No. 348, p. 564; Acts 1947, No. 364, p. 250; Acts 1951, No. 642, p. 1097.)

§ 25-2-4. Employees.

The Director of Industrial Relations shall, with the approval of the Governor, determine the number of employees needed for the efficient and economical performance of the functions and duties of the Department of Industrial Relations. The Director of Industrial Relations is authorized and empowered to make such agreements as may be necessary or proper with the Secretary of Labor or any other agency, department or bureau of the federal government with respect to the proration of salaries and expenses paid to employees of the Department of Industrial Relations whose duties are not exclusively in the performance of the functions of the unemployment compensation division. Before entering upon the duties of their respective offices, the employees of the Department of Industrial Relations shall execute to the State of Alabama bonds, to be approved by the Governor, in amounts to be fixed by the Director of Industrial Relations, for the faithful performance of their duties. (Acts 1939, No. 161, p. 232; Code 1940, T. 26, § 26; Acts 1943, No. 122, p. 123; Acts 1961, Ex. Sess., No. 208, p. 2190.)

§ 25-2-5. Applicability of merit system.

Anything in this chapter to the contrary notwithstanding, all employees and officers of the Department of Industrial Relations, including the chiefs of divisions but not including the Director of Industrial Relations, even though he be a chief of a division, shall be subject to the merit system. (Acts 1939, No. 161, p. 232; Code 1940, T. 26, § 27.)

Cross references. — As to merit system, see § 36-26-1 et seq.

§ 25-2-6. Director of Industrial Relations — Qualifications, appointment, oath of office, term of office, bond and compensation; filling of vacancies.

The Department of Industrial Relations shall be headed by and shall be under the direction, supervision and control of an officer who shall be known and designated as the Director of Industrial Relations. The Director of Industrial Relations shall be the advisor of the Governor and the legislature in matters relating to employer-employee relations and the welfare of the wage earners of the state. He shall be responsible to the Governor for the administration of the Department of Industrial Relations. The Director of Industrial Relations shall be appointed by and shall hold office at the pleasure of the Governor. Vacancies for any reason shall be filled in the same manner as original appointments are made. Before entering upon the discharge of his duties, the Director of Industrial Relations shall take the constitutional oath of office. Before entering upon the duties of his office, the Director of Industrial Relations shall execute to the State of Alabama a bond, to be approved by the Governor, in an amount to be fixed by the Governor, but not less than $10,000.00, for the faithful performance of his duties. The annual salary of the Director of Industrial Relations shall be fixed by the Governor at a sum comparable to salaries paid similar officers in other states, notwithstanding any limitation or maximum in any other law, $1,200.00 of which sum shall be paid from moneys of the State of Alabama and the remainder from grants of the United States of America to this state. Such salary shall be payable at the same time and in the same manner as the salaries of other state officers. The Director of Industrial Relations is authorized and empowered to make such agreements as may be necessary or proper with the United States of America with respect to the proration of funds from the State of Alabama and funds from the federal government for the salary paid to the Director of Industrial Relations by virtue of the provisions of this section. The Director of Industrial Relations shall devote his full time to his official duties and shall not hold another office under the government of the United States, or under any other state, or of this state or any political subdivision thereof, during his incumbency in such office, and shall not hold any position of trust or profit, or engage in any occupation or business the conduct of which shall interfere or be inconsistent with his duties as Director of Industrial Relations under the provisions of this title. (Acts 1939, No. 161, p. 232; Code 1940, T. 26, § 2; Acts 1943, No. 122, p. 123; Acts 1947, No. 527, p. 385; Acts 1951, Ex. Sess., No. 11, p. 177; Acts 1961, Ex. Sess., No. 208, p. 2190.)

§ 25-2-7. Director of Industrial Relations — Powers and duties generally.

All functions and duties of the Department of Industrial Relations shall be exercised by the Director of Industrial Relations acting by himself or by and through such administrative divisions or such officers or employees as he may designate. The Director of Industrial Relations shall have all power and authority necessary or convenient to carry out the functions and duties of the Department of Industrial Relations. It shall be the duty of the Director of Industrial Relations to administer Chapter 4 of this title and he shall have power and authority to adopt and enforce all reasonable rules and orders necessary or suitable to that end, require any reports and take any other action consistent with the provisions of said Chapter 4 necessary or suitable to that end. (Acts 1939, No. 161, p. 232; Code 1940, T. 26, § 6.)

§ 25-2-8. Director of Industrial Relations — Promulgation of rules and regulations.

The Director of Industrial Relations may prescribe such general rules and regulations for the conduct of the Department of Industrial Relations as he may deem necessary or expedient to give effect to the provisions of this chapter. (Acts 1939, No. 161, p. 232; Code 1940, T. 26, § 4.)

Collateral references. — 81 C.J.S., States, §§ 68, 72.

§ 25-2-9. Director of Industrial Relations — Right of entry.

The Director of Industrial Relations or his authorized representative shall have the power and authority to enter any place of employment, place of public assembly or public building for the purpose of collecting facts and statistics relating to the employment of workers or for the purpose of making inspections to determine whether or not the labor law and laws relating to the relationship between employer and employee and the rules and regulations adopted pursuant to the provisions of this chapter are being observed. No employer or owner shall refuse to admit the Director of Industrial Relations or his authorized representative to his place of employment, public building or place of public assembly for the purpose of making any reasonable inspection or impede or obstruct him in making any reasonable inspection. (Acts 1939, No. 161, p. 232; Code 1940, T. 26, § 21.)

§ 25-2-10. Director of Industrial Relations — Designated chief of unemployment compensation and employment service division.

The Director of Industrial Relations shall act as chief and be in immediate charge, supervision and control of the division of the Department of Industrial Relations charged with the duties arising under Chapter 4 of this title and the state employment service, thereby coordinating the functions of these two units of the Department of Industrial Relations. The Director of Industrial Relations in assuming these additional duties shall receive no remuneration for such services other than that amount specified as his salary in Section 25-2-6. (Acts 1939, No. 161, p. 232; Code 1940, T. 26, § 7.)

§ 25-2-11. Director of Industrial Relations — Agreements with federal agencies.

Nothing in this chapter shall be construed or intended to prevent the Director of Industrial Relations from conforming, if not in conflict with the provisions of this chapter, to minimum standards heretofore or hereafter adopted or promulgated by the Secretary of Labor or any other agency, department or bureau of the federal government, for the administration of Chapter 4 of this title or employment service. The director is hereby empowered and authorized to make such agreements not in conflict with the provisions of this chapter with the Secretary of Labor or any other agency of the federal government, as may be necessary to conform to such minimum standards, or as may be necessary to conform to minimum standards adopted by the Secretary of Labor or any other agency, department or bureau of the federal government in connection with grants to the Department of Industrial Relations for the administration of Chapter 4 of this title or employment service. (Acts 1939, No. 161, p. 232; Code 1940, T. 26, § 29.)

§ 25-2-12. Board of appeals — Created; composition; qualifications, appointment, terms of office, compensation and removal of members; alternate members; quorum; conflicts of interest.

There shall be a board of appeals for the Department of Industrial Relations. The board of appeals shall exercise its own judgment and discretion in all matters entrusted to it, and, to that extent, shall be entirely separate and distinct from and independent of the Department of Industrial Relations, but it shall have offices with the Department of Industrial Relations, and an employee of the Department of Industrial Relations shall act as its clerk. All proper expenses of the board of appeals shall be paid from the appropriations to the Department of Industrial Relations in the same manner as expenses of the department are paid. There shall be three members of the board of appeals, all of whom shall be appointed by the Governor, subject to confirmation by the Senate, for a term of office of six years or until their successors are appointed; except, that the first appointments of members of the board of appeals shall be for terms of two, four and six years respectively. One member of the board shall be a person who, on account of his previous employment or affiliations, shall be generally classified as a representative of employers. One member of such board shall be a person who, on account of his previous employment or affiliations, shall be generally classified as a representative of employees. One member of the board shall represent the interest of the public, shall not be generally classified as a representative of employers or of employees and shall be the chairman of the board of appeals. Before entering upon the discharge of his duties, each member of the board of appeals shall take the constitutional oath of office. No member of the board of appeals shall be employed by the federal government or the state. Members of the board of appeals shall receive no salary but shall be paid for each day or part thereof necessarily spent in the discharge of their official duties, including travel time, an amount to be agreed upon by the Director of Industrial Relations and the Governor, the same not to exceed $100.00 per day. The sum total to be paid to each member of the board in the first six months of any calendar year shall not exceed $5,000.00 with a like maximum sum total of $5,000.00 in the last six months of any calendar year, plus expense allowance as provided in Article 2 of Chapter 7 of Title 36; except, that when it has been determined by the Director of Industrial Relations that the number of appeals pending before the board of appeals shall require that the board meet and hold hearings on more than 24 days during the first six months or during the last six months of any calendar year the sum total to be paid to each member of the board during such first six months or such last six months of any calendar year shall be increased proportionally as determined by the director but in no event to exceed $6,000.00 plus travel allowance during either the first six months or the last six months of any calendar year. Members of the board of appeals shall be subject to impeachment as are other state officers. Vacancies for any reason shall be filled by appointment by the

Governor for the unexpired term, and any appointments made while the senate is not in regular session shall be effective ad interim. No member of the board of appeals shall hear or determine an appeal in any case in which he is a directly interested party. The board of appeals shall not hear or determine any appeal unless each of the three members thereof or their alternates are present. The Governor shall immediately, whenever it is shown to his satisfaction that a member of the board of appeals is disqualified for any reason or cannot attend a session of the board of appeals, appoint an alternate or alternates for the member or members so disqualified or absent. (Acts 1939, No. 161, p. 232; Code 1940, T. 26, § 8; Acts 1943, No. 410, p. 375; Acts 1949, No. 268, p. 391; Acts 1961, Ex. Sess., No. 274, p. 2298, § 1; Acts 1973, No. 1061, p. 1749, Acts 1979, No. 79-708, p. 1260; Acts 1990, No. 90-574, p. 979.)

Cited in Underwood v. State, 439 So. 2d 125 (Ala. 1983).

Collateral references. — 73 C.J.S., Public Administrative Bodies & Procedures, § 159.

Civil action for damages under state Racketeer Influenced and Corrupt Organizations Acts (RICO) for losses from racketeering activity. 62 ALR4th 654.

§ 25-2-13. Board of appeals — Powers and duties generally; appeals from findings as to dangerous condition, etc., of machines, etc.

(a) The functions and duties of the board of appeals shall be as follows:

(1) To hear and determine appeals under Chapter 4 of this title.

(2) To hold public hearings on proposed safety rules and regulations and amendments and repeals thereof, and to promulgate and publish such rules and regulations and amendments and repeals as provided in this chapter.

(3) To hear and determine appeals from the finding of any officers or employees of the Department of Industrial Relations that any machine, tool, equipment or structure is in a dangerous condition or is not properly guarded or is dangerously placed, when the discontinuance of the use thereof has been ordered.

(b) When such appeal is taken by a person affected by such order, no appeal shall be taken from such determination of the board of appeals, except on questions of law or on the ground that the determination is not supported by the preponderance of the evidence; and unless an appeal shall have been taken within 10 days after the determination of the case by the board of appeals and after notice of such determination shall have been mailed by registered or certified mail, postage prepaid, to the person affected by such order at the address furnished by him, or, if none shall have been furnished, at the address of his place of business, such an appeal shall be waived. Such appeals shall be taken to the Court of Civil Appeals.

(c) Any person affected by such order may, however, as an alternative to an appeal to the board of appeals, appeal to the circuit court of the county in which such machine, tool, equipment or structure is located, and the trial in such court shall be de novo, and in such appeal the Director of Industrial Relations shall be styled as plaintiff and the party appealing as defendant and the burden of proof shall rest upon the director. If any such person at the time of taking the appeal shall fail to request a jury, the trial shall be by the court without a jury. If any such person shall request an immediate hearing on such appeal and shall not request a jury trial, such appeal shall be a preferred case and shall be immediately heard and determined by any judge of the circuit court to whom application is made, at any location in the circuit. Either party shall have the right of appeal from the judgment or decree of the circuit court to the Court of Civil Appeals.

(d) Appeals from such finding of the board of appeals or of the circuit court shall be taken within 10 days from the effective date of the same by filing a notice of appeal with the clerk of the board, or clerk of the circuit court, as the case may be, which notice shall describe the finding from which the appeal is taken, and a copy thereof shall forthwith be mailed to the Director of Industrial Relations by the clerk. An appeal by the defendant from such finding shall operate to supersede the same if at the time of taking said appeal the party taking the same shall file with the notice of appeal a bond in such sum as the board of appeals or judge of the circuit court, as the case may be, may prescribe, with sufficient surety to be approved by the clerk of said board or court, as the case may be, payable to the Director of Industrial Relations with conditions that the party appealing will prosecute said appeal to effect and if he fail therein will pay all damage which any person may sustain on account of any injury which may be proximately caused by the dangerous condition of the machine, tool, equipment or structure affected by such finding. All court costs shall be taxed against the party or parties against whom judgment is rendered and against the state when rendered against the Director of Industrial Relations. (Acts 1939, No. 161, p. 232; Code 1940, T. 26, § 9.)

Collateral references. — Workers' compensation: injuries incurred during labor activity. 61 ALR4th 196.

§ 25-2-14. Board of appeals — Procedure; record of proceedings, etc.

The board of appeals shall have power and authority to prescribe its own procedure. A full and complete record shall be kept of all proceedings before the board of appeals by the employee of the Department of Industrial Relations designated as its clerk. All testimony in any appeal case before the board of appeals shall be taken down by a stenographer, but need not be transcribed unless an appeal is taken to the court. The testimony in hearings on safety rules and regulations, and amendments and repeals thereof, need not be recorded. (Acts 1939, No. 161, p. 232; Code 1940, T. 26, § 10.)

§ 25-2-15. Board of appeals — Sessions.

The board of appeals shall meet only at such times as the Director of Industrial Relations or the Governor shall determine a session to be in the public interest and shall notify the members thereof in writing of the time of convening. The board of appeals shall remain in session no longer than is necessary to dispose of matters pending for their consideration and determination or other action. (Acts 1939, No. 161, p. 232; Code 1940, T. 26, § 11.)

§ 25-2-16. Board of appeals — Promulgation, amendment, etc., of rules and regulations — Proposals.

Rules and regulations, or amendments or the repeal thereof, except those affecting the administration of Chapter 4 of this title, may from time to time be proposed to the board of appeals by the Director of Industrial Relations or any officer or employee of the Department of Industrial Relations designated by him or any committee of employers, employees and experts appointed by him for that purpose. All such rules, regulations and amendments shall be for the purpose of making more definite and certain the duties of employers as set forth in this chapter, and any rule, regulation or amendment, excepting those affecting administration of Chapter 4 of this title, which does not conform to the standards herein set forth, shall be invalid. The Director of Industrial Relations shall deliver to any person making application therefor a copy of all rules and regulations as from time to time promulgated under any of the provisions of this chapter. (Acts 1939, No. 161, p. 232; Code 1940, T. 26, § 14.)

Collateral references. — 73 C.J.S., Public Administrative Bodies & Procedures, §§ 92-113.

§ 25-2-17. Board of appeals — Promulgation, amendment, etc., of rules and regulations — Hearings.

Before any rule or regulation is adopted, amended or repealed by the board of appeals, there shall be a public hearing thereon, notice of which shall be published at least once, not less than 10 days prior thereto, in a daily newspaper published in Montgomery and in such other newspaper or newspapers as the board of appeals may prescribe. Any person interested shall have a right to be heard at such hearing. (Acts 1939, No. 161, p. 232; Code 1940, T. 26, § 15.)

Collateral references. — 73 C.J.S., Public Administrative Bodies & Procedures, § 98.

§ 25-2-18. Board of appeals — Promulgation, amendment, etc., of rules and regulations — Effective date; publication, etc.

All rules and regulations and all amendments and repeals thereof by the board of appeals shall, unless otherwise prescribed by the board of appeals, take effect 30 days after the first publication thereof and after a certified copy thereof shall have been filed in the office of the Secretary of State. Every such rule and regulation adopted and every amendment and repeal thereof by the board of appeals shall be published in such manner as the board of appeals may determine. The Director of Industrial Relations shall deliver a copy to every person making application therefor, and he shall include the text of each such rule or regulation, and amendment or repeal thereof, in an appendix to the annual report of the Department of Industrial Relations next following the adoption, amendment or repeal of such rule or regulation. (Acts 1939, No. 161, p. 232; Code 1940, T. 26, § 16.)

Collateral references. — 73 C.J.S., Public Administrative Bodies & Procedures, § 101.

§ 25-2-19. Variations from rules or regulations.

If there shall be practical difficulties or unnecessary hardships in carrying out a rule or regulation of the board of appeals, the board may, after a public hearing, make a variation from such requirements if the spirit of the rule and laws shall be observed. Any person affected by such rules, or his agent or attorney, may petition the board for such variations, stating the ground therefor. The board shall fix a date for hearing on such petition and give reasonable notice thereof to the petitioner. A properly indexed record of all variations made shall be kept by the clerk of the board of appeals in the office of the Department of Industrial Relations and shall be open to public inspection. (Acts 1939, No. 161, p. 232; Code 1940, T. 26, § 17.)

§ 25-2-20. Review of rules or regulations — Petition to board of appeals.

Any person in interest, his authorized agent or attorney may petition the board of appeals for a review of the validity or reasonableness of any rule or regulation adopted, amended or repealed by the board of appeals under the provisions of this chapter. The petition shall be verified, shall be filed with the board of appeals and shall state the rule or regulation proposed to be reviewed and in what respect it is claimed to be invalid or unreasonable. The board may join in one proceeding all petitions alleging the invalidity or unreasonableness of substantially similar rules or regulations. The filing of such petition shall operate to stay all proceedings under such rule or regulation until the determination of such review. The board of appeals shall order a hearing if necessary to determine the issue raised or, if the issues have been considered in a prior proceeding, the board of appeals may, without a hearing, confirm its previous determination. Notice of the time and place of hearing shall be given to the petitioner and such other person as the board of appeals may determine. If the board of appeals finds that the rule or regulation is invalid or unreasonable, it shall revoke or amend it. (Acts 1939, No. 161, p. 232; Code 1940, T. 26, § 18.)

§ 25-2-21. Review of rules or regulations — Commencement of action in circuit court.

Any employer, owner or other person in interest, being dissatisfied with any rule or regulation of the board of appeals, may commence an action in the circuit court of the county wherein such employer, owner or other person in interest resides, or has his or its principal place of business against the Director of Industrial Relations as defendant to enjoin and set aside any such rule or regulation on the ground that it is invalid or unreasonable. The defendant shall be served with a copy of the complaint. Service of the complaint may be made by serving a copy or second original by the sheriff or any deputy sheriff of any county wherein the Director of Industrial Relations may be found, or by filing a copy in the office of the Director of Industrial Relations. (Acts 1939, No. 161, p. 232; Code 1940, T. 26, § 19.)

§ 25-2-22. Employers to furnish information; access to records, accounts, etc., of employers.

Every employer or owner shall furnish to the Department of Industrial Relations or the board of appeals any information which the Department of Industrial Relations or the board of appeals is authorized to require, and shall make true and specific answers to all reasonable questions, whether submitted orally or in writing, authorized to be put to him. The Director of Industrial Relations and any authorized representative of the Department of Industrial Relations shall, for the purpose of examination, have access to and the right to copy from any book, account, record, payroll, paper or documents relating to the employment of workers in such manner as may be reasonable and at reasonable times. Information secured under the provisions of this section shall not be published or be open to public inspection in any manner revealing the employer's or owner's identity; and any officer, member or employee of the Department of Industrial Relations or the board of appeals guilty of violating this provision shall be subject to the penalties provided in this chapter. (Acts 1939, No. 161, p. 232; Code 1940, T. 26, § 20.)

Cited in United States v. Blasi, 462 F. Supp. 373 (M.D. Ala. 1979).

§ 25-2-23. Powers of director, officers of department and board of appeals as to witnesses.

The Director of Industrial Relations, any officer of the Department of Industrial Relations designated by the director and the members of the board of appeals, in the performance of any function or duty or the execution of any power prescribed by law, shall have the power to administer oaths, certify to official acts, take and cause to be taken depositions of witnesses, issue subpoenas, compel the attendance of witnesses and the production of papers, books, accounts, payrolls, documents, records and testimony. In the event of failure of any person to comply with any subpoena lawfully issued, or on the refusal of any witness to produce evidence or to testify as to any matter regarding which he may be lawfully interrogated, it shall be the duty of any court of competent jurisdiction or of the judge thereof, upon the application of the Director of Industrial Relations or any officer of the Department of Industrial Relations designated by the director or any member of the board of appeals, to compel obedience by attachment proceedings for contempt, as in the case of disobedience of the requirements of a subpoena issued for such court or a refusal to testify therein. Witness fees and other expenses involved in proceedings under this section shall be paid to the extent necessary, at rates specified by the Director of Industrial Relations, from the unemployment administration fund, when such expenses are in connection with the administration of Chapter 4 of this title. (Acts 1939, No. 161, p. 232; Code 1940, T. 26, § 22.)

§ 25-2-24. Enforcement of laws administered, etc., by department; district attorney's fee.

It shall be the duty of the qualified attorneys regularly employed by the Department of Industrial Relations, or the Attorney General of the state and any district attorney, upon the request of the Director of Industrial Relations or of any of his authorized representatives, to prosecute any violation of any law, the administration or enforcement of which has been made a duty or function of the Department of Industrial Relations, or any rule or regulation adopted pursuant thereto. A district attorney's fee of $5.00 shall be taxed as costs against any defendant convicted. (Acts 1939, No. 161, p. 232; Code 1940, T. 26, § 23.)

Collateral references. — 73 C.J.S., Public Administrative Bodies & Procedures, § 256.

§ 25-2-25. Penalties for violations of chapter or rules or regulations of board of appeals; false statements under oath.

Any person who violates or fails or refuses to comply with any requirement of this chapter or any lawful rule or regulation of the board of appeals adopted pursuant thereto, for which no penalty has been otherwise provided, shall be guilty of a misdemeanor, and upon conviction thereof shall be fined not less than $10.00 nor more than $100.00 or shall be imprisoned for not more than six months, or both so fined and imprisoned, for each such offense. Each day such violation, omission, failure or refusal continues shall be deemed a separate offense. Any person who shall knowingly testify falsely, under oath, or shall knowingly make, give or produce any false statement or false evidence under oath to the Director of Industrial Relations, or an officer of the Department of Industrial Relations designated by him or to any member of the board of appeals, shall be guilty of perjury. (Acts 1939, No. 161, p. 232; Code 1940, T. 26, § 24.)

Collateral references. — 73 C.J.S., Public Administrative Bodies & Procedures, § 110.

§ 25-2-26. Disposition and expenditure of appropriations and federal allotments.

All appropriations heretofore and hereafter to be made for the administration of Chapter 4 of this title and all moneys heretofore or hereafter to be allotted or apportioned by the federal government or the Secretary of Labor or his successor or any other federal agency, department or bureau or received from any other source to or for the State of Alabama for the administration of Chapter 4 of this title shall be held and deposited in and credited to the unemployment compensation fund and expended solely for such administration. All appropriations heretofore or hereafter to be made for the promotion or maintenance of a system of public employment offices and all moneys heretofore or hereafter to be allotted or apportioned by the federal government or the United States employment service or its successor, or any other federal agency pursuant to the provisions of the Wagner-Peyser Act or other act of Congress for the purpose of promoting or maintaining a system of public employment offices, shall be held or deposited in and credited to the employment service fund and expended solely for the purpose of promoting and maintaining such assistance. (Acts 1939, No. 161, p. 232; Code 1940, T. 26, § 5.)

CHAPTER 3.

DEPARTMENT OF LABOR.

For discussion of constitutionality of chapter. — See Alabama State Fed'n of Labor, Local 103 v. McAdory, 325 U.S. 450, 65 S. Ct. 1384, 89 L. Ed. 1725 (1945); Congress of Indus. Organizations v. McAdory, 325 U.S. 472, 65 S. Ct. 1395, 89 L. Ed. 1741 (1945).

Cited in Kaiser Aluminum & Chem. Sales, Inc. v. Crum, 402 So. 2d 995 (Ala. Civ. App.), cert. denied, 402 So. 2d 997 (Ala. 1981).

§ 25-3-1. Created.

There is hereby created the Department of Labor of the State of Alabama, which shall be an executive and administrative department of the state. (Acts 1943, No. 298, p. 252, § 3.)

§ 25-3-2. Commissioner of Labor — Appointment and term of office; oath of office and bond; filling of vacancies; full-time position.

The Department of Labor shall be headed by, and shall be under the direction, supervision and control of an officer who shall be known and designated as the Commissioner of Labor. He shall be responsible to the Governor for the administration of the Department of Labor and shall be appointed by and shall hold office at the pleasure of the Governor. Vacancies in the office for any reason shall be filled in the same manner as original appointments are made. Before entering upon the discharge of his duties the commissioner shall take the constitutional oath of office as provided for under the Constitution and shall execute bond in such penalty as may be prescribed by the Governor, conditioned upon a faithful discharge of his duties and payable to the State of Alabama. The commissioner shall devote full time to his official duties and shall not hold another office under the government of the United States, or under any other state, or of this state or any political subdivision thereof during his incumbency in such office, and shall not hold any position of trust or profit, or engage in any occupation or business the conduct of which shall interfere or be inconsistent with his duties as Director of Labor. (Acts 1943, No. 298, p. 252, § 4; Acts 1951, Ex. Sess., No. 12, p. 178.)

§ 25-3-3. Commissioner of Labor — Powers and duties generally.

(a) It shall be the duty of the Commissioner of the Department of Labor, unless otherwise expressly provided, to administer Chapter 7 of this title and such other statutes as may be provided by law, and to advise the Governor with respect to the provisions thereof. He shall have authority to employ such assistants as may be necessary in the discharge of his official duties. All such assistants shall be subject to the state merit system, and shall be paid in the same manner as other state employees.

(b) To the end that strikes, lockouts, boycotts, blacklists and discriminations may be avoided, the commissioner shall have authority and it shall be his duty to investigate labor disputes and to promote the peaceful and voluntary adjustment and settlement thereof.

(c) The commissioner shall keep a permanent record of his official acts and proceedings and shall keep the Governor fully informed with respect thereto, and shall make an annual report to the Governor in writing covering the activities and accomplishments of the Department of Labor during the preceding fiscal year.

(d) It shall be the duty of the commissioner to make available to any board of mediation appointed by the Governor pursuant to Section 25-7-4 all data and information in his custody or possession relevant or pertinent to any matter which such board of mediation may have been appointed to consider, and to render to any such board of mediation such assistance as it may request of him in the discharge of its official duties. (Acts 1943, No. 298, p. 252, § 5.)

§ 25-3-4. Commissioner of Labor — Investigation and adjustment of controversies as to wage claims.

The Commissioner of the Department of Labor shall investigate and attempt equitably to adjust controversies in respect to wage claims or alleged wage claims. (Acts 1945, No. 519, p. 760.)

§ 25-3-5. Commissioner to provide seminars for unemployed or underemployed employees regarding their rights and responsibilities; commissioner authorized to assist employee groups, communicate with creditors, etc.; state credit union may expand field of membership if adversely affected by layoffs or closings; regulations concerning financial disclosure and assistance of employees.

(a) In order to assist employees who become unemployed or underemployed as the result of a substantial layoff at or the closing of any plant or industry in Alabama, the Commissioner of Labor is hereby directed to establish a procedure to provide such unemployed or underemployed employees with seminars concerning their legal rights and responsibilities regarding their debts, to provide written material which deals with these problems and offers appropriate suggestions to such workers and to meet with management at such plants or industries and with labor organizations or other organizations including such employees in an attempt to minimize the financial burden on such employees.

(b) The Commissioner of Labor is authorized to assist and organize cooperative efforts of such employees or groups to which such employees belong in an effort to minimize the adverse impact of such plant or industry layoff or closing upon such employees and the Commissioner of Labor is further directed and authorized, to the extent he deems advisable, to engage in whatever other acts or agreements which are appropriate to assist financially such employees and groups made up of such employees, provided that the Commissioner of Labor is not authorized to require any employer or employee group to involuntarily contribute to a fund or involuntarily take any other action towards such a goal.

(c) If deemed advisable by the Commissioner of Labor, the Commissioner of Labor shall assist a plant or industry which closes or has a substantial layoff in endeavoring to communicate with the creditors of its unemployed workers concerning the financial difficulty caused to its ex-employees by such layoff or closing. If there is a substantial layoff at a plant or industry or if there is a closing of a plant or industry and if a state chartered credit union includes within its field of membership the employees of such plant or industry, then the board of directors of such state chartered credit union shall determine whether such layoff or closing has adversely affected the credit union. If the board of directors determines that such layoff or closing has adversely affected the credit union, then such credit union may include within its field of membership persons residing in the general geographic areas surrounding the plants or industries served by such credit union. Any such expansion of the field of membership of such credit union shall not be denied or restricted by any provisions of the law of Alabama heretofore enacted. Any such credit union shall endeavor to assist all such unemployed members by granting them extended periods within which to pay indebtedness owed to the credit union, to the extent deemed advisable by its board of directors.

(d) In order to stabilize the share and deposit base of credit unions which may or could be affected by plant or industry closings or by substantial layoffs, any credit union which includes in its field of membership employees of any particular company or companies shall be authorized to accept shares and deposits from such company or companies, subject to such terms and conditions as the board of directors of the credit union may establish, and such company or companies may become a member of the credit union, subject to such terms and conditions as the board of directors of the credit union may establish.

(e) The Commissioner of Labor is further directed and authorized to issue regulations, to the extent he deems advisable, concerning the instances in which employees at plants or industries which have been closed or have been the subject of substantial layoffs and organizations which include employees of such plants or industries may make appropriate disclosures of the financial situation of such employees and may assist the creditors of such workers in locating them and in arranging voluntary payment plans for their debts; provided however that nothing contained in this section shall be construed so as to authorize any activity which violates any federal act or regulation. (Acts 1983, No. 83-590, p. 922.)

Cross references. — For general provisions relating to credit unions, see chapter 17, Title 5.

CHAPTER 4.

UNEMPLOYMENT COMPENSATION.

Purpose of chapter is to insure against enforced unemployment. — The purpose of this chapter, harmonious and responsive to the social security legislation of congress, is to insure the diligent worker against vicissitudes of enforced unemployment, whether he be from office or shop, union or nonunion. Department of Indus. Relations v. Drummond, 30 Ala. App.

78, 1 So. 2d 395, cert. denied, 241 Ala. 142, 1 So. 2d 402 (1941). See also, Ex parte Alabama Textile Prods. Corp., 242 Ala. 609, 7 So. 2d 303 (1942); Tennessee Coal, Iron & R.R. v. Martin, 251 Ala. 153, 36 So. 2d 547 (1948).

The purpose of unemployment compensation is to provide an income for involuntary unemployed workers during their unemployment. Metcalf v. Department of Indus. Relations, 245 Ala. 299, 16 So. 2d 787 (1944).

It is well understood that the unemployment compensation law was enacted to relieve the consequences and vicissitudes of unavoidable and enforced unemployment which was not brought about by the voluntary creation of the worker. Department of Indus. Relations v. Mann, 35 Ala. App. 550, 50 So. 2d 780 (1950).

The prime purpose of this chapter was to provide and afford benefits for unemployed persons when this circumstance arose through no fault of the employees. Department of Indus. Relations v. Stone, 36 Ala. App. 16, 53 So. 2d 859 (1951).

The purpose of the unemployment compensation legislation is to relieve hardship caused by enforced unemployment not voluntarily created by the worker. Avondale Mills v. Burnett, 39 Ala. App. 646, 106 So. 2d 882, rev'd on other grounds, 268 Ala. 82, 106 So. 2d 885 (1958).

The design of the unemployment compensation law is to provide a worker with funds to avoid a period of destitution after having involuntarily lost his employment and thus his income. It aids in sustaining him while he looks for other employment. It provides for limitation in time and amount. It is not a gratuity. It is not insurance, but to those coming within its coverage it is in the nature of insurance. Holmes v. Cook, 45 Ala. App. 688, 236 So. 2d 352 (1970).

The Unemployment Compensation Law was enacted to relieve the consequences and vicissitudes of unavoidable and enforced unemployment which was not brought about by the voluntary creation of the worker. Landrum v. James, 425 So. 2d 1363 (Ala. Civ. App. 1982), cert. denied, 425 So. 2d 1364 (Ala. 1983).

Unemployment compensation is a creature of statute and was unknown at common law. Therefore, the legislature may lay down any reasonable and nondiscriminatory conditions it may see fit concerning eligibility and procedure. Payne v. Department of Indus. Relations, 423 So. 2d 231 (Ala. Civ. App. 1982).

This chapter is remedial in nature. Its beneficent purpose should be liberally construed and its disqualification provisions should be narrowly interpreted. State Dep't of Indus. Relations v. Deslattes, 372 So. 2d 867 (Ala. Civ. App.), cert. denied, 372 So. 2d 872 (Ala. 1979).

And it should be liberally construed. — This chapter provides a form of insurance for the unemployed worker, is remedial in nature and should be liberally construed in the worker's favor. Department of Indus. Relations v. Drummond, 30 Ala. App. 78, 1 So. 2d 395, cert. denied, 241 Ala. 142, 1 So. 2d 402 (1941); Department of Indus. Relations v. Stone, 36 Ala. App. 16, 53 So. 2d 859 (1951).

The unemployment compensation law was enacted for a beneficent purpose and it should be construed liberally in favor of the unemployed claimant. However, it was not intended to afford payment of unmerited doles or to provide vacations with pay. Department of Indus. Relations v. Wall, 34 Ala. App. 530, 41 So. 2d 611 (1949).

This chapter is remedial and is to be liberally construed to effect its beneficent purpose, and the disqualifying provisions are to be narrowly construed. Reynolds Metals Co. v. Thorne, 41 Ala. App. 331, 133 So. 2d 709 (1961).

Unemployment Compensation Act is in the nature of insurance for the unemployed worker and is intended to be a remedial measure for his benefit, and should therefore be liberally construed in claimant's favor and disqualifications from benefits narrowly construed. Department of Indus. Relations v. Smith, 360 So. 2d 726 (Ala. Civ. App. 1978).

A claimant bears the burden of proving that he is available for work during the time for which he seeks benefits. The unemployment compensation statute, however, should be liberally construed in claimant's favor. The statute is in the nature of insurance for the unemployed worker and is intended to be a remedial measure for his benefit. Polk v. State, Dep't of Indus. Relations, 413 So. 2d 1164 (Ala. Civ. App. 1982).

But construed strictly against state. — The unemployment compensation law is original and not remedial, creating rights and duties in derogation of common law, and applies taxing power of state, and hence it is to be strictly construed against taxing power. Broadway v. Alabama Dry Dock & Shipbuilding Co., 246 Ala. 201, 20 So. 2d 41 (1944).

The unemployment compensation statute is a taxing statute and, as all taxing statutes, it is to be strictly construed against the taxing authority. State Dep't of Indus. Relations v. McElrath Farms, Inc., 348 So. 2d 252 (Ala. Civ. App. 1976), rev'd on other grounds, 348 So. 2d 257 (Ala. 1977).

However, legislative intent must be sought from our Unemployment Compensation Act as a whole, and not from just a portion thereof. Department of Indus. Relations v. Chapman, 37 Ala. App. 680, 74 So. 2d 621 (1954).

Proper role of department of industrial relations is to adhere to the legal and impartial administration of the fund. It is not to be adversarial to the claimant. Crawley v. Carter, 378 So. 2d 1139 (Ala. Civ. App. 1979).

And department should not insist upon strict adherence to procedural directions. — The benevolent purpose of the Unemployment Compensation Act and the accompanying mandate for liberal construction and application of its provisions are not well served by the insistence of the department of industrial relations upon strict adherence to mere procedural directions in the statute. Crawley v. Carter, 378 So. 2d 1139 (Ala. Civ. App. 1979).

Failure to comply with an employment rule or practice is not failure to comply with this chapter, unless provided therein. Stewart v. Department of Indus. Relations, 40 Ala. App. 383, 114 So. 2d 274 (1959).

Computation of time under procedural sections of chapter. — The statutorily prescribed method of computing time under "any act," § 1-1-4, or "any applicable statute," A.R.C.P., Rule 6(a), pertains to the Unemployment Compensation Act. The court must, in construing the above quoted statutes, give the language its plain, ordinary and everyday meaning. The procedural sections of the Unemployment Compensation Act are read in pari materia with the computation of time provisions. Taylor v. Department of Indus. Relations, 409 So. 2d 447 (Ala. Civ. App. 1982).

Court authorized to order additional testimony as to eligibility for benefits. — A court's taking additional testimony should enable it to clear up any doubts it may have with regard to plaintiff's eligibility for benefits and this is in keeping with the beneficent purpose of the unemployment compensation laws. There is no abuse of discretion in either the procedure or the propriety of such a court's ordering additional testimony to do justice between the parties. Davis v. Null, 402 So. 2d 1011 (Ala. Civ. App. 1981); Davis v. McBroom, 402 So. 2d 1016 (Ala. Civ. App. 1981).

Incarceration. — Although incarceration in jail has never been construed by an Alabama appellate court to constitute voluntary departure from work, it has been held that unemployment compensation benefits are available only to those employees who leave their employment through no fault of their own. However, such absence from work is brought about solely through a voluntary act, and a person may avoid jail and also the loss of his job by not violating the law. His loss of work is directly attributable to a "voluntary" act. Landrum v. James, 425 So. 2d 1363 (Ala. Civ. App. 1982), cert. denied, 425 So. 2d 1364 (Ala. 1983).

Cited in Ex parte Miles, 248 Ala. 386, 27 So. 2d 777 (1946); Department of Indus. Relations v. Tomlinson, 251 Ala. 144, 36 So. 2d 496 (1948); Tennessee Coal, Iron & R.R. v. Martin, 33 Ala. App. 502, 36 So. 2d 535 (1948); Henderson v. Department of Indus. Relations, 252 Ala. 239, 40 So. 2d 629 (1949); Alabama Power Co. v. Atkins, 36 Ala. App. 558, 60 So. 2d 858 (1952); Carroll v. Kelly, 269 Ala. 472, 114 So. 2d 157 (1959); Carter v. Coosa Valley Youth Servs., 378 So. 2d 1145 (Ala. Civ. App. 1979); Dover Mills, Inc. v. Garrett, 384 So. 2d 1127 (Ala. Civ. App. 1980); Henley v. Housing Auth., 403 So. 2d 265 (Ala. Civ. App. 1981).

Collateral references. — Employee's refusal to take lie detector test as barring unemployment compensation. 18 ALR4th 307.

Cancer as compensable under workers' compensation acts. 19 ALR4th 639.

Employee's act or threat of physical violence as bar to unemployment compensation. 20 ALR4th 637.

Eligibility for unemployment compensation as affected by voluntary resignation because of change of location of residence. 21 ALR4th 317.

Right to unemployment compensation as affected by misrepresentation in original employment application. 23 ALR4th 1272.

Discharge from employment on ground of political views or conduct as affecting right to unemployment compensation. 29 ALR4th 287.

Conduct or activities of employees during off-duty hours as misconduct barring unemployment compensation benefits. 35 ALR4th 691.

Eligibility for unemployment compensation benefits of employee who attempts to withdraw resignation before leaving employment. 36 ALR4th 395.

ARTICLE 1.

DEFINITIONS.

§ 25-4-1. Base period.

"Base period," as used in this chapter, means the first four of the last five completed calendar quarters immediately preceding the first day of an individual benefit year. (Acts 1939, No. 497, p. 721; Code 1940, T. 26, § 193.)

Cross references. — See note under § 25-4-54.

For discussion of base period. — See Metcalf v. Department of Indus. Relations, 245 Ala. 299, 16 So. 2d 787 (1944).

Cited in Broadway v. Bolar, 33 Ala. App. 57, 29 So. 2d 687 (1947).

Collateral references. — 81 C.J.S., Social Security & Public Welfare, § 101.

Unemployment compensation: eligibility as affected by claimant's refusal to work at particular times or on particular shifts for domestic or family reasons. 2 ALR5th 475.

§ 25-4-2. Benefits.

"Benefits," as used in this chapter, means the money payable to an individual with respect to his unemployment as provided in this chapter. (Acts 1939, No. 497, p. 721; Code 1940, T. 26, § 180.)

§ 25-4-3. Benefit year.

"Benefit year," as used in this chapter with respect to any individual, means the one-year period beginning with the first day of the first week with respect to which an individual who is unemployed first files a valid claim for benefits or a claim is filed by an employer on behalf of an employee working less than full time, and thereafter the one-year period beginning with the first day of the first week with respect to which such individual next files a valid claim for benefits or such claim is filed by an employer on behalf of an employee working less than full time, after the termination of his last preceding benefit year. A claim by any such unemployed individual, or a claim filed by an employer on behalf of an employee working less than full time, made in accordance with Section 25-4-90 shall be deemed to be a "valid claim" for the purposes of this section if the individual or such employee working less than full time for whom a claim is filed by an employer, has earned the wages for insured work required under subdivision (a)(5) of Section 25-4-77. Notwithstanding the provisions of this section, if, by reason of a disqualification imposed under subdivision (3) of Section 25-4-78, the individual is not entitled to benefits on account of the wages paid to him in what normally would be his base period, no benefit year shall be established. No other disqualification under Section 25-4-78 and no holding of ineligibility under subdivision (a)(3) of Section 25-4-77 shall make a claim invalid or prevent the establishment of a benefit year. (Acts 1939, No. 497, p. 721; Code 1940, T. 26, § 194; Acts 1949, No. 525, p. 806, § 1; Acts 1955, No. 352, p. 851, § 1; Acts 1975, No. 801, § 4.)

"Valid claim" is a claim made at a time and under circumstances which qualify one for benefits and which begins his benefit year. Department of Indus. Relations v. Taylor, 54 Ala. App. 614, 311 So. 2d 438, cert. denied, 294 Ala., 770, 311 So. 2d 440 (1975). And year does not begin until claim valid. — If an individual is found to be disqualified under the claim it is not "valid"; his benefit year does not begin. Department of Indus. Relations v. Taylor, 54 Ala. App. 614, 311 So. 2d 438, cert. denied, 294 Ala., 770, 311 So. 2d 440 (1975).

§ 25-4-4. Calendar quarter; fiscal year.

(a) "Calendar quarter," as used in this chapter, means the period of three consecutive calendar months ending on March 31, June 30, September 30 or December 31, except as the director shall by regulation otherwise prescribe.

(b) "Fiscal year," as used in this chapter, shall mean the 12 consecutive month period beginning October 1 of each calendar year. (Acts 1939, No. 497, p. 721; Code 1940, T. 26, § 195; Acts 1975, No. 801, § 6.)

Cited in Broadway v. Bolar, 33 Ala. App. 57, 22 So. 2d 687 (1947).

§ 25-4-5. Contributions; payments in lieu of contributions.

(a) "Contributions," as used in this chapter, means the money payments to the state unemployment compensation fund, required by this chapter, on the basis of a percentage of wages.

(b) "Payments in lieu of contributions," as used in this chapter, means the money payments to the state unemployment compensation fund, required by this chapter, from employers who reimburse the fund for the amount of regular benefits and extended benefits paid that is attributable to service in the employ of such employers as is required by this chapter. (Acts 1939, No. 497, p. 721; Code 1940, T. 26, § 182; Acts 1971, No. 166, p. 440, § 1; Acts 1980, No. 80-756, p. 1561, § 1.)

§ 25-4-6. Director.

"Director," as used in this chapter, means the Director of Industrial Relations or his authorized representatives; except, that during any interim in which there is no duly appointed and qualified Director of Industrial Relations, the same shall mean the Director of Unemployment Compensation, provided for in Section 25-2-3. (Acts 1939, No. 497, p. 721; Code 1940, T. 26, § 182; Acts 1961, Ex. Sess., No. 274, p. 2298, § 2.)

§ 25-4-7. Employee.

Except as modified by the provisions of Section 25-4-10 defining "employment," "employee," as used in this chapter, means any individual employed by an employer subject to this chapter, in which employment the relationship of master and servant exists between the employee and the person employing him. (Acts 1939, No. 497, p. 721; Code 1940, T. 26, § 184; Acts 1971, No. 166, p. 440, § 2.)

Master-servant relationship exists where employer has right to control employee's activities, supervise him in the performance of job-related tasks, pay him a wage and discharge him at any time. State Dep't of Indus. Relations v. Montgomery Baptist Hosp., 359 So. 2d 410 (Ala. Civ. App. 1978).

Pharmacy intern was "employee" of hospital for purposes of Unemployment Compensation Act where he was carried on hospital's regular payroll just as other hospital employees were, where hospital paid him taxable wages, supervised his activities and had the power to discharge him, even though intern's immediate supervisor denominated relationship as "teacher-student" and called wages intern received a "stipend." State Dep't of Indus. Relations v. Montgomery Baptist Hosp., 359 So. 2d 410 (Ala. Civ. App. 1978).

Master-servant relationship did not exist between county commission and laid-off employee. — Where county commission did not exercise any control over laid-off employee of the probate judge of the county and it was not shown that the commission even had the right to exercise control over the employee, no master-servant relationship existed between the employee and the commission and the employee was not an "employee" of the commission under this section. Director of State Dep't of Indus. Relations v. Winston County Comm'n, 468 So. 2d 177 (Ala. Civ. App. 1985).

Cited in Carroll v. Kelly, 269 Ala. 472, 114 So. 2d 157 (1959).

Collateral references. — Who is an inde-pendent contractor rather than an employee within unemployment compensation acts. 124 ALR 682.

Tests of independent contractor relationship in the field of unemployment compensation acts. 134 ALR 1029, 147 ALR 828.

What amounts to vendor-vendee or a lessor-lessee relationship, as distinguished from employment or service relation, within unemployment compensation acts. 152 ALR 520, 164 ALR 1411.

Musicians or other entertainers as employees of establishments in which they perform, within meaning of unemployment insurance acts. 158 ALR 915, 172 ALR 325.

Outside pieceworkers as within unemployment compensation act. 1 ALR2d 555.

Taxicab driver as employee of owner of cab, or independent contractor, within unemployment insurance statutes. 10 ALR2d 369.

Salesman on commission as within act. 29 ALR2d 751.

Own projects or activities, right to unemployment compensation of one working on. 65 ALR2d 1182.

Part-time or intermittent workers as covered by or as eligible for benefits under state unemployment compensation act. 95 ALR3d 891.

Unemployment compensation: trucker as employee or independent contractor. 2 ALR4th 1219.

Eligibility for unemployment compensation as affected by voluntary resignation because of change of location of residence. 21 ALR4th 317.

§ 25-4-8. Employer.

(a) "Employer," as used in this chapter, prior to January 1, 1978, shall mean any employing unit which was so defined in this chapter prior to such date.

After December 31, 1977, except as otherwise provided in this chapter, "employer," as used in this chapter shall mean:

(1) Any employing unit which, after December 31, 1977:

a. In any calendar quarter in either the current or preceding calendar year paid, for service in employment, wages of $1,500.00 or more; or

b. For some portion of a day in each of 20 different calendar weeks, whether or not such weeks were consecutive, in either the current or the preceding calendar year, had in employment at least one individual (irrespective of whether the same individual was in employment in each such day).

(2) Any employing unit which, having become an employer under this chapter, has not under Sections 25-4-130 and 25-4-131 ceased to be an employer subject to this chapter.

(3) For the effective period of its election pursuant to Section 25-4-131, any other employing unit which has elected to become fully subject to this chapter.

(4) Any employing unit other than described in subdivision (10) of this subsection (whether or not an employing unit at the time of acquisition) which:

     a. Acquired the organization, trade or business, or substantially all the assets thereof, of another employing unit which at the time of such acquisition was an employer subject to this chapter; or

     b. Acquired a segregable part of the organization, trade or business of another employing unit which at the time of such acquisition was an employer subject to this chapter; provided, that such segregable part would have been an employer subject to this chapter if such part had constituted its entire organization, trade or business.

(5) Any employing unit which acquires the organization, trade or business, or substantially all of the assets thereof of another employing unit (not an employer subject to this chapter) and which, if the employment record of such employing unit subsequent to such acquisition, together with the employment record of the acquired unit prior to such acquisition, both within the same calendar year, would be sufficient to constitute an employing unit an employer subject to this chapter.

(6) Any employing unit not an employer by reason of any other paragraph of this section:

     a. For which, within either the current or preceding calendar year, service is or was performed with respect to which such employing unit is held liable by the federal government for any federal tax against which credit may be taken for contributions required to be paid into a state unemployment fund; or

     b. Which, as a condition for approval of this chapter for full tax credit against the tax imposed by the Federal Unemployment Tax Act, is required, pursuant to such Federal Unemployment Tax Act, to be an "employer" under this chapter.

(7) Any employing unit for which service in employment as defined in paragraph (a)(2)a of Section 25-4-10 is performed after December 31, 1971, or for which service in employment as defined in paragraph (a)(2)b of Section 25-4-10 is performed after December 31, 1977; provided, however, that such service is not excluded from the definition of "employment" by any of the provisions of subsection (b) of Section 25-4-10.

(8) Any employing unit for which service in employment as defined in subdivision (a)(3) of Section 25-4-10 is performed after December 31, 1971.

(9) Any employing unit for which agricultural labor as defined in subdivision (b)(1) of Section 25-4-10 is performed after December 31, 1977, but only if the provisions of paragraph (a)(4)a of Section 25-4-10 are met.

(10) Any employing unit for which domestic service in employment as defined in paragraph (a)(4)b of Section 25-4-10 is performed after December 31, 1977.

(11)a. In determining whether or not an employing unit for which service other than domestic service is also performed is an employer under this section other than under subdivision (10) of this subsection, the wages paid to, or the employment of, an employee performing domestic service after December 31, 1977, shall not be taken into account.

b. In determining whether or not an employing unit for which service other than agricultural labor is also performed is an employer under this section other than under subdivisions (7) and (8) of this subsection, the wages paid to, or the employment of, an employee performing service in agricultural labor after December 31, 1977, shall not be taken into account. If an employing unit is determined an employer of agricultural labor, such employing unit shall be determined an employer for the purposes of subdivision (1) of this subsection.

c. The provisions of paragraphs a and b of this subdivision notwithstanding, for the purposes of Sections 25-4-51, 25-4-52, 25-4-53 and 25-4-54, any employing unit which is or becomes subject to the provisions of any subdivision of this subsection other than subdivisions (9) or (10) shall, upon becoming subject to subdivisions (9) or (10) or if, at the time of becoming subject to any other subdivision is already subject to subdivisions (9) or (10), be a single employing unit.

(b) For the purposes of this section, if any week includes both December 31 and January 1, the days of that week up to January 1 shall be deemed one calendar week and the days beginning January 1 another such week. (Acts 1939, No. 497, p. 721; Code 1940, T. 26, § 185; Acts 1943, No. 310, p. 281, § 1; Acts 1945, No. 283, p. 449, § 7; Acts 1951, No. 644, p. 1098, § 1; Acts 1955, No. 29, p. 247; Acts 1971, No. 166, p. 440, § 3; Acts 1978, 1st Ex. Sess., No. 1, p. 5, § 1.)

Employers who act toward stabilizing employment will be rewarded with lower rate of contribution to compensation fund. It is considered advisable to reward an employer with good employment records by giving him a favorable rating and thereby reducing his payment. James v. McCoy Mfg. Co., 431 So. 2d 1147 (Ala. 1983).

An employer, under terms of paragraph (a)(4)a of this section, cannot acquire "organization" of another employer without first acquiring the management of the other employer. The management component of a business is one of the vital, integral parts required for continued operation. James v. McCoy Mfg. Co., 431 So. 2d 1147 (Ala. 1983).

Cited in Carroll v. Kelly, 269 Ala. 472, 114 So. 2d 157 (1959); State v. Gibson's Barbecue, 369 So. 2d 1229 (Ala. Civ. App. 1978); James v. Mac Del Health Care, Inc., 428 So. 2d 48 (Ala. Civ. App. 1982); Poole Furn. Mfg. Co. v. State Dep't of Indus. Relations, 474 So. 2d 692 (Ala. 1985).

Collateral references. — Election to be subject to unemployment compensation act by employer otherwise not within act. 158 ALR 601.

§ 25-4-9. Employing unit.

"Employing unit," as used in this chapter, means any individual or type of organization, including any partnership, association, trust estate, joint stock company or corporation, whether domestic or foreign, or the receiver, trustee in bankruptcy, trustee or successor thereof, or the legal representative of a deceased person, which has, or subsequent to January 1, 1935, had in its employ one or more individuals performing services for it within this state. All individuals performing services within this state for any employing unit which maintains two or more separate establishments within this state shall be deemed to be employed by a single employing unit for all the purposes of this chapter. (Acts 1939, No. 497, p. 721; Code 1940, T. 26, § 183.)

Cited in Tennessee Coal, Iron & R.R. v. Martin, 33 Ala. App. 502, 36 So. 2d 535 (1948).

Collateral references. — Provision of unemployment compensation act as to employment units which are affiliated or under a common control. 142 ALR 918, 158 ALR 1237.

State banks, insurance companies, or building and loan associations, which are members of federal reserve banks or similar federal agencies or national banks, as within state unemployment compensation act. 145 ALR 1074, 165 ALR 1250.

What amounts to presence of foreign corporation in state, so as to render it liable to actions therein to recover unemployment compensation tax. 161 ALR 1068.

Provision of unemployment compensation act subjecting to its provisions an employer purchasing or succeeding to the business of another employer. 4 ALR2d 721.

Liability of political party or its subdivision for contributions under unemployment compensation acts. 43 ALR3d 1351.

§ 25-4-10. Employment.

(a) Subject to other provisions of this chapter, "employment" means:

(1) Any service performed prior to January 1, 1978, which was employment as defined in this section prior to such date and, subject to the other provisions of this section, services performed for remuneration after December 31, 1977, including service in interstate commerce, by:

a. Any officer of a corporation; or

b. Any individual who, under the usual common law rules applicable in determining the employer-employee relationship, has the status of an employee; or

c. Any individual other than an individual who is an employee under paragraphs a or b of this subdivision who performs services for remuneration for any person:

1. As an agent-driver or commission-driver engaged in distributing meat products, bakery products, beverages (other than milk) or laundry or dry cleaning services for his principal;

2. As a traveling or city salesman engaged upon a full-time basis in the solicitation on behalf of, and the transmission to, his principal (except for sideline sales activities on behalf of some other person) of orders from wholesalers, retailers, contractors or operators of hotels, restaurants or other similar establishments for merchandise for resale or supplies for use in their business operations.

For purposes of paragraph c of this subdivision, the term "employment" shall include services described in subparagraphs 1 and 2 of paragraph c of this subdivision, performed after December 31, 1971, only if:

(i) The contract of service contemplates that substantially all of the services are to be performed personally by such individual;

(ii) The individual does not have a substantial investment in facilities used in connection with the performance of the services (other than in facilities for transportation); and

301

(iii) The services are not in the nature of a single transaction that is not part of a continuing relationship with the person for whom the services are rendered.

(2) Service performed:

a. After December 31, 1971, but prior to January 1, 1978, by an individual in the employ of this state or any of its instrumentalities or political subdivisions or their instrumentalities (or in the employ of any of the foregoing and one or more other states or their instrumentalities or political subdivisions) for a hospital or institution of higher education located in this state; provided, however, that such service is excluded from "employment" as defined in the Federal Unemployment Tax Act solely by reason of Section 3306(c)(7) of that act, and is not excluded from "employment" under subsection (b) of this section; provided further, that such service in the employ of a political subdivision or any of its instrumentalities shall be deemed to be "employment" within the meaning of this chapter only if said political subdivision or its instrumentalities has elected to become an employer subject to this chapter pursuant to Section 25-4-131 for all such service in the employ of the political subdivision and its instrumentalities and has not ceased to be an employer subject hereto pursuant to Section 25-4-130 or Section 25-4-131; and

b. After December 31, 1977, in the employ of this state or any of its instrumentalities or of any political subdivision thereof or any of its instrumentalities or any instrumentality of more than one of the foregoing or any instrumentality of any one of the foregoing and one or more other states or political subdivisions, provided, however, that such service is excluded from "employment" as defined in the Federal Unemployment Tax Act by Section 3306(c)(7) of that act and is not excluded from "employment" under subsection (b) of this section.

c. For the purposes of this chapter, the term "governmental entity" in reference to this state is defined as the entirety of state government, but for the purposes of reporting, accounting or other administrative procedures such entity shall be divided into each department, agency, board, commission and any other separately organized division or instrumentality of this state. The comptroller of this state shall make such payments to the director as are required by the other provisions of this chapter as they pertain to the various organizational components of the state. The comptroller is hereby authorized to require of such components such payments as are necessary to discharge his responsibilities and shall enforce such payments under the provisions of subsection (b) of Section 25-4-51.

d. The term "governmental entity" in reference to any political subdivision is defined as each county and its instrumentalities and each municipality and its instrumentalities, except that each instrumentality of a political subdivision which is separately incorporated or otherwise removed from the control of the governing body of the political subdivision shall be a separate governmental entity. Instrumentalities organized and operated jointly by any combination of two or more of the aforementioned entities shall be considered as constituting a separate governmental entity. The foregoing notwithstanding, each separate public school system shall constitute a separate governmental entity.

(3) Service performed after December 31, 1971, by an individual in the employ of a religious, charitable, educational or other organization but only if the following conditions are met:

a. The service is excluded from "employment" as defined in the Federal Unemployment Tax Act solely by reason of Section 3306(c)(8) of that act, and is not excluded from "employment" under subdivisions (8) and (21) of subsection (b) of this section; and

b. The organization had four or more individuals in employment for some portion of a day in each of 20 different weeks, whether or not such weeks were consecutive, within either the current or preceding calendar year, regardless of whether they were employed at the same moment of time.

(4)a. Service performed after December 31, 1977, by an individual in agricultural labor as defined in subdivision (1) of subsection (b) of this section, when:

1. Such service is performed for an employing unit which:

(i) During any calendar quarter in either the current or the preceding calendar year paid remuneration in cash of $20,000.00 or more to individuals employed in agricultural labor (not taking into account service in agricultural labor performed before January 1, 1984, by an alien referred to in subparagraph 2 of this paragraph a; or

(ii) For some portion of a day in each of 20 different calendar weeks, whether or not such weeks were consecutive, in either the current or the preceding calendar year, employed in agricultural labor (not taking into account service in agricultural labor performed before January 1, 1984, by an alien referred to in subparagraph 2 of this paragraph a, 10 or more individuals, regardless of whether they were employed at the same moment of time.

2. For the purposes of this paragraph a, such service is not considered to be performed in agricultural labor if performed before January 1, 1984, by an individual who is an alien admitted to the United States to perform service in agricultural labor pursuant to Sections 214(c) and 101(a)(15)(H) of the Immigration and Nationality Act.

3. For the purposes of this paragraph a any individual who is a member of a crew furnished by a crew leader to perform service in agricultural labor for any other person shall be treated as an employee of such crew leader.

(i) If such crew leader holds a valid certificate of registration under the Farm Labor Contractor Registration Act of 1963, or substantially all the members of such crew operate or maintain tractors, mechanized harvesting or crop dusting equipment, or any other mechanized equipment, which is provided by such crew leader; and

(ii) If such individual is not an employee of any other person within the meaning of subdivision (1) of this subsection.

4. For the purposes of this subdivision (4) in the case of any individual who is furnished by a crew leader to perform service in agricultural labor for any other person and who is not treated as an employee of such crew leader under subparagraph 3 of this paragraph a:

(i) Such other person and not the crew leader shall be treated as the employer of such individual; and

(ii) Such other person shall be treated as having paid cash remuneration to such individual in an amount equal to the amount of cash remuneration paid to such individual by the crew leader (either on his own behalf or on the behalf of such other person) for the service in agricultural labor performed for such other person.

5. For the purposes of this paragraph a, the term "crew leader" shall mean an individual who:

(i) Furnishes individuals to perform service in agricultural labor for any other persons;

(ii) Pays (either on his own behalf or on behalf of such other person) the individuals so furnished by him for the service in agricultural labor performed by them; and

(iii) Has not entered into a written agreement with the farm operator under which such crew leader is designated as an employee of such farm operator.

b. Domestic service after December 31, 1977, in a private home, local college club or local chapter of a college fraternity or sorority performed for a person who paid cash remuneration of $1,000.00 or more in any calendar quarter in the current calendar year or the preceding calendar year to individuals employed in such domestic service.

For the purposes of this paragraph b the term "domestic service" includes all service for a person in the operation and maintenance of a private household, local college club or local chapter of a college fraternity or sorority as distinguished from service as an employee in the pursuit of an employer's trade, occupation, profession, enterprise or vocation.

(5) The term "employment" shall include the service of an individual who is a citizen of the United States, performed outside the United States after December 31, 1971, (except in Canada or in the case of the Virgin Islands after December 31, 1971, and prior to January 1 of the year following the year in which the U.S. Secretary of Labor approves the Unemployment Compensation Law of the Virgin Islands under Section 3304(a) of the Internal Revenue Code of 1954) in the employ of an American employer (other than service which is deemed "employment" under the provisions of

subdivision (8) or (9) of this subsection (a) or the parallel provisions of another state's law), if:

a. The employer's principal place of business in the United States is located in this state; or

b. The employer has no place of business in the United States, but:

1. The employer is an individual who is a resident of this state; or

2. The employer is a corporation which is organized under the laws of this state; or

3. The employer is a partnership or a trust and the number of the partners or trustees who are residents of this state is greater than the number who are residents of any other state; or

c. None of the criteria of paragraphs a and b of this subdivision (5) is met but the employer has elected coverage in this state, or the employer having failed to elect coverage in any state, the individual has filed a claim for benefits, based on such service, under the law of this state.

d. An "American employer," for the purpose of this subsection, means a person who is:

1. An individual who is a resident of the United States; or

2. A partnership, if two-thirds or more of the partners are residents of the United States; or

3. A trust, if all of the trustees are residents of the United States; or

4. A corporation organized under the laws of the United States or of any state.

e. For the purposes of this subdivision (5), the term "United States" include the states of the United States, the District of Columbia, the Commonwealth of Puerto Rico, and in the case of the Virgin Islands, after December 31 of the year in which the U.S. Secretary of Labor approves the Virgin Islands' Unemployment Insurance Law for the first time.

(6) Notwithstanding subdivision (8) of this subsection (a), all service performed by an officer or a member of the crew of an American vessel on or in connection with such vessel, if the operating office from which the operations of such vessel operating on navigable waters within, or within and without, the United States are ordinarily and regularly supervised, managed, directed and controlled, is within this state.

(7) Notwithstanding any other provisions of this section, service with respect to which a tax is required to be paid under any federal law imposing a tax against which credit may be taken for contributions required to be paid into a state unemployment fund or which as a condition for full tax credit against the tax imposed by the Federal Unemployment Tax Act is required to be covered under this chapter.

(8) Subject to the other provisions of this section, the term "employment" shall include an employee's entire service, performed within or both within and without this state if:

a. The service is localized in this state; or

b. The service is not localized in any state but some of the service is performed in this state and the base of operations, or, if there is no base of operations, then the place from which such service is directed or controlled is in this state, or the base of operations or place from which such service is directed or controlled is not in any state in which some part of the service is performed, but the employee's residence is in this state;

c. Service shall be deemed to be localized within a state if the service is performed entirely within such state, or the service is performed both within and without such state, but the service performed without such state is incidental to the employee's service within the state; for example, service which is temporary or transitory in nature or consists of isolated transactions;

d. The service shall be deemed to be localized in this state wherever such service is performed within the United States, as defined in paragraph e of subdivision (5) of subsection (a) of this section, if such service is not covered under the unemployment compensation law of any other state, as defined in Section 25-4-14, and the place from which such service is directed or controlled is in this state.

(9) Services not covered under subdivision (8) of this subsection (a) and performed entirely without the state, with respect to no part of which contributions are required and paid under an unemployment compensation law of any other state or of the federal government, shall be deemed to be employment subject to this chapter if the employee performing such service is a resident of this state and the director approves the election of the employing unit for whom such services are performed. The entire service of such employee shall be deemed to be "employment" subject to this chapter.

(10) The term "employment" includes a person's entire services if such service is deemed performed in this state by virtue of reciprocal agreements pursuant to the provisions of Section 25-4-120 and does not include any service which by virtue of such agreement is deemed performed in another state.

(b) The term "employment" shall not include:

(1) Except as provided in paragraph a of subdivision (4) of subsection (a) of this section, service performed by an individual in agricultural labor. For purposes of this chapter, the term "agricultural labor" means any service performed prior to January 1, 1978, which was agricultural labor as defined in this section prior to such date, and remunerated service performed after December 31, 1977, if such service was performed:

a. On a farm, in the employ of any employing unit, in connection with cultivating the soil, or in connection with raising or harvesting any agricultural or horticultural commodity, including the raising, shearing, feeding, caring for, training and management of livestock, bees, poultry and fur-bearing animals and wildlife.

b. In the employ of the owner or tenant or other operator of a farm, in connection with the operation, management, conservation, improvement or maintenance of such farm and its tools and equipment, or in salvaging timber or clearing land of brush and other debris left by a hurricane, if the major part of such service is performed on a farm.

  c. In connection with the production or harvesting of any commodity defined as an agricultural commodity in Section 15(g) of the Agricultural Marketing Act, as amended (46 Stat. 1550, Sec. 3; 12 U.S.C. 1141j), or in connection with the ginning of cotton, or in connection with the operation or maintenance of ditches, canals, reservoirs, or waterways, not owned or operated for profit, used exclusively for supplying and storing water for farming purposes.

  d. In the employ of the operator of a farm, a group of operators of farms (or a cooperative organization of which such operators are members) in handling, planting, drying, packing, packaging, processing, freezing, grading, storing or delivering to storage or to market or to a carrier for transportation to market, in its unmanufactured state, any agricultural or horticultural commodities, but only if such operator or group of operators (or a cooperative organization of which such operators are members) produced more than one half of the commodity with respect to which service is performed; provided, however, the provisions of this paragraph shall not be deemed to be applicable with respect to service performed in connection with commercial canning or commercial freezing or in connection with any agricultural or horticultural commodity after its delivery to a terminal market for distribution for consumption.

  e. On a farm operated for profit if such service is not in the course of the employer's trade or business.

As used in this subdivision, the term "farm" includes stock, dairy, poultry, fruit, fur-bearing animal and truck farms, plantations, ranches, nurseries, ranges, greenhouses or other similar structures used primarily for the raising of agricultural or horticultural commodities, and orchards.

  (2) Prior to January 1, 1978, domestic services in a private home, local college club, or local chapter of a college fraternity or sorority and after December 31, 1977, if the provisions of paragraph b of subdivision (4) of subsection (a) of this section are not met.

  (3) Casual labor not in the usual course of the employer's trade or business performed after December 31, 1971, in any calendar quarter by an individual, unless the cash remuneration paid for such service is $50.00 or more and such service is performed by an individual who is regularly employed by such employing unit to perform such service. For the purposes of this subdivision, an individual shall be deemed to be regularly employed to perform service not in the course of an employing unit's trade or business during a calendar quarter only if:

  a. On each of some 24 days during such quarter such individual performs such service for some portion of the day; or

  b. Such individual was regularly employed (as determined under paragraph a of this subdivision) by such employing unit in the performance of such service during the preceding calendar quarter.

(4) Service performed by an individual in the employ of his son, daughter or spouse, and service performed by an individual under the age of 21 in the employ of his father or mother.

(5) Prior to January 1, 1978, except to the extent set forth in subdivision (2) of subsection (a) of this section, service performed in the employ of this state, or any political subdivision thereof, or of any instrumentality of this state or its political subdivisions.

(6) Prior to January 1, 1978, except as provided in subdivision (2) of subsection (a) of this section, service performed in the employ of any other state or any political subdivisions thereof, or any instrumentality of any one or more of the foregoing which is wholly owned by one or more such states or political subdivisions, and any service performed in the employ of any instrumentality of any one or more other states or their political subdivisions to the extent that the instrumentality is, with respect to such service, immune, under the Constitution of the United States from the tax imposed by Section 3301 of the Federal Internal Revenue Code.

(7) Service performed in the employ of the United States government or of any instrumentality wholly owned by the United States, except that if the Congress of the United States shall permit states to require any instrumentalities of the United States to make payments into an unemployment fund under this chapter, then to the extent permitted by Congress and from and after the date as of which such permission becomes effective, all of the provisions of this chapter shall be applicable to such instrumentalities and to services performed by employees for such instrumentalities in the same manner, to the same extent, and on the same terms as to all other employers and employing units; provided, however, if this state should not be certified by the Secretary of Labor under Section 3304(c) of the Federal Internal Revenue Code for any year, then the payment required of such instrumentality with respect to such year shall be deemed to have been erroneously collected within the meaning of Article 3 of this chapter and shall be refunded by the director from the fund in accordance with the provisions of Section 25-4-137.

(8) Except to the extent set forth in subdivision (3) of subsection (a) of this section, service performed in the employ of a corporation, community chest, fund or foundation organized and operated exclusively for religious, charitable, scientific, literary or educational purposes, or for the prevention of cruelty to children or animals, no part of the net earnings of which inures to the benefit of any private shareholder or individual, and no substantial part of the activities of which is carrying on propaganda, or otherwise attempting to influence legislation.

(9) Service performed after June 30, 1939, with respect to which unemployment compensation is payable under the Railroad Unemployment Insurance Act of Congress (52 Stat. 1094, as amended) and services with respect to which unemployment compensation is payable under any other unemployment compensation system established by an act of Congress; provided, however, that the director is hereby authorized and directed to

enter into agreements with the proper agencies under such act or acts of Congress, which agreements shall become effective 10 days after publication thereof in the manner provided in Section 25-4-111 for general rules to provide reciprocal treatment to individuals who have, after acquiring potential rights to benefits under this chapter acquired rights to unemployment compensation under such act or acts of Congress, or who have, after acquiring potential rights to unemployment compensation under such act or acts of Congress, acquired rights to benefits under this chapter.

(10) Service performed by an individual as an insurance agent or as an insurance solicitor, if all such service performed by such individual is performed for remuneration solely by way of commission.

(11) Service performed, in the employ of a school, college or university, if such service is performed:

a. By a student who is enrolled and is regularly attending classes at such school, college or university; or

b. By the spouse of such a student, if such spouse is advised at the time such spouse commences to perform such service, that:

1. The employment of such spouse to perform such service is provided under a program to provide financial assistance to such student by such school, college or university; and

2. Such employment will not be covered by any program of unemployment insurance.

(12) Service performed by an individual who is enrolled at a nonprofit or public educational institution which normally maintains a regular faculty and curriculum and normally has a regularly organized body of students in attendance at the place where its educational activities are carried on, as a student in a full-time program, taken for credit at such institution, which combines academic instruction with work experience, if such service is an integral part of such program, and such institution has so certified to the employer, except this paragraph shall not apply to service performed in a program established for or on behalf of an employer or group of employers.

(13) Service performed in the employ of a hospital, if such service is performed by a patient of the hospital as defined in subsection (e) of this section, or service performed as a student nurse in the employ of a hospital or a nurses' training school by an individual who is enrolled and is regularly attending classes in a nurses' training school chartered or approved pursuant to state laws, and service performed as an intern in the employ of a hospital by an individual who has completed a four-year course in a medical school chartered or approved pursuant to state law.

(14) Service performed by an individual under the age of 18 in the delivery or distribution of newspapers or shopping news, not including delivery or distribution to any point for subsequent delivery or distribution.

(15) Except as provided in subdivisions (2) and (3) of subsection (a) of this section, any employment or service which is excluded by the express statutory provisions of Section 3306 of the Federal Internal Revenue Code as amended.

(16) Service performed by an officer or member of the crew of a vessel which is not an American vessel. The term "American vessel" means any vessel documented or numbered under the law of the United States, and includes any vessel which is neither documented nor numbered under the laws of the United States nor documented under the laws of any foreign country, if its crew is employed solely by one or more citizens or residents of the United States or corporations organized under the laws of the United States or of any state.

(17) Service performed by an individual in (or as an officer or member of the crew of a vessel while it is engaged in) the catching, taking, harvesting, cultivating or farming of any kind of fish, shellfish, crustacea, sponges, seaweeds or other aquatic forms of animal and vegetable life (including service performed by any such individual as an ordinary incident to any such activity), except:

a. Service performed in connection with the catching or taking of salmon or halibut for commercial purposes; and

b. Service performed on or in connection with a vessel of more than 10 net tons (determined in the manner provided for determining the register tonnage of merchant vessels under the laws of the United States).

(18) Service performed in the employ of a foreign government (including service as a consular or other officer or employee or a nondiplomatic representative).

(19) Service performed in the employ of an instrumentality wholly owned by a foreign government if:

a. The service is of a character similar to that performed in foreign countries by employees of the United States government or of an instrumentality thereof; and

b. The director finds that the United States Secretary of State has certified to the United States Secretary of the Treasury that the foreign government, with respect to whose instrumentality exemption is claimed, grants an equivalent exemption with respect to similar service performed in the foreign country by employees of the United States government and of instrumentalities thereof.

(20) Except to the extent set forth in subdivision (3) of subsection (a) of this section, service performed in any calendar quarter in the employ of any organization exempt from income tax under Section 501(a) of the Federal Internal Revenue Code (other than organizations described in Section 401(a)) or under Section 521 of such Code, if the remuneration for such service is less than $50.00.

(21) Services performed for any governmental entity, institution or organization described in subdivisions (2) and (3) of subsection (a) of this section:

a. In the employ of:

1. A church or convention or association of churches; or

2. An organization that is operated primarily for religious purposes and which is operated, supervised, controlled or principally supported by a church or convention or association of churches; or

b. By a duly ordained, commissioned or licensed minister of a church in the exercise of his ministry or by a member of a religious order in the exercise of duties required by such order; or

c. Except as provided in subdivision (7) of subsection (a) of Section 25-4-8:

1. Prior to January 1, 1978, in the employ of a school which is not an institution of higher education;

2. After December 31, 1977, in the employ of a governmental entity referred to in paragraph b of subdivision (2) of subsection (a) of this section, if such service is performed by an individual in the exercise of duties:

(i) As an elected official;

(ii) As a member of a legislative body, or a member of the judiciary of this state or any of its political subdivisions;

(iii) As a member of the State National Guard or Air National Guard;

(iv) As an employee serving on a temporary basis in case of fire, storm, snow, earthquake, flood or similar emergency (this exclusion does not apply to permanent employees whose usual responsibilities include emergency situations);

(v) In a position which, under or pursuant to the laws of this state, is designated as a major nontenured policymaking or advisory position or a policymaking or advisory position the performance of the duties of which ordinarily does not require more than 8 hours per week; or

d. In a facility conducted for the purpose of carrying out a program of rehabilitation for individuals whose earning capacity is impaired by age or physical or mental deficiency or injury or providing remunerative work for individuals who because of their impaired physical or mental capacity cannot be readily absorbed in the competitive labor market by an individual receiving such rehabilitation or remunerative work; or

e. As part of an unemployment work relief or work training program assisted or financed in whole or in part by any federal agency or an agency of a state or political subdivision thereof, by an individual receiving such work relief or work training; or

f. For a hospital in a state prison or other state correctional institution prior to January 1, 1978, by an inmate of the prison or correctional institution and, after December 31, 1977, by an inmate of a custodial or penal institution.

(22) Services performed by an individual as a qualified real estate agent. For the purposes of this chapter the term "qualified real estate agent" shall mean an individual who is a sales person if:

a. Such individual is a licensed real estate agent; and

b. Substantially all of the remuneration for services performed as a real estate agent (whether or not paid in cash) is directly related to sales or other output (including the performance of services), rather than the number of hours worked, and

c. The services performed by the individual are performed pursuant to a written contract between such individual and the person for whom the services are performed and such contract provides that the individual will not be treated as an employee with respect to such services for federal tax purposes.

(23) Services performed by an individual as a direct seller. For the purposes of this chapter the term "direct seller" shall mean any individual who:

a. Is engaged in the trade or business of selling (or soliciting the sale of) consumer products to any buyer on a:

1. Buy-sell basis, or

2. Deposit-commission basis, or

3. Any similar basis which the U.S. Secretary of the Treasury prescribes by regulations, for resale (by the buyer or any other individual), in the home or otherwise than in a permanent retail establishment; or

b. Is engaged in the trade or business of selling (or soliciting the sale of) consumer products to a consumer in the home or otherwise than in a permanent retail establishment, and

c. Substantially all of the remuneration for the services performed by such individual as a direct seller (whether or not paid in cash) is directly related to sales or output (including the performance of services) rather than to the number of hours worked, and

d. The services performed by such individual are performed pursuant to a written contract between such individual and the person for whom the services are performed and such contract provides that the individual will not be treated as an employee with respect to such services for federal tax purposes.

(c) "Institution of higher education," for the purposes of this chapter, means an educational institution which:

(1) Admits as regular students only individuals having a certificate of graduation from a high school, or the recognized equivalent of such a certificate;

(2) Is legally authorized in this state to provide a program of education beyond high school;

(3) Provides an educational program for which it awards a bachelor's or higher degree, or provides a program which is acceptable for full credit toward such a degree, or a program of postgraduate or postdoctoral studies, or a program of training to prepare students for gainful employment in a recognized occupation.

(d) For the purposes of this chapter the term "educational institution" means an educational institution (including an institution of higher education as defined in subsection (c) of this section) in which:

(1) Participants, trainees or students are offered an organized course of study or training designed to transfer to them knowledge, skills, information, doctrines, attitudes or abilities from, by or under the guidance of an instructor(s) or teacher(s).

(2) It is approved, licensed or issued a permit to operate as a school by the State Department of Education or other government agency that is authorized within the state to approve, license or issue a permit for the operation of a school.

(3) The courses of study or training which it offers may be academic, technical, trade, or preparation for gainful employment in a recognized occupation, as opposed to study or training in the social graces or skills or whose primary purpose is to provide baby-sitting or day care services although some learning activities may be included.

In any particular case, the question of whether or not an institution is an educational institution (other than an institution of higher education) within the meaning of the criteria described above will depend on what that particular institution actually does.

(e) "Hospital" means an institution which has been licensed, certified or approved by the State Board of Health or the State Board of Mental Health as a hospital or a similar institution operated by the state or any of its political subdivisions or by an instrumentality of either of the foregoing.

(f) If the services performed during one half or more of any pay period by an employee for the employing unit employing him constitute employment, all of the services of such employee for such period shall be deemed to be employment, but if the services performed during more than one half of any such pay period by an employee for the employing unit employing him do not constitute employment, then none of the services of such employee for such period shall be deemed to be employment. As used in this subsection the term "pay period" means a period (of not more than 31 consecutive days) for which a payment or remuneration is ordinarily made to the employee by the employing unit employing him. (Acts 1939, No. 497, p. 721; Code 1940, T. 26, § 186; Acts 1945, No. 283, p. 449, § 1; Acts 1971, No. 166, p. 440, § 4; Acts 1975, No. 801, p. 1604, §§ 1, 2; Acts 1978, 1st Ex. Sess., No. 1, p. 5, § 2; Acts 1980, No. 80-756, p. 1561, § 2; Acts 1983, 2nd Ex. Sess., No. 83-155, p. 264, § 1.)

U.S. Code. — The Federal Unemployment Tax Act is codified as 26 U.S.C.A. § 3301 et seq. Section 3306 of that act is codified as 26 U.S.C.A. § 3306.

The Immigration and Nationality Act is codified as 8 U.S.C.A. § 1101 et seq. Sections 101 and 214 of that act are codified as 8 U.S.C.A. §§ 1101 and 1184, respectively.

The Farm Labor Contractor Registration Act of 1963 is codified as 7 U.S.C.A. § 2041 et seq.

The Railroad Unemployment Insurance Act (52 Stat. 1094) is codified as 42 U.S.C.A. §§ 503, 1104, 1107 and 45 U.S.C.A. § 351 et seq.

Sections 401, 501, 521, 3301, 3304 and 3306 of the Internal Revenue Code are codified as 26

U.S.C.A. §§ 401, 501, 521, 3301, 3304 and 3306, respectively.

Government service included. — Paragraphs (a)(2)b. and (a)(2)d. provide that employment, for purposes of unemployment compensation, includes service performed in the employ of a governmental entity within a political subdivision. Director of State Dep't of Indus. Relations v. Winston County Comm'n, 468 So. 2d 177 (Ala. Civ. App. 1985).

Under the clear and unambiguous language of paragraph (a)(2)d., the office of the probate judge of Winston county is a separate governmental entity from the county commission. Director of State Dep't of Indus. Relations v. Winston County Comm'n, 468 So. 2d 177 (Ala. Civ. App. 1985).

Master-servant relationship did not exist between county commission and laid-off employee. — Where county commission did not exercise any control over laid-off employee of the probate judge of the county and it was not shown that the commission even had the right to exercise control over the employee, no master-servant relationship existed between the employee and the commission and the employee was not an "employee" of the commission under § 25-4-7. Director of State Dep't of Indus. Relations v. Winston County Comm'n, 468 So. 2d 177 (Ala. Civ. App. 1985).

Farm "operator" embraces anyone actually exercising control over farm production. — The lack of a proprietary interest in the farm being managed does not disqualify one as an operator of that farm; the word embraces anyone actually exercising control over farm production. Carter v. J.P. King & Sons, 381 So. 2d 71 (Ala. Civ. App.), cert. denied, 381 So. 2d 76 (Ala. 1980).

Character of employment and not place of performance determine whether agricultural. — The whole character of the employment, not only the place of performance, determines whether an employee is engaged in

agricultural labor. A processing activity does not lose its character as agricultural labor if done at a plant some distance from the farm. Carter v. J.P. King & Sons, 381 So. 2d 71 (Ala. Civ. App.), cert. denied, 381 So. 2d 76 (Ala. 1980).

It is self-evident that egg production is a farming enterprise and a chosen device of production does not alter a corporation's status as farmer engaging in ordinary farming operations. Carter v. J.P. King & Sons, 381 So. 2d 71 (Ala. Civ. App.), cert. denied, 381 So. 2d 76 (Ala. 1980).

Cited in Opinion of Justices, 252 Ala. 527, 41 So. 2d 775 (1949); Carter v. Carter, 395 So. 2d 1020 (Ala. Civ. App. 1981); Alabama v. Marshall, 626 F.2d 366 (5th Cir. 1980).

Collateral references. — 81 C.J.S., Social Security and Public Welfare, §§ 153, 154, 165-178.

76 Am. Jur. 2d, Unemployment Compensation, §§ 23-30, 39, 40.

Provision of unemployment compensation act relating to exemption of corporations or institutions of a religious, charitable, or educational character. 136 ALR 1467, 155 ALR 369.

Salesmen on commission as within unemployment compensation acts. 138 ALR 1413, 29 ALR2d 751.

Industrial home workers as within unemployment compensation act. 143 ALR 418.

Who is "member of a crew" within meaning of unemployment compensation acts. 161 ALR 842.

What constitutes "agricultural" or "farm" labor within unemployment compensation acts. 53 ALR2d 406.

Insurance agents or salesmen as within coverage of social security or unemployment compensation acts. 39 ALR3d 872.

Part-time or intermittent workers as covered by or as eligible for benefits under State Unemployment Compensation Act. 95 ALR3d 891.

§ 25-4-11. Employment office.

"Employment office," as used in this chapter, means a free public employment office or a branch thereof operated by this or any other state as a part of a state controlled system of public employment offices or by a federal agency charged with the administration of an unemployment compensation program or free public employment offices. (Acts 1939, No. 497, p. 721; Code 1940, T. 26, § 187; Acts 1943, No. 310, p. 281, § 2.)

§ 25-4-12. Fund.

"Fund," as used in this chapter, means the unemployment compensation fund established by this chapter, to which all contributions and payments in lieu of contributions and from which all benefits required under this chapter shall be paid. All interest earned on the fund shall be credited to said fund. (Acts 1939, No. 497, p. 721; Code 1940, T. 26, § 189; Acts 1971, No. 166, p. 440, § 5.)

§ 25-4-13. Insured work.

"Insured work," as used in this chapter, means "employment" for "employers." (Acts 1939, No. 497, p. 721; Code 1940, T. 26, § 196.)

§ 25-4-14. State.

"State," as used in this chapter, includes, in addition to the states of the United States, the District of Columbia, the Virgin Islands, Puerto Rico and Canada. (Acts 1939, No. 497, p. 721; Code 1940, T. 26, § 188; Acts 1967, No. 167, p. 499, § 1; Acts 1971, No. 88, p. 349, § 1.)

§ 25-4-15. Unemployment administration fund.

"Unemployment administration fund," as used in this chapter, means the unemployment compensation administration fund established by this chapter. (Acts 1939, No. 497, p. 721; Code 1940, T. 26, § 190.)

§ 25-4-16. Wages.

(a) Prior to January 1, 1983, "wages," as used in this chapter, shall mean such remuneration as was defined in this section prior to such date.

(b) On and after January 1, 1983, "wages," as used in this chapter, shall mean every form of remuneration paid or received for personal services, including the cash value of any remuneration paid in any medium other than cash. The reasonable cash value of remuneration paid in any medium other than cash shall be determined in accordance with rules prescribed by the director; except that effective on May 28, 1980, and for the purposes of reporting and computing the amount of contributions due, back pay awarded as the result of an agreement, arbitration or order of a court of competent jurisdiction on a retroactive basis shall be considered "wages" during the calendar quarter in which such retroactive payments are made. The term "wages," however, shall not include:

(1) That part of remuneration, which after remuneration equal to $8,000.00 (or such greater amount as may be or become subject to a tax under a federal law imposing a tax against which credit may be taken for contributions required to be paid into a state unemployment fund) has been paid in a calendar year to an individual by an employer or his predecessor employer or by a combination of both the employer and his predecessor

315

employer with respect to employment during any calendar year, is paid to such individual by such employer during such calendar year except with respect to subdivisions (1) and (2) of subsection (a), subdivision (4) of subsection (b) and subsection (c) of Section 25-4-54 and Sections 25-4-71 through 25-4-75. For the purpose of this subdivision (1), the term "employment" shall include service constituting employment under any unemployment compensation law of another state or of this state.

(2) The amount of any payments (including any amount paid by an employer for insurance or annuities, or into a fund to provide for any such payment) made to, or on behalf of an employee or any of his dependents under a plan or system established by an employer which makes provisions for his employees generally (or for his employees generally and their dependents) or for a class or classes of his employees (or for a class or classes of his employees and their dependents), on account of:

a. Retirement; or

b. Sickness or accident disability; or

c. Medical or hospitalization expenses in connection with sickness or accident disability; or

d. Death.

(3) Any payment made to an employee (including any amount paid by an employer for insurance or annuities, or into a fund to provide for any such payment) on account of retirement.

(4) Any payment made by an employer to, or on behalf of, any employee or his beneficiary:

a. From or to a trust which meets the requirements of Section 401(k) of the Federal Internal Revenue Code and which is exempt from tax under Section 501(a) of the Federal Internal Revenue Code at the time of such payment unless such payment is made to an employee of the trust as remuneration for services rendered as such employee and not as a beneficiary of the trust; or

b. Under or to an annuity plan which, at the time of such payment, meets the requirements of Section 401(a) (3), (4), (5) and (6) of the Federal Internal Revenue Code.

(5) The payment by an employer (without deduction from the remuneration of the employee) of the tax imposed upon an employee under Article 3 of this chapter, or of the tax imposed upon an employee by Section 3101 of the Federal Internal Revenue Code, as amended, with respect only to remuneration paid to an employee for domestic service in a private home or for agricultural labor.

(6) Remuneration paid in any medium other than cash to an employee for agricultural or domestic services or for services not in the course of the employer's trade or business.

(7) Any payment (other than vacation or sick pay) made to an employee after the month in which he attains the age of 65, if he did not work for the employer in the period for which such payment is made.

(8) Dismissal payments which the employer is not legally required to make.

(9) Payments made into a fund by an employer to provide for supplemental unemployment benefits under a plan established to provide such benefits to employees in general, or a group or class of employees, of such employer. (Acts 1939, No. 497, p. 721; Code 1940, T. 26, § 191; Acts 1943, No. 310, p. 281, § 3; Acts 1949, No. 286, p. 412; Acts 1951, No. 644, p. 1098; Acts 1961, Ex. Sess., No. 274, p. 2298, § 3; Acts 1971, No. 166, p. 440, § 6; Acts 1075, No. 801, p. 1604, § 3; Acts 1978, 1st Ex. Sess., No. 1, p. 5, § 3; Acts 1980, No. 80-807, p. 1651, § 1; Acts 1982, No. 82-372, p. 533, § 1; Acts 1983, 2nd Ex. Sess., No. 83-155, p. 264, § 2.)

U.S. Code. — Sections 401, 501, 3101 of the federal Internal Revenue Code are codified as 26 U.S.C.A. §§ 401, 501, 3101, respectively.

Liberal construction. — A liberal construction of the unemployment compensation law is always preferred because the law itself specifically provides that there shall be no vested right of any kind against any subsequent amendment or repeal. West Point Pepperell v. Alabama Dep't of Indus. Relations, 495 So. 2d 678 (Ala. Civ. App.), cert. denied, 495 So. 2d 681 (Ala. 1986).

The unemployment compensation statute is remedial in nature by definition and should receive a liberal interpretation to best serve the purpose and intent of the legislature to avoid injustice. West Point Pepperell v. Alabama Dep't of Indus. Relations, 495 So. 2d 678 (Ala. Civ. App.), cert. denied, 495 So. 2d 681 (Ala. 1986).

Construed against taxing authority. — The unemployment compensation statute is a taxing statute and as all taxing statutes, it is to be strictly construed against the taxing authority. West Point Pepperell v. Alabama Dep't of Indus. Relations, 495 So. 2d 678 (Ala. Civ. App.), cert. denied, 495 So. 2d 681 (Ala. 1986).

Taxable wage base is basis for employer's contribution. — The use of the term "taxable wage base" in Act 83-155, which amended several sections of the Alabama Unemployment Compensation Law, as in the prior act, had reference to the amount of wages set out in this section and upon which the employer's benefit wages are computed. Thus, "taxable wage base" ultimately acted as the basis for the employer's tax contribution rate computation, as provided in former subdivision (b)(5) of § 25-4-54. West Point Pepperell v. Alabama Dep't of Indus. Relations, 495 So. 2d 678 (Ala. Civ. App.), cert. denied, 495 So. 2d 681 (Ala. 1986).

Remuneration voluntarily made is not considered "wages." State, Dep't of Indus. Relations v. Deslattes, 372 So. 2d 867 (Ala. Civ. App.), cert. denied, 372 So. 2d 872 (Ala. 1979).

"Wages," with certain express statutory exceptions, does not include remuneration which an employer is under no legal obligation to make. State, Dep't of Indus. Relations v. Deslattes, 372 So. 2d 867 (Ala. Civ. App.), cert. denied, 372 So. 2d 872 (Ala. 1979).

Holiday pay is wages. — Holiday pay received by appellants for Christmas Day and New Year's Day as provided by the union contract was "wages" within the meaning of this section. Autwell v. State Dep't of Indus. Relations, 47 Ala. App. 8, 249 So. 2d 625 (1971).

Cited in Broadway v. Bolar, 33 Ala. App. 57, 29 So. 2d 687 (1947).

Collateral references. — 81 C.J.S., Social Security and Public Welfare, § 170.

76 Am. Jur. 2d, Unemployment Compensation, §§ 21, 22.

§ 25-4-17. Week.

"Week," as used in this chapter, means such period of seven consecutive days, as the director may by regulation prescribe. The director may by regulation prescribe that a week shall be deemed to be in, within or during that benefit year which includes the greater part of such week, or that benefit year within which such week ends. (Acts 1939, No. 497, p. 721; Code 1940, T. 26, § 192.)

ARTICLE 2.

UNEMPLOYMENT COMPENSATION TRUST FUND.

§ 25-4-30. Administration and composition.

There shall be as a special fund, separate and apart from all public moneys or funds of this state, an unemployment compensation trust fund, which shall be administered by the director exclusively for the purposes of this chapter without liability on the part of the state beyond the amounts paid into and earned by the fund. This fund shall consist of:

(1) All contributions paid in or collected under this chapter;

(2) Interest earned upon any moneys in the fund;

(3) Any property or securities acquired through the use of moneys belonging to the fund;

(4) All earnings of such property or securities;

(5) Any money received from the federal unemployment account in the unemployment trust fund in accordance with Title XII of the Social Security Act;

(6) All money credited to this state's account in the unemployment trust fund pursuant to Section 903 of the Social Security Act, as amended; and

(7) All money received for the fund from any other source. (Acts 1939, No. 497, p. 721; Code 1940, T. 26, § 197; Acts 1945, No. 283, p. 449, § 2; Acts 1957, No. 303, p. 395, § 1; Acts 1963, 2nd Ex. Sess., No. 151, p. 340, § 1.)

Cited in Opinion of Justices, 252 Ala. 468, 41 So. 2d 771 (1949); Department of Indus. Relations v. West Boylston Mfg. Co., 253 Ala. 67, 42 So. 2d 787 (1949).

Collateral references. — 81 C.J.S., Social Security & Public Welfare, §§ 83, 240.

§ 25-4-31. Treasurer; separate accounts; disposition of interest and penalties.

(a) The director shall designate an employee of the unemployment compensation agency as treasurer of the fund who shall pay all vouchers or checks duly drawn upon the fund, in such manner as the director may prescribe. The director shall also designate an employee of the Unemployment Compensation Agency as alternate treasurer who, in case of extended absence of the treasurer shall, upon written notice from the director, perform all duties of the treasurer. The treasurer shall maintain within the fund the following separate accounts: a clearing account; an unemployment trust fund account; an unemployment benefit payment account; and such other account or accounts as may be necessary for the payment of any federal unemployment benefits. All moneys payable to the fund, upon receipt thereof by the director, shall be forwarded to the treasurer who shall immediately deposit them in the clearing account. Refunds payable pursuant to Section 25-4-137 (with the exception of refunds of interest and penalties collected pursuant to Sections 25-4-132, 25-4-133, and 25-4-134) may be paid from the clearing account upon warrants issued by the treasurer, as aforesaid, under the direction of the director. After clearance thereof, all other moneys in the clearing account (with the exception of said interest and penalties collected pursuant to Sections 25-4-132, 25-4-133, and 25-4-134, and any other collections required by this chapter to be transferred to the State Treasury) shall be deposited by warrants issued as aforesaid, with the Secretary of the Treasury of the United States of America to the credit of the account of this state in the unemployment trust fund established and maintained pursuant to Section 904 of the Social Security Act, any provisions of law in this state relating to the deposit, administration, release, or disbursement of moneys in the possession or custody of this state to the contrary notwithstanding. The benefit payment account shall consist of all moneys requisitioned from the state's account in the unemployment trust fund. Except as otherwise provided in this section, moneys in the clearing and benefit accounts may be deposited by the treasurer, under the direction of the director, in any bank or public depository in which general funds of the state may be deposited but no public deposit insurance charge or premium shall be paid out of the fund. The treasurer shall give bond conditioned upon the faithful performance of his duties as treasurer of the fund in a form prescribed by statute or approved by the Attorney General, and in an amount specified by the director and approved by the Governor. All premiums upon bonds required pursuant to this section when furnished by an authorized surety company or by a duly constituted governmental bonding firm shall be paid from the unemployment administration fund.

(b) Interest and penalties collected pursuant to Sections 25-4-132, 25-4-133, and 25-4-134 shall be deposited in the clearing account only for the purpose of transfer to the special employment security administration fund provided for in Section 25-4-142, and shall be spent in accordance with the provisions of said Section 25-4-142.

(c) Funds collected pursuant to the assessment made against wages paid by employers by Section 25-4-55 and Section 25-4-40.1 shall be deposited in the clearing account only for the purpose of transfer to the special interest payment fund and the employment security enhancement fund and shall be expended in accordance with the said provisions. (Acts 1939, No. 497, p. 721; Code 1940, T. 26, § 198; Acts 1945, No. 283, p. 449, § 3; Acts 1963, 2nd Ex. Sess., No. 151, p. 340, § 2; Acts 1973, No. 1057, p. 1716, § 1; Acts 1988, 1st Ex. Sess., No. 88-783, p. 195, § 3; Acts 1992, No. 92-174, § 3.)

The 1992 amendment, effective April 10, 1992, in subsection (c), substituted "and Section 25-4-40.1" for "and section 25-4-40," and inserted "the employment security enhancement fund and" preceding "shall be expended."

U.S. Code. — The Social Security Act is codified as 42 U.S.C.A. § 301.

Cited in Opinion of Justices, 252 Ala. 468, 41 So. 2d 771 (1949); Department of Indus. Relations v. West Boylston Mfg. Co., 253 Ala. 67, 42 So. 2d 787 (1949).

§ 25-4-32. Requisition of moneys from trust fund.

(a) Money shall be requisitioned from the state's account in the unemployment trust fund solely for the payment of benefits and in accordance with regulations prescribed by the director; except, that money credited to this state's account pursuant to Section 903 of the Social Security Act, as amended, shall be used exclusively as provided in this section. The director shall from time to time requisition from the unemployment trust fund such amounts, not exceeding the amounts standing to this state's account therein, as he deems necessary for the payment of benefits for a reasonable future period. Upon receipt thereof the treasurer of the fund shall deposit such moneys in the benefit payment account and shall issue his checks for the payment of benefits solely from such benefit account. Expenditures of such moneys in the benefit payment account and refunds for the clearing account shall not be subject to any provisions of law (and shall be in lieu of all provisions of law) requiring specific appropriations or other formal release by state officers of moneys in their custody. All checks issued by the treasurer of the fund for the payment of benefits shall bear the signature of said treasurer, and the countersignature of the director or his duly authorized agent, both in such manner as the director may prescribe. Any balance of moneys requisitioned from the unemployment trust fund which remains unclaimed or unexpended in the benefit payment account after the expiration of the period for which such sums were requisitioned shall either be deducted from estimates for, and may be utilized for the payment of benefits during succeeding periods, or, in the discretion of the director, shall be redeposited with the Secretary of the Treasury of the United States to the credit of this state's account in the unemployment trust fund as provided in Section 25-4-31.

(b) Money credited to the account of this state in the unemployment trust fund by the Secretary of the Treasury of the United States of America pursuant to Section 903 of the Social Security Act, as amended, may be requisitioned and used for the payment of expenses incurred for the administration of this chapter pursuant to a specific appropriation by the legislature; provided, that the expenses are incurred and the money is requisitioned after the enactment of an appropriation law which:

(1) Specifies the purposes for which such money is appropriated and the amounts appropriated therefor;

(2) Limits the period within which such money may be expended to a period ending not more than two years after the date of the enactment of the appropriation law; and

(3) Limits the amount which may be used during a 12-month period beginning on July 1, and ending on the next June 30, to an amount which does not exceed the amount by which the aggregate of the amounts credited to the account of this state pursuant to Section 903 of the Social Security Act, as amended, exceeds the aggregate of the amounts used pursuant to this section and charged against the amount credited to the account of this state.

(c) Money requisitioned for the payment of expenses of administration pursuant to this section shall be deposited in the employment security administration fund, but, until expended, shall remain a part of the unemployment fund. The director shall maintain a separate record of the deposit, obligation, expenditure, and return of funds so deposited. If any money so deposited is, for any reason, not to be expended for the purpose for which it was appropriated, or, if it remains unexpended at the end of the period specified by the law appropriating such money, it shall be withdrawn and returned to the Secretary of the Treasury of the United States for credit to this state's account in the unemployment trust fund.

(d) Money credited to the account of this state pursuant to Section 903 of the Social Security Act, as amended, may not be withdrawn or used except for the payment of benefits and for the payment of expenses for the administration of this chapter and of public employment offices pursuant to this chapter. (Acts 1939, No. 497, p. 721; Code 1940, T. 26, § 199; Acts 1957, No. 303, p. 395, § 2; Acts 1983, 2nd Ex. Sess., No. 83-155, p. 264, § 3; Acts 1992, No. 92-174, § 4.)

The 1992 amendment, effective April 10, 1992, in subdivision (b)(3), deleted "during the same 12-month period and the 34 preceding 12-month periods" following "as amended," deleted "during any of such 35 12-month periods" following "of this state," and deleted the former second sentence of this subdivision which read: "For the purposes of this subdivision, amounts used during any such 12-month period shall be charged against equivalent amounts which were first credited and which are not already so charged; except, that no amount used during any such 12-month period for administration may be charged against any amount credited during such a 12-month period earlier than the thirty-fourth preceding such period."

Collateral references. — 81 C.J.S., Social Security & Public Welfare, § 241.

ARTICLE 2A.

EMPLOYMENT SECURITY ENHANCEMENT FUNDS.

§ 25-4-40. Employment security administration enhancement fund (Expired).

Code commissioner's note. — This section expired pursuant to its own terms effective December 31, 1991. For present similar provisions, see § 25-4-40.1.

§ 25-4-40.1. Employment security enhancement fund.

(a) Retroactive to April 1, 1992, and ending March 31, 1997, there is hereby placed upon all wages so defined in Section 25-4-16, paid to employees by employers subject to pay contributions as provided in Sections 25-4-51 and 25-4-54, except as is hereinafter provided in this section, a special assessment of 0.06% (six one-hundredths of one percent) of such wages. This assessment shall not apply to wages paid during any calendar quarter of any calendar year by any employer whose rate of contribution has been computed under the provisions of said Section 25-4-54 to be at least 5.40% but not more than 5.45% for such calendar year, to any employer who for such calendar year has elected to make payments in lieu of contributions pursuant to the provisions contained in said Section 25-4-51, nor to any employer who has not had sufficient unemployment experience to qualify for a rate determination under Section 25-4-54 for such calendar year.

(1) Assessments under this section shall become due and payable at the end of each calendar quarter which begins after March 31, 1992, and shall be paid in accordance with regulations as may be prescribed by the director at the same time and in the same manner as employers are required by this chapter to file reports and pay contributions and shall not be deducted, in whole or in part, from any remuneration of individuals in the employ of the employer.

(2) The provisions of Sections 25-4-132 and 25-4-133, relating to the assessment of interest and penalties for delinquent reporting or payments and the procedures for the collection of delinquent reports and payments shall apply to the assessment prescribed by this section. Any interest or penalty so assessed and collected shall be deposited or transferred to the special employment security administration fund provided for in subsection (b) of Section 25-4-142.

(3) All moneys collected as assessments pursuant to the provisions of this section shall be promptly deposited in the clearing account of the Unemployment Compensation fund only for the purpose of transfer and, as soon as practicable to do so, shall be transferred into the "employment security enhancement fund" in the state treasury.

(b) There is hereby created in the State Treasury a special fund, to be known as "the employment security enhancement fund," into which shall be deposited or transferred all funds collected retroactive to April 1, 1992, pursuant to the assessment made by the provisions of Section 25-4-32. All moneys in this fund shall be deposited, administered, and disbursed in the same manner and under the same conditions and requirements as is provided by law for other special funds in the State Treasury. All moneys in this fund shall be continuously available to the director for expenditure in accordance with the provisions of this chapter, and shall not lapse at any time. Said funds shall not be expended or made available for expenditure in any manner which would permit their substitution for federal funds, which would, in the absence of said moneys, be available to finance expenditures for the administration of the state unemployment compensation and employment service laws.

(c) The moneys in the employment security enhancement fund are authorized and, are hereby appropriated, for use by the director as follows:

(1) Special claimant assistance program.

a. Moneys in this fund may be expended to supplement basic employment security services with special job search and job placement assistance designed to assist unemployment compensation claimants obtain employment.

b. The director shall appoint an overview committee consisting of five members and composed of the director of employment service, the director of unemployment compensation, and the chief of the research and statistical divisions of the department, one member representing employers and selected by the Business Council of Alabama (or successor organization) and one member selected to represent employees by the Alabama Labor Council (or successor organization). The committee members shall be selected as soon after approval of this amendment as is practicable.

c. The duties of the overview committee shall include the initial planning of the claimant assistance program as to content and procedures, the determination of standards, criteria, statistical requirements and reporting needs, monitoring the progress of the program and measuring the results and making recommendations to the director.

d. All members of this committee shall serve without remuneration, however, shall be reimbursed for any and all necessary expenses incurred during the performance of their duties in the same manner and under the same regulations as apply to state employees. Such expenses are to be paid from the employment security enhancement fund.

(2) General administration and enhancement of employment security. Necessary and appropriate costs of employment security enhancements, not in conflict with the foregoing or state or federal laws, rules or regulations, may be paid from this fund at the discretion of the director.

(3) The costs of the collection of revenues, for the maintenance of the fund and the repayment of advances to the fund from other sources shall be paid from this fund.

(4) The director shall submit a special report at the end of each calendar year to the Governor, Lieutenant Governor, and the Speaker of the House of Representatives giving an accounting of collections and expenditures, and an assessment of the success of programs funded from this source.

(d) Any interest earned on money in this special fund shall accrue to the employment security enhancement fund.

(e) In the event there is a cessation of the activities and purposes of the programs to be funded by moneys from this fund, all remaining moneys in the employment security enhancement fund, within 90 calendar days after all outstanding obligations of the director related to this fund have been fulfilled, shall be transferred into the state's unemployment compensation trust fund on deposit with the U.S. Treasury. (Acts 1992, No. 92-174, § 2.)

Effective date. — The act which added this section became effective April 10, 1992.

Code commissioner's note. — Acts 1992, No. 92-174, which enacted this section, in § 1 provides: "This act shall be entitled The Employment Security Enhancement Act."

ARTICLE 3.

CONTRIBUTIONS AND PAYMENTS IN LIEU OF CONTRIBUTIONS.

§ 25-4-50. Accrual; time and manner of payment by employers.

Contributions or payments in lieu of contributions shall accrue and become payable by each employer subject to this chapter. Contributions or payments in lieu of contributions shall accrue and become payable by any new employer on and after the date on which he becomes newly subject to this chapter. The contributions or payments in lieu of contributions required under this chapter shall be paid by each employer in such manner and at such times as the director may prescribe. (Acts 1939, No. 497, p. 721; Code 1940, T. 26, § 200; Acts 1971, No. 166, p. 440, § 7.)

Collateral references. — 81 C.J.S., Social Security & Public Welfare, § 148.

Service charges, made by hotels or restaurants and later distributed to waiters or similar employees, as "wages" upon which federal or state unemployment taxes or contributions are required to be paid. 83 ALR2d 1024.

Political party: liability of political party or its subdivision for contributions under unemployment compensation acts. 43 ALR3d 1351.

§ 25-4-51. Rates of contributions, etc., by employers.

(a) *Contributions.* — Except as hereinafter provided and subject to the provisions of Section 25-4-54, every employer shall pay contributions, or payments in lieu of contributions, equal to the percentages of wages payable or paid as hereinafter set out, with respect to employment by him.

(1) With respect to employment during calendar years after December 31, 1975, every employer who has been liable to the provisions of this chapter during a period of time sufficient to have his rate of contribution determined under the experience rating provisions of Section 25-4-54 shall pay contributions at the rate prescribed thereby.

(2) With respect to employment after December 31, 1975, every employer who has not been liable to the provisions of this chapter for a sufficient length of time to have his rate determined under the experience rating provisions of Section 25-4-54 shall pay contributions at the rate of 2.70 percent of such wages paid by him with respect to such employment.

(3) With respect to employment after December 31, 1971, any nonprofit organization which, pursuant to the provisions of subdivision (8) of subsection (a) of Section 25-4-8, is or becomes subject to this chapter after December 31, 1971, shall pay contributions under the provisions of subdivisions (1) and (2) of this subsection (a) of this section and Section 25-4-54, unless it elects in accordance with paragraph a of this subdivision to pay to the director for the fund an amount equal to the amount of regular benefits and one half of the extended benefits paid, that is attributable to service in the employ of such employer, to individuals for weeks of unemployment which begin during the effective period of such election.

a. Any nonprofit organization which becomes subject to this chapter on January 1, 1972, by virtue of its employment during calendar year 1971, may elect to become liable for payments in lieu of contributions for a period of not less than nine consecutive calendar quarters beginning with January 1, 1972, provided it files with the director a written notice of its election within the 30-day period immediately following such date. Any nonprofit organization which becomes subject to this chapter by virtue of its employment subsequent to calendar year 1971, may elect to become liable for payments in lieu of contributions for a period of not less than six consecutive calendar quarters, ending on the thirtieth day of September, by filing a written notice of its election with the director not later than 30 days immediately following the date on which the conditions rendering such organization subject were fulfilled.

b. Any nonprofit organization which makes an election in accordance with paragraph a of this subdivision will continue to be liable for payments in lieu of contributions until it files with the director a written notice terminating its election. Any such termination shall be effective at the end of a calendar year. Said notice shall be filed not later than the first day of December preceding the effective date of such termination.

c. Any nonprofit organization which has been paying contributions under this chapter for a period of at least one calendar year subsequent to January 1, 1972, may change to a reimbursable basis by filing with the director not later than the first day of December preceding the beginning of any calendar year a written notice of election to become liable for payments in lieu of contributions. Such election shall not be terminable by the organization during that and the next calendar year and may be terminated only at the end of a calendar year.

d. The director may for good cause extend the period within which a notice of election, or a notice of termination, must be filed and may permit an election to be retroactive but not any earlier than with respect to benefits paid after December 31, 1971.

e. The director shall notify each nonprofit organization of any determination which he makes of its status as an employer and of the effective date of any election which it makes and of any termination of such election and of benefits paid in accordance with such regulations as he may prescribe. Such notice and determination shall be subject to the provisions for review and finality as set out in subdivision (4) of subsection (c) of Section 25-4-54.

f. Any nonprofit organization which elects to make payments in lieu of contributions shall pay to the director for the fund such amounts and in such manner and at such time as is set out in subsection (b) of this section.

g. When two or more nonprofit organizations, as defined in subdivision (3) of subsection (a) of Section 25-4-10, merge or one nonprofit organization is acquired by another such organization, the method of payment for the surviving entity shall be that method elected by such surviving entity under the provisions of this section and in effect at the time of the merger or acquisition. Such method shall remain in effect until such time as it is changed as provided in paragraphs b and c of this subdivision.

(4)a. With respect to employment after December 31, 1971, and prior to January 1, 1978, any hospital or institution of higher education operated by this state or any of its instrumentalities which, pursuant to the provisions of subdivision (a)(7) of Section 25-4-8, is or becomes subject to this chapter after December 31, 1971, and prior to January 1, 1978, shall pay to the director for the fund an amount equal to the amount of regular benefits and one-half of the extended benefits paid, that is attributable to service in the employ of such employer to individuals for weeks of unemployment which begin after December 31, 1971, at the rate and in such manner and at such time as was prescribed in subdivision (2) of subsection (b) of this section prior to January 1, 1978. For the purpose of this subdivision, the governing body of any state hospital or institution of higher education may, with the approval of the director, determine the number of individual accounts for the institutions under its authority.

b. With respect to employment after December 31, 1977, any governmental entity as defined in paragraph (a)(2)b of Section 25-4-10, electing or required to make payments in lieu of contributions, shall, pursuant to the provisions of subdivision (2) of subsection (b) of this section, pay to the director for the fund an amount which:

1. Prior to January 1, 1979, is equal to the amount of regular benefits and one-half of the extended benefits paid, and

2. After December 31, 1978, is equal to the amount of regular and extended benefits paid and that is attributable to services after December 31, 1977, in the employ of such entity to individuals for weeks of unemployment which begin on or after January 1, 1979.

(5)a. With respect to employment after December 31, 1971, and prior to January 1, 1978, any political subdivision of this state (or any two or more political subdivisions) which elects, under the provisions of Section 25-4-131, to become subject to this chapter, shall pay to the director for the fund an amount equal to the amount of regular benefits and prior to January 1, 1979, one-half, and thereafter all, of the extended benefits paid, that is attributable to service in the employ of such employer, to individuals for weeks of unemployment which begin after December 31, 1971, at the rate and in such manner and at such time as was set out in subdivision (2) of subsection (b) of this section prior to January 1, 1978.

b. With respect to employment after December 31, 1977, any governmental entity, other than the state, defined in paragraph (a)(2)b of Section 25-4-10, shall pay contributions as provided in subdivision (2) of this subsection and Section 25-4-54, unless the governing body of such entity elects under the provisions of subparagraph 1 of this paragraph b to pay to the director for the fund an amount equal to the amount as is prescribed in subdivision (4) of this subsection, and at the rate and in such manner and at such time as set out in subdivision (2) of subsection (b) of this section.

1. Any governmental entity, other than the state, as defined in paragraph (a)(2)b of Section 25-4-10, which becomes subject to this chapter on January 1, 1978, may elect to become liable for payments in lieu of contributions for a period of not less than eight consecutive calendar quarters beginning with January 1, 1978, provided it files with the director a written notice of its election, officially adopted by the governing body of such entity, within the 30-day period immediately following such date. Any such entity which becomes subject to this chapter subsequent to January 1, 1978, may elect to become liable for payments in lieu of contributions for a period of not less than six, ending on the thirtieth day of September, consecutive quarters by filing with the director a written notice by the governing body of such entity of its election not later than 30 days immediately following the date on which it becomes such an entity. Such election shall remain in effect until the governing body files with the director a written notice terminating its election. Any such termination shall be effective at the end of the calendar year during which such notice is made and its acceptance by the director occurs. Said notice shall be filed not later than the first day of December preceding the effective date of such termination.

2. Any governmental entity which has been paying contributions under this chapter for a period of at least one calendar year subsequent to January 1, 1978, may, effective as of the beginning of any calendar year thereafter, change to a reimbursing basis by filing with the director not later than the first day of December preceding the beginning of such calendar year a written notice by the governing body thereof of its election to become liable for payments in lieu of contributions. Such election shall not be terminable by the governmental entity during that and the next calendar year and may be terminated only at the end of a calendar year.

3. The written notice of election or termination of election of method of payment shall be accompanied by a certified copy of the minutes of the meeting of the appropriate governing body during which the action to elect or terminate was taken.

(6)a. Any contributions or payments in lieu of contributions which are or may become due to be paid as required by this chapter which are attributable to wages paid by any governmental entity described in paragraph c of subdivision (a)(2) of Section 25-4-10 shall, upon termination in any manner or cessation of employment by such entity, be paid by the state comptroller as provided for in paragraph c of subdivision (a)(2) of Section 25-4-10.

b. Any contributions or payments in lieu of contributions which are or may become due to be paid as required by this chapter which are attributable to wages paid by any governmental entity described in paragraph d of subdivision (a)(2) of Section 25-4-10 shall, upon termination or cessation of employment by such entity, be paid by the political subdivision or subdivisions that allowed or caused the creation of such entity.

(b) *Payments in lieu of contributions.* — Payments in lieu of contributions shall be made in accordance with the provisions of subdivisions (1) and (2) of this subsection.

(1) Each nonprofit organization or group of such organizations which has elected to make payments in lieu of contributions shall at the end of each calendar quarter, or at the end of any other period as the director shall prescribe, pay to the director an amount equal to the full amount of regular benefits plus one-half of the extended benefits paid during such quarter or other prescribed period that is attributable to services in the employ of such organization. Such payments shall be made within 20 calendar days after notice of the amount due is mailed by the director.

(2) Each governmental entity which has elected to make payments in lieu of contributions shall make such payments to the director in an amount representing one of the following:

a. Any entity becoming subject to this chapter effective January 1, 1972, shall pay:

1. For the calendar quarter beginning July 1, 1972, and each succeeding calendar quarter thereafter through and including the quarter ending September 30, 1973, such amount as such employer may estimate to be equal to the amount determined pursuant to paragraph (4)b of subsection (a) of this section but the amount shall not be less than 0.25 percent of its average quarterly payroll (without regard to the limitations specified in Section 25-4-16) paid to all employees covered by this chapter in its employ during the calendar year 1971, said payments to be made not later than the tenth day of the first month of each quarter, and

2. For each calendar quarter during fiscal years beginning on and after October 1, 1973, such percentage of its average quarterly covered payroll for the four-quarter period ending on the immediately preceding June 30, as the director shall determine. Such determination, except as hereinafter provided, shall be based each year on the average quarterly benefit cost during the four-calendar-quarter period ending on the immediately preceding June 30, which is attributable to service in the employ of such entity; provided, however, that for each calendar quarter beginning on or after October 1, 1978, the rate shall be determined on the basis of its average quarterly payroll and benefit costs for the four-calendar-quarter period ending on the immediately preceding December 31.

b. Any entity becoming subject effective January 1, 1978, shall pay:

1. For the calendar quarter beginning July 1, 1978, and each succeeding calendar quarter thereafter through and including the quarter ending September 30, 1979, such amount as such employer may estimate to be equal to the amount determined pursuant to paragraph (a)(4)b of this section but the amount shall not be less than

0.25 percent of its average quarterly payroll (without regard to the limitations specified in Section 25-4-16) paid to all employees covered by this chapter in its employ during the calendar year 1977, said payments to be made not later than the tenth day of the first month of each quarter, and

2. In each calendar quarter during fiscal years beginning on and after October 1, 1979, such percentage of its average quarterly covered payroll for the four-quarter period ending on the immediately preceding December 31 as the director shall determine. Such determinations, except as hereinafter provided, shall be based each year on the average quarterly benefit cost during the four-calendar-quarter period ending on the immediately preceding December 31 which is attributable to service in the employ of such entity including benefits paid under the provisions of paragraph (b) of Section 25-4-74.

3. The director shall notify each governmental entity of its rate for the next fiscal year not later than the first day of April preceding such fiscal year.

c. Any governmental entity becoming subject to this chapter, and/or electing to make payments under this subsection, subsequent to January 1, 1978, will make the advance payment as provided in paragraph b of subdivision (2) of this subsection (b) in such amount as is therein provided within the first 10 days of the first month of the second quarter following the quarter during which the coverage and/or election becomes effective and during the first 10 days of each calendar quarter thereafter until the first day of October of the calendar year next following the calendar year during which such election became effective. Thereafter, the rate of such payment shall be computed as provided in subparagraph b 2 of this subdivision.

d. For any governmental entity which did not pay wages throughout the periods specified in paragraphs a and b, respectively, of this subdivision (2), the average quarterly covered payroll shall be as determined by the director based on that portion of such periods during which wages were paid.

(3) When a rate of payments in lieu of contributions has been set by the director for any one-year period as is provided by this subsection (b) nothing herein shall be construed as preventing the director from modifying the percentage thereafter payable by a government entity, for such entity, from the rate set in order to minimize excess or insufficient payments. In making such modification the director shall consider factors such as current benefit cost ratio and current benefit costs as may be effected by an increase or decrease in state or federal funding, reorganization of the entity, increase or decrease in the number of employees and general economic conditions which directly or indirectly affect benefits costs attributable to any entity. Any modification so made shall become effective the first day of the calendar quarter next following a notice to the employer of such modification at least 10 days prior thereto.

(4) At the end of each one-year period for which a rate for payments in lieu of contributions has been set, the director shall determine whether the total of payments for such year made by any employer is less than, or in excess of, the total amount of regular benefits plus such amount of extended benefits as is required by this section to be charged to such employer, paid to individuals during such year based on wages attributable to service in the employ of such employer. Each such employer whose total payments for such year are less than the amount so determined shall be liable for payment of the unpaid balance to the fund in accordance with this subsection. If the total payments are in excess of the amount so determined for the specified one-year period, all or a part of the excess may, at the discretion of the director, be refunded from the fund or retained in the fund as part of the payments which may be required for the next such year. Any payments due to be made under this subdivision (4) shall be made not later than 20 days after the date on which the director shall mail to the employer notice of the amount.

(5) Payments made by any organization under the provisions of this subsection shall not be deducted or deductible, in whole or in part, from the remuneration of individuals in the employ of such organizations.

(6) Any other provisions of law notwithstanding, payments in lieu of contributions as provided by this subsection shall be:

a. Subject to the same penalties, collection and enforcement proceedings and provisions for hearing and review, extensions, refunds and protections that pursuant to Sections 25-4-54, 25-4-132 through 25-4-138 and 25-4-145 apply to contributions, and

b.1. Should any amounts due from any component or instrumentality of this state remain due and unpaid for a period of 90 days after the due date, the State Comptroller shall take such action as is necessary to collect such amounts and is hereby authorized and required to levy against any funds due such component or instrumentality by any other department, agency or official of the state or against any bank account established in any bank whether or not in this state. Such department, agency or official shall deduct such amounts as are certified by the comptroller from any accounts or deposits or any funds due such delinquent component or instrumentality without regard to any prior claim and promptly forward such amounts to the comptroller.

2. Should any amounts due from any governmental entity of any county, municipality or any instrumentality thereof, as defined in paragraph (a)(2)b of Section 25-4-10, remain due and unpaid for a period of 120 days after the due date, the director shall take such action as is necessary to collect such amounts and is hereby authorized and required to levy against any funds due such governmental entity by the State Treasurer, Comptroller, Commissioner of Revenue or any other official or agency of this state or against any bank account established in any bank. Such officials, agency or bank shall deduct such amounts as are certified by the director from any accounts or deposits with or

any funds due such delinquent governmental entity without regard to any prior claim and promptly forward such amounts to the director for the fund; provided, however, that the director shall notify the delinquent entity of his intent to file such levy by certified mail at least 10 days prior to filing of a levy on any funds due the entity by any state official or agency.

(7) Any nonprofit organization which elects to become liable for payments in lieu of contributions shall, in addition to making such payments, be required within 30 days after the date the director mails notice of his approval of its election, to execute and file with the director a surety bond, or a cash deposit in lieu thereof, as approved by the director. For the purpose of this subdivision, a surety bond is a bond of surety issued by an organization licensed and authorized to issue such bond in this state. The amount of the surety bond or cash deposit required by this subdivision (7) shall be an amount as determined by the director based on a percentage (not higher than the maximum percentage provided by Section 25-4-54) of the organization's covered payroll as defined in this chapter for the four-calendar quarters immediately preceding the effective date of the election, or the renewal date in case of a bond, or the biennial anniversary in the case of a cash deposit, whichever date shall be most recent and applicable. For any such organization which did not pay wages throughout each of four such calendar quarters the amount of the bond or deposit shall be as determined by the director.

a. Any surety bond deposited under this subdivision (7) shall be in force for a period of not less than two full calendar years and shall be renewed not less frequently than at two-year intervals as long as the organization continues to be liable for payments in lieu of contributions. The director shall require adjustments to be made in a previously filed bond as he deems appropriate. If the bond is to be increased, the adjusted bond shall be filed by the organization within 30 days of the date notice of such adjustment was mailed or otherwise delivered to it. Failure of any organization covered by such bond to pay the full amount of payments in lieu of contributions when due, together with any applicable interest and penalties as provided by this chapter, shall render the surety liable on said bond to the extent of the bond, as though the surety was such organization.

b. Any deposit of money in accordance with this subdivision (7) shall be retained by the director in an escrow account until liability under the election is terminated, at which time it shall be returned to the organization, less any deductions as hereinafter provided. The director may deduct from the money deposited under this subdivision (7) by any organization to the extent necessary to satisfy any due and unpaid payments in lieu of contributions and any applicable interest and penalty. The director shall require the organization within 30 days following any deduction from a money deposit under the provisions of this subdivision (7) to deposit sufficient additional moneys to make whole the organization's deposit at the prior level. The director may, at any time, review the adequacy of the deposit made by any organization. If, as a result of such review, he determines that an adjustment is necessary, he shall require the organization to make an additional deposit within 30 days of written notice of his determination or shall return to it such portion of the deposit as he no longer considers necessary whichever action is appropriate.

c. If any organization subject to the provisions of this section fails to file a surety bond or make a cash deposit or to file a surety bond in an increased amount or to increase or make whole the amount of a previously made cash deposit, or fails to pay before the delinquency date any payments due together with any accumulated interest and penalty as provided by this chapter, the director may terminate such organization's election to make payments in lieu of contributions effective as of the end of any calendar quarter and such termination shall continue for not less than two consecutive calendar years; provided, that the director may extend for good cause the posting of a cash deposit, the filing of a surety bond or the extension of an adjustment period by not more than 30 days.

(8) If benefits paid to an individual are based on wages paid by two or more employers, the amount of benefits payable by an organization required to or electing to make payments in lieu of contributions shall be an amount which bears the same ratio to the total benefits paid to the individual as the total base period wages paid by such employer to the individual and used for the payment of benefits bears to the total base period wages paid to the individual by all his base period employers and used for payment of benefits.

The other provisions of this subsection notwithstanding, no such employer shall be required to reimburse the fund for any portion of the benefits paid to any individual whose benefits which are attributable to public service wages funded under the Comprehensive Employment and Training Act of 1973, as amended, after December 31, 1975, to the extent that such benefits are reimbursed to the fund by the federal government under the provisions of Section 220 of the Emergency Jobs Program Extension Act of 1976 (P.L. 94-444).

(9) Two or more employers that have elected to make payments in lieu of contributions in accordance with the provisions of this section may file a joint application to the director for the establishment of a group account for the purpose of sharing the cost of benefits paid that are attributable to service in the employ of such organizations. Each such application shall identify and authorize a group representative to act as the group's agent for the purposes of this subsection. Upon his approval of the application, the director shall establish a group account for such employers effective as of the beginning of the calendar quarter next following the quarter in which he received such application, and shall notify the group's representative of the effective date of the account. Such group account shall remain in effect for not less than eight calendar quarters and thereafter until terminated at the discretion of the director or upon application by the group. Upon

establishment of the account, each member of the group shall be liable for payments in lieu of contributions with respect to each calendar quarter in the amount that bears the same ratio to the total benefits paid in such quarter that are attributable to service performed in the employ of all members of the group as the total wages paid for services in employment by such member in such quarter bears to the total wages paid during such quarter for service performed in the employ of all members of the group. The director shall prescribe such regulations as he deems necessary with respect to applications for establishment, maintenance and termination of group accounts that are authorized by this subdivision (9), for addition of new members to, and withdrawal of active members from, such accounts, and for the determination of the amounts that are payable under this subdivision by members of a group and the time and manner of such payments.

(10) Notwithstanding any other provisions of this chapter, any employer who was liable for payments in lieu of contributions for the period immediately preceding the effective date of termination of its coverage pursuant to Section 25-4-130 shall nevertheless continue to be liable to pay to the director for the fund the amount of regular benefits and extended benefits paid, as required by this chapter, that is attributable to service in the employ of such employer prior to the effective date of such termination, to individuals for weeks of unemployment which begin on or after such effective date. Such payments to the director shall be made at such times and in such manner as the director shall prescribe and the director shall continue to require payments in lieu of contributions and surety in such amounts and for such period as he may deem necessary to insure restoration to the fund of the amount of such regular and extended benefits. (Acts 1939, No. 497, p. 721; Code 1940, T. 26, § 201; Acts 1971, No. 166, p. 440, § 8; Acts 1973, No. 1057, p. 1716, §§ 2, 3; Acts 1975, No. 801, p. 1604, § 5; Acts 1978, 1st Ex. Sess., No. 1, p. 5, § 4; Acts 1983, 2nd Ex. Sess., No. 83-155, p. 264, § 4; Acts 1989, No. 89-405, p. 822, § 1.)

Collateral references. — 81 C.J.S., Social Security & Public Welfare, §§ 83, 141-143. 76 Am. Jur. 2d, Unemployment Compensation, § 15 et seq.

§ 25-4-52. Contributions by employees.

(a) For each calendar year ending prior to January 1, 1986, contributions by employees shall be as was provided by this section prior to that date.

(b) Repealed by Acts 1989, No. 89-405, § 2. (Acts 1939, No. 497, p. 721; Code 1940, T. 26, § 202; Acts 1953, No. 864, p. 1163; Acts 1957, No. 304, p. 399; Acts 1961, Ex. Sess., No. 274, p. 2298; Acts 1969, No. 234, p. 559, § 1; Acts 1971, No. 166, p. 440, § 9; Acts 1983, 2nd Ex. Sess., No. 83-155, p. 264, § 5; Acts 1989, No. 89-405, p. 822, § 2.)

Cited in Carter v. J.P. King & Sons, 381 So.
2d 71 (Ala. Civ. App. 1980); Heatherly v.
Benton, 479 So. 2d 1285 (Ala. Civ. App. 1985).

§ 25-4-53. Withholding of employee contributions.

For calendar years ending prior to January 1, 1986, employee contributions, the withholding of such contributions and the penalty for an employer's failure to withhold and violations of trust shall be as was provided by this section prior to such date. (Acts 1939, No. 497, p. 721; Code 1940, T. 26, § 203; Acts 1969, No. 234, p. 559, § 2; Acts 1980, No. 80-756, p. 1561, § 3; Acts 1989, No. 89-405, p. 822, § 3.)

Collateral references. — 81 C.J.S., Social Security & Public Welfare, §§ 147-149, 152, 192.
76 Am. Jur. 2d, Unemployment Compensation, §§ 15-17.

Employee retirement pension benefits as exempt from garnishment, attachment, levy, execution, or similar proceedings. 93 ALR3d 711.

§ 25-4-54. Contribution rates for employers subject to benefit charges; determination of individual benefit charges.

(a) *Determination of contribution rates.*

(1) For the 12-month period beginning on January 1 of each year which begins after December 31, 1990, any employer whose experience rating account has been subject to benefit charges throughout at least the fiscal year, as defined in Section 25-4-4, immediately preceding such January 1, shall have his rate determined by the unemployment compensation fund's liability for benefits paid to his employees, modified by the fund's balance as of the most recent September 30. The employment record of an organization which has been making payments in lieu of contributions but which elects to change to payment of contributions shall be deemed to have been chargeable with benefits throughout the period (not to exceed three fiscal years) with respect to which it was making payments in lieu of contributions and its benefit charges and payrolls for such period shall be used in computing its benefit ratio pursuant to subsection (d) of this section.

(2) For the 12-month period beginning on January 1 of each calendar year which begins before January 1, 1991, the rates of contribution shall be determined as was prescribed by this section prior to said January 1, 1991.

(b) *Determination of individual benefit charges.*

(1) An individual's "benefit charges" shall be as follows:

a. For each week benefits are paid, an individual's "benefit charges" shall be equal to the amount of benefits he was paid for such week.

b. For each week extended benefits pursuant to Section 25-4-75 are paid to an individual, the "benefit charges" shall be equal to the state's share of such benefits paid to him for such weeks; provided, however, where an individual's "benefit charges" for extended benefits are attributable to service in the employ of any governmental entity, as defined in paragraph (a)(2)b of Section 25-4-10, the individual's "benefit charges" shall be an amount equal to the benefits he was paid for such week.

(2) Any benefits paid to an individual based on wages paid to an employee during his base period for part-time employment by an employer who continues to give the employee employment to the same extent while he is receiving benefits as he did during his base period shall not be determined to be the individual's benefit charges. The employer shall establish the continuation of work to the satisfaction of the director by submitting such information as the director may require within the time required by other provisions of this chapter after the date of notification or mailing of notice by the director that the employee has first filed a claim for benefits.

(3) If benefits paid to an individual are based on wages paid by two or more employers, the amount of the individual's benefit charges applicable to any one employer shall be an amount which bears the same ratio to the total benefit charges as the total base period wages paid by such employer to the individual and used for the payment of benefits bears to the total base period wages paid to the individual by all his base period employers and used for the payment of benefits.

(4) When, in the determination of any individual's benefits, wages have been properly included once for one benefit year or for one base period, such wages shall not thereafter be included again in the computation of his benefits for any other benefit year or in his wages for any other base period respectively.

(c) *Determination of employer benefit charges.*

(1) An employer's benefit charges for each and every fiscal year shall be the total of the regular benefits and the state's share of the extended benefits paid during such fiscal year to all of his employees or former employees which are attributable to wages paid by such employer to his employees or former employees; except as is provided by paragraph a of subdivision (a)(5) of Section 25-4-51 for governmental entities.

(2) The director shall analyze the benefit payments in each fiscal year and determine each employer's benefit charges for each fiscal year.

(3) The director shall, after the close of each calendar quarter, furnish each employer with a statement of the benefits paid to his workers, or former workers, which became his benefit charges in that calendar quarter, together with the names of such workers, or former workers, and such statement, in the absence of an application for a revision thereof within 90 days of the mailing of such statement to the employer's last known address, shall be conclusive and final upon the employer for all purposes and in all proceedings whatsoever. Such application for revision shall be in the form and manner prescribed by regulation of the director. Upon receipt of, within the time allowed, an application for revision of such statement, the director shall allow such application in whole or in part, or shall deny such application and shall serve notice upon the employer of such decision. Such decision of the director shall be final and conclusive on the employer at the

335

expiration of 30 days from the date of service of such notice, unless the employer shall within the said 30-day period file with the director a written protest and a petition for hearing, specifying his objections thereto. Upon receipt of such petition the director shall fix a time and place for a hearing and shall notify the employer thereof. At any hearing held as herein provided, the decision of the director shall be prima facie correct, and the burden shall be upon the protesting employer to prove it is incorrect. No employer shall have the right to object to the benefit charges with respect to any worker as shown on such statement, unless he shall first show that such charges arose as a result of benefits paid to such worker in accordance with a determination, or a redetermination, to which such employer was a party entitled to notice thereof, as provided by Article 5 of this chapter, and shall further show that he was not notified of such determination or redetermination in accordance with the requirements of said Article 5 of this chapter. Nothing herein contained shall affect the right of any employer at such hearing to object to such statement of benefit charges on the ground that it is incorrect by reason of a clerical error made by the director or any of his employees. The employer shall be promptly notified by mail of the director's decision. Such decision shall be final and conclusive unless an appeal is taken therefrom in the manner and within the time prescribed in subsection (h) of this section.

(4) Nothing contained in subdivision (3) of this subsection (c) shall be construed as limiting or affecting in any manner the right and authority of the director to remove benefit charges from any employer's account upon discovering or being aware of any such employer's workers or former workers having drawn benefits by reason of false representation of their earnings while filing claims for benefits nor to make any corrections resulting from any adjustment to benefits paid to the individual.

(5) Any Alabama unemployment compensation benefits paid to any claimant under the following conditions shall not be charged to the account of a contributory base period employer(s) for the state fiscal year ending September 30, 1990, and each fiscal year thereafter, if:

a. The benefits are paid for unemployment due directly to a major natural disaster, and

b. The President has declared the event a disaster pursuant to the Disaster Relief Act of 1970, 42 USC 4401, et seq., as amended, and

c. The benefits are paid from the Alabama U.I. Trust Fund to claimants who would have been eligible for disaster unemployment assistance under this act, if they have not first received Alabama unemployment insurance benefits with respect to their unemployment.

(d) *Determination of employer benefit ratio.* — Effective January 1, 1991, and each year thereafter, the benefit ratio of each employer who qualifies for a rate determination under subdivision (a)(1) of this section and has been chargeable with benefits throughout the three most recent preceding fiscal years shall be a percentage obtained by dividing the total of his benefit charges for such three-year period by that part of his total taxable payroll for the same three-year period with respect to which contributions have been paid on or before October 31, next following such period, and the benefit ratio of each employer who qualifies for a rate determination under subdivision (a) (1) of this section, but who has not been subject to this chapter for a period of time sufficient to have been chargeable with benefits throughout the three most recent preceding fiscal years, shall be a percentage obtained by dividing the total of his benefit charges for the period throughout which he has been chargeable, such period to be not less than the most recent preceding fiscal year by that part of his total taxable payroll for the same period with respect to which contributions have been paid on or before October 31 next following such period. The employers benefit ratio shall be computed to the fourth decimal and be used in determining each employer's contribution rate as prescribed in subsection (a) of this section for the next calendar year; except that:

For tax rate year beginning January 1, 1991, the employer's benefit ratio shall be determined by the employer's actual benefit charges to his account for the fiscal year ending September 30, 1990, and for fiscal years ending September 30, 1988, and September 30, 1989, the employer's benefit charges shall be determined from data accumulated by the director during such years relative to benefit wage charges and converted to benefit charges, in such manner as the director shall prescribe.

(e) *Shared costs.*

(1) For the purposes of this subsection (e) and for the determination of an employer's rate of contribution pursuant to subsection (f), "shared" or "socialized" cost for each fiscal year is defined to be:

a. Benefit charges which cannot be effectively assigned to an individual employer's experience rating account during such fiscal year because of the employer becoming inactive (in accordance with Section 25-4-130); and

b. The total amount of the difference between the benefit charges to all employers during the fiscal year who are assigned the maximum rate of contribution under any one of the rate schedules for the calendar year next following such fiscal year and the total amount of contributions received from all such maximum rated employers during the same fiscal year; and

c. Credits granted employers during such fiscal year because of the reason for separation (as provided in Section 25-4-78), continued part-time work [as provided by subdivision (b)(2) of this section] and relief from charges granted an employer under the provisions of subdivision (c)(4) of this section; and

d. Benefit overpayments which have been declared uncollectible or have been waived by the director during the fiscal year pursuant to the applicable provisions of this chapter; and

e. Contributions due from employers but not paid and which have been, during such fiscal year, declared uncollectible by the bankruptcy courts or official action by the director; and

f. Cost resulting from the relief of charges for contributory employers under Section 25-4-54(c)(5) will be included in shared cost as defined in this section.

(2) The total of the amounts determined under the provisions of subdivision (1) above shall be the statewide total shared cost for any fiscal year.

(3) Net shared costs for any fiscal year shall be the statewide total of shared costs for that fiscal year reduced (but not below zero) by the amount of:

a. Interest received by the fund from the U.S. Treasury during such fiscal year; and

b. The total amount of the difference between the contributions received from all employers during such fiscal year who are assigned the minimum rate of contributions under any one of the rate schedules for the calendar year next following such fiscal year and the total of all benefit charges made to all such minimum rated employers during the same fiscal year.

(4) To determine the "shared cost ratio" for any fiscal year, the net shared cost for such fiscal year shall be divided by the statewide total of taxable wages for the same fiscal year which have been reported by all contributory employers and upon which contributions have been timely paid (reduced by the total of the taxable wages reported and timely paid on by any employer or employers for the same fiscal year, who by the provisions of subdivision (5) of this subsection (e) are relieved of the shared cost assessment). The resulting quotient adjusted to the nearest multiple of one-thousandth shall be the "shared cost ratio" applicable for assessment to all contributory employers for the next following calendar year.

(5)a. Except as is hereinafter provided, the shared cost ratio as computed under the above provision for each fiscal year shall, for the next calendar year, be assessed each employer eligible for a rate determination under the provision of subdivision (a)(1) of this section, in addition to the rate of contributions determined by the tables contained in subsection (f) of this section.

1. Any employer whose rate of contribution has been determined to be the minimum rate allowed under Schedule A for a calendar year, shall be relieved of any shared cost assessment during that calendar year;

2. Any employer whose rate of contribution has been determined to be the minimum rate allowed under Schedule B for a calendar year and whose experience rating account has not been charged with any benefits during the three immediately preceding fiscal years, shall be relieved of any shared cost assessment for that calendar year;

3. No relief shall be granted to any employer for any portion of the shared cost assessment for a calendar year when either Schedule C or D is in effect.

b. The assessment for shared costs shall become due and payable at the same time and in the same manner as contributions.

c. The authority of the director to enforce collection of any shared cost assessment shall be the same as is provided in this chapter for the enforcement of the collections of contributions.

(f) *Notice of contribution rate, etc.; maximum rate.* — The contribution rates (expressed as a percentage of taxable wages) for each employer, as provided in subsection (a) of this section, shall be determined by the director and the director shall notify each employer of his benefit ratio and his contribution rate within 30 days after the effective date of such rate. Such employer contribution rate for the tax rate years beginning January 1, 1991, shall be determined from the appropriate rate schedule prescribed for that tax rate year by the provisions of subsection (g) of this section and shall be the rate which appears on the same horizontal line on which is found the employer's benefit ratio.

TAX RATE TABLE

EMPLOYER TAX RATE SCHEDULE:

LINE NO.	IF THE EMPLOYER'S BENEFIT RATIO IS:	A	B	C	D
1	0.00 — 0.39	0.20	0.35	0.50	0.65
2	0.40 — 0.59	0.35	0.50	0.65	0.80
3	0.60 — 0.79	0.50	0.70	0.90	1.00
4	0.80 — 0.99	0.70	0.90	1.10	1.20
5	1.00 — 1.19	0.85	1.10	1.30	1.40
6	1.20 — 1.39	1.00	1.30	1.55	1.65
7	1.40 — 1.59	1.15	1.50	1.75	1.90
8	1.60 — 1.79	1.30	1.70	1.95	2.15
9	1.80 — 1.99	1.45	1.90	2.15	2.40
10	2.00 — 2.19	1.60	2.10	2.40	2.65
11	2.20 — 2.39	1.75	2.30	2.60	2.85
12	2.40 — 2.59	1.90	2.50	2.80	3.10
13	2.60 — 2.79	2.05	2.70	3.05	3.35
14	2.80 — 2.99	2.20	2.90	3.25	3.60
15	3.00 — 3.19	2.35	3.10	3.50	3.85
16	3.20 — 3.59	2.50	3.40	3.80	4.20
17	3.60 — 3.99	2.80	3.80	4.25	4.70
18	4.00 — 4.39	3.10	4.20	4.70	5.20
19	4.40 — 4.79	3.40	4.60	5.10	5.70
20	4.80 — 5.19	3.70	5.00	5.50	6.20
21	5.20 — 5.59	4.00	5.40	6.00	6.70

EMPLOYER TAX RATE SCHEDULE:

LINE NO.	IF THE EMPLOYER'S BENEFIT RATIO IS:	A	B	C	D
22	5.60 — 5.99	4.30	5.40	6.00	6.70
23	6.00 — 6.39	4.60	5.40	6.10	6.80
24	6.40 — 6.79	4.90	5.40	6.10	6.80
25	6.80 — 7.19	5.20	5.40	6.10	6.80
26	7.20 or over	5.40	5.40	6.10	6.80

The provisions of this subsection (f) to the contrary notwithstanding, the rates of contribution shall, after having been determined as herein prescribed, be adjusted as follows for calendar quarters beginning after March 31, 1992 and ending March 31, 1997:

If the rate of contribution specified by the Tax Rate Table contained in this section is:	The employer's contribution rate shall be:
0.20	0.14
0.35	0.29
0.50	0.44
0.65	0.59
0.70	0.64
0.80	0.74
0.85	0.79
0.90	0.84
1.00	0.94
1.10	1.04
1.15	1.09
1.20	1.14
1.30	1.24
1.40	1.34
1.45	1.39
1.50	1.44
1.55	1.49
1.60	1.54
1.65	1.59
1.70	1.64
1.75	1.69
1.90	1.84
1.95	1.89
2.05	1.99

If the rate of contribution specified by the Tax Rate Table contained in this section is:	The employer's contribution rate shall be:
2.10	2.04
2.15	2.09
2.20	2.14
2.30	2.24
2.35	2.29
2.40	2.34
2.50	2.44
2.60	2.54
2.65	2.59
2.70	2.64
2.80	2.74
2.85	2.79
2.90	2.84
3.05	2.99
3.10	3.04
3.25	3.19
3.35	3.29
3.40	3.34
3.50	3.44
3.60	3.54
3.70	3.64
3.80	3.74
3.85	3.79
4.00	3.94
4.20	4.14
4.25	4.19
4.30	4.24
4.60	4.54
4.70	4.64
4.90	4.84
5.00	4.94
5.10	5.04
5.20	5.14
5.40	5.40
5.50	5.44
5.70	5.64
6.00	5.94
6.10	6.04
6.20	6.14
6.70	6.64
6.80	6.74

The adjustment in rates of contributions as are herein provided shall apply only to those employers who are required to pay contributions by the provisions of Section 25-4-51 and those nonprofit organizations, hospitals, educational institutions, agencies of the State of Alabama and political subdivisions of the state who have, under the option permitted by Section 25-4-51, for that calendar year elected to pay contributions. The adjustment shall not apply to any employer who, because of insufficient unemployment experience, has not become eligible to have his rate of contribution determined by the method prescribed under this subsection (f); whose rate of contribution is determined to be 5.4%, or is above 5.4% and by the application of the adjustment would become a rate less than 5.4%; and all employers who being eligible for such option have elected the option to make payments in lieu of contributions.

(g) *Determination of contribution rate schedule.* — Contribution rates for each employer, determined pursuant to subsection (f) of this section, shall nevertheless be subject to the contribution rate schedule as is hereinafter provided.

(1) The "benefits payroll ratio" of the state for each fiscal year shall be determined by dividing the total of benefits paid, including the state's portion of benefits paid under any extended benefit program, from the unemployment compensation fund within the preceding fiscal year, less any benefits paid for which payments in lieu of contributions have been paid or are currently due to be paid, by the statewide total payrolls of all employers upon which contributions on the taxable portion thereof have been paid during the same fiscal year, and by adjusting the quotient to the nearest multiple of one-thousandth.

(2) The desired level of unemployment compensation fund for each fiscal year shall be one and four-tenths times the amount determined by multiplying the highest statewide total of payrolls of all employers upon which contributions on the taxable portion thereof have been paid during any one of the three most recent preceding fiscal years by the highest benefits payroll ratio for any one of the 10 most recent preceding fiscal years.

(3) The director shall, on or before the December 1 next following the end of each fiscal year, declare effective for the 12-month period beginning with January 1 of the immediately succeeding calendar year, the desired level of the fund and the schedule to be in effect for that 12-month period. The contribution rate for each employer for the next calendar year shall be determined by the director as provided in subsection (f) of this section on the basis of each employer's benefit ratio as determined under the provisions of subsection (d) of this section; and whenever at the end of any fiscal year, the fund balance is:

a. One hundred twenty-five percent or more of the desired level computed for the fiscal year, contribution rates shall be determined under Schedule A;

    b. Equal to the desired level but is less than 125% thereof, contribution rates shall be determined under Schedule B.

    c. Less than the desired level but is at least 70% thereof, contribution rates shall be determined under Schedule C.

    d. Less than 70 percent of the desired level, contribution rates shall be determined under Schedule D.

    (4) Any amount credited to this state's account under Section 903 of the Social Security Act, as amended, which has been appropriated for expenses of administration, whether or not withdrawn from the trust fund, shall be included in the trust fund balance in determining whether or not such fund is greater or less than the desired level of the fund for a fiscal year; except, that any amount appropriated and withdrawn which will not be repaid to the fund shall not be included in such balances.

    (5) The director shall notify each employer of such declaration and of his benefit ratio and his contribution rate within 30 days after each such January 1. This subdivision (5) shall not apply to employers who, in lieu of contributions, reimburse the fund for benefits paid.

    (h) *Review of contribution rate, etc.* — Any employer may apply to the director for and shall be entitled to a review as to the determination of his benefit ratio and his contribution rate as fixed by his benefit ratio, provided such application is filed within 30 days of the date of the mailing by the director to the employer of the notice of such determination. Pending such review, such employer shall make all contribution payments otherwise required by this chapter at contribution rates fixed by the determination sought to be reviewed and resulting overpayments or underpayments of contributions by the employer shall, upon any redetermination, be adjusted or refunded pursuant to Section 25-4-137. Any employer may within 30 days after the date of mailing by the director to such employer of notice of the ruling of the director upon such application for review appeal such ruling to the circuit court of any county wherein the employer is engaged in doing business, upon such terms and upon giving such security for costs as the court may upon application prescribe. Trial in that court shall be de novo with respect to his benefit ratio.

    (i) *Contribution rate, etc., of successor employer.* — For the purpose of this section, an employer's benefit charges and that part of his taxable payroll with respect to which contributions have been paid, shall be deemed benefit charges and taxable payrolls of a successor employer and shall be taken into account in determining the contribution rate of such successor employer as provided in subsection (f) of this section, if such successor succeeds the employer in any of the manners set out in paragraph (a)(4)a of Section 25-4-8; provided, that an employer subject to this chapter who becomes such in any of the manners set out in paragraph (a)(4)b of Section 25-4-8 may have that portion of his predecessor's benefit charges and that part of his predecessor's total taxable payroll, with respect to which contributions have been paid which correspond to the segregable portion of the business assets and payroll thereof, acquired from his predecessor, deemed to be his benefit charges and his payroll and such shall be taken into account in determining his rates, as provided in subsection (f) of this section; provided, that he:

(1) Makes written application within 90 calendar days from the date of such acquisition; and

(2) Furnishes to the director within 120 calendar days from the date of such acquisition a transcript of such total and taxable payrolls which correspond to the segregable portion acquired from his predecessor; provided further that in the event that within the intervening 120 days a notice of his rate of contribution has been mailed to the partial successor, the 30-day finality provision set forth in subsection (h) of this section shall not prevail but, instead, be effective with respect to the subsequent notice computed on the basis of the benefit ratio and taxable payrolls of the acquired segregable portion. (Acts 1943, No. 310, p. 281, § 4; Acts 1945, No. 283, p. 449, § 8; Acts 1949, No. 527, p. 810; Acts 1951, No. 644, p. 1098, § 2; Acts 1955, No. 28, p. 238; Acts 1957, No. 299, p. 382; Acts 1961, Ex. Sess., No. 274, p. 2298, § 5; Acts 1965, No. 390, p. 548, § 1; Acts 1967, No. 167, p. 499, § 2; Acts 1969, No. 234, p. 559, §§ 3-7; Acts 1971, No. 166, p. 440, §§ 10-12; Acts 1971, No. 1201, p. 2083, § 1; Acts 1971, No. 2325, p. 3748, § 1; Acts 1973, No. 1057, p. 1716, § 4; Acts 1975, No. 801, p. 1604, § 6; Acts 1978, 1st Ex. Sess., No. 1, p. 5, § 5; Acts 1983, 2nd Ex. Sess., No. 83-155, p. 264, § 6; Acts 1985, 2nd Ex. Sess., No. 85-804, § 1; Acts 1988, 1st Ex. Sess., No. 88-783, p. 195, § 4; Acts 1989, No. 89-405, p. 822, § 4; Acts 1990, No. 90-586, p. 1022; Acts 1992, No. 92-174, § 5.)

The 1989 amendment, effective January 1, 1991, rewrote this section as amended by Acts 1988, 1st Ex. Sess., No. 88-783. See the Code commissioner's note below.

The 1992 amendment, effective April 10, 1992, in subdivision (c)(5), added "in each fiscal year thereafter" following "September 30, 1990"; in subsection (e), in paragraph (1)b inserted "total amount of the" preceding "difference," substituted "to" for "of" preceding "all employers," inserted "during the fiscal year who are" preceding "assigned," substituted "the maximum rate" for "a maximum rate," added "the calendar year next following" preceding "such fiscal year," added "total" preceding "amount of contributions," and substituted "the same fiscal year" for "a fiscal year"; rewrote paragraph (3)b which formerly read: "Contributions collected from employers who, during such fiscal year, or any part thereof, were assigned the minimum rate of contributions, under any of the rate schedules, which exceed the total of all benefit charges made to all minimum rated employers during such fiscal year."; and in subsection (f) substituted "calendar quarters beginning after March 31, 1992 and ending March 31, 1997" for "calendar years beginning after December 31, 1988 and

ending prior to January 1, 1992" in the introductory language of the second table.

Code commissioner's note. — Section 12 of Acts 1989, No. 89-405 provides: "The provisions of Sections 4, 7, and 8 of this act shall become effective immediately upon passage and approval by the Governor or its otherwise becoming law only for the purpose of implementation of the transitional provisions which will enable the full implementation of all the provisions of these sections for a complete change of system and for rate of contribution determination effective January 1, 1991; otherwise for purposes of such system change and the determination of rates of contribution, the provisions of said sections shall become effective on January 1, 1991."

Editor's note. — Many of the cases annotated below were decided under prior law.

Liberal construction. — A liberal construction of the unemployment compensation law is always preferred because the law itself specifically provides that there shall be no vested right of any kind against any subsequent amendment or repeal. West Point Pepperell v. Alabama Dep't of Indus. Relations, 495 So. 2d 678 (Ala. Civ. App.), cert. denied, 495 So. 2d 681 (Ala. 1986).

The unemployment compensation statute is

remedial in nature by definition and should receive a liberal interpretation to best serve the purpose and intent of the legislature to avoid injustice. West Point Pepperell v. Alabama Dep't of Indus. Relations, 495 So. 2d 678 (Ala. Civ. App.), cert. denied, 495 So. 2d 681 (Ala. 1986).

Rehire credit under subdivision (c)(3). — An employer was not entitled to a rehire credit for rehiring several employees who had earlier been laid off, where, although the employer mailed notice of the rehire credit within the required period of time, the notice was never received by the Alabama Department of Industrial Relations. State Dep't of Indus. Relations v. Heritage Mfg., Inc., 532 So. 2d 634 (Ala. Civ. App. 1988).

Construed against taxing authority. — The unemployment compensation statute is a taxing statute and as all taxing statutes, it is to be strictly construed against the taxing authority. West Point Pepperell v. Alabama Dep't of Indus. Relations, 495 So. 2d 678 (Ala. Civ. App.), cert. denied, 495 So. 2d 681 (Ala. 1986).

Taxable wage base is basis for employer's contribution. — The use of the term "taxable wage base" in Act 83-155, which amended several sections of the Alabama Unemployment Compensation Law, as in the prior act, had reference to the amount of wages set out in § 25-4-16 and upon which the employer's benefit wages are computed. Thus, "taxable wage base" ultimately acts as the basis for the employer's tax contribution rate computation, as provided in former subdivision (b)(5) of § 25-4-54. West Point Pepperell v. Alabama Dep't of Indus. Relations, 495 So. 2d 678 (Ala. Civ. App.), cert. denied, 495 So. 2d 681 (Ala. 1986).

Term "state experience factor" means a factor based on factual experience of all employers and their employees operating within the state coming within influence of the act. Broadway v. Alabama Dry Dock & Shipbuilding Co., 246 Ala. 201, 20 So. 2d 41 (1944).

Sufficiency of employer's notice of intent to claim rehire credit under subsection (c). — See State Dep't of Indus. Relations v. Clegg Mfg. Co., 348 So. 2d 249 (Ala. Civ. App. 1976). See also State Dep't of Indus. Relations v. McElrath Farms, Inc., 348 So. 2d 257 (Ala. 1977).

"Equal to" and "in excess of" as used in subsection (f). — In construing subsection (f), there is no occasion to impart to the unambiguous expressions "equal to" and "in excess of" any other than their commonly understood meanings, since these terms are in common use and are simple words. Department of

Indus. Relations v. Little Mfg. Co., 253 Ala. 416, 44 So. 2d 587 (1950).

Benefit wage percentage of eight and sixteen hundredths percent is a percentage in excess of eight percent within the meaning of subsection (f). Department of Indus. Relations v. Little Mfg. Co., 253 Ala. 416, 44 So. 2d 587 (1950).

Subsection (h) looks to an existing status before the contributions shall be made. Department of Indus. Relations v. West Boylston Mfg. Co., 253 Ala. 67, 42 So. 2d 787 (1949).

And it does not provide for a refund. — Subsection (h) does not provide for a refund because it does not relate to contributions which have already been made. Department of Indus. Relations v. West Boylston Mfg. Co., 253 Ala. 67, 42 So. 2d 787 (1949).

Provision relating to appeal from director is constitutional. — An appeal from the order of the director, pursuant to this section, to determine the correct rates which should govern in making contribution to the unemployment compensation fund, is not forbidden by § 14 of the Constitution, prohibiting suits against the state. Metcalf v. Department of Indus. Relations, 245 Ala. 299, 304, 16 So. 2d 787 (1944).

And does not amend section 25-4-137. — The limitation of time prescribed for review in subsection (h) of this section in no way amends § 25-4-137. Carnley v. State ex rel. West Boylston Mfg. Co., 250 Ala. 403, 34 So. 2d 681 (1948).

Review of director's determination by common-law certiorari. — The inclusion in the determination of the director of matter which is not authorized by the Constitution or law appearing on the face of the proceedings could well be made the basis of review by common-law certiorari without resorting to the remedy provided in subsection (h). Department of Indus. Relations v. West Boylston Mfg. Co., 253 Ala. 67, 42 So. 2d 787 (1949).

And section 25-4-137 is available to correct any erroneous computation on matter determined by the director which determination is conclusive by the failure to appeal under this section. Department of Indus. Relations v. West Boylston Mfg. Co., 253 Ala. 67, 42 So. 2d 787 (1949).

Subsection (h) limits the director's review to taxpayer's benefit wage percentage and his contribution rate as fixed by benefit wage percentage, and the review authorized by appeal to circuit court from director's ruling can be no broader. Broadway v. Alabama Dry Dock & Shipbuilding Co., 246 Ala. 201, 20 So. 2d 41 (1944).

And subsection (h) does not authorize a review of state's experience factor fixed by director for year within scope of taxpayer's petition for review and appeal from director's denial of his petition. Broadway v. Alabama Dry Dock & Shipbuilding Co., 246 Ala. 201, 20 So. 2d 41 (1944); Department of Indus. Relations v. West Boylston Mfg. Co., 253 Ala. 67, 42 So. 2d 787 (1949).

Employers who act toward stabilizing employment will be rewarded with lower rate of contribution to compensation fund. It is considered advisable to reward an employer with good employment records by giving him a favorable rating and thereby reducing his payment. James v. McCoy Mfg. Co., 431 So. 2d 1147 (Ala. 1983).

How rate of employer's benefit wage percentage determined on appeal. — Subsection (h) providing that the trial in circuit court on appeal shall be de novo, with respect to employer's benefit wage percentage, limited scope of hearing on appeal and contemplated that the rate would be determined anew on evidence adduced by parties, without any presumption in favor of director's previous fixation. Broadway v. Alabama Dry Dock & Shipbuilding Co., 246 Ala. 201, 20 So. 2d 41 (1944).

Subsection (h) permits a trial de novo with respect to determination of the benefit wage percentage. That contemplates that the rate will be determined anew on evidence adduced by the parties, without any presumption in favor of the director's decision or previous fixation. State Dep't of Indus. Relations v. McElrath Farms, Inc., 348 So. 2d 252 (Ala. Civ. App. 1976), rev'd on other grounds, 348 So. 2d 257 (Ala. 1977).

If an error of director in ascertaining taxpayer's contribution rate has been exposed pending hearing of taxpayer's appeal, this section does not authorize director to make an ex parte finding of fact which is binding upon court and taxpayer. Broadway v. Alabama Dry Dock & Shipbuilding Co., 246 Ala. 201, 20 So. 2d 41 (1944).

Whether director made a mistake of law held not reviewable by certiorari. Broadway v. Alabama Dry Dock & Shipbuilding Co., 246 Ala. 201, 20 So. 2d 41 (1944).

Cited in State v. Gibson's Barbecue, 369 So. 2d 1229 (Ala. Civ. App. 1978); James v. Mac Del Health Care, Inc., 428 So. 2d 48 (Ala. Civ. App. 1982); Poole Furn. Mfg. Co. v. State Dep't of Indus. Relations, 474 So. 2d 692 (Ala. 1985); Dixon v. Economy Co., 477 So. 2d 353 (Ala. 1985); Evans v. National Microsystems, 576 So. 2d 207 (Ala. 1991).

Collateral references. — 81 C.J.S., Social Security & Public Welfare, §§ 83, 142.

Unemployment compensation acts which vary rate of employer's contributions according to period in which business has been conducted. 163 ALR 1148.

Unemployment compensation benefits and incidence of tax employer where, during the base year, employee worked in different states for same employer. 9 ALR2d 646.

Right of successor in business to experience or rating of predecessor for purpose of fixing rate of contributions. 22 ALR2d 673.

Alcoholism or intoxication as ground for discharge justifying denial of unemployment compensation. 64 ALR4th 1151.

§ 25-4-55. Payment of interest on moneys advanced by federal government — Contributory employer's assessment; method of determining amount; procedures.

In addition to all other contributions required to be paid by the provisions of Sections 25-4-51 and 25-4-54, when the unemployment compensation trust fund of this state has received advances from the federal government under the provisions of 42 U.S.C. 1321, each contributory employer shall be assessed an additional rate solely for the purpose of paying interest due on such federal advances. The additional rate assessed to any employer shall be determined by dividing the estimated amount of interest to be paid on such advanced moneys minus any balance in this special fund by 95 percent of the wages as defined in Section 25-4-16 paid by all Alabama contributory employers during the immediately preceding calendar year. The amount to be paid by each employer shall be the product obtained by multiplying such employer's wages as defined in Section 25-4-16 for the calendar year immediately preceding the calendar year during which the advances became necessary by the rate as heretofore determined by provisions of this section. Each employer shall be notified of the amount of his or its assessment as required by this section not later than the fifteenth day of May next following the year in which such interest becomes due. Such amount shall be due and payable within 30 days of said notice and shall become delinquent on the day following such 30 days. Interest and penalties prescribed by the provisions of Sections 25-4-132 and 25-4-133 shall be applied to late payments to the same extent and at the same rates as is provided for delinquent contributions. Procedures for enforcing payment of amounts due including interest and penalty, by any employer shall be as prescribed by Section 25-4-134. Nothing contained herein shall prevent the Director of Industrial Relations from postponing the implementation of this section for one calendar year provided such postponement shall not delay collection later than required to pay accumulated interest when it becomes due to be paid nor shall it prevent him from making any further assessment if additional advances are made and/or additional interest becomes due. (Acts 1983, 2nd Ex. Sess., No. 83-178, p. 347, § 1; Acts 1984, No. 84-73, p. 94, § 1.)

§ 25-4-56. Payment of interest on moneys advanced by federal government — Creation of special interest payment fund; deposits; administration; disposition.

There is hereby created a special fund, to be known as the "special interest payment fund," into which shall be deposited all moneys collected under the provisions of Section 25-4-55. All moneys in the special interest payment fund shall be deposited, administered and disbursed in the same manner and under the same conditions and requirements as is provided by law in Section 25-4-31.

Moneys in this fund shall be used by the director for the payment of interest on moneys advanced by the federal government, shall be continuously available to the director for expenditures in accordance with the provisions of Sections 25-4-55 through 25-4-58 and appropriate federal laws and shall not lapse at any time. Any interest earned on moneys in this special fund shall accrue to the special fund. (Acts 1983, 2nd Ex. Sess., No. 83-178, p. 347, § 2; Acts 1984, No. 84-73, p. 94, § 2.)

§ 25-4-57. Payment of interest on moneys advanced by federal government — Assessment to discontinue when all interest paid; payment of interest on money advanced after previously borrowed funds repaid.

Payment of any assessment as provided under Section 25-4-55 shall be discontinued for the calendar year next following the calendar year during which all interest due to be paid on all advances has been paid. If it becomes necessary to borrow money from the federal government under the provisions of 42 U.S.C. 1321 subsequent to the calendar year in which all previously borrowed advances are repaid, assessments shall be made under the provisions prescribed in Section 25-4-55. (Acts 1983, 2nd Ex. Sess., No. 83-178, p. 347, § 3; Acts 1984, No. 84-73, p. 94, § 3.)

§ 25-4-58. Payment of interest on moneys advanced by federal government — Disposition of moneys in fund when assessment discontinued.

When payment of assessments have been discontinued under the provisions of Section 25-4-57, and all obligations of the director for interest on advances have been met, all remaining moneys in the special interest payment fund shall remain in this fund until such time as the balance in the unemployment trust fund equals at least 26 times the average weekly payment made from the unemployment trust fund during the immediately preceding fiscal year as defined in Section 25-4-4(b). Thereafter the director may on the immediately succeeding April 1 transfer any balances to the trust fund but in no event shall unexpended assessments remain in the special fund when the trust fund equals or exceeds 50 percent of the minimum normal amount on the preceding October 1, and may thereafter be expended only in such manner and for such purposes as other moneys in the fund may be expended. (Acts 1983, 2nd Ex. Sess., No. 83-178, p. 347, § 4; Acts 1984, No. 84-73, p. 94, § 4.)

ARTICLE 4.

BENEFITS.

The purpose of unemployment compensation law is to provide a worker with funds to avoid a period of destitution after having involuntarily lost his employment and thus his income; it is limited in time and amount; it is not a gratuity. Arrow Co. v. State Dep't of Indus. Relations, 370 So. 2d 1013 (Ala. Civ. App.), cert. denied, 370 So. 2d 1015 (Ala. 1979).

And not served by payment to claimant receiving vacation pay. — The purpose of the Unemployment Compensation Act is not served by the payment of unemployment benefits to a claimant who is receiving certain other forms of compensation, such as vacation pay, although he is not in the ordinary sense of the word employed; in such case, claimant is not suffering from disability which the act is designed to relieve, that is, financial hardship. Director of Dep't of Indus. Relations v. Butler, 367 So. 2d 496 (Ala. Civ. App. 1979).

Even if during forced lay-off. — General rule that a claimant is not eligible for unemployment compensation while he is receiving vacation pay applies regardless of whether the vacation is taken during a period of forced lay-off; the reason for this rule lies in the basic purpose of the Unemployment Compensation Act, which is to provide funds to an involuntarily unemployed worker so that he may avoid destitution during his unemployment. Director of Dep't of Indus. Relations v. Butler, 367 So. 2d 496 (Ala. Civ. App. 1979).

Collateral references. — Unemployment compensation as affected by vacation or payment in lieu thereof. 14 ALR4th 1175.

Right to unemployment compensation as affected by employee's refusal to work in areas where smoking is permitted. 14 ALR4th 1234.

Conduct or activities of employees during off-duty hours as misconduct barring unemployment compensation benefits. 35 ALR4th 691.

Eligibility for unemployment compensation benefits of employee who attempts to withdraw resignation before leaving employment. 36 ALR4th 395.

§ 25-4-70. Accrual; time and manner of payment; "reasonable assurance" defined.

(a) After contributions have been due under this chapter for two years, benefits shall become payable from the fund to any employee who thereafter is or becomes unemployed and eligible for benefits, and shall be paid through unemployment offices or such other agencies at such times and in such manner as the director may prescribe.

(b) Benefits based on service in employment defined in subdivisions (a)(2) and (a)(3) of Section 25-4-10 shall be payable in the same amount, on the same terms and subject to the same conditions as compensation payable on the basis of other service subject to this chapter; except, that:

(1) With respect to any week of unemployment beginning after December 31, 1977, benefits shall not be paid based on service in an instructional, research, or principal administrative capacity for any educational institution for any such week commencing during the period between two successive academic years, or during a similar period between two regular terms, whether or not successive, or during a period of paid sabbatical leave provided for in the individual's contract, to any individual if such individual performs such services in the first of such academic years (or terms) and if there is a contract or reasonable assurance that such individual will perform services in any such capacity for any educational institution in the second of such academic years or terms.

(2) With respect to any week of unemployment beginning after April 3, 1983, benefits shall not be paid on the basis of service in any other capacity for an educational institution, to any individual for any such week which commences during a period between two successive academic years or terms if such individual performs such services in the first of such academic years or terms and there is a reasonable assurance that such individual will perform such services in the second of such academic years or terms, except that if compensation is denied to any individual under this subdivision (2) for weeks of unemployment beginning on or after April 3, 1983 and such individual was not offered an opportunity to perform such services for the educational institution for the second of such academic years or terms, such individual shall be entitled to a retroactive payment of benefits for each week for which the individual filed a timely claim for benefits and for which benefits were denied solely by reason of this subdivision (2); provided further that such individual has given notice that the opportunity to return was not offered or was withdrawn to the director in such manner and within such time as the director by regulation shall prescribe.

(3) With respect to any week of unemployment beginning on or after April 1, 1984, benefits shall not be paid based on services in any capacity described in subdivisions (1) and (2) to any individual for any week which commences during an established and customary vacation period or holiday recess if such individual performs such services in the period immediately before such vacation period or holiday recess, and there is a reasonable

349

assurance that such individual will perform such services in the period immediately following such vacation period or holiday recess.

(4) With respect to any week of unemployment beginning on or after April 1, 1984, benefits shall not be paid on the basis of services described in subdivisions (1) and (2) of this subsection in any such capacities as specified in subdivisions (1), (2) and (3) to any individual who performed such services in an educational institution while in the employ of an educational service agency. For the purposes of this subdivision the term "educational service agency" shall mean a governmental agency or governmental entity which is established and operated exclusively for the purpose of providing such services to one or more educational institutions.

(5) With respect to weeks of unemployment beginning on or after April 1, 1984, benefits shall not be paid with respect to services to which Sections 25-4-8(a)(7), 25-4-8(a)(8), 25-4-10(a)(2) and 25-4-10(a)(3) apply, if such services are provided to or on behalf of an educational institution, under the same circumstances and subject to the same terms and conditions as described in subdivisions (1), (2), (3) and (4) of this subsection.

(6) With respect to weeks of unemployment beginning before April 1, 1984 benefits shall be paid on the basis of this section prior to that date.

(7) For the purposes of this subsection, the term "reasonable assurance" means a written, verbal or implied agreement that the employee will perform services during the ensuing academic year or term and the term "contract" is intended to include tenure status. (Acts 1943, No. 310, p. 281, § 4; Acts 1945, No. 283, p. 449, § 8; Acts 1949, No. 527, p. 810; Acts 1951, No. 644, p. 1098, § 2; Acts 1955, No. 28, p. 238; Acts 1957, No. 299, p. 382; Acts 1961, Ex. Sess., No. 274, p. 2298, § 5; Acts 1965, No. 390, p. 548, § 1; Acts 1967, No. 167, p. 499, § 2; Acts 1969, No. 234, p. 559, §§ 3-7; Acts 1971, No. 166, p. 440, §§ 10-12; Acts 1971, No. 1201, p. 2083, § 1; Acts 1971, No. 2325, p. 3748, § 1; Acts 1973, No. 1057, p. 1716, § 4; Acts 1975, No. 801, p. 1604, § 6; Acts 1978, 1st Ex. Sess., No. 1, p. 5, § 5; Acts 1979, No. 79-824, p. 1541, § 1; Acts 1983, 2nd Ex. Sess., No. 83-155, p. 264, § 7; Acts 1984, No. 84-73, p. 94, § 5.)

Cited in Ex parte Miles, 248 Ala. 386, 27 So. 2d 777 (1946); Alabama Mills, Inc. v. Carnley, 35 Ala. App. 46, 44 So. 2d 622 (1949); Department of Indus. Relations v. Haynes, 259 Ala. 238, 67 So. 2d 62 (1953).

Collateral references. — Repayment of unemployment compensation benefits erroneously paid. 90 ALR3d 987.

§ 25-4-71. When individuals deemed unemployed.

An individual shall be deemed totally unemployed in any week during which he performs no services and with respect to which no wages are payable to him, and shall be deemed partially unemployed in any week of less than full-time work if the wages payable to him with respect to such week are less than his weekly benefit amount. The director shall prescribe regulations applicable to unemployed individuals, making such distinctions in the procedures as to total unemployment, part-total unemployment, partial unemployment of individuals attached to their regular jobs and other forms of short-time work, as the director deems necessary. Wages are deemed to be payable to an individual working on a commission basis with respect to each week in which he works. (Acts 1939, No. 497, p. 721; Code 1940, T. 26, § 206.)

Purpose of the unemployment compensation law is to provide a worker with funds to avoid a period of destitution because of the loss of employment. Its goal is to sustain the worker while he looks for other employment. Hale v. Cullman County Bd. of Educ., 465 So. 2d 1143 (Ala. Civ. App. 1984).

Section expressly contemplates that claimant be unemployed though formerly an employee. — This section expressly contemplates a situation in which, although the employer-employee relationship exists between the claimant and his employer, the claimant is deemed "unemployed." Director, Dep't of Indus. Relations v. Alabama By-Products, Inc., 374 So. 2d 344 (Ala. Civ. App.), cert. denied, 374 So. 2d 347 (Ala. 1979).

Claimant is not disqualified for benefits where unemployment is not voluntary and self-imposed but is a result of a collective bargain which operates as a waiver of, and excludes him from benefits to which he is otherwise entitled. Director, Dep't of Indus. Relations v. Alabama By-Products, Inc., 374 So. 2d 344 (Ala. Civ. App.), cert. denied, 374 So. 2d 347 (Ala. 1979).

Not unemployed if receive wages attributable to weeks after termination. — An individual is not deemed unemployed even though he performs no services during a given week if he receives wages attributable to weeks after his termination from employment. State, Dep't of Indus. Relations v. Deslattes, 372 So. 2d 867 (Ala. Civ. App.), cert. denied, 372 So. 2d 872 (Ala. 1979).

Receipt of wages only disqualifies if for weeks following separation. — In order for the receipt of "wages" to disqualify a claimant under this section the payment must constitute wages for the weeks following separation as opposed to payment for services rendered prior to termination of employment. The disqualifying provisions apply to weeks with respect to which payments are made, not the week with respect to which payment is received. State, Dep't of Indus. Relations v. Deslattes, 372 So. 2d 867 (Ala. Civ. App.), cert. denied, 372 So. 2d 872 (Ala. 1979).

And that determination is a question of fact. — The determination of whether payments are made with respect to weeks following separation from employment is a question of fact. State, Dep't of Indus. Relations v. Deslattes, 372 So. 2d 867 (Ala. Civ. App.), cert. denied, 372 So. 2d 872 (Ala. 1979).

Disqualified under this section does not imply employment under another. — The fact that an individual is disqualified under this section because all the criteria of unemployment were not met does not directly imply that all the criteria of employment, as that term may be used in another context, were therefore met. Director of Dep't of Indus. Relations v. Butler, 367 So. 2d 496 (Ala. Civ. App. 1979).

A finding that unemployment compensation claimant was disqualified from receiving unemployment compensation benefits under statute because his vacation pay was deemed "wages" did not directly imply that he performed "services" required by requalification statute with respect to succeeding years. Director of Dep't of Indus. Relations v. Butler, 367 So. 2d 496 (Ala. Civ. App. 1979).

And does not mean requirements for requalification have been met. — Disqualification for a specific period does not mean that the statutory requirements for requalification in a succeeding year have thereby been met. Director of Dep't of Indus. Relations v. Butler, 367 So. 2d 496 (Ala. Civ. App. 1979).

Holiday pay considered earned in week of holiday. — Holiday pay is considered as having been earned in the week in which the holidays fell, where the union contract clearly contemplated that the holiday pay was for a day certain; this is so because the holidays were spelled out in the contract even with the hours of beginning and ending listed. Autwell v. State Dep't of Indus. Relations, 47 Ala. App. 8, 249 So. 2d 625 (1971).

Holiday pay received by employees is paid "with respect to the week in which the holiday occurs" for purposes of the unemployment compensation statute providing that an individual is totally unemployed when he receives no wages or performs no services for a particular week. Arrow Co. v. State Dep't of Indus. Relations, 370 So. 2d 1013 (Ala. Civ. App.), cert. denied, 370 So. 2d 1015 (Ala. 1979).

Receipt of vacation pay for specified time will serve to disqualify claimant from receiving unemployment compensation for that same period of time. Arrow Co. v. State Dep't of Indus. Relations, 370 So. 2d 1013 (Ala.

Civ. App.), cert. denied, 370 So. 2d 1015 (Ala. 1979).

But may not be wages to qualify for benefits in succeeding year. — The receipt of vacation pay in a prior benefit year may not be considered wages for work in insured employment so as to qualify a claimant for benefits in a succeeding year under this section. Director of Dep't of Indus. Relations v. Butler, 367 So. 2d 496 (Ala. Civ. App. 1979).

Existence of employer-employee relationship in partial unemployment case not determinative. — The existence or nonexistence of an employer-employee relationship in cases of partial unemployment is not determinative of whether an individual is "unemployed" under this section or "available for work" under § 25-4-77. Director, Dep't of

Indus. Relations v. Alabama By-Products, Inc., 374 So. 2d 344 (Ala. Civ. App.), cert. denied, 374 So. 2d 347 (Ala. 1979).

Teachers that continue to be paid wages during summer months are not eligible for unemployment compensation. Hale v. Cullman County Bd. of Educ., 465 So. 2d 1143 (Ala. Civ. App. 1984).

Collateral references. — 81 C.J.S., Social Security & Public Welfare, § 158.

Right to unemployment compensation as affected by vacation or holiday or payment in lieu thereof. 30 ALR2d 366, 3 ALR4th 557, 14 ALR4th 1175.

Unemployment compensation: eligibility of employee laid off according to employer's mandatory retirement plan. 50 ALR3d 880.

§ 25-4-72. Individual weekly benefit amount.

(a) For weeks of unemployment during benefit years which begin before the effective date of subsection (b) of this section, an individual's weekly benefit amount shall be as prescribed by this section as amended through May 2, 1989.

(b) For weeks of unemployment during benefit years beginning on or after the first Sunday of the first week which begins 30 days following approval by the Governor or its otherwise becoming law, an individual's weekly benefit amount shall be an amount equal to one twenty-fourth of the average of the wages for insured work paid to him during the two quarters of his base period in which such total wages were the highest; except, that:

(1) If the amount thus derived is not a multiple of $1.00, fractional parts of $1.00 in excess of $.50 shall be rounded to the next higher multiple of $1.00 and fractional parts of $1.00 which are $.50 or less shall be dropped to the next lower multiple of $1.00.

(2) If the amount derived before the application of subdivision (1) of this subsection is not in excess of $21.50, there shall be no weekly benefit amount.

(3) Effective with the first Sunday of the first week which begins 30 days following approval by the Governor or its otherwise becoming law, if the amount thus derived is more than $159.50, the weekly benefit amount shall be $160.00. If, for weeks of unemployment during benefit years which begin on or after January 3, 1993, if the amount thus derived is more than $164.50, the weekly benefit amount shall be $165.00.

(c) If, as a condition for approval of this section for full tax credit against the tax imposed by the Federal Unemployment Tax Act, federal law should require a greater maximum weekly benefit amount than that provided herein, then the maximum weekly benefit amount shall be the minimum required by any such federal law for such approval.

(d) Nothing herein shall serve to deprive any individual of any benefit for which he had qualified in any benefit year beginning prior to the effective date of the provisions of subsection (b) of this section. (Acts 1939, No. 497, p. 721; Code 1940, T. 26, § 207; Acts 1945, No. 283, p. 449, § 4; Acts 1951, No. 565, p. 990, § 1; Acts 1955, No. 349, p. 848, § 1; Acts 1957, No. 300, p. 392, § 1; Acts 1961, Ex. Sess., No. 274, p. 2298, § 6; Acts 1965, No. 390, p. 548, § 2; Acts 1967, No. 167, p. 499, § 3; Acts 1969, No. 234, p. 559, § 8; Acts 1971, No. 88, p. 349, § 3; Acts 1973, No. 1057, p. 1716, § 5; Acts 1975, 2nd Ex. Sess., No. 76, p. 203; Acts 1975, No. 801, p. 1604, § 7; Acts 1983, 2nd Ex. Sess., No. 83-155, p. 264, § 8; Acts 1988, 1st Ex. Sess., No. 88-784, p. 213, § 1; Acts 1989, No. 89-405, p. 822, § 5; Acts 1992, No. 92-173, § 1.)

The 1992 amendment, effective April 7, 1992, substituted "May 2, 1989" for "September, 1988" in subsection (a); in subsection (b) inserted "the first Sunday of the first week which begins 30 days following approval by the Governor or its otherwise becoming law" following "or after"; and rewrote subdivision (b)(3) which formerly read: "If the amount thus derived is more than $149.50 the weekly benefit amount shall be $150.00."

Receipt of vacation pay for specified time will serve to disqualify claimant from receiving unemployment compensation for that same period of time. Arrow Co. v. State Dep't of Indus. Relations, 370 So. 2d 1013 (Ala.

Civ. App.), cert. denied, 370 So. 2d 1015 (Ala. 1979).

Cited in Broadway v. Bolar, 33 Ala. App. 57, 29 So. 2d 687 (1947).

Collateral references. — 81 C.J.S., Social Security & Public Welfare, § 243.

Vested right of applicant for unemployment compensation in mode and manner of computing benefits in effect at time of his discharge or loss of employment. 20 ALR2d 963.

Cited in Broadway v. Bolar, 33 Ala. App. 57, 29 So. 2d 687 (1947); Department of Indus. Relations v. Little Mfg. Co., 253 Ala. 416, 44 So. 2d 587 (1950).

§ 25-4-73. Individual weekly benefit payment.

(a) Each eligible individual who is totally unemployed or partially unemployed in any week beginning on or after July 3, 1983, shall be paid with respect to such week a benefit in an amount equal to his weekly benefit amount, less that part of the wages, if any, payable to him with respect to such week which is in excess of $15.00. Such benefit, if not a multiple of $1.00, shall be computed to the nearest multiple of $1.00.

(b) With respect to weeks beginning prior to January 1, 1989, each eligible individual shall be paid with respect to such week as was provided in this section prior to such date. (Acts 1939, No. 497, p. 721; Code 1940, T. 26, § 208; Acts 1955, No. 349, p. 848, § 2; Acts 1983, 2nd Ex. Sess., No. 83-155, p. 264, § 9; Acts 1988, 1st Ex. Sess., No. 88-784, p. 213, § 2.)

Cited in Broadway v. Bolar, 33 Ala. App. 57, 29 So. 2d 687 (1947); Department of Indus. Relations v. Little Mfg. Co., 253 Ala. 416, 44 So. 2d 587 (1950).

§ 25-4-74. Maximum individual benefit entitlement during benefit year.

(a) Any otherwise eligible individual shall be entitled during any benefit year, beginning on or after July 3, 1983, to a total amount of benefits equal to whichever is the lesser of 26 times his weekly benefit amount and one third of the wages paid to him for insured work during his base period; provided, that such total amounts of benefits, if not a multiple of $1.00, shall be computed to the nearest multiple of $1.00. For the purpose of this article, wages shall be counted as "wages for insured work" with respect to any benefit year only if such wages were paid in the base period immediately preceding such benefit year; except, that any lump sum payment of wages in lieu of notice, dismissal or severance allowance or "back pay" award shall be prorated over the period or periods with respect to which such payment is made and treated as though it had been paid in such period or periods. In determining an individual's benefit rights, remuneration payable but unpaid to such individual shall, to the extent that regulations promulgated by the director prescribe, be deemed to be "wages paid" to such individual.

(b) For benefit years beginning prior to July 3, 1983, any otherwise eligible individual shall be entitled to a total amount of benefits as was provided in this section prior to such date. (Acts 1939, No. 497, p. 721; Code 1940, T. 26, § 209; Acts 1943, No. 310, p. 281, § 5; Acts 1951, No. 565, p. 990, § 2; Acts 1961, Ex. Sess., No. 274, p. 2298, § 7; Acts 1971, 1st Ex. Sess., No. 17, p. 57; Acts 1971, No. 88, p. 349, § 4; Acts 1978, 1st Ex. Sess., No. 1, p. 5, § 7; Acts 1980, No. 80-807, p. 1651, § 2; Acts 1983, 2nd Ex. Sess., No. 83-155, p. 264, § 10.)

U.S. Code. — Title II of the Emergency Jobs and Unemployment Act of 1974 is noted under 26 U.S.C.A. § 3304.

Section 121 of Public Law 94-566 is noted under 26 U.S.C.A. § 3304.

Cited in Broadway v. Bolar, 33 Ala. App. 57, 29 So. 2d 687 (1947); Caradine v. Director, Dep't of Indus. Relations, 456 So. 2d 75 (Ala. Civ. App. 1984).

§ 25-4-75. Extension of benefit period.

(a) *Applicability of section.* — Notwithstanding any other provisions of this chapter, the duration of benefits as provided in Section 25-4-74 shall be extended as provided in this section.

(b) *Definitions.* — As used in this section, unless the context clearly requires otherwise, the following terms shall mean:

(1) EXTENDED BENEFIT PERIOD. A period which:

a. Begins with the third week after a week for which there is a state "on" indicator; and

b. Ends with either of the following weeks, whichever occurs later:

1. The third week after the first week for which there is a state "off" indicator; or

2. The thirteenth consecutive week of such period;

provided, that no extended benefit period may begin by reason of a state "on" indicator before the fourteenth week following the end of a prior extended benefit period which was in effect with respect to this state.

(2) STATE "ON" INDICATOR. There is a "state 'on' indicator" for this state for a week if the director determines, in accordance with the regulations of the U.S. Secretary of Labor, that for the period consisting of such week and the immediately preceding 12 weeks, the rate of insured unemployment (not seasonally adjusted) under this section:

a. For any weeks beginning prior to September 26, 1982, equaled or exceeded that required by this section prior to such date.

b. For any week beginning on September 26, 1982, or thereafter:

1. Equaled or exceeded 120 percent of the average of such rates for the corresponding 13-week period ending in each of the preceding two calendar years; and

2. Equaled or exceeded five percent; provided, that with respect to benefits for weeks of unemployment beginning after September 25, 1982, the determination of whether there has been a "state 'on' indicator" beginning any extended benefit period shall be made under this paragraph b as if this paragraph b did not contain subparagraph 1 thereof and the "five" contained in subparagraph 2 thereof were "six".

(3) STATE "OFF" INDICATOR. There is a "state 'off' indicator" for this state for a week if the director determines, in accordance with the regulations of the U.S. Secretary of Labor, that for the period consisting of such week and the immediately preceding 12 weeks:

a. For any weeks beginning prior to September 26, 1982, the rate of insured unemployment under this section was less than that required by this section prior to such date.

b. For any weeks beginning on September 26, 1982, or thereafter, the requirements of either subparagraph 1 or 2 of paragraph (2) b of this subsection (b) were not satisfied, except that the six percent provision does not apply in determining an "off" indicator.

(4) RATE OF INSURED UNEMPLOYMENT. For the purpose of subdivisions (2) and (3) of this subsection (b), such term means the percentage derived by dividing:

a. The average weekly number of individuals filing claims for regular state benefits in this state for weeks of unemployment with respect to the most recent 13-consecutive-week period, as determined by the director on the basis of his reports to the U.S. Secretary of Labor, by

b. The average monthly employment covered under this chapter for the first four of the most recent six completed calendar quarters ending before the end of such 13-week period.

(5) REGULAR BENEFITS. Benefits payable to an individual under this chapter or under any other state law (including benefits payable to federal civilian employees and to ex-servicemen pursuant to 5 U.S.C. 85), other than extended benefits.

(6) EXTENDED BENEFITS. Benefits (incuding benefits payable to federal civilian employees and to ex-servicemen pursuant to 5 U.S.C. 85) payable to an individual under the provisions of this subsection for weeks of unemployment in his eligibility period.

(7) ELIGIBILITY PERIOD OF AN INDIVIDUAL. The period consisting of the weeks in his benefit year which begin in an extended benefit period and, if his benefit year ends within such extended benefit period, any weeks thereafter which begin in such extended benefit period.

(8) EXHAUSTEE. An individual who, with respect to any week of unemployment in his eligibility period:

a. Has received, prior to such week, all of the regular benefits that were available to him under this chapter or any other state law (including dependents' allowances and benefits payable to federal civilian employees and ex-servicemen under 5 U.S.C. 85) in his current benefit year that includes such week; provided, that for the purposes of this subdivision (8), an individual shall be deemed to have received all of the regular benefits that were available to him although as a result of a pending appeal with respect to wages and/or employment that were not considered in the original monetary determination in his benefit year, he may subsequently be determined to be entitled to added regular benefits; or

b. His benefit year having expired prior to such week, has no, or insufficient, wages on the basis of which he could establish a new benefit year that would include such week; and

c.1. Has no right to unemployment benefits or allowances, as the case may be, under the Railroad Unemployment Insurance Act, the Trade Expansion Act of 1962, the Automotive Products Trade Act of 1965 and such other federal laws as are specified in regulations issued by the U.S. Secretary of Labor; and

2. Has not received and is not seeking unemployment benefits under the unemployment compensation law of Canada; but, if he is seeking such benefits and the appropriate agency finally determines that he is not entitled to benefits under such law, he is considered an exhaustee.

(9) STATE LAW. The unemployment insurance law of any state, approved by the U.S. Secretary of Labor under Section 3304 of the Internal Revenue Code of 1954.

(c) *Effect of state law provisions relating to regular benefits on claims for, and the payment of, extended benefits.* — Except when the result would be inconsistent with the other provisions of this section, as provided in the regulations of the director, the provisions of this chapter which apply to claims for, or the payment of, regular benefits shall apply to claims for, and the payment of, extended benefits.

(d) *Eligibility requirements for extended benefits.* — An individual shall be eligible to receive extended benefits with respect to any week of unemployment in his eligibility period only if the director finds that with respect to such week:

(1) He is an "exhaustee," as defined in subdivision (b)(8) of this section.

(2) He has satisfied the requirements of this chapter for the receipt of regular benefits that are applicable to individuals claiming extended benefits, including not being subject to a disqualification for the receipts of benefits.

(e) *Weekly extended benefit amount.* — The weekly extended benefit amount payable to an individual for a week of total unemployment in his eligibility period shall be an amount equal to the weekly benefit amount payable to him during his applicable benefit year.

(f) *Total extended benefit amount.* — The total extended benefit amount payable to any eligible individual with respect to his applicable benefit year shall be 50 percent, rounded to the nearest multiple of $1.00, of the total amount of regular benefits which were payable to him under this chapter in his applicable benefit year.

(g) *Beginning and termination of extended benefit period.*

(1) Whenever an extended benefit period is to become effective in this state, as a result of a state "on" indicator, or an extended benefit period is to be terminated in this state as a result of a state "off" indicator, the director shall make an appropriate public announcement.

(2) Computations required by the provisions of subdivision (b)(4) of this section shall be made by the director, in accordance with regulations prescribed by the U.S. Secretary of Labor.

(h) *Cessation of extended benefits when paid under an interstate claim in a state where extended benefit period is not in effect.*

(1) Except as provided in subdivision (2) of this subsection (h), an individual shall not be eligible for extended benefits for any week if:

a. extended benefits are payable for such week pursuant to an interstate claim filed in any state under the interstate benefit payment plan; and

b. no extended benefit period is in effect for such week in such state.

(2) The provisions of subdivision (1) of this subsection (h) shall not apply with respect to the first two weeks for which extended benefits are payable (determined without regard to this subsection) pursuant to an interstate claim filed under the interstate benefit payment plan to the individual from his extended benefit amount established for the benefit year.

(i) *Restrictions on entitlement during eligibility period.*

(1) Notwithstanding the other provisions of this section, payment of any extended benefits under this section shall not be made to any individual for any week of unemployment in his eligibility period:

a. during which he fails to accept any offer of suitable work as defined in subdivision (3) of this subsection (i) or fails to apply for any such suitable work to which he was referred by the director; or

b. during which he fails to actively seek work, except as provided in subdivision (a)(5) of Section 25-4-77, but only with regard to the exception for the appearance for jury duty as provided therein.

(2) If any individual is ineligible for extended benefits for any week by reason of a failure described in subdivision (1) of this subsection (i), the individual shall be ineligible to receive extended benefits for any week during a period which:

a. begins with the week following the week in which such failure occurs; and

b. does not end until such individual has been employed in at least four weeks which begin after such failure and the total of the remuneration earned by the individual for being so employed is not less than four times his extended weekly benefit amount for his benefit year.

(3) For the purposes of this subsection (i), the term "suitable work" means, with respect to any individual, any work which is within such

individuals' capabilities; except that, if the individual furnishes evidence satisfactory to the director that such individual's prospects for obtaining work in his customary occupation within a reasonably short period are good, the determination of whether any work is suitable work shall be made in accordance with other provisions of this chapter.

(4) Extended benefits shall not be denied under paragraph a of subdivision (1) of this subsection (i) to any individual for any week by reason of a failure to accept an offer of, or apply for, suitable work:

a. if the gross average weekly remuneration payable to such individual for the position does not exceed the sum of

1. the individual's extended weekly benefit amount for the benefit year plus

2. the amount if any of supplemental unemployment benefits (as defined in 26 U.S.C. 501(c)(17)(D)) payable to such individual for such week;

b. if the position was not offered to such individual in writing or was not listed with the State Employment Service;

c. if such failure would not result in a denial of benefits under the other provisions of this chapter to the extent that such provisions are not inconsistent with subdivisions (4) and (5) of this subdivision (i); or

d. if the position pays wages less than the higher of the minimum wages provided under Section 6 (a) (1) of the Fair Labor Standards Act of 1938, as amended, without regard to any exemption or the applicable state or local minimum wage, if any.

(5) For purposes of this subsection (i), an individual shall be treated as actively engaged in seeking work during any week if the individual has engaged in a systematic and sustained effort to obtain work during such week, and provides tangible evidence to the director that he has engaged in such effort during such week.

(j) *Referral of extended claimant to job.* — Extended benefit claimants shall be referred to any available suitable work to which the definition in subdivision (3) of subsection (i) does not apply.

(k) *Employment required after involuntary separation.* — No provision of Section 25-4-78 which terminates a disqualification for regular or extended benefits because he or she has voluntarily left employment, was suspended or discharged for misconduct (in any of the degrees defined in Section 25-4-78) or failed to accept an offer of or apply for suitable work shall apply for purposes of determining eligibility for extended benefits unless the disqualification imposed has been terminated based upon employment in four weeks and remuneration of an amount which equals or exceeds four times the individual's weekly benefit amount subsequent to the effective date of such disqualification.

(*l*) *Effective date of added provisions.* — The provisions of subsections (h), (i), (j), (k) and (*l*) of this section shall apply to weeks of unemployment which begin after March 31, 1981.

(m) *Effect of receipt of trade readjustment allowances.* — Notwithstanding any other provisions of this section, if the benefit year of any individual ends within an extended benefit period, the remaining balance of extended benefits that such individual would, but for this subsection (m), be entitled to receive in that extended benefit period, with respect to weeks of unemployment beginning after the end of the benefit year, shall be reduced (but not below zero) by the product of the number of weeks for which the individual received any amounts as trade readjustment allowances within that benefit year, multiplied by the individual's weekly benefit amount for extended benefits. (Acts 1939, No. 497, p. 721; Code 1940, T. 26, § 209; Acts 1943, No. 310, p. 281, § 5; Acts 1951, No. 565, p. 990, § 2; Acts 1961, Ex. Sess., No. 274, p. 2298, § 7; Acts 1971, 1st Ex. Sess., No. 17, p. 57; Acts 1971, No. 88, p. 349, § 4; Acts 1978, 1st Ex. Sess., No. 1, p. 5, § 8; Acts 1981, No. 81-424, p. 665; Acts 1982, No. 82-370, p. 524, § 1; Acts 1984, No. 84-73, p. 94, § 6.)

§ 25-4-76. Maritime employment and benefit rights.

(a) As used in this section, "maritime employment" means employment in connection with the construction, repair, loading or unloading of vessels, and in connection with the handling of cargoes for vessels. The director shall, after a study of previous employment records and after investigation and hearing, determine, and may thereafter from time to time redetermine which industries are maritime industries within the meaning of this section. Until such determination by the director, no industry shall be deemed to be a maritime industry.

(b) The term "maritime worker" means an employee who is customarily or regularly employed in "maritime employment, " such as men engaged in the construction or repair of vessels and in the operation of plants at which vessels are constructed or repaired, and it shall include longshoremen, dock workers, harbor workers and other employees in occupations which, after the director has studied the nature thereof and the employment record of workers engaged therein, are found to be occupations in which employment regularly continues throughout substantially all the year.

(c) The provisions of Section 25-4-72 shall in all respects govern the benefit rights of a maritime worker, except that the weekly benefit amount of such a worker shall be determined from "the average quarterly earnings" paid such worker during his base period, instead of from the "average of the wages for insured work paid to him during the two quarters of his base period in which such total wages were the highest." If a "maritime worker" has not been engaged in maritime employment for substantially the whole of his base period, the director shall determine his average quarterly earnings on the basis of his earnings during the time he has actually been engaged in such maritime employment within his base period. (Acts 1939, No. 497, p. 721; Code 1940, T. 26, § 211; Acts 1966, Ex. Sess., No. 427, p. 571; Acts 1988, 1st Ex. Sess., No. 88-784, p. 213, § 3.)

§ 25-4-77. Benefits eligibility conditions; "suitable employment" and jury duty defined; applicability of subdivision (a)(5).

(a) An unemployed individual shall be eligible to receive benefits with respect to any week in a benefit year which begins on or after January 1, 1989, only if the director finds that:

(1) He has made a claim for benefits with respect to such week in accordance with such regulations as the director may prescribe.

(2) He has registered for work at, and thereafter continued to report at, a state employment office in accordance with such regulations as the director may prescribe; except, that the director may by regulation waive or alter either or both of the requirements of this subdivision (2) as to individuals attached to regular jobs and as to such other types of cases or situations with respect to which he finds that compliance with such requirements would be oppressive, or would be inconsistent with purposes of this chapter.

(3) He is physically and mentally able to perform work of a character which he is qualified to perform by past experience or training, and he is available for such work either at a locality at which he earned wages for insured work during his base period or at a locality where it may reasonably be expected that such work may be available. Notwithstanding any of the provisions of this subdivision (3), no otherwise eligible individual shall be denied benefits for any week because he or she is:

a. Enrolled in a course of training with the approval of the director. Such approval shall be conditioned upon the following:

1. The individual's skills are obsolete or such that there are minimal opportunities for employment;

2. Training is for an occupation for which there is a substantial and recurring demand;

3. Training is not a course of education for credit toward a degree;

4. The individual possesses aptitudes or skills which can be supplemented by retraining within a reasonable time; or

5. The individual produces satisfactory evidence of continued attendance and satisfactory progress;

b. In training approved by the director under Section 236 (a)(1) of the Trade Act of 1974, nor shall such individual be denied benefits (any other provision of this chapter requiring denial notwithstanding) by reason of leaving work to enter such training; provided,

1. The work left is not suitable employment as defined in paragraph c of this subdivision (3), or

2. Because of the application to any such week in training of provisions in this chapter (or any applicable federal unemployment compensation law) relating to availability for work, active search for work or refusal to accept work.

c. For purposes of paragraph b of this subdivision (3), and only therefor, the term "suitable employment" means with respect to an individual, work of a substantially equal or higher skill level than the individual's past adversely affected employment (as defined for purposes of the Trade Act of 1974), and wages for such work at not less than 80 percent of the individual's average weekly wage as determined for the purposes of the Trade Act of 1974.

(4) He has been totally or partially unemployed in such week.

(5) He has made a reasonable and active effort to secure work which he is qualified to perform by past experience and training, unless such failure is because the individual is before any court of the United States or any state pursuant to a lawfully issued summons to appear for jury duty. For the purposes of this subdivision (5), the entitlement to regular or extended benefits of any individual who is determined not to be actively engaged in seeking work during any week for the aforesaid reason, shall be determined pursuant to the provisions of subdivision (3) of this subsection (a) without regard to the disqualification provisions otherwise applicable under paragraph b of subdivision (i)(1) of Section 25-4-75 and subdivision (i)(2) of Section 25-4-75. Further, for the purposes of this subdivision (5), the term "jury duty" means the performance of service as a juror, during all periods of time an individual is engaged in such service, in any court of a state or the United States pursuant to the law of the state or the United States and the rules of the court in which the individual is engaged in the performance of such service.

(6) He has during his base period been paid wages for insured work equal to or exceeding one and one-half times the total of the wages for insured work paid to him in that quarter of such base period in which such total wages were the highest and in addition, qualifies for benefits under the provisions of Section 25-4-72; provided, however, that no otherwise eligible individual who shall have received benefits in a preceding benefit year shall be eligible to receive benefits in a succeeding benefit year unless and until such otherwise eligible individual, subsequent to the beginning date of the preceding benefit year, shall have worked in insured employment for which work he earned wages equal to at least eight times the weekly benefit amount established for such individual in the preceding benefit year.

(b) With respect to any week which begins prior to January 1, 1989, an unemployed individual shall be eligible to receive benefits as provided in this section prior to that date.

(c) The provisions of subdivision (5) of subsection (a) shall be applied only to any week which begins on or after March 22, 1984. (Acts 1939, No. 497, p. 721; Code 1940, T. 26, § 213; Acts 1943, No. 310, p. 281, § 7; Acts 1945, No. 283, p. 449, § 9; Acts 1949, No. 524, p. 804; Acts 1951, No. 598, p. 1029; Acts 1955, No. 353, p. 852; Acts 1961, Ex. Sess., No. 274, p. 2298, § 8; Acts 1965, No. 390, p. 548, § 4; Acts 1971, No. 88, p. 349, § 5; Acts 1975, No. 801, p. 801, § 8; Acts 1982, No. 82-372, p. 533, § 2; Acts 1983, 2nd Ex. Sess., No. 83-155, p. 264, § 11; Acts 1984, No. 84-73, p. 94, § 7; Acts 1988, 1st Ex. Sess., No. 88-784, p. 213, § 4; Acts 1989, No. 89-405, p. 822, § 6.)

U.S. Code. — As to the Trade Act of 1974 generally, see 5 U.S.C.A. §§ 5312, 5314 et seq.

Purpose of section. — The purpose of this section as a whole is to insure that claimants seeking benefits put forth a good faith effort to obtain work. Polk v. State, Dep't of Indus. Relations, 413 So. 2d 1164 (Ala. Civ. App. 1982).

This section and section 25-4-78 to be considered together. — While this section deals with the eligibility of an employee to receive benefits, and § 25-4-78 deals with his qualifications therefor, the two sections are so interrelated that consideration of one necessitates a consideration of the other, and a mechanical application of the one without consideration of the other cannot lead to satisfactory conclusions. Alabama Mills, Inc. v. Carnley, 35 Ala. App. 46, 44 So. 2d 622 (1949); Southern Bell Tel. & Tel. Co. v. Department of Indus. Relations, 42 Ala. App. 351, 165 So. 2d 128 (1964).

This section and § 25-4-78 must be read and construed together for the purpose of determining one's eligibility for unemployment compensation. Southern Bell Tel. & Tel. Co. v. Department of Indus. Relations, 42 Ala. App. 351, 165 So. 2d 128 (1964); State Dep't of Indus. Relations v. Thomas, 55 Ala. App. 712, 318 So. 2d 739 (1975); Davis v. Pickett, 412 So. 2d 1225 (Ala. Civ. App. 1981), writ quashed, 412 So. 2d 1230 (Ala. 1982).

Burden of proof is upon claimant to establish his rights to benefits under the unemployment compensation law. An unemployed individual is eligible to receive benefits only if it appears that the required conditions have been met and the burden is upon him to show that those conditions exist. The claimant assumes the risk of nonpersuasion. State, Dep't of Indus. Relations v. Downey, 380 So. 2d 906 (Ala. Civ. App. 1980).

Generally, an individual asserting a claim for unemployment benefits under this section bears the burden of establishing his right to such benefits by proving through competent evidence that he has satisfied each of the conditions precedent to obtaining such benefits. Davis v. Pickett, 412 So. 2d 1225 (Ala. Civ. App. 1981), writ quashed, 412 So. 2d 1230 (Ala. 1982).

The burden is upon the claimant for unemployment compensation to prove that he or she is available for work as required by subdivision (3) during the period for which compensation is sought. Heatherly v. Campbell, 485 So. 2d 735 (Ala. Civ. App. 1986).

Good faith and reasonable effort must be shown. — Claimant, in order to be eligible for unemployment compensation, must at least show that he acted in good faith and made a reasonable effort to secure suitable employment of a character which he is qualified to perform by past experience or training. Department of Indus. Relations v. Smith, 360 So. 2d 726 (Ala. Civ. App. 1978); Heatherly v. Campbell, 485 So. 2d 735 (Ala. Civ. App. 1986).

A claimant, in order to show that he was "available for work" during the time for which he seeks benefits, must at least show that he acted in good faith and made a reasonable effort to secure suitable employment of a character which he is qualified to perform by past experience or training. Hale v. Cullman County Bd. of Educ., 465 So. 2d 1143 (Ala. Civ. App. 1984).

Since claimant was just looking for odd jobs "to keep money in my pocket" and not seeking full-time work, claimant was ineligible for unemployment compensation benefits. Allen v. Crawford, 591 So. 2d 887 (Ala. Civ. App. 1991).

Claimant must at least show that he acted in good faith and made a reasonable effort to secure suitable employment of a character which he is qualified to perform by past experience or training. Heatherly v. Campbell, 485 So. 2d 735 (Ala. Civ. App. 1986).

Totality of circumstances must show good faith and reasonable effort. — A claimant for unemployment benefits is not required to prove the exact number of applications for employment made; there merely must be such evidence that the totality of the circumstances shows good faith and reasonable effort. State Dep't of Indus. Relations v. Singleton, 364 So. 2d 325 (Ala. Civ. App. 1978), cert. denied, 364 So. 2d 327 (Ala. 1978).

Merely registering with union and former employer or even with the state employment office did not constitute good faith effort by claimant for unemployment compensation benefits to attach himself to the labor market and make himself available for work in that employment from such sources was dependent not upon availability of jobs, but upon whether claimant was next in line to be called. State Dep't of Indus. Relations v. Harbin, 365 So. 2d 313 (Ala. Civ. App. 1978).

Must be able to work and available for work. — In order for an individual to be entitled to benefits under the unemployment compensation law he must have been able to work and available for work. Department of Indus. Relations v. Tomlinson, 251 Ala. 144, 36 So. 2d 496 (1948).

A claimant, in order to be eligible for unemployment benefits, must be available for work. Department of Indus. Relations v. Mann, 35 Ala. App. 505, 50 So. 2d 780 (1950).

It is required that claimant be physically able to do the work as well as being qualified to do it. Department of Indus. Relations v. McLeod, 55 Ala. App. 152, 314 So. 2d 72 (1975).

Where lack of proof concerning a claimant's ableness and availability for work is the only issue raised and argued by the department on appeal, proof that the claimant was able to, and available for work was necessary to sustain her case. Davis v. McBroom, 402 So. 2d 1016 (Ala. Civ. App. 1981).

The law is very clear and certain that the burden is upon a claimant who sues for unemployment compensation to establish by sufficient evidence, or by proper and adequate stipulation, that she was available for work during the time for which she seeks benefits. Quick v. Director of Dep't of Indus. Relations, 398 So. 2d 312 (Ala. Civ. App. 1981).

But a hard and fast rule as to what constitutes availability for work cannot be laid down. It depends upon the facts and circumstances of each case. However, a claimant in order to show that he was "available for work" during the time for which he seeks benefits must at least show that he acted in good faith and made a reasonable effort to secure suitable employment of a character which he is qualified to perform by past experience or training. Department of Indus. Relations v. Tomlinson, 251 Ala. 446, 36 So. 2d 496 (1946); Alabama Dep't of Indus. Relations v. Anderson, 41 Ala. App. 267, 128 So. 2d 532 (1961); Polk v. State, Dep't of Indus. Relations, 413 So. 2d 1164 (Ala. Civ. App. 1982).

There is no hard and fast rule as to what constitutes availability for work in order to establish rights to unemployment benefits, as it depends on the facts and circumstances of each case, but a claimant must at least show that he acted in good faith and made a reasonable effort to secure suitable employment of a character which he is qualified to perform by past experience or training. State Dep't of Indus. Relations v. Singleton, 364 So. 2d 325 (Ala. Civ. App. 1978), cert. denied, 364 So. 2d 327 (Ala. 1978).

There is no hard and fast rule as to what constitutes "availability" for work within the meaning of subdivision (3). Each case must be judged on its own facts and circumstances. Heatherly v. Campbell, 485 So. 2d 735 (Ala. Civ. App. 1986).

The claimant has the burden of proving he is eligible under this section and not disqualified under § 25-4-78. Department of Indus. Relations v. Jaco, 337 So. 2d 374 (Ala. Civ. App. 1976); James v. Riddle, 432 So. 2d 563 (Ala. Civ. App. 1983).

What constitutes "availability for work" depends upon the facts and circumstances of each case; a claimant must at least show that she acted in good faith and made a reasonable

effort to secure suitable employment of a character which she is qualified to perform by past experience or training, and reporting weekly to the unemployment office, even to the state employment office, is not sufficient in itself to establish "availability" for work. State Dep't of Indus. Relations v. Thompson, 359 So. 2d 1158 (Ala. Civ. App. 1978).

Claimant is ineligible to receive benefits if he fails to prove that he is physically able to do work for which he claims to be qualified. Department of Indus. Relations v McLeod, 55 Ala. App. 152, 314 So. 2d 72 (1975).

Or available for work. — Where claimant made no effort to secure suitable employment of a character which she was qualified to perform, she failed to show that she was "available for work" within the meaning and requirements of subsection (3). Department of Indus. Relations v. Wall, 34 Ala. App. 530, 41 So. 2d 611 (1949).

The claimant contented herself with filing her claim, registering with and reporting to the unemployment office, and waiting for a call from the superintendent of certain grocery stores, which call was dependent on the future and uncertain contingency of an opening developing in the said stores. This was incompatible, as a matter of law, with the concept of what would constitute a reasonable effort on the part of the claimant to secure suitable employment of a character which she was qualified to perform. Department of Indus. Relations v. Mann, 35 Ala. App. 505, 50 So. 2d 780 (1950).

Claimant was not "available for work" where he would not have accepted employment requiring him to contract for work extending past January 16, 1953, the date on which he would take office as circuit clerk of his county. Alabama Textile Prods. Corp. v. Rodgers, 38 Ala. App. 206, 82 So. 2d 267 (1955).

By voluntarily removing herself from the labor market for a specified period, for maternity reasons, the claimant was therefore, prima facie, not available for work within the purview of this section, prior to the expiration of her leave of absence. Southern Bell Tel. & Tel. Co. v. Department of Indus. Relations, 42 Ala. App. 351, 165 So. 2d 128 (1964).

Under statute requiring that one must be available for work in order to be eligible for unemployment compensation, "availability" is not satisfied by claimant being able and ready to return to the job from which she resigned if the work load is lessened to her satisfaction; "availability" under the statute is not necessarily related at all to a readiness to return to the employment she left, but rather applies to a willingness and ability to seek and accept any employment for which she may be qualified. Director of State Dep't of Indus. Relations v. Stone, 367 So. 2d 506 (Ala. Civ. App. 1979).

"Availability" to satisfy the statutory conditions for benefits, must be exemplified by continuing effort to find employment throughout the benefit period. Director of State Dep't of Indus. Relations v. Stone, 367 So. 2d 506 (Ala. Civ. App. 1979).

Failure of proof of constant availability for employment for which claimant is qualified may require a finding of ineligibility for benefits. Director of State Dep't of Indus. Relations v. Stone, 367 So. 2d 506 (Ala. Civ. App. 1979).

Where only evidence relating to the proof of "availability for work" is the fact that the claimant went to the employment office prior to leaving her employment and her statement that she needed a job and money, evidence is insufficient to meet the burden of establishing that she was "available for work" within the meaning of unemployment compensation statute. Ventress v. Coker, 361 So. 2d 591 (Ala. Civ. App. 1978).

A claimant bears the burden of proving that he is available for work during the time for which he seeks benefits. The unemployment compensation statute, however, should be liberally construed in claimant's favor. The statute is in the nature of insurance for the unemployed worker and is intended to be a remedial measure for his benefit. Polk v. State, Dep't of Indus. Relations, 413 So. 2d 1164 (Ala. Civ. App. 1982).

Claimant unavailable for work not entitled to benefits. — Alabama unemployment law provides that a claimant who has been unavailable for work since termination is not entitled to unemployment benefits. Mitchell v. Humana Hospital-Shoals, 942 F.2d 1581 (11th Cir. 1991).

There can be no presumption of availability under this section because of a claimant's past work history. Director of State Dep't of Indus. Relations v. Stone, 367 So. 2d 506 (Ala. Civ. App. 1979).

Existence of employer-employee relationship in partial unemployment case not determinative. — The existence or nonexistence of an employer-employee relationship in cases of partial unemployment is not determinative of whether an individual is "unemployed" under § 25-4-71 or "available for work" under this section. Director, Dep't of Indus. Relations v. Alabama By-Products, Inc., 374 So. 2d 344 (Ala. Civ. App.), cert. denied, 374 So. 2d 347 (Ala. 1979).

Nor does relationship's existence preclude finding claimant available for work. — The existence of an employer-employee relationship does not preclude a finding that a claimant is "available for work" as required by this section. Director, Dep't of Indus. Relations v. Alabama By-Products, Inc., 374 So. 2d 344 (Ala. Civ. App.), cert. denied, 374 So. 2d 347 (Ala. 1979).

Claimant not limited to seeking jobs in former unskilled industry. — Although claimant had been employed in the dry cleaning industry for the last nine and one-half years, she was not required to have applied for employment in that industry to establish that she was available to perform work of a character which she was qualified to perform by past experience or training, since her job as a presser at the time her employment was terminated could best be characterized as manual or unskilled labor. When she left her job with the employer, she took with her no specialized skills in the dry cleaning business. Under such circumstances, she was not limited to seeking jobs in the dry cleaning industry in order to meet the requirement of subdivision (3). Heatherly v. Campbell, 485 So. 2d 735 (Ala. Civ. App. 1986).

One who refused employment because nonunion is disqualified. — One who has refused employment for which he is qualified because he is not available for work on the ground that it is "nonunion" is disqualified because he is not available for work within the intent of the statute governing availability for work as qualification for benefits. State Dep't of Indus. Relations v. Harbin, 365 So. 2d 313 (Ala. Civ. App. 1978).

Where claimant for unemployment compensation benefits placed himself only upon union and company panels in an effort to make himself available for work and refused job for which he qualified with a different company because it paid less than union wages and would result in loss of union rights, claimant was not qualified for unemployment compensation benefits under statutes governing availability for work and refusal to accept employment for which he was qualified. State Dep't of Indus. Relations v. Harbin, 365 So. 2d 313 (Ala. Civ. App. 1978).

"Work in insured employment" required by this section is actual work and not "implied" or constructive work. Director of State Dep't of Indus. Relations v. Butler, 367 So. 2d 496 (Ala. Civ. App. 1979).

Base period wages must be paid before credited. — An employee's base period wages must be actually paid, not just earned, before they may be credited for purposes of base period eligibility to receive unemployment compensation benefits. State, Dep't of Indus. Relations v. Willard, 379 So. 2d 622 (Ala. Civ. App. 1980).

To qualify for benefits in succeeding year. — Unemployment compensation statute requires that a claimant, to qualify for benefits in a succeeding year, must have performed actual work or services during his initial benefit year. Director of State Dep't of Indus. Relations v. Butler, 367 So. 2d 496 (Ala. Civ. App. 1979).

Disqualification does not mean requirements for requalification met. — Disqualification for a specific period does not mean that the statutory requirements for requalification in a succeeding year have thereby been met. Director of State Dep't of Indus. Relations v. Butler, 367 So. 2d 496 (Ala. Civ. App. 1979).

The receipt of vacation pay in a prior benefit year may not be considered wages for work in insured employment so as to qualify a claimant for benefits in a succeeding year under this section. Director of State Dep't of Indus. Relations v. Butler, 367 So. 2d 496 (Ala. Civ. App. 1979).

As where receiving vacation pay. — A finding that unemployment compensation claimant was disqualified from receiving unemployment compensation benefits under statute because his vacation pay was deemed "wages" did not directly imply that he performed "services" required by requalification statute with respect to succeeding year. Director of Dep't of Indus. Relations v. Butler, 367 So. 2d 496 (Ala. Civ. App. 1979).

Sources of proof of qualification. — The first two requirements of this section for qualification are matters of record within the department of industrial relations. The department knows, or has available to it, knowledge of whether a claimant has filed weekly claims and has registered for work at an unemployment office in accordance with regulations. The third requirement — that of being able and available for work — may require some testimony, though the registration at the unemployment office may be said to furnish considerable proof of that fact. James v. Riddle, 432 So. 2d 563 (Ala. Civ. App. 1983).

In action for unemployment benefits, where record was devoid of any evidence supporting circuit court's finding that "... plaintiff made application for unemployment compensation benefits as prescribed by law, and continued to sign up for benefits, thereby demonstrating her availability for employment during the pendency of her appeals," claimant failed to carry the burden placed upon her by the law to prove she was eligible for benefits. State Dep't of Indus. Relations v. Page, 362 So. 2d 263 (Ala. Civ. App. 1978).

Cited in Ex parte Alabama Textile Prods. Corp., 242 Ala. 609, 7 So. 2d 303 (1942); Broadway v. Bolar, 33 Ala. App. 87, 29 So. 2d 687 (1947); Department of Indus. Relations v. Tomlinson, 251 Ala. 446, 36 So. 2d 496 (1948); Alabama Miils, Inc. v. Brand, 251 Ala. 643, 38 So. 2d 574 (1948); Department of Indus. Relations v. Haynes, 37 Ala. App. 286, 67 So. 2d 59 (1951), rev'd, 259 Ala. 238, 67 So. 2d 62 (1953); Williams v. Boyce, 42 Ala. App. 28, 151 So. 2d 254 (1963); Department of Indus. Relations v. Henry, 42 Ala. App. 573, 172 So. 2d 374 (1964); W.S. Dickey Clay Mfg. Co. v. McCleney, 46 Ala. App. 168, 239 So. 2d 304 (1968); Ventress v. Batey, 333 So. 2d 584 (Ala. Civ. App. 1976); Reichhold Chem., Inc. v. McDaniel, 361 So. 2d 363 (Ala. Civ. App. 1978); Director of State Dep't of Indus. Relations v. Bishop, 373 So. 2d 1119 (Ala. Civ. App. 1979); Davis v. Null, 402 So. 2d 1011 (Ala. Civ. App. 1981); Beatty v. Hart, 437 So. 2d 594 (Ala. Civ. App. 1983); Davis v. Department of Indus. Relations, 465 So. 2d 1140 (Ala. Civ. App. 1984).

Collateral references. — 81 C.J.S., Social Security & Public Welfare, §§ 155-171.

Alien's right to unemployment compensation benefits. 87 ALR3d 694.

Eligibility for unemployment compensation where the claimant insists on or refuses to work under certain conditions, such conditions not being common or customary to the particular employment involved. 88 ALR3d 1353.

Unemployment compensation: eligibility as affected by mental, nervous, or psychological disorder. 1 ALR4th 802.

Eligibility for unemployment compensation as affected by voluntary resignation because of change of location of residence. 21 ALR4th 317.

Eligibility for unemployment compensation of employee who left employment based on belief that involuntary discharge was imminent. 79 ALR4th 528.

Unemployment compensation: eligibility where claimant leaves employment under circumstances interpreted as a firing by the claimant but as a voluntary quit by the employer. 80 ALR4th 7.

Unemployment compensation: eligibility as affected by claimant's refusal to work at particular times or on particular shifts for domestic or family reasons. 2 ALR5th 475.

§ 25-4-78. Disqualifications for benefits.

An individual shall be disqualified for total or partial unemployment:

(1) LABOR DISPUTE IN PLACE OF EMPLOYMENT. — For any week in which his total or partial unemployment is directly due to a labor dispute still in active progress in the establishment in which he is or was last employed. For the purposes of this section only, the term "labor dispute" includes any controversy concerning terms, tenure or conditions of employment, or concerning the association or representation of persons in negotiating, fixing, maintaining, changing or seeking to arrange terms or conditions of employment, regardless of whether the disputants stand in the proximate relation of employer and employee. This definition shall not relate to a dispute between an individual worker and his employer.

(2) VOLUNTARILY QUITTING WORK. — If he has left his most recent bona fide work voluntarily without good cause connected with such work.

a.1. However, he shall not be disqualified if he was forced to leave work because he was sick or disabled, notified his employer of the fact as soon as it was reasonably practicable so to do, and returned to that employer and offered himself for work as soon as he was again able to work; provided, however, this exception shall not apply if the employer had an established leave-of-absence policy covering sickness or disability and:

(i) The individual fails to comply with same as soon as it is reasonably practicable so to do; or

(ii) Upon the expiration of a leave of absence shall fail to return to said employer and offer himself for work, if he shall then be able to work, or if he is not then able to work, he fails to so notify his employer of that fact and request an extension of his said leave of absence as soon as it is reasonably practicable so to do.

2. In case of doubt that an individual was sick or disabled, or as to the duration of any such sickness or disability, the director may, or if the employer requests it, the director shall require a doctor's certificate to establish the fact or facts in doubt.

3. An established leave-of-absence policy shall be any leave-of-absence policy covering sickness and disability communicated to the employee by the customary means used by the employer for communicating with his employees.

4. Nothing herein shall be construed or interpreted as authorizing the payment of benefits to any person during, or for, unemployment due to sickness or disability or during any period in which he is on a leave of absence granted in accordance with an established leave-of-absence policy, the duration of which leave was set in accordance with his request or in accordance with a collective bargaining agreement; except, that if such leave of absence is on account of pregnancy and extends beyond the tenth week following termination of such pregnancy, the individual shall not be denied benefits under the provisions

366

of this subdivision (2) beyond such tenth week if she has given the employer three weeks notice of her desire to return to work, is then able to work and has not refused reinstatement to a job which under the provisions of subdivision (5) of this section would be deemed suitable for her.

b. When an individual is disqualified under this subdivision (2):

1. He shall not be entitled to benefits for the week in which the disqualifying event occurs or for any week thereafter until:

(i) He has reentered insured employment or employment of the nature described in subdivisions (5), (6), (7), (8), (9), (10) or (18) of subsection (b) of Section 25-4-10; and

(ii) For which employment he has earned wages equal to at least 10 times his weekly benefit amount for the benefit year in which such disqualification is assessed; and

(iii) He has been separated from such employment under nondisqualifying conditions.

2. The total amount of benefits to which he may otherwise be entitled as determined in accordance with Sections 25-4-74 and 25-4-75 shall be reduced by an amount equal to not less than six nor more than 12 times his weekly benefit amount.

3. For the purpose of the experience rating provisions of Section 25-4-54, no portion of the benefits payable to him, based upon wages paid to him for the period of employment ending with the separation to which the disqualification applies, shall be charged to the employer's experience rating account. If the individual has been separated from employment other than his most recent bona fide work under conditions which would have been disqualifying under this subdivision (2) had the separation been from his most recent bona fide work and the employer answers a notice of payment within 15 days after it is mailed to him detailing the facts in connection with the separation, then no portion of any benefits paid to him based upon wages for the period of employment ending in such separation shall be charged to the employer's experience rating account.

c. An individual shall not be disqualified if he left his employment and immediately returned to work with his regular employer or to employment in which he had prior existing statutory or contractual seniority or recall rights. When this exception is applied, any benefits paid to such individual based upon wages paid for that period of employment immediately preceding the separation to which the exception is applied, which have not been heretofore charged to the employer's experience rating account, shall not be charged to the account of such employer.

d. For the purposes of this subdivision (2) and subdivision (3) of this section, the director in determining the "most recent bona fide work" shall consider the duration of the most recent job or jobs, the intent of the individual and his employer as to the permanence of such work and whether separation from the immediately preceding employment was under conditions which would be disqualifying in the event such immediately preceding employment should be determined to be the most recent bona fide work.

(3) DISCHARGE FOR MISCONDUCT.

a. If he was discharged or removed from his work for a dishonest or criminal act committed in connection with his work or for sabotage or an act endangering the safety of others. Disqualification under this paragraph may be applied to separations prior to separation from the most recent bona fide work only if the employer has filed a notice with the director alleging that the separation was under conditions described in this paragraph in such manner and within such time as the director may prescribe. When an individual is disqualified under this paragraph:

1. He shall not be entitled to benefits for the week in which the disqualifying event occurs or for any week thereafter until he has reentered insured employment or employment of the nature described in subdivisions (5), (6), (7), (8), (9), (10) or (18) of subsection (b) of Section 25-4-10, has earned wages equal at least to 10 times his weekly benefit amount and has been separated from such employment for a nondisqualifying reason.

2. He shall not thereafter be entitled to any benefits under this chapter on account of wages paid to him for the period of employment by the employer by whom he was employed when the disqualifying event occurred.

3. For the purposes of the experience rating provisions of Section 25-4-54:

(i) No portion of any benefits based upon wages paid to the individual for the period of employment by the employer by whom he was employed when the disqualifying event occurred shall be charged to the employer's experience rating account.

(ii) In the case of a separation prior to the separation from the most recent bona fide work, if the only reason disqualification under this paragraph a was not assessed was the failure of the employer to properly file a timely separation report with the director and the employer files such a report within 15 days after the mailing of a notice of payment, then no portion of any benefits paid based upon the wages paid for the period of employment ending in such prior separation shall be charged to the employer's experience rating account.

b. If he was discharged from his most recent bona fide work for actual or threatened misconduct committed in connection with his work (other than acts mentioned in paragraph a. of this subdivision (3)) repeated after previous warning to the individual. When an individual is disqualified under this paragraph, or exempt from disqualification for a separation under such conditions prior to his most recent bona fide work, the effect shall be the same as provided in paragraph b. of subdivision (2) of this section for disqualification or exemption from disqualification respectively.

c. If he was discharged from his most recent bona fide work for misconduct connected with his work [other than acts mentioned in paragraphs a and b of this subdivision (3)]:

1. He shall be disqualified from receipt of benefits for the week in which he was discharged and for not less than the three nor more than the seven next following weeks, as determined by the director in each case according to the seriousness of the conduct.

2. The total amount of benefits to which he may otherwise be entitled as determined in accordance with Sections 25-4-74 and 25-4-75 shall be reduced by an amount equal to the product of the number of weeks for which he shall be disqualified multiplied by his weekly benefit amount.

3. Only one-half of the benefits paid to him based upon wages for that period of employment immediately preceding the separation to which the disqualification applies shall be charged to the employer for the purposes of the experience rating provisions of Section 25-4-54. If the individual has been separated from employment, other than his most recent bona fide work, under conditions which would have been disqualifying under paragraph c of this subdivision (3), had the separation been from his most recent bona fide work and the employer answers a notice of payment within 15 days after it is mailed to him detailing the facts in connection with the separation, then only one-half of the benefits paid to him for that period of employment immediately preceding the separation shall be charged to the employer for the purposes of the experience rating provisions of Section 25-4-54.

d. If he has been suspended as a disciplinary measure connected with his work, or for misconduct connected with his work, he shall be disqualified from benefits for the week or weeks (not to exceed four weeks) in which, or for which, he is so suspended and the total amount of benefits to which he may otherwise be entitled shall be reduced in the same manner and to the same extent as provided in subparagraph 2 of paragraph c of this subdivision (3).

(4) REVOCATION OR SUSPENSION OF REQUIRED LICENSE, ETC. — For the week in which he has become unemployed because a license, certificate, permit, bond or surety which is necessary for the performance of such employment and which he is responsible to supply has been revoked, suspended or otherwise become lost to him for a cause other than one which would fall within the meaning of subdivision (3) of this section, but one which was within his power to control, guard against or prevent, and for each week thereafter until:

a. Said license, certificate, permit, bond or surety has been restored to him and he has reapplied to his employer for employment; or

b. He has reentered insured employment or employment of the nature described in subdivisions (5), (6), (7), (8), (9), (10) or (18) of subsection (b) of Section 25-4-10, whichever is the earlier.

(5) FAILURE TO ACCEPT AVAILABLE SUITABLE WORK, ETC. — If he fails, without good cause, either to apply for or to accept available suitable work or to return to his customary self-employment when so directed by the director or when he is notified of suitable work or it is offered him through a state employment office or the United States Employment Service, or directly or by written notice or offer to any such employment office or employment service by an employer by whom the individual was formerly employed. Such disqualification shall be for a period of not less than one nor more than 10 weeks from the date of said failure. This disqualification shall not apply unless the individual has an established benefit year, or is seeking to establish one or is seeking extended benefits at the time he fails without good cause, to do any of the acts set out in this subdivision (5).

a. In determining whether or not any work is suitable for an individual, the director shall consider:

1. The degree of risk involved to his health, safety and morals, his physical fitness and prior training,

2. His experience and prior earnings,

3. His length of unemployment,

4. His prospects for securing local work in his customary occupation,

5. The distance of the available work from his residence; provided, that no work or employment shall be deemed unsuitable because of its distance from the individual's residence, if such work or employment is in the same or substantially the same locality as was his last previous regular place of employment and if the employee left such voluntarily without good cause connected with such employment.

b. Notwithstanding any other provisions of this chapter, no work shall be deemed suitable and benefits shall not be denied under this chapter to any otherwise eligible individual for refusing to accept new work under any of the following conditions:

1. If the position offered is vacant due directly to a strike, lockout or other labor dispute;

2. If the wages, hours or other conditions of the work offered are substantially less favorable to the individual than those prevailing for similar work in the locality; or

3. If as a condition of being employed the individual would be required to join a company union, or to resign from or refrain from joining any bona fide labor organization.

c. Notwithstanding any other provisions of this section, benefits shall not be denied an individual, by reason of the application of the provisions of this subdivision (5), with respect to any week in which he is in training with the approval of the director as described in subdivision (a)(3) of Section 25-4-77.

(6) RECEIPT OF DISMISSAL OR SEPARATION ALLOWANCE, BACK PAY AWARD, ETC. — For any week with respect to which he is receiving or has received remuneration in the form of wages in lieu of notice, a dismissal or separation allowance or back pay award. Notwithstanding the provisions of Section 25-4-91 any benefits previously paid for weeks of unemployment with respect to which back pay awards are made shall constitute an overpayment and such amounts shall be deducted from the award by the employer prior to payment to the employee and shall be transmitted promptly to the director by the employer for application against the overpayment and credit to the claimant's maximum benefit amount and prompt deposit into the fund; provided, however, the removal of any charges made against the employer as a result of such previously paid benefits shall be applied to the calendar year and the calendar quarter in which the overpayment is received by the director and no attempt shall be made to relate such a credit to the period to which the award applies. Any amount of overpayment deducted by the employer shall be subject to the same procedures for collection as is provided for contributions by Section 25-4-134 of this chapter.

(7) RECEIPT OF OR APPLICATION FOR UNEMPLOYMENT COMPENSATION FROM ANOTHER STATE, ETC. — For any week with respect to which, or a part of which, he has received or is seeking unemployment benefits under an unemployment compensation law of any other state or of the United States; provided, that if the appropriate agency of such other state or of the United States finally determines that he is not entitled to such unemployment benefits this disqualification shall not apply.

(8) RECEIPT OF PENSION PAYMENT. — For any week with respect to which, or a part of which, an individual has received or has, except for the determination of an exact or specific amount, been determined eligible to receive (during a period for which benefits are being claimed) governmental or other pension, retirement or retired pay, annuity, or similar periodic payment which is based on the previous work of the individual; except, that

a. For weeks of unemployment which begin prior to April 26, 1982, as was prescribed by this subsection prior to such date, and

b. For weeks of unemployment which begin on or after April 26, 1982, the amount of any benefits payable to an individual for any such week which begins in a period with respect to which the disqualifying provisions of this subdivision apply, shall be reduced (but not below zero) by an amount equal to the amount of such pension, retirement or retired pay, annuity or other payment, which is reasonably attributable to such week, provided, however, such reduction required hereby shall apply to any pension, retirement or retired pay, annuity, or other similar payment only if:

1. Such payment is made under a plan maintained (or contributed to) by a base period employer, and

2. In the case of such a payment not made under the Social Security Act or the Railroad Retirement Act of 1974 (or the corresponding

provisions of prior law), services performed for such employer by the individual after the beginning of his base period (or remuneration for such services) affect eligibility for or increase the amount of, such payment.

c. The other provisions of this subdivision to the contrary notwithstanding, the amount of any pension, retirement or retired pay, annuity, or other similar periodic payment under the Social Security Act or the Railroad Retirement Act shall, prior to the deduction of such payment from any benefits due for such week, be reduced by 50 percent.

d. If in accordance with this subdivision (8) any individual is awarded pension payments retroactively covering the same period for which the individual received benefits, the retroactive payments shall constitute cause for disqualification and any benefits paid during such period shall be recovered.

(9) RECEIPT OF OR APPLICATION FOR WORKMEN'S COMPENSATION. — For any week with respect to which, or a part of which, he has received or is seeking compensation for temporary disability under any workmen's compensation law; provided, that if it is finally determined he is not entitled to such compensation, this disqualification shall not apply; and provided further, that if such compensation is less than the benefits which would otherwise be due under this chapter, he shall be entitled to receive for such week, if otherwise eligible, benefits reduced by the amount of such payment.

(10) EMPLOYMENT BY PUBLIC WORKS AGENCY, ETC. — For any week that such individual is engaged or employed by the works progress administration, the national youth administration or any federal or state unit, agency or instrumentality in charge of public works, assistance through public employment or work relief.

(11) SELF-EMPLOYMENT. — For any week in which he is self-employed and each week thereafter until he shall establish that he is no longer self-employed.

(12) RECEIPT OF, OR APPLICATION FOR, TRAINING ALLOWANCE, ETC. — For any week with respect to which, or a part of which, an individual who is enrolled in a course of training with the approval of the director, within the meaning of subdivision (a)(3) of Section 25-4-77, has applied for, or is entitled to receive, any wage or subsistence or training allowance or other form of remuneration, other than reimbursement for travel expenses, for a course of training under any public or private training program; provided, that if it is finally determined that he is not entitled to such remuneration, this disqualification shall not apply. If the remuneration, the receipt of which is disqualifying under this subdivision (12), is less than the weekly benefits which he would otherwise be due under this chapter he shall be entitled to receive, if otherwise eligible, weekly benefits reduced by the amount of such remuneration. It is further provided that receipt of training allowances under the Trade Readjustment Act shall not be cause for disqualification under this subdivision.

(13) PARTICIPATION IN PROFESSIONAL SPORTS. — For any week which commences during the period between two successive sport seasons (or similar periods) to any individual for which benefits claimed are on the basis of any services, substantially all of which consist of participating in sports or athletic events or training or preparing to so participate, if such individual performed such services in the first of such seasons (or similar periods) and there is a reasonable assurance that such individual will perform such services in the later of such seasons (or similar periods).

(14) ALIENS.

a. For any week for which benefits claimed are on the basis of services performed by an alien unless:

1. Such alien is an individual who was lawfully admitted for permanent residence at the time such services were performed, and was lawfully present for purposes of performing such services; or,

2. Such alien was permanently residing in the United States under color of law at the time such services were performed (including an alien who is lawfully present in the United States as a result of the application of the provisions of Section 203(a)(7) or Section 212(d)(5) of the Immigration and Nationality Act); or,

3. Such alien was lawfully admitted for temporary residence as provided for under the provisions of Section 245A(a) of the Immigration Reform and Control Act of 1986 (PL 99-603).

b. Any data or information required of individuals applying for benefits to determine whether benefits are not payable to them because of their alien status shall be uniformly required from all applicants for benefits.

c. In the case of an individual whose application for benefits would otherwise be approved, no determination that benefits to such individual are not payable because of his alien status shall be made except upon a preponderance of the evidence. (Acts 1939, No. 497, p. 721; Code 1940, T. 26, § 214; Acts 1943, No. 310, p. 281, § 8; Acts 1949, No. 526, p. 806; Acts 1951, No. 565, p. 990, § 3; Acts 1955, No. 360, p. 875; Acts 1965, No. 390, p. 548, § 5; Acts 1969, No. 234, p. 559, § 9, 10; Acts 1971, No. 88, p. 349, § 6-11; Acts 1971, No. 672, p. 1399; Acts 1973, No. 1057, p. 1716, § 6; Acts 1975, No. 801, p. 1604, § 9; Acts 1979, No. 79-824, p. 1541, § 2; Acts 1980, No. 80-807, p. 1651, § 3; Acts 1982, No. 82-372, p. 533, § 3; Acts 1983, 2nd Ex. Sess., No. 83-155, p. 264, § 12; Acts 1988, No. 88-265, p. 413; Acts 1989, No. 89-405, p. 822, § 7.)

The 1989 amendment, effective January 1, 1991, in subparagraph (2) b 3 in the first sentence inserted "benefits payable to him, based upon," substituted "shall be charged to the employer's experience rating account" for "shall be determined to be employee's or employer's benefit wages," and in the last sentence substituted "any benefits paid to him based upon wages" for "the wages" and "shall be charged to the employer's experience rating account" for "shall be determined to be employee's or employer's benefit wages"; in paragraph (2)(c) inserted "any benefits paid to such individual based upon," substituted "charged to the employer's experience rating account, shall not be charged to the account of such employer" for "determined to be benefit wages, shall not be determined to be employer's or

373

employee's benefit wages for the purpose of the experience rating provisions of section 25-4-54"; rewrote item (3)2.3.(i) and (ii); in subparagraph (3) c 3 substituted "Only one-half of the benefits paid to him based upon wages for that period of employment" for "Only one half of the wages paid to him for that period of employment," substituted "shall be charged to the employer" for "shall be determined to be employee's or employer's benefit wages," substituted "only one-half of the benefits" for "only one half of the wages," and substituted "shall be charged to the employer" for "shall be determined to be employee's or employer's benefit wages." See the Code commissioner's note below.

Code commissioner's note. — Section 12 of Acts 1989, No. 89-405 provides: "The provisions of Sections 4, 7, and 8 of this act shall become effective immediately upon passage and approval by the Governor or its otherwise

becoming law only for the purpose of implementation of the transitional provisions which will enable the full implementation of all the provisions of these sections for a complete change of system and for rate of contribution determination effective January 1, 1991; otherwise for purposes of such system change and the determination of rates of contribution, the provisions of said sections shall become effective on January 1, 1991."

U.S. Code. — The Immigration Reform and Control Act of 1986 is codified through Titles 7, 8, 18, 20, 29, and 42.

The Immigration and Nationality Act is codified as 8 U.S.C.A. § 1101 et seq. Sections 203 and 212 of the act are codified as 8 U.S.C.A. §§ 1153 and 1182, respectively.

The Social Security Act is codified as 42 U.S.C. § 301 et seq.

The Railroad Retirement Act of 1974 is codified as 45 U.S.C. § 231.

I. General Consideration.
II. Unemployment Due to Labor Dispute.
   A. In General.
   B. Attempt to Cross Picket Line; Apprehension of Violence.
III. Voluntarily Leaving Work.
IV. Discharge for Dishonest or Criminal Act.
V. Failure to Apply for Available Work.
VI. Receiving Pension.
VII. Receiving Separation Allowance.

I. GENERAL CONSIDERATION.

This section is distinct and unequivocal. It clearly states that an individual shall be disqualified from receiving unemployment compensation if that individual is self-employed during the time for which he claims benefits. Miller v. Director, Ala. Dep't of Indus. Relations, 460 So. 2d 1326 (Ala. Civ. App. 1984).

This section should be liberally construed in favor of the claimant and the disqualifications from benefits should be narrowly construed. Department of Indus. Relations v. Jaco, 337 So. 2d 374 (Ala. Civ. App. 1976); Department of Indus. Relations v. Nix, 381 So. 2d 651 (Ala. Civ. App. 1980).

Provisions of disqualification from benefits in the Unemployment Act should be narrowly construed. Flowers v. Director, Dep't of Indus. Relations, 435 So. 2d 76 (Ala. 1983).

Grounds for disqualification designed to encourage worker to remain employed. — This section provides specific grounds for disqualification though an employee may have otherwise been eligible. The disqualifications are designed to encourage or require the worker to remain employed and not become

unemployed voluntarily, without good cause connected with his job. They require him to avoid acts of misconduct, dishonesty and criminality while on the job. Holmes v. Cook, 45 Ala. App. 688, 236 So. 2d 352 (1970).

And they are exceptions and should be narrowly construed. Gulf Atl. Whse. Co. v. Bennett, 36 Ala. App. 33, 51 So. 2d 544 (1951); Department of Indus. Relations v. Stone, 36 Ala. App. 16, 53 So. 2d 859 (1951).

This act is remedial in character, and its beneficent purpose should be liberally construed, and its provisions of disqualification from benefits should be narrowly construed. Holmes v. Cook, 45 Ala. App. 688, 236 So. 2d 352 (1970); Davis v. Sherer, 381 So. 2d 643 (Ala. Civ. App. 1980).

The claimant has the burden of proving he is eligible under § 25-4-77 and not disqualified under this section. Department of Indus. Relations v. Jaco, 337 So. 2d 374 (Ala. Civ. App. 1976); James v. Riddle, 432 So. 2d 563 (Ala. Civ. App. 1983).

The burden of proof is upon claimant to establish his rights to benefits under the unemployment compensation law. An unemployed individual is eligible to receive benefits only if it appears that the required conditions have been met and the burden is upon him to show that those conditions exist. The claimant assumes the risk of nonpersuasion. State, Dep't of Indus. Relations v. Downey, 380 So. 2d 906 (Ala. Civ. App. 1980).

In action for unemployment benefits, where record was devoid of any evidence supporting circuit court's finding that "... plaintiff made application for unemployment compensation benefits as prescribed by law, and continued to sign up for benefits, thereby demonstrating her availability for employment during the pendency of her appeals," claimant failed to carry the burden placed upon her by the law to prove she was eligible for benefits. State, Dep't of Indus. Relations v. Page, 362 So. 2d 263 (Ala. Civ. App. 1978).

The phrase "good cause" as used in this section has been defined as, substantial reason; just ground for such action; adequate excuse that will bear the test of reason; and always the element of good faith. Department of Indus. Relations v. Lynch, 370 So. 2d 1050 (Ala. Civ. App. 1979); Lagrone v. Department of Indus. Relations, 519 So. 2d 1345 (Ala. Civ. App. 1987).

A test of good cause is whether it is reasonable when measured by what the average or normal worker would have done under similar circumstances. Lagrone v. Department of Indus. Relations, 519 So. 2d 1345 (Ala. Civ. App. 1987).

"Misconduct" defined. — Misconduct is conduct evincing a deliberate, willful, or wanton disregard of an employer's interests or of the standards of behavior which he has a right to expect of his employee. Davis v. Department of Indus. Relations, 465 So. 2d 1140 (Ala. Civ. App. 1984).

Continued failure of an employee to perform his job in a manner which previous performance indicates is contrary to his experience and ability may be found to be misconduct. Davis v. Department of Indus. Relations, 465 So. 2d 1140 (Ala. Civ. App. 1984).

Failure to comply with employment practice. — While the failure of an employee to comply with an employment rule or practice is not a failure to comply with the unemployment compensation act, if the rule is reasonable and no excuse is shown for not following it, the failure to comply may be evidence of a willful disregard of the consequences. Hadley v. Director of Dep't of Indus. Relations, 473 So. 2d 519 (Ala. Civ. App. 1985).

Employer has the burden of proving any disqualification under this section. Flowers v. Director, Dep't of Indus. Relations, 435 So. 2d 76 (Ala. 1983).

Sources of proof of qualification under § 25-4-77. — The first two requirements of § 25-4-77 for qualification are matters of record within the department of industrial relations. The department knows, or has available to it, knowledge of whether a claimant has filed weekly claims and has registered for work at an unemployment office in accordance with regulations. The third requirement — that of being able and available for work — may require some testimony, though the registration at the unemployment office may be said to furnish considerable proof of that fact. James v. Riddle, 432 So. 2d 563 (Ala. Civ. App. 1983).

Partial disqualification is a "disqualifying condition". — Nowhere did the legislature limit disqualifying reasons to totally disqualifying reasons; therefore, a partial disqualification from receipt of unemployment compensation benefits is a "disqualifying condition" for purposes of subparagraph (2)(b)(1)(iii) and persons partially disqualified under subdivision (3)(c) have not fulfilled the requirements of subparagraph (2)(b)(1)(iii) so as to requalify for such benefits. Allen v. Hawes, 539 So. 2d 273 (Ala. Civ. App. 1988).

Although the legislature chose to characterize discharge under subsection (3)(c) as a partial disqualification, it is nevertheless a disqualification and, clearly, a disqualifying condition for purposes of subsection (3)(c) cannot be a nondisqualifying condition for purposes of subsection (2)(b). Allen v. Hawes, 539 So. 2d 273 (Ala. Civ. App. 1988).

The legislature did not indicate that the subsequent separation must also have been for one of these three reasons. Instead, it stated the subsequent separation must be for a "nondisqualifying reason" in order for an individual who left a previous job under one of these three conditions to requalify for benefits. Allen v. Hawes, 539 So. 2d 273 (Ala. Civ. App. 1988).

Partial disqualification was not a nondisqualifying condition. — Employee was not entitled to any unemployment compensation benefits since he became disqualified by reason of § 25-4-78(3)(b) (misconduct after prior warning) and he did not meet the conditions necessary to requalify for benefits outlined in § 25-4-78(2)(b) because his partial disqualification under § 25-4-78(3)(c) was not a nondisqualifying condition and having failed to requalify under subsection (2)(b), employee was ineligible to receive any benefits. Allen v. Hawes, 539 So. 2d 273 (Ala. Civ. App. 1988).

Requalification provision applies to all three total disqualification reasons. — The three situations set out in the title — voluntary quit, discharge for dishonest or criminal act, and discharge for misconduct after warning — are all situations in which the employee becomes totally disqualified. However, the title and the act itself clearly state that the requalification provision of subparagraph (2)(b)(1)(iii) applies to separation from a job "subsequent to" a total disqualification for one of the three stated reasons. Allen v. Hawes, 539 So. 2d 273 (Ala. Civ. App. 1988).

Ore tenus rule applies in unemployment compensation cases. Flowers v. Director, Dep't of Indus. Relations, 435 So. 2d 72 (Ala. Civ. App. 1981), rev'd on other grounds, 435 So. 2d 76 (Ala. 1983).

Ore tenus rule has little application where material facts are substantially undisputed, although that rule usually applies in unemployment compensation cases. Flowers v. Director, Dep't of Indus. Relations, 435 So. 2d 76 (Ala. 1983).

Collection of overpayment. — The department can collect from an employee the amount of unemployment compensation benefits he has already received but for which he is subsequently disqualified due to an award of back pay where it is not possible for the employer to deduct the amount of the overpayment from future payments of the back pay award. Heatherly v. Benton, 479 So. 2d 1285 (Ala. Civ. App. 1985), decided prior to enactment of § 25-4-145(c).

Cited in Department of Indus. Relations v. Tomlinson, 251 Ala. 144, 36 So. 2d 496 (1948); Department of Indus. Relations v. Haynes, 259 Ala. 238, 67 So. 2d 62 (1953), rev'g 37 Ala. App. 286, 67 So. 2d 59 (1951); United States Steel Corp. v. Grimes, 267 Ala. 698, 104 So. 2d 330 (1958); United States Steel Corp. v. Curry, 269 Ala. 8, 114 So. 2d 532 (1959); Department of Indus. Relations v. Price, 42 Ala. App. 57, 151 So. 2d 797 (1963); Bagwell Elec. Steel Castings, Inc. v. State Dep't of Indus. Relations, 275 Ala. 677, 158 So. 2d 121 (1963); State Dep't of Indus. Relations v. Thomas, 55 Ala. App. 712, 318 So. 2d 739 (1975); Ventress v. Batey, 333 So. 2d 584 (Ala. Civ. App. 1976); Richardson Homes Corp. v. Shelton, 336 So. 2d 1367 (Ala. Civ. App. 1976); Peak v. State Dep't of Indus. Relations, 340 So. 2d 802 (Ala. 1976); State Dep't of Indus. Relations v. Thompson, 359 So. 2d 1158 (Ala. Civ. App. 1978); Lewis v. Director of State Dep't of Indus. Relations, 373 So. 2d 1147 (Ala. Civ. App. 1979); Davis v. English, 377 So. 2d 144 (Ala. Civ. App. 1979); Steele v. Carter, 390 So. 2d 299 (Ala. Civ. App. 1980); Davis v. Null, 402 So. 2d 1011 (Ala. Civ. App. 1981); Davis v. McBroom, 402 So. 2d 1016 (Ala. Civ. App. 1981); Polk v. State, Dep't of Indus. Relations, 413 So. 2d 1164 (Ala. Civ. App. 1982); Beatty v. Hart, 437 So. 2d 594 (Ala. Civ. App. 1983); Williams v. James, 446 So. 2d 631 (Ala. Civ. App. 1984); Johnson v. State, Dep't of Indus. Relations, 447 So. 2d 747 (Ala. Civ. App. 1983); Watkins v. Montgomery

Days Inn, 455 So. 2d 23 (Ala. Civ. App. 1984); Caradine v. Director, Dep't of Indus. Relations, 456 So. 2d 75 (Ala. Civ. App. 1984); Hale v. Cullman County Bd. of Educ., 465 So. 2d 1143 (Ala. Civ. App. 1984); Dixon v. Economy Co., 477 So. 2d 353 (Ala. 1985); White v. Allen, 594 So. 2d 129 (Ala. Civ. App. 1991).

Collateral references. — 81 C.J.S., Social Security & Public Welfare, §§ 98, 155, 173-208.

76 Am. Jur. 2d, Unemployment Compensation, § 52 et seq.

What amounts to misconduct which precludes benefits under unemployment compensation act. 146 ALR 243.

Power of administrative officer to limit period of disqualification for unemployment benefits. 155 ALR 411.

Circumstances of leaving employment, availability for work, or nature of excuse for refusing re-employment as affecting right to unemployment compensation. 158 ALR 396, 165 ALR 1382.

Unemployment compensation as affected by employee's or employer's removal from place of employment. 13 ALR2d 874, 21 ALR4th 317.

Leaving employment or unavailability for particular job or duties, because of sickness or disability, as affecting right to unemployment compensation. 14 ALR2d 1308.

Political views or conduct: right to compensation as affected by discharge from private employment on ground of. 51 ALR2d 742, 29 ALR4th 287.

Right to unemployment compensation of claimant who refuses nonunion employment. 56 ALR2d 1015.

Harassment or garnishment by employee's creditor as constituting misconduct connected with employment so as to disqualify employee. 86 ALR2d 1013.

Severance payments as affecting right to unemployment compensation. 93 ALR2d 1319.

Failure or delay with respect to filing or reporting requirements as ground for denial of unemployment compensation benefits. 97 ALR2d 752.

Refusal of type of work other than that in which employee was formerly engaged as affecting right to unemployment compensation. 97 ALR2d 1125, 94 ALR3d 63.

Insubordination: employee's insubordination as barring unemployment compensation. 26 ALR3d 1333, 20 ALR4th 637.

Misconduct: work-connected inefficiency or negligence as "misconduct" barring unemployment compensation. 26 ALR3d 1356.

Unemployment compensation: eligibility of employee laid off according to employer's mandatory retirement plan. 50 ALR3d 880.

Termination of employment because of pregnancy as affecting right to unemployment compensation. 51 ALR3d 254.

Right to unemployment compensation as affected by receipt of pension. 56 ALR3d 520.

Right to unemployment compensation as affected by receipt of social security benefits. 56 ALR3d 552.

Discharge for absenteeism or tardiness as affecting right to unemployment compensation. 58 ALR3d 674.

Construction of phrase "establishment" or "factory, establishment, or other premises" within unemployment compensation statute rendering employee ineligible during labor dispute or strike at such location. 60 ALR3d 11.

Construction of phrase "stoppage of work" in statutory provision denying unemployment compensation benefits during stoppage resulting from labor dispute. 61 ALR3d 693.

Unemployment compensation: eligibility of participants in sympathy strike or slowdown. 61 ALR3d 746.

Unemployment compensation: labor dispute disqualification as applicable to striking employee who is laid off subsequent employment during strike period. 61 ALR3d 766.

What constitutes participation or direct interest in, or financing of, labor dispute or strike within disqualification provisions of unemployment compensation acts. 62 ALR3d 314.

Refusal of nonstriking employee to cross picket line as justifying denial of unemployment compensation benefits. 62 ALR3d 380.

Unemployment compensation: application of labor dispute disqualification for benefits to locked-out employee. 62 ALR3d 437.

Comment note. General principles pertaining to statutory disqualification for unemployment compensation benefits because of strike or labor dispute. 63 ALR3d 88.

Unemployment compensation: harassment or other mistreatment by employer or supervisor as "good cause" justifying abandonment of employment. 76 ALR3d 1089.

Denial of unemployment compensation as affected by refusal to comply with dress, grooming or hygiene requirements of an employer or prospective employer. 88 ALR3d 150.

Entitlement to unemployment compensation benefits for an employee voluntarily retired. 88 ALR3d 274.

Eligibility for unemployment compensation where the claimant insists on or refuses to work under certain conditions, such conditions not being common or customary to the particular employment involved. 88 ALR3d 1353.

Unemployment compensation: eligibility as affected by claimant's refusal to work at reduced compensation. 95 ALR3d 449.

Unemployment compensation: eligibility as affected by mental, nervous, or psychological disorder. 1 ALR4th 802.

Right to unemployment compensation as affected by claimant's receipt of holiday pay. 3 ALR4th 557.

Leaving or refusing employment for religious reasons as barring unemployment compensation. 12 ALR4th 611.

Leaving or refusing employment because of allergic reaction as affecting right to unemployment compensation. 12 ALR4th 629.

Right to unemployment compensation of one who quit job because not given enough work to keep busy. 15 ALR4th 256.

Unemployment compensation: termination of employment, known to be for a specific, limited duration, upon expiration of period, as voluntary. 30 ALR4th 1201.

Conduct or activities of employees during off-duty hours as misconduct barring unemployment compensation. 35 ALR4th 691.

Unemployment compensation: harassment or other mistreatment by co-worker as "good cause" justifying abandonment of employment. 40 ALR4th 304.

Alcoholism or intoxication as ground for discharge justifying denial of unemployment compensation. 64 ALR4th 1151.

Unemployment compensation: burden of proof as to voluntariness of separation. 73 ALR4th 1093.

Employee's use of drugs or narcotics, or related problems, as affecting eligibility for unemployment compensation. 78 ALR4th 180.

Eligibility for unemployment compensation of employee who left employment based on belief that involuntary discharge was imminent. 79 ALR4th 528.

Unemployment compensation: eligibility where claimant leaves employment under circumstances interpreted as a firing by the claimant but as a voluntary quit by the employer. 80 ALR4th 7.

II. UNEMPLOYMENT DUE TO LABOR DISPUTE.

A. In General.

Legislative intent. — The legislative intent behind subdivision (1) of this section was to remove from the coverage of the unemployment compensation law those persons who are unemployed due to active participation in a labor dispute as that term is used in the National Labor Relations Act. Peak v. State Dep't of Indus. Relations, 340 So. 2d 796 (Ala.), writ quashed, 340 So. 2d 802 (Ala. 1976), cert. denied, 430 U.S. 984, 97 S. Ct. 1681, 52 L. Ed. 2d 379 (1977).

Definition of a "labor dispute" in subdivision (1) is in the same language as it appears in the Norris-La Guardia Act of Congress, 29 U.S.C.A. § 113(c) except that the word "tenure," found in this section, is not in the act of Congress, but it is in the exact verbiage of the definition in the National Labor Relations Act, 29 U.S.C.A. § 152(9); therefore, the federal court authorities which have construed this term will aid the court of appeals in the interpretation of this section. Department of Indus. Relations v. Stone, 36 Ala. App. 16, 53 So. 2d 859 (1951).

For cases dealing with the meaning of the term "labor dispute," but which were decided under General Acts of 1935, p. 950, etc., a predecessor of this chapter, which did not give a definition of the term "labor dispute" as now contained in subsection (1), see Department of Indus. Relations v. Pesnell, 29 Ala. App. 528, 199 So. 720, cert. denied, 240 Ala. 457, 199 So. 726 (1940); Department of Indus. Relations v. Drummond, 30 Ala. App. 78, 1 So. 2d 395, cert. denied, 241 Ala. 142, 1 So. 2d 402 (1941).

Elements of proof. — For a claimant to be disqualified under this section, five separate and distinct conditions must coincide, namely, (1) his unemployment must be directly due, (2) to a labor dispute, (3) in active progress, (4) in the establishment, (5) in which he was last employed. Flowers v. Director, Dep't of Indus. Relations, 435 So. 2d 72 (Ala. Civ. App. 1981), rev'd on other grounds, 435 So. 2d 76 (Ala. 1983).

Issue is whether dispute proximately caused unemployment. — The relevant question when considering disqualification under this section is whether the proximate cause of unemployment is the labor dispute. Flowers v. Director, Dep't of Indus. Relations, 435 So. 2d 76 (Ala. 1983).

Labor dispute must be bona fide. — A "labor dispute," to come within the meaning and interpretation of this section, must be a "bona fide," as opposed to "mala fide," difference in opinion among the disputants. In other words, good faith and fair dealing must be taken into account. Department of Indus. Relations v. Stone, 36 Ala. App. 16, 53 So. 2d 859 (1951).

And a "labor dispute" is not "bona fide" if the employer makes demands and attempts to enforce conditions that are practically impossible of fulfillment, or if undertaken will result in scarcely any remuneration for the employee. Department of Indus. Relations v. Stone, 36 Ala. App. 16, 53 So. 2d 859 (1951).

Hence, employees' refusal to accede to an unwarranted demand of the employer does not constitute a "labor dispute," within the meaning of this section. Department of Indus. Relations v. Stone, 36 Ala. App. 16, 53 So. 2d 859 (1951).

But not necessary to show strike or lockout resulted. — To establish a "labor dispute" precluding recovery of unemployment benefits, it is not necessary to show that a strike or lockout resulted. Department of Indus. Relations v. Savage, 38 Ala. App. 277, 82 So. 2d 435 (1955); Department of Indus. Relations v. Walker, 40 Ala. App. 1, 109 So. 2d 131 (1956), aff'd, 268 Ala. 507, 109 So. 2d 135 (1959); Department of Indus. Relations v. Headon, 42 Ala. App. 132, 155 So. 2d 123 (1962); Flowers v. Director, Dep't of Indus. Relations, 435 So. 2d 72 (Ala. Civ. App. 1981), rev'd on other grounds, 435 So. 2d 76 (Ala. 1983).

Unemployment must be "directly due" to labor dispute. — To disqualify an employee for receiving unemployment benefits on account of a strike, his unemployment must be "directly due" to a labor dispute still in active progress in the establishment in which he is or was last employed. Speagle v. United States Steel Corp., 268 Ala. 3, 105 So. 2d 717 (1958).

Where layoffs were made while negotiations were ongoing and before the strike, unemployment was not directly due to a labor dispute and the claimants were not disqualified from receiving unemployment benefits. Department of Indus. Relations v. Pickett, 448 So. 2d 364 (Ala. Civ. App. 1983).

Which is determined by appraisal of facts. — The answer to the question of whether the unemployment involved was due directly to a labor dispute which was in existence must be arrived at by an appraisal of the facts in the particular case. Department of Indus. Relations v. Headon, 42 Ala. App. 132, 155 So. 2d 123 (1962).

Strike attended with violence does not cease to be strike. — It would be specious to argue that, when a controversy resulting in a strike is attended with violence or lawlessness, it ceases to be a strike, and that the controversy or dispute, eo instante, loses its identity as such. It is nonetheless a dispute, a strike, even though acts of violence, etc., attend it. Ex parte McCleney, 286 Ala. 288, 239 So. 2d 311 (1970).

Burden of showing disqualification. — Under subdivision (1) the burden falls on either the director of industrial relations, as trustee, or the employer with an adverse interest, to show that an eligible claimant is disqualified. United States Steel Corp. v. Glasgow, 40 Ala. App. 424, 114 So. 2d 565 (1958), rev'd on other grounds sub nom. United States Steel Corp. v. Curry, 269 Ala. 8, 114 So. 2d 532 (1959).

Claimant entitled to compensation if unemployed after dispute ends. — The fundamental theory of unemployment compensation in connection with subsection (1) of the statute is that workers are not entitled to compensation where their unemployment was directly due to a "labor dispute" still in active progress in the establishment where last employed, but that when the strike shall have been ended if his unemployment so resulted he would be entitled to unemployment compensation if thereafter, without his fault, he should be rendered unemployed. Department of Indus. Relations v. Nix, 381 So. 2d 651 (Ala. Civ. App. 1980).

Federally protected rights not interfered with by subdivision. — Disqualification from unemployment compensation on the ground of a labor dispute does not interfere in any manner with federally protected rights to self-organization and to protection from certain unfair labor practices so as to confer preemptive jurisdiction on the National Labor Relations Board. Peak v. State Dep't of Indus. Relations, 340 So. 2d 796 (Ala.), writ quashed, 340 So. 2d 802 (Ala. 1976), cert. denied, 430 U.S. 984, 97 S. Ct. 1681, 52 L. Ed. 2d 379 (1977).

Decision of National Labor Relations Board not res judicata as to finding of department of industrial relations. — A decision by the National Labor Relations Board that an employer had committed various unfair labor practices was not res judicata so as to bar a finding by the state department of industrial relations that certain employees were disqualified from receiving benefits for unemployment caused by a labor dispute. Peak v. State Dep't of Indus. Relations, 340 So. 2d 796 (Ala.), writ quashed, 340 So. 2d 802 (Ala. 1976), cert. denied, 430 U.S. 984, 97 S. Ct. 1681, 52 L. Ed. 2d 379 (1977).

Establishment in which labor dispute is in progress. — An employer operated coal mines, ore mines, steel mills and railroads. Each unit had separate management but the ultimate control was in the office of the president. There was a strike in the steel mill and ore mines and because of this the coal mine was shut down. An employee of the coal mines sought compensation under this section. The coal mine was considered an establishment separate from the establishments in which the labor dispute was in progress. Tennessee Coal, Iron & R.R. v. Martin, 33 Ala. App. 502, 36 So. 2d 535, aff'd, 251 Ala. 153, 36 So. 2d 547 (1948).

An ore-conditioning plant connected with ore mines by a railroad system over which ore was hauled in special cars from the mines to the plant was part of the same "establishment" as the mines within the meaning of subdivision (1) of this section. United States Steel Corp. v. Wood, 40 Ala. App. 431, 114 So. 2d 533 (1958), rev'd on other grounds, 269 Ala. 5, 114 So. 2d 551 (1959).

Strike by local belonging to same parent union as claimant's local. — A member of a local union, not itself on strike, is not entitled to unemployment compensation when his unemployment is due to a strike in the establishment where he was employed, engaged in by another local union, when both locals belong to the same national or international union. United States Steel Corp. v. Wood, 269 Ala. 5, 114 So. 2d 551 (1959), rev'g 40 Ala. App. 431, 114 So. 2d 533 (1958).

Not disqualified if in no way involved in labor dispute. — The legislature never intended that one, who has purchased his protection against involuntary unemployment, should be denied those benefits because of a "labor dispute" in which he was in no way involved and the causes of which unemployment he, his agents or organization were powerless to avert. State Dep't of Indus. Relations v. Ford, 42 Ala. App. 681, 178 So. 2d 185 (1965); Ex parte McCleney, 286 Ala. 288, 239 So. 2d 311 (1970).

Where claimant's partial unemployment followed as a direct result of the strike called by his union, and claimant was "involved" in that strike or labor dispute, and his union was not powerless to avert his unemployment, claimant was disqualified from receiving unemployment compensation benefits under subdivision (1) of this section. State Dep't of Indus. Relations v. Ford, 42 Ala. App. 681, 178 So. 2d 185 (1965).

That individuals saw fit to get permits from the union during the strike period showed that they recognized the existence of the strike. There was no reason for distinguishing them from the other members of the striking union, and they should have been disqualified. Even though the management was compelled to discharge these men, still that act on the part of the employer was due to the fact that the strike reduced the work which could have been given to them, and their unemployment was due to the labor dispute which they, as members of the union, supported. State Dep't of Indus. Relations v. Ford, 278 Ala. 352, 178 So. 2d 190 (1965).

Strike by union of which claimant was not member. — Where claimant's job was abolished due to a strike by union of which claimant was not a member and neither the claimant nor his union was involved in a dispute with the employer, claimant was not disqualified from receiving benefits on ground his unemployment was "directly due to a labor dispute." Usher v. Department of Indus. Relations, 261 Ala. 509, 75 So. 2d 165 (1954), rev'g 37 Ala. App. 698, 75 So. 2d 159 (1952).

For case in which the supreme court declined to reconsider and overrule its holding in Usher v. Department of Indus. Relations, 261 Ala. 509, 75 So. 2d 165 (1954), see United States Steel Corp. v. Goodwin, 267 Ala. 612, 104 So. 2d 333 (1958).

The rule that a man out of work because of a strike is not qualified if he works in the same establishment and belongs to the same parent union (though in another local) as do the men on strike does not apply except as to fellow unionists. And where the record before the court of appeals did not show that claimant belonged to a union, the rule would not be applied. United States Steel Corp. v. Baxley, 40 Ala. App. 428, 114 So. 2d 553 (1958), rev'd on other grounds, 269 Ala. 7, 114 So. 2d 554 (1959).

Cessation of work due to apprehension of strike. — Cessation of work was not due to overproduction, but underproduction which was due to a company's apprehension of a strike or work stoppage and on this account its customers ceased active business relations with the company's warehouse. The unemployment was directly due to a misapprehension of the customers and not a labor dispute between the claimants and the company. Gulf Atl. Whse. Co. v. Bennett, 36 Ala. App. 33, 51 So. 2d 544 (1951).

Employer's ceasing operations terminates claimant's disqualification due to dispute. — A labor dispute is no longer in active progress when an employer terminates the business. An employer's decision to cease operations altogether, or at least with respect to that portion of the business affected by a claimant's strike, would operate to terminate the claimant's disqualification under the labor dispute section of the unemployment compensation statute. Department of Indus. Relations v. Nix, 381 So. 2d 651 (Ala. Civ. App. 1980).

Unemployment not due to dispute where apprehension of work delay causes work shortage. — Where the direct cause of shipyard layoffs, prior to union's vote to strike, was shortage of work caused by apprehensions on the part of both the employer and its customers as to delays in performance or work which might result should the strike occur, the unemployment of employees who were laid off while negotiations were active and in progress was not directly due to a labor dispute, but to work shortage. Flowers v. Director, Dep't of Indus. Relations, 435 So. 2d 76 (Ala. 1983).

Proper measures taken by employer for protection of property in anticipation of strike. — Where employer, in anticipation of a strike, took proper measures for the protection of its property from damage during the pendency of the strike, it was not liable for unemployment benefits even though some employees were unemployed when annealing oven was thus shut down prior to strike. Department of Indus. Relations v. Walker, 40 Ala. App. 1, 109 So. 2d 131 (1956), aff'd, 268 Ala. 507, 109 So. 2d 135 (1959).

Employees notified of layoff where contract negotiations ongoing. — The legislature did not intend that this section should act to disqualify employees given layoff notices from receipt of unemployment benefits where contract negotiations are ongoing. Flowers v. Director, Dep't of Indus. Relations, 435 So. 2d 76 (Ala. 1983).

Claimant not disqualified if unemployment is result of collective bargain. — A claimant is not disqualified for benefits where unemployment is not voluntary and self-imposed but is a result of a collective bargain which operates as a waiver of, and excludes him from benefits to which he is otherwise entitled. Director, Dep't of Indus. Relations v. Alabama By-Products, Inc., 374 So. 2d 344 (Ala. Civ. App.), cert. denied, 374 So. 2d 347 (Ala. 1979).

Layoffs caused by customers' fear of impending strike. — Where a wage reopening occurred which rendered inoperative a no-strike clause in the current labor contract and the union members had voted to empower the union leaders to call a strike when it was thought necessary, and where customers began removing their ships from the employer's shipyard because of fears that negotiations might break off, which removals caused disruption of the work schedules and temporary layoffs, the ensuing unemployment was "directly due to a labor dispute" so as to disqualify workers for unemployment benefits under this section. Department of Indus. Relations v. Headon, 42 Ala. App. 132, 155 So. 2d 123 (1962), distinguishing Gulf Atl. Whse. Co. v. Bennett, 36 Ala. App. 33, 51 So. 2d 544 (1951).

Availability of work notwithstanding strike. — There was substantial evidence to support the finding of the trial court that work was available, notwithstanding that employer's locomotive engineers were on strike, and that employees were disqualified from receiving benefits. Phelps v. United States Steel Corp., 39 Ala. App. 541, 105 So. 2d 714 (1958); Widmar v. United States Steel Corp., 39 Ala. App. 547, 105 So. 2d 716 (1958).

Presumption of continuance of unemployment status until end of strike. — See Speagle v. United States Steel Corp., 39 Ala. App. 559, 105 So. 2d 721 (1958).

Unemployment directly due to labor dispute. — Where strike was called by union representing minority group of employees in protest against closed shop contract procured by rival union designated as bargaining agent for all employees, and picket lines prevented members of controlling union from working, such unemployment of a union member that voted for closed shop agreement was due to a "labor dispute" within this section. Badgett v. Department of Indus. Relations, 30 Ala. App. 457, 10 So. 2d 872, cert. denied, 243 Ala. 538, 10 So. 2d 880 (1942).

A strike in a steel mill and ore mine caused a coal mine operated by the same corporation to be shut down. Employees of the coal mine sought compensation under this section. The employees' unemployment was held directly due to a labor dispute. Tennessee Coal, Iron & R.R. v. Martin, 33 Ala. App. 502, 36 So. 2d 535, aff'd on other grounds, supreme court refusing to pass on this point, 251 Ala. 153, 36 So. 2d 547 (1948).

Employer who bargains with employees concerning matters which under terms of bargaining agreement could not be opened for discussion at that time waives the restriction, and dispute arising from negotiations is a bona fide labor dispute. T.R. Miller Mill Co. v. Johns, 261 Ala. 615, 75 So. 2d 675 (1954). See T.R. Miller Mill Co. v. Johns, 37 Ala. App. 477, 75 So. 2d 670 (1954).

Officials of a company engaged in the manufacture of ceramic tile and brick were advised by the president of the local union that unless a new contract was signed by March 1 the men would cease work in the plant and neither kiln firemen nor foremen would stay on to "burn off" kilns that had not completed the burning cycle. The company arranged to have all kilns burned off by March 1, and beginning February 23 laid off workers in the various departments as soon as the particular jobs on which they were employed were closed down. It was held that workers so laid off before March 1 were unemployed due to a labor dispute as that term is used in subdivision (1). Department of Indus. Relations v. Savage, 38 Ala. App. 277, 82 So. 2d 435 (1955).

Evidence clearly established existence of labor dispute concerning terms, tenure or conditions of employment and that unemployment was directly due to such labor dispute, as the term is used in this section, and not to lack of work. Department of Indus. Relations v. Walker, 40 Ala. App. 1, 109 So. 2d 131 (1956), aff'd, 268 Ala. 507, 109 So. 2d 135 (1959).

Where the closing down of a company's plant was the direct result of a labor dispute then in progress between petitioners' union and the company, to hold that unemployment was "directly due" to the closing of the plant and not "directly due" to the labor dispute would be contrary to the clear purpose of this section to deny compensation when the unemployment is the direct result of a labor dispute. Department of Indus. Relations v. Walker, 268 Ala. 507, 109 So. 2d 135 (1959).

Employees who are discharged due to their attempted formation of a union are unemployed due to a "labor dispute" within the meaning of this section. Peak v. State Dep't of Indus. Relations, 340 So. 2d 796 (Ala.), writ quashed, 340 So. 2d 802 (Ala. 1976), cert. denied, 430 U.S. 984, 97 S. Ct. 1681, 52 L. Ed. 2d 379 (1977).

B. Attempt to Cross Picket Line; Apprehension of Violence.

Burden of proof is on claimant. — To qualify for unemployment compensation, the burden of proof is on the claimant to show (1) that he was willing to cross a peaceful picket line; (2) that he made a reasonable attempt to cross the picket line in question; (3) that claimant's sole reason for failing to cross the picket line was a well-founded and reasonable apprehension of violence to his person. The word "sole" is contrasted with refusing to cross a picket line because of union beliefs, sympathy with other strikers, pangs of conscience or adherence to union principles. Ex parte McCleney, 286 Ala. 288, 239 So. 2d 311 (1970); Pullman Std. v. Gamble, 377 So. 2d 1086 (Ala. Civ. App.), cert. denied, 377 So. 2d 1089 (Ala. 1979).

Only reasonable attempt to cross picket line or evidence that such an attempt would produce violence or be futile is required. Pullman Std. v. Gamble, 377 So. 2d 1086 (Ala. Civ. App.), cert. denied, 377 So. 2d 1089 (Ala. 1979).

The "reasonable attempt" to cross a picket line criterion does not contemplate that nonstriking employee must risk physical harm. There are conceivable situations in which such a violent atmosphere prevails at a strike site that no actual attempt to cross the picket line would be required. Clary v. Central Foundry Co., 333 So. 2d 824 (Ala. 1976).

The "reasonable attempt" to cross a picket line criterion could be met in certain situations by a claimant who never approached the picket line at all. For example, if several people attempting to cross had met with violence and a claimant knew of this violence, the law would not require him to do a futile act by attempting to cross the picket line. Clary v. Central Foundry Co., 333 So. 2d 824 (Ala. 1976).

Refusal to cross picket line disqualifies employee. — A voluntary refusal by an employee to cross a peaceful picket line set up in a labor dispute by some union of which claimant is not a member, to work on a job still open to him by his employer, disqualifies an employee, while so doing, for unemployment benefits under subdivision (1). Speagle v. United States Steel Corp., 268 Ala. 3, 105 So. 2d 717 (1958). See Speagle v. United States Steel Corp., 39 Ala. App. 559, 105 So. 2d 721 (1958).

A voluntary refusal by an employee to cross a peaceful picket line set up by a union of which claimant was not a member would disqualify him under subdivision (1), where his job remained open to him by his employer. Ex parte McCleney, 286 Ala. 288, 239 So. 2d 311 (1970).

Evidence that claimants refused to cross a picket line to continue work, although both crossed it to vote in their own union's election, was a voluntary refusal to cross the picket line and disqualified them for benefits. Ex parte McCleney, 286 Ala. 288, 239 So. 2d 311 (1970).

Because voluntary refusal to cross a peaceful picket line constitutes participation in a strike. Ex parte McCleney, 286 Ala. 288, 239 So. 2d 311 (1970).

But had the trial court determined that an employee had a well-founded fear of personal violence, then his refusal to cross a picket line would not have entailed his disqualification to draw unemployment compensation. Pledger v. Department of Indus. Relations, 40 Ala. App. 127, 108 So. 2d 697 (1959), holding that the evidence sustained the finding of the trial court that claimant had not such a fear and that claimant was disqualified.

Refusal to cross a picket line does not disqualify an employee from benefits when such refusal to do so results from a well-founded fear of personal violence, where his job continues to be open to him by his employer. Ex parte McCleney, 286 Ala. 288, 239 So. 2d 311 (1970).

The legislature never intended that an employee be denied unemployment benefits if his unemployment was involuntary because he was prevented by personal violence or a well-grounded fear of same from entering the premises of his employing establishment. Ex parte McCleney, 286 Ala. 288, 239 So. 2d 311 (1970).

Fear of violence exception to labor dispute disqualification. — Subdivision (1) does not disqualify an employee for benefits by reason of a labor dispute unless he is directly involved in the dispute. Such unemployment would not be directly due to a labor dispute if the employer closed the shop, in which he was engaged, on account of the fear that violence would result, even though such closing was directly due to the peaceful picketing which in turn was directly due to a labor dispute in which the claimant was not involved. Speagle v. United States Steel Corp., 268 Ala. 3, 105 So. 2d 717 (1958).

To the labor dispute disqualification provided by this section, the supreme court of Alabama by construction has established an exception. That exception is founded upon the proposition that an employee who does not participate in the strike and does not cross a picket line because he has a reasonable fear of violence is not unemployed voluntarily. Clary v. Central Foundry Co., 333 So. 2d 821 (Ala. Civ. App. 1975), modified, 333 So. 2d 824 (Ala. 1976).

It was not intended that one be denied compensation because of a labor dispute in which he was not involved, and if he showed that but for a reasonable fear of personal violence he would cross the picket line and work. Such exception to the strict construction of the statute has come to be termed the "violence exception." Pullman Std. v. Gamble, 377 So. 2d 1086 (Ala. Civ. App.), cert. denied, 377 So. 2d 1089 (Ala. 1979).

"Violence" exception to statute is a judicial interpretation which provides that if a claimant for unemployment compensation can show a well-grounded fear of personal violence, his refusal to cross a picket line would not require his disqualification for benefits. Reichhold Chem., Inc. v. McDaniel, 361 So. 2d 363 (Ala. Civ. App. 1978).

The "violence exception" to subdivision (1) of this section is a judicial interpretation which provides that if a claimant for unemployment compensation can show a well-founded fear of personal violence, his refusal to cross a picket line would not entail his disqualification. Ex parte McCleney, 286 Ala. 288, 239 So. 2d 311 (1970).

And is reasonable. — The "violence exception" to the rule concerning refusal to cross a picket line is reasonable. Ex parte McCleney, 286 Ala. 288, 239 So. 2d 311 (1970).

But fear of violence must be real and not nebulous. Just because claimants say they are afraid of the pickets is not enough and the mere presence of the pickets is not enough to excuse the claimants from crossing picket lines. Ex parte McCleney, 286 Ala. 288, 239 So. 2d 311 (1970).

In order to justify refusal to cross picket line under "violence" exceptions so as not to be disqualified for unemployment compensation, the fear of violence must be real and not nebulous, and, claimants must have made a reasonable attempt to cross the picket line. The "reasonable attempt" criterion may be met by a claimant who never approached the picket line at all if several people attempting to cross had met with violence and a claimant knew of this violence. Reichhold Chem., Inc. v. McDaniel, 361 So. 2d 363 (Ala. Civ. App. 1978).

The three requirements of proof with respect to violence exception are to be applied in the conjunctive. Pullman Std. v. Gamble, 377 So. 2d 1086 (Ala. Civ. App.), cert. denied, 377 So. 2d 1089 (Ala. 1979).

Violence exception to this section is to be "narrowly restricted." Clary v. Central Foundry Co., 333 So. 2d 821 (Ala. Civ. App. 1975), modified, 333 So. 2d 824 (Ala. 1976).

Violence exception necessarily requires an individual determination of a reasonable attempt to cross the picket line. Clary v. Central Foundry Co., 333 So. 2d 824 (Ala. 1976).

The situation existing at a strike site will dictate the standards of reasonableness to be applied to criterion of attempted crossing, and each claimant's individual attempt to cross should be examined within the context of that situation. Clary v. Central Foundry Co., 333 So. 2d 824 (Ala. 1976).

Knowledge of overriding atmosphere of violence is sufficient. — If the knowledge of the existence of an overriding atmosphere of violence arising from the labor dispute is the sole reason for the failure of the nonparticipating claimant to cross the picket line and work, he is entitled to benefit of the "violence exception" and payment of compensation. Pullman Std. v. Gamble, 377 So. 2d 1086 (Ala. Civ. App.), cert. denied, 377 So. 2d 1089 (Ala. 1979).

A claimant must show that he was willing to cross a peaceful picket line and that he made a reasonable attempt to do so. However, if there is an overriding atmosphere of violence at the strike site which would reasonably indicate a risk of physical harm to an employee attempting to enter the premises, such an attempt is unnecessary. Pullman Std. v. Gamble, 377 So. 2d 1086 (Ala. Civ. App.), cert. denied, 377 So. 2d 1089 (Ala. 1979).

A claimant need not risk violence to himself to come within the violence exception. Clary v. Central Foundry Co., 333 So. 2d 824 (Ala. 1976).

Professed intention not to cross picket line removes violence exception. — Where claimants clearly professed that they did not cross the picket line because of union membership or because of an ingrained prejudice against doing so, they are then disqualified from further opportunity to come under the "violence exception," for they could not meet the sole reason condition. Pullman Std. v. Gamble, 377 So. 2d 1086 (Ala. Civ. App.), cert. denied, 377 So. 2d 1089 (Ala. 1979).

Presumption picket line maintained in orderly manner. — In the absence of proof to the contrary, there is a presumption that a picket line is maintained and conducted in an orderly manner and with no intention to violate the law. Ex parte McCleney, 286 Ala. 288, 239 So. 2d 311 (1970).

The burden of proof is upon the claimant — to bring himself within the exception for violence. Clary v. Central Foundry Co., 333 So. 2d 821 (Ala. Civ. App. 1975), modified, 333 So. 2d 824 (Ala. 1976).

To escape the statutory disqualification, the burden rests upon the claimants to establish that their failure to pursue employment and to cross a picket line was essentially attributable to a real and genuine fear to do so rather than to a desire to abide by the traditional principles and policies of union solidarity. Ex parte McCleney, 286 Ala. 288, 239 So. 2d 311 (1970).

Claimants failed to meet the burden of proof to establish the violence exception to the provisions of this section. — See Clary v. Central Foundry Co., 333 So. 2d 821 (Ala. Civ. App. 1975), modified, 333 So. 2d 824 (Ala. 1976).

Employee's statement of his apprehension of violence to his person if he were to cross a picket line would not be legal evidence. Speagle v. United States Steel Corp., 268 Ala. 3, 105 So. 2d 717 (1958). See Speagle v. United States Steel Corp., 39 Ala. App. 559, 105 So. 2d 721 (1958); Evergreen Textiles, Inc. v. State Dep't of Indus. Relations, 42 Ala. App. 364, 165 So. 2d 716 (1964).

And fact that violence erupted after the claimants had refused to cross a picket line cannot bolster their claim for benefits. Ex parte McCleney, 286 Ala. 288, 239 So. 2d 311 (1970).

The mere fact that, during the pendency of an action for benefits and while the strike was in progress, there was lawlessness, "defiance of law" –– or by whatever term the acts which prevented free ingress and egress of claimant and others to and from the mill, because of a refusal to cross a picket line may be characterized — does not militate against the conclusion that the strike — the labor dispute — was the primary and direct cause of the claimant's inability to work at the mill. Ex parte McCleney, 286 Ala. 288, 239 So. 2d 311 (1970).

Evidence of violence which occurred prior to the issuance of an injunction against violence in a strike is not sufficient to support a claim of fear of violence as the basis for not crossing a picket line after the issuance of the injunction. Ex parte McCleney, 286 Ala. 288, 239 So. 2d 311 (1970).

Legal evidence of the presence or absence of violence after the issuance of an injunction against violence in a strike is admissible in determining whether an employee was justified in refusing to cross a picket line. Ex parte McCleney, 286 Ala. 288, 239 So. 2d 311 (1970).

Even after issuance of injunction. — After the issuance of an injunction against further violence in a strike, the burden is still on the claimant to show that he was willing to cross the picket line, that he attempted to or that the sole reason for his failure to return to work was because of a real and genuine fear of personal violence. Ex parte McCleney, 286 Ala. 288, 239 So. 2d 311 (1970).

III. VOLUNTARILY LEAVING WORK.

Unemployment compensation act was intended to insure a diligent worker against the vicissitudes of enforced unemployment not voluntarily created by the worker. West Point Mfg. Co. v. Keith, 35 Ala. App. 414, 47 So. 2d 594 (1950).

The Unemployment Compensation Law was enacted to relieve the consequences and vicissitudes of unavoidable and enforced unemployment which was not brought about by the voluntary creation of the worker. Landrum v. James, 425 So. 2d 1363 (Ala. Civ. App. 1982), cert. denied, 425 So. 2d 1364 (Ala. 1983).

Thus, voluntary abandonment of employment disqualifies employee. — A claimant for unemployment compensation benefits is disqualified from benefits for the week in which she has left her work voluntarily without good cause connected with such work. Ex parte Alabama Textile Prods. Corp., 242 Ala. 609, 7 So. 2d 303 (1942).

A reason for voluntary termination, no matter how well justified, will not satisfy subdivision (2) of this section if it is personal and in no way connected with the employment. Davis v. Hoggle, 392 So. 2d 1190 (Ala. Civ. App. 1980), cert. denied, 392 So. 2d 1194 (Ala. 1981).

Although incarceration in jail has never been construed by an Alabama appellate court to constitute voluntary departure from work, it has been held that unemployment compensation benefits are available only to those employees who leave their employment through no fault of their own. However, where such absence from work is brought about solely through a voluntary act, a person may avoid jail and also the loss of his job by not violating the law, loss of work is directly attributable to a "voluntary" act. Landrum v. James, 425 So. 2d 1363 (Ala. Civ. App. 1982), cert. denied, 425 So. 2d 1364 (Ala. 1983).

And disqualification found in subdivision (2) contemplates a complete severance of employer-employee relations rather than its mere temporary suspension due to strike. T.R. Miller Mill Co. v. Johns, 261 Ala. 615, 75 So. 2d 675 (1954).

"Reasonable cause" defined. — For an employee to be eligible for unemployment benefits, he must have terminated his employment for reasonable cause. Reasonable cause is defined as a material and substantial cause in light of the circumstances. State, Dep't of Indus. Relations v. Nyco, Inc., 513 So. 2d 650 (Ala. Civ. App. 1987).

Reasonable cause required. — This section requires an employee to terminate employment for a reasonable cause, a cause that is material and substantial under the circumstances. Carlisle v. Director, Dep't of Indus. Relations, 494 So. 2d 437 (Ala. Civ. App. 1986).

Reasonable cause is question of fact. — It is well settled that the determination of whether an employee is disqualified from receiving unemployment compensation benefits because he left work voluntarily without good cause attributable to the employer is a question of fact, the resolution of which is governed by the ore tenus rule, where the court sits without a jury. Thus, it is the duty of the trial court in unemployment cases to resolve conflicts in testimony of the claimant and his supervisor and to determine weight and inferences to be drawn from that testimony. Lagrone v. Department of Indus. Relations, 519 So. 2d 1345 (Ala. Civ. App. 1987).

Burden is on employee to show that he had good cause connected with his work for leaving his employment. Department of Indus. Relations v. Wall, 34 Ala. App. 530, 41 So. 2d 611 (1949); West Point Mfg. Co. v. Keith, 35 Ala. App. 414, 47 So. 2d 594 (1950); Morrison v. Department of Indus. Relations, 35 Ala. App. 475, 48 So. 2d 72 (1950); Evergreen Textiles, Inc. v. State Dep't of Indus. Relations, 42 Ala. App. 364, 165 So. 2d 716 (1964).

When a claimant admits that he voluntarily left his employment but seeks to avoid the disqualifications from receiving benefits set up in this section, the burden is upon him to show that he had good cause connected with his work for leaving such employment. Henderson v. Department of Indus. Relations, 252 Ala. 239, 40 So. 2d 629 (1949); West Point Mfg. Co. v. Keith, 35 Ala. App. 414, 47 So. 2d 594 (1950); Morrison v. Department of Indus. Relations, 35 Ala. App. 475, 48 So. 2d 72 (1950); Department of Indus. Relations v. Mann, 35 Ala. App. 505, 50 So. 2d 780 (1950); Alabama Power Co. v. Atkins, 36 Ala. App. 558, 60 So. 2d 858 (1952); Davis v. Sherer, 381 So. 2d 643 (Ala. Civ. App. 1980).

An unemployed individual is eligible to receive benefits only if it appears that required conditions have been met, and the burden is upon him to show that those conditions exist. Craig v. Department of Indus. Relations, 35 Ala. App. 377, 47 So. 2d 286 (1950).

Where it was admitted that claimant voluntarily quit his job, the burden was cast upon him to show that he had good cause, connected with such work, for leaving. Alabama Textile Prods. Corp. v. Rodgers, 38 Ala. App. 206, 82 So. 2d 267 (1955); Nowell v. Mobile County Health Dep't, 501 So. 2d 468 (Ala. Civ. App. 1986).

When the evidence shows that a claimant left his or her most recent bona fide work voluntarily, claimant has the burden of showing good cause connected with such work for leaving. Department of Indus. Relations v. Meeks, 40 Ala. App. 231, 110 So. 2d 643 (1959).

Where an employee leaves his work of his own volition, he has the burden of proving facts to avoid the requirements of the statutory provision. Andala Co. v. Ganus, 269 Ala. 571, 115 So. 2d 123 (1959).

An employee who leaves her work voluntarily has the burden of proving good cause connected with her work. Department of Indus. Relations v. Curenton, 42 Ala. App. 242, 160 So. 2d 14 (1964).

Where an employee leaves his work of his own volition, he has the burden of proving facts to avoid the requirement of the statutory provision. He must show that he left most recent bona fide work for good cause connected with the work. Avondale Mills v. Burnett, 268 Ala. 82, 106 So. 2d 885, rev'd 39 Ala. App. 646, 106 So. 2d 882 (1958); Evergreen Textiles, Inc. v. State Dep't of Indus. Relations, 42 Ala. App. 364, 165 So. 2d 716 (1964).

When a claimant admits that he left his most recent bona fide work voluntarily, but seeks to avoid the disqualification from receiving unemployment compensation benefits under subdivision (2) of this section, the burden is then cast upon him to show that he had good cause connected with his work for leaving such work. Department of Indus. Relations v. Estes, 45 Ala. App. 360, 231 So. 2d 137 (1970).

The burden of proving that he is not disqualified from receiving unemployment compensation benefits pursuant to this section is on the claimant. In order to sustain this burden, the claimant must prove: (1) that he was compelled to leave his work because he was sick or disabled, (2) that he notified his employer of his sickness or disability as soon as was practicable to do so, and (3) that he returned to his employer and offered himself for work. Davis v. Stewart, 410 So. 2d 62 (Ala. Civ. App. 1981), cert. quashed as improvidently granted, 410 So. 2d 64 (Ala. 1982).

Burden of showing good cause. — If an employee voluntarily left her employment, the burden is upon the employee to show that she had good cause connected with her work for leaving her employment. Nowell v. Mobile County Health Dep't, 501 So. 2d 468 (Ala. Civ. App. 1986).

Test in determining whether reason to terminate is sufficient. — In determining whether the reason to terminate employment is sufficient for unemployment compensation, the applicable test is whether an average or normal worker would have similarly terminated employment under the facts. State Dep't of Indus. Relations v. Prance, 369 So. 2d 289 (Ala. Civ. App. 1979).

The employee is disqualified from receiving unemployment benefits if she left her employment voluntarily without good cause connected with her work. A "test of good cause is whether it is reasonable when measured by what the average or normal worker would have done under similar circumstances." Hadley v. Director of Dep't of Indus. Relations, 473 So. 2d 519 (Ala. Civ. App. 1985).

Determination of leaving work without good cause is question of fact. — The determination of whether the employee is disqualified for benefits because he left his most recent bona fide work voluntarily without good cause connected with such work under subdivision (2) is a question of fact, the resolution of which by the trial court sitting without a jury is governed by the ore tenus rule. Taylor v. Director, Dep't of Indus. Relations, 491 So. 2d 964 (Ala. Civ. App. 1986).

"Bona fide work" is to be determined by circumstances of leaving of next preceding employment and whether the last job was taken with the intention that it was to be permanent rather than just temporary until he could return to the next preceding employment. Department of Indus. Relations v. Taylor, 54 Ala. App. 614, 311 So. 2d 438, cert. denied, 294 Ala. 770, 311 So. 2d 440 (1975).

Plaintiff out of work because of strike has not "left his employment". — When a person goes or is forced out on a strike because of a labor dispute, he has not "left his employment" within the meaning of subdivision (2). It is well settled that such a strike does not sever the employer-employee relationship. T.R. Miller Mill Co. v. Johns, 261 Ala. 615, 75 So. 2d 675 (1954); Greene v. Department of Indus. Relations, 38 Ala. App. 199, 83 So. 2d 360 (1955); Department of Indus. Relations v. Lynch, 370 So. 2d 1050 (Ala. Civ. App. 1979); Davis v. Sherer, 381 So. 2d 643 (Ala. Civ. App. 1980).

Where claimant's employment was terminated by the employer's act of hiring a permanent replacement for her job while she was out on strike and not by her failure to report back to the company at the end of the strike, she was not disqualified under subdivision (2) of this section. Greene v. Department of Indus. Relations, 38 Ala. App. 199, 83 So. 2d 360 (1955).

But wife voluntarily abandons employ-

ment to assume new domicile with husband. — Act of wife in leaving her employment, which continued to be available, in Alabama and moving to New York to join her husband at newly selected domicile, was a "voluntary" abandonment of employment, precluding an award of benefits under this chapter. Ex parte Alabama Textile Prods. Corp., 242 Ala. 609, 7 So. 2d 303 (1942).

Where a wife leaves her most recent bona fide work to reside with her husband in another locality than that of her work, her leaving is for a "personal reason" and she is not entitled to unemployment benefits — as she left voluntarily without good cause connected with her work. Department of Indus. Relations v. Curenton, 42 Ala. App. 242, 160 So. 2d 14 (1964).

And employee who found that he was unable to live on compensation earned under the contract of employment, the terms of which were met by the employer in every respect, who voluntarily quit his employment, was disqualified from receiving unemployment benefits. Department of Indus. Relations v. Scott, 36 Ala. App. 184, 53 So. 2d 882 (1951).

Unemployment compensation law contains no provisions defining the phrase "good cause" as used in subdivision (2) of this section. Andala Co. v. Ganus, 269 Ala. 571, 115 So. 2d 123 (1959).

But "good cause" as used in subdivision (2) is defined as substantial reason; just ground for such action; adequate excuse that will bear the test of reason; and always the element of good faith. Department of Indus. Relations v. Estes, 45 Ala. App. 360, 231 So. 2d 137 (1970).

The word "voluntarily" as it appears in subdivision (2) must be taken in connection with the term "without good cause." "Good cause" in the quoted phrase connotes substantial reason; just ground for such action; adequate excuse that will bear the test of reason; and always the element of good faith. Dwight Mfg. Co. v. Long, 36 Ala. App. 387, 56 So. 2d 685 (1952).

And means reasonable cause. — There are no provisions in our unemployment compensation law defining or indicating what constitutes "good cause" under this section. The supreme court therefore concluded that the legislature meant a reasonable cause, one that is material and substantial as applied to a particular set of facts. Department of Indus. Relations v. Mann, 35 Ala. App. 505, 50 So. 2d 780 (1950); Andala Co. v. Ganus, 269 Ala. 571, 115 So. 2d 123 (1959).

By "good cause" legislature meant a reasonable cause, one that is material and substantial as applied to a particular set of facts.

Avondale Mills v. Burnett, 268 Ala. 82, 106 So. 2d 885, rev'd 39 Ala. App. 646, 106 So. 2d 882 (1958); Evergreen Textiles, Inc. v. State Dep't of Indus. Relations, 42 Ala. App. 364, 165 So. 2d 716 (1964).

Hence, criterion of reasonableness is test whether an employee "left his most recent bona fide work voluntarily without good cause." Ex parte McCleney, 286 Ala. 288, 239 So. 2d 311 (1970).

The pertinent consideration is whether or not claimant acted reasonably in quitting his job. In other words, a test of good cause is whether it is reasonable when measured by what the average or normal worker would have done under similar circumstances. The question is whether it be said that a claimant, under the facts, acted reasonably, that is, as an average or normal worker. Ex parte McCleney, 286 Ala. 288, 239 So. 2d 311 (1970).

And standards that must be used by law are standards of reasonableness as applied to average man or woman, and not to the supersensitive. Department of Indus. Relations v. Mann, 35 Ala. App. 505, 50 So. 2d 780 (1950); Andala Co. v. Ganus, 269 Ala. 571, 115 So. 2d 123 (1959).

A test of good cause is whether it is reasonable when measured by what the average or normal worker would have done under similar circumstances. Evergreen Textiles, Inc. v. State Dep't of Indus. Relations, 42 Ala. App. 364, 165 So. 2d 716 (1964).

One of the factors to be considered in determining what is good cause for leaving one's job is the consistency of one's conduct with a reasonably evidenced intent and desire to work and be self-supporting. Department of Indus. Relations v. Mann, 35 Ala. App. 505, 50 So. 2d 780 (1950).

When the unemployment compensation claimant has proven "good cause" for voluntarily leaving his employment, thus exempting him from disqualification under this section, the exception contained in subdivision (2) of this section has no application. Vulcan Materials Co. v. Holst, 418 So. 2d 152 (Ala. Civ. App. 1982).

If disability is connected with work. — A justifiable cause for leaving work, unless connected with the work, is not a "good cause" within the meaning of our statute. Ill health is of course a compelling reason for quitting work, but if such ill health does not result from, or is unconnected with, the work, it will not be considered a good cause. Department of Indus. Relations v. Chapman, 37 Ala. App. 680, 74 So. 2d 621 (1954).

Ill health is a compelling reason for quitting one's work, but if it is not connected with the work, it will not be "good cause" for avoiding the disqualification set out in subdivision (2). Department of Indus. Relations v. Estes, 45 Ala. App. 360, 231 So. 2d 137 (1970).

Physical inability to perform the only job available because of aggravation of bursitis condition resulting from the nature of that job is more than sufficient evidence to satisfy the claimant's burden in showing "good cause" for leaving connected with her work. Polk v. State, Dep't of Indus. Relations, 398 So. 2d 722 (Ala. Civ. App. 1981).

Employee must show ill health resulted from employment. — Ill health or physical infirmity is, of course, good cause for employees to cease working. But unless the illness or physical infirmity is shown to have resulted from or to have been caused by the employment, the employee is disqualified from receiving benefits when he voluntarily leaves his employment on account of such illness or physical infirmity. Henderson v. Department of Indus. Relations, 252 Ala. 239, 40 So. 2d 629 (1949); Alabama Mills v. Carnley, 35 Ala. App. 46, 44 So. 2d 622 (1949), citing Ex parte Alabama Textile Prods. Corp., 242 Ala. 609, 7 So. 2d 303 (1942); Department of Indus. Relations v. Chapman, 37 Ala. App. 680, 74 So. 2d 621 (1954); Department of Indus. Relations v. Henry, 42 Ala. App. 573, 172 So. 2d 374 (1964).

"Good cause" for leaving one's employment may well be prompted by the claimant's ill health or physical infirmity where the illness or infirmity results from, is connected with, or is caused by the employment. Polk v. State, Dep't of Indus. Relations, 398 So. 2d 722 (Ala. Civ. App. 1981).

Pregnancy must be deemed a good cause for quitting work, though not within the usual reach of this section. Alabama Mills v. Carnley, 35 Ala. App. 46, 44 So. 2d 622 (1949).

Substantial reduction in earnings is generally regarded as good cause for leaving one's employment, but the surrounding circumstances should be considered in determining whether a particular reduction in pay constitutes good cause for leaving one's employment. Alabama Textile Prods. Corp. v. Rodgers, 38 Ala. App. 206, 82 So. 2d 267 (1955); Andala Co. v. Ganus, 40 Ala. App. 455, 115 So. 2d 119 (1958), rev'd on other grounds, 269 Ala. 571, 115 So. 2d 123 (1959); Carlisle v. Director, Dep't of Indus. Relations, 494 So. 2d 437 (Ala. Civ. App. 1986).

A substantial reduction in earnings is regarded as good cause for leaving one's employment. Tombigbee Lightweight Aggregate Corp. v. Roberts, 351 So. 2d 1388 (Ala. Civ. App. 1977); Davis v. Prestwood, 381 So. 2d 85 (Ala. Civ. App. 1980); Carlisle v. Director, Dep't of Indus. Relations, 494 So. 2d 437 (Ala. Civ. App. 1986).

A substantial reduction in earnings is generally regarded as good cause for leaving one's employment, and, hence, one who leaves for such reason is not disqualified for unemployment compensation on the ground of leaving his work voluntarily without good cause; but in this connection the surrounding circumstances should be considered in determining whether a particular reduction in pay constitutes good cause for leaving one's employment. Department of Indus. Relations v. Lynch, 370 So. 2d 1050 (Ala. Civ. App. 1979).

Reductions in pay for employees, the lowest reduction being $100.00 and the highest $132.00 per month, could constitute a substantial reduction, so as to be regarded as good cause for leaving their jobs. Davis v. Prestwood, 381 So. 2d 85 (Ala. Civ. App. 1980).

The general rule in Alabama is that a substantial reduction in an employee's earnings establishes good cause for the employee's leaving his employment. However, the court must examine the facts of each case to determine whether the pay reduction in question actually constituted good cause. This inquiry into good cause focuses on whether a normal worker, faced with similar circumstance, would have also terminated his employment. State, Dep't of Indus. Relations v. Nyco, Inc., 513 So. 2d 650 (Ala. Civ. App. 1987).

Elimination of overtime work. — When the basis of employment includes the guarantee of overtime, an employee can leave his job with good cause when the employer eliminates his overtime. Tombigbee Lightweight Aggregate Corp. v. Roberts, 351 So. 2d 1388 (Ala. Civ. App. 1977).

Discharge for absenteeism not tantamount to leaving without good cause. — It would require a very strained interpretation of facts to hold that discharge for absenteeism or tardiness was tantamount to voluntarily leaving employment without good cause. Department of Indus. Relations v. Jaco, 337 So. 2d 374 (Ala. Civ. App. 1976).

Disability justifying refusal of job would also justify quitting job. — If a disability would justify a refusal of a proffered job, such disability must also be considered as a good cause for quitting a job of the same nature as the proffered one, provided of course that there is a causal connection between the work and the disability. Department of Indus. Relations v. Chapman, 37 Ala. App. 680, 74 So. 2d 621 (1954); Department of Indus. Relations v. Henry, 42 Ala. App. 573, 172 So. 2d 374 (1964).

A claimant cannot be disqualified for refusing to accept employment which may be a risk to or endanger his health. If this be true, then certainly it is unreasonable to hold that a claimant must lose credits or be denied benefits where he has been compelled to terminate his most recent bona fide work because such work has resulted in a physical condition or disease likewise dangerous to health and personal safety. Department of Indus. Relations v. Henry, 42 Ala. App. 573, 172 So. 2d 374 (1964).

Work-related depression ruled good cause. — Evidence supported the trial court's findings that correction officer's resignation was for good cause connected with the work and was reasonable under the circumstances; work-related depression caused hospitalization and intensive outpatient treatment that resulted in her physician's advising her not to return to work. State Dep't of Cors. v. Stokes, 558 So. 2d 955 (Ala. Civ. App. 1990).

Employee who is retired pursuant to terms of a collective bargaining agreement between his employer and the union of which the employee is a member, despite the fact that he wishes to continue at his work, has not "left his most recent bona fide work voluntarily without good cause connected with such work," within the meaning of this section, and is entitled to benefits. Reynolds Metals Co. v. Thorne, 41 Ala. App. 331, 133 So. 2d 709 (1961).

Unwritten agreement between unions had no connection with job. — The claimants, upon their own initiative and without any cause connected with their work, voluntarily quit their employment in order to follow union custom based upon "unwritten" agreements between locals. Certainly the employer may not be caused to be assessed a higher rate of contribution to the compensation fund because of a custom between unions. A personal reason, without any connection with conditions or circumstances of the job, does not satisfy the requirements of the statute. Allen v. Stewart, 560 So. 2d 1067 (Ala. Civ. App. 1990).

Part-time employee who wanted to work only certain hours to qualify for subsidized housing. — Where the claimant was aware that as a part-time employee the number of hours she would be scheduled to work would vary from week to week, during the claimant's employment, she experienced a varying number of assigned work hours, she lived in subsidized housing and paid a rent based on her estimated income, there was evidence presented that the employer refused to sign a statement for the housing authority that she worked only one day a week because the claimant was subject to being called in to work more than she was scheduled to work and because the claimant would possibly be scheduled to work a greater number of hours in the following two-week pay period, and there was conflicting evidence presented as to whether or not the employee had requested that her hours

be cut, claimant voluntarily left work with the employer without good cause. Carlisle v. Director, Dep't of Indus. Relations, 494 So. 2d 437 (Ala. Civ. App. 1986).

Evidence held to establish justifiable cause for quitting job. — In the present case there is evidence to the effect that claimant's disability was caused by having to stand on a concrete floor in order to perform the duties of his job. He was advised by his physician to seek other work. Thus, there is evidence tending to establish a justifiable cause for quitting work, and a direct causal connection between the work and the disability. Department of Indus. Relations v. Chapman, 37 Ala. App. 680, 74 So. 2d 621 (1954).

Evidence warranted a finding that although the employee voluntarily left his work, he had good cause connected with such work for leaving and, therefore, was not disqualified from receiving benefits by virtue of this section. Alabama Mills, Inc. v. Brand, 251 Ala. 643, 38 So. 2d 574 (1948).

Evidence held to show that claimant had good cause for declining to remain at his job after the indicated changes were made in the character of employment. Dwight Mfg. Co. v. Long, 36 Ala. App. 387, 56 So. 2d 685 (1952).

The evidence was sufficient to sustain the finding of the trial court that claimant was not disqualified for benefits on the ground that she voluntarily left her most recent bona fide work without good cause connected with the work. Zac Smith Stationery Co. v. Reynolds, 39 Ala. App. 389, 101 So. 2d 573 (1958).

Where claimant was reinstated after voluntarily leaving job. — Where the claimant voluntarily quit her job without good cause, but a few days later, however, she went to the employer, apologized, and was reinstated or rehired, the evidence as to the latter being in conflict, the record clearly contained evidence to support the circuit court's conclusion that the claimant was reinstated, where the claimant testified that, when she returned to work, she performed the same job she had performed before she quit, and she further testified that she was not required to fill out employment papers as a new employee and that she was not required to train new employees. Although there was also evidence to support the conclusion that the claimant was rehired only on a temporary basis, to train or oversee new employees who had been hired in her absence, it was the circuit court's responsibility to weigh such conflicting evidence and reach a conclusion. Heatherly v. Campbell, 485 So. 2d 735 (Ala. Civ. App. 1986).

Payment of back wages within three days was reasonable. — As a matter of law, payment of plaintiff's back wages only three working days after she was reinstated, and given to her on the second working day after she returned to work, was not unreasonable and did not constitute good cause for her resignation. Nowell v. Mobile County Health Dep't, 501 So. 2d 468 (Ala. Civ. App. 1986).

Where claimant was absent from work in order to care for a sick baby she failed to meet the burden upon her to show to the reasonable satisfaction of the court that she had a good cause connected with her work for voluntarily leaving her employment, and she was disqualified under this section. Craig v. Department of Indus. Relations, 35 Ala. App. 377, 47 So. 2d 286 (1950).

Leaving employment to campaign for public office not good cause. — Claimant's leaving his employment to campaign for the office of circuit clerk was a factor connected with that office and was not the "good cause connected with such work" which under our statute would justify him in quitting his job. Alabama Textile Prods. Corp. v. Rodgers, 38 Ala. App. 206, 82 So. 2d 267 (1955).

Decrease in the number of hours worked did not constitute good cause for quitting work where there did not appear to have been a decrease in the wage rate and it was stipulated that the employer's policy was to transfer employees to other jobs when their jobs were eliminated because of a change in operations and that claimant's seniority would in all probability have placed him in line for transfer to another full time job. Alabama Textile Prods. Corp. v. Rodgers, 38 Ala. App. 206, 82 So. 2d 267 (1955).

It cannot be said with justification that an alleged speedup of a machine on which a claimant was working some nine years before was the substantial reason for some as yet unproved mental or physical disease or illness causing him to leave his most recent bona fide work for purposes of subdivision (2) of this section. Department of Indus. Relations v. Estes, 45 Ala. App. 360, 231 So. 2d 137 (1970).

Voluntary termination of employment due to antiquated machinery not good cause. — Where the only reason given for the sale of business and the voluntary termination of employment was antiquated machinery, such is not "good cause" within the meaning of unemployment compensation law and does not entitle claimant to benefits. Davis v. Sherer, 381 So. 2d 643 (Ala. Civ. App. 1980).

Employee who had left her job because of change in her job assignment failed to meet the burden cast upon her to show to the reasonable satisfaction of the court that she had good cause connected with her work for voluntarily leaving her employment, under subdivision (2). Department of Indus. Relations

v. Garrett, 38 Ala. App. 213, 81 So. 2d 691 (1955).

Assignment of additional duties. — Evidence failed to establish that claimant had good cause for leaving his most recent bona fide work on account of additional duties assigned to him. Avondale Mills v. Burnett, 268 Ala. 82, 106 So. 2d 885, rev'g 39 Ala. App. 646, 106 So. 2d 882 (1958).

Dividing work up not cause to impel reasonable man to give up work. — Dividing the work up is certainly within managerial prerogative. Without showing oppression or reduction in earnings, this circumstance is not a cause to impel a reasonable man to give up work. Evergreen Textiles, Inc. v. State Dep't of Indus. Relations, 42 Ala. App. 364, 165 So. 2d 716 (1964).

Refusal to comply with reasonable job directives of employer. — If the employee, of his own volition, refuses to comply with a reasonable job direction by his employer, the employer is entitled to release him from employment. To hold otherwise would place an illogical duty upon the employer to retain recalcitrant employees or discharge them at its own risk. Avondale Mills v. Burnett, 268 Ala. 82, 106 So. 2d 885, rev'g 39 Ala. App. 646, 106 So. 2d 882 (1958).

Disqualification for unreasonably resisting changes in working conditions. — A breakdown of the cases under the unemployment insurance law on claims of workers alleged to have unreasonably resisted changes of wages, working conditions, introduction of new or different machines or techniques and the like brings out no fixed rule. The only test of whether the employee is disqualified for benefits is what the reasonable man or woman similarly circumstanced would do. Williams v. Boyce, 42 Ala. App. 28, 151 So. 2d 254 (1963).

Failure to give new work techniques a fair trial. — Claimant failed to give new work techniques a fair trial, as an average or normal worker would have done under similar circumstances, and therefore, not having acted reasonably in voluntarily leaving most recent bona fide work, was not entitled to benefits. Andala Co. v. Ganus, 269 Ala. 571, 115 So. 2d 123 (1959).

Failure to take up complaint according to company practice. — Failure to take up complaint of abusive language according to company practice held to raise inference that employee was indifferent as to whether or not she worked and this would bear on the matter of good cause. Stewart v. Department of Indus. Relations, 40 Ala. App. 383, 114 So. 2d 274 (1959).

Inconsistency in reasons given for leaving employment held sufficient to affirm judgment reciting that employee failed to show good cause for leaving connected with work. Stewart v. Department of Indus. Relations, 40 Ala. App. 383, 114 So. 2d 274 (1959).

Good marital cause not equated as nondisqualifying reason to leave work. — The supreme court has refused to equate a good marital cause as a nondisqualifying reason to leave work. Evergreen Textiles, Inc. v. State Dep't of Indus. Relations, 42 Ala. App. 364, 165 So. 2d 716 (1964).

Failure to ask for sick leave adds to burden cast upon claimant to show that he had good cause connected with his work for leaving such most recent bona fide work. Department of Indus. Relations v. Estes, 45 Ala. App. 360, 231 So. 2d 137 (1970).

And claimant's nonaction and lack of diligence in not applying for sick leave before voluntarily leaving her job was incompatible with any rational concept of involuntary unemployment, and removed her from the liberal scope of beneficent influences of the act. West Point Mfg. Co. v. Keith, 35 Ala. App. 414, 47 So. 2d 594 (1950).

Failure to return to work following leave of absence. — Had his employment been terminated at the end of a leave of absence for failure of the claimant to report for work, if he was able to work or for failure to request an extension of his leave of absence should he not be able to work, he would have been disqualified under the terms of this section. Department of Indus. Relations v. McLeod, 55 Ala. App. 156, 314 So. 2d 72 (1975).

Word "expiration" means "cessation; close; end; conclusion; termination of a contract or agreement." Southern Bell Tel. & Tel. Co. v. Department of Indus. Relations, 42 Ala. App. 351, 165 So. 2d 128 (1964).

Expiration of a leave-of-absence does not occur until after the period for which the leave-of-absence was granted. Southern Bell Tel. & Tel. Co. v. Department of Indus. Relations, 42 Ala. App. 351, 165 So. 2d 128 (1964).

Evidence sufficient to show voluntary abandonment of employment. — Evidence held to show that claimant did not get a leave of absence but voluntarily severed his employment relationship. Alabama Power Co. v. Atkins, 36 Ala. App. 558, 60 So. 2d 858 (1952).

Evidence held not to show that employee left most recent bona fide work for good cause connected with the work. Department of Indus. Relations v. Meeks, 40 Ala. App. 231, 110 So. 2d 643 (1959).

Evidence held to support trial court's conclusion that employee who had been employed by employer at its plant in Fayette for approximately nine years when the employer relocated its plant to Decatur, and who was given the option of transferring to Decatur or of not transferring and drawing unemployment and severance pay, chose to transfer to Decatur since he was close to having a vested interest in his retirement plan, and who commuted to Decatur from Fayette for approximately six months after the plant was closed, and sometime after being told by the employer's plant manager that he would be terminated if he didn't move to Decatur by the first of April and also learning that his pension had vested, simply did not report for work after March 31, 1984, voluntarily left his employment without good cause connected with his work. Taylor v. Director, Dep't of Indus. Relations, 491 So. 2d 964 (Ala. Civ. App. 1986).

Employees not required to prove pay checks worthless. — Where employees received payroll checks drawn on insufficient funds, employees were not required to prove that payroll checks in question were "worthless checks" under Worthless Check Act, in order to constitute reasonable cause for leaving employment. State Dep't of Indus. Relations v. Prance, 369 So. 2d 289 (Ala. Civ. App. 1979).

Where employer had knowledge that payroll checks were drawn on insufficient funds, fact known when they left employment, did not preclude finding that employees left employment for good cause. State Dep't of Indus. Relations v. Prance, 369 So. 2d 289 (Ala. Civ. App. 1979).

Where request for extension denied. — Pharmacy intern did not voluntarily leave his job at hospital where record showed that he agreed to accept a position as a pharmacy intern with the hospital for a specified term and that the nature of the work compelled him to leave at the end of this term, at which time his requested extension was denied. Intern was therefore not disqualified from receiving unemployment compensation benefits on that basis. State Dep't of Indus. Relations v. Montgomery Baptist Hosp., 359 So. 2d 410 (Ala. Civ. App. 1978).

Claimant's incorrect belief that she should not have been transferred not good cause. — Claimant's incorrect belief that she should not have been subject to a temporary transfer to the night shift on seniority grounds did not constitute good cause connected with her work to justify leaving her employment. Davis v. Director, Dep't of Indus. Relations, 507 So. 2d 942 (Ala. Civ. App. 1986).

IV. DISCHARGE FOR DISHONEST OR CRIMINAL ACT.

Word "dishonest" is defined as characterized by lack of truth, honesty, probity or trustworthiness or by an inclination to mislead, lie, cheat or defraud. Scott v. Scott Paper

Co., 280 Ala. 486, 195 So. 2d 540 (1967), rev'g 43 Ala. App. 532, 195 So. 2d 536 (1966); Payne v. Carter, 406 So. 2d 433 (Ala. Civ. App. 1981).

The term "misconduct," absent modifying words in this section indicates legislative intent that "deliberate misconduct" and "misconduct" are two separate and distinct categories of employee behavior, authorizing either total disqualification or partial disqualification, respectively. McClain v. State Dep't of Indus. Relations, 405 So. 2d 34 (Ala. Civ. App. 1981).

"Dishonest" and "criminal," as used in this section, are not synonymous, either generally or in connection with the unauthorized possession of company property. Scott v. Scott Paper Co., 280 Ala. 486, 195 So. 2d 540 (1967), rev'g 43 Ala. App. 532, 195 So. 2d 536 (1966).

And dishonest act need not be violation of criminal law. — There is no question but that an employee can be disqualified for benefits if he was discharged because of a criminal act committed in connection with his work, but the legislature did not intend that all dischargeable acts must amount to a violation of the criminal law. If such were the case, there would have been no need to add the word "dishonest." Scott v. Scott Paper Co., 280 Ala. 486, 195 So. 2d 540 (1967), rev'g 43 Ala. App. 532, 195 So. 2d 536 (1966).

The legislature did not intend that every time company property was found in the unauthorized possession of an employee, and there was proof that the possession was dishonest and unauthorized, the proof was to no avail unless it also was sufficient to support a conviction for larceny or embezzlement. Scott v. Scott Paper Co., 280 Ala. 486, 195 So. 2d 540 (1967), rev'g 43 Ala. App. 532, 195 So. 2d 536 (1966).

Sufficient evidence of dishonest act. — Where an employee was discovered with a package of finished bond paper concealed in his clothing as he was leaving the plant, his explanation was not plausible and his conduct was in conflict with company rules, there was sufficient evidence to classify his action as a dishonest act committed in connection with his work. Scott v. Scott Paper Co., 280 Ala. 486, 195 So. 2d 540 (1967), rev'g 43 Ala. App. 532, 195 So. 2d 536 (1966).

Factual question. — Whether misconduct was totally disqualifying under paragraphs a or b of subdivision (3) or was misconduct under paragraph c of subdivision (3) was for the trier of fact according to the evidence. Department of Indus. Relations v. Jaco, 337 So. 2d 374 (Ala. Civ. App. 1976).

Absenteeism as misconduct. — Claimant's termination for absenteeism with notice did not constitute voluntary departure from work without good cause that would disqualify her from receiving unemployment compensation benefits, but, rather, constituted discharge for misconduct connected with her work, and she was entitled to reduced benefits rather than no benefits. Department of Indus. Relations v. Smith, 360 So. 2d 726 (Ala. Civ. App. 1978).

But only partially disqualified. — Where unemployment compensation claimant's discharge from his employment was due to unsatisfactory attendance record attributable to alcoholism, trial court found that claimant was not discharged for deliberate misconduct and was therefore only partially disqualified from receiving unemployment compensation. Department of Indus. Relations v. Baldwin, 363 So. 2d 100 (Ala. Civ. App. 1978), cert. denied, 363 So. 2d 101 (Ala. 1978).

Strike by public employees as misconduct. — A strike by public employees and their failure to report to work for 23 days constitutes deliberate misconduct in violation of the statute. This is especially true since they knowingly broke the rule of the city and county of Montgomery personnel board, which authorizes the dismissal of any city or county employee who, without authority, fails to report to work for more than three days. Their strike and unauthorized absence from their public employment for that long period of time falls within the classic definition of misconduct. That misconduct was deliberate. Henley v. Housing Auth., 403 So. 2d 365 (Ala. Civ. App. 1981).

Continued failure of employee to perform his job in a manner which previous performance indicates is contrary to his experience and ability may be found to be misconduct under subdivision (3)b of this section. Rubin v. Department of Indus. Relations, 494 So. 2d 82 (Ala. Civ. App. 1986).

Evidence sufficient to support disqualification for misconduct. — Decision of the trial court disqualifying claimant from unemployment benefits for seven weeks pursuant to subsection (3)c for misconduct held amply supported by the evidence. Williams v. Department of Indus. Relations, 490 So. 2d 1246 (Ala. Civ. App. 1986).

An employee who has been terminated for misconduct repeated after warning loses all unemployment benefits. — If, however, he is terminated for misconduct without warning, he is entitled to partial benefits. Fuller v. State, Dep't of Indus. Relations, 445 So. 2d 925 (Ala. Civ. App. 1984).

Sufficient warning before firing. — Under subdivision (3)(b) of this section, a sufficient warning does not require the employer to state that the employee will be fired if the misconduct continues; thus, the warning was sufficient where the employer made several requests for the employee to cease her course of conduct. Johnson v. Director, Dep't of Indus. Relations, 470 So. 2d 1274 (Ala. Civ. App. 1985).

Discharge for misconduct. — Evidence justified a finding that an employee, who was discharged for reckless driving of employer's truck after drinking, was guilty of misconduct in the performance of his work, but not to the extent that he should be wholly and totally disqualified for any and all unemployment compensation. Department of Indus. Relations v. Rich, 42 Ala. App. 80, 152 So. 2d 692 (1963).

Evidence supported finding that claimant was terminated for misconduct, where she left work without clocking out and argued with her supervisor after having been warned about such misconduct. Sanders v. Department of Indus. Relations, 509 So. 2d 908 (Ala. Civ. App. 1987).

V. FAILURE TO APPLY FOR AVAILABLE WORK.

Refusal of suitable work closely akin to voluntarily leaving without good cause. — Under this section there is a close kinship between disqualification because of refusal of suitable work, and disqualification for voluntarily leaving recent bona fide work without good cause connected with the work. Department of Indus. Relations v. Henry, 42 Ala. App. 573, 172 So. 2d 374 (1964).

Law presupposes some effort to secure work. — The unemployment compensation law does not contemplate that a job must seek out a man and coax him to work, but presupposes some effort on his part to secure work. Broadway v. Bolar, 33 Ala. App. 87, 29 So. 2d 687 (1947).

And justification for refusal of work diminishes as period of unemployment lengthens. — Under subdivision (5), a skilled laborer is justified in refusing as unsuitable work offered immediately after separation from his last job, when the offered work is of a type that would require less skill and training than he possesses, and less remuneration. Such justification for refusal however, even for a skilled worker, diminishes as the period of unemployment lengthens. The unemployment compensation laws were not passed as an invitation to idleness. Broadway v. Bolar, 33 Ala. App. 87, 29 So. 2d 687 (1947).

Factors to be considered in determining whether job suitable. — Under subdivision (5), the factors pertinent to be considered by the director of the department of industrial relations in determining whether available job

was suitable for claimant were (1) degree of risk to health involved, (2) safety, (3) morals, (4) physical fitness of applicant, (5) prior training of applicant, (6) applicant's experience and prior earnings, (7) length of applicant's unemployment and prospect for securing local work in customary occupation, and (8) distance of available work from applicant's residence. Broadway v. Bolar, 33 Ala. App. 87, 29 So. 2d 687 (1947).

Latitude in determining whether offered work is suitable. — This section gives the director and the appeal tribunal much latitude in determining whether offered work is suitable to an unemployed claimant seeking benefits. Ex parte Alabama Textile Prods. Corp., 242 Ala. 609, 7 So. 2d 303 (1942).

If director and appeal tribunal find that unemployed claimant seeking benefits under this chapter is not physically able to perform the duties of employment, or that employment is not morally fit for the employee, or the employee does not have the skill to do the work, or that it is not reasonably safe for the employee, and that finding is based on competent evidence, and is not arbitrary or unreasonable, there is nothing for the supreme court to review on certiorari in that respect. Ex parte Alabama Textile Prods. Corp., 242 Ala. 609, 7 So. 2d 303 (1942).

Claimant not qualified where refused nonunion work. — Where claimant for unemployment compensation benefits placed himself only upon union and company panels in an effort to make himself available for work and refused job for which he qualified with a different company because it paid less than union wages and would result in loss of union rights, claimant was not qualified for unemployment compensation benefits under statutes governing availability for work and refusal to accept employment for which he was qualified. State Dep't of Indus. Relations v. Harbin, 365 So. 2d 313 (Ala. Civ. App. 1978).

VI. RECEIVING PENSION.

Literal construction of section not permitted to defeat spirit of act. — If the required elements for a contract exist in fact, saying therein that it is not a contract is not conclusive, and if the pension of claimant is paid pursuant to this contract, or agreement or plan, provided and entered into as a result of his employment, it is a pension paid within the intent and meaning of subdivision (8). A literal construction of the words of this section is not to be permitted to defeat the spirit of the act. Holmes v. Cook, 45 Ala. App. 688, 236 So. 2d 352 (1970).

Intent of subdivision. — Intent of subdivision (8) of this section is to disqualify an individual from receiving the unemployment compensation to which he would have otherwise been entitled, when he is receiving a pension paid, or largely provided, by the employer from whose employment his right to benefits was derived. Holmes v. Cook, 45 Ala. App. 688, 236 So. 2d 352 (1970).

"Pension," as it appears in subdivision (8), imports within its meaning retirement pay or annuity. Holmes v. Cook, 45 Ala. App. 688, 236 So. 2d 352 (1970).

The word "pension" as found in the statute does not have the narrow meaning commonly given. That is, the meaning is not confined to a gratuity, wholly given or financed by an employer. It is not a mere bounty springing from the appreciation and graciousness of an employer. It may be these, but in modern or recent terminology, it has been used broadly in the sense of retirement pay or an annuity. Such retirement or annuity may be wholly financed by the employer or may have been contributed to by the employee. Holmes v. Cook, 45 Ala. App. 688, 236 So. 2d 352 (1970).

And payments made to a claimant out of a pension fund, until they equal his contributions, are pension payments, and not a return of his own funds. Holmes v. Cook, 45 Ala. App. 688, 236 So. 2d 352 (1970).

Hence, contributions by an employee to a fund from which a pension is being paid do not matter when it is shown that the pension payments represent considerably more than the amount contributed by the employee. Such payments are substantially compensation paid by the employer for loss of wages due to involuntary retirement. Holmes v. Cook, 45 Ala. App. 688, 236 So. 2d 352 (1970).

Employer may compensate either by pension payments or benefits under the compensation act. — It is the purpose of the Unemployment Compensation Act that an employer shall compensate for loss of wages of an employee who has lost his job through no fault of his own, either by providing a pension or retirement pay equal to or in excess of benefits due because of his employment, or that he receive benefits under the compensation act. The employee cannot receive both. The remedial and beneficent purpose of the act is fulfilled by either. Holmes v. Cook, 45 Ala. App. 688, 236 So. 2d 352 (1970).

Disqualification dependent upon pension being paid by last employer. — Disqualification under subdivision (8) due to receipt of a pension or retirement payment is dependent upon such pension or retirement payment being paid by his last employer. Holmes v. Cook, 45 Ala. App. 688, 236 So. 2d 352 (1970).

Pension is a substitute for wages lost by employee by reason of loss of his job and is payment made "by way of compensation for loss of wages." Holmes v. Cook, 45 Ala. App. 688, 236 So. 2d 352 (1970).

Claimant not due unemployment where retirement amounts exceed benefits. — Where the accrued retirement sum paid to the claimant was a pension that arose out of the employer-employee relationship based on the previous work of the claimant, and the sum, when divided into weekly paydays, exceeded the benefits allowable by the Unemployment Compensation Act, the claimant was not due any unemployment compensation benefits, pursuant to subdivision (8) of this section. Wright v. State Dep't of Indus. Relations, 470 So. 2d 1246 (Ala. Civ. App. 1985).

VII. RECEIVING SEPARATION ALLOWANCE.

Subsection (6) of this section was intended to disqualify claimant only when he receives remuneration in the form of wages. The disqualification obtains where the wages received are in lieu of (1) notice (to terminate), (2) a dismissal allowance, or (3) a separation allowance. State, Dep't of Indus. Relations v. Deslattes, 372 So. 2d 867 (Ala. Civ. App.), cert. denied, 372 So. 2d 872 (Ala. 1979).

Disqualification does not result by mere receipt of separation allowance, payment must be in the form of wages in lieu of the allowance. State, Dep't of Indus. Relations v. Deslattes, 372 So. 2d 867 (Ala. Civ. App.), cert. denied, 372 So. 2d 872 (Ala. 1979).

Disqualification results only if termination allowance was legally required. — Construing subsections (6) and (8) of this section consistently, disqualification under subsection (6) can only result when a termination allowance is paid by an employer under a legal obligation to do so. State, Dep't of Indus. Relations v. Deslattes, 372 So. 2d 867 (Ala. Civ. App.), cert. denied, 372 So. 2d 872 (Ala. 1979).

ARTICLE 5.

PROCEDURE FOR CLAIMS FOR BENEFITS.

Collateral references. — Discharge from employment on ground of political views or conduct as affecting right to unemployment compensation. 29 ALR4th 287.

Conduct or activities of employees during off-duty hours as misconduct barring unemployment compensation benefits. 35 ALR4th 691.

Eligibility for unemployment compensation benefits of employee who attempts to withdraw resignation before leaving employment. 36 ALR4th 395.

§ 25-4-90. Filing claims for benefits.

Claims for benefits shall be made in accordance with such general rules as the director may prescribe. (Acts 1939, No. 497, p. 721; Code 1940, T. 26, § 215.)

Cited in Ex parte Miles, 248 Ala. 386, 27 So. 2d 777 (1946); Department of Indus. Relations v. Haynes, 259 Ala. 238, 67 So. 2d 62 (1953); Department of Indus. Relations v. Headon, 42 Ala. App. 132, 155 So. 2d 123 (1962).

Collateral references. — 81 C.J.S., Social Security & Public Welfare, § 217.

Discharge from employment on ground of political views or conduct as affecting right to unemployment compensation. 29 ALR4th 287.

§ 25-4-91. Determinations and redeterminations upon claims for benefits.

(a) *Determination by examiner.* — A determination upon a claim filed pursuant to Section 25-4-90 shall be made promptly by an examiner designated by the director, and shall include a statement as to whether and in what amount a claimant is entitled to benefits and, in the event of denial, shall state the reasons therefor; except, that where he deems additional evidence to be needed, the examiner may refer such claim or any question involved therein to an appeals tribunal who shall make this decision with respect thereto in accordance with the proceeding prescribed in Section 25-4-93. A determination with respect to the first week of a benefit year shall also include a statement as to whether the claimant has been paid the wages specified under subdivision (a)(5) of Section 25-4-77 and if so, the first day of the benefit year, his weekly benefit amount, and the maximum total amount of benefits payable to him with respect to a benefit year.

(b) *Redeterminations and reconsiderations.*

(1) The director may reconsider any determination which has not become final as provided in subsection (d) of this section and may issue a redetermination. The director may reconsider a determination which has become final whenever he finds that an error or omission in base period wages, computation of benefits or identity of the claimant or the employer for whom the claimant worked during the base period of his claim has occurred in connection therewith and may issue a redetermination. No such redetermination shall be made after the expiration of the benefit year within which the claim was filed; except, that the director may, within one year after the end of such benefit year, reconsider any determination which

394

has become final and issue a redetermination upon a finding that the determination was based on false statements or misrepresentation of material facts, whether or not intentional. Notice of any such redetermination shall be promptly given to the parties entitled to notice of the original determination in the manner prescribed in this section with respect to notice of an original determination. Such redetermination shall be subject to review upon appeal in the same manner and under the same conditions as original determinations. Except when the director has written documentation that an interested party has made false statements or a misrepresentation of material facts or such party admits to such in writing or waives his right to a hearing, no redetermination shall be effectuated so as to interrupt the benefit status of a claimant until after the determination has become final.

(2) An appeal tribunal or the board of appeals may reconsider any decision which has not become final as provided by Sections 25-4-92 and 25-4-94 and may issue an amended decision. An appeals tribunal or the board of appeals may, within one year after the end of the benefit year, reconsider any decision which has become final and issue an amended decision upon a finding that the decision was based on false statements or misrepresentation of material facts, whether or not intentional and the director may petition the body which issued the decision for a rehearing and amended decision.

(3) In the event that an appeal involving an original determination is pending as of the date a redetermination thereof is issued, such appeal, unless withdrawn, shall be treated as an appeal from such redetermination.

(c) *Notice of determination and notice of payment.*

(1) Notice of determination or decision upon a claim shall be promptly given to the claimant and the claimant's last employing unit by delivery thereof or by mailing such notices to their last known addresses.

(2) Notice of payment will be promptly given to every employer in the claimant's base period who is not entitled to a notice of determination when the claimant has been paid any amount of benefits which may result in a charge to the employers' experience rating accounts pursuant to Section 25-4-54 by delivery thereof or by mailing such notice to their last known addresses.

(d) *Finality of determinations and notice of payment.*

(1) Unless any party to whom notice of determination is required to be given shall, within seven calendar days after delivery of such notice or within 15 calendar days after such notice was mailed to his last known address, file an appeal from such decision, such decision shall be deemed final.

   a. If an appeal is duly filed, any disputed benefits which may have been paid at any time prior to the final decision, which would not have been payable under the terms of the final decision, shall be determined to be an overpayment and the claimant shall be required to repay to the fund any such benefits and the director shall have the authority to enforce collections of overpayments as is contained in Section 25-4-145.

b. If an appeal is duly filed by an interested employer, any benefits based upon wages in the base period paid by that employer shall not be charged under the experience rating provisions of Section 25-4-54 until the decision on such appeal becomes final and in event the final decision allows benefits the charge to the employer's experience rating record will be made in the calendar quarter in which such decision becomes final.

(2) Unless any party to whom notice of payment is required to be given shall, within seven calendar days after delivery of such notice or within 15 calendar days after such notice was mailed to his last known address, request the director to review the decision determining the benefits to be chargeable, such decision shall become final. If the final decision provides for the removal of benefit charges, such a credit shall be applied to the calendar year and calendar quarter in which such decision becomes final and no attempt shall be made to relate the credit to the period in which the benefits were previously determined to be chargeable. (Acts 1939, No. 497, p. 721; Code 1940, T. 26, § 216; Acts 1943, No. 310, p. 281, § 9; Acts 1945, No. 283, p. 449, § 10; Acts 1957, No. 301, p. 393; Acts 1971, No. 1201, p. 2083, §§ 2-4; Acts 1971, No. 2325, p. 3748, §§ 2-4; Acts 1973, No. 1716, p. 1057, § 7; Acts 1975, No. 801, p. 1604, § 10; Acts 1981, No. 81-842, p. 1508; Acts 1983, 2nd Ex. Sess., No. 83-155, p. 264, § 13; Acts 1989, No. 89-405, p. 822, § 8.)

The 1989 amendment, effective January 1, 1991, rewrote subdivision (c)(2); in paragraph (d)(1)b inserted "any benefits based upon," substituted "charged under the experience rating provisions" for "determined to be employee's or employer's benefit wages for the purpose of the experience rating provisions"; in subdivision (d)(2) substituted "the benefits to chargeable" for "wages to be benefit wages" in the first sentence, and substituted "benefit charges" for "benefit wages," substituted "benefits" for "wages," and substituted "chargeable" for "benefit wages" in the second sentence. See the Code commissioner's note below.

Code commissioner's note. — Section 12 of Acts 1989, No. 89-405: "The provisions of Sections 4, 7, and 8 of this act shall become effective immediately upon passage and approval by the Governor or its otherwise becoming law only for the purpose of implementation of the transitional provisions which will enable the full implementation of all the provisions of these sections for a complete change of system and for rate of contribution determination effective January 1, 1991; otherwise for purposes of such system change and the determination of rates of contribution, the provisions of said sections shall become effective on January 1, 1991."

"Final decision" defined. — "Final decision," although not defined in the Unemployment Compensation Act, is deemed to be a decision from which an appeal will lie to an appellate court. Cargill v. State, Dep't of Indus. Relations, 428 So. 2d 62 (Ala. Civ. App. 1982).

This section creates a legal obligation on claimants to repay any benefits received by them during a period of ineligibility. This obligation springs forth by operation of law when a "final decision" as to eligibility is reached. Cargill v. State, Dep't of Indus. Relations, 428 So. 2d 62 (Ala. Civ. App. 1982).

But, section does not provide a procedure for the collection of overpayment; consequently, the department is relegated to any one of the methods authorized by law to collect the amount owed by claimants as the result of the overpayment of benefits. Cargill v. State, Dep't of Indus. Relations, 428 So. 2d 62 (Ala. Civ. App. 1982).

An appeal can be duly taken under subdivision (d)(1) of this section, by simply identifying the claim, stating the party taking the appeal, writing the words "we appeal" thereon and timely filing it with the department. The method or procedure for taking an appeal under that code section is not detailed therein. The magic word "appeal" need not appear in such a writing, although, without it, an interpretation of the entire instrument must be made to determine the intent of the party in filing the document. Donaldson v. State Dep't of Indus. Relations, 439 So. 2d 1301 (Ala. Civ. App. 1983).

Particularity in pleading is not required as to appeals by employer of an award of unemployment compensation. This is just and fair because laymen, both employers and claimants, ordinarily represent themselves at this stage in unemployment compensation proceedings. Donaldson v. State Dep't of Indus. Relations, 439 So. 2d 1301 (Ala. Civ. App. 1983).

It has been held that, in case of an appeal to the circuit court from a determination by the board, all that need be stated is that the decision of the board of appeals is incorrect under the facts or the law. Donaldson v. State Dep't of Indus. Relations, 439 So. 2d 1301 (Ala. Civ. App. 1983).

For discussion of whether letter was sufficient to file an appeal as is required by this section, see Donaldson v. State Dep't of Indus. Relations, 439 So. 2d 1301 (Ala. Civ. App. 1983).

An appeal under this section may be mailed, but it must be received within the time limit. Olsen v. Moffat Rd. Veterinary Clinic, 441 So. 2d 971 (Ala. Civ. App. 1983).

Merely mailing notice of appeal within the time provided is not a "filing" as intended by subdivision (d)(1) of this section. The historical definition of the term in other areas of the law, the definition other jurisdictions apply in connection with unemployment compensation laws, and the context in which the word is used in relation to Alabama's unemployment compensation laws leads the court to the conclusion that the notice of appeal must be received to be considered filed. Olsen v. Moffat Rd. Veterinary Clinic, 441 So. 2d 971 (Ala. Civ. App. 1983).

To hold that the appeal is filed when mailed would be to, in effect, extend the time provided by the statute. This is so especially since the legislature recognized that use of the mails should allow a longer time period in which to appeal. Olsen v. Moffat Rd. Veterinary Clinic, 441 So. 2d 971 (Ala. Civ. App. 1983).

Cited in Crawley v. Carter, 378 So. 2d 1139 (Ala. Civ. App. 1979); Caradine v. Director, Dep't of Indus. Relations, 456 So. 2d 75 (Ala. Civ. App. 1984); Heatherly v. Benton, 479 So. 2d 1285 (Ala. Civ. App. 1985).

Collateral references. — 81 C.J.S., Social Security & Public Welfare, § 223.

Discharge from employment on ground of political views or conduct as affecting right to unemployment compensation. 29 ALR4th 287.

Alcoholism or intoxication as ground for discharge justifying denial of unemployment compensation. 64 ALR4th 1151.

§ 25-4-92. Appeals tribunals — Appointment; procedure; when decisions final.

(a) To hear and decide disputed claims the director shall appoint one or more impartial appeals tribunals, consisting in each instance of an officer or an employee of the department of industrial relations. No person shall participate in the hearing or disposition of any claim upon appeal thereof as an appeals tribunal, if he has an interest therein. At any such hearing all testimony shall be taken down, but need not be transcribed unless an appeal is applied for or taken.

(b) The manner in which disputed claims before appeals tribunals shall be presented and the conduct of hearings and appeals before appeals tribunals shall be in accordance with regulations prescribed by the director for determining the rights of the parties.

(c) The decision of an appeals tribunal shall become final 15 days after notice of such decision has been mailed, postage prepaid, to the claimant and other parties to the proceedings, at the addresses furnished, or, if none shall have been furnished, at their last known addresses, unless within that time application be made to the board of appeals for permission to appeal to the board of appeals. (Acts 1939, No. 497, p. 721; Code 1940, T. 26, § 218; Acts 1971, No. 1201, p. 2083, § 6; Acts 1971, No. 2325, p. 3748, § 6; Acts 1975, No. 801, p. 1604, § 11.)

Testimony part of public record. — Generally, §§ 25-4-92(a), 25-4-94(c) and 25-4-95 indicate that the record would have been transcribed and would have become part of the public record if defendant had appealed to the state circuit court the department of industrial relations' decision granting plaintiff unemployment compensation. Surely the Alabama legislature did not intend to bar an employer or an employee from obtaining such testimony because the losing party elected not to appeal. Thorne v. Big "D" Discount Auto Parts of Daleville, Inc., 92 F.R.D. 55 (M.D. Ala. 1981).

Particularity in pleading is not required as to appeals by employer of an award of unemployment compensation. This is just and fair because laymen, both employers and claimants, ordinarily represent themselves at this stage in unemployment compensation proceedings. Donaldson v. State Dep't of Indus. Relations, 439 So. 2d 1301 (Ala. Civ. App. 1983).

It has been held that, in case of an appeal to the circuit court from a determination by the board, all that need be stated is that the decision of the board of appeals is incorrect under the facts or the law. Donaldson v. State Dep't of Indus. Relations, 439 So. 2d 1301 (Ala. Civ. App. 1983).

Filing is not complete until notice is delivered and mere mailing is not enough. The mail is only an agent of the party involved and the chance of delay is always a contingency, the happening of which an applicant must assume. Haigler v. Department of Indus. Relations, 512 So. 2d 113 (Ala. Civ. App. 1987).

No good cause exception for late filing. — The appeal procedure is exclusive and Alabama's unemployment compensation law does not contain a good cause exception for late filing with the board of appeals base upon equity. Haigler v. Department of Indus. Relations, 512 So. 2d 113 (Ala. Civ. App. 1987).

Summary judgment in favor of department where application for leave to appeal not timely received. — Where claimant's application for leave to appeal to the board of appeals was not received by the board until after the time for filing such application had expired, and she then filed a complaint and notice of appeal in the circuit court, summary judgment was properly granted by the circuit court in favor of the department. Haigler v. Department of Indus. Relations, 512 So. 2d 113 (Ala. Civ. App. 1987).

Cited in Davis v. Black, 406 So. 2d 408 (Ala. Civ. App. 1981).

§ 25-4-93. Appeals tribunals — Power to affirm, modify or set aside decision; notification of parties.

Unless such appeal is withdrawn, an appeals tribunal, after affording the parties reasonable opportunity for fair hearing, shall affirm, modify or set aside the findings of fact and decision of the deputy. The parties shall be promptly notified in writing of such tribunal's decision, together with his reasons therefor. (Acts 1939, No. 497, p. 721; Code 1940, T. 26, § 217; Acts 1971, No. 1201, p. 2083, § 5; Acts 1971, No. 2325, p. 3748, § 5.)

Cited in Department of Indus. Relations v. Haynes, 259 Ala. 238, 67 So. 2d 62 (1953).

Collateral references. — 81 C.J.S., Social Security & Public Welfare, § 225.

§ 25-4-94. Powers and duties of board of appeals for Department of Industrial Relations.

(a) The board of appeals for the Department of Industrial Relations, created by Section 25-2-12, may, on its own motion at any time before a decision of an appeals tribunal becomes final, affirm, modify or set aside any such decision on the basis of the evidence previously submitted in such case, or direct the taking of additional evidence, or may permit any party in interest to initate an appeal to it. The board of appeals may remove to itself or transfer to another appeals tribunal the proceedings on any claim pending before an appeals tribunal. The board of appeals shall promptly notify in writing the parties to any proceedings of its findings and decision, together with the reasons therefor.

(b) Unless the application for appeal described in subsection (c) of Section 25-4-92 is granted by the board of appeals within 10 days after its filing with it, the applicant may, within the following 10 days, take an appeal from the decision of the appeals tribunal to the circuit court of the county of the residence of the claimant.

(c) The manner in which disputed claims before the board of appeals shall be presented and the conduct of hearing and appeals before it shall be in accordance with the regulations prescribed by the board of appeals for determining the rights of the parties. At any such hearing the parties shall be afforded a reasonable opportunity for fair hearing and all testimony shall be taken down or recorded but need not be transcribed except at the direction of the board of appeals in the exercise of its judgment and discretion. No person shall participate in the hearing or disposition of any claim as a member of the board if he has an interest therein.

(d) Any decision of the board of appeals, in the absence of an appeal therefrom as provided in this article, shall become final 10 days after the date notification thereof shall have been mailed, postage prepaid, to the parties to the proceeding, at their last known addresses. The director shall be deemed to be a party to all such proceedings and to any judicial action involving any such decision. (Acts 1939, No. 497, p. 721; Code 1940, T. 26, §§ 219, 220; Acts 1982, No. 82-372, p. 533, § 4.)

Appeal time periods not unconstitutionally vague and overbroad. — Statutory time periods for perfecting an appeal from the board of appeals of department of industrial relations to a circuit court are not unconstitutionally "vague and overbroad." Quick v. Utotem of Ala., Inc., 365 So. 2d 1245 (Ala. Civ. App. 1979).

Testimony part of public record. — Generally, §§ 25-4-92(a), 25-4-94(c) and 25-4-95 indicate that the record would have been transcribed and would have become part of the public record if defendant had appealed to the state circuit court the department of industrial relations' decision granting plaintiff unemployment compensation. Surely the Alabama legislature did not intend to bar an employer or an employee from obtaining such testimony because the losing party elected not to appeal.

Thorne v. Big "D" Discount Auto Parts of Daleville, Inc., 92 F.R.D. 55 (M.D. Ala. 1981).

Costs of an appeal to the circuit court under the provisions of this section are not a part of the costs of administering the unemployment compensation claims, and it is not error to tax costs against an unsuccessful claimant. Morrison v. Department of Indus. Relations, 35 Ala. App. 475, 48 So. 2d 72 (1950).

Cited in United States Steel Corp. v. Wood, 40 Ala. App. 431, 114 So. 2d 533 (1958); Crawley v. Carter, 378 So. 2d 1139 (Ala. Civ. App. 1979); Davis v. Black, 406 So. 2d 408 (Ala. Civ. App. 1981); Taylor v. Department of Indus. Relations, 409 So. 2d 447 (Ala. Civ. App. 1982); Payne v. Department of Indus. Relations, 423 So. 2d 231 (Ala. Civ. App. 1982); Donaldson v. State Dep't of Indus. Relations, 439 So. 2d 1301 (Ala. Civ. App. 1983).

§ 25-4-95. Appeals from final decisions of board of appeals or appeals tribunal.

Within 10 days after the decision of the board of appeals has become final, any party to the proceeding including the director who claims to be aggrieved by the decision may secure a judicial review thereof by filing a notice of appeal in the circuit court of the county of the residence of the claimant; except, that if the claimant does not reside in this state at the time the appeal is taken, the notice of appeal shall be filed in the circuit court of the county in this state in which the claimant last resided, or in the circuit court of the county in this state wherein the claimant last worked. In such action, the notice of appeal need not be verified, but shall state the grounds upon which a review is sought. A copy shall be served upon the director or upon such person as the director may designate (and for the purpose hereof, mailing a copy addressed to the director at Montgomery by registered or certified mail shall be deemed service on the director), and such service shall be deemed completed service on all parties, but there shall be left with the parties so served as many copies of the notice of appeal as there are defendants, and the director shall forthwith mail one copy to each defendant. The director shall cause to be certified and filed in the said court all documents and papers introduced in evidence before the board of appeals or appeals tribunal, together with the findings of fact and the decision of the board of appeals or the appeals tribunal, as the case may be. No circuit court shall permit an appeal from a decision allowing or disallowing a claim for benefits unless the decision sought to be reviewed is that of an appeals tribunal or of the board of appeals and unless the person filing such appeal has exhausted his administrative remedies as provided by this chapter. Trial in the circuit court shall be de novo. Actions under this chapter shall be tried by any judge of the circuit court to whom application is made at any location in said circuit, and shall be given precedence over all other civil cases except cases arising under Chapter 5 of this title. An appeal may be taken from the decision of the circuit court in the same manner as is provided in civil cases. It shall not be necessary in any judicial proceeding, under this section, to enter exceptions to the rulings of the board of appeals or the appeals tribunals, as the case may be, and no bond shall be required before entering such appeal. Upon the final determination of such judicial proceeding, the board of appeals shall enter an order in accordance with such determination. (Acts 1939, No. 497, p. 721; Code 1940, T. 26, § 221; Acts 1957, No. 298, p. 381.)

This section is the exclusive method for appeal of the decisions of the board of appeals to the circuit court. Davis v. Black, 406 So. 2d 408 (Ala. Civ. App. 1981).

This section preempted by AAPA. — Because § 41-22-25 provides that the Alabama Administrative Procedure Act (AAPA) shall take precedence over any other statute which diminishes the rights created by the AAPA, this section is preempted and the 30-day appeal deadline contained in § 41-22-20 should apply. Ex parte Varner, 571 So. 2d 1108 (Ala. 1990).

This section requires appeal to be filed within 10 days, and § 1-1-4 and A.R.C.P., Rule 6(a) provide a method for computing the 10 days. Taylor v. Department of Indus. Relations, 409 So. 2d 447 (Ala. Civ. App. 1982).

This section mandates that the notice of appeal be filed in the circuit court within 10 days after Department of Industrial Relations' decision becomes final, and that the notice be filed in the county in which the claimant resides. White v. Allen, 567 So. 2d 295 (Ala. Civ. App. 1989), rev'd on other grounds sub nom. Ex parte White, 567 So. 2d 300 (Ala. 1990).

Section construed liberally. — A narrow interpretation of this section, that which demands that the director be served with a notice of appeal within 10 days after the decision of the board of appeals becomes final, is contrary to the benevolent purpose of the Unemployment Compensation Act and the accompanying mandate for liberal construction and application of its provisions. Taylor v. Department of Indus. Relations, 409 So. 2d 447 (Ala. Civ. App. 1982).

Time period for appeal not unconstitutionally vague or overbroad. — Statutory time periods for perfecting an appeal from the board of appeals of department of industrial relations to a circuit court are not unconstitutionally "vague and overbroad." Quick v. Utotem of Ala., Inc., 365 So. 2d 1245 (Ala. Civ. App. 1979).

This statute clearly details the method to seek judicial review, i.e., who may appeal, where to appeal, and the time limitation imposed, which is within 10 days after the decision. White v. Allen, 594 So. 2d 129 (Ala. Civ. App. 1991).

This section means trial without a jury when it says that the actions shall be tried "by any judge of the circuit court." Ex parte Miles, 248 Ala. 386, 27 So. 2d 777 (1946).

And claimant not entitled to trial by jury. — Upon an appeal under this section to the circuit court, from an adverse decision of the board of appeals on claim for benefits, claimant is not entitled to a trial by jury of the controversy in the circuit court. Ex parte Miles, 248 Ala. 386, 27 So. 2d 777 (1946).

Requirements of this section are jurisdictional and failure to comply will necessitate dismissal of appeal. Director of State Dep't of Indus. Relations v. Nolin, 374 So. 2d 903 (Ala. Civ. App. 1979).

The requirements of this section are jurisdictional and require dismissal of an appeal when it is filed in the wrong county. Cruce v. Demarco Concrete & Block Co., 380 So. 2d 900 (Ala. Civ. App. 1980).

The requirements of this section are jurisdictional and failure to file in the proper county requires dismissal. Security Eng'rs, Inc. v. Anderson, 421 So. 2d 1298 (Ala. Civ. App. 1982).

The requirements of this section are jurisdictional and provide the exclusive method for appealing the decision of the board of appeals

to the circuit court. Payne v. Department of Indus. Relations, 423 So. 2d 231 (Ala. Civ. App. 1982).

Presumption that jurisdictional facts were shown. — Where record omitted various matters required to be filed by the director of industrial relations with the circuit court under this section, the court of appeals would presume from the judgment that the jurisdictional facts had been shown. United States Steel Corp. v. Wood, 40 Ala. App. 431, 114 So. 2d 533 (1958), rev'd on other grounds, 269 Ala. 5, 114 So. 2d 551 (1959).

Legislature may set reasonable and nondiscriminatory conditions concerning procedure. — Unemployment compensation is a creature of statute and was unknown at common law. Therefore, the legislature may lay down any reasonable and nondiscriminatory conditions it may see fit concerning eligibility and procedure. Director of State Dep't of Indus. Relations v. Nolin, 374 So. 2d 903 (Ala. Civ. App. 1979).

Timely filing of notice of appeal with director invokes jurisdiction of circuit court under this section. Failure to comply with other statutory procedural requirements does not affect the jurisdiction of the court to hear the appeal, but may be ground for sanctions including dismissal of the appeal. Crawley v. Carter, 378 So. 2d 1139 (Ala. Civ. App. 1979).

The employee's failure to serve the director of the Department of Industrial Relations with a copy of her complaint was a jurisdictional defect requiring the dismissal of her appeal. Craig v. Department of Indus. Relations, 470 So. 2d 1278 (Ala. Civ. App. 1985).

Timely filing of notice of appeal with circuit court clerk pursuant to this section invokes jurisdiction of circuit court; the failure to pay the filing fees initially or to obtain a waiver of such filing fee from the court may warrant sanctions, including dismissal of the appeal, at a later time, but when the notice of appeal is timely filed, the circuit court has jurisdiction of the appeal. Rubin v. Department of Indus. Relations, 469 So. 2d 657 (Ala. Civ. App. 1985).

This section does not require action on the part of a circuit clerk, sheriff, or any other court personnel, and the appealing party must bear the responsibility for serving the notice of appeal on the director. White v. Allen, 567 So. 2d 295 (Ala. Civ. App. 1989), rev'd on other grounds sub nom. Ex parte White, 567 So. 2d 300 (Ala. 1990).

Ten-day period does not apply for notice to director. — The notice of an appeal to the director need not be filed within the 10-day period provided for the filing of a notice of appeal since this section does not specify a time period for filing with the director, the law requires filing within a reasonable time. Eggleston v. Heatherly, 553 So. 2d 618 (Ala. Civ. App. 1989).

And reasonable time determination. — A reasonable time is to be determined by the judicial discretion of the trial judge in every case, keeping in mind the beneficent purpose of the unemployment statutes. Eggleston v. Heatherly, 553 So. 2d 618 (Ala. Civ. App. 1989).

Where the director was served by certified mail immediately after the judge granted the order of hardship, it was not unreasonable for the clerk to delay the expense of service upon the director until the order of hardship was granted and as a matter of law such delay was not unreasonable. Eggleston v. Heatherly, 553 So. 2d 618 (Ala. Civ. App. 1989).

Ten day period does not apply for appeals from denial of workers' compensation benefits. — The supreme court determined that an appeal from a decision denying a claim for unemployment compensation benefits is governed by the 30-day appeal deadline found in the Administrative Procedure Act, § 41-22-20, rather than the 10-day deadline previously applied to such appeals. White v. Allen, 594 So. 2d 129 (Ala. Civ. App. 1991).

Completion of administrative process gives court jurisdiction. — Completion of the administrative process in industrial relations board along with the notice of appeal, gives to the circuit court jurisdiction to try unemployment compensation case. State Dep't of Indus. Relations v. Page, 362 So. 2d 263 (Ala. Civ. App. 1978).

All documents must be certified to court. — Statute requiring exhaustion of administrative remedies prior to circuit court review of unemployment compensation claim requires that all documents and papers introduced into evidence before department of industrial relations board, as well as findings of fact and decision, be certified to the circuit court in order to establish that the administrative process has been completed. State Dep't of Indus. Relations v. Page, 362 So. 2d 263 (Ala. Civ. App. 1978).

Affidavit of substantial hardship. — When an unemployment compensation claimant timely presented a notice of appeal and affidavit of substantial hardship to the circuit court clerk, the case was deemed to have been filed, notwithstanding that the clerk failed to enter the case on the docket until the judge signed the affidavit. Rubin v. Department of Indus. Relations, 469 So. 2d 657 (Ala. Civ. App. 1985).

A final judgment in an unemployment compensation case is necessary to give the appellate courts of this state jurisdiction on appeal. Department of Indus. Relations v. Burgett, 336 So. 2d 1375 (Ala. Civ. App. 1976).

Particularity in pleading is not required as to appeals by employer of an award of unemployment compensation. This is just and fair because laymen, both employers and claimants, ordinarily represent themselves at this stage in unemployment compensation proceedings. Donaldson v. State Dep't of Indus. Relations, 439 So. 2d 1301 (Ala. Civ. App. 1983).

Designation of all interested parties as defendants not prerequisite. — Claimant's failure to designate as defendants all interested parties in his notice of appeal to circuit court is not prerequisite to the circuit court obtaining jurisdiction of the appeal and is not a requirement under this section. Crawley v. Carter, 378 So. 2d 1139 (Ala. Civ. App. 1979).

Appeal from board of appeals is for trial de novo. — An "appeal" from the board of appeals of the department of industrial relations to the circuit court is for a trial de novo. Davis v. Department of Indus. Relations, 465 So. 2d 1140 (Ala. Civ. App. 1984).

In a de novo proceeding the circuit court, rather than affirming or reversing the board of appeals, renders a new, distinct, and independent judgment as may be required by the merits of the case. Heatherly v. Carter, 485 So. 2d 769 (Ala. Civ. App. 1986).

As appeal is to a trial de novo, there is not a review on appeal, but in fact, another trial. Department of Indus. Relations v. Jaco, 337 So. 2d 374 (Ala. Civ. App. 1976); Security Eng'rs, Inc. v. Department of Indus. Relations, 414 So. 2d 975 (Ala. Civ. App. 1982).

On review by circuit court of decision made by board of appeals of department of industrial relations, circuit court does not affirm or reverse the board's decision, but rather, renders a new, distinct and independent judgment as may be required by the merits shown on the trial. State Dep't of Indus. Relations v. Page, 362 So. 2d 263 (Ala. Civ. App. 1978); Security Eng'rs, Inc. v. Department of Indus. Relations, 414 So. 2d 975 (Ala. Civ. App. 1982).

Claimant's appeal of administrative denial of her claim for unemployment benefits to the circuit court for a trial de novo vacated the decision made by the board of appeals of department of industrial relations. State Dep't of Indus. Relations v. Page, 362 So. 2d 263 (Ala. Civ. App. 1978).

All that need be stated in an appeal is that the decision of the board is incorrect under the facts or the law. Department of Indus. Relations v. Jaco, 337 So. 2d 374 (Ala. App. 1976).

It has been held that, in case of an appeal to

the circuit court from a determination by the board, all that need be stated is that the decision of the board of appeals is incorrect under the facts or the law. Donaldson v. State Dep't of Indus. Relations, 439 So. 2d 1301 (Ala. Civ. App. 1983).

Dismissal of appeal should not be granted for reasons of particularity in pleading. Department of Indus. Relations v. Jaco, 337 So. 2d 374 (Ala. Civ. App. 1976).

Court's findings presumed correct. — When an unemployment compensation case is heard orally before the court sitting without a jury, the court's findings are presumed correct unless shown to be clearly contrary to the great weight of the evidence. Steele v. Carter, 390 So. 2d 299 (Ala. Civ. App. 1980).

When an unemployment compensation case is tried orally before the court sitting without a jury, the court's findings are presumed correct and will not be reversed on appeal unless they are clearly contrary to the great weight of the evidence. Williams v. Department of Indus. Relations, 490 So. 2d 1246 (Ala. Civ. App. 1986).

Where the facts are undisputed, no presumption of correctness applies to the circuit court's findings. Heatherly v. Carter, 485 So. 2d 769 (Ala. Civ. App. 1986).

Testimony part of public record. — Generally, §§ 25-4-92(a), 25-4-94(c) and this section indicate that the record would have been transcribed and would have become part of the public record if defendant had appealed to the state circuit court the department of industrial relations' decision granting plaintiff unemployment compensation. Surely the Alabama legislature did not intend to bar an employer or an employee from obtaining such testimony because the losing party elected not to appeal.

Thorne v. Big "D" Discount Auto Parts of Daleville, Inc., 92 F.R.D. 55 (M.D. Ala. 1981).

Where the state department of industrial relations denied a claim under the Trade Act of 1974, 19 U.S.C.A. § 2271, this section governs the appropriate method of judicial review. James v. Ballard, 418 So. 2d 140 (Ala. Civ. App. 1982).

Cited in Ex parte Alabama Textile Prods. Corp., 242 Ala. 609, 7 So. 2d 303 (1942); Alabama Mills, Inc. v. Brand, 251 Ala. 643, 38 So. 2d 574 (1948); Henderson v. Department of Indus. Relations, 252 Ala. 239, 40 So. 2d 629 (1949); Department of Indus. Relations v. Haynes, 259 Ala. 238, 67 So. 2d 62 (1953); Ex parte Darnell, 262 Ala. 71, 76 So. 2d 770 (1954); Thompson v. Department of Indus. Relations, 48 Ala. App. 303, 264 So. 2d 528 (1972); Clary v. Central Foundry Co., 333 So. 2d 821 (Ala. Civ. App. 1975), modified, 333 So. 2d 824 (Ala. 1976); Ventress v. Batey, 333 So. 2d 584 (Ala. Civ. App. 1976); Reichhold Chem., Inc. v. McDaniel, 361 So. 2d 363 (Ala. Civ. App. 1978); Davis v. Prestwood, 381 So. 2d 85 (Ala. Civ. App. 1980); Payne v. Director of Dep't of Indus. Relations, 405 So. 2d 1322 (Ala. Civ. App. 1981); Fuller v. State, Dep't of Indus. Relations, 445 So. 2d 925 (Ala. Civ. App. 1984); Williams v. James, 446 So. 2d 631 (Ala. Civ. App. 1984); Johnson v. Director, Dep't of Indus. Relations, 470 So. 2d 1274 (Ala. Civ. App. 1985).

Collateral references. — 81 C.J.S., Social Security & Public Welfare, §§ 226-235.

Declaratory relief with respect to unemployment compensation. 14 ALR2d 826.

Alcoholism or intoxication as ground for discharge justifying denial of unemployment compensation. 64 ALR4th 1151.

§ 25-4-96. Procedure exclusive.

The procedure provided in this article for the making of determinations with respect to claims for unemployment compensation benefits and for appealing from such determinations shall be exclusive. (Acts 1939, No. 497, p. 721; Code 1940, T. 26, § 222.)

Procedure confined to article. — Under the provisions of this section the procedure for making claims in unemployment compensation cases is confined to the statutes included in this article of this title. Ex parte Miles, 248 Ala. 386, 27 So. 2d 777 (1946), holding that the legislature had authority to so restrict or limit the procedure.

Procedure for pursuing unemployment compensation claim is completely governed by statute. Director of State Dep't of Indus. Rela-

tions v. Nolin, 374 So. 2d 903 (Ala. Civ. App. 1979).

Cited in Ventress v. Batey, 333 So. 2d 584 (Ala. App. 1976); Quick v. Utotem of Ala., Inc., 365 So. 2d 1245 (Ala. Civ. App. 1979); Taylor v. Department of Indus. Relations, 409 So. 2d 447 (Ala. Civ. App. 1982); Johnson v. Gary, 443 So. 2d 924 (Ala. 1983); Haigler v. Department of Indus. Relations, 512 So. 2d 113 (Ala. Civ. App. 1987).

§ 25-4-97. Powers of appeals tribunal, board of appeals and officers of Department of Industrial Relations as to witnesses; witness fees.

In the discharge of their duties under this chapter any deputy, any appeals tribunal, any member of the board of appeals and any officer of the Department of Industrial Relations authorized and designated by the director shall have power to administer oaths, certify to official acts, take and cause to be taken depositions of witnesses, issue and serve subpoenas, compel the attendance of witnesses and the production of papers, books, accounts, payrolls, documents, records and testimony. In the event of failure of any person to comply with any subpoena lawfully issued, or on the refusal of any witness to produce evidence or to testify as to any matter regarding which he may be lawfully interrogated, it shall be the duty of any court of competent jurisdiction or of the judge thereof, upon the application of the director or any officer of the Department of Industrial Relations designated by the director, or any member of the board of appeals, to compel obedience by attachment proceedings for contempt as in the case of disobedience of the requirements of a subpoena issued for such court or a refusal to testify therein. Witness fees and other expenses involved in the proceedings under this article shall be paid to the extent necessary at rates specified by the director. Such expenses shall be deemed a part of the expense of administering this chapter. (Acts 1939, No. 497, p. 721; Code 1940, T. 26, § 223; Acts 1945, No. 283, p. 449.)

Cited in Quick v. Utotem of Ala., Inc., 365 So. 2d 1245 (Ala. Civ. App. 1979).

Collateral references. — Propriety of telephone testimony or hearings in unemployment compensation proceedings. 90 ALR4th 532.

ARTICLE 6.

ADMINISTRATION.

Collateral references. — Discharge from employment on ground of political views or conduct as affecting right to unemployment compensation. 29 ALR4th 287.

Eligibility for unemployment compensation benefits of employee who attempts to withdraw resignation before leaving employment. 36 ALR4th 395.

§ 25-4-110. Powers and duties of director as to administration of chapter generally.

It shall be the duty of the director to administer this chapter. He shall have power and authority to adopt, amend or rescind such lawful rules and regulations, to employ such persons, make such expenditures, require such reports, make such investigations and take such other action as may be necessary or suitable to that end. The director shall determine his own organization and methods of procedure in accordance with the provisions of this chapter and the industrial relations law. Annually, the director shall submit to the Governor a summary report covering the administration and operation of this chapter during the preceding fiscal year, and make such recommendations as he deems proper. Whenever the director believes that a change in contribution or benefit rates will become necessary to protect the solvency of the fund, he shall at once inform the Governor and the legislature thereof, and make recommendations accordingly. The director shall fully cooperate with the agencies of other states, and shall make every proper effort within his means to oppose and prevent any action which would in his judgment tend to effect complete or substantial federalization of state unemployment compensation funds or of the state employment security program. (Acts 1939, No. 497, p. 721; Code 1940, T. 26, § 227; Acts 1943, No. 310, p. 281, § 12.)

Collateral references. — 73 C.J.S., Public Administrative Bodies & Procedure, §§ 48-113.

§ 25-4-111. Adoption, etc., of general rules and regulations.

General rules interpreting or applying this chapter and affecting all, or classes of, employers, or other employing units, shall be adopted by the director only after a public hearing thereon, notice of which shall be published at least once, not less than 10 days prior thereto in daily newspapers published in Montgomery, Birmingham and Mobile, Alabama, and in such other newspaper or newspapers as the director may prescribe. Prior to such hearing the director shall furnish to any person upon his application therefor a copy of the proposed general rules to be considered at the hearing. Such general rules shall, upon adoption by the director, be filed with the secretary of state and, subject to the provisions of Section 25-4-112, shall take legal effect 10 days thereafter, unless a later date is specified by the director, which rules may be amended or repealed in the same manner as is above provided for their adoption. The director shall by general rule prescribe the manner in which regulations may be adopted, amended or rescinded. (Acts 1939, No. 497, p. 721; Code 1940, T. 26, § 228.)

Collateral references. — 73 C.J.S., Public Administrative Bodies & Procedure, § 99.

§ 25-4-112. Publication and distribution of general rules and regulations, etc.

The director shall cause to be printed in proper form for distribution to the public the text of this chapter, general rules, his annual report to the governor and any other material he deems relevant and suitable, and shall furnish the same to any person upon application therefor, and such printing and availability upon application shall be deemed a sufficient publication of the same. Copies of all general rules and regulations, as and when adopted, amended or repealed, shall be forwarded by the director to all employers subject to this chapter, who request in writing that they be placed on the mailing list therefor. Such rules and regulations shall in no event become effective until after the requirements of this section have been complied with. (Acts 1939, No. 497, p. 721; Code 1940, T. 26, § 229.)

Collateral references. — 73 C.J.S., Public
Administrative Bodies & Procedure, § 101.

§ 25-4-113. Employees; immunity from civil suit; exception.

The director shall, with the approval of the Governor, determine the number of employees needed for the efficient and economical performance of the functions and duties of administering this chapter. All positions in the administration of this chapter shall be filled subject to the provisions of the merit system. The minimum standards that may be prescribed by the United States Secretary of Labor or his successor with respect to the selection and classification of officers and employees engaged in the performance of any of the functions and duties of the Department of Industrial Relations having to do with the administration of this chapter in this state shall be observed. The director shall fix the duties and powers of all persons thus employed, and may authorize any such person to do any act or acts which could lawfully be done by the director. The director, his employees and members of the board of appeals shall be immune from civil suits for damages in their individual capacities for acts in the performance of their duties under this chapter other than for wanton or malicious conduct. (Acts 1939, No. 497, p. 721; Code 1940, T. 26, § 230; Acts 1980, No. 80-756, p. 1561, § 4.)

Cross references. — As to merit system,
see § 36-26-1 et seq.

§ 25-4-114. Advisory council.

The Governor shall appoint an advisory council of not less than nine members, composed of equal numbers of employer representatives and employee representatives, who may be fairly regarded as representative because of their vocation, employment or affiliations, and of members representing the public generally. Such council shall aid the director in formulating policies and discussing problems related to the administration of this chapter, and in assuring impartiality and freedom from political influence in the solution of such problems, and shall perform such other duties and functions as may be assigned to it by the director, and as it may, on its own initiative, undertake within the limits of this section. Such advisory council shall serve at the pleasure of the Governor, and without compensation, but shall be reimbursed for any necessary expenses pursuant to Article 2 of Chapter 7 of Title 36. Said council shall from time to time prepare recommendations as to the administration of this chapter, and as to changes, amendments or modifications of such acts and laws of the State of Alabama, and particularly this chapter, as such council may deem proper, and said recommendations shall be submitted to the Governor and to the legislature at its next session and at such succeeding sessions. (Acts 1939, No. 497, p. 721; Code 1940, T. 26, § 231.)

§ 25-4-115. Duties of director, etc., with respect to reduction of unemployment, etc.

It shall be one of the purposes of this chapter to promote the regularization of employment in enterprises, localities, industries and the state. The director, with the advice and aid of the advisory council, shall take all appropriate steps within his means to reduce and prevent unemployment; to encourage and assist in the adoption of practical methods of vocational training, retraining and vocational guidance; to investigate, recommend, advise and assist in the establishment and operation, by municipalities, counties, school districts and the state, of reserves for public works to be used in times of business depression and unemployment; to promote the reemployment of unemployed workers throughout the state in every other way that may be feasible; and, to these ends, to employ experts and to carry on and publish the results of investigations and research studies. (Acts 1939, No. 497, p. 721; Code 1940, T. 26, § 232.)

§ 25-4-116. Records and reports of employing units.

Every employing unit shall keep true and accurate work records containing such information as is necessary for the administration of this chapter. Such records shall be open to inspection and be subject to being copied by the director or his authorized representatives at any reasonable time and as often as may be necessary. The director, an appeals tribunal, any member of the board of appeals created by the industrial relations law or any authorized representative of the director may require from such employer or employing unit such reports covering persons employed by him or it, or employment, wages, hours, unemployment and related matters as are necessary to the effective administration of this chapter. Information thus obtained shall be held confidential, except to the extent necessary for the proper presentation of the contest of a claim, and shall not be published or be open to public inspection in any manner revealing the employers' or employing units' identity. Any person violating any provision of this section shall be fined not less than $20.00 nor more than $200.00 or imprisoned for not longer than 30 days or both. All letters, reports, communications and other matters, written or oral, from employer or employee to each other or to the director or any of his agents, representatives or employees, or to any official or board functioning under this chapter, which shall have been written, sent, delivered or made in connection with the requirements and administration of this chapter, shall be absolutely privileged and shall not be made the subject matter or basis for any civil action for slander or libel in any court. The director may cause to be made such summaries, compilations, photographs, duplications or reproductions of any records, reports or transcripts thereof or cancelled benefit payment checks as he may deem advisable for the effective and economical preservation of the information contained therein, and such summaries, compilations, photographs, duplications or reproductions, duly authenticated, shall be admissible in any proceeding under this chapter if the original record or records would have been admissible therein. The director may provide by regulations for the destruction or disposition, after reasonable periods, of any records, reports, transcripts or reproductions thereof or other papers in his custody, the preservation of which is no longer necessary for the establishment of contribution liability or benefit rights or for any purpose necessary for the proper administration of this chapter, including any required audit thereof. (Acts 1939, No. 497, p. 721; Code 1940, T. 26, § 233; Acts 1943, No. 310, p. 281, § 13.)

Scope of section. — This section lists several groups of documentary evidence designated as confidential. These groups include work records from the employer, reports on employment, wages, and hours required by the department of industrial relations, and all letters, reports, or communications between employer and employee to each other or the department. Although this section includes "written or oral" communications in this last group, the records and other communications appear to be those collected for the purpose of supervising the unemployment compensation program or preparing for a hearing on a disputed claim. Neither category would include the record of the testimonial evidence given at the hearing on the claim. Thorne v. Big "D" Discount Auto Parts of Daleville, Inc., 92 F.R.D. 55 (M.D. Ala. 1981).

Cited in United States v. Blasi, 462 F. Supp. 373 (M.D. Ala. 1979); Cole v. Cooper, 437 So. 2d 1257 (Ala. 1983); Dixon v. Economy Co., 477 So. 2d 353 (Ala. 1985).

Collateral references. — Statutory provisions requiring filing of payroll report or other statistics for purposes of unemployment insurance. 174 ALR 410.

§ 25-4-117. Representation in court actions.

The director and the state, in any court action relating to this chapter or its administration and enforcement, shall be represented by any qualified attorney regularly employed by the Department of Industrial Relations, and who is designated by the director for such purpose; provided, however, that the director may request the Attorney General or such special counsel as he deems necessary to represent him in any such action. (Acts 1939, No. 497, p. 721; Code 1940, T. 26, § 234.)

§ 25-4-118. Cooperation with state and federal agencies, institutions of higher education, public and law enforcement officials, etc.; penalty for wrongfully securing or misusing information.

(a) In the administration of this chapter, the director shall cooperate to the fullest extent consistent with the provisions of this chapter with the U.S. Secretary of Labor and his successors, and the Federal Internal Revenue Service, and, notwithstanding any other provisions of this chapter, shall make such reports in such form and containing such information as either may from time to time require, and shall comply with such provisions as the U.S. Secretary of Labor, or his successors, or the Federal Internal Revenue Service may from time to time find necessary to insure the correctness and verification of such reports, and shall comply with the regulations prescribed by the U.S. Secretary of Labor, and his successors, governing the expenditures of such sums as may be allotted and paid to this state under Title III of the Social Security Act for the purpose of assisting in the administration of this chapter. Upon request therefor the director shall furnish to any agency of the United States charged with the administration of public works or assistance through public employment, the name, address, ordinary occupation and employment status of each recipient of benefits and such recipient's rights to further benefits under this chapter.

(b)(1) The director may make the state's records relating to the administration of this chapter available to the United States Railroad Retirement Board and may furnish the railroad retirement board, at the expense of such board, such copies thereof as the railroad retirement board deems necessary for its purposes. Notwithstanding any other provisions of this chapter, the director may also, upon request therefor, furnish to any public agency the name, address, ordinary occupation, unemployment status and wage information of a recipient of benefits or of a recipient's rights to further benefits under this chapter and shall upon specific request furnish such information as is necessary (as determined by the U.S. Secretary of Agriculture or the U.S. Secretary of Health, Education and Welfare or their successors in regulations) for the purpose of determining eligibility of an individual for aid or services, or such information regarding any recipient of or party to such aid or services, or the amount of such aid or services, to needy families with children, or in connection with child support or food stamps provided such agencies make reimbursement for the administrative cost involved.

(2) For the purpose of establishing and maintaining free public employment offices, the director is authorized to enter into agreements with the United States Railroad Retirement Board or any other agency of the United States, with any political subdivision of this state or with any private nonprofit organization, and as a part of such arrangement the director may accept moneys, services or quarters as a contribution to the employment service account.

(3) Moneys received from the United States Railroad Retirement Board as compensation for service or facilities supplied to said board shall be paid into the unemployment compensation administration fund and the employment service fund on the same basis as expenditures are made for such services or facilities from such funds.

(c) The director may afford reasonable cooperation with any agency of the United States charged with the administration of any unemployment insurance law.

(d) The director may, at his discretion, release information regarding employment, wages, wage rates and unemployment to institutions of higher education of this state, or a federal governmental corporation upon payment of reasonable cost therefor, for the purpose of making economic analyses; provided, that such institution or corporation agrees that information so obtained will not be published or released by it to any person or persons in such manner as to permit the identification of any specific individual or employing unit.

(e) The director may release any information authorized to be released under the provision of subsection (b) of this section to any public or law enforcement official as may be necessary for the performance of his official duties in accordance with such regulations as the director may prescribe and subject to the provision of subsection (f) of this section.

(f) Whoever willfully makes a false statement or representation to obtain any information under the authority of subsection (e) of this section, either for himself or for any other person, or uses any information for any purpose other than in the performance of his official duties or in any other manner misuses such information, shall be guilty of a misdemeanor and upon conviction therefor, shall be punished by a fine of not less than $200.00 nor more than $1,000.00, or by imprisonment for not less than three nor more than 12 months or by both such fine and imprisonment. (Acts 1939, No. 497, p. 721; Code 1940, T. 26, § 235; Acts 1967, No. 170, p. 528; Acts 1980, No. 80-756, p. 1561, § 5; Acts 1982, No. 82-372, p. 533, § 5.)

U.S. Code. — Title III of the Social Security Act is codified as 42 U.S.C.A. § 501 et seq.

Cited in Steward Mach. Co. v. Davis, 301 U.S. 548, 57 S. Ct. 883, 81 L. Ed. 1279 (1937); United States v. Blasi, 462 F. Supp. 373 (M.D. Ala. 1979).

Collateral references. — Construction and application of state unemployment compensation act as affected by terms of the federal act or judicial or administrative rulings thereunder. 139 ALR 892.

§ 25-4-119. Compromise or waiver of civil penalties or interest charges.

The director may compromise or waive any civil penalty or interest charge arising under the provisions of this chapter instead of commencing a civil action thereon and may compromise any such penalty or interest charge after a civil action thereon has been commenced. In such cases the director shall keep on file in the office of the Department of Industrial Relations at Montgomery, Alabama, the reasons for settlement by compromise, together with a statement of the amount of contribution imposed, the amount of additional contribution or penalty or interest imposed by law in consequence of neglect or delinquency and the amount actually paid in accordance with the terms of the compromise. (Acts 1939, No. 497, p. 721; Code 1940, T. 26, § 236.)

Collateral references. — 73 C.J.S., Public Administrative Bodies & Procedure, § 52.

§ 25-4-120. Reciprocal arrangements with state and federal agencies.

(a) *Interstate benefit payments.* — The director is hereby authorized to enter into reciprocal arrangements with appropriate and duly authorized agencies of other states or of the federal government, or both, whereby potential rights to benefits under this chapter may constitute the basis for payment of benefits by another state or the federal government, and potential rights to benefits accumulated under the law of another state or the federal government may constitute the basis for the payment of benefits by this state. Such benefits shall be paid under such provisions of the law of the state wherein the wages, upon the basis of which such benefits are determined, were issued. No such arrangement shall be entered into unless it contains provision for reimbursement to the fund for such benefits as are paid on the basis of wages and service subject to the law of another state or the federal government, and provision for reimbursement from the fund for such benefits as are paid by another state or the federal government on the basis of wages and service subject to this chapter. Reimbursements paid from the fund pursuant to this subsection shall be deemed to be benefits for the purposes of this chapter.

(b) *Combination of wage credits.* — The director shall participate in any arrangements for the payment of compensation on the basis of combining an individual's wages and employment covered under this chapter with his wages and employment covered under the unemployment compensation laws of other states, which are approved by the United States Secretary of Labor in consultation with the state unemployment compensation agencies as reasonably calculated to assure the prompt and full payment of compensation in such situations, and which include provisions for

(1) Applying the base period of a single state law to a claim involving the combining of an individual's wage and employment covered under two or more state unemployment compensation laws, and

(2) Avoiding the duplicate use of wages and employment by reason of such combining.

(c) *Reciprocal coverage.* — The director is hereby authorized to enter into reciprocal arrangements with appropriate and duly authorized agencies of other states or of the federal government or both, whereby, notwithstanding any other provisions of this chapter:

(1) Service performed by an individual for a single employing unit for which service is customarily performed by such individual in more than one state shall be deemed to be service performed entirely within any one of the states in which

a. Any part of such individual's service is performed, or

b. Such individual has his residence, or

c. The employing unit maintains a place of business; provided, that there is in effect, as to such service an approved election by an employing unit with the consent of such individual, pursuant to which service performed by such individual for such employing unit is deemed to be performed entirely within such state; and

(2) Service performed by not more than three individuals, on any portion of a day but not necessarily simultaneously, for a single employing unit which customarily operates in more than one state shall be deemed to be service performed entirely within the state in which such employing unit maintains the headquarters of its business; provided, that there is in effect, as to such service, an approved election by an employing unit with the

consent of each such individual, pursuant to which service performed by such individual for such employing unit is deemed to be performed entirely within such state.

(d) *Reexamination of reciprocal arrangements.* — If, after entering into an arrangement provided for by this section, the director finds that the employment security law of any state or of the federal government participating in such arrangement has been changed in a material respect, the director shall make a new finding as to whether such arrangement shall be continued with such state or with the federal government. (Acts 1939, No. 497, p. 721; Code 1940, T. 26, § 237; Acts 1949, No. 287, p. 414; Acts 1971, No. 88, p. 349, § 12.)

Collateral references. — 81 C.J.S., States, § 10.

ARTICLE 7.

GENERAL PROVISIONS.

Collateral references. — Eligibility for unemployment compensation benefits of employee who attempts to withdraw resignation before leaving employment. 36 ALR4th 395.

§ 25-4-130. Duration of employer's coverage under this chapter; termination of coverage.

(a) Except as otherwise provided in subsection (b) of this section, any employing unit which is or becomes an employer subject to this chapter within any calendar year, shall be an employer subject thereto during the whole of such calendar year.

(b) Except as otherwise provided in Section 25-4-131, an employer (except governmental entities) shall cease to be an employer subject to this chapter:

(1) As of January 1 of any calendar year if he files with the director, prior to April 1 of such year, a written application for termination of coverage and he has not, during the preceding calendar year, met any of the conditions for remaining subject to this chapter.

(2)a. As of the date of transfer of his organization, trade or business, or substantially all the assets thereof to a successor as provided by paragraph (a)(4)a of Section 25-4-8; provided, that he shall have ceased to employ any individual or individuals in employment subject to this chapter; provided further, however, should the disposing employer reacquire all or substantially all of the same employing unit during the same or next succeeding calendar year without the predecessor having employed individuals, thereby succeeding to the employment experience, he shall be deemed not to have ceased operation and shall have his rate of contribution computed based upon that portion of his and his successor's employment experience occurring during the period specified in Section 25-4-54.

b. If, immediately subsequent to the date of transfer of his organization, trade or business, or substantially all the assets thereof to a successor as provided by paragraph (a)(4)a of Section 25-4-8, he shall cease to be an employer subject to this chapter as of the date of such transfer. If, however, subsequent to the date of transfer, he employs or continues to employ any individual or individuals he shall again become an employer subject to this chapter when any of the provisions of Section 25-4-8 are met and shall be considered an employer first becoming subject for the purposes of Sections 25-4-16 and 25-4-54.

(3) As of January 1, next following two consecutive calendar years ending on the preceding December 31, during which he employed no individuals in employment subject to this chapter.

(c) Any political subdivision which has made an election may, prior to January 1, 1978, terminate said election after the two-year period called for in subsection (b) of Section 25-4-131 has been completed by filing with the director written notice not later than the December 1, of any calendar year, such termination to be effective as of the first day of the next ensuing calendar year with respect to services performed on and after that date.

(d) When an employer's coverage is terminated under the provisions of this section, such employer shall not, except as otherwise provided in this section, thereafter become subject to the provisions of this chapter on the basis of any employment by such employer prior to the effective date of such termination. (Acts 1939, No. 497, p. 721; Code 1940, T. 26, § 224; Acts 1943, No. 310, p. 281, § 10; Acts 1951, No. 642, p. 1097; Acts 1955, No. 30, p. 249; Acts 1965, No. 390, p. 548, § 6; Acts 1971, No. 166, p. 440, § 13; Acts 1975, No. 801, p. 1604, § 12; Acts 1978, 1st Ex. Sess., No. 1, p. 5, § 9; Acts 1983, 2nd Sess., No. 83-155, p. 264, § 14.)

Collateral references. — 81 C.J.S., Social Security & Public Welfare, § 111.

§ 25-4-131. Election of coverage under chapter by employing units and political subdivisions.

(a) Any employing unit (except one whose employment is specifically exempt under the provisions of subsection (b) of Section 25-4-10) not otherwise subject to this chapter which files with the director its written election to become an employer subject hereto for not less than two calendar years shall, with the written approval of such election by the director, become an employer subject hereto to the same extent as all other employers as of the date stated in such approval.

(b) Prior to January 1, 1978, any political subdivision of this state may elect at the beginning of any calendar quarter beginning on or after January 1, 1972, for a period of not less than two calendar years, to cover under this chapter service performed by employees in all of the hospitals and institutions of higher education, as defined in subsections (c) and (e) of Section 25-4-10, operated by such political subdivision. Election is to be made by filing with the director a notice of such election at least 30 days prior to the effective date of such election. (Acts 1939, No. 497, p. 721; Code 1940, T. 26, § 225; Acts 1943, No. 310, p. 281, § 11; Acts 1945, No. 283, p. 449, § 11; Acts 1955, No. 30, p. 249; Acts 1965, No. 390, p. 548, § 7; Acts 1971, No. 166, p. 440, § 14; Acts 1978, 1st Ex. Sess., No. 1, p. 5, § 10.)

Collateral references. — 81 C.J.S., Social Security & Public Welfare, § 108.
Election to be subject to unemployment compensation act by employer otherwise not within act. 158 ALR 601.

§ 25-4-132. Assessment of interest on delinquent contribution payments.

Contributions unpaid on the date when they are due and payable, as provided in this chapter, or as may be provided by rules or regulations in this chapter, shall bear interest at the rate of one percent per month from and after such date until payment is received by the director. (Acts 1939, No. 497, p. 721; Code 1940, T. 26, § 238.)

Cited in Opinion of Justices, 252 Ala. 468, 41 So. 2d 771 (1949).

§ 25-4-133. Penalties for delinquent contribution payments and reports.

(a) Any employer without good cause failing to pay any contribution within the time required by this chapter or the rules and regulations of the director shall be required by the director to pay, in addition thereto, a penalty of 10 percent of the amount thereof, together with interest on said contributions at the rate prescribed in Section 25-4-132. If the failure to pay on the part of the employer is due to fraud, an additional penalty of 15 percent shall be assessed against, and collected from, such defaulting employer.

(b) Any employer without good cause failing to file any quarterly wage and contribution report within the time required by this chapter or the rules and regulations of the director shall be required by the director to pay a penalty of $5.00 for his or its failure to file such report when due. Such penalty shall be in addition to any penalty assessed under the provisions of subsection (a) of this section and shall apply for each report's due date separately. (Acts 1939, No. 497, p. 721; Code 1940, T. 26, § 239; Acts 1973, No. 1057, p. 1716, § 8.)

Cited in Opinion of Justices, 252 Ala. 468, 41 So. 2d 771 (1949).

Collateral references. — 81 C.J.S., Social Security & Public Welfare, § 252.

§ 25-4-134. Procedures for collection of delinquent contribution payments.

(a) *Generally.* — The contributions, interest and penalties required to be paid under this chapter shall be a first and prior lien upon all property and rights to property, real or personal, of any employer subject to this chapter. The lien shall arise at the time the contribution report, or the payment of the contributions, as the case may be, was due to have been filed with or made to the Department of Industrial Relations. The director may file in the office of the judge of probate of any county in this state a certificate which shall show the name of the department for which it is filed, the amount and nature of the contributions, interest and penalties for which a lien is claimed together with any costs that may have accrued, the name of the employer against whose property a lien for such contributions, interest and penalties is claimed and the date thereof. An error in the certificate of the amount shall not invalidate the lien for the amount actually due. Such certificates shall be indexed and recorded under the same provision of law of this state relating to the filing and recording of certificates of judgment and without costs; provided, however, that such lien shall be effective as to purchasers, mortgagees and judgment creditors only from the time a certificate shall have been duly filed for record in the office of the judge of probate in the county wherein is located the property to be subjected to such lien.

(b) *Civil actions.*

(1) LIEN. — The director shall insure the payment of the amount of any contributions, interest and penalties required to be paid under this chapter by filing a lien as prescribed in subsection (a) of this section against any employer who has not made such payments by the due date.

(2) ATTACHMENT, ETC. — If, after due notice, an employer defaults in the payment of contributions, interest or penalties provided by this chapter, the amount due may be collected by civil suit in the name of the director, which shall include the right of attachment. Civil actions brought under this section to collect contributions, interest and penalties thereon from an employer shall be heard by the court at the earliest possible date, and shall be entitled to preference upon the calendar of the court over all other civil actions, except cases arising under Chapter 5 of this title and Article 5 of this chapter. In addition to or independently of the above remedy by civil action, the director may proceed in the manner set out hereinafter.

(3) INJUNCTION AGAINST EMPLOYMENT. — After due notice an employer failing to make reports or defaulting in any payment of contribution or interest thereon, as levied under this chapter, for a period of 90 days after the date such reports or contributions are due, and who has not ceased to be an employer, as provided in Sections 25-4-130 and 25-4-131, may be enjoined from employing individuals in employment, as defined in this chapter, upon the complaint of the director filed in the circuit court of any county in which the employer has his or its headquarters or his or its primary place of doing business; and such employer so failing to make

reports or to pay contributions levied hereunder shall, as part of the court judgment or order, be enjoined from employing individuals in employment until such returns shall have been made and the contributions shown by any proceedings provided by this chapter to be due thereunder shall have been paid to the director.

(4) GARNISHMENT. — The director shall have authority to issue writs of garnishment directed to any sheriff of Alabama on any final assessment made by the director and upon such garnishment the sheriff shall proceed the same as though the garnishment was issued by a circuit court, and he shall make due return thereof to the director within 60 days after the issuance thereof.

(5) LEVY UPON EXECUTION. — Whenever any contributions, interest and penalties required to be paid under this chapter are not paid within 30 days of the date due and upon final assessment in any of the manners provided in this section, the director is authorized to issue an execution therefor directed to any sheriff of the State of Alabama, commanding him to levy upon and sell the real and personal property of the employer against whom such execution is directed, found in his county, for the payment of contributions and interest due, together with penalties assessed. The sheriff shall, within five days after the receipt thereof, file with the clerk of the circuit court of his county a copy thereof and thereupon the circuit clerk shall enter in the judgment roll in the column of judgment debtors the name of the employer named in the execution, the amount of contributions, interest and penalties for which the execution is issued and the date when such copy is filed. The sheriff shall thereupon levy upon any property of the employer with like effect and in the manner prescribed by law in respect to executions issued upon judgments of the circuit court and the remedies of attachment and garnishment shall apply fully to such executions and the officer shall be entitled to the same fees for his services as now allowed by law for like services, to be collected in the same manner as now provided by law for like services. The sheriff shall make due return of such execution within 60 days of the issuance thereof to the director and upon such return alias executions may be issued by the director and such shall be executed in the same manner. Whenever any execution is issued by the Department of Industrial Relations for the collection of any unemployment compensation taxes owing said department by an employer, such execution, duly attested by the director of said department or his authorized agent, shall be sufficient warrant to the sheriff to whom the same is directed to levy on the property of the employer against whom said execution is directed and the sheriff shall forthwith execute such writ without demanding or requiring any indemnifying bond or other protective obligation, and the said writ of execution issued by the department for the collection of unemployment taxes due it shall be sufficient defense to any civil action for damages on any grounds other than the willful, wanton or malicious conduct of the officer making the levy. Sales under executions issued hereunder shall be held as provided by the laws of Alabama. At any such sale the director or

his authorized agent shall be empowered to act on behalf of the State of Alabama in bidding at any such sale.

(c) *Assessments.*

(1) ASSESSMENT OF CONTRIBUTIONS AND PENALTIES DUE.

a. If an employer fails to make and file with the department any report as and when required by the terms and provisions of this chapter or by any rule and regulation of the director for the purpose of determining the amount of contributions due by said employer under this chapter, the director may issue a written notice by registered or certified mail to such employer, addressed to his last known address or place of business, to make such report or reports forthwith, and if such employer fails or refuses to make such report within 15 days from the date of such notice, then the director shall make a report for such employer upon such information as he may reasonably obtain, and shall assess the contributions and penalties due thereon and interest at the rate of one percent per month, or fraction thereof, from the date such contributions were due.

b. If an employer who has made and filed with the department any report required and such report is signed by the employer or his duly authorized representative but he has not paid, or has not paid in the correct amount, any contribution due within 30 days from the date due, then the director shall assess the correct amount of contributions due to be paid, along with penalties due thereon and interest at the rate of one percent per month, or fraction thereof, from the date such contributions were due, without any further notice or hearing as is provided for in subdivision (2) of this subsection (c) and such assessment shall be final unless an appeal is taken as is provided in subdivision (3) of this subsection (c).

c. If any report which is filed is deemed by the director to be incorrect, incomplete or insufficient, the director may issue a written notice by registered or certified mail to such employer, addressed to his last known address or place of business, to make such report correct, complete or sufficient forthwith, and if such employer fails or refuses to do so within 15 days from the date of such notice, then the director shall make such corrections or completions upon such information as he may reasonably obtain and shall, without further notice or hearing, assess the contribution and penalties due thereon and interest at the rate of one percent per month or fraction thereof from the date such contributions were due and such assessment shall be final unless an appeal is taken as is provided in subdivision (3) of this subsection (c).

(2) NOTICE OF ASSESSMENT AND HEARING: REVISION OF ASSESSMENT.

a. Whenever the director shall make an assessment against an employer as provided in this section, the director shall notify the employer by registered or certified mail of the amount of such assessment and shall notify the employer to appear before him on a day named not less than 15 days from the date of such notice and show cause why such assessment should not be made final. Such appearance may be made by agent or attorney. If no showing is made on or before the date fixed in said notice or if such showing is not sufficient in the judgment of the director, such assessment shall be made final in the amount originally fixed or in such other amount as is determined by the director to be correct. If, upon such hearing, the director finds the amount due to be different from that originally assessed, he shall make the assessment final in the correct amount and in all cases shall notify the employer of the assessment as finally fixed. A notice by the United States registered or certified mail addressed to the employer's last known address or place of business shall be sufficient. Any assessment made by the director shall be prima facie correct upon appeal.

b. If, after the assessment has become final, the employer files the report for the period covered by the assessment and the report is substantiated by reasonable evidence, the director may, for good cause and at his discretion correct the assessment, either upward or downward, provided the report and substantiation is filed with him not later than four years after the date on which the report originally became due.

(3) APPEAL FROM ASSESSMENTS.

a. Whenever any employer who has duly appeared and protested an assessment by the director under the provisions of paragraph a. of subdivision (2) of this subsection (c), is dissatisfied with the assessment as finally made, he may appeal as provided in this subdivision; provided, however, that no appeal shall lie in cases where the employer has failed to appear and protest.

b. If an employer against whom an assessment is made by the director is dissatisfied with the final assessment as fixed by the director under any of the provisions of subdivision (1) of this subsection (c) and duly protests the fixing of the same, he may appeal from said final assessment to the circuit court of Montgomery County, or to the circuit court of the county in which the employer resides or has his principal place of business, if the employer has within the state a permanent residence, at the option of the employer, by filing notice of appeal with the director and with the register of the circuit court of the county to which appeal shall be taken, within 30 days of the date of the final assessment made and entered on the minutes of the department, and in addition thereto by giving bond conditioned to pay all costs, to be filed with and approved by the register or clerk of the court to which the appeal shall be taken. The employer shall pay the assessment so made before the appeal is filed, or the court shall upon motion dismiss such appeal, unless at the time of taking the appeal the employer has executed a supersedeas bond with sufficient sureties to be approved by the register or clerk of the court to which the appeal shall be taken in double the amount of contributions, interest and penalties, payable to the director, conditioned to pay all contributions, interest, penalties and costs found to be due the department of industrial relations. In such appeal, the employer shall be styled the appellant and the director shall be styled the appellee. The assessment made by the director shall be prima facie correct, and the burden shall be on the employer to show that such assessment is incorrect. The circuit court, or court of civil appeals or the Supreme Court of Alabama on appeal, may, if it be of the opinion from all the evidence that the assessment as made is either too high or too low, fix the amount of such assessment. The court shall hear such appeals according to its own rules and methods of procedure so far as practicable and shall decide all questions both as to legality of the assessment and the amount thereof. No court shall have the power to enjoin the payment of any contributions, interest or penalty due on such assessment so appealed or to suspend the payment thereof. From the judgment of the circuit court, the employer or the director may appeal to the court of civil appeals if the amount involved, exclusive of interest and costs, does not exceed $10,000.00, or to the Supreme Court of Alabama if said amount exceeds $10,000.00, within 30 days of the rendition of the judgment upon giving such security for the cost of such appeal as approved by the register or clerk of the circuit court from which the appeal shall be taken. If upon such appeal the assessment made by the director is reduced, the court, upon proof of payment of said contributions, interest and penalties, shall ascertain and recite such fact in the judgment and shall ascertain and determine by its judgment and order the amount of contributions, interest and penalties which was invalid and the director shall thereupon refund to the employer the amount so ascertained by the court to be invalid.

(4) COLLECTION OF ASSESSMENTS. If contributions, interest or penalties are not paid within 15 days from the date of final assessment where no appeal is taken, or within 15 days of the date upon which any decision is issued upon an appeal is made final, the director shall take any action to collect as he may be authorized by any of the provisions of this section.

(d) *Bonds.*

(1) SURETY BOND OR CASH DEPOSIT FROM CONTRACTOR. — Any contractor primarily engaged in contract construction who is or becomes an employer, as defined by this chapter, and who is or becomes delinquent for any contributions due under this chapter may be required to post with the director a blanket surety bond by a licensed surety company authorized to do business in the State of Alabama in any amount which the director shall determine to be sufficient for the payment of all unemployment compensation taxes which will be due to the state for a period of not less than one year by virtue of its operations. In the alternative, said contractor may file a surety bond with respect to each contract. Further, in lieu of such security bond, he or it may deposit with the director in cash an amount equal thereto. These deposits shall be held by the director in a special deposit fund account established for that purpose; provided further, no bond or cash deposit shall be required for an amount to exceed $10,000.00 unless in the opinion of the director a larger amount is necessary.

(2) WITHHOLDING OF LICENSE FROM CONTRACTOR. — The Alabama state licensing board for general contractors or any other licensing agency of the

State of Alabama is hereby authorized to, and upon petition by the director shall, withhold any license from any contractor subject to the provisions of this section until the provisions of this subsection (d) have been complied with.

(3) RELEASE OF CONTRACTOR. — Any "employer" contractor shall cease to be subject to the provisions of this subsection (d) after he or it has been an employer as defined in this chapter within this state for a period of 12 calendar quarters and has paid all contributions due under the provisions of this chapter. Any employer who ceases to be subject to the provisions of this subsection (d) as provided in this subdivision or was excepted under the provisions of subdivision (1) of this subsection (d) and who later became delinquent for any contributions shall again become subject to such provisions until he or it again becomes eligible for release in accordance with the provisions of this subsection (d). When any contractor ceases operations or is otherwise released from the requirements under this section, he or it shall be entitled to have his or its bond cancelled or cash deposit refunded upon payment of all contributions, interest and penalties due under the provisions of this chapter.

(4) PROCEEDINGS AGAINST SURETY, ETC. — If an "employer" contractor fails to pay any contributions, interest and penalties provided for in this chapter when they become due, the director may call upon the surety company for the payment thereof or cause them to be paid by deducting the amount due from the contractor's cash deposit. Any employer subject to the provisions of this subsection (d) who fails to comply thereto shall be enjoined from any further operations until the provisions of this subsection (d) have been complied with. (Acts 1939, No. 497, p. 721; Code 1940, T. 26, § 240; Acts 1945, No. 283, p. 449, § 6; Acts 1951, No. 566, p. 995; Acts 1967, No. 169, p. 522; Acts 1971, No. 1201, p. 2083, §§ 7, 8; Acts 1971, No. 2325, p. 3748, §§ 7, 8; Acts 1973, No. 1057, p. 1716, § 9; Acts 1979, No. 79-824, p. 1541, § 3.)

This section denominates action to be taken by employer dissatisfied with assessment as an appeal to the circuit court. This section also provides that the assessment made by the director of the department shall be prima facie correct and casts the burden on the employer to show it is incorrect. Carter v. J.P. King & Sons, 381 So. 2d 71 (Ala. Civ. App.), cert. denied, 381 So. 2d 76 (Ala. 1980).

Under this section introduction of independent evidence and reconsideration of facts is permissible. Carter v. J.P. King & Sons, 381 So. 2d 71 (Ala. Civ. App.), cert. denied, 381 So. 2d 76 (Ala. 1980).

This section requires as a condition precedent to appeal in an unemployment compensation tax assessment that the employer pay the amount of tax claimed or execute a supersedeas bond for double the amount of the tax. However, the Alabama Unemployment Compensation Act is silent as to the payment of interest on a subsequent refund. James v. Mac Del Health Care, Inc., 428 So. 2d 48 (Ala. Civ. App. 1982).

When appeal is of right, time periods are procedural and thus covered by the Alabama Rules of Appellate Procedure, any inconsistent statutory provisions notwithstanding. Carter v. J.P. King & Sons, 381 So. 2d 71 (Ala. Civ. App.), cert. denied, 381 So. 2d 76 (Ala. 1980).

On appeal, employer must prove that assessment was incorrect. — The scope of review in the circuit court is not limited to a mere determination of whether there is any evidence to support the assessment. The employer is to prove, through appeal, that the assessment was incorrect; not that there was no evidence at all to support it. Carter v. J.P. King & Sons, 381 So. 2d 71 (Ala. Civ. App.), cert. denied, 381 So. 2d 76 (Ala. 1980).

When a tax refund statute is silent as to interest, it does not imply that interest should be paid. James v. Mac Del Health Care, Inc., 428 So. 2d 48 (Ala. Civ. App. 1982).

The trial court erred in denying the department's motion to dismiss employer's notice of appeal for failure to timely serve the department of industrial relations, and,

therefore, acted without jurisdiction in subsequently determining the case on its merits. Allen v. John Baker Hauling, Inc., 545 So. 2d 771 (Ala. Civ. App. 1989).

Cited in Poole Furn. Mfg. Co. v. State Dep't of Indus. Relations, 474 So. 2d 692 (Ala. 1985).

Collateral references. — 81 C.J.S., Social Security & Public Welfare, §§ 149-151.

§ 25-4-135. Effect of bankruptcy or liquidation of employer.

In the event of bankruptcy of any employer, or of liquidation of an employer under any law of this state by reason of insolvency or inability to pay his debts, the amount due for contributions on behalf of the employer shall have the same status and priority as other taxes due the state; provided, that in the event of an employer's adjudication in bankruptcy, a judicially confirmed extension proposal or a composition of creditors under the Federal Bankruptcy Act of 1898, as amended, contributions then or thereafter due shall be entitled to such priority as is provided therein for other taxes due and owing this state. (Acts 1939, No. 497, p. 721; Code 1940, T. 26, § 241.)

Collateral references. — 81 C.J.S., Social Security & Public Welfare, § 147.

76 Am. Jur. 2d, Unemployment Compensation, § 20.

Rank or priority of lien or claim for unpaid

employer's contribution under unemployment compensation act. 140 ALR 1042.

Unemployment taxes as payable in respect of claims for wages earned before bankruptcy of employer. 174 ALR 1295.

§ 25-4-136. Director may extend time for payment of contributions.

The director, for good cause may extend the time for payment of any contributions required by this chapter, without interest or penalty, for a period not to exceed 90 days, subject to such conditions and restrictions as the director may impose. (Acts 1939, No. 497, p. 721; Code 1940, T. 26, § 242.)

§ 25-4-137. Adjustments or refunds.

(a) If, not later than four years after the date on which any contributions, penalties or interest became due, an employer who has paid such contributions, penalties or interest thereon shall make application for an adjustment thereof in connection with subsequent contribution payments, or for a refund thereof because such adjustment cannot be made, and the director shall determine that such contributions, penalties or interest, or any portion thereof, was erroneously collected, the director shall allow such employer to make an adjustment thereof in connection with subsequent contribution liability, or, if such adjustment cannot be made, the director may refund such contributions, interest and penalties from the clearing account. Any refund of interest and/or penalties which have been transferred to the special employment security administration fund shall be made from the special employment security administration fund, provided for in Section 25-4-142. If the director shall deny, in whole or in part, any such application, the applicant may within 60 days after notice of such action, to be given by the director by mail, appeal to the circuit court of the county wherein is the principal place of business of the applicant, and the trial in that court shall be without a jury, and the court shall render such judgment as the facts and circumstances warrant. For like cause and within four years, adjustment or refund may be made on the director's own initiative.

(b) The amount of any adjustments or refunds made under this section shall be reduced by the sum of any benefits that shall have been paid based on the wages on which contributions are to be refunded. Such reduction shall be made first from the employee contributions withheld from wages of those employees to whom such benefits were paid and the remainder from the employer contributions; provided, however, that no such reduction in the amount of any adjustment or refund under this section shall be made if such contributions were paid under protest and such benefits were paid prior to final adjudication of such protest.

(c) Before any adjustment or refund may be made under the provisions of this section, the employer must conform to applicable rules and regulations of the director with respect to the refund to the employees entitled thereto of any moneys deducted by the employer in accordance with the provisions of this chapter. (Acts 1939, No. 497, p. 721; Code 1940, T. 26, § 243; Acts 1963, 2nd Ex. Sess., No. 151, p. 340, § 3; Acts 1965, No. 390, p. 548, § 8.)

Application of section. — This section is not without application to situations such as overpayments because the amount had been incorrectly figured according to the rate established, or because of a mistake in figuring the number of employees for whom payments had to be made, or any other overpayments from any general cause, as by the inclusion in the determination of a statutory burden which is in violation of the constitution. Department of Indus. Relations v. West Boylston Mfg. Co., 253 Ala. 67, 42 So. 2d 787 (1949).

Limitation of time not affected by section 25-4-54. — The limitation of time prescribed for review in subsection (h) of § 25-4-54 in no way amends this section. Carnley v. State ex rel. West Boylston Mfg. Co., 250 Ala. 403, 34 So. 2d 681 (1948).

Application filed on August 18, 1947, with director of department of industrial relations for an adjustment or refund under the provisions of this section, in respect to a payment made on May 4, 1944, estimated on taxable wages accruing and paid by petitioner to employees from January 22 to March 31, 1944, was timely and was governed by the limitation fixed by this section rather than by § 25-4-54(h). Carnley v. State ex rel. West Boylston Mfg. Co., 250 Ala. 403, 34 So. 2d 681 (1948).

Failure to apply for redetermination under section 25-4-54(h). — A right that has been foreclosed by a failure to apply for a redetermination of excess wages under § 25-4-54(h) cannot be made the basis of an application under this section. Department of Indus. Relations v. West Boylston Mfg. Co., 253 Ala. 67, 42 So. 2d 787 (1949).

The legislature did not intend that by failure to apply for review and redetermination of excess wages under § 25-4-54(h) an employer would be concluded from seeking review under this section as to a matter over which the judicial power of the director could not be made conclusive when that want of authority appeared on the face of the proceeding. Department of Indus. Relations v. West Boylston Mfg. Co., 253 Ala. 67, 42 So. 2d 787 (1949).

It must be conclusively assumed that contribution rate fixed by director is correct where applications for adjustments and refunds are made, and whether there are erroneous payments or contributions, interest and penalties must be determined in light of contribution rates previously fixed. Broadway v. Alabama Dry Dock & Shipbuilding Co., 246 Ala. 201, 20 So. 2d 41 (1944).

Except as to errors not going to the basis of the computation. — Both the benefit wage percentage and the state experience factor when determined by the director are conclusive, except that the percentage may be reviewed under § 25-4-54(h), subject to errors in computation reviewable under this section.

Department of Indus. Relations v. West Boylston Mfg. Co., 253 Ala. 67, 42 So. 2d 787 (1949).

In Department of Indus. Relations v. West Boylston Mfg. Co., 253 Ala. 67, 42 So. 2d 787 (1949), the court stated that its holding concerning applications for adjustments and refunds under this section in Broadway v. Alabama Dry Dock & Shipbuilding Co., 246 Ala. 201, 20 So. 2d 41 (1944), meant that to the extent that redetermination and review are available under § 25-4-54(h), a failure to exercise the right as provided has the effect of conclusively making effective the director's primary determination and it is not subject to review under this section, except for some erroneous computation or other error not going to the basis of the computation.

And in cases of want of jurisdiction or plain violation of law. — Where a controversy concerning a petition by an employer for redetermination and review of excess wages relates to the claim of want of jurisdiction or plain violation of law which, appearing on the face of the proceeding, is not foreclosed by a failure to apply for a redetermination under § 25-4-54(h), there is no reason why this section should not be available for relief as is common-law certiorari. Department of Indus. Relations v. West Boylston Mfg. Co., 253 Ala. 67, 42 So. 2d 787 (1949).

Personal judgment not proper for collection of overpayment. — Where it was determined that employer had made an overpayment of contributions, form of judgment should have been one requiring director to allow adjustment by giving credit on current taxes due or refund sum of money resulting from such overpayment, and pay the cost of the proceedings, and it was error to enter personal judgment against director and authorize issuance of execution for its collection. Broadway v.

Alabama Dry Dock & Shipbuilding Co., 246 Ala. 201, 20 So. 2d 41 (1944); Department of Indus. Relations v. West Boylston Mfg. Co., 253 Ala. 67, 42 So. 2d 787 (1949).

This section does not provide for a refund of money out of the state treasury. The money subject to refund payments is collected and administered for certain purposes as directed by law, and that is one of them, and it does not become subject to the restrictions of § 72 of the Constitution. Department of Indus. Relations v. West Boylston Mfg. Co., 253 Ala. 67, 42 So. 2d 787 (1949).

In addition to authorizing no personal judgment for the amount of the refund, this section does not direct payment thereof out of the general treasury upon the basis of the result of an application for a refund brought under this section. Department of Indus. Relations v. West Boylston Mfg. Co., 253 Ala. 67, 42 So. 2d 787 (1949).

It only makes provision for determining the true amount of the obligation. It does not release or extinguish a liquidated claim. Department of Indus. Relations v. West Boylston Mfg. Co., 253 Ala. 67, 42 So. 2d 787 (1949).

Effect of payment of refund. — The payment of a refund by the director of industrial relations under the provisions of this section is in no sense a release or discharge of an obligation or liability to the state, except by its payment in full as required by § 100 of the Constitution. Department of Indus. Relations v. West Boylston Mfg. Co., 253 Ala. 67, 42 So. 2d 787 (1949).

Cited in Opinion of Justices, 252 Ala. 468, 41 So. 2d 771 (1949).

Collateral references. — 81 C.J.S., Social Security & Public Welfare, § 152.

Repayment of unemployment compensation benefits erroneously paid. 90 ALR3d 987.

§ 25-4-138. Agreement to waive right to benefits; agreement to pay employer's contributions; reduction of wages to finance employer's contributions.

Any agreement by an employee to waive or release his rights to benefits or any other rights under this chapter shall be void. Any agreement by an employee to pay all or any portion of his employer's contributions, required under this chapter from such employer, shall be void. No employer shall directly or indirectly make or require or accept any reduction from wages to finance the employer's contributions required of him, or require or accept any waiver of any right hereunder by any employee in his employ. Any employer or officer or agent of an employer who violates any provision of this section shall be guilty of a misdemeanor and upon conviction, for each offense be fined not less than $25.00 nor more than $100.00 or be imprisoned for not more than 60 days, or both. (Acts 1939, No. 497, p. 721; Code 1940, T. 26, § 244.)

Section to be strictly interpreted. — Because the purpose of this act is remedial, the disqualifying provisions set forth in this section are to be strictly interpreted. Director, Dep't of Indus. Relations v. Alabama By-Products, Inc., 374 So. 2d 344 (Ala. Civ. App.), cert. denied, 374 So. 2d 347 (Ala. 1979).

§ 25-4-139. Fees in proceedings under chapter.

No individual shall be charged fees of any kind by the director or his representatives, in any proceeding under this chapter. Any individual claiming benefits in any proceeding or court action may be represented by counsel or other duly authorized agent but no such counsel or agents shall together charge or receive for such services more than 10 percent of the maximum benefits at issue in such proceeding or court action. (Acts 1939, No. 497, p. 721; Code 1940, T. 26, § 245.)

§ 25-4-140. Certain assignments, etc., of right to benefits void; exemption from attachment, etc.; exception.

Any assignment, pledge or encumbrance of any right to benefits which are or may become due or payable under this chapter, except as is provided by this chapter, shall be void, and such rights to benefits shall be exempt from levy, execution, attachment or any other remedy whatsoever provided for the collection of debts. Any waiver of any exemption herein provided, unless expressly permitted by this section, shall be void. (Acts 1939, No. 497, p. 721; Code 1940, T. 26, § 246; Acts 1982, No. 82-370, p. 524, § 2.)

Collateral references. — Employee retirement pension benefits as exempt from garnishment, attachment, levy, execution, or similar proceedings. 93 ALR3d 711.

§ 25-4-141. Protection against self-incrimination. Repealed by Acts 1980, No. 80-756, p. 1561, § 6, effective May 28, 1980.

§ 25-4-142. Employment security administration fund; special employment security administration fund; replacement of certain funds.

(a) There shall be in the state treasury a fund to be known as the employment security administration fund. All moneys which are deposited or paid into this fund are hereby appropriated and made available to the director for expenditure in accordance with the provisions of this chapter, and shall not lapse at any time or be transferred to any other fund. All moneys in this fund, which are received from the federal government or any agency thereof, or which are appropriated by this state for the administration of this chapter, except money received pursuant to the provisions of subdivision (6) of Section 25-4-30, shall be expended solely for the purposes and in the amounts found necessary by the authorized cooperating federal agencies for the proper and efficient administration of this chapter. The fund shall consist of all moneys appropriated by this state and all moneys received from the United States or any agencies thereof and all moneys received from any other source for such purposes. Notwithstanding any provisions of this section, all money requisitioned and deposited in this fund pursuant to subsection (b) of Section 25-4-32 shall remain part of the fund until encumbered, and shall be used only in accordance with the conditions specified in said section. All moneys in this fund shall be deposited, administered and disbursed in the same manner and under the same conditions and requirements as are provided by law for other special funds in the State Treasury. Any balances in this fund shall not lapse at any time, but shall be continuously available to the director for expenditure consistent with this chapter. The treasurer shall give separate and additional bonds conditioned upon the faithful performance of his duties in connection with the employment security administration fund and the special employment security administration fund, described in subsection (b) of this section, in amounts to be fixed by the director, and in a form prescribed by law or approved by the Attorney General. The premiums for such bonds of the treasurer for the employment security administration fund shall be paid from the moneys in the employment security administration fund. The premiums for such bonds of the treasurer for the special employment security administration fund shall be paid from the special employment security administration fund.

(b) There is hereby created in the State Treasury a special fund, to be known as the "special employment security administration fund," into which shall be deposited or transferred all interest and penalties collected after May 9, 1963, pursuant to Sections 25-4-132 through 25-4-134. Interest and penalties collected on delinquent contribution payments deposited during any calendar quarter in the clearing account in the unemployment compensation fund shall, as soon as practicable after the close of such calendar quarter, be transferred to the special employment security administration fund. All moneys in this fund shall be deposited, administered and disbursed in the same manner and under the same conditions and requirements as is provided by law for other special funds in the state treasury. Said moneys shall not be expended or made available for expenditure in any manner which would permit their substitution for (or permit a corresponding reduction in) federal funds, which would, in the absence of said moneys, be available to finance expenditures for the administration of the state unemployment compensation and employment service laws. Nothing in this section shall prevent said moneys in this fund from being used as a revolving fund to cover expenditures necessary and proper under the law for which federal funds have been duly requested but not yet received, subject to the charging of such expenditures against such funds when necessary. The moneys in this fund may be used by the director for the payment of costs of administration of the employment security laws of this state which are found not to be or not to have been properly and validly chargeable against funds obtained from federal sources. All moneys in this special employment administration fund shall be continuously available to the director for expenditure in accordance with the provisions of this chapter, and shall not lapse at any time. The moneys in this fund are hereby specifically made available to replace, as contemplated by subsection (c) of this section, expenditures from the employment security administration fund established by subsection (a) of this section, which have been found by the bureau of employment security (or other authorized agency or authority) because of any action or contingency, to have been lost or improperly expended.

The director, whenever he is of the opinion that the money in the special employment security administration fund is more than ample to pay for all foreseeable needs for which such special fund is set up, may, by written order, order the transfer therefrom to the trust fund of such amount of money in the said special employment security administration fund as he deems proper, and the same shall thereupon be immediately transferred to the trust fund.

(c) All moneys received after June 30, 1941, from the Secretary of Labor, or his successor or successors, under Title III of the Social Security Act, or any unencumbered balances in the unemployment compensation administration fund as of that date, or any moneys granted after that date to this state pursuant to the provisions of the Wagner-Peyser Act, or any moneys made available by the state or its political subdivisions and matched by such moneys granted to this state pursuant to the provisions of the Wagner-Peyser Act, shall be expended solely for the purposes and in the amounts found necessary by the Secretary of Labor, or his successor or successors, for the proper and efficient administration of this chapter. If any of such moneys are found by the Secretary of Labor, or his successor or successors, because of any action or contingency, to have been lost or been expended for the purposes other than or in the amounts in excess of those found necessary by the Secretary of Labor, or his successor or successors, for the proper administration of this chapter, it is the policy of this state that such moneys, if not replaced from other sources, shall be replaced by moneys appropriated for such purpose from the general funds of this state to the unemployment compensation administration fund for expenditure as provided in subsection (a) of this section. Upon receipt of such finding by the Secretary of Labor, or his successor or successors, the director shall promptly report the amount required for such replacement to the Governor and the Governor shall at the earliest opportunity, submit to the legislature a request for the appropriation of such amount. This subsection shall not be construed to relieve this state of its obligation with respect to funds received prior to July 1, 1941, pursuant to the provisions of Title III of the Social Security Act; provided, however, that funds which have been expended by the director or his predecessors in office, in accordance with a budget approved by the Secretary of Labor, or his successor or successors, and in accordance with the general standards and limitations promulgated by the Secretary of Labor, or his successor or successors, prior to such expenditure (where proposed expenditures have not been specifically disapproved by the Secretary of Labor, or his successor or successors) shall not be deemed to require replacement. (Acts 1939, No. 497, p.

721; Code 1940, T. 26, § 248; Acts 1943, No. 310, p. 281, § 14; Acts 1957, No. 303, p. 395, § 3; Acts 1963, 2nd Ex. Sess., No. 151, p. 340, § 4.)

§ 25-4-143. Appropriations.

All moneys in the unemployment administration fund, the special employment security administration fund, the special federal advance interest repayment fund and the employment security enhancement fund, or any appropriated by the state or granted by the federal government in accordance with the provisions of the Wagner-Peyser Act or other federal or state laws at any time are hereby appropriated to the director for the administration of this chapter. (Acts 1939, No. 497, p. 721; Code 1940, T. 26, § 249; Acts 1988, 1st Ex. Sess., No. 88-783, p. 195, § 4; Acts 1992, No. 92-174, § 6.)

The 1992 amendment, effective April 10, 1992, added "and the employment security enhancement fund" following "interest repayment fund."

Purpose of section. — Apparently to be sure that there is no violation of § 72 of the Constitution, this section in terms makes an appropriation to the director of all moneys for the administration of this chapter of the Code. Department of Indus. Relations v. West Boylston Mfg. Co., 253 Ala. 67, 42 So. 2d 787 (1949).

Cited in Department of Indus. Relations v. West Boylston Mfg. Co., 253 Ala. 67, 42 So. 2d 787 (1949).

§ 25-4-144. Reservation of right to repeal or amend chapter.

The legislature reserves the right to amend or repeal all or any part of this chapter at any time. There shall be no vested private right of any kind against such amendment or repeal. All the rights, privileges or immunities conferred by this chapter or by acts done pursuant thereto shall exist subject to the power of the legislature to amend or repeal this chapter at any time. (Acts 1939, No. 497, p. 721; Code 1940, T. 26, § 250.)

Cited in United States Steel Corp. v. Wood, 40 Ala. App. 431, 114 So. 2d 533 (1958).

§ 25-4-145. Penalties; limitation of actions; collection of overpayments; waiver of overpayments.

(a) *Penalties.*

(1) Whoever willfully makes a false statement or representation or who willfully fails to disclose a material fact to obtain or increase any benefit or payment under this chapter, or under an unemployment insurance law of any other state or government, either for himself or for any other person, whether such benefit or payment is actually received or not, shall be guilty of a misdemeanor and upon such conviction shall be punished by a fine of not less than $50.00 nor more than $500.00, or by imprisonment for not longer than 12 months, or by both such fine and imprisonment, and each such false statement or representation shall constitute a separate and distinct offense.

(2) Any officer or agent of employer, or any employer who is an individual, who willfully makes a false statement or representation to avoid his employer or himself becoming or remaining subject to this chapter for contributions, or to reduce any contribution or other payment required of such employer or him under this chapter, or who willfully fails or refuses to make any such contributions or other payments as lawfully required under this chapter, or who induces any employee to waive any rights under this chapter, or any officer or agent of an employing unit, or any employing unit who is an individual, who refuses to furnish any reports duly required under this chapter or to appear or testify or produce records as lawfully required hereunder shall, upon conviction, be punished by a fine of not less than $50.00 nor more than $500.00, or by imprisonment for not longer than 12 months, or by both such fine and imprisonment, and each such false statement or representation and each day of such failure or refusal, and each such inducement shall constitute a separate and distinct offense.

(3) If the director finds that any fraudulent misrepresentation has been made by a claimant with the object of obtaining benefits under this chapter to which he was not entitled, then, in addition to any other penalty or prosecution provided under this chapter, the director may make a determination that there shall be deducted from any benefits to which such claimant might become entitled during his present benefit year and/or next subsequent benefit year, an amount not less than four times his weekly benefit amount and not more than the maximum benefit amount payable in a benefit year, as determined under Sections 25-4-72, 25-4-74 and 25-4-75, at the time the director makes the determination. The director shall notify the claimant of his findings and determination either by delivering a copy thereof to him or by mailing a copy, postage prepaid, to his last known address. Unless the claimant shall appeal from said finding or from said determination, or both, within seven calendar days after delivery of such notice to him, or within 15 calendar days after such notice was mailed to his last known address, postage prepaid, such finding and determination shall become final. If such claimant shall appeal from such finding or determination, or both, within the time specified, the issue or issues shall be referred to an appeals tribunal for hearing, as in other benefit cases, and thereafter the procedure shall be the same as set forth in Article 5 of this chapter.

(4) Any violation of any provisions of this chapter, for which a penalty is neither prescribed above nor provided by any other applicable statute, shall be punished by a fine of not less than $50.00 nor more than $500.00, or by imprisonment for not longer than twelve months, or by such fine and imprisonment.

(b) *Limitation of actions.* — Prosecution under this section must be begun within three years from the date of the commission of the offense or offenses described herein.

(c) *Collection of overpayments.*

(1) Any individual who has received any sum as benefits or payments under this chapter while any conditions for the receipt of benefits or

payment imposed by this chapter were not fulfilled by such person, or while he was disqualified from receipt of benefits; or by reason of non-disclosure or misrepresentation by him or another of a material fact (irrespective of whether such non-disclosure was known or fraudulent) or for any other reason causing him to receive benefits to which he was not entitled, shall be required to repay such sum in cash or by offset against any future benefits if payable or a combination of both.

(2) Such person shall be promptly notified of the determination of overpayment and the reasons therefor. Unless such person, within 15 calendar days immediately following the date such notification was mailed to his last known address, files an appeal from such determination, such determination shall be final. Any appeal therefrom pursuant to the provisions of this chapter shall be limited solely to the overpayment issue.

(3) If the indebtedness is not paid by such person within 30 calendar days after the determination has become final, the director shall proceed to effect collection of the overpayment and shall have available to him all civil actions available to him under the laws of this state to collect the overpayment as well as those provisions contained in subsection (b) of Section 25-4-134 applying to the collection of contributions.

(d) *Waiver of overpayment; limitations.*

(1) The director is hereby authorized to waive overpayments under such procedure and conditions as he may by regulation prescribe.

(2) The other provisions of this section to the contrary notwithstanding, no action to enforce recovery or recoupment of any overpayment shall begin after six years from the date of the final determination as is provided for in subsection (c) of this section. (Acts 1939, No. 497, p. 721; Code 1940, T. 26, § 251; Acts 1951, No. 568, p. 1000; Acts 1961, Ex. Sess., No. 274, p. 2298, § 9; Acts 1978, 1st Ex. Sess., No. 1, p. 5, § 11; Acts 1980, No. 80-756, p. 1561, § 7; Acts 1983, 2nd Ex. Sess., No. 83-155, p. 264, § 15.)

This section applies only to a claimant who received benefits by misrepresentation or nondisclosure of a material fact. Cargill v. State, Dep't of Indus. Relations, 428 So. 2d 62 (Ala. Civ. App. 1982).

This section prescribes the offense as being the willful making of a false statement in order to obtain payment. Pierce v. State, 42 Ala. App. 53, 151 So. 2d 793 (1963).

And whether payment is actually received is immaterial. Pierce v. State, 42 Ala. App. 53, 151 So. 2d 793 (1963).

But name of person to whom alleged statement made must be given. — In a false pretense case or case similar to false pretense, the name of the person to whom the alleged statement is made must be given in order to enable the defendant to prepare his defense. Pierce v. State, 42 Ala. App. 53, 151 So. 2d 793 (1963).

Offender disqualified from voting. — The offense of receiving unemployment compensation benefits by reason of misrepresentations is one which disqualifies the offender from voting under Alabama law. It has been determined in a prior unappealed case that the offense is a crime involving "moral turpitude." Waddy v. Davis, 445 F.2d 1 (5th Cir. 1971).

Collection of overpayment. — The department can collect from an employee the amount of unemployment compensation benefits he has already received but for which he is subsequently disqualified due to an award of back pay where it is not possible for the employer to deduct the amount of the overpayment from future payments of the back pay award. Heatherly v. Benton, 479 So. 2d 1285 (Ala. Civ. App. 1985), decided prior to enactment of § 25-4-145(c).

Cited in Hollenquest v. State, 431 So. 2d 1364 (Ala. Crim. App. 1983).

Collateral references. — 73 C.J.S., Public

Administrative Bodies & Procedure, § 90. 81
C.J.S., Social Security and Public Welfare,
§§ 271-290.
  76 Am. Jur. 2d, Unemployment Compensation, §§ 91-96.
  Construction, application, and effect, with
respect to withholding, social security, and
unemployment taxes, of statutes imposing penalties for tax evasion or default. 22 ALR3d 8.
  Criminal liability for wrongfully obtaining
unemployment benefits. 80 ALR3d 1280.

§ 25-4-146. Certain employees of Department of Industrial Relations constituted peace officers to enforce unemployment compensation law and other specified state criminal laws.

  (a) Employees of the Department of Industrial Relations classified as unemployment insurance claims investigators and those supervisors charged with the direct enforcement of the fraud provisions of the Alabama Unemployment Compensation Law, as designated in writing by the Director of the Department of Industrial Relations, are hereby constituted peace officers of the State of Alabama with full and unlimited police powers and jurisdiction as any other state police officers in this state, to enforce the provisions of the Alabama Unemployment Compensation Law and those provisions of state criminal law relating to forgery, larceny, embezzlement and fraud when the offense of forgery, larceny, embezzlement or fraud is directly related to a check issued by the Department of Industrial Relations or a check issued in conjunction with a program administered by the Department of Industrial Relations and to maintain order in offices operated by said department.

  (b) All claim investigators given arrest powers by this section shall be required to comply with the minimum standard requirements now in effect relating to state troopers and deputy sheriffs in this state. (Acts 1971, No. 1142, p. 1966, § 1; Acts 1981, No. 81-565, p. 950.)

§ 25-4-147. Arrest fee; disposition of fees collected.

  In all cases where arrests are made by any of said unemployment insurance fraud investigators or other supervisors charged with the direct enforcement of the fraud provisions of the law, as designated in writing by the director of the department, designated by Section 25-4-146 as peace officers, an arrest fee of $5.00 for an arrest resulting in a conviction shall be collected by the proper authorities and promptly turned over to the Director of Industrial Relations, who shall pay the same into the State Treasury to the credit of the Department of Industrial Relations' unemployment compensation agency's interest and penalty fund. (Acts 1971, No. 1142, p. 1966, § 2.)

§ 25-4-148. Disposition of trust funds, etc., in event of invalidity of provisions pertaining to payment of contributions and benefits.

  If at any time the Governor shall find that the provisions of this chapter requiring the payment of contributions and benefits have been held invalid under the Constitution of this state by the supreme court of this state or under the United States Constitution by the Supreme Court of the United States in such manner that any person or concern required to pay contributions under this chapter might secure a similar decision, or that the tax imposed by Title IX of the Social Security Act, as amended, or any other federal tax against which contributions under this chapter may be credited has been amended or repealed by Congress or has been held unconstitutional by the Supreme Court of the United States, with the result that no portion of the contributions required by this chapter may be credited against such federal tax, the Governor shall publicly so proclaim and upon the date of such proclamation the provisions of this chapter requiring the payment of contributions and benefits shall be suspended. The director (and for the purposes of this section, the director shall remain or become the agency for carrying out the provisions hereof) shall thereupon forthwith requisition from the unemployment trust fund all moneys therein standing to its credit and shall direct the treasurer to deposit such moneys, together with any other moneys in the fund, as a special fund in any banks or public depositories in this state in which general funds of the state may be deposited. The director shall thereupon forthwith and within 60 days after receipt of such moneys, refund, without interest and in accordance with regulations prescribed by him, to each person or concern by whom contributions have been paid, his pro rata share of the total contributions paid under this chapter. After the expiration of said 60 days, the duties imposed by this section upon said director shall cease and determine and all powers conferred and duties imposed not then executed shall be conferred upon and executed by the treasurer. Any interest or earnings of the fund shall be available to the director to pay for the costs of making such refunds. When the director shall have executed the duties prescribed in this section and performed such other acts as are incidental to the termination of his duties under this chapter, the Governor shall by proclamation declare that the provisions of this chapter shall cease to be operative. (Acts 1939, No. 497, p. 721; Code 1940, T. 26, § 252.)

§ 25-4-149. Appropriation of funds for payment of benefits for state employees generally.

Such moneys as are needed to pay the state's portion of benefits provided in this chapter are hereby appropriated from such funds as the salaries of the several state's employees are paid. (Acts 1978, 1st Ex. Sess., No. 1, p. 5, § 12.)

Collateral references. — 81 C.J.S., Social Security, § 183.

§ 25-4-150. Appropriation of funds for payment of benefits for employees of local school systems.

Such moneys as are necessary to finance the benefit costs for employees of local school systems shall be paid by the local school system from funds allocated from the special educational trust fund, and such amounts are hereby appropriated from the special educational trust fund for this purpose. (Acts 1978, 1st Ex. Sess., No. 1, p. 5, § 13.)

Collateral references. — 81 C.J.S., Social Security, § 194.

§ 25-4-151. Effect of challenges to or invalidation of federal unemployment compensation amendments of 1976.

In the event any portion of Section 115 of the unemployment compensation amendments of 1976 (Public Law 94-566, 94th Congress, dated October 20, 1976), as it applies to the requirement for states to provide coverage of certain services performed for local governmental entities under the various states' unemployment compensation law, is determined to be unconstitutional or invalid in a final adjudication by the courts of the United States, then from and after the date of such final adjudication, no local governmental entity of any county or municipality in the State of Alabama or their instrumentalities, or any separate public primary and secondary school system, as defined in Section 25-4-10, shall be required to participate in the unemployment compensation program; provided, that nothing herein shall be construed as invalidating the entitlement of such entities to elect coverage for their hospitals or institutions of higher education; provided further, that nothing herein shall be construed as relieving any entity of the responsibility for any contributions or payments in lieu of contributions incurred during the period prior to the date of the final adjudicational determination by the courts; provided further, that in the event any local governmental entity shall become a part of any suit in the courts of the United States challenging the constitutionality of the provisions of Section 115 of PL 94-566 and such court, of competent jurisdiction, shall temporarily stay the implementation of said provision of federal law, then during the effective period of such stay, the coverage of said services shall be stayed in this state but shall be applicable only to those entities that are, or are made, a party to the suit or included in the stay. (Acts 1978, 1st Ex. Sess., No. 1, p. 5, § 16.)

U.S. Code. — Section 115 of the federal unemployment compensation amendments of 1976, Pub. L. 94-566, referred to in this section, is codified as 26 U.S.C.A. § 3309.

Collateral references. — 81 C.J.S., Social Security, § 150.

§ 25-4-152. Deduction of child support obligations; procedures; reimbursement for administrative costs; time of implementation.

(a)(1) An individual filing a new claim for unemployment compensation shall, at the time of filing such claim, disclose whether or not the individual owes child support obligations as defined under subdivision (7). If any such individual discloses that he or she owes child support obligations, and is determined to be eligible for unemployment compensation, the director shall notify the state or local child support enforcement agency enforcing such obligation that the individual has been determined to be eligible for unemployment compensation.

(2) The director shall deduct and withhold from any unemployment compensation payable to an individual who owes child support obligations as defined under subdivision (7).

a. The amount specified by the individual to the director to be deducted and withheld under this subdivision, if neither paragraph b. nor c. is applicable; or

b. The amount (if any) determined pursuant to an agreement submitted to the director under Section 454 (20) (B) (i) of the Social Security Act by the state or local child support enforcement agency, unless paragraph c. is applicable; or

c. Any amount otherwise required to be so deducted and withheld from such unemployment compensation pursuant to legal process (as that term is defined in Section 462 (e) of the Social Security Act) properly served upon the director.

(3) Any amount deducted and withheld under subdivision (2) shall be paid by the director to the appropriate state or local child support enforcement agency.

(4) Any amount deducted and withheld under subdivision (2) shall for all purposes be treated as if it were paid to the individual as unemployment compensation and paid by such individual to the state or local child support enforcement agency in satisfaction of the individual's child support obligations.

(5) For purposes of subdivisions (1) through (4), the term "unemployment compensation" means any compensation payable under this section (including amounts payable by the director pursuant to an agreement under any federal law providing for compensation, assistance, or allowances with respect to unemployment).

(6) The provisions of this section shall apply only if appropriate arrangements have been made for reimbursement by the state or local child support enforcement agency for the administrative costs incurred by the director under this section which are attributable to child support obligations being enforced by the state or local child support enforcement agency.

(7) The term "child support obligations" is defined for purposes of these provisions as including only obligations which are being enforced pursuant to a plan described in Section 454 of the Social Security Act which has been approved by the U.S. Secretary of Health and Human Services under Part D of Title IV of the Social Security Act.

(8) The term "state or local child support enforcement agency" as used in these provisions means any agency of this state or a political subdivision thereof operating pursuant to a plan as described in subdivision (7).

(b) The provisions of subsection (a) shall become effective for implementation with respect to benefits paid on or after September 25, 1982. (Acts 1982, No. 82-371, p. 531, §§ 1, 2.)

U.S. Code. — Section 454 of the Social Security Act, referred to in this section, is codified as 42 U.S.C.A. § 654. Section 462 of the Social Security Act, also referred to in this section, is codified as 42 U.S.C.A. § 662.

CHAPTER 5.

WORKERS' COMPENSATION.

437

I. General Consideration.
II. Construction.
III. Employees Covered by Act.

I. GENERAL CONSIDERATION.

Constitutionality. Smith v. West Point-Pepperell, Inc., 431 So. 2d 1268 (Ala. Civ. App. 1983).

For discussion of the relationship between Ala. Const. § 13 and the Workmen's Compensation Act, see Smith v. West Point-Pepperell, Inc., 431 So. 2d 1268 (Ala. Civ. App. 1983).

Workmen's Compensation Act is not invalid because more than one purpose s expressed in title. Chapman v. Railway Fuel Co., 212 Ala. 106, 101 So. 879 (1924).

In title of Workmen's Compensation Act, expression of subject of liability to make compensation for "injuries received," includes injuries resulting in death, and act is valid, under Constitution 1901, § 45, requiring title of law to express subject thereof. Chapman v. Railway Fuel Co., 212 Ala. 106, 101 So. 879 (1924).

Purpose of workmen's compensation is to place upon industry the burden of disability and death resulting from industrial accidents. Ford v. Mitcham, 53 Ala. App. 102, 298 So. 2d 34 (1974).

The purpose of compensation laws is to require industry to bear part of the burden of disability and death, resulting from the hazards of industry. Pow v. Southern Constr. Co., 235 Ala. 580, 180 So. 288 (1938).

The primary goal of workmen's compensation legislation is to aid the injured person, but not to allow a double recovery. Holder v. Weatherly, 456 So. 2d 812 (Ala. Civ. App. 1984).

Court in construing Workmen's Compensation Act should give effect to legislative purpose and policy. Woodward Iron Co. v. Horton, 267 Ala. 449, 103 So. 2d 717 (1958).

Designed as substitute for tort action. — And workmen's compensation was designed as a substitute for common-law tort actions for personal injuries between master and servant. Ford v. Mitcham, 53 Ala. App. 102, 298 So. 2d 34 (1974).

Workmen's Compensation Act was intended, in general, as in the nature of a substitute, between master and servant, who elect to come within its provisions, for actions of tort for personal injuries at common law and under other statutes. Gentry v. Swann Chem. Co., 234 Ala. 313, 174 So. 530 (1937); Harris v. Louisville & N.R.R., 237 Ala. 366, 186 So. 771 (1939).

But it does not deny a remedy to those not within its provisions. — In the light of the provisions of § 13 of the Constitution "that all courts shall be open; that every person, for any injury done him, in his lands, goods, person, or reputation, shall have a remedy by due process of law" it cannot be said that for an injury done a person, not within the provisions of the Workmen's Compensation Act, it was the legislative intent by the enactment of said law, to deny such person a remedy, if under the common law or the Employer's Liability Act, § 25-6-1 et seq., or other statute he was entitled to maintain an action therefor. Gentry v. Swann Chem. Co., 234 Ala. 313, 174 So. 530 (1937).

Amendments did not affect elective option. — The 1973 amendments to Workmen's Compensation Act, which, as written, only repealed those sections of the code pertaining to the election procedures governing whether or not the employer and employee would be bound by the provisions of the act, in no way affected the elective option between employer and employee existing under the act. The constitutional validity of the act rests upon the same being elective rather than compulsory. Pipkin v. Southern Elec. & Pipefitting Co., 358 So. 2d 1015 (Ala. 1978).

Action under workmen's compensation laws is purely statutory. Boatright v. Dothan Aviation Corp., 278 Ala. 142, 176 So. 2d 500 (1965); Slagle v. Reynolds Metals Co., 344 So. 2d 1216 (Ala. 1977).

Workmen's compensation is a creature of statute. Freeman v. Blue Mt. Indus., 395 So. 2d 1049 (Ala. Civ. App. 1981).

This chapter sets forth operating conditions of the compensation laws. Ivey v. Dixon Inv. Co., 283 Ala. 590, 219 So. 2d 639 (1969).

Workmen's Compensation Act and Employer's Liability Act are mutually exclu-

sive. — Because the Workmen's Compensation Act and the Employer's Liability Act are mutually exclusive and cannot apply to the same set of facts, an employee who seeks to recover damages from his employer under the Employer's Liability Act must bring himself within an exception to the Workmen's Compensation Act by alleging in his complaint facts sufficient to establish that exception. Veterans of Foreign Wars Post 7320 v. Sheffield, 398 So. 2d 262 (Ala. 1981).

Generally, the Employers' Liability Act, § 25-6-1 et seq., was superseded by the Workmen's Compensation Act, and any injuries sustained by an employee are presumed to come under the compensation act. Pound v. Gaulding, 237 Ala. 387, 187 So. 468 (1939). See Jackson v. United Cigar Stores Co., 228 Ala. 220, 153 So. 422 (1934).

Alabama workmen's compensation laws were adopted from the Minnesota laws of workmen's compensation, M.S.A., § 176.01 et seq. Brunson Milling Co. v. Grimes, 267 Ala. 395, 103 So. 2d 315 (1958); Eley v. Brunner-Lay S. Corp., 289 Ala. 120, 266 So. 2d 276 (1972).

And Minnesota construction of such law presumed adopted. — The legislature, in adopting the Minnesota compensation law as the compensation law of Alabama, is presumed to have adopted the construction given such law by the Minnesota court at the time of its adoption. Pow v. Southern Constr. Co., 235 Ala. 580, 180 So. 288 (1938); Swift & Co. v. Rolling, 252 Ala. 536, 42 So. 2d 6 (1949).

Hence, Minnesota construction of that law is of persuasive value to the Alabama court. Brunson Milling Co. v. Grimes, 267 Ala. 395, 103 So. 2d 315 (1958); Eley v. Brunner-Lay S. Corp., 289 Ala. 120, 266 So. 2d 276 (1972).

Cases decided prior to Code of 1940 are considered sound. — The cases construing and applying compensation statutes, decided before the readoption of the statutes into the Code of 1940, would be considered sound and would be followed after readoption of the statutes. Sloss-Sheffield Steel & Iron Co. v. Nations, 243 Ala. 107, 8 So. 2d 833 (1942).

When federal decision not binding. — A finding by the federal compensation commission as to whether a person is an employee of the United States is not binding upon Alabama court, so far as concerns the application of our own compensation laws. Humphrey v. Poss, 245 Ala. 11, 15 So. 2d 732 (1943).

The workmen's compensation statutes create rights and remedies and procedures all their own. Riley v. Perkins, 282 Ala. 629, 213 So. 2d 796 (1968); Gilmore v. Rust Eng'r Co., 45 Ala. App. 626, 235 So. 2d 673 (1970);

Freeman v. Blue Mt. Indus., 395 So. 1049 (Ala. Civ. App. 1981).

Workmen's compensation statutes are sui generis and create rights, remedies and procedure all their own, being based on a new theory of compensation distinct from previously existing theories of damages and are not rested upon any theory of wrongful conduct or neglect of employer. Pound v. Gaulding, 237 Ala. 387, 187 So. 468 (1939).

And attempt to make employee's relief more certain. — The Workmen's Compensation Act is sui generis and superseded and replaced many previously existing theories of personal injury damages arising out of common law and statutory actions. The terms and provisions of the act attempt to make more certain the relief to the employee who comes under its influence. Alabama By-Products Co. v. Landgraff, 32 Ala. App. 343, 27 So. 2d 209, aff'd, 248 Ala. 253, 27 So. 2d 215 (1946).

Rights and remedies exclusive. — The rights and remedies granted by Alabama Workmen's Compensation Act are exclusive in those cases coming within the influence of that act. Steagall v. Sloss-Sheffield Steel & Iron Co., 205 Ala. 100, 87 So. 787 (1920); Georgia Cas. Co. v. Haygood, 210 Ala. 56, 97 So. 87 (1923); Smith v. Southern Ry., 237 Ala. 372, 187 So. 195 (1939).

The Alabama Workmen's Compensation Act intends to, and does, provide the exclusive remedy for death damages in cases of employee-employer injuries. It confines the remedy to those who, within the meaning of the act, are dependents of the deceased; and if there are no dependents to sue, there is no action, since the remedy is furnished not to the administrator of the estate of a decedent but to his dependents. Patterson v. Sears-Roebuck & Co., 196 F.2d 947 (5th Cir. 1952).

In death damage cases the compensation act is exclusive, and where provision is made only for actions by dependents, no others may predicate an action upon an allegation that there are no dependents. Patterson v. Sears-Roebuck & Co., 196 F.2d 947 (5th Cir. 1952); De Arman v. Ingalls Iron Works Co., 258 Ala. 205, 61 So. 2d 764 (1952).

The "exclusive remedy" sections of the Workmen's Compensation Act stand as an impenetrable barrier to claims outside the act asserted by the employee against his employer. Wilkins v. West Point-Pepperell, Inc., 397 So. 2d 115 (Ala. 1981).

Where injured employee has been compensated for injuries sustained during his employment, employer has satisfied whatever implied contractual duty he owed to employee at will in regard to the workmen's compensation law. Martin v. Tapley, 360 So. 2d 708 (Ala. 1978).

439

The Workmen's Compensation Act provides that the rights and remedies granted to an employee shall exclude all other rights and remedies of said employee. However, if the injury is caused by some conduct on the part of the employer which results from a separate, independent relationship between the employer and the employee, the doctrine of dual capacity may remove the action from the exclusive provisions of the Workmen's Compensation Act. Windham v. Blount Int'l, Ltd., 423 So. 2d 194 (Ala. 1982).

Compensation intended where job kills worker. — The Workmen's Compensation Act as enacted in this state does not write a life insurance policy covering every employee covered under it, but in cases where it is established that the job killed the worker, the legislature intended that his widow and minor children would be compensated. B.F. Goodrich Co. v. Martin, 47 Ala. App. 244, 253 So. 2d 37 (1971).

Effect on death by wrongful act statute. — Sections 6-5-390, 6-5-391 and 6-5-410 are affected by the compensation act to the extent only, if at all, they apply to cases arising between employer and employee. Chapman v. Railway Fuel Co., 212 Ala. 106, 101 So. 879 (1924).

Compensation not limited to those in perfect health. — The benefits of the workmen's compensation law are not limited to those in perfect health. The test is: Was the accident a proximate contributing cause acting upon the particular individual to produce the disability to work, whether directly or through disease? New River Coal Co. v. Files, 215 Ala. 64, 109 So. 360 (1926); Alabama Pipe Co. v. Wofford, 253 Ala. 610, 46 So. 2d 404 (1950); Irby v. Republic Creosoting Co., 228 F.2d 195 (5th Cir.), rev'g 129 F. Supp. 92 (S.D. Ala. 1955); Southern Cotton Oil Co. v. Wynn, 266 Ala. 327, 96 So. 2d 159 (1957); B.F. Goodrich Co. v. Martin, 47 Ala. App. 244, 253 So. 2d 37 (1971).

And that employee has reached retirement age does not destroy right to compensation. — An employee's right to compensation for loss of earning capacity resulting from occupational pneumoconiosis may not be challenged on the ground that he had reached retirement age. Black Diamond Coal Mining Co. v. Wilson, 274 Ala. 220, 147 So. 2d 810 (1962).

"Double recovery" has been defined as recovering from two sources an amount that exceeds the damages. It could also mean any recovery from two sources whether or not the amount recovered exceeds the losses. Holder v. Weatherly, 456 So. 2d 812 (Ala. Civ. App. 1984).

Workmen's compensation statute does not write a life insurance policy covering every employee covered under it, but in cases where it is established that the job killed the worker, the legislature intended that his widow and minor children would be compensated. Reynolds Metals Co. v. Gray, 278 Ala. 309, 178 So. 2d 87 (1965).

And does not govern recovery in excess of benefits it confers. — While the Workmen's Compensation Act is designed to provide for the dependents of a deceased working man by affording them the benefits allowed by that statute, it is not intended to govern the distribution of that portion of a recovery from a negligent third party which is in excess of the benefits conferred by operation of the act. Sanders v. Shockley, 468 F.2d 88 (5th Cir. 1972).

The social and financial policies of this chapter are met if the carrier is subrogated to the extent of all required compensation payments, and if the dependents are entitled to recover, either directly or through the carrier, from the negligent third party any difference between the full death compensation benefits and the subrogation recovery. Sanders v. Shockley, 468 F.2d 88 (5th Cir. 1972).

Thus, excess sums may be distributed under wrongful death statute. — It is immaterial to any purpose of the Workmen's Compensation Act that all sums in excess of amounts specified in the act are distributed in accordance with the wrongful death statute. Sanders v. Shockley, 468 F.2d 88 (5th Cir. 1972).

Requirements for compensability. — In order for an accident or death to be compensable under the Workmen's Compensation Act, the following two requirements must be met: (1) the accident or death must arise out of the employment and (2) the accident or death must occur in the course of employment. Slimfold Mfg. Co. v. Martin, 417 So. 2d 199 (Ala. Civ. App. 1981), cert. quashed, 417 So. 2d 203 (Ala. 1982).

In order for an employee to recover benefits under Alabama's workmen's compensation laws, his injuries or death must be "caused by an accident arising out of and in the course of his employment." Montgomery Lincoln-Mercury, Inc. v. Neal, 423 So. 2d 846 (Ala. Civ. App.), rev'd on other grounds, 423 So. 2d 850 (Ala. 1982).

Court must find a loss of ability to earn. — The Workmen's Compensation Act requires a finding by the trial court that the employee has suffered a loss of ability to earn. Martin Indus., Inc. v. Dement, 435 So. 2d 85 (Ala. Civ. App. 1983).

Employee had been fully compensated for his

injury and was not entitled to recover any additional sums where there was no evidence that he had suffered any permanent physical impairment or loss of ability to earn a living due to injury. Pike v. Heil Co., 529 So. 2d 1020 (Ala. Civ. App. 1988).

Post-injury earnings do create a presumption of earning capacity commensurate with earnings; that presumption may be rebutted by other evidence which shows incapacity or explains why the amount of post-injury earnings is an unreliable basis for determining capacity. Harrison v. Champion Int'l Corp., 550 So. 2d 1001 (Ala. Civ. App. 1989).

The unreliability of post-injury earnings may be due to such factors as a general increase in wage levels, an increase in the employee's maturity or training, longer hours worked by the employee, sympathetic payment of wages disproportionate to capacity, and the temporary and unpredictable character of post-injury earnings. Harrison v. Champion Int'l Corp., 550 So. 2d 1001 (Ala. Civ. App. 1989).

Where worker performs same job after injury. — If worker performed the same job after his injury as he did before for the same wages or higher, a finding that he suffered a reduction in earning capacity was not necessarily precluded, but he must rebut the presumption that he did not sustain a loss of ability to earn. Russell Coal Co. v. Williams, 550 So. 2d 1007 (Ala. Civ. App. 1989).

Presumption of earning capacity was not overcome where there was evidence which supported the trial court's finding that worker had suffered no loss of ability to earn since he had been working since 1987 in the same job that he had before the accident and although his physical restrictions prevented him from performing some tasks that he did before the accident, he worked regularly to the apparent satisfaction of his employer. Harrison v. Champion Int'l Corp., 550 So. 2d 1001 (Ala. Civ. App. 1989).

Failure to present evidence medical expenses reasonable or necessary. — Worker was precluded from recovering medical expenses because he failed to present any evidence that they were reasonable, necessary, or directly related to the accident. Russell Coal Co. v. Williams, 550 So. 2d 1007 (Ala. Civ. App. 1989).

Injuries presumed to come within Act. — Injuries to employee presumably come under the Workmen's Compensation Act. W.B. Davis & Son v. Ruple, 222 Ala. 52, 130 So. 772 (1930); De Arman v. Ingalls Iron Works Co., 258 Ala. 205, 61 So. 2d 764 (1952).

Suits brought by an employee against his employer for injuries sustained in the course of his employment are presumed to fall within the provisions of the Workmen's Compensation Act. Veterans of Foreign Wars Post 7320 v. Sheffield, 398 So. 2d 262 (Ala. 1981).

Legal test of causation does not require proof of some unusual exertion, strain or exposure not ordinary to the job, but the strenuous activity, exposure or other risk must be different from that to which others not employed in the same capacity are exposed. Montgomery Lincoln-Mercury, Inc. v. Neal, 423 So. 2d 846 (Ala. Civ. App.), rev'd on other grounds, 423 So. 2d 850 (Ala. 1982).

But-for test is clearly not the test for causation under Alabama's Workmen's Compensation Act. Instead, the burden is on the claimant to establish a definite causal connection between the work and the injury. Slimfold Mfg. Co. v. Martin, 417 So. 2d 199 (Ala. Civ. App. 1981), cert. quashed, 417 So. 2d 203 (Ala. 1982).

Heat exposure cases. — The following two-pronged test applies to heat exposure cases: the harmful condition does arise out of the employment, if, in the performance of the duties for which he was engaged, in the manner required or contemplated by the employer, it is necessary for the employee to expose himself to a danger, materially in excess of that to which people commonly in that locality are exposed, when not situated as he is when thus performing his service, and that such excessive exposure may be found to have been the direct cause of the injury, though operating upon other conditions of common exposure. This principle has been specifically thus applied to sunstroke or heat prostration or heat exhaustion in many varying conditions. Montgomery Lincoln-Mercury, Inc. v. Neal, 423 So. 2d 846 (Ala. Civ. App.), rev'd on other grounds, 423 So. 2d 850 (Ala. 1982).

The two-pronged test has been cited as controlling in cases dealing with death or injury arising from a heart attack allegedly caused by strain or exertion on the job. Montgomery Lincoln-Mercury, Inc. v. Neal, 423 So. 2d 846 (Ala. Civ. App.), rev'd on other grounds, 423 So. 2d 850 (Ala. 1982).

Clarification of two-pronged test. — If in the performance of his job the employee has to exert or strain himself or is exposed to conditions of risk or hazard and he would not have strained or exerted himself or been exposed to such conditions had he not been performing his job and the exertion or strain or the exposure to the condition was, in fact, a contributing cause to his injury or death, the test whether the job caused the injury or death is satisfied. Montgomery Lincoln-Mercury, Inc. v. Neal, 423 So. 2d 846 (Ala. Civ. App.), rev'd on other grounds, 423 So. 2d 850 (Ala. 1982).

441

The occupational disease statutes, by definition and reason, relate to a particular occupation or industry. Each of the specific occupational diseases provided by statute relates to a general classification or occupation, i.e., coal miners, textile workers, radiation workers, and workers exposed to dust and silica regularly and peculiarly as an incident of their job. Chrysler Corp. v. Henley, 400 So. 2d 412 (Ala. Civ. App. 1981).

Effect of insurance policy clauses excluding liability for injuries covered by act. — It is common for hospital and public liability policies to exclude benefits or liability for injuries covered by the workmen's compensation law; and where the policy states that it excludes benefits for injuries covered by the workmen's compensation law, even though the benefits claimed are in excess of those provided by that law, it has been held to exclude liability or benefits for injuries covered by the workmen's compensation law. This is because it is the type of disease or injury that calls into play the exclusion rather than the amount of benefits that may be received. Phillips v. Prudential Ins. Co. of Am., 285 Ala. 472, 233 So. 2d 480 (1970).

Where the invocation of an exclusionary clause in an insurance policy depends upon whether the type of injury places the injured workman within the provisions of the workmen's compensation law, the cases uniformly hold that effect must be accorded the exclusionary clause. Phillips v. Prudential Ins. Co. of Am., 285 Ala. 472, 233 So. 2d 480 (1970).

Worker's compensation carrier may be liable when it voluntarily undertakes to inspect employer's premises for safety. However, in a suit of this nature, a plaintiff bears the burden of proving (1) that the defendant had a duty, or assumed a duty by voluntarily undertaking the inspection; (2) the scope of that duty; (3) whether the duty was breached; (40) whether there was damage or injury; and (5) whether the injury was proximately caused by that breach. Barnes v. Liberty Mut. Ins. Co., 472 So. 2d 1041 (Ala. 1985).

Direct action by employee. — Provision in a policy providing workmen's compensation which allows a direct action on the policy by the injured employee is valid and enforceable and is not invalidated by the Workmen's Compensation Act. Wilson v. Central Foundry Co., 414 So. 2d 963 (Ala. 1982).

Widow's right to benefits under the Workmen's Compensation Act is "a right of property" within the rule established in Fox v. Fox, 235 Ala. 338, 179 So. 237 (1938), that a decree of divorce may be attacked for fraud after the death of the party procuring it

where rights of property are concerned. Lucas v. Lucas, 258 Ala. 515, 64 So. 2d 70 (1953).

Relief granted against award obtained by fraud. — Petition to enjoin enforcement of judgment at law for fraud in its procurement, alleging that defendant by falsely representing and testifying that she was wife of a deceased employee obtained an award of compensation under workmen's compensation law, was held not demurrable (subject to motion to dismiss now), the very existence of defendant's cause of action having been simulated. Bolden v. Sloss-Sheffield Steel & Iron Co., 215 Ala. 334, 110 So. 574 (1925).

Claims based on tort of bad faith refusal to pay an insurance claim in the workmen's compensation context, are not barred by the exclusivity provisions of the Workmen's Compensation Act. Gibson v. Fidelity & Cas. Co., 454 So. 2d 526 (Ala. 1984).

The tort of outrageous conduct is a valid claim in the workmen's compensation context. However, in attempting to prove such a claim, the plaintiff has the burden of showing that the conduct is so outrageous in character and so extreme in degree as to be regarded as atrocious and utterly intolerable in a civilized society. Gibson v. Fidelity & Cas. Co., 454 So. 2d 526 (Ala. 1984).

A claim based upon the tort of outrageous conduct is not barred under the exclusivity provisions of the Workmen's Compensation Act. Gibson v. Fidelity & Cas. Co., 454 So. 2d 526 (Ala. 1984).

An injured employee's claim based on intentional infliction of emotional distress or outrageous conduct against an employer is not barred by the exclusivity provisions of the Workmen's Compensation Act. Jackson v. Roberts, 485 So. 2d 1116 (Ala. 1986).

Injury resulting from willful and criminal assault upon employee by fellow employee may be considered accident compensable under the workmen's compensation statutes. However, the fact that the assault occurred on the employer's premises during work hours does not conclusively establish that the assault arose out of and in the course of the employment. That determination is to be drawn from the circumstances of the individual case. Thompson v. Anserall, Inc., 522 So. 2d 284 (Ala. Civ. App. 1988).

Assault based solely upon personal ill will, hatred, or anger does not arise out of and in course of employment. If the rational mind could determine that the proximate cause of the injury was set in motion by the employment, then the assault arose out of and in the course of the employment. Thompson v. Anserall, Inc., 522 So. 2d 284 (Ala. Civ. App. 1988).

Alabama's Workmen's Compensation Act does not extend coverage to mental disorders or injuries that were neither produced nor proximately caused by some physical injury to the claimant's body. Belcher v. Pinkerton's, Inc., 519 So. 2d 529 (Ala. Civ. App. 1987).

Personal representative of a deceased person cannot maintain an action under this chapter. There is a total lack of statutory authority for such a procedure. The compensation law being in derogation of the common law, as the homicide act, in the absence of statutory authority the personal representative cannot maintain such an action. DeBardeleben Coal Corp. v. Richards, 251 Ala. 324, 37 So. 2d 121 (1948).

Act merely requires that adopted child be able to inherit as deceased's child. — There is no statement in the Workmen's Compensation Act which indicates that the act of adoption takes a child out of the terminology of "children" of his natural father. All that is required is that the adopted child be entitled to inherit as a child of the deceased. Central Foundry Co. v. Brown, 381 So. 2d 635 (Ala. Civ. App. 1979), cert. denied, 381 So. 2d 637 (Ala. 1980).

If a trial court awards an attorney's fee for more than the statutory amount in a workmen's compensation case, the error would be solely related to the employee and not to the employer since the employee must bear the whole fee out of compensation awarded. Rush v. Heflin, 411 So. 2d 1295 (Ala. Civ. App. 1982).

When attorney's fees recoverable. — It is well settled in Alabama that attorney's fees are recoverable only when authorized by statute, when a contract exists, or in certain equitable proceedings. Cowgill v. Bowman Transp., Inc., 587 So. 2d 1000 (Ala. Civ. App.), writ quash improvidently granted, 587 So. 2d 1002 (Ala. 1991).

Counsel not entitled to fee for obtaining payment of expenses. — In the absence of willful or contumacious conduct by the employer, the employee's counsel is not entitled under the Workmen's Compensation Act to an award of an attorney's fee for obtaining the payment of medical and surgical expenses. Cowgill v. Bowman Transp., Inc., 587 So. 2d 1000 (Ala. Civ. App.), writ quashed improvidently granted, 587 So. 2d 1002 (Ala. 1991).

Workmen's Compensation Act mandates suspension of employee's benefits if employee refuses to comply with any reasonable request for examination or refuses to accept rehabilitation. Beatrice Foods Co. v. Gray, 431 So. 2d 1299 (Ala. Civ. App. 1983). The reasonableness or unreasonableness of employee's refusal to undergo further treatment is a question of fact for the trier of fact. Moreover, whether an employee can be rehabilitated is also a question of fact for the trial court. Beatrice Foods Co. v. Gray, 431 So. 2d 1299 (Ala. Civ. App. 1983).

Back injury from on-the-job accident. — Evidence in workmen's compensation action that claimant, while unloading truck, picked up a box and immediately felt a stinging sensation and then numbness in his back, was sufficient to support finding that claimant's physical disability was caused by an arthritic condition incurred as the result of an injury to his back suffered in an on-the-job accident or was caused by an on-the-job accident which aggravated an existing arthritic condition in his back, and thus supported award of compensation. Hellums v. Hager, 360 So. 2d 721 (Ala. Civ. App. 1978).

Second injury to same eye does not give employer a defense where sight is lost. — Evidence that compensation claimant received second injury to eye several months after original injury held not to relieve employer from liability for loss of sight of eye, where eye became gradually worse from time of original injury. Agricola Furnace Co. v. Bowen, 26 Ala. App. 106, 154 So. 121 (1934).

Standard of review. — The standard of review in workmen's compensation cases is limited to a determination of whether there is any legal evidence or reasonable inferences therefrom to support the findings of fact of the trial court. Where the findings of fact by the trial court are meager or omissive, this court will look to the evidence to see if, on any reasonable view of the evidence, the judgment of the court can be sustained. On appeal, however, this court will not weigh the evidence to determine if it reasonably satisfies the issue in question; that is for the trial court. Sun Papers, Inc. v. Jerrell, 411 So. 2d 790 (Ala. Civ. App. 1981).

The standard of review in workmen's compensation cases is limited to a determination of whether there is any legal evidence to support the trial court's findings of fact. The appellate court does not weigh the evidence. If any reasonable view of the evidence supports the findings of the trial court, it is then determined if the correct legal conclusions have been drawn therefrom. Montgomery Lincoln-Mercury, Inc. v. Neal, 423 So. 2d 850 (Ala. 1982).

In workmen's compensation cases the appellate court looks at the record only to determine if the findings of fact by the trial court are supported by any legal evidence and if the law has been properly applied to the facts. It will not consider the weight of the evidence. Hall v.

Teledyne Firth Sterling, 448 So. 2d 395 (Ala. Civ. App. 1984).

On certiorari to review workmen's compensation cases, the appeals court will not undertake an examination of the weight or preponderance of the evidence presented to the trial court. Instead, the court will look to see if there is any evidence to support the facts found by the trial court. Lankford v. International Paper Co., 454 So. 2d 988 (Ala. Civ. App. 1984).

The standard of review in a workmen's compensation case is very narrow. Dodson v. Atrax Div. of Wallace-Murray Corp., 437 So. 2d 1294 (Ala. Civ. App. 1983).

Appellate court's review of the judgment in workmen's compensation cases is limited to determining if there is any legal evidence to support the trial court's finding of fact and if the correct law was applied to such facts. Martin Indus., Inc. v. Dement, 435 So. 2d 85 (Ala. Civ. App. 1983).

On appeal, review of a workmen's compensation case is limited to questions of law, and to examination of the evidence to determine if there is any legal evidence to support the findings of the trial court. Dodson v. Atrax Div. of Wallace-Murray Corp., 437 So. 2d 1294 (Ala. Civ. App. 1983).

The standard of appellate review in workmen's compensation cases is a two-step process. Initially, the reviewing court will look to see if there is any legal evidence to support the trial court's findings. If such evidence is found, then the reviewing court determines whether any reasonable view of that evidence supports the trial court's judgment. Ex parte Eastwood Foods, Inc., 575 So. 2d 91 (Ala. 1991).

Condition within a supersedeas bond requiring satisfaction of a judgment by the appellant in a workmen's compensation case, wherein the judgment includes amounts to be paid in future installments, is satisfied by the appellant's payment of so much of the judgment that represents workmen's compensation payments, interest, costs, and affirmance penalties accrued up to the time of termination of the appeal. Employers Ins. Co. v. American Liberty Ins. Co., 495 So. 2d 1039 (Ala. 1986).

Cited in Hill v. Metal Reclamation, Inc., 348 So. 2d 493 (Ala. 1977); Haney v. Dunlop Tire & Rubber Corp., 373 So. 2d 334 (Ala. Civ. App. 1979); Mission Ins. Co. v. Barnett, 476 F. Supp. 925 (S.D. Ala. 1979); Dover Mills, Inc. v. Garrett, 384 So. 2d 1127 (Ala. Civ. App. 1980); Stauffer Chem. Co. v. McIntyre Elec. Serv., Inc., 401 So. 2d 745 (Ala. 1981); Therrell v. Scott Paper Co., 428 So. 2d 33 (Ala. 1983); Parker v. Thyssen Mining Constr., Inc., 428 So. 2d 615 (Ala. 1983); Lockett v. Thermal Components, Inc., 460 So. 2d 1352 (Ala. Civ. App.

1984); Bailey v. Collier, 465 So. 2d 381 (Ala. 1985).

Collateral references. — Cancer as compensable under workers' compensation acts. 19 ALR4th 639.

Right of health or accident insurer to intervene in workers' compensation proceeding to recover benefits previously paid to claimant or beneficiary. 38 ALR4th 355.

II. CONSTRUCTION.

Workmen's Compensation Act must be liberally construed. Alabama By-Products Co. v. Landgraff, 32 Ala. App. 343, 27 So. 2d 209, aff'd, 248 Ala. 253, 27 So. 2d 215 (1946); Alabama Pipe Co. v. Wofford, 253 Ala. 610, 46 So. 2d 404 (1950); Hamilton Motor Co. v. Cooner, 254 Ala. 422, 47 So. 2d 270 (1950); Baggett Transp. Co. v. Holderfield, 260 Ala. 56, 68 So. 2d 21 (1953); Kroger Co. v. Millsap, 280 Ala. 531, 196 So. 2d 380 (1967); Riley v. Perkins, 282 Ala. 629, 213 So. 2d 796 (1968); Cement Prods. Co. v. Martin, 397 So. 2d 149 (Ala. Civ. App. 1981).

Workmen's Compensation Act and phrase "arising out of and in the course of his employment," should be construed broadly and liberally, so as to advance beneficent objects of act, so far as it will permit. Ex parte Majestic Coal Co., 208 Ala. 86, 93 So. 728 (1922); Ex parte Louisville & N.R.R., 208 Ala. 216, 94 So. 289 (1922); Ex parte Rosengrant, 213 Ala. 202, 104 So. 409 (1925); Ex parte Taylor, 213 Ala. 282, 104 So. 527 (1925); Ex parte Little Canaba Coal Co., 213 Ala. 596, 105 So. 648 (1925); Edwards v. Doster-Northington Drug Co., 214 Ala. 640, 108 So. 862 (1926); Mobile Liners v. McConnell, 220 Ala. 562, 126 So. 626 (1930); Sloss-Sheffield Steel & Iron Co. v. Brown, 228 Ala. 460, 153 So. 642 (1934); Sloss-Sheffield Steel & Iron Co. v. Nations, 236 Ala. 571, 183 So. 871 (1938); Southern Cotton Oil Co. v. Bruce, 249 Ala. 675, 32 So. 2d 666 (1947); Wells v. Morris, 33 Ala. App. 497, 35 So. 2d 54 (1948); Swift & Co. v. Rolling, 252 Ala. 536, 42 So. 2d 6 (1949); Hamilton Motor Co. v. Cooner, 254 Ala. 422, 47 So. 2d 270 (1950); Baggett Transp. Co. v. Holderfield, 260 Ala. 56, 68 So. 2d 21 (1953); Irby v. Republic Creosoting Co., 228 F.2d 195 (5th Cir.), rev'g 129 F. Supp. 92 (S.D. Ala. 1955).

Practically all courts are agreed that there should be accorded to the workmen's compensation law a broad and liberal construction. But it is also agreed that this law does not mean one thing when it is to the advantage of an employee so to maintain, and something else when an employer invokes the protection of the law in his favor. Carraway Methodist Hosp. v. Pitts, 256 Ala. 665, 57 So. 2d 96 (1952).

The Workmen's Compensation Act should be liberally construed to the end that its beneficent objects may be advanced. United States Steel Corp. v. Baker, 266 Ala. 538, 97 So. 2d 899 (1957).

The Workmen's Compensation Act should be given a liberal construction to accomplish its beneficent purposes. Benson-Jackson-Mathers Post No. 5106 v. Donaldson, 267 Ala. 60, 99 So. 2d 688 (1957); Brunson Milling Co. v. Grimes, 267 Ala. 395, 103 So. 2d 315 (1958); Kroger Co. v. Millsap, 280 Ala. 531, 196 So. 2d 380 (1967); Bell v. Driskill, 282 Ala. 640, 213 So. 2d 806 (1968); Aluminum Workers Int'l v. Champion, 45 Ala. App. 570, 233 So. 2d 511 (1970); Dale Motels, Inc. v. Crittenden, 50 Ala. App. 251, 278 So. 2d 370 (1973).

The compensation law should be liberally construed in furtherance of the humanitarian purposes leading to its enactment. City of Foley v. Terry, 278 Ala. 30, 175 So. 2d 461 (1965); Gilmore v. Rust Eng'r Co., 45 Ala. App. 626, 235 So. 2d 673 (1970).

The workmen's compensation laws are special and remedial and to be construed and applied liberally to effect the beneficent purposes, and reasonable doubts are to be resolved in favor of claimants. Tiger Motor Co. v. Winslett, 278 Ala. 108, 176 So. 2d 39 (1965).

The Workmen's Compensation Act, being remedial in nature, should be given liberal construction to accomplish the beneficent purposes, and all reasonable doubts must be resolved in favor of the employee. Riley v. Perkins, 282 Ala. 629, 213 So. 2d 796 (1968); Lankford v. Redwing Carriers, Inc., 344 So. 2d 515 (Ala. Civ. App.), cert. denied, 344 So. 2d 522 (Ala. 1977); American Tennis Courts, Inc. v. Hinton, 378 So. 2d 235 (Ala. Civ. App.), cert. denied, 378 So. 2d 239 (Ala. 1979).

In line with the authorities generally, that the Workmen's Compensation Act should be construed liberally in favor of the employee to advance its benevolent objects, the court of appeals (now court of civil appeals) has been very liberal in its own interpretation of facts to sustain an injury in such cases. Myers v. Juneman Elec. Co., 46 Ala. App. 529, 244 So. 2d 809 (1971).

Liberal construction of the workmen's compensation law has been favored to effectuate its purposes and eliminate procedural technicalities. Defense Ordinance Corp. v. England, 52 Ala. App. 565, 295 So. 2d 419 (1974).

The act should be liberally construed to carry out its beneficent purposes. Ford v. Mitcham, 53 Ala. App. 102, 298 So. 2d 34 (1974); Lauderdale County Coop. v. Shook, 376 So. 2d 199 (Ala. Civ. App.), cert. denied, 376 So. 2d 202 (Ala. 1979).

Alabama workmen's compensation laws should be liberally construed in order to effectuate the purpose behind the act and to eliminate procedural technicalities. This liberal construction is in line with the intent of the procedural rules relating to amendments under A.R.C.P., Rule 15. Sun Papers, Inc. v. Jerrell, 411 So. 2d 790 (Ala. Civ. App. 1981).

An employee covered under the workmen's compensation law is entitled to be fully compensated for a job-related injury and the provisions of that law should be liberally construed to accomplish just such a result. Haggard v. Uniroyal, Inc., 423 So. 2d 865 (Ala. Civ. App. 1982).

An amendment adding a child posthumously as another party to the complaint is properly allowed where evidence indicates that the employer paid medical insurance for both the widow and the child until the child was three months old. Although the child was not included as a party plaintiff in the complaint itself, both the widow and the child were in essence before the court as dependents seeking compensation under the workmen's compensation law. Thus the filing of the petition in the name of the widow only does not preclude a subsequent amendment to include the child's name on the face of the complaint. Sun Papers, Inc. v. Jerrell, 411 So. 2d 790 (Ala. Civ. App. 1981).

Terms of the Workmen's Compensation Act are a legislative matter. Slagle v. Reynolds Metals Co., 344 So. 2d 1216 (Ala. 1977).

And reasonable doubts should be resolved in favor of the workman. Alabama By-Products Co. v. Landgraff, 32 Ala. App. 343, 27 So. 2d 209, aff'd, 248 Ala. 253, 27 So. 2d 215 (1946); Alabama Pipe Co. v. Wofford, 253 Ala. 610, 46 So. 2d 404 (1950); Hamilton Motor Co. v. Cooner, 254 Ala. 422, 47 So. 2d 270 (1950); Baggett Transp. Co. v. Holderfield, 260 Ala. 56, 68 So. 2d 21 (1953); Kroger Co. v. Millsap, 280 Ala. 531, 196 So. 2d 380 (1967); Riley v. Perkins, 282 Ala. 629, 213 So. 2d 796 (1968); Ford v. Mitcham, 53 Ala. App. 102, 298 So. 2d 34 (1974).

But liberality of construction should not proceed to such a point as to amount to judicial legislation. Ford v. Mitcham, 53 Ala. App. 102, 298 So. 2d 34 (1974).

And statute not to be extended. — The provisions of the workmen's compensation law cannot be extended to cover persons or occupations not within its scope. Birmingham Post Co. v. Sturgeon, 227 Ala. 162, 149 So. 74 (1933).

The court cannot extend statute beyond its legitimate scope. Nichols v. St. Louis & S.F.R.R., 227 Ala. 592, 151 So. 347 (1933); United States Steel Corp. v. Baker, 266 Ala. 538, 97 So. 2d 899 (1957).

While the Workmen's Compensation Act should be liberally construed to accomplish its beneficent purposes, it should not be given a construction extending it beyond its legitimate scope, nor one which the language of the act does not fairly and reasonably support. City of Jasper v. Sherer, 273 Ala. 356, 141 So. 2d 202 (1962).

Nor is rule as to evidence changed. — Liberality of construction does not mean that the rule as to the measure of proof, or the sufficiency of the evidence, is different from the rule in ordinary cases. Kroger Co. v. Millsap, 280 Ala. 531, 196 So. 2d 380 (1967).

III. EMPLOYEES COVERED BY ACT.

This act does not extend its benefits to employees of the state or of its agencies and departments, and those employees must depend on such relief as may be had through the state board of adjustment. (§§ 41-9-60 through 41-9-73). Breeding v. TVA, 243 Ala. 240, 9 So. 2d 6 (1942). See also Humphrey v. Poss, 245 Ala. 11, 15 So. 2d 732 (1943); Employer's Ins. Co. v. Harrison, 250 Ala. 116, 33 So. 2d 264 (1947).

Nor to employee of Tennessee Valley Authority. — An employee of the Tennessee Valley Authority is not entitled to benefits of this act in case of accidental injuries arising out of and in course of his employment. Breeding v. TVA, 243 Ala. 240, 9 So. 2d 6 (1942).

Nor to post exchange employees. — A fort post exchange operated as arm of government was entitled to immunities of federal government against action or liability under this section. Humphrey v. Poss, 245 Ala. 11, 15 So. 2d 732 (1943).

Application of chapter not limited to municipalities while engaged only in proprietary functions. — The legislature did not intend to limit the application of the Workmen's Compensation Act to municipalities while engaged only in proprietary functions. City of Foley v. Terry, 278 Ala. 30, 175 So. 2d 461 (1965).

This chapter is not applicable to employees engaged in interstate commerce. —

Railroad yard policeman, who was shot while attempting to arrest person who broke into freight car of interstate train which policeman was watching held engaged in "interstate commerce," and action for injuries was governed by Federal Employers' Liability Act, and not by compensation statute. Nichols v. St. Louis & S.F.R.R., 227 Ala. 592, 151 So. 347 (1933).

Yard policeman, if engaged in interstate commerce when removing hobos from interstate train, held not so engaged after taking them to station for search. Southern Ry. v. Varnell, 222 Ala. 237, 131 So. 803 (1930).

Nor is it applicable to maritime workers. — Repair work on vessels used on navigable waters, in dry dock on shore of such waters, is maritime service, and Workmen's Compensation Act cannot be applied to injury sustained therein without violating U.S. Const., article III, § 2. Baker Tow Boat Co. v. Langner, 218 Ala. 34, 117 So. 915 (1928).

Nor to workers in former state territory ceded to United States. — Where employee was injured while working on federal government building located on land ceded to federal government prior to passage of Workmen's Compensation Act and at time when Employer's Liability Act, § 25-6-1 et seq., was in force, employee was entitled to recover under Employer's Liability Act instead of Workmen's Compensation Act, since the compensation act was without effect in the ceded territory. Pound v. Gaulding, 237 Ala. 387, 187 So. 468 (1939).

Employee injured on building way which is used in construction of vessels. — A building way, which is used exclusively in the construction of vessels and subsequent launching and is not used to remove a vessel from the water, does not fall within the statutory meaning of "and dry dock" under § 3(a) of the Longshoremen's & Harbor Workers' Compensation Act, and an employee injured on a building way would be covered under the Workmen's Compensation Act of Alabama. American Mut. Liab. Ins. Co. v. Neuman, 318 F. Supp. 398 (S.D. Ala. 1969).

ARTICLE 1.

GENERAL PROVISIONS.

§ 25-5-1. Definitions.

Throughout this chapter, the following words and phrases as used therein shall be considered to have the following meanings, respectively, unless the context shall clearly indicate a different meaning in the connection used:

(1) COMPENSATION. The money benefits to be paid on account of injury or death, as provided in Articles 3 and 4. The recovery which an employee may receive by action at law under Article 2 of this chapter is termed "recovery of civil damages," as provided for in Sections 25-5-31 and 25-5-34. "Compensation" does not include medical and surgical treatment and attention, medicine, medical and surgical supplies, and crutches and apparatus furnished an employee on account of an injury.

(2) CHILD or CHILDREN. The terms include posthumous children and all other children entitled by law to inherit as children of the deceased; stepchildren who were members of the family of the deceased, at the time of the accident, and were dependent upon him or her for support; a grandchild of the deceased employee, whose father is dead or is an invalid, and who was supported by and a member of the family of the deceased grandparent at the time of the accident.

(3) DEPENDENT CHILD or ORPHAN. An unmarried child under the age of 18 years or one over that age who is physically or mentally incapacitated from earning.

(4) EMPLOYER. Every person who employs another to perform a service for hire and pays wages directly to the person. The term shall include a service company for a self-insurer or any person, corporation, copartnership, or association, or group thereof, and shall, if the employer is insured, include his or her insurer, the insurer being entitled to the employer's rights, immunities, and remedies under this chapter, as far as applicable. The inclusion of an employer's insurer within the term shall not provide the insurer with immunity from liability to an injured employee, or his or her dependent in the case of death to whom the insurer would otherwise be subject to liability under Section 25-5-11. Notwithstanding the provisions of this chapter, in no event shall a common carrier by motor vehicle operating pursuant to a certificate of public convenience and necessity be deemed the "employer" of a leased-operator or owner-operator of a motor vehicle or vehicles under contract to the common carrier.

(5) EMPLOYEE or WORKER. The terms are used interchangeably, have the same meaning throughout this chapter, and shall be construed to mean the same. The terms include the plural and all ages and both sexes. The terms include every person in the service of another under any contract of hire, express or implied, oral or written, including aliens and also including minors who are legally permitted to work under the laws of this state, and also including all employees of Tannehill Furnace and Foundry Commis-

sion. Any reference in this chapter to a "worker" or "employee" shall, if the worker or employee is dead, include his or her dependent, as defined in this chapter, if the context so requires.

(6) WAGES or WEEKLY WAGES. The terms shall in all cases be construed to mean "average weekly earnings", based on those earnings subject to federal income taxation and reportable on the Federal W-2 tax form which shall include voluntary contributions made by the employee to a tax-qualified retirement program, voluntary contributions to a Section 125 cafeteria program, and fringe benefits as defined herein. Average weekly earnings shall not include fringe benefits if and only if the employer continues the benefits during the period of time for which compensation is paid. "Fringe benefits" shall mean only the employer's portion of health, life, and disability insurance premiums.

(7) ACCIDENT. The term, as used in the phrases "personal injuries due to accident" or "injuries or death caused by accident" shall be construed to mean an unexpected or unforeseen event, happening suddenly and violently, with or without human fault, and producing at the time injury to the physical structure of the body or damage to an artificial member of the body by accidental means.

(8) INJURIES BY AN ACCIDENT ARISING OUT OF AND IN THE COURSE OF THE EMPLOYMENT. Without otherwise affecting either the meaning or interpretation of the clause, the clause does not cover workers except while engaged in or about the premises where their services are being performed or where their service requires their presence as a part of service at the time of the accident and during the hours of service as workers.

(9) INJURY. "Injury and personal injury" shall mean only injury by accident arising out of and in the course of the employment, and shall not include a disease in any form, except for an occupational disease or where it results naturally and unavoidably from the accident. Injury shall include physical injury caused either by carpal tunnel syndrome disorder or by other cumulative trauma disorder if either disorder arises out of and in the course of the employment, and breakage or damage to eyeglasses, hearing aids, dentures, or other prosthetic devices which function as part of the body, when injury to them is incidental to an on-the-job injury to the body. Injury does not include an injury caused by the act of a third person or fellow employee intended to injure the employee because of reasons personal to him or her and not directed against him or her as an employee or because of his or her employment. Injury does not include a mental disorder or mental injury that has neither been produced nor been proximately caused by some physical injury to the body.

(10) SINGULAR and PLURAL. Wherever the singular is used, the plural shall be included.

(11) GENDER. Where the masculine gender is used, the feminine and neuter shall be included.

(12) LOSS OF HAND OR FOOT. Amputation between the elbow and wrist shall be considered as the equivalent to the loss of a hand, and the

amputation between the knee and ankle shall be considered as the equivalent of the loss of a foot.

(13) PROVIDERS. A medical clinic, pharmacist, dentist, chiropractor, psychologist, podiatrist, physical therapist, pharmaceutical supply company, rehabilitation service, or other person or entity providing treatment, service, or equipment, or person or entity providing facilities at which the employee receives treatment.

(14) MEDICAL. All services, treatment, or equipment provided by a provider.

(15) PREVAILING. The most commonly occurring reimbursements for health services, other than those provided by federal and state programs for the elderly (Medicare) and economically disadvantaged (Medicaid). "Prevailing" shall include not only amounts per procedure code, but also commonly used adjudication rules as applied to multiple procedures, global procedures, use of assistant surgeons, and others as appropriate. For hospitals, "prevailing" rate of reimbursement or payment shall be established by the method contained in Section 25-5-77.

(16) PARTICIPATING AND NONPARTICIPATING HOSPITALS. Those hospitals that have a negotiated rate of reimbursement or payment with the Department of Industrial Relations. "Nonparticipating hospitals" means those hospitals that have not negotiated a rate of reimbursement or payment with the Department of Industrial Relations.

(17) HOSPITAL. A hospital, ambulatory surgical center, outpatient rehabilitation center licensed by the State of Alabama, and diagnostic facilities accredited by the Commission on Accreditation of Rehabilitation Facilities.

(18) THE COURT. The circuit court that would have jurisdiction in an ordinary civil action involving a claim for the injuries or death in question, and "the judge" means a judge of that court.

(19) UTILIZATION REVIEW. The determination of medical necessity for medical and surgical in-hospital, out-patient, and alternative settings treatments for acute and rehabilitation care. It includes precertification for elective treatments. Concurrent review and, if necessary, retrospective review are required for emergency cases.

(20) BILL SCREENING. The evaluation and adjudication of provider bills for appropriateness of reimbursement relative to medical necessity and prevailing rates of reimbursement, duplicate charges, unbundling of charges, relativeness of services to injury or illness, necessity of assistant surgeons, adjudication of multiple procedures, number of modalities, global procedures, and any other prevailing adjudication issues that may apply.

(21) ADJUDICATION. The review of claims to apply prevailing rules that adjust reimbursements for the amount of work required when multiple procedures are performed at the same time, when assisting surgeons are present, to eliminate duplicate billing from the unbundling of global fees, and to adjust for the most commonly occurring method adopted for total reimbursement.

449

(22) OMBUDSMAN. An individual who assists injured or disabled employees, persons claiming death benefits, employers, and other persons in protecting their rights and obtaining information available under the workers' compensation law. (Code 1923, § 7396; Acts 1939, No. 661, p. 1036, § 18; Code 1940, T. 26, § 262; Acts 1949, No. 36, p. 47; Acts 1971, No. 667, p. 1376, §§ 1, 2; Acts 1973, No. 1062, p. 1750, § 4; Acts 1975, 4th Ex. Sess., No. 86, p. 2729, § 2; Acts 1984, 1st Ex. Sess., No. 84-787, p. 177; Acts 1984, 2nd Ex. Sess., No. 85-41, p. 44, § 2; Acts 1992, No. 92-537, § 2.)

The 1992 amendment, effective May 19, 1992, rewrote this section. As to the implementation date for the amendments to subdivisions (4) and (6), see the Code commissioner's note.

Code commissioner's note. — Acts 1984, 2nd Ex. Sess., No. 85-41, § 14 provides: "This act shall become effective immediately upon its passage and approval by the governor [January 9, 1985], or upon its otherwise becoming a law, provided it shall have no effect whatsoever with respect to the right of any injured employee to bring an action with respect to or upon any cause of action which arose or accrued prior to February 1, 1985. Provided further, it shall have no effect on and shall not apply to any accident or exposure to injurious condition occurring before the effective date of this Act."

Acts 1985, No. 85-77, provides that Acts 1985, No. 85-41, shall be named the Bishop-Cooley-Johnson Act.

Acts 1992, No. 92-537, § 1 provides: "It is the intent of the Legislature that the Department of Industrial Relations and the Alabama judicial system shall administer the Alabama Workers' Compensation Act to provide a workers' benefit system to insure the quick and efficient payment of compensation and medical benefits to injured and disabled workers at a reasonable cost to the employers who are subject to the Alabama Workers' Compensation Act. It is the specific intent of the Legislature that workers' compensation benefit claim cases be decided on their merits. The Alabama Workers' Compensation Act is remedial in nature and should be liberally construed to effectuate the intended beneficial purposes. However, even a liberality of construction does not abrogate the measure of proof or sufficiency of evidence.

It is also the intent of the Legislature in adopting this workers' compensation scheme to address difficulties in the current scheme that are producing a debilitating and adverse effect on the state's ability to retain existing industry and attract new industry. The Legislature finds that the current Workmen's Compensation Law of Alabama and other means of compensation or remedy for injury in the workplace has unduly increased cost to employers in the state, driven away jobs, and produced no concomitant benefit. There is a total absence of any reliable evidence that the current act has resulted in fewer injuries on the job, and a considerable body of evidence that any added benefit to the worker is significantly offset by the resulting reduction in job opportunities.

The Legislature has reviewed substantial evidence related to various types of cumulative physical stress disorders, cumulative trauma disorders and certain "natural aging" disorders, including carpal tunnel syndrome, repetitive motion syndrome, and even back and neck infirmities that result from gradual deterioration or the natural process of aging. The Legislature has concluded that it is extremely difficult for the adjudicator of fact to determine whether these disorders are related to work or whether they result from some congenital defect, aging processes, or simply the routine activities of daily living.

These claims also account for a substantial percentage of the workers' compensation claims in this state and are one of the contributing causes of the current workers' compensation crisis facing this state.

It is the finding and expressed intent of the Legislature that the existence of a fair and affordable workers' compensation system within the State of Alabama materially contributes to the economic growth and prosperity of the state and all its citizens. It is the further finding of the Legislature that the provision of quality medical services to employees injured in the workplace at a reasonable and fair cost to employers is an important part of a workers' compensation system. The establishment of a Workers' Compensation Medical Services Board as constituted in this amendatory act is considered by the Legislature to be the most appropriate mechanism for insuring that high quality medical services are provided in a cost-effective manner to employees injured in the workplace."

Section 52 of Acts 1992, No. 92-537 provides: "The term 'Alabama Workmen's Compensation Law,' as provided for in the Code of Alabama

1975, shall henceforth be known as 'The Alabama Workers' Compensation Law.'"

Section 53 of Acts 1992, No. 92-537 provides that subdivisions (4) and (6) of this section shall be implemented on August 1, 1992.

U.S. Code. — Section 125 cafeteria program, referred to in subdivision (6), is codified as 26 U.S.C. § 125.

I. General Consideration.
II. Particular Words and Phrases.
    A. Accident.
    B. Children.
    C. Course of Employment.
    D. Employer and Employee or Independent Contractor.
    E. Personal Injury.
    F. Premises.

I. GENERAL CONSIDERATION.

Editor's note. — The cases annotated below were decided under prior law.

The workmen's compensation laws are remedial in nature and are to be liberally construed and applied in order to effect their beneficent purposes. Hilyard Drilling Co. v. Janes, 462 So. 2d 942 (Ala. Civ. App. 1985); Middleton v. Dan River, Inc., 617 F. Supp. 1206 (M.D. Ala. 1985), modified, 834 F.2d 903 (11th Cir. 1987).

An employee covered under the workmen's compensation law is entitled to be fully compensated for his job-related injury, and provisions of the law should be liberally construed to accomplish that result. Hilyard Drilling Co. v. Janes, 462 So. 2d 942 (Ala. Civ. App. 1985).

The exclusive remedy provisions were not designed to shield an employer or its insurer from the entire field of tort law, and these provisions apply only to limit the liability of an employer or its insurer to the statutorily prescribed claims for job-related injuries. Lowman v. Piedmont Executive Shirt Mfg. Co., 547 So. 2d 90 (Ala. 1989).

No protection for injuries not caused by job-related accident. — The exclusivity provisions of the act do not afford protection for injuries not caused by a job-related accident. Lowman v. Piedmont Executive Shirt Mfg. Co., 547 So. 2d 90 (Ala. 1989).

"Compensation" does not include hospital, medical or surgical payments. — Under the majority holding in Ingalls Shipbuilding Corp. v. Cahela, 251 Ala. 163, 36 So. 2d 513 (1948), "compensation," under the act then extant, included hospital, medical or surgical payments, at least for the purposes of the third sentence of § 25-5-80. However, the legislature quite promptly abolished the effect of the Cahela doctrine by adding the last sentence to subdivision (1) of this section. This exclusion cuts across the entire law and is not restricted merely to § 25-5-80. Sam's Place v. Middleton, 39 Ala. App. 481, 103 So. 2d 812 (1958).

The introductory language of Workmen's Compensation Act makes clear that the definitions contained therein apply throughout the act unless the context clearly indicates a different meaning should apply, and a plain reading of the language in one-year limitations provision of act does not indicate that the word "compensation," as used in that section, should be given a different meaning than that provided in introductory provision. Cunningham v. Milstead Pulpwood Co., 366 So. 2d 737 (Ala. Civ. App. 1979).

Medical payments, unlike compensation payments, do not toll the statute of limitations. Blackmon v. R.L. Zeigler Co., 390 So. 2d 628 (Ala. Civ. App.), cert. denied, 390 So. 2d 635 (Ala. 1980).

And applies to § 25-5-11. — The context of § 25-5-11 does not indicate that the word "compensation" as there used is to be given a meaning different from that spelled out in this section. Liberty Mut. Ins. Co. v. Manasco, 271 Ala. 124, 123 So. 2d 527 (1960).

A check sent not as payment of compensation but as an attempt to correct an underpayment of compensation benefits is compensation under this section and, if the last such payment, begins the running of the limitation under § 25-5-80. Cement Prods. Co. v. Martin, 397 So. 2d 149 (Ala. Civ. App. 1981).

Causation. — To establish requisite causation, a medical-factual causal connection must be demonstrated. That is, that the employee in performance of his duties on the job must have been exposed to a danger or risk materially in excess of that to which people not so employed were exposed, and this danger must have been the cause of death. Leaseway Transp. Corp. v. Burgett, 500 So. 2d 1091 (Ala. Civ. App. 1986).

Plaintiff in compensation proceedings has burden to prove injuries to employee by accident arising out of and in course of employment, as provided by this section, subdivision (9). Sloss-Sheffield Steel & Iron Co. v. Harris, 218 Ala. 130, 117 So. 755 (1928); Dean v.

Stockham Pipe & Fittings Co., 220 Ala. 25, 123 So. 225 (1929).

Plaintiff has burden of proof to show that deceased employee met death by accident arising out of and in course of employment. Sloss-Sheffield Steel & Iron Co. v. Jones, 220 Ala. 10, 123 So. 201 (1929); Republic Iron & Steel Co. v. Ingle, 223 Ala. 127, 134 So. 878 (1931).

Fact that a decedent was an officer, director, and shareholder of the defendant corporation does not, in and of itself, bar recovery. Read News Agency, Inc. v. Moman, 383 So. 2d 840 (Ala. Civ. App.), cert. denied, 383 So. 2d 847 (Ala. 1980).

The corporate executive, in discharging his duties, must necessarily be an employee of the corporation. Read News Agency, Inc. v. Moman, 383 So. 2d 840 (Ala. Civ. App.), cert. denied, 383 So. 2d 847 (Ala. 1980).

Documents purporting to release employer prospectively from any liability under workmen's compensation act for injuries suffered by employee were void as against public policy. Kennedy v. Cochran ex rel. Cochran, 475 So. 2d 872 (Ala. Civ. App. 1985).

The legislature in enacting the workmen's compensation law declared a principle of public policy that employees be covered by this law, and any attempt to modify the act's provision by contract or agreement would abrogate the act and its purpose. Kennedy v. Cochran ex rel. Cochran, 475 So. 2d 872 (Ala. Civ. App. 1985).

The tort of outrageous conduct is not barred by the exclusivity of the act. Moore v. Liberty Mut. Ins. Co., 468 So. 2d 122 (Ala. 1985), overruled on other grounds, Lawman v. Piedmont Exec. Shirt Mfg. Co., 547 So. 2d 90 (Ala. 1989).

But bad faith or negligent conduct is not actionable. — Bad faith or negligent conduct upon the part of the employer or its compensation carrier is not actionable. Relief is barred because of the exclusivity of the compensation remedy. Moore v. Liberty Mut. Ins. Co., 468 So. 2d 122 (Ala. 1985), overruled on other grounds, Lawman v. Piedmont Exec. Shirt Mfg. Co., 547 So. 2d 90 (Ala. 1989).

However, employee may seek relief in case of fraud. — Claims for fraudulent misrepresentation and fraudulent suppression of facts in connection with settlement of a workers' compensation claim were not ones for which relief might be granted in a subsequent court suit, because of the exclusivity of the Alabama Workmen's Compensation Act; employee's remedy, if indeed there was fraud infecting the settlement of his compensation claim, was to have it set aside under the provisions of § 25-5-56, and seek relief from the settlement judgment under the provisions of Rule 60, A.R.C.P. Moore v. Liberty Mut. Ins.

Co., 468 So. 2d 122 (Ala. 1985), overruled on other grounds, Lawman v. Piedmont Exec. Shirt Mfg. Co., 547 So. 2d 90 (Ala. 1989).

Employee must present clear and convincing evidence of fraud. — In regard to a fraud claim against an employer, a fellow employee, or an employer's insurer, in order to present a claim to the jury, the plaintiff must present evidence that, if accepted and believed by the jury, would qualify as clear and convincing proof of fraud. Lowman v. Piedmont Executive Shirt Mfg. Co., 547 So. 2d 90 (Ala. 1989).

Failure to warn of potential health hazards. — The mere fact that workmen's compensation carrier may have had some knowledge of the potential health hazards associated with cotton dust exposure did not, without more, impose a legal duty upon it as the insurance carrier to disclose such knowledge to its insured employees, and absent any legal duty, mere silence would not support a claim for fraudulent concealment. Likewise, the fact that the carrier was a member of a trade organization that allegedly encouraged its members to block scientific investigation into byssinosis would not give rise to any inference of a conspiracy or liability for failure to warn of potential health hazards. Barnes v. Liberty Mut. Ins. Co., 468 So. 2d 124 (Ala. 1985).

When trial court used word "convinced" in judgment, it only placed required reasonable satisfaction measure of proof upon employee. Additionally, that was the only reasonable conclusion that the court of civil appeals could reach after a fair reading of the entire judgment. Hammons v. Cheesebrough-Pond's Inc., 516 So. 2d 713 (Ala. Civ. App. 1987).

Trial court's inference that the employee's failure to inform anyone of his alleged injury for a substantial length of time after alleged date of the injury meant that the injury did not occur on that date was a natural and reasonable inference based upon the facts as set out in great detail in the trial court's opinion. Eddy v. Dunlop Tire & Rubber Corp., 516 So. 2d 709 (Ala. Civ. App. 1987).

As to the burden of employee bringing claim against workman's compensation insurance carrier in occupational disease case, see Barnes v. Liberty Mut. Ins. Co., 468 So. 2d 124 (Ala. 1985); Alabama Power Co. v. Beam, 472 So. 2d 619 (Ala. 1985).

Election of compensation estops other remedies. — The acceptance of compensation payments under the Workers' Compensation Act constitutes an election that estops the employee from resorting to any other remedy. Thompson v. Town of Killen, 583 So. 2d 1337 (Ala. 1991).

Attorney fee for obtaining payment of

medical expenses not authorized. — Nothing in § 25-5-90 or this section or the other workmen's compensation statutes provides for the assessment or payment of an attorney fee for obtaining the payment of medical and surgical expenses. Day v. Ramada Inn S., 527 So. 2d 130 (Ala. Civ. App. 1987).

There is no provision for the assessment of attorney's fees for the obtaining of medical and surgical expenses. Ex parte Cowgill, 587 So. 2d 1002 (Ala. 1991).

The injured employee's right to sue for accrued medical expenses is totally independent of the employee's right to sue for workmen's compensation benefits; thus, the commencement of an employee's action, whether for compensation benefits or for medical expenses, or for both, within two years was not a condition precedent to the employee's right to sue for accrued medical expenses, whether such expenses are incurred during the period of limitations for compensation benefits or after the expiration of such period. Tuscaloosa County v. INA/Aetna Ins. Co., 522 So. 2d 782 (Ala. 1988).

"Compensation" affected by § 25-5-80 time limitation does not include "medical expenses." Tuscaloosa County v. INA/Aetna Ins. Co., 522 So. 2d 782 (Ala. 1988).

Disability rating upheld. — Trial court did not contort or strain the construction of the Workmen's Compensation Act unfairly by allowing an eight percent physical impairment rating to translate into a 100 percent employment disability rating since a finding of a physical disability is not the controlling factor in determining employability ratings or disability ratings for the purpose of compensation. Redi Roast Prods., Inc. v. Burnham, 531 So. 2d 664 (Ala. Civ. App. 1988).

Cited in Ex parte Central Iron & Co., 212 Ala. 367, 102 So. 797 (1925); Ex parte Big Four Coal Mining Co., 213 Ala. 305, 104 So. 764 (1925); Bagwell v. Woodward Iron Co., 236 Ala. 668, 184 So. 692 (1938); Ingalls Shipbuilding Corp. v. Cahela, 251 Ala. 163, 36 So. 2d 513 (1948); Floyd v. Barrentine, 275 Ala. 432, 155 So. 2d 598 (1963); Williams v. Alco Mining Co., 46 Ala. App. 333, 241 So. 2d 893 (1970); Grantham v. Denke, 359 So. 2d 785 (Ala. 1978); Hayes v. City of Lanett, 418 So. 2d 907 (Ala. Civ. App. 1982); McLain v. GAF Corp., 424 So. 2d 1329 (Ala. Civ. App. 1982); Garvin v. Shewbart, 442 So. 2d 80 (Ala. 1983); Johnson v. Gary, 443 So. 2d 924 (Ala. 1983); St. Paul Ins. Co. v. Harris, 758 F.2d 1450 (11th Cir. 1985); Stokes v. Atrax Div. of Wallace-Murray Corp., 466 So. 2d 967 (Ala. Civ. App. 1985); Fontenot v. Bramlett, 470 So. 2d 669 (Ala. 1985); Alabama Power Co. v. Beam, 472 So. 2d 619 (Ala. 1985); Sexton v. Prisock, 495 So. 2d 581 (Ala. 1986); Hughes v. Decatur Gen. Hosp., 514 So. 2d 935 (Ala. 1987); Middleton v. Dan River, Inc., 834 F.2d 903 (11th Cir. 1987); Maryland Cas. Co. v. Tiffin, 537 So. 2d 469 (Ala. 1988); Morrow v. Travelers Ins. Co., 550 So. 2d 1015 (Ala. Civ. App. 1989); Bonner v. Union Camp, Inc., 559 So. 2d 183 (Ala. Civ. App. 1989), cert. denied, 559 So. 2d 185 (Ala. 1990).

Collateral references. — 99 C.J.S., Workmen's Compensation, §§ 1, 38, 60, 141(2).

58 Am. Jur. 2d, Workmen's Compensation, § 26 et seq.

Charitable institutions as within workmen's compensation act. 30 ALR 600.

Public officer as within workmen's compensation act. 44 ALR 1477.

Municipal corporation as an employer within workmen's compensation act. 54 ALR 788.

One employed by servant in emergency as servant of the master. 76 ALR 971.

Helper, assistant, or substitute for an employee as himself an employee. 80 ALR 522.

Misrepresentations in obtaining employment as affecting status as employee or servant. 136 ALR 1124.

Partnership as distinguished from employment. 137 ALR 6.

One temporarily impressed into public service in emergency as within act. 142 ALR 657.

Posthumous children and children born after accident as dependents. 18 ALR3d 900.

Workmen's compensation: injury sustained while attending employer-sponsored social affair as arising out of and in the course of employment. 47 ALR3d 566.

Exchange of labor by farmers as creating an employment relationship for liability insurance purposes. 89 ALR3d 834.

Modern status: "dual capacity doctrine" as basis for employee's recovery from employer in tort. 23 ALR4th 1151.

Workers' compensation: Liability of successive employers for disease or condition allegedly attributable to successive employments. 34 ALR4th 958.

Workers' compensation: sexual assaults as compensable. 52 ALR4th 731.

Workers' compensation: student athlete as "employee" of college or university providing scholarship or similar financial assistance. 58 ALR4th 1259.

Workers' compensation: injuries incurred during labor activity. 61 ALR4th 196.

Workers' compensation: injuries incurred while traveling to or from work with employer's receipts. 63 ALR4th 253.

Employer's liability to employee for failure to provide work environment free from tobacco smoke. 63 ALR4th 1021.

Workers' compensation: effect of allegation

that injury was caused by, or occurred during course of, worker's illegal conduct. 73 ALR4th 270.

Ownership interest in employer business as affecting status as employee for workers' compensation purposes. 78 ALR4th 973.

Workers' compensation: compensability of injuries incurred traveling to or from medical treatment of earlier compensable injury. 83 ALR4th 110.

II. PARTICULAR WORDS AND PHRASES.

A. Accident.

Legislative requirements must be upheld. — Where the legislature has expressly required some physical trauma before an injury can be held compensable, that requirement must be upheld by the courts. To do otherwise would be to ignore well established rules of statutory construction. Magouirk v. UPS, 496 So. 2d 55 (Ala. Civ. App. 1986).

The term "accident" is not a characterization of the method of injury, but the result thereof. Ex parte Harris, 590 So. 2d 285 (Ala. 1991).

"Accident" occurs if injury was unexpected, unforeseen and caused by the job. — The requirement that there must be shown a violent and unusual event which causes the injury has been replaced by the principle that there was an accident if the result was unexpected and unforeseen and it was caused by the job. Ex parte Harris, 590 So. 2d 285 (Ala. 1991).

Test as to whether injury is unexpected and unforeseen so if received on a single occasion occurs "by accident" is that the sufferer did not intend or expect that the injury would on that particular occasion result from what he was doing. What was actually probable, or even inevitable, because of circumstances unknown to the sufferer, is unimportant. De Arman v. Ingalls Iron Works Co., 258 Ala. 205, 61 So. 2d 764 (1952).

And accident may be an event not expected or designed by the workman himself although it may have been designed by another, and be the result of willful, intentional or designed acts on the part of others. De Arman v. Ingalls Iron Works Co., 258 Ala. 205, 61 So. 2d 764 (1952).

Employee not required to prove violent and unusual event. — An employee is not required, under the Act, to prove the existence of some violent and unusual event that resulted in his or her injury—if the job caused the injury, then the injury is an accident within the intent of the Act. Ex parte Harris, 590 So. 2d 285 (Ala. 1991).

Plaintiff's injury was an accident under the Act; the fact that the injury did not manifest itself within a definite time period in no way diminishes the fact that plaintiff's injury was an accident, for it was her job that caused her injury. Ex parte Harris, 590 So. 2d 285 (Ala. 1991).

But word "accident" as defined in subdivision (8) is not synonymous with "disability." When the legislature defines the word "accident" as meaning an unexpected or unforeseen event producing at the time injury to the physical structure of the body by accidental means, the legislature clearly is not saying that the word "accident" shall be construed to mean disability produced by injury to the physical structure of the body. Davis v. Standard Oil Co., 261 Ala. 410, 74 So. 2d 625 (1954).

And accident concept includes element of reasonable definiteness in time. — It has generally been assumed that the accident concept includes an element of reasonable definiteness in time, as distinguished from gradual disintegration or deterioration. United Tel. & Tel. Co. v. Culiver, 271 Ala. 568, 126 So. 2d 119 (1961); City of Florence v. Gallien, 484 So. 2d 1095 (Ala. Civ. App. 1986).

Clearly, this definition contemplates a reasonably definite period of time during which the injury manifests itself. Blackmon v. R.L. Zeigler Co., 390 So. 2d 628 (Ala. Civ. App.), cert. denied, 390 So. 2d 635 (Ala. 1980).

Test of whether there is an accident is: if in the performance of the duties for which he is employed an employee is exposed to a danger or risk materially in excess of that to which people not so employed are exposed, and an injury occurs, such injury may legally be determined to have arisen from his employment and be an accident under the statute. Young v. City of Huntsville, 342 So. 2d 918 (Ala. Civ. App. 1976), cert. denied, 342 So. 2d 924 (Ala. 1977).

Test must be considered in context with "any evidence" rule. — In order for there to be an "accident" within the intent of the Workmen's Compensation Act, the injury suffered by the claimant must be legally caused by the performance of his duties and a causal relationship of a medical nature must exist between claimant's injury and his job. However, this two-pronged test must be considered in context with the "any evidence" rule under which the court reviews workmen's compensation cases. Martin Indus., Inc. v. Dement, 435 So. 2d 85 (Ala. Civ. App. 1983).

Accident arises out of employee's employment when the rational mind can trace the injury to a proximate cause set in motion by the employment, rather than some other agency. Phenix Medical Park Hosp. v. Kozub, 575 So. 2d 1162 (Ala. Civ. App. 1991).

No accident where there was no evidence of physical injury. — Where employee was dismissed from her position as personnel supervisor and was instructed to "clean out her desk," where employee testified that she then became very upset, and that she proceeded to her office and was in the process of cleaning out her desk when she became dizzy and disoriented, and where she further testified that her husband told her that she fell out of her chair and was taken by an ambulance to the hospital, trial court erred in awarding the employee any workmen's compensation benefits since there was no evidence that the employee suffered any physical injury to her body and there was nothing in the medical records to indicate any physical injury, nor did the employee testify that she suffered any physical injury. J.C. Penney Co. v. Pigg, 544 So. 2d 169 (Ala. Civ. App. 1989).

Tortious conduct which occurred in hospital was not "accident." — Where the allegedly tortious conduct in question occurred while employee was hospitalized as a result of the initial injury to her back, this tortious conduct was not an "accident" compensable under workmen's compensation. Lowman v. Piedmont Executive Shirt Mfg. Co., 547 So. 2d 90 (Ala. 1989).

Mental disorders or injuries. — Only those "accidents" in which some physical injury or harm to the body is produced should be held compensable. Therefore, the Alabama's Workmen's Compensation Act does not extend coverage to mental disorders or injuries that have neither produced nor been proximately caused by some physical injury to the body. Magouirk v. UPS, 496 So. 2d 55 (Ala. Civ. App. 1986).

Attack of allergens in the air was unexpected and unforeseen because the employee had been removed from direct contact with the material believed to have caused prior and similar injury or disease. B.F. Goodrich Co. v. Martin, 47 Ala. App. 244, 253 So. 2d 37 (1971).

Death from disease caused by exposure resulted from accident. — Where the duties of an engineer required long-continued exposure to wetting and chill of water accumulated in excavations, materially in excess of exposure to which other people in locality were subject, death from pneumonia because of exposure resulted from an "accident" within subdivision (8) of this section and was compensable under the workmen's compensation law. Pow v. Southern Constr. Co., 235 Ala. 580, 180 So. 288 (1938).

Also harmful effect caused by heat exhaustion. — Where heat exhaustion arises out of and in course of employment, any harmful effect on physical structure of employee proximately resulting therefrom is "accident" under statute. Gulf States Steel Co. v. Christison, 228 Ala. 622, 154 So. 565 (1934); Gadsden Iron Works, Inc. v. Beasley, 249 Ala. 115, 30 So. 2d 10 (1947).

If heat exhaustion arises out of the employment, as well as in its course, it is clear that any harmful effect upon the physical structure of the body of the employee, which is a proximate result of it, is an accident under this section. B.F. Goodrich Co. v. Martin, 47 Ala. App. 244, 253 So. 2d 37 (1971).

And breathing gas due to insufficient ventilation. — Injury to miner by breathing carbon monoxide or carbon dioxide gas, due to insufficient ventilation and passing of current of such air through opening he was making into room where other workmen had been shooting, held due to "accident" within subdivision (8) of this section. New River Coal Co. v. Files, 215 Ala. 64, 109 So. 360 (1926).

But injury from working in unventilated room may not be an accident. — Injuries to employee from working in an unventilated room filled with fumes, dust and small particles of chemical mixture, which did not appear suddenly and violently, but grew progressively worse, held not an "accident" within Workmen's Compensation Act, and hence employee's remedy was at common law and under Employer's Liability Act (§§ 25-6-1 through 25-6-4). Gentry v. Swann Chem. Co., 234 Ala. 313, 174 So. 530 (1937).

Absorption of paint fumes an accident. — The absorption of paint fumes over a two-day period constitutes an "accident" as that term is used in Alabama Workmen's Compensation Act, and thus employee's exclusive remedy was under the Workmen's Compensation Act. Kane v. South Cent. Bell Tel. Co., 368 So. 2d 3 (Ala. 1979).

Dermatitis contracted by garage employee as a result of contact with substance used in undercoating automobiles held result of accident. Mitchell Motor Co. v. Burrow, 37 Ala. App. 222, 66 So. 2d 198 (1953).

Heart attack caused by strenuous activity. — Evidence supported the trial court's conclusion that the death of employee who died suddenly while putting a tarpaulin over the loaded truck was the result of a sudden and unexpected heart attack brought on by the strenuous exertion of placing the tarpaulin over the truck and was accidental within the meaning of Alabama workmen's compensation laws. Leaseway Transp. Corp. v. Burgett, 500 So. 2d 1091 (Ala. Civ. App. 1986).

Willful assault upon an employee may be an "accident" within the definition of this section. Ex parte Coleman, 211 Ala. 248, 100 So. 114 (1924); Mallory S.S. Co. v. Higgins, 22 Ala. App. 26, 111 So. 758 (1927); W.B. Davis & Son v. Ruple, 222 Ala. 52, 130 So. 772 (1930).

The fact that an injury is the result of a willful or criminal assault upon the employee does not prevent the injury from being accidental within the meaning of workmen's compensation acts. Garrett v. Gadsden Cooperage Co., 209 Ala. 223, 96 So. 188 (1923); Tiger Motor Co. v. Winslett, 278 Ala. 108, 176 So. 2d 39 (1965).

Arthritis as accident. — If an incident occurring during the performance of claimant's job is deemed to have caused his arthritic condition or aggravated an existing arthritic condition, the trial court may properly hold that the claimant is the victim of an accident and that he is entitled to receive workmen's compensation benefits. Martin Indus., Inc. v. Dement, 435 So. 2d 85 (Ala. Civ. App. 1983).

An injury that manifests itself over time as a result of repetitive, continuous motions of lifting, pushing, and pulling, while discharging the duties of a particular job, is not an accident covered under these statutes. Bradley v. Springhill Manor, 580 So. 2d 1355 (Ala. Civ. App. 1991).

Gradual deterioration held not an "accident". — Where employee was not injured by a fall, gradual deterioration of his physical ability could not constitute an "accident" under the workmen's compensation act, and employee could not be awarded compensation benefits. Buchanan Lumber Co. v. Edwards, 531 So. 2d 1 (Ala. Civ. App. 1988).

Lung problem that gradually came on. — A worker's testimony that his lung problem was a problem that "gradually came on me" and that his problem was caused by gradual exposure to certain chemicals with which he worked was legal evidence from which the trial court could conclude that the worker's lung condition was not due to an "accident" as defined by this section, but rather a gradual deterioration. Terry v. Webb Div. Marmon Indus., Inc., 582 So. 2d 558 (Ala. Civ. App. 1991).

The progressive aggravation of worker's back problems did not entitle him to workmen's compensation benefits since gradual deterioration cannot constitute an "accident" under the Workmen's Compensation Act. Russell Coal Co. v. Williams, 550 So. 2d 1007 (Ala. Civ. App. 1989).

B. Children.

Constitutionality. — See Foy v. Vann, 386 So. 2d 1141 (Ala. Civ. App. 1979), cert. quashed, 386 So. 2d 1144 (Ala. 1980).

"Child" or "children". — Only stepchil-

dren and grandchildren must be dependent, in fact, upon the deceased for support in order to be considered a child under the Workmen's Compensation Act. Ragsdale v. Altec Indus., Inc., 456 So. 2d 54 (Ala. 1984).

Posthumous children and all other children entitled by law to inherit as children of the deceased are dependents if they qualify under the provisions of subdivision (3). Ragsdale v. Altec Indus., Inc., 456 So. 2d 54 (Ala. 1984).

The definitions for the Workmen's Compensation Act, do not require that the child receive financial support from her father in order to be deemed his dependent. Ragsdale v. Altec Indus., Inc., 456 So. 2d 54 (Ala. 1984).

The case of Central Foundry Co. v. Brown, 381 So. 2d 635 (Ala. Civ. App. 1979), which held that every child under the age of 18 is conclusively presumed to be wholly dependent upon its natural parent, even though at the time of death of the parent, the child had been adopted by and is living with adoptive parents, is applicable to the entire Workmen's Compensation Act. Ragsdale v. Altec Indus., Inc., 456 So. 2d 54 (Ala. 1984).

A child adopted six months prior to the decedent's death may inherit from or through either natural parent. Ragsdale v. Altec Indus., Inc., 456 So. 2d 54 (Ala. 1984).

Definition of child in this section is much broader than the accepted customary or legal definition. Browning v. City of Huntsville, 46 Ala. App. 503, 244 So. 2d 378 (1971).

But "mother" and "parent" have usual meaning. — Since the words mother and parent were not expressly broadened by statutory definition, it appears clear that the usual and accepted definition was intended to apply. Browning v. City of Huntsville, 46 Ala. App. 503, 244 So. 2d 378 (1971).

Adoption does not remove child from "children" of natural father. — There is no statement in the Workmen's Compensation Act which indicates that the act of adoption takes a child out of the terminology of "children" of his natural father. All that is required is that the adopted child be entitled to inherit as a child of the deceased. Central Foundry Co. v. Brown, 381 So. 2d 635 (Ala. Civ. App. 1979), cert. denied, 381 So. 2d 637 (Ala. 1980).

Adopted children within section. — Provision of subdivision (2) of this section that child or children include "all other children entitled by law to inherit as children of deceased" is broad enough to include adopted children. Ex parte Cline, 213 Ala. 599, 105 So. 686 (1925).

But child merely receiving support is not. — A child merely receiving support and standing toward deceased in no other relation than that of person in loco parentis is not included within subdivision (2) of this section. Ex parte Cline, 213 Ala. 599, 105 So. 686 (1925). See note to same case under § 25-5-62 of this title.

Stepchildren are included within statutory definition of "children" only if they are members of the family of the decedent at the time of the accident and are dependent upon him for support. Pate v. Miller Transporters, Inc., 381 So. 2d 64 (Ala. Civ. App. 1979), aff'd, 381 So. 2d 68 (Ala. 1980).

Stepchildren considered dependent if deceased furnished more than court-ordered support. — Stepchildren are dependent upon the decedent for support although the stepchildren receive court-ordered support of $100.00 per month from their natural father where the evidence shows that the deceased had furnished more than this amount monthly in support of his stepchildren. Pate v. Miller Transporters, Inc., 381 So. 2d 64 (Ala. Civ. App. 1979), aff'd, 381 So. 2d 68 (Ala. 1980).

Illegitimate children. The terms "child" and "children," as used in this section, include an illegitimate child or children in order to be constitutional. Foy v. Vann, 386 So. 2d 1141 (Ala. Civ. App. 1979), cert. quashed, 386 So. 2d 1144 (Ala. 1980).

Nephew living with maternal aunt not dependent child. — Under the definition of child as expressed in this section, a nephew living with his maternal aunt could not have qualified as a dependent child, whether he had been minor or adult at the time the claim for compensation arose. Browning v. City of Huntsville, 46 Ala. App. 503, 244 So. 2d 378 (1971).

Minor claimant was not dependent child of his deceased grandfather, where claimant's father was alive and able to work. Black v. Freeman Lumber Co., 509 So. 2d 914 (Ala. Civ. App. 1987).

C. Course of Employment.

Cross references. — For other cases on "course of employment," see note to § 25-5-31.

Phrase refers to cause and source of accident. — It is usually said that the phrase "arise out of" employment refers to employment as the cause and source of the accident. Carraway Methodist Hosp. v. Pitts, 256 Ala. 665, 57 So. 2d 96 (1952).

Also refers to time, place and circumstances. — The phrase "in the course of his employment" refers to the time, place and circumstances under which the accident took place. Carraway Methodist Hosp. v. Pitts, 256 Ala. 665, 57 So. 2d 96 (1952); Massey v. United States Steel Corp., 264 Ala. 227, 86 So. 2d 375 (1955).

An injury to an employee arises in the course of his employment when it occurs, within the period of his employment, at a place where he may reasonably be and while he is reasonably fulfilling the duties of his employment or engaged in doing something incident to it. Carraway Methodist Hosp. v. Pitts, 256 Ala. 665, 57 So. 2d 96 (1952); Massey v. United States Steel Corp., 264 Ala. 227, 86 So. 2d 375 (1955).

If an injury occurs within the period of employment, at a place where employee may reasonably be while he is reasonably performing the duties assigned, such injury may be said to have occurred in the course of his employment. Wiregrass Comprehensive Mental Health Clinic, Inc. v. Price, 366 So. 2d 725 (Ala. Civ. App. 1978), cert. denied, 366 So. 2d 728 (Ala. 1979).

And includes entering and leaving premises and terminating services. — An accident is compensable if the employee was either doing the work or performing the service he was engaged to do or perform or was engaged in an act or service naturally related thereto, which includes the movement of the employee in entering at the appropriate time, the employer's premises to discharge his function, his preparation to begin and to terminate his actual service, and to leave the premises at an appropriate time after completion of his actual service. Hayes v. Alabama By-Products Corp., 242 Ala. 148, 5 So. 2d 624 (1942).

In order to show that an injury arose out of his employment, an employee must establish a definite causal connection between his employment and his injury. It is not enough to show that the injury would not have occurred "but for" the employment. Pope v. Golden Rod Broilers, Inc., 539 So. 2d 313 (Ala. Civ. App. 1989).

Whether case arose out of "course of employment" depends upon particular facts and circumstances. See Prayther v. Deepwater Coal & Iron Co., 216 Ala. 579, 114 So. 194 (1927); Baggett Transp. Co. v. Holderfield, 260 Ala. 56, 68 So. 2d 21 (1953); Wooten v. Roden, 260 Ala. 606, 71 So. 2d 802 (1954).

The employee's accident arose out of and in the course of her employment, where the employee had lived in Russellville for five years while working at the local store, she had only had one other temporary assignment during that period, she was informed by her employer that she would be working in a distant store and required to clock in at her normal working hour at that store location 30 miles away, and her employer helped her to arrange a carpool back and forth from Russellville to the Moulton store with another employee under a similar temporary assignment. Winn-Dixie Stores, Inc. v. Smallwood, 516 So. 2d 716 (Ala. Civ. App. 1987).

And no exact formula can be laid down which will automatically solve every case of personal injuries arising under subdivision (9) of this section. Benoit Coal Mining Co. v. Moore, 215 Ala. 220, 109 So. 878 (1926); Baggett Transp. Co. v. Holderfield, 260 Ala. 56, 68 So. 2d 21 (1953); Wooten v. Roden, 260 Ala. 606, 71 So. 2d 802 (1954).

Danger materially in excess of normal. — A harmful condition "arises out of employment" if in performing duties in manner required or contemplated by employer, employee must expose himself to danger materially in excess of that to which people commonly in that locality are exposed, and such excessive exposure may be direct cause of injury though operating on other conditions of common exposure. Pullman-Standard Car Mfg. Co. v. Lively, 239 Ala. 648, 196 So. 870 (1940).

If an injury is to be one "arising out of employment" it is necessary that the duties of the employment expose employee to a danger materially in excess of that to which people commonly in that locality are exposed when not situated as he was in the course of his employment. Dallas Mfg. Co. v. Kennemer, 243 Ala. 42, 8 So. 2d 519 (1942).

Determination of aggravated risk or unusual condition. — The aggravated risk or unusual condition arising out of employment is determined by a comparison of the conditions existing at the place of employment with those existing in the same general locality, but unassociated with the place and performance of the employment. B.F. Goodrich Co. v. Martin, 47 Ala. App. 244, 253 So. 2d 37 (1971).

Rule providing that but for claimant's employment he would not have been where he was at the time of accident and would not have been subjected to the danger which killed him is not appropriate as a basis for determining whether deceased was in the course of his employment at the time he was killed; it certainly cannot be a valid indicator of "arising out of" his employment. Wiregrass Comprehensive Mental Health Clinic, Inc. v. Price, 366 So. 2d 725 (Ala. Civ. App. 1978), cert. denied, 366 So. 2d 728 (Ala. 1979).

The but-for test is clearly not the test for causation under Alabama's Workmen's Compensation Act. Instead, the burden is on the claimant to establish a definite causal connection between the work and the injury. Middleton v. Dan River, Inc., 617 F. Supp. 1206 (M.D. Ala. 1985), modified, 834 F.2d 903 (11th Cir. 1987).

Determination of medical causation is not an exact science and may be viewed in light of attending circumstances. Valley Steel Constr. v. Prater, 479 So. 2d 1259 (Ala. Civ. App. 1985), upholding trial court's finding of medical causation between claimant's back injury and the condition of his right leg.

It is immaterial and merely a matter of semantics as to whether the cause or the result is unforeseen and unexpected so long as the cause or origin of the injury can be proximately connected with the course of employment. B.F. Goodrich Co. v. Martin, 47 Ala. App. 244, 253 So. 2d 37 (1971).

Provision as to injuries on premises construed in connection with section 25-5-31. — Subdivision (9), under this section, providing injuries arising from employment covers only injuries on premises where services are performed, does not affect meaning or interpretation of general clause under § 25-5-31 and must be construed in connection with legal meaning of said section. Jett v. Turner, 215 Ala. 352, 110 So. 702 (1926).

And employee furnished transportation may recover for injury while riding from work. — Where employer furnished auto transportation to and from servants' place of work, injury to employee while riding back from work held compensable under § 25-5-31, as injury arising in "course of employment," because it was incident to and part of relation of master and servant, though subdivision (9) of this section provides injuries arising out of course of employment cover only those sustained on or about premises where services are performed. Jett v. Turner, 215 Ala. 352, 110 So. 702 (1926).

Where employee was injured some five or six miles from the job site while being transported from work by employer the injury was not compensable under subdivision (9) since the transportation furnished by employer was not a part of the work contract. Blair v. Greene, 247 Ala. 104, 22 So. 2d 834 (1945); Wooten v. Roden, 260 Ala. 606, 71 So. 2d 802 (1954).

But not for injury while alighting from street car. — Where deceased, a track layer for defendant street railway company, boarded its street car to go home, riding on transportation ticket furnished him by company, an injury to him from passing automobile while he was alighting from car held not one arising out of and in course of employment within Workmen's Compensation Act, subdivision (9) of this section. Ex parte Taylor, 213 Ala. 282, 104 So. 527 (1925).

Traveling to and from work not in course of employment. — It is the general rule that accidents occurring while an employee is traveling to and from work are not considered as arising out of and in course of employment; exceptions to the general rule have arisen where the employer furnishes

458

transportation to and from work, or where the employee performs some service en route or at home. Wiregrass Comprehensive Mental Health Clinic, Inc. v. Price, 366 So. 2d 725 (Ala. Civ. App. 1978), cert. denied, 366 So. 2d 728 (Ala. 1979).

Travel to receive pay was held to be in the course of employee's employment; therefore, employee's injury in auto accident resulted from a work-related accident, since the trip did not fall within the general rule that commuting to and from work is not covered by the workmen's compensation laws. Oliver v. Faulkner Wood Co., 531 So. 2d 675 (Ala. Civ. App. 1988).

Injury while traveling a different route to work. — Employee was not engaged in a personal mission which so deviated from his business journey that his accident was noncompensable; the employee simply happened to be traveling a different route and transporting one of his coworkers to a different destination than normal on the day of the accident; even if this "deviation" could be considered "personal," it was not "personal" as to the injured employee; further, the "deviation," which was for the benefit of a coworker, had not even occurred at the time of the accident. Worthington v. Moore Elec. Co., 563 So. 2d 617 (Ala. Civ. App. 1990).

Clearly identifiable side trip beyond the course of employment. — Employee's accident may be found noncompensable if the only reasonable view of the evidence was that the employee took a clearly identifiable side trip and so deviated from his business journey that he unquestionably went beyond the course of his employment in going away from his business route and toward a personal objective. Worthington v. Moore Elec. Co., 563 So. 2d 617 (Ala. Civ. App. 1990).

Injury in employer's truck traveling to work arose out of employment. — Where employee's testimony was that the truck he drove to and from work was furnished by his employer, and further, the employee was given $25.00 a day for expenses related to the truck, and he had a practice of picking up his two coworkers and transporting them to work, also, the employee, while driving to and from work every day, was on a journey that arose out of and occurred in the course of his employment. Worthington v. Moore Elec. Co., 563 So. 2d 617 (Ala. Civ. App. 1990).

Injuries sustained at home are not generally compensable. — Where miner furnished his own explosives and kept them at his home furnished by employer, injuries sustained when testing dynamite cap before leaving home in morning held not, under subdivision (9) of this section, to "arise out of and in course

of employment." Sloss-Sheffield Steel & Iron Co. v. Thomas, 220 Ala. 686, 127 So. 165 (1930).

Where claimant had contract with mining company to haul timber to mines for which he was paid so much per stack or per load, and furnished his own mules and wagon and lived at home, injuries sustained while feeding mules at home, after having completed work for day, did not arise out of and in course of employment, under subdivision (9) of this section. Prayther v. Deepwater Coal & Iron Co., 216 Ala. 579, 114 So. 194 (1927).

Where employee's death ensues from heat exhaustion, death does not "arise out of employment" unless employment exposes employee to a risk in excess of that to which other people commonly in locality are exposed because of hot weather. Pullman-Standard Car Mfg. Co. v. Lively, 239 Ala. 684, 196 So. 870 (1940).

An employee, suffering heat exhaustion while performing manual work in operating a press in employer's plant, did not sustain an injury caused by a compensable "accident arising out of and in course of his employment," where employee was exposed to no unusual or excess heat other than state of weather, and there was no finding of unusual strain or overexertion attending work employee was engaged in. Pullman-Standard Car Mfg. Co. v. Lively, 239 Ala. 684, 196 So. 870 (1940).

In connection with the sort of accident such as heat exhaustion, the principle to which most authorities give assent is that the harmful condition does arise out of the employment, if, in the performance of the duties for which he was engaged, in the manner required or contemplated by the employer, it is necessary for the employee to expose himself to a danger, materially in excess of that to which people commonly in that locality are exposed, when not situated as he is when thus performing his service, and that such excessive exposure may be found to have been the direct cause of the injury, though operating upon other conditions of common exposure. B.F. Goodrich Co. v. Martin, 47 Ala. App. 244, 253 So. 2d 37 (1971).

Court cannot speculate that job brought on heart attack. — Where there was no evidence that the activity and conditions of deceased's employment produced or triggered his fatal attack, the trial court was not at liberty to guess or speculate that the job brought on the heart attack. Durr v. State, 46 Ala. App. 532, 244 So. 2d 811 (1970).

Nonparticipating victim of horseplay may recover. — It seems to be the rule in practically all jurisdictions that a nonparticipating victim of horseplay may recover compensation. McKnight v. Consolidated Concrete Co., 279 Ala. 430, 186 So. 2d 144 (1966).

To render employee's injury as result of horseplay with fellow employee compensable, such horseplay must not be instigated by injured workman and he must be engaged in duties of his employment at time of injury. Stockham Pipe & Fittings Co. v. Williams, 245 Ala. 570, 18 So. 2d 93 (1943), wherein it was held injury did not "arise out of employment." McKnight v. Consolidated Concrete Co., 279 Ala. 430, 186 So. 2d 144 (1966).

Fall resulting from epileptic seizure was compensable. — Disability from a fractured neck which resulted directly from a fall from a three foot platform while in an epileptic seizure was caused by an accident arising out of appellant's employment. Irby v. Republic Creosoting Co., 228 F.2d 195 (5th Cir.), rev'g 129 F. Supp. 92 (M.D. Ala. 1955).

Injuries by assault may be compensable. — Under § 25-5-31 et seq. and subdivision (9) of this section, a willful assault intended to injure employee is a compensable accident, and, if a hazard peculiar to the employment is a contributing cause, it is immaterial whether violence was directed to him as an employee. Dean v. Stockham Pipe & Fittings Co., 220 Ala. 25, 123 So. 225 (1929).

Where wife of one employee shot at a second employee against whom she had a personal grievance, but missed him and struck a third employee accidentally causing the latter's death, provisions of subdivision (9) of this section did not preclude payment of compensation to deceased employee, since there had been no intent to injure him. Dallas Mfg. Co. v. Kennemer, 243 Ala. 42, 8 So. 2d 519 (1942).

A willful assault by a coemployee may be compensable under the Alabama workmen's compensation statute. However, the fact of a willful assault alone does not conclusively establish that the assault arose out of the employee's employment. That conclusion must be drawn from the circumstances of each case. McGaughy v. Allied Prods. Co., 412 So. 2d 803 (Ala. Civ. App. 1982).

But only if they arise out of or in course of employment. — The death of an employee killed while on duty by willful act of someone on a personal ground not connected with employment is not compensable. Dallas Mfg. Co. v. Kennemer, 243 Ala. 42, 8 So. 2d 519 (1942).

Hence, assault committed solely to gratify personal ill will, not compensable. — If an assault on an employee is committed by another, whether co-employee or stranger, solely to gratify personal ill will, anger or hatred, the injury done cannot be said to arise out of the employment within the meaning of

the Workmen's Compensation Act. Garrett v. Gadsden Cooperage Co., 209 Ala. 223, 96 So. 188 (1923).

Death caused by act of third person intended to injure deceased employee for personal reasons is not within subdivision (9) of this section. Harris v. Sloss-Sheffield Steel & Iron Co., 222 Ala. 470, 132 So. 727 (1931).

If an assault on an employee is committed by another, whether co-employee or stranger, solely to gratify personal ill will, anger or hatred, the injury done cannot be said to arise out of the employment within the meaning of the Workmen's Compensation Act. To justify recovery the rational mind must be able to trace the resultant personal injury to a proximate cause set in motion by the employment, and not by some other agency. Tiger Motor Co. v. Winslett, 278 Ala. 108, 176 So. 2d 39 (1965).

From the fact alone of a willful assault upon a workman, it cannot be presumed that it arose out of his employment. That conclusion must be drawn, if at all, from the circumstances of the case, or from the testimony of witnesses, tending to show the causal relation of the employment to the injury; and the rational mind must be able to trace the resultant personal injury to a proximate cause set in motion by the employment and not by some other agency. Tiger Motor Co. v. Winslett, 278 Ala. 108, 176 So. 2d 39 (1965).

Also when an employee steps aside from his work to renew a quarrel for purely personal reasons and because of personal anger, in view of subdivision (9) of this section the employer is not liable for damages resulting from his death at the hand of a fellow employee, while continuing such quarrel. See Martin v. Sloss-Sheffield Steel & Iron Co., 216 Ala. 500, 113 So. 578 (1927).

However, employer should be responsible for conduct of an excitable and impetuous supervisor in the prosecution of his duties, until there is sufficient interruption in the performance of such duties to justify the conclusion that the supervisor had abandoned his employment, and that any assault committed by him upon the claimant was an independent and undivided act, free from any association or connection with his employment. Tiger Motor Co. v. Winslett, 278 Ala. 108, 176 So. 2d 39 (1965).

Injuries from assault were not compensable. — Intentional shooting of electrician by fellow employee in course of altercation between some of employees and watchman was held not injury by accident arising out of or in course of electrician's employment under subdivision (9), where shooting was prompted by assailant's belief that electrician had attacked him, and occurred without any relation to fact or duties of electrician's employment, though electrician at the time was on duty awaiting trouble signals. Sloss-Sheffield Steel & Iron Co. v. Harris, 218 Ala. 130, 117 So. 755 (1928).

Where wife of one employee went through gate to exit of cotton mill and shot at a second employee against whom she had a personal grievance, but missed him and killed a third employee who was within the enclosed premises awaiting blowing of factory whistle to change shifts, third employee's death did not "arise out of employment" and was not compensable, since it did not result from a hazard which was a natural incident to his work. Dallas Mfg. Co. v. Kennemer, 243 Ala. 42, 8 So. 2d 519 (1942).

Injuries from assault were compensable. — An assault and resultant injuries to a claimant were held to have arisen from a risk that was incidental to employment, where the supervisor who committed the assault was the person to whom defendant intrusted the duty of assigning repair work on motor vehicles to the employed mechanics, it was the supervisor's duty to supervise the mechanics, check the payroll sheets for accuracy and to remove therefrom any listing of mechanical work improperly or erroneously listed, and mechanics had the right, under their method of employment, to discuss their grievances concerning the payroll with the supervisor, and to protest his action adversely affecting the mechanic's compensation claim. Tiger Motor Co. v. Winslett, 278 Ala. 108, 176 So. 2d 39 (1965).

Death of night watchman slain by trespasser in lumber yard he was employed to watch while engaged in discharge of his duty to employer, held to have arisen in course of his employment within this section. McLaughlin v. Davis Lumber Co., 220 Ala. 440, 125 So. 608 (1929).

Murder and robbery of night watchman while engaged in his regular occupation on night following his pay day was held compensable under subdivision (9). Dean v. Stockham Pipe & Fittings Co., 220 Ala. 25, 123 So. 225 (1929).

Unexplained accident arose out of employment. — Where the record showed that employee suffered a broken jaw, the loss of part of a finger, and back injuries while performing the duties of his employment, and that these injuries were the kind that normally occur suddenly and traumatically, the only reasonable view of the evidence required a finding that employee's injuries were the result of an accident that was causally connected to his employment, nothwithstanding the fact that the circumstances surrounding the accident itself remained largely unexplained. Ex parte Patterson, 561 So. 2d 236 (Ala. 1990).

Where bending, lifting, and twisting motions required by employee's work were a contributing cause to her injury and but for her employment, employee would not have exerted herself in this way, employee's back pain was caused by her employment and was not, as employer suggested, a lingering malady. Avondale Mills, Inc. v. Webster, 574 So. 2d 51 (Ala. Civ. App. 1990).

Illustrative cases. — Where a drug store, to carry out agency contract with telegraph company for transmission of telegrams, employed plaintiff's son to deliver telegrams, and the son was killed when struck by train while delivering a telegram, the son's death was caused by an accident "arising out of and in the course of employment" by telegraph company. Western Union Tel. Co. v. George, 239 Ala. 80, 194 So. 183 (1940).

Plaintiff's intestate, who met his death by electrocution while engaged in the performance of his duties as a welder for the corporate defendants, was killed by an accident arising out of and in the course of his employment and was within the purview of the Alabama Workmen's Compensation Act. De Arman v. Ingalls Iron Works Co., 258 Ala. 205, 61 So. 2d 764 (1952).

Where a truck driver met his death in the performance of his obligation under a written agreement to keep a truck owned by him and leased to defendant, his employer, in good repair at his own expense, and the driver was not under the direction and control of the defendant, nor subject to defendant's supervision in the manner, place and time in which he made repairs, and was free to accomplish his duty of properly maintaining the vehicle as he, in his own discretion, deemed necessary subject only to the end result being satisfactory to the defendant, it was held that death did not come in the course of his employment. Deaton Truck Line v. Acker, 266 Ala. 611, 98 So. 2d 429 (1957).

Where, eliminating the testimony of a physician who gave it as her opinion that deceased died of heart disease, the evidence showed only that deceased dropped dead on the job early in the morning while talking to his boss, there was no evidence that deceased died of a heat stroke and that his death arose out of and in the course of his employment. Benson-Jackson-Mathers Post No. 5106 v. Donaldson, 267 Ala. 60, 99 So. 2d 688 (1957).

Deceased employee deliberately and substantially stepped outside his employment in getting upon a crane bucket and remaining thereon to the point where he was injured. This conduct was, indeed, a substantial deviation from his employment, and his death was not compensable. McKnight v. Consolidated Concrete Co., 279 Ala. 430, 186 So. 2d 144 (1966).

D. Employer and Employee or Independent Contractor.

Cross references. — As to right of action for damages for injuries or death of employee, see § 25-5-31.

Statutory definitions of words "employer" and "employee" must control in compensation cases, so far as they tend to modify common law governing master and servant. Birmingham Post Co. v. Sturgeon, 227 Ala. 162, 149 So. 74 (1933); Baggett Transp. Co. v. Holderfield, 260 Ala. 56, 68 So. 2d 21 (1953).

And as to cases coming within purview of Employer's Liability Act (§§ 25-6-1 through 25-6-4), statutory definitions of "employer" and "employee" prevail over common-law definitions, but as to cases not coming within purview of act, common law still obtains. Daves v. Rain, 28 Ala. App. 54, 178 So. 59 (1937).

The terms "employee" and "workman" are expressly made interchangeable, and it is mandated they shall be construed to mean the same. There is clearly no distinction drawn here between those who live by the sweat of their brow and those who enjoy the title, "executive." Read News Agency, Inc. v. Moman, 383 So. 2d 840 (Ala. Civ. App.), cert. denied, 383 So. 2d 847 (Ala. 1980).

When interpreting the statutory definitions of "employer" and "employee" the courts must use criteria which will help apply these general definitions to the specific situation at bar. Terry v. Read Steel Prods., 430 So. 2d 862 (Ala. 1983).

Insurance carrier not immune for negligent inspection. — The legislature may not constitutionally immunize from tort liability a workmen's compensation carrier and its employees for injuries resulting to employees of the insured from negligent inspections performed by the carrier. Johnson v. American Mut. Liab. Ins. Co., 394 So. 2d 1 (Ala. 1980).

Statutory definition of employer not only basis for determining relationship of employer and employee. American Tennis Courts, Inc. v. Hinton, 378 So. 2d 235 (Ala. Civ. App.), cert. denied, 378 So. 2d 239 (Ala. 1979).

One of the essentials of the relation of employee and employer is the voluntary rendition of service by the employee. Downey v. Bituminous Cas. Corp., 349 So. 2d 1153 (Ala. 1977).

"Master" is one who has supreme choice, control and direction of servant and whose will servant represents, not merely in ultimate results of his work, but in all its details.

Birmingham Post Co. v. Sturgeon, 227 Ala. 162, 149 So. 74 (1933); United States Steel Corp. v. Mathews, 261 Ala. 120, 73 So. 2d 239 (1954).

To be a "servant," other party must retain right to direct manner in which business shall be done, as well as result to be accomplished. Birmingham Post Co. v. Sturgeon, 227 Ala. 162, 149 So. 74 (1933); United States Steel Corp. v. Mathews, 261 Ala. 120, 73 So. 2d 239 (1954).

And that employee is "discharged" does not so completely sever master-servant relationship as to render compensation statute inapplicable, until after reasonable time for employee's departure. W.B. Davis & Son v. Ruple, 222 Ala. 52, 130 So. 772 (1930).

Complaint for employee being wrongfully discharged and forcibly ejected, if stating action ex delicto, was held subject to motion to dismiss in not averring facts to take it outside compensation statute. W.B. Davis & Son v. Ruple, 222 Ala. 52, 130 So. 772 (1930).

Act does not apply to independent contractor. — The Workmen's Compensation Act does not apply when the injured person is an independent contractor. Birmingham Post Co. v. Sturgeon, 227 Ala. 162, 149 So. 74 (1933).

Hence, law of independent contractor has not been changed by the Workmen's Compensation Act. Birmingham Post Co. v. Sturgeon, 227 Ala. 162, 149 So. 74 (1933).

And section 25-5-10 inferentially recognizes continued existence of rule as to independent contractors by guarding against any fraudulent scheme tending to an evasion of liability. Birmingham Post Co. v. Sturgeon, 227 Ala. 162, 149 So. 74 (1933).

Test for determining relationship is reservation of right of control. — If the employee is an independent contractor, then deceased could not have been an employee. The test to be used in determining the relationship is whether the employer had a reserved right of control over the means and agencies by which the work was done or the result produced, not the actual exercise of such control. American Tennis Courts, Inc. v. Hinton, 378 So. 2d 235 (Ala. Civ. App.), cert. denied, 378 So. 2d 239 (Ala. 1979); Dennis v. Huff, 406 So. 2d 412 (Ala. Civ. App. 1981).

In deciding whether the employer-employee relationship exists, the deciding factor is the reserved right of control. Ford v. Mitcham, 53 Ala. App. 102, 298 So. 2d 34 (1974).

Whether laborer is employee or independent contractor depends on right of control, as shown by all the circumstances. Birmingham Post Co. v. Sturgeon, 227 Ala. 162, 149 So. 74 (1933). See also, V.P. Brown & Sons Lumber Co. v. Crossley, 230 Ala. 403, 161 So. 536

(1935), holding that whether laborer helping another who was cutting and skidding timber for lumber company was employee of company so as to be entitled to compensation for injury held for trial court.

Whether relation of "independent contractor" or that of "servant" exists depends upon whether person for whom one is working has control over means and agencies by which work is done, or over means and agencies by which result is produced. Birmingham Post Co. v. Sturgeon, 227 Ala. 162, 149 So. 74 (1933); Western Union Tel. Co. v. George, 239 Ala. 80, 194 So. 183 (1940).

Test whether relation of employer and employee or of independent contractor exists is reserved right of control rather than actual exercise of control. Tuscaloosa Veneer Co. v. Martin, 233 Ala. 567, 172 So. 608 (1937).

But failure of contract of hire to provide for supervision and control of employee is not of itself determinative of question whether relation established between parties was that of employer and employee or that of independent contractor. Tuscaloosa Veneer Co. v. Martin, 233 Ala. 567, 172 So. 608 (1937).

Finding that woodcutter who was employed to cut timber at rate of 75 cents per 1,000 feet under contract which contained no expression as to supervision and control was an employee, entitled to compensation for injuries, and not independent contractor, would not be disturbed where supported by inferences to be drawn from the evidence. Tuscaloosa Veneer Co. v. Martin, 233 Ala. 567, 172 So. 608 (1937).

However, contractual relationship between parties essential. — The definitions in our statute of employer and employee are not totally clear but they do indicate that a contractual relationship between two parties is essential. Ford v. Mitcham, 53 Ala. App. 102, 298 So. 2d 34 (1974).

A necessary prerequisite for recovery under the Workmen's Compensation Act is the existence of the relation of employer and employee. In order for that relation to exist, there must be a valid contract of service together with the right or power in the employer to control the employee with respect to the transaction out of which the injury arose. Blair v. Greene, 247 Ala. 104, 22 So. 2d 834 (1945).

"Regularly employs" does not mean constant employment of the requisite number of persons, but rather is a function of the frequency, regularity and duration of the occurrences in which that number is employed. LaPoint v. Barton, 57 Ala. App. 352, 328 So. 2d 605 (1976).

The criteria in definition of the term "regular employment" indicate that the totality of circumstances concerning the employment practices of the business must be examined. This necessitates that regard must be had to the number of persons employed over a reasonable time. LaPoint v. Barton, 57 Ala. App. 352, 328 So. 2d 605 (1976).

Whether relation of employer and employee or of independent contractor exists is question for jury, where there is no evidence except inference from circumstances that alleged employer reserved no control. Tuscaloosa Veneer Co. v. Martin, 233 Ala. 567, 172 So. 608 (1937).

If there is no evidence that defendant reserved no control, except an inference from the circumstances, the question is one for the trier of fact. Tidwell v. Walker County Mining & Inv. Co., 256 Ala. 547, 56 So. 2d 641 (1952).

And burden rests on claimant to show that relation of master and servant existed between deceased and alleged employer. Birmingham Post Co. v. Sturgeon, 227 Ala. 162, 149 So. 74 (1933).

Thus, facts must show supervision. — Where issue was whether relation of master and servant existed between newspaper publisher and newsboy, omission from stipulated facts that any district manager supervised newsboys justified conclusion that there was none. Birmingham Post Co. v. Sturgeon, 227 Ala. 162, 149 So. 74 (1933).

Employee's helpers covered if their need to employee reasonably contemplated. — If it was reasonably contemplated by an employer that it would be necessary for an employee to have helpers in his work, the employment of such helpers would make them employees of such employer within the meaning of the Workmen's Compensation Law. American Tennis Courts, Inc. v. Hinton, 378 So. 2d 235 (Ala. Civ. App.), cert. denied, 378 So. 2d 239 (Ala. 1979).

Implied contract of employment. — Even though contract between power company and contracting company designated ironworker as employee of contracting company, and even though contracting company had on-site supervision of its employees, it was undisputed that power company retained control of the manner or methods of work performed by the workers hired by contracting company and that ironworker submitted to power company's control and supervision of his work; there was an implied contract of employment between ironworker and power company, and therefore, power company was immune from suit under § 25-5-53. Pinson v. Alabama Power Co., 557 So. 2d 1236 (Ala. 1990).

Worker assigned by temporary employment agency. — Paint company to which worker was assigned by temporary employment agency was worker's special employer, despite the fact that the agency, and not the company, paid workers, and was thus immune from suit for injuries received by worker on the job. Pettaway v. Mobile Paint Mfg. Co., 467 So. 2d 228 (Ala. 1985).

Newsboy held "independent contractor". — Newsboy, required to call at stated time for papers, to be at stand to receive other editions, to sell at prescribed price in defined area and to account daily at specified rate for all papers not returned, held "independent contractor." Birmingham Post Co. v. Sturgeon, 227 Ala. 162, 149 So. 74 (1933).

"Required" and "permitted," as used in stipulation respecting duties of newsboy, meant, not that relation of master and servant existed between publisher and newsboy, but that newsboy was under duty or obligation to do certain things and was at liberty to do others. Birmingham Post Co. v. Sturgeon, 227 Ala. 162, 149 So. 74 (1933).

Automobile salesmen held not to be "employees". — Where automobile salesmen worked solely on a commission basis, had no regular working hours, no prescribed work rules, and the employer maintained no control over their individual actions in consummating sales, they were held not to be "employees" for the purpose of determining whether their employer was subject to the workmen's compensation law. Horton v. DeLoach, 276 Ala. 357, 162 So. 2d 453 (1964).

Partner cannot be an employee of his partnership for the purposes of workmen's compensation. Ford v. Mitcham, 53 Ala. App. 102, 298 So. 2d 34 (1974).

Worker held not employee of corporation but was employee of owner. — Where worker was injured while roofing a house of owner of a construction company, but brought his action against the owner's corporation, summary judgment was proper in favor of corporation since worker was not an employee of the corporation and whatever was done by owner appeared to have been done in his individual capacity and not in behalf of his construction company. Ray v. Rigsby Constr. Co., 549 So. 2d 1355 (Ala. Civ. App. 1989).

Because contract implicit in definitions of employer and employee is lacking in case of a working partner unless the partnership is considered to be a separate legal entity. Ford v. Mitcham, 53 Ala. App. 102, 298 So. 2d 34 (1974).

Convict performing forced labor while leased to custody of highway department by board of corrections held not an employee of highway department. See Downey v. Bituminous Cas. Corp., 349 So. 2d 1153 (Ala. 1977).

Joint employment liability. — In cases where there is evidence of joint employment, both employers may be liable for workmen's compensation. Jackson v. Weaver, 516 So. 2d 702 (Ala. Civ. App. 1987).

In determining which of two putative employers was the employee's employer for workmen's compensation purposes, federal law and regulations did not preempt state law, although under federal law and regulations one of the two employers, a common carrier, was deemed to be the employer of drivers of trucks it leased. The federal law and regulations may govern the liability of a common carrier to the public for injury or damage it or its employees may cause, but they did not govern the liability of such carrier as opposed to another putative employer for an injured driver's workmen's compensation benefits. Jackson v. Weaver, 516 So. 2d 702 (Ala. Civ. App. 1987).

Control test inappropriate to cases involving two putative employers. — The control test is inappropriate in cases where the issue is not whether the workmen's compensation claimant is an employee (as opposed to an independent contractor), but who among two or more putative employers is liable for the employee's workmen's compensation benefits. Rather, in cases such as this, the finder of fact should concentrate not solely on control, but also on additional indicia of the employment relationship in determining an employee's status. Jackson v. Weaver, 516 So. 2d 702 (Ala. Civ. App. 1987).

Instances of "employees". — One engaged to dig test pits, paying his own labor and working on "piecework" basis, held "employee," where contract was terminable for violation of rules or "carelessness or incapacity." Martin v. Republic Steel Co., 226 Ala. 209, 146 So. 276 (1933).

Payment of compensation to woodcutter at rate of $.75 per 1,000 feet of timber cut, and his employment of helper to do piecework, held not to make woodcutter an "independent contractor" rather than an "employee" within Workmen's Compensation Act. Tuscaloosa Veneer Co. v. Martin, 233 Ala. 567, 172 So. 608 (1937).

In proceeding against telegraph company for compensation for death of plaintiff's son while delivering telegram for drug store which had entered into agency contract with telegraph company for transmission of telegrams, evidence warranted conclusion that son was "employee" of telegraph company and not an "independent contractor" at time of accident. Western Union Tel. Co. v. George, 239 Ala. 80, 194 So. 183 (1940).

Relationship between a student nurse and a hospital held to be that of employee and employer. Carraway Methodist Hosp. v. Pitts, 256 Ala. 665, 57 So. 2d 96 (1952).

Injury during attempt to pass physical agility test. — Plaintiff was not an employee of the city when she was injured during her second attempt to pass a physical agility test, and had signed a form, releasing the city from any liability in the event of her injury as a result of the agility test. Boyd v. City of Montgomery, 515 So. 2d 6 (Ala. Civ. App. 1987).

Where timber company designated tract to be cut and size and type of tree to be cut, but did not control or affect how the work was to be done, the woodcutter was an independent contractor; therefore, the worker hired by the woodcutter was not an employee of the timber company. Gallery v. J.B. Jones Timber, Inc., 514 So. 2d 1033 (Ala. Civ. App.), writ denied, 514 So. 2d 1035 (Ala. 1987).

Employee of temporary service agency working for client company. — Where the plaintiff, admittedly an employee of a temporary service agency, was, for workmen's compensation purposes, also an employee of the company she was sent to work for, her exclusive remedy against company was the benefits provided by Workmen's Compensation Act and the trial court was correct in ruling that she could not maintain an independent action for damages against the company she was working for at the time of injury. Marlow v. Mid S. Tool Co., 535 So. 2d 120 (Ala. 1988).

E. Personal Injury.

Disease resulting from accident is an injury. — It is settled by our decisions that a disease which results proximately from an accident is an injury within the meaning of the compensation act of Alabama and is included within the phrase "injuries by an accident arising out of and in the course of his employment" as that phrase is used in the act. Davis v. Standard Oil Co., 261 Ala. 410, 74 So. 2d 625 (1954).

Thus, arthritis caused by an accidental injury arising out of and in the course of employment must be considered an injury. Davis v. Standard Oil Co., 261 Ala. 410, 74 So. 2d 625 (1954).

Traumatic arthritis, even though a disease, is covered by the act as a personal injury under subdivision (9) if it resulted from an accident arising out of and in the course of appellant's employment. Davis v. Standard Oil Co., 261 Ala. 410, 74 So. 2d 625 (1954).

Arthritis caused by an accidental injury arising out of and in the course of employment must be considered an injury. Martin Indus., Inc. v. Dement, 435 So. 2d 85 (Ala. Civ. App. 1983).

Injury from working in unventilated room held personal injury. — Injury to employee from working in an unventilated room filled with fumes, dust and small particles of chemical mixture, which did not appear suddenly and violently, but grew progressively worse, was held a "personal injury." Gentry v. Swann Chem. Co., 234 Ala. 313, 174 So. 530 (1937).

Employee victim of assault. — An employee may be the victim of an assault and his injury or death may still be compensable; however, the fact of a willful assault alone does not conclusively establish that the assault arose out of the employee's employment. That conclusion must be drawn from the circumstances of each case. Powell v. Jack Ingram Motors, Inc., 537 So. 2d 37 (Ala. Civ. App. 1988).

Disease induced or aggravated by lowered air resistance caused by accident. — Employee's disease results proximately from accident, so as to be "personal injury" under subdivision (9) of this section, if it is induced by lowered air resistance caused by accident in a mine, or is aggravated or accelerated by it. New River Coal Co. v. Files, 215 Ala. 64, 109 So. 360 (1926).

F. Premises.

The term "premises" must be related to the control or to the right of control of the employer over the employee. Turner v. Drummond Co., 349 So. 2d 598 (Ala. Civ. App.), cert. denied, 349 So. 2d 605 (Ala. 1977).

Under subdivision (9) of this section, the term "premises" has reference to premises at or near which service is to be rendered. Sloss-Sheffield Steel & Iron Co. v. Thomas, 220 Ala. 686, 127 So. 165 (1930); Hayes v. Alabama By-Products Corp., 242 Ala. 148, 5 So. 2d 624 (1942); Blair v. Greene, 247 Ala. 104, 22 So. 2d 834 (1945); Ammons v. McClendon, 263 Ala. 651, 83 So. 2d 239 (1955); Glens Falls Ins. Co. v. Anderson, 280 Ala. 626, 197 So. 2d 276 (1967).

But word "premises" is an elastic and inclusive term and it does not have one definite and fixed meaning, but its meaning is to be determined by its context and is dependent on circumstances in which used; the term may mean a room, shop, building or any definite area. Russellville Gas Co. v. Duggar, 47 Ala. App. 661, 260 So. 2d 393 (1971); Turner v. Drummond Co., 349 So. 2d 598 (Ala. Civ. App.), cert. denied, 349 So. 2d 605 (Ala. 1977).

However, its definition cannot negate requirement of existing master-servant relationship at moment of accident. — The definition of the term "premises" cannot be allowed to negate the requirement of the existence of a master-servant relationship at the moment of the accident. Russellville Gas

Co. v. Duggar, 47 Ala. App. 661, 260 So. 2d 393 (1971).

Premises includes entering or leaving place of services. — Under the provisions of subdivision (9) of this section excluding from compensation all injuries except while employees are engaged in, on or about the premises, etc., an employee who is leaving or entering the place of service is still so engaged for a reasonable time and space while he is at or near his place of employment. Knight Iron & Metal Co. v. Ardis, 240 Ala. 305, 199 So. 716 (1940).

An employee while in the act of leaving his employer's premises where his services have been performed at an appropriate time after the completion of his actual services is engaged in an act naturally related and incidental to the service or work which he was engaged to perform. The same rule applied to an employee who at the time he was stricken was taking a bath in preparation for his homeward journey. Massey v. United States Steel Corp., 264 Ala. 227, 86 So. 2d 375 (1955). But see, Hayes v. Alabama By-Products Corp., 242 Ala. 148, 5 So. 2d 624 (1942).

When definition of premises applicable to employee's home. — There would be no difficulty in applying the "elastic" definition of premises to the home of a worker in the instant case had he been engaged in the service of his employer at the time of his injury. However, to permit the home of the worker to be categorically designated as the premises of the employer at all times when occupied by the worker would, in effect, provide protection of workmen's compensation to the worker at all times without any means of control of his activities by the employer; the benevolent purposes of workmen's compensation were not intended to be extended so far. Russellville Gas Co. v. Duggar, 47 Ala. App. 661, 260 So. 2d 393 (1971).

Fact that a worker, injured at home, had at home as his means of transportation a vehicle provided by his employer, which might have been used by him to perform a service for his employer if called, is merely incidental. Russellville Gas Co. v. Duggar, 47 Ala. App. 661, 260 So. 2d 393 (1971).

Injury on highway not excluded where duties required regular use of highway. — The duties of plaintiff required him to make regular trips over the highways in an automobile, stop at hotels and visit branch offices. These were his workshop, the places where he spent his time and worked for his employer. His injury on a highway was not excluded from compensation under subdivision (9) of this section. United Serv. Ins. Co. v. Donaldson, 254 Ala. 204, 48 So. 2d 3 (1950).

Injury did not occur in or about premises. — That some time prior to accident deceased's work as track layer was about place of accident, occurring when he alighted from employer's street car transporting him from work, held not to make such place premises where his service was "being performed" at the time within subdivision (9) of this section. Ex parte Taylor, 213 Ala. 282, 104 So. 527 (1925).

Where it appeared that supplyman had no further services to perform for employer after checking out at lamp house, that after leaving the lamp house the supplyman went to shower house, which was maintained by a tenant of a house of employer about 612 feet from the lamp house, and that while the supplyman was preparing to take a bath a hot water tank exploded, causing fatal injury, the accident did not occur about the employer's "premises" and the supplyman's injuries did not "arise out of and in the course of his employment" and were, therefore, not compensable. Hayes v. Alabama By-Products Corp., 242 Ala. 148, 5 So. 2d 624 (1942). But see, Massey v. United States Steel Corp., 264 Ala. 227, 86 So. 2d 375 (1955).

When a state highway department employee on her coffee break left the premises of the state highway building, on a purely personal mission to another state building, unconnected with her employment, she was off-premises. The mere fact that the other building was also a state building and part of the capitol complex does not make it the premises where she worked. Glens Falls Ins. Co. v. Anderson, 280 Ala. 626, 197 So. 2d 276 (1967).

§ 25-5-2. Powers and duties of Director of Industrial Relations with respect to administration of chapter generally; "director" defined.

The Director of the Department of Industrial Relations of the State of Alabama shall gather statistics on accidents and their causes and shall generally be responsible for the efficient administration of this chapter. To this end, the director shall make the necessary investigations and examinations in connection with the settlement of all workers' compensation claims.

As used in this chapter, the word "director" shall mean the Director of the "Department of Industrial Relations". (Code 1923, § 7589; Acts 1939, No. 661, p. 1036, § 9; Code 1940, T. 26, § 264; Acts 1992, No. 92-537, § 3.)

The 1992 amendment, effective May 19, 1992, divided the former first sentence into the present first and second sentences by substituting "of this chapter. To this end" for "of this chapter and, to this end," in the present second sentence substituted "the director shall make" for "shall have full power to make or cause to be made" and "workers'" for "workmen's," in the last sentence deleted "be construed to" following "shall," inserted "Director of the," and deleted "or the director thereof unless a contrary meaning plainly appears" at the end of the sentence, and made changes in capitalization throughout the section.

§ 25-5-3. Director to prepare and distribute forms, etc.

The director shall prepare and cause to be printed, at the expense of the state, and to be paid for as other supplies are paid for, and upon request furnish free sample copies to any employer or employee the blank forms and literature as he or she shall deem requisite to facilitate or promote the efficient administration of Articles 2, 3, and 4 of this chapter, other than the papers relating to court proceedings. The director shall adopt and cause a standardized claim reimbursement form to be used by providers. The director shall also assist providers in developing a system for electronic reporting, billing, and payment in workers' compensation cases. Standardized claim reimbursement forms for physicians licensed to practice medicine and for other providers shall be approved by the director and the Workers' Compensation Medical Services Board. If the board and the director are unable to agree on a standardized claim reimbursement form for physicians within three months following May 19, 1992, then the form shall be established under Section 27-1-16. (Code 1923, § 7590; Acts 1939, No. 661, p. 1036, § 10; Code 1940, T. 26, § 265; Acts 1992, No. 92-537, § 4.)

The 1992 amendment, effective May 19, 1992, in the first sentence deleted "of the department of industrial relations" following "The director," substituted "sample copies" for "of charge," substituted "the blank forms" for "such blank forms," inserted "or she" and substituted "Articles 2, 3, and 4" for "articles 2 and 3," and added the second through the fifth sentences.

Editor's note. — The cases annotated below were decided under prior law.

Compensation not controlled by exact form prepared by director. — Although the director of the department of industrial relations is delegated authority to prepare and distribute such blank forms and literature as he shall deem requisite to facilitate or promote the efficient administration of this chapter, fact that director drafted form to be used when filing an election of coverage under § 25-5-50 did not mean that workmen's compensation for farm laborers should have been controlled by whether or not this exact form appeared in the files of the department of industrial relations. Smith v. Thrower Nursery, Inc., 360 So. 2d 741 (Ala. 1978).

Consistent pattern of behavior as evidence of intent. — While a single act of taking out insurance or paying a claim may not be sufficient evidence of intent to come under Workmen's Compensation Act, a consistent pattern of behavior on the part of the employer, his employees and the department of industrial relations will suffice, despite failure to comply with technical filing requirements. Smith v. Thrower Nursery, Inc., 360 So. 2d 741 (Ala. 1978).

Cited in Waldon v. Hartford Ins. Group, 435 So. 2d 1271 (Ala. 1983); Gibson v. Fidelity & Cas. Co., 454 So. 2d 526 (Ala. 1984).

§ 25-5-4. Reports and records of injuries for which compensation claimed.

An employer shall keep a record of all injuries, fatal or otherwise, received by his or her employees arising out of and in the course of their employment and for which compensation is claimed or paid. Within 15 days after the occurrence of the injuries and knowledge thereof by the employer, a report of the same shall be made to the department on forms approved by the department. At the discretion of the director, reports received under this chapter may be destroyed after 12 years. (Code 1923, § 7591; Acts 1939, No. 661, p. 1036, § 11; Code 1940, T. 26, § 266; Acts 1957, No. 334, p. 436; Acts 1992, No. 92-537, § 5.)

The 1992 amendment, effective May 19, 1992, in the first sentence substituted "An employer" for "Every employer," inserted "received by his or her employees arising out of and in the course of their employment and," and deleted "received by his employees in the course of their employment" at the end of the sentence, in the second sentence substituted "the injuries" for "such injuries," deleted "of industrial relations" following "made to the department," substituted "by the department" for "by said department," and deleted "the provisions of" preceding "this chapter" in the last sentence.

Cited in Waldon v. Hartford Ins. Group, 435 So. 2d 1271 (Ala. 1983); Gibson v. Fidelity & Cas. Co., 454 So. 2d 526 (Ala. 1984).

Collateral references. — 101 C.J.S., Workmen's Compensation, § 915.

§ 25-5-5. Reports of settlements.

Every employer shall, within 10 days after the settlement of any case, other than a settlement approved by the court, make a report thereof in writing, giving the details of such settlement, and shall mail the same to the Department of Industrial Relations on forms approved by said department. (Code 1923, § 7592; Acts 1939, No. 661, p. 1036, § 12; Code 1940, T. 26, § 267.)

Collateral references. — Mental disorders as compensable under Workmen's Compensation Acts. 97 ALR3d 161.

§ 25-5-6. Circuit court clerks to report disposition of cases.

The clerk of the circuit court shall, within 10 days after the disposition of any case in his court, make a report in writing, giving the details of such disposition, and shall mail the same to the Department of Industrial Relations on forms approved by said department. (Code 1923, § 7593; Acts 1939, No. 661, p. 1036, § 13; Code 1940, T. 26, § 268.)

§ 25-5-7. Supplementary reports as to initiation, cessation, etc., of compensation payments.

In all cases, upon making the first payment of compensation and upon cessation or termination of payment of compensation, for any reason whatever, the employer shall make a supplementary report within 10 days to the Department of Industrial Relations on forms approved by said department. If the first installment of compensation is not paid within 30 days after the employer has knowledge of a claim for compensation, the employer shall file a report, within 10 days of the expiration of the 30-day period, setting out the reason for such nonpayment with the Department of Industrial Relations on forms approved by said department. (Code 1923, § 7594; Acts 1939, No. 661, p. 1036, § 14; Code 1940, T. 26, § 269; Acts 1949, No. 36, p. 47; Acts 1973, No. 1062, p. 1750, § 6.)

§ 25-5-8. Employers' options to secure payment of compensation.

(a) *Option to insure risks.* — An employer subject to this chapter may secure the payment of compensation under this chapter by insuring and keeping insured his or her liability in some insurance corporation, association, organization, insurance association, corporation, or association formed of employers and workers or formed by a group of employers to insure the risks under this chapter, operating by mutual assessment or other plans or otherwise. Notwithstanding the foregoing, the insurance association, organization, or corporation shall have first had its contract and plan of business approved in writing by the Commissioner of the Department of Insurance of Alabama and have been authorized by the Department of Insurance to transact the business of workers' compensation insurance in this state and under the plan. Notwithstanding any other provision of the law to the contrary, the obligations of employers under law for workers' compensation benefits for injury of employees may be insured by any combination of life, disability, accident, health, or other insurance provided that the coverages insure without limitation or exclusion the workers' compensation benefits of this state.

(b) *Option to operate as self-insurer.* — An employer subject to this chapter who elects not to insure his or her liability thereunder shall furnish satisfactory proof to the director of his or her financial ability to pay directly compensation in the amount and manner and when due as provided by this chapter. Upon receiving satisfactory proof, the director shall authorize the employer to operate as a self-insurer. The director may prescribe other reasonable rules and regulations for the purpose of protecting the injured employee or the employee's dependents and set reasonable fees to accompany self-insurance applications.

(c) *Evidence of compliance.* — An employer subject to this chapter shall file with the director, on a form prescribed by the director, annually or as often as the director in his or her discretion deems necessary, evidence of compliance with the requirements of this section. In cases where insurance is taken with a carrier duly authorized to write such insurance in this state, notice of insurance coverage filed by the carrier shall be sufficient evidence of compliance by the insured.

(d) *Certificate of compliance.*

(1) ISSUANCE, REVOCATION. — Upon the employer's complying with subsection (b) of this section relating to self-insurance, the director shall issue to the employer a certificate, which shall remain in force for a period fixed by the director. Upon 60 days' notice and hearing to the employer, the director may, for financial reasons, for failure of the employer to faithfully discharge his or her obligations according to the agreements contained in his or her application for self-insurance, or for the violation of any reasonable rule or regulation prescribed by the director, revoke the self-insurance certificate, in which case the employer shall immediately insure his or her liability. Certificates of self-insurance issued prior to September 17, 1973, shall continue in force but shall become subject to revocation as provided in this subsection. At any time after the revocation, the director may grant a new certificate to the employer upon application by the employer.

(2) APPEALS. — An appeal may be taken from any ruling of the director under subsection (b) of this section or under this subsection to the circuit court. The presiding judge shall, within 10 days after notification of appeal, assign a member of the court to hear the case and the matter shall be set for hearing at the earliest available time. Trial shall be de novo. The taking of an appeal shall not stay the ruling or order appealed from unless good and sufficient bond approved by the judge of the court to which the appeal is taken shall be filed with the court, conditioned on complying with such order as may be legally made effective and further conditioned upon payment by the employer of all final orders for compensation that may be rendered against the employer pending the disposition of the appeal.

(e) *Penalties for failure to secure payment of compensation; injunctions.* — An employer required to secure the payment of compensation under this section who fails to secure compensation shall be guilty of a misdemeanor, and upon conviction thereof, shall be subject to a fine of not less than $100.00 nor more than $1,000.00. In addition, an employer required to secure the payment of compensation under this section who fails to secure the compensation shall be liable for two times the amount of compensation which would have otherwise been payable for injury or death to an employee. The director may apply to a court of competent jurisdiction for an injunction to restrain threatened or continued violation of any provisions relating to the requirements of insurance or self-insurance. The court may impose civil penalties against an employer in noncompliance with this amendatory act, in an amount not to exceed $100.00 per day. Subsequent compliance with this amendatory act shall not be a defense.

(f) *Employer insurance policies.*

(1) REQUIRED and PROHIBITED PROVISIONS. — Insurance policies written pursuant to this section shall contain a clause to the effect that, as between

the worker and the insurer, notice to and knowledge by the employer of the occurrence of the injury shall be deemed notice and knowledge on the part of the insurer; that jurisdiction of the employer for the purpose of this chapter shall be jurisdiction of the insurer; and that the insurer will in all things be bound by and subject to the award or judgment rendered against the employer upon the risk so insured. The policies shall provide that the worker shall have an equitable lien upon any amount that shall become owing, on account of the policy, to the employer from the insurer, and in case of legal incapacity or inability of the employer to receive the amount owing and pay it over to the worker or his or her dependent, that the insurer will pay the same direct to the worker or dependent, thereby discharging all obligations under the policy to the employer and all the obligations of the employer and the insurer to the worker. Such policies, however, shall contain no obligations relieving the insurance company from payment of obligations if the employer becomes insolvent or discharged in bankruptcy or otherwise during the period the policy is in force, if the compensation remains owing. The insurer shall be one authorized by law to conduct business in the State of Alabama, and all insurance companies writing such insurance may include in their policies, in addition to the requirements now provided by law, the additional requirements, terms, and conditions provided in this section.

(2) FILING OF AND APPROVAL OF PREMIUM AND RISK CLASSIFICATIONS. — An insurance corporation, mutual corporation, reciprocal exchange, or association authorized to transact the business of workers' compensation insurance in this state and which insures employers against liability for compensation under this chapter shall file with the Department of Insurance its classification of risks and premiums relating thereto and any subsequent proposed classification of risks and premiums, together with the basic rates and merit-rating schedules, if a system of schedule rating or merit rating is used by the insurance corporation, exchange, or association, none of which shall take effect until the Commissioner of the Department of Insurance shall have approved the same as reasonable, adequate, and not excessive. All filings with the Department of Insurance containing aggregate industry data of classifications of risks and premiums, rates, and merit-rating schedules pertaining to workers' compensation insurance shall be public records, notwithstanding any other provisions of Alabama law. The Commissioner of the Department of Insurance shall convene a public hearing with reasonable public notice for the purpose of considering public testimony and other evidence relevant to any filing prior to approval of any bureau loss cost or rate filing related to workers' compensation insurance. Within 10 days after approval, the Commissioner of the Department of Insurance shall make or cause to be made a sufficient number of copies of same for that purpose, and shall mail at least one copy of each of the same to every insurance carrier writing workers' compensation business in the State of Alabama, at the carrier's last address or at the last address of its designated agent to receive the same. The insurance carrier shall (or if it is

a member of or associated with a rating or inspection bureau, either or both of them, or a concern or aggregation of like character, it shall cause the rating and inspection bureau, either or both, or concern or aggregation of like character with which it is affiliated to do so) file with the Department of Insurance a full and complete statement of the actuarial and underwriting experience data and the like in its possession, from which and upon which the rates, schedules, and systems so filed were ascertained, calculated, and constructed, and within six months after the expiration of each succeeding six months, shall file a like statement of all actuarial and underwriting data and the like, pertaining to the rates, schedules, and system accumulated or acquired by it during the preceding six months. Upon failure to file the statement within the time specified above, the rates, schedules, and systems may be presumed by the Commissioner of the Department of Insurance, without more, to be excessive, unreasonable, inadequate to provide the necessary reserves, or discriminatory, as the case may be. The Commissioner of the Department of Insurance may withdraw his or her approval of any premium rate or schedule made by an insurance corporation, association, mutual corporation, or reciprocal exchange, if, in his or her judgment, the premium rate or schedule is excessive, unreasonable, discriminatory, or inadequate to provide the necessary reserves. The commissioner shall withdraw approval of any premium rate or schedule shown by a motor common carrier employer to be conditioned on the motor common carrier accepting the coverage of owner-operators or lease-operators as a condition to providing coverage for the motor common carrier employer's employees.

Nothing contained in this chapter or in any other law of this state shall affect the right of an insurance corporation or a mutual or reciprocal insurance corporation or association to issue participating policies or contracts or to pay savings, refunds, or dividends upon the policies or contracts.

(3) PAYMENT OF INSURANCE COSTS BY EMPLOYEES. — No agreement by an employee to pay to an employer any portion of the cost of insuring his or her risk under this chapter shall be valid unless the agreement between the employer and employee, the plan of which is part of a contract, is approved in writing by the commissioner. But the employer and the worker may agree to carry the risks and to provide other and greater benefits, such as additional compensation; accident, sickness, or old age insurance; or benefits, and the fact that the plan involves a contribution by the worker shall not prevent its validity if the plan has been approved in writing by the commissioner. An employer who makes any charge or deduction prohibited by this section is guilty of a misdemeanor.

(4) DIRECT ACTIONS AGAINST INSURERS. — If the employer insures the payment of the compensation provided by this chapter and according to the full benefits thereof and with full coverage under this chapter in a corporation or association authorized to do business in Alabama and approved by the commissioner, and if the employer posts a notice or notices

in a conspicuous place or in conspicuous places about his or her place of employment, stating that he or she is insured and by whom insured; and if the employer files a copy of the notice with the Department of Insurance, then, and in such case, any civil actions brought by an injured employee or the employee's dependent shall be brought directly against the insurer, and the employer, or insured, shall be released from any further liability. If the insurance company is insolvent or bankrupt, or if it cannot be reached by due diligence by process in this state, the employer shall not be released from liability under this chapter. Should any recovery be had in excess of the amount of the insurance carried, the employer shall be liable for the excess. The return of execution upon a judgment of an employee against an insurance company, unsatisfied in whole or in part, shall be conclusive evidence of the insolvency of the insurance company for the purposes of this chapter, and if the insurance company is adjudged to be bankrupt or insolvent by a court of competent jurisdiction, proceedings may be brought by the employee against the employer in the first instance or against the employer and the insurance company jointly or severally or in a pending proceeding against the insurance company, and the employer may be joined at any time after the adjudication.

(g) *Employer bill of rights — Penalty.*

(1) Every insurance carrier and self-insurer, individual and group, shall, on written request of the insured employer, provide the employer with a list of claims made against the employer. The information provided to the employer shall include amounts paid for closed claims and, if requested, details regarding the treatment and condition of the injured or disabled worker. The employer shall also receive notice of any proposed settlement of any claim against the employer if the employer so requests in writing.

(2) In the event the court determines and makes a finding that a worker has filed a fraudulent claim for workers' compensation benefits under this amendatory act, Section 25-5-11.1 shall not apply to the employer. In addition to the denial of workers' compensation benefits under this amendatory act, the employer, upon such a finding that a worker has filed a fraudulent claim for workers' compensation benefits under this amendatory act, may terminate the worker.

(3) Failure to comply with subdivision (1) may subject the violator to a fine, upon hearing by a court, of not less than $25.00 nor more than $100.00. (Code 1923, § 7584; Acts 1939, No. 661, p. 1036, § 7; Code 1940, T. 26, § 309; Acts 1955, No. 308, p. 707; Acts 1971, No. 667, p. 1376, § 9; Acts 1973, No. 1062, p. 1750, §§ 23-25; Acts 1992, No. 92-537, § 6.)

The 1992 amendment, effective May 19, 1992, rewrote this section.

Code commissioner's note. — The phrase "this amendatory act," as used in the section above, refers to Acts 1992, No. 92-537, which amended this section. Act No. 92-537 also amended §§ 25-5-1 through 25-5-4, 25-5-8, 25-5-10, 25-5-11, 25-5-13, 25-5-50 through 25-5-57, 25-5-59, 25-5-60, 25-5-66 through 25-5-68, 25-5-77, 25-5-78, 25-5-80, 25-5-81, 25-5-83, 25-5-85, 25-5-86, 25-5-90, 25-5-110, 25-5-116, 25-5-117, 25-5-120, 25-5-251, enacted §§ 25-5-15.1, 25-5-290 through 25-5-294, and 25-5-310 through 25-5-318, and repealed

§§ 25-5-16, 25-5-70 through 25-5-75, 25-5-140 through 25-5-152, and 25-5-170 through 25-5-180.

Editor's note. — The cases annotated below were decided under prior law.

Constitutionality. — See Hester v. Ridings, 388 So. 2d 1218 (Ala. Civ. App. 1980).

In the absence of some applicable statute there can be no direct action against an employer's insurer by an injured employee. Subsection (f)(4), provides the only instance where such direct suit may be maintained. Den-Tal-Eze Mfg. Co. v. Gosa, 388 So. 2d 1006 (Ala. Civ. App. 1980).

Employer can provide that action be brought against insurer directly. — An employer, if he be insured according to the Workmen's Compensation Act, can provide that the action be brought against the insurer directly. Hale v. United States Fid. & Guar. Co., 45 Ala. App. 379, 231 So. 2d 156 (1970).

Provision in a policy providing workmen's compensation which allows a direct action on the policy by the injured employee is valid and enforceable and is not invalidated by the Workmen's Compensation Act. Wilson v. Central Foundry Co., 414 So. 2d 963 (Ala. 1982).

Where a workmen's compensation policy expressly provides for a direct action by the employee or his dependent against the insurer, neither subsection (f)(4) of this section nor section 25-5-53 precludes such suits. Wilson v. Central Foundry Co., 414 So. 2d 963 (Ala. 1982).

Employee's action against insurance carrier. — An employee injured in Alabama could not maintain proceeding for compensation against employer's insurance carrier in absence of employer over whom jurisdiction had not been obtained. Pounds v. Travelers Ins. Co., 239 Ala. 573, 196 So. 108 (1940).

A procedure for an employee to sue an insurance carrier directly is provided by this section and mandates a direct action only if certain requirements are met. Read News Agency, Inc. v. Moman, 383 So. 2d 840 (Ala. Civ. App.), cert. denied, 383 So. 2d 847 (Ala. 1980).

Interpretation of group accident insurance policy in relation to workmen's compensation insurance. — See Mutual Benefit Health & Accident Ass'n v. Bullard, 270 Ala. 558, 120 So. 2d 714 (1960).

Burden of establishing whether employer is self-insured is on employer. — Although the provisions of this section do not set out who has the burden of establishing whether an employer is self-insured, because proof of self-insurance would prevent an employer from having to pay the double penalty provision, establishing such proof should prop-

erly be the employer's burden. Hastings v. Hancock, 576 So. 2d 666 (Ala. Civ. App. 1991).

For construction of such terms as "incidental" and "connected" in reference to operations covered by workmen's compensation policy. — See Tuscaloosa Veneer Co. v. American Mut. Liab. Ins. Co., 240 Ala. 444, 199 So. 868 (1941).

Employer does not lose its employer status — for immunity purposes — by qualifying under the Workmen's Compensation Act as a self-insurer and, in that capacity, performing or failing to perform safety inspections. Adair v. Moretti-Harrah Marble Co., 381 So. 2d 181 (Ala. 1980).

This section has two penalty provisions. The first is a criminal penalty for failure to secure compensation as required even though no award has been granted. Second is a civil penalty awarded to a worker, or in event of his death, his dependents, after there has been an injury or death for which compensation has been granted but for which payment has not been secured. There appears no reason why both penalties could not be assessed in the proper case. Harris v. Vaughan, 373 So. 2d 1111 (Ala. Civ. App.), cert. denied, 373 So. 2d 1113 (Ala. 1979).

The penalty was designed to promote compliance with the workmen's compensation law. Hester v. Ridings, 388 So. 2d 1218 (Ala. Civ. App. 1980).

The double award penalty provision of this section is mandatory. Naturally, there is some hardship upon any employer where the penalty of the double award must be assessed; however, there is no legal right to relief from a penalty which is required to be imposed by law. Rush v. Heflin, 411 So. 2d 1295 (Ala. Civ. App. 1982).

The penalty provided in subsection (e) is permissible in that it promotes compliance with a valid legislative objective. Hester v. Ridings, 388 So. 2d 1218 (Ala. Civ. App. 1980).

Employee is entitled to have the compensation first computed, then the penalty assessed thereon and the credit for any payment by the employer thereafter given. Rush v. Heflin, 411 So. 2d 1295 (Ala. Civ. App. 1982).

Employee may recover double penalty despite failure to specifically ask for such relief. — Employee proved such facts as would entitle him to recover the double penalty, regardless of the fact that he failed to specifically request this relief in his complaint. Hastings v. Hancock, 576 So. 2d 666 (Ala. Civ. App. 1991).

This section does authorize direct suit against insurer, but this right exists only if the conditions therein set forth are met. Therefore, if the proper notices are not posted and filed as contemplated by the statute, the employee's only recourse is direct suit against the employer. Thomason v. Midland Ins. Co., 380 So. 2d 902 (Ala. Civ. App. 1980).

Cited in Lawrence v. United States Fid. & Guar. Co., 226 Ala. 161, 145 So. 577 (1933); Alabama Dry Dock & Shipbuilding Co. v. Henderson, 98 F. Supp. 1001 (S.D. Ala. 1951); Universal Underwriters Ins. Co. v. Marriott Homes, Inc., 286 Ala. 231, 238 So. 2d 730 (1970); Price Ceiling, Inc. v. Ray, 394 So. 2d 58 (Ala. Civ. App. 1981); Stinson v. Liberty Mut. Ins. Co., 395 So. 2d 1032 (Ala. Civ. App. 1981); Baird v. Spradlin, 409 So. 2d 820 (Ala. 1982); Wilson v. Central Foundry Co., 414 So. 2d 962 (Ala. Civ. App. 1981); Bentley v. Arnold, 431 So. 2d 549 (Ala. Civ. App. 1983); Bechtel v. Crown Cent. Petro. Corp., 495 So. 2d 1052 (Ala. 1986); Jackson v. Weaver, 516 So. 2d 702 (Ala. Civ. App. 1987).

Collateral references. — 100 C.J.S., Workmen's Compensation, § 353(1).

58 Am. Jur. 2d, Workmen's Compensation, § 555 et seq.

Provisions directed against noninsuring or self-insuring employers. 18 ALR 267.

Insurer's right to recover from employer, who has breached warranty, the amount it has been obliged to pay employee. 22 ALR 1481.

Insurance carrier as bound by findings upon claim for compensation. 28 ALR 882.

Insurance under compensation act coextensive with insurance liability under act. 45 ALR 1329, 108 ALR 812.

Provisions of compensation insurance policy with respect to notice of accident, claim, etc. 76 ALR 23, 123 ALR 950, 18 ALR2d 443, 32 ALR4th 141.

Injuries for which insured is liable in representative capacity only as within coverage of policy issued to him in another capacity. 78 ALR 1333.

Voluntary payment or other relief by insurance carrier as estoppel to deny issuance of policy or that case is within coverage. 91 ALR 1530.

Right of insurance company as to rejection of applications for insurance in view of its public interest. 107 ALR 1421, 123 ALR 139.

Cancellation or attempt at cancellation of insurance. 107 ALR 1514.

Policy of compensation insurance issued to individual as covering employees of partnership of which he is a member. 114 ALR 724.

Right to indemnity, or contribution as between insurance carriers under compensation laws of different states. 126 ALR 881.

Proper tribunal for determination of questions relating to insurance under compensation act. 127 ALR 473.

Refusal of compensation insurer to act upon claim against employer, or delay or repudiation of liability in that regard, as justifying payment or compromise by employer without complying with provisions of policy that make judgment against employer or agreement with insurer's consent a condition of its liability. 128 ALR 565.

Antedating policy of compensation insurance as affecting liability for loss that had already occurred. 132 ALR 1325.

Liability of insurance carrier where because of relationship between employee and employer recovery would inure in whole or in part to employer. 147 ALR 115.

Reinsurance of self-insurer. 153 ALR 967.

Insurance carrier's liability for part of employer's liability attributable to violation of law or other misconduct on his part. 1 ALR2d 407.

Crediting employer or insurance carrier with earnings of employee reemployed, or continued in employment, after injury. 84 ALR2d 1108.

Renewal of policy, insurer's denial of, waiver and estoppel. 85 ALR2d 1410.

Homeowners' or personal liability insurance as providing coverage for liability under workmen's compensation laws. 41 ALR3d 1306.

Tort liability of worker's compensation insurer for wrongful delay or refusal to make payments due. 8 ALR4th 902.

§ 25-5-9. Pooling of employers' liabilities for qualification as self-insurers.

(a) The Director of Industrial Relations may, under such rules and regulations as he may prescribe, permit two or more employers, as such term is defined in Section 25-5-1, to enter into agreements to pool their liabilities under this chapter for the purpose of qualifying as self-insurers under this chapter. Each employer member of such approved group shall be authorized to operate as a self-insurer under this chapter.

(b) Two or more employer groups as described in (a) above may enter into agreements to pool their liabilities under this chapter for the purpose of providing excess coverage above the self insured retention levels maintained by the individual employer groups.

(c) This section is supplemental and shall insofar as possible be construed in pari materia with this chapter; however, any law or part thereof in conflict herewith is repealed. (Acts 1965, No. 407, p. 587; Acts 1987, No. 87-559, p. 842.)

Cross references. — As to registration of judgments generally, see § 6-9-210 et seq. As to the immunity from suit and civil liability of not-for-profit corporations, associations or organizations, see T. 10, ch. 11.

§ 25-5-10. Liabilities of persons engaged in schemes, etc., to avoid liability to workers.

(a) A person who creates or carries into operation any fraudulent scheme, artifice, or device to execute work without being responsible to the worker for the benefits provided by this chapter shall be included in the term "employer" and shall be subject to all the liabilities of employers under this chapter.

(b) When compensation is claimed from or proceedings taken against a person under subsection (a) of this section, the compensation shall be calculated with reference to the wage the worker was receiving from the person by whom he or she was immediately employed at the time of the injury.

(c) The employer shall not be liable or required to pay compensation for injuries due to the acts or omissions of third persons not at the time in the service of the employer nor engaged in the work in which the injury occurs, except as provided in Section 25-5-11. (Acts 1919, No. 245, p. 206; Code 1923, § 7585; Code 1940, T. 26, § 310; Acts 1992, No. 92-537, § 7.)

The 1992 amendment, effective May 19, 1992, rewrote subsection (a), in subsection (b) substituted "worker" for "workmen" and inserted "or she," and substituted "or omissions" for "of omissions" in subsection (c).

Editor's note. — The cases annotated below were decided under prior law.

This section inferentially recognizes the continued existence of the rule as to independent contractors by guarding against any fraudulent scheme tending to an evasion of liability. Birmingham Post Co. v. Sturgeon, 227 Ala. 162, 149 So. 74 (1933).

Test determining relationship between parties. — It is the reserved right of control rather than its exercise that furnishes the true test of whether the relationship between the parties is that of an independent contractor or of employer and employee. Calvert v. Funderburg, 284 Ala. 311, 224 So. 2d 664 (1969).

"Employees". — If one performed his work upon employer's premises and with employer's tools or appliances and under the employer's directions, or did piecework, where the system of employment used merely provided a method of fixing the workman's wages, he was an "employee." Majors v. Jackson Lumber Co., 244 Ala. 418, 13 So. 2d 885 (1943).

If one was an employee of defendant and employment contemplated the use of other persons, such persons were also "employees" of defendant. Majors v. Jackson Lumber Co., 244 Ala. 418, 13 So. 2d 885 (1943).

Employee of independent contractor. — See Majors v. Jackson Lumber Co., 244 Ala. 418, 13 So. 2d 885 (1943).

Person hired by independent contractor was not employee. — Where there was legal evidence to support the trial court's determination that the individual who contracted with pulpwood company to haul logs was an independent contractor, then a fortiori, he could not be classified as a piece-worker. In light of this determination, assertion of plaintiff truck driver, who had been hired by such individual, that he was the pulpwood company's employee was without merit. McCraney v. Bigger Pulpwood Co., 500 So. 2d 1116 (Ala. Civ. App. 1986).

Contract provision that employee should hold employer harmless by reason of claims for injuries was held not to avoid liability for compensation. J.E. Ross & Co. v. Collins, 224 Ala. 453, 140 So. 764 (1932); Martin v. Republic Steel Co., 226 Ala. 209, 146 So. 276 (1933).

Cited in Ex parte Big Four Coal Mining Co., 213 Ala. 305, 104 So. 764 (1925); Sloss-Sheffield Steel & Iron Co. v. Crim, 219 Ala. 148, 121 So. 408 (1929); DeBardeleben Coal Corp. v. Richards, 251 Ala. 324, 37 So. 2d 121 (1948).

Collateral references. — 58 Am. Jur. 2d, Workmen's Compensation, §§ 57, 58.

Rights and remedies where employee was injured by third person's negligence. 19 ALR 766, 27 ALR 493, 37 ALR 838, 67 ALR 249, 88 ALR 665, 106 ALR 1040.

Modern status of effect of workmen's compensation act on right of third-person tortfeasor to contribution or indemnity from employer of injured or killed workman. 100 ALR3d 350.

Recovery for discharge from employment in retaliation for filing workers' compensation claim. 32 ALR4th 1221.

Workers' compensation: third-party tort liability of corporate officer to injured workers. 76 ALR4th 365.

§ 25-5-11. Actions against third parties jointly liable with employers for injuries or death; actions for injury or death resulting from willful conduct; attorney's fees in settlements with third parties.

(a) If the injury or death for which compensation is payable under Articles 3 or 4 of this chapter was caused under circumstances also creating a legal liability for damages on the part of any party other than the employer, whether or not the party is subject to this chapter, the employee, or his or her dependents in case of death, may proceed against the employer to recover compensation under this chapter or may agree with the employer upon the compensation payable under this chapter, and at the same time, may bring an action against the other party to recover damages for the injury or death, and the amount of the damages shall be ascertained and determined without regard to this chapter. If a party, other than the employer, is a workers' compensation insurance carrier of the employer or any person, firm, association, trust, fund, or corporation responsible for servicing and payment of workers' compensation claims for the employer, or any officer, director, agent, or employee of the carrier, person, firm, association, trust, fund, or corporation, or is a labor union, or any official or representative thereof, or is a governmental agency providing occupational safety and health services, or an employee of the agency, or is an officer, director, agent, or employee of the same employer, or his or her personal representative, the injured employee, or his or her dependents in the case of death, may bring an action against any workers' compensation insurance carrier of the employer or any person, firm, association, trust, fund, or corporation responsible for servicing and payment of workers' compensation claims for the employer, labor union, or the governmental agency, or person, or his or her personal representative, only for willful conduct which results in or proximately causes the injury or death. If the injured employee, or in case of death, his or her dependents, recovers damages against the other party, the amount of the damages recovered and collected shall be credited upon the liability of the employer for compensation. If the damages recovered and collected are in excess of the compensation payable under this chapter, there shall be no further liability on the employer to pay compensation on account of the injury or death. To the extent of the recovery of damages against the other party, the employer shall be entitled to reimbursement for the amount of compensation theretofore paid on account of injury or death. If the employee who recovers damages is receiving or entitled to receive compensation for permanent total disability, then the employer shall be entitled to reimbursement for the amount of compensation theretofore paid, and the employer's obligation to pay further compensation for permanent total disability shall be suspended for the number of weeks which equals the quotient of the total damage recovery, less the amount of any reimbursement for compensation already paid, divided by the amount of the weekly benefit for permanent total disability which the employee was receiving or to which the employee was entitled. For purposes of this amendatory act, the employer shall be entitled to subrogation for medical and vocational benefits expended by the employer on behalf of the employee; however, if a judgment in an action brought pursuant to this section is uncollectible in part, the employer's entitlement to subrogation for such medical and vocational benefits shall be in proportion to the ratio the amount of the judgment collected bears to the total amount of the judgment.

(b) If personal injury or death to any employee results from the willful conduct, as defined in subsection (c) herein, of any officer, director, agent, or employee of the same employer or any workers' compensation insurance carrier of the employer or any person, firm, association, trust, fund, or corporation responsible for servicing any payment of workers' compensation claims for the employer, or any officer, director, agent, or employee of the carrier, person, firm, association, trust, fund, or corporation, or of a labor union, or an official or representative thereof, the employee shall have a cause of action against the person, workers' compensation carrier, or labor union.

(c) As used herein, "willful conduct" means any of the following:

(1) A purpose or intent or design to injure another; and if a person, with knowledge of the danger or peril to another, consciously pursues a course of conduct with a design, intent, and purpose of inflicting injury, then he or she is guilty of "willful conduct."

(2) The willful and intentional removal from a machine of a safety guard or safety device provided by the manufacturer of the machine with knowledge that injury or death would likely or probably result from the removal; provided, however, that removal of a guard or device shall not be willful conduct unless the removal did, in fact, increase the danger in the use of the machine and was not done for the purpose of repair of the machine or was not part of an improvement or modification of the machine which rendered the safety device unnecessary or ineffective.

(3) The intoxication of another employee of the employer if the conduct of that employee has wrongfully and proximately caused injury or death to the plaintiff or plaintiff's decedent, but no employee shall be guilty of willful

478

conduct on account of the intoxication of another employee or another person.

(4) Willful and intentional violation of a specific written safety rule of the employer after written notice to the violating employee by another employee who, within six months after the date of receipt of the written notice, suffers injury resulting in death or permanent total disability as a proximate result of the willful and intentional violation. The written notice to the violating employee shall state with specificity all of the following:

a. The identity of the violating employee.

b. The specific written safety rule being violated and the manner of the violation.

c. That the violating employee has repeatedly and continually violated the specific written safety rule referred to in b. above with specific reference to previous times, dates, and circumstances.

d. That the violation places the notifying employee at risk of great injury or death.

A notice that does not contain all of the above elements shall not be valid notice for purposes of this section. An employee shall not be liable for the willful conduct if the injured employee himself or herself violated a safety rule, or otherwise contributed to his or her own injury. No employee shall be held liable under this section for the violation of any safety rule by any other employee or for failing to prevent any violation by any other employee.

(d) In the event the injured employee, or his or her dependents, in case of death, do not file a civil action against the other party to recover damages within the time allowed by law, the employer or the insurance carrier for the employer shall be allowed an additional period of six months within which to bring a civil action against the other party for damages on account of the injury or death. In the event the employer or the insurance carrier has paid compensation to the employee or his or her dependent, or in the event a proceeding is pending against the employer to require the payment of the compensation, the civil action may be maintained either in the name of the injured employee, his or her dependent in case of death, the employer, or the insurance carrier. In the event the damages recovered in the civil action are in excess of the compensation payable by the employer under this chapter and costs, attorney's fees, and reasonable expenses incurred by the employer in making the collection, the excess of the amount shall be held in trust for the injured employee or, in case of death, for the employee's dependents. If the injured employee has no dependent, the personal representative, in the event of death, may bring a civil action against the other party to recover damages without regard to this chapter.

(e) In a settlement made under this section with a third party by the employee or, in case of death, by his or her dependents, the employer shall be liable for that part of the attorney's fees incurred in the settlement with the third party, with or without a civil action, in the same proportion that the amount of the reduction in the employer's liability to pay compensation bears to the total recovery had from the third party. For purposes of the subrogation provisions of this subsection only, "compensation" includes medical expenses, as defined in Section 25-5-77, if and only if the employer is entitled to subrogation for medical expenses under subsection (a) of this section.

(f) For the purpose of this section, a carrier, person, firm, association, trust, fund, or corporation includes a company or a governmental agency making a safety inspection on behalf of a self-insured employer or its employees, and an officer, director, agent, or employee of the company or a governmental agency. (Acts 1919, No. 245, p. 206; Code 1923, § 7587; Acts 1939, No. 661, p. 1036, § 8; Code 1940, T. 26, § 312; Acts 1947, No. 635, p. 484, § 1; Acts 1961, Ex. Sess., No. 272, p. 2289, § 4; Acts 1973, No. 1062, p. 1750, § 26; Acts 1975, 4th Ex. Sess., No. 86, p. 2729, § 10; Acts 1984, 2nd Ex. Sess., No. 85-41, p. 44, § 3; Acts 1992, No. 92-537, § 8.)

The **1992 amendment,** effective May 19, 1992, rewrote this section. As to the implementation of this amendment, see the Code commissioner's note.

Code commissioner's note. — Acts 1984, 2nd Ex. Sess., No. 85-41, § 14 provides: "This act shall become effective immediately upon its passage and approval by the governor [January 9, 1985], or upon its otherwise becoming a law, provided it shall have no effect whatsoever with respect to the right of any injured employee to bring an action with respect to or upon any cause of action which arose or accrued prior to February 1, 1985. Provided further, it shall have no effect on and shall not apply to any accident or exposure to injurious condition occurring before the effective date of this Act."

The phrase "this amendatory act," as used in the section above, refers to Acts 1992, No. 92-537, which amended this section. Act No. 92-537 also amended §§ 25-5-1 through 25-5-4, 25-5-8, 25-5-10, 25-5-11, 25-5-13, 25-5-50 through 25-5-57, 25-5-59, 25-5-60, 25-5-66 through 25-5-68, 25-5-77, 25-5-78, 25-5-80, 25-5-81, 25-5-83, 25-5-85, 25-5-86, 25-5-90, 25-5-110, 25-5-116, 25-5-117, 25-5-120, 25-5-251, enacted §§ 25-5-15.1, 25-5-290 through 25-5-294, and 25-5-310 through 25-5-318, and repealed §§ 25-5-16, 25-5-70 through 25-5-75, 25-5-140 through 25-5-152, and 25-5-170 through 25-5-180.

Section 53 of Acts 1992, No. 92-537, provides that the amendments to this section made by § 8 of the act shall be implemented on August 1, 1992.

Cross references. — For statute of limitations as to actions brought under subsection (b), see § 6-2-38.

I. General Consideration.
II. Co-employees.
III. Wrongful Death.
IV. Capacity to Sue.
V. Subrogation.
VI. Attorneys' Fees.

I. GENERAL CONSIDERATION.

Editor's note. — The cases annotated below were decided under prior law.

Constitutionality of 1973 amendment. — See Childers v. Couey, 348 So. 2d 1349 (Ala. 1977); Atchison v. Horton, 348 So. 2d 1358 (Ala. 1977).

This section does not violate the Constitution of the United States. Reed v. Brunson, 527 So. 2d 102 (Ala. 1988).

This section, as amended, is not a violation of § 13, Constitution of Alabama 1901. Rudolph v. Gwin, 526 So. 2d 581 (Ala. 1988).

The limited immunity granted to co-employees under this section is constitutional. Reed v. Brunson, 527 So. 2d 102 (Ala. 1988).

For a review of the constitutionality of **Alabama's Workmen's Compensation Act** in view of Ala. Const., Art. I, § 13 and Art. IV, § 45, see, Reed v. Brunson, 527 So. 2d 102 (Ala. 1988).

The immunity test under § 13 of the Alabama Constitution is equally applicable to all parties other than the employer, including the workmen's compensation insurance carrier. Fireman's Fund Am. Ins. Co. v. Coleman, 394 So. 2d 334 (Ala. 1980).

Duty to provide co-employees with a safe workplace naturally encompasses a duty to provide co-employees with machines that function properly and safely. Creel v. Bridewell, 535 So. 2d 95 (Ala. 1988).

Insurance carrier not immune from making negligent inspection. — The legislature may not constitutionally immunize from tort liability a workmen's compensation carrier and its employees for injuries resulting to employees of the insured from negligent inspections performed by the carrier. Johnson v. American Mut. Liab. Ins. Co., 394 So. 2d 1 (Ala. 1980).

Worker's compensation carrier may be liable when it voluntarily undertakes to inspect employer's premises for safety. However, in a suit of this nature, a plaintiff bears the burden of proving (1) that the defendant had a duty, or assumed a duty by voluntarily undertaking the inspection; (2) the scope of that duty; (3) whether the duty was breached; (4) whether there was damage or injury; and (5) whether the injury was proximately caused by that breach. Barnes v. Liberty Mut. Ins. Co., 472 So. 2d 1041 (Ala. 1985).

Retrospective application of 1973 amendment. — There was no apparent legislative intent in the 1973 amendment to subsection (a) of this section that it should be applied retrospectively. Sewell v. Harris, 351 So. 2d 566 (Ala. 1977).

This section was drafted to ease burden of expense to employee in bringing the third-party action. Had the drafters of this section intended that attorney's fees be deducted from the third-party recovery before the insurer's right to reimbursement was computed, there would be no need for the inclusion of subsection (c) of this section in the provision. Fitch v. Insurance Co. of N. Am., 408 So. 2d 1017 (Ala. Civ. App. 1981).

In arriving at legislative intent in enacting statute regarding liability of party other than employer for employee's injuries, as codified in this section, every part of the statute as disclosed by its context and spirit will be given consideration. Harris v. Louisville & N.R.R., 237 Ala. 366, 186 So. 771 (1939).

Action under the workmen's compensation laws is purely statutory. Hartford Accident & Indem. Co. v. Rigdon, 418 F. Supp. 540 (S.D. Ala. 1976).

An action under this section is purely statutory in form and remedial in nature. Garren v. Commercial Union Ins. Co., 340 So. 2d 764 (Ala. 1976).

This section creates a remedy, not a right. Hartford Accident & Indem. Co. v. Rigdon, 418 F. Supp. 540 (S.D. Ala. 1976).

This section does not provide an action against an employer; subdivision (a) provides that actions may be maintained against those parties that may be jointly liable with the employer, provided that if the other party is a coemployee, then his actions, in order to give rise to liability, must be willful. However, this section does not affect the immunity provided by §§ 25-5-52 and 25-5-53. Padgett v. Neptune Water Meter Co., 585 So. 2d 900 (Ala. 1991).

"Manufacturer" defined. — The term "manufacturer" may include not only the original manufacturer (one who produces articles for use or trade), but also a subsequent entity that substantially modifies or materially alters the product through the use of different components and/or methods of assembly. Harris v. Gill, 585 So. 2d 831 (Ala. 1991).

The terms "safety device" and "safety guard" mean an invention or contrivance intended to protect against injury, damage, or loss that insures or gives security that an accident will be prevented. Moore v. Reeves, 589 So. 2d 173 (Ala. 1991).

A "safety device" or "safety guard" is that which is provided, principally, but not exclusively, as protection to an employee, which provides some shield between the employee and danger so as to prevent the employee from incurring injury while he is engaged in the performance of the service required of him by the employer; it is not something that is a component part of the machine whose principal purpose is to facilitate or expedite the work. Moore v. Reeves, 589 So. 2d 173 (Ala. 1991).

"Bypassing" safety device is "removal". — The act of "bypassing" a safety device of a particular machine that would prevent an injury is encompassed within the word "removal." Harris v. Gill, 585 So. 2d 831 (Ala. 1991).

Failure to maintain or repair safety device tantamount to removal. — The failure to maintain and/or repair a safety guard or device provided by the manufacturer of a particular machine would be tantamount to the "removal of" or the "failure to install" a safety guard or device; to hold otherwise would allow supervisory employees to neglect the maintenance and repair of safety equipment provided to protect coemployees from injury, which by its very nature is a clear violation of public policy. Moore v. Reeves, 589 So. 2d 173 (Ala. 1991).

Word "compensation" as used in this section does note include "medical and hospital expenses." Liberty Mut. Ins. Co. v. Manasco, 271 Ala. 124, 123 So. 2d 527 (1960).

And given same meaning as spelled out

in § 25-5-1. — The context of this section, as amended, does not indicate that the word "compensation" as there used is to be given a meaning different from that spelled out in § 25-5-1. Liberty Mut. Ins. Co. v. Manasco, 271 Ala. 124, 123 So. 2d 527 (1960).

"Dependents" construed. — It is apparent that the legislature intended that the word "dependents", as used in this section, mean dependents at the time of the employee's death. Braxton v. Dixie Elec. Coop., 409 So. 2d 822 (Ala. 1982).

The word "intoxication" in this section should be given its plain and ordinary meaning, unless the context of the word or the intent of the legislature suggests otherwise. Rudolph v. Gwin, 526 So. 2d 581 (Ala. 1988).

Notice of employee's intoxication. — The legislature did not intend that the officer or director who has been put on notice of an employee's intoxication at work should be protected from liability when he acquiesces in the intoxication. Hobden v. Snow, 551 So. 2d 317 (Ala. 1989).

Evidence insufficient to find intoxication. — Even if a jury was convinced that employee had taken two sips of beer, or even that he drank the entire 16-ounce beer, this would have been insufficient, without additional evidence, for the jury to find intoxication. Rudolph v. Gwin, 526 So. 2d 581 (Ala. 1988).

This section grants two separate and distinct rights of action to an employee or his dependents, and prosecution of one is not dependent upon the prosecution of the other. Baggett v. Webb, 46 Ala. App. 666, 248 So. 2d 275 (1971).

And employee may pursue both at once. — It is not intended that action or settlement against the employer must precede or coincide with a third-party action; it is merely made clear that it is permissible and proper for an employee or his dependents to pursue two rights of action at the same time. Baggett v. Webb, 46 Ala. App. 666, 248 So. 2d 275 (1971).

Filing action against employer not prerequisite to third-party action. — This section does not require the filing of action against the employer, or the entry of an agreement with the employer as to compensation due, by the employee, or his dependents in case of death, as a prerequisite to the bringing of the third-party action authorized by the section. Baggett v. Webb, 46 Ala. App. 666, 248 So. 2d 275 (1971).

Failure to sue or reach agreement with his employer as to workmen's compensation and amount due, prior to or in conjunction with the third-party liability action, did not disqualify the employee's action, nor the settlement therein, from being one brought or made under this section. Baggett v. Webb, 46 Ala. App. 666, 248 So. 2d 275 (1971).

Subsection (a) allows third-party wrongful death action and third-party breach of warranty action. — The principle that allows the dependent to bring a third-party claim for wrongful death under subsection (a) of this section, i.e., to avoid the necessity of administration of the estate, also allows the dependent to bring a third-party claim for breach of warranty under subsection (a) of this section. Industrial Chem. & Fiberglass Corp. v. Chandler, 547 So. 2d 812 (Ala. 1988).

Third-party action is not workmen's compensation claim. — An action against third parties or coemployees as allowed by this section is not a claim for workmen's compensation, but is a tort action for damages that is removed from the exclusive remedy provisions of §§ 25-5-52 and 25-5-53 by virtue of the exceptions set forth in this section. Johnson v. Asphalt Hot Mix, 565 So. 2d 219 (Ala. 1990).

Employer does not lose its employer status — for immunity purposes — by qualifying under the Workmen's Compensation Act as a self-insurer and, in that capacity, performing or failing to perform safety inspections. Adair v. Moretti-Harrah Marble Co., 381 So. 2d 181 (Ala. 1980).

Dual capacity of corporate officer. — An officer may exercise a dual function and enjoy a dual capacity in a corporation. Depending on his, or her, function at the time of injury, he, or she, may not be immune from suit by an injured employee. Jones v. Watkins, 364 So. 2d 1144 (Ala. 1978).

For purposes of immunity from suit under Workmen's Compensation Act, which function the officer is fulfilling is a matter of fact. Jones v. Watkins, 364 So. 2d 1144 (Ala. 1978).

Dual capacity such as to subject an employer to tort liability outside the Workmen's Compensation Act will not be found merely because an employer has a number of departments or divisions that perhaps are quite separate in their functions and operations. Stone v. United States Steel Corp., 384 So. 2d 17 (Ala. 1980).

Where plaintiff, an employee of defendant's corporate division, brought suit for damages arising from injuries sustained on the division's job site, the defendant was not operating in a dual capacity as employer-safety inspector, or employer-manufacturer, or employer-owner in a sense that would bring the dual capacity doctrine into play and the trial court properly granted defendant's motion for summary judgment because the action was barred by §§ 25-5-52 and 25-5-53. Stone v. United States Steel Corp., 384 So. 2d 17 (Ala. 1980).

Employer's recovery under subsection (a). — Subsection (a) does not limit an employer's reimbursement for sums paid under the Workmen's Compensation Act only when an employee, or his dependents in case of his death, has recovered from two sources an amount that exceeds the employee's damages, since the words of subsection (a) do not limit an employer's recovery in such a way. Maryland Cas. Co. v. Tiffin, 537 So. 2d 469 (Ala. 1988).

Sums recovered by plaintiffs in their action against third parties had to be credited against the liability of insurance company for compensation, and since they exceeded the amount of compensation payable under the workmen's compensation laws, insurance company had no further liability on account of employee's death and was entitled to reimbursement for the amount of compensation already paid subject to insurance company liability for attorney fees under subsection (e). Maryland Cas. Co. v. Tiffin, 537 So. 2d 469 (Ala. 1988).

Common fund doctrine. — There is a statutorily prescribed common fund doctrine involved in a third-party recovery in the workmen's compensation context. Maryland Cas. Co. v. Tiffin, 537 So. 2d 469 (Ala. 1988).

Plaintiff was unable to show willful conduct by his supervisor in not repairing vehicle that had a damaged door and broken seat which caused plaintiff to be flung out of the vehicle at 40 to 45 m.p.h., since the evidence failed to show that a reasonable man in the supervisor's position would have known that injury or death to driver was substantially certain to occur because of the failure to have the vehicle repaired. Turnbow v. Kustom Kreation Vans, 535 So. 2d 132 (Ala. 1988).

The willful and intentional failure to install an available safety guard equates to the willful and intentional removal of a safety guard for the purposes of subdivision (c)(2) of this section. Bailey v. Hogg, 547 So. 2d 498 (Ala. 1989).

Failure to add guard can constitute willful conduct. — The failure to add a guard provided by the manufacturer can constitute willful conduct under subdivision (c)(2), but there is no duty under subdivision (c)(2) on coemployees to add safety guards that the manufacturer fails to provide. Harris v. Simmons, 585 So. 2d 906 (Ala. 1991).

Door and door closure mechanism of vehicle constituted safety device. — Where machine was the vehicle security officer was driving to patrol campus, and the peril was the set of circumstances that caused the security officer to sustain injuries, the door and door closure mechanism of the vehicle in which the security officer was driving constituted a safety device or safety guard; it constituted a shield between security officer and danger so as to protect him from the injuries he sustained while he was patrolling the campus in performance of the services required of him by the college. Moore v. Reeves, 589 So. 2d 173 (Ala. 1991).

Willful removal of safety guards does not have higher burden of proof. — By making the willful and intentional removal of a safety guard the basis for a cause of action without the higher burden of proof of "intent to injure" found in subsection (a), the legislature acknowledged the important public policy of promoting safety in the workplace and the importance of such guards in providing such safety; the same dangers are present when an available safety guard is not installed as are present when the same guard has been removed. Bailey v. Hogg, 547 So. 2d 498 (Ala. 1989).

No willful conduct found on part of injured forklift operator's supervisors for neck injuries sustained while working under a procedure implemented and instituted by those supervisors; although supervisors knew of worker's history of back and neck problems, they were not aware that he had been restricted by his doctor as to the amount of weight he could lift. Lee v. Ledsinger, 577 So. 2d 900 (Ala. 1991).

Employees of federal government. — The fact that the Alabama legislature has relieved employees of employers covered by the Alabama Workmen's Compensation Act from certain liabilities does not imply that they wished to relieve employees of the federal government of the same liability. In the first situation, the relief is part of one compensation scheme enacted by the state; the second situation would involve applying part of that scheme to an unrelated compensation scheme. Heathcoat v. Potts, 790 F.2d 1540 (11th Cir. 1986), cert. denied, 484 U.S. 1025, 108 S. Ct. 747, 98 L. Ed. 2d 761 (1988).

Action on the case for injuries caused by negligence of party other than employer. — The only action for recovery of damages for personal injuries proximately resulting from the negligence of a party other than the employer is an action on the case. In such action the basis of the liability of any party other than the employer rests in tort for negligently injuring the workman. State Farm Mut. Auto. Ins. Co. v. Cahoon, 287 Ala. 462, 252 So. 2d 619 (1971).

Whether action is brought as third-party action determined by allegations of complaint. — Whether action is brought under this section as a third-party liability action is to be determined by the allegations of the complaint and not by whether action is pending or settlement has been made with the employer for compensation. Baggett v. Webb, 46 Ala. App. 666, 248 So. 2d 275 (1971).

When insured does not receive any workmen's compensation benefits due to a settlement with a third-party tort-feasor, the insurer is not allowed to reduce the payments it is obligated to make to the insured under a salary continuation insurance policy by the amount the insured would have received under the Workmen's Compensation Act if there had been no third-party recovery merely because the insured's injury fortuitously occurred while the insured was acting in the line and scope of his employment. Antram v. Stuyvesant Life Ins. Co., 291 Ala. 716, 287 So. 2d 837 (1973).

Alabama disapproves of unencumbered intervention when the insurance company occupies a dual role because it gives the jury the impression that plaintiff has already been compensated and is now attempting to recover again from defendants. Southern v. Plumb Tools, 696 F.2d 1321 (11th Cir. 1983).

Alabama law precludes the introduction of evidence that a plaintiff has received workmen's compensation benefits. It also requires conditions to be imposed on an intervening insurance company's participation at trial, particularly when the same company has the defendant's liability coverage and is the workmen's compensation carrier for the plaintiff's employer, unless the carrier can meet certain narrow conditions. Southern v. Plumb Tools, 696 F.2d 1321 (11th Cir. 1983).

Conditions requiring submission to a jury. — A careful reading of the Workmen's Compensation Act reveals that the act was promulgated to ensure that cases where a plaintiff was compelled to work under circumstances that posed foreseeable risks of harm to himself or others or under circumstances from which harm could likely or even probably would result would not be submitted to a jury without evidence sufficient to show either 1) the reason why the co-employee defendant would want to intentionally injure the plaintiff, or 2) that a reasonable man in the position of the defendant would have known that a particular result (i.e., injury or death) was substantially certain to follow from his action. Lee v. Ledsinger, 577 So. 2d 900 (Ala. 1991).

Instruction not curing error in admitting papers filed in compensation proceedings. — In action by employee for injuries sustained when employer's truck, on which employee was riding, collided with defendant's truck, court's error in admitting papers which were filed in a proceeding in which employee obtained a settlement with employer's insurer under Workmen's Compensation Act was not cured by instruction that insurer was subrogated to all rights of employee in the action, and that insurer was entitled to come in and intervene to the extent of the settlement. Coleman v. Hamilton Storage Co., 235 Ala. 553, 180 So. 553 (1938).

Averments held insufficient. — Averments held not to supply basis for plaintiffs' right to bring an action under this section. Murphy v. Louisville & N.R.R., 258 Ala. 138, 61 So. 2d 3 (1952).

Testimony on obligation to pay medical bills excluded. — In third party tort action brought by injured employee of painting subcontractor, to whom workmen's compensation benefits had been paid, to recover from prime contractor for injuries sustained in fall on ground that prime contractor had failed to provide a safe place to work, trial court acted correctly in ruling defendants' attorney would not be permitted to cross-examine plaintiff as to whether he paid or became obligated to pay the medical bills for which he sought compensation in damages. Jones v. Crawford, 361 So. 2d 518 (Ala. 1978).

Right of intervention of employer's insurance carrier in third-party action under section. — See Hughes v. Newton, 295 Ala. 117, 324 So. 2d 270 (1975).

This section does not give the employee the right to intervene in the employer's action. Hartford Accident & Indem. Co. v. Rigdon, 418 F. Supp. 540 (S.D. Ala. 1976).

Liability of employer or his insurer is no defense against third party's liability under this section, either as to right to recover or the quantum of recovery. Coleman v. Hamilton Storage Co., 235 Ala. 553, 180 So. 553 (1938).

And judgment against third party does not preclude recovery from employer. — An employee is entitled to recover of his employer his medical and hospital expenses after having recovered a judgment against a third party in an action in which medical and hospital expenses were claimed since neither the court of appeals nor the trial court is authorized to resort to speculation or guesswork to determine what proportion, if any, of the judgment recovered against the third-party tort-feasor was for hospital and medical expenses. Poultry & Egg Co. v. Smith, 41 Ala. App. 665, 149 So. 2d 838 (1962).

Also settlement with third party does not preclude prosecution of claim for compensation. — Where widow of deceased employee settled with railway causing his death, she was not precluded by the settlement from prosecuting a claim for compensation. Benoit Coal Mining Co. v. Moore, 215 Ala. 220, 109 So. 878 (1926).

Distribution of third-party recovery. — Where the identity of the heirs and the dependents differ, the Workmen's Compensation Act is the primary basis of recovery — but only as to the monetary limits and payment conditions specified therein. After the disposition of these amounts has been accomplished, any remainder of a third-party recovery is available for distribution to the heirs-at-law as their rights are defined by the statute of distributions. Sanders v. Shockley, 468 F.2d 88 (5th Cir. 1972).

Where plaintiff pursued worker's compensation claim, he could not maintain respondeat superior action. — Where the plaintiff had pursued his claim for compensation from the employer through a workers' compensation action, he could not maintain a separate action based upon respondeat superior to impose civil liability upon the employer for injuries compensable under the Workers' Compensation Act. Padgett v. Neptune Water Meter Co., 585 So. 2d 900 (Ala. 1991).

When summary judgment for defendant proper. — Without evidence that the defendant had reason to injure the plaintiff or someone else or evidence that the plaintiff's injury was substantially certain to follow, a summary judgment for the defendant was proper. Padgett v. Neptune Water Meter Co., 585 So. 2d 900 (Ala. 1991).

Deduction allowed from award of compensation. — Money received by a deceased employee's administratrix in settlement of an action to recover damages for deceased's death should be deducted from award of compensation and only the balance is payable. Benoit Coal Mining Co. v. Moore, 215 Ala. 220, 109 So. 878 (1926); Western Union Tel. Co. v. George, 239 Ala. 80, 194 So. 183 (1940).

Where a third-party action had been brought by administrator of deceased employee's estate and money recovered therein distributed to employee's dependents, in a subsequent proceeding under compensation act by employee's father, the amount recovered in third-party action and distributed to the father should have been deducted from judgment. Western Union Tel. Co. v. George, 239 Ala. 80, 194 So. 183 (1940).

Reimbursement to which employer and insurance carrier entitled. — The employer or insurance carrier is entitled to be reimbursed, out of any judgment recovered by the employee or his representative in an action against a third-party wrongdoer, all payments made by the employer or the insurance carrier which are included within the meaning of the word "compensation" as used in this section, irrespective of the type of damages claimed in the complaint in the action against the third-

party wrongdoer. Liberty Mut. Ins. Co. v. Manasco, 271 Ala. 124, 123 So. 2d 527 (1960).

Injured employee must reimburse his employer's workmen's compensation carrier for benefits received upon obtaining a settlement from a third-party tort-feasor. Orum v. Employers Cas. Co., 348 So. 2d 792 (Ala. Civ. App. 1977).

In the provision of subsection (a) for the recovery of damages by the employee against the third-party tort-feasor, the term "damages" does not mean only a money judgment, and therefore does not preclude reimbursement of the employer's insurance carrier from a settlement. Orum v. Employers Cas. Co., 348 So. 2d 792 (Ala. Civ. App. 1977).

Statute of limitations runs from date of injury. — In a negligence action brought by an injured employee against third parties pursuant to this section and § 25-5-117 the statute of limitations begins to run from the date of the injury, which is defined in § 25-5-117 as the date of the last exposure to the hazards or the disease which gave rise to the injury. Garren v. Commercial Union Ins. Co., 340 So. 2d 764 (Ala. 1976).

In actions by employees against third parties under former § 6-2-39 (see now § 6-2-38) for injuries sustained as a result of continuous exposure to harmful events such as blasting or flooding the statute of limitations begins to run when injury occurs or damage accrues, not from the date of the act causing injury or damage, and the date of injury is the last day on which plaintiff was exposed to the danger. Garren v. Commercial Union Ins. Co., 340 So. 2d 764 (Ala. 1976).

Statute of limitations in third-party action where injuries resulted from continuous exposure to harmful events. — Former § 6-2-39 (see now § 6-2-38) is applicable to actions by employees under this section against third parties where recovery is sought for injuries sustained as a result of continuous exposure to harmful events, such as repeated blasting or flooding. Garren v. Commercial Union Ins. Co., 340 So. 2d 764 (Ala. 1976).

This section does not extend the statute of limitations for the employee. Hartford Accident & Indem. Co. v. Rigdon, 418 F. Supp. 540 (S.D. Ala. 1976).

This section neither creates nor enlarges the substantive rights of the injured employee nor does it extend the period of limitation for the employee. Garren v. Commercial Union Ins. Co., 340 So. 2d 764 (Ala. 1976).

The intervention of the employer's insurance carrier in an employee's negligence action against a third party under this section did not entitle the employee to an additional six month recovery period beyond the period defined by the statute of limitations. Garren v. Commercial Union Ins. Co., 340 So. 2d 764 (Ala. 1976).

Question raised for first time on appeal. — It did not appear from an examination of the record that the question of whether plaintiff should have amount of settlement from a third party deducted from her recovery under the Workmen's Compensation Act was raised either on the trial of the case or by a motion to set aside the award for excessiveness after the trial court had acted. Since the trial court should have had an opportunity to pass on the question, the supreme court would not put the court in error in this regard. Hamilton Motor Co. v. Cooner, 254 Ala. 422, 47 So. 2d 270 (1950).

Cited in Scott v. Birmingham Elec. Co., 250 Ala. 61, 33 So. 2d 344 (1948); Johnson v. Pullman Co., 200 F.2d 751 (5th Cir. 1952); Blackmon v. United States, 130 F. Supp. 498 (S.D. Ala. 1955); City of Birmingham v. Walker, 267 Ala. 150, 101 So. 2d 250 (1958); Southern Ry. v. McCamy, 270 Ala. 510, 120 So. 2d 695 (1960); Glens Falls Indem. Co. v. Boutwell, 274 Ala. 258, 147 So. 2d 476 (1962); Blount Bros. Constr. Co. v. Rose, 274 Ala. 429, 149 So. 2d 821 (1962); Head v. Triangle Constr. Co., 274 Ala. 519, 150 So. 2d 389 (1963); Green v. Reynolds Metals Co., 328 F.2d 372 (5th Cir. 1964); Alabama Power Co. v. Johnson, 281 Ala. 259, 201 So. 2d 514 (1967); Prather v. Nashville Bridge Co., 286 Ala. 3, 236 So. 2d 322 (1970); King v. Winslett, 287 Ala. 98, 248 So. 2d 566 (1971); Lingo v. Young & Vann Supply Co., 288 Ala. 80, 257 So. 2d 328 (1971); Johnson v. Lee, 460 F.2d 1053 (5th Cir. 1972); White v. Great Am. Ins. Co., 343 F. Supp. 1112 (M.D. Ala. 1972); C.F. Halstead Contractor v. Lowery, 51 Ala. App. 86, 282 So. 2d 909 (1973); Hubbard v. Cutts, 331 So. 2d 632 (Ala. 1976); Knight v. Burns, Kirkley & Williams Constr. Co., 331 So. 2d 651 (Ala. 1976); Beloit Corp. v. Harrell, 339 So. 2d 992 (Ala. 1976); Gunter v. United States Fid. & Guar. Co., 340 So. 2d 749 (Ala. 1976); Hutto v. Vanity Fair Mills, 350 So. 2d 417 (Ala. 1977); R.L. Reid, Inc. v. Plant, 350 So. 2d 1022 (Ala. 1977); United States Fid. & Guar. Co. v. Jones, 356 So. 2d 596 (Ala. 1977); Hathcock v. Commercial Union Ins. Co., 576 F.2d 653 (5th Cir. 1978); Marshall v. Kopesky, 361 So. 2d 76 (Ala. 1978); Evans v. Kendred, 362 So. 2d 206 (Ala. 1978); Hughes v. Hughes, 367 So. 2d 1384 (Ala. 1979); King v. Landrum, 370 So. 2d 945 (Ala. 1979); Phillips v. Unijax, Inc., 625 F.2d 54 (5th Cir. 1980); McGaha v. Steadman, 410 So. 2d 420 (Ala. Civ. App. 1981); Glenn v. United States Steel Corp., 423 So. 2d 152 (Ala. 1982); Reynolds Metals Co. v. Jeffreys, 425 So. 2d 457 (Ala. 1983); Clements v. Webster, 425 So. 2d 1058 (Ala. 1982); Howell v. Leiman, 447 So. 2d 661 (Ala. 1984); Welch v. Jones, 470 So. 2d 1103 (Ala. 1985); Cofer v. Ensor, 473 So. 2d 984 (Ala. 1985); Lott v. Toomey, 477 So. 2d 316 (Ala. 1985); Alabama Power Co. v. Brooks, 479 So. 2d 1169 (Ala. 1985); Littleton v. Gold Kist, Inc., 480 So. 2d 1236 (Ala. Civ. App. 1985); Rice v. Deas, 504 So. 2d 220 (Ala. 1986); Gray v. Rider, 510 So. 2d 209 (Ala. 1987); Pierce v. Orr, 540 So. 2d 1364 (Ala. 1989); Waters ex rel. Alabama Forest Prods. Indus. Workmen's Comp. Self-Insurer's Fund v. J.I. Case Co., 548 So. 2d 454 (Ala. 1989); Thompson v. Liberty Mut. Ins. Co., 552 So. 2d 129 (Ala. 1989); Johnson v. Niagara Mach. & Tool Works, 555 So. 2d 88 (Ala. 1989); Means v. International Sys., 555 So. 2d 142 (Ala. 1989); Pressley v. Wiltz, 565 So. 2d 26 (Ala. 1990); Beville v. Spencer, 568 So. 2d 1224 (Ala. 1990); Farley v. CNA Ins. Co., 576 So. 2d 158 (Ala. 1991); Alexander v. Lyon, 582 So. 2d 1096 (Ala. 1991); O'Neal v. Kennamer, 958 F.2d 1044 (11th Cir. 1992).

Collateral references. — 101 C.J.S., Workmen's Compensation, §§ 983-1045.

58 Am. Jur. 2d, Workmen's Compensation, § 357 et seq.

Rights and remedies where employee was injured by third person's negligence. 19 ALR 766, 27 ALR 493, 37 ALR 838, 67 ALR 249, 88 ALR 665, 106 ALR 1040.

Claim or action against one as third party as precluding action or claim against him as employer, or vice versa. 98 ALR 416.

Deduction on account of recovery from third person responsible for injury. 142 ALR 170.

Right of employee who has not received award to maintain malpractice action against physician. 154 ALR 315.

Workmen's compensation: attorney's fee or other expenses of litigation incurred by employee in action against third-party tortfeasor as charge against employer's distributive share. 74 ALR3d 854.

Modern status of effect of state Workmen's Compensation Act on right of third-person tort-feasor to contribution or indemnity from employer of injured or killed workman. 100 ALR3d 350.

Third-party tort-feasor's right to have damages recovered by employee reduced by amount of employee's worker's compensation benefits. 43 ALR4th 849.

Willful, wanton, or reckless conduct of coemployee as ground of liability despite bar of workers' compensation law. 57 ALR4th 888.

Workers' compensation: effect of allegation that injury was caused by, or occurred during course of, worker's illegal conduct. 73 ALR4th 270.

Workers' compensation: third-party tort liability of corporate officer to injured workers. 76 ALR4th 365.

Workers' compensation: compensability of injuries incurred traveling to or from medical treatment of earlier compensable injury. 83 ALR4th 110.

II. CO-EMPLOYEES.

Suits against co-employees for negligence or wantonness constitutionally abolished. — Whether tested by the traditional test of the vested rights approach or by either prong of the common-law rights approach, the Workmen's Compensation Act is not violative of § 13 of the Alabama Constitution insofar as it abolishes suits against co-employees for negligence or wantonness. Reed v. Brunson, 527 So. 2d 102 (Ala. 1988).

Immunity of coemployee from suit by injured employee under 1973 and 1975 amendments unconstitutional. — Legislature's grant of immunity to a coemployee from suit by an injured employee by the 1973 amendments to this section is unconstitutional. Pipkin v. Southern Elec. & Pipefitting Co., 358 So. 2d 1015 (Ala. 1978).

Amendments to Workmen's Compensation Act which were enacted in 1975 and which eliminated an injured employee's action against her or his fellow employee, if the injuries were also covered under the Workmen's Compensation Act, were unconstitutional in violation of constitutional provision that every person, for any injury done him, in his lands, goods, person or reputation shall have a remedy by due process of law. Grantham v. Denke, 359 So. 2d 785 (Ala. 1978).

The legislature does have the police power to eliminate co-employee suits by the Workmen's Compensation Act in an attempt to eradicate or ameliorate what it perceives to be a social evil. Reed v. Brunson, 527 So. 2d 102 (Ala. 1988).

But legislature can grant immunity from suit for wrongful death. — The legislature can grant immunity to coemployees of a decedent covered by the Workmen's Compensation Act from suit for wrongful death where the death arose out of a job-related accident. Slagle v. Parker, 370 So. 2d 947 (Ala.), appeal dismissed, 444 U.S. 804, 100 S. Ct. 24, 62 L. Ed. 2d 17 (1979).

The 1973 or 1975 amendments to this section which granted immunity to coemployees in wrongful death actions are not violative of the due process clause of the Fourteenth Amendment to the United States Constitution, or of any due process provision of the Alabama Constitution. Slagle v. Parker, 370 So. 2d 947 (Ala.), appeal dismissed, 444 U.S. 804, 100 S. Ct. 24, 62 L. Ed. 2d 17 (Ala. 1980).

Requirements for submission of question to jury. — A careful reading of the Workmen's Compensation Act reveals that the act was promulgated to ensure that cases where a plaintiff was compelled to work under circumstances that posed foreseeable risks of harm to himself or others or circumstances from which harm could likely or even probably result would not be submitted to a jury without some evidence tending to show either 1) the reason why the co-employee defendant would want to intentionally injure the plaintiff, or 2) that a reasonable man in the position of the defendant would have known that a particular result (i.e., injury or death) was substantially certain to follow from his action. Williams v. Price, 564 So. 2d 408 (Ala. 1990).

Actual knowledge or substantial certainty required. — A co-employee must either have actual knowledge that an injury will occur from his actions or have substantial certainty that injury will occur. Bean v. Craig, 557 So. 2d 1249 (Ala. 1990).

Purpose, intent or design not inferable from knowledge and appreciation of risk. — Short of substantial certainty that injury or death would occur, a purpose, intent, or design to injure another was not intended to be reasonably inferable from evidence showing only knowledge and appreciation of a risk of injury or death. Williams v. Price, 564 So. 2d 408 (Ala. 1990).

Evidence showing only a knowledge or an appreciation of a risk of injury will not entitle a plaintiff to a jury determination of whether the co-employee acted with a purpose, intent, or design to injure another. Bean v. Craig, 557 So. 2d 1249 (Ala. 1990).

Intent to inflict injury. — The intent to inflict injury required for in subdivision (c)(1) is shown by evidence tending to show either (1) the reason why the co-employee defendant would want to intentionally injure the plaintiff, or someone else, or (2) that a reasonable man in the position of the defendant would have known that a particular result (i.e., injury or death) was substantially certain to follow from his actions. Burkett v. Loma Mach. Mfg., Inc., 552 So. 2d 134 (Ala. 1989).

No evidence of motive to injure. — Summary judgment was properly entered for supervising coemployee, where, although he may have been aware that the practice of pinning a gas torch oxygen control lever in the open position might pose some risk to the safety of employees, there was no evidence tending to indicate that he had a motive to injure claimant, who was burned when he dropped his torch. Sharit v. Harkins, 564 So. 2d 876 (Ala. 1990).

Intent to injure "someone". — The plaintiff need not show that the co-employee defendant specifically intended to injure the person who was injured; what must be shown, however, is that the co-employee defendant set out purposefully, intentionally, or by design to injure someone, and that his actions in furtherance of that purpose, intent, or design, resulted in, or proximately caused, the injury or death upon which suit was brought. Williams v. Price, 564 So. 2d 408 (Ala. 1990).

Action against co-employee must be based on willful conduct. — Under this section, an employee may be liable in damages for the death of, or injuries sustained by, a fellow employee; however, such liability can be based only on injury or death proximately caused by the offending employee's willful conduct. Reed v. Brunson, 527 So. 2d 102 (Ala. 1988).

Willful conduct defined for an action against co-employee. — The plaintiff need not show that the co-employee defendant specifically intended to injure the person who was injured. What must be shown, however, is that the co-employee defendant set out purposefully, intentionally, or by design to injure someone, and that his actions in furtherance of that purpose, intent, or design, resulted in, or proximately caused, the injury or death upon which suit was brought. In defining "willful conduct" in these terms, the legislature recognized the clear distinction that has developed in Alabama between wanton conduct and willful conduct. Reed v. Brunson, 527 So. 2d 102 (Ala. 1988).

Evidence necessary to show willful conduct. — In § 25-5-14 the legislature sought to ensure that cases involving willfulness of co-employee would not be submitted to a jury without at least some evidence tending to show either (1) the reason why the co-employee defendant would want to intentionally injure the plaintiff, or someone else, or (2) that a reasonable man in the position of the defendant would have known that a particular result (i.e., injury or death) was substantially certain to follow from his actions. Reed v. Brunson, 527 So. 2d 102 (Ala. 1988).

Complaint did not state actionable claim. — Where complaint alleged that defendants, co-employees, had negligently or wantonly injured plaintiff when they played a prank on her by pulling out her chair, the complaint did not state an actionable claim against co-employees under this section, since plaintiff did not prove willful conduct with intent to injure. Sanford v. Brasher, 549 So. 2d 29 (Ala. 1989).

Willful conduct not shown. — Design and installation of wiring of a mechanized drum which short-circuited and resulted in employee's death did not amount to "willful conduct" within the meaning of subsection (c)

of this section. Landers v. O'Neal Steel, Inc., 564 So. 2d 925 (Ala. 1990).

Where supervisor did not replace tractor part because the tractor was going to be transferred to another district and he did not want to spend money on a tractor that was not to be used in his district, it was not supervisor's design, intent, and purpose to inflict injury upon the employee by not replacing the plates. It was his design, intent, and purpose to avoid spending money on a tractor that was not going to be used in his district; thus, employee's subsequent death when the runaway tractor's blades struck him did not create an action under this section against the supervisor. Merritt v. Cosby, 578 So. 2d 1242 (Ala. 1991).

Negligence and wantonness. — Although evidence tended to show that plant manager was negligent, and perhaps even wanton, in his conduct towards employee, it failed to show that plant manager set out purposefully, intentionally, or by design to injure anyone; in other words, there was no evidence tending to show the existence of a state of mind on plant manager's part above and beyond that required to establish negligence or wantonness. Williams v. Price, 564 So. 2d 408 (Ala. 1990).

Wrongful death action against coemployees of deceased may not be maintained in this state. Actions against third parties may be maintained, however, under the provisions of this section. Corbin v. Allen, 505 So. 2d 339 (Ala. 1987).

Tort action against coemployees for personal injuries survives if death results from those injuries while the action is pending. Mattison v. Kirk, 497 So. 2d 120 (Ala. 1986).

An injured employee may sue a director for intoxicating his employee, but he cannot sue another employee who helped intoxicate that employee. Hobden v. Snow, 551 So. 2d 317 (Ala. 1989).

An injured employee may recover against an officer if that officer's conduct resulted in the intoxication of another employee who, in turn, caused the injury. Hobden v. Snow, 551 So. 2d 317 (Ala. 1989).

Loss of consortium. — The husband's claim for loss of consortium had its origins in common law. Common law is decisional law, not written on unchangeable tablets of stone, and the wife's cause of action for loss of consortium caused by a tortious act of a third party is recognized. Thus, wife's loss of consortium claim against the co-employee defendants is a common-law claim and not a statutory claim. Thus, wife's third-party claim for loss of consortium survives the death of the injured spouse. Mattison v. Kirk, 497 So. 2d 120 (Ala. 1986).

Coemployee's responsibility for providing safe work place. — Where the judge's instructions informed the jury that the employer is primarily responsible for providing employees a safe place to work, but that such duty may be assumed by or delegated to a coemployee, who may be liable for its breach, and it was clear from the instructions that without personal fault on the part of a coemployee defendant, regardless of the liability of some other person, the coemployee defendant must be absolved, the trial judge's charge, when taken as a whole, did not constitute reversible error. Kennemer v. McFann, 470 So. 2d 1113 (Ala. 1985).

Section 25-1-1 imposes on employers the duty to provide reasonably safe employment. A co-employee is not liable to another employee unless he (1) voluntarily assumed or (2) was delegated his employer's duty to provide a reasonably safe workplace. A plaintiff must also prove that his co-employee breached the assumed (or delegated) duty by failure to exercise reasonable care and that this breach proximately caused injury to the plaintiff. Harris v. Hand, 530 So. 2d 191 (Ala. 1988).

The fact that a co-employee is in an administrative or supervisory position alone does not make that person liable. Neither does the imposition of liability arise out of the amount of control which the co-employee exerts at the workplace, or his overall role with regard to the jobsite. Harris v. Hand, 530 So. 2d 191 (Ala. 1988).

No duty to add safety guards not provided. — There is no duty under subdivision (c)(2) on a co-employee to add safety guards that the manufacturer failed to provide. Burkett v. Loma Mach. Mfg., Inc., 552 So. 2d 134 (Ala. 1989).

Subdivision (c)(2) does not require co-employees to add a safety device to compensate for the willful removal of one by previous co-employees. Burkett v. Loma Mach. Mfg., Inc., 552 So. 2d 134 (Ala. 1989).

Safety procedure instructions. — Where case dealt with a co-employee's instructions concerning a safety procedure, although this section was extended in Bailey v. Hogg, 547 So. 2d 498 (Ala. 1989) to equate the term "removal" with "failure to install," this section could not be extended to include instructions, whether given or not given, pertaining to safety procedures. Williams v. Price, 564 So. 2d 408 (Ala. 1990).

While coemployees may raise applicable defenses, they are not entitled to immunity provided to their employer, as a matter of law, by the Workmen's Compensation Act.

Fontenot v. Bramlet, 470 So. 2d 669 (Ala. 1985).

Injured worker's release preserving "any claim for workmen's compensation" barred all tort actions that this section would otherwise allow him to bring against his co-employees, while preserving his claims for workmen's compensation. Johnson v. Asphalt Hot Mix, 565 So. 2d 219 (Ala. 1990).

III. WRONGFUL DEATH.

This section and § 6-5-410 are to be construed together. Smith v. Southern Ry., 237 Ala. 372, 187 So. 195 (1939); Robinson v. Western Ry., 243 Ala. 278, 9 So. 2d 885 (1942); Baggett v. Webb, 46 Ala. App. 666, 248 So. 2d 275 (1971).

Workmen's Compensation Act merely creates a right of compensation against the employer on account of the death of an employee arising out of and in the course of employment. Liberty Mut. Ins. Co. v. Lockwood Greene Eng'rs, Inc., 273 Ala. 403, 140 So. 2d 821 (1962).

It does not purport to create a cause of action for wrongful death against any other person. It is only because the Wrongful Death Act creates such an actionable claim that the provisions for election and subrogation of the employer are operative at all. Liberty Mut. Ins. Co. v. Lockwood Greene Eng'rs, Inc., 273 Ala. 403, 140 So. 2d 821 (1962).

And there is only one cause of action for wrongful death. Liberty Mut. Ins. Co. v. Lockwood Greene Eng'rs, Inc., 273 Ala. 403, 140 So. 2d 821 (1962).

This section gives to the dependents of an employee killed under circumstances creating liability against a third party a right to bring an action against such third party, but such action, when brought, must be deemed to arise under the wrongful death statute (§ 6-5-410); for there can be only one action for wrongful death. Nicholson v. Lockwood Greene Eng'rs, Inc., 278 Ala. 497, 179 So. 2d 76 (1965); Alabama Power Co. v. White, 377 So. 2d 930 (Ala. 1979).

Which arises under the wrongful death statute (§ 6-5-410). Liberty Mut. Ins. Co. v. Lockwood Greene Eng'rs, Inc., 273 Ala. 403, 140 So. 2d 821 (1962).

Right to bring action for wrongful death vested in dependents. — Since the enactment of this section, if an employee covered by workmen's compensation met his death due to an act of a negligent third party and has dependents as defined under the Workmen's Compensation Act, the right to bring an action for wrongful death is vested in the dependents and not in a personal representative under

§ 6-5-410. Baggett v. Webb, 46 Ala. App. 666, 248 So. 2d 275 (1971).

The fact that a right to bring a third-party action is vested in the dependents by the Workmen's Compensation Act is no more than an added means of assuring that negligent third parties pay the damages their negligence may occasion, thus reducing the portion of the compensation risk which must be funded by covered employers and carriers. Sanders v. Shockley, 468 F.2d 88 (5th Cir. 1972).

Wrongful death action where no dependents survive. — It is obvious that if there were no dependents of the employee at the time of his death, there would be no compensation benefits or wrongful death damages payable to any dependent, and consequently, there would be no right of subrogation by the employer or the carrier to any recovery obtained in a third-party suit; therefore, the right to sue would logically be in the personal representative of the deceased employee. If there were no dependents of a deceased workman, in the case of a minor employee, the suit would be maintainable as provided in § 6-5-391; in the case of an adult employee, the suit would be maintainable by the personal representative of the deceased employee. Braxton v. Dixie Elec. Coop., 409 So. 2d 822 (Ala. 1982).

Wrongful death action against co-employees of deceased may not be maintained in this state. Actions against third parties may be maintained, however, under the provisions of this section. Corbin v. Allen, 505 So. 2d 339 (Ala. 1987).

Wrongful death suit was sufficient to toll statute of limitations. — The wrongful death suit instituted by employee's widow as administratrix of the estate of the decedent was sufficient to toll the statute of limitations so that she could amend to sue as widow and dependent; the spirit of A.R.Civ.P. 15 would have been offended if this amendment were disallowed. Swindle v. Jack B. Kelly, Inc., 549 So. 2d 21 (Ala. 1989).

Tort action against co-employees for personal injuries survives if death results from those injuries while the action is pending. Mattison v. Kirk, 497 So. 2d 120 (Ala. 1986).

Effect of section on father's right to bring action for death of minor child. — There is nothing in this section, as amended, clearly indicating an intention to take away the father's existing right to bring an action for the death of a minor child, expressly given by § 6-5-391. Daniel Constr. Co. v. Pierce, 270 Ala. 522, 120 So. 2d 381 (1959).

Action for wrongful death after unsuccessful action against another third party. — The widow of decedent, an alighting Pull-man passenger killed by a freight train, was awarded workmen's compensation for his death and thereafter brought an action against the railroad under this section providing a remedy over against third parties legally liable for wrongful death. After a judgment in favor of the railroad the widow brought an action against the Pullman Company, which contended that because the Wrongful Death Act, § 6-5-410, provides for only one recovery for a wrongful death the widow could not bring a second action. It was held that this contention was without merit as there had been no recovery by her against a third party, and under the last-mentioned statute the mere adverse determination of the action against the railroad would not bar the action against the Pullman Company. Johnson v. Pullman Co., 200 F.2d 751 (5th Cir. 1952).

Right to maintain wrongful death action not assignable. — The right in the dependents of a deceased employee to maintain an action for wrongful death under this section within the time provided by law could not be assigned by the widow to a compensation carrier, since a right of action for wrongful death is not assignable. Liberty Mut. Ins. Co. v. Lockwood Greene Eng'rs, Inc., 273 Ala. 403, 140 So. 2d 821 (1962).

Period for bringing suit prescribed by § 6-5-410 (the wrongful death statute) governs in an action under this section. Plant v. R.L. Reid, Inc., 294 Ala. 155, 313 So. 2d 518 (1975).

Nor can it be waived in favor of insurer. — This section conferred no right on a widow to waive the right to bring an action and to authorize the compensation carrier to bring an action, and only by the subrogative provisions of this section would the compensation carrier have any right to maintain an action at all. Liberty Mut. Ins. Co. v. Lockwood Greene Eng'rs, Inc., 273 Ala. 403, 140 So. 2d 821 (1962).

An assignment or waiver by a widow, for herself and her minor children, of the right to bring an action and authorizing a compensation carrier to bring an action, was totally ineffectual to confer on the carrier any right of action not granted by this section, and no such right was thus granted. Liberty Mut. Ins. Co. v. Lockwood Greene Eng'rs, Inc., 273 Ala. 403, 140 So. 2d 821 (1962).

Statute of limitations provided by the wrongful death statute (two years) governs. Liberty Mut. Ins. Co. v. Lockwood Greene Eng'rs, Inc., 273 Ala. 403, 140 So. 2d 821 (1962).

There is no saving clause in this section, or in § 6-5-410, suspending or excepting the operation of the two-year requirement in which action must be brought under § 6-5-410 (wrongful death statute), even as to those claimants under disability at the time the cause of action accrues. Nicholson v. Lockwood Greene Eng'rs, Inc., 278 Ala. 497, 179 So. 2d 76 (1965).

Timeliness of wrongful death action is not controlled by statute of limitations but, rather, by the two-year period contained within the provision creating the right of recovery. Shirley v. Getty Oil Co., 367 So. 2d 1388 (Ala. 1979).

IV. CAPACITY TO SUE.

Party need not prove his capacity to bring action until that capacity is challenged. Alabama Power Co. v. White, 377 So. 2d 930 (Ala. 1979).

And plea to merits not challenging capacity waives that defense. — Proof of capacity is not required until capacity is challenged and a plea to the merits which does not challenge capacity waives that defense. Alabama Power Co. v. White, 377 So. 2d 930 (Ala. 1979).

Thus general denial does not challenge capacity. — A general denial does not meet the requirement that capacity must be challenged by specific negative averment. Alabama Power Co. v. White, 377 So. 2d 930 (Ala. 1979).

And if not raised at trial cannot be raised on appeal. — When the issue of capacity is not raised until after judgment has been rendered at trial, then the issue has been raised too late to be considered by the trial court and thus too late to be raised on appeal. Alabama Power Co. v. White, 377 So. 2d 930 (Ala. 1979).

V. SUBROGATION.

Right of subrogation depends entirely upon statute and cannot otherwise be created. Liberty Mut. Ins. Co. v. Lockwood Greene Eng'rs, Inc., 273 Ala. 403, 140 So. 2d 821 (1962); Hartford Accident & Indem. Co. v. Rigdon, 418 F. Supp. 540 (S.D. Ala. 1976).

The employer's right to a set-off or credit under subsection (a) depends entirely upon the terms of the statute. Jackson v. Weaver, 516 So. 2d 702 (Ala. Civ. App. 1987).

Section permits action by subrogee against third party. — This section permits a subrogee to bring an action against a third party if the injured party does not bring such an action. Garren v. Commercial Union Ins. Co., 340 So. 2d 764 (Ala. 1976).

Statutory right of subrogation created by this section is in favor of the employer when compensation is due an injured employee, and the injury is caused to the employee under circumstances also creating a legal liability for damages on the part of any party other than the employer. State Farm Mut. Auto. Ins. Co. v. Cahoon, 287 Ala. 462, 252 So. 2d 619 (1971).

Subrogation extends only to cases where compensation is payable under this chapter. — The right of subrogation granted by this section extends only to instances where injury or death occurs under circumstances for which compensation is payable under this chapter of the Workmen's Compensation Act. Steele v. Aetna Cas. & Sur. Co., 46 Ala. App. 705, 248 So. 2d 745 (1971).

Employer not subrogated against employee's insurer. — Subrogation of the employer was against the person who was driving the other car, but not against the employee's insurance company, since the insurance company's liability arose from contract. State Farm Mut. Auto. Ins. Co. v. Cahoon, 287 Ala. 462, 252 So. 2d 619 (1971).

Subrogation effects an assignment by operation of law, administered on equitable principles and has been designated in Groom v. Federal Land Bank, 240 Ala. 335, 199 So. 237 (1940), as an "equitable assignment." Liberty Mut. Ins. Co. v. Manasco, 41 Ala. App. 110, 123 So. 2d 525 (1959), rev'd on other grounds, 271 Ala. 124, 123 So. 2d 527 (1960).

Which requires strict compliance. — To avail itself of the right to bring an action, a compensation carrier must bring itself precisely within the terms of this section. Liberty Mut. Ins. Co. v. Lockwood Greene Eng'rs, Inc., 273 Ala. 403, 140 So. 2d 821 (1962).

Action need not be in insurance carrier's name. — This section, which authorizes an action by the insurance carrier, does not provide that such an action shall be in the carrier's name for the use of anyone. Trammell v. Glens Falls Indem. Co., 259 Ala. 430, 66 So. 2d 537 (1953).

Under this section the subrogated insurance carrier is not required to bring legal proceedings in the name of the injured employee for the use of the insurance carrier. Sloss-Sheffield Steel & Iron Co. v. Metropolitan Cas. Ins. Co., 28 Ala. App. 366, 185 So. 395 (1938).

Nature of the action brought under this section by an insurance carrier which paid compensation to a deceased employee's widow, as to its form and applicable principles, was as though it were by the personal representative of the deceased under the wrongful death statute, § 6-5-410. Louisville & N.R.R. v. American Mut. Liab. Ins. Co., 254 Ala. 128, 47 So. 2d 206 (1950).

Right of compensation carrier to recover under wrongful death statute. — Under this section the compensation carrier of the employer, which had paid and was paying compensation to the widow of a deceased employee under the Workmen's Compensation Act, might recover from a third party for the benefit of the widow such punitive damages as could be recovered under the wrongful death statute, § 6-5-410. American Mut. Liab. Ins. Co. v. Louisville & N.R.R., 250 Ala. 354, 34 So. 2d 474 (1948).

Only one action by subrogee is contemplated. — Under this section only one action is contemplated and subrogee cannot make successive compensation payments and bring repeated actions and recover the amount so paid, and costs and attorney's fees in such actions. Metropolitan Cas. Ins. Co. v. Sloss-Sheffield Steel & Iron Co., 241 Ala. 545, 3 So. 2d 306 (1941).

Where insurance carrier, as subrogee, instituted action against tort-feasor, subrogee's action was "action in tort" and not an "action on a contract," and § 6-5-280 authorizing action for each breach of a severable contract was not applicable so as to permit successive actions for amounts paid by subrogee. Metropolitan Cas. Ins. Co. v. Sloss-Sheffield Steel & Iron Co., 241 Ala. 545, 3 So. 2d 306 (1941).

Insurer must allege payment of compensation. — In a proceeding by the workmen's compensation insurer of the employer to recover damages from the negligent third party a necessary allegation by the insurer is that the insurer has paid compensation to the injured employee or his dependents. In such a proceedings counsel for the insurer is entitled to ask the widow of the deceased employee if she is receiving compensation from the insurer. Foster & Creighton Co. v. St. Paul Mercury Indem. Co., 264 Ala. 581, 88 So. 2d 825 (1956).

Excess over insurer's interest was brought for widow's benefit. — Statement of insurer's counsel in third-party proceeding by workmen's compensation insurer that "any excess over and above their interest is being brought for the benefit of widow of deceased employee" was a correct statement of the law. Foster & Creighton Co. v. St. Paul Mercury Indem. Co., 264 Ala. 581, 88 So. 2d 825 (1956).

Deduction of settlement from award did not destroy employer's right. — Where amount recovered by widow of deceased employee, in settlement with railway causing employee's death, was deducted from compensation awarded under this section, employer's right of subrogation to claim against railway was not thereby destroyed. Benoit Coal Mining Co. v. Moore, 215 Ala. 220, 109 So. 878 (1926).

Right arises after employee fails to bring action within statutory time period. — The employer or its insurance carrier has a right of action only after the employee fails to bring action within the statutory time period. Hart-

ford Accident & Indem. Co. v. Rigdon, 418 F. Supp. 540 (S.D. Ala. 1976).

A subrogee cannot bring an action against a third party under this section until the period within which the injured party has to bring action has lapsed. Garren v. Commercial Union Ins. Co., 340 So. 2d 764 (Ala. 1976).

Set-off not allowed where no proof of damages. — Where there was no proof of damages suffered by the employee and hence no evidence that the employee enjoyed a double recovery, there was no error on the part of the trial court in refusing to grant employer a set-off as to the amounts the employee received under uninsured motorist and medical benefits insurance policies. Jackson v. Weaver, 516 So. 2d 702 (Ala. Civ. App. 1987).

Credit not allowed where no claim made against employer. — Where the medical benefits paid for all of the employee's medical expenses, and he made no claim against employer for them, there was no authority for giving employer a credit for the amount of medical benefits received against the employee's workmen's compensation benefits. Jackson v. Weaver, 516 So. 2d 702 (Ala. Civ. App. 1987).

Jurisdiction lacking. — While the United States District Court, as a federal court sitting in diversity, was bound to recognize a carrier's right to sue in the additional six-month period provided by subsection (d), it could not give recognition to the provision allowing carriers to sue in the name of the injured employee and it could not allow the statute, via its collateral effect, to operate so as to vest the court with diversity jurisdiction where the pecuniary interest of the real party plaintiff in interest did not meet the requisite jurisdictional amount. Ryan v. Flame Refractories, Inc., 759 F. Supp. 774 (S.D. Ala. 1991).

VI. ATTORNEYS' FEES.

Awarding of attorney's fee constitutional. — The amendment of this section by the legislature in 1961 was not in violation of Constitution, § 45. Baggett v. Webb, 46 Ala. App. 666, 248 So. 2d 275 (1971).

Purpose of awarding attorney's fee. — At least one of the purposes of the addition of the 1961 amendment was to grant to the employee or his dependents some relief from the expense of their bringing the third-party action and thus saving the employer or his carrier from paying some or all of the due compensation, or if compensation had been paid, recovery of some or all of it. Baggett v. Webb, 46 Ala. App. 666, 248 So. 2d 275 (1971).

It would be patently unfair and unjust to allow recovery of attorney's fees from the employer if a third-party claim or action was settled with a nominal effort by the employee or his dependents, but disallow recovery of more substantial fees incurred by prolonged and difficult action by trial and judicial determination. Baggett v. Webb, 46 Ala. App. 666, 248 So. 2d 275 (1971).

To the extent a workmen's compensation insurance company paid attorneys fees, the sickness and accident policy insurer is entitled to a credit, this being workmen's compensation benefits "paid or payable"; the fact that such payment is designated as attorneys fees is of no consequence since the end result inures to the direct benefit of the injured employee and third-party plaintiff. Antram v. Stuyvesant Life Ins. Co., 291 Ala. 716, 287 So. 2d 837 (1973).

Damages "recovered and collected" do not include only that amount which plaintiff retains after payment of attorney's fees. It is clear that the statute presupposes that the entire money judgment recovered is the sum to which the insurer's claim for reimbursement attaches. Nowhere is it mentioned that only the "net" recovery, after payment of attorney's fees, is intended. The purpose behind this section is to preclude the employee from recovering twice for the same injury. Fitch v. Insurance Co. of N. Am., 408 So. 2d 1017 (Ala. Civ. App. 1981).

Employer not entitled to expenses incurred by employee's attorney. — Since subsection (e) does not specifically mention "expenses," employer was not entitled to a pro rata share of the expenses incurred by the employee's attorney in prosecuting the third party claim. Insurance Co. of N. Am. v. Phillips, 523 So. 2d 447 (Ala. Civ. App. 1988).

"Attorney's fees" under subsection (e) does not include attorney's expenses. — Although an attorney's "reasonable expenses" are recoverable, in addition to the attorney's fees, by an employer in an action against a third party under subsection (d), absence of the phrase "reasonable expenses" in subsection (e) renders attorney expenses unrecoverable by an employee, and therefore unrecoverable in pro rata share by employer, in an action against a third party. Insurance Co. of N. Am. v. Phillips, 523 So. 2d 447 (Ala. Civ. App. 1988).

Employee cannot reduce reimbursement to employer by pro rata share of expenses. — When an employee has recovered for his or her on the job injury from a third party, the employee must reimburse the employer the amount of compensation paid less a pro rata share of attorney's fees and cannot further reduce that reimbursement to the employer by a pro rata share of expenses incurred in prosecuting the third-party claim. Simply, the employee cannot reduce the reimbursement to the employer by a pro rata share of expenses incurred in prosecuting the third-party claim by the employee and his or her attorney. Insurance Co. of N. Am. v. Phillips, 523 So. 2d 447 (Ala. Civ. App. 1988).

§ 25-5-11.1. Employee not to be terminated solely for action to recover benefits nor for filing notice of safety rule violation.

No employee shall be terminated by an employer solely because the employee has instituted or maintained any action against the employer to recover workers' compensation benefits under this chapter or solely because the employee has filed a written notice of violation of a safety rule pursuant to subdivision (c)(4) of Section 25-5-11. (Acts 1984, 2nd Ex. Sess., No. 85-41, p. 44, § 11.)

Code commissioner's note. — Acts 1984, 2nd Ex. Sess., No. 85-41, § 14 provides: "This act shall become effective immediately upon its passage and approval by the governor [January 9, 1985], or upon its otherwise becoming a law, provided it shall have no effect whatsoever with respect to the right of any injured employee to bring an action with respect to or upon any cause of action which arose or accrued prior to February 1, 1985. Provided further, it shall have no effect on and shall not apply to any accident or exposure to injurious condition occurring before the effective date of this Act."

Section is to be liberally construed. — Because this was remedial legislation, intended to prevent an employee's termination solely because the employee had instituted or maintained an action against the employer to recover worker's compensation benefits, this section would be construed liberally to effect its purposes. Twilley v. Daubert Coated Prods., Inc., 536 So. 2d 1364 (Ala. 1988).

Legislative intent. — This section was clearly designed to prohibit employers from terminating employees in retaliation for their decision to file a claim for worker's compensation benefits. In order for the beneficent goals of the worker's compensation chapter to be realized, the employee must be able to exercise his right to be compensated for work-related injuries in an unfettered fashion without being subject to reprisal. McClain v. Birmingham Coca-Cola Bottling Co., 578 So. 2d 1299 (Ala. 1991).

"Action". — The legislature's choice of the word "action" in this section was not intended to restrict the cause of action to cases where the employee is terminated in retaliation for his decision to file a lawsuit, as opposed to merely filing a claim, to recover worker's compensation benefits. Viewed pragmatically, such a literal interpretation of this section would not only encourage some employers to terminate injured employees who file claims for worker's compensation benefits, but it would also effectively discourage employees from ever filing a claim in the first place. Such an interpretation also would be unreasonable because it would obviously circumvent the purpose behind this section and ultimately deprive it of any meaningful effect. McClain v. Birmingham Coca-Cola Bottling Co., 578 So. 2d 1299 (Ala. 1991).

"Termination". — The word "termination" in this section is broad enough to include a "constructive termination." Twilley v. Daubert Coated Prods., Inc., 536 So. 2d 1364 (Ala. 1988).

Jury trial available. — An action for wrongful termination is of a sort that has traditionally been tried to a jury, even though it may have arisen out of a workmen's compensation factual setting. Twilley v. Daubert Coated Prods., Inc., 536 So. 2d 1364 (Ala. 1988).

Burden of proof. — An employee may establish a prima facie case of retaliatory discharge by proving that he was terminated because he sought to recover workmen's compensation benefits, which would be an impermissible reason. The burden would then shift to the defendant employer to come forward with evidence that the employee was terminated for a legitimate reason, whereupon the plaintiff would have to prove that the reason was not true but a pretext for an otherwise impermissible termination. Twilley v. Daubert Coated Prods., Inc., 536 So. 2d 1364 (Ala. 1988).

Although this section omits specific reference to damages for violation of its provisions, damages can be awarded in accordance with the general law of torts. Caraway v. Franklin Ferguson Mfg. Co., 507 So. 2d 925 (Ala. 1987).

The absence from this section of a provision for damages is not a basis for dismissing a plaintiff's complaint for wrongful dismissal on the grounds that she has failed to state a claim upon which relief can be granted. The cause of action is clearly established by this section. Caraway v. Franklin Ferguson Mfg. Co., 507 So. 2d 925 (Ala. 1987).

Plaintiff's claim for relief or cause of action for retaliatory discharge "arises under" Alabama's Workmen's Compensation Act and is therefore barred by federal statute from removal to federal court. Kilpatrick v. Martin K. Eby Constr. Co., 708 F. Supp. 1241 (N.D. Ala. 1989).

Cited in Hoffman-La Roche, Inc. v. Campbell, 512 So. 2d 725 (Ala. 1987).

§ 25-5-12. Chief Justice of supreme court to prepare uniform rules for circuit courts.

The Chief Justice of the Supreme Court of Alabama, from time to time as he deems it is necessary, may prepare uniform rules for the circuit judges and circuit courts which may be necessary for carrying out the provisions of this chapter, including such forms for orders and judgments as said chief justice of the supreme court deems best. Such rules and forms when so prepared and promulgated by the chief justice shall be followed and used by the said judges and courts. (Acts 1919, No. 245, p. 206; Code 1923, § 7588; Code 1940, T. 26, § 313.)

Cross references. — As to rule-making authority of supreme court generally, see § 12-2-7. As to filing and publication of rules promulgated by supreme court, see § 12-2-19.

§ 25-5-13. Applicability of chapter.

(a) This chapter shall be applicable to the employees of all counties and all municipalities having populations greater than 2,000 according to the most recent federal decennial census, and shall govern in their employment. This chapter shall be applicable also to the employees of all county and city boards of education, the Alabama Institute for the Deaf and Blind, and all employees of the two-year colleges under the control of the State Board of Education, and shall govern in their employment. The employees of all school systems and institutions, counties, and each municipality covered under this section shall have available to them all the rights and remedies provided under this chapter. The governing bodies of all school systems and institutions, counties, and of each municipality covered under this section shall file all necessary employer reports and notices required at the times and in the manner prescribed in this chapter.

(b) Notwithstanding subsection (a) of this section, this chapter shall not apply to any city (excepting school districts and institutions) which has a population of 250,000 or more according to the last or any subsequent decennial federal census, to any park and recreation board now or hereafter established for those cities, to any board or agency now or hereafter authorized and established by the governing body of those cities, nor to employees of the city or of any board or agency. (Acts 1975, No. 565, p. 1299, § 1; Acts 1975, 4th Ex. Sess., No. 29, p. 2645, § 1; Acts 1984, No. 84-322, p. 741, § 1; Acts 1992, No. 92-537, § 9.)

The 1992 amendment, effective May 19, 1992, in subsection (a), in the first and second sentences, deleted "The provisions of" at the beginning of the sentence and deleted "the provisions of this chapter" preceding "shall govern," inserted "the" preceding "Alabama Institute" in the second sentence, substituted "under this section" for "under the provisions of this section" in the third sentence, and deleted "the provisions of" preceding "this section" in the last sentence, and in subsection (b) deleted "the provisions of" preceding "subsection (a)" and preceding "this chapter," substituted "those cities" for "such cities" in two places, substituted "the city" for "any such city," and deleted "such" preceding "board or agency," and made some changes in capitalization within the section.

Code commissioner's note. — Acts 1984, No. 84-322, s. 4, provides: "The provisions of this act shall become effective on August 15,

1984 provided, however, the provisions of this amendatory act shall not be in effect until sufficient funds are appropriated from the special educational trust fund to implement said provisions; and further provided that nothing contained herein shall prohibit any school board that voluntarily elects to provide such coverage from doing so with local or other available funds."

Although employees of cities with populations in excess of 250,000 are not covered by workmen's compensation, such employees are covered under Ala. Acts 1973, Act No. 1272, at 2124 (Pension Act). Board of Managers v. Elliott, 532 So. 2d 1019 (Ala. Civ. App. 1988).

Cited in City of Montgomery v. Johnson, 403 So. 2d 244 (Ala. Civ. App. 1981); City of Montgomery v. Robinson, 441 So. 2d 857 (Ala. 1983); Robinson v. City of Montgomery, 485 So. 2d 695 (Ala. 1986).

§ 25-5-14. Legislative findings and intent as to actions filed by injured employee against officers, etc., of same employer.

The legislature finds that actions filed on behalf of injured employees against officers, directors, agents, servants or employees of the same employer seeking to recover damages in excess of amounts received or receivable from the employer under the workers' compensation statutes of this state and predicated upon claimed negligent or wanton conduct resulting in injuries arising out of and in the course of employment are contrary to the intent of the legislature in adopting a comprehensive workers' compensation scheme and are producing a debilitating and adverse effect upon efforts to retain existing, and to attract new industry to this state. Specifically, the existence of such causes of action places this state at a serious disadvantage in comparison to the existing laws of other states with whom this state competes in seeking to attract and retain industrial operations which would provide better job opportunities and increased employment for people in this state. The existence of such causes of action, and the consequent litigation resulting therefrom, results in substantial costs and expenses to employers which, as a practical matter, must either procure additional liability insurance coverage for supervisory and management employees or fund the costs of defense, judgment or settlement from their own resources in order to retain competent and reliable personnel. The existence of such causes of action has a disruptive effect upon the relationship among employees and supervisory and management personnel. There is a total absence of any reliable evidence that the availability of such causes of action has resulted in any reduction of the number or severity of on-the-job accidents or of any substantial improvement on providing safe working conditions and work practices. The intent of the legislature is to provide complete immunity to employers and limited immunity to officers, directors, agents, servants or employees of the same employer and to the workers' compensation insurance carrier and compensation service companies of the employer or any officer, director, agent, servant or employee of such carrier or company and to labor unions and to any official or representative thereof, from civil liability for all causes of action except those based on willful conduct and such immunity is an essential aspect of the workers' compensation scheme. The legislature hereby expressly reaffirms its intent, as set forth in Section 25-5-53, as amended herein, and Sections 25-5-144 and 25-5-194, regarding the exclusivity of the rights and remedies of an injured employee, except as provided for herein. (Acts 1984, 2nd Ex. Sess., No. 85-41, p. 44, § 1.)

Code commissioner's note. — Acts 1984, 2nd Ex. Sess., No. 85-41, § 14 provides: "This act shall become effective immediately upon its passage and approval by the governor [January 9, 1985], or upon its otherwise becoming a law, provided it shall have no effect whatsoever with respect to the right of any injured employee to bring an action with respect to or upon any cause of action which arose or accrued prior to February 1, 1985. Provided further, it shall have no effect on and shall not apply to any accident or exposure to injurious condition occurring before the effective date of this Act."

Section 25-5-144, referred to in the last sentence, was repealed by Acts 1992, No. 92-537, § 51.

For a review of the constitutionality of

Alabama's **Workmen's Compensation Act** in view of Ala. Const., Art. I, § 13 and Art. IV, § 45, see, Reed v. Brunson, 527 So. 2d 102 (Ala. 1988).

The legislature does have the police power to eliminate co-employee suits by the Workmen's Compensation Act in an attempt to eradicate or ameliorate what it perceives to be a social evil. Reed v. Brunson, 527 So. 2d 102 (Ala. 1988).

Evidence necessary to show willfulness. — In this section the legislature sought to insure that cases involving willfulness of co-employee would not be submitted to a jury without at least some evidence tending to show either (1) the reason why the co-employee

defendant would want to intentionally injure the plaintiff, or someone else, or (2) that a reasonable man in the position of the defendant would have known that a particular result (i.e., injury or death) was substantially certain to follow from his actions. Reed v. Brunson, 527 So. 2d 102 (Ala. 1988).

No actionable cause where no proof of willful conduct. — Where the complaint alleged that the defendants, co-employees, had negligently or wantonly injured plaintiff when they played a prank on her by pulling out her chair, the complaint did not state an actionable claim against co-employees, since plaintiff did not prove willful conduct with intent to injure. Sanford v. Brasher, 549 So. 2d 29 (Ala. 1989).

§ 25-5-15. Safety committee.

Upon the written request of any employee, each employer subject to the workers' compensation law shall appoint a safety committee. The safety committee shall consist of not less than three committee members, one of whom must be a nonsupervisory employee. The safety committee shall advise the employer regarding safety in the work place, including suggestions from employees regarding safety conditions in the work place. Any employee shall have the right to notify the safety committee of a safety condition in the work place. The safety committee shall develop procedures by which an employee may give such notification. The provisions of this section shall not apply to any employer who now or in the future has an established safety committee pursuant to contract or agreement with its employees or their representative. (Acts 1984, 2nd Ex. Sess., No. 85-41, p. 44, § 10.)

Code commissioner's note. — Acts 1984, 2nd Ex. Sess., No. 85-41, § 14 provides: "This act shall become effective immediately upon its passage and approval by the governor [January 9, 1985], or upon its otherwise becoming a law, provided it shall have no effect whatsoever with respect to the right of any injured

employee to bring an action with respect to or upon any cause of action which arose or accrued prior to February 1, 1985. Provided further, it shall have no effect on and shall not apply to any accident or exposure to injurious condition occurring before the effective date of this Act."

§ 25-5-15.1. State safety program; legislative intent; creation.

(a) It is the intent of the legislature to promote safety education, safety planning, and to provide any needed technical assistance.

(b) The Director of the Department of Industrial Relations shall coordinate with the safe state program, the safety and health consulting service, to establish a safety program for cooperating with industry to promote safety and provide technical assistance. Emphasis shall be placed on unsafe acts in both small industry and high risk industry.

(c) Qualified safety management specialists shall be employed in the safe state program to assist employers in developing or improving their safety programs. Safe state program personnel shall, upon referral by the director of an employer's request, make inspections for safety monitoring and report the resulting findings and recommendations to the employer and to the director.

(d) The safe state program shall establish and collect reasonable fees for technical and consultative safety services that are not required by law, provided to persons requesting the services from or through the Workers' Compensation Division of the Department of Industrial Relations. (Acts 1992, No. 92-537, § 31.)

Effective date. — The act which added this section became effective May 19, 1992.

§ 25-5-16. Applicability as to occupational diseases, pneumoconiosis, and exposure to radiation. Repealed by Acts 1992, No. 92-537, § 31, effective May 19, 1992.

Code commissioner's note. — The phrase "this act," as used in this section, refers to Acts 1984, 2nd Ex. Sess., No. 85-41, which amended §§ 25-5-1, 25-5-11, 25-5-51, 25-5-53, 25-5-57, 25-5-68, 25-5-77, and 25-5-80, and added §§ 25-5-11.1 and 25-5-14 through 25-5-17.

Acts 1984, 2nd Ex. Sess., No. 85-41, § 14 provides: "This act shall become effective immediately upon its passage and approval by the governor [January 9, 1985], or upon its otherwise becoming a law, provided it shall have no effect whatsoever with respect to the right of any injured employee to bring an action with respect to or upon any cause of action which arose or accrued prior to February 1, 1985. Provided further, it shall have no effect on and shall not apply to any accident or exposure to injurious condition occurring before the effective date of this Act."

§ 25-5-17. Severability.

The provisions of this act are expressly declared not to be severable. If any provision of this act shall be adjudged to be invalid by any court of competent jurisdiction, then this entire act shall be invalid and held for naught. (Acts 1984, 2nd Ex. Sess., No. 85-41, p. 44, § 13.)

Code commissioner's note. — The phrase "this act," as used in this section, refers to Acts 1984, 2nd Ex. Sess., No. 85-41, which amended §§ 25-5-1, 25-5-11, 25-5-51, 25-5-53, 25-5-57, 25-5-68, 25-5-77, and 25-5-80, and added §§ 25-5-11.1 and 25-5-14 through 25-5-17.

Acts 1984, 2nd Ex. Sess., No. 85-41, § 14 provides: "This act shall become effective immediately upon its passage and approval by the governor [January 9, 1985], or upon its otherwise becoming a law, provided it shall have no effect whatsoever with respect to the right of any injured employee to bring an action with respect to or upon any cause of action which arose or accrued prior to February 1, 1985. Provided further, it shall have no effect on and shall not apply to any accident or exposure to injurious condition occurring before the effective date of this Act."

For a review of the constitutionality of Alabama's Workmen's Compensation Act in view of Ala. Const., Art. I, § 13 and Art. IV, § 45, see, Reed v. Brunson, 527 So. 2d 102 (Ala. 1988).

ARTICLE 2.

COMPENSATION BY CIVIL ACTION.

Lack of dependents did not entitle administratrix to bring civil action. — Fact that employee, whose death arose out of and in the course of his employment, had no dependents did not entitle administratrix of employee's estate to seek compensation by civil action against employer, even though maximum compensation benefits payable otherwise were medical expenses, burial expenses and payment to secondary trust fund. Holliday v. C.T. Thackston Sand & Gravel Co., 361 So. 2d 13 (Ala. Civ. App. 1978).

The determination of the proper percentage of disability rests with the trial court. The trial judge has the opportunity to observe the courtroom demeanor of the employee and other witnesses. Jefferson County v. Pitts, 448 So. 2d 958 (Ala. Civ. App. 1984).

Collateral references. — What conduct is willful, intentional, or deliberate within Workmen's Compensation Act provision authorizing tort action for such conduct. 96 ALR3d 1064.

§ 25-5-30. Applicability of article; article deemed extension or modification of common law.

This article shall not apply in cases where Article 3 of this chapter becomes operative in accordance with the provisions thereof, but shall apply in all other cases, and in such cases shall be an extension or modification of the common law. (Acts 1939, No. 661, p. 1036, § 18; Code 1940, T. 26, § 262; Acts 1949, No. 36, p. 47, § 2; Acts 1971, No. 667, p. 1376, §§ 1, 2; Acts 1973, No. 1062, p. 1750, § 4.)

Cited in Lackey v. Jefferson Energy Corp., 439 So. 2d 1290 (Ala. Civ. App. 1983).

§ 25-5-31. Right of action for damages for injuries or death of employee.

When personal injury or death is caused to an employee by an accident arising out of and in the course of his employment, of which injury the actual or lawfully imputed negligence of the employer is the natural and proximate cause, he, or in case of death, his personal representative, for the exclusive benefit of the surviving spouse and next of kin, shall receive compensation by way of damages therefor from the employer; provided, that the injury or death was not caused by the wilful misconduct of the employee or was not due to misconduct on his part, as defined in Section 25-5-51. (Acts 1919, No. 245, p. 206; Code 1923, § 7534; Code 1940, T. 26, § 253.)

I. General Consideration.
II. Course of Employment.
    A. In General.
    B. Employee Going to and from Work.
III. Employer-Employee Relationship.
IV. Accident.
V. Pleading.
VI. Evidence.

I. GENERAL CONSIDERATION.

Cross references. — For further cases on usual course of employment, see § 25-5-1.

Appellate review in workers' compensation cases is a two-step process. First, the court will look to see if there is any legal evidence to support the trial court's findings. If such evidence is found, the court will then determine whether any reasonable view of that evidence supports the trial court's judgment. Wiley Sanders Truck Lines v. McLain, 591 So. 2d 527 (Ala. Civ. App. 1991).

Cited in United States Cast Iron Pipe & Foundry Co. v. Fuller, 212 Ala. 177, 102 So. 25 (1924); Ex parte Sloss-Sheffield Steel & Iron Co., 212 Ala. 699, 103 So. 920 (1925); Boris Constr. Co. v. Haywood, 214 Ala. 162, 106 So. 799 (1925); Gulf States Steel Co. v. Witherspoon, 214 Ala. 130, 106 So. 900 (1926); Indian Head Mills v. Ashworth, 215 Ala. 348, 110 So. 565 (1926); Vida Lumber Co. v. Courson, 216 Ala. 248, 112 So. 737 (1926); Poe v. Pate, 216 Ala. 264, 113 So. 234 (1927); Sloss-Sheffield Steel & Iron Co. v. Greer, 216 Ala. 267, 113 So. 271 (1927); Carothers v. McNabb, 216 Ala. 366, 113 So. 298 (1927); Prayther v. Deepwater Coal & Iron Co., 216 Ala. 579, 114 So. 194 (1927); Dean v. Stockham Pipe & Fittings Co., 220 Ala. 25, 123 So. 225 (1929); Tennessee Coal, I. & R.R. v. Jordan, 223 Ala. 430, 136 So. 820 (1931); Board of Revenue v. Puckett, 227 Ala. 374, 149 So. 850 (1933); Webb v. French, 228 Ala. 43, 152 So. 215 (1934); Ex parte Carlisle, 27 Ala. App. 142, 168 So. 598 (1936); Hardy v. City of Dothan, 234 Ala. 664, 176 So. 449 (1937); Posey v. TVA, 93 F.2d 726 (5th Cir. 1937); Bagwell v. Woodward Iron Co., 236 Ala. 668, 184 So. 692 (1938); Wilkey v. State ex rel. Smith, 244 Ala. 568, 14 So. 2d 536 (1943); Sloss-Sheffield Steel & Iron Co. v. Watford, 245 Ala. 425, 17 So. 2d 166 (1944); Bonner v. Alexander, 34 Ala. App. 89, 36 So. 2d 533 (1948); DeBardeleben Coal Corp. v. Richards, 251 Ala. 324, 37 So. 2d 121 (1948); Wade & Richey v. Oglesby, 251 Ala. 356, 37 So. 2d 596 (1948); Lingo v. Crews, 253 Ala. 227, 43 So. 2d 815 (1950); Ex parte Arrington, 253 Ala. 501, 45 So. 2d 466 (1950); Bennett v. Walsh Stevedoring Co., 253 Ala. 685, 46 So. 2d 834 (1950); Dunning v. Republic Steel Corp., 257 Ala. 1, 59 So. 2d 606 (1950); Bass v. Cowikee Mills, 257 Ala. 280, 58 So. 2d 589 (1952); Jackson v. Baldwin, 37 Ala. App. 254, 66 So. 2d 838 (1953); Wooten v. Roden, 260 Ala. 606, 71 So. 2d 802 (1954); Lucas v. Black Diamond Coal Mining Co., 262 Ala. 368, 79 So. 2d 26 (1955); United States Steel Corp. v. Danner, 263 Ala. 310, 82 So. 2d 404 (1955); Johnson v. Cox, 38 Ala. App. 222, 82 So. 2d 562 (1955); Goodyear Tire & Rubber Co. v. Downey, 266 Ala. 344, 96 So. 2d 278 (1957); American Fid. & Cas. Co. v. St. Paul-Mercury Indem. Co., 248 F.2d 509 (5th Cir. 1957); State v. Anderson, 39 Ala. App. 380, 101 So. 2d 96 (1958); Tennessee Coal & Iron Div., United States Steel Corp. v. Hubbert, 268 Ala. 674, 110 So. 2d 260 (1959); Daniel Constr. Co. v. Pierce, 270 Ala. 522, 120 So. 2d 381 (1959); Bell v. Brooks, 270 Ala. 691, 121 So. 2d 911 (1960); Nashville Bridge Co. v. Ritch, 276 F.2d 171 (5th Cir. 1960); Crider v. Zurich Ins. Co., 224 F. Supp. 87 (N.D. Ala. 1963); Centraal Stikstof Verkoopkanter, N.V. v. Walsh Stevedoring Co., 380 F.2d 523 (5th Cir. 1967); Agee v. Lloyd, 282 Ala. 224, 210 So. 2d 699 (1968); Brown v. Cerco Enters., Inc., 286 Ala. 421, 240 So. 2d 671 (1970); Boaz Nursing Home, Inc. v. Recovery Inns of Am., Inc., 289 Ala. 144, 266 So. 2d 588 (1972); Stewart v. Busby, 51 Ala. App. 242, 284 So. 2d 269 (1973); Sabino v. Independent Life & Accident Ins. Co., 52 Ala. App. 368, 292 So. 2d 662 (1974); Thompson-Hayward Chem. Co. v. Peterson, 56 Ala. App. 432, 322 So. 2d 723 (1975); Hendrix v. National Life & Accident Ins. Co., 356 So. 2d 1199 (Ala. 1978); Holliday v. C.T. Thackston Sand & Gravel Co., 361 So. 2d 13 (Ala. Civ. App. 1978); Porter v. International Paper Co., 466 So. 2d 146 (Ala. Civ. App. 1985); St. Paul Ins. Co. v. Harris, 758 F.2d 1450 (11th Cir. 1985).

Collateral references. — 99 C.J.S., Workmen's Compensation, §§ 152-265, 336. 100 C.J.S., Workmen's Compensation, §§ 488-581, 587. 101 C.J.S., Workmen's Compensation, §§ 944, 955-958.

58 Am. Jur., Workmen's Compensation, § 26 et seq.

Compensation to workman injured through smoking. 5 ALR 1521.

Injury producing insanity as proximate cause of suicide. 6 ALR 570.

Applicability of compensation acts to watchman. 6 ALR 578, 13 ALR 512.

Injury received during lunch hour on employer's premises. 6 ALR 1151.

Recovery for death or injury from excitement. 6 ALR 1256.

Injury from fumes or gases as accident or occupational disease. 6 ALR 1466, 23 ALR 335, 90 ALR 619.

Injuries received while performing service for employer before or after hours as arising out of and in the course of employment. 7 ALR 1078.

Injury through curiosity as arising out of and in the course of employment. 7 ALR 1305.

Hemorrhage as an accident. 7 ALR 1614, 13 ALR 438.

Compensation for death of or injury to peace officer employed in private plant. 8 ALR 190.

Injury while riding to or from work in

employer's conveyance. 10 ALR 169, 21 ALR 1223, 24 ALR 1233, 62 ALR 1438, 145 ALR 1033.

Right of firemen and policemen to recover under workmen's compensation acts. 10 ALR 201, 81 ALR 478.

Injury or death due to elements. 13 ALR 974, 16 ALR 1038, 25 ALR 146, 40 ALR 400, 46 ALR 1218, 53 ALR 1084, 82 ALR 234.

Injury from assault. 15 ALR 588, 21 ALR 758, 29 ALR 437, 40 ALR 1122, 72 ALR 110, 112 ALR 1258.

Interest in the business or in corporation or firm owning the business as affecting right to compensation. 15 ALR 1288, 81 ALR 644.

Death from heart disease. 19 ALR 110, 28 ALR 204, 60 ALR 1299.

Circumstances under which existence of relationship of employer and independent contractor is predictable. 19 ALR 1169, 60 ALR 303.

Injury received while doing prohibited act. 23 ALR 1161, 26 ALR 166, 58 ALR 197, 83 ALR 1211, 119 ALR 1409.

Applicability of state compensation act to injury within admiralty jurisdiction. 25 ALR 1029, 31 ALR 518, 56 ALR 352.

Injury to solicitor, collector, or outside salesman, as arising out of and in the course of the employment. 29 ALR 120, 36 ALR 474.

Injury to muscles or nerves attributable to occupation, but not due to a sudden event. 29 ALR 510.

Lead or other occupational poisoning as within workmen's compensation act. 29 ALR 691, 44 ALR 371.

Charitable institutions as within workmen's compensation act. 30 ALR 600.

Effect of kinship or family relationship between parties. 33 ALR 585.

Injury to employee while engaged in employer's work but outside the scope of his usual duty. 33 ALR 1335, 82 ALR 1251.

Applicability of workmen's compensation act to piece workers. 38 ALR 839.

External infection as accident or an accidental injury. 39 ALR 871.

Injury or illness due to artificial temperature. 41 ALR 1124, 53 ALR 1095, 61 ALR 218.

Public officer as within workmen's compensation act. 44 ALR 1477.

Injury while entering or leaving place of employment as arising out of or in course of employment. 49 ALR 424, 82 ALR 1043.

Street risks incurred in course of employment. 51 ALR 509, 80 ALR 126.

Municipal corporation as an employer within workmen's compensation act. 54 ALR 788.

Injury after discharge. 56 ALR 859, 69 ALR 1121.

Injury to employee while temporarily en-gaged in personal business. 59 ALR 370, 66 ALR 756.

Injury accidentally inflicted on employee while on employer's premises by one not an employee nor connected with the work. 60 ALR 1401.

Condition of bodily organs due to particles of dust or other material incident to work, as compensable within workmen's compensation act not covering occupational diseases. 62 ALR 1460, 97 ALR 1412.

Workmen's compensation as insurance. 63 ALR 728, 100 ALR 1449, 119 ALR 1241.

Injury to or incapacity of employee as the result of vaccination or inoculation as compensable. 69 ALR 863.

Juror as within workmen's compensation act. 70 ALR 1248.

Test in determining whether one is an independent contractor. 75 ALR 725.

Deviation on personal errand as affecting question whether injury to employee on street or highway arose out of and in the course of employment. 76 ALR 356.

One employed by servant in emergency as servant of the master. 76 ALR 971.

Helper, assistant, or substitute for an employee as himself an employee. 80 ALR 522.

Employee's use of his own motor vehicle as affecting question whether injury or death was within act. 85 ALR 978, 96 ALR 467.

Termination of employment before disability or disease attributable to employment as affecting right to compensation. 104 ALR 1210.

Fright or shock without visible impact as accidental injury. 109 ALR 892.

Gradual occurrence of bruise or other traumatic injury or condition as an accident. 122 ALR 839.

Violation of statute in connection with his employment as affecting status of one as employee. 128 ALR 1310.

"Workmen" or "operatives" within workmen's compensation act. 129 ALR 990.

Responsibility of seller or purchaser of business or plant in respect of employee's claims under compensation act. 131 ALR 1362.

Misrepresentations in obtaining employment as affecting status as employee or servant. 136 ALR 1124.

Partnership as distinguished from employment. 137 ALR 6.

School teacher as an employee. 140 ALR 1383.

Injury to employee away from employer's premises during lunch hour. 141 ALR 862.

Compensation for injury or illness from contaminated water. 141 ALR 1490.

One temporarily impressed into public service in emergency as within act. 142 ALR 657.

Industrial home workers as within workmen's compensation act. 143 ALR 418.

Injury due to character or quality of material or equipment used for cleansing or other personal conveniences of employees. 148 ALR 1017.

Transfer of business as affecting compensation in respect of injury subsequently sustained by employee. 150 ALR 1166.

Workmen's compensation act as applicable to person in military or naval service. 150 ALR 1456.

Applicability of state workmen's compensation act to injury occurring on, or in connection with contracts in relation to, federal property within state. 153 ALR 1050.

Living on employer's premises as affecting question whether injury to servant arises out of or in the course of employment. 158 ALR 606.

Musicians or other entertainers as employees of hotel or restaurant in which they perform. 158 ALR 915, 172 ALR 325.

Injury sustained through horseplay or fooling around. 159 ALR 319.

Injury to employee while in automobile parking lot. 159 ALR 1395.

Accidental injury to employee while doing private work for his own benefit, following a continuous practice in that regard, in employer's plant. 161 ALR 1461.

Coverage of industrial or business employee when performing, under orders, services for private benefit of employer or superior, or officer, representative, or stockholder of corporate employer. 172 ALR 378.

Statutory provision referring to employees as including public officers. 5 ALR2d 418.

Railroad tracks: injury while crossing or walking along railroad or street railway tracks, going to or from work, as arising out of and in the course of employment. 50 ALR2d 363.

Status, under workmen's compensation act, of gasoline and oil distributor or dealer as agent, employee, independent dealer. 83 ALR2d 1290, 1300.

Suicide as compensable under workmen's compensation act. 15 ALR3d 616.

Storms: injury or death due to storms. 42 ALR3d 385.

Social affair: injury sustained while attending employer-sponsored social affair as arising out of and in the course of employment. 47 ALR3d 566.

Employer's right of action for loss of services or the like against third person tortiously killing or injuring employee. 4 ALR4th 504.

Modern status: "dual capacity doctrine" as basis for employee's recovery from employer in tort. 23 ALR4th 1151.

Intoxicating liquors: employer's liability for furnishing or permitting liquor on social occasion, 51 ALR4th 1048.

Liability of employer, supervisor, or manager for intentionally or recklessly causing employee emotional distress. 52 ALR4th 853.

Workers' compensation: injuries incurred during labor activity. 61 ALR4th 196.

Employer's liability to employee for failure to provide work environment free from tobacco smoke. 63 ALR4th 1021.

II. COURSE OF EMPLOYMENT.

A. In General.

Liberal construction in favor of claimant. — The provision of this section that employee's death must have arisen out of his employment to entitle dependent to compensation should be construed liberally in favor of claimant. McLaughlin v. Davis Lumber Co., 220 Ala. 440, 125 So. 608 (1929).

This section, making compensable personal injury or death caused to an employee by accident arising out of and in course of employment, refers to distinct conceptions, and their concurrent existence is essential to invoke benefits of workmen's compensation law, but overwrought refinements in administration should be avoided. American Fuel & Clay Prods. Co. v. Gilbert, 221 Ala. 44, 127 So. 540 (1930).

Injury must arise out of and in the course of employment. — In order for an accident to be compensable under the workmen's compensation law, it must arise out of and in the course of employment. Deaton Truck Line v. Acker, 261 Ala. 468, 74 So. 2d 717 (1954), overruled on other grounds, Pritchett v. G & B Log Co., 424 So.2d 620 (Ala. 1982); United States Fid. & Guar. Co. v. Dunlap, 276 Ala. 616, 165 So. 2d 404 (1963); Anderson v. Custom Caterers, Inc., 279 Ala. 360, 185 So. 2d 383 (1966); McKnight v. Consolidated Concrete Co., 279 Ala. 430, 186 So. 2d 144 (1966); Ragland Brick Co. v. Campbell, 409 So. 2d 443 (Ala. Civ. App. 1982); Kennedy v. Cochran ex rel. Cochran, 475 So. 2d 872 (Ala. Civ. App. 1985).

The test is not whether the employee's conduct has created a greater risk, but whether at the time of the accident he was acting within the sphere of his employment. Malbis Bakery Co. v. Collins, 245 Ala. 84, 15 So. 2d 705 (1943).

An employee's injury is within the act if, when the injury was received, the employee was either doing the work or performing the service he was engaged to do or perform, or was engaged in an act or service naturally related thereto, such as a reasonable judgment would refer either to the express or the implied elements of the contract of employment, such as a reasonable conception would conclude to be a natural incident of the employee's engagement. Within the purview of such naturally related and incidental acts in the course of the employment is the movement of the employee in entering, at the appropriate time, the employer's premises to discharge his function; his preparation to begin and to terminate his actual service; and to leave the premises at an appropriate time after the completion of his actual service. United States Steel Corp. v. Martin, 267 Ala. 634, 104 So. 2d 475 (1958).

To bring plaintiff's case within the scope of the act it must appear, not only that his injury was caused by accident, but that it arose out of and in the course of his employment. Tiger Motor Co. v. Winslett, 278 Ala. 108, 176 So. 2d 39 (1965).

And both terms must be satisfied. — While an accident arising out of an employment usually occurs in the course of it, such is not invariably true. Likewise, an accident which occurs in the course of an employment does not necessarily arise out of it. The words "arising out of" involve the idea of causal relationship between the employment and the injury, while the term "in the course of" relates more particularly to the time, place and circumstances under which the injury occurred. The phrases are not synonymous; where both are used conjunctively a double condition has been imposed, and both terms must be satisfied in order to bring a case within the act. Wooten v. Roden, 260 Ala. 606, 71 So. 2d 802 (1954).

The words "arising out of" involve the idea of a causal relationship between the employment and the injury, while the term "in the course of" relates more particularly to the time, place and circumstances under which the injury occurred. The phrases are not synonymous; where both are used conjunctively a double condition has been imposed, and both terms must be satisfied in order to bring a case within the act. Queen City Furn. Co. v. Hinds, 274 Ala. 584, 150 So. 2d 756 (1963).

The phrases "arising out of" and "in the course of" are not synonymous and where, as in this section, they are used conjunctively, a double condition has been imposed and both terms must be satisfied in order to put an injury under the coverage of the workmen's compensation law. Anderson v. Custom Caterers, Inc., 279 Ala. 360, 185 So. 2d 383 (1966).

Lunch breaks, whether compensated or not, are periods of activity instrumental to employment just as would be a coffee break or a visit to the toilet, and when taken on the employer's premises in an area provided for

that purpose, either expressly or impliedly, they may reasonably be assumed to be of some benefit or advantage to the employer in the operation of its business or the advancement of its interest. Gold Kist, Inc. v. Jones, 537 So. 2d 39 (Ala. Civ. App. 1988).

Where the employee was on his lunch break, and as was customary he was eating his lunch on his car hood in the parking lot, and while preparing to return to his work duties, the employee either pushed himself, or slipped, off the hood of his car and twisted his back and hip and ruptured a disc in his spine, his injury occurred on the premises during a lunch break and, thus, was in the course of his employment. Gold Kist, Inc. v. Jones, 537 So. 2d 39 (Ala. Civ. App. 1988).

Subdivision (9) of section 25-5-1 places a limitation upon the phrase of "arising out of and in the course of his employment," contained in this section. Russellville Gas Co. v. Duggar, 47 Ala. App. 661, 260 So. 2d 393 (1971).

Phrase refers to time, place and circumstances of accident. — The phrase "in the course of his employment" refers to the time, place and circumstances under which the accident took place. An injury to an employee arises in the course of his employment when it occurs within the period of his employment, at a place where he may reasonably be and while he is reasonably fulfilling the duties of his employment or engaged in doing something incident to it. Mobile Liners v. McConnell, 220 Ala. 562, 126 So. 626 (1930); Southern Cotton Oil Co. v. Bruce, 249 Ala. 675, 32 So. 2d 666 (1947); Wells v. Morris, 33 Ala. App. 497, 35 So. 2d 54 (1948); Baggett Transp. Co. v. Holderfield, 260 Ala. 56, 68 So. 2d 21 (1953); Foster v. Continental Gin Co., 261 Ala. 366, 74 So. 2d 474 (1954); Alabama Textile Prods. Corp. v. Grantham, 263 Ala. 179, 82 So. 2d 204 (1955); Anderson v. Custom Caterers, Inc., 279 Ala. 360, 185 So. 2d 383 (1966); Riley v. Perkins, 282 Ala. 629, 213 So. 2d 796 (1968); Kennedy v. Cochran ex rel. Cochran, 475 So. 2d 872 (Ala. Civ. App. 1985).

And is narrower than "while employed". — "While employed" covers a wider field than "arising out of and in the course of his employment." Central of Ga. R.R. v. Rush, 286 Ala. 333, 239 So. 2d 763 (1970).

The following criteria are considered in determining whether an activity is within the course of employment: (1) the customary nature of the activity, (2) the employer's encouragement or subsidization of the activity, (3) the extent to which the employer managed or directed the activity, (4) the presence of substantial pressure or actual compulsion upon the employee to attend and participate, (5) the fact that the employer expects or receives a benefit from the employees' participation in the activity. The foregoing enumeration is not exclusive of other factors which might appear in a given case. What is required in each case is an evaluation of the significance of each factor found to be present in relation to the enterprise as a whole. Kennedy v. Cochran ex rel. Cochran, 475 So. 2d 872 (Ala. Civ. App. 1985).

Injuries compensable where acts incident to employment and benefit employer. — In general, injuries which occur while an employee is acting solely for his own benefit and where his acts are not incident to his employment are not compensable. However, where the acts of the employee are incident to the employment or where there is a benefit to the employer, compensation may be awarded. Lauderdale County Coop. v. Shook, 376 So. 2d 199 (Ala. Civ. App.), cert denied, 376 So. 2d 202 (Ala. 1979).

Injury must be due to employment. — Both the American and British courts hold that, for an injury to arise "out of and in the course of" the employment, the accident must, in some sense, be due to the employment. McLaughlin v. Davis Lumber Co., 220 Ala. 440, 125 So. 608 (1929).

And the phrase "arises out of" employment refers to employment as the cause and source of the accident. Garrett v. Gadsden Cooperage Co., 209 Ala. 223, 96 So. 188 (1923); Southern Cotton Oil Co. v. Bruce, 249 Ala. 675, 32 So. 2d 666 (1947); Wells v. Morris, 33 Ala. App. 497, 35 So. 2d 54 (1948); Alabama Pipe Co. v. Wofford, 253 Ala. 610, 46 So. 2d 404 (1950); Anderson v. Custom Caterers, Inc., 279 Ala. 360, 185 So. 2d 383 (1966).

The phrase "arising out of" employment denotes employment as the source and cause of the accident. In order to satisfy this requisite the rational mind must be able to trace the resultant injury to a proximate cause set in motion by the employment and not otherwise. Alabama Pipe Co. v. Wofford, 253 Ala. 610, 46 So. 2d 404 (1950); Wooten v. Roden, 260 Ala. 606, 71 So. 2d 802 (1954); Williams v. Tennessee Valley Butane Co., 265 Ala. 145, 90 So. 2d 84 (1956); Southern Cotton Oil Co. v. Wynn, 266 Ala. 327, 96 So. 2d 159 (1957).

For an accident "to arise out of employment" the employment must have been the cause and source of the accident and the resultant injuries must be traceable to a proximate cause set in motion by the employment, not by some other agency. Foster v. Continental Gin Co., 261 Ala. 366, 74 So. 2d 474 (1954); Alabama Textile Prods. Corp. v. Grantham, 263 Ala. 179, 82 So. 2d 204 (1955).

To justify recovery under the Alabama act, the particular employment must be the cause and source of the accident. Collins v. Central Foundry Co., 263 F.2d 712 (5th Cir. 1959).

This section expresses intent that the injury or death suffered by an employee be the natural and proximate cause of an action arising from the employment. Lankford v. Redwing Carriers, Inc., 344 So. 2d 515 (Ala. Civ. App.), cert. denied, 344 So. 2d 522 (Ala. 1977).

And not that the injury must be one which ought to have been foreseen, but it must be one which, after the event, may be seen to have had its origin in the nature of the employment. Tiger Motor Co. v. Winslett, 278 Ala. 108, 176 So. 2d 39 (1965).

And the injury is included within the statute if there is some causal relation between the employment and the injury. Tiger Motor Co. v. Winslett, 278 Ala. 108, 176 So. 2d 39 (1965).

Generally, an injury arises out of an employment only when there is a causal connection between the injury and the conditions under which the work is required to be performed. Wooten v. Roden, 260 Ala. 606, 71 So. 2d 802 (1954).

Where servant, employed to do certain service, is injured in performance of different service voluntarily undertaken by him, master is not liable for compensation for his resulting death. Morgan v. City of Guntersville, 239 Ala. 669, 196 So. 877 (1940), holding that evidence sustained trial court's finding that servant was acting outside course of his employment at time of fatal injury.

In order to show that an injury arose out of his employment, an employee must establish a definite causal connection between his employment and his injury. It is not enough to show that the injury would not have occurred "but for" the employment. Pope v. Golden Rod Broilers, Inc., 539 So. 2d 313 (Ala. Civ. App. 1989).

A traveling salesman who was injured during his lunch break alongside a gravel road was within the course of employment at the time of the accident. Young v. Mutual Sav. Life Ins. Co., 541 So. 2d 24 (Ala. Civ. App. 1989).

But where a voluntary act is acquiesced in by the employer, and an accident results from such voluntary act, it may be said to arise "out of and in the course of" the employment. Fair Park Amusement Co. v. Kimbrough, 221 Ala. 488, 129 So. 275 (1930).

And injury contemplated by act must have had its origin in some risk of the employment. It must arise out of and in the course of the employment or be incident thereto. A risk is incident to the employment when it belongs to or is connected with the duties a workman has to perform under his contract of service. It is not enough that the injured person may be present at the place of the accident because of his work, unless the injury is the result of some risk of the employment. Wooten v. Roden, 260 Ala. 606, 71 So. 2d 802 (1954); Russellville Gas Co. v. Duggar, 47 Ala. App. 661, 260 So. 2d 393 (1971).

Question is whether employment specially subjected employee to hazard. — In determining whether the injury is one arising out of employment the question is whether the employment specially subjected the employee to a hazard of the sort causing injury and one which might be supposed would be a natural consequence of it. United Serv. Ins. Co. v. Donaldson, 254 Ala. 204, 48 So. 2d 3 (1950).

Claimant's injury may be said to "arise out of" his employment when it had its origin in some risk of the employment. Lauderdale County Coop. v. Shook, 376 So. 2d 199 (Ala. Civ. App.), cert. denied, 376 So. 2d 202 (Ala. 1979).

And if the hazard of accident was peculiar to the employment as a contributing cause and flowed from that as a rational consequence, it was within the protective scope of the statute. Alabama Pipe Co. v. Wofford, 253 Ala. 610, 46 So. 2d 404 (1950).

Causation consists of two distinct tests: legal and medical, and both of these tests must be satisfied before the employment can be said to have caused the injury. The legal test requires that the employee demonstrate that in the performance of the duties of the job, the employee is exposed to a danger or risk materially in excess of that to which people not so employed are exposed. The medical test requires the employee to demonstrate that the exertion or strain or the exposure to conditions was, in fact, a contributing cause of the injury. Fordham v. Southern Phenix Textiles, Inc., 387 So. 2d 204 (Ala. Civ. App.), cert. denied, 387 So. 2d 206 (Ala. 1980); Ragland Brick Co. v. Campbell, 409 So. 2d 443 (Ala. Civ. App. 1982).

Once legal causation has been established, medical causation must be established through medical testimony. Stated differently, once the law has determined that an accident arose out of the employment, doctors must determine whether the accident caused the injury for which recovery is sought. Ragland Brick Co. v. Campbell, 409 So. 2d 443 (Ala. Civ. App. 1982).

Injury having origin in act benefiting employer compensable to employee acting in dual capacity. — Where an employee is acting in a dual capacity such as employee and customer and the employer derives a benefit from his actions, an injury having its origin in such act may be found to have arisen out of and in the course of employment. Lauderdale County Coop. v. Shook, 376 So. 2d 199 (Ala. Civ. App.), cert. denied, 376 So. 2d 202 (Ala. 1979).

Injury during trip where employee acting in dual capacity. — Where the employee is acting in a dual capacity, i.e., the employee's trip served the purposes of both herself and the employer, and the employer derives a benefit from her actions, an injury to the employee during the performance of such acts may be found to have arisen out of and in the course of employment. American Auto. Ins. Co. v. Hinote, 498 So. 2d 848 (Ala. Civ. App. 1986).

Pre-existing disease or infirmity of the employee does not qualify a claim under the "arising out of employment" requirement if the employment aggravated, accelerated or combined with the disease or infirmity to produce the death or disability for which compensation is sought. Southern Cotton Oil Co. v. Wynn, 266 Ala. 327, 96 So. 2d 159 (1957).

And claimant must establish logical causal connection between work and injury. — In order to show that the injury was caused by an accident arising out of employment, the plaintiff must establish a logical causal connection between his work and the injury. Southern Cotton Oil Co. v. Wynn, 266 Ala. 327, 96 So. 2d 159 (1957).

Excessive exposure to common hazard. — The harmful condition does arise out of the employment, if, in the performance of the duties for which he was engaged, in the manner required or contemplated by the employer, it is necessary for the employee to expose himself to a danger, materially in excess of that to which people commonly in that locality are exposed, when not situated as he is when thus performing his service, and that such excessive exposure may be found to have been the direct cause of the injury, though operating upon other conditions of common exposure. Alabama Pipe Co. v. Wofford, 253 Ala. 610, 46 So. 2d 404 (1950).

The rule which can be drawn from the cases is that when an injury to an employee results from exposure the injury cannot be regarded as arising out of his employment unless he is subjected to unusual risk and excessive exposure because of the nature of his work. However, the court has limited application of this rule to injuries resulting from exposure. Gulf States Steel Co. v. Christison, 228 Ala. 622, 154 So. 565 (1934) (heat exhaustion); Pow v. Southern Constr. Co., 235 Ala. 580, 180 So. 288 (1938) (pneumonia resulting from exposure to cold and dampness); Pullman-Standard Car

Mfg. Co. v. Lively, 239 Ala. 684, 196 So. 870 (1940) (heat exhaustion); Southern Cotton Oil Co. v. Wynn, 266 Ala. 327, 96 So. 2d 159 (1957).

Perils of street or highway. — In the case of workmen whose duties require them to be continually or frequently in or upon the street or highway and who are injured as a result thereof, the injury is one arising out of their employment. United Serv. Ins. Co. v. Donaldson, 254 Ala. 204, 48 So. 2d 3 (1950).

Strain or exertion. — Where the proximate cause of the plaintiff's injury was the strain or exertion of his work (as distinguished from exposure), a finding by the trial court that the plaintiff had been subjected to unusual strain or overexertion is not necessary to support a conclusion that the injury was caused by an accident arising out of his employment. Southern Cotton Oil Co. v. Wynn, 266 Ala. 327, 96 So. 2d 159 (1957).

Where the circumstances of the plaintiff's injury, considered in conjunction with the medical testimony, supported a fair inference that his cerebral hemorrhage was caused by the exertion of his work, the finding of the trial court awarding compensation must be sustained. Southern Cotton Oil Co. v. Wynn, 266 Ala. 327, 96 So. 2d 159 (1957).

Brain tumor aggravated by accidental injury. — While testimony of a brain specialist tended to show that the employee's death was due to the inexorable progress of a brain tumor, there was other medical testimony that the employee's injury aggravated his condition and was a proximate contributing cause of his death, and the evidence was held sufficient to support the award. Braswell v. Brooks, 266 Ala. 141, 94 So. 2d 879 (1957).

Employment is not limited to the actual time employee begins or ceases work. — The rule is that employee's death is not compensable if sustained while going to or from some point not visited for discharge of duty arising out of employment, or while in use of public highway used by public generally, but is subject to exception that the employment includes reasonable time, space and opportunity before and after actual work while employee is at or near place of employment. Exchange Distrib. Co. v. Oslin, 229 Ala. 547, 158 So. 743 (1935).

Work must be reasonably necessary or related for proper performance of duties. — Whether work being done by employee when injured was reasonable necessity in proper performance of his ordinary duties, or reasonably related thereto, and done in good faith in furtherance of employer's business, are tests for determining whether injury is one arising out of employment within workmen's

compensation law. Vickers v. Alabama Power Co., 218 Ala. 107, 117 So. 650 (1928); Hamilton Motor Co. v. Cooner, 254 Ala. 422, 47 So. 2d 270 (1950).

The firmly established principle is, based of course upon the theory of a liberal rather than a strict or narrow construction, that an employee's injury may be properly held to have arisen out of his employment notwithstanding that the act or conduct of the employee to which the injury is proximately referable was not within the scope of his authority nor strictly within the line of his duty, provided it was reasonably related to the service he was employed to render and was in good faith done or undertaken in furtherance of the employer's business; and notwithstanding, also, that the injury in question was not one of the anticipated risks of the service. Houser v. Young, 247 Ala. 562, 25 So. 2d 421 (1946); Foster v. Continental Gin Co., 261 Ala. 366, 74 So. 2d 474 (1954); Riley v. Perkins, 282 Ala. 629, 213 So. 2d 796 (1968).

Injury to street car cleaner while constructing tool box for his own tools and clothing with lumber dressing machine in workroom where his duties did not require his presence held not one arising out of his employment within workmen's compensation law, particularly in view of employer's statement that he could not have locker until one became vacant. Vickers v. Alabama Power Co., 218 Ala. 107, 117 So. 650 (1928).

It certainly would not comport with the beneficent purposes of the workmen's compensation law of Alabama to penalize a widow by holding that her husband was not obedient to a custom, if there were such a custom, in the performance of a service that was closely identified with or related to the activity he was employed to perform. Riley v. Perkins, 282 Ala. 629, 213 So. 2d 796 (1968).

Or naturally related to work for which employee was engaged. — Employee's injury arises out of and in the course of his employment when he is either doing the work or performing the services he was engaged to do or is engaged in an act or service naturally related thereto such as a reasonable judgment would refer to the express or implied elements of the contract of employment. Hamilton Motor Co. v. Cooner, 254 Ala. 422, 47 So. 2d 270 (1950).

Acts made necessary by emergency are within scope of employment. Performance of any act made necessary to employer's business by reason of emergency is within scope of employee's duty under Workmen's Compensation Act. Mobile Liners v. McConnell, 220 Ala. 562, 126 So. 626 (1930).

Workman disobeying a rule or order

which limits the sphere of employment cannot recover. Moss v. Hamilton, 234 Ala. 181, 174 So. 622 (1937).

In Sloss-Sheffield Steel & Iron Co. v. Jones, 220 Ala. 10, 123 So. 201 (1929), the employee had gone into the slope of the mine, a dangerous, unlighted and narrow place upon which trip cars were operated frequently and rapidly without lights, and which was forbidden to be used either to ride the trip cars or walk upon it. This prohibition was known to the employee, and the employer provided a walkway, called "man-way, " as a means of ingress and egress to and from the mine for the use of the employees. The court held that the employee had thus voluntarily placed himself in a prohibited zone of danger and outside the sphere of his employment. Moss v. Hamilton, 234 Ala. 181, 174 So. 622 (1937).

That sales manager, killed while unloading steel against instructions, deemed his act beneficial to employer, would not render employer liable under compensation statute. Cohen v. Birmingham Fabricating Co., 224 Ala. 67, 139 So. 97 (1932).

But may recover if the rule deals only with his misconduct within the sphere of his employment. Moss v. Hamilton, 234 Ala. 181, 174 So. 622 (1937). See Blocton Cahaba Coal Co. v. Campbell, 219 Ala. 529, 122 So. 806 (1929); Alabama Concrete Pipe Co. v. Berry, 226 Ala. 204, 146 So. 271 (1933).

Where employee, in violation of employer's rule, passed in harmony with this section, rode motor rather than car from a place near the entry of the mine to his working place, employee was not precluded from recovering workmen's compensation on ground that he had left the sphere of his employment, especially where violations of rule were constantly permitted by foreman in charge of men. Moss v. Hamilton, 234 Ala. 181, 174 So. 622 (1937).

That truck helper violated employer's rule in stepping off truck while moving, which resulted in his death, did not prevent recovery of compensation. Alabama Concrete Pipe Co. v. Berry, 226 Ala. 204, 146 So. 271 (1933).

Working by the day does not render such work casual. — Fact that employee was recently employed or was working by day instead of by job does not render employment casual and not in usual course of business or trade within Workmen's Compensation Act. Mobile Liners v. McConnell, 220 Ala. 562, 126 So. 626 (1930).

A traveling salesman who was injured during his lunch break alongside a gravel road was within the course of employment at the time of the accident. Young v. Mutual Sav. Life Ins. Co., 541 So. 2d 24 (Ala. Civ. App. 1989).

A traveling salesman who was injured during his lunch break when he fell into a roadside ditch while looking for blackberries was not eligible for benefits since the salesman's injuries did not arise out of his employment; he had departed on his own personal enterprise and his action was not necessary to his life, comfort, or convenience. Young v. Mutual Sav. Life Ins. Co., 541 So. 2d 24 (Ala. Civ. App. 1989).

Injury during lunch period. — Nourishment being essential to the continued efficiency of the employee in the performance of his work the courts have been liberal in protecting the workers during the lunch hour, and have almost unanimously concluded that where the employee is eating his lunch on the employer's premises that such lunch period is considered in the course of employment. Wells v. Morris, 33 Ala. App. 497, 35 So. 2d 54 (1948).

Plaintiff, because of his remoteness in the woods at the lunch hour and the limited time of the lunch period, had no choice as a practical matter but to eat in the woods where he was working. Such a situation not only suggested but invited the heating of coffee to accompany the eating under such circumstances. His employment was therefore a contributing cause to the injury he sustained (burns), and the injury was reasonably related to his employment. Wells v. Morris, 33 Ala. App. 497, 35 So. 2d 54 (1948).

Stepping aside to answer call of nature. — The death of a workman occurred during his hours of service and there were tendencies of the evidence going to show that he suffered from retention of urine and that he stepped aside to relieve himself and walked into the place where his body was found. Such act was not such as to warrant a holding, as a matter of law, that he had abandoned his work and was not entitled to compensation. Jackson v. Tennessee Coal, I. & R.R., 259 Ala. 85, 65 So. 2d 167 (1953).

Fall sustained while dancing at Christmas party. — An employee who was injured as a result of a fall which she sustained while dancing at a Christmas party given by her employer for its employees was not entitled to compensation because the accident which produced her injury "did not occur during the course of her employment." Anderson v. Custom Caterers, Inc., 279 Ala. 360, 185 So. 2d 383 (1966).

Where employee injured her back in picking up a 20 pound Christmas ham given to her by her employer, which injury occurred on the employer's premises, only a few minutes after work hours, and within a few feet of employee's normal working area, it was error for the court to grant employer's motion for summary judgment on grounds that the injury did not arise out of and in the course of employment. Moesch v. Baldwin County Elec. Membership Corp., 479 So. 2d 1271 (Ala. Civ. App. 1985).

Injury may be compensable even though employee had stepped aside from his usual work. — If the work being done at the time of the accident may properly be regarded as within the ordinary expectation or contemplation of the parties, as being necessary or proper for the employee to do, to aid in carrying out, either directly or indirectly, the main purpose or business of the employer, even though the workman steps aside from his usual work to do it, the accident may be said to be one arising out of his employment. Foster v. Continental Gin Co., 261 Ala. 366, 74 So. 2d 474 (1954).

Cases illustrating injuries within scope of employment. — Death of employee by accidental discharge of pistol, in hands of member of crew of tug waiting to remove barge, while deceased was checking lumber being unloaded from latter, held to have arisen out of and in course of his employment, within Workmen's Compensation Act. Ex parte Rosengrant, 213 Ala. 202, 104 So. 409 (1925), aff'd, Rosengrant v. Harvard, 273 U.S. 664, 47 S. Ct. 454, 71 L. Ed. 829 (1927).

Broken arm sustained by employee engaged to cut and haul props on mine company's land, when hauling timber for purpose of stacking is within "scope of employment" and compensable. Stith Coal Co. v. Alvis, 224 Ala. 603, 141 So. 663 (1932).

Injury to employee who slipped on sidewalk just outside only entrance to employer's premises just before time to start to work held to "arise out of and in the course of employment." Barnett v. Britling Cafeteria Co., 225 Ala. 462, 143 So. 813 (1932).

That truck helper left disabled truck to go after drink of water did not remove him from "course of employment." Alabama Concrete Pipe Co. v. Berry, 226 Ala. 204, 146 So. 271 (1933).

Employee suffered heat exhaustion while working near machines. Gulf States Steel Co. v. Christison, 228 Ala. 622, 154 So. 565 (1934).

Evidence that night watchman, employed to protect property against trespassers and permitted to sleep on premises, was found unconscious with crushed skull near office in which safe was located on morning after a robbery and that he died on day after robbery, warranted award of compensation on ground that death was caused by accident "arising out of and in the course of employment." Howard Odorless Cleaners v. Belvins, 237 Ala. 210, 186 So. 141 (1939).

In Valley Coal & Lumber Co. v. Hopkins, 32 Ala. App. 522, 27 So. 2d 700 (1946), it was held that undertakings of lumber company employee at time of injury in attempting to make surveyor's stake was reasonably related to the services which he was employed to perform and was in good faith an undertaking to act in furtherance of employer's business, thus injury sustained in so acting was compensable under the Workmen's Compensation Act.

Death of employee by accidental discharge of company's pistol, in hands of minor son of employee's immediate superior, while employee was on duty as night watchman, was held to have arisen out of and in the course of his employment within Workmen's Compensation Act. Southern Cotton Oil Co. v. Bruce, 249 Ala. 675, 32 So. 2d 666 (1947).

Deceased was acting within the course of his employment when he met his untimely end in traveling to inform wife of fellow employee that fellow employee would work overtime. Hamilton Motor Co. v. Cooner, 254 Ala. 422, 47 So. 2d 270 (1950).

In Wilson & Co. v. Curry, 259 Ala. 685, 68 So. 2d 548 (1953), it was held that an injury received while the employee was away from the place of employment on an errand for his superior arose out of and in the course of his employment.

Where an employee was injured while retrieving his cigarettes, which had fallen into a pit under the conveyor belt at which he worked, the injury arose out of and in the course of his employment. Natco Corp. v. Mallory, 262 Ala. 595, 80 So. 2d 274 (1955).

Evidence supported finding that employee died from "myelo radiculitis" caused by an accident which arose out of and in the course of his employment. Davis Lumber Co. v. Self, 263 Ala. 276, 82 So. 2d 291 (1955).

An employee, while changing his clothes before going to work in a place furnished employees for the purpose, got a catch in his back. It was held that his injury was one "arising out of or in the course of his employment." United States Steel Corp. v. Martin, 267 Ala. 634, 104 So. 2d 475 (1958).

Plaintiff's employment included reading meters, some of which were located on dirt roads that become muddy and slippery during and after rainstorms, and getting stuck is clearly a special hazard of that type employment. An act is incidental to employment when it is necessary to the life, comfort, or convenience of the employee, and [i]njuries which occur during the performance of such acts are compensable. It is clear that plaintiff's act of getting out of the stuck vehicle was necessary to his comfort or convenience. Alabama Power

Co. v. Mackey, 594 So. 2d 1238 (Ala. Civ. App. 1991).

Evidence sustained the finding of the lower court that employee did not die as a result of an accident arising out of and in the course of his employment. Collins v. Central Foundry Co., 263 F.2d 712 (5th Cir. 1959).

Where claimant sustained injury when struck by an automobile while alighting from a street car when on way from employer's main store to branch office under orders of employer to relieve other employees at branch office, claimant's injury "arose out of and in course of employment" and was compensable. Hardie Sales Co. v. Astrachan, 239 Ala. 558, 196 So. 135 (1940).

B. Employee Going to and from Work.

Generally employee is not protected when going to and from work. — Generally, employee injured while on way home or to work, or to place not required by duty to employer, is not covered by compensation act. Barnett v. Britling Cafeteria Co., 225 Ala. 465, 143 So. 813 (1932); Baggett Transp. Co. v. Holderfield, 260 Ala. 56, 68 So. 2d 21 (1953).

As a general rule, accidents occurring while an employee is traveling to and from work are not considered "arising out of and in the course of his employment." Bell v. General Am. Transp. Corp., 52 Ala. App. 123, 290 So. 2d 184 (1973).

But he is protected if he is at or near his place of employment. — Workman is within protection of compensation law while going to work or returning to his home, where injury occurs on master's premises or for a "reasonable time, space, and opportunity before and after while he is at or near his place of employment." Barnett v. Britling Cafeteria Co., 225 Ala. 462, 143 So. 813 (1932); Overton v. Belcher, 232 Ala. 396, 168 So. 442 (1936); Knight Iron & Metal Co. v. Ardis, 240 Ala. 305, 199 So. 716 (1940); Baggett Transp. Co. v. Holderfield, 260 Ala. 56, 68 So. 2d 21 (1953).

And he is protected when he is going to certain assigned work. — See Benoit Coal Mining Co. v. Moore, 215 Ala. 220, 109 So. 878 (1926).

But adjusting route to assigned work location not deviation outside scope of employment. — When travelling to certain assigned work at another location by direction of employer, employee's selection of route may be considered not to have deviated outside scope of employment where employee adjusted route to avoid unfavorable traffic conditions. Vulcan Materials Co. v. Belcher, 49 Ala. App. 61, 268 So. 2d 843 (1972).

Also when employer furnishes the transportation. — Where employer furnished auto transportation to and from servants' place of work, injury to employee while riding back from work held compensable under this section, as injury arising in "course of employment," because incident to and part of relation of master and servant, though subdivision (9) of § 25-5-1, provides injuries arising out of course of employment cover only those sustained on or about premises where services are performed. Jett v. Turner, 215 Ala. 352, 110 So. 702 (1926).

Injuries causing employee's death arise out of and in course of employment where employee was injured on master's premises while leaving place of employment at end of day's services on master's truck on which employees were permitted to ride to and from work. Overton v. Belcher, 232 Ala. 396, 168 So. 442 (1936).

Employee who was killed while en route home in employer's truck driven by co-employee was covered by the act where the evidence supported a finding that the transportation was a part of the business and that there was an implied contract that employees would be carried to and from their work. Ammons v. McClendon, 263 Ala. 651, 83 So. 2d 239 (1955).

Whether the transportation to and from work furnished by an employer to one in his employ is an incident of that employment is, when the evidence on the question is disputed, a question of fact dependent upon the particular circumstances of the case. United States Fid. & Guar. Co. v. Byrd, 273 Ala. 207, 137 So. 2d 743 (1962).

Another exception to the general rule is when the transportation constitutes a part of the consideration paid to the employee for his services. Bell v. General Am. Transp. Corp., 52 Ala. App. 123, 290 So. 2d 184 (1973).

If by contract, express or implied, the transportation constituted a part of the consideration paid or to be paid employee for his services, then, in that event, the mutual duties of employer and employee were being performed at the time of the accident and the workmen's compensation laws would be applicable. Bell v. General Am. Transp. Corp., 52 Ala. App. 123, 290 So. 2d 184 (1973).

Where an employee during his travel to and from work is engaged in some duty for the employer which is in furtherance of the employer's business, accidents occurring during such travel arise out of and in the course of the employment. Patterson v. Whitten, 57 Ala. App. 297, 328 So. 2d 301 (1976).

Accidents occurring during journeys arise out of and in the course of employment if the trip involves performance of a service for the employer which would have necessitated a trip by someone if the employee had been unable to perform that service in connection with his personal journey. Patterson v. Whitten, 57 Ala. App. 297, 328 So. 2d 301 (1976).

If a journey is considered as having both a business and a personal purpose, the business purpose is such that an accident on that journey arose out of and in the course of the employment. Patterson v. Whitten, 57 Ala. App. 297, 328 So. 2d 301 (1976).

Where travel is an incidental part of the service performed by the employee an injury occurring while the employee is traveling arises out of and is in the course of his employment. Bell v. General Am. Transp. Corp., 52 Ala. App. 123, 290 So. 2d 184 (1973).

Assault by striking employee. — In Baggett Transp. Co. v. Holderfield, 260 Ala. 56, 68 So. 2d 21 (1953), it was held that injuries received when the employee was on his way home and was assaulted by a striking employee were in the course of employment.

Travel to receive pay was held to be in the course of employment; therefore, employee's injury in auto accident resulted from a work-related accident, since the trip did not fall within the general rule that commuting to and from work is not covered by the workmen's compensation laws. Oliver v. Faulkner Wood Co., 531 So. 2d 675 (Ala. Civ. App. 1988).

III. EMPLOYER-EMPLOYEE RELATIONSHIP.

Liberal statutory definitions of employer and employee control in incidents pertaining to workmen's compensation to the extent that they modify the common law governing master and servant. Hamilton Motor Co. v. Cooner, 254 Ala. 422, 47 So. 2d 270 (1950).

"Employment" relationship exists when one employs another to perform service for hire, and to whom employer directly pays wages. Stith Coal Co. v. Alvis, 224 Ala. 603, 141 So. 663 (1932).

Where plaintiff was directly paid fixed prices by mine company for cutting and hauling certain props from company's land he was held to be an "employee" of company within this section. Stith Coal Co. v. Alvis, 224 Ala. 603, 141 So. 663 (1932).

And person is deemed "master" who has supreme choice, control and direction of servant, and whose will servant represents, not merely in ultimate result of work, but in all its details. North Ala. Motor Express v. Whiteside, 27 Ala. App. 223, 169 So. 335 (1936); United States Steel Corp. v. Mathews, 261 Ala. 120, 73 So. 2d 239 (1954); Jeffrey Mfg. Co. v. Hannan, 268 Ala. 262, 105 So. 2d 672 (1958).

Employee of motor freight company employed to pick up and deliver freight at local stations and perform odd jobs on instructions of local manager to whose control he was subject held "servant" and not "independent contractor," so as to be entitled to compensation for injuries received in course of employment, notwithstanding that employee used his own truck and furnished additional labor necessary in performing service. North Ala. Motor Express v. Whiteside, 27 Ala. App. 223, 169 So. 335 (1936); United States Steel Corp. v. Mathews, 261 Ala. 120, 73 So. 2d 239 (1954).

Determining factor is reserved right of control. — The factor determining whether relationship is employee or independent contractor is the reserved right of control rather than the actual exercise of such control. Riddle v. Smith, 252 Ala. 369, 41 So. 2d 288 (1949); Tidwell v. Walker County Mining & Inv. Co., 256 Ala. 574, 56 So. 2d 641 (1952); United States Steel Corp. v. Mathews, 261 Ala. 120, 73 So. 2d 239 (1954); Jeffrey Mfg. Co. v. Hannah, 268 Ala. 262, 105 So. 2d 672 (1958); Weeks v. C.L. Dickert Lumber Co., 270 Ala. 713, 121 So. 2d 894 (1960).

For one to be an employee, the other party must retain the right to direct the manner in which the business shall be done, as well as the result to be accomplished or, in other words, not only what shall be done, but how it shall be done. Greenwald v. Russell, 233 Ala. 502, 172 So. 895 (1937); Weeks v. C.L. Dickert Lumber Co., 270 Ala. 713, 121 So. 2d 894 (1960); Stewart v. Baker's Ice Cream Co., 272 Ala. 147, 130 So. 2d 42 (1961).

And employee's helpers are also employees. — If an employee, within the meaning of this section, has to have helpers, the latter are also employees of the employer for compensation purposes. Riddle v. Smith, 252 Ala. 369, 41 So. 2d 288 (1949).

Expert machinist as employee. — Expert machinist who was employed by the hour on special job to repair compress company's broken-down compress and, at time of injuries, was working on company's premises in cooperation with its superintendent, held "employee," not original "contractor," and hence was entitled to compensation. Tuscaloosa Compress Co. v. Hagood, 229 Ala. 284, 156 So. 633 (1934).

Employee in service of general employer may be transferred and become employee of special employer. — It is a well-recognized fact that one may be in the service of a general master and nevertheless with respect to particular work may be transferred to the service of another in such a way that he becomes for the time being the servant of the special master. Martin v. Anniston Foundry Co., 259 Ala. 633, 68 So. 2d 323 (1953), and authorities there cited. See also Jeffrey Mfg. Co. v. Hannah, 268 Ala. 262, 105 So. 2d 672 (1958).

An employee may be in the general service of another, and, nevertheless, with respect to particular work, may be transferred, with his own consent or acquiescence, to the service of a third person, so that the employee becomes the servant of such third person with all the legal consequences of the new relation. Counts v. Monsanto Co., 278 F. Supp. 655 (N.D. Ala. 1966).

Question arises, in considering loaned servant doctrine, as to what is meant by "control." It is said that there must be careful distinguishing "between authoritative direction and control, and mere suggestion as to details or the necessary cooperation, where the work furnished is part of a large undertaking." And the fact that the borrower gives information and directions to the servant as to details of work or the manner of doing it does not make the general servant of the employer the servant of such other person. United States Steel Corp. v. Mathews, 261 Ala. 120, 73 So. 2d 239 (1954); Jeffrey Mfg. Co. v. Hannah, 268 Ala. 262, 105 So. 2d 672 (1958).

General employer must suspend relationship with employee to be relieved. — In order to relieve the general master from the legal relation of master and servant, it must appear that that relation for the time had been suspended, and a new relation between the servant and the special master had been created. In the absence of evidence to the contrary, there is an inference that the servant remains in his general employment so long as, by the service rendered another, he is performing the business entrusted to him by the general employer. United States Steel Corp. v. Mathews, 261 Ala. 120, 73 So. 2d 239 (1954).

In order to relieve the general master from the legal relationship of master and servant, it must appear that that relation, for the time, had been suspended, and a new like relation between the servant and the special master had been created. Counts v. Monsanto Co., 278 F. Supp. 655 (N.D. Ala. 1966).

And there must be consensual relationship to transfer employer-employee relationship. — It seems to be quite generally agreed that in order to transfer the employer-employee relationship from the general employer to the one to whom the employee is loaned there must be some consensual relationship between the loaned employee and the employer whose service he enters sufficient to create a new employer-employee relationship. Where an employee enters the service of another at the command and pursuant to the direction of the master, no new relationship is necessarily created, particularly where the employee was assured of his continuing status as an employee of the general employer and was given the new assignment for the purpose of becoming better equipped to perform services for the general employer. Jeffrey Mfg. Co. v. Hannah, 268 Ala. 262, 105 So. 2d 672 (1958).

There must be some consensual relationship between the loaned employee and the employer whose service he enters sufficient to create a new employer-employee relationship. Counts v. Monsanto Co., 278 F. Supp. 655 (N.D. Ala. 1966).

Whether new relationship created question of fact. — Whether one who is usually and normally the servant of one master has become specially and temporarily the servant of another is ordinarily a question of fact. If under the circumstances only one inference can properly be drawn, the court will determine it, but if reasonable men may fairly come to different conclusions respecting the inference to be drawn from the fact, the case will be one for the jury. Jeffrey Mfg. Co. v. Hannah, 268 Ala. 262, 105 So. 2d 672 (1958).

By answering whose work was the servant doing and under whose control was he doing it will the result be determined in such a case. United States Steel Corp. v. Mathews, 261 Ala. 120, 73 So. 2d 239 (1954); Jeffrey Mfg. Co. v. Hannah, 268 Ala. 262, 105 So. 2d 672 (1958).

Considerations when evidence does not establish who employer is. — Where the evidence does not clearly establish who the employer is, consideration must be given to the character of the service to be rendered, the duration of employment and the one who is paying the employee. United States Steel Corp. v. Mathews, 261 Ala. 120, 73 So. 2d 239 (1954).

It is only where the evidence does not clearly establish who the employer is that consideration must be given to the character of service to be rendered, the duration of the employment and the one who is paying the employee, and then these factors are merely aids in determining the relation and do not necessarily determine the relationship. Counts v. Monsanto Co., 278 F. Supp. 655 (N.D. Ala. 1966).

Where nature of employment is controlled by contract. — Rule that, in determination of liability, question of nature of employment is controlled by circumstances without regard to expression in contract under workmen's compensation law, is inapplicable, where there is no connection between contractor and alleged employer, and rule will not be given strained construction to give consideration to evidence having no bearing on case. W.P. Brown & Sons Lumber Co. v. Yarbrough, 27 Ala. App. 229, 169 So. 337 (1936).

Compensation law does not apply where the injured person is an independent contractor, and the relation of employer and employee does not exist. It is not possible to lay down a hard and fast rule or state definite facts by which the status of men working and contracting together can be definitely defined in all cases as employee or independent contractor. Each case must depend on its own facts. Ordinarily, no one feature of the relation is determinative, but all must be considered together. Birmingham Post Co. v. Sturgeon, 227 Ala. 162, 149 So. 74 (1933); Stewart v. Baker's Ice Cream Co., 272 Ala. 147, 130 So. 2d 42 (1961).

Partner cannot be an employee of his partnership for the purposes of workmen's compensation. Ford v. Mitcham, 53 Ala. App. 102, 298 So. 2d 34 (1974).

In view of the present state of the law concerning partnerships, the court cannot hold that a working partner is entitled to benefits under the Workmen's Compensation Act. Ford v. Mitcham, 53 Ala. App. 102, 298 So. 2d 34 (1974).

Ice cream vendor, whose name appeared neither on alleged employer's payroll nor application for workmen's compensation insurance, who was subject to no control or suspension while on his assigned route, and whose sole compensation was the difference between the price at which he purchased the confections on one day's credit and that at which he sold it was an independent contractor to whom the compensation law did not apply. Stewart v. Baker's Ice Cream Co., 272 Ala. 147, 130 So. 2d 42 (1961).

IV. ACCIDENT.

Under this section the employer is liable for injuries from accidents to employees arising out of and in the course of their employment. The statute is concerned to afford protection against accidental results. In the sense of the statute, broadly speaking, the employment itself is the means of the accident and the employment, of course, is never accidental. New River Coal Co. v. Files, 215 Ala. 64, 109 So. 360 (1926); Pow v. Southern Constr. Co., 235 Ala. 580, 180 So. 288 (1938); Adkins v. Metropolitan Life Ins. Co., 235 Ala. 417, 179 So. 382 (1938).

And injury must result proximately from an accident. — The law requires that disease or death for which compensation is sought result proximately from an accident. Pow v. Southern Constr. Co., 235 Ala. 580, 180 So. 288 (1938).

If the job caused the injury, it was "by accident" within the intent of the section. Causation has two parts, a legal part and a

medical part. If, in the performance of the duties of the job, an employee is exposed to a danger or risk materially in excess of that to which people not so employed are exposed, and an injury occurs, such injury may be legally determined to have arisen from the job and be termed an accident. It then must be determined whether the medical test of causation can be shown: that the conditions, dangers or risks on the job precipitated or contributed to the injury. Newman Bros. v. McDowell, 354 So. 2d 1138 (Ala. Civ. App.), cert. denied, 354 So. 2d 1142 (Ala. 1977).

Unusual strain or exertion not ordinary to the job is not required to be shown. Newman Bros. v. McDowell, 354 So. 2d 1138 (Ala. Civ. App.), cert. denied, 354 So. 2d 1142 (Ala. 1977).

No preexisting condition where employee able to perform work duties in normal manner. — An employee able to perform his work duties in a normal manner prior to time of the disabling injury has no preexisting condition for compensation purposes. Alabama Power Co. v. Mackey, 594 So. 2d 1238 (Ala. Civ. App. 1991).

Actual aggravation of existing infirmity compensable. — An actual aggravation of an existing infirmity, caused by an accident in the course of employment, is compensable even though the accident would have caused no injury in a normal person. Mitchell Motor Co. v. Burrow, 37 Ala. App. 222, 66 So. 2d 198 (1953).

Fact that the workman had preexisting disease does not affect an award of compensation if the job combined with the disease to produce the death. Newman Bros. v. McDowell, 354 So. 2d 1138 (Ala. Civ. App.), cert. denied, 354 So. 2d 1142 (Ala. 1977).

Heart attacks may be caused by accidents within the meaning of the statute when the employee is shown to have been engaged in strenuous activity connected with his employment prior to or at the time of the fatal attack. Reynolds Metals Co. v. Gray, 278 Ala. 309, 178 So. 2d 87 (1965).

Back injuries held caused by accident. — Evidence supported a finding that a back injury was caused by an "accident" within the meaning of our compensation law, although there was no finding of a fall, slip or blow or that the injury resulted from unusual strain or exertion. Alabama Textile Prods. Corp. v. Grantham, 263 Ala. 179, 82 So. 2d 204 (1955); Davis Lumber Co. v. Self, 263 Ala. 276, 82 So. 2d 291 (1955).

Injury from rupture of intervertebral disc held an accidental injury within the meaning of the Alabama Workmen's Compensation Act.

Dorsey Trailers, Inc. v. Weaver, 263 Ala. 229, 82 So. 2d 261 (1955).

Finding that injury caused by blow, etc., unnecessary to show injury caused "by accident". — Finding by the trial court that the injury was caused by a blow, slip, fall or that it resulted from any unusual strain or exertion is not necessary to support the conclusion that an injury was caused "by an accident" within the meaning of the workmen's compensation law. Reynolds Metals Co. v. Gray, 278 Ala. 309, 178 So. 2d 87 (1965).

Neither is it essential that an external traumatic injury occur. Reynolds Metals Co. v. Gray, 278 Ala. 309, 178 So. 2d 87 (1965).

Mental disorders and injuries. — Only those "accidents" in which some physical injury or harm to the body is produced should be held compensable. Therefore, the Alabama's Workmen's Compensation Act does not extend coverage to mental disorders or injuries that have neither produced nor been proximately caused by some physical injury to the body. Magourik v. UPS, 496 So. 2d 55 (Ala. Civ. App. 1986).

Injury resulting from willful or criminal assault not prevented from being "accidental". — The fact that an injury is the result of a willful or criminal assault upon the employee does not prevent the injury from being accidental within the meaning of Workmen's Compensation Act. Tiger Motor Co. v. Winslett, 278 Ala. 108, 176 So. 2d 39 (1965).

Absorption of paint fumes an accident. — The absorption of paint fumes over a two-day period constitutes an "accident" as that term is used in Alabama Workmen's Compensation Act, and thus employee's exclusive remedy was under the Workmen's Compensation Act. Kane v. South Cent. Bell Tel. Co., 368 So. 2d 3 (Ala. 1979).

"Accidents" illustrated. — Death of employee, slain by trespasser while engaged in discharge of his duty as night watchman, was "accidental" within meaning of Workmen's Compensation Act. McLaughlin v. Davis Lumber Co., 220 Ala. 440, 125 So. 608 (1929).

Death of grocery store employee from valvular heart disease accelerated by electric shock received while operating electric sausage grinder held compensable as "accident" within compensation law. Great Atl. & Pac. Tea Co. v. Davis, 226 Ala. 626, 148 So. 309 (1933).

Injuries to employee from working in an unventilated room filled with fumes, dust and small particles of chemical mixture, which did not appear suddenly and violently, but grew progressively worse, held not a "personal injury" but an "accident" within this section. Gentry v. Swann Chem. Co., 234 Ala. 313, 174 So. 530 (1937).

Where the duties of an engineer required long-continued exposure to wetting and chill of water accumulated in excavations materially in excess of exposure to which other people in locality were subject, death from pneumonia because of exposure resulted from an "accident" and was compensable under the workmen's compensation law. Pow v. Southern Constr. Co., 235 Ala. 580, 180 So. 288 (1938).

Death of employee, shot accidentally by minor son of his immediate superior, while he was on duty as night watchman, was "accidental" within the meaning of the Workmen's Compensation Act. Southern Cotton Oil Co. v. Bruce, 249 Ala. 675, 32 So. 2d 666 (1947).

Death of an employee from a ruptured aortic aneurysm was due to an accident where the court found that the rupture was caused by exertion and strain as the result of the employee running at a dog trot for a distance equivalent to two city blocks to a bathhouse and then taking a cold shower. Massey v. United States Steel Corp., 264 Ala. 227, 86 So. 2d 375 (1955).

Where the proximate cause of the plaintiff's injury was the strain or exertion of his work (as distinguished from exposure), a finding by the trial court that the plaintiff had been subjected to unusual strain or overexertion was not necessary to support a conclusion that the injury was caused by an accident arising out of his employment and compensable under our workmen's compensation statute. Reynolds Metals Co. v. Gray, 278 Ala. 309, 178 So. 2d 87 (1965).

If deceased, while engaged in work or heavy lifting, and great strain, with no evidence of chronic cough or other cause of hernia, suddenly develops it in a very acute and painful state, which continues unabated, and he dies the following day, it is not mere surmise or conjecture to find that his condition was produced by the nature of his work, but that it was so produced is rather a fair, if not conclusive, inference from those circumstances. Reynolds Metals Co. v. Gray, 278 Ala. 309, 178 So. 2d 87 (1965).

Plaintiff who was engaged in coal mining and was overcome by, and rendered unconscious as a result of, breathing carbon dioxide or carbon monoxide gas or both, suffered an accident within the meaning of the workmen's compensation law. Nason v. Jones, 278 Ala. 532, 179 So. 2d 281 (1965).

Mental disorders and injuries. — Only those "accidents" in which some physical injury or harm to the body is produced should be held compensable. Therefore, the Alabama's Workmen's Compensation Act does not extend coverage to mental disorders or injuries that have neither produced nor been proximately caused by some physical injury to the body. Magourik v. UPS, 496 So. 2d 55 (Ala. Civ. App. 1986).

Disability not due to accident. — Under testimony of electric refrigerator repairman that he did not consider that disability from breathing methyl chloride gas was due to accident, but that effect of breathing gas became noticeable gradually, disability held not compensable as resulting from "accident." Birmingham Elec. Co. v. Meacham, 27 Ala. App. 471, 175 So. 316 (1937).

Death caused by a heart attack because of alleged emotional strain when deceased saw another employee approaching him on the day following which the two had had a controversy was not an "accident." City of Jasper v. Sherer, 273 Ala. 356, 141 So. 2d 202 (1962).

V. PLEADING.

Compliance with the technical rules as to pleading is not required in actions under the Workmen's Compensation Act. Alabama Concrete Pipe Co. v. Berry, 226 Ala. 204, 146 So. 271 (1933); Randle v. Dumas, 229 Ala. 396, 157 So. 218 (1934); Sloss-Sheffield Steel & Iron Co. v. Watts, 236 Ala. 636, 184 So. 201 (1938); Humphrey v. Poss, 245 Ala. 11, 15 So. 2d 732 (1943); Consolidated Coal Co. v. Dill, 248 Ala. 5, 26 So. 2d 88 (1946); Gadsden Iron Works, Inc. v. Beasley, 249 Ala. 115, 30 So. 2d 10 (1947); Swift & Co. v. Rolling, 252 Ala. 536, 42 So. 2d 6 (1949); Herndon v. Slayton, 263 Ala. 677, 83 So. 2d 726 (1955); Southern Cotton Oil Co. v. Wynn, 266 Ala. 327, 96 So. 2d 159 (1957).

Pleading under the act was not intended to be "cast in the technical precision of the common law, or tested by the refined objections of hypercriticism." Ex parte Coleman, 211 Ala. 248, 100 So. 114 (1924); Ex parte National Pipe & Foundry Co., 213 Ala. 605, 105 So. 693 (1925); City of Foley v. Terry, 278 Ala. 30, 175 So. 2d 461 (1965); Gilmore v. Rust Eng'r Co., 45 Ala. App. 626, 235 So. 2d 673 (1970).

Technical rules of procedure are to be disregarded as far as practicable in workmen's compensation cases. Braswell v. Brooks, 266 Ala. 141, 94 So. 2d 879 (1957).

Compliance with technical rules and precision as to pleading is not required in actions under the workmen's compensation statutes. Riley v. Perkins, 282 Ala. 629, 213 So. 2d 796 (1968).

In action under Workmen's Compensation Act by the widow and children of a deceased employee, mistaken reference in complaint to employee as "plaintiff" instead of "plaintiff's intestate" was amendable and not objectionable in view of the fact that the case throughout was tried upon the sole theory that the action was for the death of the plaintiff's intestate. Sloss-Sheffield Steel & Iron Co. v. Watts, 236 Ala. 636, 184 So. 201 (1938).

The Minnesota court in State ex rel. London & Lancashire Guar. & Accident Co. of Can. v. District Court, 133 Minn. 402, 158 N.W. 615 (1916), speaking of the matter of procedure in the workmen's compensation law of that state (from which ours was largely borrowed), held in effect that if the real parties are before the court, it is immaterial who may have brought the action in the first instance. Humphrey v. Poss, 245 Ala. 11, 15 So. 2d 732 (1943).

But proceedings are clothed with all indicia of conventional action at law. — Under the law of this state, proceedings under this and the following sections of the Workmen's Compensation Act are clothed with all of the indicia of the conventional action at law. While compliance with the technical rules as to pleading is not required, a complaint appropriate to the right to recover thereunder is necessary to obtain its benefits; a defective complaint is subject to motion to dismiss; it is the duty of the trial court to enter a final judgment upon the pleadings and proof. Barrett v. Consolidated Coal Co., 65 F. Supp. 291 (N.D. Ala. 1946).

Complaint. — When an action is brought by an employee against the employer for injuries arising since the workmen's compensation law became effective, the complaint should conform to said law or else set up a state of facts showing the inapplicability of same and bringing it within the influence of the law upon which the complaint is grounded and upon which reliance is had for a recovery. Thompson Tractor Co. v. Cobb, 283 Ala. 100, 214 So. 2d 558 (1968).

Act seems designed to afford employer opportunity to ascertain nature of injury. — The Workmen's Compensation Act seems designed to eliminate the requirements of technical pleading but seems also designed to give to the employer full opportunity to ascertain the true nature of plaintiff's alleged injury. Semmes Nurseries, Inc. v. McVay, 279 Ala. 42, 181 So. 2d 331 (1965).

Complaint alleging breach of common-law duty. — Plaintiff in action for personal injuries, founded on alleged breach of common-law duty to furnish reasonably safe tools for servant's use, should aver facts which bring it within one of the exceptions of workmen's compensation law. Kaplan v. Sertell, 217 Ala. 413, 116 So. 112 (1928).

There is no necessity to specifically deny coverage of workmen's compensation law in a common-law action when the complaint is based upon the allegation that plaintiff is an invitee. Butler Mfg. Co. v. Standifer, 268 Ala. 181, 105 So. 2d 57 (1958).

Complaint for breach of common-law duty to provide reasonably safe place to work was held to show that the Workmen's Compensation Act did not apply. Foreman v. Dorsey Trailers, Inc., 256 Ala. 253, 54 So. 2d 499 (1951).

Employee bringing action ex delicto against employer must aver facts removing case from act. — If a complaint filed by an employee against his employer should be interpreted to state an action ex delicto, it would be defective in failing to aver facts that take it without the workmen's compensation law. Johnson v. Ralls, 286 Ala. 565, 243 So. 2d 673 (1971).

In an action under § 6-5-410, by a personal representative, proof that the relationship of master and servant existed between plaintiff's intestate and defendant at the time of the injuries that caused the death of the intestate has the effect of imposing on plaintiff the duty to aver facts which would bring the case within the exceptions of the workmen's compensation law. Johnson v. Ralls, 286 Ala. 565, 243 So. 2d 673 (1971).

Employee, in action against later employer, is not estopped by his answers in action against former employer. — Employer held not entitled to judgment in injured employee's compensation proceeding on theory of claimant's estoppel by his answers to interrogatories in action against former employer; later employer not being party to, interested in nor influenced in his conduct by, such action. Randle v. Dumas, 229 Ala. 396, 157 So. 218 (1934).

As injuries to employee presumably come under act. — Injuries to an employee, where the relation of employer and employee exists, presumably come under the workmen's compensation statutes. Johnson v. Ralls, 286 Ala. 565, 243 So. 2d 673 (1971).

Question whether employee's death was caused by accident within meaning of statute may be presented by record on appeal and brief (formerly bill of exceptions) setting out evidence before trial court. Great Atl. & Pac. Tea Co. v. Davis, 226 Ala. 626, 148 So. 309 (1933).

Amendment of complaint properly allowed. — See Southern Cotton Oil Co. v. Wynn, 266 Ala. 327, 96 So. 2d 159 (1957).

VI. EVIDENCE.

Burden of proof rests upon plaintiff to sustain the allegations of his complaint. Simpson v. Alabama Dry Dock & Shipbuilding Co., 269 Ala. 635, 114 So. 2d 918 (1959); Big "B"

Disct. Drugs, Inc. v. Parker, 401 So. 2d 115 (Ala. Civ. App. 1981).

In proceeding under the Workmen's Compensation Act, plaintiff must reasonably satisfy trial court that accident was within provisions of the act, and rational mind must be able to trace result in personal injury to a proximate cause set in motion by the employment, and not by some other agency. Ex parte Alabama Dry Dock & Shipbuilding Co., 213 Ala. 88, 104 So. 251 (1925); Ex parte Big Four Coal Mining Co., 213 Ala. 305, 104 So. 764 (1925); New River Coal Co. v. Files, 215 Ala. 64, 109 So. 360 (1926).

Claimant had burden of showing that employee's death was caused by accident arising out of and in course of his employment. McLaughlin v. Davis Lumber Co., 220 Ala. 440, 125 So. 608 (1929); Mobile Liners v. McConnell, 220 Ala. 562, 126 So. 626 (1930); Exchange Distrib. Co. v. Oslin, 229 Ala. 547, 158 So. 743 (1935); Emonds v. Standard Brands, 233 Ala. 315, 171 So. 751 (1937); Southern Cotton Oil Co. v. Wynn, 266 Ala. 327, 96 So. 2d 159 (1957).

The burden rested on the claimant to prove by competent evidence that the death of her husband resulted from a compensable injury, and only when it is shown that there is a causal connection between such injury and the conditions of hazard under which the work was required to be performed does liability attach. Alabama Pipe Co. v. Wofford, 253 Ala. 610, 46 So. 2d 404 (1950).

The burden was upon the plaintiff to present evidence sufficient to reasonably satisfy the trial court (1) that she suffered a personal injury; (2) that such personal injury was caused by an accident; and (3) that the accident which caused the personal injury arose out of and in the course of her employment. And there should have been an express finding by the trial court that each of those facts was established by the evidence. Alabama Textile Prods. Corp. v. Grantham, 263 Ala. 179, 82 So. 2d 204 (1955).

The burden was on plaintiff to reasonably satisfy the trial court by competent evidence (1) that her husband sustained a personal injury, (2) which was caused by an accident arising out of and in the course of his employment, and (3) to show by the same character of evidence a causal connection between the injury so received and death. Davis Lumber Co. v. Self, 263 Ala. 276, 82 So. 2d 291 (1955).

The burden is on the plaintiff to reasonably satisfy the trial court that the accident arose out of and in the course of the workman's employment. Tiger Motor Co. v. Winslett, 278 Ala. 108, 176 So. 2d 39 (1965); Kroger Co. v. Millsap, 280 Ala. 531, 196 So. 2d 380 (1967).

The burden of claimant was to present sufficient evidence to reasonably satisfy the trial court that the death of deceased was due to accident arising out of and in the course of his employment. Myers v. Juneman Elec. Co., 46 Ala. App. 529, 244 So. 2d 809 (1971).

Claimant was required to prove by competent evidence that the death of her husband was due to an accident proximately caused by the conditions and hazards of his employment. Myers v. Juneman Elec. Co., 46 Ala. App. 529, 244 So. 2d 809 (1971).

The burden of proof in workmen's compensation cases is upon the employee to reasonably satisfy the trial court by the evidence of the truth of the elements of the cause of action. Big "B" Disct. Drugs, Inc. v. Parker, 401 So. 2d 115 (Ala. Civ. App. 1981).

The claimant bears the burden of proving a causal connection between his work and his injuries to be compensable under the Alabama Workmen's Compensation Act. B.F. Goodrich Co. v. Skelton, 473 So. 2d 539 (Ala. Civ. App. 1985).

And burden is no less than in other actions. — The burden of proof on plaintiff in a workmen's compensation case, in spite of its benevolent purpose and liberality of rules of pleading, is no less than in any other action for compensation for injury or death. Myers v. Juneman Elec. Co., 46 Ala. App. 529, 244 So. 2d 809 (1971).

Decision upheld where any legal evidence supports findings. — In a workmen's compensation case, the decision of the trial court will be upheld upon review if there is any legal evidence to support the trial court's findings. Dees v. Daleville Florist, 408 So. 2d 155 (Ala. Civ. App. 1981); Ragland Brick Co. v. Campbell, 409 So. 2d 443 (Ala. Civ. App. 1982); Tidwell Indus., Inc. v. Kennedy, 410 So. 2d 109 (Ala. Civ. App. 1982).

The appellate court can consider neither the weight of the evidence nor the propriety of the trial court's finding of fact for its inquiry is limited to a determination of whether there is any evidence to support the trial court's finding. Tidwell Indus., Inc. v. Kennedy, 410 So. 2d 109 (Ala. Civ. App. 1982).

Where there is a conflict in the evidence as to whether the employee was reasonably fulfilling duties of his employment, the trial court's decision in this regard is conclusive, and all reasonable doubt in the evidence must be resolved in favor of the employee. Kennedy v. Cochran ex rel. Cochran, 475 So. 2d 872 (Ala. Civ. App. 1985).

Evidence held sufficient in Sloss-Sheffield Steel & Iron Co. v. House, 217 Ala. 422, 116 So. 167 (1928); Mobile Liners v. McConnell, 220 Ala. 562, 126 So. 626 (1930); Williams Bros. v. Staggs, 221 Ala. 625, 130 So. 334 (1930); W.T. Smith Lumber Co. v. Raines, 271 Ala. 671, 127 So. 2d 619 (1961); Kroger Co. v. Millsap, 280 Ala. 531, 196 So. 2d 380 (1967).

Evidence held to sustain judgment for compensation claimant on ground claimant was at time of injury employee of oil company, and not employee of official of oil company personally. Shell Petro. Corp. v. Lucas, 232 Ala. 654, 169 So. 291 (1936).

Evidence sustained finding that employee sustained accidental injury which arose out of and in the course of his employment and which proximately resulted in the loss of index finger of his left hand. Republic Steel Corp. v. Willis, 243 Ala. 127, 9 So. 2d 297 (1942).

Evidence held insufficient in Hearn v. United States Cast Iron Pipe & Foundry Co., 217 Ala. 352, 116 So. 365 (1928); Bullard v. Cullman Heading Co., 220 Ala. 143, 124 So. 200 (1929); Williams v. Tennessee Valley Butane Co., 265 Ala. 145, 90 So. 2d 84 (1956); Simpson v. Alabama Dry Dock & Shipbuilding Co., 269 Ala. 635, 114 So. 2d 918 (1959). See Simmons v. F.W. Dodge Corp., 270 Ala. 616, 120 So. 2d 921 (1960).

Evidence held insufficient to support judgment awarding employee of timber owner compensation for injuries against lumber company purchasing timber from owner on ground that employee was employed by lumber company. W.P. Brown & Sons Lumber Co. v. Yarbrough, 27 Ala. App. 229, 169 So. 337 (1936).

Testimony as to mere possibilities is generally insufficient to sustain an award under the workmen's compensation law. Davis Lumber Co. v. Self, 263 Ala. 276, 82 So. 2d 291 (1955).

And experts' opinions are not conclusive on triers of fact. — In compensation proceeding, experts' opinions are not conclusive on triers of fact, though uncontroverted, and may be disregarded unless the matter is one for experts only, and the triers of fact cannot be assumed to have or be able to form a correct opinion concerning such matter. Warrior Stone & Contracting Co. v. De Foor, 241 Ala. 227, 2 So. 2d 430 (1941).

In workmen's compensation proceedings experts' opinions are not conclusive on triers of facts even though uncontroverted. Pinto Island Metals Co. v. Edwards, 275 Ala. 351, 155 So. 2d 304 (1963); Kroger Co. v. Millsap, 280 Ala. 531, 196 So. 2d 380 (1967); Unexcelled Mfg. Corp. v. Ragland, 52 Ala. App. 57, 289 So. 2d 626 (1974).

But testimony of claimant himself is of probative value to trial court in determining disability even in the absence of medical testimony. Unexcelled Mfg. Corp. v. Ragland, 52 Ala. App. 57, 289 So. 2d 626 (1974).

New trial not awarded on evidence merely cumulative. Great Atl. & Pac. Tea Co. v. Davis, 226 Ala. 626, 148 So. 309 (1933).

But circuit court may set aside judgment, and re-examine facts, for good cause shown. Birmingham Clay Prods. Co. v. White, 226 Ala. 89, 145 So. 668 (1933).

It may proceed summarily in ascertaining facts. Birmingham Clay Prods. Co. v. White, 226 Ala. 89, 145 So. 668 (1933).

Circumstantial evidence is a recognized form of proof in compensation cases as in others. W.T. Smith Lumber Co. v. Raines, 271 Ala. 671, 127 So. 2d 619 (1961).

It is true that testimony as to mere possibilities is generally insufficient to sustain an award under the workmen's compensation law, and that the defendant cannot be guessed into liability. It is equally clear, however, that all of the essential facts in a workmen's compensation case, including the question of causal relation, can be proved by circumstantial evidence. Southern Cotton Oil Co. v. Wynn, 266 Ala. 327, 96 So. 2d 159 (1957).

Evidence of instruction given by employer to deceased employee not inadmissible under dead man's statute. — Evidence in a compensation case concerning giving of instruction by employer to deceased employee is not in inadmissible under § 12-21-163 (the dead man's statute), for the reason that an action under the Workmen's Compensation Act is purely statutory and the estate of the deceased is not interested in the results of the action. Boatright v. Dothan Aviation Corp., 278 Ala. 142, 176 So. 2d 500 (1965).

§ 25-5-32. Excluded defenses.

In all cases brought under this article, it shall not be a defense:

(1) That the employee was negligent, unless and except it shall also appear that such negligence was wilful or that such employee was guilty of wilful misconduct as defined in Section 25-5-51.

(2) That the injury was caused by the negligence of a fellow employee.

(3) That the employee had assumed the risks inherent in or incidental to the work, or arising out of his employment, or arising from the failure of the employer to provide and maintain safe premises and suitable appliances, which grounds of defense are hereby abolished. (Acts 1919, No. 245, p. 206; Code 1923, § 7535; Code 1940, T. 26, § 254.)

Cited in Sloss-Sheffield Steel & Iron Co. v. Nations, 236 Ala. 571, 183 So. 871 (1938); Gadsden Iron Works, Inc. v. Beasley, 249 Ala. 115, 30 So. 2d 10 (1947); B.F. Goodrich Co. v. Martin, 47 Ala. App. 244, 253 So. 2d 37 (1971).

Collateral references. — 58 Am. Jur., Workmen's Compensation, § 200 et seq.

Serious and wilful misconduct of employee as bar to compensation. 4 ALR 116.

Effect of employee's intoxication. 43 ALR 421.

Intoxicating liquors: employer's liability for furnishing or permitting liquor on social occasion, 51 ALR4th 1048.

Workers' compensation: injuries incurred during labor activity. 61 ALR4th 196.

Employer's liability to employee for failure to provide work environment free from tobacco smoke. 63 ALR4th 1021.

§ 25-5-33. Applicability of Sections 25-5-31 and 25-5-32 to other claims for personal injury or death.

The provisions of Sections 25-5-31 and 25-5-32 shall apply to any claims for death of an employee as covered by Sections 6-5-391, 6-5-410 and 25-6-3, and to personal injuries arising under Sections 6-5-390 and 25-6-1. (Acts 1919, No. 245, p. 206; Code 1940, T. 26, § 257; Acts 1973, No. 1062, p. 1750, § 3.)

Section makes sections 25-5-31 and 25-5-32 applicable to Employer's Liability Act. — This section makes §§ 25-5-31 and 25-5-32, which are part of the Workmen's Compensation Act, applicable to the Employer's Liability Act. Johnson v. Brinker, 289 Ala. 240, 266 So. 2d 851 (1972).

§ 25-5-34. Applicability of this article and Article 3 of chapter to minors; double compensation when minor illegally employed.

The provisions of this article and Article 3 of this chapter shall apply to employees who are minors and who have been employed in accordance with or contrary to laws regulating the employment of minors. If at the time of injury the minor was employed in violation of or contrary to the law regulating the employment or any part thereof, then the compensation shall be two times what it would be if the employment had been legal. (Acts 1919, No. 245, p. 206; Code 1923, § 7539; Acts 1931, No. 357, p. 415; Code 1940, T. 26, § 258.)

Policy of the law is determined by legislature. — Whether inclusion of minors, employed in violation of child labor law, §§ 25-8-1 through 25-8-30, within workmen's compensation law, by this section, is a wise or just policy, is for the legislature to determine, not the courts. Ivey v. Railway Fuel Co., 218 Ala. 407, 118 So. 583 (1928).

Employment contrary to child labor law does not remove employee from protection of Workmen's Compensation Act. Ward v. State Farm Mut. Auto. Ins. Co., 241 F.2d 134 (5th Cir. 1957).

But this section does not strike down, nor conflict with child labor law, §§ 25-8-1 through 25-8-30, which makes its violation a misdemeanor, and does not deal with civil remedies of injured child or representative of deceased child, employed in violation thereof, as in mine, contrary to § 25-8-2. Ivey v. Railway Fuel Co., 218 Ala. 407, 118 So. 583 (1928).

Violation of purely procedural statutes does not give right to additional compensation. — In view of the strict construction which is given penal provisions, and the fact that there appears to have been no legislative intent to apply the penalty in this section to the violation of purely procedural statutes, it is held that unless the employer has permitted or suffered the minor to work at an employment banned by the Child Labor Act, no right arises for additional compensation under this section. There must be some relationship between the act violated by the employer and the injury suffered by the minor employee. Willis v. Storey, 268 Ala. 205, 105 So. 2d 128 (1958).

And failure to have required employment certificate on file did not justify double compensation. — The failure of an employer to have on file an employment certificate for an employee between 16 and 17 years of age as required by § 25-8-13 was not such a violation of the Child Labor Act as would justify an award of double compensation under this section. Willis v. Storey, 268 Ala. 205, 105 So. 2d 128 (1958).

Whether employer-employee relationship exists is question for jury. — Whether relation of employer and employee existed between child and defendant company within provisions of workmen's compensation was held a question for the jury. Nichols v. Smith's Bakery, Inc., 218 Ala. 607, 119 So. 638 (1928).

In 16 year old boy's action against ice company for injuries sustained while riding on delivery truck on which the boy had taken part in delivery of ice, evidence whether boy was invitee, or was employee whose rights were governed by workmen's compensation statute, was for jury. Birmingham Ice & Cold Storage Co. v. McFarling, 240 Ala. 479, 200 So. 110 (1941).

Cited in Larry v. Taylor, 227 Ala. 90, 149 So. 104 (1933).

Collateral references. — 99 C.J.S., Workmen's Compensation, §§ 112-114.

58 Am. Jur., Workmen's Compensation, § 152.

Applicability and effect of workmen's compensation act in case of injury to minors. 14 ALR 818, 33 ALR 337, 49 ALR 1435, 60 ALR 847, 83 ALR 416, 142 ALR 1018.

Status of minor employed by parent as regards provision of workmen's compensation act relating to compensation thereunder. 132 ALR 1030.

Worker's compensation statute as barring illegally employed minor's tort action. 77 ALR4th 844.

§ 25-5-35. Recovery where accident occurs outside state; effect of compensation under law of another state, etc., upon compensation under this article and Article 3 of chapter, etc.; recovery under this article and Article 3 of chapter for accident occurring within state where employment principally localized outside state.

(a) As used in this section:

(1) The term "United States" includes only the states of the United States and the District of Columbia; and

(2) The term "state" includes any state of the United States or the District of Columbia.

(b) For the purposes of this section, a person's employment is principally localized in this or another state when his employer has a place of business in this or such other state and he regularly works at or from such place of business, or if he is domiciled and spends a substantial part of his working time in the service of his employer in this or such other state.

(c) An employee whose duties require him to travel regularly in the service of his employer in this and one or more other states may, by written agreement with his employer, provide that his employment is principally localized in this or another such state; and, unless such other state refuses jurisdiction, such agreement shall be given effect under this section.

(d) If an employee, while working outside of this state, suffers an injury on account of which he or, in the event of his death, his dependents, would have been entitled to the benefits provided by this article and Article 3 of this chapter had such injury occurred within this state, such employee or, in the event of his death resulting from such injury, his dependents, shall be entitled to the benefits provided by this article and Article 3 of this chapter, provided that at the time of such injury:

(1) His employment was principally localized in this state;

(2) He was working under a contract of hire made in this state in employment not principally localized in any state;

(3) He was working under a contract of hire made in this state in employment principally localized in another state whose workmen's compensation law was not applicable to his employer; or

(4) He was working under a contract of hire made in this state for employment outside the United States.

(e) The payment or award of benefits under the workers' compensation law of another state, territory, province or foreign nation to an employee or his dependents otherwise entitled on account of such injury or death to the benefits of this article and Article 3 of this chapter shall not be a bar to a claim for benefits under this article and Article 3 of this chapter; provided that claim under this article is filed within the time limits set forth in Section 25-5-80. If compensation is paid or awarded under this article and Article 3 of this chapter:

(1) The medical and related benefits furnished or paid for by the employer under such other workers' compensation law on account of such injury or death shall be credited against the medical and related benefits to which the employee would have been entitled under this article and Article 3 of this chapter had claim been made solely under this article and Article 3 of this chapter;

(2) The total amount of compensation paid or awarded the employee under such other workers' compensation law shall be credited against the total amount of compensation which would have been due the employee under this article and Article 3 of this chapter, had claim been made solely under this article and Article 3 of this chapter; and

(3) The total amount of death benefits paid or awarded under such other workers' compensation law shall be credited against the total amount of death benefits due under this article and Article 3 of this chapter.

(f) The recovery of any compensation benefits under the law of any other state shall bar any common-law or statutory right of action for damages that an employee or his dependents might otherwise have had against the employer or the officers, directors or employees of the employer as a result of the injury or death on account of which such compensation benefits were paid.

(g) If, as a result of an employment principally localized in another state, an employee of an employer who would have been subject to this article or Article 3 of this chapter, had the contract of employment been entered into in this state for performance in this state, suffers injury or death as a result of an accident occurring in this state, compensation and medical, surgical and hospital benefits on account of such injury or death may be recovered under this article or Article 3 of this chapter. (Acts 1919, No. 245, p. 206; Code 1923, § 7540; Code 1940, T. 26, § 259; Acts 1975, 4th Ex. Sess., No. 86, p. 2729, § 1.)

Principal localization of employment. — This section requires for principal localization of employment that employee be domiciled in Alabama and spend substantial part of his working time in Alabama; this implies a current, ongoing employment status where it is foreseeable that the employee will continue to spend a substantial part of his working time in this state. Seales ex rel. Seales ex rel. Seales v. Daniel Constr. Co., 469 So. 2d 629 (Ala. Civ. App. 1985).

The phrase "spends a substantial part of his working time in the service of his employer in this . . . state," which is set forth in subsection (b) of this section, implies a current, ongoing employment status where it is foreseeable that the employee will continue to spend a substantial part of his working time in this state. Mills v. Tri-State Motor Transit Co., 541 So. 2d 557 (Ala. Civ. App. 1989).

Mere quantity of time spent in any single state or locale in the past is not the control-

ling factor in a determination of the principal localization of employment. Seales ex rel. Seales v. Daniel Constr. Co., 469 So. 2d 629 (Ala. Civ. App. 1985).

Where all of the essential ingredients which usually precede an employment relationship, such as filling out an application for employment and completing the necessary payroll, tax and insurance forms, were all performed in Mississippi, as a matter of law the contract of employment was made in Mississippi. Seales ex rel. Seales v. Daniel Constr. Co., 469 So. 2d 629 (Ala. Civ. App. 1985).

Settlement of workmen's compensation claim in another state is not bar to an action in Alabama to determine right to and amount of benefits due under Alabama law. Sager v. Royce Kershaw Co., 359 So. 2d 398 (Ala. Civ. App. 1978).

Claimant, who had made settlement in release of claim in another state was entitled to further prosecute his suit in Alabama even though he had previously received payments in Illinois. Sager v. Royce Kershaw Co., 359 So. 2d 398 (Ala. Civ. App. 1978).

Workmen's compensation claimants whose homes were in Alabama were not eligible for benefits under Alabama law where they were hired by a transit company headquartered in Missouri, their work was not principally localized in Alabama and their contracts for hire were made in Missouri. Mills v. Tri-State Motor Transit Co., 541 So. 2d 557 (Ala. Civ. App. 1989).

Cited in St. Louis-San Francisco Ry. v. Carros, 207 Ala. 535, 93 So. 445 (1922); National Cast Iron Pipe Co. v. Higginbotham, 216 Ala. 129, 112 So. 734 (1927); Holcomb v. Arma, Inc., 575 So. 2d 575 (Ala. Civ. App. 1991).

Collateral references. — 99 C.J.S., Workmen's Compensation, § 24.

58 Am. Jur., Workmen's Compensation, § 70.

Extraterritorial operation of workmen's compensation of statutes; conflict of laws, 3 ALR 1351, 18 ALR 292, 28 ALR 1345, 35 ALR 1414, 45 ALR 1234, 59 ALR 735, 82 ALR 709, 90 ALR 119.

Award under workmen's compensation act as bar to or ground for reduction of claim under act of another state. 169 ALR 1185.

§ 25-5-36. Burden of proof as to misconduct of employee.

In all actions of law brought pursuant to this article, the burden of proof to establish the wilful misconduct or other misconduct as defined in Section 25-5-51, of the injured employee shall be upon the defendant. (Acts 1919, No. 245, p. 206; Code 1923, § 7541; Code 1940, T. 26, § 260.)

Collateral references. — 100 C.J.S., Workmen's Compensation, §§ 516-524, 547(1). 101 C.J.S., Workmen's Compensation, § 956.

58 Am. Jur., Workmen's Compensation, § 433.

Workers' compensation: injuries incurred during labor activity. 61 ALR4th 196.

Workers' compensation: injuries incurred while traveling to or from work with employer's receipts. 63 ALR4th 253.

Workers' compensation: effect of allegation that injury was caused by, or occurred during course of, worker's illegal conduct. 73 ALR4th 270.

ARTICLE 3.

ELECTIVE COMPENSATION UNDER CONTRACT OF EMPLOYMENT.

Lack of dependents did not entitle administratrix to bring civil action. — Fact that employee, whose death arose out of and in the course of his employment, had no dependents did not entitle administratrix of employee's estate to seek compensation by civil action against employer, even though maximum compensation benefits payable otherwise were medical expenses, burial expenses and payment to secondary trust fund. Holliday v. C.T. Thackston Sand & Gravel Co., 361 So. 2d 13 (Ala. Civ. App. 1978).

§ 25-5-50. This article and Article 2 not applicable to certain employments; exemption for corporate officer; when school boards to provide coverage; coverage for volunteer fire departments and rescue squads.

This article and Article 2 of this chapter shall not be construed or held to apply to an employer of a domestic employee; an employer of a farm laborer; an employer of a person whose employment at the time of the injury is casual and not in the usual course of the trade, business, profession, or occupation of the employer; an employer who regularly employs less than five employees in any one business, other than the business of constructing or assisting on-site in the construction of single-family, detached residential dwellings; or a

521

municipality having a population of less than 2,000 according to the most recent federal decennial census. An employer who regularly employs less than five employees in any one business; a farm-labor employer; an employer of a domestic employee; or a municipality having a population of less than 2,000 according to the most recent federal decennial census, may accept and become subject to this article and Article 4 of this chapter by filing written notice thereof with the Department of Industrial Relations, a copy thereof to be posted at the place of business of the employer; provided further, that an employer who has so elected to accept this article and Article 4 of this chapter may at any time withdraw the acceptance by giving like notice of withdrawal. Notwithstanding the foregoing, an employer electing not to accept coverage under this article and Article 4 of this chapter shall notify in writing each employee of the withdrawal of coverage. Additionally, the employer shall post a notice in a conspicuous place notifying all employees and applicants for employment that workers' compensation insurance coverage is not available.

Notwithstanding the foregoing paragraph, an officer of a corporation may elect annually to be exempt from coverage by filing written certification of the election with the department and the employer's insurance carrier.

At the end of any calendar year, a corporate officer who has been exempted, by proper certification from coverage, may revoke the exemption and thereby accept coverage by filing written certification of his or her election to be covered with the department and the employer's insurance carrier.

The certification for exemption or reinstatement of coverage shall become effective on the first day of the calendar month following the filing of the certification of exemption or reinstatement of coverage with the department.

If the corporate officer elects to be exempt from coverage, the election shall not relieve the employer from continuing coverage for all other eligible employees who may have been covered prior to the election or who may subsequently be employed by the firm.

This section shall not be construed to mandate any school board to provide coverage until sufficient funds are appropriated from the special educational trust fund to implement the provisions. Nothing contained herein shall prohibit any school board that voluntarily elects to provide such coverage from doing so with local or other available funds.

This section shall provide for voluntary coverage of certified volunteer fire departments as described in Section 9-3-17 and legally organized rescue squads that meet the minimum personnel and equipment standards as established by the Alabama Association of Rescue Squads, that are engaged in fighting a fire or performing other duties involving any emergency incident and while performing any official supervised duties of the organization, including maintaining equipment and attending official training classes, and while traveling to and from an emergency incident.

In all cases where an injury that is compensable under the terms of the Alabama workers' compensation law is received by a volunteer fire fighter or rescue squad member, the wages for purposes of computing the average weekly wage shall be equal to $66^2/_3$ percent of what he or she is earning at his or her regular place of employment or 66²/₃ percent of the minimum wage, whichever is greater.

State certified volunteer fire departments and legally organized rescue squads are herein granted the right to purchase workers' compensation medical or disability insurance, or both, but in no event are they required to do so.

In no event shall the regular employer of a volunteer fire fighter or rescue squad member be liable for a compensable injury under this section. (Code 1923, § 7543; Acts 1939, No. 661, p. 1036, § 2; Code 1940, T. 26, § 263; Acts 1971, No. 667, p. 1376, § 3; Acts 1973, No. 1062, p. 1750, § 5; Acts 1975, No. 565, p. 1299, § 2; Acts 1975, 4th Ex. Sess., No. 86, p. 2622, § 3; Acts 1979, No. 79-325, p. 488; Acts 1983, No. 83-592, p. 925, § 1; Acts 1984, No. 84-322, p. 741, § 2; Acts 1992, No. 92-537, § 10.)

The 1992 amendment, effective May 19, 1992, rewrote the first paragraph, in the second paragraph substituted "an officer" for "any officer," "of the election" for "of such election," and "and the employers" for "of industrial relations and his," in the third paragraph substituted "At the end of any calendar year, a corporate officer who has been exempted, by proper" for "A corporate officer who has exempted himself by proper," substituted "coverage, may revoke the exemption" for "coverage may at the end of any calendar year revoke such exemption," inserted "or her" and substituted "department and the employer's" for "department of industrial relations and his," deleted "of industrial relations" following "department" in the fourth paragraph, substituted "If the corporate officer elects to be exempt from coverage, the election" for "In the event that the corporate officer

election occurs such election," and added the last five paragraphs.

Code commissioner's note. — Section 1 of Acts 1979, No. 325, p. 488, which amended this section, provides that it is the legislative intent by the passage of this amendment that an individual employer may elect to cover himself as well as his employees under the provisions of workmen's compensation.

Acts 1984, No. 84-322, s. 4, provides: "The provisions of this act shall become effective on August 15, 1984 provided, however, these provisions of this amendatory act shall not be in effect until sufficient funds are appropriated from the special educational trust fund to implement said provisions; and further provided that nothing contained herein shall prohibit any school board that voluntarily elects to provide such coverage from doing so with local or other available funds."

I. General Consideration.
II. Particular Employments.
   A. Casual Employment.
   B. Employment of Less Than Three Employees.

I. GENERAL CONSIDERATION.

Editor's note. — The cases annotated below were decided under prior law.

Amendments do not affect elective option. — The 1973 amendments to Workmen's Compensation Act, which, as written, only repealed those sections of the code pertaining to the election procedures governing whether or not the employer and employee would be bound by the provisions of the act, in no way affected the elective option between employer and employee existing under the act. The constitutional validity of the act rests upon the same being elective rather than compulsory.

Pipkin v. Southern Elec. & Pipefitting Co., 358 So. 2d 1015 (Ala. 1978).

Intent of section is to exempt specific employers-employees. — It is clear that the intent of the legislature in enacting this section was to exempt specific employers-employees from the operation of the act. It is equally clear that the employer which the legislature intended to exempt by its use of the term "school district" is the agency empowered by statute to administer primary-secondary education in a defined area. Mills v. Ozark City Bd. of Educ., 376 So. 2d 747 (Ala. Civ. App. 1979).

This section and section 25-5-51 are in

pari materia. Ivey v. Dixon Inv. Co., 283 Ala. 590, 219 So. 2d 639 (1969).

And section 25-5-51 does not provide for qualification of those previously disqualified by this section, but is merely expressive of conditions precedent to becoming subject to the act if not disqualified from acceptance. Steele v. Aetna Cas. & Sur. Co., 46 Ala. App. 705, 248 So. 2d 745 (1971).

Workmen's Compensation Act superseded the Employer's Liability Act. C.F. Halstead Contractor v. Lowery, 51 Ala. App. 86, 282 So. 2d 909 (1973).

Except in cases excepted from Workmen's Compensation Act by this section and which would otherwise come within the Employer's Liability Act. C.F. Halstead Contractor v. Lowery, 51 Ala. App. 86, 282 So. 2d 909 (1973).

Term "school district" as used in this section is synonymous with "school system," a more common designation. The agencies empowered by statute to administer the public schools of Alabama are county and city boards of education. The term "school district" has a geographical connotation in respect to the limits of the jurisdiction of those administrative bodies. Mills v. Ozark City Bd. of Educ., 376 So. 2d 747 (Ala. Civ. App. 1979).

No denial of remedy for injury not within provisions of Workmen's Compensation Act. — In the light of the provisions of § 13 of the Constitution "That all courts shall be open; and that every person, for any injury done him, in his lands, goods, person, or reputation, shall have a remedy by due process of law," it cannot be said that for an injury done a person not within the provisions of the Workmen's Compensation Act, that it was the legislative intent by the enactment of said law to deny such person a remedy if under the common law or the Employer's Liability Act, or other statute, he was entitled to maintain an action therefor. Ivey v. Dixon Inv. Co., 283 Ala. 590, 219 So. 2d 639 (1969).

Application of act not limited to municipalities while engaged only in proprietary functions. — The legislature did not intend to limit the application of the Workmen's Compensation Act to municipalities while engaged only in proprietary functions. City of Foley v. Terry, 278 Ala. 30, 175 So. 2d 461 (1965).

Burden of proving applicability of workmen's compensation coverage. — The burden of alleging and proving the applicability of workmen's compensation coverage should be on a municipality after general inapplicability of such coverage has been alleged in the complaint. McCarroll v. City of Bessemer, 289 Ala. 449, 268 So. 2d 731 (1972).

Broadly speaking, test of employment under this section is the relation of the employment in question to the general line of business in which the employer is engaged. Aluminum Workers Int'l v. Champion, 45 Ala. App. 570, 233 So. 2d 511 (1970).

Exemption of domestic servants. — Domestic servants are exempted in the Alabama Workmen's Compensation Law and in the Alabama Unemployment Compensation Act, and it does not appear that the classification in those statutes has ever been held to offend the law of equality and uniformity. Estes v. City of Gadsden, 266 Ala. 166, 94 So. 2d 744 (1957), holding valid a municipal ordinance imposing a license tax on salaried or wage-earning employees and exempting domestic servants.

Children within child labor law. — Where a child coming within the prohibition of § 25-8-2 is injured at the defendant's lumber plant it is not necessary that he be an employee and within the provisions of this chapter to recover damages as such child should not be permitted to work at such plant under certain conditions, regardless of employment or nonemployment. Vida Lumber Co. v. Courson, 216 Ala. 248, 112 So. 737 (1926).

Wrongful death barred by accepting compensation benefits. — Where widow of employee killed in automobile accident had accepted workmen's compensation benefits from employer and had not returned payments she received, wrongful death action against employer was barred. Phillips v. Unijax, Inc., 462 F. Supp. 942 (S.D. Ala. 1978), rev'd on other grounds, 625 F.2d 54 (5th Cir. 1980).

Compensation not controlled by exact form prepared by director. — Although the director of the department of industrial relations is delegated authority to prepare and distribute such blank forms and literature as he shall deem requisite to facilitate or promote the efficient administration of this chapter, fact that director drafted form to be used when filing an election of coverage under this section does not mean that workmen's compensation for farm laborers should be controlled by whether or not this exact form appears in the files of the department of industrial relations. Smith v. Thrower Nursery, Inc., 360 So. 2d 741 (Ala. 1978).

Under this section, absolute compliance with technical filing requirements is not necessary for an effective election of coverage by an exempt employer where the employer's actions clearly and consistently manifest an intent to come under the act. Smith v. Thrower Nursery, Inc., 360 So. 2d 741 (Ala. 1978).

Consistent pattern of behavior as evidence of intent. — While a single act of taking out insurance or paying a claim may not be sufficient evidence of intent to come under Workmen's Compensation Act, a consistent pattern of behavior on the part of the employer, his employees and the department of industrial relations will suffice, despite failure to comply with technical filing requirements. Smith v. Thrower Nursery, Inc., 360 So. 2d 741 (Ala. 1978).

Exemption of farm labor. — The exemption of farm labor from workmen's compensation coverage is construed according to the character of the work regularly performed by the employee, not according to the nature of the employer's business. In other words, it is the nature of the work the employee does that determines whether he is a "farm laborer" for purposes of this section. Patrick v. Miller, 440 So. 2d 1096 (Ala. Civ. App. 1983).

The employer's business can be agricultural in nature, but if the employee's work is nonagricultural or significantly disassociated from the normal routine of running a farm, the farm laborer exemption will not apply. On the other hand, if the specific employee's work is nonagricultural, but is such an indispensable part of the normal routine of running a farm that the job is not merely incidental to the farming operation, then the farm laborer exemption will apply. Patrick v. Miller, 440 So. 2d 1096 (Ala. Civ. App. 1983).

The controlling consideration in determining whether an employee is a farm laborer for purposes of this section is the nature of the work performed by the employee. Buchanan v. Pankey, 531 So. 2d 1225 (Ala. Civ. App. 1988).

A farm laborer at a commercial dairy was subject to exemption pursuant to workmen's compensation. Buchanan v. Pankey, 531 So. 2d 1225 (Ala. Civ. App. 1988).

Estoppel. — An employer was estopped to deny that he was covered by the Workmen's Compensation Act, where the evidence showed that he told his agent that he was covered by the act, and the agent in turn informed an employee whom he hired for the employer that the employer was covered by the act, and, in reliance on this assertion, the employee accepted dangerous employment that resulted in his death. Herndon v. Slayton, 263 Ala. 677, 83 So. 2d 726 (1955).

Since the plaintiff had no action under the Workmen's Compensation Act, his acceptance of compensation payments voluntarily made by the defendant's insurer did not estop him from pursuing his remedy under the common law or the Employer's Liability Act. Ivey v. Dixon Inv. Co., 283 Ala. 590, 219 So. 2d 639 (1969).

Cited in Ex parte Big Four Coal Mining Co., 213 Ala. 305, 104 So. 764 (1925); Ex parte Louisville & N.R.R., 214 Ala. 489, 108 So. 379 (1926); Martin v. Republic Steel Co., 226 Ala. 209, 146 So. 276 (1933); Birmingham Post Co.

v. Sturgeon, 227 Ala. 162, 149 So. 74 (1933); Bonner v. Alexander, 34 Ala. App. 89, 36 So. 2d 533 (1948); Louisville & N.R.R. v. American Mut. Liab. Ins. Co., 254 Ala. 128, 47 So. 2d 206 (1950); Sinclair Ref. Co. v. Howell, 222 F.2d 637 (5th Cir. 1955); West Point Mfg. Co. v. Bennett, 263 Ala. 571, 83 So. 2d 303 (1955); Ward v. State Farm Mut. Auto. Ins. Co., 241 F.2d 134 (5th Cir. 1957); Bullard v. Murdock, 271 Ala. 378, 124 So. 2d 263 (1960); Ellison v. Butler, 271 Ala. 399, 124 So. 2d 88 (1960); Fleet Transp. Co. v. Insurance Co. of N. Am., 340 F. Supp. 158 (M.D. Ala. 1972); City of Tuscaloosa v. Howard, 55 Ala. App. 701, 318 So. 2d 729 (1975); Harris v. National Truck Serv., 56 Ala. App. 350, 321 So. 2d 690 (1975); Veterans of Foreign Wars Post 7320 v. Sheffield, 398 So. 2d 262 (Ala. 1981); City of Montgomery v. Robinson, 441 So. 2d 857 (Ala. 1983); Fluker v. Sunnyland Foods, 469 So. 2d 586 (Ala. 1985); Miles v. Tennessee River Pulp & Paper Co., 519 So. 2d 562 (Ala. Civ. App. 1987).

Collateral references. — 99 C.J.S., Workmen's Compensation, §§ 26, 42, 69.

58 Am. Jur., Workmen's Compensation, § 81 et seq.

Application of compensation act to employees engaged in farming. 7 ALR 1296, 13 ALR 955, 35 ALR 208, 43 ALR 954, 107 ALR 977, 140 ALR 399.

What is "casual" employment. 33 ALR 1452, 60 ALR 1195, 107 ALR 934.

Applicability of workmen's compensation act to intrastate employee where railroad company is engaged in both interstate and intrastate commerce. 80 ALR 1418.

Requirement of act making application dependent on number of persons employed. 81 ALR 1232.

"Seasonal" employment within provisions of workmen's compensation act. 93 ALR 308.

Workmen's compensation act as applicable to motor carriers and their employees engaged in interstate commerce. 133 ALR 956, 148 ALR 873.

Workers' compensation: injuries incurred during labor activity. 61 ALR4th 196.

II. PARTICULAR EMPLOYMENTS.

A. Casual Employment.

Provision excepting casual employment is liberally construed. — The part of this section reading, "Casual and not in the usual course of the trade, business," etc., is liberally construed to attain the end in view, and with reference to the hardships and evils to be corrected. See National Cast Iron Pipe Co. v. Higginbotham, 216 Ala. 129, 112 So. 734 (1927).

Hence, doubts and implications resolved in favor of rule rather than exception. — If there is any doubt about an exception or proviso in such a statute it must be judged on the assumption that the rule is broader than the exception, and all doubts and implications should be resolved in favor of the rule rather than the exception. National Cast Iron Pipe Co. v. Higginbotham, 216 Ala. 129, 112 So. 734 (1927). See also, Summit Coal Co. v. Walker, 214 Ala. 332, 107 So. 905 (1926).

"Casual" and "not in usual course of business" are used conjunctively. — This section is of that class in which "casual" and "not in the usual course of the business of the employer" are used conjunctively. Both conditions must concur to exclude the employee from compensation. It may be said both terms are interrelated and together define a status of employment outside the field covered by this state's compensation laws. Aluminum Workers Int'l v. Champion, 45 Ala. App. 570, 233 So. 2d 511 (1970).

And employment must be both casual and not in usual course of employer's business, in order to exclude from compensation an employee sustaining injuries arising out of employment. Tuscaloosa Compress Co. v. Hagood, 229 Ala. 284, 156 So. 633 (1934).

To exclude an employee from coverage of the workmen's compensation law on the theory that he is not a regular employee, his employment must be both "casual" and outside "the usual course of the trade, business, profession or occupation of the employer." Aluminum Workers Int'l v. Champion, 45 Ala. App. 570, 233 So. 2d 511 (1970).

Test in determining whether injured employee's employment was "casual" is relation of employment in question to general line of business in which employer is engaged. Tuscaloosa Compress Co. v. Hagood, 229 Ala. 284, 156 So. 633 (1934).

That an employee was recently employed or was employed by the day instead of for the job does not make the employment casual and not in the usual course of trade. National Cast Iron Pipe Co. v. Higginbotham, 216 Ala. 129, 112 So. 734 (1927).

Employments held not casual. — Finding that decedent, a carpenter by trade, who was employed to cover house of coal company with shingles, which house was leased to vice president of coal company, was not engaged in a "casual employment" within Workmen's Compensation Act, so as to deprive claimants of compensation for his death, held warranted by evidence that defendant kept and had at that time a regular crew of carpenters to do carpenter work in its business. Ex parte Little

Cahaba Coal Co., 213 Ala. 596, 105 So. 648 (1925).

Where superintendent of compress company's plant made ordinary repairs of machinery, but, because of breakdown in compress, expert machinist was employed on special repair job on hourly wage, such machinist was held employed in "usual course of business of employer." Tuscaloosa Compress Co. v. Hagood, 229 Ala. 284, 156 So. 633 (1934).

It is within the usual course of business of a labor union to seek to enlist new members and organize new locals. Aluminum Workers Int'l v. Champion, 45 Ala. App. 570, 233 So. 2d 511 (1970).

Carpenter hired to aid in the remodeling of his employer's private residence was engaged in employment which was casual in nature and which was outside the scope of his employer's normal course of business as the proprietor of a hardware store, and was consequently precluded from recovering workmen's compensation benefits. Craft v. Owens, 359 So. 2d 390 (Ala. Civ. App. 1978).

B. Employment of Less Than Three Employees.

Burden is upon employer to bring himself within terms of exception, of this section, that he employs less than 16 (now three) employees. Mobile Liners v. McConnell, 220 Ala. 562, 126 So. 626 (1930).

This section does not require a continuous employment of eight (now three) men in order to come within its terms, but it does require as many as eight (now three) men to be employed either constantly or on constantly recurring conditions of the business which require an increase in the number of employees at recurring periods necessarily brought about by the nature and character of the business in which the employer is engaged. Lingo v. Crews, 253 Ala. 227, 43 So. 2d 815 (1950).

And term "regularly" has no reference to constancy of occurrence. — The word "regularly" used in this section refers to question whether occurrence is established mode or plan in operation of business and has no reference to constancy of occurrence. Mobile Liners v. McConnell, 220 Ala. 562, 126 So. 626 (1930); Lingo v. Crews, 253 Ala. 227, 43 So. 2d 815 (1950).

In determining whether employer regularly employed less than 16 (now three) employees it is immaterial that periods of employment are not definite and at stipulated times. Mobile Liners v. McConnell, 220 Ala. 562, 126 So. 626 (1930); Lingo v. Crews, 253 Ala. 227, 43 So. 2d 815 (1950).

The question cannot be affected by the fact

that the identity of men employed remains same or changes from time to time. Mobile Liners v. McConnell, 220 Ala. 562, 126 So. 626 (1930); Lingo v. Crews, 253 Ala. 227, 43 So. 2d 815 (1950).

And all acts respecting "one business" need not be done at same place, but all must contribute to that as one independent enterprise. Jackson v. United Cigar Stores Co., 228 Ala. 220, 153 So. 422 (1934).

On motion to strike answer (formerly motion to dismiss pleas), allegations therein that three stores operated by company constituted "one business" was not conclusive of question whether company employed more than 16 (now three) employees in one business, if answer (formerly pleas) and complaint taken together had different meaning. Jackson v. United Cigar Stores Co., 228 Ala. 220, 153 So. 422 (1934).

§ 25-5-51. Right to compensation for injuries or death; grounds for denial of compensation.

If an employer is subject to this article, compensation, according to the schedules hereinafter contained, shall be paid by the employer, or those conducting the business during bankruptcy or insolvency, in every case of personal injury or death of his or her employee caused by an accident arising out of and in the course of his or her employment, without regard to any question of negligence. Notwithstanding the foregoing, no compensation shall be allowed for an injury or death caused by the willful misconduct of the employee, by the employee's intention to bring about the injury or death of himself or herself or of another, his or her willful failure or willful refusal to use safety appliances provided by the employer or by an accident due to the injured employee being intoxicated from the use of alcohol or being impaired by illegal drugs.

A positive drug test conducted and evaluated pursuant to standards adopted for drug testing by the U.S. Department of Transportation in 49 C.F.R. Part 40 shall be a conclusive presumption of impairment resulting from the use of illegal drugs. No compensation shall be allowed if the employee refuses to submit to or cooperate with a blood or urine test as set forth above after the accident after being warned in writing by the employer that such refusal would forfeit the employee's right to recover benefits under this chapter.

No compensation shall be allowed if, at the time of or in the course of entering into employment or at the time of receiving notice of the removal of conditions from a conditional offer of employment, the employee knowingly and falsely misrepresents in writing his or her physical or mental condition and the condition is aggravated or reinjured in an accident arising out of and in the course of his or her employment.

At the time an employer makes an unconditional offer of employment or removes conditions previously placed on a conditional offer of employment, the employer shall provide the employee with the following written warning in bold type print, "Misrepresentations as to preexisting physical or mental conditions may void your workers' compensation benefits." If the employer defends on the ground that the injury arose in any or all of the last above-stated ways, the burden of proof shall be on the employer to establish the defense. (Acts 1919, No. 245, p. 206; Code 1923, § 7544; Code 1940, T. 26, § 270; Acts 1973, No. 1062, p. 1750, § 7; Acts 1984, 2nd Ex. Sess., No. 85-41, p. 44, § 4; Acts 1992, No. 92-537, § 11.)

The 1992 amendment, effective May 19, 1992, in the first paragraph, in the first sentence substituted "If an employer" for "When an employer," substituted "paid by the employer" for "paid by every such employer," inserted "or her" preceding "employee" and "employment," in the second sentence substituted "Notwithstanding the foregoing" for "except, that," deleted "or" following "of the employee," inserted "or herself," substituted "his or her" for "or due to his own intoxication or his," and added the language beginning "or by an accident due to the injured employee," added the second and third paragraphs, and in the last paragraph added the first sentence, and substituted "the defense" for "such defense" in the second sentence. As to the implementation of this amendment, see Code commissioner's note.

Code commissioner's note. — Acts 1984, 2nd Ex. Sess., No. 85-41, § 14 provides: "This act shall become effective immediately upon its passage and approval by the governor [January 9, 1985], or upon its otherwise becoming a law, provided it shall have no effect whatsoever with respect to the right of any injured employee to bring an action with respect to or upon any cause of action which arose or accrued prior to February 1, 1985. Provided further, it shall have no effect on and shall not apply to any accident or exposure to injurious condition occurring before the effective date of this Act."

Section 53 Acts 1992, No. 92-537 provides that the amendment to this section by § 11 of the 1992 act will be implemented August 1, 1992.

I. General Consideration.
II. Acts of Employee Precluding Compensation.
    A. Violation of Law.
    B. Violation of Rules of Employer.
    C. Willful Misconduct.
III. Judicial Review.

I. GENERAL CONSIDERATION.

Editor's note. — The cases annotated below were decided under prior law.

Compensation Act is elective, and to be constitutionally valid must be accepted by both employer and employee. Ellison v. Butler, 271 Ala. 399, 124 So. 2d 88 (1960).

Workmen's compensation law is an elective remedy merely substituted at the election of both employer and employee for other existing remedies under the Employer's Liability Act and common law. Steele v. Aetna Cas. & Sur. Co., 46 Ala. App. 705, 248 So. 2d 745 (1971).

This section and section 25-5-50 are in pari materia. Ivey v. Dixon Inv. Co., 283 Ala. 590, 219 So. 2d 639 (1969).

Liberal construction. — The Alabama workmen's compensation laws should be liberally construed in order to effectuate the purpose behind the act and to eliminate procedural technicalities. This liberal construction is in line with the intent of the procedural rules relating to amendments under A.R.C.P., Rule 15. Sun Papers, Inc. v. Jerrell, 411 So. 2d 790 (Ala. Civ. App. 1981).

An amendment adding a posthumous child as another party to the complaint is properly allowed where evidence indicates that the employer paid medical insurance for both the widow and the child until the child was three months old. Although the child was not included as a party plaintiff in the complaint itself, both the widow and the child were in essence before the court as dependents seeking compensation under the workmen's compensation law. Thus the filing of the petition in the name of the widow only does not preclude a subsequent amendment to include the child's name on the face of the complaint. Sun Papers, Inc. v. Jerrell, 411 So. 2d 790 (Ala. Civ. App. 1981).

After an election to come under the Workmen's Compensation Act of this state, coverage cannot be altered or modified by an individual or private contract. Bell v. General Am. Transp. Corp., 52 Ala. App. 123, 290 So. 2d 184 (1973).

Proximate cause standard intended. — By inference from the language of § 25-5-31, a proximate cause standard was intended under this section. Lankford v. Redwing Carriers, Inc., 344 So. 2d 515 (Ala. Civ. App.), cert. denied, 344 So. 2d 522 (Ala. 1977).

Injury as to time and place of employment. — If an injury occurs within the period of employment, at a place where employee may reasonably be while he is reasonably performing the duties assigned, such injury may be said to have occurred in the course of his employment. Wiregrass Comprehensive Mental Health Clinic, Inc. v. Price, 366 So. 2d 725 (Ala. Civ. App. 1978), cert. denied, 366 So. 2d 728 (Ala. 1979).

Rule providing that but for claimant's employment he would not have been where he was at the time of accident and would not have been subjected to the danger which killed him is not appropriate as a basis for determining whether deceased was in the course of his employment at the time he was killed; it certainly cannot be a valid indicator of "arising out of" his employment. Wiregrass Comprehensive Mental Health Clinic, Inc. v. Price, 366 So. 2d 725 (Ala. Civ. App. 1978), cert. denied, 366 So. 2d 728 (Ala. 1979).

In order to come within the terms of the act, and therefore, have liability limited to the benefits paid thereunder, it is essential that the person seeking to limit the remedy of the injured party be in an employer-employee relationship with that party. Kilgore v. C.G. Canter, Jr. & Assocs., 396 So. 2d 60 (Ala. 1981).

The Alabama Workmen's Compensation Act makes it clear that it is an exclusive remedy only in situations where an employee is suing his employer for injury in the course of his employment. Kilgore v. C.G. Canter, Jr. & Assocs., 396 So. 2d 60 (Ala. 1981).

Whether an accident arises out of and in the course of employment depends upon the facts and circumstances of each case. Havelin v. Poole Truck Lines, 395 So. 2d 75 (Ala. Civ. App. 1980), cert. denied, 395 So. 2d 77 (Ala. 1981).

An employee's right to recover benefits under workmen's compensation law depends primarily upon the employee's injury or disability resulting from an accident arising out of and in the course of his employment. Havelin v. Poole Truck Lines, 395 So. 2d 75 (Ala. Civ. App. 1980), cert. denied, 395 So. 2d 77 (Ala. 1981).

If the job causes the injury, it is an "accident" within the meaning of the act. Clanton v. Hudson Foods, Inc., 594 So. 2d 141 (Ala. Civ. App. 1991).

Proper test to determine whether a claimant's job caused his injury is: if in the performance of his job he has to exert or strain himself or is exposed to conditions of risk or hazard and he would not have strained or exerted himself or been exposed to such conditions had he not been performing his job and the exertion or strain or the exposure to the conditions was, in fact, a contributing cause to his injury or death, the test whether the job caused the injury or death is satisfied. Albertville Nursing Home v. Upton, 383 So. 2d 544 (Ala. Civ. App. 1980).

An injury to an employee arises in the course of his employment when it occurs within the period of his employment, at a place where he may reasonably be and while he is reasonably fulfilling the duties of his employment or doing something incident to it. Havelin v. Poole Truck Lines, 395 So. 2d 75 (Ala. Civ. App. 1980), cert. denied, 395 So. 2d 77 (Ala. 1981).

The legal test of causation does not require proof of some unusual exertion, strain or exposure not ordinary to the job, but the strenuous activity, exposure or other risk must be different from that to which others not employed in the same capacity are exposed. Montgomery Lincoln-Mercury, Inc. v. Neal, 423 So. 2d 846 (Ala. Civ. App.), rev'd on other grounds, 423 So. 2d 850 (Ala. 1982).

Injury to employee must arise out of and in course of employment in order to be compensable. Jones v. Sloss-Sheffield Steel & Iron Co., 221 Ala. 547, 130 So. 74 (1930); Republic Iron & Steel Co. v. Ingle, 223 Ala. 127, 134 So. 878 (1931).

Trial court's finding that plaintiff's blindness did not result from an accident arising out of and in course of his employment, so as to be compensable, but resulted from atrophy of optic nerves, held sufficiently sustained by evidence. Taylor v. Tennessee Coal, I. & R.R., 219 Ala. 614, 123 So. 78 (1929).

An accident may occur in the course of employment without arising out of it. In order to be compensable the accident must have the two concurring incidents. Bell v. Tennessee Coal, I. & R.R., 247 Ala. 394, 24 So. 2d 443 (1945).

In order for a claimant's injuries to be compensable under the Alabama workmen's compensation laws, the accident must arise out of and occur in the course of his employment. Sun Papers, Inc. v. Jerrell, 411 So. 2d 790 (Ala. Civ. App. 1981).

In order for an employee to recover benefits under Alabama's workmen's compensation laws, his injuries or death must be "caused by an accident arising out of and in the course of his employment." Montgomery Lincoln- Mercury, Inc. v. Neal, 423 So. 2d 846 (Ala. Civ. App.), rev'd on other grounds, 423 So. 2d 850 (Ala. 1982).

And burden of proof is on claimant. — In proceedings, under workmen's compensation law, burden of proving that injury arose out of and in the course of employment, which is condition precedent in all cases, is on the claimant when put in issue by answer. Ex parte Little Cahaba Coal Co., 213 Ala. 244, 104 So. 422 (1925).

When an employee deviates from his business route by taking a side trip that is clearly identifiable as such, he is unquestionably beyond the course of his employment while going away from the business route and toward the personal objective. Havelin v. Poole Truck Lines, 395 So. 2d 75 (Ala. Civ. App. 1980), cert. denied, 395 So. 2d 77 (Ala. 1981).

Test in heat-exposure cases. — The following two-pronged test applies to heat exposure cases: the harmful condition does arise out of the employment, if, in the performance of the duties for which he was engaged, in the manner required or contemplated by the employer, it is necessary for the employee to expose himself to a danger, materially in excess of that to which people commonly in that locality are exposed, when not situated as he is when thus performing his service, and that such excessive exposure may be found to have been the direct cause of the injury, though operating upon other conditions of common exposure. This principle has been specifically thus applied to sunstroke or heat prostration or heat exhaustion in many varying conditions. Montgomery Lincoln-Mercury, Inc. v. Neal, 423 So. 2d 846 (Ala. Civ. App.), rev'd on other grounds, 423 So. 2d 850 (Ala. 1982).

The two-pronged test has been cited as controlling in cases dealing with death or injury arising from a heart attack allegedly caused by strain or exertion on the job. Montgomery Lincoln-Mercury, Inc. v. Neal, 423 So. 2d 846 (Ala. Civ. App.), rev'd on other grounds, 423 So. 2d 850 (Ala. 1982).

Clarification of two-pronged test. — If in the performance of his job the employee has to exert or strain himself or is exposed to conditions of risk or hazard and he would not have strained or exerted himself or been exposed to such conditions had he not been performing his job and the exertion or strain or the exposure to the condition was, in fact, a contributing cause to his injury or death, the test whether the job caused the injury or death is satisfied. Montgomery Lincoln-Mercury, Inc. v. Neal, 423 So. 2d 846 (Ala. Civ. App.), rev'd on other grounds, 423 So. 2d 850 (Ala. 1982).

Traveling to and from work not in course of employment. — It is the general rule that accidents occurring while an employee is traveling to and from work are not considered as arising out of and in the course of employment; exceptions to the general rule have arisen where the employer furnishes transportation to and from work, or where the employee performs some service en route or at home. Wiregrass Comprehensive Mental Health Clinic, Inc. v. Price, 366 So. 2d 725 (Ala. Civ. App. 1978), cert. denied, 366 So. 2d 728 (Ala. 1979).

As a general rule, accidents which occur while the employee is traveling to and from work are not considered "arising out of and in the course of" his employment. There are, however, several well-recognized exceptions to the general rule, among which is the following exception: where the employee is engaged in some duty to his employer in connection with his employment or en route. Sun Papers, Inc. v. Jerrell, 411 So. 2d 790 (Ala. Civ. App. 1981).

An employee injured while on the way home or to work or to a place not required by duty is generally not covered by the Workmen's Compensation Act. Hughes v. Decatur Gen. Hosp., 514 So. 2d 935 (Ala. 1987).

Injury while crossing street to reach employer's parking lot. — Where the accident occurred as the employee was leaving the main premises of the employer and crossing a public street in order to reach a parking lot owned and maintained by the employer for use by its employees and visitors, the employee's injury arose out of and in the course of her employment. Hughes v. Decatur Gen. Hosp., 514 So. 2d 935 (Ala. 1987).

In a case involving temporary total disability, where the claimant is totally disabled at the time of trial, it becomes the duty of the court to make some estimate from the evidence as to its probable duration and fix the compensation to be payable until such estimated time, not exceeding the maximum in making that determination. The trial court is not bound by expert medical testimony, but must consider all of the evidence, including its own observation, and interpret it to its own best judgment. Albertville Nursing Home v. Upton, 383 So. 2d 544 (Ala. Civ. App. 1980).

A preexisting disease does not affect an award of compensation if the job combined with the disease to produce an injury or death. Hightower v. Brammall, Inc., 435 So. 2d 1295 (Ala. Civ. App. 1982).

Award of compensation is not affected by pre-existing conditions and diseases if the job-related injury combined with the pre-existing condition to produce the disability. Associated Forest Materials v. Keller, 537 So. 2d 957 (Ala. Civ. App. 1988).

Settlement waives other remedies. — Under this and the two following sections and § 25-5-56, injured employee's acceptance of compensation installments under Workmen's Compensation Act constituted an election which estopped him from resorting to any other remedy, in absence of repudiation of agreement or partial settlement and restoration of status quo by return of payments received. National Cast Iron Pipe Co. v. Higginbotham, 216 Ala. 129, 112 So. 734 (1927).

An action brought under the Workmen's Compensation Act is the exclusive remedy in situations where the employee sues his employer for injury in the course of his employment. Parker v. Thyssen Mining Constr., Inc., 428 So. 2d 615 (Ala. 1983).

Cited in Virginia-Carolina Chem. Co. v. Cherry, 233 Ala. 582, 173 So. 86 (1937); Harris v. Louisville & N.R.R., 237 Ala. 366, 186 So. 771 (1939); Foster v. Continental Gin Co., 261 Ala. 366, 74 So. 2d 474 (1954); West Point Mfg.

Co. v. Bennett, 263 Ala. 571, 83 So. 2d 303 (1955); Riley v. Perkins, 282 Ala. 629, 213 So. 2d 796 (1968); Phillips v. Unijax, Inc., 462 F. Supp. 942 (S.D. Ala. 1978); Moses v. Pitney Bowes, Inc., 368 So. 2d 543 (Ala. Civ. App. 1978); McGaughy v. Allied Prods. Co., 412 So. 2d 803 (Ala. Civ. App. 1982); Baggett v. Builders Transp., Inc., 457 So. 2d 413 (Ala. Civ. App. 1984); Hyster Co. v. Chandler, 461 So. 2d 828 (Ala. Civ. App. 1984); Lowman v. Piedmont Executive Shirt Mfg. Co., 547 So. 2d 90 (Ala. 1989); Cooper v. Western Supermarkets, 553 So. 2d 1153 (Ala. Civ. App. 1989); Hooper v. Denney, 587 So. 2d 340 (Ala. Civ. App. 1991).

Collateral references. — 99 C.J.S., Workmen's Compensation, §§ 258-261.

Employer's taking out of insurance covering employees not otherwise within act as an election to accept the act. 103 ALR 1523.

What amounts to acceptance or election to come within act by employer as to whom act is not mandatory. 136 ALR 899.

Workers' compensation: sexual assaults as compensable. 52 ALR4th 731.

Workers' compensation: injuries incurred during labor activity. 61 ALR4th 196.

Workers' compensation: injuries incurred while traveling to or from work with employer's receipts. 63 ALR4th 253.

II. ACTS OF EMPLOYEE PRECLUDING COMPENSATION.

A. Violation of Law.

Employer has burden of proving defense that employee was injured as result of willful violation of law. Sloss-Sheffield Steel & Iron Co. v. Nations, 236 Ala. 571, 183 So. 871 (1938).

What constitutes "willful violation" of law depends upon circumstances. — Under provision of this section that compensation shall not be allowed for injury caused by "willful violation" of law by employee, what amounts to a willful failure or refusal to comply with a statutory regulation is dependent upon the circumstances, and is to be determined upon the particular facts to each case. Sloss-Sheffield Steel & Iron Co. v. Nations, 236 Ala. 571, 183 So. 871 (1938).

And presumed knowledge of the law will not serve to make a statutory violation a "willful violation" of the law within the meaning of this section. Sloss-Sheffield Steel & Iron Co. v. Nations, 236 Ala. 571, 183 So. 871 (1938).

But "willful violation" may be shown by evidence that employee was informed and knew of the statute which was violated.

Sloss-Sheffield Steel & Iron Co. v. Nations, 236 Ala. 571, 183 So. 871 (1938).

Question for jury. — In action to recover compensation for injuries sustained by mine employee while riding on loaded cars when a derailment occurred on way to top of mine, where riding on cars violated statute and rule of employer, question whether employee's conduct amounted to "willful violation of the law" within compensation act, so as to bar recovery of compensation, was for jury. Sloss-Sheffield Steel & Iron Co. v. Nations, 236 Ala. 571, 183 So. 871 (1938).

Instruction regarding whether mine employee's injuries resulted from his willful violation of law, so as to bar recovery, held not objectionable. Sloss-Sheffield Steel & Iron Co. v. Nations, 236 Ala. 571, 183 So. 871 (1938).

B. Violation of Rules of Employer.

Employer has burden of proving breach of rules to defeat recovery of compensation. Rockwood Ala. Stone Co. v. Lawler, 223 Ala. 336, 135 So. 569 (1931).

Violation of rule may constitute willful misconduct. — See cases under succeeding analysis line.

Safety rule held reasonable. — Safety rule which required coal car drivers at mine to stop cars before entering on main haulageway of mine to observe whether way was clear held reasonable, as respects employer's liability under compensation act for death of driver caused by collision resulting from failure to stop car before entering main haulageway. Trannon v. Sloss-Sheffield Steel & Iron Co., 233 Ala. 312, 171 So. 898 (1937).

Sufficiency of evidence. — Evidence sustained finding that "joining saw" operator, injured while operating cutoff saw, was not knowingly violating employer's rule. Rockwood Ala. Stone Co. v. Lawler, 223 Ala. 336, 135 So. 569 (1931).

C. Willful Misconduct.

Burden of proving employee's willful misconduct is on employer pleading it, under § 25-5-31, and this section. Ex parte Little Cahaba Coal Co., 213 Ala. 244, 104 So. 422 (1925); Sloss-Sheffield Steel & Iron Co. v. Greer, 216 Ala. 267, 113 So. 271 (1927); Jones v. Sloss-Sheffield Steel & Iron Co., 221 Ala. 547, 130 So. 74 (1930).

"Willful misconduct" includes all conscious or intentional violations of definite law or definitely prescribed rules of conduct as to which obedience is not discretionary, as contradistinguished from inadvertent, unconscious or involuntary violations thereof.

Sloss-Sheffield Steel & Iron Co. v. Nations, 236 Ala. 571, 183 So. 871 (1938).

Conscious and intentional violation of a known reasonable rule is willful misconduct under § 25-5-31, and this section, and it is not necessary to show specific intent. Sloss-Sheffield Steel & Iron Co. v. Greer, 216 Ala. 267, 113 So. 271 (1927).

"Willful misconduct" of employee, within § 25-5-31, and this section, is more than a mere negligent, inadvertent, unconscious or involuntary act or violation of a known reasonable rule or regulation of employer. Sloss-Sheffield Steel & Iron Co. v. Greer, 216 Ala. 267, 113 So. 271 (1927).

Usually willful disobedience of rules and orders amounts to willful misconduct under this section, but there are cases where in a continuation of employment and under unusual circumstances violation of rules and orders does not amount to willful misconduct. See Ex parte Little Cahaba Coal Co., 213 Ala. 244, 104 So. 422 (1925), and examples cited.

"Willful" misconduct, as used in this section, includes all conscious or intentional violations of definite law or definitely prescribed rules of conduct, as to which obedience is not discretionary, as contradistinguished from inadvertent, unconscious, or involuntary violations thereof. Sun Papers, Inc. v. Jerrell, 411 So. 2d 790 (Ala. Civ. App. 1981).

Failure to observe traffic and to yield the right-of-way when such traffic is obstructed by sunlight does not, without more, establish willful misconduct within the meaning of this section. Sun Papers, Inc. v. Jerrell, 411 So. 2d 790 (Ala. Civ. App. 1981).

But where employee lacked knowledge of rule, breach thereof held not willful. — A bakery salesman, without knowledge of employer's rule which prohibited anyone except employees from riding in employer's trucks, was not precluded from recovering workmen's compensation because he violated the rule. Malbis Bakery Co. v. Collins, 245 Ala. 84, 15 So. 2d 705 (1943).

And willful misconduct referred to in this section is such misconduct which occurs within the sphere of employment as pointed out in Jones v. Sloss-Sheffield Steel & Iron Co., 221 Ala. 547, 130 So. 74 (1930); Trannon v. Sloss-Sheffield Steel & Iron Co., 233 Ala. 312, 171 So. 898 (1937).

The willful misconduct and willful violations referred to in § 25-5-31 and defined by this section are those which occur within the sphere of employment. Johnson v. Brinker, 289 Ala. 240, 266 So. 2d 851 (1972).

But employee's willful misconduct outside sphere of employment precludes compensation for his resulting death, though not pleaded. Jones v. Sloss-Sheffield Steel & Iron Co., 221 Ala. 547, 130 So. 74 (1930).

And there is no liability if the employee disobeys a rule or condition which in effect limits the sphere of his employment. Johnson v. Brinker, 289 Ala. 240, 266 So. 2d 851 (1972).

Intoxication defense available only where accident proximately caused by intoxication. — The legislature intended a successful defense on the ground of the employee's intoxication only where it appears that the accident producing the injury or death was proximately caused by the employee's intoxication. Lankford v. Redwing Carriers, Inc., 344 So. 2d 515 (Ala. Civ. App.), cert. denied, 344 So. 2d 522 (Ala. 1977).

Burden of establishing intoxication on employer. — Where an employer raises an employee's intoxication as a defense to a workmen's compensation claim, the employer has the burden of establishing the intoxication. Lankford v. Redwing Carriers, Inc., 344 So. 2d 515 (Ala. Civ. App.), cert. denied, 344 So. 2d 522 (Ala. 1977).

Sufficiency of evidence. — In compensation proceeding where miner, in attempting to assist in putting out fire in mine, went into return air course after being told not to by foreman, and was killed by explosion, finding that he was not guilty of willful misconduct was sustained under evidence. Ex parte Little Cahaba Coal Co., 213 Ala. 244, 104 So. 422 (1925).

Evidence was ample to support a finding by the trial court that at the time employee was killed he was knowingly violating a reasonable rule, regulation or order of his employer which constituted willful misconduct of the deceased. Boatright v. Dothan Aviation Corp., 278 Ala. 142, 176 So. 2d 500 (1965).

III. JUDICIAL REVIEW.

Standard of review. — The standard of review in workmen's compensation cases is limited to a determination of whether there is any legal evidence to support the trial court's findings-of-fact. This court will not weigh the evidence. If any reasonable view of the evidence supports the findings of the trial court, the court may then determine if the correct legal conclusions have been drawn therefrom. Montgomery Lincoln-Mercury, Inc. v. Neal, 423 So. 2d 846 (Ala. Civ. App.), rev'd on other grounds, 423 So. 2d 850 (Ala. 1982).

On certiorari to review judgments in workmen's compensation cases, a court will not look to weight of evidence as to any fact found by the trial court, but simply to see if there is any evidence or any reasonable inference therefrom to support facts found by the trial court regardless of whether award of compensation has been denied or granted. Padgett v. Neptune Water Meter Co., 510 So. 2d 277 (Ala. Civ. App. 1987).

When finding as to loss of ability to earn is absent from judgment. — When a finding as to an employee's loss of ability to earn is absent from the judgment, there are no grounds for awarding compensation benefits and courts will reverse and remand such a case for a determination of whether the employee suffered a loss of ability to earn as a result of her back injury. Kroger Co. v. Daniel, 582 So. 2d 552 (Ala. Civ. App. 1991).

§ 25-5-52. Manner of compensation, etc., provided by chapter exclusive.

Except as provided in this chapter, no employee of any employer subject to this chapter, nor the personal representative, surviving spouse, or next of kin of the employee shall have a right to any other method, form, or amount of compensation or damages for an injury or death occasioned by an accident or occupational disease proximately resulting from and while engaged in the actual performance of the duties of his or her employment and from a cause originating in such employment or determination thereof. (Acts 1919, No. 245, p. 206; Code 1923, § 7545; Code 1940, T. 26, § 271; Acts 1973, No. 1062, p. 1750, § 8; Acts 1992, No. 92-537, § 12.)

The 1992 amendment, effective May 19, 1992, added "Except as provided in this chapter" at the beginning of the section, substituted "chapter" for "article," substituted "the employee" for "any such employee," "a right" for "any right," "an injury" for "any injury," and "an accident or occupational disease" for "any accident," inserted "or her," and deleted "other than as provided in this article" at the end of this section.

Constitutionality. — See Lackey v. Jefferson Energy Corp., 439 So. 2d 1290 (Ala. Civ. App. 1983).

Exclusivity provision does not violate Art. I, § 1, of the Constitution. — Because no suspect class is involved, that portion of the act that limits benefits available to the estates of employees who die leaving no dependents to funeral and medical expenses must have rational basis to withstand constitutional scrutiny under art. I, § 1, of the Constitution. The classification at issue here is rationally related to a legitimate state interest: to provide, after an employee's death, only for those individuals who were dependent upon the decedent's salary when he or she was alive. Yarchak v. Munford, Inc., 570 So. 2d 648 (Ala. 1990), cert. denied, — U.S. —, 111 S. Ct. 2237, 114 L. Ed. 2d 478 (1991).

This section and § 25-5-53 are not arbitrary or capricious and they do not violate art. I, § 13, of the Constitution. Yarchak v. Munford, Inc., 570 So. 2d 648 (Ala. 1990), cert. denied, — U.S. —, 111 S. Ct. 2237, 114 L. Ed. 2d 478 (1991).

Intent of legislature. — The act is designed to financially aid an employee and/or his dependents in the event of a job-related injury or death. Yarchak v. Munford, Inc., 570 So. 2d 648 (Ala. 1990), cert. denied, — U.S. —, 111 S. Ct. 2237, 114 L. Ed. 2d 478 (1991).

Election to come under act is an acceptance of all provisions of the act. Bell v. General Am. Transp. Corp., 52 Ala. App. 123, 290 So. 2d 184 (1973).

And no provisions are provided by legislature allowing modification of the provisions enumerated under the act. Bell v. General Am. Transp. Corp., 52 Ala. App. 123, 290 So. 2d 184 (1973).

Therefore, after election to come under Workmen's Compensation Act, coverage cannot be altered or modified by an individual or private contract. Bell v. General Am. Transp. Corp., 52 Ala. App. 123, 290 So. 2d 184 (1973).

Proceeding under this section has been construed as an action ex contractu. Sabino v. Independent Life & Accident Ins. Co., 52 Ala. App. 368, 292 So. 2d 662 (1974).

Rights of employee are purely statutory. Owens v. Ward, 49 Ala. App. 293, 271 So. 2d 251 (1972).

And right to benefits not transferable. — Benefits are in lieu of wages intended for the personal benefit of the employee, and the right thereto is not transferable to others. Owens v. Ward, 49 Ala. App. 293, 271 So. 2d 251 (1972).

Also certain rights of dependents being specified by this chapter, such dependents possess only those rights so specified.

Owens v. Ward, 49 Ala. App. 293, 271 So. 2d 251 (1972).

Employer does not lose its employer status — for immunity purposes — by qualifying under the Workmen's Compensation Act as a self-insurer and, in that capacity, performing or failing to perform safety inspections. Adair v. Moretti-Harrah Marble Co., 381 So. 2d 181 (Ala. 1980); Stone v. United States Steel Corp., 384 So. 2d 17 (Ala. 1980).

Under the doctrine of dual capacity, an employer, normally shielded from tort liability by the exclusive remedy principle enunciated within this section, may become liable in tort to his own employee if he occupies, in addition to his capacity as employer, a second capacity that confers on him obligations independent of those imposed on him as employer. Stone v. United States Steel Corp., 384 So. 2d 17 (Ala. 1980).

Dual capacity such as to subject an employer to tort liability outside the Workmen's Compensation Act will not be found merely because an employer has a number of departments or divisions that perhaps are quite separate in their functions and operations. Stone v. United States Steel Corp., 384 So. 2d 17 (Ala. 1980).

Where plaintiff, an employee of defendant's corporate division, brought suit for damages arising from injuries sustained on the division's job site, the defendant was not operating in a dual capacity as employer-safety inspector, or employer-manufacturer, or employer-owner in a sense that would bring the dual capacity doctrine into play and the trial court properly granted defendant's motion for summary judgment because the action was barred by this section and § 25-5-53. Stone v. United States Steel Corp., 384 So. 2d 17 (Ala. 1980).

The court has authority to judicially engraft an exception into the immunity provisions applicable to the employer. Gibson v. Fidelity & Cas. Co., 454 So. 2d 526 (Ala. 1984).

Section 25-5-11 does not affect immunity provided in this section. — Section 25-5-11 does not provide an action against an employer; § 25-5-11(a) provides that actions may be maintained against those parties that may be jointly liable with the employer, provided that if the other party is a coemployee, then his actions, in order to give rise to liability, must be willful. However § 25-5-11 does not affect the immunity provided by this section and § 25-5-53. Padgett v. Neptune Water Meter Co., 585 So. 2d 900 (Ala. 1991).

Compensation would exceed purpose of act. — Compensation which is any greater than compensation for disability caused by injuries sustained while in the performance of his duties and which is intended as compensa-

tion to him for loss of earnings, or compensation to his dependents for his death if caused by the injury, which is intended as compensation for loss of the support which they would have received from him if he had lived — in the form of benefits to or a cause of action for wrongful death by the estate of an employee who leaves no dependents — would clearly exceed the purpose of the act. Yarchak v. Munford, Inc., 570 So. 2d 648 (Ala. 1990), cert. denied, — U.S. —, 111 S. Ct. 2237, 114 L. Ed. 2d 478 (1991).

Intentional tort claim not barred by exclusivity provisions. — Exclusive remedy provisions of the Workmen's Compensation Act are not designed to shield an employer or its insurer from the entire field of tort law. These provisions apply only to limit the liability of an employer or its insurer to the statutorily prescribed claims for job-related injuries, thus, employee's intentional fraud claim against employer should not be barred as a matter of law; such intentional tort claim against employer or fellow employee fall outside the scope of workmen's compensation coverage. Lowman v. Piedmont Executive Shirt Mfg. Co., 547 So. 2d 90 (Ala. 1989).

The exclusivity provisions of the Act do not prohibit an action for intentional tortious conduct, i.e., intentional fraud and outrageous conduct. Tittle v. Custard Ins. Adjusters, 590 So. 2d 880 (Ala. 1991).

The Act should not be an impervious barrier, insulating a wrongdoer from the payment of just and fair damages for intentional tortious acts only very tenuously related to workplace accidents. Tittle v. Custard Ins. Adjusters, 590 So. 2d 880 (Ala. 1991).

In carving out this exception for allowing intentional tort claims, the court is constrained, in accommodation to the exclusivity provisions of the Act, to rule out all questionable claims. Tittle v. Custard Ins. Adjusters, 590 So. 2d 880 (Ala. 1991).

Only intentional frauds would be actionable outside of the exclusive remedy provision, and a higher burden of proof would be imposed in accommodation to the exclusivity provisions of the act. Garvin v. Shewbart, 564 So. 2d 428 (Ala. 1990).

Where plaintiff pursued worker's compensation claim, he could not maintain respondeat superior action. — Where plaintiff had pursued his claim for compensation from the employer through a workers' compensation action, he could not maintain a separate action based upon respondeat superior to impose civil liability upon the employer for injuries compensable under the Workers' Compensation Act. Padgett v. Neptune Water Meter Co., 585 So. 2d 900 (Ala. 1991).

Acceptance of payment barred suit. —

Because employee's wife accepted payments from company's workmen's compensation carrier, she was barred by this section and § 25-5-53 from bringing an action against employee's company based on employee's wrongful death. Davis v. M.C. Dixon Lumber Co., 551 So. 2d 305 (Ala. 1989).

The plaintiffs' claims of psychological injuries by her supervisor were not barred by the exclusivity provisions of the Alabama Workmen's Compensation Act. Busby v. Truswall Sys. Corp., 551 So. 2d 322 (Ala. 1989).

Action for bad faith in paying claims barred by exclusivity provision. — An independent tort action of an employee against the employer or workmen's compensation carrier for bad faith in processing or paying claims is barred by the exclusivity provision of the Workmen's Compensation Act. Garnett v. Neumann, 507 So. 2d 496 (Ala. 1987), overruled on other grounds, Lowman v. Piedmont Executive Shirt Mfg. Co., 547 So. 2d 90 (Ala. 1989).

The viability of a separate bad faith action against the workmen's compensation carrier is controlled by Waldon v. Hartford Ins. Group, 435 So. 2d 1271 (Ala. 1983), which held that the employee's action against the employer or its carrier for bad faith in processing or paying claims was barred under the exclusivity provisions of the Workmen's Compensation Act. Bearden v. Equifax Servs., 455 So. 2d 836 (Ala. 1984).

Action against manager for failure to obtain benefits for employee barred by exclusivity provisions. — The exclusivity provisions of the Workmen's Compensation Act are applicable to an employee's suit against his employer's plant manager for an alleged failure of the plant manager to obtain workmen's compensation benefits for the employee. Garnett v. Neumann, 507 So. 2d 406 (Ala. 1987).

In order to ensure against borderline or frivolous claims, plaintiff must meet a higher **burden** or make a stronger showing that than required by the "substantial evidence rule" as it applies to issues in regard to tort claims generally. In order for her claim to go to the jury, plaintiff must present evidence that, if accepted and believed by the jury, would qualify as clear and convincing proof of the claim. Tittle v. Custard Ins. Adjusters, 590 So. 2d 880 (Ala. 1991).

Evidence did not support fraud claim. — Evidence tended at least as much to show that employee's difficulties in obtaining further medical care were the result of ordinary delays, misunderstandings, and breakdowns in communication as it showed that her difficulties were the result of any deliberate attempt by insurer to deny her further medical care; therefore, the evidence could not be said to support the fraud claim by clear and convincing proof. Garvin v. Shewbart, 564 So. 2d 428 (Ala. 1990).

Cited in United States Cas. Co. v. Hoage, 77 F.2d 542 (D.C. Cir. 1935); Smith v. West Point-Pepperell, Inc., 431 So. 2d 1268 (Ala. Civ. App. 1983); Waldon v. Hartford Ins. Group, 435 So. 2d 1271 (Ala. 1983); City of Montgomery v. Robinson, 441 So. 2d 857 (Ala. 1983); Garvin v. Shewbart, 442 So. 2d 80 (Ala. 1983); Strickland v. Birmingham Bldg. & Remodeling, 449 So. 2d 1242 (Ala. 1984); Alabama Power Co. v. Beam, 472 So. 2d 619 (Ala. 1985); Glenn v. Vulcan Materials Co., 534 So. 2d 598 (Ala. 1988).

Collateral references. — 100 C.J.S., Workmen's Compensation, § 410.

58 Am. Jur., Workmen's Compensation, §§ 48, 49.

Insured's receipt of or right to compensation benefits as affecting recovery under accident, hospital, or medical expense policy. 40 ALR3d 1012.

Workers' compensation immunity as extending to one owning controlling interest in employer corporation. 30 ALR4th 948.

Workers' compensation law as precluding employee's suit against employer for third person's criminal attack. 49 ALR4th 926.

§ 25-5-53. Rights and remedies of employees, etc., exclusive; civil and criminal liability of employers, etc.

The rights and remedies granted in this chapter to an employee shall exclude all other rights and remedies of the employee, his or her personal representative, parent, dependent, or next of kin, at common law, by statute, or otherwise on account of injury, loss of services, or death. Except as provided in this chapter, no employer shall be held civilly liable for personal injury to or death of the employer's employee, for purposes of this chapter, whose injury or death is due to an accident or to an occupational disease while engaged in the service or business of the employer, the cause of which accident or occupational disease originates in the employment. In addition, immunity from civil liability for all causes of action except those based upon willful conduct shall also extend to the workers' compensation insurance carrier of the employer; to a person, firm, association, trust, fund, or corporation responsible for servicing and payment of workers' compensation claims for the employer; to an officer, director, agent, or employee of the carrier, person, firm, association, trust, fund, or corporation; to a labor union, an official, or representative thereof; to a governmental agency providing occupational safety and health services, or an employee of the agency; and to an officer, director, agent, or employee of the same employer, or his or her personal representative. Nothing in this section shall be construed to relieve a person from criminal prosecution for failure or neglect to perform a duty imposed by law.

For the purpose of this section, a carrier, person, firm, association, trust, fund, or corporation shall include a company or a governmental agency making a safety inspection on behalf of a self-insured employer or its employees and an officer, director, agent, or employee of the company or a governmental agency. (Acts 1919, No. 245, p. 206; Code 1923, § 7546; Code 1940, T. 26, § 272; Acts 1975, 4th Ex. Sess., No. 86, p. 2729, § 4; Acts 1984, 2nd Ex. Sess., No. 85-41, p. 44, § 5; Acts 1992, No. 92-537, § 13.)

The 1992 amendment, effective May 19, 1992, rewrote the first paragraph, and in the second paragraph substituted "a carrier" for "any carrier," "a company or a governmental agency" for "any company," "a self-insured" for "any self-insured," "an officer" for "any officer," deleted "servant" following "agent," and substituted "the company or a governmental agency" for "such company."

Code commissioner's note. — Acts 1984, 2nd Ex. Sess., No. 85-41, § 14 provides: "This act shall become effective immediately upon its passage and approval by the governor [January 9, 1985], or upon its otherwise becoming a law, provided it shall have no effect whatsoever with respect to the right of any injured employee to bring an action with respect to or upon any cause of action which arose or accrued prior to February 1, 1985. Provided further, it shall have no effect on and shall not apply to any accident or exposure to injurious condition occurring before the effective date of this Act."

I. General Consideration.
II. Statutory Requirements.
III. Employer Immunity.
IV. Exclusivity Provisions.

I. GENERAL CONSIDERATION.

Editor's note. — The cases annotated below were decided under prior law.

Constitutionality. — See Lackey v. Jefferson Energy Corp., 439 So. 2d 1290 (Ala. Civ. App. 1983).

Exclusivity provision does not violate Ala. Const., art. I, § 13. — The legislature has taken from employees, through the Workmen's Compensation Act, the right to bring certain common-law actions against employers and their workmen's compensation insurance carriers. It is clear, however, there is a quid pro quo. The employee has been given the right, where there is a dispute regarding recovery from the carrier, to sue and recover damages for injuries related to employment; this, without proof of the employer's negligent action in causing the injury. Waldon v. Hartford Ins. Group, 435 So. 2d 1271 (Ala. 1983), overruled on other grounds, Lowman v. Redmont Exec. Shirt Mfg. Co., 547 So. 2d 90 (Ala. 1989).

Section 25-5-52 and this section of the act are not arbitrary or capricious and they do not violate art. I, § 13, of the Constitution. Yarchak v. Munford, Inc., 570 So. 2d 648 (Ala.

1990), cert. denied, — U.S. —, 111 S. Ct. 2237, 114 L. Ed. 478 (1991).

Because no suspect class is involved, that portion of the act that limits benefits available to the estates of employees who die leaving no dependents to funeral and medical expenses must have rational basis to withstand constitutional scrutiny under art. I, § 1, of the Constitution. The classification at issue here is rationally related to a legitimate state interest: to provide, after an employee's death, only for those individuals who were dependent upon the decedent's salary when he or she was alive. Yarchak v. Munford, Inc., 570 So. 2d 648 (Ala. 1990), cert. denied, — U.S. —, 111 S. Ct. 2237, 114 L. Ed. 478 (1991).

The barring of a claim for loss of consortium under the exclusivity provisions of this section does not offend Ala. Const., art. I, § 13 under either the vested rights approach or the common-law approach set forth in Reed v. Brunson. This is because there is a quid pro quo between the spouse and the employer, and the legislature has exercised its police power by adopting the exclusivity provisions of this section to eradicate a perceived social evil. Murdock v. Steel Processing Servs., Inc., 581 So. 2d 846 (Ala. 1991).

Intent of legislature. — The act is designed to financially aid an employee and/or his dependents in the event of a job-related injury or death. Yarchak v. Munford, Inc., 570 So. 2d 648 (Ala. 1990), cert. denied, — U.S. —, 111 S. Ct. 2237, 114 L. Ed. 478 (1991).

Workmen's Compensation Act is a contract between employer and employee insofar as rights or remedies for injury in employment are concerned, and all others, whether common-law or statutory, are waived. Owens v. Ward, 49 Ala. App. 293, 271 So. 2d 251 (1972).

Workmen's Compensation Act creates rights, remedies and procedure all its own, being based on a new theory of compensation distinct from previously existing theories of damages, and it is not rested upon any theory of wrongful conduct or neglect of employer. Pound v. Gaulding, 237 Ala. 387, 187 So. 468 (1939); Read News Agency, Inc. v. Moman, 383 So. 2d 840 (Ala. Civ. App.), cert. denied, 383 So. 2d 847 (Ala. 1980); Baird v. Spradlin, 409 So. 2d 820 (Ala. 1982).

And it is the criterion of rights and liabilities of all parties affected thereby and within its terms. Such was its purpose and scope, embracing as it does the employer, employee, dependents, insurance carriers and third persons liable for injuries or deaths, falling within and compensable thereunder. Steagall v. Sloss-Sheffield Steel & Iron Co., 205 Ala. 100, 87 So. 787 (1920); Georgia Cas. Co. v.

Haygood, 210 Ala. 56, 97 So. 87 (1923); Sloss-Sheffield Steel & Iron Co. v. Greek, 211 Ala. 95, 99 So. 791 (1924); Harris v. Lousiville & N.R.R., 237 Ala. 366, 186 So. 771 (1939); Carraway Methodist Hosp. v. Pitts, 256 Ala. 665, 57 So. 2d 96 (1952).

Thus, common-law right of action of an employee or his heirs against his employer is abolished by the statutory right in the employee or certain of his dependents substituted in the respects indicated by the Workmen's Compensation Act in all cases in which the employee elects to proceed under the act. Harris v. Louisville & N.R.R., 237 Ala. 366, 186 So. 771 (1939).

And actions presumed to come under Workmen's Compensation Act. — All actions for injury or death brought by an employee or his personal representative against his employer are presumed to come under the Workmen's Compensation Act. C.F. Halstead Contractor v. Lowery, 51 Ala. App. 86, 282 So. 2d 909 (1973).

Where a workmen's compensation policy expressly provides for a direct action by the employee or his dependent against the insurer, neither this section nor § 25-5-8(f)(4) precludes such suits. Wilson v. Central Foundry Co., 414 So. 2d 963 (Ala. 1982).

Provision in a policy providing workmen's compensation which allows a direct action on the policy by the injured employee is valid and enforceable and is not invalidated by the Workmen's Compensation Act. Wilson v. Central Foundry Co., 414 So. 2d 963 (Ala. 1982).

Injury from assault by fellow servant on employee, while engaged in performance of work on employer's premises, being accident arising out of course of employment, held not subject of civil action for damages under this section, exceptions mentioned in § 25-5-30, not being applicable. Mallory S.S. Co. v. Higgins, 22 Ala. App. 26, 111 So. 758 (1927).

Action against coemployee disallowed. — Where a workman's death resulted from injuries he received during the course of his employment, the principles of law that neither a personal representative nor a dependent of an employee can sue a coemployee for the alleged wrongful death of the employee applied. Baird v. Spradlin, 409 So. 2d 820 (Ala. 1982).

Tort action against coemployees for personal injuries survives if death results from those injuries while the action is pending. Mattison v. Kirk, 497 So. 2d 120 (Ala. 1986).

Survival of cause of action for benefits. — The Workmen's Compensation Act has no provision as to survival of a cause of action for benefits and thus ordinarily the answer as to whether a survivor can bring an action for a former employee's benefits would be supplied by the general act as to survival of causes of action which provides that causes of action sounding in contract survive, but those sounding in tort do not. Owens v. Ward, 49 Ala. App. 293, 271 So. 2d 251 (1972).

Employee's acceptance of employer's payment same as accepting workmen's compensation. — Acceptance by an employee of payment from an employer, in settlement of his workmen's compensation claim, should be considered as having the same effect as the acceptance of compensation payments under the Workmen's Compensation Act. This constitutes an election estopping him from resorting to any other remedy. Kelley v. Dupree, 376 So. 2d 1371 (Ala. 1979).

Acceptance of payment barred suit. — Because employee's wife accepted payments from company's workmen's compensation carrier, whe was barred by § 25-5-52 and this section from bringing an action against employee's company based on employee's wrongful death. Davis v. M.C. Dixon Lumber Co., 551 So. 2d 305 (Ala. 1989).

Compensation would exceed purpose of act. — Compensation which is any greater than compensation for disability caused by injuries sustained while in the performance of workman's duties and which is intended as compensation to him for loss of earnings, or compensation to his dependents for his death if caused by the injury, which is intended as compensation for loss of the support which they would have received from him if he had lived — in the form of benefits to or a cause of action for wrongful death by the estate of an employee who leaves no dependents — would clearly exceed the purpose of the act. Yarchak v. Munford, Inc., 570 So. 2d 648 (Ala. 1990), cert. denied, — U.S. —, 111 S. Ct. 2237, 114 L. Ed. 478 (1991).

Dismissal of claim alleging bad faith. — Trial court did not err in granting the defendants' motion to dismiss her claim alleging bad faith refusal to pay workmen's compensation benefits. Wooley v. Shewbart, 569 So. 2d 712 (Ala. 1990).

Complaint. — When an action is brought by an employee against the employer for injuries, the complaint should conform to the workmen's compensation law or should state facts showing that it did not apply. Bell v. Brooks, 270 Ala. 691, 121 So. 2d 911 (1960); Whatley v. Alabama Dry Dock & Shipbuilding Co., 279 Ala. 403, 186 So. 2d 117 (1966).

When an action is brought by an employee or by his personal representative against the employer for injuries or death, the complaint should conform to the Workmen's Compensa-

tion Act or should state facts showing the relationship to be within the exceptions to the Act as provided in § 25-5-50. C.F. Halstead Contractor v. Lowery, 51 Ala. App. 86, 282 So. 2d 909 (1973).

Questions for jury. — In action under the wrongful death statute for death of minor, sustained while riding on road contractor's truck, whether minor had been employed by contractor, so that exclusive remedy was under the compensation law, was for jury. Couch v. Hutcherson, 243 Ala. 47, 8 So. 2d 580 (1942).

Act held not applicable. — See Sinclair Oil Ref. Co. v. Howell, 222 F.2d 637 (5th Cir. 1955).

Cited in United States Cas. Co. v. Hoage, 77 F.2d 542 (D.C. Cir. 1935); Harris v. Louisville & N.R.R., 237 Ala. 366, 186 So. 771 (1939); Daniel Constr. Co. v. Pierce, 270 Ala. 522, 120 So. 2d 381 (1959); Southern Ry. v. McCamy, 270 Ala. 510, 120 So. 2d 695 (1960); Fleet Transp. Co. v. Insurance Co. of N. Am., 340 F. Supp. 158 (M.D. Ala. 1972); Hubbard v. Cutts, 331 So. 2d 632 (Ala. 1976); Redwing Carriers, Inc. v. Crown Cent. Petro. Corp., 356 So. 2d 1203 (Ala. 1978); Phillips v. Unijax, Inc., 462 F. Supp. 942 (S.D. Ala. 1978); Mapson v. Montgomery White Trucks, Inc., 357 So. 2d 971 (Ala. 1978); Stauffer Chem. Co. v. McIntyre Elec. Serv., Inc., 401 So. 2d 745 (Ala. 1981); Wilson v. Central Foundry Co., 414 So. 2d 962 (Ala. Civ. App. 1981); Smith v. West Point-Pepperell, Inc., 431 So. 2d 1268 (Ala. Civ. App. 1983); City of Montgomery v. Robinson, 441 So. 2d 857 (Ala. 1983); Bailey v. Collier, 465 So. 2d 381 (Ala. 1985); Alabama Power Co. v. Beam, 472 So. 2d 619 (Ala. 1985); Glenn v. Vulcan Materials Co., 534 So. 2d 598 (Ala. 1988).

Collateral references. — 99 C.J.S., Workmen's Compensation, § 6. 101 C.J.S., Workmen's Compensation, §§ 917-935. Mapson v. Montgomery White Trucks, Inc., 357 So. 2d 971 (Ala. 1978).

58 Am. Jur., Workmen's Compensation, §§ 48, 49. Stauffer Chem. Co. v. McIntyre Elec. Serv., Inc., 401 So. 2d 745 (Ala. 1981).

Workmen's compensation act as providing exclusive remedy for injury by assault. 72 ALR 117, 112 ALR 1258.

Compensation act as precluding common-law action by husband or wife of injured employee. 104 ALR 346.

Application for, or award, denial, or acceptance of, compensation under state workmen's compensation act as precluding action under federal employers' liability act by one engaged in interstate commerce within that act. 6 ALR2d 581.

Common-law action: right of employee to maintain common-law action for negligence against workmen's compensation insurance carrier. 93 ALR2d 598.

Malpractice: right to maintain malpractice suit against injured employee's attending physician notwithstanding receipt of workmen's compensation award. 28 ALR3d 1066.

Workmen's compensation provision as precluding employee's action against employer for fraud, false imprisonment, defamation, or the like. 46 ALR3d 1279.

Workers' compensation immunity as extending to one owning controlling interest in employer corporation. 30 ALR4th 948.

Workers' compensation act as precluding tort action for injury to or death of employee's unborn child. 55 ALR4th 792.

II. STATUTORY REQUIREMENTS.

Essential that employer-employee relationship exist. — In order to come within the terms of the act, and therefore, have liability limited to the benefits paid thereunder, it is essential that the person seeking to limit the remedy of the injured party be in an employer-employee relationship with that party. Kilgore v. C.G. Canter, Jr. & Assocs., 396 So. 2d 60 (Ala. 1981).

The Alabama Workmen's Compensation Act makes it clear that it is an exclusive remedy only in situations where an employee is suing his employer for injury in the course of his employment. Kilgore v. C.G. Canter, Jr. & Assocs., 396 So. 2d 60 (Ala. 1981).

When a general employer lends an employee to a special employer, the special employer becomes liable for workmen's compensation only if (a) the employee has made a contract of hire, express or implied, with the special employer; (b) the work being done is essentially that of the special employer; and (c) the special employer has the right to control the details of the work. Terry v. Read Steel Prods., 430 So. 2d 862 (Ala. 1983).

For discussion as to whether an employer-employee relationship is created where a general employer such as Manpower merely provides laborers to special employers and performs clerical payroll tasks, see Terry v. Read Steel Prods., 430 So. 2d 862 (Ala. 1983).

When interpreting the statutory definitions of "employer" and "employee" the courts must use criteria which will help apply these general definitions to the specific situation at bar. Terry v. Read Steel Prods., 430 So. 2d 862 (Ala. 1983).

Provisions limit liability to prescribed claims for job-related injuries. — The exclusive remedy provisions were not designed to shield an employer or its insurer from the entire field of tort law, and these provisions apply only to limit the liability of an employer

or its insurer to the statutorily prescribed claims for job-related injuries. Lowman v. Piedmont Executive Shirt Mfg. Co., 547 So. 2d 90 (Ala. 1989).

No protection for injuries not caused by job-related accidents. — The exclusivity provisions of the act do not afford protection for injuries not caused by a job-related accident. Lowman v. Piedmont Executive Shirt Mfg. Co., 547 So. 2d 90 (Ala. 1989).

III. EMPLOYER IMMUNITY.

Immunity provided for employer by section. — This section provides immunity for an employer for injuries arising out of and in the course of employment. Slagle v. Reynolds Metals Co., 344 So. 2d 1216 (Ala. 1977).

The employer has immunity under this section from liability for injuries to his employee arising out of the course of employment. Gunter v. United States Fid. & Guar. Co., 340 So. 2d 749 (Ala. 1976).

And such immunity not violative of Constitution. — The legislature's purposes are met by the terms of the act and the legislative grant of immunity is neither violative of Constitution 1901, § 13 or of the fourteenth amendment to the Constitution of the United States. Slagle v. Reynolds Metals Co., 344 So. 2d 1216 (Ala. 1977).

Legislature may not constitutionally immunize from tort liability a workmen's compensation carrier and its employees for injuries resulting to employees of the insured from negligent inspections performed by the carrier. Johnson v. American Mut. Liab. Ins. Co., 394 So. 2d 1 (Ala. 1980).

Employer does not lose its employer status — for immunity purposes — by qualifying under the Workmen's Compensation Act as a self-insurer and, in that capacity, performing or failing to perform safety inspections. Adair v. Moretti-Harrah Marble Co., 381 So. 2d 181 (Ala. 1980).

Section 25-5-11 does not affect immunity provided in this section. — Section 25-5-11 does not provide an action against an employer; § 25-5-11(a) provides that actions may be maintained against those parties that may be jointly liable with the employer, provided that if the other party is a coemployee, then his actions, in order to give rise to liability, must be willful. However § 25-5-11 does not affect the immunity provided by § 25-5-52 and this section. Padgett v. Neptune Water Meter Co., 585 So. 2d 900 (Ala. 1991).

Implied contract of employment created immunity. — Even though contract between power company and contracting company designated ironworker as employee of contracting company, and even though contracting company had on-site supervision of its employees, it was undisputed that power company retained control of the manner or methods of work performed by the workers hired by contracting company and that ironworker submitted to power company's control and supervision of his work; there was an implied contract of employment between ironworker and power company, and therefore, power company was immune from suit under this section. Pinson v. Alabama Power Co., 557 So. 2d 1236 (Ala. 1990).

The court has authority to judicially engraft an exception into the immunity provisions applicable to the employer. Gibson v. Fidelity & Cas. Co., 454 So. 2d 526 (Ala. 1984).

Employer's statutory immunity from actions on account of injury to employees protects the employer from actions by third parties seeking indemnity (under contractual provisions) from claims arising out of injuries sustained by employees of the same employer. Paul Krebs & Assocs. v. Matthews & Fritts Constr. Co., 356 So. 2d 638 (Ala. 1978); Union Camp Corp. v. McAbee Constr. Co., 465 So. 2d 390 (Ala. 1985).

An employer who voluntarily agrees to indemnify a third party against whom an injured workman files an action is not liable under the indemnity agreement. Paul Krebs & Assocs. v. Matthews & Fritts Constr. Co., 356 So. 2d 638 (Ala. 1978).

This section, as interpreted by the Alabama supreme court in Paul Krebs & Assocs. v. Matthews & Fritts Constr. Co., 356 So. 2d 638 (Ala. 1978), did not create a public policy in Alabama sufficiently strong to bar an indemnity provision of a 1975 sublicense agreement between the employer (an Ohio corporation) and a third-party tort-feasor domiciled in Michigan, notwithstanding the legality of the indemnity provision under the laws of Michigan and the agreement between the parties to apply Michigan law to any dispute. Goodwin v. George Fischer Foundry Sys., 769 F.2d 708 (11th Cir. 1985).

Worker assigned by temporary employment agency. — Paint company to which worker was assigned by temporary employment agency was worker's special employer, despite the fact that the agency, and not the company, paid workers, and was thus immune from suit for injuries received by worker on the job. Pettaway v. Mobile Paint Mfg. Co., 467 So. 2d 228 (Ala. 1985).

Legal duty upon truck rental. — Employer, which rented dump truck from rental corporation pursuant to lease providing that employer would indemnify or hold harmless rental corporation with respect to any claim for property damage or personal injuries instituted against corporation, owed no legal duty to corporation upon which corporation could sue, with respect to personal injury action brought against corporation by injured employee, in light of statute providing that employer was civilly immune from such personal injury suits by employees, and of rule that one of several joint tort-feasors cannot enforce contribution from other joint tort-feasors. Hertz Equip. Rental Corp. v. Dravo Corp., 360 So. 2d 325 (Ala. 1978).

Employer's affirmative defense was appropriated pleaded and was properly considered by the trial court Where the employer based its motion for summary judgment on the defense of statutory employer immunity and also included that defense in its answer, filed prior to the hearing on its motion for summary judgment, prior to the trial court's ruling thereon, and therefore that defense was before the court at the time it considered the summary judgment motion. Marlow v. Mid S. Tool Co., 535 So. 2d 120 (Ala. 1988).

IV. EXCLUSIVITY PROVISIONS.

Employee forfeits all other rights against his employer, whether common law or statutory, for the rights granted under the act. Slagle v. Reynolds Metals Co., 344 So. 2d 1216 (Ala. 1977).

An action brought under the Workmen's Compensation Act is the exclusive remedy in situations where the employee sues his employer for injury in the course of his employment. Parker v. Thyssen Mining Constr., Inc., 428 So. 2d 615 (Ala. 1983).

Where plaintiff was an instrumentation technician, whose job was to repair and adjust the controls on certain machines at employer's plant, he did not regularly work at the machine that caused his injury, but he had worked on that machine a "good many times" in his position as instrumentation technician, the machine was owned by the employer, it was in employer's plant, and the employer made the machine, in which plaintiff caught his hand, for the exclusive use of its employees, the dual capacity doctrine had no application, and the exclusive remedy provisions of our Workmen's Compensation Act barred claimant's claim against the employer. Bowen v. Goodyear Tire & Rubber Co., 516 So. 2d 570 (Ala. 1987).

Employee's death subject to this article although employee left no dependents. — The employee's death arising out of and in the course of employment was subject to this article even though the employee died leaving no dependents; therefore, the administratrix of the estate is not entitled to bring a wrongful death action against employer because the Workmen's Compensation Act provided the exclusive remedies. Hughes v. Decatur Gen. Hosp., 514 So. 2d 935 (Ala. 1987).

While employer may implead manufacturer of defective product causing injuries to his employee, the reverse is not true. Sherman Concrete Pipe Mach., Inc. v. Gadsden Concrete & Metal Pipe Co., 335 So. 2d 125 (Ala. 1976).

Employee may not bring common-law action where carrier refuses to pay claim. — Where an employee's dispute is with the carrier's failure to supply the financial responsibility required under the act, its refusal to pay a claim, his common-law claim is so interwoven with the compensation award under the provisions of the act, that to allow an independent common-law action would circumvent the statutory provisions and the policy behind the statute. Waldon v. Hartford Ins. Group, 435 So. 2d 1271 (Ala. 1983), overruled on other grounds, Lowman v. Redmont Exec. Shirt Mfg. Co., 547 So. 2d 90 (Ala. 1989).

Employee of temporary service agency injured while working for client company. — Where the plaintiff, admittedly an employee of a temporary service agency, was, for workmen's compensation purposes, also an employee of the company she was sent to work for, her exclusive remedy against such a company was the benefits provided by Alabama's Workmen's Compensation Act, and the trial court was correct in ruling that she could not maintain an independent action for damages against the company she was working for at the time of injury. Marlow v. Mid S. Tool Co., 535 So. 2d 120 (Ala. 1988).

The exclusivity provision of this section bars an action for loss of consortium by a dependent spouse. Murdock v. Steel Processing Servs., Inc., 581 So. 2d 846 (Ala. 1991).

The question of whether to exclude loss of consortium claims against employers was for the legislature. The legislature spoke by enacting the exclusivity provisions. There is nothing in the Alabama Constitution that bars the legislature from treating a husband and wife as an entity for such purposes. Murdock v. Steel Processing Servs., Inc., 581 So. 2d 846 (Ala. 1991).

And excludes rights of dependents for loss of services. — This section provides that workmen's compensation benefits are the exclusive remedy for an employee and his or her dependents. This includes his or her spouse. In addition, the section expressly excludes any rights and remedies of a dependent for "loss of services." Murdock v. Steel Processing Servs., Inc., 581 So. 2d 846 (Ala. 1991).

Employer not liable for physician's malpractice. — This section and § 25-5-77, relating to medical treatment, confine injured employee to remedy under statute, precluding action against employer for physician's malpractice. Nall v. Alabama Util. Co., 224 Ala. 33, 138 So. 411 (1931).

Forgery claim arising from employer's mishandling of report was barred. — Workmen's Compensation Act barred employee's forgery claim, where the claim arose from the employer's compensation first suit report. Cummings v. Food World, Brunos, Inc., 510 So. 2d 160 (Ala. 1987).

The viability of a separate bad faith action against the workmen's compensation carrier is controlled by Waldon v. Hartfor Ins. Group, 435 So. 2d 1271 (Ala. 1983), which held that the employee's action against the employer or its carrier for bad faith in processing or paying claims barred under the exclusivity provisions of the Workmen's Compensation Act. Bearden v. Equifax Servs., 455 So. 2d 836 (Ala. 1984).

Where plaintiff pursued workers' compensation claim, he could not maintain respondeat superior action. — Where plaintiff had pursued his claim for compensation from the employer through a workers' compensation action; he could not maintain a separate action based upon respondeat superior to impose civil liability upon the employer for injuries compensable inder the Workers' Compensation Act. Padgett v. Neptune Water Meter Co., 585 So. 2d 900 (Ala. 1991).

Only intentional frauds would be actionable outside of the exclusive remedy provision, and a higher burden of proof would be imposed in accommodation to the exclusivity provisions of the act. Garvin v. Shewbart, 564 So. 2d 428 (Ala. 1990).

Injured employee's claim based on intentional infliction of emotional distress or outrageous conduct against an employer is not barred by the exclusivity provisions of the Workmen's Compensation Act. Jackson v. Roberts, 485 So. 2d 1116 (Ala. 1986).

The plaintiffs' claims of psychological injuries by her supervisor were not barred by the exclusivity provisions of the Alabama Workmen's Compensation Act. Busby v. Truswall Sys. Corp., 551 So. 2d 322 (Ala. 1989).

Wife's third-party claim for loss of consortium survived death of injured spouse. — The husband's claim for loss of consortium had its origins in common law. Common law is decisional law, not written on unchangeable tablets of stone, and the wife's cause of action for loss of consortium caused by a tortious act of a third party is recognized. Thus, wife's loss of consortium claim against the coemployee defendants is a common law claim and not a statutory claim. Thus, wife's third-party claim for loss of consortium survives the death of the injured spouse. Mattison v. Kirk, 497 So. 2d 120 (Ala. 1986).

Exclusive remedy provisions of this section do not exclude medical benefits for hernia on the theory that the denial (if there is a denial) of "compensation" by paragraph a of Subdivision (6) of subsection (a) of § 25-5-57 extinguishes also the medical claim. This is a remedial statute and exemptions from it are to be strictly construed. Sam's Place v. Middleton, 39 Ala. App. 481, 103 So. 2d 812 (1958).

Dual-capacity test. — The decisive test to determine if the dual-capacity doctrine is invocable is not whether the second function or capacity of the employer is different and separate from the first. Rather, the test is whether the employer's conduct in the second role or capacity has generated obligations that are unrelated to those flowing from the company's or individual's first role as an employer. If the obligations are related, the doctrine is not applicable. Bowen v. Goodyear Tire & Rubber Co., 516 So. 2d 570 (Ala. 1987).

Under the doctrine of dual capacity, an employer, normally shielded from tort liability by the exclusive remedy principle enunciated within this section, may become liable in tort to his own employee if he occupies, in addition to his capacity as employer, a second capacity that confers on him obligations independent of those imposed on him as employer. Stone v.

United States Steel Corp., 384 So. 2d 17 (Ala. 1980).

The Workmen's Compensation Act provides that the rights and remedies granted to an employee shall exclude all other rights and remedies of said employee. However, if the injury is caused by some conduct on the part of the employer which results from a separate, independent relationship between the employer and the employee, the doctrine of dual capacity may remove the action from the exclusive provisions of the Workmen's Compensation Act. Windham v. Blount Int'l, Ltd., 423 So. 2d 194 (Ala. 1982).

Dual capacity such as to subject an employer to tort liability outside the Workmen's Compensation Act will not be found merely because an employer has a number of departments or divisions that perhaps are quite separate in their functions and operations. Stone v. United States Steel Corp., 384 So. 2d 17 (Ala. 1980).

Where plaintiff, an employee of defendant's corporate division, brought suit for damages arising from injuries sustained on the division's job site, the defendatnt was not operating in a dual capacity as employer-safety inspector, or employer-manufacturer, or employer-owner in a sense that would bring the dual capacity doctrine into play and the trial court properly granted defendant's motion for summary judgment because the action was barred by § 25-5-52 and this section. Stone v. United States Steel Corp., 384 So. 2d 17 (Ala. 1980).

§ 25-5-54. Presumptions as to applicability and acceptance of provisions of articles.

Every employer and employee, except as otherwise specifically provided in this article, shall be presumed to have accepted and come under this article and Article 4 of this chapter and the provisions thereof relating to the payment and acceptance of compensation. (Acts 1919, No. 245, p. 206; Code 1923, § 7547; Acts 1935, No. 387, p. 831; Acts 1936, Ex. Sess., No. 29, p. 9; Acts 1939, No. 661, p. 1036, § 15; Code 1940, T. 26, § 273; Acts 1973, No. 1062, p. 1750, § 9; Acts 1992, No. 92-537, § 14.)

The 1992 amendment, effective May 19, 1992, deleted the former first two sentences which read: "All contracts of employment made on or after January 1, 1920, shall be presumed to have been made with reference to and subject to the provisions of this article. All contracts of employment made prior to, and existing on, January 1, 1920, shall be presumed to continue from and after January 1, 1920, subject to and under the provisions of

this article," and inserted "and Article 4 of this chapter" in the present section.

Editor's note. — The cases below were decided under prior law.

Section does not invade province of judiciary. — The provision of this section, relating to presumption of acceptance of terms of act from failure to signify election not to be bound, is not invasive of province of judiciary, as giving evidence conclusive effect. Chapman v.

Railway Fuel Co., 212 Ala. 106, 101 So. 879 (1924).

Employer presumed subject to compensation law. — In action by subrogee of injured employee to recover sums paid under workmen's compensation law to employee of independent contractor as result of defendant's negligence where it was not proven that defendant at time of employee's injury was subject to the workmen's compensation law and it appeared that defendant was an employer, it would be presumed that defendant was subject to the workmen's compensation law in absence of evidence to the contrary. Sloss-Sheffield Steel & Iron Co. v. Metropolitan Cas. Ins. Co., 28 Ala. App. 366, 185 So. 395 (1938).

Where the relationship of employer and employee exists in Alabama, an injury to the employee is presumably subject to the Alabama Workmen's Compensation Act. Phillips v. Unijax, Inc., 462 F. Supp. 942 (S.D. Ala. 1978), reversed on other grounds, 625 F.2d 54 (5th Cir. 1980).

Lack of dependents did not entitle administratrix to bring civil action. — Fact that employee, whose death arose out of and in the course of his employment, had no dependents did not entitle administratrix of employee's estate to seek compensation by civil action against employer, even though maximum compensation benefits payable otherwise were medical expenses, burial expenses and payment to secondary trust fund. Holliday v. C.T. Thackston Sand & Gravel Co., 361 So. 2d 13 (Ala. Civ. App. 1978).

Employer's right to terminate employee not restricted. — While contracts for employment at will are presumed to be made with reference to and subject to the provisions of the workmen's compensation law, this does not mean that the employer's right to terminate employees at will has been restricted. Martin v. Tapley, 360 So. 2d 708 (Ala. 1978), rev'd on other grounds, 625 F.2d 54 (5th Cir. 1980).

Complaint must allege relation of employer and employee. — Unless a complaint alleges facts showing the relation of employer and employee the parties will not be presumed to be within the application of the article as provided by this section. Garrett v. Gadsden Cooperage Co., 209 Ala. 223, 96 So. 188 (1923).

Words "all contracts of employment" in this section are necessarily modified by the exclusionary provision in § 25-5-50, and provision in § 25-5-50 for withdrawal of acceptance by either party. Ellison v. Butler, 271 Ala. 399, 124 So. 2d 88 (1960); Steele v. Aetna Cas. & Sur. Co., 46 Ala. App. 705, 248 So. 2d 745 (1971) (decided prior to 1992 amendment).

Cited in United States Cas. Co. v. Hoage, 77 F.2d 542 (D.C. Cir. 1935); Gentry v. Swann Chem. Co., 234 Ala. 313, 174 So. 530 (1937).

Collateral references. — 99 C.J.S., Workmen's Compensation, § 2. 100 C.J.S., Workmen's Compensation, § 519.

58 Am. Jur., Workmen's Compensation, § 39 et seq.

Workers' compensation: incarceration as terminating benefits. 54 ALR4th 241.

§ 25-5-55. Rights and powers of minors under article generally; effect of payment of awards to minors.

For the purposes of this article and Article 4 of this chapter, minors shall have the same power to contract, make settlements and receive compensation as adult employees, subject to the power of the court, in its discretion, to require the appointment of a guardian to make the settlement and to receive moneys thereunder or under an award. Payments of awards made to minors or their guardians shall exclude any further compensation either to the minors or to their parents for loss of services or otherwise. (Acts 1919, No. 245, p. 206; Code 1923, § 7549; Code 1940, T. 26, § 277; Acts 1973, No. 1062, p. 1750, § 13; Acts 1992, No. 92-537, § 15.)

The 1992 amendment, effective May 19, 1992, in the first sentence deleted "Minor shall" at the beginning of the sentence, inserted "and Article 4 of this chapter, minors shall," deleted "at any time" preceding "to require the," and substituted "the settlement" for "such settlement."

Minors may be joined so as to be bound

by judgment. — Where widow's petition for compensation in her own behalf disclosed existence of minors without naming them, insurer, being party defendant, could bring in minors on record so as to bind them by judgment. Lawrence v. United States Fid. & Guar. Co., 226 Ala. 161, 145 So. 577 (1933).

Cited in Ex parte Central Iron & Coal Co.,

212 Ala. 367, 102 So. 797 (1925); Larry v. Taylor, 227 Ala. 90, 149 So. 104 (1933).

Collateral references. — 99 C.J.S., Workmen's Compensation, §§ 112-114.

Applicability and effect of workmen's compensation act in case of injury to minors. 14 ALR 818, 33 ALR 337, 49 ALR 1435, 60 ALR 847, 83 ALR 416, 142 ALR 1018.

Who may assert claim of minor. 120 ALR 395.

Status of minor employed by parent as regards provision of workmen's compensation act relating to compensation thereunder. 132 ALR 1030.

Workers' compensation statute as barring illegally employed minor's tort action. 77 ALR4th 844.

§ 25-5-56. Settlements between parties.

The interested parties may settle all matters of benefits, whether involving compensation, medical payments, or rehabilitation, and all questions arising under this article and Article 4 of this chapter between themselves, and every settlement shall be in amount the same as the amounts or benefits stipulated in this article. No settlement for an amount less than the amounts or benefits stipulated in this article shall be valid for any purpose, unless a judge of the court where the claim for compensation under this chapter is entitled to be made, or upon the written consent of the parties, a judge of the court determines that it is for the best interest of the employee or the employee's dependent to accept a lesser sum and approves the settlement. The court shall not approve any settlement unless and until it has first made inquiry into the bona fides of a claimant's claim and the liability of the defendant; and if deemed advisable, the court may hold a hearing thereon. Settlements made may be vacated for fraud, undue influence, or coercion, upon application made to the judge approving the settlement at any time not later than six months after the date of settlement. Upon settlements being approved, judgment shall be entered thereon and duly entered on the records of the court in the same manner and have the same effect as other judgments or as an award if the settlement is not for a lump sum. All moneys voluntarily paid by the employer or insurance carrier to an injured employee in advance of agreement or award shall be treated as advance payments on account of the compensation. In order to encourage advance payments, it is expressly provided that the payments shall not be construed as an admission of liability but shall be without prejudice. (Code 1923, § 7550; Acts 1939, No. 661, p. 1036, § 3; Code 1940, T. 26, § 278; Acts 1992, No. 92-537, § 16.)

The 1992 amendment, effective May 19, 1992, in the first sentence substituted "may settle" for "shall have the right to settle," substituted "benefits, whether involving compensation, medical payments, or rehabilitation" for "compensation," inserted "and Article 4 of this chapter," and deleted "made under this article" following "every settlement," in the second sentence substituted "judge of the court" for "judge of the circuit court of the county," substituted "judge of the court" for "judge of the circuit court of any county" preceding "determines," and substituted "the employee's dependent" for "his dependent," and "the settlement" for "such settlement," in the third sentence deleted "such" preceding

"settlement," and inserted "a" preceding "claimants," substituted "Settlements made" for "Any settlements hereunder" in the fourth sentence, in the fifth sentence deleted "such" preceding "settlements," and substituted "the court" for "said court," deleted the former sixth and seventh sentences which read: "The costs of the proceedings shall not exceed $2.00 and shall be borne by the employer. Such proceedings shall not be deemed subject to state trial, library or other taxes, general or local," and substituted "the payments" for "such payments" in the last sentence.

This section does not preempt the operation of A.R.C.P., Rule 60(b), with respect to setting aside vel non workmen's compensation settlements. Fabarc Steel Supply, Inc. v. Davis, 422 So. 2d 797 (Ala. Civ. App. 1982).

Compensation claims removed from ordinary settlement principles. — This section clearly removes settlement of workmen's compensation claims from the ambit of the principles applicable to the settlement and release of ordinary personal injury claims. Sager v. Royce Kershaw Co., 359 So. 2d 398 (Ala. Civ. App. 1978).

Employer and injured employee have right to settle all matters relating to payment, subject to limitations of statute which requires compensation to be paid substantially as fixed by statute. Tennessee Coal, I. & R.R. v. King, 26 Ala. App. 581, 164 So. 757 (1935).

Except contingent liability in favor of dependents. — Continuing and contingent liability in favor of dependents of injured employee may not be abrogated by agreement as to compensation payments to which they were not parties or their rights determined by judicial proceedings. Tennessee Coal, I. & R.R. v. King, 26 Ala. App. 581, 164 So. 757 (1935).

And settlement waives other remedies. — See National Cast Iron Pipe Co. v. Higginbotham, 216 Ala. 129, 112 So. 734 (1927).

Counsel is not required for settlement of a claim under this section. Porter v. Mobile Pulley & Mach. Works, 507 So. 2d 529 (Ala. Civ. App. 1987).

Timely filing required. — Motion for independent action filed by former employee as an appeal from a denial of his motion for relief from a prior judgment, which approved a settlement of the employees' workmen's compensation, was filed too late for consideration under this section and was not a Rule 60(b) motion because the employee had earlier been denied a Rule 60(b) motion and had failed to timely appeal that denial. Hollins v. Beverly Enters., 532 So. 2d 1025 (Ala. Civ. App. 1988).

Court approval needed if settlement not equal to benefits due. — This section requires court approval of a settlement between an employer and an injured employee for workmen's compensation benefits only if the settlement is not equal to the benefits due under the Workmen's Compensation Act. Johnson v. Asphalt Hot Mix, 565 So. 2d 219 (Ala. 1990).

Finality of judgment or award. — Whether judgment or award entered pursuant to this section would be final as to all matters anterior thereto, quaere. Sloss-Sheffield Steel & Iron Co. v. Lang, 213 Ala. 412, 104 So. 770 (1925). See note to same case under § 25-5-88.

Distinction is made between lump sum award and award payable in installments. — The clear legislative purpose of this section is to make a distinction between the effect of a lump sum award and an award payable in installments. United States Steel Corp. v. Baker, 266 Ala. 538, 97 So. 2d 899 (1957).

When there is a lump sum award it has the same effect as the usual judgment for money, that is, it becomes vested on entry of the judgment just as would be the situation if all compensation installments to which an employee is entitled shall have accrued at the time of an award. See Goodyear Tire & Rubber Co. v. Downey, 266 Ala. 344, 96 So. 2d 278 (1957).

In such cases the awards are vested and not subject to the contingencies prescribed by the act when payment is made in installments. United States Steel Corp. v. Baker, 266 Ala. 538, 97 So. 2d 899 (1957).

Section encourages payment in advance of determination of liability. — Even though the words "to encourage advance payments" appear in the last sentence, it is plain that the purpose of the last two sentences is to encourage the employer, or his insurance carrier when there is insurance, to make advance payments to the disabled employee without waiting for a determination of the question of liability, the length of the disability or the extent of the injuries. March v. City of Huntsville, 45 Ala. App. 480, 232 So. 2d 662 (1970).

And employer may, even though it is insured, make payments later deductible as compensation, if such intention clearly appears. March v. City of Huntsville, 45 Ala. App. 80, 232 So. 2d 662 (1970).

If employer is not insured, employer may take credit for voluntary advance payments against the amount of the ultimate liability. March v. City of Huntsville, 45 Ala. App. 80, 232 So. 2d 662 (1970).

And when there is insurance, carrier may take credit for any advance payments made by it. March v. City of Huntsville, 45 Ala. App. 80, 232 So. 2d 662 (1970).

But insurance carrier may not take credit for advance payments made by employer. March v. City of Huntsville, 45 Ala. App. 80, 232 So. 2d 662 (1970).

Payments made in fulfillment of a contractual obligation owed by appellant to claimant arising from a union contract were in no wise paid as advance payments of workmen's compensation where paid for accrued sick pay; there were two separate obligations. Beatrice Foods Co. v. Clemons, 54 Ala. App. 150, 306 So. 2d 18 (1975).

Advance payments must be pleaded. — Where employer had made payments to dependents prior and subsequent to death of employee, but did not set such payments out in answer, as required by § 25-5-88, it was held that he was not entitled to have same considered as advance payment on account of compensation due, under this section. Southern Cement Co. v. Walthall, 217 Ala. 645, 117 So. 17 (1928). See also Braswell v. Brooks, 266 Ala. 141, 94 So. 2d 879 (1957).

Section 25-5-84 applies only to settlements approved by court. — Statute relating to modification of award of compensation (§ 25-5-84) applies only to settlement made between parties and approved by the court in Davis v. Birmingham Trussville Iron Co., 223 Ala. 259, 135 So. 455 (1931); Sloss-Sheffield Steel & Iron Co. v. Nations, 243 Ala. 107, 8 So. 2d 833 (1942).

A settlement for less than the amount established by the Workmen's Compensation Act must be approved by the court in order to be binding. Phillips v. Opp & Micolas Cotton Mills, Inc., 445 So. 2d 927 (Ala. Civ. App. 1984); Kennedy v. Cochran ex rel. Cochran, 475 So. 2d 872 (Ala. Civ. App. 1985).

Payments made pursuant to an inadequate settlement which was not court approved may be considered as advance payments upon the amount of compensation actually due under the statute. The reverse is also true regarding settlements, for if the noncourt-approved compensation which an employee was paid was the same as, or exceeded, that compensation as fixed by the statute, the provisions of this section have been completely satisfied. The employer and the employee have a right to settle all matters relating to payment, subject to any restrictions or limitations contained in the act. Phillips v. Opp & Micolas Cotton Mills, Inc., 445 So. 2d 927 (Ala. Civ. App. 1984).

Where court approval was never obtained, the compensation paid to the employee constituted advance payments, which are due to be credited against the total compensation which the employer was actually supposed to pay to the employee as compensation under the act if that amount exceeds the total permanent partial compensation actually paid. However, a right of action rests with the employee to have the court decide if the payments actually made were less than that which he should have received under the act. Phillips v. Opp & Micolas Cotton Mills, Inc., 445 So. 2d 927 (Ala. Civ. App. 1984).

Where workmen's compensation payments are voluntarily made without court approval by an employer to an injured employee in the same weekly amounts and for the same period of time as are provided for a particular injury by the statute, those advance payments would fully pay the compensation obligation of the employer to the employee for that injury. However, if the moneys so voluntarily paid without court approval amounted to less than the total amount which should have been paid under the statute, the employer would be liable to the employee for the difference between those total figures, and the employee could institute a timely civil action for that balance. Phillips v. Opp & Micolas Cotton Mills, Inc., 445 So. 2d 927 (Ala. Civ. App. 1984).

When court approval not required. — If the settlement is equal to or exceeds the benefits due under the Alabama Workmen's Compensation Act, then the settlement does not require court approval. King v. Travelers Ins. Co., 513 So. 2d 1023 (Ala. 1987).

Mandamus is appropriate remedy to review order of circuit court vacating settlement under this section. Burger-Phillips Co. v. Phillips, 234 Ala. 563, 176 So. 181 (1937).

And when brought precludes certiorari. — Where employer had brought mandamus to review order vacating order approving lump-sum settlement, employer was precluded by that proceeding from having question re-examined in certiorari proceeding. Burger-Phillips Co. v. Phillips, 234 Ala. 563, 176 So. 181 (1937).

No error in court's denial to set aside judgment entered upon agreement. — Trial court did not err in denying motion of claimant to set aside a judgment entered upon agreement in settlement of a workmen's compensation claim on grounds that the settlement was agreed to by claimant without benefit of counsel, that he believed his injury was greater than stated by his physician, as he continued to suffer pain, and that he mistakenly understood that he could not recover future benefits if his injury was greater than first determined. Porter v. Mobile Pulley & Mach. Works, 507 So. 2d 529 (Ala. Civ. App. 1987).

Findings have force of verdict. — Findings of circuit court, on motion to vacate order approving settlement on conflicting evidence given ore tenus in compensation case, have force of verdict of jury and will not be disturbed unless plainly and palpably unsupported by evidence. Burger-Phillips Co. v. Phillips, 234 Ala. 563, 176 So. 181 (1937).

Authority to vacate approval of settlement within 30 days was granted to court by Code 1940, Tit. 13, § 119 (now covered by A.R.C.P., Rule 59(b)). Ex parte Ingalls Shipbuilding Corp., 32 Ala. App. 609, 28 So. 2d 808 (1947).

And is motion for new trial. — When a motion is made to set aside the approval of a settlement made under this section, within the 30-day period, it is motion for a new trial and is not limited to fraud, undue influence or coercion, but it may include any statutory ground, Code 1940, Tit. 7, § 276 (now covered by A.R.C.P., Rule 59(a)), or any common-law ground, such as fraud, etc., and it would be subject to the privileges of § 12-22-10, and to the burdens of Code 1940, Tit. 13, § 119 (now covered by A.R.C.P., Rule 59(b)), so that an appeal would lie under § 12-22-10. Ingalls Shipbuilding Corp. v. Cahela, 251 Ala. 163, 36 So. 2d 513 (1948).

Employee cannot waive benefits. — If the employee is prohibited from concluding a settlement of his claim with his employer for less than the benefits stipulated in the act, it would seem clear that he cannot, ex parte, waive such benefits. An attempted waiver is contrary to the letter and spirit of the compensation act. Griffith v. Alabama By-Products Corp., 120 F. Supp. 219 (N.D. Ala. 1954).

Settlement agreement held valid. — An agreement to settle a workmen's compensation case is valid, where a circuit judge of the county in which the claimant was injured approved the settlement, he had before him the claimant's settlement offer stating that "there would be no further Workmen's Compensation due" other than the payments to be made in accordance with the settlement, the trial court found that the parties entered into a binding contract in which there was a definite offer, acceptance and consideration; and the parties had the capacity and authority to agree as they did which was set out in writing, and claimant received an amount far in excess of any amount of benefits a workmen's compensation claimant is entitled to receive for the injury claimed. Although the trial court's order did not specifically state that the workmen's compensation claim was within the schedule of benefits prescribed by the act, such a finding was implicit in the trial court's judgment. King v. Travelers Ins. Co., 513 So. 2d 1023 (Ala. 1987).

Cited in National Cast Iron Pipe Co. v. Higginbotham, 216 Ala. 129, 112 So. 734 (1927); Lawrence v. United States Fid. & Guar. Co., 226 Ala. 161, 145 So. 577 (1933); Tennessee Coal, I. & R.R. v. King, 231 Ala. 303, 164 So. 760 (1935); Ex parte Carlisle, 27 Ala. App. 142, 168 So. 598 (1936); Harris v. Louisville & N.R.R., 237 Ala. 366, 186 So. 771 (1939); Wade & Richey v. Oglesby, 251 Ala. 356, 37 So. 2d 596 (1948); Tennessee Coal & Iron Div. v. Hubbert, 268 Ala. 674, 110 So. 2d 260 (1959); Phillips v. Unijax, Inc., 462 F. Supp. 942 (S.D. Ala. 1978); Sparks v. Delta Masonry Contractors, 411 So. 2d 808 (Ala. Civ. App. 1982); Wilson v. Berry Indus. Co., 451 So. 2d 339 (Ala. Civ. App. 1984); Erwin v. Erwin, 459 So. 2d 928 (Ala. Civ. App. 1984); Chenault Motor Co. v. Chenault, 522 So. 2d 293 (Ala. Civ. App. 1988).

Collateral references. — 100 C.J.S., Workmen's Compensation, §§ 402-413.

58 Am. Jur., Workmen's Compensation, § 389 et seq.

Right to credit for amounts paid under invalid settlement or compromise. 10 ALR 1016.

Waiver or compromise of claims. 65 ALR 160.

Release or waiver of claim by employee as affecting right of dependents in event of his death as result of injury. 101 ALR 1410.

Fraud or mistake respecting amount of compensation to which employee was entitled as ground for release from settlement or compromise of claim. 121 ALR 1270.

Time and jurisdiction for review, reopening, modification, or reinstatement of agreement. 165 ALR 9.

OPINIONS OF THE SUPREME COURT CLERK

The filing of a settlement under this chapter should be treated as an original filing for cost purposes under § 12-19-71. Op. No. 11, 356 So. 2d 636 (1978).

The docket fee for filing settlements in workmen's compensation cases is $33.00. Op. No. 11, 356 So. 2d 636 (1978).

§ 25-5-57. Compensation for disability.

(a) *Compensation schedule.* — Following is the schedule of compensation:

(1) TEMPORARY TOTAL DISABILITY. — For injury producing temporary total disability, the compensation shall be 66²/₃ percent of the average weekly earnings received at the time of injury, subject to a maximum and minimum weekly compensation as stated in Section 25-5-68, but if at the time of injury the employee received average weekly earnings of less than

the minimum stated in Section 25-5-68, then he or she shall receive the full amount of the average weekly earnings per week. This compensation shall be paid during the time of the disability, but at the time as a temporary total disability shall become permanent, compensation for the continued total disability shall be governed by (a)(4) of this section with respect to permanent total disability. Payments are to be made at the intervals when the earnings were payable, as nearly as may be, unless the parties otherwise agree.

(2) TEMPORARY PARTIAL DISABILITY.

a. Amount and Duration of Compensation. — For temporary partial disability, the compensation shall be 66²/₃ percent of the difference between the average weekly earnings of the worker at the time of the injury and the average weekly earnings he or she is able to earn in his or her partially disabled condition. This compensation shall be paid during the period of the disability, but not beyond 300 weeks. Payments shall be made at the intervals when the earnings were payable, as nearly as may be, unless the parties otherwise agree, and shall be subject to the same maximum weekly compensation as stated in Section 25-5-68.

b. Effect of Change in Employment. — If the injured employee who is receiving compensation for temporary partial disability leaves the employment of the employer by whom he or she was employed at the time of the accident for which the compensation is being paid, he or she shall, upon securing employment elsewhere, give to the former employer an affidavit in writing containing the name of his or her new employer, the place of employment, and the amount of wages being received at the new employment, and until he or she gives the affidavit, the compensation for temporary partial disability shall cease. The employer for whom the employee was employed at the time of the accident for which the compensation is being paid may also at any time demand of the employee an additional affidavit, in writing, containing the name of his or her employer, the place of his or her employment, and the amount of wages he or she is receiving; and if the employee upon demand fails or refuses to make and furnish the affidavit, his or her right to compensation for temporary partial disability shall cease until the affidavit is made and furnished.

(3) PERMANENT PARTIAL DISABILITY.

a. Amount and Duration of Compensation. — For permanent partial disability, the compensation shall be based upon the extent of the disability. In cases included in the following schedule, the compensation shall be 66²/₃ percent of the average weekly earnings, during the number of weeks set out in the following schedule:

1. For the loss of a thumb, 62 weeks.

2. For the loss of a first finger, commonly called the index finger, 43 weeks.

3. For the loss of a second finger, 31 weeks.

4. For the loss of a third finger, 22 weeks.

5. For the loss of a fourth finger, commonly called the little finger, 16 weeks.

6. The loss of the first phalange of the thumb or of any finger shall be considered as equal to the loss of one half of the thumb or finger, and compensation shall be paid at the prescribed rate during one half of the time specified above for the thumb or finger.

7. The loss of two or more phalanges shall be considered as the loss of the entire finger or thumb, but in no case shall the amount received for more than one finger exceed the amount provided in this schedule for the loss of a hand.

8. For the loss of a great toe, 32 weeks.

9. For the loss of any of the toes other than the great toe, 11 weeks.

10. The loss of the first phalange of any toe shall be considered to be equal to the loss of one half of the toe, and compensation shall be paid at the prescribed rate during one half the time prescribed above for the toe.

11. The loss of two or more phalanges shall be considered as the loss of an entire toe.

12. For the loss of a hand, 170 weeks.

13. For the loss of an arm, 222 weeks.

14. For the loss of a foot, 139 weeks.

15. Amputation between the elbow and wrist shall be considered as the equivalent to the loss of a hand, and amputation between the knee and ankle shall be considered as the equivalent of the loss of a foot.

16. For the loss of a leg, 200 weeks.

17. For the loss of an eye, 124 weeks.

18. For the complete and permanent loss of hearing in both ears, 163 weeks.

19. For the complete and permanent loss of hearing in one ear, 53 weeks.

20. For the loss of an eye and a leg, 350 weeks.

21. For the loss of an eye and one arm, 350 weeks.

22. For the loss of an eye and a hand, 325 weeks.

23. For the loss of an eye and a foot, 300 weeks.

24. For the loss of two arms, other than at the shoulder, 400 weeks.

25. For the loss of two hands, 400 weeks.

26. For the loss of two legs, 400 weeks.

27. For the loss of two feet, 400 weeks.

28. For the loss of one arm and the other hand, 400 weeks.

29. For the loss of one hand and one foot, 400 weeks.

30. For the loss of one leg and the other foot, 400 weeks.

31. For the loss of one hand and one leg, 400 weeks.

32. For the loss of one arm and one foot, 400 weeks.

33. For the loss of one arm and one leg, 400 weeks.

34. For serious disfigurement, not resulting from the loss of a member or other injury specifically compensated, materially affecting

the employability of the injured person in the employment in which he or she was injured or other employment for which he or she is then qualified, 66²/₃ percent of the average weekly earnings for the period as the court may determine, but not exceeding 100 weeks.

b. Successive or Concurrent Temporary Total and Permanent Partial Disabilities Resulting from Same Injury. — When a permanent partial disability, the number of weeks compensation for which is scheduled in subdivision (a)(3) of this section, follows or accompanies a period of temporary total disability resulting from the same injury, the number of weeks of the temporary total disability shall not be deducted from the number of weeks payable for the permanent partial disability.

c. Concurrent Disabilities. — If an employee sustains concurrent injuries resulting in concurrent disabilities, he or she shall receive compensation only for the injury which entitled him or her to the largest amount of compensation, but this paragraph shall not affect liability for the concurrent loss of more than one member for which members compensation is provided in the specific schedule.

d. Loss of Use of Member. — The permanent and total loss of the use of a member shall be considered as equivalent to the loss of that member, but in such cases the compensation specified in the schedule for such injury shall be in lieu of all other compensation, except as otherwise provided herein. For permanent disability due to injury to a member resulting in less than total loss of use of the member not otherwise compensated in this schedule, compensation shall be paid at the prescribed rate during that part of the time specified in the schedule for the total loss or total loss of use of the respective member which the extent of the injury to the member bears to its total loss.

e. Effect of Refusal of Suitable Employment. — If an injured employee refuses employment suitable to his or her capacity offered to or procured for him or her, he or she shall not be entitled to any compensation at any time during the continuance of the refusal, unless at any time, in the opinion of the judge of the circuit court of the county of his or her residence, the refusal is justifiable.

f. Maximum and Minimum Compensation Awards. — Compensation provided in this subsection (a) for loss of members or loss of use of members is subject to the same limitations as to maximum and minimum weekly compensation as stated in Section 25-5-68.

g. Compensation for Permanent Partial Disabilities Not Enumerated. — For all other permanent partial disabilities not above enumerated, the compensation shall be 66²/₃ percent of the difference between the average weekly earnings of the worker at the time of the injury and the average weekly earnings he or she is able to earn in his or her partially disabled condition, subject to the same maximum weekly compensation as stated in Section 25-5-68. If a permanent partial disability, compensation for which is not calculated by use of the schedule in subdivision (a)(3) of this section, follows a period of temporary total disability resulting from the same injury, the number of weeks of the temporary total disability shall be deducted from the number of weeks payable for the permanent partial disability. Compensation shall continue during disability, but not beyond 300 weeks.

h. Affidavit of New Employment. — If the injured employee leaves the services of the employer for whom he or she was working at the time of the accident and accepts employment elsewhere, he or she shall make and furnish affidavit as to his or her new employment in the manner as required in (a)(2) of this section.

i. Return to Work. — If, on or after the date of maximum medical improvement, except for scheduled injuries as provided in Section 25-5-57(a)(3), an injured worker returns to work at a wage equal to or greater than the worker's pre-injury wage, the worker's permanent partial disability rating shall be equal to his or her physical impairment and the court shall not consider any evidence of vocational disability. Notwithstanding the foregoing, if the employee has lost his or her employment under circumstances other than any of the following within a period of time not to exceed 300 weeks from the date of injury, an employee may petition a court within two years thereof for reconsideration of his or her permanent partial disability rating:

(i) The loss of employment is due to a labor dispute still in active progress in the establishment in which he or she is or was last employed. For the purposes of this section only, the term "labor dispute" includes any controversy concerning terms, tenure, or conditions of employment, or concerning the association or representation of persons in negotiating, fixing, maintaining, changing, or seeking to arrange terms or conditions of employment, regardless of whether the disputants stand in the proximate relation of employer and employee. This definition shall not relate to a dispute between an individual worker and his or her employer.

(ii) The loss of employment is voluntary, without good cause connected with such work.

(iii) The loss of employment is for a dishonest or criminal act committed in connection with his or her work, for sabotage, or an act endangering the safety of others.

(iv) The loss of employment is for actual or threatened misconduct committed in connection with his or her work after previous warning to the employee.

(v) The loss of employment is because a license, certificate, permit, bond, or surety which is necessary for the performance of such employment and which he or she is responsible to supply has been revoked, suspended, or otherwise become lost to him or her for a cause.

The burden of proof is on the employer to prove, by clear and convincing evidence, that an employee's loss of employment was due to one of the causes (i) through (v) above. At the hearing, the court may consider evidence as to the earnings the employee is or may be able to earn in his or her partially disabled condition, and may consider any evidence of vocational disability. The fact the employee had returned to work prior to his or her loss of employment shall not constitute a presumption of no vocational impairment. In making this evaluation, the court shall consider the permanent restriction, if any, imposed by the treating physician under Section 25-5-77, as well as all available reasonable accommodations that would enable the employee in his or her condition following the accident or onset of occupational disease to perform jobs that he or she in that condition otherwise would be unable to perform, and shall treat an employee able to perform with such accommodation as though he or she could perform without the accommodation. Nothing contained in this section shall be construed as having any effect upon any evidentiary issues or claims made in third party actions pursuant to Section 25-5-11.

(4) PERMANENT TOTAL DISABILITY.

a. Amount, Duration, and Payment of Compensation. — For permanent total disability, as defined in paragraph d. of this subdivision, the employee shall receive 66²/₃ percent of the average weekly earnings received at the time of the injury, subject to a maximum and minimum weekly compensation as stated in Section 25-5-68. Notwithstanding the foregoing, if at the time of injury the employee was receiving earnings of less than the minimum as stated in Section 25-5-68, then he or she shall receive the full amount of his or her earnings per week. This compensation shall be paid during the permanent total disability, as defined in paragraph d. of this subdivision. Payment of the compensation shall be made at the intervals when the earnings were payable, as nearly as may be, unless the parties otherwise agree. The payments, with the approval of the circuit judge or by the agreement of the parties, may be made monthly, quarterly, or otherwise as the parties may agree. Payments for permanent total disability shall not be ordered to be paid in a lump sum without the consent of both the employer and the employee.

b. Alteration, Amendment, or Revision of Compensation. — At any time, the employer may petition the court that awarded or approved compensation for permanent total disability to alter, amend, or revise the award or approval of the compensation on the ground that as a result of physical or vocational rehabilitation, or otherwise, the disability from which the employee suffers is no longer a permanent total disability and, if the court is so satisfied after a hearing, it shall alter, amend, or revise the award accordingly. If compensation for permanent total disability is being paid pursuant to a written agreement between employer and employee without approval, the employer may make application to the court that would have had jurisdiction to award the compensation to the employee to alter, amend, or revise the agreement on such grounds. If an employee is receiving benefits for permanent total disability other than as a result of an award or a written agreement between the employer and employee and if the employer terminates the payment of the benefits, the employee may, within two years of the last payment, petition the court to reinstate the benefits and, upon a showing that the permanent total disability still exists, shall be entitled to have the benefits reinstated effective the date of the last payment.

c. Employees in Public Institutions. — In case an employee who is permanently and totally disabled becomes an inmate of a public institution, no compensation shall be payable unless the employee has wholly dependent on him or her for support a person or persons named in Sections 25-5-61 and 25-5-62, whose dependency shall be determined as if the employee were deceased, in which case the compensation provided for in this subdivision shall be paid for the benefit of the person so dependent, during dependency, in the manner so ordered by the court, while the employee is an inmate in the institution. Nothing contained herein shall be construed to deprive a permanently and totally disabled employee who has no dependent named in Sections 25-5-61 and 25-5-62 from receiving benefits to which he or she would otherwise be entitled if the employee, although an inmate of a public institution, is paying or on whose behalf funds are paid from any source to the public institution the normal and customary charge for the services rendered by the public institution. Normal and customary charge shall mean that charge actually made by the public institution to persons able to pay for the services rendered them whether the charge actually covers the expense of the upkeep of the inmate or not. If the employee has had a guardian appointed by a court of competent jurisdiction, the workers' compensation payments shall be directly paid to the guardian.

d. Definition. — The total and permanent loss of the sight of both eyes or the loss of both arms at the shoulder or any physical injury or mental impairment resulting from an accident, which injury or impairment permanently and totally incapacitates the employee from working at and being retrained for gainful employment, shall constitute prima facie evidence of permanent total disability but shall not constitute the sole basis on which an award of permanent total disability may be based. Any employee whose disability results from an injury or impairment and who shall have refused to undergo physical or vocational rehabilitation or to accept reasonable accommodation shall not be deemed permanently and totally disabled.

e. Second Permanent Injuries Generally. — If an employee has a permanent disability or has previously sustained another injury than that in which the employee received a subsequent permanent injury by accident, as is specified in this section defining permanent injury, the employee shall be entitled to compensation only for the degree of injury that would have resulted from the latter accident if the earlier disability or injury had not existed.

f. Second Permanent Injury in Same Employment Resulting in Permanent Total Disability. — If an employee receives a permanent injury as specified in this section after having sustained another permanent injury in the same employment, and if the previous and subsequent injuries result in permanent total disability, compensation shall be payable for permanent total disability only.

g. Concurrent Compensation Payments. — If an employee receives an injury for which compensation is payable while he or she is still receiving or entitled to receive compensation for a previous injury in the same employment, he or she shall not at the same time be entitled to compensation for both injuries, unless the later injury is a permanent injury, as specified in this section, but he or she shall be entitled to compensation for that injury and from the time of that injury which will cover the longest period and the largest amount payable under this article and Article 4 of this chapter.

If an employee receives a permanent injury as specified in this section, after having sustained another permanent injury in the same employment, he or she shall be entitled to compensation for both injuries, subject to paragraph e. of this subdivision, but the total compensation shall be paid by extending the period and not by increasing the amount of weekly compensation, and in no case for permanent partial disability exceeding 700 weeks.

h. Effect of Rehabilitation or Recovery on Permanent Total Disability Benefits. — If an employee who is receiving benefits for permanent total disability shall, as a result of physical or vocational rehabilitation or otherwise, obtain gainful employment, the obligation to pay permanent total disability benefits shall thereupon terminate; provided, that at any time that the employee's weekly wage from the employment shall be less than the employee's average weekly wage at the time of injury, the employer shall remain obligated to pay to the employee as compensation an amount equal to $66^2/_3$ percent of the difference, subject to each of the following limitations:

1. The employer's liability for the payment of $66^2/_3$ percent of the difference shall continue for 200 weeks from the date of reemployment or 300 weeks from the date of injury, whichever is the longer period.

2. In no event shall the amount of weekly benefits paid by the employer to the employee exceed the weekly benefit the employee was receiving for permanent total disability.

3. No payments shall be due for any week the employee earns as much as or more than his or her average weekly wage at the time of injury. If the employee who obtains gainful employment suffered a permanent partial disability as specified in subsection (a), subdivision (3) of this section, the total amount of compensation paid for permanent total disability shall not be less than that amount which would have been payable for the permanent partial disability.

i. Affidavit of Gainful Employment. — If an employee who is receiving benefits for permanent total disability shall, as the result of physical or vocational rehabilitation, accommodation, or otherwise, obtain gainful employment with an employer other than with his or her former employer, he or she shall, upon securing employment, give to his or her former employer an affidavit in writing containing the name of his or her new employer, the place of employment and the amount of wages being received at the new employment. Until he or she gives the affidavit, the compensation for permanent total disability shall cease. The employer for whom the employee was employed at the time of the accident for which compensation is being paid may also at any time demand of the employee additional affidavit, in writing, containing the name of his or her employer, the place of his or her employment, and the amount of wages he or she is receiving. If the employee, upon demand, fails or refuses to make and furnish the affidavit, his or her rights to compensation shall cease until the affidavit is made and furnished.

(5) DEATH FOLLOWING DISABILITY. — If an employee sustains an injury occasioned by an accident arising out of and in the course of his or her employment and, during the period of disability caused thereby, death results proximately therefrom, all payments previously made as compensation for the injury shall be deducted from the compensation, if any, due on account of death. If an employee who sustains a permanent partial or permanent total disability, the degree of which has been agreed upon by the parties or has been ascertained by the court, and death results not proximately therefrom, the employee's surviving spouse or dependent children or both shall be entitled to the balance of the payments which would have been due and payable to the worker, whether or not the decedent employee was receiving compensation for permanent total disability, not exceeding, however, the amount that would have been due the surviving spouse or dependent children or both if death had resulted proximately from an injury on account of which compensation is being paid to an employee.

(6) HERNIA.

a. Proof. — For hernia resulting from injury by an accident arising out of and in the course of the employee's employment, it must be definitely proven to the satisfaction of the court all of the following:

1. That there was an injury resulting in hernia.
2. That the hernia appeared suddenly.
3. That it was accompanied by pain.
4. That the hernia immediately followed an accident.
5. That the hernia did not exist prior to the accident for which compensation is claimed.

b. Treatment. — All hernia, inguinal, femoral, or otherwise, proved to be the result of an injury by accident arising out of and in the course of the employment, shall be treated in a surgical manner by radical operation. If the injured employee refuses to undergo the radical operation for the cure of the hernia, no compensation will be allowed during the time the refusal continues. If, however, it is shown that the employee has some chronic disease or is otherwise in physical condition that the court considers it unsafe for the employee to undergo the operation, the employee shall be paid as otherwise provided in this chapter.

(b) *Computation of compensation; determination of average weekly earnings.* — Compensation under this section shall be computed on the basis of the average weekly earnings. Average weekly earnings shall be based on the wages, as defined in Section 25-5-1(6) of the injured employee in the employment in which he or she was working at the time of the injury during the period of 52 weeks immediately preceding the date of the injury divided by 52, but if the injured employee lost more than seven consecutive calendar days during the period, although not in the same week, then the earnings for the remainder of the period, although not in the same week, then the earnings for the remainder of the 52 weeks shall be divided by the number of weeks remaining after the time so lost has been deducted. Where the employment prior to the injury extended over a period of less than 52 weeks, the method of dividing the earnings during that period by the number of weeks and parts thereof during which the employee earned wages shall be followed, provided results just and fair to both parties will thereby be obtained. Where by reason of the shortness of the time during which the employee has been in the employment of his or her employer or the casual nature or terms of the employment it is impracticable to compute the average weekly earnings as above defined, regard shall be had to the average weekly amount which during the 52 weeks prior to the injury was being earned by a person in the same grade, employed at the same work by the same employer, and if there is no person so employed, by a person in the same grade employed in the same class of employment in the same district. Whatever allowances of any character made to an employee in lieu of wages are specified as part of the wage contract shall be deemed a part of his or her earnings.

(c) *Setoff for other recovery.* — In calculating the amount of workers' compensation due:

(1) The employer may reduce or accept an assignment from an employee of the amount of benefits paid pursuant to a disability plan, retirement plan, or other plan providing for sick pay by the amount of compensation paid, if and only if the employer provided the benefits or paid for the plan or plans providing the benefits deducted.

(2) The employee shall forfeit to the employer all compensation paid for any period to which is attributed any award of back pay either by a court, administrative agency, arbitration, or settlement, provided, however, social security payments shall not be included herein.

(3) If an employer continues the salary of an injured employee during the benefit period or pays similar compensation during the benefit period, the employer shall be allowed a setoff in weeks against the compensation owed under this article. For the purposes of this section, voluntary contributions to a Section 125-cafeteria plan for a disability or sick pay program shall not be considered as being provided by the employer. (Acts 1919, No. 245, p. 206; Code 1923, § 7551; Acts 1935, No. 387, p. 831; Acts 1936, Ex. Sess., No. 29, p. 9; Code 1940, T. 26, § 279; Acts 1949, No. 36, p. 47; Acts 1951, No.

563, p. 978, § 1; Acts 1955, No. 110, p. 355; Acts 1957, No. 337, p. 438; Acts 1963, No. 578, p. 1252, § 1; Acts 1967, No. 168, p. 509; Acts 1969, No. 233, p. 557, § 1; Acts 1973, No. 1062, p. 1750, § 14; Acts 1975, 4th Ex. Sess., No. 86, p. 2729, § 5; Acts 1984, 2nd Ex. Sess., No. 85-41, p. 44, § 6; Acts 1992, No. 92-537, § 17.)

The 1992 amendment, effective May 19, 1992, rewrote this section. As to the implementation of this amendment, see the Code commissioner's note.

Code commissioner's note. — Acts 1984, 2nd Ex. Sess., No. 85-41, § 14 provides: "This act shall become effective immediately upon its passage and approval by the governor [January 9, 1985], or upon its otherwise becoming a law, provided it shall have no effect whatsoever with respect to the right of any injured employee to bring an action with respect to or upon any cause of action which arose or accrued prior to February 1, 1985. Provided further, it shall have no effect on and shall not apply to any accident or exposure to injurious condition occurring before the effective date of this Act."

Section 53 of Acts 1992, No. 92-537, provides that the amendment of this section by § 17 of the 1992 act shall be implemented on August 1, 1992.

U.S. Code. — Section 125-cafeteria plan, referred to in subdivision (c)(3), is codified as 26 U.S.C. § 125.

I. GENERAL CONSIDERATION.

Editor's note. — The cases annotated below were decided under prior law.

The purpose of this section, which is entitled "Compensation for disability," is obviously to set forth practical guidelines, including specific amounts and terms, for compensation for a work-related disability. Adkins v. Gold Kist, Inc., 531 So. 2d 890 (Ala. Civ. App. 1987), writ quashed as improvidently granted, ; 531 So. 2d 893 (Ala. 1988).

This section is a literal copy of the Minnesota Act. Wilborn Constr. Co. v. Parker, 281 Ala. 626, 206 So. 2d 872 (1968).

Claim of workman and claim of dependents separate and distinct. — This section is an express recognition of the principle that the claim of the workman and the claim of his dependents on his death are separate and distinct, except that all payments previously made to him as compensation for his injury shall be deducted from the compensation, if any, due on account of death. Wade & Richey v. Oglesby, 251 Ala. 356, 37 So. 2d 596 (1948).

Final determination of the employee's rights under the Workmen's Compensation Act does not conclude his dependents' rights under said act. Wade & Richey v. Oglesby, 251 Ala. 356, 37 So. 2d 596 (1948).

The phrase "judicially ascertained" requires that a court of competent jurisdiction consider the matter and then enter a final order setting forth the extent of the injured employee's disability, and this particular statutory language reflects legislative intent to ensure that disability determinations not be made following an employee's death. Vann Express, Inc. v. Phillips, 539 So. 2d 296 (Ala. Civ. App. 1988).

Basis for compensation is capacity to earn. — While generally no workmen's compensation can be had for partial disability unless employee is as result of injury unable to earn as much thereafter as he did before, his actual earnings after the injury are not always to be taken as the criterion, since the basis for compensation is the capacity to earn. Nashville Bridge Co. v. Honeycutt, 246 Ala. 319, 20 So. 2d 591 (1945).

Compensation cannot be awarded in cases where subsection (a)(3) of this section is operative unless the workman suffered a loss of ability to earn. Black v. Alabama Dry Dock & Shipbuilding Co., 249 Ala. 209, 30 So. 2d 456 (1947).

A finding that an employee, who lost the sight of one eye and 20 percent of the other, was unable to earn anything is not a finding that he was incapacitated from working at an occupation which would bring him an income. Tennessee Coal, Iron & R.R. v. Long, 251 Ala. 492, 38 So. 2d 18 (1948).

Trial court's finding that total loss of the sight of one eye and the loss of 20 percent of that of the other disabled employee to earn anything in his partially disabled condition, and fixing the allowance under this section was correct. Tennessee Coal, I. & R.R. v. Long, 251 Ala. 492, 38 So. 2d 18 (1948).

Under the Alabama workmen's compensation laws, compensation is awarded on the basis of loss of ability to earn. Without a finding of fact as to the loss of ability to earn, there can be no award. Ashley v. Blue Bell, Inc., 401 So. 2d 112 (Ala. Civ. App. 1981).

Compensation under Alabama's workmen's compensation laws for permanent disability can be awarded only when there is a loss of ability to earn. Lankford v. International Paper Co., 454 So. 2d 988 (Ala. Civ. App. 1984).

An employee may not be compensated for an undisputed disability where there is not actual impairment of earnings. Lankford v. International Paper Co., 454 So. 2d 988 (Ala. Civ. App. 1984).

Lost earning capacity is not determined by a worker's loss of actual earnings but by his loss of ability to earn. An injured worker's loss of actual earnings is one of many factors a trial court may consider in determining lost earning capacity. Wilde v. Taco Bell Corp., 531 So. 2d 918 (Ala. Civ. App. 1988).

Which must be measured by average earnings. — While it is sometimes said that the purpose is to compensate the worker for decreased earning capacity, it also appears that such capacity must be measured by his average earnings, representing the reasonable value of his services, when he is making an honest effort to secure and perform work to the extent of his capacity to do so. Alabama By-Products Co. v. Landgraff, 248 Ala. 253, 27 So. 2d 215 (1946).

And statute does not prescribe comparative wages received before and after the injury as the test of the employee's ability to earn. Instead, the test is the difference between the average weekly earnings at the time of the injury and the average weekly earnings the employee "is able to earn in his partially disabled condition." Goodyear Tire & Rubber Co. v. Downey, 266 Ala. 344, 96 So. 2d 278 (1957).

Where scheduled benefits are provided for compensation for loss of a member, they are not dependent on actual wage loss. There may be no loss of time involved. But when there is a clean-cut loss of a scheduled member, with no complications, many jurisdictions hold that the schedule allowance for that member is exclusive. Leach Mfg. Co. v. Puckett, 284 Ala. 209, 224 So. 2d 242 (1969).

Medical testimony is not only factor trial court may consider in determining loss of ability to earn. Orkin Exterminating Co. v. Williams, 389 So. 2d 935 (Ala. Civ. App. 1980).

Factors in determining loss of earning capacity. — In workmen's compensation cases, the trial court has much discretion in determining an employee's loss of earning capacity; many factors are considered by the trial court in determining loss of earning capacity including age, education, past work history, and the effect of the injury on the employee's earning ability. Hayes Int'l Corp. v. Johnson, 563 So. 2d 1052 (Ala. Civ. App. 1990).

Ability to earn does not always mean earning capacity. But it carries the idea of ability to secure as well as to perform profitable employment, which may or may not be to the full extent of earning capacity. Alabama By-Products Co. v. Landgraff, 248 Ala. 253, 27 So. 2d 215 (1946).

Thus, inability to earn may result from inability to find employment. — The inability of the employee to earn anything may result from inability to find employment which he was capable of performing, though he was capable of doing a limited amount of work for hire, if he could get it. Tennessee Coal, I. & R.R. v. Long, 251 Ala. 492, 38 So. 2d 18 (1948).

And wages received are not necessarily a fair criterion. — The Workmen's Compensation Act fixes the liability as of the time of the injury and is referable to the employee's decreased physical efficiency to work, and wages received are not necessarily a fair criterion of a person's ability to labor. Alabama By-Products Co. v. Landgraff, 32 Ala. App. 343, 27 So. 2d 209, aff'd, 248 Ala. 253, 27 So. 2d 215 (1946).

And not sole determining factor. — The fact that the employee, after his injury, received the same salary which he received prior thereto, does not exclude the idea that his ability to earn has been decreased as a result of his disability. While this might presumptively indicate that his ability to earn has not been impaired, it is not the sole determining factor. Goodyear Tire & Rubber Co. v. Downey, 266 Ala. 344, 96 So. 2d 278 (1957).

But the fact that a person does work and earns compensation for his labor after he has suffered an injury should become a

consideration of evidential value in determining the extent of his disability under the Workmen's Compensation Act. Alabama By-Products Co. v. Landgraff, 32 Ala. App. 343, 27 So. 2d 209, aff'd, 248 Ala. 253, 27 So. 2d 215 (1946).

Where there was no finding of fact as to loss of ability to earn, but there was evidence in the record as to the earnings of respondent at the time of his injury, his earnings at the time of trial, his limited education, the limitation of his work experience to manual skills, his constant suffering and pain from the injury and the prediction by the attending physician that respondent could not do manual labor, there is no basis for the award. Brooks v. Crimson Homes, Inc., 51 Ala. App. 252, 284 So. 2d 279 (1973).

Trial court made provision for cessation of employee's disability. — There is no violation of this section where the trial court's award to the employee was "for the rest of her life or until further order of the court". Clearly, by such language the trial court made provision for the termination of benefits should the employee's disability cease. Drummond Co. v. Lolley, 528 So. 2d 885 (Ala. Civ. App. 1988).

Difference in earnings as indication of loss of earning capacity. — Benefits in cases in which there is evidence of average weekly earnings before and after injury is determined by the difference between such earnings. However, in some injuries such difference in earnings may not accurately indicate loss of earning capacity. Littleton v. Gold Kist, Inc., 480 So. 2d 1236 (Ala. Civ. App. 1985).

Second sentence of subsection (a)(5) created new substantive rights — in favor of the widow and dependent children, on the one hand, by giving them a right to money which they did not theretofore have and, on the other hand, by adding to the employer's obligation a requirement that it pay money which theretofore it was not obligated to pay to anyone. Tennessee Coal & Iron Div. v. Hubbert, 268 Ala. 674, 110 So. 2d 260 (1959).

But second sentence of subsection (a)(5) was not retrospective, and does not cover cases where injuries were suffered and awards made prior to its passage, since it would then impair the obligations of contracts in violation of Ala. Const., art. 1, § 22 and art. 4, § 95, as well as the federal Constitution. Tennessee Coal & Iron Div. v. Hubbert, 268 Ala. 674, 110 So. 2d 260 (1959); Woodward Iron Co. v. Newell, 268 Ala. 673, 110 So. 2d 266 (1959).

And right limited to where prior to death benefits due have been determined. — The legislature granted to widows or dependents of injured workmen, subject to the Workmen's Compensation Act, who subsequently died from unrelated causes, the right to bring an action to collect benefits, but chose to limit such right to those cases where there had, prior to death, been a determination of benefits due for the injury. Owens v. Ward, 49 Ala. App. 293, 271 So. 2d 251 (1972).

Court of civil appeals is restricted to determining whether award given by trial court was supported by evidence. McCarty v. Campbell Plumbing Co., 45 Ala. App. 617, 234 So. 2d 895 (1970).

But it is not within province of the court of civil appeals to determine the percentage of disability of an injured employee. McCarty v. Campbell Plumbing Co., 45 Ala. App. 617, 234 So. 2d 895 (1970).

Employment of casual nature. — Employment of 10 year old boy, who ground sausage for grocery at odd times during summer vacation whenever he was needed, working on an average of three days a week, and receiving about 25 cents for each time he helped grind sausage, held "employment of casual nature" as respects fixing of compensation. Hill Grocery Co. v. Ligon, 26 Ala. App. 584, 164 So. 216, rev'd on another point, 231 Ala. 141, 164 So. 219 (1935).

Compensation of child same as any person doing same work. — Compensation of 10 year old boy injured while casually employed to do work that should have been done by a man should be same as for a person employed in same grade, at same work, by same employer, and, if there was no such person, then the same as a person in same grade employed in same class of work in that district. Hill Grocery Co. v. Ligon, 26 Ala. App. 584, 164 So. 216, rev'd on another point, 231 Ala. 141, 164 So. 219 (1935).

Mental disability. — In appropriate circumstances, an award may be made for mental disability even though medical testimony relating to its existence or cause is inconclusive, or even nonexistent. Federal Mogul Corp. v. Campbell, 494 So. 2d 443 (Ala. Civ. App. 1986).

Future medical expenses. — Where the trial court found that the employee was not entitled to permanent disability and that his temporary disability had ended, no award of future medical expenses would be justified. Therefore, the trial court did not err in not issuing a ruling that decided whether the employee was entitled to future necessary medical treatment. Davis v. City of Tuscaloosa, 494 So. 2d 643 (Ala. Civ. App. 1986).

Discretion to make lump-sum attorney fee award. — The trial court has the discretion to make a lump-sum attorney fee award to be paid from the Second Injury Trust Fund. Second Injury Trust Fund v. Stanton, 512 So. 2d 1377 (Ala. Civ. App. 1987). But see Ex parte

St. Regis Corp., 535 So. 2d 160 (Ala. 1988), holding that to the extent this case and others hold that it is not an abuse of discretion to award a lump sum attorney fee without reducing the payments to their present value, and that the employer does not have standing to appeal such an award, this case and the others are expressly overruled.

Award reversed absent findings as to loss of earning ability. — Trial court's award of compensation based upon its finding of a 23 percent impairment to employee's upper extremity, where the trial court made no specific findings that the employee had sustained a loss of ability to earn, would be reversed and the case would be remanded to the trial court for it to ascertain whether the employee had sustained a loss of ability to earn, since the trial court did not treat the employee as having a scheduled injury. Gibson v. Southern Stone Co., 500 So. 2d 32 (Ala. Civ. App. 1986).

Case was reversed and remanded where the trial court made no specific finding that the employee sustained any loss of ability to earn; compensation is awarded on the basis of loss of ability to earn, and without such a finding, no compensation could be awarded. Tyson Foods, Inc. v. Calloway, 568 So. 2d 811 (Ala. Civ. App. 1990).

Trial court erred in awarding the employee benefits without finding that he suffered a loss of ability to earn. Piggly Wiggly Ala. Distrib. Co. v. Barnes, 571 So. 2d 1197 (Ala. Civ. App. 1990).

Cited in Ex parte Little Cahaba Coal Co., 213 Ala. 244, 104 So. 422 (1925); Tennessee Coal, I. & R.R. v. Shelby, 214 Ala. 87, 106 So. 499 (1925); Woodstock Cotton Mills v. Gilmer, 216 Ala. 256, 113 So. 83 (1927); Armour & Co. v. White, 23 Ala. App. 515, 128 So. 119 (1930); Tuscaloosa Compress Co. v. Hagood, 229 Ala. 284, 156 So. 633 (1934); Ex parte Johnston, 231 Ala. 458, 165 So. 108 (1935); Ex parte Carlisle, 27 Ala. App. 142, 168 So. 598 (1936); Alabama By-Products Corp. v. Winters, 234 Ala. 566, 176 So. 183 (1937); Sloss-Sheffield Steel & Iron Co. v. Metropolitan Cas. Ins. Co., 28 Ala. App. 366, 185 So. 395 (1938); Sloss-Sheffield Steel & Iron Co. v. Metropolitan Cas. Ins. Co., 237 Ala. 43, 185 So. 399 (1938); Daniels Constr. Co. v. Phillips, 241 Ala. 537, 3 So. 2d 304 (1941); Tombrello Coal Co. v. Fortenberry, 248 Ala. 640, 29 So. 2d 125 (1947); H.C. Price Co. v. Lee, 249 Ala. 230, 30 So. 2d 579 (1947); Dunning v. Republic Steel Corp., 257 Ala. 1, 59 So. 2d 606 (1950); Birmingham Post Co. v. McGinnis, 256 Ala. 473, 55 So. 2d 507 (1951); C.E. Adams & Co. v. Harrell, 257 Ala. 25, 57 So. 2d 83 (1952); Wilson & Co. v. Curry, 259 Ala. 685, 68 So. 2d 548 (1953); West Point Mfg. Co. v. Bennett, 263 Ala. 571, 83 So. 2d 303 (1955); Sam's Place v. Middleton, 271 Ala. 226, 122 So. 2d 925 (1960); Shepard v. Chrysler Corp., 314 F. Supp. 1179 (N.D. Ala. 1969); Dale Motels, Inc. v. Crittenden, 49 Ala. App. 51, 268 So. 2d 834 (1972); Henderson v. Johnson, 49 Ala. App. 191, 269 So. 2d 905 (1972); Bell v. Mar-Mil Steel & Supply Co., 54 Ala. App. 432, 309 So. 2d 471 (1975); Harris v. National Truck Serv., 56 Ala. App. 350, 321 So. 2d 690 (1975); B.F. Goodrich Co. v. Butler, 336 So. 2d 1357 (Ala. Civ. App. 1976); Romine v. McDuffie, 341 So. 2d 952 (Ala. Civ. App. 1977); Federal Mogul Corp. v. Taylor, 345 So. 2d 1366 (Ala. Civ. App. 1977); Conagra v. White, 348 So. 2d 502 (Ala. Civ. App. 1977); Russell v. H.K. Porter Co., 357 So. 2d 154 (Ala. Civ. App. 1978); Belcher v. Vulcan Materials Co., 359 So. 2d 386 (Ala. 1978); Jamestown Corp. v. Ward, 373 So. 2d 1136 (Ala. Civ. App. 1979); Thompson & Co. Contractors v. Cole, 391 So. 2d 1042 (Ala. Civ. App. 1980); Sunnyland Foods, Inc. v. Catrett, 395 So. 2d 1005 (Ala. Civ. App. 1980); Cement Prods. Co. v. Martin, 397 So. 2d 149 (Ala. Civ. App. 1981); Turner v. Birmingham Clay Co., 399 So. 2d 856 (Ala. Civ. App. 1981); Ray Motels, Inc. v. Griffin, 428 So. 2d 107 (Ala. Civ. App. 1983); Smith v. West Point-Pepperell, Inc., 431 So. 2d 1268 (Ala. Civ. App. 1983); Butler v. Moretti-Harrah Marble Co., 431 So. 2d 1291 (Ala. Civ. App. 1983); Ashland Chem. Co. v. Watkins, 435 So. 2d 1301 (Ala. Civ. App. 1983); Henson v. Estes Health Care Ctr., Inc., 439 So. 2d 74 (Ala. 1983); City of Montgomery v. Robinson, 441 So. 2d 857 (Ala. 1983); Allen v. Diversified Prods., 453 So. 2d 1063 (Ala. Civ. App. 1984); Lawler Mobile Homes, Inc. v. Hinkle, 459 So. 2d 903 (Ala. Civ. App. 1984); Erwin v. Erwin, 459 So. 2d 928 (Ala. Civ. App. 1984); Hilyard Drilling Co. v. Janes, 462 So. 2d 942 (Ala. Civ. App. 1985); Fruehauf Corp. v. Keenum, 466 So. 2d 137 (Ala. Civ. App. 1984); Hurt v. Pullman, Inc., 764 F.2d 1443 (11th Cir. 1985); Elbert Greeson Hosiery Mills, Inc. v. Ivey, 472 So. 2d 1049 (Ala. Civ. App. 1985); Middleton v. Dan River, Inc., 617 F. Supp. 1206 (M.D. Ala. 1985); Guy v. Southwest Ala. Council on Alcoholism, 495 So. 2d 77 (Ala. Civ. App. 1986); King v. Travelers Ins. Co., 513 So. 2d 1023 (Ala. 1987); Coan v. Lawrence County Comm'n, 537 So. 2d 937 (Ala. Civ. App. 1988); Smither v. International Paper Co., 540 So. 2d 760 (Ala. Civ. App. 1989); Drummond Co. v. Wilson, 547 So. 2d 564 (Ala. Civ. App. 1989); Patterson v. Clarke County Motors, Inc., 551 So. 2d 412 (Ala. Civ. App. 1989); Jowers v. Williams, 567 So. 2d 359 (Ala. Civ. App. 1990); Stevison v. Qualified Personnel, Inc., 571 So. 2d 1178 (Ala. Civ. App. 1990); Gilbreath v. Eastwood Foods, Inc., 575 So. 2d 87 (Ala. Civ. App. 1990); Ex parte Eastwood Foods, Inc., 575 So. 2d 91 (Ala. 1991); Bowman Transp., Inc. v.

Blackwell, 586 So. 2d 913 (Ala. Civ. App. 1991).

Collateral references. — 99 C.J.S., Workmen's Compensation, §§ 306-317.

58 Am. Jur., Workmen's Compensation, §§ 281-320.

Right to consider rise or fall in wages since date of accident in fixing compensation. 2 ALR 1642, 92 ALR 1188.

Insanity as terminating right to compensation. 6 ALR 570.

Survival of right to compensation upon death of person entitled to award. 15 ALR 821, 24 ALR 441, 29 ALR 1426, 51 ALR 1446, 87 ALR 864, 95 ALR 254.

What amounts to loss of member. 18 ALR 1350.

Necessity and sufficiency of evidence that hernia is attributable to employment. 20 ALR 48, 73 ALR 488.

Previous loss or mutilation of member as affecting amount or basis of compensation. 30 ALR 979.

Phrase "incapacity for work" or the like, as including inability to obtain work following an injury. 33 ALR 115.

Mental state or nervous condition following injury as factor in determining amount or duration of compensation. 44 ALR 500, 86 ALR 961.

Neglect or improper self-treatment as affecting right to or amount of compensation. 54 ALR 637.

Effect of refusal to accept, or failure to seek, other employment, or entering into business for oneself after injury. 63 ALR 1241.

What amounts to total incapacity. 67 ALR 785, 98 ALR 729.

Change of status as regards relationship or dependence after injury as ground for modification of amount of compensation to employee. 73 ALR 1016.

Tips or gratuities as factor in determining amount of compensation. 75 ALR 1223.

Compensation for disfigurement. 80 ALR 970, 116 ALR 712.

Deduction for lost time in computing wages as basis for workmen's compensation. 82 ALR 889.

Time as of which earnings are to be considered in computing compensation for injury or incapacity ultimately from causes not immediately operative. 86 ALR 524.

Right to compensation for temporary total disability in addition to compensation for permanent partial disability. 88 ALR 385.

Expense money as a factor in computing one's earnings as basis for award. 94 ALR 763.

Marriage as terminating right to future payment of compensation to injured female employee. 96 ALR 976.

Computation of compensation as affected by compensation allowed for previous injury. 96 ALR 1080.

Payment, or period of payment, for separate compensable injuries as concurrent or consecutive. 99 ALR 896.

Rate of discount to be considered in computing present value of future earning or benefits lost on account of personal injuries. 105 ALR 234.

Basis for computation of compensation in case of intermittent employment. 112 ALR 1094.

Provisions of workmen's compensation act relating to hernia. 114 ALR 1337.

Deduction of pension, insurance, gratuities, or other benefits not derived from compensation act. 119 ALR 920.

Right to compensation as affected by fact that injured employee earns, or is offered as much as or more than, before the injury. 149 ALR 413.

Right to compensation as for total or partial disability in case of abnormal condition of body or member which results from or is incident to specific injury for which the act makes special allowance. 156 ALR 1344.

Crediting employer or insurance carrier with earnings of employee reemployed, or continued in employment, after injury. 175 ALR 725, 84 ALR2d 1108.

Excessiveness or adequacy of damages awarded for injuries to, or conditions induced in, sexual organs and processes. 13 ALR4th 183.

Excessiveness or adequacy of damages awarded for injuries to legs and feet. 13 ALR4th 212.

Workers' compensation: value of home services provided by victim's relative. 65 ALR4th 142.

Workers' compensation: recovery for home service provided by spouse. 67 ALR4th 765.

Workers' compensation: compensability of injuries incurred traveling to or from medical treatment of earlier compensable injury. 83 ALR4th 110.

Workers' compensation: bonus as factor in determining amount of compensation. 84 ALR4th 1055.

Workers' compensation as covering cost of penile or similar implants related to sexual or reproductive activity. 89 ALR4th 1057.

II. RIGHT TO COMPENSATION IN GENERAL.

Right of action of dependents is separate from that accruing to injured employee. — The right of action accruing under this section to the dependents is separate and distinct from that accruing to the injured workman. One results from the death of the workman, the other from his injury. The right of the surviving dependents does not arise until the death of the workman, while his right accrued immediately upon his injury. Tennessee Coal, I. & R.R. v. King, 231 Ala. 303, 164 So. 760 (1935).

And right of surviving dependents does not arise until death of workman. Ex parte Woodward Iron Co., 277 Ala. 133, 167 So. 2d 702 (1964).

While workman's right accrues immediately upon his injury. — See Ex parte Woodward Iron Co., 277 Ala. 133, 167 So. 2d 702 (1964).

Hence, claims are separate and distinct causes of action. — A claim of an employee for compensation for injuries, and the claim of his widow or other dependents after his death on account of such injuries are separate and distinct causes of action. Ex parte Woodward Iron Co., 277 Ala. 133, 167 So. 2d 702 (1964).

Wife has no right to be substituted as plaintiff in original action. — Wife's cause of action did not arise and had not accrued when her husband's original workmen's compensation action was filed, and she had no right to be substituted as plaintiff in the original action when he died. The two different claims, the husband's and the wife's, could not exist at the same time. His rights terminated at his death, and hers did not exist prior to his death. Ex parte Woodward Iron Co., 277 Ala. 133, 167 So. 2d 702 (1964).

Overpayment to employee cannot be deducted from amount due dependents. — Amount of intentional overpayment of compensation made by employer at request of injured employee prior to employee's death could not be deducted from compensation due dependents of employee after his death. Tennessee Coal, I. & R.R. v. King, 231 Ala. 303, 164 So. 760 (1935).

No right to succeed to deceased employee's cause of action for determination of benefits. — Where there had been no agreement nor ascertainment by the trial court as to the amount of benefits due for the employee's injury prior to his death there is no right given by the section to the widow or dependent children to succeed to the deceased employee's cause of action for determination of benefits. Owens v. Ward, 49 Ala. App. 293, 271 So. 2d 251 (1972).

Right given by this section is only to proceed for collection of benefits already determined to be due and payable for the injury suffered but unpaid because of death. Owens v. Ward, 49 Ala. App. 293, 271 So. 2d 251 (1972).

Cause of action of employee does not survive, nor for that matter does the em-

ployee's action survive under the statute, but a separate cause of action is granted the widow or dependents to recover the fruits of the action of the employee remaining unpaid after his death. Owens v. Ward, 49 Ala. App. 293, 271 So. 2d 251 (1972).

Factors other than strict medical physical disability may be properly considered in determining disability in workmen's compensation cases; however, where the only evidence of disability offered was subjective complaints, with no organic or physical disorders either caused or aggravated by the worker's work-related injury and the trial court considered the expert testimony, but simply did not believe that the claimant actually suffered from a permanent psychological disability, the trial court properly denied benefits. Armstrong v. Lewis & Assocs. Constr. Co., 469 So. 2d 605 (Ala. Civ. App. 1984).

Subsection (a)(3)g should not be considered in making awards for loss of use of member. — Subsections (a)(3)a and (a)(3)d govern compensation for the loss of or the loss of use of a scheduled member, and subsection (a)(3)g, which governs the amount to be awarded in loss of ability to earn cases, should not be considered in making awards for loss of use of a member. Jackson v. Dunlop Tire & Rubber Corp., 487 So. 2d 940 (Ala. Civ. App. 1986).

Unrelated pain not compensable. — Where testimony by an orthopedic specialist, who treated the plaintiff's finger injuries, emphatically stated that the shoulder pain could not be related to the finger injuries with sound medical judgment, and another physician testified that the plaintiff did not complain about his shoulder until a month after the accident which injured the plaintiff's fingers, the trial court could properly find that the shoulder injury did not arise from the finger injury sustained in an employment accident and was therefore not compensable. Davis v. Fabarc Steel Supply, Inc., 469 So. 2d 114 (Ala. Civ. App. 1985).

Termination of temporary benefits. — Termination of the temporary benefits payments by insurer to employee when insurer receives a copy of a letter that was sent to employee by her doctor stating that she had reached maximum recovery and had a 20 percent permanent disability to the body as a whole is in accord with subsection (a)(1) of this section. Floyd v. Housing Auth., 397 So. 2d 136 (Ala. Civ. App.), cert. denied, 397 So. 2d 139 (Ala. 1981).

The workmen's compensation law does not require notice of termination of temporary total benefits before they can be stopped. The cessation of payments should be sufficient notice that the temporary total benefits have been terminated. Floyd v. Housing Auth., 397 So. 2d 136 (Ala. Civ. App.), cert. denied, 397 So. 2d 139 (Ala. 1981).

Disability for neurosis. — If it is established by legal evidence that an employee has suffered a physical injury or trauma in the line and scope of his employment and he develops a neurosis as a proximate result of such injury or trauma which neurosis causes or contributes to an occupational or physical disability, such disability is compensable. Fruehauf Corp. v. Prater, 360 So. 2d 999 (Ala. Civ. App. 1978); Abex Corp. v. Coleman, 386 So. 2d 1160 (Ala. Civ. App. 1980).

Employee not limited to schedule where greater incapacity. — Where an injury to one part of the body leads to greater incapacity than that which normally results from the specific injury, the employee is not limited in his recovery to the amount allowed for the member in the schedule. Republic Steel Corp. v. Kimbrell, 370 So. 2d 294 (Ala. Civ. App.), cert. denied, 370 So. 2d 297 (Ala. 1979).

Even though there is an injury to a scheduled member, if the effects of that injury extend to other parts of the body and produce a greater or more prolonged incapacity than that which results from the specific injury, then the employee may recover the greater benefits allowed by subsection (a)(3)g of this section for a permanent partial disability rather than be limited to the benefits allowed for a scheduled member. J.S. Walton & Co. v. Reeves, 396 So. 2d 699 (Ala. Civ. App. 1981).

For discussion of right to compensation for loss of a sightless eye, see Gold Kist, Inc. v. Barnett, 439 So. 2d 703 (Ala. Civ. App. 1983).

Provision that an employee is not entitled to compensation if he refuses suitable employment during continuance of such refusal, unless circuit judge finds refusal justifiable, is inapplicable to cases involving permanent partial disability enumerated in the schedule, since compensation for injuries coming within the enumerated scheduled class is given without qualification or restriction. Agricola Furnace Co. v. Smith, 239 Ala. 488, 195 So. 743 (1940).

Claimant may have compensation for permanent injury after receiving compensation for temporary disability. — Our courts have always construed the Workmen's Compensation Act as allowing a claimant to recover compensation for a permanent injury although he has already received compensation for temporary incapacity because of the same injury. And there is no reason to believe that it was intended that a permanently disfigured claimant should be placed in a worse position in this respect than one suffering any of the other permanent injuries specifically compensated by subdivision (a)(3) of this section. Johnson v. Cox, 38 Ala. App. 222, 82 So. 2d 562 (1955).

Offer of required operation for hernia by employer. — Under subsection (a)(6) of this section, relating to denial of compensation where injured employee refuses to undergo operation for hernia, offer of required operation by employer should be accompanied with averment of fact that employer was ready, willing and able to furnish required medical and surgical skill. Where employer's answer was mere denial of liability for employee's hernia, but doctor testified that he proposed that they operate, but employee said he wanted compensation, there was no compliance with the subsection. Woodward Iron Co. v. Vines, 217 Ala. 369, 116 So. 514 (1928).

Fact that employee had resumed work after injury could be considered for its evidentiary value in determining percentage of disability, but the mere fact that such work had been resumed for a given time and at same wage as employee received before injury did not disentitle employee to compensation. Agricola Furnace Co. v. Smith, 239 Ala. 488, 195 So. 743 (1940).

Compensation to wife of deceased employee does not cease upon her being committed to public institution for insane, paragraph (a)(4)b of this section applying only to injured employee without dependents. Ex parte Gude & Co., 213 Ala. 584, 105 So. 657 (1925).

III. PARTICULAR PROVISIONS AND INJURIES.

A. Temporary Total Disability.

Temporary total disability refers to period of time employee is recuperating, as distinguished from permanent partial disability, which is based on the medical condition after maximum improvement has been reached. Defense Ordinance Corp. v. England, 52 Ala. App. 565, 295 So. 2d 419 (1974).

Temporary total disability is ordinarily established by direct evidence of actual wage loss. Defense Ordinance Corp. v. England, 52 Ala. App. 565, 295 So. 2d 419 (1974).

And fact a person is unemployed does not necessarily in and of itself mean he is temporarily totally disabled. Defense Ordinance Corp. v. England, 52 Ala. App. 565, 295 So. 2d 419 (1974).

"Healing period" or "period of recovery" are descriptive and definitional terms as to what period temporary total disability applies.

Defense Ordinance Corp. v. England, 52 Ala. App. 565, 295 So. 2d 419 (1974).

And temporary total disability may occur at different times during recuperative period of healing until maximum medical improvement is reached or can be ascertained depending upon the circumstances of each case. Defense Ordinance Corp. v. England, 52 Ala. App. 565, 295 So. 2d 419 (1974).

B. Temporary Partial Disability.

Where injury to an employee is temporary and partial, the general compensation formula for temporary partial disability under paragraph (a)(2) is applicable although the injury was to a member, but if such injury is permanent, it is controlled by paragraph (a)(3)d for "loss of a member." If the injury is permanent and partial, but not of a member, it is controlled by paragraph (a)(3)g, using the same formula as paragraph (a)(2)a. Alabama By-Products Co. v. Landgraff, 248 Ala. 253, 27 So. 2d 215 (1946).

Employee's percentage of decreased earning capacity ascertained first. — In determining what is the average weekly earnings the employee is able to earn in his partially disabled condition, employee's percentage of decreased earning capacity must first be ascertained. All relevant evidence should be considered, including without being limited to the evidence of experts and the amount of his earnings after the accident. Alabama By-Products Co. v. Landgraff, 248 Ala. 253, 27 So. 2d 215 (1946).

And the greater the difference in earnings the greater the compensation. — The greater the spread is between the average earnings of a partially disabled employee before his injury and his average earnings afterward under the second factor of the formula, the greater will be the amount of his compensation under paragraph (a)(2)a. So that if his earnings after the injury are taken as the second factor of the formula and are less than he was able to earn, the result would be favorable to him. If his earnings are more than is justified by his earning capacity, the amount should be reduced to that of his earning capacity. Such reduction would increase the spread, operating to his interest. If his earnings are less than his earning capacity, a fixation of that factor at his earning capacity operates in favor of his employer in fixing his compensation under paragraph (a)(2)a. So that to use his earning capacity, rather than his average earnings, as the second factor in the formula cannot be prejudicial to the employer but may be to the employee. Alabama By-Products Co. v. Landgraff, 248 Ala. 253, 27 So. 2d 215 (1946).

But if employee's earnings after injury exceed his decreased earning capacity they are more than "he is able to earn," and the second factor in the formula in paragraph (a)(2)a of this section is based upon the proportionate loss of earning capacity. Alabama By-Products Co. v. Landgraff, 248 Ala. 253, 27 So. 2d 215 (1946).

However, if employee's earnings after injury are less than his decreased earning capacity could produce, the amount of his average earnings after the accident is to be taken as the second factor in the formula in paragraph (a)(2)a of this section provided he was making an honest effort to obtain and perform lucrative employment to the extent of his capacity, for they are then as much as "he is able to earn": But his proportionate loss of earning capacity is to be taken as the measure of the second factor, when he is earning less than his earning capacity could produce, if he is not making an honest effort to obtain and perform such employment to the extent of his capacity, for then he is not earning what "he is able to earn." Alabama By-Products Co. v. Landgraff, 248 Ala. 253, 27 So. 2d 215 (1946).

And if employee after injury is earning an amount equal to what his earning capacity can produce, his average earnings and his earning capacity would represent the same figure as the second factor of the formula in paragraph (a)(2)a of this section. Alabama By-Products Co. v. Landgraff, 248 Ala. 253, 27 So. 2d 215 (1946).

Paragraph (a)(2)b must be construed in connection with paragraph (a)(2)a. Alabama By-Products Co. v. Landgraff, 32 Ala. App. 343, 27 So. 2d 209 (1946).

Paragraph (a)(2)b safeguard to shield employer against overpayment. — The provisions of paragraph (a)(2)b of this section requiring an employee receiving temporary partial disability compensation, upon securing new employment, to furnish affidavits to former employer, are safeguards to shield the employer against overpayment of compensation for partial disability benefits. The necessity for the protection is not immediate or urgent unless the injured person is in fact receiving compensation from the employer by whom he was employed at the time of the accident — and this is the status when he receives wages elsewhere. Alabama By-Products Co. v. Landgraff, 32 Ala. App. 343, 27 So. 2d 209 (1946), holding that injured employee, who was not receiving compensation at time of securing new employment, was not required to furnish affidavits to former employer under subsection (a)(2)b of this section.

C. Permanent Partial Disability.

Subdivision (a)(3) provides a schedule of compensation for disability resulting from the loss of certain members. Dale Motels, Inc. v. Crittenden, 50 Ala. App. 251, 278 So. 2d 370 (1973).

When compensation required under subdivision (a)(3). — Compensation under subdivision (a)(3) of this section is required where there is an injury resulting in the loss of the use of a member and where the loss is not accompanied by any other physical disability of the body. Loggins v. Mallory Capacitor Co., 344 So. 2d 522 (Ala. Civ. App. 1977).

The criteria for determining permanent partial disability for the purpose of compensation is not controlled by a finding of physical disability of the body as a whole. Such physical disability may be involved, but is not necessarily or exclusively so. Littleton v. Gold Kist, Inc., 480 So. 2d 1236 (Ala. Civ. App. 1985).

Loss of fingers rendering hand useless. — Compensation for injury to child's hand necessitating amputation of index, middle and third fingers held to be aggregate of allowances fixed for loss of such fingers separately, notwithstanding statement of medical witness that injury rendered hand practically useless. Hill Grocery Co. v. Ligon, 231 Ala. 141, 164 So. 219, rev'g 26 Ala. App. 584, 164 So. 216 (1935).

Complete arm, in common parlance, extends from where it connects with the shoulder blade to the hand. McCarty v. Campbell Plumbing Co., 45 Ala. App. 627, 234 So. 2d 895 (1970).

Shoulder is not a part of the arm. McCarty v. Campbell Plumbing Co., 45 Ala. App. 617, 234 So. 2d 895 (1970); M.R. Thomason & Assocs. v. Jones, 48 Ala. App. 67, 261 So. 2d 899 (1972).

Where defendant suffered an injury at the sternoclavicular junction (end of the collarbone at the chest bone), this junction is not part of the arm. McCarty v. Campbell Plumbing Co., 45 Ala. App. 617, 234 So. 2d 895 (1970).

Fact that arm's use is impaired does not of itself bring injury within category of a scheduled injury and warrant award for partial loss of the use of the arm. McCarty v. Campbell Plumbing Co., 45 Ala. App. 617, 234 So. 2d 895 (1970).

Disease contributing to loss of arm. — An employee can recover specific compensation fixed for loss of arm, notwithstanding existence of disease which contributed to necessity for amputation. Stith Coal Co. v. Alvis, 224 Ala. 603, 141 So. 663 (1932).

Loss of foot. — If claimant's injury was below the knee and that was the only part of the leg physically affected so that its usefulness was materially impaired, compensation was payable for a period of time based upon that fixed by law for total loss of the member, a "total loss of the member" as distinguished from "total loss of use of the member" involving substantially its amputation, and therefore if the partial loss of use is of the portion of the leg defined as a foot when amputated, the definition fixes the name of the member whose loss fixes the basic period of compensation. Nolan v. Ernest Constr. Co., 243 Ala. 460, 10 So. 2d 547 (1942).

Where claimant had sustained a temporary total disability of 40 weeks followed by a 50 percent, permanent loss of use by a fracture of a leg at a point a short distance above the ankle and below the knee, with the fracture extending into the ankle, all of the leg below the knee was denominated "foot" so as to fix the basic compensation period under the provisions of this section providing for compensation for loss of use of a member and defining loss of a foot as an amputation between the knee and ankle. Nolan v. Ernest Constr. Co., 243 Ala. 460, 10 So. 2d 547 (1942).

Loss of a "leg". — Under compensation schedule defining loss of a "foot" as an amputation between the knee and ankle, amputation at or above the knee is the loss of a "leg." Nolan v. Ernest Constr. Co., 243 Ala. 460, 10 So. 2d 547 (1942).

Permanent partial disability due to injury to eyes was governed by paragraph (a)(3)d and paragraph (a)(4)a considered in connection with paragraph (a)(4)c. Consolidated Coal Co. v. Dill, 248 Ala. 5, 26 So. 2d 88 (1946).

For partial permanent disability to sight, the award is governed by the provisions of subdivision (a)(4) and paragraph (a)(3)d of this section, and not by the provisions of paragraph (a)(3)g of this section. Pinto Island Metals Co. v. Edwards, 275 Ala. 304, 155 So. 2d 304 (1963).

Disfigurement. — The evidence supported the finding by the trial court that claimant's disfigurement was of a type "materially affecting his employability in the employment in which he was injured, or other employment for which he was qualified." Johnson v. Cox, 38 Ala. App. 222, 82 So. 2d 562 (1955).

Where there was no disability other than the loss of four fingers, the petitioner was due no compensation for any disfigurement. Leach Mfg. Co. v. Puckett, 284 Ala. 209, 224 So. 2d 242 (1969).

Summary judgment improper where question of fact as to disfigurement. — Where the employee's own deposition testimony created a question of fact as to whether his disfigurement materially affected his employability with either the employer or subsequently with the United States Army, summary judgment as to the employee's entitlement to benefits under subdivision (a)(3)a.34 was improper. Shoney's Restaurants v. Biddle, 496 So. 2d 70 (Ala. Civ. App. 1986).

Extension of effect of injury to other parts of body. — Although the injury itself is to only one part or member of the body, if the effect of such injury extends to other parts of the body, and produces a greater or more prolonged incapacity than that which naturally results from the specific injury, or the injury causes an abnormal and unusual incapacity with respect to the member, then the employee is not limited in his recovery under the workmen's compensation law to the amount allowed under the schedule for injury to the one member. Bell v. Driskill, 282 Ala. 640, 213 So. 2d 806 (1968).

The many variations that occur when there are resulting injuries that extend to other parts of the body and interfere with their efficiency are recognized; then the schedule is and should not be exclusive. Leach Mfg. Co. v. Puckett, 284 Ala. 209, 224 So. 2d 242 (1969); Avondale Mills, Inc. v. Tollison, 52 Ala. App. 52, 289 So. 2d 621 (1974).

A variation from the scheduled benefits under paragraph (a)(3)a may be allowed when there are resulting injuries, the effects of which extend to other parts of the body and interfere with their efficiency. Dale Motels, Inc. v. Crittenden, 50 Ala. App. 251, 278 So. 2d 370 (1973).

Even though the injury is to a scheduled member, if the effects of such injury extend to other parts of the body, and produce a greater or more prolonged incapacity than that which naturally results from the specific injury, then the employee is not limited in his recovery to the amount allowed for the member in the schedule. Unexcelled Mfg. Corp. v. Ragland, 52 Ala. App. 57, 289 So. 2d 626 (1974); Richardson Homes Corp. v. Shelton, 336 So. 2d 1367 (Ala. Civ. App. 1976).

Even though an injury itself is to only one part or member of the body, if the effect of such injury extends to other parts of the body, and produces a greater or more prolonged incapacity than that which naturally results from the specific injury, or the injury causes an abnormal and unusual incapacity with respect to the member, then the employee is not limited in his recovery under the workmen's compensation law to the amount allowed under the schedule for injury to one member. City of Moulton v. Pearson, 54 Ala. App. 340, 308 So. 2d 252 (1975).

Minimum rate under § 25-5-68 inapplicable under subdivision (a)(3)g. — The minimum weekly compensation rate as established pursuant to § 25-5-68 does not apply in non-scheduled permanent partial disability cases where compensation is provided and governed by subdivision (a)(3)g of this section. Winston Furn., Inc. v. Kirkpatrick, 495 So. 2d 1092 (Ala. Civ. App. 1985), aff'd, 495 So. 2d 1095 (Ala. 1986).

The minimum benefit provision of § 25-5-68(b) does not apply to injury falling under subdivision (a)(3)g of this section. T.G. & Y. Stores v. Stringfellow, 500 So. 2d 1133 (Ala. Civ. App. 1986).

Determining compensation for loss of use of a member. — In regard to loss of, or loss of use of, a scheduled member, the loss of wages or earning ability is not directly concerned in determining compensation. Patrick v. Femco S.E., Inc., 565 So. 2d 644 (Ala. Civ. App. 1990).

Percent of disability does not automatically translate into same percent loss of earning ability. — A 15 percent permanent partial disability does not automatically translate into a 15 percent loss of ability to earn for the purpose of calculating compensation under this section. Weaver v. Shook & Fletcher Insulation Co., 568 So. 2d 1229 (Ala. Civ. App. 1990).

Double compensation is not payable for two concurrent injuries to employee but for two such injuries, specifically compensated in schedule of this section the basis of computation is separate and the compensation periods are to run consecutively, not concurrently. Herron v. Williams & Voris Lumber Co., 30 Ala. App. 510, 8 So. 2d 593 (1942).

Under paragraph (a)(3)d, loss of use of a member is tied into a definition of the member set forth in paragraph (a)(3)a, relating to permanent partial disability. Nolan v. Ernest Constr. Co., 243 Ala. 460, 10 So. 2d 547 (1942); Swift & Co. v. Rolling, 252 Ala. 536, 42 So. 2d 6 (1949).

And an eye is included in the schedule as "a member" and when the schedule has prescribed the compensation to be paid for the loss of a member, paragraph (a)(3)d controls and determines the compensation due for such loss, and that provision also controls and determines the compensation to be paid for its partial loss. Swift & Co. v. Rolling, 252 Ala. 536, 42 So. 2d 6 (1949).

But compensation for loss of use of a member should not exceed compensation for loss of the same member. Nolan v. Ernest Constr. Co., 243 Ala. 460, 10 So. 2d 547 (1942).

The supreme court held that where there was an injury resulting in the loss of a member, or the loss of the use of a member, so as to invoke payment of compensation as provided in paragraph (a)(3)a, and where this was not accompanied by other physical disability (of the body), the payment of the specified sum is intended to fully compensate the injured employee for the injury sustained. This would certainly include loss of earning capacity or inability to secure employment. True, in many cases the amount awarded (allowed) seems insufficient or inadequate, but this is a matter entirely within the function of the legislature. Leach Mfg. Co. v. Puckett, 284 Ala. 209, 224 So. 2d 242 (1969).

Permanent disability due to partial loss of member compensated at full rate. — Under paragraph (a)(3)d of this section, an employee sustaining a permanent partial loss of a member is entitled to compensation at full rate prescribed for loss of that member for that proportion of full prescribed compensation period as extent of loss bears to total loss. Galloway Coal Co. v. Stanford, 215 Ala. 79, 109 So. 377 (1926).

Under said paragraph, time of total disability of employee sustaining a permanent partial disability must be deducted from compensation period fixed for permanent partial disability rather than from period allowed for total loss in determining period during which compensation for partial disability is payable. Galloway Coal Co. v. Stanford, 215 Ala. 79, 109 So. 377 (1926).

Injury extending to or impairing use of second member material in fixing compensation. — Under paragraph (a)(3)d, that the injury extends to some other member whose use is thereby impaired would be material in fixing compensation, and to be compensable there must be an injury to a member followed by a partial loss of use of the member, a distinction being made where one member cannot function so well because the use of another is impaired by an injury to the latter, and where the injury extends in physical form to them both. Nolan v. Ernest Constr. Co., 243 Ala. 460, 10 So. 2d 547 (1942).

Paragraph (a)(3)g catchall. — Paragraph (a)(3)g is placed at the end of the provisions relating to partial disability, apparently as a sort of catchall to cover those cases which otherwise might be omitted, and by its terms applies only to those cases not before enumerated. Swift & Co. v. Rolling, 252 Ala. 536, 42 So. 2d 6 (1949); Dearmon v. C.L. Guild Constr. Co., 44 Ala. App. 152, 204 So. 2d 497 (1967).

And an award under paragraph (a)(3)g must be based upon a finding of a permanent partial loss of an ability to earn. Misco, Inc. v. Driver, 50 Ala. App. 256, 278 So. 2d 374 (1973).

Compensation awarded on basis of permanent partial loss of ability to earn. —

The criteria for determining permanent partial disability for purpose of compensation is not controlled by a finding of physical disability of the body as a whole. Compensation is awarded on the basis of permanent partial loss of ability to earn. Without such finding of fact there can be no award. Physical disability may be inextricably involved but not necessarily or exclusively so. B.F. Goodrich Co. v. Martin, 47 Ala. App. 244, 253 So. 2d 37 (1971).

Where there was no evidence as to a permanent partial disability affecting the ability of the employee to earn upon which an award of compensation could be made, the judgment of the trial court as to the award of compensation for permanent partial disability was reversed, and remanded to the trial court for further hearing and the presentation of evidence as to the existence of a permanent partial disability to earn. B.F. Goodrich Co. v. Martin, 47 Ala. App. 244, 253 So. 2d 37 (1971).

Where there was evidence in the record as to the earnings of employee at the time of her injury, her limited education, the limitation of her work experience to manual skills and her inability to work at her job since the injury, but there was no finding of a loss of ability to earn, there was no basis for an award. Lingo v. Dixie Veneer Co., 349 So. 2d 591 (Ala. Civ. App. 1977).

Effect upon finding of permanent partial disability of post-injury earnings greater in amount than preinjury earnings. — See Federal Mogul Corp. v. Moses, 341 So. 2d 162 (Ala. Civ. App. 1976).

Implied finding of loss of ability to earn. — In workman's compensation proceeding, judgment, which found the plaintiff to be 25 percent permanently partially disabled and then continued to apply that finding of disability to average weekly earnings before the injury sufficiently implied a finding that plaintiff suffered a loss of ability to earn, and thus circuit court was empowered to clarify its judgment and cause it to speak specifically what it previously spoke by implication. Ohio Ferro-Alloys Corp. v. Whaley, 366 So. 2d 287 (Ala. Civ. App. 1979).

Finding that a three percent injury to claimant's body as a whole translated into a three percent loss of ability to earn was erroneous and was not supported by the evidence. Littleton v. Gold Kist, Inc., 480 So. 2d 1236 (Ala. Civ. App. 1985), remanding case for proper determination of loss of ability to earn and determination of benefits due.

Back injuries are nonscheduled injuries subject to paragraph (a)(3) of this section. T.G. & Y. Stores v. Stringfellow, 500 So. 2d 1133 (Ala. Civ. App. 1986).

Injury to pelvic bone falls within para-

graph (a)(3)g. — There is no schedule specifically covering an injury to the pelvic bone and to the back above the uppermost part of the lower limb. The court properly held that the injury fell within the provisions of paragraph (a)(3)g. Malbis Bakery Co. v. Collins, 245 Ala. 84, 15 So. 2d 705 (1943).

And not within paragraphs (a)(3)a or (a)(3)d. — Pelvic bone permanently forced upward and out of line did not come within the schedule providing for loss of a leg and a permanent disability due to injury to a member. McCarty v. Campbell Plumbing Co., 45 Ala. App. 617, 234 So. 2d 895 (1970).

Also partial loss of hearing falls within paragraph (a)(3)g. — If the only disability which plaintiff suffered was a 50 percent loss of hearing in one ear, his right to compensation must be determined by the application of paragraph (a)(3)g of this section since there is no specific schedule covering a permanent partial disability of that nature. Black v. Alabama Dry Dock & Shipbuilding Co., 249 Ala. 209, 30 So. 2d 456 (1947).

Permanent partial disability of 35 percent. — The evidence was sufficient to support the finding of the trial court that the employee "sustained trauma which resulted in osteoarthritis in and about his lumbar spine and a partial collapse of two intervertebral discs of his lumbar spine, which resulted in his permanent partial disability to the extent of 35%." Goodyear Tire & Rubber Co. v. Downey, 266 Ala. 344, 96 So. 2d 278 (1957).

References to section 25-5-68. — While there is a reference in paragraph (a)(3)g to § 25-5-68, it is also true that this section is included in a number of other subdivisions and paragraphs of this section to expressly provide and limit all awards to minimum and maximum compensation therein provided. Rowell v. Doss, 284 Ala. 500, 226 So. 2d 157 (1969).

D. Permanent Total Disability.

A trial court may make a finding of permanent total disability or a percentage of disability without medical testimony. Bankhead Forest Indus., Inc. v. Lovett, 423 So. 2d 899 (Ala. Civ. App. 1982).

Total disability within the Workers' Compensation Act does not mean absolute helplessness or entire physical disability but means inability to perform the work of one's trade or inability to obtain reasonably gainful employment. Brunson Milling Co. v. Grimes, 267 Ala. 395, 103 So. 2d 315 (1958); Bell v. Driskill, 282 Ala. 640, 213 So. 2d 806 (1968); Edwards v. City of Huntsville, 49 Ala. App. 498, 273 So. 2d 475 (1973); Stewart v. Busby, 51 Ala. App. 242, 284 So. 2d 269 (1973); City of Moulton v. Pearson, 54 Ala. App. 340, 308 So.

2d 252 (1975); Vulcraft, Inc. v. Wilbanks, 54 Ala. App. 393, 309 So. 2d 105 (1975); B.F. Goodrich Co. v. Butler, 56 Ala. App. 635, 324 So. 2d 776, cert. quashed, 295 Ala. 401, 324 So. 2d 788 (1975), aff'd, 336 So. 2d 1357 (Ala.), cert. denied, 336 So. 2d 1360 (Ala. 1976); Carroll Constr. Co. v. Hutcheson, 347 So. 2d 527 (Ala. Civ. App. 1977); Blue Bell, Inc. v. Nichols, 479 So. 2d 1264 (Ala. Civ. App. 1985).

Total disability does not mean absolute helplessness or entire physical disability, but refers instead to the injured employee's inability to perform the work of his trade or an inability to obtain reasonable gainful employment. Den-Tal-Eze Mfg. Co. v. Gosa, 388 So. 2d 1006 (Ala. Civ. App. 1980).

The test for a permanent total disability is not absolute helplessness or entire physical disability but inability to perform one's trade or inability to obtain gainful employment. J.S. Walton & Co. v. Reeves, 396 So. 2d 699 (Ala. Civ. App. 1981); Health-Tex, Inc. v. West, 401 So. 2d 88 (Ala. Civ. App.), cert. denied, 401 So. 2d 90 (Ala. 1981); City of Muscle Shoals v. Davis, 406 So. 2d 919 (Ala. Civ. App.), cert. denied, 406 So. 2d 923 (Ala. 1981); Bankhead Forest Indus., Inc. v. Lovett, 423 So. 2d 899 (Ala. Civ. App. 1982); Kline v. Combined Ins. Co. of Am., 570 So. 2d 1238 (Ala. Civ. App. 1990); Southeastern Com. Printing Corp. v. Sallas, 575 So. 2d 1151 (Ala. Civ. App. 1991).

Paragraph (a)(4)d does not require that an employee be absolutely helpless or suffer total physical disability in order to be totally and permanently disabled for workmen's compensation purposes. Rather, it requires that the employee be unable to perform his trade or unable to obtain reasonably gainful employment. Boyd Bros. Transp. v. Asmus, 540 So. 2d 757 (Ala. Civ. App. 1988).

The law is well settled in Alabama that to suffer permanent total disability, an employee does not have to be absolutely helpless or entirely physically disabled, only that the employee be unable to perform his trade or unable to obtain gainful employment. Campbell Piping Contractors v. Parker, 590 So. 2d 326 (Ala. Civ. App. 1991).

Subdivision (a)(4)b does not deny the employee equal protection and is not otherwise unconstitutional. Adkins v. Gold Kist, Inc., 531 So. 2d 890 (Ala. Civ. App. 1987), writ quashed as improvidently granted, Ex parte Adkins, 531 So. 2d 893 (Ala. 1988); Adkins v. Gold Kist, Inc., 565 So.2d 632 (Ala. Civ. App. 1989), aff'd, 565 So. 2d 633 (Ala. 1990).

The term "disability" in paragraph (a)(4)e and infirmity in § 25-5-58 refer to a condition which affects his ability to work as a normal man at the time of and prior to the accident, or which would probably so affect him within the compensable period. Ingalls Shipbuilding Corp. v. Cahela, 251 Ala. 163, 36 So. 2d 513 (1948); Kroger Co. v. Millsap, 280 Ala. 531, 196 So. 2d 380 (1967).

The term "disability" in subsections (a)(4)e and (a)(4)f refers to a condition which affects the ability to work as a normal man at the time of and prior to the accident. Thompson & Co. Contractors v. Cole, 391 So. 2d 1042 (Ala. Civ. App. 1980).

Total permanent disability under subdivision (4) may occur without loss of specific members of the body; in that case the court considers the education and training of the individual and the effect of the injury on his earning ability. Carroll Constr. Co. v. Hutcheson, 347 So. 2d 527 (Ala. Civ. App. 1977).

Subsection (a)(4)d requires that an employee must suffer from an injury that totally incapacitates him from working and being retrained for gainful employment in order to be classified as totally and permanently disabled. Thompson & Co. Contractors v. Cole, 391 So. 2d 1042 (Ala. Civ. App. 1980).

Failure to apply subdivision (a)(4)e held error where claimant suffered prior disability. — The evidence was clear that claimant suffered from a disability prior to her injury, where although she had returned to work, she had done so only with specific limitations placed upon her, she was not allowed to return to her old position, but was placed in the ultrasound department, where she could work within her limitations, and while she subsequently transferred to the emergency room, with all limitations removed, she reinjured her back after only three months of work. Therefore, the trial judge was in error for his failure to apply subdivision (a)(4)e of this section and § 25-5-58. Druid City Hosp. Regional Medical Ctr. v. Junkins, 495 So. 2d 69 (Ala. Civ. App. 1986).

Subdivision (a)(4)g clearly states necessity of employee's having suffered "two" permanent injuries. Davis v. City of Tuscaloosa, 494 So. 2d 643 (Ala. Civ. App. 1986).

Where there is loss of scheduled member with no complications, claimant is not entitled to permanent total benefits. Bentley v. Arnold, 431 So. 2d 549 (Ala. Civ. App. 1983).

The test for determining permanent total disability is the inability to perform one's trade or to obtain reasonably gainful employment. Smith v. O'Neal Steel, Inc., 571 So. 2d 1148 (Ala. Civ. App. 1990).

Amount of disability to body as whole is not determinative of the extent of loss of ability to earn. Tidwell Indus., Inc. v. Kennedy, 410 So. 2d 109 (Ala. Civ. App. 1982).

A finding of physical disability of the body as a whole does not necessarily coincide with loss of ability to earn. Wheeler v. Lake Forest Property Owners' Ass'n, 523 So. 2d 1083 (Ala. Civ. App. 1988).

Search for gainful employment includes retraining for another job; moreover, a person cannot refuse to be retrained if he or she is a proper candidate for retraining. Mead Paper Co. v. Brizendine, 575 So. 2d 571 (Ala. Civ. App. 1990).

Two permanent partial disabilities. — Although paragraph (a)(4)(h) falls under the subtitle "Permanent Total Disability," and although employee's problems concerned not a permanent total disability, but rather two permanent partial disabilities, the statute applied to the fact situation; first, the last sentence of paragraph (a)(4)(h) specifically mentions "permanent partial disability" as being the subject matter of the statute, and second, paragraph (a)(4)(g), which precedes the applicable statute in question, totally disposes of any case wherein a second injury results in permanent total disability. Chrysler Motor Corp. v. Cole, 563 So. 2d 1040 (Ala. Civ. App. 1990).

The prior adjudication of a five percent permanent loss of earning ability did not preclude the trial court from later finding complainant to be permanently totally disabled as a result of another injury in the same employment. Wright v. Goodyear Tire & Rubber Co., 591 So. 2d 518 (Ala. Civ. App. 1991).

Employee rendered incapable of doing only work for which he was suited. — Due to the loss of three fingers of his right hand and injury to his right wrist and other injuries, causing loss of the use of his right arm for manual labor, and considering the fact that the appellee was unsuited for work other than manual labor, the circuit court did not err in adjudging the appellee as totally and permanently disabled. Brunson Milling Co. v. Grimes, 267 Ala. 395, 103 So. 2d 315 (1958).

Where the evidence revealed that the employee obviously injured his back and was in the line and scope of his employment when the accident occurred and the testimony showed that the employee's only trade was as an iron worker and that he could no longer perform the work of his trade nor obtain reasonably gainful employment, while the trial court might well have been better informed by having the employee examined by a physician, the evidence was sufficient for the trial court's finding of total permanent disability in this instance under the Workmen's Compensation Act.

Stewart v. Busby, 51 Ala. App. 242, 284 So. 2d 269 (1973).

Employee who refuses physical or vocational rehabilitation not deemed permanently and totally disabled. — An employee who suffers a physical injury as a result of an accident arising out of and in the course of his employment which permanently and totally incapacitates him from both working at his preinjury trade or profession and being retrained for gainful employment in a new trade or profession commensurate with his education and post-injury physical limitations may be considered permanently and totally disabled; however, an employee whose disability results from such injury and who has refused to undergo physical or vocational rehabilitation shall not be deemed permanently and totally disabled. J.S. Walton & Co. v. Reeves, 396 So. 2d 699 (Ala. Civ. App. 1981).

Legal evidence supported the trial court's finding that employee could not currently perform gainful employment where two vocational experts testified that employee could not return to her former work as a truck driver and one of those vocational experts testified on deposition that employee could not perform any gainful employment. Although employee worked for several months after her accident, that work was part time and she was frequently absent due to health problems and her health had deteriorated significantly over the past three years and she was in constant pain. Boyd Bros. Transp. v. Asmus, 540 So. 2d 757 (Ala. Civ. App. 1988).

Evidence held sufficient to support finding of permanent total disability, see Olin Corp. v. Snow, 582 So. 2d 566 (Ala. Civ. App. 1991).

Claimant was entitled to recover even though claimant had 20/400 vision in right eye at time of employment. -- Where it was clear from the record and the trial court's order that the claimant sustained the loss of vision itself when he injured his left eye, the claimant was entitled to recover permanent total disability under paragraph (a)(4)d even though the claimant suffered from 20/400 vision in his right eye at the time of employment since an employee was not required to bear the risk of his own physical infirmities when sustaining a job-related injury and since prior to the injury, the employee was able to perform his job. Speegle v. Dobbs Bros., 545 So. 2d 777 (Ala. Civ. App. 1989).

Evidence supported determination of trial court. — For case holding that trial court did not err in finding employee permanently and totally disabled as a result of a work-related injury, see Hayes Int'l Corp. v. Johnson, 563 So. 2d 1052 (Ala. Civ. App. 1990).

Attorney's fees deducted when calculating weekly benefits award. — A trial court, when exercising its discretion to order payment of a lump sum attorney's fee in a total permanent disability case, must deduct that fee from the present value of the aggregate award in order to calculate the amount of weekly benefits to which the employee is entitled. Jim Walter Resources, Inc. v. Bentley, 560 So. 2d 1072 (Ala. Civ. App. 1990).

E. Hernia.

Development of inguinal hernia is accident compensable by workmen's compensation law, provided requirements of this section and § 25-5-1(8) are met. Gulf States Creosoting Co. v. Walker, 224 Ala. 104, 139 So. 261 (1932).

Sufficiency of proof. — Proof of hernia is sufficient when it is such as to reasonably satisfy court that plaintiff received physical injury arising out of and in course of employment, which injury resulted in hernia. Woodward Iron Co. v. Vines, 217 Ala. 369, 116 So. 514 (1928).

Paragraph (a)(6)a relating to proof of hernia, does not change rule in supreme court on review by certiorari. Woodward Iron Co. v. Vines, 217 Ala. 369, 116 So. 514 (1928).

Hernia must be accompanied by pain. — The statute requires that in claims for compensation for hernia, it must be proved to the satisfaction of the court that "it was accompanied by pain." Semmes Nurseries, Inc. v. McVay, 279 Ala. 42, 181 So. 2d 331 (1965).

A conflict in plaintiff's own testimony with respect to his suffering pain does not prevent the court from finding that the hernia "was accompanied by pain." Semmes Nurseries, Inc. v. McVay, 279 Ala. 42, 181 So. 2d 331 (1965).

Employer who seeks to require employee to submit to hernia operation must raise such defensive matter before the trial. Before the trial means by answer showing that the employer has offered to provide and is ready, willing and able to provide the hernia operation and that the other requirements of the statute in respect to the operation have been complied with. Semmes Nurseries, Inc. v. McVay, 279 Ala. 42, 181 So. 2d 331 (1965).

Where the employer was fully advised of the nature of plaintiff's injury prior to the trial, the statute does not permit the employer to have a new trial or an amended judgment requiring an operation, by offering to furnish the operation for the first time on motion for new trial. Semmes Nurseries, Inc. v. McVay, 279 Ala. 42, 181 So. 2d 331 (1965).

Finding that plaintiff's hernia appeared suddenly was supported by a reasonable view of the evidence, where plaintiff testified that he was lifting some trees, felt a sudden pain and "it just felt like a drop in my intestine back there. Like it dropped down." Semmes Nurseries, Inc. v. McVay, 279 Ala. 42, 181 So. 2d 331 (1965).

And did not previously exist. — Evidence favorable to plaintiff supported an inference that plaintiff's hernia did not exist prior to the accident. Semmes Nurseries, Inc. v. McVay, 279 Ala. 42, 181 So. 2d 331 (1965).

Hospital, medical and surgical benefits for hernia not excluded by subdivision (a)(6). — Since the provisions of subdivision (a)(6) are confined to "claims for compensation for hernia," and under § 25-5-1(1) the word "compensation" does not include hospital, medical or surgical payments, any exclusory effect of the five conditions would not apply to medical, surgical and other benefits required of the employer under § 25-5-77, if the other terms of the statute apply to the injury. Sam's Place v. Middleton, 39 Ala. App. 481, 103 So. 2d 812 (1958).

The exclusive remedy provisions of § 25-5-53 do not exclude the medical benefits on the theory that the denial of "compensation" by subdivision (a)(6) extinguishes also the medical claim. This is a remedial statute and exemptions from it are to be strictly construed. Sam's Place v. Middleton, 39 Ala. App. 481, 103 So. 2d 812 (1958).

Pre-existing nondisabling hernia. — An employee who had had a hernia for some years but was not incapacitated by it from performing the usual duties of his work was disabled when a cylinder head was thrown by a grinding wheel against his stomach, rendering a hernia operation necessary. On remanding the case to the trial court, the court of appeals (now court of civil appeals) said that if the trial court made up an issue based on how much of the disability was attributable to the pre-existing hernia — which seemed to have been virtually nondisabling — and the quantum of disability because of the blow to the stomach, together with the disability resulting from the surgical treatment which the stomach trauma required, then the disqualifying conditions of subdivision (a)(6) could be balanced against the effect of the second injury as required by the provisions of § 25-5-58. The fact that the "benign" hernia "flared up" as a consequence of the blow — the problem of causation — would be for the trial court's reconsideration. Sam's Place v. Middleton, 39 Ala. App. 481, 103 So. 2d 812 (1958).

Where evidence showed that an employee who had a pre-existing and nondisabling hernia condition suffered a blow in the stomach requiring surgery for the hernia, the trial court's conclusion that the employee's tempo-

rary disability was not attributable to the pre-existing hernia but resulted from the surgery required by the blow in the stomach was supported by the evidence. Sam's Place v. Middleton, 41 Ala. App. 13, 122 So. 2d 924 (1959), aff'd, 271 Ala. 226, 122 So. 2d 925 (1960).

Evidence that manual laborer who sustained a hernia was required to wear a truss to perform any manual labor sustained finding that he was suffering from a permanent partial disability. Nashville Bridge Co. v. Honeycutt, 246 Ala. 319, 20 So. 2d 591 (1945).

F. Death Following Disability.

Surviving spouse and dependent children entitled to benefits. — When an employee is injured and then subsequently dies from unrelated causes, not being survived by a spouse or by dependent children, the legislature does not require the employer to pay the compensation benefits to other heirs. The right to that employee's benefits is not determined by dependency alone. The employer is not obligated to pay the benefits to just any relative; it must be the employee's surviving spouse or dependent children. The act is clear in this regard. Harris v. Kimerling Truck & Parts Co., 504 So. 2d 304 (Ala. Civ. App. 1986).

Degree of disability must be determined. — This section provides for payment to a spouse or dependent children only in the event the degree of disability has been agreed upon or judicially ascertained. Harris v. Kimerling Truck & Parts Co., 504 So. 2d 304 (Ala. Civ. App. 1986).

IV. DETERMINATION AND PROCEEDINGS.

A trial court must look to the entire evidence and to its own observations in determining the extent of disability. Blue Bell, Inc. v. Nichols, 479 So. 2d 1264 (Ala. Civ. App. 1985).

In determining the extent of disability, it is the duty of the trial court to review the entire evidence, as well as to consider its own observations. Smith v. O'Neal Steel, Inc., 571 So. 2d 1148 (Ala. Civ. App. 1990).

Statutory formula must be observed. — When the court proceeds to make determination of the amount of compensation, the statutory formula must be observed; likewise when the parties do so by negotiation. Alabama By-Products Co. v. Landgraff, 248 Ala. 253, 27 So. 2d 215 (1946).

Method of computing "average weekly earnings" under subsection (b) of this section for an injured employee by dividing his earnings during the 52 weeks he worked preceding the accident by 52 is mandatory and exclusive. Odell v. Myers, 52 Ala. App. 558, 295 So. 2d 413 (1974).

The application of this section in determining the average weekly earnings of an injured employee who has worked in the same employment for more than 52 weeks is mandatory. Orkin Exterminating Co. v. Williams, 389 So. 2d 935 (Ala. Civ. App. 1980).

The statutory formulas for computing the average weekly earnings are mandatory. However, it has been held that the trial court may exercise its discretion when the computation is not practicable and will cause an unjust and unfair result. Holder v. Weatherly, 456 So. 2d 812 (Ala. Civ. App. 1984).

Application of subsection (b) in determining the average weekly wage of an employee who has worked more than 52 weeks in the same employment is mandatory. International Paper Co. v. Murray, 490 So. 2d 1234 (Ala. Civ. App. 1985), aff'd in part and rev'd in part on other grounds, 490 So. 2d 1238 (Ala. 1986).

Subsection (b) requires that employee's average weekly wage be computed by dividing by 52 the amount of his earnings during the 52-week period immediately preceding his injury. International Paper Co. v. Murray, 490 So. 2d 1234 (Ala. Civ. App. 1985), aff'd in part and rev'd in part on other grounds, 490 So. 2d 1238 (Ala. 1986).

Where a practice or procedure which is specifically provided by the Workmen's Compensation Act of the State of Alabama is appropriate for use in a particular case, it is improper to resort to Rule 60(b) as to the issue, since that rule would not be applicable under Rule 81(a). St. Regis Corp. v. Parnell, 531 So. 2d 911 (Ala. Civ. App. 1988).

Determination of the proper percentage of disability rests with the trial court. — The trial judge has the opportunity to observe the courtroom demeanor of the employee and other witnesses. The trial court also takes note of the evidence concerning the employee's skills and marketability for part-time employment. Dees v. Daleville Florist, 408 So. 2d 155 (Ala. Civ. App. 1981).

Subdivision (a)(4)b does not deny the employee equal protection and is not otherwise unconstitutional. Adkins v. Gold Kist, Inc., 531 So. 2d 890 (Ala. Civ. App. 1987), writ quashed as improvidently granted, Ex parte Adkins, 531 So. 2d 893 (Ala. 1988); Adkins v. Gold Kist, Inc., 565 So. 2d 632 (Ala. Civ. App. 1989), aff'd, 565 So. 2d 633 (Ala. 1990).

Under subsection (b), the term "earnings" is comprised of three elements: (1) allowances of any character; (2) made to the employee in lieu of wages; and (3) specified as part of the wage contract. International Paper Co. v. Murray, 490 So. 2d 1238 (Ala. 1986).

Employer-paid insurance premiums constitute "allowances of any character." — Under subsection (b), employer-paid fringe benefits in the nature of employer-paid premiums on insurance policies constitute "allowances of any character" and are includable in the computation of the employee's average weekly wage. International Paper Co. v. Murray, 490 So. 2d 1238 (Ala. 1986); W.Y. Shugart & Son v. Cox, 578 So. 2d 1332 (Ala. Civ. App. 1990).

Fringe benefits may be included in computing average weekly wage. Goodyear Tire & Rubber Co. v. Gilbert, 521 So. 2d 991 (Ala. Civ. App. 1987), writ denied, 521 So. 2d 992 (Ala. 1988).

Method for employment less than 52 weeks to be used if fair and just. — Method for determining "average weekly earnings" under subsection (b) of this section for an injured employee employed less than 52 weeks, by dividing his total earnings by weeks and parts thereof worked is not mandatory, but unless the court determines that for some valid reason the use of such method will not produce just and fair results, this method is not merely optional and should be used. Brunson Milling Co. v. Grimes, 267 Ala. 395, 103 So. 2d 315 (1958); Willis v. Storey, 268 Ala. 205, 105 So. 2d 128 (1958); Odell v. Myers, 52 Ala. App. 558, 295 So. 2d 413 (1974).

There is no indication of an intention of the legislature to extend to the trial court the power whereby the court, after computing the compensation as prescribed in this section, can then adjust for a raise in pay received by the injured employee on the last week of his employment next preceding his injury. In so doing the court exceeds its discretionary power. Brunson Milling Co. v. Grimes, 267 Ala. 395, 103 So. 2d 315 (1958).

If, by reason of the shortness of the time of employment or the casual nature of such employment, it is impractical to use such method and its use would not produce results fair and just to both parties, this method may be abandoned, and average weekly earnings for the injured may be computed by considering the average weekly earnings of a coemployee of the same grade doing the same work for the same employer who has been employed for the prior 52 weeks, or the average weekly earnings of a worker of the same grade, doing the same work in the same district. Odell v. Myers, 52 Ala. App. 558, 295 So. 2d 413 (1974).

However, if not practical much left to judicial discretion and judgment. — If the formulas for determining average weekly earnings set out in subsection (b) are impracticable to apply in a particular case so as to arrive at a just and fair result to both parties, much must be left to the sound judgment and judicial discretion of the trial court. Aluminum Workers Int'l v. Champion, 45 Ala. App. 570, 233 So. 2d 511 (1970); Unexcelled Mfg. Corp. v. Ragland, 52 Ala. App. 57, 289 So. 2d 626 (1974).

Where the trial court found that petitioner's average weekly earnings were approximately $37.00 per week, but that this was not a fair basis to determine his earnings because of the irregularity of his employment during the time he was employed, and that the hourly rate paid for work of the same character would justify a finding that petitioner's average weekly earnings would be $50.00, it was held on appeal that the award was within the judicial discretion of the trial court and provided "results just and fair to both parties" under subsection (b). Willis v. Storey, 268 Ala. 205, 105 So. 2d 128 (1958).

The tenor of the Alabama decisions dealing with this Code section seems to be that if the formulas set forth are impracticable to apply in a particular case so as to arrive at a result which is fair and just to both parties, much must be left to the trial court's sound judgment and judicial discretion. Patterson v. Whitten, 57 Ala. App. 297, 328 So. 2d 301 (1976).

But result must be fair and just to both parties. — If such consideration is given, and a determination made of average weekly earnings to be used as a base for payment of compensation, the result must be fair and just to both parties. Odell v. Myers, 52 Ala. App. 558, 295 So. 2d 413 (1974).

There is no provision as to whether there must be actual payment or merely an obligation for payment. Farmers Gin Co. v. Rose, 374 So. 2d 351 (Ala. Civ. App. 1979).

Only consecutive off days considered. — In calculating average weekly wages of employee, under subsection (b), only periods of off days to be considered are those found by trial court to be of consecutive days. Ex parte Hodges, 213 Ala. 388, 104 So. 829 (1925).

In determining the average weekly wages of employees, under subsection (b), only off day periods of more than seven consecutive days can be considered, and off periods should be first aggregated, and whole number of days then reduced to weeks and deducted from 52, to ascertain number of weeks employee has worked. Ex parte Hodges, 213 Ala. 388, 104 So. 829 (1925).

Subsection (b) substantially complied with. — Where injured employee had not been in present employment for 52 consecutive weeks, but worked intermittently during pe-

riod preceding injury, finding of fact giving in detail wages earned and striking average weekly earning, being supported by legal evidence, held substantial compliance with subsection (b) of this section. Ex parte DeBardeleben Coal Co., 212 Ala. 533, 103 So. 548 (1925).

Factors which indicate the unreliability of post-injury earnings include an increase in general wage levels since the time of the claimant's accident; claimant's own greater maturity; receipt of additional training by claimant; longer hours worked by claimant after the accident; payment of wages disproportionate to the claimant's ability to perform work-related tasks because of sympathy for the claimant; and the temporary and unpredictable character of post-injury earnings received by the claimant. Abex Corp. v. Coleman, 386 So. 2d 1160 (Ala. Civ. App. 1980).

Where post-injury earnings equal or exceed preinjury earnings, there exists a presumption that the claimant's earning ability has not been reduced; however, this presumption may be rebutted by (1) independent evidence which demonstrates incapacity, or (2) evidence which tends to indicate that the post-injury earnings are an unreliable basis for estimating earning capacity. Abex Corp. v. Coleman, 386 So. 2d 1160 (Ala. Civ. App. 1980).

Where actual post-injury earnings equal or exceed the pre-injury earnings, a presumption arises that the claimant has suffered no reduction in earning ability. This presumption can, however, be overcome by showing either independent evidence of incapacity or evidence tending to indicate the unreliability of the post-injury earnings as an estimate of earning capacity. Goodyear Tire & Rubber Co. v. Mitchell, 459 So. 2d 901 (Ala. Civ. App. 1984).

While it is true that an injured worker's post-injury earnings are a factor for the trial court to consider in assessing the degree of disability, Alabama courts have consistently rejected the notion that these earnings are the determinative factor as to loss of ability to earn. Goodyear Tire & Rubber Co. v. Mitchell, 459 So. 2d 901 (Ala. Civ. App. 1984), Overruled on other grounds, Ex parte St. Regis Corp., 535 So. 2d 160 (Ala. 1988).

Absent evidence showing that the employee's post-injury earnings were an unreliable basis for estimating the employee's earning capacity, the presumption raised that the employee's actual post-injury earnings, which were greater than his pre-injury earnings, are commensurate with his earning capacity was unrebutted. Jim Walter Resources, Inc. v. Hall, 516 So. 2d 690 (Ala. Civ. App. 1987).

The fact that employee's present weekly

earnings exceed his earnings at the time of his injury does not necessarily preclude a finding that he has an 80 percent reduction in his earning capacity. Such evidence creates a presumption of earning capacity commensurate with earnings, but the presumption may be rebutted by other evidence showing incapacity or explaining why evidence of higher earnings is an unreliable basis for determining capacity. Jim Walter Resources, Inc. v. Hall, 516 So. 2d 690 (Ala. Civ. App. 1987).

It is an established rule of law that in situations where an employee's wages following a work-related accident are the same or higher than his pre-injury wages, a presumption will arise that no loss of earning capacity has occurred; this presumption may be rebutted, however, by other evidence which demonstrates incapacity or which explains why the higher wages are an unreliable basis for determining the employee's earning capacity. Winn-Dixie of Montgomery, Inc. v. Nobles, 571 So. 2d 1174 (Ala. Civ. App. 1990); Southeastern Com. Printing Corp. v. Sallas, 575 So. 2d 1151 (Ala. Civ. App. 1991).

Statute does not set forth comparative wages test. — Concerning employee's earnings before and after her injury, the workmen's compensation statute does not set forth a comparative wages test as the mechanism for determining the employee's ability to earn. Southeastern Com. Printing Corp. v. Sallas, 575 So. 2d 1151 (Ala. Civ. App. 1991).

This section does not prescribe comparative wages received before and after the injury as the test of the employee's ability to earn. Instead, the test is the difference between the average weekly earnings at the time of the injury and the average weekly earnings the employee "is able to earn in his partially disabled condition." It seems that this clearly excludes any notion of limiting the determination of a loss in ability to earn to the one question of wages actually earned after the injury as compared with those earned before. Goodyear Tire & Rubber Co. v. Corfman, 424 So. 2d 1326 (Ala. Civ. App. 1982).

Court determines earning capacity. — Actual earnings and earning capacity are not the same for workmen's compensation purposes; it is the latter that the court determines from the evidence. Ohio Ferro-Alloys Corp. v. Whaley, 366 So. 2d 287 (Ala. Civ. App. 1979).

The trial court has much discretion in determining the loss of earning capacity and may consider such factors as age, education, past work history, and the effect of the injury on the employee's earning ability; in arriving at its decision, the trial court may consider all the evidence, including its own observations, and interpret it according to its own best judgment;

the trial court is not bound by the opinions of expert witnesses, even if their opinions are uncontroverted. Alverson v. Fontaine Fifth Wheel Co., 586 So. 2d 216 (Ala. Civ. App. 1991).

Award of compensation at rate of maximum amount provided for by § 25-5-68 was sustained as to employee who came within the third sentence of subsection (b). H.C. Price Co. v. Lee, 249 Ala. 230, 30 So. 2d 579 (1947).

Determining weekly benefits employee entitled to during period of life expectancy. — Once the present value of the compensation awarded has been reduced by the amount of attorney fee, this reduced amount is then used to calculate, at the 6 percent annual discount rate, the amount of weekly benefits the employee is entitled to during the period of his life expectancy. Southeastern Com. Printing Corp. v. Sallas, 575 So. 2d 1151 (Ala. Civ. App. 1991).

"Weekly earnings" of deceased employed in mine for four months, but not every day because of slack season, held to be total earnings divided by number of days actually worked, multiplied by six, in view of subsection (b). County Coal Co. v. Bush, 215 Ala. 25, 109 So. 151 (1926).

Disability compensation payments made to the employee during his lifetime must be specially pleaded in order for the employer to get the benefit of them under subdivision (a)(5). Braswell v. Brooks, 266 Ala. 141, 94 So. 2d 879 (1957), holding that in the case at bar the fact that disability payments were made was clearly brought to the court's attention by the defendant's answer.

Employer, not second injury trust fund, to compensate employee. — Where employer failed to report the "second injury," as required by this section; did not seek to make the trust fund a party to this action for apportionment purposes; and failed to raise any issue at trial concerning the liability of the trust fund, compensation will not be paid by the second injury trust fund. James River Corp. v. Mays, 572 So. 2d 469 (Ala. Civ. App. 1990).

Award apportioned where employees changed theory of their case. — The trial court did not err by apportioning the amount of scheduled benefits to be awarded to employees where on appeal they asserted that each suffered an occupational hearing loss which was compensable under § 25-5-110; at trial, the employees asserted their claims as ones for recovery from injuries sustained by accident, and since recovery for those types of scheduled losses is governed by this section, the trial court specifically based its award on that provision; employee's argument on appeal that they suffered from an occupational disease, as opposed to sustaining accidental injuries, was an attempt to change their theory of the case after a decision had already been rendered. Parden v. City of Mobile, 570 So. 2d 1233 (Ala. Civ. App. 1990).

Sufficiency of complaint. — The employer was not prejudiced because it was not given notice, in haec verba, that plaintiff had suffered a prolapse of the rectum, or a hernia where the complaint alleged that: (1) Plaintiff was lifting trees, (2) he was stooping over, (3) he strained, (4) he felt a sudden pain in back and spine and (5) since the injury he had been totally and permanently disabled. Semmes Nurseries, Inc. v. McVay, 279 Ala. 42, 181 So. 2d 331 (1965).

Burden was on plaintiff to show that he received his injury as a result of accident arising out of and in the course of his employment, and as a basis for computation of allowance under the statute to show the average weekly wage earned by him in said employment, and in the absence of proof of these facts the defendant was entitled to a judgment. Bennett v. Walsh Stevedoring Co., 253 Ala. 685, 46 So. 2d 834 (1950).

The burden rests upon the plaintiff to reasonably satisfy the trial court that he has in fact sustained permanent injuries to his thigh, or other parts of the body not covered in the schedule, so as to bring his case under paragraph (a)(3)g. Dearmon v. C.L. Guild Constr. Co., 44 Ala. App. 152, 204 So. 2d 497 (1967).

Trial court estimates duration of total disability and compensation therefor. — Under the Workmen's Compensation Act where an employee at time of trial is totally disabled, the trial court must from the evidence estimate the probable duration of the disability and determine the compensation, not exceeding the maximum, to be paid during disability period. Ford v. Crystal Laundry Co., 238 Ala. 187, 189 So. 730 (1939); Champion Int'l Corp. v. Simmons, 398 So. 2d 305 (Ala. Civ. App. 1981).

In compensation proceeding involving question as to duration of period of employee's total disability, the trial judge was not obliged to accept either the contention of the employee or employer where both were expressions of expert opinion but aided by such expert opinion he could consider all the evidence and interpret it according to his best judgment. Ford v. Crystal Laundry Co., 238 Ala. 187, 189 So. 730 (1939).

And expert medical testimony not required. — A trial court may make a finding of permanent total disability or a percentage of disability without expert medical testimony. Stewart v. Busby, 51 Ala. App. 242, 284 So. 2d 269 (1973).

Weight of expert medical testimony. — Expert medical opinion as to the nature, extent and permanency of a disability in a workmen's compensation case is not conclusive on the trier of fact even if the testimony is uncontroverted. Carroll Constr. Co. v. Hutcheson, 347 So. 2d 527 (Ala. Civ. App. 1977).

An expert's opinion as to the percent of disability is not binding upon the trial court in workmen's compensation cases. Blue Bell, Inc. v. Nichols, 479 So. 2d 1264 (Ala. Civ. App. 1985).

Experienced employment supervisor's testimony material and relevant. — If reasonably stable employment is not available for an employee by reason of certain injuries which have crippled him physically or neurologically, evidence of that fact, through the testimony of an experienced employment supervisor, is both material and relevant in determining whether the employee's disability is of such a character that he has no reasonable likelihood, while such disability continues, of being able to obtain and pursue an income-yielding occupation with reasonable continuity. Unexcelled Mfg. Corp. v. Ragland, 52 Ala. App. 57, 289 So. 2d 626 (1974).

It is duty of trial court to set forth sufficient findings of fact in support of its decision. Furthermore, the trier of fact may not completely disregard evidence and render judgment contrary thereto. Littleton v. Gold Kist, Inc., 485 So. 2d 1180 (Ala. Civ. App. 1986).

To sustain an award of permanent partial disability, the trial court must make a specific finding of a permanent partial loss of an ability to earn. Cook v. Munn, 521 So. 2d 1341 (Ala. Civ. App. 1988).

Effect of finding as to injury sustained. — A finding by the trial court that employee's injury was for the loss of her right thumb constituted an exclusion of her claim that she was also disabled as the result of the loss of use of her right arm. The failure of the trial court to mention the claimed disability from the loss of use of the right arm did not render the finding of fact so meager or omissive as to require a reversal of the case. Jackson v. W.L. Smith Poultry Co., 264 Ala. 184, 85 So. 2d 893 (1955).

In determining loss of ability to earn trial court may properly consider the employee's education and vocational training. Tidwell Indus., Inc. v. Kennedy, 410 So. 2d 109 (Ala. Civ. App. 1982).

Where there was evidence that tips were part of waitress's wage contract, it was not error to include the "tips" of the employee in the court's determination of the employee's average weekly earnings. S.M., Inc. v. Wise, 373 So. 2d 868 (Ala. Civ. App. 1979).

Finding of 60 percent disability. — There was reasonable basis in the evidence to support the finding that plaintiff had suffered a 60 percent permanent disability of his whole body. Semmes Nurseries, Inc. v. McVay, 279 Ala. 42, 181 So. 2d 331 (1965).

The law does not demand testimony, expert or otherwise, in the words "sixty percent permanent partial disability," or any other number of percent, in order to sustain a finding that plaintiff had a permanent partial disability amounting to 60 percent of his body as a whole. Semmes Nurseries, Inc. v. McVay, 279 Ala. 42, 181 So. 2d 331 (1965).

Employee has the burden to prove his weekly wage. — The computation of compensation and the determination of average weekly earnings are governed by this section and the employee has the burden of presenting evidence for computation of his average weekly wage. Cook Transports, Inc. v. Beavers, 528 So. 2d 875 (Ala. Civ. App. 1988).

The employee has the burden of presenting evidence for computing his average weekly wage. H.C. Moore & Sons v. Middlebrooks, 567 So. 2d 1359 (Ala. Civ. App. 1990).

Trial court is not bound by experts' opinions in workmen's compensation cases. It may consider all evidence, including its own observations, and interpret the evidence according to its own best judgment. Wilde v. Taco Bell Corp., 531 So. 2d 918 (Ala. Civ. App. 1988).

V. REVIEW.

Review in workmen's compensation cases is limited to a determination of whether there is any legal evidence to support the trial court's findings. If any reasonable view of the evidence supports the findings of the trial court, this court may then determine whether the correct legal conclusions have been drawn therefrom. Adkins v. Morton Thiokol, Inc., 560 So. 2d 1090 (Ala. Civ. App. 1990).

Decision of trial court upheld if any evidence to support findings. — It is well settled in workmen's compensation cases that the decision of the trial court will be upheld upon review by writ of certiorari if there is any legal evidence to support the trial court's findings of fact. This rule prevails where some testimony at trial indicates that the percentage of disability may be greater than the percentage ultimately determined by the court while other testimony indicates that it may be less. Hill v. J.P. Stevens & Co., 360 So. 2d 1035 (Ala. Civ. App. 1978).

In a workmen's compensation case the appellate court's inquiry is limited to a determina-

tion of whether there is any legal evidence to support the findings of the trial court. The trial court is not bound by the opinion of expert witnesses. However, the trial court may not fail to consider legal evidence in making its determination. Littleton v. Gold Kist, Inc., 485 So. 2d 1180 (Ala. Civ. App. 1986).

Court of Appeals review on workmen's compensation cases in limited to a determination of whether there is any legal evidence to support the trial court's conclusions; if, however, a reasonable review of the evidence supports the findings of the trial court, the court may then determine whether the correct legal conclusions have been drawn therefrom. Smith v. O'Neal Steel, Inc., 571 So. 2d 1148 (Ala. Civ. App. 1990).

Trial court not required to make specific finding that worker cannot be retrained for gainful employment. Such a finding is implicit when the trial court concludes that employee is totally, permanently disabled. Mead Paper Co. v. Brizendine, 575 So. 2d 571 (Ala. Civ. App. 1990).

A subsection (a)(4)(b) argument for the first time on appeal is too late. Jasper Community Hosp. v. Hyde, 397 So. 2d 153 (Ala. Civ. App. 1981).

A post trial motion for a new trial on the ground of newly discovered evidence is not a petition to modify pursuant to subsection (a)(4)(b) of this section. Jasper Community Hosp. v. Hyde, 397 So. 2d 153 (Ala. Civ. App. 1981).

Right to reopen case under Alabama Rules of Civil Procedure. — Although this section does not specifically provide that an employee may petition to reopen his case upon a change in his disability subsequent to the award, he has such a right, in effect, under Rules 59 and 60, A.R.Civ.P. Adkins v. Gold Kist, Inc., 531 So. 2d 890 (Ala. Civ. App. 1987), writ quashed as improvidently granted, Ex parte Adkins, 531 So. 2d 893 (Ala. 1988).

Appellate court will not disturb the finding of the trial court where legal evidence exists to support its conclusion of total and permanent disability. Den-Tal-Eze Mfg. Co. v. Gosa, 388 So. 2d 1006 (Ala. Civ. App. 1980).

The weight of evidence before the trial court is not before the appellate court on appeal in a workmen's compensation case. Den-Tal-Eze Mfg. Co. v. Gosa, 388 So. 2d 1006 (Ala. Civ. App. 1980).

Upon review by certiorari, rulings on admission of evidence will not be considered if it appears that the judgment is supported by legal evidence. Den-Tal-Eze Mfg. Co. v. Gosa, 388 So. 2d 1006 (Ala. Civ. App. 1980).

Judgment in a worker's compensation proceeding will not be disturbed upon review by certiorari if there is any legal evidence to support the trial court's findings. Bankhead Forest Indus., Inc. v. Lovett, 423 So. 2d 899 (Ala. Civ. App. 1982).

In reviewing workmen's compensation awards, the Alabama court of criminal appeals is limited to a determination of whether there is any legal evidence, or reasonable inferences therefrom, to support the facts as found by the trial court. If those findings are supported by any legal evidence, they shall be conclusive and will not be disturbed on appeal. Glenn v. Kent Corp., 416 So. 2d 1066 (Ala. Civ. App. 1982).

With a plaintiff being restricted in physical activity to little more than simple walking, with his lack of education or training, with his job history and limited mental acuity, with his already having suffered two heart attacks and being dependent upon a permanent pacemaker, and with his injury undoubtedly having a profound adverse effect upon his earning ability, the appellate court does not disturb the holding of the trial court that the plaintiff was totally and permanently disabled, for lawful evidence upheld that adjudication. City of Muscle Shoals v. Davis, 406 So. 2d 919 (Ala. Civ. App.), cert. denied, 406 So. 2d 923 (Ala. 1981).

The question whether an employee can be rehabilitated is a question of fact, and where the weight of the evidence was not before the court it was not within appellate court's purview; therefore, since the trial court's finding that employee had not refused to undergo rehabilitation was supported by the evidence, there was no error. Redi Roast Prods., Inc. v. Burnham, 531 So. 2d 664 (Ala. Civ. App. 1988).

Provisional judgment properly set aside. — Judgment denying plaintiff compensation under this section subject to consideration of any evidence which plaintiff should introduce within 60 days from judgment date concerning disability, amounting merely to continuation of trial with provisional finding and judgment on uncompleted evidence, was properly set aside, and new trial granted upon plaintiff's

motion. Indian Head Mills v. Ashworth, 215 Ala. 348, 110 So. 565 (1926).

Judgment not reopened for changes in plaintiff's condition. — Under the Workmen's Compensation Act, after the court has determined the period of disability and fixed the compensation to be paid, the judgment cannot be reopened because of subsequent changes in the condition of plaintiff. Ford v. Crystal Laundry Co., 238 Ala. 187, 189 So. 730 (1939).

In determining whether compensation should be increased after remand directing that compensation is applicable, trial court may hear further testimony from both parties. Alabama By-Products Corp. v. Winters, 234 Ala. 566, 176 So. 183 (1937).

Where there was no inquiry as to employee's expenses, trial court's determination of average weekly wage was affirmed. — In workman's compensation case, evidence of the amount of expenses deducted from the employee's gross income could have reduced the average weekly wage claimed by the employee; but where the employee was questioned on cross-examination as to what expenses were deducted from his gross income but no inquiry was made as to the amount of those expenses, the trial court's determination that the employee's average weekly wage was in excess of $500 was affirmed where the evidence supported the trial court's determination. H.C. Moore & Sons v. Middlebrooks, 567 So. 2d 1359 (Ala. Civ. App. 1990).

Clinical decibel test rejected for hearing loss analysis on appeal. — Question of whether employee suffered a "complete and permanent loss of hearing" during his employment was a question of fact for the trial court, not, as employer suggested, a question to be answered by the appellate court taking a clinical approach and setting a certain decibel level to indicate when a "complete and permanent loss of hearing" has occurred. James River Corp. v. Mays, 572 So. 2d 469 (Ala. Civ. App. 1990).

§ 25-5-58. Effect of preexisting injuries or infirmities.

If the degree or duration of disability resulting from an accident is increased or prolonged because of a preexisting injury or infirmity, the employer shall be liable only for the disability that would have resulted from the accident had the earlier injury or infirmity not existed. (Acts 1919, No. 245, p. 206; Code 1923, § 7561; Code 1940, T. 26, § 288.)

Liberal construction. — This section is to be liberally construed so as not to apply if the previous injury or infirmity has not demonstrated itself as disabling and prevented the employee from performing his job in a normal manner. Robinson Foundry, Inc. v. Tinsley, 510 So. 2d 825 (Ala. Civ. App. 1987); Merico, Inc. v. Sparks, 567 So. 2d 315 (Ala. Civ. App. 1990).

This section is to be liberally construed and does not apply if any previous injury has not demonstrated itself as disabling or has not prevented the employee from performing his job in a normal manner. Merico, Inc. v. Sparks, 567 So. 2d 315 (Ala. Civ. App. 1990).

This section does not apply to death cases, and compensation allowable in such cases is not subject to abatement or deduction on account of the contribution of pre-existing disease to result. United States Cast Iron Pipe & Foundry Co. v. Hartley, 217 Ala. 462, 116 So. 666 (1928).

Where abscessed condition of miner's abdomen existed before injury, and physical shock and injury aggravated such condition and eventuated in death, there is full liability under the Workmen's Compensation Act, this section not applying. Crescent Coal Co. v. Simmons, 217 Ala. 367, 116 So. 512 (1928).

Where workman died as result of injury arising out of and in course of his employment, coupled with arteriosclerosis, this section was held inapplicable. Southern Cement Co. v. Walthall, 217 Ala. 645, 117 So. 17 (1928).

Section inapplicable where claimant performing job normally prior to injury. — Where the evidence supported the conclusion that claimant was performing his job normally and clearly to the satisfaction of his employer prior to the time of the injury to his back and that the permanent partial disability found by the trial court resulted from the injury, this section did not apply. Robinson Foundry, Inc. v. Tinsley, 510 So. 2d 825 (Ala. Civ. App. 1987).

"Affirmity" and "disability" defined. — An "affirmity," as well as a "disability," pursuant to this section is simply a condition affecting the employee's ability to work as a normal man, both prior to and at the time of a job-related accident, or as probably affecting the employee during the period of compensation. Gold Kist, Inc. v. Nix, 519 So. 2d 556 (Ala. Civ. App. 1987).

"Infirmity" defined. — The term "infirmity" under this section means a condition which affects the employee's ability to work as a normal man at the time of and prior to the accident, or which would probably so affect him within the compensable period. International

Paper Co. v. Rogers, 500 So. 2d 1102 (Ala. Civ. App. 1986).

The key words in this section are "infirmity" and "disability". These terms have been defined as "simply a condition affecting the employee's ability to work as a normal man." Drummond Co. v. Lolley, 562 So. 2d 1320 (Ala. Civ. App. 1989), writ quashed as improvidently granted, 562 So. 2d 1322 (Ala. 1990).

Infirmity refers to condition affecting ability to work. — The term disability in paragraph (a)(4)e of § 25-5-57, and infirmity in this section refer to a condition which affects his ability to work as a normal man at the time of and prior to the accident, or which would probably so affect him within the compensable period. Ingalls Shipbuilding Corp. v. Cahela, 251 Ala. 163, 36 So. 2d 513 (1948); Kroger Co. v. Millsap, 280 Ala. 531, 196 So. 2d 380 (1967).

The term "infirmity" refers to a condition which affects the ability to work as a normal man at the time of and prior to the accident. Thompson & Co. Contractors v. Cole, 391 So. 2d 1042 (Ala. Civ. App. 1980).

Latent conditions. — This section does not refer to latent conditions which might not spring into action during the compensable period, and at the time of the accident are not causing any apparent physical effect on the health or activity of the employee. International Paper Co. v. Rogers, 500 So. 2d 1102 (Ala. Civ. App. 1986).

The terms of this section do not refer to latent conditions which may not spring into activity during the compensable period, and at the time of the accident are causing no apparent physical effect on the health or activity of the employee. North Ala. Nursing Home, Inc. v. Borden, 442 So. 2d 112 (Ala. Civ. App. 1983); International Paper Co. v. Rogers, 500 So. 2d 1102 (Ala. Civ. App. 1986).

Under this section, liability may be apportioned only among different diseases, not among different causes of a disease. Middleton v. Dan River, Inc., 617 F. Supp. 1206 (M.D. Ala. 1985), modified, 834 F.2d 903 (11th Cir. 1987).

A preexisting condition is defined in terms of its effect on the employee's ability to earn. Drummond Co. v. Lolley, 562 So. 2d 1320 (Ala. Civ. App. 1989), writ quashed as improvidently granted, 562 So. 2d 1322 (Ala. 1990).

Preexisting disability does not disqualify claim. — Workmen's compensation is not limited to those in perfect health; if the employment aggravated, accelerated, or combined with a latent disease or infirmity to produce disability, the preexisting disability does not disqualify the claim under the "arising out of employment" requirement of the statute. The rule is applicable to cases where a work-related heart attack renders arteriosclerosis symptomatic. Lewis v. 4-E Corp., 469 So. 2d 599 (Ala. 1985).

A preexisting condition will not affect a workmen's compensation award if a job-related injury combined with that preexisting condition to produce disability. Reynolds Metals Co. v. Stults, 532 So. 2d 1035 (Ala. Civ. App. 1988).

Failure to take into account employee's preexisting injuries. — Where the trial court, in awarding the employee benefits for a permanent and total disability, failed to take into account the employee's preexisting injuries, the award violated this section and must be remanded for such consideration. Drummond Co. v. Lolley, 528 So. 2d 885 (Ala. Civ. App. 1988).

No preexisting condition where able to perform duties. — Regardless of the existence of a preexisting condition or disease, if the employee was able to perform his duties prior to the subject injury, no preexisting condition is present for compensation purposes. International Paper Co. v. Rogers, 500 So. 2d 1102 (Ala. Civ. App. 1986); Phenix Medical Park Hosp. v. Kozub, 575 So. 2d 1162 (Ala. Civ. App. 1991).

The trial court did not err in refusing to apply res judicata or collateral estoppel to the employee's claim for benefits due to his second injury where the trial court's order contained this specific factual finding: "the employee was satisfactorily performing his duties subsequent to the first injury and prior to this second injury." Blue Circle, Inc. v. Williams, 579 So. 2d 630 (Ala. Civ. App. 1991).

If condition is aggravated by accident occurring in course of employment, the condition is still compensable even though the accident may not have caused the same injury in a normal person. International Paper Co. v. Rogers, 500 So. 2d 1102 (Ala. Civ. App. 1986).

In determining employee's compensation, the trial court must determine that there has been loss of earning capacity. That loss in earning capacity must be expressed as a percentage. International Paper Co. v. Murray, 490 So. 2d 1234 (Ala. Civ. App. 1985), aff'd in part and rev'd in part on other grounds, 490 So. 2d 1238 (Ala. 1986).

Court must assign percentage loss of ability to earn. — Because the "before and after" wages and the loss of earnings capacity may be quite different, the trial court must assign a percentage loss of ability to earn before any award of compensation can be calculated. International Paper Co. v. Murray, 490 So. 2d 1234 (Ala. Civ. App. 1985), aff'd in

part and rev'd in part on other grounds, 490 So. 2d 1238 (Ala. 1986).

The trial court may consider all of the evidence, and is not even bound by the testimony of experts in its determination of the percentage of loss of ability to earn. International Paper Co. v. Murray, 490 So. 2d 1234 (Ala. Civ. App. 1985), aff'd in part and rev'd in part on other grounds, 490 So. 2d 1238 (Ala. 1986).

The percentage of disability and the percentage of loss of ability to earn may be different. International Paper Co. v. Murray, 490 So. 2d 1234 (Ala. Civ. App. 1985), aff'd in part and rev'd in part on other grounds, 490 So. 2d 1238 (Ala. 1986).

Section 25-5-57(a)(3)g does not prescribe comparative wages received before and after the injury as the test of the employee's ability to earn. International Paper Co. v. Murray, 490 So. 2d 1234 (Ala. Civ. App. 1985), aff'd in part and rev'd in part on other grounds, 490 So. 2d 1238 (Ala. 1986).

The trial court may use the difference between wages recovered before and after the injury as one of the factors it considers to arrive at the percentage of the employee's loss of ability to earn. However, there are many other factors that may also be considered, including age, experience, education, etc. International Paper Co. v. Murray, 490 So. 2d 1234 (Ala. Civ. App. 1985), aff'd in part and rev'd in part on other grounds, 490 So. 2d 1238 (Ala. 1986).

Injured employee's answers to interrogatories in former action against former employer for hernia caused by lifting held properly considered by court on matter of his credibility in proceedings against later employer to recover compensation for enlarged hernia caused by lifting log. Randle v. Dumas, 229 Ala. 396, 157 So. 218 (1934).

Proof insufficient to enable court to make finding. — Assuming (without deciding) the pertinency of this section in a proceeding to recover benefits for disability resulting from cerebral hemorrhage, the defendant offered no proof which would have enabled the court to make a finding under this section. Southern Cotton Oil Co. v. Wynn, 266 Ala. 327, 96 So. 2d 159 (1957).

Where arteriosclerosis was aggravated and rendered symptomatic by work-related injury and the worker's ability to work was unaffected by the arteriosclerosis prior to the accident, and there was no evidence to indicate that the condition would have become symptomatic during the compensable period but for the injury, apportionment of an award for permanent disability between the work-related injury and the preexisting infirmity was improper. Lewis v. 4-E Corp., 469 So. 2d 599 (Ala. 1985).

Employer held liable for full extent of employee's disability. — Where the date of employee's injury, under former § 25-5-147, was when she was last exposed to cotton dust, which was her last day of work in 1982, and there was no evidence before the court that her heart or brain disease had an apparent physical effect on her ability to work at that time, her employer was liable for the full extent of her disability. Middleton v. Dan River, Inc., 617 F. Supp. 1206 (M.D. Ala. 1985), modified, 834 F.2d 903 (11th Cir. 1987).

Evidence was clear that claimant suffered from disability prior to her injury, where although she had returned to work, she had done so only with specific limitations placed upon her, she was not allowed to return to her old position, but was placed in the ultrasound department, where she could work within her limitations, and while she subsequently transferred to the emergency room, with all limitations removed, she reinjured her back after only three months of work. Therefore, the trial judge was in error for his failure to apply § 25-5-57(a)(4)e and this section. Druid City Hosp. Regional Medical Ctr. v. Junkins, 495 So. 2d 69 (Ala. Civ. App. 1986).

Trial court properly considered evidence of preexisting infirmity. — Where it was undisputed that the employee was able to perform her job normally and satisfactorily prior to employee's back injury, it appeared from the record that the trial court properly considered evidence of the existence of any preexisting infirmity. Price's Bar-B-Que v. Carter, 541 So. 2d 38 (Ala. Civ. App. 1989).

Physician's testimony supported finding of loss of earning capacity. — Where employee was declared totally disabled and employee's physician testified that employee suffered 65 percent bodily impairment based on reduced pulmonary function, and the impairment was due, in part, to asbestosis, there was support for the court's finding that employee's asbestosis caused a 45 percent loss of earning capacity. Reynolds Metal Co. v. Stults, 532 So. 2d 1035 (Ala. Civ. App. 1988).

Compensation not reduced where spondylolisthesis did not cause employee to miss work. — Although the employee who had a back deformity known as spondylolisthesis, had discussed the possibility of back surgery with his doctor prior to this accident, where the uncontradicted proof was that the employee never missed any work nor was he limited in any way in his activities prior to his accident, the trial court was correct in not allowing his spondylolisthesis to reduce his compensation award. International Paper Co. v. Rogers, 500 So. 2d 1102 (Ala. Civ. App. 1986).

Pre-existing nondisabling hernia. — An employee who had had a hernia for some years but was not incapacitated by it from performing the usual duties of his work was disabled when a cylinder head was thrown by a grinding wheel against his stomach, rendering a hernia operation necessary. On remanding the case to the trial court, the court of appeals (now court of civil appeals) said that if the trial court made up an issue based on how much of the disability was attributable to the pre-existing hernia — which seemed to have been virtually nondisabling — and the quantum of disability because of the blow to the stomach, together with the disability resulting from the surgical treatment which the stomach trauma required, then the disqualifying conditions of subdivision (a)(6) of § 25-5-57 could be balanced against the effect of the second injury as required by the provisions of this section. The fact that the "benign" hernia "flared up" as a consequence of the blow — the problem of causation — would be for the trial court's reconsideration. Sam's Place v. Middleton, 39 Ala. App. 481, 103 So. 2d 812 (1958).

Cited in Ingalls Shipbuilding Corp. v. Cahela, 251 Ala. 163, 36 So. 2d 513 (1948); Sam's Place v. Middleton, 39 Ala. App. 481, 103 So. 2d 812 (1958); Den-Tal-Eze Mfg. Co. v. Gosa, 388 So. 2d 1006 (Ala. Civ. App. 1980); Smith v. Capps, 414 So. 2d 102 (Ala. Civ. App. 1982); Miller v. Childers, 421 So. 2d 118 (Ala. Civ. App. 1982); McKinney Petro. Equip., Inc. v. Connell, 453 So. 2d 1044 (Ala. Civ. App. 1984); Baggett v. Builders Transp., Inc., 457 So. 2d 413 (Ala. Civ. App. 1984); Vann Express, Inc. v. Phillips, 539 So. 2d 296 (Ala. Civ. App. 1988); Drummond Co. v. Wilson, 547 So. 2d 564 (Ala. Civ. App. 1989); Bowman Transp., Inc. v. Blackwell, 586 So. 2d 913 (Ala. Civ. App. 1991).

Collateral references. — 99 C.J.S., Workmen's Compensation, §§ 164, 173.

Preexisting physical condition of employee which causes or contributes to injury or death. 19 ALR 95, 28 ALR 204, 60 ALR 1299.

Pleading aggravation of a preexisting physical condition in compensation cases. 32 ALR2d 1459.

§ 25-5-59. Waiting period for compensation; penalty for overdue compensation payments.

(a) For purposes of this article, except for scheduled injuries as provided in Section 25-5-57(a)(3), compensation for the first three days of disability shall not be payable, nor shall compensation be paid in any case unless the employer has actual knowledge of the injury or is notified thereof within the period specified in Section 25-5-78.

(b) Compensation shall begin with the fourth day after disability, and if the disability from the injury exists for a period as much as 21 days, compensation for the first three days after the injury shall be added to and payable with the first installment due the employee after the expiration of the 21 days. If any installment of compensation payable is not paid without good cause within 30 days after it becomes due, there shall be added to the unpaid installment an amount equal to 15 percent thereof, which shall be paid at the same time as, but in addition to, the installment. (Code 1923, § 7566; Acts 1939, No. 661, p. 1036, § 5; Code 1940, T. 26, § 292; Acts 1955, No. 351, p. 850; Acts 1971, No. 667, p. 1376, § 7; Acts 1973, No. 1062, p. 1750, § 20; Acts 1992, No. 92-537, § 18.)

The 1992 amendment, effective May 19, 1992, added the subsection designations (a) and (b), substituted the language beginning "For purposes of this article" and ending "nor shall compensation be paid" for "In cases of temporary total or temporary partial disability, no compensation shall be allowed for the first three days after disability, except as provided by section 25-5-77, nor" in subsection (a), and in subsection (b) substituted "if the disability" for "and, in the event the disability" in the first sentence, and in the second sentence substituted "the unpaid" for "such unpaid," "equal to 15 percent" for "equal to 10 percent," and "the installment" for "such installment."

Purpose of this section is to prevent malingering. Morris v. Dickson, 252 Ala. 588, 42 So. 2d 337 (1949).

Section does not apply in death case. — Nothing in this section specifically mentions recovery of a penalty in a death case, therefore, this section does not apply in a death case. Read News Agency, Inc. v. Moman, 383 So. 2d 840 (Ala. Civ. App.), cert. denied, 383 So. 2d 847 (Ala. 1980).

This provision does not provide for assessment of 10 percent (now 15 percent) penalty on medical bills. Turnipseed v. McCafferty, 521 So. 2d 31 (Ala. Civ. App. 1987).

Proof to recover penalty. — Under the provisions of this section, it is not necessary to allege or prove any element beyond the statutorily proscribed delay in payment of benefits, in order to recover the prescribed penalty. Lowman v. Piedmont Executive Shirt Mfg. Co., 547 So. 2d 90 (Ala. 1989).

"Good cause" exists when there is a good faith dispute as to the employer's liability to its employee. Crown Textile Co. v. Dial, 507 So. 2d 522 (Ala. Civ. App. 1987).

Where there was evidence that the employee's fall might have been caused by a condition not arising out of and in the course of his employment, there was a good faith dispute as to the employer's liability to the employee, and thus the employer was not liable for a penalty. Crown Textile Co. v. Dial, 507 So. 2d 522 (Ala. Civ. App. 1987).

No waiting period where disability is permanent. — While this section provides for a waiting period of seven (now three) days in case of a temporary total or temporary partial disability, and also that compensation shall begin with the eighth (now fourth) day after disability, there is no provision herein for a waiting period in case of a permanent partial disability. Morris v. Dickson, 252 Ala. 588, 42 So. 2d 337 (1949) (decided prior to the 1992 amendment).

Thus, compensation period for permanent disability begins on day after disability. Morris v. Dickson, 252 Ala. 588, 42 So. 2d 337 (1949) (decided prior to the 1992 amendment).

Mere delay is not actionable as separate tort claim. — A mere delay in payment of workmen's compensation benefits is not actionable as a separate tort claim since the penalty for untimely payment of workmen's compensation benefits is provided in this section. Lowman v. Piedmont Executive Shirt Mfg. Co., 547 So. 2d 90 (Ala. 1989).

This section clearly imports that actual knowledge is equivalent of the statutory notice. Ex parte Stith Coal Co., 213 Ala. 399, 104 So. 756 (1925).

This section provides a 10 percent (now 15 percent) penalty where any installment of compensation payable is not paid without good cause within 30 days after it becomes due. Read News Agency, Inc. v. Moman, 383 So. 2d 840 (Ala. Civ. App.), cert. denied, 383 So. 2d 847 (Ala. 1980).

Evidence showed delay was result of good faith dispute. — Evidence in case clearly showed that the delay in the employer's payment of workmen's compensation benefits to the employee was the result of a good faith dispute between the parties regarding the amount of workmen's compensation benefits due; therefore, there was no error in trial court's refusal to impose the ten percent penalty against the employer under these circumstances. Stevison v. Qualified Personnel, Inc., 571 So. 2d 1178 (Ala. Civ. App. 1990).

Cited in Garvin v. Shewbart, 442 So. 2d 80 (Ala. 1983); Wallace Roofing Co. v. Ganley, 442 So. 2d 118 (Ala. Civ. App. 1983); Lewis v. 4-E Corp., 469 So. 2d 594 (Ala. Civ. App. 1984); Glenn v. Vulcan Materials Co., 534 So. 2d 598 (Ala. 1988); Lowman v. Piedmont Executive Shirt Mfg. Co., 547 So. 2d 90 (Ala. 1989).

Collateral references. — 99 C.J.S., Workmen's Compensation, § 296.

Construction of provision of act regarding waiting period. 81 ALR 1261.

§ 25-5-60. Compensation for death.

In death cases, where the death results proximately from the accident within three years, compensation payable to dependents shall be computed on the following basis and shall be paid to the persons entitled thereto without administration, or to a guardian or other person as the court may direct, for the use and benefit of the person entitled thereto.

(1) PERSONS ENTITLED TO BENEFITS; AMOUNT OF BENEFITS.

a. If the deceased employee leaves one dependent, there shall be paid to the dependent 50 percent of the average weekly earnings of the deceased.

b. If the deceased employee leaves two or more dependents, there shall be paid to the dependents $66^{2}/_{3}$ percent of the average weekly earnings of the deceased.

c. If one of two or more dependents is a widow or widower, the compensation may be paid to the widow or widower for the benefit of herself or himself and the dependent child or children. In its discretion and when it considers appropriate to do so, the court shall at any time have the power to determine, without the appointment of any guardian or guardians, what portion of the compensation shall be applied for the benefit of any child or children and may order the same paid to a guardian or custodian of the child or children.

d. Partial dependents shall be entitled to receive only that proportion of the benefits provided for total dependents which the average amount of the earnings regularly contributed by the deceased employee to the partial dependent, at and for a reasonable time immediately prior to the injury, bore to the total income of the dependent during the same time. If there is one dependent and one or more partial dependents and the dependent is not entitled to the maximum amount of compensation provided in Section 25-5-68, there shall be paid to the partial dependent or partial dependents that percentage of the benefit paid to a full dependent which the contribution of the decedent to the partial dependent's support bears to the total income of the partial dependent. Notwithstanding the foregoing, the compensation payable to the partial dependent or dependents shall not exceed the lesser of 16²/₃ percent of the decedent's average weekly wage or the difference between the compensation payable to the full dependent and the maximum weekly compensation benefit payable as provided in Section 25-5-68.

e. If compensation is being paid under this article to any dependent, the compensation shall cease upon the death or marriage of the dependent, unless otherwise provided in this article.

f. Upon the cessation of compensation to or for any dependent, for any cause, the compensation of the remaining dependents entitled to compensation shall, for the unexpired period during which their compensation is payable, be that which would have been payable to them had they been the only persons entitled to compensation at the time of death of the deceased employee.

g. If, however, the deceased employee at the time of his or her death has no dependents as herein defined, then within 60 days of his or her death, the employer shall pay a one-time lump sum payment of seven thousand five hundred dollars ($7,500) to the deceased worker's estate.

(2) MAXIMUM AND MINIMUM COMPENSATION AWARDS. — The compensation payable in case of death to persons wholly dependent shall be subject to a maximum and minimum weekly compensation as stated in Section 25-5-68, but if at the time of injury the employee receives earnings of less than the minimum stated in Section 25-5-68, then the compensation shall be the full amount of such earnings per week. The compensation payable to partial dependents shall be subject to a maximum and minimum weekly compensation as stated in Section 25-5-68, but if the income loss of the partial dependents by the death is less than the minimum weekly compensation stated in Section 25-5-68, then the dependents shall receive the full amount of their income loss. This compensation shall be paid during dependency, not exceeding 500 weeks. Payments shall be made at the intervals when the earnings were payable, as nearly as may be, unless the parties otherwise agree. (Acts 1919, No. 245, p. 206; Code 1923, §§ 7554, 7556, 7558; Acts 1935, No. 387, p. 831; Acts 1936, Ex. Sess., No. 29, p. 9; Code 1940, T. 26, § 283; Acts 1949, No. 36, p. 47, § 5; Acts 1949, No. 544, p. 855; Acts 1951, No. 563, p. 978; Acts 1955, No. 356, p. 864; Acts 1957, No. 338, p. 446; Acts 1967, No. 168, p. 509; Acts 1973, No. 1062, p. 1750, § 16; Acts 1992, No. 92-537, § 19.)

The 1992 amendment, effective May 19, 1992, deleted "such" preceding "other person as" in the introductory paragraph, in subdivision (1), in the second sentence of paragraph c deleted "such" following "benefit of any," and substituted "the child" for "such child," in paragraph d substituted "the partial" for "such partial" in the first sentence, and in the third sentence substituted "Notwithstanding the foregoing, the compensation" for "provided, that the compensation," and substituted "the partial" for "such partial," in paragraph e substituted "the compensation" for "such compensation," and "the dependent" for "such dependent," added paragraph g, and in subdivision (2) substituted "the partial dependents by the death" for "said partial dependents by such death" in the second sentence.

Constitutionality. — This section furthers a legitimate state purpose, it does not violate the due process or equal protection clauses, and it is constitutional. Guy v. Southwest Ala. Council on Alcoholism, 495 So. 2d 77 (Ala. Civ. App. 1986).

Statutory requirement that death must occur within three years of injury. — Former section 25-5-178 provided in part that claims for benefits for death due to pneumoconiosis shall be considered timely filed if brought within three years of the date of death. While it is true action was timely filed, the time of filing was not the basis for the trial court's ruling; the trial court properly dismissed the action because of the additional statutory requirement that the death must have occurred within three years of the date of the injury. See this section and § 25-5-80. That is, the statute sets a three-year time limit for the employee to die after the occurrence of the injury as a condition precedent for having a cause of action under the Workmen's Compensation Act. Kilgore v. Alabama By-Prods. Corp., 581 So. 2d 872 (Ala. Civ. App. 1991).

This section and § 25-5-80 place a limit on the time that may elapse between the time of injury and the time of death for there to be a claim, whereas former § 25-5-178 placed a limit on the time for filing a claim. Kilgore v. Alabama By-Prods. Corp., 581 So. 2d 872 (Ala. Civ. App. 1991).

No presumption that death more than three years after injury is not related to it. — The legislature did not intend that there be a presumption that a death occurring more than three years after an injury is not related to the injury. This section is so clear that it does not need any such interpretation. Guy v. Southwest Ala. Council on Alcoholism, 495 So. 2d 77 (Ala. Civ. App. 1986).

Compensation intended where job kills worker. — The Workmen's Compensation Act does not write a life insurance policy covering every employee covered under it, but in cases where it is established that the job killed the worker, the legislature intended that his widow and minor children would be compensated. Hannah v. Kellerman Mining Co., 46 Ala. App. 63, 237 So. 2d 867 (1970).

Workmen's Compensation Act is not to be construed in such a manner as to disinherit heirs at law of a decedent simply because he was subject to a compensation act at the time of his death; proceeds from a recovery should be distributed under the Alabama descent and distribution statute as the wrongful death statute directs. Sanders v. Hertz Equip. Rental Corp., 339 F. Supp. 777 (S.D. Ala. 1972), modified sub nom. Sanders v. Shockley, 468 F.2d 88 (5th Cir. 1972).

Where identity of heirs and dependents differs, Workmen's Compensation Act is primary basis of recovery, but only as to the monetary limits and payment conditions specified therein. After the disposition of these amounts has been accomplished, any remainder of a third party recovery is available for distribution to the heirs-at-law as their rights are defined by the statute of distributions. Sanders v. Shockley, 468 F.2d 88 (5th Cir. 1972).

Section does not allow lump-sum death payments to deceased's widow. — This section which allows payment of death benefits to the deceased's widow, does not provide for lump-sum payments of such benefits. Jamestown Corp. v. Ward, 373 So. 2d 1136 (Ala. Civ. App.), cert. denied, 373 So. 2d 1142 (Ala. 1979).

Intended beneficiaries are real parties in interest. — While § 6-5-410 of the Alabama Code requires a "personal representative" of the decedent to commence a wrongful death action, the real parties in interest, and the intended beneficiaries under the statute, are the heirs of the decedent determined by the statute of distribution (former § 43-3-1 et seq. (now § 43-8-42)). The descent and distribution statute clearly identifies the decedent's children as intended beneficiaries. Blansit v. Cornelius & Rush Coal Co., 380 So. 2d 859 (Ala. 1980).

Court's discretion to apportion benefits does not extend to outright exclusion of one statutorily presumed to be wholly dependent upon the decedent. Frawley ex rel. Frawley v. U.S. Steel Mining Co., 496 So. 2d 731 (Ala. 1986).

Trial court is given discretion of dividing benefits among claimants under this section. Pate v. Miller Transporters, Inc., 381 So. 2d 64 (Ala. Civ. App. 1979), aff'd, 381 So. 2d 68 (Ala. 1980).

This statute provides that a partial dependent is to receive benefits in the same proportion that the employee's contributions bear to the dependent's income for the same time period. Once this proportion is established, it is then applied to the amount a total dependent would receive. Griffin Wood Co. v. Jones, 425 So. 2d 486 (Ala. Civ. App. 1983).

Minimum weekly compensation apportioned among multiple dependents. — Three dependents of deceased worker were not each entitled to the full amount of the 66⅔ percent of the deceased average weekly earnings, rather, the aggregate amount was properly apportioned between the three dependents. Grant v. Bracewell-Grant Timber, Inc., 576 So. 2d 1278 (Ala. Civ. App. 1991).

Child is statutorily presumed to have

been wholly dependent upon her natural father, and is entitled to an appropriate share of the workmen's compensation benefits. Frawley ex rel. Frawley v. U.S. Steel Mining Co., 496 So. 2d 731 (Ala. 1986).

Remarriage and nondependency relieved employer from payments. — In garnishment proceeding filed by widow against her late husband's employer when the employer ceased making weekly workmen's compensation payments, finding that remarriage of employee's widow and nondependency of employee's children relieved employer from further payments of workmen's compensation benefits pursuant to judgment for installment payments was proper. Belcher v. Vulcan Materials Co., 359 So. 2d 383 (Ala. Civ. App. 1978).

Trial court does not have to provide for reapportionment of compensation award in the event of death or remarriage of the decedent's widow or of death or marriage of a dependent since such occurrences are covered by statute. Pate v. Miller Transporters, Inc., 381 So. 2d 64 (Ala. Civ. App. 1979), aff'd, 381 So. 2d 68 (Ala. 1980).

Heart attacks may be caused by accidents within the meaning of the statute when the employee is shown to have engaged in strenuous activity connected with his employment prior to or at the time of the fatal attack. Hannah v. Kellerman Mining Co., 46 Ala. App. 63, 237 So. 2d 867 (1970).

Compensation for widow and children may be paid to widow. The question of apportionment of this compensation is a matter left to the discretion of the court. The court may order the payment of the whole sum to the widow, or may apportion the same as is deemed advisable. Ex parte Central Iron & Coal Co., 212 Ala. 367, 102 So. 797 (1925).

And she may maintain action therefor. — Where decedent, whose death was alleged to have been caused by an accident arising out of and in course of his employment, left a widow and two dependent children, she was a proper person to maintain for herself and them an action under Workmen's Compensation Act for compensation for his death. Ex parte Little Cahaba Coal Co., 213 Ala. 596, 105 So. 648 (1925).

Proceeding under Workmen's Compensation Act by plaintiff for compensation for death of decedent for herself and children, and pending action by her as administratrix of decedent's estate for damages for his death, held not subject to abatement (now dismissal) as being between the same parties. Ex parte Little Cahaba Coal Co., 213 Ala. 596, 105 So. 648 (1925).

And res judicata bars subsequent action by minors. — Widow could bring action for compensation for benefit of herself and minor children without other legal or personal representation. Such judgment is res judicata of subsequent action by minor children. Lawrence v. United States Fid. & Guar. Co., 226 Ala. 161, 145 So. 577 (1933).

Burden was on widow to reasonably satisfy the trial court by competent evidence (1) that her husband sustained a personal injury, (2) which was caused by an accident arising out of and in the course of his employment, and (3) to show by the same character of evidence a causal connection between the injury so received and death. There must be legal evidence of the facts necessary to relief. The conclusion of the trial court must not be allowed to rest on surmise. Hannah v. Kellerman Mining Co., 46 Ala. App. 63, 237 So. 2d 867 (1970).

Overexertion or unusual strain is not necessary to be proved. Hannah v. Kellerman Mining Co., 46 Ala. App. 63, 237 So. 2d 867 (1970).

Evidence held insufficient. — Where there was not evidence that the deceased had overexerted himself or had been overexposed to extreme heat prior to his death, and where there was no medical evidence of what caused the deceased's death, and where, for aught that appeared from the evidence, the deceased died from natural causes, the wife failed to carry the burden of proving that deceased's death was the result of a job-connected accident. Hannah v. Kellerman Mining Co., 46 Ala. App. 63, 237 So. 2d 867 (1970).

Right to accruing installments continues only during dependency. — All of the provisions of the Workmen's Compensation Act with reference to payment of an award to dependents in installments are to the effect that such payments continue only so long as the widow and children are dependent. In other words, the widow, on remarriage or death, ceases to be a dependent; a child, on reaching the age of 18 years (if not physically or mentally incapacitated from earning) or dying, ceases to be a dependent. The provisions of the act manifest a clear legislative intent that the right of dependents to accruing installments continues only during dependency. United States Steel Corp. v. Baker, 266 Ala. 538, 97 So. 2d 899 (1957).

But right to compensation does not rest upon dependency alone. There must be the existence of the relationship specified in the statute. Hunt v. United States Steel Corp., 274 Ala. 328, 148 So. 2d 618 (1963).

The right to benefits under the Workmen's Compensation Act does not rest upon dependency alone. There must also exist the relationship specified in the statute. Browning v. City of Huntsville, 46 Ala. App. 503, 244 So. 2d 378 (1971).

Payment so long as any dependent survives within designated period. — Compensation is payable under §§ 25-5-62, 25-5-63 and 25-5-69, read in connection with this section, so long as any named dependent survives throughout period of 300 (now 500) weeks. Ex parte Todd Shipbuilding & Dry Docks Co., 212 Ala. 477, 103 So. 447 (1925).

Paragraph (1)e of this section and section 25-5-66 are to be construed together and each has a separate field of operation. Kilby Steel Co. v. Robshaw, 242 Ala. 351, 6 So. 2d 427 (1942).

Effect of marriage of dependents. — Paragraph (1)e and the like provisions of § 25-5-69 relate to marriage of widow as well as to other dependents, and, when construed in connection with § 25-5-66, the only effect of such provisions is to intercept compensation from passing to personal representative in case of death of one or more of dependents, and in case of relief from dependency by marriage of dependent to direct its application to dependents remaining. Central Iron & Coal Co. v. Coker, 217 Ala. 472, 116 So. 794 (1928).

Where deceased employee left surviving dependent widow and more than four dependent children, thereby authorizing compensation to his dependents on basis of 65 (now 66 and two-thirds) percent of his average weekly earnings, under this section, remaining dependents, after widow remarried and other dependent children married and others passed the age of 18 years, were held entitled to the benefit of the full award. Central Iron & Coal Co. v. Coker, 217 Ala. 472, 116 So. 794 (1928).

Aunt of deceased does not come within any class enumerated in this section as entitled to benefits. Browning v. City of Huntsville, 46 Ala. App. 503, 244 So. 2d 378 (1971).

It was error for the trial court to amend its finding that employee contributed $75.00 per week to his parents' income to reduce the amount of the employee's contribution by $7.00 to $68.00 ($1.00 below the statutory minimum), in order to enable parents to take advantage of this section and receive $68.00 per week compensation, rather than merely $37.85, the amount they would have received under § 25-5-68, where it was apparent from the trial court's own statements that it did not determine that $68.00 was in its best judgment the true or most likely amount the evidence showed that the employee had contributed to his parents each week. W.S. Newell, Inc. v. Thurmond, 481 So. 2d 398 (Ala. Civ. App. 1985).

Case within declaratory judgment act. — Even though an action brought by an employee's widow for workmen's compensation death benefits was not initiated as a declaratory judgment action or as an attack on the validity of a state statute, when the widow defended the employer's motion to dismiss by contending that this section, the compensation statute, was unconstitutional, the case then came within the Declaratory Judgment Act and its requirement that the attorney general be served with notice of the widow's constitutional challenge. Guy v. Southwest Ala. Council on Alcoholism, 475 So. 2d 1190 (Ala. Civ. App. 1985).

Minimum weekly benefit held payable. — Where the weekly benefits payable to decedent's parents, who had been partially dependent on him, was computed by the trial judge at $37.85, and since that figure is less than the minimum weekly compensation of $69.00 stated in § 25-5-68 and since the income loss of $75.00 per week to the partially dependent parents was more than the minimum weekly compensation, the minimum weekly compensation was the weekly benefit which was payable to the parents by the employer. Thurmond v. W.S. Newell, Inc., 500 So. 2d 13 (Ala. Civ. App. 1986).

Cited in Ex parte Central Iron & Coal Co., 212 Ala. 367, 102 So. 797 (1925); Ex parte Todd Shipbuilding & Dry Docks Co., 212 Ala. 477, 103 So. 447 (1925); Ex parte Du Pont De Nemours & Co., 213 Ala. 604, 105 So. 592 (1925); Birmingham Slag Co. v. Johnson, 214 Ala. 131, 106 So. 806 (1926); Morgan-Hill Paving Co. v. Evans, 214 Ala. 125, 106 So. 869 (1926); Locke v. Centennial Ice & Coal Co., 214 Ala. 411, 108 So. 46 (1926); Larry v. Taylor, 227 Ala. 90, 149 So. 104 (1933); Sloss-Sheffield Steel & Iron Co. v. Brown, 228 Ala. 460, 153 So. 642 (1934); Braswell v. Brooks, 266 Ala. 141, 94 So. 2d 879 (1957); American Tennis Courts, Inc. v. Hinton, 378 So. 2d 235 (Ala. Civ. App. 1979); Central Foundry Co. v. Brown, 381 So. 2d 635 (Ala. Civ. App. 1979); Baird v. Spradlin, 409 So. 2d 820 (Ala. 1981); Boles v. Hooper & McDonald, Inc., 424 So. 2d 634 (Ala. Civ. App. 1982); Lackey v. Jefferson Energy Corp., 439 So. 2d 1290 (Ala. Civ. App. 1983); Maryland Cas. Co. v. Tiffin, 537 So. 2d 469 (Ala. 1988); Mobile Water & Sewer Bd. v. Wilson, 555 So. 2d 1081 (Ala. Civ. App. 1989).

Collateral references. — 99 C.J.S., Workmen's Compensation, §§ 130-151, 204, 321-329.

58 Am. Jur., Workmen's Compensation, §§ 281-320.

Anticipation of increase in wages of minor as element in fixing death benefit. 21 ALR 1531.

Deductions allowable in computing earnings as basis of death benefit. 22 ALR 864.

Gifts or gratuities as factor in determining amount of compensation. 75 ALR 1223.

Board and lodging as factor in determining amount of compensation. 85 ALR 188, 72 ALR2d 191.

Expense money as factor in computing one's earnings as a basis for award. 94 ALR 763.

Right of woman who marries injured workman to compensation as his widow or surviving wife. 98 ALR 993.

Rate of discount to be considered in comput-

ing present value of future earnings or benefits lost on account of death. 105 ALR 234.

Right and remedies of secondary or deferred class of beneficiaries of death benefits as affected by act of one in primary class of beneficiaries. 105 ALR 1232.

Prejudicial effect of bringing to jury's attention fact that plaintiff in personal injury or death action is entitled to workers' compensation benefits. 69 ALR4th 131.

§ 25-5-61. Persons presumed wholly dependent.

For the purposes of this article, the following described persons shall be conclusively presumed to be wholly dependent:

(1) The wife, unless it is shown that she was voluntarily living apart from her husband at the time of his injury or death, or unless it is shown that the husband was not in any way contributing to her support and had not in any way contributed to her support for more than 12 months next preceding the occurrence of the injury causing his death;

(2) The husband, unless it is shown that he was voluntarily living apart from his wife at the time of her injury or death, or unless it is shown that the wife was not in any way contributing to his support and had not in any way contributed to his support for more than 12 months next preceding the occurrence of the injury causing her death; and

(3) Minor children under the age of 18 years and those over 18, if physically or mentally incapacitated from earning. (Acts 1919, No. 245, p. 206; Code 1923, § 7552; Acts 1935, No. 387, p. 831; Acts 1936, Ex. Sess., No. 29, p. 9; Code 1940, T. 26, § 280; Acts 1973, No. 1062, p. 1750, § 15.)

Section constitutional. — Such legislative declarations of dependency are not offensive to the provisions of the Constitution. Ex parte Thomas, 209 Ala. 276, 96 So. 233 (1923); Gulf States Steel Co. v. Griffin, 214 Ala. 126, 106 So. 898 (1926); Woodward Iron Co. v. Jones, 217 Ala. 361, 116 So. 425 (1928).

And it is mainly remedial. Ex parte Cline, 213 Ala. 599, 105 So. 686 (1925).

To define dependents and to fix an employer's liability in respect thereto is for legislature and not for the court. Briggs v. Tennessee Coal, I. & R.R., 240 Ala. 44, 197 So. 17 (1940).

And difference made by legislature as to dependency between wife and children is founded in reason, the result of common observation and experience. Gulf States Steel Co. v. Griffin, 214 Ala. 126, 106 So. 898 (1926).

Dependency of wife is based on status at time of injury or death. — Under this section providing that wife shall be "conclusively presumed" to be wholly dependent, legal dependency thus declared is based on the status at time of injury or death. Ex parte Gude & Co., 213 Ala. 584, 105 So. 657 (1925).

And is declared as matter of law subject to exceptions. — Under this section providing that wife shall be "conclusively presumed" to be wholly dependent, the words quoted merely declare dependency as matter of law subject to exceptions named in statute. Ex parte Gude & Co., 213 Ala. 584, 105 So. 657 (1925); Royster & Haardt v. Morgan, 245 Ala. 496, 17 So. 2d 582 (1944).

Such as living apart. — Compensation for death of workman cannot be claimed under this section by his wife, who without divorce had taken another husband, and at time of workman's death was living apart from him and not receiving contribution to her support. Wilson v. Birmingham Elec. Co., 219 Ala. 436, 122 So. 411 (1929).

Phrase "living with" has usually been given constructive meaning going well beyond physical presence under the same roof. If a wife is living apart from her husband and if this separation is a result of the husband's deserting the wife, she may still be constructively living with him and entitled to benefits. Further, if the husband's cruelty justifiably causes the wife to leave him, it will be treated the same way as desertion and will not break the "continuity of living with" the husband. Robinson Foundry, Inc. v. Moon, 503 So. 2d 863 (Ala. Civ. App. 1987).

Wife deemed living with husband absent complete severance of marital relations. — The wife will be deemed to be living with the husband unless there has been an actual severance of marital relations so deliberate and complete that it is obvious that the wife no longer looks to the husband for support. Robinson Foundry, Inc. v. Moon, 503 So. 2d 863 (Ala. Civ. App. 1987).

Words "in any way" refer to character of husband's support. — Nature and extent of husband's support may be evidence to confirm or refute character and intent, under this section, of husband's "in any way" making contributions to his wife; the words "in any way," as used in such statute, referring to the character, intent and purpose of support by the husband giving, providing and contributing, and not merely to the nature and extent thereof. Woodward Iron Co. v. Jones, 217 Ala. 361, 116 So. 425 (1928).

The words "in any way" in this section refer to the character and intent of the purpose of support by the spouse giving and contributing and not merely to the nature and extent thereof. Read News Agency, Inc. v. Moman, 383 So. 2d 840 (Ala. Civ. App.), cert. denied, 383 So. 2d 847 (Ala. 1980).

When presumption of dependency broken. — If the living apart from the deceased employee is without justifiable cause, the presumption of dependency is broken. Robinson Foundry, Inc. v. Moon, 503 So. 2d 863 (Ala. Civ. App. 1987).

Substantial evidence is not required to support a conclusion of nondependency. Rather, the findings are conclusive if there is any evidence to support them. Lucas v. Black Diamond Coal Mining Co., 262 Ala. 368, 79 So. 2d 26 (1955).

Seventy-five-dollar remittance made by husband within the 12 months next preceding the occurrence of the injury causing his death was a gift and not a contribution to his wife's support. Lucas v. Black Diamond Coal Mining Co., 262 Ala. 368, 79 So. 2d 26 (1955).

Voluntariness is fact question. — The question of voluntariness was a question of fact which had to be determined by the trial court. Robinson Foundry, Inc. v. Moon, 503 So. 2d 863 (Ala. Civ. App. 1987).

Where wife's dependency a question of fact. — If it be shown that the wife was voluntarily living apart from her husband at the time of his injury or death, the question of dependency, total or partial, becomes an issue

of fact. Royster & Haardt v. Morgan, 245 Ala. 496, 17 So. 2d 582 (1944).

Higher salary does not make spouse nondependent. — Where all of decedent's salary was placed in joint-checking account, fact that plaintiff-husband also put money into the account and earned a considerably higher salary than decedent does not, as a matter of law, make plaintiff-husband nondependent under this section. Read News Agency, Inc. v. Moman, 383 So. 2d 840 (Ala. Civ. App.), cert. denied, 383 So. 2d 847 (Ala. 1980).

Employee not contributing to support of insane wife. — Where deceased employee had not contributed to the support or maintenance of his insane wife for more than two years prior to his death as result of injuries sustained in an accident arising out of and in the course of his employment, no recovery could be had by wife under the compensation act, though wife was an indigent patient in insane hospital and an object of charity. Briggs v. Tennessee Coal, I. & R.R., 240 Ala. 44, 197 So. 17 (1940).

Dissolution of marriage. — Where evidence established that deceased employee had obtained divorce from compensation claimant, claimant could not obtain compensation for employee's death as a "dependent" of the employee. Hallmark v. Virginia Bridge Co., 241 Ala. 283, 2 So. 2d 447 (1941).

Sufficiency of evidence as to common-law marriage. — Evidence supported finding that deceased employee and compensation claimant contending to be employee's dependent common-law wife entered into a common-law marriage contract. Sloss-Sheffield Steel & Iron Co. v. Alexander, 241 Ala. 476, 3 So. 2d 46 (1941).

Evidence held to establish invalidity of plaintiff's alleged common-law marriage to decedent because of his previous undissolved ceremonial marriage to another woman still living, so as to bar recovery. Bell v. Tennessee Coal, I. & R.R., 240 Ala. 422, 199 So. 813 (1941).

Compensation for death of workman cannot be claimed by woman living with him at time when both had spouses by marriages not dissolved by death or divorce. Wilson v. Birmingham Elec. Co., 219 Ala. 436, 122 So. 411 (1929).

Children as indicated are presumed to be dependent. Gulf States Steel Co. v. Griffin, 214 Ala. 126, 106 So. 898 (1926).

But only first degree children are included in the presumption. — It is manifest that children within this conclusive presumption of dependency include only those of the first degree; children born into the family of the deceased; dependents by nature, for whose care, support and training the law makes the father responsible. Ex parte Cline, 213 Ala. 599, 105 So. 686 (1925).

In a summary proceeding under the workmen's compensation law, circuit court could not assume jurisdiction to determine question whether grandchild living with grandfather and dependent wholly on him for support was entitled to inherit from him as an adopted child. Ex parte Cline, 213 Ala. 599, 105 So. 686 (1925).

Minor children under age of 18 years are conclusively presumed to be wholly dependent upon a decedent. Pate v. Miller Transporters, Inc., 381 So. 2d 64 (Ala. Civ. App. 1979), aff'd, 381 So. 2d 68 (Ala. 1980).

Even though adopted and living with adoptive parents. — Every child under the age of 18 is conclusively presumed to be "wholly dependent" upon its natural parent, even though at the time of the death of the parent, the child had been adopted by and is living with the adoptive parents. Central Foundry Co. v. Brown, 381 So. 2d 635 (Ala. Civ. App. 1979), cert. denied, 381 So. 2d 637 (Ala. 1980).

And all that is required is that adopted child be able to inherit. — There is no statement in the Workmen's Compensation Act which indicates that the act of adoption takes a child out of the terminology of "children" of his natural father. All that is required is that the adopted child be entitled to inherit as a child of the deceased. Central Foundry Co. v. Brown, 381 So. 2d 635 (Ala. Civ. App. 1979), cert. denied, 381 So. 2d 637 (Ala. 1980).

Child held not entitled to share in trust. — Child who had previously been adopted by her mother's second husband was not entitled to a distributive share in a private trust, funded by public donations, which had been established for the benefit of the widows and children of two police officers killed in the line of duty, one of whom was the child's natural father, as she had not been intended by the settlors to be included. Barnett ex rel. Barnett v. Beck, 481 So. 2d 348 (Ala. 1985).

Minor claimant was not dependent child

of his deceased grandfather, where claimant's father was alive and able to work. Black v. Freeman Lumber Co., 509 So. 2d 914 (Ala. Civ App. 1987).

In cases not covered by this section claimant has burden of proof to show actual dependency. Ex parte Cline, 213 Ala. 599, 105 So. 686 (1925); Morgan-Hill Paving Co. v. Stewart, 220 Ala. 480, 126 So. 116 (1930).

Finding as to dependency, or lack thereof, is conclusive on review, if there is any substantial evidence to support the conclusion announced. Gulf States Steel Co. v. Griffin, 214 Ala. 126, 106 So. 898 (1926), and cases cited.

Cited in Larry v. Taylor, 227 Ala. 90, 149 So. 104 (1933); Sloss-Sheffield Steel & Iron Co. v. Brown, 228 Ala. 460, 153 So. 642 (1934); Trammell v. Glens Falls Indem. Co., 259 Ala. 430, 66 So. 2d 537 (1953); Birmingham Belt R.R. v. Ellenburg, 215 Ala. 395, 111 So. 219 (1926); United States Steel Corp. v. Baker, 266 Ala. 538, 97 So. 2d 899 (1957); Whatley v. Lewis, 46 Ala. App. 18, 237 So. 2d 503 (1970); Blansit v. Cornelius & Rush Coal Co., 380 So. 2d 859 (Ala. 1980); Boles v. Hooper & McDonald, Inc., 424 So. 2d 634 (Ala. Civ. App. 1982); Fluker v. Sunnyland Foods, 469 So. 2d 586 (Ala. 1985); McCain v. Capital Veneer Works, Inc., 571 So. 2d 1215 (Ala. Civ. App. 1990); Allen v. Deaton, Inc., 587 So. 2d 344 (Ala. Civ. App. 1991).

Collateral references. — 100 C.J.S., Workmen's Compensation, §§ 512, 520.

58 Am. Jur., Workmen's Compensation, § 161 et seq.

"Dependency" within workmen's compensation act. 13 ALR 686, 30 ALR 1253, 35 ALR 1066, 39 ALR 313, 53 ALR 218, 62 ALR 160, 86 ALR 865, 100 ALR 1090.

Bigamous character of marriage as affecting right of one party thereto to compensation for death of other. 80 ALR 1428.

Children of one with whom deceased workman was living in illicit relations as dependents. 154 ALR 698.

§ 25-5-62. Total dependents — Designated; order of compensation.

A wife, child, husband, mother, father, grandmother, grandfather, sister, brother, mother-in-law or father-in-law who was wholly supported by the deceased workman at the time of his death and for a reasonable period of time immediately prior thereto shall be considered his total dependents, and payment of compensation shall be made to such total dependents in the order named. (Acts 1919, No. 245, p. 206; Code 1923, § 7553; Code 1940, T. 26, § 281.)

Purpose of section's separate listing of wife and children. — The separate listing of wife and children in this section is less to establish the priority between them than to establish the priority of each over the potential beneficiaries listed subsequently. Blansit v. Cornelius & Rush Coal Co., 380 So. 2d 859 (Ala. 1980).

Compensation not payable concurrently. — Under this section and §§ 25-5-60 and 25-5-63, compensation is not payable concurrently to more than one of the classes or grades of dependent relatives designated in § 25-5-60, and allowance to grandmother in addition to allowance to mother was erroneous. Ex parte Todd Shipbuilding & Dry Docks Co., 212 Ala. 477, 103 So. 447 (1925).

Widow and minor children not classes exclusive to each other. — The legislature did not intend to make a widow and minor children separate classes of total dependents to the exclusion of each other. Blansit v. Cornelius & Rush Coal Co., 380 So. 2d 859 (Ala. 1980).

Partial dependents eligible only if total dependents disqualified. — Partial dependents as a class may be eligible for benefits only after demonstrating that those classified as total dependents are ineligible for such benefits. Blansit v. Cornelius & Rush Coal Co., 380 So. 2d 859 (Ala. 1980).

Stepchildren are included within statutory definition of "children" only if they are members of the family of the decedent at the time of the accident and are dependent upon him for support. Pate v. Miller Transporters, Inc., 381 So. 2d 64 (Ala. Civ. App. 1979), aff'd, 381 So. 2d 68 (Ala. 1980).

Stepchildren dependents if deceased furnished more than court ordered support. — Stepchildren are dependent upon the decedent for support although the stepchildren receive court-ordered support of $100.00 per month from their natural father where the evidence shows that the deceased had furnished more than this amount monthly in support of his stepchildren. Pate v. Miller Transporters, Inc., 381 So. 2d 64 (Ala. Civ. App. 1979), aff'd, 381 So. 2d 68 (Ala. 1980).

Dependent mother was not entitled to compensation. — Under this section and §§ 25-5-61 and 25-5-64, wholly dependent mother of deceased employee leaving dependent widow and minor children, is entitled to no compensation. Locke v. Centennial Ice & Coal Co., 214 Ala. 411, 108 So. 46 (1926).

To justify an award to a deceased employee's half sister as a dependent, the evidence must show the death or nondependency of all those dependents in a class ahead of the half sister. Sloss-Sheffield Steel & Iron Co. v. Alexander, 241 Ala. 476, 3 So. 2d 46 (1941).

Grandchild was actual dependent. — In view of this section and §§ 25-5-1(3), 25-5-61, 25-5-64 and 25-5-65, when grandchild, made an orphan by death of his father, becomes member of family of grandfather, to be supported as one of his children, and is entitled to inherit his estate, he is within list of dependents having status of actual dependent. Ex parte Cline, 213 Ala. 599, 105 So. 686 (1925). See note to same case under § 25-5-1.

Minor claimant was not dependent child of his deceased grandfather, where claimant's father was alive and able to work. Black v. Freeman Lumber Co., 509 So. 2d 914 (Ala. Civ App. 1987).

Cited in Trammell v. Glens Falls Indem. Co., 259 Ala. 430, 66 So. 2d 537 (1953); Browning v. City of Huntsville, 46 Ala. App. 503, 244 So. 2d 378 (1971); Frawley ex rel. Frawley v. U.S. Steel Mining Co., 496 So. 2d 731 (Ala. 1986).

Collateral references. — 99 C.J.S., Workmen's Compensation, §§ 134, 322, 324. 100 C.J.S., Workmen's Compensation, § 520.

58 Am. Jur., Workmen's Compensation, § 161 et seq.

Posthumous children and children born after accident as dependents. 18 ALR3d 900.

§ 25-5-63. Total dependents — Maximum compensation.

Total dependents shall be entitled to take compensation in the order named in Section 25-5-62 until the percentage of the average weekly earnings of the deceased, during the time and as specified in Section 25-5-60, shall have been exhausted; but the total compensation to be paid to all total dependents of a deceased employee shall not exceed in the aggregate the maximum weekly compensation stated in Section 25-5-68, except as otherwise provided in this article. (Acts 1919, No. 245, p. 206; Code 1923, § 7560; Acts 1935, No. 387, p. 831; Acts 1936, Ex. Sess., No. 29, p. 9; Code 1940, T. 26, § 287; Acts 1949, No.

36, p. 47; Acts 1951, No. 563, p. 978; Acts 1955, No. 350, p. 849; Acts 1957, No. 339, p. 449.)

Cited in Ex parte Todd Shipbuilding & Dry Docks Co., 212 Ala. 477, 103 So. 447 (1925); Blansit v. Cornelius & Rush Coal Co., 380 So. 2d 859 (Ala. 1980); Frawley ex rel. Frawley v. U.S. Steel Mining Co., 496 So. 2d 731 (Ala. 1986).

Collateral references. — 99 C.J.S., Workmen's Compensation, § 324.

§ 25-5-64. Partial dependents.

Any member of a class named in Section 25-5-62 who regularly derived part of his support from the earnings of the deceased workman at the time of his death and for a reasonable period of time immediately prior thereto shall be considered his partial dependent, and payment of compensation shall be made to such partial dependents in the order named. (Acts 1919, No. 245, p. 206; Code 1923, § 7554; Acts 1935, No. 387, p. 831; Acts 1936, Ex. Sess., No. 29, p. 9; Code 1940, T. 26, § 282.)

The purpose of the statute is to provide compensation for the financial loss suffered by dependents because of the death of the decedent. Hopper v. Hale Constr. Co., 571 So. 2d 1160 (Ala. Civ. App. 1990).

Section liberally construed. — In ascertaining whether the plaintiffs were partially dependent on the deceased son and brother, as provided in this section, the trier of fact should give a liberal interpretation to the terms of the section and resolve all reasonable doubts in favor of the deceased employee. Hayles v. Ray E. Loper Lumber Co., 46 Ala. App. 58, 237 So. 2d 862 (1970).

Test of partial dependency under this section is not whether members of classes named could support life without contribution of deceased, but whether they regularly received from his wages part of their "support," meaning income used as means of living. Ex parte Sloss-Sheffield Sheffield Steel & Iron Co., 212 Ala. 3, 101 So. 608 (1924); Hayles v. Ray E. Loper Lumber Co., 46 Ala. App. 58, 237 So. 2d 862 (1970).

The question of partial dependency is determined by the actual support rendered to a family on a fairly consistent basis so that they not only can enjoy the necessities of life, but reasonably maintain their standard of living. Hayles v. Ray E. Loper Lumber Co., 46 Ala. App. 58, 237 So. 2d 862 (1970).

Mere fact of contributions standing alone does not prove support. Contributions, to constitute support, must be used as a means of living for the dependent in a manner in which he was accustomed to live. Ex parte Sloss-Sheffield Steel & Iron Co., 212 Ala. 3, 101 So. 608 (1924).

The receipt of contributions does not necessarily prove support. Such contributions must be used by the recipient to maintain himself in a manner to which he had become accustomed. Griffin Wood Co. v. Jones, 425 So. 2d 486 (Ala. Civ. App. 1983).

And income tax withholding exemption certificates have no probative value. — The income tax withholding exemption certificates relied on by defendant to show nondependency were neither relevant nor material, nor did they have any probative value. Hayles v. Ray E. Loper Lumber Co., 46 Ala. App. 58, 237 So. 2d 862 (1970).

The finding of fact by the trial court that the plaintiffs were not partially dependent upon the deceased son-brother because the income tax withholding exemption certificates revealed that deceased claimed only one exemption for income tax purposes was insufficient to support a judgment for the defendant. Hayles v. Ray E. Loper Lumber Co., 46 Ala. App. 58, 237 So. 2d 862 (1970).

What constitutes a reasonable time is a conclusion of fact. If deceased was contributing to support of the plaintiff at the time of his death and for such time prior to it as to raise a reasonable inference that he would continue, this is a reasonable time. American Tennis Courts, Inc. v. Hinton, 378 So. 2d 235 (Ala. Civ. App.), cert. denied, 378 So. 2d 239 (Ala. 1979).

Where parents' son was killed in a work-related accident while employed by construction company, trial court did not err in failing to find parents to be partial dependents within the contemplation of the Workmen's Compensation Act; the parents did not rely upon son's assistance to maintain their accustomed mode of living; son's assistance, though commendable, failed to establish dependency within the meaning of this section. Hopper v. Hale Constr. Co., 571 So. 2d 1160 (Ala. Civ. App. 1990).

Cited in Trammell v. Glens Falls Indem. Co., 259 Ala. 430, 66 So. 2d 537 (1953); Belcher v. Vulcan Materials Co., 359 So. 2d 386 (Ala. 1978); Frawley ex rel. Frawley v. U.S. Steel Mining Co., 496 So. 2d 731 (Ala. 1986); Mobile Water & Sewer Bd. v. Wilson, 555 So. 2d 1081 (Ala. Civ. App. 1989).

Collateral references. — 99 C.J.S., Workmen's Compensation, §§ 133, 134, 143, 322-324, 331. 100 C.J.S., Workmen's Compensation, §§ 520, 552, 608.

58 Am. Jur., Workmen's Compensation, § 161 et seq.

§ 25-5-65. Compensation of orphans or other children.

In computing and paying compensation to orphans or other children, in all cases, only those under 18 years of age or those over 18 years of age who are physically or mentally incapacitated from earning shall be included; the former to receive compensation only during the time they are under 18, the latter for the time they are so incapacitated, within the applicable period for which benefits are payable. (Acts 1919, No. 245, p. 206; Code 1923, § 7559; Code 1940, T. 26, § 286; Acts 1973, No. 1062, p. 1750, § 18.)

Cited in Ex parte Cline, 213 Ala. 599, 105 So. 686 (1925); Belcher v. Vulcan Materials Co., 359 So. 2d 386 (Ala. 1978).

Collateral references. — 99 C.J.S., Workmen's compensation, § 141(2).

§ 25-5-66. Disposition of compensation upon remarriage of widow of employee who has another dependent.

In case of the remarriage of a widow of an employee who has another dependent, the unpaid balance of compensation, which would otherwise become due her, shall be paid to the dependent or may, on approval by the court, be paid to some suitable person designated by the court for the use and benefit of the dependent. Payment to that person shall discharge the employer from any further liability. (Code 1923, § 7555; Acts 1939, No. 661, p. 1036, § 4; Code 1940, T. 26, § 284; Acts 1992, No. 92-537, § 20.)

The 1992 amendment, effective May 19, 1992, in the first sentence substituted "who has another dependent" for "who has dependent children," and "the dependent" for "such children," and substituted "that person" for "such person" in the second sentence.

Stepchild entitled to widow's share. — Upon remarriage of widow of deceased employee, dependent stepchild was entitled to have all of widow's share of compensation payments added to his payments. Kilby Steel Co. v. Robshaw, 242 Ala. 351, 6 So. 2d 427 (1942).

Remarriage and nondependency relieved employer from payments. — In garnishment proceeding filed by widow against her late husband's employer when the employer ceased making weekly workmen's compensation payments, finding that remarriage of employee's widow and nondependency of employee's children relieved employer from

further payments of workmen's compensation benefits pursuant to judgment for installment payments was proper. Belcher v. Vulcan Materials Co., 359 So. 2d 383 (Ala. Civ. App. 1978).

Trial court does not have to provide for reapportionment of compensation award in the event of death or remarriage of the decedent's widow or of death or marriage of a dependent since such occurrences are covered by statute. Pate v. Miller Transporters, Inc., 381 So. 2d 64 (Ala. Civ. App. 1979), aff'd, 381 So. 2d 68 (Ala. 1980).

Future-due installments do not become vested in dependent. — This section and §§ 25-5-65 and 25-5-69 clearly indicate that future-due installments of an award do not become vested in the dependent-payee. United States Steel Corp. v. Baker, 266 Ala. 538, 97 So. 2d 899 (1957).

Cited in Ex parte Central Iron & Coal Co., 212 Ala. 367, 102 So. 797 (1925).

Collateral references. — 99 C.J.S., Workmen's Compensation, §§ 141(1), 148, 321.

58 Am. Jur., Workmen's Compensation, § 187.

§ 25-5-67. Burial expenses.

If death results to an employee as the result of an accident or an occupational disease arising out of and in the course of the employment, the employer shall pay, in addition to the medical and hospital expenses provided for in Section 25-5-77, the expenses of burial, not exceeding in amount $3,000.00. If a dispute arises as to the reasonable value of the services rendered in connection with the burial, the same shall be approved by the court before payment after reasonable notice to interested parties as the court may require. (Acts 1919, No. 245, p. 206; Code 1923, § 7557; Acts 1935, No. 387, p. 831; Acts 1936, Ex. Sess., No. 29, p. 9; Code 1940, T. 26, § 285; Acts 1945, No. 469, p. 704; Acts 1957, No. 336, p. 437; Acts 1961, Ex. Sess., No. 272, p. 2289, § 1; Acts 1971, No. 667, p. 1376, § 5; Acts 1973, No. 1062, p. 1750, § 17; Acts 1992, No. 92-537, § 21.)

The 1992 amendment, effective May 19, 1992, in the first sentence substituted "If death" for "In all cases where death," "as the result of an accident or an occupational disease" for "caused by an accident, the employment" for "his employment," and "three thousand dollars ($3,000)" for "$1,000.00," and in the second sentence substituted "If a dispute" for "In case dispute," and deleted "such" following "payment after."

Burden is on plaintiff to show expenses incurred. — This section fixes a maximum and not a flat allowance for expenses of burial. And the burden is on plaintiff to show the amount incurred for such purpose. Paramount Coal Co. v. Williams, 214 Ala. 394, 108 So. 7 (1926).

And nonliability of insurer or benefit association. — To bring expenses of burial within this section, the burden is also on plaintiff to show no insurer or benefit association is liable therefor. This is a condition to recovery within the special knowledge of the plaintiff. Paramount Coal Co. v. Williams, 214 Ala. 394, 108 So. 7 (1926).

Better practice is to set out facts in complaint to support claim for burial expenses. Paramount Coal Co. v. Williams, 214 Ala. 394, 108 So. 7 (1926).

And if no issue is made by answer no proof is required. — When facts to support claim for burial expenses are set out in plaintiff's complaint and no issue is made by answer, no proof is required. Paramount Coal Co. v. Williams, 214 Ala. 394, 108 So. 7 (1926).

When defendant's liability is not presented in pleading or proof court should not of its own motion include in judgment maximum sum allowed by this section for burial expenses. Paramount Coal Co. v. Williams, 214 Ala. 394, 108 So. 7 (1926).

Agreement held not admission of liability. — Agreement in compensation case, waiving all questions going to right of recovery save that of ultimate cause of death, held not an admission of employer's liability for burial expenses, under this section, where it was not made an issue in pleadings or evidence. Paramount Coal Co. v. Williams, 214 Ala. 394, 108 So. 7 (1926).

Cited in Baird v. Spradlin, 409 So. 2d 820 (Ala. 1982).

Collateral references. — 99 C.J.S. Workmen's Compensation, §§ 266-288.

58 Am. Jur., Workmen's Compensation, §§ 327-333.

§ 25-5-68. Maximum and minimum weekly compensation.

(a) The compensation paid under this article shall be not less than, except as otherwise provided in this article, 27½ percent of the average weekly wage of the state as determined by the director, rounded to the nearest dollar, pursuant to subsection (b) of this section and, in any event, no more than 100 percent of the average weekly wage. Notwithstanding the foregoing, the maximum compensation payable for permanent partial disability shall be no more than the lesser of $220.00 per week or 100 percent of the average weekly wage.

(b) For the purpose of this section, the average weekly wage of the state shall be determined by the director as follows: On or before June 1 of each year, the total wages reported on contribution reports to the unemployment compensation division of the department for the preceding calendar year shall be divided by the average monthly number of insured workers, which shall be determined by dividing the sum of the number of insured workers reported for each month of the preceding year by 12. The average annual wage thus obtained shall be divided by 52, and the average weekly wage thus determined rounded to the nearest cent. The average weekly wage as so determined shall be applicable for the 12-month period beginning July 1 following the June 1 determination. If the determination shall not be made on or before June 1, the effective date of the average weekly wage when determined shall be the first day of the month next following 30 days after the determination is made.

(c) The maximum and minimum weekly benefit shall not be changed on any July 1 or as a result of any annual determination, unless the computation provided for in subsection (b) of this section results in an increase or decrease of two dollars ($2) or more in the amount of either the maximum or minimum benefit.

(d) In no event, except as provided for permanent total disability in subdivision (a)(4) of Section 25-5-57 or except for compensation benefits payable for permanent partial and temporary total disability in connection with a disability scheduled in subdivisions (1) and (3) of subsection (a) of Section 25-5-57, shall the total amount of compensation payable for an accident or an occupational disease exceed the product of 500 times the maximum weekly benefit applicable on the date of the accident.

(e) The minimum and maximum benefits that are in effect on the date of the accident which results in injury or death shall be applicable for the full period during which compensation is payable. (Acts 1919, No. 245, p. 206; Code 1923, § 7563; Acts 1935, No. 387, p. 831; Acts 1936, Ex. Sess., No. 29, p. 9; Acts 1939, No. 661, p. 1036; Code 1940, T. 26, § 289; Acts 1949, No. 36, p. 47, § 6; Acts 1951, No. 563, p. 978, § 4; Acts 1955, No. 359, p. 874; Acts 1957, No. 340, p. 449; Acts 1961, Ex. Sess., No. 272, p. 2289, § 2; Acts 1963, No. 578, p. 1252; Acts 1967, No. 168, p. 509, § 3; Acts 1969, No. 233, p. 557, § 2; Acts 1971, No. 667, p. 1376, § 6; Acts 1973, No. 1062, p. 1750, § 19; Acts 1975, 4th

Ex. Sess., No. 86, p. 2729, § 7; Acts 1984, 2nd Ex. Sess., No. 85-41, p. 44, § 7; Acts 1992, No. 92-537, § 22.)

The 1992 amendment, effective May 19, 1992, deleted former subsection (a) which pertained to injury or death resulting from accidents occurring before February 1, 1985, redesignated former subsections (b) through (f) as subsections (a) through (e), in present subsection (a), in the first sentence deleted "With respect to injury or death resulting from an accident occurring on or after February 1, 1985" at the beginning of the sentence, substituted "director, rounded to the nearest dollar" for "director of industrial relations (rounded to the nearest dollar)," "subsection (b)" for "subsection (c)," and "the average" for "such average," and in the second sentence substituted "Notwithstanding the foregoing" for "except that," "the average" for "such average," and inserted "two hundred twenty dollars," in subsection (b), in the first sentence deleted "of industrial relations" following "director" and "department," and inserted "which shall be," and substituted "the determination" for "such determination" in two places in the last sentence, in subsection (c) substituted "subsection (b)" for "subsection (c)" and inserted "two dollars," and substituted "an accident or an occupational disease" for "any accident" in subsection (d).

Code commissioner's note. — Acts 1984, 2nd Ex. Sess., No. 85-41, § 14 provides: "This act shall become effective immediately upon its passage and approval by the governor [January 9, 1985], or upon its otherwise becoming a law, provided it shall have no effect whatsoever with respect to the right of any injured employee to bring an action with respect to or upon any cause of action which arose or accrued prior to February 1, 1985. Provided further, it shall have no effect on and shall not apply to any accident or exposure to injurious condition occurring before the effective date of this Act."

Section referred to in section 25-5-57. — While there is a reference in § 25-5-57 (a) (3)g to this section, it is also true that this section is included in a number of other subdivisions and paragraphs of § 25-5-57 to expressly provide and limit all awards to minimum and maximum compensation therein provided. Rowell v. Doss, 284 Ala. 500, 226 So. 2d 157 (1969).

Determination of percentage loss of earning capacity. — Disability of the body is not the only determinative factor in reaching the required factual conclusion of percentage loss of earning capacity. The court may consider other factors, including the claimant's age, education and experience, as they affect his employability and earning capacity. Bickerstaff Clay Prods. Co. v. Dixon, 444 So. 2d 390 (Ala. Civ. App. 1983).

Limitation is to apply to permanent partial disability benefits only. — Subsection (b) (now subsection (a)) limits compensation payable for permanent partial disability to $200.00 per week but it does not place such a limitation on compensation payable for temporary total disability. Clearly, the legislature intended this limitation to apply to permanent partial disability benefits only. Smither v. International Paper Co., 540 So. 2d 760 (Ala. Civ. App. 1989).

Minimum weekly compensation apportioned among multiple dependents. — Three dependents of deceased worker were not each entitled to the full amount of the 66²/₃ percent of the deceased average weekly earnings, rather, the aggregate amount was properly apportioned between the three dependents. Grant v. Bracewell-Grant Timber, Inc., 576 So. 2d 1278 (Ala. Civ. App. 1991).

Minimum rate inapplicable under § 25-5-57(a)(3)g. — The minimum weekly compensation rate as established pursuant to this section does not apply in nonscheduled permanent partial disability cases where compensation is provided and governed by § 25-5-57(a)(3)g. Winston Furn., Inc. v. Kirkpatrick, 495 So. 2d 1092 (Ala. Civ. App. 1985), aff'd, 495 So. 2d 1095 (Ala. 1986).

Minimum benefit provision of subsection (b) of this section does not apply to injury falling under § 25-5-57(a)(3)g. T.G. & Y. Stores v. Stringfellow, 500 So. 2d 1133 (Ala. Civ. App. 1986).

It was error for the trial court to amend its finding that employee contributed $75.00 per week to his parents' income to reduce the amount of the employee's contribution by $7.00 to $68.00 ($1.00 below the statutory minimum), in order to enable the parents to take advantage of § 25-5-60 and receive $68.00 per week compensation, rather than merely $37.85, the amount they would have received under this section, where it was apparent from the trial court's own statements that it did not determine that $68.00 was in its best judgment the true or most likely amount the evidence showed that the employee had contributed to his parents each week. W.S. Newell, Inc. v. Thurmond, 481 So. 2d 398 (Ala. Civ. App. 1985).

Cited in H.C. Price Co. v. Lee, 249 Ala. 230, 30 So. 2d 579 (1947); Southern Cotton Oil Co. v. Wynn, 266 Ala. 327, 96 So. 2d 159 (1957);

Sanders v. Hertz Equip. Rental Corp., 339 F. Supp. 777 (S.D. Ala. 1972); Shepard v. Chrysler Corp., 314 F. Supp. 1179 (N.D. Ala. 1969); M.R. Thomason & Assocs. v. Jones, 48 Ala. App. 67, 261 So. 2d 899 (1972); Carroll Constr. Co. v. Hutcheson, 347 So. 2d 527 (Ala. Civ. App. 1977); Middleton v. Dan River, Inc., 617 F. Supp. 1206 (M.D. Ala. 1985); King v. Travelers Ins. Co., 513 So. 2d 1023 (Ala. 1987);

Mobile Water & Sewer Bd. v. Wilson, 555 So. 2d 1081 (Ala. Civ. App. 1989).

Collateral references. — Limit of compensation as inclusive or exclusive of medical or hospitalization expense. 128 ALR 136.

Workers' compensation: value of home services provided by victim's relative. 65 ALR4th 142.

§ 25-5-69. Compensation to cease upon death or marriage of dependent; proportional benefits for dependents.

If compensation is being paid under this article to any dependent, such compensation shall cease upon the death or marriage of such dependent. Where compensation is being paid under this chapter to any dependent, in no event shall such dependent receive more than the proportion which the amount received of the deceased employee's income during his life bears to the compensation provided under this article. (Acts 1919, No. 245, p. 206; Code 1923, § 7564; Code 1940, T. 26, § 290.)

First sentence of this section is a practical repetition of section 25-5-60(1)e. Ex parte Todd Shipbuilding & Dry Docks Co., 212 Ala. 477, 103 So. 447 (1925). See also, Central Iron & Coal Co. v. Coker, 217 Ala. 472, 116 So. 794 (1928).

And specifies only grounds for stopping compensation. — Continued compensation under the compensation act during the statutory period is not conditioned upon the continued dependency upon the bounty thus provided, and such compensation ceases only upon the happening of the events named in statute. Ex parte Gude & Co., 213 Ala. 584, 105 So. 657 (1925).

Status of a wife as a dependent having been fixed under Workmen's Compensation Act at the time of the employee's death, compensation continues for the period named in the statute until her marriage or death as expressly provided by this section. Ex parte Gude & Co., 213 Ala. 584, 105 So. 657 (1925).

Right to compensation for employee's death did not continue after remarriage of partially dependent mother, though she had a husband living when son died. Sloss-Sheffield Steel & Iron Co. v. Brown, 228 Ala. 460, 153 So. 642 (1934), holding that court cannot add limitations upon provision terminating compensation upon marriage because court surmises that legislature may have so wished, when it did not so enact.

Compensation does not cease upon void marriage. — Second marriage of employee's widow to one who was not allowed to remarry by divorce decree obtained by his former wife is a nullity, and hence does not work discontinuance of compensation under this section. Gulf States Steel Co. v. Witherspoon, 214 Ala. 529, 108 So. 573 (1926).

Notwithstanding dependent's wrongful intent. — Whether deceased employee's widow was guilty of wrong intent in marrying one not allowed to remarry by decree of divorce from former wife, or any subsequent decree, does not affect her legal status as dependent under Workmen's Compensation Act. Gulf States Steel Co. v. Witherspoon, 214 Ala. 529, 108 So. 573 (1926).

Trial court does not have to provide for reapportionment of compensation award in the event of death or remarriage of the decedent's widow or of death or marriage of a dependent since such occurrences are covered by statute. Pate v. Miller Transporters, Inc., 381 So. 2d 64 (Ala. Civ. App. 1979), aff'd, 381 So. 2d 68 (Ala. 1980).

Provision limiting compensation does not affect those wholly dependent. — The second sentence of this section was held not to affect compensation of those wholly dependent who were as family group receiving in home full benefit of workman's earning power at time of his death. Central Iron & Coal Co. v. Coker, 217 Ala. 472, 116 So. 794 (1928).

The last sentence of this section applies when the dependent was a member of a family group receiving in the home full benefit of the workman's earning power at the time of his death. Central Iron & Coal Co. v. Coker, 217 Ala. 472, 116 So. 794 (1928); Kilby Steel Co. v. Robshaw, 242 Ala. 351, 6 So. 2d 427 (1942).

Cited in Brack v. State, 19 Ala. App. 258, 96 So. 727 (1923).

Collateral references. — 99 C.J.S., Workmen's Compensation, §§ 146-148.

Divorce as affecting right of spouse to compensation. 8 ALR 1113, 13 ALR 729.

§§ 25-5-70 through 25-5-75. Repealed by Acts 1992, No. 92-537, § 51, effective May 19, 1992.

§ 25-5-76. Liability of joint employers.

In case any employee for whose injury or death compensation is payable under this article shall, at the time of the injury, be employed and paid jointly by two or more employers subject to this chapter, such employers shall contribute the payment of such compensation in the proportion of their several earnings liability to such employee. If one or more, but not all of such employers, should be subject to this article, and otherwise subject to liability for compensation hereunder, then the liability of such of them as are so subject shall be to pay the proportion of the entire compensation which their proportionate earnings liability bears to the entire earnings of the employee. Nothing in this section shall prevent any arrangement between such employers for a different distribution, as between themselves, of the ultimate burden of such compensation. (Acts 1919, No. 245, p. 206; Code 1923, § 7565; Code 1940, T. 26, § 291.)

Compensation for death of employee who had worked at several employments was proportioned to earnings received from employer liable under this section and § 25-5-57(b). Odom v. Galloway Coal Co., 223 Ala. 118, 134 So. 855 (1931).

Collateral references. — 99 C.J.S., Workmen's Compensation, §§ 46, 51.

58 Am. Jur., Workmen's Compensation, § 341.

Concurrent or joint employment by several. 30 ALR 1000, 58 ALR 1395.

§ 25-5-77. Expenses of medical and surgical treatment, vocational rehabilitation, medicine, etc.; medical examinations; review by ombudsman of medical services.

(a) In addition to the compensation provided in this article and Article 4 of this chapter, the employer, where applicable, shall pay the actual cost of the repair, refitting, or replacement of artificial members damaged as the result of an accident arising out of and in the course of employment, and the employer, except as otherwise provided in this amendatory act, shall pay an amount not to exceed the prevailing rate or maximum schedule of fees as established herein of reasonably necessary medical and surgical treatment and attention, physical rehabilitation, medicine, medical and surgical supplies, crutches, artificial members, and other apparatus as the result of an accident arising out of and in the course of the employment, as may be obtained by the injured employee or, in case of death, obtained during the period occurring between the time of the injury and the employee's death therefrom. If the employee is dissatisfied with the initial treating physician selected by the employer and if further treatment is required, the employee may so advise the employer, and the employee shall be entitled to select a second physician from a panel or list of four physicians selected by the employer. If surgery is required and if the employee is dissatisfied with the designated surgeon, he or she may so advise the employer, and the employee shall be entitled to select a second surgeon from a panel or list of four surgeons selected by the employer. If four physicians or surgeons are not available to be listed, the employer shall include on the list as many as are available. The four physicians or surgeons selected by the employer hereunder shall not be from or members of the same firm, partnership, or professional corporation. The total liability of the employer shall, unless otherwise provided in this chapter, not exceed the prevailing rate or the maximum schedule of fees as established herein. Notwithstanding the foregoing, in ascertaining the prevailing rate of reimbursement or payment with regard to participating hospitals and ambulatory surgical centers or outpatient rehabilitation centers licensed by the State of Alabama, as well as diagnostic facilities accredited by the Commission on Accreditation of Rehabilitation Facilities, the prevailing rate shall be negotiated with each individual hospital, ambulatory surgical center, licensed outpatient rehabilitation facility, or diagnostic facility based on that institution's treatment of comparable type cases for the 12-month period immediately preceding May 19, 1992. These rates shall be updated every 12 months thereafter. Initial rates shall be established within six months of May 19, 1992. For those non-participating hospitals the prevailing rate shall be determined by a committee. In the first year following May 19, 1992, the committee shall be composed of five members. The director shall appoint one member from the Department of Industrial Relations and two members from the community in which the non-participating hospital is located. The non-participating hospital shall appoint two members. This committee shall by a majority vote establish the maximum rates of reimbursement or payment for the non-participating hospital, and the hospital shall be bound for one year by the determined rates of reimbursement or payment for workers' compensation cases. If, following the first year after the rates were established by this committee, the hospital is again non-participating, then another committee shall be appointed. This second committee shall have three members selected by the non-participating hospital and two members selected by the director. The committee composition shall alternate as above described each year the hospital is non-participating. The total liability of the employer shall not exceed the rates established by the committee. This committee, in determining the rates of reimbursement or payments to the hospital, may consider such factors as the size, staffing, and medical equipment of the hospital, and any other factors which the committee may consider relevant. If an insurer of the employee or a benefit association has paid or is liable for the employee's medical, surgical, and hospital service or for a part thereof, or if the employee is entitled to the same or a part thereof, from any source whatever by virtue of any agreement or understanding or law, state or federal, without any loss of benefit to the employee, the employer shall not be required to pay any part of the expense. If the benefits are insufficient to pay all the employee's expense, the employer shall be liable for the deficiency only. All cases of dispute as to the necessity and value of the services shall be determined by the tribunal having jurisdiction of the claim of the injured employee for compensation.

(b) If requested to do so by the employer, the injured employee shall submit to examination by the employer's physician at all reasonable times, but the employee shall have the right to have a physician of his or her own selection present at the examination, in which case the employee shall be liable to the physician of his or her own selection for his or her services. The employer shall pay for the services of the physician making the examination at the instance of the employer. If a dispute arises as to the injury, or as to the extent of the disability therefrom, the court may, at the instance of either party or of its own motion, appoint a neutral physician of good standing and ability to make an examination of the injured employee and to report his or her findings to the court, the expense of which examination shall be borne equally by the parties. If the injured employee refuses to comply with reasonable request for examination, or refuses to accept the medical service or physical rehabilitation, which the employer elects to furnish under this chapter, the employee's right to compensation shall be suspended and no compensation shall be payable for the period of the refusal. A physician whose services are furnished or paid for by the employer, or a physician of the injured employee who treats or makes or is present at any examination of an injured employee may be required to testify as to any knowledge obtained by him or her in the course of the treatment or examination as the treatment or examination related to the injury or the disability arising therefrom. The physician shall, upon written request of the injured employee or his or her employer and without consent of or notice to the employee or employer not making the request, furnish the injured employee or his or her employer a written statement of his or her professional opinion as to the extent of the injury and disability. In all death claims where the cause of death is obscure or is disputed, any interested party may require an autopsy, the cost of which is to be borne by the party demanding the autopsy. The term "physicians" shall include medical doctor, surgeon, and chiropractor. A hospital, medical clinic, rehabilitation service, or other person or entity providing treatment to an employee or providing facilities at which the employee receives treatment shall, upon the written request of the employee or of the employer, furnish, at a reasonable cost, the employee or the employer a copy of the records, including X-rays and laboratory reports, relating to the treatment of the injured employee. The copy may be furnished without the consent of or notice to the employee or employer not making the request. A physician, hospital, medical clinic, rehabilitation service, or other person or entity providing written statement of professional opinion or copies of records pursuant to this subsection shall not be liable to any person for a claim arising out of the release of medical information concerning the employee.

(c) If the employer so elects, the employee shall submit to and undergo vocational rehabilitation at the employer's expense through a vocational rehabilitation specialist, who shall be qualified to render competent vocational rehabilitation service. If an employee who is unable in the opinion of the treating physician to return to his or her former employment shall request vocational rehabilitation and if both a vocational rehabilitation specialist and a treating physician, the cost of whose service is the obligation of the employer under this section, shall express their opinions in writing that in the judgment of each of them vocational rehabilitation is reasonably calculated to restore the employee to gainful employment and is in the best interest of the employee, the cost of the rehabilitation shall be borne by the employer. The cost, where rehabilitation requires residence at or near a facility or institution away from the employee's customary residence, shall include reasonable charges for the employee's necessary board, lodging, and travel.

(d) If an employee refuses, without the consent of the court, to accept vocational rehabilitation at the employer's request, the refusal shall result in loss of compensation for the period of refusal.

(e) All disputes with regard to vocational rehabilitation may be submitted to the court for resolution.

(f) The employer shall pay mileage costs to and from medical and rehabilitation providers at the same rate as provided by law for official state travel.

(g) In a compensable workers' compensation claim, the injured employee shall not be liable for payment of any authorized and compensable medical expenses associated with the workers' compensation claim.

(h) All undisputed medical reimbursements or payments shall be made within 25 working days of receipt of claims in the form specified in Section 25-5-3. There shall be added to any undisputed medical invoice which is not paid within 25 working days an amount equal to 10 percent of the unpaid balance.

If the employer or insurer responsible for payment of the claim fails to add the additional 10 percent to the claim as required by this section, the person, firm, corporation, or partnership providing the medical service for which payment has been delayed beyond the period specified in this section may file a written complaint stating that fact with the director. Upon investigation, if the director determines that the facts stated in the complaint are true, then in that event the director shall order the employer or insurer to pay to the provider the amount of the claim and any applicable penalty, and in addition may assess a civil monetary penalty in amount not to exceed five hundred dollars ($500) against the employer or insurer, payment of which shall be made to the director within 30 days of the notice of assessment.

(i) Any party, including a health care provider, is entitled to a review by an ombudsman of medical services that are provided or for which authorization of payment is sought if any party or the health care provider has any of the following:

(1) Been denied payment or had the charge reduced for medical services rendered.

(2) Been denied authorization for the payment of services requested or performed when authorization is required.

(3) Been ordered by the director to refund payments received for the provision of medical services.

(4) A party to a medical dispute that remains unresolved after a review of medical services as provided by this section may petition the court for relief.

(5) In any review under this subsection of medical services provided by a physician, any party to a dispute may request that the ombudsman consult with an independent medical expert for the purpose of obtaining advice and consultation on the resolution of any issue involving medical practice. If such a request is made, the ombudsman shall select an independent medical expert from among a list of at least three names provided by the Workers' Compensation Medical Services Board in a medical specialty appropriate to the issues raised in the dispute and shall secure a written opinion from the independent medical expert. In rendering a decision or recommendation, the ombudsman shall give full consideration to the opinion of the independent medical expert but shall not be bound by that opinion. The independent medical expert shall be compensated at a rate set by the Workers' Compensation Medical Services Board and approved by the director. (Acts 1919, No. 245, p. 206; Code 1923, § 7567; Acts 1935, No. 387, p. 831; Acts 1936, Ex. Sess., No. 29, p. 9; Acts 1939, No. 661, p. 1036, § 17; Code 1940, T. 26, § 293; Acts 1949, No. 36, p. 47, § 8; Acts 1955, No. 354, p. 853; Acts 1957, No. 341, p. 450; Acts 1961, Ex. Sess., No. 272, p. 2289, § 3; Acts 1963, No. 578, p. 1252, § 3; Acts 1967, No. 168, p. 509, § 4; Acts 1969, No. 233, p. 557, § 3; Acts 1971, No. 667, p. 1376, § 8; Acts 1973, No. 1062, p. 1750, § 21; Acts 1975, 4th Ex. Sess., No. 86, p. 2729, § 8; Acts 1984, 2nd Ex. Sess., No. 85-41, p. 44, § 8; Acts 1992, No. 92-537, § 23.)

The 1992 amendment, effective May 19, 1992, rewrote this section. As to the implementation of this amendment, see the Code commissioner's note.

Code commissioner's note. — Acts 1984, 2nd Ex. Sess., No. 85-41, § 14 provides: "This act shall become effective immediately upon its passage and approval by the governor [January 9, 1985], or upon its otherwise becoming a law, provided it shall have no effect whatsoever with respect to the right of any injured employee to bring an action with respect to or upon any cause of action which arose or accrued prior to February 1, 1985. Provided further, it shall have no effect on and shall not apply to any accident or exposure to injurious condition occurring before the effective date of this Act."

The phrase "this amendatory act," as used in the section above, refers to Acts 1992, No. 92-537, which amended this section. Act No. 92-537 also amended §§ 25-5-1 through 25-5-4, 25-5-8, 25-5-10, 25-5-11, 25-5-13, 25-5-50 through 25-5-57, 25-5-59, 25-5-60, 25-5-66 through 25-5-68, 25-5-77, 25-5-78, 25-5-80, 25-5-81, 25-5-83, 25-5-85, 25-5-86, 25-5-90, 25-5-110, 25-5-116, 25-5-117, 25-5-120, 25-5-251, enacted §§ 25-5-15.1, 25-5-290 through 25-5-294, and 25-5-310 through 25-5-318, and repealed §§ 25-5-16, 25-5-70 through 25-5-75, 25-5-140 through 25-5-152, and 25-5-170 through 25-5-180.

Section 53 of Acts 1992, No. 92-537, provides that the amendment to this section by § 23 of the act shall be implemented on August 1, 1992.

I. GENERAL CONSIDERATION.

Editor's note. — The cases annotated below were decided under prior law.

Clear import of section is that an employer shall be liable to an employee for expenses incurred in the treatment of a compensable injury unless a statutory exception precludes liability on the employer's part. United States v. Bear Bros., 355 So. 2d 1133 (Ala. Civ. App. 1978).

Physical therapists are not physicians. — The term "physician," as defined under subsection (b), only refers to medical doctors, surgeons, and chiropractors and not physical therapists. Interstate Truck Leasing v. Bryan, 537 So. 2d 53 (Ala. Civ. App. 1988).

Examination by employer's physicians. — Language found in subsection (b), which states that injured employee must submit himself to examination by employer's physician at all reasonable times, applies only to pending cases before final judgment of the circuit court, or after such judgment is procedurally reopened for alteration, amendment, or revision. Cerrock Wire & Cable Co. v. Johnson, 533 So. 2d 622 (Ala. Civ. App. 1988).

Where employer's motion simply moved circuit court to require employee to submit to physical examinations and vocational rehabilitation, but nothing was presented to the trial court upon which it could reasonably have concluded that employee's condition had improved in any way since trial, the trial court did not err in its denial of post-judgment motion to require employee to submit himself for physical examination and vocational rehabilitation as provided by subsections (b) and (c). Cerrock Wire & Cable Co. v. Johnson, 533 So. 2d 622 (Ala. Civ. App. 1988).

Request to trial court for an order to employee to submit to medical examination some seven months after trial court's judgment finding employee permanently and totally disabled did not have same effect as if presented to trial court before or during the pendency of the original trial and before judgment. Cerrock Wire & Cable Co. v. Johnson, 533 So. 2d 622 (Ala. Civ. App. 1988).

Taking of medical benefits does not constitute election against common-law remedy. — The taking of medical benefits for hernia where compensation proper is precluded by § 25-5-57(a)(6) does not constitute an election against a common-law remedy or one conferred by the Employer's Liability Act, §§ 25-6-1 through 25-6-4, except as to the medical expense thereby avoided. Sam's Place v. Middleton, 39 Ala. App. 481, 103 So. 2d 812 (1958).

Employee's right to compensation for accrued medical expenses independent of workmen's compensation benefits. — The injured employee's right to sue for accrued medical expenses, is totally independent of the employee's right to sue for workmen's compensation benefits; thus, the commencement of an employee's action, whether for compensation benefits or for medical expenses, or for both, within two years was not a condition precedent to the employee's right to sue for accrued medical expenses, whether such expenses are incurred during the period of limitations for compensation benefits or after the expiration of such period. Tuscaloosa County v. INA/Aetna Ins. Co., 522 So. 2d 782 (Ala. 1988).

The Workmen's Compensation Act does not prescribe, as a condition precedent to the right to sue for accrued medical expenses, that the injured employee be entitled to weekly compensation benefits. Tuscaloosa County v. INA/Aetna Ins. Co., 522 So. 2d 782 (Ala. 1988).

Recovery of accrued medical expenses not time-barred. — The filing of a suit to enforce payment of compensation benefits was not required in order to vest jurisdiction in the circuit court to adjudicate a claim for accrued medical expenses. To recover medical expenses, whether incurred within the two-year period of limitations or at any time thereafter, the injured employee, of course, must meet the statutorily imposed burden of proof with respect to "notice," "accident," causal relation of the injury and resultant medical expenses, etc.; but such a claim is not time-barred merely because the injured employee has not complied with the statutorily prescribed period of limitations for a compensation claim. Tuscaloosa County v. INA/Aetna Ins. Co., 522 So. 2d 782 (Ala. 1988).

Payments by the employer for medical treatment and medicine are not considered compensation. Carroll Constr. Co. v. Hutcheson, 347 So. 2d 527 (Ala. Civ. App. 1977).

Compensation begins on day employee decides to submit to treatment. — If and when plaintiff decides to submit to surgery on his back such benefits as he is then entitled to receive will on that day commence to flow to him. Scott v. Alabama Mach. & Supply Co., 52 Ala. App. 459, 294 So. 2d 160 (1974).

No evidence of contract to pay for medical services. — Neither employer nor its insurance carrier were required to pay for employee's medical bills; there was no evidence before the trial court that a contract, either express or implied, existed between health care provider and employer to pay for employee's medical services. Radiology Assocs. v. St. Clair Timber Co., 563 So. 2d 1020 (Ala. 1990).

Jurisdiction in dispute over failure to pay medical expenses. — Should a dispute arise in the future over the failure of the employer to pay medical expenses that may be due the employee, such dispute can be resolved by the court that awarded compensation benefits to employee. Champion Int'l Corp. v. Simmons, 398 So. 2d 305 (Ala. Civ. App. 1981).

Medical expenses paid by Medicare or Medicaid. — This section does not operate to reduce the employer's liability for reimbursement of medical expenses which were paid by Medicare or Medicaid in view of subrogation provisions in the applicable federal statutes. Kimberly-Clark Corp. v. Golden, 486 So. 2d 435 (Ala. Civ. App. 1986).

Employer not entitled to credit when no claim made against employer. — Where the medical benefits paid for all of the employee's medical expenses, and he made no claim against employer for them, there was no authority for giving employer a credit for the amount of medical benefits received against the employee's workmen's compensation benefits. Jackson v. Weaver, 516 So. 2d 702 (Ala. Civ. App. 1987).

Testimony on obligation to pay medical bills excluded. — In third party tort action brought by injured employee of painting subcontractor, to whom workmen's compensation benefits had been paid, to recover from prime contractor for injuries sustained in fall on ground that prime contractor had failed to provide a safe place to work, trial court acted correctly in ruling defendants' attorney would not be permitted to cross-examine plaintiff as to whether he paid or became obligated to pay the medical bills for which he sought compensation in damages. Jones v. Crawford, 361 So. 2d 518 (Ala. 1978).

Claimant was entitled to further medical benefits for a second injury to a knee, where he had suffered a prior, compensable injury which resulted in a weakened left knee and was still undergoing treatment at the time of his second injury, and claimant's doctor testified that if the original knee injury had never occurred, the subsequent knee injury would not have occurred. Erwin v. Harris, 474 So. 2d 1125 (Ala. Civ. App. 1985).

Judgment against third party does not preclude recovery from employer. — An employee is entitled to recover of his employer his medical and hospital expenses after having recovered a judgment against a third party in an action in which medical and hospital expenses were claimed since neither the court of appeals (now court of civil appeals) nor the trial court is authorized to resort to speculation or guesswork to determine what proportion, if any, of the judgment recovered against the third-party tort-feasor was for hospital and medical expenses. Poultry & Egg Co. v. Smith, 41 Ala. App. 665, 149 So. 2d 838 (1962).

May not recover for or on behalf of United States government. — Claimant is not legally authorized to attempt to recover from his employer under the provisions of this section for and on behalf of the United States government pursuant to 42 U.S.C. §§ 2651 through 2653. Sabino v. Independent Life & Accident Ins. Co., 52 Ala. App. 368, 292 So. 2d 662 (1974).

There is no provision for the assessment of attorney's fees for the obtaining of medical and surgical expenses. Ex parte Cowgill, 587 So. 2d 1002 (Ala. 1991).

Cited in Shepard v. Chrysler Corp., 314 F. Supp. 1179 (N.D. Ala. 1969); Misco, Inc. v. Driver, 50 Ala. App. 256, 278 So. 2d 374 (1973); United States v. Reyes, 595 F.2d 275 (5th Cir. 1979); Den-Tal-Eze Mfg. Co. v. Gosa, 388 So. 2d 1006 (Ala. Civ. App. 1980); Price Ceiling, Inc. v. Ray, 394 So. 2d 58 (Ala. Civ. App. 1981); Sunnyland Foods, Inc. v. Catrett, 395 So. 2d 1005 (Ala. Civ. App. 1980); Baird v. Spradlin, 409 So. 2d 820 (Ala. 1982); L.W. Limbaugh Mining & Constr. Co. v. Youngblood, 413 So. 2d 1146 (Ala. 1981); L.W. Limbaugh Mining & Constr. Co. v. Youngblood, 413 So. 2d 1151 (Ala. Civ. App. 1981); Ward v. King, 415 So. 2d 1095 (Ala. Civ. App. 1982); Wimbs v. El Biscuit Village, Inc., 418 So. 2d 129 (Ala. Civ. App. 1982); Therrell v. Scott Paper Co., 428 So. 2d 33 (Ala. 1983); TG & Y Stores Co. v. Higdon, 437 So. 2d 1035 (Ala. Civ. App. 1983); City of Montgomery v. Robinson, 441 So. 2d 857 (Ala. 1983); Marion Homes of Bear Creek, Div. of Tidwell Indus., Inc. v. Dulaney, 441 So. 2d 955 (Ala. Civ. App. 1983); Hurt v. Pullman, Inc., 764 F.2d 1443 (11th Cir. 1985); Kennedy v. Cochran ex rel. Cochran, 475 So. 2d 872 (Ala. Civ. App. 1985); Hudson Indus. v. Harrell, 484 So. 2d 1099 (Ala. Civ. App. 1986); Wheeler v. Lake Forest Property Owners' Ass'n, 523 So. 2d 1083 (Ala. Civ. App. 1988); Glenn v. Vulcan Materials Co., 534 So. 2d 598 (Ala. 1988); Smither v. International Paper Co., 540 So. 2d 760 (Ala. Civ. App. 1989); Harrison v. Champion Int'l Corp., 550 So. 2d 1001 (Ala. Civ. App. 1989); Moore Elec. Co., Inc. v. Worthington, 586 So. 2d 5 (Ala. Civ. App. 1991); Wiley Sanders Truck Lines v. McLain, 591 So. 2d 527 (Ala. Civ. App. 1991).

Collateral references. — 99 C.J.S., Workmen's Compensation, §§ 266-268.

58 Am. Jur., Workmen's Compensation, §§ 327-333.

Duty of injured employee to submit to operation or to take other measure to restore earning capcity. 6 ALR 1260, 18 ALR 431, 73 ALR 1303, 105 ALR 1470.

Duty of injured employee to submit to examination. 6 ALR 1270, 41 ALR 866.

Liability of employer or insurance company for medical and hospital aid furnished to injured employee. 7 ALR 545.

Failure to seek or refusal to accept medical treatment. 54 ALR 639.

Impossibility of cure as affecting application of provisions of compensation act relating to duty of employer or insurer, as to medical, surgical, or hospital service. 88 ALR 1192.

Misstatement to employee by physician as imputable to employer. 129 ALR 344.

Selection or change of physican, surgeon, or hospital. 142 ALR 1205.

Award with respect to operation performed to make use of corrective appliance possible or more effective. 143 ALR 581.

Workers' compensation: value of home services provided by victim's relative. 65 ALR4th 142.

Workers' compensation: vocational rehabilitation statutes. 67 ALR4th 612.

Workers' compensation: reasonableness of employee's refusal of medical services tendered by employer. 72 ALR4th 905.

What amounts to failure or refusal to submit to medical treatment sufficient to bar recovery of workers' compensation. 3 ALR5th 907.

II. REASONABLE AND NECESSARY TREATMENT AND EXPENSES.

This section requires the employer to pay the actual cost of reasonably necessary medical expenses incurred by the employee, and it sets out the procedure for selecting the treating physicians. Champion Int'l Corp. v. Simmons, 398 So. 2d 305 (Ala. Civ. App. 1981).

Plaintiff must show reasonableness of medical expenses. — It was incumbent upon plaintiff to introduce evidence tending to show the reasonableness of the medical expenses he incurred, these expenses being matters not of common knowledge, and where he failed to do so there was no basis for a finding by the court allowing such expenses. Mitchell Motor Co. v. Burrow, 37 Ala. App. 222, 66 So. 2d 198 (1953).

Where there is no evidence that a medical charge is reasonable, there is no basis for awarding judgment on the charge because it is not a matter of common knowledge. Carroll Constr. Co. v. Hutcheson, 347 So. 2d 527 (Ala. Civ. App. 1977).

Where there is no evidence that a medical charge is reasonable, there is no basis for awarding judgment thereon, because it is not a matter of common knowledge. Lowe v. Walters, 491 So. 2d 962 (Ala. Civ. App. 1986).

Where there is no evidence that a medical charge is reasonable, there is no basis for

awarding judgment on the charge, because the reasonableness of medical charges is not a matter of common knowledge. Alverson v. Fontaine Fifth Wheel Co., 586 So. 2d 216 (Ala. Civ. App. 1991).

Future medical expenses. — When disability is determined, it carries with it as a matter of law that the employer must provide for payment of all future medical expenses that may be reasonable and necessary for the treatment of the injury. Conley v. SCI Sys., 495 So. 2d 698 (Ala. Civ. App. 1986).

Future medical expenses are recoverable if they are related to the injury, are "reasonable" and "necessary," and are obtained with the authorization of the employer. Jones v. Pickens County Health Care, 589 So. 2d 754 (Ala. Civ. App. 1991).

Subsequent injury. — If an injury occurs as the direct and natural result of the original, compensable injury, it is a reasonable conclusion that any medical expenses incurred by the employee for the subsequent injury are those that the employer is required to pay as "reasonably necessary" under subsection (a) of this section. Erwin v. Harris, 474 So. 2d 1125 (Ala. Civ. App. 1985).

Psychiatric treatment as reasonably necessary. — Cost of psychiatric treatment of claimant who as a result of work-related trauma was found to be suffering from depressive neurosis was required to be borne by employer since such treatment was reasonably necessary. Fruehauf Corp. v. Prater, 360 So. 2d 999 (Ala. Civ. App. 1978).

In suit alleging the tort of outrage, where jury instructions stated that workmen's compensation insurance carrier is required to pay the cost of reasonable necessary medical treatment and that the burden of proving that certain medical treatments are not reasonably necessary is on the defendant insurance company, such instructions were proper because the respective rights and duties of the parties were crucial to the question of whether the defendant insurance company had done no more than insist upon its legal rights under this section in a permissible way. Continental Cas. Ins. Co. v. McDonald, 567 So. 2d 1208 (Ala. 1990).

III. AUTHORIZATION AND NOTIFICATION.

Employer not liable for treatment obtained without notice or justification. — Under the language of this section requiring an employee to advise his employer if he is dissatisfied with the employer's physician and permitting the employer to select the medical or surgical attendant of his choice, the employer is not liable for the costs of medical or surgical treatment obtained by employee without justification or notice to the employer. Condry v. Jones Farm Equip. Co., 358 So. 2d 1030 (Ala. Civ. App. 1978).

It is clear from this section that the selection of the initial physician and of other physicians in the event of employee dissatisfaction is a decision for the employer. It is also clear from this section that the employee must notify the employer before consulting a physician or before changing physicians except in the case of an emergency. Jasper Community Hosp. v. Hyde, 419 So. 2d 594 (Ala. Civ. App. 1982); Allen v. Diversified Prods., 453 So. 2d 1063 (Ala. Civ. App. 1984).

An employee may avail himself of medical services if the employer has expressly or impliedly conveyed to him the impression that the employee has authorization to proceed in this fashion, or with full knowledge has over a sustained period of time failed to object to claimant's change of physician. Jasper Community Hosp. v. Hyde, 419 So. 2d 594 (Ala. Civ. App. 1982).

Employer is not liable for medical or surgical treatment obtained by employee without justification or notice to employer. Genpak Corp. v. Gibson, 534 So. 2d 312 (Ala. Civ. App. 1988).

An employee may avail himself of medical services if the employer has expressly or impliedly conveyed to the employee the impression that the employee is authorized to go to a physician of the employee's choosing or if the employer, with full knowledge, has failed to object thereto over a sustained period of time. Blue Bell, Inc. v. Nichols, 479 So. 2d 1264 (Ala. Civ. App. 1985).

Authorization for treatment where employer's physician admits employee. — Where doctor, employer's physician, admitted employee into hospital and subsequently requested hospital doctor to perform myelogram, the myelogram procedure performed by hospital doctor was authorized. Genpak Corp. v. Gibson, 534 So. 2d 312 (Ala. Civ. App. 1988).

Mere misdiagnosis of cause of ailment does not excuse adherence to notice requirements of this section, since this section does not anticipate excuse of the notice requirement except in an emergency situation. Grantham v. AMOCO Fabrics Co., 514 So. 2d 1385 (Ala. 1987).

Defendant justified in seeking medical treatment without notification. — Evidence, though disputed, supported the trial court's finding that defendant was justified in seeking medical treatment without notification or authorization by the employer, because the employer had neglected or refused to provide necessary medical care. Kimberly-Clark Corp. v. Golden, 486 So. 2d 435 (Ala. Civ. App. 1986).

The appellate courts of this state have set out several instances of justification for an employee not obtaining authorization from the employer before incurring medical expenses. Among such instances are (1) where the employer has neglected or refused to provide the necessary medical care, (2) where notice of and request for alternative care would be futile, and (3) where other circumstances exist which justify the selection of alternative care by the employee. Combustion Eng'g, Inc. v. Walley, 541 So. 2d 560 (Ala. Civ. App. 1989).

Employee was justified in not obtaining authorization from employer before incurring medical expenses where employee was in contact with employer or its insurance carrier on numerous occasions requesting authorization, where the employer did not grant authorization and stated that authorization would not have been granted even if further requests had been made, and where there was testimony from numerous, qualified physicians that the treatment in question was reasonable and necessary and was directly related to employee's work-related injuries. Combustion Eng'g, Inc. v. Walley, 541 So. 2d 560 (Ala. Civ. App. 1989).

Employer to pay expenses although employer attempted later to withdraw authorization for physician. — Where employee was authorized by the employer to choose his own physician and the employer later attempted to withdraw its delegated authorization, since the evidence conclusively proved that the employee was authorized to seek treatment from his personal physician, and the employee never voiced dissatisfaction with that choice, subsection (a) simply did not apply. The trial court did not err in ordering the employer to pay medical expenses to the employee's treating physician, which he clearly had the authority to select. G.C. Colyer & Co. v. McAdams, 562 So. 2d 1326 (Ala. Civ. App. 1990).

Failure to notify employer of inability to work or to obtain authorization to consult another physician. — Where an injured employee was examined and treated by several doctors over a period of several weeks, then released by the attending doctors to return to work, and the employer notified the employee that he was expected to return to work and he did not notify his employer that he was physically unable to work nor did he attempt to get authorization from employer to consult another physician, the evidence failed to demonstrate that the employee complied with the requirements of this section, or that he fell within any of the exceptions. Grantham v. AMOCO Fabrics Co., 514 So. 2d 1383 (Ala. Civ. App. 1986); 514 So. 2d 1385 (Ala. 1987).

IV. REFUSAL TO SUBMIT TO TREATMENT.

Compensation suspended for unreasonable refusal to submit to treatment. — This section requires that compensation be suspended in the presence of an unreasonable refusal to submit to examination or surgical treatment and no award of compensation may be founded upon speculative results of compliance while such unreasonable refusal continues. Daniel Ornamental Iron Co. v. Black, 47 Ala. App. 608, 259 So. 2d 291 (1971), aff'd, 288 Ala. 736, 259 So. 2d 295 (1972); Avondale Mills, Inc. v. Tollison, 52 Ala. App. 52, 289 So. 2d 621 (1974).

This section requires that right to compensation be suspended for unreasonable refusal to submit to examination and treatment and that no compensation be paid during such refusal. Black v. Daniel Ornamental Iron Co., 351 So. 2d 575 (Ala. Civ. App.), cert. denied, 351 So. 2d 576 (Ala. 1977).

During the period of unreasonable refusal, benefits are forever lost. Black v. Daniel Ornamental Iron Co., 351 So. 2d 575 (Ala. Civ. App.), cert. denied, 351 So. 2d 576 (Ala. 1977).

Compensation not terminated. — The trial court's judgment providing that should plaintiff refuse to submit to the surgery as ordered, his compensation benefits would be terminated is contrary to this section which provides that his right thereto would be suspended until such time as he agrees to submit to the surgery. Scott v. Alabama Mach. & Supply Co., 52 Ala. App. 459, 294 So. 2d 160 (1974).

Compensation not suspended if refusal reasonable. — Subsection (b) does not suspend the payment of compensation if the refusal of surgery is reasonable. Weatherly v. Republic Steel Corp., 391 So. 2d 662 (Ala. Civ. App. 1980).

Reasonable refusal to undergo treatment. — If employee's refusal to undergo proposed medical or surgical treatment is reasonable, his workmen's compensation benefits may not be terminated on the basis of subsection (b). Lewis G. Reed & Sons v. Wimbley, 533 So. 2d 628 (Ala. Civ. App. 1988).

Injured employee receiving compensation benefits may refuse medical treatment or surgical procedures only where his refusal is not unreasonable, and for the reasonableness standard to come into play, trial court must have before it some evidence upon which it could base judgment requiring physical examination and rehabilitation. Cerrock Wire & Cable Co. v. Johnson, 533 So. 2d 622 (Ala. Civ. App. 1988).

Standard required by this section is one of reasonableness in evaluating a refusal to undergo medical or surgical treatment. Scott v. Alabama Mach. & Supply Co., 52 Ala. App. 459, 294 So. 2d 160 (1974).

Employee not required to submit to operation as condition to compensation unless success reasonably assured. — This section, authorizing suspension of compensation where employee refuses to submit to an operation, is not to be construed as requiring employee to submit to an operation as a condition to compensation, unless success is reasonably assured and operation is free from serious danger. Gulf States Steel Co. v. Cross, 214 Ala. 155, 106 So. 870 (1926); Scott v. Alabama Mach. & Supply Co., 52 Ala. App. 459, 294 So. 2d 160 (1974).

This section has been interpreted to mean that for an employee to be deprived of future benefits because of his refusal to submit to proposed medical treatment, there must be some reasonable expectation that the employee's condition will improve as a result. The treatment required must also be reasonably danger-free. The employee's subjective fear of surgery, alone, is not a reasonable basis for refusal of such an operation. Elbert Greeson Hosiery Mills, Inc. v. Ivey, 472 So. 2d 1049 (Ala. Civ. App. 1985).

Compensation will not be suspended where expert witnesses are equally divided as to probability of success. — Where expert witnesses were equally divided as to nature and cause of cataract in injured employee's eye, and whether an operation would be successful, court properly declined to suspend compensation under this section for employee's refusal to submit to an operation. Gulf States Steel Co. v. Cross, 214 Ala. 155, 106 So. 870 (1926).

And if the evidence presented in a case were to indicate that treatment extended would not remove or modify an existing disability, it would appear that refusal of such treatment would not be unreasonable, and denial of compensation would not be proper. Avondale Mills, Inc. v. Tollison, 52 Ala. App. 52, 289 So. 2d 621 (1974).

Employee to be given reasonable opportunity to be properly advised. — A motion made upon the trial to suspend compensation until the employee submits to surgical treatment, which had not been tendered theretofore, may well be overruled, unless the tender of treatment is so made as to give the employee reasonable opportunity to be properly advised in that regard. Gulf States Steel Co. v. Cross, 214 Ala. 155, 106 So. 870 (1926); Semmes Nurseries, Inc. v. McVay, 279 Ala. 42, 181 So. 2d 331 (1965).

While employee's subjective fear alone is not proper basis for refusal of proposed medical treatment, subsection (b) will not preclude award of workmen's compensation benefits unless (1) there is reasonable expectation that the employee's condition will improve as result of treatment, and (2) treatment is reasonably danger free. Lewis G. Reed & Sons v. Wimbley, 533 So. 2d 628 (Ala. Civ. App. 1988).

No evidence that employee refused to submit to medical treatment. — No evidence supported employer's argument that employee refused to submit to medical treatment where the record reflected that subsequent to the injury, employee was advised by the employer to report to the emergency room, that while at emergency room employee was advised to see a doctor for follow-up care, that this doctor then referred employee to another doctor, and that the latter doctor subsequently requested another doctor to perform myelogram. Genpak Corp. v. Gibson, 534 So. 2d 312 (Ala. Civ. App. 1988).

Refusal to submit to surgery held reasonable. — See Federal Mogul Corp. v. Moses, 341 So. 2d 162 (Ala. Civ. App. 1976).

There was ample legal evidence to support trial court's finding that employee's refusal of surgery was reasonable where doctor who proposed surgery told employee it would probably relieve some of his pain but he would not be able to return to heavy labor even after surgery, and where surgery (a bone fusion) was not minor and there was some danger of making pain worse, and where doctor would not know whether the surgery had been successful for about six months. Lewis G. Reed & Sons v. Wimbley, 533 So. 2d 628 (Ala. Civ. App. 1988).

The employee's right to benefits is not terminated by subsection (b), unless (1) a reasonable expectation exists that the employee's condition will improve due to treatment and (2) the proposed treatment is reasonably danger-free, and employee's refusal to submit to surgery was not unreasonable since evidence was presented which indicated that with this type of knee injury the proposed reparative effect of surgery was only short term and the doctor testified that employee's pain and disability rating might be worse following surgery. Flame Refractories, Inc. v. Cole, 539 So. 2d 1062 (Ala. Civ. App. 1988).

V. AUTOPSY.

Autopsy is not condition precedent to suit. — The provision of this section that any interested party may require an autopsy, where cause of death is obscure or disputed, may be enforced in and of a pending case, and not be made a condition precedent to bringing of an action founded on the pertinent facts. Summit Coal Co. v. Walker, 214 Ala. 332, 107 So. 905 (1926).

Nor to valid judgment. — Judgment on the facts in proceedings for compensation for death under Workmen's Compensation Act held not invalid because court did not enforce order under this section requiring autopsy to ascertain cause of death. Summit Coal Co. v. Walker, 214 Ala. 332, 107 So. 905 (1926).

Court ordering autopsy has jurisdiction throughout state. — Judge of circuit court, granting order for autopsy under this section, has jurisdiction as circuit court throughout state. Summit Coal Co. v. Walker, 214 Ala. 332, 107 So. 905 (1926).

And may continue trial pending autopsy. — Where court has jurisdiction, it may, on due application and notice, exercise its judicial discretion as to continuance of trial pending compliance with its order requiring an autopsy under this section, where cause of death is obscure, and may compel enforcement of the statute. Summit Coal Co. v. Walker, 214 Ala. 332, 107 So. 905 (1926).

Trial judge has much discretion in matter of autopsy. Ex parte Gadsden Iron Works, Inc., 247 Ala. 180, 24 So. 2d 540 (1945).

VI. VOCATIONAL REHABILITATION.

Inclusion of the phrase "restore ... to gainful employment" in subsection (c) of this section means that because of the injury, the employee must no longer be capable of gainful employment. Beaver Valley Corp. v. Priola, 477 So. 2d 408 (Ala. 1985).

"Gainful employment" in subsection (c) of this section means employment similar in remuneration to that earned prior to the injury. Implicit in this is that the gainful employment sought to be restored must be "suitable," that is, must be compatible with the employee's preinjury occupation, age, education and aptitude. Beaver Valley Corp. v. Priola, 477 So. 2d 408 (Ala. 1985).

In deciding whether an employee is entitled to vocational rehabilitation, the trial court must determine if the employee has the ability to obtain suitable gainful employment. If the employee has lost the ability to obtain suitable gainful employment due to a compensation injury, then, barring any other reasonable basis to deny vocational rehabilitation, he should be entitled to have that ability restored through an appropriate plan of vocational rehabilitation. Beaver Valley Corp. v. Priola, 477 So. 2d 408 (Ala. 1985).

The trial court must make two determinations before awarding vocational rehabilitation. First, the court must determine if the work is a proper candidate for vocational rehabilitation. Second, if the worker is a proper candidate, the court must determine the type of vocational rehabilitation which is most appropriate to restore the worker to gainful employment. Beaver Valley Corp. v. Priola, 477 So. 2d 408 (Ala. 1985).

Nature of vocational rehabilitation program chosen. — Under subsection (c) of this section, the program of vocational rehabilitation chosen should be reasonably calculated to restore the employee to suitable employment providing an income comparable to that earned prior to the injury. In making its determination, the trial court should also consider the type of work done by the employee at the time of the injury, his vocational aptitude, his physical and mental abilities, and such other factors as the court may deem relevant. Beaver Valley Corp. v. Priola, 477 So. 2d 408 (Ala. 1985).

The award of undergraduate and master's degrees in computer science was not an appropriate program of vocational rehabilitation. Such a program far exceeded the purpose of subsection (c) of this section, which is to restore the injured employee to suitable gainful employment. Rather than restoring the employee of his preinjury economic status, such program would allow him to improve his station in life at the expense of the employer. Beaver Valley Corp. v. Priola, 477 So. 2d 408 (Ala. 1985).

Employee who refuses vocational rehabilitation to lose permanent total disability benefits. — If an employee is receiving permanent total disability benefits and refuses to undergo vocational rehabilitation when requested by the employer, he shall lose his benefits during the period of refusal. J.S. Walton & Co. v. Reeves, 396 So. 2d 699 (Ala. Civ. App. 1981).

The Workmen's Compensation Act mandates suspension of employee's benefits if the employee refuses to comply with any reasonable request for examination or refuses to accept rehabilitation. Beatrice Foods Co. v. Gray, 431 So. 2d 1299 (Ala. Civ. App. 1983).

The reasonableness or unreasonableness of employee's refusal to undergo further treatment is a question of fact for the trier of fact. Moreover, whether an employee can be rehabilitated is also a question of fact for the trial court. Beatrice Foods Co. v. Gray, 431 So. 2d 1299 (Ala. Civ. App. 1983).

§ 25-5-78. Written notice to employer of accident — Required.

For purposes of this article only, an injured employee or the employee's representative, within five days after the occurrence of an accident, shall give or cause to be given to the employer written notice of the accident. If the notice is not given, the employee or the employee's dependent shall not be entitled to physician's or medical fees nor any compensation which may have accrued under the terms of this article, unless it can be shown that the party required to give the notice had been prevented from doing so by reason of physical or mental incapacity, other than minority, fraud or deceit, or equal good reason. Notwithstanding any other provision of this section, no compensation shall be payable unless written notice is given within 90 days after the occurrence of the accident or, if death results, within 90 days after the death. (Acts 1919, No. 245, p. 206; Code 1923, § 7568; Code 1940, T. 26, § 294; Acts 1992, No. 92-537, § 24.)

The 1992 amendment, effective May 19, 1992, in the first sentence substituted "For purposes of this article only, an injured employee or the employee's representative" for "Every injured employee or his representative shall," and inserted "shall," in the second sentence substituted "If the notice is not given, the employee or the employee's dependent" for "and the employee, if he fails to give such notice," deleted "and article 2 of this chapter" following "this article," and substituted "the notice" for "such notice," and in the last sentence substituted "Notwithstanding any other provision of this section" for "but," substituted "the written notice" for "such written notice," and "if death results" for "where death results."

I. General Consideration.
II. Necessity and Sufficiency of Notice.
III. Pleading, Proof and Review.

I. GENERAL CONSIDERATION.

Purpose of this section is to enable an employer to make a speedy examination, afford proper treatment and protect himself against simulated or exaggerated claims. Gold Kist, Inc. v. Dumas, 442 So. 2d 115 (Ala. Civ. App. 1983).

Object of prompt notice of injury under this section and § 25-5-79 is to enable employer to make speedy examination, afford proper treatment and protect himself against simulated or exaggerated claims. Ex parte Stith Coal Co., 213 Ala. 399, 104 So. 756 (1925).

That the notice must be written is for certainty; that it is to be given promptly is to enable the employer to make speedy examination, afford proper treatment and protect himself against simulated or exaggerated claims. B.F. Goodrich Co. v. Martin, 47 Ala. App. 244, 253 So. 2d 37 (1971).

The aim of the notice is to advise the employer that a certain employee, by name, received a specified injury in the course of his employment on or about a specified time, at or near a certain place specified. B.F. Goodrich Co. v. Martin, 47 Ala. App. 244, 253 So. 2d 37 (1971).

Judicial construction of this section has, to a great extent, abrogated its literal application. Beatrice Foods Co. v. Clemons, 54 Ala. App. 150, 306 So. 2d 18 (1975); Ragland Brick Co. v. Campbell, 409 So. 2d 443 (Ala. Civ. App. 1982).

Cited in Ex parte Sloss-Sheffield Steel & Iron Co., 212 Ala. 699, 103 So. 920 (1925); Ex parte Big Four Coal Mining Co., 213 Ala. 305, 104 So. 764 (1925); Larry v. Taylor, 227 Ala. 90, 149 So. 104 (1933); Bass v. Cowikee Mills, 259 Ala. 391, 67 So. 2d 12 (1953); Fairfax Mfg. Co. v. Bragg, 342 So. 2d 17 (Ala. Civ. App. 1977); Thompson & Co. Contractors v. Cole, 391 So. 2d 1042 (Ala. Civ. App. 1980); Wimbs v. El Biscuit Village, Inc., 418 So. 2d 129 (Ala. Civ. App. 1982); Middleton v. Dan River, Inc., 617 F. Supp. 1206 (M.D. Ala. 1985); International Paper Co. v. Murray, 490 So. 2d 1234 (Ala. Civ. App. 1985).

Collateral references. — 100 C.J.S., Workmen's Compensation, §§ 445, 448.

58 Am. Jur., Workmen's Compensation, § 375 et seq.

Requirements as to notice of accident or injury. 78 ALR 1232, 92 ALR 505, 107 ALR 816, 145 ALR 1263.

May notice of injury or claim be waived. 78 ALR 1306.

Mental incompetence as obviating effect of failure to comply with provisions as to giving notice. 91 ALR 1400.

Action by employee for injury as notice of claim. 98 ALR 529.

War as suspending time for notice. 137 ALR 1465, 140 ALR 1518, 141 ALR 1511.

Provision limiting time for giving notice of injury or presenting claim as applied to infant. 142 ALR 1035.

Excuses for want of notice. 145 ALR 1283.

II. NECESSITY AND SUFFICIENCY OF NOTICE.

This section specifies two time periods with respect to notice. International Paper Co. v. Murray, 490 So. 2d 1230 (Ala. 1984).

The aim of written notice is to advise the employer that a certain employee, by name, received a specified injury in the course of his employment on or about a specified time, at or near a certain specified place, so that the employer may verify the injury by its own investigation. International Paper Co. v. Murray, 490 So. 2d 1228 (Ala. Civ. App.), remanded on other grounds, 490 So. 2d 1230 (Ala. 1984).

This requirement of notice is mandatory, and a failure to give it, in a proper case, defeats the claim to compensation. Ex parte Sloss-Sheffield Steel & Iron Co., 207 Ala. 531, 93 So. 425 (1922); Ex parte Harper, 210 Ala. 134, 97 So. 140 (1923); Ex parte Sloss-Sheffield Steel & Iron Co., 212 Ala. 699, 103 So. 920 (1925); Ex parte Stith Coal Co., 213 Ala. 399, 104 So. 756 (1925); Ex parte Big Four Coal Mining Co., 213 Ala. 305, 104 So. 764 (1925).

No recovery can be had under workmen's compensation law for death of employee, where giving notice of death, as required by this and the following section is not shown. Ex parte Big Four Coal Mining Co., 213 Ala. 305, 104 So. 764 (1925).

In proceeding for compensation for disability of electric refrigerator repairman resulting from breathing methyl chloride gas, where cause of injury was not discovered by claimant until one year after he left employment, and evidence failed to show that employer had actual knowledge of any compensable accident, or that written notice was given before expiration of statutory period, claimant was not entitled to compensation. Birmingham Elec. Co. v. Meacham, 27 Ala. App. 471, 175 So. 316 (1937).

Employee precluded from giving effec-

tual notice after expiration of 90 days. — The concluding clause of this section, "but no compensation shall be payable unless such written notice is given within 90 days after the occurrence of the accident," is not followed by a "saving clause," and for this reason the injured employee is precluded from giving effectual notice after the expiration of 90 days. Ex parte Harper, 210 Ala. 134, 97 So. 140 (1923).

Where employee did not serve employer with written notice for more than 90 days after receiving his alleged injury, he could not insist that sufficient excuse was shown for such failure in that the employer's physician had advised him that he was suffering from a disease and not the injury. The question of fraud on the part of the attending physician was not presented, and § 6-5-101, dealing with actions for fraud, was manifestly without application. Ex parte Harper, 210 Ala. 134, 97 So. 140 (1923).

Unless waived or circumstances dispense with it. — The statutory notice of injury required to be given employer by Workmen's Compensation Act may be waived, or the circumstances may be such that it is not required. Ex parte National Pipe & Foundry Co., 213 Ala. 605, 105 So. 693 (1925).

Notice of the accident was waived by the city's admission that decedent's immediate supervisor took him to the hospital the day after he was injured, and the city, through its workmen's compensation insurance carrier, paid a part of his doctor, medical and hospital bills until he died. City of Foley v. Terry, 278 Ala. 30, 175 So. 2d 461 (1965).

Oral notice which informs employer of accident and injury is sufficient. — Oral notice which places the employer on notice that an accident has occurred and that a resultant injury of some degree has occurred is sufficient to satisfy the requirements of the statute. American Tennis Courts, Inc. v. Hinton, 378 So. 2d 235 (Ala. Civ. App.), cert. denied, 378 So. 2d 239 (Ala. 1979); Gold Kist, Inc. v. Dumas, 442 So. 2d 115 (Ala. Civ. App. 1983).

Actual notice is equivalent to statutory notice and, in that regard, oral notice which places the employer on notice that an accident occurred whereby the employee was injured is sufficient to satisfy the requirement of this section. Blue Bell, Inc. v. Nichols, 479 So. 2d 1264 (Ala. Civ. App. 1985).

Notice was sufficient even though employee incorrectly diagnosed injury. — Where employee told his supervisors he had gotten a blister on the top of his big toe from use of a piece of equipment but employee saw a doctor and found out the blister was actually frostbite, the notice requirements of this section were met since employee's initial conversation with supervisors put the employer on reasonable notice to investigate further. Robbins Tire & Rubber Co. v. Jackson, 551 So. 2d 1079 (Ala. Civ. App. 1989).

Delayed discovery of injury. — There was evidence to support the trial court's award of benefits from June 7, 1986 where claimant injured his back on that day but did not report the injury until June 17, 1986 since, the injury did not manifest itself until June 17 and claimant was away from job until then. Cook Transports, Inc. v. Beavers, 528 So. 2d 875 (Ala. Civ. App. 1988).

Actual knowledge is equivalent to statutory notice. — Section 25-5-59 clearly imports that actual knowledge is the equivalent of the statutory notice required under this section and § 25-5-79. Ex parte Stith Coal Co., 213 Ala. 399, 104 So. 756 (1925); Swift & Co. v. Rolling, 252 Ala. 536, 42 So. 2d 6 (1949).

If written notice of an accident is not given, actual knowledge is the equivalent of the required statutory notice. Tripple M. Homes, Inc. v. Pickens, 46 Ala. App. 643, 248 So. 2d 139 (1971).

It has long been the rule in this state that actual notice is the equivalent of statutory notice. Price Ceiling, Inc. v. Ray, 394 So. 2d 58 (Ala. Civ. App. 1981); City of Montgomery v. Johnson, 403 So. 2d 244 (Ala. Civ. App. 1981); Suit v. Hudson Metals, Inc., 414 So. 2d 115 (Ala. Civ. App. 1982).

And written notice is not required if the employer had actual knowledge of the injury and circumstances out of which it arose. B.F. Goodrich Co. v. Martin, 47 Ala. App. 244, 253 So. 2d 37 (1971).

Written notice to employer of employee's injury, under Workmen's Compensation Act, held not necessary, where trial court found that employer had knowledge of accident on the day it occurred. Ex parte Stith Coal Co., 213 Ala. 399, 104 So. 756 (1925); Ex parte E.I. Du Pont De Nemours & Co., 213 Ala. 604, 105 So. 592 (1925); Sloss-Sheffield Steel & Iron Co. v. Keefe, 216 Ala. 379, 113 So. 400 (1927); Alabama Marble Co. v. Jones, 217 Ala. 300, 116 So. 147 (1928).

Written notice will not be required where it is shown that the employer has actual knowledge of the injury. Legg v. Americold Compressor Co., 336 So. 2d 1121 (Ala. Civ. App. 1976); Stinson v. Liberty Mut. Ins. Co., 395 So. 2d 1032 (Ala. Civ. App. 1981).

Written notice is not required where it is shown that the employer had actual notice of the injury. International Paper Co. v. Murray, 490 So. 2d 1228 (Ala. Civ. App.), remanded on other grounds, 490 So. 2d 1230 (Ala. 1984).

If acquired within time required for written notice. — Although written notice of accident and injury to employee as required by compensation act can be dispensed with when actual knowledge of the employer is shown, it is essential that the knowledge must have been acquired within the time required for the written notice. Sloss-Sheffield Steel & Iron Co. v. Foote, 231 Ala. 275, 164 So. 379 (1935); Sloss-Sheffield Steel & Iron Co. v. Watts, 236 Ala. 636, 184 So. 201 (1938); Nashville Bridge Co. v. Honeycutt, 246 Ala. 319, 20 So. 2d 591 (1945).

Where the employer has actual knowledge that an accident has occurred to an employee in the course of his employment, from which, after the lapse of the five-day period, an injury does result, this is sufficient actual knowledge under the statute, providing the employer has actual notice or knowledge of such injury within the 90-day period. Swift & Co. v. Rolling, 252 Ala. 536, 42 So. 2d 6 (1949).

If all the facts are brought to the knowledge of the employer within the prescribed period, written notice is not necessary. But verbal notice alone given by the employee is not the same as actual knowledge. C.E. Adams & Co. v. Harrell, 257 Ala. 25, 57 So. 2d 83 (1952).

If the employer obtained "actual knowledge" of the employee's death within a 90-day period subsequent to the accident, there was no obligation to give written notice of the accident. C.E. Adams & Co. v. Harrell, 257 Ala. 25, 57 So. 2d 83 (1952).

The written notice required by this section is not necessary where the employer has actual knowledge of the accidental injury within the time written notice is provided for in this section. Calvert v. Funderburg, 284 Ala. 311, 224 So. 2d 664 (1969).

Where appellee orally informed his employer that he had injured his back while on the job, there was sufficient information brought to the knowledge of appellant to place it on notice that an accident had occurred to its employee. Speigner v. McGhee, 55 Ala. App. 384, 316 So. 2d 215, 294 Ala. 769, 316 So. 2d 221 (1975).

If the injury occurs under the eye of the employer, or if all the facts are brought to his knowledge within the time written notice is required, the employer can suffer no injury. Price Ceiling, Inc. v. Ray, 394 So. 2d 58 (Ala. Civ. App. 1981).

Written notice is not required if the employer receives actual notice of an injury. Oral notification of an injury is sufficient to give an employer actual notice. Bonner v. Union Camp, Inc., 559 So. 2d 183 (Ala. Civ. App. 1989), cert. denied, 559 So. 2d 185 (Ala. 1990).

Since opportunity for investigation and protection against exaggerated claim is presented. — Once actual knowledge of an accident and injury is imparted to an employer, the opportunity for investigation of the accident and injury and to protect against simulated and exaggerated claims is presented. The statute does not require further notice nor continuing information be provided by the claimant without request. Beatrice Foods Co. v. Clemons, 54 Ala. App. 150, 306 So. 2d 18 (1975).

And the compensation act and evidence are liberally construed as to actual knowledge if it is had within statutory period. Nashville Bridge Co. v. Honeycutt, 246 Ala. 319, 20 So. 2d 591 (1945).

Where written notice is not given, the question to be decided is whether the employer had such actual knowledge of the accident and injury of the employee as to remove the necessity of, or to substitute for, the statutory requirement of written notice. B.F. Goodrich Co. v. Martin, 47 Ala. App. 244, 253 So. 2d 37 (1971).

What constitutes actual knowledge depends upon particular facts. Nashville Bridge Co. v. Honeycutt, 246 Ala. 319, 20 So. 2d 591 (1945); Bedford v. Gulsby, 257 Ala. 312, 58 So. 2d 892 (1952).

What constitutes "actual knowledge" is scarcely capable of more exact definition than the words import, and each case where that question is involved must be determined on its own facts. C.E. Adams & Co. v. Harrell, 257 Ala. 25, 57 So. 2d 83 (1952); Calvert v. Funderburg, 284 Ala. 311, 224 So. 2d 664 (1969); Stinson v. Liberty Mut. Ins. Co., 395 So. 2d 1032 (Ala. Civ. App. 1981).

Actual knowledge sufficient to remove the requirement of giving written notice is a question of fact in each case. B.F. Goodrich Co. v. Martin, 47 Ala. App. 244, 253 So. 2d 37 (1971).

Actual knowledge can exist without a compliance with all requirements of written notice. It is not necessary that the employer know at first hand that the injury arose out of and in the course of employment. C.E. Adams & Co. v. Harrell, 257 Ala. 25, 57 So. 2d 83 (1952).

Essential facts necessary to constitute "actual knowledge" by employer of accidental injuries sustained by employee which is equivalent of written notice of the accident is knowledge that employee received a specified injury in the course of his employment in or about a specified time at or near a certain place, and depends on circumstances of each case. Republic Steel Corp v. Willis, 243 Ala. 127, 9 So. 2d 297 (1942); Bedford v. Gulsby, 257 Ala. 312, 58 So. 2d 892 (1952).

In order for there to be knowledge, accident need not occur under eye of

employer or his alter ego. C.E. Adams & Co. v. Harrell, 257 Ala. 25, 57 So. 2d 83 (1952).

An employer, to have "actual knowledge" of injury sustained by employee as required by compensation act, need not have seen occurrence, but it is sufficient if employer observes injuries upon employee's person under circumstances which are known to him, and which are sufficient to impress a reasonable man that they were the result of an accident which arose out of and in the course of employment. Virginia-Carolina Chem. Co. v. Cherry, 233 Ala. 582, 173 So. 86 (1937); Nashville Bridge Co. v. Honeycutt, 246 Ala. 319, 20 So. 2d 591 (1945).

Actual knowledge does not necessarily mean that an accident must be seen firsthand by the employer. Price Ceiling, Inc. v. Ray, 394 So. 2d 58 (Ala. Civ. App. 1981).

Actual knowledge of an accident and injury suffered by an employee while on the job may be obtained from fellow employees who witnessed the accident. Price Ceiling, Inc. v. Ray, 394 So. 2d 58 (Ala. Civ. App. 1981).

Where a claimant testified that he told a supervisor of the injury and showed him the swollen knee on the day of the injury, such notice satisfies the actual notice rule. City of Montgomery v. Johnson, 403 So. 2d 244 (Ala. Civ. App. 1981).

If injury occurs under eye of employer, or if all the facts are brought to his knowledge within the time written notice is required, he can suffer no injury; the giving of notice becomes a matter of technical form, a trap for the helpless and unadvised. B.F. Goodrich Co. v. Martin, 47 Ala. App. 244, 253 So. 2d 37 (1971).

Where the evidence disclosed that the accident from which the employee suffered injury occurred under the eye of the defendant's superintendent or foreman, employer had actual knowledge and the written notice was not necessary. Swift & Co. v. Rolling, 252 Ala. 536, 42 So. 2d 6 (1949).

Employer had actual notice of injury through the medium of safety engineers, whose duty it was to make investigations and receive actual notice of accidents and injuries, where they received actual oral notice within five days after the accident. Jack Cole Co. v. Crawford, 285 Ala. 440, 233 So. 2d 225 (1970).

Where a company maintains a safety engineering department to promote safety among its employees and to make investigations of injuries, and the safety engineer makes an investigation of an injury, the information he acquires is actual notice to the company of an injury to an employee. Statutory written notice is not then necessary. Jack Cole Co. v. Crawford, 285 Ala. 440, 233 So. 2d 225 (1970).

And knowledge of agent may be imputed to employer. — That grocery store manager was present, learned of employee's accident and its nature immediately after occurrence and later called on employee at his home, held sufficient to show employer's notice or actual knowledge of injury. Great Atl. & Pac. Tea Co. v. Davis, 226 Ala. 626, 148 So. 309 (1933).

Where employee, a few days after pipe had fallen on his foot and acid had burned it, showed foot to employer's manager on employer's premises and told him how injury was sustained, and manager told employee to see a physician about it, manager, and employer by imputation, acquired "actual knowledge" of injury as required by compensation act. Virginia-Carolina Chem. Co. v. Cherry, 233 Ala. 582, 173 So. 86 (1937).

As where employer's surgeon has notice. — Where employee on receipt of injury to eye had presented himself to employer's surgeon pursuant to instructions of general nature given by employer to employees, his physical condition had manifested recent occurrence of an injury and he had told surgeon circumstances of occurrence which showed that injuries arose out of and in course of employment, surgeon, and employer by imputation, acquired "actual knowledge" of such injury within this section so requiring as condition to right to compensation. Sloss-Sheffield Steel & Iron Co. v. Foote, 231 Ala. 275, 164 So. 379 (1935).

But proof that fellow servant knew of injury was held not binding on employer, so as to dispense with necessity of written notice of injury under this section and § 25-5-79. Sloss-Sheffield Steel & Iron Co. v. Keefe, 217 Ala. 409, 116 So. 424 (1928).

And a letter between third persons was held not required notice to employer of employee's injury, where relations of persons sending and receiving letter to parties were not shown. Poe v. Pate, 216 Ala. 264, 113 So. 234 (1927).

Copy of verified complaint cannot serve purpose of notice. — A copy of the verified complaint filed in court under § 25-5-88, served on employer within 90 days after employee's injury, cannot serve the purpose of the written notice required by this section and § 25-5-79. Alabama Marble Co. v. Jones, 217 Ala. 300, 116 So. 147 (1928).

Written complaint filed within three months of the alleged injury is not the kind of notice envisioned by this section. Speigner v. McGhee, 55 Ala. App. 384, 316 So. 2d 215, cert. denied, 294 Ala. 769, 316 So. 2d 221 (1975).

And notice to insurance company is not sufficient notice to employer. See Poe v. Pate, 216 Ala. 264, 113 So. 234 (1927).

Employer's answer to interrogatories

held not to dispense with notice. — Employer's answer to interrogatories, even if his knowledge of employee's injury was inferable from them, held not sufficient to dispense with the notice required by this section and § 25-5-79, where not indicating that the employer had had such knowledge within 90 days of the injury. Alabama Marble Co. v. Jones, 217 Ala. 300, 116 So. 147 (1928).

"Good reason" for failure to give notice. — There was a very "good reason" why the employer did not receive notice of the plaintiff's actual injury within the five-day period required by this section where the serious injury to plaintiff's back had not manifested itself within five days from the time of the accident. Alabama Textile Prods. Corp. v. Grantham, 263 Ala. 179, 82 So. 2d 204 (1955).

Forfeiture can be effective only where no "good reason" can be shown for failure to notify the employer within five days of the injury. In that event, if the employer received actual notice within 90 days of the injury, the employee would forfeit only those payments accrued up to the time of notification. International Paper Co. v. Murray, 490 So. 2d 1230 (Ala. 1984).

The saving clause in this section is a means by which an employee may avoid sanction of forfeiture. International Paper Co. v. Murray, 490 So. 2d 1230 (Ala. 1984).

Oral notice is sufficient to give the employer actual notice. Nevertheless, oral notification must be given within the time periods provided by this section and must sufficiently inform the employer that an accident had occurred to its employee and that a resultant injury of some degree occurred or was likely to occur. The employer must also be notified that the employee was injured while in the scope of his employment. International Paper Co. v. Murray, 490 So. 2d 1228 (Ala. Civ. App.), remanded on other grounds, 490 So. 2d 1230 (Ala. 1984).

Employer had required actual notice that incident was work related. — Where there was testimony that the employer's foreman was with the employee earlier on the day of the incident when the employee complained of weakness and was forced to rest, and the foreman was summoned to the hospital by the employee's wife within minutes after the workday ended, and where the employer knew that the employee was a 58-year-old man who had worked, at the employer's request, in the hot July weather cutting grass for several hours that day and had to request a rest due to weakness earlier in the day, the finding of the trial court that the employer had the required actual notice that the incident was work-related was supported by the evidence. Brown-

Ray Dev., Inc. v. Murphy, 568 So. 2d 814 (Ala. Civ. App. 1990).

Actual notice present where employee spoke with employer's personnel manager two months after injury occurred to inform him of her injury and resultant surgery and also told the personnel manager that her doctor attributed the injury to her job. Avondale Mills, Inc. v. Webster, 574 So. 2d 51 (Ala. Civ. App. 1990).

III. PLEADING, PROOF AND REVIEW.

Plaintiff must aver employer's notice or knowledge of injury. Sloss-Sheffield Steel & Iron Co. v. Watts, 236 Ala. 636, 184 So. 201 (1938). See note under § 25-5-88.

And employee had burden of proving that employer had notice or knowledge of injury. Poe v. Pate, 216 Ala. 264, 113 So. 234 (1927).

In action to recover compensation for death of employee, plaintiff was required to prove employer's notice or knowledge of accident and injury. Sloss-Sheffield Steel & Iron Co. v. Watts, 236 Ala. 636, 184 So. 201 (1938).

But employer need not specially plead want of notice or knowledge. — In action to recover compensation for death of employee, general denial of the answer was sufficient to make an issue as to whether employer had knowledge or notice of accident as required by compensation act, and to require proof thereof by plaintiff, and want of knowledge or notice was not required to be specially pleaded by employer. Sloss-Sheffield Steel & Iron Co. v. Watts, 236 Ala. 636, 184 So. 201 (1938).

Evidence of employer's knowledge of injury held not sufficient to dispense with proving written notice of injury. Sloss-Sheffield Steel & Iron Co. v. Keefe, 217 Ala. 409, 116 So. 424 (1928).

Evidence showing "actual knowledge" by employer. — See Birmingham Post Co. v. McGinnis, 256 Ala. 473, 55 So. 2d 507 (1951); Bedford v. Gulsby, 257 Ala. 312, 58 So. 2d 892 (1952).

Evidence held to show that the employer had actual knowledge of employee's death within 90 days after the accident. C.E. Adams & Co. v. Harrell, 257 Ala. 25, 57 So. 2d 83 (1952).

Evidence that immediately after appearance of hernia employee notified his foreman, who immediately sent the employee to employer's timekeeper who took employee to physician who had examined the employee on behalf of the employer at time of application for employment, sustained finding that employer had actual knowledge or notice of injury, notwithstanding employee failed to file timely written notice of the accident. Nashville Bridge Co. v. Honeycutt, 246 Ala. 319, 20 So. 2d 591 (1945).

Evidence showing that employer had no

"actual knowledge" of injury. — Where evidence disclosed that, for a period of more than 90 days after accident, employee concealed fact that he was injured while engaged in scope of employment, and only evidence of knowledge of employer was that within 90-day period employer's foreman and physician knew that employee had a splinter in his finger, which subsequently resulted in amputation of the finger, employer had no "actual knowledge" of injury which would entitle employee to workmen's compensation even though he failed to file timely written notice of the accidental injury. Republic Steel Corp. v. Willis, 243 Ala. 127, 9 So. 2d 297 (1942).

In situations where the notice requirement is at issue there must be a finding of fact in the trial court's judgment which notes the existence or absence of notice to the employer. Harbin v. United States Steel Corp., 356 So. 2d 179 (Ala. Civ. App. 1978).

And failure of trial court to make a finding on the notice issue cannot be corrected by amending its judgment pursuant to Rule 60(a), A.R.C.P., because the error is judicial, not clerical. Harbin v. United States Steel Corp., 356 So. 2d 179 (Ala. Civ. App. 1978).

When question of notice not raised on trial. — In proceeding under Workmen's Compensation Act, employer's objection as to notice given held not tenable, in view of finding of fact by trial court that there was no controversy with respect thereto, and it appearing that the giving of notice had not been challenged on the trial. Ex parte Nat'l Pipe & Foundry Co., 213 Ala. 605, 105 So. 693 (1925).

Raising question of variance on appeal. — Where evidence was offered by both sides on question of employer's knowledge of injury within meaning of § 25-5-88, without objection because of variance from verified complaint alleging the giving of written notice under this and § 25-5-79, and the matter of variance was not otherwise raised so as to call for amendment in court below, it cannot be raised in court on appeal. American Radiator Co. v. Andino, 217 Ala. 424, 116 So. 121 (1928).

§ 25-5-79. Written notice to employer of accident — Service and contents.

The notice referred to in Section 25-5-78 may be served personally upon the employer or upon any agent of the employer upon whom a summons may be served in civil actions or by sending it by registered or certified mail to the employer at his last known residence or business place within the state and shall be substantially in the following form:

"Notice — You are hereby notified that an injury was received by .... who was in your employ at .... while engaged as ...., under the superintendency of ...., on or about the ... day of ......, 19.., at about .. o'clock, ..m., and who is now located at .... (give town, street and number), that so far as now known, the nature of the injury was .... and that compensation may be claimed therefor. (Signed .... (giving address) ...., dated ......, 19.." No variation from this form shall be material if the notice is sufficient to advise the employer that a certain employee, by name, received a specified injury in the course of his employment on or about a specified time, at or near a certain place specified. (Acts 1919, No. 245, p. 206; Code 1923, § 7569; Code 1940, T. 26, § 295.)

Cited in Ex parte Sloss-Sheffield Steel & Iron Co., 212 Ala. 699, 103 So. 920 (1925); Sloss-Sheffield Steel & Iron Co. v. Foote, 229 Ala. 189, 155 So. 629 (1934); Sloss-Sheffield Steel & Iron Co. v. Watts, 236 Ala. 636, 184 So. 201 (1938); Pass v. Cowikee Mills, 259 Ala. 391, 67 So. 2d 12 (1953).

Collateral references. — 99 C.J.S., Workmen's Compensation, §§ 447, 448.

58 Am. Jur., Workmen's Compensation, §§ 377, 378.

Form and contents of notice of accident or injury. 145 ALR 1269.

Excuses for defects in notice. 145 ALR 1283.

§ 25-5-80. Limitation period for claims or actions for compensation.

In case of a personal injury not involving cumulative physical stress, all claims for compensation under this article shall be forever barred unless within two years after the accident the parties shall have agreed upon the compensation payable under this article or unless within two years after the accident one of the parties shall have filed a verified complaint as provided in Section 25-5-88. In cases involving personal injury due to cumulative physical stress, compensation under this article shall be forever barred unless within two years after the date of the injury one of the parties shall have filed a verified complaint as provided in Section 25-5-88. In cases involving claims for lost earning capacity under Section 25-5-57(a)(3)i., other than those involving cumulative physical stress, following termination of employment as outlined therein, compensation under this article and Article 4 shall be forever barred unless brought within two years of the termination. In case of death, all claims for compensation shall be forever barred unless within two years after death, when the death results proximately from the accident within three years, the parties shall have agreed upon the compensation under this article or unless within two years after the death one of the parties shall have filed a verified complaint as provided in Section 25-5-88. Where, however, payments of compensation, as distinguished from medical or vocational payments, have been made in any case, the period of limitation shall not begin to run until the time of making the last payment. In case of physical or mental incapacity, other than the minority of the injured person or his or her dependents, to perform or cause to be performed any act required within the time in this section specified, the period of limitation in any case shall be extended to become effective two years from the date when the incapacity ceases. (Acts 1919, No. 245, p. 206; Code 1923, § 7570; Code 1940, T. 26, § 296; Acts 1984, 2nd Ex. Sess., No. 85-41, p. 44, § 9; Acts 1992, No. 92-537, § 25.)

The **1992 amendment,** effective May 19, 1992, in the first sentence inserted "not involving cumulative physical stress," and deleted "and article 2 of this chapter" following "this article" in two places, added the second and third sentences, in the fourth sentence deleted "and article 2 of this chapter" following "this article," and substituted "the death" for "such death," substituted "compensation, as distinguished from medical or vocational payments, have been made in any case, the period of limitation shall not begin to run until the time" for "compensation have been made in any case, said limitations shall not take effect until the expiration of two years from the time" in the fifth sentence, and in the last sentence inserted "or her," deleted "such" preceding "case," and substituted "the incapacity" for "such incapacity." As to the implemen-

tation of this amendment, see the Code commissioner's note.

Code commissioner's note. — Acts 1984, 2nd Ex. Sess., No. 85-41, § 14 provides: "This act shall become effective immediately upon its passage and approval by the governor [January 9, 1985], or upon its otherwise becoming a law, provided it shall have no effect whatsoever with respect to the right of any injured employee to bring an action with respect to or upon any cause of action which arose or accrued prior to February 1, 1985. Provided further, it shall have no effect on and shall not apply to any accident or exposure to injurious condition occurring before the effective date of this Act."

Section 53 of Acts 1992, No. 92-537 provides that the amendment to this section by § 25 of the 1992 act shall be implemented on August 1, 1992.

I. General Consideration.
II. Tolling of Statute of Limitations.
III. Amendment of Complaint.
IV. Physical or Mental Incapacity.
V. Compensation Payments.
   A. In General.
   B. Tolling of Statute of Limitations.

I. GENERAL CONSIDERATION.

Editor's note. — The cases annotated below were decided under prior law.

Section should be read in pari materia with § 1-1-4. — The one-year (now two-year) statute of limitations of this section is subject to and should be read in pari materia with the statutory method for computing time set forth in § 1-1-4. Young v. Michael Dwain Mfg., Inc., 504 So. 2d 287 (Ala. Civ. App. 1986).

Section 14, Alabama Acts 1984-85, No. 85-41 remains viable and applicable, though not codified. — Failure of publisher to incorporate § 14 of Act No. 85-41 into the Code of Alabama did not affect its validity. Section 14, dealing with the effective date of Act No. 85-41, preserving already accrued causes of action, and restricting the act's application to causes of action arising after the act's effective date, belongs in that category of provisions that customarily are not codified but remain viable and applicable provisions of the legislative enactment. In such cases, it is customary for the publisher to include a code commissioner's note, referring to the omitted provision, which was done in this instance. Hodges v. Rheem Mfg., 524 So. 2d 631 (Ala. 1988).

Plain language of section should be given effect. — It was within the province of the legislature in adopting the compensation act to provide for a period of limitations within which actions thereunder must be brought and courts should give effect to the plain language of the statute as enacted by the legislature. Davis v. Standard Oil Co., 261 Ala. 410, 74 So. 2d 625 (1954).

This section is a limitation on the right itself and not alone upon the remedy, and the time limitations within which such actions must be brought constitute a condition precedent to the right to maintain such action and is jurisdictional. Shepard v. Chrysler Corp., 430 F.2d 161 (5th Cir. 1970).

The commencement of the action within the time prescribed is an indispensable condition to the liability of the defendant and to the plaintiff's right to sue. Morgan v. Rheem Mfg. Co., 395 So. 2d 1030 (Ala. Civ. App. 1981); Harris v. Speedee Food Mart, 410 So. 2d 113 (Ala. Civ. App. 1982).

Statutory requirement that death must occur within three years of injury. — Former section 25-5-178 provided in part that claims for benefits for death due to pneumoconiosis would be considered timely filed if brought within three years of the date of death. While it was true the action was timely filed, the time of filing was not the basis for the trial court's ruling; the trial court properly dismissed the action because of the additional statutory requirement that the death had to have occurred within three years of the date of the injury. See § 25-5-60 and this section. That is, the statute set a three-year time limit for the employee to die after the occurrence of the injury as a condition precedent for having a cause of action under the Workmen's Compensation Act. Kilgore v. Alabama By-Prods. Corp., 581 So. 2d 872 (Ala. Civ. App. 1991).

Section 25-5-60 and this section, place a limit on the time that may elapse between the time of injury and the time of death for there to be a claim, whereas former § 25-5-178 placed a limit on the time for filing a claim. Kilgore v. Alabama By-Prods. Corp., 581 So. 2d 872 (Ala. Civ. App. 1991).

Statute of limitations runs from date of injury. — This section sets forth a one-year (now two-year) statute of limitations for claims requesting workmen's compensation benefits, which begins to run from the date of the injury. Kimberly-Clark Corp. v. Golden, 486 So. 2d 435 (Ala. Civ. App. 1986).

One-year statute (now two-year) of limitations for workmen's compensation claims begins to run from the date of the injury. Cunningham v. Milstead Pulpwood Co., 366 So. 2d 737 (Ala. Civ. App. 1979); Morgan v. Rheem Mfg. Co., 395 So. 2d 1030 (Ala. Civ. App. 1981); City of Florence v. Gallien, 484 So. 2d 1095 (Ala. Civ. App. 1986).

Limitation runs from time of accident and not from time injury becomes apparent. — The courts have uniformly held that the time for filing an action begins to run from the time of the happening or occurrence which later produced disability and not from the time a compensable injury or disability becomes apparent, where the act provides that the period of limitation runs from the date of the accident, as distinguished from the time of disability or other date. Davis v. Standard Oil Co., 261 Ala. 410, 74 So. 2d 625 (1954).

Where injury occurred earlier than em-

ployee claimed. — Where evidence showed that employee's disability was caused by an injury which occurred 21 months earlier than employee claimed, his workmen's compensation claim was barred by the statute of limitations. Poole v. Ellard Contracting Co., 527 So. 2d 1327 (Ala. Civ. App. 1988).

Section does not apply to an action under an insurance policy procured by the state highway department as authorized by § 23-1-41. Employers Ins. Co. v. Harrison, 33 Ala. App. 199, 33 So. 2d 260 (1947), rev'd, Employers Ins. Co. v. Harrison, 250 Ala. 116, 33 So. 2d 264 (1947).

Section applies to employees of department of state docks. — Section 33-1-25 extends to employees of the department of state docks and terminals (now state docks department) all of the benefits of the Workmen's Compensation Act, and in so doing, it makes the acquisition of those benefits subject to the time limitation contained in this section and not the longer time limitation in § 6-2-34. Hale v. United States Fid. & Guar. Co., 45 Ala. App. 379, 231 So. 2d 156 (1970).

Section applies in case of disease resulting from accident. — This section applies alike to cases where disability from disease results from an accident as to cases where liability for an injury results from an accident. It cannot be said that a claim for disability resulting from an accidental injury to a member of the body, such as a broken leg, is barred unless action is brought within one year (now two years) after the accident causing the injury, while a claim for disability resulting from a disease likewise caused by an accidental injury would not be so barred. Davis v. Standard Oil Co., 261 Ala. 410, 74 So. 2d 625 (1954).

Section did not apply to subsequent action seeking resolution of dispute. — Where previously defendant properly invoked the jurisdiction of the court when he brought suit against the employer on a workmen's compensation claim, which action resulted in a consent final judgment which held that defendant was entitled to certain workmen's compensation benefits, and payment of necessary medical treatment, this section did not apply to a subsequent action brought by defendant seeking resolution of a dispute as to necessity, reasonableness and the proper authorization of treating physicians. Kimberly-Clark Corp. v. Golden, 486 So. 2d 435 (Ala. Civ. App. 1986).

Two statutes of limitation apply where case involves third-party action for wrongful death. — In a case involving a third-party action for wrongful death, there are two different applicable statutes of limitations: The third-party action has a two-year statute of

limitation and the action against the employer has a one-year (now two-year) limitation. Baggett v. Webb, 46 Ala. App. 666, 248 So. 2d 275 (1971).

The representations of an employer or its insurance carrier may be such as to estop them from asserting the statute of limitations as a bar to a claim for workmen's compensation, if the employer or the carrier, or their representatives, in their dealings with the claimant, conduct themselves in such a manner, whether innocently or fraudently, as to mislead the claimant into believing that he can postpone the filing of his claim until the period of limitation has expired. Whether the employer or the carrier, or their representatives were primarily responsible for the delay is a fact question for the factfinder at the trial level. L.W. Limbaugh Mining & Constr. Co. v. Youngblood, 413 So. 2d 1146 (Ala. 1981).

If an employer or carrier, or their representatives, in dealing with the employee conduct themselves in such a manner as to mislead the claimant into believing he can postpone the filing of his claim beyond one year (now two years), the employer is estopped from asserting the statute of limitations. Mayes v. Dake, 434 So. 2d 271 (Ala. Civ. App. 1983).

An employer may be estopped from asserting the statue of limitations in a workmen's compensation case if the employer or the carrier, or their representatives, in their dealings with the claimant conduct themselves in such a manner, whether innocently or fraudently, as to mislead the claimant into believing that he can postpone the filing of his claim until the period of limitation has expired. Wadsworth Contractors v. Uptain, 504 So. 2d 1217 (Ala. Civ. App. 1987).

Overt act required for employer to be estopped. — There must be some overt act on the part of the employer or his carrier or representatives that lulls employee into inaction before estoppel can be asserted. Mayes v. Dake, 434 So. 2d 271 (Ala. Civ. App. 1983); J.B. Constr. Co. v. Horton, 472 So. 2d 1085 (Ala. Civ. App. 1985).

Effect of employer's actions where claimant represented by counsel. — There is merit in the contention that the securing of legal representation for the purpose of prosecuting a claim for workmen's compensation should be an element for consideration in determining whether actions or representations of the employer are primarily responsible for a delay in bringing suit. Certainly, there would be a duty upon the attorney in such a case to bring suit before the expiration of the statute of limitations or to secure a waiver of the statute. Mayes v. Dake, 434 So. 2d 271 (Ala. Civ. App. 1983).

Instance of recovery barred. — In proceeding filed July 25, 1929, for compensation for disability of electric refrigerator repairman from breathing methyl chloride gas, where injury was result of gradual breathing and was not incurred at any particular time of employment, and employment was terminated July 27, 1928, recovery was barred by one-year (now two-year) limitation. Birmingham Elec. Co. v. Meacham, 27 Ala. App. 471, 175 So. 316 (1937).

Cited in Birmingham Elec. Co. v. Meacham, 234 Ala. 506, 175 So. 322 (1937); Sam's Place v. Middleton, 39 Ala. App. 481, 103 So. 2d 812 (1958); Pinkney v. James B. Clow & Sons, 277 Ala. 648, 173 So. 2d 811 (1965); City of Foley v. Terry, 278 Ala. 30, 175 So. 2d 461 (1965); Nicholson v. Lockwood Greene Eng'rs, Inc., 278 Ala. 497, 179 So. 2d 76 (1965); Shepard v. Chrysler Corp., 314 F. Supp. 1179 (N.D. Ala. 1969); Dorsey v. United States Pipe & Foundry Co., 353 So. 2d 797 (Ala. Civ. App. 1977); Hellums v. Hager, 360 So. 2d 721 (Ala. Civ. App. 1978); Barfield v. General Steel Tank Co., 370 So. 2d 1005 (Ala. Civ. App. 1979); City of Prichard v. Box, 396 So. 2d 58 (Ala. 1981); Wilkins v. West Point-Pepperell, Inc., 397 So. 2d 115 (Ala. 1981); Agan v. Union Foundry Co., 404 So. 2d 71 (Ala. Civ. App. 1981); Mason v. County of Mobile, 410 So. 2d 19 (Ala. 1982); Sun Papers, Inc. v. Jerrell, 411 So. 2d 790 (Ala. Civ. App. 1981); Lee v. Kimberly-Clark Corp., 418 So. 2d 164 (Ala. Civ. App. 1982); Rhett v. Southland Broilers, Inc., 421 So. 2d 126 (Ala. Civ. App. 1982); Reynolds Metals Co. v. Jeffreys, 425 So. 2d 457 (Ala. 1983); Baggett v. Builders Transp., Inc., 457 So. 2d 413 (Ala. Civ. App. 1984); Lockett v. Thermal Components, Inc., 460 So. 2d 1352 (Ala. Civ. App. 1984); Weaver v. Redwing Carriers, Inc., 475 So. 2d 869 (Ala. Civ. App. 1985); Federal Mogul Corp. v. Campbell, 494 So. 2d 443 (Ala. Civ. App. 1986); Malone v. Temporary Placement Servs., 508 So. 2d 275 (Ala. Civ. App. 1987); Russell Coal Co. v. Williams, 550 So. 2d 1007 (Ala. Civ. App. 1989).

Collateral references. — 100 C.J.S., Workmen's Compensation, §§ 468(1)-482.

58 Am. Jur., Workmen's Compensation, § 411.

Limitation of time for filing claim as jurisdictional. 78 ALR 1294.

Action by employee for injury as claim. 98 ALR 529.

War as suspending time for filing of claim. 137 ALR 1465, 140 ALR 1518, 141 ALR 1511.

Provision limiting time for presenting claim as applied to infant. 142 ALR 1035.

Payments, or furnishing medical or hospital services, or burial, by employer or his insurer, to employee after injury, as affecting time for filing claim. 144 ALR 606.

When limitation period begins to run against cause of action or claim for contracting of disease, 11 ALR2d 277.

When statute of limitations begins to run as to cause of action for development of latent industrial or occupational disease. 1 ALR4th 117.

II. TOLLING OF STATUTE OF LIMITATIONS.

When running of statute of limitations may be tolled. — When acts are done by the employer which lead the employee to believe that liability under the statute is admitted and will not be contested, or where the acts of the employer either falsely misrepresent to the employee or fraudulently conceal from him the truth of the facts upon which the liability of the employer depends, the running of the statute of limitations may be tolled, and it is immaterial whether the employee relies upon actual fraud or mere estoppel. Dorsey v. United States Pipe & Foundry Co., 353 So. 2d 800 (Ala. 1977); Langham Small Motors v. Thomas, 390 So. 2d 1055 (Ala. Civ. App.), cert. denied, 390 So. 2d 1058 (Ala. 1980); L.W. Limbaugh Mining & Constr. Co. v. Youngblood, 413 So. 2d 1143 (Ala. Civ. App. 1980), rev'd on other grounds, 413 So. 2d 1146 (Ala. 1981).

A nonfraudulent representation by the employer's representative which unintentionally misled an employee to delay the filing of a workmen's compensation claim may toll the limitations period set out in this section. L.W. Limbaugh Mining & Constr. Co. v. Youngblood, 413 So. 2d 1151 (Ala. Civ. App. 1981), rev'd on other grounds, 413 So. 2d 1153 (Ala. 1982).

Fraud can toll the running of the statute of limitations, but there must first be found acts by the employer which lead the employee to believe liability is admitted and will not be contested, or acts of the employer which either falsely misrepresent to the employee or falsely conceal from him the truth of the facts which liability depends. Blackmon v. R.L. Zeigler Co., 390 So. 2d 628 (Ala. Civ. App.), cert. denied, 390 So. 2d 635 (Ala. 1980).

III. AMENDMENT OF COMPLAINT.

Amendment of complaint under federal act to present a case under state act permitted. — A complaint erroneously alleging a cause of action for injuries under the Federal Employers' Liability Act (U.S. Comp. St. §§ 8657-8665), may be amended more than one year (now two years) after the accident so as to present a case under this chapter, notwithstanding the instant section. Birmingham Belt R.R. v. Ellenburg, 215 Ala. 395, 111 So. 219 (1926); Shepard v. Chrysler Corp., 430 F.2d 161 (5th Cir. 1970).

Amending complaint after expiration of two years does not bar action. — A proceeding brought within year after plaintiff's injury was not barred by one-year (now two-year) statute of limitations because plaintiff amended complaint by adding required certification after such time. Lovelady v. Belcher, 31 Ala. App. 408, 18 So. 2d 109 (1944).

Amendment after expiration of two years did not add new party. — An amendment of the complaint in a workmen's compensation proceeding which changed the party plaintiff from "Elbert N. Brooks, as administrator of the estate of Morey Pits Brooks," to "Elbert N. Brooks, individually, for the use and benefit of Iris Tint Brooks, Ethel Brooks and Bobby Ray Brooks, minor children of Morey Pits Brooks, deceased," did not add an entirely new party plaintiff in the action so that the claim was barred because the amendment was made after the running of the one-year (now two-year) statute of limitations. The amendment referred to the same parties in interest as the original complaint and properly related back to the commencement of the action. Braswell v. Brooks, 266 Ala. 141, 94 So. 2d 879 (1957).

Where the amended complaint was filed after, but on the same day, the summary judgment was granted as to the original complaint, and the trial court, in granting summary judgment, expressly stated that it was granted after being held up for the preparation of an amended complaint and without prejudice to the filing of such an amended complaint, the amended complaint was in point of fact nothing more than an amendment to the original action. Shepard v. Chrysler Corp., 430 F.2d 161 (5th Cir. 1970).

IV. PHYSICAL OR MENTAL INCAPACITY.

This section does not contemplate that proceedings by minor dependents shall be delayed until disability of minority has passed. Larry v. Taylor, 227 Ala. 90, 149 So. 104 (1933), holding section's application to minors not invalid.

Physical or mental incapacity exemption to statute of limitations. — The court interpreted the language of this section to provide for an exemption to the statute of limitations in the case of physical or mental incapacity only when such incapacity prevents the employee from taking action to obtain workmen's compensation benefits "within the time in this

section specified." In other words, such incapacity must exist for such a length of time as will prevent the employee from filing suit to obtain benefits within the one-year limitations period. Stewart v. Carter Realty Co., 518 So. 2d 122 (Ala. Civ. App.), writ denied, 518 So. 2d 125 (Ala. 1987).

Where the record showed that the employee returned to her job as resident manager of an apartment complex approximately four and one-half months after the accident, and that she continued in that position for five months and where the employee testified that she was unable to perform all of her former duties and that she continued to require assistance with her bandages and with certain "daily functions." The evidence did not indicate that the employee's incapacity continued to such an extent or for such a period of time as to prevent her filing suit within one year following the accident. Stewart v. Carter Realty Co., 518 So. 2d 122 (Ala. Civ. App.), writ denied, 518 So. 2d 125 (Ala. 1987).

Finding, that evidence did not present a case of physical or mental incapacity to perform the act of filing a verified complaint under § 25-5-88 so as to bring it within exception declared in this section to requirement that action for compensation be instituted within one year (now two years) after injury, held sufficiently sustained by evidence. Taylor v. Tennessee Coal, Iron & R.R., 219 Ala. 614, 123 So. 78 (1929).

Finding of incapacity supported by evidence. — There was ample evidence to support the finding that the employee was physically and mentally incapacitated from filing a complaint within the one year (now two years) provided by this section so as to bring the time of filing within the influence of the exemption declared in this section. Southern Cotton Oil Co. v. Wynn, 266 Ala. 327, 96 So. 2d 159 (1957).

V. COMPENSATION PAYMENTS.

A. In General.

Meaning of "compensation". — See Liberty Mut. Ins. Co. v. Manasco, 271 Ala. 124, 123 So. 2d 527 (1960).

The introductory language of Workmen's Compensation Act makes clear that the definitions contained therein apply throughout the act unless the context clearly indicates a different meaning should apply, and a plain reading of the language in one-year (now two-year) limitations provision of act does not indicate that the word "compensation," as used in that section, should be given a different meaning than that provided in introductory provision. Cunningham v. Milstead Pulpwood Co., 366 So. 2d 737 (Ala. Civ. App. 1979).

When an injured employee receives the same wages for lighter work upon returning to his job, such payment can be compensation under appropriate circumstances. Blackmon v. R.L. Zeigler Co., 390 So. 2d 628 (Ala. Civ. App.), cert. denied, 390 So. 2d 635 (Ala. 1980).

In determining whether payments constitute compensation, and, consequently, toll the statute, three factors are to be considered: (1) was the employer aware, or should he have been aware, that the payments were compensation, (2) did the payments have the effect of recognizing the employee's claim, and (3) did the evidence indicate that the employer paid for more than what he received? Godwin v. Scott Paper Co., 571 So. 2d 1126 (Ala. Civ. App. 1990).

Payment, for purposes of this section, is the receipt by the workman of an instrument of payment, and payment is deemed to have ceased as of the day the last instrument of payment was received. Cement Prods. Co. v. Martin, 397 So. 2d 149 (Ala. Civ. App. 1981).

Payment of temporary total benefits by insurer until advised that employee has reached maximum recovery does not estop insurer from asserting the one-year (now two-year) statute of limitation. Floyd v. Housing Auth., 397 So. 2d 136 (Ala. Civ. App.), cert. denied, 397 So. 2d 139 (Ala. 1981).

Where compensation payments have been made, the statutory limitation of one year (now two years) within which an employee may file a complaint does not take effect until the expiration of one year (now two years) from the time of the making of the last payment. Phillips v. Opp & Micolas Cotton Mills, Inc., 445 So. 2d 927 (Ala. Civ. App. 1984).

Where the last payment of compensation was alleged to have been made on July 14, 1981 and the employee's complaint was filed on May 25, 1982, which was within one year (now two years) from the date of the last payment of compensation, insofar as this section is concerned, the complaint was filed within the prescribed time. Phillips v. Opp & Micolas Cotton Mills, Inc., 445 So. 2d 927 (Ala. Civ. App. 1984).

The filing of an action more than one year (now two years) after the last payment of workmen's compensation benefits comes too late and must be dismissed. Boling v. Delchamps, Inc., 451 So. 2d 342 (Ala. Civ. App. 1984).

Bar of right of subsequent claimant. — Under this section claim for compensation for death of employee, who was paid compensation for over three years after injury, is not barred

until one year (now two years) after last payment, limitation of § 25-5-60 not applying. Moss v. Standridge, 215 Ala. 237, 110 So. 17 (1926).

Medical expenses not time-barred. — The filing of a suit to enforce payment of compensation benefits was not required in order to vest jurisdiction in the circuit court to adjudicate a claim for accrued medical expenses. To recover medical expenses, whether incurred within the two-year period of limitations or at any time thereafter, the injured employee, of course, must meet the statutorily imposed burden of proof with respect to "notice," "accident," causal relation of the injury and resultant medical expenses, etc.; but such a claim is not time-barred merely because the injured employee has not complied with the statutorily prescribed period of limitations for a compensation claim. Tuscaloosa County v. INA/Aetna Ins. Co., 522 So. 2d 782 (Ala. 1988).

Agreement that compensation was payable in proceedings timely brought by other could not remove bar of limitation in favor of different parties seeking compensation. Larry v. Taylor, 227 Ala. 90, 149 So. 104 (1933).

Fixing compensation when status of dependents changed. — Where deceased left widow and five dependent minors, subsequent remarriage of widow after birth of posthumous child, which is expressly included by § 25-5-1, and one of dependent children reaching 18, justified court in ordering widow's portion of compensation distributed to remaining dependent children under 18, including such posthumous child, and limitation of one year (now two years) provided for by this section does not affect such case. Ex parte Central Iron & Coal Co., 212 Ala. 367, 102 So. 797 (1925).

B. Tolling of Statute of Limitations.

Statute of limitations tolled by the employer's payment of compensation to employee in the form of full pay for less work. County of Mobile v. Benson, 521 So. 2d 992 (Ala. Civ. App. 1988).

Tolled limitation runs when last compensation payment made. — One-year (now two-year) limitation period for workmen's compensation claims is tolled where the employer makes compensation payments to the injured employee, in which event the one-year (now two-year) limitation begins to run at the time the last compensation payment is made. Cunningham v. Milstead Pulpwood Co., 366 So. 2d 737 (Ala. Civ. App. 1979); Cement Prods. Co. v. Martin, 397 So. 2d 149 (Ala. Civ. App. 1981).

Conditions to extension of limitations. — Payment of compensation does not extend the statute of limitation for any injury unless payment is made or liability acknowledged for that injury. Leslie v. Republic Steel Corp., 273 Ala. 586, 143 So. 2d 442 (1962).

Payments for medical benefits should be construed as payments for compensation. The statute of limitations would run from the date of such payment. Ingalls Shipbuilding Corp. v. Cahela, 251 Ala. 163, 36 So. 2d 513 (1948).

A medical payment made by an employer is not a payment of compensation so as to toll the statute of limitations set forth in Workmen's Compensation Act. Cunningham v. Milstead Pulpwood Co., 366 So. 2d 737 (Ala. Civ. App. 1979).

Medical payments, unlike compensation payments, do not toll the statute of limitations. Blackmon v. R.L. Zeigler Co., 390 So. 2d 628 (Ala. Civ. App.), cert. denied, 390 So. 2d 635 (Ala. 1980); Harris v. Speedee Food Mart, 410 So. 2d 113 (Ala. Civ. App. 1982).

Payment of medical expenses does not toll the statute of limitations. Welborn v. GTE Communication Sys. Corp., 526 So. 2d 600 (Ala. Civ. App. 1988).

Determining whether payment of wages constitutes compensation that will toll statute. — It is only just that under the appropriate circumstances payment of wages by an employer to an injured employee, who was put on lighter work when he returned to work, constitutes compensation that will toll the statute; but the correct rule for deciding the question involves the issues of (1) whether the employer was aware, or should have been aware, that such payments were compensation, (2) whether the payments had the effect of recognition of the employee's claim, and (3) whether or not the evidence indicates that the employer paid for more than he received. Head v. Triangle Constr. Co., 274 Ala. 519, 150 So. 2d 389 (1963).

The general rule seems to be that when an injured employee receives the same wage rate for lighter work after returning to his job, it is "compensation" if the employer was aware, or should have been aware, that such wages constituted compensation. The correct rule for deciding the question involves the issues of (1) whether the employer was aware, or should have been aware, that such payments were compensation, (2) whether the payments had the effect of recognition of the employee's claim, and (3) whether or not the evidence indicates that the employer paid for more than he received. B.F. Goodrich Co. v. Parker, 282 Ala. 151, 209 So. 2d 647 (1967).

It is only just that under the appropriate circumstances payment of wages constitutes compensation that will toll the statute. To hold otherwise would allow an employer to lull an injured employee into a false sense of security by paying him full wages for less than normal work. The statute of limitations would be defeated, for an employer could simply pay wages for one year (now two years) and then rely on the bar to relieve him from further liability. On the other hand, the court would probably be hesitant to announce an absolute rule that wages paid under such conditions were always compensation that tolled the statute. Such an announcement would make employers who did not feel that they were liable hesitate to reemploy their injured workers. B.F. Goodrich Co. v. Parker, 282 Ala. 151, 209 So. 2d 647 (1967).

There is a three-pronged test to determine whether payment of wages constitutes compensation. The prongs are: (1) Whether the employer was aware, or should have been aware, that the payments were compensation, (2) whether the payments had the effect of a recognition of the employee's claim, and (3) whether the employer paid for more than he received. Welborn v. GTE Communication Sys. Corp., 526 So. 2d 600 (Ala. Civ. App. 1988).

Full pay for lighter work may constitute payment of compensation. — In Alabama our courts have long recognized that the payment of full pay for lighter work may constitute the payment of compensation that will toll the statute of limitations. For such wages to toll the running of the statute of limitations depends upon three factors: (1) whether the employer was aware, or should have been aware, that such payments were compensation, (2) whether the payments had the effect of recognition of the employee's claim, and (3) whether or not the evidence indicates that the employer paid for more than he received. County of Mobile v. Benson, 521 So. 2d 992 (Ala. Civ. App. 1988).

Sick pay does not constitute payments of compensation or payments in lieu of compensation for the purpose of tolling the statute of limitations. Belser v. American Cast Iron Pipe Co., 356 So. 2d 659 (Ala. Civ. App. 1978).

Although sick pay is generally not recognized as compensation, it may be so classified if certain conditions are met. Blackmon v. R.L. Zeigler Co., 390 So. 2d 628 (Ala. Civ. App.), cert. denied, 390 So. 2d 635 (Ala. 1980).

§ 25-5-81. Determination of disputed compensation claims generally.

(a) *Commencement of action in circuit court.*

(1) PROCEDURE. — In case of a dispute between employer and employee or between the dependents of a deceased employee and the employer with respect to the right to compensation under this article and Article 2 of this chapter, or the amount thereof, either party may submit the controversy to the circuit court of the county which would have jurisdiction of a civil action in tort between the parties. The controversy shall be heard and determined by the judge who would hear and determine a civil action between the same parties arising out of tort, and, in case there is more than one judge of the court, the controversies shall be set and assigned for hearing under the same rules and statutes that civil actions in tort are set and assigned. The court may hear and determine the controversies in a summary manner. The decision of the judge hearing the same shall be conclusive and binding between the parties, subject to the right of appeal provided for in this article.

(2) RIGHT TO JURY TRIAL. — When willful misconduct on the part of the employee is set up by the employer, as it is provided for in this article, the employer may, upon appearing, demand a jury to hear and determine, under the direction of the court, the issues involved in this defense. If the employer fails to demand a jury upon appearing, the employee may demand a jury to try the issues by filing a demand within five days after the appearance of the employer. When a jury is demanded by either party, the court shall submit the issues of fact as to willful misconduct set up by the employer to the jury, for a special finding of the facts subject to the usual powers of the court over verdicts rendered contrary to the evidence or the law, but the judge shall determine all other questions involved in the controversy without a jury. Upon setting up the defense, the employer shall serve a copy of the answer, setting up the defense, upon the employee or the attorney of record.

(b) *Court deemed open at all times.* — For the purpose of hearing and determining controversies between an employer and employee or the dependents of a deceased employee and the employer arising under this article and Article 2 of this chapter, the circuit court shall be deemed always in session.

(c) *Evidence.* — The decision of the court shall be based on a preponderance of the evidence as contained in the record of the hearing, except in cases involving injuries which have resulted from gradual deterioration or cumulative physical stress disorders, which shall be deemed compensable only upon a finding of clear and convincing proof that those injuries arose out of and in the course of the employee's employment.

For the purposes of this amendatory act, "clear and convincing" shall mean evidence that, when weighted against evidence in opposition, will produce in the mind of the trier of fact a firm conviction as to each essential element of the claim and a high probability as to the correctness of the conclusion. Proof by clear and convincing evidence requires a level of proof greater than a preponderance of the evidence or the substantial weight of the evidence, but less than beyond a reasonable doubt.

(d) *Interpleader of adverse claimants to compensation.* — If at any time there are adverse claimants to compensation under this article, the employer, in submitting the claim to the circuit court, may suggest in writing the claimants, and they shall be required to interplead. The court shall determine and order to which claimant or claimants compensation is justly due, and the employer, upon complying with the order of the judge, shall be released from the claims of any other claimants thereto.

(e) *Review.* — From an order or judgment, any aggrieved party may, within 42 days thereafter, appeal to the Court of Civil Appeals and review shall be as in cases reviewed as follows:

(1) In reviewing the standard of proof set forth herein and other legal issues, review by the Court of Civil Appeals shall be without a presumption of correctness.

(2) In reviewing pure findings of fact, the finding of the circuit court shall not be reversed if that finding is supported by substantial evidence.

(f) *Discovery.* — Methods of discovery shall be determined and established in rules promulgated by this amendatory act and the rules established by the Alabama Rules of Civil Procedure with the limitations of pre-trial discovery as set forth below. Additionally, the following rules of discovery shall apply to workers' compensation cases:

(1) Two depositions for each side shall be permitted without leave of court, however, any additional depositions shall not be permitted except with leave of court for good cause shown including, but not limited to, a claim by the employee for permanent total disability.

(2) Notwithstanding the limitations in (1) above, each party may take the deposition of every other party.

(3) No more than 25 interrogatory questions with each sub-part to be considered a question shall be permitted without leave of court for good cause shown.

(4) Certified sealed copies of records of medical treatment and charges therefor, whether from a physician, hospital, clinic, or other provider, shall be authenticated in accordance with Alabama Rules of Civil Procedure, Rule 44(h), without further need for authenticating testimony. Copies of records obtained by one party shall be furnished by certified mail to the other party not less than 21 days prior to trial, unless the party offering the records can establish unusual circumstances justifying their admission despite the failure to make the exchange after receiving the records of a physician's treatment prior to trial, the party not offering the records of a physician's treatment shall, without regard to the limitation set forth herein, have the right to depose prior to trial the physician whose records of treatment are to be offered by any other party.

It is the intent of this section that limited discovery shall be available. (Acts 1919, No. 245, p. 206; Code 1923, § 7571; Code 1940, T. 26, § 297; Acts 1992, No. 92-537, § 26.)

The 1992 amendment, effective May 19, 1992, rewrote this section. As to the implementation of this amendment, see the Code commissioner's note.

Code commissioner's note. — The phrase "this amendatory act," as used in the section above, refers to Acts 1992, No. 92-537, which amended this section. Act No. 92-537 also amended §§ 25-5-1 through 25-5-4, 25-5-8, 25-5-10, 25-5-11, 25-5-13, 25-5-50 through 25-5-57, 25-5-59, 25-5-60, 25-5-66 through 25-5-68, 25-5-77, 25-5-78, 25-5-80, 25-5-81,

25-5-83, 25-5-85, 25-5-86, 25-5-90, 25-5-110, 25-5-116, 25-5-117, 25-5-120, 25-5-251, enacted §§ 25-5-15.1, 25-5-290 through 25-5-294, and 25-5-310 through 25-5-318, and repealed §§ 25-5-16, 25-5-70 through 25-5-75, 25-5-140 through 25-5-152, and 25-5-170 through 25-5-180.

Section 53 of Acts 1992, No. 92-537 provides that the amendment to this section by § 26 of the 1992 act shall be implemented on August 1, 1992.

I. General Consideration.
II. Jury Trial.
III. Review by Certiorari.
  A. In General.
  B. Cross Assignment of Errors.
  C. Limitations on Scope of Review.
    1. Standard of Review Defined.
    2. Limited to Questions of Law.
    3. Factfinding Determination Not Reviewed.
  D. Conclusiveness of Trial Court's Findings.

I. GENERAL CONSIDERATION.

Editor's note. — The cases annotated below were decided under prior law.

This section must be construed in pari materia with section 25-5-88. Lawrence v. United States Fid. & Guar. Co., 226 Ala. 161, 145 So. 577 (1933).

And in connection with the common law. — This section and § 25-5-88 must be construed in connection with the common law as it existed when they were enacted. Ex parte Pittman Constr. Co., 28 Ala. App. 134, 180 So. 725 (1938).

Alabama workmen's compensation law provides a very simple civil action for the determination of controversies or disputes with respect to the right to compensation. Collins v. Central Foundry Co., 263 F.2d 712 (5th Cir. 1959).

Workmen's compensation cases are required to be brought in circuit court regardless of amount sought. Baggett v. Webb, 46 Ala. App. 666, 248 So. 2d 275 (1971).

And section makes findings and conclusions of trial court conclusive between parties. — Findings of fact and conclusions of the trial court, prescribed by § 25-5-88 of this title, unlike the finding in an ordinary action, are made conclusive as between the parties by this section, subject to a limited review by certiorari. Hardisty v. Woodward Iron Co., 214 Ala. 256, 107 So. 837 (1926); Paramount Coal Co. v. Williams, 214 Ala. 394, 108 So. 7 (1926); Bryant v. Central Foundry Co., 217 Ala. 332, 116 So. 345 (1928).

Under this section A and § 25-5-88, award of compensation in adversary proceedings prosecuted by employee held conclusive between parties. Davis v. Birmingham Trussville Iron Co., 223 Ala. 259, 135 So. 455 (1931); Sloss-Sheffield Steel & Iron Co. v. Nations, 243 Ala. 107, 8 So. 2d 833 (1942).

The trial court's finding in workmen's compensation proceedings is conclusive, if there is any evidence in the record that will support it. Purser Steel, Inc. v. McEwen, 47 Ala. App. 263, 253 So. 2d 56 (1971).

However, judgment must contain finding of fact and law. — If a judgment entered in a workmen's compensation case does not contain a finding of fact and law and the conclusion of the court, the matter must be reversed. It matters not whether the judgment is in favor of the employer or employee. Kearley v. Peterman Lumber Co., 46 Ala. App. 204, 239 So. 2d 776 (1970).

Compensation can be awarded only after the trial court makes a determination based on a sufficient finding of facts and conclusions of law that such an award is warranted. Eddons Drug Co. v. Wright, 46 Ala. App. 645, 248 So. 2d 140 (1971).

Purpose of requirement for filing of a finding of fact and law with or in the judgment is clear when it is considered that the only method for review of the proceedings is by writ of certiorari as provided by this section. Such method of review would be worthless without the findings and conclusions of the trial court as to the facts and the law. Kearley v. Peterman Lumber Co., 46 Ala. App. 204, 239 So. 2d 776 (1970).

Proceedings in federal courts simple and subject to limited review. — In a purely statutory action such as one under the Alabama Workmen's Compensation Act, the proceedings in the federal courts, like those provided in the state courts, should be kept simple and subject to limited review only. Collins v. Central Foundry Co., 263 F.2d 712 (5th Cir. 1959).

Venue in action against foreign corporation. — Under this section and § 25-5-88, a foreign corporation that has qualified to do business in state by designating agent and known place of business is not subject to an action in compensation case in county where it is not doing business at time of commencement of the action. Tennessee Valley Oil & Gas Co. v. Martin, 224 Ala. 348, 140 So. 429 (1932).

Cited in Ex parte Big Four Coal Mining Co., 213 Ala. 305, 104 So. 764 (1925); Woodward Iron Co. v. Jones, 217 Ala. 361, 116 So. 425 (1928); Davis v. Birmingham Trussville Iron Co., 223 Ala. 259, 135 So. 455 (1931); Birmingham Clay Prods. Co. v. White, 226 Ala. 89, 145 So. 668 (1933); Aetna Life Ins. Co. v. Copeland, 25 Ala. App. 383, 147 So. 206 (1933); Ex parte Johnston, 231 Ala. 458, 165 So. 108 (1935); Ex parte Carlisle, 27 Ala. App. 142, 168 So. 598 (1936); Tombrello Coal Co. v. Fortenberry, 248 Ala. 640, 29 So. 2d 125 (1947); Wade & Richey v. Oglesby, 251 Ala. 356, 37 So. 2d 596 (1948); Morris v. Dickson, 252 Ala. 588, 42 So. 2d 337 (1949); Ex parte Arrington, 253 Ala. 501, 45 So. 2d 466 (1950); Bedford v. Gulsby, 257 Ala. 312, 58 So. 2d 892 (1952); Jackson v. Tennessee Coal, Iron & R.R., 259 Ala. 85, 65 So. 2d 167 (1953); United States Steel Corp. v. Baker, 266 Ala. 538, 97 So. 2d 899 (1957); Pinkney v. James B. Clow & Sons, 277 Ala. 648, 173 So. 2d 811 (1965); Alabama Hide & Tallow Co. v. Pincheon, 282 Ala. 404, 211 So. 2d 896 (1968); Calvert v. Funderburg, 284 Ala. 311, 224 So. 2d 664 (1969); Jack Cole Co. v. Crawford, 285 Ala. 440, 233 So. 2d 225 (1970); Gilmore v. Rust Eng'r Co., 45 Ala. App. 626, 235 So. 2d 673 (1970); Whatley v. Lewis, 46 Ala. App. 18, 237 So. 2d 503 (1970); Hannah v. Kellerman Mining Co., 46 Ala. App. 63, 237 So. 2d 867 (1970); Sabino v. Independent Life & Accident Ins. Co., 52 Ala. App. 368, 292 So. 2d 662 (1974); Bell v. Mar-Mil Steel & Supply Co., 54 Ala. App. 432, 309 So. 2d 471 (1975); Romine v. McDuffie, 341 So. 2d 952 (Ala. Civ. App. 1977); Strickland v. National Gypsum Co., 348 So. 2d 496 (Ala. 1976); Freeman v. Blue Mt. Indus., 395 So. 2d 1049 (Ala. Civ. App. 1981); Wilkins v. West Point-Pepperell, Inc., 397 So. 2d 115 (Ala. 1981); Butler v. Moretti-Harrah Marble Co., 431 So. 2d 1291 (Ala. Civ. App. 1983); Hightower v. Brammall, Inc., 435 So. 2d 1295 (Ala. Civ. App. 1982); Waldon v. Hartford Ins.

Group, 435 So. 2d 1271 (Ala. 1983); Padgett v. International Paper Co., 470 So. 2d 1287 (Ala. Civ. App. 1985); Hurt v. Pullman, Inc., 764 F.2d 1443 (11th Cir. 1985); Arrow Trucking Lines v. Robinson, 507 So. 2d 1332 (Ala. Civ. App. 1987); Gibson v. Southern Stone Co., 518 So. 2d 730 (Ala. Civ. App. 1987); Nor, Inc. v. Smith, 519 So. 2d 534 (Ala. Civ. App. 1987); Miles v. Tennessee River Pulp & Paper Co., 519 So. 2d 562 (Ala. Civ. App. 1987); Jefferson County v. Cunningham, 521 So. 2d 37 (Ala. Civ. App. 1987); County of Mobile v. Benson, 521 So. 2d 992 (Ala. Civ. App. 1988); Maxie Carroll Seafood, Inc. v. Howard, 521 So. 2d 1342 (Ala. Civ. App. 1988); Wilson v. William Wilson Co., 537 So. 2d 930 (Ala. Civ. App. 1988).

Collateral references. — 100 C.J.S., Workmen's Compensation, §§ 621-624, 672, 770.

58 Am. Jur., Workmen's Compensation, § 396 et seq.

Serious and wilful misconduct of employee as question of law or fact. 4 ALR 127.

Review of finding as to dependency of beneficiary. 13 ALR 722, 30 ALR 1253, 35 ALR 1066, 39 ALR 313, 53 ALR 218, 62 ALR 160, 86 ALR 865, 100 ALR 1090.

Review of finding as to excuse or failure to give, or as to prejudice to employer because of failure to give, notice of injury. 78 ALR 1281, 92 ALR 505, 107 ALR 816, 145 ALR 1263.

Time and jurisdiction for review of award or agreement. 165 ALR 9.

Admissibility of opinion evidence as to employability on the issue of disability in insurance and workmen's compensation cases. 89 ALR3d 783.

Workers' compensation: injuries incurred during labor activity. 61 ALR4th 196.

Workers' compensation: injuries incurred while traveling to or from work with employer's receipts. 63 ALR4th 253.

Workers' compensation: effect of allegation that injury was caused by, or occurred during course of, worker's illegal conduct. 73 ALR4th 270.

II. JURY TRIAL.

Section gives right to demand jury trial of issue as to employee's misconduct. — This section secured to both employer and employee the right to demand that a jury shall hear and determine the issue as to whether the injury and death of the employee arose from the willful breach of a reasonable rule or regulation of the employer, of which rule or regulation the employee had knowledge. Trannon v. Sloss-Sheffield Steel & Iron Co., 233 Ala. 312, 171 So. 898 (1937).

And only issue upon which a jury trial can be demanded is that of willful miscon-

duct on the part of the employee. Collins v. Central Foundry Co., 263 F.2d 712 (5th Cir. 1959).

But in absence of demand trial court properly determines issue. — In compensation proceeding wherein defense was that employee's death resulted from willful misconduct and wherein neither employer nor claimant demanded jury trial, trial court properly heard and determined issue. Trannon v. Sloss-Sheffield Steel & Iron Co., 233 Ala. 312, 171 So. 898 (1937).

Verdict under this section is subject to usual powers of court and the appellate court as to verdicts entered contrary to the evidence or the law. Sloss-Sheffield Steel & Iron Co. v. Greer, 216 Ala. 267, 113 So. 271 (1927).

Verdict held sufficient. — Verdict, "We, the jury impaneled to try the issue of willful misconduct of" employee, "in a willful breach of a reasonable rule or regulation of" employer, "find that said" employee "did not willfully contribute to the cause of the accident," etc., held in form provided by this section. Sloss-Sheffield Steel & Iron Co. v. Greer, 216 Ala. 267, 113 So. 271 (1927).

III. REVIEW BY CERTIORARI.

A. In General.

Method of review in workmen's compensation cases is directed by this section. Odell v. Myers, 52 Ala. App. 558, 295 So. 2d 413 (1974).

Only method of review in workmen's compensation cases is by certiorari. Fordham v. Southern Phenix Textiles, Inc., 387 So. 2d 204 (Ala. Civ. App.), cert. denied, 387 So. 2d 206 (Ala. 1980).

Workmen's compensation cases come before the court of civil appeals by way of certiorari. On certiorari its review is limited; if there is any legal evidence to support the trial court's findings and conclusions, it must affirm. Jim Walter Resources, Inc. v. Hall, 516 So. 2d 690 (Ala. Civ. App. 1987).

Legislature may restrict or abolish appeal, as is done in this section and § 25-5-88, so long as it does not attempt to restrict the right of the appellate courts to exercise superintendence and control over inferior tribunals. Ex parte Louisville & N.R.R., 214 Ala. 489, 108 So. 379 (1926).

And remedy by appeal is not available to review the judgment of the trial court in a case under this chapter. Carothers v. McNabb, 216 Ala. 366, 113 So. 298 (1927); Bessemer Eng'r & Constr. Co. v. Smith, 216 Ala. 348, 113 So. 290 (1927); Guntner v. Wofford & Co., 223 Ala.

420, 137 So. 27 (1931); Faddis v. Woodward Iron Co., 276 Ala. 283, 161 So. 2d 486 (1964).

Only method of review is by certiorari, as provided in this section. Bessemer Eng'r & Constr. Co. v. Smith, 216 Ala. 348, 113 So. 290 (1927); Carothers v. McNabb, 216 Ala. 366, 113 So. 298 (1927); Guntner v. Wofford & Co., 223 Ala. 420, 137 So. 27 (1931); Ex parte Pittman Constr. Co., 28 Ala. App. 134, 180 So. 725 (1938); Hallmark v. Virginia Bridge Co., 241 Ala. 283, 2 So. 2d 447 (1941); Smith v. Wilson, 248 Ala. 436, 28 So. 2d 182 (1946); Mitchell Motor Co. v. Burrow, 37 Ala. App. 222, 66 So. 2d 198 (1953); Collins v. Central Foundry Co., 263 F.2d 712 (5th Cir. 1959); Faddis v. Woodward Iron Co., 276 Ala. 283, 161 So. 2d 486 (1964).

The only kind of review provided in the state courts is by certiorari. Upon such review, if there is any reasonable view of the evidence that will support the conclusion below the judgment will not be disturbed. The conclusions must be based on legal evidence, but, where there is any legal evidence to support the finding of the trial court, such finding is conclusive, and no technical questions as to the admissibility of evidence will be considered on appeal. Collins v. Central Foundry Co., 263 F.2d 712 (5th Cir. 1959).

The review procedure of a workmen's compensation case is by writ of certiorari. Eddons Drug Co. v. Wright, 46 Ala. App. 645, 248 So. 2d 140 (1971); Odell v. Myers, 52 Ala. App. 558, 295 So. 2d 413 (1974).

But certiorari under this section cannot be made to serve purpose of an appeal. Summit Coal Co. v. Walker, 214 Ala. 332, 107 So. 905 (1925); Gulf States Steel Co. v. Christison, 228 Ala. 622, 154 So. 565 (1934).

Though it is to be considered in the nature of a limited appeal. — While appeal and certiorari are not identical (Ex parte Woodward Iron Co., 211 Ala. 74, 99 So. 97 (1924)), yet this section by its language indicates a legislative intent that the method of review be considered in the nature of a limited appeal. Agricola Furnace Co. v. Smith, 239 Ala. 488, 195 So. 743 (1940).

However, writ of certiorari is not regarded as one of right, but rather one which is discretionary with the court, in order to promote the ends of justice as effectively as possible. And, while the right to the writ has been given by this section, the discretion of the court has not been taken away. Ex parte Pittman Constr. Co., 28 Ala. App. 134, 180 So. 725 (1938).

And indemnifying bond may be made a condition precedent to its issuance. — The court of civil appeals (formerly court of appeals) may require the employer, petitioning for certiorari to review an award of workmen's compensation, to execute an indemnifying bond as a condition precedent. Ex parte Pittman Constr. Co., 28 Ala. App. 134, 180 So. 725 (1938).

Which is not regulated by statute. — As there is no provision regulating the issuance of the writ of certiorari, the provision of this section authorizing the writ must have been made in consonance with the requirements of the common law. And the provision must be construed in connection with the common law as it existed when the section was enacted. Ex parte Pittman Constr. Co., 28 Ala. App. 134, 180 So. 725 (1938).

Time of taking appeal by certiorari is jurisdictional. Bessemer Eng'r & Constr. Co. v. Smith, 216 Ala. 348, 113 So. 290 (1927); Exchange Distrib. Co. v. Oslin, 229 Ala. 547, 158 So. 743 (1935).

And an attempted review will be dismissed for delay. — An attempted review under the Workmen's Compensation Act will be dismissed if not sought within 42 (formerly 30) days as required by this section. Bessemer Eng'r & Constr. Co. v. Smith, 216 Ala. 348, 113 So. 290 (1927); Kidd v. Roberts, 238 Ala. 446, 191 So. 243 (1939).

Time for review by certiorari is counted from date of filing with clerk of written expression of decision and judgment of judge. Langston v. Louisville & N.R.R., 214 Ala. 489, 108 So. 379 (1926).

And time for review of amended judgment dates from original judgment. — Where a judgment, even though defective, has been entered by the court, and a motion is made to amend such judgment nunc pro tunc to correct clerical errors, the corrected judgment relates back to the defective judgment, that is, the date it was originally entered, and the time for taking an appeal, and review by writ of certiorari under the compensation statutes, dates from the date of the original judgment. Faddis v. Woodward Iron Co., 276 Ala. 283, 161 So. 2d 486 (1964).

Petition for extension of time for filing record on certiorari. — When the clerk of the trial court in a workmen's compensation case finds himself in the position of not being able to comply with the time limits prescribed in the writ of certiorari for filing the record with the court of civil appeals, he may petition that court for an extension of time within which the record can be prepared and filed with the court as directed. Eddons Drug Co. v. Wright, 46 Ala. App. 645, 248 So. 2d 140 (1971).

Statutes construed together in determining nature of judgment from which writ lies. — Sections 25-5-81 and 25-5-91, providing for filing and entry of judgment in compensation case, are to be considered in pari materia with this section in ascertaining nature of "judgment" from which aggrieved party may "appeal" by certiorari within 42 (formerly 30) days after its entry. Langston v. Louisville & N.R.R., 214 Ala. 489, 108 So. 379 (1926); Lawrence v. United States Fid. & Guar. Co., 226 Ala. 161, 145 So. 577 (1933).

Costs of appeal. — Where employer brought certiorari to review unsatisfactory judgment in compensation case, and employer's theory of nonliability could not be sustained but trial court erroneously failed to deduct from judgment against employer an amount recovered by employee's administrator in a third-party action, costs of appeal were adjudged two thirds against employer and one third against claimant. Western Union Tel. Co. v. George, 239 Ala. 80, 194 So. 183 (1940).

Nature of judgment. — The judgment against a defendant in a workmen's compensation case, certainly to the extent of the accrued payments, is a judgment for the payment of money which, except for the right of "appeal by certiorari," is then due to be paid the plaintiff, and if not paid execution must be issued thereon "unless otherwise directed by the court or the judge presiding at the trial of the case or by the written direction of owner of the judgment or his attorney of record" under § 6-9-21. Goodyear Tire & Rubber Co. v. Downey, 266 Ala. 344, 96 So. 2d 278 (1957).

Application of procedures prescribed for direct appeals. — The authorized "appeal by certiorari" in workmen's compensation cases is subject, at least for some purposes, to procedures prescribed for cases coming to the court of civil appeals by direct appeal. Goodyear Tire & Rubber Co. v. Downey, 266 Ala. 344, 96 So. 2d 278 (1957).

Supersedeas bond. — Code 1940, Tit. 7, § 793 (now covered by A.R.A.P., Rule 8), providing for supersedeas bonds, applies to a judgment in workman's compensation case. Accordingly, the giving of a supersedeas bond is essential to a stay of the judgment. This means that the granting of the writ of certiorari in these cases does not, ipso facto, operate as a stay as does the granting of the common-law writ. If the order granting the writ calls for such bond, the execution of the bond is not a condition to the issuance of the writ. Rather, it is the fixing of the amount of the supersedeas bond. If the appellant declines to give the bond, the writ may nevertheless issue; but in that situation there is no stay of the judgment. Goodyear Tire & Rubber Co. v. Downey, 266 Ala. 344, 96 So. 2d 278 (1957), wherein it was said that the court was not passing on the question whether the court was without authority, in its discretion, to require, as a condition to the issuance of the writ in compensation cases, the giving by appellant of a bond to indemnify the appellee against loss, in event appellant declines to give a supersedeas bond.

The practice is for a justice of the appellate court to grant the writ of certiorari as a matter of course, at the same time fixing the amount of the bond, to be approved by the clerk of the circuit court. Such bond has generally been fixed in double the amount of the judgment for accrued compensation payments and the estimated number of payments to accrue between the time of the judgment and a decision here. As a rule such estimate has included payments accruing within 12 months after the judgment. Goodyear Tire & Rubber Co. v. Downey, 266 Ala. 344, 96 So. 2d 278 (1957).

"Interlocutory decree". — Although the trial court's judgment was styled as an "interlocutory decree," which is by definition not a final judgment, the test of a judgment's finality is whether it sufficiently ascertains and declares the rights of the parties; the "interlocutory decree" entered by the trial court contained the findings necessary to support an appeal without undue hardship to the employer; moreover, the fact that the trial court retained jurisdiction over the award of temporary disability did not bar such an appeal. Ex parte DCH Regional Medical Ctr., 571 So. 2d 1162 (Ala. Civ. App. 1990).

"Interlocutory order" was conclusive and appealable since trial court was not required to estimate the probable duration of the temporary total disability and fix a specific number of weeks that the employee was to be paid; the legislature amended § 25-5-57 to ensure that a claimant would be compensated throughout the time of recovery, regardless of the time it takes to reach maximum medical recovery; with this amendment, the legislature had effectively overruled the cases which required a trial court to estimate the period of temporary total disability for which a claimant may receive benefits; it was now unnecessary to make this estimate for the sake of a "conclusive" judgment. Ex parte DCH Regional Medical Ctr., 571 So. 2d 1162 (Ala. Civ. App. 1990).

Trial court's judgment was conclusive even though it left the question of permanent disability open to further proceedings; since the statute provides a remedy for the employee if a permanent disability does result from the period of temporary total disability, the trial court's reservation of jurisdiction was mere surplusage. Ex parte DCH Regional Medical Ctr., 571 So. 2d 1162 (Ala. Civ. App. 1990).

Damages included in judgment of affirmance. — Since the case of DeBardeleben Coal Corp. v. Richards, 251 Ala. 324, 37 So. 2d 121 (1948), straight judgments of affirmance in workmen's compensation cases have consistently included the 10 percent damages provided for in § 12-22-72. The 10 percent damages have been assessed against the defendant appellant and the surety on the supersedeas bond on all payments which have accrued up to the time of affirmance. The procedure followed since the DeBardeleben case is proper. Goodyear Tire & Rubber Co. v. Downey, 266 Ala. 344, 96 So. 2d 278 (1957).

B. Cross Assignment of Errors.

Employee had right to cross-assign errors. — Where employer brought certiorari to review judgment awarding compensation, employee had the right to cross-assign errors (present issues for review now) and hence employer's motion to dismiss its case and vacate writ of certiorari would be denied where employee had assigned cross-errors (presented issues for review now). Agricola Furnace Co. v. Smith, 239 Ala. 488, 195 So. 743 (1940).

C. Limitations on Scope of Review.

1. Standard of Review Defined.

The standard of review in workmen's compensation cases is whether there is any legal evidence to sustain the trial court's finding or conclusion or judgment. Young v. City of Huntsville, 342 So. 2d 918 (Ala. Civ. App. 1976), cert. denied, 342 So. 2d 924 (Ala. 1977).

Under the standard of review on certiorari the appellate court may not look to the weight of the evidence presented to the trial court. Rather, it reviews the record only to determine if there is any legal evidence which supports the trial court's judgment and if there is any such evidence it will affirm. Poole v. Ellard Contracting Co., 527 So. 2d 1327 (Ala. Civ. App. 1988).

Standard of review in a workmen's compensation case is very narrow. Allen v. Metro Contract Servs., Inc., 421 So. 2d 1289 (Ala. Civ. App. 1982); Dodson v. Atrax Div. of Wallace-Murray Corp., 437 So. 2d 1294 (Ala. Civ. App. 1983).

The scope of review and the duty of the court in a workmen's compensation case is simply to ascertain whether there was any legal evidence to sustain the conclusion of the trial court. If any reasonable view of the evidence supports such conclusion, then the judgment will not be disturbed. Aluminum Workers Int'l v. Champion, 45 Ala. App. 570, 233 So. 2d 511 (1970); Glover v. Howell Plywood Co., 50 Ala. App. 22, 276 So. 2d 608 (1973).

Review on petition for certiorari in a compensation case is limited. Bryant v. Central Foundry Co., 217 Ala. 332, 116 So. 345

(1928); Agricola Furnace Co. v. Smith, 239 Ala. 488, 195 So. 743 (1940).

The limited review by certiorari involves determination whether there is any legal evidence to support findings of fact and conclusions of trial court in compensation cases. Bryant v. Central Foundry Co., 217 Ala. 332, 116 So. 345 (1928); Bass v. Cowikee Mills, 259 Ala. 391, 67 So. 2d 12 (1953); Southern Cotton Oil Co. v. Wynn, 266 Ala. 327, 96 So. 2d 159 (1957).

On certiorari the court's review is limited to questions of law and to a determination of whether there is any legal evidence to support the findings of the trial court. Under this standard of review, the court will affirm the findings and conclusions of the trial court if there is any legal evidence to support them. Valley Steel Constr. v. Prater, 479 So. 2d 1259 (Ala. Civ. App. 1985).

On review by certiorari the appellate court will not weigh the evidence nor consider its preponderance but will review the evidence only to determine if any reasonable view of it supports the conclusions of fact of the trial court; if there is any legal support for the findings of fact of the trial court the appellate court may then determine if the correct legal conclusions have been drawn therefrom. Newman Bros. v. McDowell, 354 So. 2d 1138 (Ala. Civ. App.), cert. denied, 354 So. 2d 1142 (Ala. 1977).

On review by certiorari, the court of civil appeals does not look to the weight of the evidence as to any fact found by the trial court, but looks to see if there is any evidence to support the facts which the trial court found; if any reasonable view of the evidence supports the conclusion of fact made by the trial court and the correct law was applied to such facts, the court of civil appeals will not disturb the trial court's judgment. Fordham v. Southern Phenix Textiles, Inc., 387 So. 2d 204 (Ala. Civ. App.), cert. denied, 387 So. 2d 206 (Ala. 1980).

Under the Workmen's Compensation Act, a finding of the trial court will be sustained if it has support in the evidence. Ford v. Crystal Laundry Co., 238 Ala. 187, 189 So. 730 (1939). And some evidence is all that is required. Ex parte Paramount Coal Co., 213 Ala. 281, 104 So. 753 (1925); Ex parte National Pipe & Foundry Co., 213 Ala. 605, 105 So. 693 (1925); Tripple M. Homes, Inc. v. Pickens, 46 Ala. App. 643, 248 So. 2d 139 (1971).

A compensation judgment sustained by any evidence will be affirmed. Wilson v. Birmingham Elec. Co., 219 Ala. 436, 122 So. 411 (1929).

2. Limited to Questions of Law.

Review limited to questions of law. — On certiorari to review order granting new trial in proceeding under Workmen's Compensation Act, review is limited to questions of law. Birmingham Clay Prods. Co. v. White, 226 Ala. 89, 145 So. 668 (1933).

Review under this section is limited to questions of law; whether the finding of fact required by statute and entered in judgment is sufficient to support the judgment and whether there is any legal evidence tending to support said finding of fact. Bagwell Steel Co. v. Tinker, 256 Ala. 585, 56 So. 2d 114 (1951).

A total lack of evidence on trial, to support finding of material fact in compensation proceeding, becomes question of law. Ex parte Big Four Coal Mining Co., 213 Ala. 305, 104 So. 764 (1925); Birmingham Post Co. v. McGinnis, 256 Ala. 473, 55 So. 2d 507 (1951).

On certiorari review the court is confined to questions of law apparent upon the face of the record. Simpson v. Alabama Dry Dock & Shipbuilding Co., 269 Ala. 632, 114 So. 2d 918 (1959); Head v. Triangle Constr. Co., 274 Ala. 519, 150 So. 2d 389 (1963); Boatright v. Dothan Aviation Corp., 278 Ala. 142, 176 So. 2d 500 (1965); Dearmon v. C.L. Guild Constr. Co., 44 Ala. App. 152, 204 So. 2d 497 (1967).

On certiorari the court's review is limited to questions of law and to an examination of the evidence to determine if there is any legal evidence to support the findings of the trial court. Lowe v. Walters, 491 So. 2d 962 (Ala. Civ. App. 1986).

In a workmen's compensation case the appellate court reviews the judgment of the trial court by writ of certiorari, i.e., the reviewing court will look to see if there are errors of law apparent from the face of the record and will only be concerned with whether or not there is legal evidence to support the findings of fact. Young v. City of Huntsville, 342 So. 2d 918 (Ala. Civ. App. 1976), cert. denied, 342 So. 2d 924 (Ala. 1977).

On appeal, review of a workmen's compensation case is limited to questions of law and to examination of the evidence to determine if there is any legal evidence to support the findings of the trial court. The reviewing court may, however, examine the trial court's application of the law to the facts. Allen v. Metro Contract Servs., Inc., 421 So. 2d 1289 (Ala. Civ. App. 1982); Dodson v. Atrax Div. of Wallace-Murray Corp., 437 So. 2d 1294 (Ala. Civ. App. 1983).

Review is limited to questions of law and to an examination of the evidence to determine if there is any legal evidence to support the findings of the trial court. If there is any legal evidence that supports those findings, the appellate court will affirm. American Auto.

Ins. Co. v. Hinote, 498 So. 2d 848 (Ala. Civ. App. 1986).

Where a case is before the court of appeals on certiorari, review is limited to questions of law and to an examination of the evidence to determine if there is any legal evidence to support the findings of the trial court. If there is any legal evidence that supports the findings, the court of appeals will affirm. Robinson Foundry, Inc. v. Moon, 503 So. 2d 863 (Ala. Civ. App. 1987); Wadsworth Contractors v. Uptain, 504 So. 2d 1217 (Ala. Civ. App. 1987); Bradley v. Nelson, 507 So. 2d 958 (Ala. Civ. App. 1987).

Review by the court of civil appeals of workmen's compensation cases is by certiorari. The review in such cases "is limited to questions of law and to an examination of the evidence to determine if there is any legal evidence to support the findings of the trial court." Under this narrow standard of review, if there is any legal evidence which supports the trial court's findings of fact, the court will affirm those findings. Benefield v. Goodwill Indus., 473 So. 2d 505 (Ala. Civ. App. 1985).

Review under subsection (d) of this section is limited to questions of law and to an examination of the evidence to determine if there is any legal evidence to support the findings of the trial court. Stewart v. Carter Realty Co., 518 So. 2d 122 (Ala. Civ. App.), writ denied, 518 So. 2d 125 (Ala. 1987).

3. Factfinding Determination Not Reviewed.

Court will not review weight or preponderance of evidence. — In every workmen's compensation case coming for review before an appellate court, the court will not review the weight or preponderance of the evidence. Aluminum Workers Int'l v. Champion, 45 Ala. App. 570, 233 So. 2d 511 (1970).

On certiorari to review judgments in workmen's compensation cases, the court of civil appeals does not look to the weight of the evidence as to any fact found by the trial court, but looks to see if there is any evidence to support the facts which the trial court found. Mobile Paint Mfg. Co. v. Crowley, 56 Ala. App. 673, 325 So. 2d 182 (1975).

If trial judge's finding of facts in a compensation case is supported by any legal evidence the conclusion and judgment will not be disturbed. Hearn v. United States Cast Iron Pipe & Foundry Co., 217 Ala. 352, 116 So. 365 (1928); Morgan v. City of Gunthersville, 239 Ala. 669, 196 So. 877 (1940); Majors v. Jackson Lumber Co., 244 Ala. 418, 13 So. 2d 885 (1943).

On certiorari to review judgments in compensation cases, the appellate court will not look to the weight of the evidence as to any fact

found by the trial court, and this rule applies when the award or compensation is denied as well as where there has been a judgment favorable to the plaintiff. Ellis v. Woodward Iron Co., 274 Ala. 226, 147 So. 2d 801 (1962); Campbell v. United States Steel Corp., 274 Ala. 326, 148 So. 2d 484 (1962); Head v. Triangle Constr. Co., 274 Ala. 519, 150 So. 2d 389 (1963); Floyd v. Barrentine, 274 Ala. 432, 155 So. 2d 598 (1963); Boatright v. Dothan Aviation Corp., 278 Ala. 142, 176 So. 2d 500 (1965); Dearmon v. C.L. Guild Constr. Co., 44 Ala. App. 152, 204 So. 2d 497 (1967); Hayles v. Ray E. Loper Lumber Co., 46 Ala. App. 58, 237 So. 2d 862 (1970).

The reviewing court merely looks to see if there is any evidence supporting the finding of facts by the trial court in a workmen's compensation case. Summit Coal Co. v. Walker, 214 Ala. 332, 107 So. 905 (1926); Benoit Coal Mining Co. v. Moore, 215 Ala. 220, 109 So. 878 (1926). See Ex parte Little Cahaba Coal Co., 213 Ala. 596, 105 So. 648 (1925); Hearn v. United States Cast Iron Pipe & Foundry Co., 217 Ala. 352, 116 So. 365 (1928); Trannon v. Sloss-Sheffield Steel & Iron Co., 233 Ala. 312, 171 So. 898 (1937); Lucas v. Black Diamond Coal Mining Co., 262 Ala. 368, 79 So. 2d 26 (1955); Sam's Place v. Middleton, 41 Ala. App. 13, 122 So. 2d 924 (1959), aff'd, 271 Ala. 226, 122 So. 2d 925 (1960); Birson v. Decatur Transf. & Storage, Inc., 271 Ala. 240, 122 So. 2d 917 (1960).

On certiorari to review judgments in workmen's compensation cases, the court will not look to weight of evidence as to any fact found by the trial court, but simply to see if there is any evidence to support facts found by trial court regardless of whether an award of compensation has been denied or granted. Davis-Day Timber Co. v. Gentry, 54 Ala. App. 385, 309 So. 2d 97 (1975).

On certiorari to review judgments in compensation cases, the court does not look to the weight of the evidence as to facts found by the trier of fact, and will only determine if there is any evidence, or reasonable inference therefrom, to support the finding. Queen City Furn. Co. v. Hinds, 274 Ala. 584, 150 So. 2d 756 (1963); Thomas v. Gulf States Paper Corp., 276 Ala. 660, 166 So. 2d 104 (1964); City of Foley v. Terry, 278 Ala. 30, 175 So. 2d 461 (1965); Dale Motels, Inc. v. Crittenden, 50 Ala. App. 251, 278 So. 2d 370 (1973).

The court will not look to the evidence to ascertain the weight or preponderance thereof as to any fact found by the trial court, but simply to see if there is any evidence, or reasonable inference from evidence, to support the facts found by the trial court. Simpson v. Alabama Dry Dock & Shipbuilding Co., 269

Ala. 635, 114 So. 2d 918 (1959); Bullard v. Murdock, 271 Ala. 378, 124 So. 2d 263 (1960); Pinto Island Metals Co. v. Edwards, 275 Ala. 351, 155 So. 2d 304 (1963); Horton v. DeLoach, 276 Ala. 357, 162 So. 2d 453 (1964); Reynolds Metals Co. v. Gray, 278 Ala. 309, 178 So. 2d 87 (1965); Nason v. Jones, 278 Ala. 532, 179 So. 2d 281 (1965).

In workmen's compensation cases the reviewing court does not consider the weight of the evidence supporting a fact or facts found by the trial court, but only ascertains whether or not there is any evidence to support the fact so found. Colvin v. Lee Turzillo Contracting Co., 54 Ala. App. 401, 309 So. 2d 112 (1975).

On certiorari to review judgments in compensation cases, the court is not concerned with the weight of the evidence as to any fact found by the trial court. Anderson v. Custom Caterers, Inc., 279 Ala. 360, 185 So. 2d 383 (1966); McKnight v. Consolidated Concrete Co., 279 Ala. 430, 186 So. 2d 144 (1966).

On certiorari to review judgments, in compensation cases, the court does not look to the weight of the evidence as to any fact found by the trial court, but looks to see if there is any evidence to support the facts found by the trial court. Bell v. Driskill, 282 Ala. 640, 213 So. 2d 806 (1968); Vulcraft, Inc. v. Wilbanks, 54 Ala. App. 393, 309 So. 2d 105 (1975).

In every review, by certiorari of a workmen's compensation case, the court of civil appeals is bound by the findings of fact of the trial court if such findings are supported by legal evidence. Misco, Inc. v. Driver, 50 Ala. App. 256, 278 So. 2d 374 (1973).

On review in a workmen's compensation case, the court will not review the weight or preponderance of the evidence taken by the trial court to support the findings of fact, but will only review the record to ascertain if there is any legal evidence or reasonable inference to be gathered therefrom to support said findings; and where such evidence is found, the findings of the trial court will be deemed conclusive and will not be disturbed on appeal. Eddons Drug Co. v. Wright, 46 Ala. App. 645, 248 So. 2d 140 (1971).

On certiorari to review workmen's compensation cases, the court will not review the preponderance of the evidence, but will look to see if there is any evidence to support the facts found by the trial court. Avondale Mills, Inc. v. Tollison, 52 Ala. App. 52, 289 So. 2d 621 (1974); Unexcelled Mfg. Corp. v. Ragland, 52 Ala. App. 57, 289 So. 2d 626 (1974); Defense Ordinance Corp. v. England, 52 Ala. App. 565, 295 So. 2d 419 (1974).

Appellate court reviews the evidence, but will neither weigh the evidence nor consider its preponderance in workmen's compensation cases. Wilson v. American Cast Iron Pipe Co., 528 So. 2d 338 (Ala. Civ. App. 1988).

Weight of evidence not passed on to determine question of liability. — Court in reviewing judgment in compensation case on certiorari will not pass on weight of evidence to determine question of liability; but this is for trial judge. Hearn v. United States Cast Iron Pipe & Foundry Co., 217 Ala. 352, 116 So. 365 (1928); Bass v. Cowikee Mills, 259 Ala. 391, 67 So. 2d 12 (1953); Goodyear Tire & Rubber Co. v. Downey, 266 Ala. 344, 96 So. 2d 278 (1957).

A contention that the court of civil appeals (formerly court of appeals) was in error in holding that there was evidence to support a finding that claimant's injury arose out of and in course of employment involved a finding of fact and application of law to the facts not within the range of review of the court of civil appeals (formerly court of appeals) by certiorari. Hardie Sales Co. v. Astrachan, 239 Ala. 558, 196 So. 135 (1940).

But court will review legal conclusion drawn from evidence. — The reviewing court will not weigh the evidence and if on any reasonable view of the evidence the conclusion of the trial court is supported, then the finding and judgment of the trial court will not be disturbed. But this does not mean that the court will not review the legal conclusion of the court drawn from the evidence. Dorsey Trailers, Inc. v. Weaver, 263 Ala. 229, 82 So. 2d 261 (1955).

Where testimony is conflicting, but there is testimony supporting the findings of the trial court in proceedings under the Workmen's Compensation Act, such finding is conclusive, and this principle applies in reviewing the trial court's finding of fact with respect to the employee's "physical or mental incapacity ... to perform or cause to be performed" the act of filing a verified complaint as provided in § 25-5-88 the same as other findings of fact. Southern Cotton Oil Co. v. Wynn, 266 Ala. 327, 96 So. 2d 159 (1957).

Where finding of fact is meager or omissive court looks to evidence. — Where the finding of fact in a compensation case is meager or omissive the court will look to the evidence in the case to see if on any reasonable view of the evidence the judgment of the court can be sustained. Bass v. Cowikee Mills, 257 Ala. 280, 58 So. 2d 589 (1952); Alabama Textile Prods. Corp. v. Grantham, 263 Ala. 179, 82 So. 2d 204 (1955); West Point Mfg. Co. v. Bennett, 263 Ala. 571, 83 So. 2d 303 (1955); Birson v. Decatur Transf. & Storage, Inc., 271 Ala. 240, 122 So. 2d 917 (1960); Pinkney v. James B. Clow & Sons, 277 Ala. 648, 173 So. 2d 811 (1965); Calvert v. Funderburg, 284 Ala. 311, 224 So. 2d 664 (1969); M.R. Thomason &

Assocs. v. Jones, 48 Ala. App. 67, 261 So. 2d 899 (1972); Defense Ordinance Corp. v. England, 52 Ala. App. 565, 295 So. 2d 419 (1974).

Where the trial court's findings of fact are merely meager or omissive, the reviewing court may look to the evidence to see if it can find any support for the judgment. Avondale Mills, Inc. v. Tollison, 52 Ala. App. 52, 289 So. 2d 621 (1974).

Where there was an omission in the trial court's "determination" as to the existence or nonexistence of the employer-employee relationship, the court had to go to the evidence to determine if the judgment of the trial court could be sustained. Calvert v. Funderburg, 284 Ala. 311, 224 So. 2d 664 (1969).

And statement in brief of what evidence showed will not be considered by the court in determining the issues before it in a compensation case. Trannon v. Sloss-Sheffield Steel & Iron Co., 233 Ala. 312, 171 So. 898 (1937).

And rulings on admission of evidence not considered. — On reviewing by certiorari a workmen's compensation case, rulings on admission of evidence will not be considered if it appears the conclusion and judgment are supported by legal evidence. Defense Ordinance Corp. v. England, 52 Ala. App. 565, 295 So. 2d 419 (1974).

On certiorari in compensation cases, the court will not disturb the findings of the trial court because of mere errors in the admission or rejection of evidence, where there is legal evidence to support the judgment entered. Majors v. Jackson Lumber Co., 244 Ala. 418, 13 So. 2d 855 (1943).

Upon review by certiorari in the state courts, if there is any reasonable view of the evidence that will support the conclusion below the judgment will not be disturbed. The conclusions must be based on legal evidence, but, where there is any legal evidence to support the finding of the trial court, such finding is conclusive, and no technical questions as to the admissibility of evidence will be considered on appeal. Collins v. Central Foundry Co., 263 F.2d 712 (5th Cir. 1959).

The appellate court will not review technical questions regarding the trial court's rulings on objections to the admission of evidence. Young v. City of Huntsville, 342 So. 2d 918 (Ala. Civ. App. 1976), cert. denied, 342 So. 2d 924 (Ala. 1977).

D. Conclusiveness of Trial Court's Findings.

Finding of trial court is conclusive if supported by any evidence in compensation proceeding. Exchange Distrib. Co. v. Oslin, 229 Ala. 547, 158 So. 743 (1935);

Trannon v. Sloss-Sheffield Steel & Iron Co., 233 Ala. 312, 171 So. 898 (1937); Edmonds v. Standard Brands, Inc., 233 Ala. 315, 171 So. 751 (1937); Alabama By-Products Corp. v. Winters, 234 Ala. 566, 176 So. 183 (1937); Ford v. Crystal Laundry Co., 238 Ala. 187, 189 So. 730 (1939); Herndon v. Slayton, 263 Ala. 677, 83 So. 2d 726 (1955); Jackson v. W.L. Smith Poultry Co., 264 Ala. 184, 85 So. 2d 893 (1955); Simmons v. F.W. Dodge Corp., 270 Ala. 616, 120 So. 2d 921 (1960).

Questions of law. — If there is any legal evidence tending to support finding of court under Workmen's Compensation Act, such finding is conclusive, and review by certiorari is upon questions of law. Woodward Iron Co. v. Dean, 217 Ala. 530, 117 So. 52 (1928); Bass v. Cowikee Mills, 259 Ala. 391, 67 So. 2d 12 (1953); Southern Cotton Oil Co. v. Wynn, 266 Ala. 327, 96 So. 2d 159 (1957); Goodyear Tire & Rubber Co. v. Downey, 266 Ala. 344, 96 So. 2d 278 (1957).

Workmen's compensation cases are not triable de novo in the appellate court on the evidence taken below nor reviewed even as the finding of a judge sitting without a jury, as in ordinary trials upon testimony of witnesses examined before the court. The court's duty in this type of case is simply to ascertain whether there was any legal evidence to sustain the conclusion of the trial court. If any reasonable view of the evidence supports such conclusion, then the judgment will not be disturbed. Alabama Textile Prods. Corp. v. Grantham, 263 Ala. 179, 82 So. 2d 204 (1955).

Where there is any legal evidence of employer's actual knowledge of injury to employee the finding of the trial court thereon is conclusive, as on other issues. American Radiator Co. v. Andino, 217 Ala. 424, 116 So. 121 (1928).

The finding and judgment in a compensation case will not be disturbed on appeal if any reasonable view of evidence supports trial court's conclusion. Ex parte Little Cahaba Coal Co., 213 Ala. 596, 105 So. 648 (1925); Summit Coal Co. v. Walker, 214 Ala. 332, 107 So. 905 (1926); Benoit Coal Mining Co. v. Moore, 215 Ala. 220, 109 So. 878 (1926); Mobile Liners v. McConnell, 220 Ala. 562, 126 So. 626 (1930); Republic Iron & Steel Co. v. Ingle, 223 Ala. 127, 134 So. 878 (1931); Warrior Stone & Contracting Co. v. De Foor, 241 Ala. 227, 2 So. 2d 430 (1941); Sloss-Sheffield Steel & Iron Co. v. Alexander, 241 Ala. 476, 3 So. 2d 46 (1941); Birmingham Post Co. v. McGinnis, 256 Ala. 473, 55 So. 2d 507 (1951).

The court's finding in workmen's compensation proceedings is conclusive, if there is any evidence in the record that will support it. Ex parte Smith Lumber Co., 206 Ala. 485, 90 So.

807 (1921); Ex parte Sloss-Sheffield Steel & Iron Co., 207 Ala. 219, 92 So. 458 (1922); Ex parte Nunnally Co., 209 Ala. 82, 95 So. 343 (1923); Ex parte Woodward Iron Co., 211 Ala. 74, 99 So. 97 (1924); Morgan-Hill Paving Co. v. Stewart, 220 Ala. 480, 126 So. 116 (1930); Trannon v. Sloss-Sheffield Steel & Iron Co., 233 Ala. 312, 171 So. 898 (1937). See (any legal evidence or reasonable inferences therefrom) Ex parte Little Cahaba Coal Co., 213 Ala. 596, 105 So. 648 (1925); (conflicting testimony) Martin v. Sloss-Sheffield Steel & Iron Co., 216 Ala. 500, 113 So. 578 (1927); Woodward Iron Co. v. Dean, 217 Ala. 530, 117 So. 52 (1928); Bass v. Cowikee Mills, 259 Ala. 391, 67 So. 2d 12 (1953); Lucas v. Black Diamond Coal Mining Co., 262 Ala. 368, 79 So. 2d 26 (1955).

On certiorari in compensation cases, if on any reasonable view of the evidence it will support the conclusion reached in the trial court the finding and judgment will not be disturbed. Majors v. Jackson Lumber Co., 244 Ala. 418, 13 So. 2d 885 (1943); Valley Coal & Lumber Co. v. Hopkins, 32 Ala. App. 522, 27 So. 2d 700 (1946); Southern Cotton Oil Co. v. Bruce, 249 Ala. 675, 32 So. 2d 666 (1947); Wells v. Morris, 33 Ala. App. 497, 35 So. 2d 54 (1948); Riddle v. Smith, 252 Ala. 369, 41 So. 2d 288 (1949); Mitchell Motor Co. v. Burrow, 37 Ala. App. 222, 66 So. 2d 198 (1953); Davis Lumber Co. v. Self, 263 Ala. 276, 82 So. 2d 291 (1955); Ammons v. McClendon, 263 Ala. 651, 83 So. 2d 239 (1955); Southern Cotton Oil Co. v. Wynn, 266 Ala. 327, 96 So. 2d 159 (1957); B.F. Goodrich Co. v. Lee, 271 Ala. 312, 123 So. 2d 117 (1960); W.T. Smith Lumber Co. v. Raines, 271 Ala. 671, 127 So. 2d 619 (1961); Anderson v. Custom Caterers, Inc., 279 Ala. 360, 185 So. 2d 383 (1966); McKnight v. Consolidated Concrete Co., 279 Ala. 430, 186 So. 2d 144 (1966).

The primary court's findings of facts in workmen's compensation cases are exclusive and will not be disturbed by the appellate courts on review if there is any legal evidence to support the findings. Alabama By-Products Co. v. Landgraff, 32 Ala. App. 343, 27 So. 2d 209, aff'd, 248 Ala. 253, 27 So. 2d 215 (1946).

Where testimony is conflicting, but there is testimony supporting the finding of the trial court in proceedings under the Workmen's Compensation Act, such finding is conclusive. Bass v. Cowikee Mills, 259 Ala. 391, 67 So. 2d 12 (1953); Braswell v. Brooks, 266 Ala. 141, 94 So. 2d 879 (1957); Simpson v. Alabama Dry Dock & Shipbuilding Co., 269 Ala. 635, 114 So. 2d 918 (1959); Bullard v. Murdock, 271 Ala. 378, 124 So. 2d 263 (1960); Boatright v. Dothan Aviation Corp., 278 Ala. 142, 176 So. 2d 500 (1965); Reynolds Metals Co. v. Gray, 278 Ala. 309, 178 So. 2d 87 (1965).

Where there is any legal evidence or reasonable inference from any legal evidence to support the findings of the trial court, such finding is conclusive and the judgment of the court will not be disturbed. United States Steel Corp. v. Danner, 263 Ala. 310, 82 So. 2d 404 (1955); Horton v. DeLoach, 276 Ala. 357, 162 So. 2d 453 (1964); Nason v. Jones, 278 Ala. 532, 179 So. 2d 281 (1965); Semmes Nurseries, Inc. v. McVay, 279 Ala. 42, 181 So. 2d 331 (1965); Bell v. Driskill, 282 Ala. 640, 213 So. 2d 806 (1968); Aluminum Workers Int'l v. Champion, 45 Ala. App. 570, 233 So. 2d 511 (1970); Merrill Co. v. Butler, 46 Ala. App. 447, 243 So. 2d 710 (1971); Dale Motels, Inc. v. Crittenden, 50 Ala. App. 251, 278 So. 2d 370 (1973); Avondale Mills, Inc. v. Tollison, 52 Ala. App. 52, 289 So. 2d 621 (1974); Unexcelled Mfg. Corp. v. Ragland, 52 Ala. App. 57, 289 So. 2d 626 (1974); Defense Ordinance Corp. v. England, 52 Ala. App. 565, 295 So. 2d 419 (1974); Davis-Day Timber Co. v. Gentry, 54 Ala. App. 385, 309 So. 2d 97 (1975); Turner v. Drummond Co., 349 So. 2d 598 (Ala. Civ. App.), cert. denied, 349 So. 2d 605 (Ala. 1977).

If, upon any reasonable view of the evidence, it will support the findings and conclusion of the trial court, the judgment entered thereon will not be disturbed. Tiger Motor Co. v. Winslett, 278 Ala. 108, 176 So. 2d 39 (1965).

If, on any reasonable view of the evidence, it will support the conclusion reached by the trial court, the finding and judgment will not be disturbed. Horton v. DeLoach, 276 Ala. 357, 162 So. 2d 453 (1964); Nason v. Jones, 278 Ala. 532, 179 So. 2d 281 (1965).

Where testimony in workmen's compensation proceedings is conflicting, and there is testimony supporting the trial court's finding, such finding is conclusive. Young v. City of Huntsville, 342 So. 2d 918 (Ala. Civ. App. 1976), cert. denied, 342 So. 2d 924 (Ala. 1977).

Conclusiveness applies where the award is denied as well as where granted. Cohen v. Birmingham Fabricating Co., 224 Ala. 67, 139 So. 97 (1932); Simpson v. Alabama Dry Dock & Shipbuilding Co., 269 Ala. 635, 114 So. 2d 918 (1959); Bullard v. Murdock, 271 Ala. 378, 124 So. 2d 263 (1960); Reynolds Metals Co. v. Gray, 278 Ala. 309, 178 So. 2d 87 (1965).

Where there is any substantial legal evidence in support of the finding of the trial court, the judgment, whether affirmative or negative, will not be disturbed on appeal. Tiger Motor Co. v. Winslett, 278 Ala. 108, 176 So. 2d 39 (1965).

Court would not disturb finding that employer had actual knowledge of employee's injury where there was evidence tending to show knowledge. Sloss-Sheffield Steel & Iron Co. v. Watts, 236 Ala. 636, 184 So. 201 (1938).

But in the absence of sufficient evidence the judgment will be reversed. — If there is no legal evidence to support trial judge's findings of facts in a compensation case the judgment will be reversed. Hearn v. United States Cast Iron Pipe & Foundry Co., 217 Ala. 352, 116 So. 365 (1928).

And judgment reached by considering illegal evidence reversed. — If it affirmatively appears from the record that the judgment of the trial court was reached after consideration of a substantial quantity of illegal evidence the judgment may be reversed. Odell v. Myers, 52 Ala. App. 558, 295 So. 2d 413 (1974); Defense Ordinance Corp. v. England, 52 Ala. App. 565, 295 So. 2d 419 (1974).

§ 25-5-82. Compensation for death to be paid only to United States residents.

Compensation for the death of an employee shall be paid only to dependents who, at the time of the death of the injured employee, were actually residents of the United States. No right of action to recover damages for the death of an employee shall exist in favor or for the benefit of any person who was not a resident of the United States at the time of the death of such employee. (Acts 1919, No. 245, p. 206; Code 1923, § 7572; Code 1940, T. 26, § 298.)

Collateral references. — Right to maintain action under workmen's compensation acts, based upon death of employee, for benefit of nonresident aliens. 138 ALR 695.

§ 25-5-83. Commutation of compensation to lump sum payments.

By agreement of the parties and with approval of the court, the amounts of compensation payable periodically, under this article and Article 4 of this chapter, may be commuted to one or more lump sum payments. No commutation shall be approved by the court unless the court is satisfied that it is in the best interest of the employee or the employee's dependent, in case of death, to receive the compensation in a lump sum rather than in periodic payments. In making the commutations, the lump sum payment shall, in the aggregate, amount to a sum equal to the present value of all future installments of compensation calculated on a six percent basis. (Acts 1919, No. 245, p. 206; Code 1923, § 7573; Acts 1939, No. 661, p. 1036, § 6; Code 1940, T. 26, § 299; Acts 1949, No. 36, p. 47; Acts 1957, No. 336, p. 437; Acts 1969, No. 233, p. 557, § 4; Acts 1975, 4th Ex. Sess., No. 86, p. 2729, § 9; Acts 1992, No. 92-537, § 27.)

The 1992 amendment, effective May 19, 1992, inserted "and Article 4 of this chapter" in the first sentence, in the second sentence deleted "such" preceding "commutation," and substituted "dependent" for "dependents," and substituted "the commutations" for "such commutations" in the last sentence.

Parties must agree, and court must approve, lump sum payment. — This section provides that workmen's compensation benefits may be paid in one or more lump sums if the parties agree to such method of payment and the agreement is approved by the court. Jamestown Corp. v. Ward, 373 So. 2d 1136

(Ala. Civ. App.), cert. denied, 373 So. 2d 1142 (Ala. 1979).

This section has consistently been construed as requiring the agreement of the parties in order for a lump sum payment to be made. United States Steel Corp. v. Baker, 266 Ala. 538, 97 So. 2d 899 (1957); Jamestown Corp. v. Ward, 373 So. 2d 1136 (Ala. Civ. App.), cert. denied, 373 So. 2d 1142 (Ala. 1979).

Hence, employer must agree to lump sum settlement. — In absence of agreement by employer, the court is without jurisdiction to award a lump sum settlement to claimant. Edwards v. Doster-Northington Drug Co., 214 Ala. 640, 108 So. 862 (1926). See also, County

Coal Co. v. Bush, 215 Ala. 25, 109 So. 151 (1926).

And where payment is agreed upon and approved, right thereto becomes vested in employee. — If the employer and employee agree to a lump sum payment, and such payment is approved by the court, the obvious inference to be drawn is that the right thereto becomes vested in the employee, because, by commuting, all installments are made presently due. United States Steel Corp. v. Baker, 266 Ala. 538, 97 So. 2d 899 (1957).

But insurer not party to proceeding cannot object to lump sum payment. — Agreement between employer and dependents of deceased employee, who were only parties to compensation proceeding, that compensation should be paid in lump sum, held to justify such award, notwithstanding objection of insurer, in view of § 25-5-8, since "agreement of the parties" in this section, relative to lump sum settlements, embraces only parties to proceeding. County Coal Co. v. Bush, 215 Ala. 25, 109 So. 151 (1926).

Lump sum judgment is erroneous in absence of a showing that parties agreed, with the approval of the court, that such a judgment could be entered. Richardson Lumber Co. v. Pounders, 254 Ala. 285, 48 So. 2d 228 (1950); Jamestown Corp. v. Ward, 373 So. 2d 1136 (Ala. Civ. App.), cert. denied, 373 So. 2d 1142 (Ala. 1979).

There is nothing to indicate this section should be read in connection with awarding of attorney's fees. Ashland Chem. Co. v. Watkins, 435 So. 2d 1301 (Ala. Civ. App. 1983), overruled on other grounds, Ex parte St. Regis Corp., 535 So. 2d 160 (Ala. 1988).

Lump sum payments of unaccrued benefits. — If the parties agree, with approval of the court, to a lump sum payment of unaccrued benefits, the amount of compensation payable periodically may be commuted to a lump sum payment, using an annual discount rate of six percent. St. Regis Corporation-Champion Int'l Corp. v. Parnell, 535 So. 2d 160 (Ala. 1988).

As to the method of computing lump sum attorney's fees, see St. Regis Corporation-Champion Int'l Corp. v. Parnell, 535 So. 2d 160 (Ala. 1988).

Discretion of trial court. — The trial court has the discretion to order a lump sum pay-

ment of the attorney's fee, and when the trial court orders such a payment of the attorney's fee, the provisions of this section providing for computation of present value are fully applicable to this part of the award. Ciba-Geigy Corp. v. Kelly, 579 So. 2d 662 (Ala. Civ. App. 1991).

The trial court's discretion to order a lump sum payment of the attorney fee is but an exception to the employer's otherwise exclusive right to elect whether to pay the award in a lump sum. Thus, when the employer elects not to pay the full award of compensation in a lump sum, and the trial court orders a lump sum payment of the attorney fee (which represents up to 15 percent of the award), the provisions of this section providing for computation of present value are fully applicable to this part of the award. St. Regis Corporation-Champion Int'l Corp. v. Parnell, 535 So. 2d 160 (Ala. 1988).

This section requires court approval only where the employer wishes to commute the benefits payable to the employee to one or more lump sum payments. Johnson v. Asphalt Hot Mix, 565 So. 2d 219 (Ala. 1990).

Cited in Lawrence v. United States Fid. & Guar. Co., 226 Ala. 161, 145 So. 577 (1933); Consolidated Coal Co. v. Dill, 248 Ala. 5, 26 So. 2d 88 (1946); Griffith v. Alabama By-Products Corp., 120 F. Supp. 219 (N.D. Ala. 1954); Sanders v. Shockley, 468 F.2d 88 (5th Cir. 1972); Harris v. National Truck Serv., 56 Ala. App. 350, 321 So. 2d 690 (1975); B.F. Goodrich Co. v. Butler, 336 So. 2d 1357 (Ala. Civ. App.), cert. denied, 336 So. 2d 1360 (Ala. 1976); Fairfax Mfg. Co. v. Bragg, 342 So. 2d 17 (Ala. 1977); Cochrum v. Kinro Indus., Inc., 352 So. 2d 456 (Ala. Civ. App. 1977); Sparks v. Delta Masonry Contractors, 411 So. 2d 808 (Ala. Civ. App. 1982); Cox v. Republic Steel Corp., 459 So. 2d 886 (Ala. Civ. App. 1984); Robinson Foundry, Inc, v. Tinsley, 510 So. 2d 825 (Ala. Civ. App. 1987).

Collateral references. — 99 C.J.S., Workmen's Compensation, §§ 337-352.

58 Am. Jur., Workmen's Compensation, § 548.

Specific grounds for commutation of payments under workmen's compensation acts. 69 ALR 547.

Workers' compensation: recovery for home service provided by spouse. 67 ALR4th 765.

§ 25-5-84. Modification of payments.

All amounts paid by the employer and received by the employee or his dependents under settlements made under Section 25-5-56 shall be final, but the amount of any award payable periodically for more than six months may be modified at any time by agreement of the parties and approved by the court. (Acts 1919, No. 245, p. 206; Code 1923, § 7574; Code 1940, T. 26, § 300; Acts 1967, No. 168, p. 509, § 5.)

This section applies only to settlements made between the parties and approved by the court under § 25-5-56. Davis v. Birmingham Trussville Iron Co., 233 Ala. 259, 135 So. 455 (1936); Sloss-Sheffield Steel & Iron Co. v. Nations, 243 Ala. 107, 8 So. 2d 833 (1942); Tombrello Coal Co. v. Fortenberry, 248 Ala. 640, 29 So. 2d 125 (1947).

Court may reapportion distribution of compensation. — Although where amount of compensation is once vested it cannot be changed except as provided by statute, court may always reapportion distribution of compensation; the 30 days statute (Code 1940, Tit. 7, § 276, now covered by A.R.C.P., Rule 59(b)), not applying to reapportionment of compensation, and there being nothing in § 25-5-56, and this section to the contrary. Ex parte Central Iron & Coal Co., 212 Ala. 367, 102 So. 797 (1925).

Remarriage and nondependency relieved employer from payments. — In garnishment proceeding filed by widow against her late husband's employer when the employer ceased making weekly workmen's compensation payments, finding that remarriage of employee's widow and nondependency of employee's children relieved employer from further payments of workmen's compensation benefits pursuant to judgment for installment payments was proper. Belcher v. Vulcan Materials Co., 359 So. 2d 383 (Ala. Civ. App. 1978).

Cited in Ex parte Central Iron & Coal Co., 212 Ala. 367, 102 So. 797 (1925); Standard Chem. Co. v. Barbaree, 239 Ala. 601, 195 So. 892 (1940); United States Steel Corp. v. Baker, 266 Ala. 538, 97 So. 2d 899 (1957); Faddis v. Woodward Iron Co., 276 Ala. 283, 161 So. 2d 486 (1964).

Collateral references. — 101 C.J.S., Workmen's Compensation, § 864.

58 Am. Jur., Workmen's Compensation, § 395.

Right to credit for amounts paid under invalid settlement or compromise. 10 ALR 1016.

Inability to obtain work because of an injury as ground for modification of original award. 33 ALR 115.

Provision as to waiver or compromise of claims. 65 ALR 160.

Release or waiver of claim by employee as affecting right of dependents in event of his death as result of injury. 101 ALR 1410.

Fraud or mistake respecting amount of compensation to which employee was entitled as ground for release from settlement or compromise of claim. 121 ALR 1270.

Right of employer or insurance carrier to discontinue, without an order or ruling in that regard, payments provided for by agreement. 129 ALR 418.

Time and jurisdiction for modification of award or agreement. 165 ALR 9.

§ 25-5-85. Procedure for and effect of payment of compensation to court appointed trustee.

At any time after the amount of an award has been agreed upon by the parties or found and ordered by the court, a sum equal to the present value of all future installments of compensation calculated on a six percent basis may, where death or the nature of the injury renders the amount of future payments certain, by leave of court, be paid by the employer to a bank or trust company of this state or a national bank doing business in this state to be approved and designated by the court, and the sum, together with all interest thereon, shall thereafter be held in trust for the employee or dependent of the employee, who shall have no further recourse against the employer. The payment of the sum by the employer, evidenced by the receipts in duplicate of the trustees, one of which shall be filed with the probate judge of the county in which the injury or death occurred and the other filed with the court, shall operate as a satisfaction of the award as to the employer, and the trustee designated by the court shall be allowed to pay itself from the fund a reasonable compensation for acting as the trustee, which compensation shall be fixed by the court in the order making the designation. Payments from the fund shall be made by the trustee in the same amounts and at the same time as are required in this article of the employer until the fund, after deducting the trustee's compensation as above provided, and interest shall be exhausted. In the appointment of the trustee, preference shall be given, in the discretion of the court, to the choice of the injured employee or the dependent of the deceased employee. If the right to receive compensation should terminate on account of death, becoming of age, or marriage, or for any other cause as provided in this article, the balance remaining in the bank or trust company after the termination should be returned by them to the employer, his or her successor, or assigns. (Acts 1919, No. 245, p. 206; Code 1923, § 7575; Acts 1939, No. 149, p. 225; Code 1940, T. 26, § 301; Acts 1949, No. 36, p. 47; Acts 1973, No. 1062, p. 1750, § 22; Acts 1992, No. 92-537, § 28.)

The 1992 amendment, effective May 19, 1992, in the first sentence, substituted "the amount of an award" for "the amount of any award," "a bank or trust" for "any savings bank or trust," "a national bank" for "any national bank," "the sum" for "such sum," and "dependent" for "dependents," in the second sentence substituted "the sum" for "such sum," deleted "clerk of the circuit" preceding "court," substituted "the award" for "said award," "the fund" for "said fund," "the trustee" for "such trustee," and "the designation" for "such designation," substituted "the fund" for "said fund" in two places in the third sentence, in the fourth sentence substituted "dependent" for "dependents" and deleted "as the case may be" at the end of the sentence, and in the last sentence substituted "If the right" for "In the event the right," "the bank" for "said bank," "the termination" for "such termination," and inserted "or her."

Cited in United States Steel Corp. v. Baker, 266 Ala. 538, 97 So. 2d 899 (1957).

Collateral references. — 101 C.J.S., Workmen's Compensation, § 829.

§ 25-5-86. Remedy for default upon periodic compensation payments; exemption of compensation claims, etc., from garnishment, etc.

For purposes of this article and Article 4 of this chapter:

(1) If the award, order, or settlement agreement is payable in installments and default has been made in the payment of an installment, the owner or interested party may, upon the expiration of 30 days from the default and upon five days' notice to the defaulting employer or defendant, move for a modification of the award or settlement agreement by ascertaining the present value of the case, including the 15 percent penalty provision of Section 25-5-59, under the rule of computation contained in Section 25-5-85, and upon which execution may issue. The defaulting employer may relieve itself of the execution by entering into a good and sufficient bond, to be approved by the judge, securing the payment of all future installments, and forthwith paying all past due installments with interest and penalty thereon since due. The bond shall be recorded upon the minutes of the court.

(2) Claims for compensation, awards, judgments, or agreements to pay compensation owned by an injured employee or his or her dependent shall not be assignable and shall be exempt from seizure or sale or garnishment for the payment of any debt or liability. (Acts 1919, No. 245, p. 206; Code 1923, § 7576; Code 1940, T. 26, § 302; Acts 1992, No. 92-537, § 29.)

The 1992 amendment, effective May 19, 1992, added the introductory language, redesignated former subsections (a) and (b) as subdivisions (1) and (2), in subdivision (1), in the first sentence substituted "If the award, order, or settlement agreement" for "In all cases in which the award or judgment," substituted "an installment" for "any installment," substituted "the default" for "said default," substituted "award or settlement agreement" for "judgment or award," and substituted "present value of the case, including the 15 percent penalty provision of section 25-5-59" for "cash or present value of same," in the second sentence substituted "The defaulting employer may relieve itself of the execution by entering" for "unless the defaulting employer enters," deleted "circuit" preceding "judge," and inserted "and penalty," and in the last sentence substituted "The bond" for "Said bond," and deleted "circuit" preceding "court," and in subdivision (2) substituted "compensation, awards, judgments, or agreements" for "compensation or awards, or judgments or agreements," substituted "or her dependent" for "dependents," and deleted the former second sentence which read: "There shall be no right to waive this exemption."

Workers' compensation plans are within ambit of state's police power. — Regarding state workers' compensation plans, Employment Retirement Income Security Act is inapplicable by its own terms, because workers' compensation plans fall within the ambit of the state's police power. Richardson v. Lahood & Assocs., 571 So. 2d 1082 (Ala. 1990).

It was clearly the Congressional intent to leave the administration of ordinary worker's compensation programs that do no more than the law sets out to the states. Richardson v. Lahood & Assocs., 571 So. 2d 1082 (Ala. 1990).

This section is not preempted by ERISA. — Because this section only prohibits reduction of workers' compensation plan benefits by the amount of Employment Retirement Income Security Act (ERISA) plan payments received and does not purport to regulate ERISA plans and payments, this section is not preempted by ERISA. Richardson v. Lahood & Assocs., 571 So. 2d 1082 (Ala. 1990).

Cited in Griffith v. Alabama By-Products Corp., 120 F. Supp. 219 (N.D. Ala. 1954); Birson v. Decatur Transf. & Storage, Inc., 271 Ala. 240, 122 So. 2d 917 (1960).

Collateral references. — 101 C.J.S., Workmen's Compensation, § 846.

58 Am. Jur., Workmen's Compensation, §§ 549, 576.

Constitutionality of prohibition of assignment or release of claim under compensation acts. 47 ALR 799.

Exemption of compensation award as affected by deposit thereof. 67 ALR 1205.

Exemptions: construction and effect of statutory exemptions of proceeds of workmen's compensation awards. 31 ALR3d 532.

§ 25-5-87. Preference of right to compensation, etc.

The right to compensation and of compensation awarded any injured employee or for death claims to his dependents shall have the same preference against the assets of the employer as other unpaid wages for labor; but such compensation shall not become a lien upon the property of third persons by reason of such preference. (Acts 1919, No. 245, p. 206; Code 1923, § 7577; Code 1940, T. 26, § 303.)

Collateral references. — 101 C.J.S., Workmen's Compensation, § 839.

58 Am. Jur., Workmen's Compensation, § 551.

Claim for compensation as provable in bankruptcy. 86 ALR 770.

Receivership of employer as affecting claim by employees under compensation act. 111 ALR 328.

§ 25-5-88. Proceedings for determination of disputed claims for compensation — Commencement of action, etc.

Either party to a controversy arising under this article and Article 2 of this chapter may file a verified complaint in the circuit court of the county which would have jurisdiction of an action between the same parties arising out of tort, which shall set forth the names and residences of the parties and the circumstances relating to the employment at the time of the injury, with a full description of the injury, its nature and extent, the amount of the average earnings received by the employee which would affect his compensation under this article and Article 2 of this chapter, the knowledge of the employer of the injury or the notice to him thereof, which must be of the kind provided for in this article and Article 2 of this chapter and such other facts as may be necessary to enable the court to determine what, if any, compensation the employee or, in case of a deceased employee, his dependents, are entitled to under this article and Article 2 of this chapter. The complaint shall be filed with the clerk of the circuit court, who shall cause summons to be issued thereon requiring the defendant to come in and answer said complaint within 30 days of the service thereof. Thereafter, said action shall proceed in accordance with and shall be governed by the same rules and statutes as govern civil actions, except as otherwise provided in this article and Article 2 of this chapter, and except that all civil actions filed hereunder shall be preferred actions and shall be set down and tried as expeditiously as possible. At the hearing or any adjournment thereof the court shall hear such witnesses as may be presented by each party, and in a summary manner without a jury, unless one is demanded to try the issue of willful misconduct on the part of the employee, shall decide the controversy. This determination shall be filed in writing with the clerk of said court, and judgment shall be entered thereon in the same manner as in civil actions tried in the said circuit court and shall contain a statement of the law and facts and conclusions as determined by said judge. Subsequent proceedings thereon shall only be for the recovery of moneys thereby determined to be due, but nothing in this section contained shall be construed as limiting the jurisdiction of the Court of Civil Appeals to review questions of law by certiorari. (Acts 1919, No. 245, p. 206; Code 1923, § 7578; Code 1940, T. 26, § 304; Acts 1957, No. 350, p. 460.)

I. General Consideration.
II. Pleading.
    A. In General.
    B. Plea or Answer and Variance.
III. Determination, Judgment and Subsequent Proceedings.

I. GENERAL CONSIDERATION.

Workmen's Compensation Act looks to a prompt disposition of controversies arising thereunder and with as little formality as is consistent with its administration. Agricola Furnace Co. v. Smith, 239 Ala. 488, 195 So. 743 (1940).

And compensation due may not be split up in separate actions. — Cause of compensation claimant's action is his injury, and compensation due thereon may not be split up in separate actions. Ex parte Carlisle, 27 Ala. App. 142, 168 So. 598 (1934).

Section establishes procedure in disputed claims. — Procedure in disputed claims or actions arising under the Workmen's Compensation Act is set out in this section, and it must be complied with. Kearley v. Peterman Lumber Co., 46 Ala. App. 204, 239 So. 2d 776 (1970).

And section inapplicable where judgment relates solely to right to maintain action. — Where the judgment relates solely to the right to maintain an action under the act, and not to the merits of whether recovery, and how much, is due under the act, the provisions of this section are not applicable. Browning v. City of Huntsville, 46 Ala. App. 503, 244 So. 2d 378 (1971).

Procedure under the act is governed by its terms and requirements and not by ordinary methods of procedure. Pittman Constr. Co. v. Boles, 233 Ala. 187, 171 So. 268 (1936).

And technical rules of procedure are disregarded as far as practicable in compensation cases. However, no reason is thereby afforded why an order granting a rehearing to employee on motion for new trial, after denial of relief under the workmen's compensation law, should not be reviewed in view of this section. Continental Gin Co. v. Eaton, 214 Ala. 224, 107 So. 209 (1926).

Technical rules of procedure are not followed in workmen's compensation cases. Semmes Nurseries, Inc. v. McVay, 279 Ala. 42, 181 So. 2d 331 (1965).

Circuit courts and judges thereof are invested with plenary power in proceedings under Workmen's Compensation Act, and may proceed summarily in ascertaining facts. Birmingham Clay Prods. Co. v. White, 226 Ala. 89, 145 So. 668 (1933).

This section must be construed in pari materia with section 25-5-81. Ex parte Louisville & N.R.R., 214 Ala. 489, 108 So. 379 (1926); Lawrence v. United States Fid. & Guar. Co., 226 Ala. 161, 145 So. 577 (1933).

And this section must be construed in connection with the common law as it existed when the section was enacted. Ex parte Pittman Constr. Co., 28 Ala. App. 134, 180 So. 725 (1938).

"Knowledge" construed. — In view of the liberal construction given to this chapter, the "knowledge" of injury required to be possessed by employer by this section, as alternative to the requirement of §§ 25-5-78 and 25-5-79 for written notice, will be construed in the sense in which it is used in ordinary parlance. American Radiator Co. v. Andino, 217 Ala. 424, 116 So. 121 (1928).

Effect of accepting compensation paid in many installments. — Where plaintiff accepts compensation under the Workmen's Compensation Act, paid him in many installments, he is precluded by this agreement from resorting to another remedy, if such other remedy exists. Thompson Tractor Co. v. Cobb, 283 Ala. 100, 214 So. 2d 558 (1968).

Cited in Ex parte Stith Coal Co., 213 Ala. 399, 104 So. 756 (1925); Gulf States Steel Co. v. Griffin, 214 Ala. 126, 106 So. 898 (1926); Birmingham Clay Prods. Co. v. White, 226 Ala. 89, 145 So. 668 (1933); Aetna Life Ins. Co. v. Copeland, 25 Ala. App. 383, 147 So. 206 (1933); Larry v. Taylor, 227 Ala. 90, 149 So. 104 (1933); Sloss-Sheffield Steel & Iron Co. v. Foote, 231 Ala. 275, 164 So. 379 (1935); Ex parte Johnston, 231 Ala. 458, 165 So. 108 (1935); Sloss-Sheffield Steel & Iron Co. v. Wilkes, 236 Ala. 173, 181 So. 276 (1938); Howard Odorless Cleaners, Inc. v. Blevins, 237 Ala. 210, 186 So. 141 (1939); Tombrello Coal Co. v. Fortenberry, 248 Ala. 640, 29 So. 2d 125 (1947); Ingalls Shipbuilding Corp. v. Cahela, 251 Ala. 163, 36 So. 2d 513 (1948); Wade & Richey v. Oglesby, 251 Ala. 356, 37 So. 2d 596 (1948); Morris v. Dickson, 252 Ala. 588, 42 So. 2d 337 (1949); Bennett v. Walsh Stevedoring Co., 253 Ala. 685, 46 So. 2d 834 (1950); United Serv. Ins. Co. v. Donaldson, 254 Ala. 204, 48 So. 2d 3 (1950); Bass v. Cowikee Mills, 259 Ala. 391, 67 So. 2d 12 (1953); Lucas v. Black Diamond Coal Mining Co., 262 Ala. 368, 79 So. 2d 26 (1955); Goodyear Tire & Rubber Co. v. Downey, 266 Ala. 344, 96 So. 2d 278 (1957); Sam's Place v. Middleton, 41 Ala. App. 13, 122 So. 2d 924 (1959), aff'd, 271 Ala. 226, 122 So. 2d 925 (1960); Liberty Mut. Ins. Co. v. Manasco, 271 Ala. 124, 123 So. 2d 527 (1960); City of Jasper v. Sherer, 273 Ala. 356, 141 So. 2d 202 (1962); Horton v. DeLoach, 276 Ala. 357, 162 So. 2d 453 (1964); Ex parte Woodward Iron Co., 277 Ala. 133, 167 So. 2d 702 (1964); Hale v. United States Fid. & Guar. Co., 45 Ala. App. 379, 231 So. 2d 156 (1970); Jack Cole Co. v. Crawford, 285 Ala. 440, 233 So. 2d 225 (1970); B.F. Goodrich Co. v. Martin, 47 Ala. App. 244, 253 So. 2d 37 (1971); Dale Motels, Inc. v. Crittenden, 50 Ala. App. 251, 278 So. 2d 370 (1973); Misco, Inc. v. Driver, 50 Ala. App. 256, 278 So. 2d 374 (1973); Unexcelled Mfg. Corp. v. Ragland, 52 Ala. App. 57, 289 So. 2d 626 (1974); Young v. City of Huntsville, 342 So. 2d 918 (Ala. Civ. App. 1976); Strickland v. National Gypsum Co., 348 So. 2d 496 (Ala. 1976); Lingo v. Dixie Veneer Co., 349 So. 2d 591 (Ala. Civ. App. 1977); Condry v. Jones Farm Equip. Co., 358 So. 2d 1030 (Ala. Civ. App. 1978); City of Enterprise v. Herring, 372 So. 2d 358 (Ala. Civ. App. 1979); Dover Mills, Inc. v. Garrett, 384 So. 2d 1127 (Ala. Civ. App. 1980); Dennis v. Gamble's, Inc., 389 So. 2d 142 (Ala. Civ. App. 1980); Smith v. Capps, 414 So. 2d 102 (Ala. Civ. App. 1982); Abercrombie v. Hunter's R & O Cafe, Inc., 414 So. 2d 124 (Ala.

Civ. App. 1982); Ward v. King, 415 So. 2d 1095 (Ala. Civ. App. 1982); Smith v. West Point-Pepperell, Inc., 431 So. 2d 1268 (Ala. Civ. App. 1983); Waldon v. Hartford Ins. Group, 435 So. 2d 1271 (Ala. 1983); Garvin v. Shewbart, 442 So. 2d 80 (Ala. 1983); Scott v. Harley Davidson Motor Co., 450 So. 2d 133 (Ala. Civ. App. 1984); Hurt v. Pullman, Inc., 764 F.2d 1443 (11th Cir. 1985); Wallace v. Springs Indus., Inc., 503 So. 2d 853 (Ala. Civ. App. 1987); Brooks v. Bobby Kitchens, Inc., 536 So. 2d 81 (Ala. Civ. App. 1988); Monroe v. West Point Pepperell, 545 So. 2d 785 (Ala. Civ. App. 1989); Clark Bros. Transp. v. Perry, 554 So. 2d 1056 (Ala. Civ. App. 1989); Mobile Water & Sewer Bd. v. Wilson, 555 So. 2d 1081 (Ala. Civ. App. 1989).

Collateral references. — 99 C.J.S., Workmen's Compensation, § 287, 100 C.J.S., Workmen's Compensation, §§ 488-580, 638-659. 101 C.J.S., Workmen's Compensation, §§ 947-963.

58 Am. Jur., Workmen's Compensation, § 396 et seq.

Workers' compensation: injuries incurred during labor activity. 61 ALR4th 196.

II. PLEADING.

A. In General.

Section establishes procedure and necessary averments. — This section specifically establishes the procedure and the necessary averments for the filing of a verified complaint under the Workmen's Compensation Act. Baggett v. Webb, 46 Ala. App. 666, 248 So. 2d 275 (1971).

Allegations of a complaint in a workmen's compensation case should be accorded a liberal construction leading to the resolution of all reasonable doubts in favor of the employee. Gilmore v. Rust Eng'r Co., 289 Ala. 46, 265 So. 2d 591 (1972).

And compliance with the technical rules as to pleading is not required in actions under the Workmen's Compensation Act. Ex parte National Pipe & Foundry Co., 213 Ala. 605, 105 So. 693 (1925); Sloss-Sheffield Steel & Iron Co. v. Watts, 236 Ala. 636, 184 So. 201 (1938).

In workmen's compensation cases technical accuracy as to pleading is not required where the complaint meets all substantial requirements and fully advises the defendant of the relief sought and the grounds upon which it was based. Gilmore v. Rust Eng'r Co., 45 Ala. App. 626, 235 So. 2d 673 (1970).

A complaint under the Workmen's Compensation Act is not a common-law action and is not required to meet common-law niceties or requirements of pleading. Baggett v. Webb, 46 Ala. App. 666, 248 So. 2d 275 (1971).

The workmen's compensation statutes create rights and remedies and procedure all their own, and it is for this reason that complaints in such cases are not subject to as rigorous a requirement with regard to specificity as they otherwise would be. Gilmore v. Rust Eng'r Co., 289 Ala. 46, 265 So. 2d 591 (1972).

In an effort to effectuate the humanitarian purposes of the compensation law the technical rules of pleading are not followed in workmen's compensation cases. Gilmore v. Rust Eng'r Co., 289 Ala. 46, 265 So. 2d 591 (1972).

But a complaint appropriate to right to recover under Workmen's Compensation Act is necessary to obtain benefits thereof. McDuff v. Kurn, 233 Ala. 619, 172 So. 886 (1937).

The complaint should conform to the Workmen's Compensation Act, or else set up a state of facts showing the inapplicability of same and bringing the case within the influence of the law upon which the complaint is grounded and upon which reliance is had for recovery. Steagall v. Sloss-Sheffield Steel & Iron Co., 205 Ala. 100, 87 So. 787 (1920); Kasulka v. Louisville & N.R.R., 213 Ala. 463, 105 So. 187 (1925); Bell v. Brooks, 270 Ala. 691, 121 So. 2d 911 (1960).

Complaint which did not conform to this section or state facts showing that the Workmen's Compensation Act did not apply to the case, and that State Employers' Liability Act (§ 25-6-1) applied was held demurrable (subject to motion to dismiss now). Kasulka v. Louisville & N.R.R., 213 Ala. 463, 105 So. 187 (1925).

The complaint should conform to this section or should state facts showing that it did not apply. Thompson Tractor Co. v. Cobb, 283 Ala. 100, 214 So. 2d 558 (1968).

Though not strictly an action seeking compensation in the usual sense, a cause of action which is one authorized by the Workmen's Compensation Act is subject to no more strict rules of pleading than that for injuries. Baggett v. Webb, 46 Ala. App. 666, 248 So. 2d 275 (1971).

This section covers situations where there is a disputed claim for compensation, and requires the filing of a verified complaint alleging certain facts as may be necessary to enable the court to determine what, if any, compensation the employee or, in case of a deceased employee, his dependents are entitled to. Read News Agency, Inc. v. Moman, 383 So. 2d 840 (Ala. Civ. App.), cert. denied, 383 So. 2d 847 (Ala. 1980).

And complaint must aver employer's notice or knowledge of injury. Sloss-Sheffield Steel & Iron Co. v. Watts, 236 Ala. 636, 184 So. 201 (1938).

Or it is subject to motion to dismiss. — In proceeding under Workmen's Compensation Act for death of plaintiff's decedent, complaint failing to allege any facts showing knowledge of defendant of the injury or notice to defendant, in accordance with this section is subject to motion to dismiss on that ground. Ex parte Little Cahaba Coal Co., 213 Ala. 596, 105 So. 648 (1925).

But the motion to dismiss may be waived. — Motion to dismiss to complaint because it failed to allege statutory notice held waived, where judgment and finding showed no ruling thereon. Dixie Coal Mining & Mfg. Co. v. Williams, 221 Ala. 331, 128 So. 799 (1930).

And overruling motion to dismiss for lack of notice of injury not prejudicial where evidence shows notice. — In proceeding under Workmen's Compensation Act for death of plaintiff's decedent, defendant was not prejudiced by error in overruling of motion to dismiss complaint for failure to allege defendant's knowledge or notice of injury, in view of supreme court Rule 45 (now covered by A.R.A.P., Rule 45) where evidence sufficiently showed due and legal notice. Ex parte Little Cahaba Coal Co., 213 Ala. 596, 105 So. 648 (1925).

This section does not require an ad damnum averment. Baggett v. Webb, 46 Ala. App. 666, 248 So. 2d 275 (1971).

Complaint may be amended. — In action under the Workmen's Compensation Act by the widow and children of a deceased employee, mistaken reference in complaint to employee as "plaintiff" instead of "plaintiffs' intestate" was amendable and not objectionable in view of the fact that the case throughout was tried upon the sole theory that the action was for the death of plaintiffs' intestate. Sloss-Sheffield Steel & Iron Co. v. Watts, 236 Ala. 636, 184 So. 201 (1938).

In proceeding under Workmen's Compensation Act, it was held that complaint as amended sufficiently complied with this section as to statement of nature and extent of injury, amendment going to proximate result of injury and the resulting compensation under the statute, and fact that amendment was not reverified not being sufficiently called to court's attention. Ex parte Nat'l Pipe & Foundry Co., 213 Ala. 605, 105 So. 693 (1925).

Even more than a year after accident. — Complaint erroneously setting up cause of action for injuries under Federal Employers' Liability Act may be amended more than a year after accident to present case under Workmen's Compensation Act, notwithstanding § 25-5-80. The section is a statute of limitation, and action begun within that limitation may be amended so long as the rules in regard to amendments are conformed to. Birmingham Belt R.R. v. Ellenburg, 215 Ala. 395, 111 So. 219 (1926).

Statement of conclusion is insufficient. — There was no allegation of fact in the complaint to negate the applicability of the workmen's compensation law. There was an averment as a conclusion that defendant did not come within that statute, but statement of a conclusion is not sufficient. Facts must be alleged. Thompson Tractor Co. v. Cobb, 283 Ala. 100, 214 So. 2d 558 (1968).

A complaint or a count thereof which shows on its face that an employee seeks to recover damages from his employer does not sufficiently show the inapplicability of the workmen's compensation law by only alleging that on the date of the injury to the employee, he was not directly being paid wages by the defendant. Facts should be alleged going to show why such a condition existed. Thompson Tractor Co. v. Cobb, 283 Ala. 100, 214 So. 2d 558 (1968).

Sufficiency of complaint not using "prolapse of rectum" or "hernia". — A plaintiff should not be permitted to allege, for example, an injury to a foot and prove loss of an eye, but in the instant case the employer was not prejudiced by the failure of plaintiff to use the words "prolapse of the rectum" or "hernia" in the complaint. The employer here did fully advise itself of the nature of plaintiff's injury prior to the trial. Semmes Nurseries, Inc. v. McVay, 279 Ala. 42, 181 So. 2d 331 (1965).

B. Plea or Answer and Variance.

Want of notice need not be specially pleaded. — See note under § 25-5-78.

Answer may admit allegations of complaint. — In complaint in compensation proceeding, allegations that workman had dependents not denied in answer, which merely denied defendant's knowledge of matter, held properly treated as confessed (now admitted). Fair Park Amusement Co. v. Kimbrough, 221 Ala. 488, 129 So. 275 (1930).

Defendant pleading res judicata, and filing no plea of general issue (answer generally denying the allegations of the complaint now) or other verified answer denying allegations of complaint, admitted allegations of fact therein. Lawrence v. United States Fid. & Guar. Co., 226 Ala. 161, 145 So. 577 (1933).

Question of variance not arising. — Where, though verified complaint of workmen's compensation claimant under this section alleged that notice was given as required by §§ 25-5-78 and 25-5-79, no evidence of such notice was offered, but employer's answer put in issue fact of its knowledge of the injury, the alternative requirement of this section, and the evidence and finding of fact were directed to that issue, no question of variance arose. American Radiator Co. v. Andino, 217 Ala. 424, 116 So. 121 (1928).

III. DETERMINATION, JUDGMENT AND SUBSEQUENT PROCEEDINGS.

Entry of determination is essential to reviewable judgment. — Under this section the act of entry of determination of judge in compensation case must be performed by its due enrollment "filed in writing with the clerk" before there is a determination that becomes a judgment, within meaning of § 25-5-81, reviewable by certiorari. Ex parte Louisville & N.R.R., 214 Ala. 489, 108 So. 379 (1926); Woodward Iron Co. v. Bradford, 206 Ala. 447, 90 So. 803 (1921); Ex parte Sloss-Sheffield Steel & Iron Co., 207 Ala. 219, 92 So. 458 (1922); Hearn v. United States Cast Iron Pipe & Foundry Co., 217 Ala. 352, 116 So. 365 (1928); Richardson Lumber Co. v. Pounders, 254 Ala. 285, 48 So. 2d 228 (1950).

This determination, like unto the verdict of a jury, is the warrant of authority for the clerk to enroll upon the minutes of the court a final judgment, and its filing with the clerk of the court is essential to the regularity of the proceedings. Under the rulings here, a judgment, though previously entered, does not become effective for the purpose of review until "determination" of the judge is filed with the clerk. Woodward Iron Co. v. Bradford, 206 Ala. 447, 90 So. 803 (1921); Ex parte Sloss-Sheffield Steel & Iron Co., 207 Ala. 219, 92 So. 458 (1922); Hearn v. United States Cast Iron Pipe & Foundry Co., 217 Ala. 352, 116 So. 365 (1928); Richardson Lumber Co. v. Pounders, 254 Ala. 285, 48 So. 2d 228 (1950).

And compensation can be awarded only after trial court makes a determination based on a sufficient finding of facts and conclusions of law that such an award is warranted. Gilmore v. Rust Eng'r Co., 45 Ala. App. 626, 235 So. 2d 673 (1970).

And omission of determination reversible error. — The court below failed to make the written determination required by this section. This omission of the written determination is reversible error. Sam's Place v. Middleton, 39 Ala. App. 481, 103 So. 2d 812 (1958).

It is duty of trial court to enter final judgment for one or the other of parties in case according to prevailing evidence. Indian Head Mills v. Ashworth, 215 Ala. 348, 110 So. 565 (1926).

And conditional or provisional judgment is properly set aside. — Judgment denying plaintiff compensation subject to consideration

of any evidence which plaintiff should introduce within 60 days from judgment date concerning disability, amounting merely to continuation of trial with provisional finding and judgment on uncompleted evidence, was properly set aside, and new trial granted upon plaintiff's motion. Indian Head Mills v. Ashworth, 215 Ala. 348, 110 So. 565 (1926).

Parties as well as court must see that judgment is moulded so as to preserve finality. — Under this and § 25-5-81, it is duty of parties as well as court to see that judgment is moulded so as to preserve its integrity and finality and limit subsequent proceedings to question of money awarded and applying it to needs of dependent. Central Iron & Coal Co. v. Coker, 217 Ala. 472, 116 So. 794 (1928).

Except for enforcement and collection of moneys recovered. — An award in compensation proceeding, which was entered under this section and not under § 25-5-56 is, under the terms of this section, final, except for enforcement and collection of moneys recovered. Sloss-Sheffield Steel & Iron Co. v. Lang, 213 Ala. 412, 104 So. 770 (1925).

Purpose of requirement for filing of a finding of fact and law with or in the judgment is clear when it is considered that the only method for review of the proceedings below is by writ of certiorari as provided by § 25-5-81. Such method of review would be worthless without the findings and conclusions of the trial court as to the facts and the law. Kearley v. Peterman Lumber Co., 46 Ala. App. 204, 239 So. 2d 776 (1970).

The required statement of law, facts and conclusions is necessary to make serviceable the review by certiorari which the statute provides. Calvert v. Funderburg, 284 Ala. 311, 224 So. 2d 664 (1969).

This section provides essentially that the judgment of the trial court in a workmen's compensation case shall contain a statement of the law applicable to the case, the facts as they relate to the law, and the resulting conclusion. The purpose of this section is to ensure sufficiently detailed findings so that the appellate court can determine whether the judgment is supported by the facts. Substantial compliance with this section will suffice. Elbert Greeson Hosiery Mills, Inc. v. Ivey, 472 So. 2d 1049 (Ala. Civ. App. 1985).

It is helpful if a trial judge cites the applicable sections which control his decision as to whether to award or deny compensation and the amount, if awarded, but there is not any requirement that he do so. Wilson v. William Wilson Co., 537 So. 2d 930 (Ala. Civ. App. 1988).

A final judgment in a workmen's compensation case must contain a statement of

the law, the facts, and the conclusions as determined by the trial court, and the court was required to reverse this case since the judgment totally omitted a finding of facts as is mandated by this section. Morton v. Blue Bell, Inc., 540 So. 2d 79 (Ala. Civ. App. 1989).

What the employee contends is not a finding of fact. Pinkney v. James B. Clow & Sons, 277 Ala. 648, 173 So. 2d 811 (1965).

There must be a finding of every fact necessary to sustain the judgment of the court under this section. Bryant v. Central Foundry Co., 217 Ala. 332, 116 So. 345 (1928); Richardson Lumber Co. v. Pounders, 254 Ala. 285, 48 So. 2d 228 (1950); Alabama Textile Prods. Corp. v. Grantham, 263 Ala. 179, 82 So. 2d 204 (1955); West Point Mfg. Co. v. Bennett, 263 Ala. 571, 83 So. 2d 303 (1955); M.R. Thomason & Assocs. v. Jones, 48 Ala. App. 67, 261 So. 2d 899 (1972).

It is the duty of the trial court to make sufficiently detailed findings of fact so that the appellate court can determine whether the judgment or award is supported by the facts. If no findings are made by the lower court, it is impossible for the appellate court to say whether the judgment is supported by the findings or whether there is any evidence to support the findings. Richardson Lumber Co. v. Pounders, 254 Ala. 285, 48 So. 2d 228 (1950); Diamond Coal Co. v. White, 262 Ala. 112, 77 So. 2d 372 (1955); Reynolds v. Kirby, 273 Ala. 252, 139 So. 2d 341 (1962).

Statute contemplates, not a recital of the evidence, with its conflicting lights and tendencies, but a determination by the trial judge of the facts established by the evidence, responsive to the issues presented, with the conclusion as to whether the facts found established or failed to establish the liability asserted; and there should be a finding of every fact necessary to sustain the judgment of the court. Jackson v. Tennessee Coal, Iron & R.R., 259 Ala. 85, 65 So. 2d 167 (1953); Boatright v. Dothan Aviation Corp., 278 Ala. 142, 176 So. 2d 500 (1965); Calvert v. Funderburg, 284 Ala. 311, 224 So. 2d 664 (1969).

The finding of fact should include all the facts necessary to sustain a judgment except what is admitted in the answer. West Point Mfg. Co. v. Bennett, 263 Ala. 571, 83 So. 2d 303 (1955); Head v. Triangle Constr. Co., 274 Ala. 519, 150 So. 2d 389 (1963); Boatright v. Dothan Aviation Corp., 278 Ala. 142, 176 So. 2d 500 (1965).

The trial judge should make a finding of every fact necessary to sustain the judgment of the court. United Tel. & Tel. Co. v. Culiver, 271 Ala. 568, 126 So. 2d 119 (1961).

It is the duty of the trial court to make sufficiently detailed findings of fact so that the

appellate court can determine whether the judgment is supported by the facts. Fordham v. Southern Phenix Textiles, Inc., 387 So. 2d 204 (Ala. Civ. App.), cert. denied, 387 So. 2d 206 (Ala. 1980).

Since it is part of judicial duty of court. — The entry of the findings of fact and conclusions of law are a part of the judicial duty of the court. Alabama Hide & Tallow Co. v. Pincheon, 282 Ala. 404, 211 So. 2d 896 (1968).

And finding of fact must conform to the issue. — Trial judge's finding of fact in compensation case, required by this section, is similar to special finding of fact under Code 1940, Tit. 7, § 262 (now covered by A.R.C.P., Rule 52) in ordinary law action where trial is by court without jury, and if finding varies from issue in a substantial manner, it is a nullity and will not be aided by intendment nor by reference to extrinsic facts. Hearn v. United States Cast Iron Pipe & Foundry Co., 217 Ala. 352, 116 So. 365 (1928). See Bryant v. Central Foundry Co., 217 Ala. 332, 116 So. 345 (1928).

Section places on trial judge a duty to make findings responsive to the issue presented; and where this is not done, the case must be reversed whether the judgment is in favor of the defendant or the plaintiff. Pinkney v. James B. Clow & Sons, 277 Ala. 648, 173 So. 2d 811 (1965).

Such findings are conclusive. — Findings of fact and conclusions of the trial court prescribed by this section, unlike the finding in an ordinary action at law, are made conclusive as between the parties by § 25-5-81, subject to a limited review by certiorari. Hardisty v. Woodward Iron Co., 214 Ala. 256, 107 So. 837 (1926); Paramount Coal Co. v. Williams, 214 Ala. 394, 108 So. 7 (1926); Bryant v. Central Foundry Co., 217 Ala. 332, 116 So. 345 (1928); West Point Mfg. Co. v. Bennett, 263 Ala. 571, 83 So. 2d 303 (1955); Hinkle v. Schott Indus., Inc., 53 Ala. App. 412, 301 So. 2d 174 (1974).

And burden of proof is on plaintiff to show that his injuries were caused by an accident or accidents arising out of or in the course of his employment. Hinkle v. Schott Indus., Inc., 53 Ala. App. 412, 301 So. 2d 174 (1974).

The burden was upon the plaintiff to present evidence sufficient to reasonably satisfy the trial court (1) that she suffered a personal injury; (2) that such personal injury was caused by an accident; and (3) that the accident which caused the personal injury arose out of and in the course of her employment. And there should have been an express finding by the trial court that each of those facts was established by the evidence. Alabama Textile

Prods. Corp. v. Grantham, 263 Ala. 179, 82 So. 2d 204 (1955).

Statement as to what testimony did not show is not a ruling shifting burden of proof. — In proceedings under Workmen's Compensation Act, the statement by trial court, in setting out evidence on which findings were based, as to what expert testimony did not show, when considered with other testimony, was not a ruling that shifted burden of proof from plaintiff to defendant, but was in the nature of an assignment of a reason by the court in support of the finding. Ex parte Ala. Dry Dock & Shipbuilding Co., 213 Ala. 88, 104 So. 251 (1925).

Rule of res adjudicata applies. — Where pleadings in compensation action were broad enough to bring within issue extent of claimant's injuries and their probable duration, award of definite sum from which claimant did not appeal held to bar further action based upon same injuries, notwithstanding future compensation was erroneously expressly excluded in award which would have been ground for reversal on appeal. Ex parte Carlisle, 27 Ala. App. 142, 168 So. 598 (1936).

And judgment cannot be reopened because of changes in plaintiff's condition. — Under the Workmen's Compensation Act, after the court has determined the period of disability and fixed the compensation to be paid, the judgment cannot be reopened because of subsequent changes in the condition of plaintiff. Ford v. Crystal Laundry Co., 238 Ala. 187, 189 So. 730 (1939).

But court may set aside judgment and re-examine facts on timely application and for good cause. — The circuit court, in a proceeding under the Workmen's Compensation Act, has the power, on timely application and for good cause, to set aside the judgment and re-examine the facts. Birmingham Clay Prods. Co. v. White, 226 Ala. 89, 145 So. 668 (1933).

However, where employee was awarded compensation for temporary total disability in adversary proceedings by employee, circuit court could not, on employer's motion more than 18 months after final judgment, re-examine facts and redetermine degree of employee's disability, notwithstanding retention of case on docket for "further and necessary orders." Ex parte Johnston, 231 Ala. 458, 165 So. 108 (1935).

Mandamus lies to require a trial judge to vacate and annul an unauthorized order in a workmen's compensation case. Ex parte Woodward Iron Co., 277 Ala. 133, 167 So. 2d 702 (1964).

Substantial compliance with this section will suffice. Alabama Textile Prods. Corp. v. Grantham, 263 Ala. 179, 82 So. 2d 204 (1955); Calvert v. Funderburg, 284 Ala. 311, 224 So. 2d 664 (1969); Defense Ordinance Corp. v. England, 52 Ala. App. 565, 295 So. 2d 419 (1974); Republic Steel Corp. v. Kimbrell, 370 So. 2d 294 (Ala. Civ. App.), cert. denied, 370 So. 2d 297 (Ala. 1979); Fordham v. Southern Phenix Textiles, Inc., 387 So. 2d 204 (Ala. Civ. App.), cert. denied, 387 So. 2d 206 (Ala. 1980); Dees v. Daleville Florist, 408 So. 2d 155 (Ala. Civ. App. 1981); Littleton v. Gold Kist, Inc., 480 So. 2d 1236 (Ala. Civ. App. 1985); American Auto. Ins. Co. v. Hinote, 498 So. 2d 848 (Ala. Civ. App. 1986); Bradley v. Nelson, 507 So. 2d 958 (Ala. Civ. App. 1987); Jackson v. Weaver, 516 So. 2d 702 (Ala. Civ. App. 1987).

Where it has been stated that the case is a workmen's compensation case, that plaintiff's injury is compensable under said law, and a determination of the amounts due to be paid for the injury has been made pursuant to said law, a substantial compliance with that portion of this section requiring the trial judge to file a statement of the law has been made. Henderson v. Johnson, 49 Ala. App. 191, 269 So. 2d 905 (1972).

Where a review of the record clearly indicates substantial compliance with this section, there is no reversible error. Dees v. Daleville Florist, 408 So. 2d 155 (Ala. Civ. App. 1981).

This section "provides essentially that the judgment of the trial court shall contain a statement of the law applicable to the case, the facts as they relate to the law, and the resulting conclusions. Substantial compliance with this section will suffice." B.F. Goodrich Co. v. Skelton, 473 So. 2d 539 (Ala. Civ. App. 1985).

While the court of civil appeals has reversed workmen's compensation decisions in which the trial court's findings of fact were completely unresponsive to the issues, the court has also held that substantial compliance with this section will suffice. Benefield v. Goodwill Indus., 473 So. 2d 505 (Ala. Civ. App. 1985).

The learned trial judge in this case rendered a six and one-half page "Findings of Fact, Conclusions of Law and Final Judgment"; at a minimum, this document substantially complies with the requirements of this section and would not be grounds for reversal. City of Mobil v. Benson, 521 So. 2d 992 (Ala. Civ. App. 1988).

Where the court did misstate the name of the physician who gave testimony at trial, but did not misstate the substance of that testimony, such error was not so "unresponsive to the issues" as to warrant reversal. McGough v. Arvin Indus., Inc., 569 So. 2d 410 (Ala. Civ. App. 1990).

This section mandates only substantial compliance with its requirements. Terry v. Webb

Div. Marmon Indus., Inc., 582 So. 2d 558 (Ala. Civ. App. 1991).

But where trial court completely fails to comply case will be reversed. — Where the trial court completely fails to comply with the provisions of this section, the judgment of the trial court will be reversed by the appellate court. Alabama Textile Prods. Corp. v. Grantham, 263 Ala. 179, 82 So. 2d 204 (1955); Calvert v. Funderburg, 284 Ala. 311, 224 So. 2d 664 (1969); Defense Ordinance Corp. v. England, 52 Ala. App. 565, 295 So. 2d 419 (1974).

Case must be reversed in absence of "finding of facts". Where the trial court in a workmen's compensation case does not make a "finding of facts" in accordance with the requirements of this section, the case must be reversed no matter whether the judgment is in favor of the defendant or employee. Bass v. Cowikee Mills, 257 Ala. 280, 58 So. 2d 589 (1952); Diamond Coal Co. v. White, 262 Ala. 112, 77 So. 2d 372 (1955).

Findings of fact and conclusions of law are required to be entered with the judgment entry. The failure of the trial court to make and enter these findings must result in a reversal of the case. Alabama Hide & Tallow Co. v. Pincheon, 282 Ala. 404, 211 So. 2d 896 (1968).

Omission to file a statement of law and facts as required by this section can cause a reversal. Leach Mfg. Co. v. Puckett, 284 Ala. 209, 224 So. 2d 242 (1969).

If a judgment entered in a workmen's compensation case does not contain a finding of fact and law and the conclusion of the court, the matter must be reversed. It matters not whether the judgment is in favor of the employer or employee. Kearley v. Peterman Lumber Co., 46 Ala. App. 204, 239 So. 2d 776 (1970).

When the trial court completely fails to comply with the provisions of this section, the judgment of the trial court will be reversed. Dale Motels, Inc. v. Crittenden, 49 Ala. App. 51, 268 So. 2d 834 (1972); Henderson v. Johnson, 49 Ala. App. 191, 269 So. 2d 905 (1972).

Complete failure to abide by this section requires a reversal of the case. Avondale Mills, Inc. v. Tollison, 52 Ala. App. 52, 289 So. 2d 621 (1974).

Standard for review. — On certiorari to review judgments in workmen's compensation cases, the court of civil appeals does not look to the weight of the evidence as to any fact found by the trial court, but looks to see if there is any evidence to support the facts which the trial court found. Mobile Paint Mfg. Co. v. Crowley, 56 Ala. App. 673, 325 So. 2d 182 (1975).

This section provides essentially that the judgment of the trial court shall contain a statement of the law applicable to the case, the facts as they relate to the law and the resulting conclusions. Republic Steel Corp. v. Kimbrell, 370 So. 2d 294 (Ala. Civ. App.), cert. denied, 370 So. 2d 297 (Ala. 1979); Dees v. Daleville Florist, 408 So. 2d 155 (Ala. Civ. App. 1981).

Court must make findings of fact and conclusions of law. — This section requires a judgment in a workmen's compensation case to contain findings of fact and conclusions of law. Littleton v. Gold Kist, Inc., 480 So. 2d 1236 (Ala. Civ. App. 1985).

When the trial court's findings are merely meager or omissive, the court of Civil Appeals will look to the evidence to see if the trial court's judgment can be sustained. Littleton v. Gold Kist, Inc., 480 So. 2d 1236 (Ala. Civ. App. 1985).

No requirement that decree must expressly state relevant provisions of act upon which recovery is granted. Republic Steel Corp. v. Kimbrell, 370 So. 2d 294 (Ala. Civ. App.), cert. denied, 370 So. 2d 297 (Ala. 1979).

Analogous to special findings. — The findings of facts and conclusions prescribed by this section in cases under the Workmen's Compensation Act have an analogy in the special findings of fact under Code 1940, Tit. 7, § 262 (now covered by A.R.C.P., Rule 52). Richardson Lumber Co. v. Pounders, 254 Ala. 285, 48 So. 2d 228 (1950).

Objection to finding of fact by trial court in compensation case on the ground of its insufficiency may be presented to the trial court for correction. Bass v. Cowikee Mills, 257 Ala. 280, 58 So. 2d 589 (1952).

Insufficient "finding of fact". — Order of trial court in compensation proceedings that "plaintiff is not entitled to compensation under the facts of the case" was not a "finding of facts" as required by this section. Bass v. Cowikee Mills, 257 Ala. 280, 58 So. 2d 589 (1952).

"Interlocutory decree". — Although the trial court's judgment was styled as an "interlocutory decree", which is by definition not a final judgment, the test of a judgment's finality is whether it sufficiently ascertains and declares the rights of the parties; the "interlocutory decree" entered by the trial court contained the findings necessary to support an appeal without undue hardship to the employer; moreover, the fact that the trial court retained jurisdiction over the award of temporary disability did not bar such an appeal. Ex parte DCH Regional Medical Ctr., 571 So. 2d 1162 (Ala. Civ. App. 1990).

Appellate court may refer to record. — If the trial court's findings are merely meager or omissive, the appellate court may refer to the record to determine if the judgment should be upheld. American Auto. Ins. Co. v. Hinote, 498 So. 2d 848 (Ala. Civ. App. 1986); Bradley v. Nelson, 507 So. 2d 958 (Ala. Civ. App. 1987); Harbison Walker Refractories v. McKaig, 567 So. 2d 324 (Ala. Civ. App. 1990).

Remarriage and nondependency relieved employer from payments. — In garnishment proceeding filed by widow against her late husband's employer when the employer ceased making weekly workmen's compensation payments, finding that remarriage of employee's widow and nondependency of employee's children relieved employer from further payments of workmen's compensation benefits pursuant to judgment for installment payments was proper. Belcher v. Vulcan Materials Co., 359 So. 2d 383 (Ala. Civ. App. 1978).

Where the critical issue in the case was whether common-law marriage existed between plaintiff and the deceased employee, the trial court's factual finding that the plaintiff failed to meet the burden of proof "that she was the common law wife of the employee" was adequate under the statute to meet the issue made. Luther v. M & M Chem. Co., 475 So. 2d 191 (Ala. Civ. App. 1985).

Employer not bound to make payments until trial court decision. — Where there is a good faith dispute, the defendant employer is not bound to make compensation payments until the trial court has made its decision, and in appropriate cases where the requisite bond has been posted, that decision has been confirmed on the appellate level. Read News Agency, Inc. v. Moman, 383 So. 2d 840 (Ala. Civ. App.), cert. denied, 383 So. 2d 847 (Ala. 1980).

Order held not in compliance with requirements of this section, see Curry v. Interstate-Express, Inc., 582 So. 2d 565 (Ala. Civ. App. 1991).

§ 25-5-89. Proceedings for determination of disputed claims for compensation — Costs and fees.

Costs may be awarded by said court in its discretion, and, when so awarded, the same costs shall be allowed, taxed and collected as for like services and proceedings in civil cases, but if it shall appear that the employer, prior to the commencement of the action, made to the person or persons entitled thereto a written offer of compensation in specific terms, which terms were in accordance with the provisions of this article and Article 2 of this chapter, then no costs shall be awarded or taxed against such employer. (Acts 1919, No. 245, p. 206; Code 1923, § 7579; Code 1940, T. 26, § 305.)

In workmen's compensation cases, this section supersedes the seemingly mandatory cost taxing provision of ARCP Rule 68. Stated differently, the taxation of costs in a workmen's compensation case is within the discretion of the trial court even when the employee refuses an offer of judgment and later fails to obtain a judgment more favorable than the offer. Kaiser Aluminum & Chem. Sales, Inc. v. Crum, 402 So. 2d 995 (Ala. Civ. App.), cert. denied, 402 So. 2d 997 (Ala. 1981).

A provision requiring mandatory taxation of costs against an employee in a workmen's compensation action might in some instances deprive an injured employee of a large portion, if not all, of his compensation benefits and in some instances such a provision would place an injured employee in a position where he owes his employer money, namely when the amount of costs exceeds the amount of the award of benefits. In addition, a mandatory cost taxing provision would have a chilling effect on the pursuit of claims by injured employees and would tend to defeat the beneficent purposes of the Workmen's Compensation Act. Kaiser Aluminum & Chem. Sales, Inc. v. Crum, 402 So. 2d 995 (Ala. Civ. App.), cert. denied, 402 So. 2d 997 (Ala. 1981).

The assessment of costs is merely incidental to the judgment and may be done at any time prior to the issuance of execution. Littleton v. Gold Kist, Inc., 480 So. 2d 1236 (Ala. Civ. App. 1985).

Discretion of trial court. — Under this section and § 12-21-144, the taxing of costs in a case is within the discretion of the trial court, subject to the guideline of Rule 54(d), A.R.C.P. Littleton v. Gold Kist, Inc., 480 So. 2d 1236 (Ala. Civ. App. 1985).

Costs taxed against defendant. — In proceeding under Workmen's Compensation Act, provision in judgment awarding compensation that "defendants shall pay all costs of this proceeding" held proper. Ex parte Paramount Coal Co., 213 Ala. 281, 104 So. 753 (1925).

Cited in United States Steel Corp. v. Baker, 266 Ala. 538, 97 So. 2d 899 (1957); B.F. Goodrich Co. v. Campbell, 445 So. 2d 920 (Ala. Civ. App. 1984); Godwin v. Scott Paper Co., 571 So. 2d 1126 (Ala. Civ. App. 1990).

Collateral references. — 101 C.J.S., Workmen's Compensation, § 823.

58 Am. Jur., Workmen's Compensation, § 543.

Costs or expenses on appeal or review. 79 ALR 678.

§ 25-5-90. Proceedings for determination of disputed claims for compensation — Attorney's fees.

(a) Unless otherwise provided in this chapter, no part of the compensation payable under this article and Article 4 of this chapter shall be paid to an attorney for the plaintiff for legal services, unless upon the application of the plaintiff, the judge shall order or approve of the employment of an attorney by the plaintiff; and in such event, the judge, upon the hearing of the complaint for compensation, either by law or by settlement, shall fix the fee of the attorney for the plaintiff for his or her legal services and the manner of its payment, but the fee shall not exceed 15 percent of the compensation awarded or paid.

(b) All expenses of litigation and attorney's fees charged by any attorney in any representation under this chapter while representing any employer, insurance company, or self-insurer shall be reported to the Department of Industrial Relations. (Acts 1919, No. 245, p. 206; Code 1923, § 7542; Acts 1939, No. 661, p. 1036, § 1; Code 1940, T. 26, § 261; Acts 1949, No. 36, p. 47, § 1; Acts 1992, No. 92-537, § 30.)

The 1992 amendment, effective May 19, 1992, redesignated the former section as subsection (a), in subsection (a) added "Unless otherwise provided in this chapter" at the beginning of the subsection, inserted "and Article 4 of this chapter," substituted "an attorney" for "attorneys", substituted "the judge" for "to a judge of the circuit court, such judge," inserted "either by law or by settlement," inserted "or her," substituted "the fee" for "such fee," and added subsection (b). As to the implementation of this amendment, see the Code commissioner's note.

Code commissioner's note. — Section 53 of Acts 1992, No. 92-537 provides that the amendment to this section by § 30 of the act shall be implemented on August 1, 1992.

Constitutionality. — The fee-limitation provision of this section has been upheld against constitutional attack. Sokoll v. Humphrey, Lutz & Smith, 337 So. 2d 362 (Ala. Civ. App.), cert. denied, 337 So. 2d 365 (Ala. 1976).

Limitation of attorneys' fees in workmen's compensation cases has been upheld as a valid exercise of the police power by the United States Supreme Court. Sokoll v. Humphrey, Lutz & Smith, 337 So. 2d 362 (Ala. Civ. App.), cert. denied, 337 So. 2d 365 (Ala. 1976).

There is nothing to indicate § 25-5-83 should be read in connection with awarding of attorney's fees. Ashland Chem. Co. v. Watkins, 435 So. 2d 1301 (Ala. Civ. App. 1983), overruled on other grounds, Ex parte St. Regis Corp., 535 So. 2d 160 (Ala. 1988).

Manner of payment of attorney's fees within discretion of trial judge. — The most clear and reasonable construction of this section suggests that it is left to the sound discretion of the trial judge to direct the manner of payment of attorney's fees. Lawler Mobile Homes, Inc. v. Hinkle, 459 So. 2d 903 (Ala. Civ. App. 1984), overruled on other grounds, Ex parte St. Regis Corp., 535 So. 2d 160 (Ala. 1988).

A trial judge's determination of the manner of payment of attorney fees in workmen's compensation cases is discretionary by statute. Lawler Mobile Homes, Inc. v. Hinkle, 459 So. 2d 903 (Ala. Civ. App. 1984), overruled on other grounds, Ex parte St. Regis Corp., 535 So. 2d 160 (Ala. 1988).

In a workmen's compensation case, the manner of payment of the attorney's fees is left to the discretion of the trial court. Hardin's Bakery, Inc. v. Higgins, 480 So. 2d 1252 (Ala. Civ. App. 1985), overruled on other grounds,

Ex parte St. Regis Corp., 535 So. 2d 160 (Ala. 1988); Southern Prestressed Concrete, Inc. v. Thomas, 485 So. 2d 772 (Ala. Civ. App. 1986), overruled on other grounds, Ex parte St. Regis Corp., 535 So. 2d 160 (Ala. 1988).

The manner of payment of attorney's fees in a workmen's compensation case pursuant to this section is a matter within the discretion of the trial court. This discretion includes the determination of whether or not to award a lump sum attorney's fee. Lowe v. Walters, 491 So. 2d 962 (Ala. Civ. App. 1986).

Possibility of later change in compensation award does not affect fee award. — The fact that there is a possibility of a later change in the compensation award has no effect on the award of attorney's fees. The attorney has earned the fee regardless of subsequent changes. The computation of attorney's fees is based on the facts as to the attorney's services as of the time the services are rendered. Ashland Chem. Co. v. Watkins, 435 So. 2d 1301 (Ala. Civ. App. 1983), overruled on other grounds, Ex parte St. Regis Corp., 535 So. 2d 160 (Ala. 1988); Lawler Mobile Homes, Inc. v. Hinkle, 459 So. 2d 903 (Ala. Civ. App. 1984), overruled on other grounds, Ex parte St. Regis Corp., 535 So. 2d 160 (Ala. 1988).

Compensation of each attorney shall be based on compensation awarded his particular client. Pate v. Miller Transporters, Inc., 381 So. 2d 64 (Ala. Civ. App. 1979), aff'd, 381 So. 2d 68 (Ala. 1980).

This section mandates that 15 percent of the amount of recovery is the maximum fee which an attorney may receive in a workmen's compensation case where the fee is to be paid from the award. Sokoll v. Humphrey, Lutz & Smith, 337 So. 2d 362 (Ala. Civ. App.), cert. denied, 337 So. 2d 365 (Ala. 1976).

Litigation costs and expenses not included within 15 percent limit. — The legislature did not intend that cost and expenses of litigation should be included within the 15 percent maximum of fee for legal services. Sokoll v. Humphrey, Lutz & Smith, 380 So. 2d 845 (Ala. 1980).

The mandatory operation of this section renders ineffectual any contract between claimant and attorney as to fees. Sokoll v. Humphrey, Lutz & Smith, 337 So. 2d 362 (Ala. Civ. App.), cert. denied, 337 So. 2d 365 (Ala. 1976); Sokoll v. Humphrey, Lutz & Smith, 380 So. 2d 840 (Ala. Civ. App. 1979), aff'd in part and rev'd in part on other grounds, 380 So. 2d 845 (Ala. 1980).

That part of a contract between plaintiff and defendants which specified a 50 percent contingent fee arrangement was of no force and effect once plaintiff's claim was prosecuted under the Workmen's Compensation Act. Accordingly, the maximum fee to which defendants were entitled was 15 percent of plaintiff's recovery. Sokoll v. Humphrey, Lutz & Smith, 337 So. 2d 362 (Ala. Civ. App.), cert. denied, 337 So. 2d 365 (Ala. 1976).

Lump-sum award from back end of compensation benefits. — The trial court is permitted to order that attorney's fees be paid in a lump sum to be deducted by the employer from the back end of the compensation benefits. Ashland Chem. Co. v. Watkins, 435 So. 2d 1301 (Ala. Civ. App. 1983), overruled on other grounds, Ex parte St. Regis Corp., 535 So. 2d 160 (Ala. 1988).

The Workmen's Compensation Act allows for a lump-sum payment of attorney fees. Goodyear Tire & Rubber Co. v. Mitchell, 459 So. 2d 901 (Ala. Civ. App. 1984), overruled on other grounds, Ex parte St. Regis Corp., 535 So. 2d 160 (Ala. 1988).

This statute permitting lump sum attorney fees within the discretion of the trial judge applies to all workmen's compensation cases. Lawler Mobile Homes, Inc. v. Hinkle, 459 So. 2d 903 (Ala. Civ. App. 1984), overruled on other grounds, Ex parte St. Regis Corp., 535 So. 2d 160 (Ala. 1988).

Lump-sum attorney fee. — The trial court's discretion to order a lump sum payment of the attorney fee is but an exception to the employer's otherwise exclusive right to elect whether to pay the award in a lump sum. Thus, when the employer elects not to pay the full award of compensation in a lump sum, and the trial court orders a lump sum payment of the attorney fee (which represents up to 15 percent of the award), the provisions of this section providing for computation of present value are fully applicable to this part of the award. Ex parte St. Regis Corp., 535 So. 2d 160 (Ala. 1988).

Although former § 25-5-74 made no provision for the payment of attorneys' fees, the award of lump-sum attorneys' fees from the fund are allowed pursuant to this section, the general section relating to the award of lump-sum attorneys' fees in workers' compensation cases. Allen v. Brooks, 591 So. 2d 504 (Ala. Civ. App. 1991).

This section permits circuit courts to make discretionary lump-sum attorney fee awards in all workers' compensation cases. Allen v. Brooks, 591 So. 2d 504 (Ala. Civ. App. 1991).

Discretion to make lump-sum attorney fee award. — The trial court has the discretion to make a lump-sum attorney fee award to be paid from the Second Injury Trust Fund. Second Injury Trust Fund v. Stanton, 512 So. 2d 1377 (Ala. Civ. App. 1987), overruled on other grounds, Ex parte St. Regis Corp., 535 So. 2d 160 (Ala. 1988).

As to the method of computing lump sum attorney's fees, see Ex parte St. Regis Corp., 535 So. 2d 160 (Ala. 1988).

There is no requirement in statute that record contain competent evidence upon which court can make determination of a reasonable fee. Southern Prestressed Concrete, Inc. v. Thomas, 485 So. 2d 772 (Ala. Civ. App. 1986). But see Ex parte St. Regis Corp., 535 So. 2d 160 (Ala. 1988), holding that to the extent this case and others hold that it is not an abuse of discretion to award a lump sum attorney fee without reducing the payments to their present value, and that the employer does not have standing to appeal such an award, this case and the others are expressly overruled.

This section gives the trial court broad discretion in its award of attorney's fees, and there is no requirement that the record contain competent evidence upon which the court can make a determination of a reasonable fee; therefore, where the trial court awarded a 15 percent attorney's fee award, which was within the maximum allowed by statute, there was no abuse of the trial court's discretion. Merico, Inc. v. Sparks, 567 So. 2d 315 (Ala. Civ. App. 1990).

Computation of attorney's fees. — Any award of attorney's fees must be computed according to the following instructions: The periodic monthly payment award must be reduced to present value. Only then can attorney's fees be calculated. Next, the present value of the fees should be deducted from the present value of the aggregate of the payments. Once the present value of the compensation has been reduced by the fee award, the reduced amount of the compensation should then be used to calculate the amount of the weekly benefits to which the employee is entitled. Russell Coal Co. v. Williams, 550 So. 2d 1007 (Ala. Civ. App. 1989).

Discretion of trial court. — The trial court has the discretion to order a lump sum payment of the attorney's fee, and when the trial court orders such a payment of the attorney's fee, the provisions of § 25-5-83 providing for computation of present value are fully applicable to this part of the award. Ciba-Geigy Corp. v. Kelly, 579 So. 2d 662 (Ala. Civ. App. 1991).

Benefits must accurately reflect reduction for attorney's fees. — Where judgment did not state that worker's award of accrued weekly benefits was to be reduced by the amount of attorney's fees awarded relative thereto, the court's judgment was incorrect since the benefits awarded did not accurately reflect a reduction to account for payment of

attorney's fees. Russell Coal Co. v. Williams, 550 So. 2d 1007 (Ala. Civ. App. 1989).

Error regarding fee is matter between employee and his attorney. — Since the employer pays no portion of attorney fee but the employee must bear the whole fee out of compensation awarded, any error regarding the attorney's fee award is a matter for correction between the employee and his attorney. It is no basis for complaint on appeal by the employers. Topline Retreads of Decatur, Inc. v. Moore, 484 So. 2d 1090 (Ala. Civ. App. 1985).

No attorney fee for obtaining payment of medical expenses. — Nothing in this section or § 25-5-1(1) or the other workmen's compensation statutes provides for the assessment or payment of an attorney fee for obtaining the payment of medical and surgical expenses. Day v. Ramada Inn S., 527 So. 2d 130 (Ala. Civ. App. 1987).

Employer did not have standing appeal award to employee's attorney of 15 percent of total estimated compensation benefits, to be paid in a lump sum to be deducted by the employer from the back end of the compensation benefits. Topline Retreads of Decatur, Inc. v. Moore, 484 So. 2d 1090 (Ala. Civ. App. 1985).

Motion for relief where attorney not aware of lump sum fees. — Where attorney was unaware of a case that would have permitted him to recover his attorney fees in a lump sum, due to his own mistake and inadvertence, he failed to request that his fees be awarded in a lump sum. His motion thus shows grounds for relief under Rule 60(b)(1), and he may not seek relief under Rule 60(b)(6). Nor may he characterize his motion as a 60(b)(6) motion and thereby escape the four month time limitation of Rule 60(b)(1). Rebel Oil Co. v. Pike, 473 So. 2d 529 (Ala. Civ. App. 1985).

Court did not abuse discretion in failing to award lump sum. — The hard work that counsel for the employee put into the case in order to obtain a judgment of 100 percent disability did not indicate that the trial court abused its discretion in failing to award a lump sum attorney's fee. Lowe v. Walters, 491 So. 2d 962 (Ala. Civ. App. 1986).

Where it was clear from the stipulation of the parties that the employee was receiving maximum benefits prior to initiation of suit, the employee's lawyer was not entitled to any fee for the benefits received by the employee before the date of trial. Ex parte St. Regis Corp., 535 So. 2d 160 (Ala. 1988).

Credit for uncashed drafts. — Trial court did not err in calculating employee's attorney's fee on judgment which failed to give credit for amount of uncashed drafts, since whether the trial court ordered uncashed drafts returned to employee or ordered new payment based on correct average weekly wage calculation, money would have been a part of compensation awarded for purposes of award of attorney's fees pursuant to this section and either method involved an award of benefits by trial court. Lewis G. Reed & Sons v. Wimbley, 533 So. 2d 628 (Ala. Civ. App. 1988).

Cited in Lawrence v. United States Fid. & Guar. Co., 226 Ala. 161, 145 So. 577 (1933); Gulf States Steel Co. v. Christison, 228 Ala. 622, 154 So. 565 (1934); Frazer v. First Nat'l Bank, 235 Ala. 252, 178 So. 441 (1938); Shepard v. Chrysler Corp., 314 F. Supp. 1179 (N.D. Ala. 1969); Fruehauf Corp. v. Keenum, 466 So. 2d 137 (Ala. Civ. App. 1984); Middleton v. Dan River, Inc., 617 F. Supp. 1206 (M.D. Ala. 1985).

Collateral references. — 58 Am. Jur., Workmen's Compensation, § 544.

Compensation of attorneys for services in connection with claims. 159 ALR 912.

§ 25-5-91. Forwarding of copy of judgment, etc., to probate court; creation of judgment lien.

Whenever any decision or order is made and filed by the court upon any matter arising under this article, the clerk of the court shall forthwith make and forward to the judge of probate of the county in which the complaint was filed a certified copy of such decision or order with any memorandum of the judge and of any judgment entered. No fee or other charge shall be collected therefor. The plaintiff or owner of any judgment so certified may have the same registered by the probate judge upon the payment of the fee fixed by law for registering judgments, and the same shall become a lien in like manner as other registered judgments, unless the same is made a preferred lien by other provisions of some law. (Acts 1919, No. 245, p. 206; Code 1923, § 7580; Code 1940, T. 26, § 306.)

Employee's appearance not constructive filing of appeal. — Employees's contention that his appearance at the department's office within the time limit should be regarded as a constructive filing of his appeal within the statutorily mandated period of time was wrong, since he had received and signed several documents which clearly explained the time limits for appeal of the initial determination. Furthermore, the appeal time cannot be extended for good cause based upon equity as the procedure in the unemployment compensation law for appealing determinations is exclusive. Kirk v. Department of Indus. Relations, 521 So. 2d 1343 (Ala. Civ. App. 1988).

Cited in United States Steel Corp. v. Baker, 266 Ala. 538, 97 So. 2d 899 (1957).

§ 25-5-92. Discharge of lien upon judgment payable periodically.

When the judgment, however, is for a sum not due, that is, payable periodically, the defendant may discharge the registered lien by giving a bond for the payment of same to be approved by the probate judge and recorded, and he shall receive the same for registration. No execution shall issue where such judgment is payable periodically unless default is made in the payment of one or more of such periodical payments. (Acts 1919, No. 245, p. 206; Code 1923, § 7581; Code 1940, T. 26, § 307.)

Cited in United States Steel Corp. v. Baker, 266 Ala. 538, 97 So. 2d 899 (1957).

§ 25-5-93. Judgments discharged and marked satisfied upon proof of release or satisfaction of judgment.

Any judgment entered under the provisions of this article and Article 2 of this chapter, either by award or by settlement, and entered on the minutes of any court, shall be discharged by said court and marked satisfied upon presentment to said court or the clerk thereof of a release or discharge of said judgment, executed by the party in whose favor the same runs and acknowledged in the same manner as conveyances are acknowledged or upon presentment by the employer or his representative of an affidavit that said judgment has been, in accordance with its terms, fully satisfied and discharged, together with satisfactory proof in the way of vouchers or checks duly endorsed by the party in whose favor such judgment ran. (Acts 1919, No. 245, p. 206; Code 1923, § 7582; Code 1940, T. 26, § 308.)

This section applies only when payment is made direct to plaintiff, and not when payment is made to clerk of court. Hayes v. Waldrop, 214 Ala. 534, 108 So. 333 (1926).

Cited in United States Steel Corp. v. Baker, 266 Ala. 538, 97 So. 899 (1957); Topline Retreads of Decatur, Inc. v. Moore, 484 So. 2d 1090 (Ala. Civ. App. 1985).

Collateral references. — 101 C.J.S., Workmen's Compensation, § 844.

ARTICLE 4.

COMPENSATION FOR OCCUPATIONAL DISEASES.

Requirement as to proof of injury by accident. — One effect of this article is to remove the strict requirement of proof that the injury occurred by accident. City of Tuscaloosa v. Howard, 55 Ala. App. 701, 318 So. 2d 729 (1975).

Requirement as to proof of contraction of disease out of and in course of employment. — Proof of the contraction of an occupational disease does not remove the burden of proving that the contraction of the disease arose out of and in the course of employment and resulted from the nature of the employment. City of Tuscaloosa v. Howard, 55 Ala. App. 701, 318 So. 2d 729 (1975).

This article requires that there be evidence that plaintiff has a disease which may be directly caused by or result from exposure over a period of time to a hazard recognized as peculiar to the normal working conditions of his particular occupation. There must be further evidence that plaintiff's disease was in fact contracted from the nature of his employment or was aggravated thereby, and that the contraction or aggravation arose out of and in the course of his employment. It then must be shown that the disability claimed resulted from the disease. City of Tuscaloosa v. Howard, 55 Ala. App. 701, 318 So. 2d 729 (1975).

Claim against coemployee. — An occupational disease claim against a coemployee is to be treated by traditional tort standards. Wilkins v. West Point-Pepperell, Inc., 397 So. 2d 115 (Ala. 1981).

Arteriosclerosis as occupational disease of firemen. — See City of Tuscaloosa v. Howard, 55 Ala. App. 701, 318 So. 2d 729 (1975).

Cited in Dan River Mills, Inc. v. Foshee, 365 So. 2d 1232 (Ala. Civ. App. 1979).

Collateral references. — Excessiveness or adequacy of damages awarded for injuries causing particular diseases or conditions. 16 ALR4th 736.

Workers' compensation: Liability of successive employers for disease or condition allegedly attributable to successive employments. 34 ALR4th 958.

§ 25-5-110. Definitions.

For the purposes of this article, the following terms shall have the meanings respectively ascribed to them by this section:

(1) OCCUPATIONAL DISEASE. A disease arising out of and in the course of employment, including occupational pneumoconiosis and occupational exposure to radiation as defined in subdivisions (2) and (3), respectively, of this section, which is due to hazards in excess of those ordinarily incident to employment in general and is peculiar to the occupation in which the employee is engaged but without regard to negligence or fault, if any, of the employer. A disease, including, but not limited to, loss of hearing due to noise, shall be deemed an occupational disease only if caused by a hazard recognized as peculiar to a particular trade, process, occupation, or employment as a direct result of exposure, over a period of time, to the normal working conditions of the trade, process, occupation, or employment.

(2) OCCUPATIONAL PNEUMOCONIOSIS. A disease of the lungs caused by inhalation of minute particles of dust over a period of time, which dust is due to causes and conditions arising out of and in the course of the employment, without regard to whether the causes or conditions are inherent in the employment or can be eliminated or reduced by due care on the part of the employer. The term "occupational pneumoconiosis" shall include, but without limitation, such diseases as silicosis, siderosis, anthracosis, anthrasilicosis, anthracosilicosis, anthraco-tuberculosis, tuberculosilicosis, silico-tuberculosis, aluminosis, and other diseases of the lungs resulting from causes enumerated in this section.

(3) OCCUPATIONAL EXPOSURE TO RADIATION. Gradual exposure to radiation over a period of time from the use of or direct contact with radium, radioactive substances, roentgen rays (X-rays), or ionizing radiation, arising out of and in the course of the employment and resulting from the nature of the employment in which the employee is engaged, without regard to whether the exposure is inherent in the employment or can be eliminated or reduced by due care on the part of the employer.

(4) NATURE OF EMPLOYMENT. With respect to subdivisions (2) and (3) above, this term shall mean that, as to the industry in which the employee is engaged, there is attached a particular hazard of the exposure that distinguishes it from the usual run of occupations and is in excess of the hazards of the exposure attending employment in general.

(5) CONTRACTION OF AN OCCUPATIONAL DISEASE. This term shall include any aggravation of the disease without regard to the employment in which the disease was contracted. (Acts 1971, No. 668, p. 1379; Acts 1992, No. 92-537, § 32.)

The 1992 amendment, effective May 19, 1992, in subdivision (1), in the first sentence substituted "including" for "other than," and "subsection 2 and 3, respectively, of this section" for "articles 5 and 7, respectively, of this chapter," substituted "the trade" for "such trade" near the end of the second sentence, and deleted the former third sentence which read: "The term 'occupational disease' shall not include accidents within the meaning of articles 3, 5 and 7 of this chapter," added subdivisions (2) through (4), redesignated former subdivision (2) as subdivision (5), and in subdivision (5) substituted "This term" for "Such term," and "the disease" for "such disease."

Editor's note. — The cases annotated below were decided under prior law.

Disease means more than a temporary disorder, it denotes a serious disorder which has impaired the constitution or left in its wake some organic or chronic effect which has undermined the general health. Chrysler Corp. v. Henley, 400 So. 2d 412 (Ala. Civ. App. 1981).

Occupational disease. — In order for a disease to be occupational the plaintiff must be exposed by his or her employment to the risk causing the disease in a measurably greater degree and in a substantially different manner than are persons in employment generally. Young v. City of Huntsville, 342 So. 2d 918 (Ala. Civ. App. 1976), cert. denied, 342 So. 2d 924 (Ala. 1977); Chrysler Corp. v. Henley, 400 So. 2d 412 (Ala. Civ. App. 1981).

In order for a disease to be occupational it must be due to hazards which are (1) in excess of those ordinarily incident to employment in general and (2) different in character from those found in the general run of occupations. Young v. City of Huntsville, 342 So. 2d 918 (Ala. Civ. App. 1976), cert. denied, 342 So. 2d 924 (Ala. 1977).

In order for a disease to be occupational it must be due to hazards which are (1) in excess of those ordinarily incident to employment in general and (2) different in character from those found in the general run of occupations. To state the matter succinctly, the employee must be exposed by his or her employment to the risk causing the disease in a measurably greater degree and in a substantially different manner than are persons in employment generally. Dodson v. Atrax Div. of Wallace-Murray Corp., 437 So. 2d 1294 (Ala. Civ. App. 1983).

An occupational disease is one which is more than temporary, one which denotes a serious disorder which has impaired the constitution or left in its wake some organic or chronic effect which has undermined the employee's general health. Dodson v. Atrax Div. of Wallace-Murray Corp., 437 So. 2d 1294 (Ala. Civ. App. 1983).

It is axiomatic that an occupational disease is not compensable if it is not caused or aggravated by the nature of the employment. However, if there is evidence to support a trial court's findings that a plaintiff's employment caused respiratory problems, such findings must be upheld. Chrysler Corp. v. Henley, 400 So. 2d 412 (Ala. Civ. App. 1981).

Bronchitis and bronchial asthma are diseases within the meaning of this section.

Chrysler Corp. v. Henley, 400 So. 2d 412 (Ala. Civ. App. 1981).

The general definition of occupational disease contained in this section was not intended to apply to one worker employed on an assembly line who is exposed to an element or a condition not common to his fellow employees, which causes him to develop a common disease such as bronchitis. Chrysler Corp. v. Henley, 400 So. 2d 412 (Ala. Civ. App. 1981).

To be deemed "occupational," a disease must result from hazards recognized as peculiar to the normal working conditions of the employee's particular occupation. "Peculiar to the occupation" means that: the conditions of the employment must result in a hazard which distinguishes it in a character from the general run of occupations. Alatex, Inc. v. Couch, 449 So. 2d 1254 (Ala. Civ. App. 1984).

To fall within the definitional parameters of this section, a disease must be caused or aggravated by the nature of the employment. Alatex, Inc. v. Couch, 449 So. 2d 1254 (Ala. Civ. App. 1984).

In order for the employee to recover under the occupational disease or the occupational pneumoconiosis sections of the Workmen's Compensation Act, she must prove the disease arose out of and in the course of employment. Hall v. Teledyne Firth Sterling, 448 So. 2d 395 (Ala. Civ. App. 1984).

An "occupational disease" must be a serious disorder which has impaired the worker's constitution or left in its wake some organic or chronic effect which has undermined the general health. Stokes v. Atrax Div. of Wallace-Murray Corp., 466 So. 2d 967 (Ala. Civ. App. 1985).

Bronchitis and bronchial asthma are occupational diseases within the meaning of this section. Dodson v. Atrax Div. of Wallace-Murray Corp., 437 So. 2d 1294 (Ala. Civ. App. 1983).

"Sitting," as required of deputy sheriff in driving his motor vehicle, did not fit under requirements of an occupational disease, since there was no evidence that it was a hazard in excess of those ordinarily incidental to employment in general and different in character from those found in the general run of occupations. Elmore County v. Hornsby, 533 So. 2d 620 (Ala. Civ. App. 1988).

Hearing loss classified as occupational disease where employee worked large amount of overtime, in addition to regular work hours which increased the duration of the exposure and the extent of hearing loss; expert witness testified as to noise levels in the plant and the causation of the noise induced deafness in the employee by such excessive noise levels and expert testified that employee's earlier hearing loss would have stabilized at that time without further noxious stimuli. James River Corp. v. Mays, 572 So. 2d 469 (Ala. Civ. App. 1990).

Tenosynovitis. — Where sock seamer's job required repetitive hand movements such as pulling socks on tubes as they passed on a conveyor belt, where employee's rate of pay was based on production level, inducing her to rapidly repeat the movements peculiar to her job, and where there was no conflict in the testimony regarding the existence of tenosynovitis in employee's left wrist, evidence clearly supported trial court's finding that employee suffered a compensable occupational disease within the statutory meaning of the term. W.Y. Shugart & Son v. Cox, 578 So. 2d 1332 (Ala. Civ. App. 1990).

Lung ailment. — For a case in which a worker suffering from a lung ailment failed to establish that he suffered an occupational disease that was either contracted from or aggravated by the nature of his employment, see Terry v. Webb Div. Marmon Indus., Inc., 582 So. 2d 558 (Ala. Civ. App. 1991).

Error to award compensation for occupational pneumoconiosis. — Where, in a workman's compensation case, the trial judge expressly found that hazards in the plaintiff's work aggravated a lung disease resulting in disability to the plaintiff and since former § 25-5-140 et seq., is all comprehensive and exclusive (except as to coal mines) as to compensate for such diseases, or the aggravation of such diseases, so caused; and because this section expressly excludes occupational pneumoconiosis from the very definition of occupational disease, the trial judge was in error to award compensation to the plaintiff under this article. Dover Mills, Inc. v. Garrett, 384 So. 2d 1127 (Ala. Civ. App. 1980).

An occupational disease is not compensable if it is not caused or aggravated by the nature of the employment. Dodson v. Atrax Div. of Wallace-Murray Corp., 437 So. 2d 1294 (Ala. Civ. App. 1983); Hall v. Teledyne Firth Sterling, 448 So. 2d 395 (Ala. Civ. App. 1984); Taylor v. United States Steel Corp., 456 So. 2d 831 (Ala. Civ. App. 1984).

A preexisting disease does not affect an award of compensation if the job combined with the disease to produce an injury or death. Hightower v. Brammall, Inc., 435 So. 2d 1295 (Ala. Civ. App. 1982).

The fact that an employee had a preexisting disease does not affect an award of compensation if the job combined with the disease to produce injury or death. To recover benefits under this view, however, the claimant must prove aggravation or combination. It is axiomatic that an occupational disease is not compensable if it is not caused or aggravated by

the nature of the employment. Taylor v. United States Steel Corp., 456 So. 2d 831 (Ala. Civ. App. 1984).

Temporary allergic reaction to exposure to powdered metals. — Finding of the trial court that workers exposed to powdered metals (tungsten carbide) in the course of their employment suffered only a temporary allergic reaction, leaving no residual impairment, would be upheld under the evidence. Stokes v. Atrax Div. of Wallace-Murray Corp., 466 So. 2d 967 (Ala. Civ. App. 1985).

Award apportioned where employees changed theory of their case. — Trial court did not err by apportioning the amount of scheduled benefits to be awarded to employees where on appeal they asserted that each suffered an occupational hearing loss which was compensable under this section; at trial, the employees asserted their claims as ones for recovery from injuries sustained by accident, and since recovery for those types of scheduled losses is governed by § 25-5-57, the trial court specifically based its award on that provision; employee's argument on appeal that they suffered from an occupational disease, as opposed to sustaining accidental injuries, was an attempt to change their theory of the case after a decision had already been rendered. Parden v. City of Mobile, 570 So. 2d 1233 (Ala. Civ. App. 1990).

Cause of the disease of occupational pneumoconiosis is, by definition, the inhalation of minute particles of dust over a period of years. Nason v. Jones, 278 Ala. 532, 179 So. 2d 281 (1965).

Disease permanent. — Occupational pneumoconiosis not only is contracted over a long period of time but is permanent. Nason v. Jones, 278 Ala. 532, 179 So. 2d 281 (1965).

In order for the employee to recover under this article she must prove the disease arose out of and in the course of employment. Hall v. Teledyne Firth Sterling, 448 So. 2d 395 (Ala. Civ. App. 1984).

An occupational disease is not compensable if it is not caused or aggravated by the nature of the employment. Hall v. Teledyne Firth Sterling, 448 So. 2d 395 (Ala. Civ. App. 1984).

"Occupational pneumoconiosis," the subject of former §§ 25-5-140 through 25-5-152, does not refer to any single disease or finite set of diseases, but rather, encompasses the range of impairments caused by the inhalation of minute particles of dust over a period of time. Middleton v. Dan River, Inc., 617 F. Supp. 1206 (M.D. Ala. 1985), modified, 834 F.2d 903 (11th Cir. 1987).

Visualization of at least pinpoint nodules in X-rays of the chest is required before finding that a coal miner has contracted occupational pneumoconiosis. Colvert v. Alabama By-Products Corp., 115 F. Supp. 493 (N.D. Ala. 1953).

Error to award compensation for occupational pneumoconiosis under section 25-5-110. — Where, in a workman's compensation case, the trial judge expressly found that hazards in the plaintiff's work aggravated a lung disease resulting in disability to the plaintiff and since this article is all comprehensive and exclusive (except as to coal mines) as to compensate for such diseases, or the aggravation of such diseases, so caused; and because

§ 25-5-110 expressly excludes occupational pneumoconiosis from the very definition of occupational disease, the trial judge was in error to award compensation to the plaintiff under § 25-5-110, et seq. Dover Mills, Inc. v. Garrett, 384 So. 2d 1127 (Ala. Civ. App. 1980).

Cited in City of Tuscaloosa v. Howard, 55 Ala. App. 701, 318 So. 2d 729 (1975); Missildine v. Avondale Mills, Inc., 415 So. 2d 1040 (Ala. 1981); Hyster Co. v. Chandler, 461 So. 2d 828 (Ala. Civ. App. 1984); Fluker v. Sunnyland Foods, 469 So. 2d 586 (Ala. 1985); Middleton v. Dan River, Inc., 617 F. Supp. 1206 (M.D. Ala. 1985).

§ 25-5-111. Right to compensation for death or disablement.

Where the employer and employee are subject to this chapter, the disablement or death of an employee caused by the contraction of an occupational disease, as defined in Section 25-5-110, shall be treated as an injury by accident, and the employee or, in case of his death, his dependents shall be entitled to compensation as provided in this article. In no case, however, shall an employer be liable for compensation by reason of the contraction of an occupational disease, as defined in Section 25-5-110, or for disability or death resulting therefrom unless such disease arose out of and in the course of the employment and resulted from the nature of the employment in which the employee was engaged. (Acts 1971, No. 668, p. 1379.)

Editor's note. — The cases annotated below were decided under former § 25-5-141.

Hazard of disease attached to coal mining industry. — Once the court is reasonably satisfied that occupational pneumoconiosis has been contracted, it requires little evidence and less imagination to persuade that, as to the industry of mining coal underground, there is attached a particular hazard of such disease that distinguishes it from the usual run of occupations and is in excess of the hazards of such disease attending employment in general. Colvert v. Alabama By-Products Corp., 115 F. Supp. 493 (N.D. Ala. 1953).

When disease compensable. — The disease of occupational pneumoconiosis is compensable as an injury by accident under the workmen's compensation law only if (1) the disease arose out of and in the course of the employment; (2) the disease resulted from the nature of the employment in which the employee was engaged under such employment; (3) as to the industry in which the employee was engaged there was attached (a) a particular hazard of such disease, (b) the hazard attached to such employment was such as distinguished such employment from the usual run of occupations, and (c) the hazards of such disease in the employment in which the em-

ployee was engaged are in excess of the hazards of such disease attending employment in general. Nason v. Jones, 278 Ala. 532, 179 So. 2d 281 (1965).

This section sets forth two requirements for compensation for occupational pneumoconiosis or dust-induced disease. First, the employee must show that the industry in which he or she works presents a particular hazard of the disease in excess of what employment in general presents; this is the requirement of legal causation. Second, the employee must have a disease that arose out of and in the course of the employment; this is the requirement of medical causation. Middleton v. Dan River, Inc., 617 F. Supp. 1206 (M.D. Ala. 1985), modified, 834 F.2d 903 (11th Cir. 1987).

Lung disease caused by exposure to cotton dust is an occupational pneumoconiosis, compensable according to this section. Middleton v. Dan River, Inc., 617 F. Supp. 1206 (M.D. Ala. 1985), modified, 834 F.2d 903 (11th Cir. 1987).

Defenses. — In defense of the claim of the occupational disease, the defendant could assert, among other things, that plaintiff was not exposed, within a period of five years prior to the date of injury, to the hazards of such disease in each of at least 12 months; that as to the industry in which plaintiff was employed by defendant, there was not attached a particular hazard of such disease that distinguished it from the usual run of occupations and is in excess of the hazards of such disease attending employment in general; that plaintiff did not, in fact, have such disease. Nason v. Jones, 278 Ala. 532, 179 So. 2d 281 (1965).

Evidence supporting finding of unusual hazards. — The evidence supported the finding of the trial court that the plaintiff, who had been employed in a tin mill, had been exposed to the hazards of the disease of occupational pneumoconiosis that distinguished it from the usual run of occupations and was in excess of the hazards of such disease attending employment in general as required by this section. United States Steel Corp. v. Danner, 263 Ala. 310, 82 So. 2d 404 (1955).

Evidence sufficient to support finding of occupational pneumoconisis. — See Woodward Iron Co. v. King, 268 Ala. 680, 110 So. 2d 270 (1959).

Finding that employees exposed to agent causing byssinosis supported by evidence. — Where the district court found that the textile industry presents a hazard peculiar to the industry and that the plaintiffs had contracted a disabling form of byssinosis, and the district court also found that controversy exists regarding the exact part of cotton dust which causes byssinosis and therefore adopted a broader definition, a finding that is also supported by substantial record evidence, there was ample support for the district court's finding that the employees were exposed to an agent causing byssinosis. Middleton v. Dan River, Inc., 834 F.2d 903 (11th Cir. 1987).

Evidence sufficient to support finding of occupational pneumoconisis. Where employee testified that he had been exposed to asbestos throughout his employment with employer, the maintenance supervisor of employer's plant corroborated this testimony as to a significant portion of employee's employment and a physician specializing in pulmonary diseases testified on deposition that employee's lung disease was asbestos-related and stated the dangers of breathing asbestos fibers, this proof was sufficient to meet the requirements of this section. Reynolds Metals Co. v. Stults, 532 So. 2d 1035 (Ala. Civ. App. 1988).

Cited in City of Tuscalossa v. Howard, 55 Ala. App. 701, 318 So. 2d 729 (1975).

§ 25-5-112. Presumptions as to applicability and acceptance of provisions of article.

All contracts of employment made on or after September 1, 1971, shall be presumed to have been made with reference to and subject to the provisions of this article. All contracts of employment made prior to and existing on September 1, 1971, shall be presumed to continue from and after said date, subject to and under the provisions of this article. Every employer and every employee shall be presumed to have accepted and come under this article and the provisions thereof relating to the payment and acceptance of compensation. (Acts 1971, No. 668, p. 1379; Acts 1973, No. 1062, p. 1750, § 37.)

Collateral references. — 99 C.J.S., Workmen's Compensation, § 2. 101 C.J.S., Workmen's Compensation, § 519.

§ 25-5-113. Manner of compensation, etc., provided by article exclusive.

No employee of any employer subject to this article, nor the personal representative, surviving spouse or next of kin of any such employee shall have any right to any other method, form or amount of compensation or damages for the contraction of an occupational disease, as defined in this article, or for injury, disability, loss of service or death resulting from such disease, arising out of and in the course of employment, or determination thereof, in any manner other than as provided in this article. (Acts 1971, No. 668, p. 1379; Acts 1973, No. 1062, p. 1750, § 39.)

Cited in City of Tuscaloosa v. Howard, 55 Ala. App. 701, 318 So. 2d 729 (1975); Smith v. West Point-Pepperell, Inc., 431 So. 2d 1268 (Ala. Civ. App. 1983); Fluker v. Sunnyland Foods, 469 So. 2d 586 (Ala. 1985).

Collateral references. — 99 C.J.S., Workmen's Compensation, § 128.
Malpractice: right to maintain malpractice suit against injures employee's attending physician notwithstanding receipt of workmen's compensation award. 28 ALR3d 1066.

§ 25-5-114. Rights and remedies of employees, etc., under article exclusive; civil and criminal liability of employers, etc.

The rights and remedies granted in this article shall exclude all other rights and remedies of an employee, his personal representative, parent, surviving spouse, dependents or next of kin, at common law, by statute, contract or otherwise on account of the contraction of an occupational disease, as defined in this article, and on account of any injury, disability, loss of service or death resulting from an occupational disease, as defined in this article. Except as provided in this article, no employer included within the terms of this chapter and no officer, director, agent, servant or employee of such employer shall be held civilly liable for the contraction of an occupational disease, as defined in this article, or for injury, disability, loss of service or death of any employee due to an occupational disease while engaged in the service or business of the employer, the cause of which occupational disease originates in the employment; but nothing in this section shall be construed to relieve any person from criminal prosecution for failure or neglect to perform any duty imposed by law. The immunity from civil liability shall extend to any workers' compensation insurance carrier of such employer and to any officer, director, agent, servant or employee of such carrier, and such immunity shall further extend to any labor union, or any official or representative thereof, making a safety inspection for the benefit of the employer or the employees. (Acts 1971, No. 668, p. 1379; Acts 1975, 4th Ex. Sess., No. 86, p. 2729, § 17.)

Cited in Smith v. West Point-Pepperell, Inc., 431 So. 2d 1268 (Ala. Civ. App. 1983); Fluker v. Sunnyland Foods, 469 So. 2d 586 (Ala. 1985).

Collateral references. — 101 C.J.S., Workmen's Compensation, §§ 918, 931.

§ 25-5-115. False written representation to employer as to previous compensation for occupational disease.

If an employee, at the time of or in the course of entering into the employment of the employer by whom the compensation would otherwise be paid, wilfully and falsely represented himself in writing to such employer as not having previously been compensated in damages, or under this article, because of occupational disease, as defined in this article, such employee, his personal representative, parents, surviving spouse, dependents and next of kin shall be barred from compensation or other benefits provided by this article or from recovery at common law by statute, contract or otherwise on account of occupational disease as defined in this article, resulting from exposure to the hazards of such disease subsequent to such representation and while in the employ of such employer. (Acts 1971, No. 668, p. 1379.)

Section not applied beyond occupational disease to include injury due to accidents. — Court of appeals would not apply section beyond the limited situation of occupational disease to extend the bar from compensation to include injury due to accidents, where there was willful misrepresentation of the employee's physical condition. Builders Transp., Inc. v. Jochum, 585 So. 2d 52 (Ala. Civ. App. 1991).

§ 25-5-116. Which employer liable for compensation of employee; contribution.

(a) If compensation is payable for an occupational disease other than pneumoconiosis or radiation, the only employer liable, if any, shall be the employer in whose employment the employee was last exposed to the hazards of the disease. The employer who is liable shall not be entitled to contribution from any other employer of the employee except one who furnished workers' compensation for the employee during the employment of last exposure.

(b) If compensation is payable for pneumoconiosis or radiation, the only employer liable, if any, shall be the employer in whose employment the employee was last exposed in each of at least 12 months, within a period of five years prior to the date of the injury, to the hazards of the disease and, in addition, any employer who furnished workers' compensation coverage during this period. (Acts 1971, No. 668, p. 1379; Acts 1992, No. 92-537, § 33.)

The 1992 amendment, effective May 19, 1992, designated the former section as subsection (a), in subsection (a), in the first sentence substituted "If compensation is payable for an occupational disease other than pneumoconiosis or radiation" for "Where compensation is payable under this article," and "the disease" for "said disease," and in the second sentence substituted the language beginning "the employee except one who furnished" for "such employee," and added subsection (b).

Editor's note. — The cases annotated below were decided under prior law.

Apportioning loss between two employers not permitted. — In Alabama, there is no apportionment of benefits in an occupational disease case among multiple employers. James River Corp. v. Mays, 572 So. 2d 469 (Ala. Civ. App. 1990).

Trial court did not err by apportioning the amount of scheduled benefits to be awarded to employees where on appeal they asserted that each suffered an occupational hearing loss which was compensable under Section 25-5-110; at trial, the employees asserted their claims as ones for recovery from injuries sustained by accident, and since recovery for those types of scheduled losses is governed by Section 25-5-57, the trial court specifically based its award on that provision; employee's argument on appeal that they suffered from an occupational disease, as opposed to sustaining accidental injuries, was an attempt to change their theory of the case after a decision had already been rendered. Parden v. City of Mobile, 570 So. 2d 1233 (Ala. Civ. App. 1990).

Collateral references. — 101 C.J.S., Workmen's Compensation, § 982.

§ 25-5-117. Limitation period for claims or actions for compensation.

(a) In case of the contraction of an occupational disease, as defined in this article, or of injury or disability resulting therefrom, a claim for compensation, as defined in Section 25-5-1, shall be forever barred, unless within two years after the date of the injury, as hereinafter defined, the parties shall have agreed upon the compensation payable under this article, or unless within two years after the date of the injury, one of the parties shall have filed a verified complaint as provided in Section 25-5-88. In case of death, the claim shall be forever barred, unless within two years after death, if death results proximately from the occupational disease, as defined in this article, and death occurs within three years of the date of the injury, as hereinafter defined, the parties have agreed upon the compensation under this article, or unless within two years after death, one of the parties shall have filed a verified complaint as provided in Section 25-5-88. Notwithstanding the foregoing, if upon the date of death the employee's claim is barred, any claim by his or her dependents likewise shall be barred. If, however, payments of compensation have been made, the limitations as to compensation shall not take effect until the expiration of two years from the time of making the last payment. In case of physical or mental incapacity, other than the minority of the injured employee or his or her dependent, to perform or cause to be performed any act required within the time specified in this section, the period of limitation in any case shall be extended to become effective two years from the date when the incapacity ceases. No agreement, express or implied, to shorten or to extend the limitations shall be valid or binding on either of the parties if the employment, at the time of the exposure, is or was subject to this article.

(b) For the purposes of occupational diseases other than pneumoconiosis or radiation, "the date of the injury" shall mean the date of the last exposure to the hazards of the disease in the employment of the employer in whose employment the employee was last exposed to the hazards of the disease.

(c) For purposes of pneumoconiosis and radiation, "the date of the injury" shall mean the date of the last exposure to the hazards of the disease in the employment of the employer in whose employment the employee was last exposed to the hazards of the disease in each of at least 12 months, within a period of five years prior to the date of the injury. (Acts 1971, No. 668, p. 1379; Acts 1992, No. 92-537, § 34.)

The **1992 amendment,** effective May 19, 1992, rewrote and redesignated the former section as subsection (a), and added subsections (b) and (c).

Editor's note. — The cases annotated below were decided under former § 25-5-147 and prior law.

Statutory requirement that death must occur within three years of injury. — This section, provides in part that claims for benefits for death due to pneumoconiosis shall be

considered timely filed if brought within three years of the date of death. While it is true action was timely filed, the time of filing was not the basis for the trial court's ruling; the trial court properly dismissed the action because of the additional statutory requirement that the death must have occurred within three years of the date of the injury. See §§ 25-5-60 and 25-5-80. That is, the statute sets a three-year time limit for the employee to die after the occurrence of the injury as a condition precedent for having a cause of action under the Workmen's Compensation Act. Kilgore v. Alabama By-Prods. Corp., 581 So. 2d 872 (Ala. Civ. App. 1991) (decided under former § 25-5-178).

Sections 25-5-60 and 25-5-80, place a limit on the time that may elapse between the time of injury and the time of death for there to be a claim, whereas this section, places a limit on the time for filing a claim. Kilgore v. Alabama By-Prods. Corp., 581 So. 2d 872 (Ala. Civ. App. 1991) (decided under former § 25-5-178).

This section does not limit or even purport to limit the amount of compensation an injured employee may be entitled to receive from his employer to that portion of the disabling disease accruing in the period of one year next preceding the filing of the complaint and the date of last exposure to the hazards causing the disease. Chrysler Corp. v. Henley, 400 So. 2d 412 (Ala. Civ. App. 1981).

Sections were not amended and statute of limitations remains one year. — According to the mandates of Ala. Const., Art. IV, § 45, those parts of an original act of the legislature which are to be amended shall be re-enacted or published at length; although the legislature may have intended to amend the statute of limitations in all workmen's compensation cases to two years, it clearly did not follow the mandates of Ala. Const., Article IV, § 45, and since this section and former § 25-5-147 were not published in the amendatory bill, Act No. 85-41 did not amend this section nor former § 25-5-147, and the statute of limitations under these sections is still one year. Sims v. Union Underwear Co., 551 So. 2d 1078 (Ala. Civ. App. 1989).

There is no apportionment of benefits in a workmen's compensation case. Chrysler Corp. v. Henley, 400 So. 2d 412 (Ala. Civ. App. 1981).

Thus an employee seeking workmen's compensation benefits is entitled to all of the benefits permitted by law regardless of the date of filing of his claim within the statutory period. Chrysler Corp. v. Henley, 400 So. 2d 412 (Ala. Civ. App. 1981).

Trial court's judgment was conclusive even though it left the question of permanent disability open to further proceedings; since the statute provides a remedy for the employee if a permanent disability does result from the period of temporary total disability, the trial court's reservation of jurisdiction was mere surplusage. Ex parte DCH Regional Medical Ctr., 571 So. 2d 1162 (Ala. Civ. App. 1990).

Sick pay does not constitute payment of compensation or in lieu of compensation for purpose of tolling the statute of limita-

tions. Belser v. American Cast Iron Pipe Co., 356 So. 2d 659 (Ala. Civ. App. 1978).

Statute not tolled by incapacity of employee. — The one-year limitation period of this section barred recovery for an occupational disease notwithstanding the fact that the employee was prevented from filing the claim by virtue of confinement in a hospital. Geter v. United States Steel Corp., 264 Ala. 94, 84 So. 2d 770 (1956).

Former section 25-5-152 does not have the effect of adding to this section the provision of § 25-5-80 for an extension of the one-year limitation period in case of physical or mental incapacity, since the incapacity was apparently intentionally omitted from this section. Geter v. United States Steel Corp., 264 Ala. 94, 84 So. 2d 770 (1956).

And statute not tolled by plaintiff's discovery of disease after one year. — The fact that plaintiff did not discover that he was suffering from occupational pneumoconiosis until after the expiration of one year from the date of injury did not toll the running of the statute. Nason v. Jones, 278 Ala. 532, 179 So. 2d 281 (1965).

Nor by amended complaint adding new cause not relating back to commencement of original suit. — Where the original cause of action was for an injury due to the inhalation of carbon monoxide fumes during a period of several hours and amendments to the original complaint sought to recover for occupational pneumoconiosis, it was held that the amendments added a new cause of action, which did not relate back to the commencement of the action, and the statute of limitations was therefore not tolled. Nason v. Jones, 278 Ala. 532, 179 So. 2d 281 (1965).

Statute may be tolled by fraudulent concealment or false representation. — While, under this section, an employee must file a claim for compensation for occupational pneumoconiosis within one year of "the date of the last exposure to the hazards of the disease," there are two ways by which the running of the statute of limitations may be tolled: Fraudulent concealment and false representation. Middleton v. Dan River, 617 F. Supp. 1206 (M.D. Ala. 1985), modified, 834 F.2d 903 (11th Cir. 1987).

Statute tolled when employer misleads employee in postponing claim. — Running of the statute of limitations is tolled when the employer or its agent innocently or fraudulently misleads the claimant in the postponing of the filing of his or her claim, regardless of whether the employee relies upon actual fraud or mere estoppel. Middleton v. Dan River, Inc., 834 F.2d 903 (11th Cir. 1987).

To establish fraudulent concealment, an

employee must prove four facts: (1) That the employer knew or should have known that the employee was suffering from a disease or infirm condition; (2) That the employer knew or should have known that the employee did not know of this disease or condition; (3) That the employee did not have reason to understand either the nature and gravity of the condition or its relation to the employment; and (4) That the employer failed to disclose to the employee the nature and extent of the employee's condition. Middleton v. Dan River, Inc., 617 F. Supp. 1206 (M.D. Ala. 1985), modified, 834 F.2d 903 (11th Cir. 1987).

False representation is an issue of whether the employer is "primarily responsible" for the employee's delay in filing the claim. The employer must commit an overt act that lulls the employee into inaction. Middleton v. Dan River, Inc., 617 F. Supp. 1206 (M.D. Ala. 1985), modified, 834 F.2d 903 (11th Cir. 1987).

More than a confused and uninformed suspicion of disease on employee's part is required to warrant barring a claim. Middleton v. Dan River, Inc., 617 F. Supp. 1206 (M.D. Ala. 1985), modified, 834 F.2d 903 (11th Cir. 1987).

Employer's conduct warranted tolling of the limitation of this section, where employer knew or should have known that exposure to cotton dust could cause permanent lung disease, and operated a medical department, and thus had a duty to disclose or have its medical department disclose a condition which its medical staff had determined to exist or which the staff in exercise of reasonable care should have diagnosed, and where in view of cotton workers' circumstances, including their education, they did not have reason to understand the nature and gravity of their condition and its relationship to their employment. Middleton v. Dan River, Inc., 617 F. Supp. 1206 (M.D. Ala. 1985), modified, 834 F.2d 903 (11th Cir. 1987).

Employer held to have knowledge of employee's condition. — Where, in determining whether the statute of limitations was tolled because of the employer's misrepresentation, the district court found that there is a chronic form of byssinosis and the employer had sufficient indicators that the plaintiffs were suffering from such a disease, there was sufficient consistent evidence to support a finding that the employer knew or should have known of the plaintiff's condition. Middleton v. Dan River, Inc., 834 F.2d 903 (11th Cir. 1987).

Sending of medical reports to physician held not to disclose employees' condition. — In determining whether the statute of limitations was tolled because of the em-

ployer's misrepresentation, the employer's sending of the employees' medical reports to their personal physician did not disclose to the employees the nature and extent of their condition, where the personal physician was expressly told that the employees did not have the one disease that could be attributed to cotton dust exposure, there was nothing whatsoever in the employer's transmittal letters to alert personal physician that he even needed to read the reports, much less challenge their ultimate conclusions, and even assuming that the reports themselves were disclosures of the employees' conditions, the district court had sufficient reason to find that the personal physician was not acting as the employees' representative for the purpose of disclosure. Middleton v. Dan River, Inc., 834 F.2d 903 (11th Cir. 1987).

Employer held not to have knowledge of condition of employee who falsely answered questionnaire. — Where the employee testified that she answered the employer's questionnaire falsely because she feared the company would fire her if it appeared she had byssinosis, and her pulmonary function test scores were normal enough that she was not referred to the physician, it could not be said that the employer knew or should have known that she had byssinosis, and her claim that the statute of limitations should have been equitably tolled based on fraudulent concealment failed. Middleton v. Dan River, Inc., 834 F.2d 903 (11th Cir. 1987).

Claim held timely. — Where employee's last day of work was October 26, 1982, and he filed his claim on October 26, 1983, his claim was not time barred, even though employer offered evidence that production in the card room where employee worked stopped on October 21, 1982, as even if this was true, this did not mean that employee's exposure to cotton dust stopped on that day. Middleton v. Dan River, Inc., 617 F. Supp. 1206 (M.D. Ala. 1985), modified, 834 F.2d 903 (11th Cir. 1987).

Employer held liable for full extent of employee's disability.'— Where the date of employee's injury, under this section, was when she was last exposed to cotton dust, her last day of work in 1982, and there was no evidence before the court that her heart or brain disease had an apparent physical effect on her ability to work at that time, her employer was liable for the full extent of her disability. Middleton v. Dan River, Inc., 617 F. Supp. 1206 (M.D. Ala. 1985), modified, 834 F.2d 903 (11th Cir. 1987).

Cited in Garren v. Commercial Union Ins. Co., 340 So. 2d 764 (Ala. 1976); Garrett v. Raytheon Co., 368 So. 2d 516 (Ala. 1979); Smith v. West Point-Pepperell, Inc., 431 So. 2d

1268 (Ala. Civ. App. 1983); Russell Coal Co. v. Williams, 550 So. 2d 1007 (Ala. Civ. App. 1989).

Collateral references. — 101 C.J.S., Workmen's Compensation, § 844.

When limitation period begins to run against claim under workmen's compensation or occupational diseases act for contracting of disease. 11 ALR2d 297.

When statute of limitations begins to run as to cause of action for development of latent industrial or occupational disease. 1 ALR4th 117.

§ 25-5-118. Rights and remedies as to exposures to hazards of occupational disease occurring prior to September 1, 1971.

All exposures of the employee occurring prior to September 1, 1971, to the hazards of an occupational disease, as defined in this article, while in the employ of the employer, shall be deemed for all purposes to be subject to the provisions of this article, and the employee, his personal representative, parents, surviving spouse, dependents and next of kin shall be entitled to compensation or other benefits and barred from other rights and remedies as provided in this article for exposures occurring after September 1, 1971. (Acts 1971, No. 668, p. 1379; Acts 1973, No. 1062, p. 1750, § 41.)

§ 25-5-119. Computation of compensation and benefits payable under article.

The compensation payable for death or disability caused by an occupational disease, as defined in this article, shall be computed in the same manner and in the same amounts as provided in Article 3 of this chapter for computing compensation for disability or death resulting from an accident arising out of and in the course of the employment and the medical, surgical, hospital and burial benefits payable under this article caused by said disease shall be computed in the same manner and in the same amounts as provided in Article 3 of this chapter for computing like benefits. The date of injury, as defined in Section 25-5-117, shall be considered the date of the accident for determining the applicable medical, surgical and hospital benefits, the minimum and maximum weekly benefits and the limitation on the total amount of compensation payable for such occupational disease. (Acts 1971, No. 668, p. 1379; Acts 1975, 4th Ex. Sess., No. 86, p. 2729, § 18.)

§ 25-5-120. Presumptions and burden of proof as to right to compensation.

There shall not be a presumption that disablement or death from any cause or infirmity is the result of an occupational disease, nor that an occupational disease will result in disablement or death, and any person claiming compensation or other benefits under this article shall have the burden of establishing that he or she is entitled to the benefits. (Acts 1971, No. 668, p. 1379; Acts 1992, No. 92-537, § 35.)

The 1992 amendment, effective May 19, 1992, substituted "not be a presumption" for "be no presumption," inserted "or she," and substituted "the benefits" for "such."

Collateral references. — Admissibility of opinion evidence as to employability on the issue of disability in insurance and workmen's compensation cases. 89 ALR3d 783.

§ 25-5-121. Settlements between parties; determination of disputed compensation claims.

The interested parties shall have the right to settle all matters of compensation and all questions arising hereunder between themselves in accordance with and subject to the provisions of Article 3 of this chapter, and, in case of a dispute, either party may submit the controversy to the circuit court in accordance with and subject to the provisions of Article 3 of this chapter. (Acts 1971, No. 668, p. 1379.)

§ 25-5-122. Applicability of article.

The provisions of this article shall apply to all cases of occupational disease, as defined in this article, or injury, disability or death therefrom, in which the last exposure to hazards of such disease occurred after September 1, 1971, except as otherwise provided in this article. (Acts 1971, No. 668, p. 1379.)

§ 25-5-123. Applicability of other provisions of chapter to article.

All of the provisions of Articles 1, 2, 3 and 8 of this chapter, except Section 25-5-78, shall be applicable to this article, unless otherwise provided or inconsistent herewith. (Acts 1971, No. 668, p. 1379; Acts 1975, 4th Ex. Sess., No. 86, p. 2729, § 19.)

Cited in Fluker v. Sunnyland Foods, 469 So. 2d 586 (Ala. 1985).

ARTICLE 5.

COMPENSATION FOR OCCUPATIONAL PNEUMOCONIOSIS GENERALLY.

§§ 25-5-140 through 25-5-152. Repealed by Acts 1992, No. 92-537, § 51, effective May 19, 1992.

ARTICLE 6.

COMPENSATION FOR PNEUMOCONIOSIS OF COAL MINERS.

§§ 25-5-170 through 25-5-180. Repealed by Acts 1992, No. 92-537, § 51, effective May 19, 1992.

ARTICLE 7.

COMPENSATION FOR OCCUPATIONAL EXPOSURE TO RADIATION.

Cross references. — As to radiation generally, see § 22-14-1 et seq.

Collateral references. — Excessiveness or adequacy of damages awarded for injuries causing particular diseases or conditions. 16 ALR4th 736.

§ 25-5-190. Definitions.

For the purposes of this article, the following terms shall have the meanings respectively ascribed to them by this section:

(1) OCCUPATIONAL EXPOSURE TO RADIATION. Gradual exposure to radiation over a period of time from the use of or direct contact with radium, radioactive substances, roentgen rays (X rays) or ionizing radiation, arising out of and in the course of the employment and resulting from the nature of the employment in which the employee is engaged, without regard to whether or not said exposure is inherent in the employment or can be eliminated or reduced by due care on the part of the employer. The term "occupational exposure to radiation" shall not include accidents involving sudden and violent injuries within the meaning of subdivision (9) of Section 25-5-1, such accidents being covered by such section.

(2) NATURE OF EMPLOYMENT. Such term shall mean that, as to the industry in which the employee is engaged, there is attached a particular hazard of such exposure that distinguishes it from the usual run of occupations and is in excess of the hazards of such exposure attending employment in general. (Acts 1967, No. 521, p. 1245.)

Collateral references. — Tort liability for nonmedical radiological harm. 73 ALR4th 582.

§ 25-5-191. Right to compensation for injury or death.

Where the employer and employee are subject to the provisions of this chapter, the disablement or death of an employee caused by occupational exposure to radiation, as defined in this article, shall be treated as an injury by accident, and the employee or, in case of his death, his dependents shall be entitled to compensation as provided in this article. In no case, however, shall an employer be liable under this article for compensation by reason of exposure to radiation or for disability or death resulting therefrom unless such exposure arose out of and in the course of the employment and resulted from the nature of the employment in which the employee was engaged. (Acts 1967, No. 521, p. 1245.)

§ 25-5-192. Presumptions as to applicability and acceptance of provisions of article.

All contracts of employment made on or after September 7, 1967, shall be presumed to have been made with reference to and subject to the provisions of this article. All contracts of employment made prior to and existing on September 7, 1967, shall be presumed to continue from and after said date, subject to and under the provisions of this article. Every employer and every employee shall be presumed to have accepted and come under this article and the provisions thereof relating to the payment and acceptance of compensation. (Acts 1967, No. 521, p. 1245; Acts 1973, No. 1062, p. 1750, § 32.)

Collateral references. — 99 C.J.S., Workmen's Compensation, § 2. 101 C.J.S., Workmen's Compensation, § 519.

§ 25-5-193. Manner of compensation, etc., provided by article exclusive.

No employee of any employer subject to this article, nor the personal representative, surviving spouse or next of kin of any such employee shall have any right to any other method, form or amount of compensation or damages for occupational exposure to radiation, or for injury, disability, loss of service or death resulting from such exposure, arising out of and in the course of employment, or determination thereof, in any manner other than as provided in this article. (Acts 1967, No. 521, p. 1245; Acts 1973, No. 1062, p. 1750, § 34.)

Collateral references. — 99 C.J.S., Workmen's Compensation, § 128.

§ 25-5-194. Rights and remedies of employees, etc., under article exclusive; civil and criminal liability of employers, etc.

The rights and remedies granted in this article shall exclude all other rights and remedies of an employee, his personal representative, parent, surviving spouse, dependents or next of kin, at common law, by statute, contract or otherwise on account of occupational exposure to radiation and on account of any injury, disability, loss of service or death resulting from occupational exposure to radiation. Except as provided in this article, no employer included within the terms of this chapter and no officer, director, agent, servant or employee of such employer shall be held civilly liable for the occupational exposure to radiation or for injury, disability, loss of service or death of any employee due to occupational exposure to radiation while engaged in the service or business of the employer, the cause of which occupational exposure to radiation originates in the employment, but nothing in this section shall be construed to relieve any person from criminal prosecution for failure or neglect to perform any duty imposed by law; provided, however, that nothing in this article shall be interpreted so as to deprive an employee or, in case of

666

death, his dependents of any rights or remedies he may have under Articles 2 and 3 of this chapter. The immunity from civil liability shall extend to any workmen's compensation insurance carrier of such employer and to any officer, director, agent, servant or employee of such carrier, and such immunity shall further extend to any labor union, or any official or representative thereof, making a safety inspection for the benefit of the employer or its employees. (Acts 1967, No. 521, p. 1245; Acts 1975, 4th Ex. Sess., No. 86, p. 2729, § 14.)

Collateral references. — 101 C.J.S., Workmen's Compensation, §§ 918, 931.

§ 25-5-195. False written representation to employer as to previous compensation for exposure to radiation.

If any employee, at the time of or in the course of entering into the employment of the employer by whom the compensation would otherwise be paid, wilfully and falsely represented himself in writing to such employer as not having previously been disabled, laid off or compensated in damages, workmen's compensation or otherwise, because of occupational exposure to radiation, or as not having previously been subjected to occupational exposure to radiation, such employee, his personal representative, parents, surviving spouse, dependents and next of kin shall be barred from compensation or other benefits provided by this article or from recovery at common law, by statute, contract or otherwise on account of occupational exposure to radiation subsequent to such representation and while in the employ of such employer. (Acts 1967, No. 521, p. 1245.)

§ 25-5-196. Which employer liable for compensation of employee; contribution not required from nonliable employer.

Where compensation is payable under this article, the only employer liable, if any, shall be the employer in whose employment the employee was last exposed within a period of five years prior to the date of the injury, to the hazards of said radiation, in each of at least 12 months. The employer who is liable shall not be entitled to contribution from any other employer of such employee. (Acts 1967, No. 521, p. 1245.)

§ 25-5-197. Limitation period for claims or actions for compensation.

In case of occupational exposure to radiation, as defined in this article, or of injury or disability resulting therefrom, all claims for compensation shall be forever barred, unless within one year after the employee first suffered disability therefrom and either knew or in the exercise of reasonable diligence should have known that the disability was caused therefrom, but in no event more than three years after date of the injury as hereinafter defined, the parties shall have agreed upon the compensation payable under this article, or unless within such period of time one of the parties shall have filed a verified complaint as provided in Section 25-5-88. In case of death, all claims for compensation shall be forever barred, unless the death results proximately from occupational exposure to radiation, as defined in this article, and occurs within three years of the date of the injury, as hereinafter defined, and unless within one year after such death the parties shall have agreed upon the compensation under this article, or unless within one year after such death one of the parties shall have filed a verified complaint as provided in Section 25-5-88; provided, however, that if upon the date of the death of the employee the employee's claim is barred, any claim by or for his dependents shall likewise be barred. Where, however, payments of compensation have been made in any case, said limitations shall not take effect until the expiration of one year from the time of making the last payment. In case of the mental incapacity of the injured employee or his dependents to perform or cause to be performed any act required within the time in this section specified, the period of limitation in any such case shall be extended to become effective one year from the date when such incapacity ceases. No agreement, express or implied, to shorten or to extend said limitations shall be valid or binding on either of the parties when said employment, at the time of said exposure, is or was subject to the provisions of this article. The "date of the injury" shall mean, for all purposes of this article, the date of the last exposure to the hazards of radiation in the employment of the employer in whose employment the employee was last exposed, within a period of five years prior to the date of the injury, to the hazards of radiation in each of at least 12 months. (Acts 1967, No. 521, p. 1245.)

Collateral references. — When statute of limitations begins to run as to cause of action for development of latent industrial or occupational disease. 1 ALR4th 117.

§ 25-5-198. Rights and remedies as to exposures to hazards of radiation occurring prior to September 7, 1967.

All exposures of the employee occurring prior to September 7, 1967, to the hazards of radiation while in the employ of the employer shall be deemed for all purposes to be subject to the provisions of this article, and the employee, his personal representative, parents, surviving spouse, dependents and next of kin shall be entitled to compensation, or other benefits and barred from other rights and remedies as provided in this article for exposures occurring after September 7, 1967. (Acts 1967, No. 521, p. 1245; Acts 1973, No. 1062, p. 1750, § 36.)

§ 25-5-199. Computation of compensation and benefits payable under article.

The compensation payable for death or disability caused by occupational exposure to radiation shall be computed in the same manner and in the same amounts as provided in Article 3 of this chapter for computing compensation for disability or death resulting from an accident arising out of and in the course of the employment, and the medical, surgical, hospital and burial benefits payable under this article caused by said exposure shall be computed in the same manner and in the same amounts as provided in Article 3 of this chapter for computing like benefits. The date of injury, as defined in Section 25-5-197, shall be considered the date of the accident for determining the applicable medical, surgical and hospital benefits, the minimum and maximum weekly benefits and the limitation on the total amount of compensation payable for occupational exposure to radiation. (Acts 1967, No. 521, p. 1245; Acts 1975, 4th Ex. Sess., No. 86, p. 2729, § 15.)

§ 25-5-200. Presumptions and burden of proof as to right to compensation.

There shall be no presumption that disablement or death from any cause or infirmity is the result of occupational exposure to radiation, nor that occupational exposure to radiation will result in disablement or death, and any person claiming compensation or other benefits under this article shall have the burden of establishing that he is entitled to such. (Acts 1967, No. 521, p. 1245.)

§ 25-5-201. Settlements between parties; determination of disputed compensation claims.

The interested parties shall have the right to settle all matters of compensation and all questions arising under this article between themselves in accordance with and subject to the provisions of Article 3 of this chapter, and, in case of a dispute, either party may submit the controversy to the circuit court in accordance with and subject to the provisions of Article 3 of this chapter. (Acts 1967, No. 521, p. 1245.)

§ 25-5-202. Applicability of article.

The provisions of this article shall apply to all cases of occupational exposure to radiation, or injury, disability or death therefrom, in which the last exposure to hazards of such radiation occurred after September 7, 1967, except as provided in Section 25-5-198. (Acts 1967, No. 521, p. 1245.)

§ 25-5-203. Applicability of other provisions of chapter to article.

All of the provisions of Articles 1, 2, 3 and 8 of this chapter, except Section 25-5-78, shall be applicable to this article, unless otherwise provided or inconsistent herewith. (Acts 1967, No. 521, p. 1245; Acts 1975, 4th Ex. Sess., No. 86, § 16.)

ARTICLE 8.

OFFENSES AND PENALTIES.

§§ 25-5-220 through 25-5-225. Repealed by Acts 1977, No. 607, p. 812, § 9901, as amended, effective January 1, 1980.

§ 25-5-226. Solicitation of employment or acceptance of solicited employment by attorneys.

Any attorney who in person solicits employment to collect for a consideration any claim of any employee for compensation under this chapter, or who solicits for a consideration employment to defend such claims, or who knowingly accepts such claim after it has been solicited by some other person, or who employs any other person for the purpose of soliciting or obtaining such claim or claims shall be guilty of a misdemeanor and, on conviction, may be imprisoned in the county jail or sentenced to hard labor for the county for not more than 12 months and must also be fined not more than $500.00. Any attorney convicted under this section must be removed and disbarred from the practice of law in this state, and the record of his conviction is conclusive evidence thereof. The commission by any attorney of any of such acts shall also be a cause for the removal and disbarment of such attorney. (Acts 1919, No. 245, p. 206; Code 1923, § 3998; Code 1940, T. 26, § 320.)

§ 25-5-227. Solicitation of claims or representation of claimants by persons not authorized to practice law.

Any person who is not authorized by law to practice the profession of law within this state, who solicits for a consideration or traffics in for a consideration or represents for a consideration any claimant, claimants or claim for compensation under this chapter, shall be guilty of a misdemeanor and, on conviction, may be imprisoned in the county jail or sentenced to hard labor for the county for not more than 12 months and must also be fined not more than $500.00. (Acts 1919, No. 245, p. 206; Code 1923, § 3999; Code 1940, T. 26, § 321.)

§ 25-5-228. False statement in affidavit. Repealed by Acts 1977, No. 607, p. 812, § 9901, as amended, effective January 1, 1980.

§ 25-5-229. Solicitation or writing of workers' compensation insurance by insurance companies, etc., not in compliance with Code.

Any insurance corporation, organization or association, or any officer, employee or agent of such insurance corporation, organization or association who solicits or writes any workers' compensation insurance in this state without complying with the law as set forth in this Code in reference to filing with the Commissioner of Insurance its classifications of risks and premiums relating thereto or without having received from said Commissioner of Insurance approval of its plan of business or who fails to comply with any other requisites set out in this chapter to make reports in writing, who conducts business in the State of Alabama, shall be guilty of a misdemeanor and, on conviction, may be imprisoned in the county jail or sentenced to hard labor for the county for not more than 12 months and must also be fined not more than $500.00. (Acts 1919, No. 245, p. 206; Code 1923, § 4001; Code 1940, T. 26, § 323.)

§ 25-5-230. Failure to make written reports required under chapter.

Repealed by Acts 1977, No. 607, p. 812, § 9901, as amended, effective January 1, 1980.

§ 25-5-231. Acceptance of assignment of employee compensation claim, etc.

Any person, other than a beneficiary under this chapter, who for a consideration takes or accepts from an employee an assignment of his claim or award or judgment for, or agreement to pay, compensation, or who accepts or takes same as security for a loan or a debt, or who takes a power of attorney to collect the same, retaining any interest in the amount to be collected, shall be guilty of a misdemeanor and, on conviction, may be imprisoned in the county jail or sentenced to hard labor for the county for not more than 12 months and must also be fined not more than $500.00. (Acts 1919, No. 245, p. 206; Code 1923, § 4003; Code 1940, T. 26, § 325.)

Cited in Griffith v. Alabama By-Products Corp., 120 F. Supp. 219 (N.D. Ala. 1954).

ARTICLE 9.

ALABAMA WORKMEN'S COMPENSATION SELF-INSURERS GUARANTY ASSOCIATION.

§ 25-5-250. Creation; purpose; powers.

There is created a nonprofit corporation to be known as the "Alabama Workmen's Compensation Self-Insurers Guaranty Association, Incorporated," hereinafter referred to as "the association." The purpose of the association shall be to create and fund an insolvency fund to assure payment of workmen's compensation claims due from self-insuring employers who are members of the association and who become insolvent. The association shall have those powers granted or permitted nonprofit corporations, as provided in Title 10. In addition, the corporation shall have the power to borrow funds as necessary to carry out its purposes, and to purchase such insurance and reinsurance as is deemed necessary. (Acts 1989, No. 89-533, p. 1092, § 1.)

§ 25-5-251. Membership requirements.

(a) All employers who elect to be self-insurers for workers' compensation as provided in Article 1, other than self-insurers which are governmental entities, or public utilities, shall be members of the association as a condition of their authority to self-insure. Membership shall be sufficient security for self-insurance.

(b) Membership in the association shall cease when the employer terminates its self-insurance election. However, terminating members shall be and remain liable for the period of time in which they were members of the association and for any subsequent assessments made for that period.

(c) Membership in the association may be terminated for nonpayment of assessments.

(d) The association shall not issue stock and its members shall not, as such, be liable for its obligations. (Acts 1989, No. 89-533, p. 1092, § 2; Acts 1992, No. 92-537, § 36.)

The **1992 amendment,** effective May 19, 1992, in subsection (a), in the first sentence substituted "workers' compensation" for "workmen's compensation," and "Article 1" for "section 25-5-8(b), as amended," and substituted "nonpayment" for "non-payment" in subsection (c).

§ 25-5-252. Board of directors; eligibility; length of term; vacancies; reimbursement; registered agent.

The affairs of the association shall be managed by a board of directors which shall consist of nine persons appointed by the Director of the Department of Industrial Relations. To be eligible for appointment, a person must be an owner, employee or agent of a member self-insurer, and should be experienced in the field. In the initial appointments, four directors shall be appointed for a two year term and five shall be appointed for a four year term. Subsequent terms shall be for a period of four years. Vacancies on the board shall be filled for the unexpired portion of the term in the same manner. Directors shall be entitled to no compensation for their services as such, but shall be entitled to reimbursement from the association of expenses incurred in carrying out their duties. The board of directors shall designate a registered office and appoint a registered agent and shall continuously maintain the same, and shall file with the Secretary of State a certification thereof. (Acts 1989, No. 89-533, p. 1092, § 3.)

§ 25-5-253. Bylaws.

(a) Within 120 days after their appointment, the board of directors shall propose to the Director of the Department of Industrial Relations a set of bylaws for the operation and administration of the association. The bylaws shall not be effective until approved by the Director of the Department of Industrial Relations. If the board of directors fails to submit bylaws or if the Director of the Department of Industrial Relations does not approve the submitted bylaws, then the Director of the Department of Industrial Relations may promulgate, subject to the provisions of the Administrative Procedures Act, appropriate rules and regulations for the administration of the association.

(b) The bylaws may be amended from time to time by proposal of the board of directors approved by the Director of the Department of Industrial Relations.

(c) The bylaws shall contain:

(1) Provisions governing the administration of the association.

(2) Provisions governing managing the assets of the association and its financial record keeping.

(3) Procedures by which claims may be filed with the association.

(4) Provisions for the times and places for call of and conduct of meetings of the board of directors.

(5) Procedures for terminating the membership of a member who does not pay assessments when due.

(6) Procedures for recommendations by members of candidates for the board of directors for submission to the Director of the Department of Industrial Relations.

(7) Such additional provisions as are necessary or proper for carrying out the purposes of the association. (Acts 1989, No. 89-533, p. 1092, § 4.)

§ 25-5-254. Annual assessments for administration of association.

(a) To the extent necessary to secure funds for the payment of covered claims and costs of administration, the association may levy annual assessments on members of the association at a rate not to exceed $15.00 per $1,000.00 of security amount established by the department for the respective members. Assessments shall be remitted to and administered by the association as provided in the bylaws. The rate of annual assessments against members of the association may vary by duration of membership so that the cumulative contribution rate of recently admitted members becomes the same as previously admitted members.

(b) If, at any time, the insolvency fund is not sufficient to make the payments or reimbursements then owing, the association may levy a special assessment on members of the association at a rate not to exceed $15.00 per $1,000.00 of security amount established by the department for each member, but such special assessment may not be levied more than once in each calendar year.

(c) No state funds shall be allocated or paid to the association except those funds which may accrue to the association by or through assignments of rights of an insolvent employer. All moneys in the fund shall be held in trust and shall not be money or property of the state or the participants in the association. (Acts 1989, No. 89-533, p. 1092, § 5.)

§ 25-5-255. Insolvency fund.

Upon receipt of the funds assessed on members, the association may set aside funds for the administration of its affairs, and the balance of the funds shall be deposited to an insolvency fund under the following terms:

(1) The fund is created for the purpose of assuring payment of workers' compensation claims against members of the association who become insolvent; but only those claims which accrue while the insolvent employer is a member of the association and accrue prior to the determination of insolvency or within 30 days thereafter. The obligation of the fund shall be limited to the obligation of the insolvent employer under the Workers' Compensation Act, in an amount not to exceed 150 percent of the amount of security as determined by the department as of the last annual financial review. The fund shall have all defenses of and shall be subrogated to all rights of the insolvent employer. The fund shall not be liable for any penalties or interest assessed against the employer.

(2) It shall be the duty of the Department of Industrial Relations to determine insolvency of any self-insurer employers, and to notify the association of its determination. Members and directors of the association are specifically forbidden to be given information on the financial condition of any members except the fact of determination of insolvency.

(3) The Director of the Department of Industrial Relations, or his representative, will at all reasonable times have full and free access to the books and records of the association and may audit the association's financial affairs as he deems necessary. Should the director deem the balance in the insolvency fund insufficient to meet projected liabilities, he shall inform the board of directors, and after consultation with them, he shall set the amount which he deems sufficient and the board of directors shall levy assessments as provided herein to secure that amount.

(4) The association shall be subrogated to all rights of any claimant whose claim it pays and shall have a claim against the member employer for all such claims and expenses of administration.

(5) If at any time the insolvency fund is insufficient to pay all claims then owing, the funds available shall be prorated and the unpaid portion shall be paid as soon thereafter as sufficient funds become available. (Acts 1989, No. 89-533, p. 1092, § 6.)

§ 25-5-256. Association subject to examination and regulation by Department of Industrial Relations.

The association shall be subject to examination and regulation by the Department of Industrial Relations. No later than March 30 of each year, the board of directors shall submit a financial report for the preceding calendar year in a form approved by the department. (Acts 1989, No. 89-533, p. 1092, § 7.)

§ 25-5-257. Assessments deductible as business expenses.

A member may deduct as a business expense for state income tax purposes any assessment levied under Section 25-5-254 in the year such assessments are paid. (Acts 1989, No. 89-533, p. 1092, § 8.)

ARTICLE 10.

INSURANCE WITH OPTIONAL DEDUCTIBLES.

Effective date. — The act which added this article became effective July 29, 1991.

§ 25-5-270. Certain employers authorized to purchase insurance with optional deductibles.

(a) Each insurer issuing a policy under this article shall offer, as a part of the policy or as an optional endorsement to the policy, deductibles optional to the policyholder for benefits payable under this article. Deductible amounts offered shall be fully disclosed to the prospective policyholder in writing in the amount of $100.00, $200.00, $300.00, $400.00, $500.00, or increments of $500.00 up to a maximum of $2,500.00 per compensable claim. The policy-holder exercising the deductible option shall choose only one deductible amount.

(b) If the policyholder exercises the option and chooses a deductible, the insured employer shall be liable for the amount of the deductible for benefits paid for each compensable claim of work injury suffered by an employee. The insurer shall pay all or part of the deductible amount, whichever is applicable to a compensable claim, to the person or medical provider entitled to the benefits conferred by this article and then seek reimbursement from the insured employer for the applicable deductible amount. The payment or nonpayment of deductible amounts by the insured employer to the insurer shall be treated under the policy insuring the liability for workers' compensation in the same manner as payment or nonpayment of premiums. (Acts 1991, No. 91-472, p. 856, § 1.)

§ 25-5-271. Optional deductibles to be offered in policy; exception.

Optional deductibles shall be offered in each policy insuring liability for workers' compensation that is issued, delivered, issued for delivery, or renewed under this article on or after July 29, 1991, unless an insured employer and insurer agree to renegotiate a workers' compensation policy in effect on July 29, 1991, so as to include a provision allowing for a deductible. (Acts 1991, No. 91-472, p. 856, § 2.)

§ 25-5-272. Premium reduction to be determined before application of experience modification, premium surcharge, etc.

Premium reduction for deductibles shall be determined before the application of any experience modification, premium surcharge, or premium discounts. To the extent that an employer's experience rating or safety record is based on benefits paid, money paid by the insured employer under a deductible as provided in this article shall not be included as benefits paid so as to harm the experience rating of such employer. (Acts 1991, No. 91-472, p. 856, § 3.)

§ 25-5-273. Applicability.

This article shall not apply to employers who are approved to self-insure against liability for workers' compensation or group self-insurance funds for workers' compensation established pursuant to this chapter. (Acts 1991, No. 91-472, p. 856, § 4.)

ARTICLE 11.

OMBUDSMAN PROGRAM.

Effective date. — The act which added this article became effective May 19, 1992.

§ 25-5-290. Ombudsman program, creation; purpose; members; notification of service; benefit review conferences.

(a) The Department of Industrial Relations shall establish an Ombudsman Program to assist injured or disabled employees, persons claiming death benefits, employers, and other persons in protecting their rights and obtaining information available under the Workers' Compensation Law.

(b) Providing that the employer and the employee agree to participate in the benefit review conference, the ombudsmen shall meet with or otherwise provide information to injured or disabled employees, investigate complaints, and communicate with employers, insurance carriers, and health care providers on behalf of injured or disabled employees.

(c) Ombudsmen shall be merit system employees and demonstrate familiarity with the Workers' Compensation Law. An ombudsman shall not be an advocate for any person who shall assist a claimant, employer, or other person in any proceeding beyond the benefit review conference, but may, at all times, provide appropriate information regarding this chapter and rules and regulations promulgated thereunder.

(d) Each employer shall notify his or her employees of the ombudsman's service in a manner prescribed by the Director of the Department of Industrial Relations. The notice shall include the posting of a notice in one or more conspicuous places. The director shall also describe clearly the availability of the ombudsman on the first report of accident form required by this article.

The ombudsman shall give each employee with a lost-time accident claim written notice of workers' compensation assistance that is available. The notice shall include a toll-free phone number for employees to reach an ombudsman.

(e) Ombudsmen may conduct benefit review conferences. A benefit review conference may be held between the parties involved in a dispute over any claim arising after January 1, 1993. Such benefit review conference shall be held only by agreement of the employer and employee and shall not be deemed mandatory. The director shall institute and maintain an education and training program for ombudsmen. The ombudsmen shall be trained in the principles and procedures of dispute mediation and the director may consult or contract with the federal mediation and conciliation service or other appropriate organizations to accomplish this purpose.

(f) In conducting benefit review conferences, the ombudsman:

(1) Shall mediate disputes between the parties and assist with the claim consistent with this article and the policies of the department.

(2) Shall inform all parties of their rights and responsibilities under this article, especially in cases in which either party is not represented by an attorney or other representative. An employee shall be advised, in writing which shall be notarized, of his or her right to be represented by counsel and of his or her right to have any settlement of his or her claim reviewed by a court of competent jurisdiction at any time within 60 days after the date of the settlement and at the end of 60 days it shall be final and irrevocable.

(3) Shall ensure that all documents and information relating to the employee's wages, medical condition, and any other information pertinent to the resolution of disputed issues are contained in the claim file at the conference, especially in cases in which the employee is not represented by an attorney or other representative.

(4) May reschedule a benefit review conference if he or she determines that available information pertinent to the resolution of disputed issues is not produced at the benefit review conference.

(5) May not take testimony but may direct questions to an employee, an employer, or a representative of an insurance carrier to supplement or clarify information in a claim file.

(6) May not make a formal record.

(7) May issue a statement with regard to an award of attorney fees in accordance with the amount as provided by Section 25-5-90. (Acts 1992, No. 92-537, § 37.)

§ 25-5-291. Benefit review conferences.

A benefit review conference is a nonadversarial, informal dispute resolution proceeding designed to:

(1) Explain, orally and in writing, the rights of the respective parties to a workers' compensation claim and the procedures necessary to protect those rights.

(2) Discuss the facts of the claim, review available information in order to evaluate the claim, and delineate the disputed issues.

(3) Mediate and resolve disputed issues by mutual agreement of the parties in accordance with this article and the policies of the department. (Acts 1992, No. 92-537, § 38.)

§ 25-5-292. Resolution of disputes, settlement agreements; written reports; interlocutory orders; final determinations of liability.

(a) A dispute may be resolved either in whole or in part at the benefit review conference. If the conference results in the resolution of some of the disputed issues by mutual agreement or in a settlement, the ombudsman shall reduce the agreement or the settlement to writing. The ombudsman and each party or the designated representative of the party shall sign the agreement or settlement. A settlement reached hereunder shall, unless otherwise provided herein, be effective on the date the settlement is signed unless one of the parties submits the settlement to the court for approval as provided in this article.

(b) An agreement signed pursuant to this section shall be binding on all parties through the final conclusion of all matters relating to the claim, unless within 60 days after the agreement is signed or approved the court on a finding of fraud, newly discovered evidence, or other good cause, shall relieve all parties of the effect of the agreement.

(c) If the dispute is entirely resolved at the benefit review conference, the ombudsman shall prepare a written report, which shall not be admissible into evidence in any court, that includes:

(1) A statement of each resolved issue.

(2) The ombudsman's recommendations regarding the payment or denial of benefits.

(3) No permission of the court is required by an attorney to represent any party before an ombudsman.

(d) If there is a dispute as to which of two or more insurance carriers is liable for compensation for one or more compensable injuries, the ombudsman may issue an interlocutory order directing each insurance carrier to pay a proportionate share of benefits due pending a final decision on liability. The proportionate share shall be determined by dividing the compensation due by the number of insurance carriers involved.

(e) On final determination of liability, any insurance carrier that has been determined not to be liable for the payment of benefits is entitled to reimbursement from the share paid by the insurance carrier that has been determined to be liable.

(f) The ombudsman shall file the signed agreement and the report with the Department of Industrial Relations. (Acts 1992, No. 92-537, § 39.)

§ 25-5-293. Duties of director; continuing education, accounting; recovery of expenses; advisory committees; legislative intent regarding reimbursements.

(a) The Director of the Department of Industrial Relations may prescribe rules and regulations for the purpose of conducting continuing education seminars for all personnel associated with workers' compensation claims and collect registration fees in order to cover the related expenditures. The director may adopt rules and regulations setting continuing education standards for workers' compensation claims personnel employed by insurance companies and self-insured employers and groups.

(b) The director shall file annually with the Governor and the presiding officer of each house of the legislature a complete and detailed written report accounting for all funds received and disbursed during the preceding fiscal year. The annual report shall be in the form and reported in the time provided by law.

(c) The director shall establish reasonable charges to recover expenses for services not required by law or rule provided to persons requesting the services from the Department of Industrial Relations.

(d) The director shall appoint appropriate advisory committees on workers' compensation matters, including: an advisory committee consisting of three administrators who are members of the Alabama Hospital Association, who shall be selected by the director from nominations submitted by the Alabama Hospital Association; an advisory committee consisting of three chiropractors who are members in good standing with the Alabama State Chiropractic Association, who shall be selected by the director from nominations submitted by the Alabama State Chiropractic Association; an advisory committee consisting of three pharmacists who are members in good standing with the Alabama Pharmaceutical Association who shall be selected by the director from nominations submitted by the Alabama Pharmaceutical Association; and an advisory committee consisting of three optometrists who are members in good standing with the Alabama Optometric Association who shall be selected by the director from nominations submitted by the Alabama Optometric Association. These committees shall guide the director and make recommendations to ascertain the prevailing rate of reimbursement or payment of medical costs in the State of Alabama. These committees shall make recommendations with regard to the implementation of all other rules and regulations, including, but not limited to, utilization review by like peers. These committees shall also advise and guide the director in determining all other rules and regulations required to accomplish the intent of the legislature in assuring the quality of medical care and achieving medical cost control.

The director shall also appoint a vocational rehabilitation advisory committee consisting of at least five professional licensed rehabilitation specialists. These rehabilitation specialists shall be selected by the director from nominations from the rehabilitation associations in the state of Alabama, including, but not limited to, the Alabama Physical Therapy Association. The committee shall guide the director and make recommendations to ascertain the prevailing rate of reimbursement or payment of rehabilitation costs in the State of Alabama. The committee shall also make recommendations with regard to the implementation of all other rules and regulations, including but not limited to, utilization review, and with regard to rehabilitation policies as provided by this article. The committee shall also advise and guide the director in determining all other rules and regulations required to accomplish the intent of the legislature in assuring the quality of rehabilitation care and achieving rehabilitation cost control.

(e) The director shall appoint an advisory committee consisting of attorneys who are members in good standing of the Alabama State Bar. This committee shall guide and assist the director in creating and promulgating rules and regulations for the efficient administration of the Ombudsman Program.

Members of the advisory committee shall receive State of Alabama mileage expense which shall be paid by the Department of Industrial Relations.

(f) It is the intent of the legislature that final reimbursements related to workers' compensation claims be commensurate and in line with the prevailing rate of reimbursement or payment in the State of Alabama, or as otherwise provided in this article. The director shall conduct field audits as necessary to assist the private sector to gain compliance with the legislative intent. The department shall develop administrative rules to facilitate implementation and continuity of the legislative intent of this article. The director, except as otherwise provided in this article, shall not establish the prevailing rate of payment or reimbursement, but may collect data which are construed to be statistically significant as defined by an independent, disinterested consultant. By definition, the prevailing rate of payment or reimbursement is self-defining and self-setting and shall be updated annually. The director may create a statistically valid data base from which prevailing rates of reimbursement or payment shall be ascertained. Except as otherwise provided herein, the prevailing rate of reimbursement or payment for medical services provided under this article shall be effective 30 days after the prevailing rate of reimbursement or payment is discovered, but in no event earlier than six months from May 19, 1992.

(g) Insurance carriers and self-insurers, individual and group, are required to make appropriate payment for services provided under this article. Unless otherwise provided in this article, an insurance carrier or self-insurer, individual or group, shall not pay more than the applicable prevailing rate of reimbursement for medical services. Insurance carriers and self-insurers, individual and group, shall have utilization review and medical bill screenings. Utilization review and bill screening shall be performed by qualified individuals or entities to insure the integrity of the services and the quality of cost containment. It is the express legislative intent of this article to ensure that the highest quality health care is available to employees who become injured or ill as the result of employment, at an appropriate rate of provider reimbursement. All insurers, claims adjusters, self-administered employers, and any entity involved in the administration or payment of workers' compensation claims are mandated to implement utilization review and bill screening for health services provided to employees covered under this article. In this regard, employers' liability for reimbursement shall be limited to the prevailing rate or maximum fee schedule established by the Workers' Compensation Services Board for similar treatment. All services will be reviewed by utilization review for medical necessity and bills for such services screened for appropriateness of charges. Services provided that are deemed not medically necessary are not reimbursable and the employer is held harmless. In no event is the employee responsible or held liable for any charges associated with an authorized workers' compensation claim. To ensure compliance of providers, insurance carriers, and self-insurers, the director may provide by rule for the review and audit of insurance carriers and self-insurers, individual and group, of payments for medical services. The director may maintain a statewide data base from insurance carriers and self-insurers, individual and group, on medical charges, actual payments, and adjudication methods for use in administering this article.

(h) Claims payors, and insurers operating in Alabama shall, at the director's request, provide the director such data as he or she deems necessary to evaluate costs and quality. The data shall be provided in the form and content to the director's specifications and in a manner deemed timely by the director. The director may gather from health care claims intermediaries that operate in Alabama any claims data related to diagnoses and procedures encountered in the treatment of workers'-compensation-type injury and illness in Alabama. Results from all data gathered shall be made available to employers or their representatives for use in decisions regarding the direction of care or to determine appropriateness of reimbursement.

(i) Beginning immediately after May 19, 1992, and to be completed within six months thereafter, the director may engage an independent firm to identify the initial costs for the program. These initial expenses shall include, but not be limited to, the establishment of a data base to determine prevailing rates, and the conducting of cost analysis for appropriate reimbursement rates to hospitals and other facilities.

(j) A person who performs services for the director pertaining to the policies of any advisory committee or board is immune from civil liability against any claim arising out of, or related to, any decision made in good faith, and without malice, and predicated upon information which was then available to the person. Immunity from liability under this section does not apply to a person providing medical treatment to an injured employee.

(k) Notwithstanding any other provision of this section to the contrary, it is the intent of this section that any and all utilization review, bill screening, medical necessity determinations, or audits which relate to the services of physicians as defined in Section 25-5-310 shall only be conducted under and in accordance with policies, guidelines, or regulations which have been jointly approved by the Workers' Compensation Medical Services Board and the director under the provisions of Section 25-5-312, as and when such policies, guidelines, criteria, and regulations are adopted in a final and effective form pursuant to the Alabama Administrative Procedure Act. Not later than six months from May 19, 1992, the director, with the approval of the board, shall publish a notice of the intended action in Alabama Administrative Monthly to adopt initial policies, guidelines, criteria, or regulations for utilization review, medical necessity determinations, and bill screenings; however, each insurer, self-insured employer, claims administrator, or other payor may continue utilization review, medical necessity determinations, and bill screenings unaffected by this article during the first six months from May 19, 1992, or until such policies, guidelines, criteria, or regulations may become effective in a final adopted form within that initial six month period. If such above referenced pending policies, guidelines, criteria, or regulations have not become effective in a final form pursuant to the Administrative Procedure Act after six months from May 19, 1992, then until such time as they are finally adopted, each insurer, self-insured employer, or claims administrator shall conduct utilization review, medical necessity determinations, and bill screenings in a manner that is consistent with similar practices of a majority of commercial insurance companies authorized to issue policies of health insurance in this state. Any amendments, including additions or deletions, to the initial policies, guidelines, criteria, or regulations shall be adopted in accordance with the requirements of this section and Section 25-5-312. (Acts 1992, No. 92-537, § 40.)

§ 25-5-294. Communications, etc. privileged; documentation; release of records or information; penalty for obtaining information under false pretenses.

(a) All letters, reports, communications, and other matters, written or oral, from employer or employee to each other, to the Director of the Department of Industrial Relations, any of his or her agents, representatives, or employees, or to any official or board functioning under this article, which have been written, sent, delivered, or made in connection with the requirements and administration of this article, shall be absolutely privileged. Information obtained from the above mentioned matters shall be held confidential, except to the extent necessary for the proper presentation of the contest of a claim, and shall not be published or open to public inspection in any manner. Any person violating this section shall be fined not less than $20.00 nor more than $200.00, or imprisoned for not longer than 30 days, or both.

(b) The director may make summaries, compilations, photographs, duplications, or reproductions of any records as he or she may deem advisable for the effective and economical preservation of the information contained therein. The documentation, duly authenticated, shall be admissible in any proceeding under this article if the original record or records would have been admissible therein.

(c) The director may, upon specific request therefor, furnish to any public agency a workers' compensation record in his or her custody, if the agency makes payment of a reasonable cost therefor.

(d) At his or her discretion, the director may release information for the purpose of making economic analyses to institutions of higher education, or a federal government corporation upon payment of a reasonable cost therefor. The institution or federal government corporation shall agree in writing that information so obtained shall not be published or released by it to any person in a manner to permit the identification of any specific individual or employing unit.

(e) The director may afford reasonable cooperation with any agency of the United States or any state agency charged with the administration of any workers' compensation laws.

(f) The director may upon specific request release a workers' compensation record or information therein to any public official or to any law enforcement officer if the release is deemed by the director to be necessary for the performance of the official's or officer's duties and upon payment of a reasonable cost therefor in accordance with any regulations the director may prescribe.

(g) Any person who willfully makes a false statement or representation to obtain any information under this section, either for himself or herself or for any other person, who uses any information for any purpose other than in the performance of his or her official duties, or in any other manner misuses the information, shall be guilty of a misdemeanor and upon conviction, shall be punished by a fine of not less than $200.00 nor more than $1,000.00, or by imprisonment for not less than three nor more than 12 months, or by both fine and imprisonment. (Acts 1992, No. 92-537, § 41.)

ARTICLE 12.

WORKERS' COMPENSATION MEDICAL SERVICES BOARD.

Effective date. — The act which added this article became effective May 19, 1992.

§ 25-5-310. Definitions.

For the purposes of this article the following words and phrases have the following meanings:

(1) BOARD. The Workers' Compensation Medical Services Board.

(2) MEDICAL or MEDICAL SERVICES. Any and all medical or surgical services provided by physicians under this new article.

(3) PHYSICIAN. A doctor of medicine or doctor of osteopathy licensed to practice medicine. (Acts 1992, No. 92-537, § 42.)

§ 25-5-311. Workers' Compensation Medical Services Board; creation, members, functions.

There is established a Workers' Compensation Medical Services Board composed of five physicians licensed to practice medicine in the State of Alabama who shall be appointed by the Director of the Department of Industrial Relations. The initial board shall be selected from a list of 15 physicians who are members of the Medical Association of the State of Alabama, submitted by the association.

Members of the board shall serve terms of five years. In order that the appointments be staggered, one member shall serve an initial term of six years, one member shall serve an initial term of two years, one member shall serve an initial term of three years, one member shall serve an initial term of four years, and the remaining member shall serve an initial term of five years. Thereafter, successors shall be appointed by the director from among a list of three nominees submitted by the Medical Association of the State of Alabama to serve full five-year terms. A member of the board shall continue to serve beyond the expiration of his or her term of office until his or her successor is legally appointed. Members of the Workers' Compensation Medical Services Board shall be eligible to serve two five-year terms of office in addition to an initial or unexpired term of less than three years, but shall not serve thereafter. Members of the board shall be entitled to receive per diem at the rate of $100.00 for each day or portion thereof spent in the performance of the duties of their office, and in addition, shall be reimbursed for expenses of travel in the same manner as employees of the State of Alabama.

The Workers' Compensation Medical Services Board shall function as a part of the Department of Industrial Relations and shall have the authority, duties, and responsibilities as prescribed in this article. The board may meet quarterly at a time and place designated by the chair, and may meet more frequently at the call of the chair. The board shall elect one of its members as chair who shall serve a term of one year. The board may adopt rules governing its own proceedings. The department shall provide the board with necessary meeting and office space, secretarial and clerical support, reimbursement for travel expenses and per diem as specified in this article. Upon approval of the director, the Lieutenant Governor, and the Speaker of the House of Representatives, additional funding as required by the board for the employment of consultants, attorneys, and other professional staff necessary to accomplish the purposes and objectives stated in this article may be provided. (Acts 1992, No. 92-537, § 43.)

§ 25-5-312. Powers and duties of the board.

The board shall exercise general supervision in all matters related to the provision of medical services provided by physicians, as defined in Section 25-5-310, rendered to workers under this article. The duties of the board shall include, but are not limited to, the following:

(1) Study, develop, and implement any necessary and reasonable guidelines for medical services and physician care provided by physicians. In addition, with respect to services provided by physicians, the board shall study, develop, and recommend to the director uniform medical criteria and policies for the conduct of utilization review, bill screenings, and medical necessity determinations for use by insurance carriers, self-insurers, and claims administrators.

(2) Study, design, and implement standardized uniform claims processing forms and forms for the reporting of medical information to employers and insurance companies by physicians.

(3) Address and give consideration to those matters referred to it by the director.

(4) The board shall contract with physicians, health care providers, professional associations of physicians, and health-related organizations to provide the board with consultation, and research and development expertise in discharging its duties and responsibilities under this article. Any contract entered into by the board shall be approved by the director and submitted as are other state contracts.

(5) The board may establish, by regulations promulgated by the department, regional committees of physicians appointed by the board to perform any duties and responsibilities specified by the board in programs established for the delivery of medical services under this article. In addition the board shall appoint board certified physicians in any of the medical or surgical specialties to act as independent expert medical consultants to the ombudsman in connection with the resolution of disputes involving physicians providing medical services to injured workers. Members of the regional committees shall be physicians and shall serve at the pleasure of the board. Physicians serving as members of the regional committees as constituted under this section or independent expert medical consultants to the ombudsman shall be granted the same immunities as provided members of the board under this article and existing state law.

(6) Implementation of this section shall be governed by and subject to the Alabama Administrative Procedure Act. Rules and regulations relating to the duties and authority of the board, enumerated herein, may be promulgated only with the consent of both the director and the board. (Acts 1992, No. 92-537, § 44.)

§ 25-5-313. Schedule of maximum fees.

Within 60 days from May 19, 1992, the Workers' Compensation Medical Services Board shall submit to the Governor an initial schedule of maximum fees for medical services covered by this article, which schedule shall become effective immediately upon submission to the Governor. The initial schedule of maximum fees shall be established by the board in the manner prescribed in this section. The fee for each service in the schedule shall be exactly equal to an amount derived by multiplying the preferred provider reimbursement customarily paid on May 19, 1992, by the largest health care service plan incorporated pursuant to Sections 10-4-100 to 10-4-115, inclusive, by a factor of 1.075, which product shall be the maximum fee for each such service. In addition the board may submit to the Governor for approval on or before January 31, 1993, a revised schedule of selected fees for medical services covered by this article, which fees shall not exceed the fees established in the initial schedule of fees by more than $2^1/_2$ percent. The revised schedule of fees, but not individual fees or separate portions thereof, shall be subject to acceptance or rejection by the Governor. If the revised schedule of fees is rejected by the Governor, it shall be referred to the board for further consideration and the initial schedule of maximum fees shall continue to be in effect until the Governor and the board reach agreement; provided, however, the schedule of maximum fees in effect on January 31, 1993, shall not be subject to further revision through this process.

The schedule of maximum fees and any additions, deletions, corrections, or changes thereto shall not be considered a rule or regulation requiring publication under the Alabama Administrative Procedure Act. It is the express legislative intent that the Workers' Compensation Medical Services Board may establish a system of maximum fees under this section for services rendered by physicians to employees covered by the Workers' Compensation Law and that the schedule of fees shall replace and supplant traditional competitive market mechanisms in the interest of obtaining quality physician services in a cost effective manner. The board shall annually adjust the schedule of fees established pursuant to this section by increases which shall be no more than the annual increase in the cost of living as reflected by the U. S. Department of Labor consumer price index. The board may, from time to time, add to or adjust the schedule of fees in response to changes in technology and medical practice, subject only to the right of the Governor to accept or reject the addition or adjustment made by the board, and to refer to the board for further consideration any additions or adjustments which he or she may reject. In the event that at any time a state or federal tax, levy, fee, or assessment is imposed or assessed on physicians licensed to practice medicine which tax, levy, fee, or assessment is based in whole or in part upon the provision of professional services in connection with the practice of medicine, then, in that event, the board may, subject to the approval of the Governor, within three months of the effective date of the tax, levy, fee, or assessment issue a revised schedule of maximum fees which increases the maximum fee for each service reflected therein by an amount which shall be no more than the rate fixed by law of the tax, levy, fee, or assessment. This provision shall not be construed to include income or sales tax increases. The liability of the employer for the payment of services rendered by physicians shall not exceed those maximum fees established by the board and approved by the Governor. The employees shall not be liable to the physician for any amount in excess of the schedule of maximum fees established by the board and approved by the Governor. (Acts 1992, No. 92-537, § 45.)

§ 25-5-314. Contracts for medical services at mutually agreed rates.

Notwithstanding any other provisions of this article to the contrary, any employer, workers' compensation insurance carrier, self-insured employer, or group fund, may contract with physicians, hospitals, and any other health care provider for the provision of medical services to injured workers at any rates, fees, or levels of reimbursement which shall be mutually agreed upon between the physician, hospitals, and any other health care provider and the employer, workers' compensation insurance carrier, self-insured employer, or group fund. (Acts 1992, No. 92-537, § 46.)

§ 25-5-315. Immunity from liability.

The Workers' Compensation Medical Services Board, the individual members thereof, the agents, servants, employees, consultants, or attorneys of the board, and any person, firm, or corporation contracting with the board for the specific purpose of implementing the duties, obligations, and responsibilities of the board under this article, shall each be immune from civil liability against the claims of any and all individuals, firms, corporations, institutions, or other entities for any claims of any nature whatsoever arising out of or related to the decisions, opinions, deliberations, reports, or publications which are made, rendered, or entered by the board, the individual members of the board, or the agents, servants, employees, consultants, or attorneys of the board or any person, firm, or corporation contracting with the board which decisions, opinions, deliberations, reports, or publications were made in good faith, without malice, and predicated upon information which was then available to the board. (Acts 1992, No. 92-537, § 47.)

§ 25-5-316. Workers' compensation administrative trust fund; creation; management; trustee and custodian; assessments; penalties.

(a) There is established in the State Treasury a fund entitled the workers' compensation administrative trust fund, into which shall be deposited certain assessments provided under Chapter 5 (commencing with Section 25-5-1) of Title 25 collected by the Department of Industrial Relations. The fund shall constitute a separate fund to be disbursed by the State Comptroller on order of the Director of the Department of Industrial Relations. All expenses incurred by the department under the Workers' Compensation Law, including the salaries of all employees, travel cost, and any other cost of administration and enforcement as may become necessary, either within or without the state, shall be paid from the separate fund in the State Treasury upon warrants of the State Comptroller drawn upon the State Treasury from time to time when vouchers therefor are approved by the director. The State Treasurer shall pay moneys from the separate fund upon the order of the director. The total expense for every purpose incurred shall not exceed the total assessment collected and paid into the fund. The total expense for every purpose incurred in implementing this article shall not exceed the amount appropriated by the legislature in the general fund appropriation act. No funds shall be withdrawn or expended except those budgeted and allocated in accordance with Article 4 (commencing with Section 41-4-80) of Chapter 4 of Title 41. All moneys remaining unexpended in the separate fund at the end of the fiscal year shall remain in the State Treasury to be expended as herein provided. Included in the budget shall be an amount of money allocated for the specific and exclusive purpose of paying only benefits to the claimants who have qualified to receive benefits from the second injury trust fund on May 19, 1992. Payments of these benefits shall be made weekly. The director shall each week make requisitions to the State Comptroller who shall draw warrants on the State Treasurer for the weekly compensation amount. The warrants shall be drawn only if there are sufficient moneys in the treasury for immediate payment. Claims shall take priority in an ascending numerical order according to the time of the accident, and the time shown in the settlement between the employer and employee shall be prima facie evidence of the time of the accident. No funds allocated for the payment of benefits from the fund shall be used to pay lump-sum attorney's fees. Payment shall resume at the end of the first week of the fiscal year in which the legislature approves the requested budget for the workers' compensation administrative trust fund. The claimants who were receiving weekly benefits from the second injury trust fund as of August 31, 1991, shall be paid all weekly benefits due to date and the benefits shall be continued for the duration of claim. Those amounts shall be paid from the moneys as allocated.

(b) The State Treasurer shall determine if the money in the trust fund shall be kept in cash or invested. The moneys in the fund may be invested by the State Treasurer and all moneys and interest remaining unexpended in the separate fund provided at the end of the fiscal year shall remain in the State Treasury to be expended as herein provided.

(c) The director is designated as trustee of the fund and the State Treasurer is designated as custodian of the fund, and both shall furnish bonds in amounts deemed appropriate. The cost of bonds for the trustee, custodian, and other employees or officials required to post bond in connection with the program shall be paid out of the fund.

(d) Each insurance carrier, self-insured employer, and group fund shall be assessed $250.00. The gross claims for compensation and medical payments paid by the carriers, self-insured employers, and group funds are the basis for computing the amount to be assessed. The amount of assessment shall be based upon the proportion that the total gross claims for compensation and medical payments paid by the carrier, self-insured employer, or group fund during the preceding calendar year bore to the total gross claims for compensation and medical payments paid by all carriers, self-insured employers, and group funds during that period. The total assessment shall not exceed $5,000,000.00 per year. The director shall determine if the assessment shall be a specific amount or shall be a percentage of gross claims for compensation and medical payments paid by the insurance carriers, self-insured employers, and group funds. An assessment shall not exceed an amount reasonably necessary to defray the necessary administration expense.

(e) The department shall provide by regulation for the collection of the amounts assessed against each insurance carrier, self-insured employer, and group fund. The amounts shall be paid within 30 days from the date that the notice is served upon the insurance carrier, self-insured employer, and group fund. If the amounts are not paid within that period, there may be assessed, for each 30 days that the amount so assessed remains unpaid, a civil penalty equal to 10 percent of the amount unpaid. The amount of the civil penalty shall be collected at the same time the amount assessed is collected.

(f) If an insurance carrier, self-insured employer, or group fund fails to pay the amounts assessed against it within 60 days from the time the notice is served, the department may suspend or revoke the authorization to the self-insurer and may request that the Department of Insurance revoke the authority of the insurance company to insure workers' compensation.

(g) The department may require from each insurance carrier, self-insured employer, and group fund reports with respect to all payments of compensation and medical payments by the insurance carriers, self-insured employers, or group funds during each calendar year, and may determine the amounts paid by each insurance carrier, self-insured employer, and group fund and may determine the amounts paid by all insurance carriers, self-insured employers, and group funds during the period.

(h) On or before the first day of March of each year, every insurance carrier, self-insured employer, and group fund shall file with the department a statement on the prescribed forms showing the gross claims for compensation and medical payments paid by the insurance carrier, self-insured employer, or group fund during the preceding one-year period ending on the 31st day of December. Any insurance carrier, self-insured employer, or group fund which neglects to file its annual written statement within the time provided in this manner shall pay to the workers' compensation administrative trust fund a penalty for each day's neglect in an amount prescribed by rule of the director.

(i) All money collected under this section shall be deposited in the workers' compensation administrative trust fund. (Acts 1992, No. 92-537, § 48.)

§ 25-5-317. Assessment of pro rata share; disposition of unexpended balance.

(a) Within 60 days after May 19, 1992, the Director of the Department of Industrial Relations shall assess each insurance carrier, self-insured employer, and group fund its pro rata share of the total amount of up to $4,500,000.00 according to the method set out in Section 25-5-316(d). Of the total amount, $800,000.00 shall be allocated to pay weekly benefits to the claimants of the second injury trust fund until an appropriate budget is approved in accordance with Chapter 4 of Title 41. The assessment shall be deposited into the workers' compensation administrative trust fund and disbursed by the State Comptroller on order of the director.

(b) The assessment is appropriated and made available for the initial implementation costs and expenses of the workers' compensation program to fund activities not included in the general fund appropriation for fiscal year 1991-1992 and fiscal year 1992-1993, which are peculiar to this article.

(c) Any unexpended balance remaining at the end of the fiscal year will be credited to the insurance carriers and self-insured employers at the end of the next fiscal year. (Acts 1992, No. 92-537, § 49.)

§ 25-5-318. One-time discount to small employers.

(a) For purposes of this article, "small employer" means an employer who is not experienced-rated for workers' compensation insurance purposes and whose annual workers' compensation premium is less than $5,000.00.

(b) The Department of Insurance shall promulgate a plan by which all insurance companies writing workers' compensation insurance in this state shall grant a one-time discount to small employers who qualify under this article and by which surcharges are assessed against small employers who experience two or more employee on-the-job injuries resulting in payment of indemnity or medical payments during a one-year period.

(c) A small employer who has not experienced an employee on-the-job injury resulting in payment of indemnity or medical payments during the most recent one-year period for which statistics are available shall receive a one-time discount of 10 percent on the amount of the employer's workers' compensation insurance premium.

(d) A small employer who has not experienced an employee on-the-job injury resulting in payment of indemnity or medical payments during the most recent two-year period for which statistics are available shall receive a one-time discount of 15 percent on the amount of the employer's workers' compensation insurance premium.

(e) A small employer who has experienced one employee on-the-job injury resulting in payment of indemnity or medical payments during the most recent one-year period for which statistics are available is not eligible for a discount on the amount of the employer's workers' compensation insurance premium, as otherwise would be available under subsections (c) or (d) of this section.

(f) A small employer who has experienced two or more employee on-the-job injuries resulting in payment of indemnity or medical payments during the most recent one-year period for which statistics are available shall be assessed a surcharge of 10 percent on the amount of the employer's workers' compensation premium; provided, however, no surcharge shall be assessed unless the small employer has received a discount, under subsections (c) or (d) of this section for the previous policy year.

(g) The discounts and surcharges under this article are not cumulative. For any annual workers' compensation premium, a small employer may not receive a discount of more than 15 percent, and a small employer may not be required to pay a surcharge of more than 10 percent.

(h) Within 30 days after one year following May 19, 1992, the Insurance Commissioner shall make a report to the Governor, with copies to the Lieutenant Governor and the Speaker of the House of Representatives on the Premium Incentives for Small Employers Program. This report shall include, but not be limited to, the number of employers participating in this program, the numbers and amounts of discounts and surcharges and any recommendations regarding this program. (Acts 1992, No. 92-537, § 50.)

CHAPTER 6.

EMPLOYER'S LIABILITY FOR CERTAIN INJURIES.

Consistent pattern of behavior as evidence of intent. — While a single act of taking out insurance or paying a claim may not be sufficient evidence of intent to come under Workmen's Compensation Act, a consistent pattern of behavior on the part of the employer, his employees and the department of industrial relations will suffice, despite failure to comply with technical filing requirements. Smith v. Thrower Nursery, Inc., 360 So. 2d 741 (Ala. 1978).

Cited in Carter v. Cincinnati Ins. Co., 435 So. 2d 42 (Ala. 1983).

Collateral references. — Excessiveness or adequacy of damages awarded for injuries causing particular diseases or conditions. 16 ALR4th 736.

Liability of private citizen or his employer for injury or damage to third person resulting from firing of shots at fleeing criminal. 29 ALR4th 144.

Employer's liability for injury to babysitter in home or similar premises. 29 ALR4th 304.

State or local governmental unit's liability for injury to private highway construction worker based on its own negligence. 29 ALR4th 1188.

§ 25-6-1. Liability of master or employer; effect of servant's or employee's knowledge of defect or negligence causing injury.

(a) Except as otherwise provided by law, when a personal injury is received by a servant or employee in the service or business of the master or employer, the master or employer is liable to answer in damages to such servant or employee, as if he were a stranger and not engaged in such service or employment, provided such liability is enforced in a court of competent jurisdiction, in the cases following:

(1) When the injury is caused by reason of any defect in the condition of the ways, works, machinery or plant connected with or used in the business of the master or employer.

(2) When the injury is caused by reason of the negligence of any person in the service or employment of the master or employer who has any superintendence intrusted to him, while in the exercise of such superintendence.

(3) When such injury is caused by reason of the negligence of any person in the service or employment of the master or employer, to whose orders or directions the servant or employee at the time of the injury was bound to conform and did conform, if such injuries resulted from his having so conformed.

(4) When such injury is caused by reason of the act or omission of any person in the service or employment of the master or employer, done or

made in obedience to the rules and regulations or bylaws of the master or employer, or in obedience to particular instructions given by any person delegated with the authority of the master or employer in that behalf.

(5) When such injury is caused by reason of the negligence of any person in the service or employment of the master or employer, who has charge or control of any signal, points, locomotive, engine, electric motor, switch, car or train, upon a railway or any part of the track of a railway.

(b) The master or employer is not liable under this section, if the servant or employee knew of the defect or negligence causing the injury and failed in a reasonable time to give information thereof to the master or employer, or to some person superior to himself engaged in the service or employment of the master or employer, unless the master or employer, or such superior, already knew of such defect or negligence, nor is the master or employer liable under subdivision (a) (1) unless the defect therein mentioned arose from, or had not been discovered or remedied, owing to the negligence of the master or employer, or of some person in the service of the master or employer, and intrusted by him with the duty of seeing that the ways, works, machinery or plant were in proper condition, but in no event shall it be contributory negligence or an assumption of the risk on the part of a servant to remain in the employment of the master or employer after knowledge of the defect or negligence causing the injury, unless he be a servant whose duty it is to remedy the defect or who committed the negligent act causing the injury complained of. (Code 1886, § 2590; Code 1896, § 1749; Code 1907, § 3910; Acts 1911, No. 456, p. 485; Code 1923, § 7598; Code 1940, T. 26, § 326.)

I. General Consideration.
II. Ways, Works, Machinery or Plant.
III. Pleading, Proof and Trial.

I. GENERAL CONSIDERATION.

Enactment of Employer's Liability Act created a new cause of action by the employee against the employer for injury from the negligent conduct of a fellow employee occurring under specified circumstances. C.F. Halstead Contractor, Inc. v. Lowery, 51 Ala. App. 86, 282 So. 2d 909 (1973).

Injuries to employee are presumed to come under the Workmen's Compensation Act. Pound v. Gaulding, 237 Ala. 387, 187 So. 468 (1939); Kasulka v. Louisville & N.R.R., 213 Ala. 463, 105 So. 187 (1925).

And generally, the Employer's Liability Act was superseded by the Workmen's Compensation Act. Pound v. Gaulding, 237 Ala. 387, 187 So. 468 (1939).

The Workmen's Compensation Act superseded the Employer's Liability Act except in cases excepted from the Workmen's Compensation Act by this section thereof and which would otherwise come within the Employer's Liability Act. C.F. Halstead Contractor v. Lowery, 51 Ala. App. 86, 282 So. 2d 909 (1973).

But employees not covered under workmen's compensation may, if applicable, bring an action under Employer's Liability Act. Fleet Transp. Co. v. Insurance Co. of N. Am., 340 F. Supp. 158 (M.D. Ala. 1972).

Injuries to employee from working in an unventilated room filled with fumes, dust and small particles of chemical mixture, which did not appear suddenly and violently, but grew progressively worse, held a "personal injury" but not an "accident" within Workmen's Compensation Act, and hence employee's remedy was at common law and under this section. Gentry v. Swann Chem. Co., 234 Ala. 313, 174 So. 530 (1937).

However, it does not apply to a case controlled by the Workmen's Compensation Act. McDuff v. Kurn, 233 Ala. 619, 172 So. 886 (1937).

In view of §§ 25-5-53 and 25-5-54, actions for injuries to employee when brought against the employer must be brought under the Workmen's Compensation Act, if the relation is not within the exceptions of § 25-5-50. An action under this section is subject to motion to dismiss if the relations of the parties come under the application of the compensation act. Garrett v. Gadsden Cooperage Co., 209 Ala. 223, 96 So. 188 (1923).

Facts showed that cigar company employed more than 16 (now three) employees in its "one business" consisting of three stores, thereby making Workmen's Compensation Act applicable, and barring employee's action for injuries under Employer's Liability Act. Jackson v. United Cigar Stores Co., 228 Ala. 220, 153 So. 422 (1934).

Because the Workmen's Compensation Act and the Employer's Liability Act are mutually exclusive and cannot apply to the same set of facts an employee who seeks to recover damages from his employer under the Employer's Liability Act must bring himself within an exception to the Workmen's Compensation Act by alleging in his complaint facts sufficient to establish that exception. VFW Post 7320 v. Sheffield, 398 So. 2d 262 (Ala. 1981).

Or by the Federal Employer's Liability Act. McDuff v. Kurn, 233 Ala. 619, 172 So. 886 (1937).

But injury within territory ceded to federal government prior to passage of Workmen's Compensation Act and at time when Employer's Liability Act was in force, employee was entitled to recover under Employer's Liability Act instead of Workmen's Compensation Act, since the compensation act was without effect in the ceded territory. Pound v. Gaulding, 237 Ala. 387, 187 So. 468 (1939).

Where employee was injured while working on federal goverment building located on land ceded to federal government prior to passage of Workmen's Compensation Act and at time when Employer's Liability Act was in force, employee was entitled to recover under Employer's Liability Act instead of Workmen's Compensation Act, since the compensation act was without effect in the ceded territory. Pound v. Gaulding, 237 Ala. 387, 187 So. 468 (1939).

And no denial of remedy for injury not within Workmen's Compensation Act. — In the light of the provisions of § 13 of the Constitution "That all courts shall be open; and that every person, for any injury done him, in his lands, goods, person, or reputation, shall have a remedy by due process of law," it cannot be said that for an injury done a person, not within the provisions of the Workmen's Compensation Act, that it was the legislative intent by the enactment of said law to deny such

person a remedy if, under the common law or the Employer's Liability Act, or other statute, he was entitled to maintain an action therefor. Ivey v. Dixon Inv. Co., 283 Ala. 590, 219 So. 2d 639 (1969).

Employer's Liability Act was not rendered inapplicable as a whole to municipalities by §§ 11-47-190 through 11-47-192. Hillis v. City of Huntsville, 274 Ala. 663, 151 So. 2d 240 (1963).

But is inapplicable in conflict therewith. — The Employer's Liability Act is inapplicable to a municipality where in conflict with § 11-47-190, giving literal effect thereto. Hillis v. City of Huntsville, 274 Ala. 663, 151 So. 2d 240 (1963).

Employee's negligence not issue under compensation act. — In action under this chapter for injuries to employee of defendant who had elected not to come under or be bound by Workmen's Compensation Act, plaintiff's negligence was not an issue. Belcher v. Chapman, 242 Ala. 653, 7 So. 2d 859 (1942).

While this statute refers in terms to negligence, it also includes wantonness. Foreman v. Dorsey Trailers, Inc., 256 Ala. 253, 54 So. 2d 499 (1951). See Dorsey Trailers, Inc. v. Foreman, 260 Ala. 141, 69 So. 2d 459 (1953).

Both superintendent and plaintiff must be acting within the line and scope of their employment on the occasion of the accident. Lipscomb v. Chisenhall, 285 Ala. 512, 234 So. 2d 280 (1970).

Lack of ventilation. — If the place of employment was not reasonably safe as a place in which to work because not properly ventilated, defendant employer can be made liable if employee's injury was caused by the negligence of a fellow servant and without the aid of this section. Foreman v. Dorsey Trailers, Inc., 256 Ala. 253, 54 So. 2d 499 (1951).

Taking of medical benefits for hernia under the Workmen's Compensation Act, where compensation proper is precluded under § 25-5-57(a)(6), does not constitute an election against a common-law remedy or one conferred by this chapter, except as to the medical expense thereby avoided. Sam's Place v. Middleton, 39 Ala. App. 481, 103 So. 2d 812 (1958).

Injury arising out of and in the course of employment. — Before an employee can recover from his employer under the Employer's Liability Act, it is clear that it must be shown that the injury to the employee arose "out of and in the course of his employment." Johnson v. Brinker, 289 Ala. 240, 266 So. 2d 851 (1972).

Estoppel. — Since the plaintiff had no action under the Workmen's Compensation Act, his acceptance of compensation payments voluntarily made by the defendant's insurer did not estop him from pursuing his remedy under the common law or the Employer's Liability Act. Ivey v. Dixon Inv. Co., 283 Ala. 590, 219 So. 2d 639 (1969).

Cited in Posey v. TVA, 93 F.2d 726 (5th Cir. 1937); Bagwell v. Woodward Iron Co., 236 Ala. 668, 184 So. 692 (1938); American Mut. Liab. Ins. Co. v. Agricola Furnace Co., 236 Ala. 535, 183 So. 677 (1938); Humphrey v. Poss, 245 Ala. 11, 15 So. 2d 732 (1943); Herndon v. Slayton, 263 Ala. 677, 83 So. 2d 726 (1955); City of Athens v. Cook, 269 Ala. 364, 113 So. 2d 133 (1958); Boeing Co. v. Shipman, 389 F.2d 507 (5th Cir. 1968); Parker v. Kellum, 284 Ala. 701, 228 So. 2d 16 (1969); Shephard v. Chrysler Corp., 314 F. Supp. 1179 (N.D. Ala. 1969); Boeing Co. v. Shipman, 411 F.2d 365 (5th Cir. 1969); Hardy v. Sawyer, 352 So. 2d 1104 (Ala. 1977); Parham v. Taylor, 402 So. 2d 884 (Ala. 1981); Roper v. Campbell, 496 So. 2d 754 (Ala. 1986).

Collateral references. — 56 C.J.S., Master and Servant, §§ 171-481. 57 C.J.S., Master and Servant, §§ 482-554.

53 Am. Jur. 2d, Master & Servant, §§ 482-554.

Liability of master for injury to servant from unknown danger where he failed to inform him of known danger. 4 ALR 488.

Master's liability for injury of one servant by another in enforcing rules. 8 ALR 1432, 156 ALR 640.

"Works," "ways," "equipment," "machinery," etc., what is embraced by such words in employer's liability act. 24 ALR 716.

Liability of employer for injury to employee as affected by expiration of statutory hours of labor before injury. 71 ALR 861.

Statute denying to employer defense of assumption of risk as affecting simple tool rule. 91 ALR 786.

Constitutionality of statute which imposes liability upon employer not within workmen's compensation act, for injury to or death of employee without fault on employer's part. 129 ALR 1124.

Right to maintain action under employer's liability act for wrongful death for benefit of nonresident aliens. 138 ALR 695.

Employer's compliance with specific legal standard prescribed by or pursuant to statute for equipment, structure, or material, as defense to charge of negligence. 159 ALR 870.

Failure to furnish assistance to employee as affecting employer's liability for injury or death of employee. 36 ALR2d 8.

Liability of employer to domestic servant for personal injury or death. 49 ALR2d 317.

Act of God: servant's injury or death caused in whole or in part by. 62 ALR2d 796.

Action by employee against employer for injury by dog. 66 ALR2d 916.

Hours: liability of master for injury or death of servant on master's premises where injury occurred outside working hours. 76 ALR2d 1215.

Doctor: employer's liability to employee for malpractice of physician supplied by employer. 16 ALR3d 564.

Smoking: master's liability for injury to or death of person, or damage to property, resulting from fire allegedly caused by servant's smoking. 20 ALR3d 893.

Exchange of labor by farmers as creating an employment relationship for liability insurance purposes. 89 ALR3d 834.

Employer's tort liability to worker for concealing workplace hazard or nature or extent of injury. 9 ALR4th 778.

What constitutes duress by employer or former employer vitiating employee's release of employer from claims arising out of employment. 30 ALR4th 294.

Validity and enforceability of provision that employer shall be liable for stipulated damages on breach of employment contract. 40 ALR4th 285.

Intoxicating liquors: employer's liability for furnishing or permitting liquor on social occasion, 51 ALR4th 1048.

Liability of employer, supervisor, or manager for intentionally or recklessly causing employee emotional distress. 52 ALR4th 853.

Employer's liability to employee for failure to provide work environment free from tobacco smoke. 63 ALR4th 1021.

II. WAYS, WORKS, MACHINERY OR PLANT.

Temporary contrivances are not part of ways, works, machinery or plant. — Windlass supported on one end by tree at brink of well, a temporary contrivance for digging well, which caused earth to become loose and fall in upon employee, was not part of "ways, works, machinery or plant," within the meaning of subdivision (1) of subsection (a) of this section. Riley v. Chancey Bros., 216 Ala. 176, 112 So. 830 (1927).

A boom or gin pole consisting of timbers fastened to the top of a coal mine trestle or tipple and put up temporarily for use with a block and tackle to hoist timbers to be used in constructing the tipple is not a part of the master's "ways, works, machinery or plant" connected with or used in his business, within subdivision (1) of subsection (a) of this section. Corona Coal Co. v. Davis, 208 Ala. 358, 94 So. 532 (1922).

And complaint showing lack of permanency is insufficient. — A complaint is not sufficient although it alleges that the contrivance was a part of ways, works, machinery or plant of the defendant if another part of the complaint shows lack of permanency in the contrivance. Riley v. Chancey Bros., 216 Ala. 176, 112 So. 830 (1927).

However, tools, etc., furnished for general use are part of employer's "plant". — It is master's nondelegable common-law duty to supply for servant's use, and keep in proper condition, tools, implements and appliances necessary and reasonably adequate to carry on master's business, and such tools, etc., so furnished for general or permanent use, are part of employer's "plant" within meaning of this section. Belcher v. Chapman, 242 Ala. 653, 7 So. 2d 859 (1942).

Particular defects must be alleged and proven. — While this section makes the master liable for an injury to one of his servants on account of any defect in his ways, etc., some particular defect must be alleged and proven. It is not sufficient merely to follow the language of the statute without describing any defect. Lipscomb v. Paul, 277 Ala. 182, 168 So. 2d 214 (1964).

A complaint under the Employer's Liability Act containing allegations that employee was injured by reason of a defect in the condition of the ways, works, machinery or plant connected with or used in the business of his employers, to-wit, a grain auger having fallen on him, was not sufficient to state a cause of action under the act, where it lacked any allegation that the auger was defective, or that any other tool or appliance was defective, or that the auger fell as the proximate result of a defect in the auger or any other tool, appliance or device. Lipscomb v. Paul, 277 Ala. 182, 168 So. 2d 214 (1964).

And described in complaint with particularity. — When based on defects in the ways, works or machinery of the employer, the complaint should describe the defects with such particularity as to inform the defendant of what he is called on to defend. Lipscomb v. Paul, 277 Ala. 182, 168 So. 2d 214 (1964).

Also burden of proof is upon plaintiff to show that a contrivance is a part of ways, works, machinery or plant of the defendant as provided by subdivision (1) of subsection (a) of this section. Corona Coal Co. v. Davis, 208 Ala. 358, 94 So. 532 (1922).

III. PLEADING, PROOF AND TRIAL.

Complaint declaring on negligence should conform to rules applying to pleading generally. — A complaint declaring on negligence under the Employer's Liability Act should, in respect of certainty, conform to rules which, under our system, apply to pleading generally. Lipscomb v. Paul, 277 Ala. 182, 168 So. 2d 214 (1964).

And should allege breach of duty owed plaintiff. — In order to maintain an action based on negligence, the complaint must show the existence of some duty which defendants owed to plaintiff, and, in addition, must allege a breach of such duty. Lipscomb v. Paul, 277 Ala. 182, 168 So. 2d 214 (1964).

Insufficient allegation of negligence under subdivision (a)(3). — A count framed under subdivision (a)(3), of this section, alleging that plaintiff, a minor, was ordered to grind meat with an electric power machine, and that injuries to his hand, caught in the grinder, were caused by the negligence of defendant's employee, to whose orders plaintiff was bound to conform, held fatally defective in not alleging that such employee was negligent in ordering plaintiff to grind the meat. Richardson v. Vaughn, 208 Ala. 422, 94 So. 514 (1922).

Allegations where injuries due to lack of ventilation. — In action for injuries to employee from working in unventilated room filled with fumes, dust and small particles of a chemical mixture, count charging that defendant's servants and agents wantonly, willfully and intentionally caused plaintiff to work in such room instead of alleging that his injury was so caused, held subject to motion to dismiss. Gentry v. Swann Chem. Co., 234 Ala. 313, 174 So. 530 (1937).

In action for injuries sustained by employee while working in plant where trisodium phosphate was manufactured, allegedly due to lack of ventilation resulting in room being filled with fumes, dust and small particles of the mixture, which would stick to the skin, and which plaintiff was forced to breathe and inhale, counts based on common-law negligence, on defects in employer's ways, works, machinery or plant, and on negligence of person in employ of defendant to whom superintendent of the work and the men engaged in the work was entrusted, held to state causes of action. Gentry v. Swann Chem. Co., 234 Ala. 313, 174 So. 530 (1937).

Action against municipality based on subdivision (a)(1) fails to state cause of action. — In an action against a municipality, a count, framed under subdivision (a)(1) of this section, would not be within the purview of § 11-47-190, and as such would be subject to motion to dismiss for failing to state a cause of action. Hillis v. City of Huntsville, 274 Ala. 663, 151 So. 2d 240 (1963).

But action against municipality based on subdivision (a)(2) does state cause of action. — A count, framed under subdivision (a)(2) of this section, alleging that the injury was caused by reason of the negligence of the city's agents and employees entrusted with the superintendence of the work in allowing defective brakes to exist on a tractor would not be in conflict with § 11-47-190 as it would be within the purview of the first class of municipal liability contemplated by the latter, i.e., ". . . said injury or wrong was done or suffered through the neglect, carelessness or unskillfullness of some agent, officer or employee of the municipality engaged in work therefor." Hillis v. City of Huntsville, 274 Ala. 663, 151 So. 2d 240 (1963).

Employer must establish defensive matter. — In employee's action under Employer's Liability Act to recover for injuries sustained while working on federal government building located on land ceded to federal government prior to passage of Workmen's Compensation Act, if, upon any theory of conflict of laws or otherwise, employee was not entitled to recover, employer would be required to establish such defensive matter. Pound v. Gaulding, 237 Ala. 387, 187 So. 468 (1939).

Contributory negligence is a defense under this section, and questions of contributory negligence may rest upon facts or inferences from facts within the province of the factfinder to draw. Lee v. Shrader, 502 So. 2d 741 (Ala. 1987).

When name of negligent coemployee to be stated. — When the complaint counts on one of the alternatives of this section, other than the first, it should either name the negligent coemployee or allege that his name is unknown to plaintiff. This does not apply to alternative No. 1, which relates to a defect in the ways, works, machinery or plant of defendant, since the injured party has no better opportunity than the common employer to know the name of the negligent employee under this alternative. Atlantic Coast Line R.R. v. Winn, 259 Ala. 184, 66 So. 2d 184 (1953).

General averment of negligence by fellow servant not sufficient. — Except as modified by statute, a servant assumes the risk of injury caused by a fellow servant. This is the common-law doctrine. This section modifies such principle insofar as the negligence of a fellow servant is concerned. So that if the complaint counts on the negligence of a fellow servant, it should allege the existence of matter made necessary to that end by the statute, and a general averment of negligence by a fellow servant is not sufficient. Foreman v. Dorsey Trailers, Inc., 256 Ala. 253, 54 So. 2d 499 (1951).

Complaint charging breach of common-law duty. — Where the complaint charges the injury of employee to the wantonness of the

employer in not providing a reasonably safe place in which to work, knowing the danger to employee by not doing so, it undertakes to charge to the employer the breach of a common-law duty to provide a reasonably safe place in which employee must work. It was not controlled, therefore, by the Employer's Liability Act, and the complaint also shows that the Workmen's Compensation Act does not apply. Foreman v. Dorsey Trailers, Inc., 256 Ala. 253, 54 So. 2d 499 (1951).

When the common-law duty to provide a safe place in which to work is shown by the complaint to exist, it is not necessary to make the allegations required by this section, which are necessary when the complaint may be proven by showing the negligence of a fellow servant. Foreman v. Dorsey Trailers, Inc., 256 Ala. 253, 54 So. 2d 499 (1951).

Burden of proof on plaintiff. — See case under preceding analysis line.

Evidence properly admitted. — In employee's action under this section for injuries sustained in fall in open freight elevator shaft, evidence as to the method of the elevator's use by the employer and its employees, and the precautions taken to prevent injury, was properly admitted. Johnson v. Johns Serv. Funeral Parlor, 240 Ala. 231, 198 So. 357 (1940).

Sufficiency of evidence. — In employee's action under this section for injuries sustained when scaffold gave way, evidence sustained jury's verdict for employee based on negligence of employer's superintendent. Pound v. Gaulding, 237 Ala. 387, 187 So. 468 (1939).

In employee's action under this section for injuries sustained while working on land ceded to government prior to passage of Workmen's Compensation Act, evidence authorized jury's finding that there was a new hiring each day on ceded land as respects whether compensation act or this section applied. Pound v. Gaulding, 237 Ala. 387, 187 So. 468 (1939).

In an action by employee to recover for injuries sustained due to a defective truck, the employer was not entitled to the affirmative charge where the evidence was in conflict as to whose duty it was to keep the truck repaired. Parkinson v. Hudson, 265 Ala. 4, 88 So. 2d 793 (1956).

There was sufficient evidence to require submission to the jury, and therefore to preclude a directed verdict on the negligence of employer, where employer testified that he knew of the dangerous conditions on the roof of new building that required a "toe board" to prevent a fall and that he knew he had a duty to provide a reasonably safe place for plaintiff to work. Bellew v. Sloan, 536 So. 2d 917 (Ala. 1988).

In action by administratrix of firefighter's

estate, evidence was sufficient to support jury verdict for the estate where regulations requiring firefighters to wear full "turn-out equipment" at all times while fighting a fire burdened the deceased with excessive and foreseeably unhealthy equipment, which, in combination with the 90-degree temperature caused him to suffer a heat stroke and to die while responding to a brushfire. City of Birmingham v. Hale, 574 So. 2d 784 (Ala. 1991).

Questions for jury. — In employee's action under this section for injuries sustained when scaffold gave way, question whether scaffold was in safe condition on evening preceding accident, as respects duty of employer's superintendent to inspect, and question of negligence of superintendent in failure properly to inspect were for jury. Pound v. Gaulding, 237 Ala. 387, 187 So. 468 (1939).

In action under this act for injuries to employee as result of negligence of superintendent of plaintiff's work, whether such superintendent was independent contractor or employee of defendant held for jury under evidence. Belcher v. Chapman, 242 Ala. 653, 7 So. 2d 859 (1942).

In employee's action under this section for injuries sustained in fall into open elevator shaft while carrying equipment, whether employee was contributorily negligent was for jury under the evidence. Johnson v. Johns Serv. Funeral Parlor, 240 Ala. 231, 198 So. 357 (1940).

§ 25-6-2. Damages recovered not subject to debts, etc., of servant or employee.

Damages recovered by the servant or employee, of and from the master or employer, are not subject to the payment of debts or any legal liabilities incurred by him, except judgments in favor of the wholly dependent, or dependents, as defined in Section 25-5-61. (Code 1886, § 2592; Code 1896, § 1750; Code 1907, § 3911; Code 1923, § 7599; Acts 1933, Ex. Sess., No. 126, p. 118; Code 1940, T. 26, § 327.)

Cited in Posey v. TVA, 93 F.2d 726 (5th Cir. 1937); American Mut. Liab. Ins. Co. v. Agricola Furnace Co., 236 Ala. 535, 183 So. 677 (1938).

Collateral references. — Employer's liability to employee for failure to provide work environment free from tobacco smoke. 63 ALR4th 1021.

§ 25-6-3. Maintenance of action by personal representative; disposition of damages recovered.

If such injury results in the death of the servant or employee, his personal representative is entitled to maintain an action therefor in a court of competent jurisdiction, and the damages recovered are not subject to the payment of debts or liabilities but shall be distributed according to the statute of descent and distributions. (Code 1886, § 2591; Code 1896, § 1751; Code 1907, § 3912; Acts 1911, No. 454, p. 483; Code 1923, § 7600; Code 1940, T. 26, § 328.)

Cross references. — As to descents and distributions generally, see § 43-8-40 et seq.

This section provides the remedy when the employee dies from an injury specified in § 25-6-1. United States Cast Iron Pipe & Foundry Co. v. McCoy, 196 Ala. 45, 71 So. 406 (1916); McDuff v. Kurn, 233 Ala. 619, 172 So. 886 (1937).

And it is an extension of the employee's right of action for injury from negligence of fellow employee, if it resulted in death, to the personal representative. C.F. Halstead Contractor v. Lowery, 51 Ala. App. 86, 282 So. 2d 909 (1973).

If the parties are not covered by Workmen's Compensation Act. — The denial of the right of action under this section, where the parties have been brought within the field of operation covered by the Workmen's Compensation Act, is manifestly germane and cognate. Chapman v. Railway Fuel Co., 212 Ala. 106, 101 So. 879 (1924).

Or the Federal Employers' Liability Act. — Count against employer for employee's death, based on State Employer's Liability Act, held not to authorize recovery, where evidence showed that plaintiff's rights were controlled either by Federal Employers' Liability Act or workmen's compensation law. McDuff v. Kurn, 233 Ala. 619, 172 So. 886 (1937).

But right of action under section distinct from wrongful death action. — The purpose of the wrongful death statute is punitive, but the purpose of the action for death under the Employer's Liability Act is compensatory. Both statutes created new actions unknown at common law, but for different purposes, and there is an entirely different measure of damages and an entirely different basis for establishing liability in the two actions. C.F. Halstead Contractor v. Lowery, 51 Ala. App. 86, 282 So. 2d 909 (1973).

Election of remedies and joinder of parties. — Where the right of action for wrongful death arises out of a personal breach of a common-law duty of the master to the servant, whether such duty is nondelegable or not, or a breach of such duty by the master's vice principal or alter ego, of a nondelegable common-law duty, and the case is not within the Workmen's Compensation Act, the personal representative may at his or her election proceed against the master alone under this section, or proceed under the Wrongful Death Act and join as parties defendant joint tortfeasors, whose negligence or wrongful acts concurred with that of the master in producing the death. Hardy v. City of Dothan, 234 Ala. 664, 176 So. 449 (1937).

But if the right of action is predicated on the negligence of a fellow servant, not cognizable at common law, but for which liability is imposed on the master by the Employer's Liability Act, such joinder is not premissible for the reason that the measure of damages against one would be punitive and as to the other compensatory only. Hardy v. City of Dothan, 234 Ala. 664, 176 So. 449 (1937).

Applicable statute of limitations. — The Employer's Liability Act does not provide a limitation upon the time for bringing action by the personal representative; therefore, in the absence of such provision, the general statute for the bringing of such action for injury by the employee had he not died must be looked to: that statute is former § 6-2-39 (see now § 6-2-38). C.F. Halstead Contractor v. Lowery, 51 Ala. App. 86, 282 So. 2d 909 (1973).

The limitation of two years as provided for in § 6-5-410, does not apply to an action for death under the Employer's Liability Act because the two actions are separate and distinct. C.F. Halstead Contractor v. Lowery, 51 Ala. App. 86, 282 So. 2d 909 (1973).

Distributee may compromise claim. — Action by administrator for wrongful death of intestate, under this section or § 6-5-410, is for benefit of distributees of estate, and not for estate, and distributee who is sui juris may compromise claim and give release valid equity. Irwin v. Alabama Fuel & Iron Co., 215 Ala. 328, 110 So. 566 (1925).

Cited in Posey v. TVA, 93 F.2d 726 (5th Cir. 1937); American Mut. Liab. Ins. Co. v. Agricola Furnace Co., 236 Ala. 535, 183 So. 677 (1938); City of Athens v. Cook, 269 Ala. 364, 113 So. 2d 133 (1958).

Collateral references. — Employer's liability to employee for failure to provide work environment free from tobacco smoke. 63 ALR4th 1021.

§ 25-6-4. Acceptance of insurance benefits, etc., not to bar action, etc.; setoff.

No contract of employment, insurance, relief benefit or indemnity for injury or death entered into by or on behalf of any employee, nor the acceptance of any such insurance, relief benefit or indemnity by the person entitled thereto shall constitute any bar or defense to any action brought to recover damages for personal injuries to or death of such employee, but, upon the trial of such action against any employer, the defendant may set off therein any sum he has contributed toward any such insurance, relief benefit or indemnity that may have been paid to the injured employee or, in case of death, to his personal representative. (Code 1907, § 3913; Code 1923, § 7601; Code 1940, T. 26, § 329.)

No denial of remedy for injury not within Workmen's Compensation Act. — In the light of the provisions of § 13 of the Constitution "That all courts shall be open; and that every person, for any injury done him, in his lands, goods, person, or reputation, shall have a remedy by due process of law," it cannot be said that for an injury done a person, not within the provisions of the Workmen's Compensation Act, that it was the legislative intent by the enactment of said law to deny such person a remedy if, under the common law or the Employer's Liability Act, or other statute, he was entitled to maintain an action therefor. Ivey v. Dixon Inv. Co., 283 Ala. 590, 219 So. 2d 639 (1969).

Estoppel. — Since the plaintiff had no action under the Workmen's Compensation Act, his acceptance of compensation payments voluntarily made by the defendant's insurer did not estop him from pursuing his remedy under the common law or the Employer's Liability Act. Ivey v. Dixon Inv. Co., 283 Ala. 590, 219 So. 2d 639 (1969).

Cited in Posey v. TVA, 93 F.2d 726 (5th Cir. 1937); American Mut. Liab. Ins. Co. v. Agricola Furnace Co., 236 Ala. 535, 183 So. 677 (1938).

Collateral references. — Employer's liability to employee for failure to provide work environment free from tobacco smoke. 63 ALR4th 1021.

CHAPTER 7.

LABOR UNIONS AND LABOR RELATIONS.

Collateral references. — What constitutes unfair labor practice under state public employee relations acts. 9 ALR4th 20.

ARTICLE 1.

GENERAL PROVISIONS.

For discussion of constitutionality of chapter. — See Alabama State Fed'n of Labor, Local 103 v. McAdory, 325 U.S. 450, 65 S. Ct. 1384, 89 L. Ed. 1725 (1945); Congress of Indus. Orgs. v. McAdory, 325 U.S. 472, 65 S. Ct. 1395, 89 L. Ed. 1741 (1945).

This chapter does not violate the provision of the Constitution, § 45, that each law shall contain but one subject which shall be clearly expressed in its title. Alabama State Fed'n of Labor v. McAdory, 246 Ala. 1, 18 So. 2d 810 (1944).

Nor is it repugnant to the National Labor Relations Act. Alabama State Fed'n of Labor v. McAdory, 246 Ala. 1, 18 So. 2d 810 (1944).

Nor does it impose a burden on interstate commerce, and is within the state's police power. Alabama State Fed'n of Labor v. McAdory, 246 Ala. 1, 18 So. 2d 810 (1944).

And it is not invalid because of a capricious discrimination, in that it expressly

701

excludes organizations coming within the influence of the Railway Labor Act, 45 U.S.C.A. § 151 et seq. Alabama State Fed'n of Labor v. McAdory, 246 Ala. 1, 18 So. 2d 810 (1944); Alabama State Fed'n of Labor v. McAdory, 325 U.S. 450, 65 S. Ct. 1384, 89 L. Ed. 1725 (1945).

However, certain sections were invalid. — See Alabama State Fed'n of Labor v. McAdory, 246 Ala. 1, 18 So. 2d 810 (1944);

Alabama State Fed'n of Labor v. Lusk, 246 Ala. 32, 18 So. 2d 833 (1944).

Cited in Klibanoff v. Tri-Cities Retail Clerks' Union, Local 1678, 258 Ala. 479, 64 So. 2d 393 (1953).

Collateral references. — Liability of labor union for injury or death allegedly resulting from unsafe working conditions. 14 ALR4th 1161.

§ 25-7-1. Declaration of policy.

The right to live involves the right to work. The public and working men and women must be protected. The activities of labor organizations affect the social and economic conditions of the state and the welfare of its citizens. It is declared to be the policy of this state, in the exercise of its police power and in the protection of the public interest, to promote voluntary and peaceful settlement and adjustment of labor disputes and to regulate the activities and affairs of labor organizations, their officers, agents and other representatives in the manner and to the extent provided in this article. (Acts 1943, No. 298, p. 252, § 1.)

Collateral references. — Procedural rights of union members in union disciplinary proceedings — modern state cases. 79 ALR4th 941.

§ 25-7-2. Definitions.

When used in this article, the terms defined in this section shall have the meanings herein ascribed to them, unless it clearly appears from the context that some other meaning is indicated:

(1) LABOR ORGANIZATION or LABOR UNION. Every organization, association, group, union, lodge, local, branch or subdivision thereof, whether incorporated or not, having within its membership employees working in the State of Alabama, organized for the purpose of dealing with employer or employers concerning hours of employment, rates of pay or the tenure or other terms or conditions of employment, but such term or terms shall not include any labor organization or labor union the members of which are subject to the Act of Congress known as the Railway Labor Act.

(2) LABOR DISPUTE. Any controversy concerning terms, tenure or conditions of employment or concerning the association or representation of persons in negotiating, fixing, maintaining, changing or seeking to arrange terms or conditions of employment, regardless of whether the disputants stand in the proximate relation of employer and employee; provided, that this definition shall not relate to a dispute between an individual worker and his employer. (Acts 1943, No. 298, p. 252, § 2.)

§ 25-7-3. Construction of article.

Except as otherwise specifically provided in this article, nothing contained in this article shall be construed to interfere with or impede or diminish in any way the right to strike or the right to individuals to work, nor shall anything in this chapter be construed so as to invade unlawfully the right to freedom of speech. (Acts 1943, No. 298, p. 252, § 13.)

Collateral references. — 51A C.J.S., Labor Relations, § 275.
48 Am. Jur. 2d, Labor & Labor Relations, § 1360.

Right of labor union to strike to compel payment by employer of fine or other penalty. 32 ALR2d 342.

§ 25-7-4. Boards of mediation.

The Governor may, whenever he considers it expedient, appoint a board of mediation, consisting of three members, for the purpose of gathering facts and information and hearing evidence concerning the cause of any strike, lockout or other dispute or disagreement between employees or between any employer and his employees, for the purpose of making recommendations for the peaceable solution thereof, and, if the parties involved in such strike, lockout or other dispute or disagreement shall in writing submit to such board such strike, lockout or other dispute or disagreement for arbitration, which written submission must contain an agreement to abide by the determination or award of the board, then also for the purpose of arbitrating such strike, lockout or other dispute or disagreement. One member of the board shall be a person who, on account of his previous employment or affiliations, shall be generally classified as a representative of employers. One member of the board shall be a person who, on account of his previous employment or affiliations, shall be generally classified as a representative of employees. One member of the board shall represent the interest of the public, shall not be generally classified as a representative of employers or of employees and shall be chairman of the board. The Governor may, if he so elects, serve as one of the three members thereof, in which event the Governor shall represent the interests of the public and serve as chairman of the board. Members of such board shall be paid their expenses, as provided in Article 2 of Chapter 7 of Title 36, and $20.00 per day for each day the board is necessarily in session, except, that the Governor shall not be entitled to any such per diem allowance. The board of mediation shall have the same power and authority to subpoena witnesses and to compel the production of books, records, documents and papers as the Director of Industrial Relations or the members of the board of appeals have under Chapter 2 of this title, and the same power and authority to enter any place of employment, place of public assembly or public building as the Director of Industrial Relations has under Chapter 2 of this title. The board of mediation shall make a finding of facts and a recommendation for settling such strike, lockout or other dispute or disagreement, and, if such strike, lockout or other dispute or disagreement shall have been submitted for arbitration, a determination or award, which may be enforced by any circuit court in the same manner as other determinations or awards of matters submitted for arbitration. Such board shall remain in session no longer than is necessary to accomplish the purposes for which it was appointed, and in no event more than 30 days in which to make a determination, but the board shall be allowed an additional 10 days time to make their findings of fact and recommendation for settling such strike, lockout or other dispute or disagreement, and, as soon as it shall have rendered its findings of fact, recommendation, determination or award, it shall be discharged. Copies of each finding of facts, recommendation, determination and award shall be submitted to the Governor, to the Commissioner of the Department of Labor and to each party or a representative of each party to such strike, lockout, dispute or disagreement. (Acts 1943, No. 298, p. 252, § 6.)

Cross references. — As to local boards of arbitration, see § 25-7-50.

Collateral references. — 51A C.J.S., Labor Relations, §§ 460, 468, 475.

§ 25-7-5. Labor organizations to file copies of constitutions, bylaws and amendments thereto; annual reports.

(a) Every labor organization functioning in Alabama, and every labor organization hereafter desiring to function in Alabama shall, before doing so, file a copy of its constitution and its bylaws and a copy of the constitution and bylaws of the national or international union, if any, to which the labor organization belongs, with the Department of Labor, but this provision shall not be construed to require the filing of any ritual relating solely to the initiation or reception of members. All changes or amendments to the constitution or bylaws, local, national or international, adopted subsequent to their original filing must be filed with the Department of Labor within 30 days after the adoption thereof.

(b) Every labor organization functioning in the State of Alabama and having 25 or more members in any calendar year shall file annually, on or before March 31, or, if the organization's fiscal year does not coincide with the calendar year, within 90 days after the close of the organization's fiscal year, with every member of their respective labor organizations and with the Commissioner of the Department of Labor, a report in writing showing certain facts hereinafter required as of the close of business on the last day of the previous calendar or fiscal year. Such report shall be filed by the secretary or business agent of such labor organization and shall show the following facts:

(1) The name of the labor organization;

(2) The location of its principal office and its offices in Alabama;

(3) The name of the president, secretary, treasurer and other officers and business agents, together with the salaries, wages, bonuses and other remuneration paid each and post office address of each;

(4) The date of the regular election of officers of such labor organization;

(5) The number of its paid up members;

(6) A complete financial statement of all fees, dues, fines or assessments levied and/or received, together with an itemized list of all disbursements, with the names of recipients and purpose therefor, covering the preceding 12 months; and

(7) A complete statement of all property owned by the labor organization, including any moneys on hand or accredited to such labor organization. Said report shall be duly verified by the oath of the president, secretary or some other regularly selected and acting officer of such labor organization having knowledge of the facts therein stated. It shall be the duty of the Commissioner of Labor to cause to be printed and to make available to the public forms for making such report. At the time of filing each such report it shall be the duty of every such labor organization to pay the Commissioner of Labor an annual fee therefor in the sum of $2.00. The Commissioner of Labor shall receive, file and index the reports provided for in this section.

(c) The records provided for in this section shall be made available by the Commissioner of Labor in his office to the Governor of Alabama for examination.

(d) It shall be unlawful for any fiscal or other officer or agent of any labor organization to collect or accept payment of any dues, fees, assessments, fines or any other moneys from any member while such labor organization is in default with respect to filing the annual report required in this section. (Acts 1943, No. 298, p. 252, § 7; Acts 1961, Ex. Sess., No. 262, p. 2278.)

This section does not violate the constitutional provisions of free speech and assembly. Alabama State Fed'n of Labor v. McAdory, 246 Ala. 1, 18 So. 2d 810 (1944); Bordon v. Sparks, 54 F. Supp. 300 (M.D. Ala. 1944).

Nor is it invalid as requiring issuance of a license to a labor organization as a condition precedent to functioning in the state. Alabama State Fed'n of Labor v. McAdory, 246 Ala. 1, 18 So. 2d 810 (1944).

And filing of reports required by this section is a reasonable regulation under the police power of the state. The requirement for a financial statement may be fully justified as a regulation for the benefit of the members of the

organization, and no claimed right of privacy in any manner affects the validity of this section. Alabama State Fed'n of Labor v. McAdory, 246 Ala. 1, 18 So. 2d 810 (1944).

"Function" as used in this section simply means a labor organization, whether incorporated or not, engaged in business in this state, and in the character of business thus indicated, for the promotion of the interests of its members. True, as a part of its functioning, and a part only, the assemblage of its members for discussion is had, but this is merely incidental. Alabama State Fed'n of Labor v. McAdory, 246 Ala. 1, 18 So. 2d 810 (1944).

Cited in Shiland v. Retail Clerks, Local 1657, 259 Ala. 277, 66 So. 2d 146 (1953).

§ 25-7-6. Freedom to join or refrain from joining labor organizations.

Every person shall be free to join or to refrain from joining any labor organization, except as otherwise provided in Section 25-7-13, and, in the exercise of such freedom, shall be free from interference by force, coercion or intimidation, by threats of force or coercion or by the intimidation of or injury to his family. (Acts 1943, No. 298, p. 252, § 8.)

Cross references. — As to right to work, see § 25-7-30.

This section is valid. — See Walter v. State, 34 Ala. App. 268, 38 So. 2d 609 (1949), holding both this section and former § 25-7-7 constitutional.

And this section and former § 25-7-7 have not made illegal a contract calling for a closed shop. Hotel & Restaurant Employees, Int'l Alliance v. Greenwood, 249 Ala. 265, 30 So. 2d 696 (1947).

This section and former § 25-7-7 only denounce the imposition of restraint on one regarding his attitude toward affiliation with a labor organization by force, coercion, intimidation or by threats thereof, or by intimidation of or injury to his family. Hotel & Restaurant Employees, Int'l Alliance v. Greenwood, 249 Ala. 265, 30 So. 2d 696 (1947).

And make unlawful interference with person's freedom of choice. — The essence of this section and former § 25-7-7 is not to ban a closed shop but to make unlawful interference, by the stated methods, with a person's freedom of choice in regard to such affiliation. Hotel & Restaurant Employees, Int'l Alliance v. Greenwood, 249 Ala. 265, 30 So. 2d 696 (1947).

Maintenance of membership clause in a contract is understood to mean that all employees who are members of the union at a specified time after the contract is executed and all who later join the union must, as a condition of employment, remain as members in good standing for the duration of the agreement between the employer and the union. Therefore, if a contract between employer and union contained a maintenance of membership clause, employee was obligated to retain his union membership standing by the payment of the required dues. And the company was also bound by the terms of the contract. Walter v. State, 34 Ala. App. 268, 38 So. 2d 609 (1949), reversing conviction for discharge of employee as a result of failure to pay union dues.

Cited in Klibanoff v. Tri-Cities Retail Clerks' Union, Local 1678, 258 Ala. 479, 64 So. 2d 393 (1953).

Collateral references. — 51 C.J.S., Labor Relations, § 61.

Union security arrangements in state public employment. 95 ALR3d 1102.

Workers' compensation: injuries incurred during labor activity. 61 ALR4th 196.

§§ 25-7-7, 25-7-8. Repealed by Acts 1977, No. 607, p. 812, § 9901, as amended, effective January 1, 1980.

§ 25-7-9. Interference, etc., with peaceable exercise of lawful industry, business, etc.

Any person who, by force or threats of violence to person or property, or who, by any means of duress prevents, or seeks to prevent, another from doing work or furnishing materials or from contracting to do work or furnish materials for or to any person engaged in any lawful business, or who disturbs, interferes with or prevents, or in any manner attempts to prevent the peaceable exercise of any lawful industry, business or calling by any other person shall, on conviction, be fined not less than $10.00 nor more than $500.00, and may also be imprisoned in the county jail or sentenced to hard labor for the county for not more than 12 months. (Code 1886, § 3763; Code 1896, § 5514; Code 1907, § 6856; Code 1923, § 3990; Code 1940, T. 26, § 336.)

This section seems to be constitutional. — See Hardie-Tynes Mfg. Co. v. Cruse, 189 Ala. 66, 66 So. 657 (1914).

It prohibits picketing and even peaceable persuasions. — This section prohibits picketing by members of a labor union, and even peaceable persuasion of persons not to become employees of one transacting a lawful business, or to induce employees to quit the service of such person, where the intention and

effect of such act is to prevent the operation of a lawful business or enterprise, and to interfere with the operation thereof. Hardie-Tynes Mfg. Co. v. Cruse, 189 Ala. 66, 66 So. 657 (1914).

Also threats, intimidation or violence to induce employees to leave or not to enter service of employer. — Employees may rightfully organize themselves into associations for mutual protection and betterment, and having so organized, may, by confederated action, withdraw from or declare to enter the service of a particular employer, but in such self-protection they may not employ threats, intimidation or violence against or on employers or their employees, or on strangers, to induce them to leave, or not to enter the service of a particular employer. Hardie-Tynes Mfg. Co. v. Cruse, 189 Ala. 66, 66 So. 657 (1914).

Cited in Carlton v. Musicians Protective Ass'n, Local 479, 276 Ala. 128, 159 So. 2d 831 (1963).

Collateral references. — 51A C.J.S., Labor Relations, § 284.

45 Am. Jur. 2d, Interference, § 45 et seq. 48

Am. Jur. 2d, Labor & Labor Relations, §§ 2, 3, 7, 8, 45-48, 342.

Fines: right of labor union to strike, picket, or impose boycott to compel payment by employer of fine or other penalty. 32 ALR2d 342.

Right of public employees to strike or engage in work stoppage. 37 ALR3d 1147.

State criminal prosecutions of union officer or member for specific physical threats to employer's property or person, in connection with labor dispute — modern cases. 43 ALR4th 1141.

Civil action for damages under state Racketeer Influenced and Corrupt Organizations Acts (RICO) for losses from racketeering activity. 62 ALR4th 654.

§ 25-7-10. Interference with acquisitions, use or disposition of materials, etc., by operator of place of employment. Repealed by Acts 1977, No. 607, p. 812, § 9901, as amended, effective January 1, 1980.

§ 25-7-11. Use or threats of use of force, etc., to secure or prevent attendance at strike votes or to influence votes.

It shall be unlawful for any person at any time or place, by force or the threat of force, to seek to secure or prevent attendance at any meeting or voting place at which any strike vote is taken, or to influence the vote of such employee at such meeting or voting place by the use of force, coercion or intimidation or by threat of force or coercion or by the offering of a reward or the threat of loss of employment or membership in a labor organization. Any person using such force, coercion or threats or offering of rewards or withholding of membership from labor organizations or any person encouraging, aiding or abetting in such prohibited conduct shall be guilty of a misdemeanor. (Acts 1943, No. 298, p. 252, § 13.)

There is no private cause of action implied from this section. Hester v. International Union of Operating Eng'rs, 742 F. Supp. 1522 (N.D. Ala. 1990), aff'd in part and rev'd in part on other grounds, 941 F.2d 1574 (11th Cir. 1991).

Collateral references. — Civil action for damages under state Racketeer Influenced and Corrupt Organizations Acts (RICO) for losses from racketeering activity. 62 ALR4th 654.

§ 25-7-12. Collection, etc., by labor organization, etc., of fee, etc., as work permit or condition of work.

It shall be unlawful for any labor organization, any labor organizer, any officer, agent, representative or member of any labor organization or any other person to collect, receive or demand, directly or indirectly, from any person, any fee, assessment or sum of money whatsoever, as a work permit or as a condition for the privilege of work; provided, however, this shall not prevent the collection of initiation fees or dues. (Acts 1943, No. 298, p. 252, § 15.)

For discussion of section, see Alabama State Fed'n of Labor, Local 103 v. McAdory, 325 U.S. 450, 65 S. Ct. 1384, 89 L. Ed. 1725 (1945).

This section is proper exercise of the police power. Alabama State Federation of Labor v. McAdory, 246 Ala. 1, 18 So. 2d 810 (1944).

Cited in Klibanoff v. Tri-Cities Retail Clerks' Union, Local 1678, 258 Ala. 479, 64 So. 2d 393 (1953).

Collateral references. — Union security arrangements in state public employment. 95 ALR3d 1102.

§ 25-7-13. Membership of executive, administrative, etc., employees in labor organizations; effect of section on existing insurance contracts.

It shall be unlawful for any executive, administrative, professional or supervisory employee to be a member in, or to be accepted for membership by, any labor organization, the constitution and bylaws of which permit membership to employees other than those in executive, administrative, professional or supervisory capacities or which is affiliated with any labor organization which permits membership to employees other than those in an executive, administrative, professional or supervisory capacity. The provisions of this section shall not be construed so as to interfere with or void any insurance contract in existence and in force on June 29, 1943. (Acts 1943, No. 298, p. 252, § 16.)

For discussion of section, see Alabama State Fed'n of Labor, Local 103 v. McAdory, 325 U.S. 450, 65 S. Ct. 1384, 89 L. Ed. 1725 (1945); Congress of Indus. Orgs. v. McAdory, 325 U.S. 472, 64 S. Ct. 1395, 89 L. Ed. 1741 (1945).

This section is valid. Alabama State Fed'n of Labor v. McAdory, 246 Ala. 1, 18 So. 2d 810 (1944).

This section applies to an employee, not to an employer, and it cannot render unlawful an agreement between a barbershop proprietor and a barbers' union permitting the former to display a union shop card provided he complied with certain imposed conditions.

Head v. Local Union 83, Journeymen Barbers, 262 Ala. 84, 77 So. 2d 363 (1955).

Cited in Klibanoff v. Tri-Cities Retail Clerks' Union, Local 1678, 258 Ala. 479, 64 So. 2d 393 (1953).

Collateral references. — Union security arrangements in state public employment. 95 ALR3d 1102.

Who are supervisors for purposes of bargaining—unit determinations. 96 ALR3d 723.

Civil action for damages under state Racketeer Influenced and Corrupt Organizations Acts (RICO) for losses from racketeering activity. 62 ALR4th 654.

§ 25-7-14. Adoption and use of labels or devices by unions or associations of workingmen.

Any union or association of workingmen may adopt and use a label or device for the purpose of designating and distinguishing any goods, wares or merchandise or other product of the labor of the association or union of workingmen or of a member or members of the association or union. A copy of any such label or device may be filed in the Office of the Secretary of State upon payment of a fee of $1.00. (Code 1907, § 4876; Code 1923, § 8990; Code 1940, T. 26, § 330.)

Collateral references. — 51 C.J.S., Labor Relations, § 125.
48 Am. Jur. 2d, Labor & Labor Relations, §§ 284-291.

Rights in union label, shop card, or other insignia denoting union shop or workmanship. 42 ALR2d 709.

§ 25-7-15. Provisions of article cumulative.

The provisions of this article shall be cumulative of all other laws in force on June 29, 1943, upon the subject, and, in the event of a conflict between laws in force on June 29, 1943, and the provisions of this article, then and in that event the provisions, offenses and punishments set forth in this article shall prevail over such laws. (Acts 1943, No. 298, p. 252, § 19.)

§ 25-7-16. Penalty for violations of article.

If any labor organization violates any provision of this article, it shall be penalized civilly in a sum not exceeding $1,000.00 for each such violation, to be recovered as a penalty in the circuit court of the county in which the violation occurred, the action being brought in the name of the State of Alabama by the district attorney of the circuit in which the violation occurred, and it shall be the duty of the district attorney of any circuit in which any such violation occurs to institute and prosecute such action. The doing of any act forbidden or declared unlawful by the provisions of this article, except where a penalty is specifically provided in this article, or the commission of any offense declared in this article to be a misdemeanor shall constitute a misdemeanor and shall be punishable by a fine not exceeding $500.00, by imprisonment at hard labor for not more than 12 months, or by both. (Acts 1943, No. 298, p. 252, § 18.)

Cited in Shiland v. Retail Clerks, Local 1657, 259 Ala. 277, 66 So. 2d 146 (1953).
Collateral references. — 51B C.J.S., Labor Relations, §§ 1002-1016.
Damage liability of state or local public employee's union or union officials for unlaw-

ful work stoppage. 84 ALR3d 236.
Civil action for damages under state Racketeer Influenced and Corrupt Organizations Acts (RICO) for losses from racketeering activity. 62 ALR4th 654.

ARTICLE 2.

RIGHT TO WORK.

Cross references. — As to freedom of workers to join or refrain from joining labor organizations, see § 25-7-6.

Collateral references. — 51 C.J.S., Labor Relations, §§ 6, 10. 51B C.J.S., Labor Relations, § 1009.

§ 25-7-30. Declaration of policy.

It is hereby declared to be the public policy of Alabama that the right of persons to work shall not be denied or abridged on account of membership or nonmembership in any labor union or labor organization. (Acts 1953, No. 430, p. 535, § 1.)

State possesses jurisdiction to enjoin picketing for an unlawful purpose, although peaceful, when in contravention of the public policy as declared in the state's right to work law. Alabama Hwy. Express, Inc. v. Teamsters, Local 612, 268 Ala. 392, 108 So. 2d 350 (1959). See Radio Broadcast Technicians, Local 1264 v. Jemcon Broadcasting Co., 281 Ala. 515, 205 So. 2d 595 (1967).

Cited in Carlton v. Musicians Protective Ass'n, Local 479, 276 Ala. 128, 159 So. 2d 831 (1963); Allen v. International Alliance of Theatrical Employees, 338 F.2d 309 (5th Cir. 1964); Moving Picture Mach. Operators, Local 236 v. Cayson, 281 Ala. 468, 205 So. 2d 222 (1967).

Collateral references. — 48 Am. Jur. 2d, Labor & Labor Relations, §§ 14-21.

§ 25-7-31. Agreement or combination to deny right to work on account of membership or nonmembership in labor union, etc., prohibited.

Any agreement or combination between any employer and any labor union or labor organization whereby persons not members of such union or organization shall be denied the right to work for said employer, or whereby such membership is made a condition of employment or continuation of employment by such employer, or whereby any such union or organization acquires an employment monopoly in any enterprise, is hereby declared to be against public policy and an illegal combination or conspiracy. (Acts 1953, No. 430, p. 535, § 2.)

Cited in Moving Picture Mach. Operators, Local 236 v. Cayson, 281 Ala. 468, 205 So. 2d 222 (1967).

§ 25-7-32. Employers not to require union membership as condition of employment, etc.

No person shall be required by an employer to become or remain a member of any labor union or labor organization as a condition of employment or continuation of employment. (Acts 1953, No. 430, p. 535, § 3.)

Longevity of union membership as condition of continued employment. — A contract between an employer and a union which makes longevity of union membership a condition of continuation of employment makes union membership itself a condition of continuation of employment in violation of this section. Moving Picture Mach. Operators, Local 236 v. Cayson, 281 Ala. 468, 205 So. 2d 222 (1967).

Collateral references. — Union security arrangements in state public employment. 95 ALR3d 1102.

Civil action for damages under state Racketeer Influenced and Corrupt Organizations Acts (RICO) for losses from racketeering activity. 62 ALR4th 654.

§ 25-7-33. Employers not to require abstention from union membership as condition of employment, etc.

No person shall be required by an employer to abstain or refrain from membership in any labor union or labor organization as a condition of employment or continuation of employment. (Acts 1953, No. 430, p. 535, § 4.)

§ 25-7-34. Employer not to require payment of union dues, etc., as condition of employment, etc.

No employer shall require any person, as a condition of employment or continuation of employment, to pay any dues, fees or other charges of any kind to any labor union or labor organization. (Acts 1953, No. 430, p. 535, § 5.)

Cited in United States Gypsum Co. v. United Steelworkers, 384 F.2d 38 (5th Cir. 1967); United Steelworkers v. United States Gypsum Co., 339 F. Supp. 302 (N.D. Ala. 1972); Mumford v. Glover, 503 F.2d 878 (5th Cir. 1974).

Collateral references. — Union security arrangements in state public employment. 95 ALR3d 1102.

§ 25-7-35. Right of action for damages for denial of employment in violation of provisions of article.

Any person who may be denied employment or be deprived of continuation of his employment in violation of Sections 25-7-32, 25-7-33 or 25-7-34 or of one or more of such sections, shall be entitled to recover from such employer and from any other person, firm, corporation or association acting in concert with him by appropriate action in the courts of this state such damages as he may have sustained by reason of such denial or deprivation of employment. (Acts 1953, No. 430, p. 535, § 6.)

Cited in Moving Pictures Mach. Operators, Local 236 v. Cayson, 281 Ala. 468, 205 So. 2d 222 (1967).

Collateral references. — Failure to pursue or exhaust remedies under union contract as affecting employee's right of state civil action

for retaliatory discharge. 32 ALR4th 350.

Civil action for damages under state Racketeer Influenced and Corrupt Organizations Acts (RICO) for losses from racketeering activity. 62 ALR4th 654.

§ 25-7-36. Applicability of article.

The provisions of this article shall not apply to any lawful contract in force on August 28, 1953, but they shall apply in all respects to contracts entered into after August 28, 1953, and to any renewal or extension of an existing contract. (Acts 1953, No. 430, p. 535, § 7.)

Cited in Head v. Local Union 83, Journeymen Barbers, 262 Ala. 84, 77 So. 2d 363 (1955).

ARTICLE 3.

LOCAL BOARDS OF ARBITRATION.

§ 25-7-50. Composition; appointment of members.

A grievance or dispute between an employer and his employees may be submitted to a local board of arbitrators, consisting of three persons, for hearing and settlement. When the employees concerned are members in good standing of a labor organization, one arbitrator may be appointed by such organization and one by the employer. The two so designated shall appoint a third, who shall be chairman of the board. If such employees are not members of a labor organization, a majority thereof at a meeting duly called for that purpose may designate one arbitrator for such board. (Acts 1911, No. 234, p. 320; Code 1923, § 7608; Code 1940, T. 26, § 338.)

§ 25-7-51. Oath and consent of members; secretary; notice of board proceedings; powers of board as to witnesses.

Before entering upon his duties, each arbitrator so selected shall sign a consent to act and take and subscribe an oath to faithfully and impartially discharge his duties as such arbitrator, which consent and oath shall be filed in the office of the clerk of the circuit court of the county or counties where the controversy arose. When such board is ready for the transaction of business, it shall select one of its members to act as secretary, and notice of the time, place and hearing shall be given to the parties to the controversy. The local board may, through its chairman, subpoena witnesses, compel their attendance and take and hear testimony as is provided in Section 25-7-4 for the board of mediation. (Acts 1911, No. 234, p. 320; Code 1923, § 7609; Code 1940, T. 26, § 339.)

§ 25-7-52. Compensation of members.

Each member of such local board shall receive as compensation for his services, $4.00 for each day actually engaged in such hearing. (Acts 1911, No. 234, p. 320; Code 1923, § 7610; Code 1940, T. 26, § 340.)

§ 25-7-53. Decision of board.

The local board shall, within 10 days after the close of the hearing, render a written decision signed by them, giving such details as clearly show the nature of the controversy and the questions decided by them. One copy of the decision shall be filed in the office of the clerk of the circuit court of the county or counties where the controversy arose. One copy shall be forwarded to the department of labor, to the governor, and to each of the parties to the controversy. (Acts 1911, No. 234, p. 320; Code 1923, § 7611; Code 1940, T. 26, § 341.)

§ 25-7-54. Costs.

The witness fees and the fees of the local arbitrators as provided in this article shall be taxed against the parties to said arbitrations equally. (Acts 1911, No. 234, p. 320; Code 1923, § 7613; Acts 1939, No. 161, p. 232; Code 1940, T. 26, § 342.)

CHAPTER 8.

CHILD LABOR.

§ 25-8-1. Employment of children under 16 years of age — Prohibited generally; exceptions as to agricultural and domestic employment; employment of children between 14 and 16 years of age outside school hours.

No child under 16 years of age shall be employed, permitted or suffered to work in any gainful occupation, except in agricultural or in domestic service, and except as provided in this chapter; provided, however, that any child between 14 and 16 years of age may be employed outside school hours and during school vacation periods, but shall not be so employed, permitted or suffered to work in, about or in connection with any manufacturing or mechanical establishment or cannery or in any occupation or place of employment otherwise prohibited by law; provided further, that work in connection with or around any mechanical device for sorting, grading or preparing any agricultural product for market shall be considered agricultural labor. (Acts 1919, No. 629, p. 867; Code 1923, § 3494; Code 1940, T. 26, § 343; Acts 1947, No. 613, p. 460, § 1.)

Employment of a child in violation of Child Labor Act is negligence per se, but civil liability does not follow unless child suffers from injury which is in a legal sense the proximate result of the violation of the statute, and therefore within its protective purpose. Birmingham News Co. v. Andrews, 204 Ala. 649, 87 So. 168 (1920).

In cases where the minor is not employed in a place inherently dangerous or where such employment is entirely prohibited, the employment of a child in violation of the child labor law does not render the employer liable in tort unless injury can be traced to the violation of the statute as its proximate cause. Ward v. State Farm Mut. Auto. Ins. Co., 241 F.2d 134 (5th Cir. 1957).

Violation of this section renders party liable for injuries to child resulting proximately therefrom, whether injury resulted from inherent dangers of work or from hazards of environment. Nichols v. Smith's Bakery, Inc., 218 Ala. 607, 119 So. 638 (1928).

Cited in Hoyt v. United States, 286 F.2d 356 (5th Cir. 1961).

Collateral references. — 43 C.J.S., Infants, § 12. 56 C.J.S., Master & Servant, §§ 14, 194.

48A Am. Jur. 2d, Labor & Labor Relations, §§ 1866-1874.

Constitutionality of child labor law. 12 ALR 1216, 21 ALR 1437.

Right of parent who consents to or acquiesces in employment of child under statutory age to recover for latter's injury or death while in such employment. 23 ALR 635, 40 ALR 1206.

Constitutionality of statutes limiting hours of labor in private industry. 90 ALR 814.

Lawn mowing by minors as violation of child labor statutes. 56 ALR3d 1166.

§ 25-8-2. Employment of children under 16 years of age — Prohibited occupations and places of employment.

No child under the age of 16 years shall be employed, permitted or suffered to work at any of the following occupations, positions or places:

(1) Operating or assisting in operating any of the following machines:
  a. Circular or band saws;
  b. Wood shapers;
  c. Wood jointers;
  d. Planers;
  e. Sand paper or wood polishing machinery;
  f. Wood turning or boring machinery;
  g. Machines used in picking wool, cotton, hair or any other material;

h. Job or cylinder printing presses;

i. Boring or drilling presses;

j. Stamping machines used in sheet metal or tin ware, or in paper or leather manufacturing or in washer or nut factories;

k. Metal or paper cutting machines;

l. Corner staying machines;

m. Steam boilers;

n. Dough brakes or cracker machinery of any description;

o. Wire or iron straightening or drawing machinery;

p. Rolling mill machinery;

q. Power punches or shears;

r. Washing, grinding or mixing machinery;

s. Laundry machinery;

(2) In any work in or about a rolling mill, machine shop or manufacturing establishment which is hazardous, or dangerous to health, limb or life;

(3) In proximity to any hazardous or unguarded gearing;

(4) Upon any railroad, whether steam, electric or hydraulic;

(5) Upon any vessel or boat engaged in navigation or commerce within the jurisdiction of this state;

(6) In, about or in connection with any processes in which dangerous or poisonous acids are used;

(7) In the manufacture or packing of paints, colors or white or red lead;

(8) In soldering or welding;

(9) In occupations causing dust in injurious quantities;

(10) In the manufacture or use of poisonous dyes;

(11) In the manufacture or preparation of compositions with dangerous or poisonous gases;

(12) In the manufacture or use of compositions of lye in which the quantity is injurious to health;

(13) On scaffolding;

(14) In the building trades;

(15) In any tunnel or excavation;

(16) Assorting, manufacturing or packing tobacco;

(17) Operating any automobile, motor car or truck;

(18) As fire fighters;

(19) In airport hangars or landing strips or taxi and maintenance aprons;

(20) In any place or occupation which the state board of health may declare dangerous to life or limb or injurious to the health or morals of children under 16 years of age. (Acts 1919, No. 629, p. 867; Code 1923, § 3499; Code 1940, T. 26, §§ 348, 349; Acts 1961, Ex. Sess., No. 273, p. 2293, § 3; Acts 1980, No. 80-748, p. 1520.)

Employer is liable for all injuries during prohibited employment. Employment of a child in an occupation or place regarded as inherently dangerous so that employment is absolutely prohibited under the Child Labor Act makes the employer liable for all injuries to the child during his employment, whether resulting from performance of services or of contact with some agency associated with the employer's business or inherent in its environment. Birmingham News Co. v. Andrews, 204 Ala. 649, 87 So. 168 (1920).

Injuries from such sources it is the purpose of the statute to prevent, and they are regarded as the proximate result of the wrongful employment whether suffered at work or in irrelevant and forbidden play. Birmingham News Co. v. Andrews, 204 Ala. 649, 87 So. 168 (1920); Vida Lumber Co. v. Courson, 216 Ala. 248, 112 So. 737 (1926).

And it is immaterial whether child had entered on work on morning of death if he was there to work as his employer should direct. Nichols v. Smith's Bakery, Inc., 218 Ala. 607, 119 So. 638 (1928).

Permitting minor to work in proximity to unguarded gearing with knowledge or notice of those in charge thereof would constitute a violation of this section. Vida Lumber Co. v. Courson, 216 Ala. 248, 112 So. 737 (1926).

Precluding affirmative charge. — In action under this section for death of minor when caught in unguarded gearing at defendant's sawmill, conflicting evidence relative to whether minor was employed or knowingly permitted to work with his father, an employee, held to preclude affirmative charge on theory employment was without workmen's compensation statute. Vida Lumber Co. v. Courson, 216 Ala. 248, 112 So. 737 (1926).

Fifteen year old was held to standard of responsibility of child. — Where issue was whether 15-year-old child's negligence contributed to his injury, the supreme court did not hold the child to the same standard of responsibility as an adult since the legislature recognized that there are certain positions of employment from which a child under 16 should be barred and the Child Labor Act prohibits children age 15 and under from employment where dangerous acids are used. Jones ex rel. Jones v. Power Cleaning Contractors, 551 So. 2d 996 (Ala. 1989).

Questions for jury. — Question whether deceased went to place of work to presently engage therein and whether his presence there for such purpose unlawfully permitted by defendant had causal connection with death held for jury. Nichols v. Smith's Bakery, Inc., 218 Ala. 607, 119 So. 638 (1928).

Cited in Ward v. State Farm Mut. Auto. Ins. Co., 241 F.2d 134 (5th Cir. 1957).

Collateral references. — 43 C.J.S., Infants, § 99. 56 C.J.S., Master & Servant, § 14.

48A Am. Jur. 2d, Labor & Labor Relations, §§ 1874, 2653-2661.

§ 25-8-3. Employment of children under 16 years of age — State Board of Health may declare place or occupation dangerous or injurious.

The State Board of Health may declare any place or occupation dangerous to life or limb or injurious to health or morals of children under 16 years of age. (Acts 1919, No. 629, p. 867; Code 1923, § 3501; Code 1940, T. 26, § 351.)

§ 25-8-4. Employment of children under 16 years of age — Hours of employment; evidence of employment.

No child under 16 years of age shall be employed, permitted or suffered to work in any gainful occupation, except agricultural or domestic service, for more than six days in any one week, or for more than 40 hours in any one week, or for more than eight hours in any one day, or before 7:00 A.M. or after 7:00 P.M., except that during the summer school vacation such children may work until 9:00 P.M. No child under 18 years of age who is enrolled in any public or private primary or secondary school system shall work between 10:00 P.M. and 5:00 A.M. on any night preceding a school day; provided, however, that those students who are enrolled in certified training programs as authorized by the State Department of Education shall be allowed to work past 10:00 P.M. The appropriate county or city superintendent of schools (or where there is no superintendent, the school headmaster) shall have authority to grant exemptions to the 10:00 P.M. provisions; provided, however, that such exemptions shall not be granted routinely but only when the individual circumstances are found to be in the best interests of the child. It is further provided that information of such exceptions shall be transmitted to the chief child labor inspector of Alabama on a form authorized by him. The presence of any child under 16 years of age in any mill, factory, cannery, workshop, laundry or mechanical establishment shall be prima facie evidence of his employment therein; provided, however, that work in connection with or around any mechanical device for sorting, grading or preparing any agricultural product for market shall be considered agricultural labor. (Acts 1919, No. 629, p. 867; Code 1923, § 3495; Code 1940, T. 26, § 344; Acts 1947, No. 613, p. 460, § 2; Acts 1961, Ex. Sess., No. 273, p. 2293, § 1; Acts 1987, No. 87-673, p. 1203, § 1.)

This section was intended to protect the health of children, and not to prevent physical injuries to them. Birmingham News Co. v. Andrews, 204 Ala. 649, 87 So. 168 (1920).

And does not apply to injuries while playing. — The employment of a boy under 16 at hours prohibited by this section, in the circulating room of a newspaper, which is not a place inherently dangerous or where such employment is prohibited at all times, does not make the master liable for injuries to the boy resulting from falling or jumping down a chute while playing, since such injury might have occurred at any hour, and the violation of the statute had no causal connection therewith. Birmingham News Co. v. Andrews, 204 Ala. 649, 87 So. 168 (1920).

Collateral references. — 51B C.J.S., Labor Relations, §§ 1186, 1190, 1192. 56 C.J.S., Master & Servant, § 16.

48A Am. Jur. 2d, Labor & Labor Relations, § 1840.

§ 25-8-5. Employment of children under 16 years of age — Employment during school hours; employment of children 14 and 15 years of age upon waiver of school attendance.

No child under 16 years of age shall be employed, permitted or suffered to work in any gainful occupation during the hours in which the public schools of the district in which the child resides are in session, unless such child has completed the course of study required for secondary schools. Minors 14 and 15 years of age, when school attendance has been waived, may, upon recommendation of the superintendent of education in the area, and the chief child labor inspector, be issued a certificate for employment in nonhazardous occupations. The hours restriction will not be waived. None of the provisions of this section shall apply to agricultural workers or domestic service workers. (Acts 1919, No. 629, p. 867; Code 1923, § 3504; Code 1940, T. 26, § 354; Acts 1947, No. 613, p. 460, § 6; Acts 1961, Ex. Sess., No. 273, p. 2293, § 5.)

Code commissioner's note. — Acts 1980, No. 80-748, p. 1520, § 1, reenacted this section without change.

Collateral references. — 48A Am. Jur. 2d, Labor & Labor Relations, § 1840.

§ 25-8-6. Employment of children under 16 years of age — Posting of notice of law.

Every employer shall post and keep posted in a conspicuous place in every room where any child under the age of 16 years is employed, permitted or suffered to work, a printed notice stating the maximum number of hours such persons may be required or permitted to work on each day of the week, the hours of commencing and stopping work and the hours allowed for meals. The printed form of such notice shall be furnished by the Department of Industrial Relations, and the employment of any minor for a longer time in any day so stated, or at any time other than as stated in such printed form of notice, shall be deemed a violation of the provisions of this chapter. (Acts 1919, No. 629, p. 867; Code 1923, § 3496; Code 1940, T. 26, § 345.)

§ 25-8-7. Working in public places — Persons under 12 years of age not to engage in certain occupations; exceptions.

No person under 12 years of age shall distribute, sell, expose or offer for sale newspapers, magazines, periodicals, handbills or circulars, or be so employed or permitted or suffered to work in any other trade or occupation performed in any street or public place; provided, that persons 10 years of age or over may engage in the distribution of newspapers and periodicals on fixed routes and persons 12 years of age or over may engage in the occupation of bootblacks and caddies on golf links. (Acts 1919, No. 629, p. 867; Code 1923, § 3512; Code 1940, T. 26, § 362; Acts 1961, Ex. Sess., No. 273, p. 2293, § 7.)

Cited in Ward v. State Farm Mut. Auto. Ins. Co., 241 F.2d 134 (5th Cir. 1957).

Collateral references. — 48A Am. Jur. 2d, Labor & Labor Relations, § 1873.

§ 25-8-8. Working in public places — Hours persons under 16 years of age may work.

(a) No person under 16 years of age shall engage in any of the occupations mentioned in Section 25-8-7 after 7:00 P.M. of any day or before 5:00 A.M. of any day.

(b) No person, firm or corporation shall employ, permit or suffer a person under 16 years of age to work at any of the occupations mentioned in Section 25-8-7 after 7:00 P.M. of any day or before 5:00 A.M. of any day. (Acts 1919, No. 629, p. 867; Code 1923, §§ 3513, 3516; Code 1940, T. 26, §§ 363, 366; Acts 1961, Ex. Sess., No. 273, p. 2293, §§ 8, 10; Acts 1987, No. 87-673, p. 1203, § 2.)

§ 25-8-9. Working in public places — Permits for persons under 16 years of age engaged in authorized occupations.

(a) No person under 16 years of age shall engage in such occupations mentioned in Section 25-8-7 unless he has secured and has with him a permit as required by this section. Such permit shall be issued by the superintendent or principal of schools, or some person designated by him in writing, and shall be granted only after the child has applied to him personally, and has established in the manner provided in this article for procuring an employment certificate that he is 12 years of age or over, or if engaged only in distributing papers or periodicals on fixed routes, that he is 10 years of age or over, and is a regular attendant at school.

(b) The official charged with enforcement of this chapter shall have authority to investigate each case where he believes that the child holding a permit under this section is not entitled to its possession, and if he is satisfied from the evidence obtained that the child has secured the permit through misrepresentation or fraud, such official shall have authority to revoke the permit and return it to the official who issued it. Use of a permit shall be revoked or suspended in case the child's school record is not satisfactory to the principal of the school which he attends, by either the officer who issued the permit or by any official charged with the enforcement of this article. (Acts 1919, No. 629, p. 867; Code 1923, §§ 3513, 3516; Code 1940, T. 26, §§ 363, 366; Acts 1961, Ex. Sess., No. 273, p. 2293, §§ 8, 10; Acts 1980, No. 80-748, p. 1520.)

Collateral references. — 43 C.J.S., Infants, § 99. 56 C.J.S., Master & Servant, § 14.   48A Am. Jur. 2d, Labor & Labor Relations, §§ 2653-2661.

§ 25-8-10. Working in public places — Child violating provisions as to street occupations deemed delinquent.

Any child who shall engage in any street occupation in violation of the provisions of Sections 25-8-7, 25-8-8 or 25-8-9 may be deemed delinquent and brought before any court having jurisdiction over juvenile delinquents, and shall be dealt with according to law. (Acts 1919, No. 629, p. 867; Code 1923, § 3515; Code 1940, T. 26, § 365; Acts 1961, Ex. Sess., No. 273, p. 2293, § 9.)

§ 25-8-11. Prohibited places of employment for persons under 18 years of age.

No person under 18 years of age shall be employed or permitted or suffered to work at any of the following occupations, positions or places:

(1) In or about or in connection with any mine, coke breaker, coke oven or quarry in any capacity.

(2) In wrecking, demolition and shipbreaking.

(3) In that part of any establishment where alcoholic beverages are sold, served or dispensed for consumption on the premises; provided, that this subdivision shall not prohibit the employment of persons 16 years of age or

older as busboys, dishwashers, janitors or cooks, or as hostesses and seaters restricted to that occupation of leading patrons to seats. Persons age 16 and 17 who are in the above named occupations are prohibited from performing any other occupation in such establishments. This subdivision shall not apply to any member of the immediate family of the owner or operator of such establishment if said member does not serve, sell, dispense or handle alcoholic beverages. (Acts 1919, No. 629, p. 867; Code 1923, §§ 3498, 3500; Code 1940, T. 26, §§ 347, 350; Acts 1947, No. 613, p. 460, § 3; Acts 1961, Ex. Sess., No. 273, p. 2293, § 2; Acts 1980, No. 80-748, p. 1520.)

Cross references. — As to prohibition against persons under 18 years of age working in or about coal mines, see § 25-9-30.

Complaint held to sufficiently charge a violation of subdivision (1). Ivey v. Railway Fuel Co., 211 Ala. 10, 99 So. 177 (1924).

Cited in Ward v. State Farm Mut. Auto. Ins. Co., 241 F.2d 134 (5th Cir. 1957); Kelley v. Moretti-Harrah Marble Co., 414 So. 2d 1 (Ala. 1982).

Collateral references. — 43 C.J.S., Infants, § 99. 56 C.J.S., Master & Servant, §§ 14, 194. 48A Am. Jur. 2d, Labor & Labor Relations, §§ 1874, 2653-2661.

§ 25-8-12. Employment of persons under 19 years of age in certain establishments.

No person under 19 years of age shall be employed, permitted or suffered to serve or dispense alcoholic beverages in any establishment where alcoholic beverages are sold, served or dispensed for consumption on the premises. (Acts 1919, No. 629, p. 867; Code 1923, § 3498; Code 1940, T. 26, § 347; Acts 1947, No. 613, p. 460, § 3; Acts 1961, Ex. Sess., No. 273, p. 2293, § 2.)

Cited in Ward v. State Farm Mut. Auto. Ins. Co., 241 F.2d 134 (5th Cir. 1957).

Collateral references. — Social host's lia-bility for injuries incurred by third parties as a result of intoxicated guest's negligence. 62 ALR4th 16.

§ 25-8-13. Employment and age certificates — When required.

No person, firm or corporation shall employ, permit or suffer any person under 16 years of age to work in any gainful occupation, except agriculture or domestic service, unless such person, firm or corporation procures and keeps on file for the inspection of the officials charged with the enforcement of this chapter, an employment certificate, as provided in this chapter, for every such person under 16 years of age, and unless such person, firm or corporation keeps on file for the inspection of the officials charged with the enforcement of this chapter a complete list of all such persons under 16 years of age employed therein. No firm, person or corporation shall employ, permit or suffer any person between 16 and 17 years of age to work in any gainful occupation, except agriculture or domestic service, unless such person, firm or corporation procures and keeps on file for the inspection of the officials charged with the enforcement of this chapter, an age certificate, as provided in this chapter, for every person between 16 and 17 years of age, and every person between 18 and 19 years of age who works in any capacity in, about or in connection with any mine, coke breaker, coke oven or quarry. (Acts 1919, No. 629, p. 867; Code 1923, § 3502; Code 1940, T. 26, § 352.)

Absence of certificate did not prevent person from being "employee". — The Alabama statutory provisions regarding child labor did not prevent a 16-year-old boy employed by a newspaper distributor from becoming an "employee of the insured" within the meaning of an exclusion provision in a liability insurance policy issued to the distributor, notwithstanding the absence of an employment certificate as required by this section. Ward v. State Farm Mut. Auto. Ins. Co., 241 F.2d 134 (5th Cir. 1957).

Absence of certificate not such violation as to justify double compensation payment. The failure of an employer to have on file an employment certificate for an employee between 16 and 17 years old, as required by this section, was not such a violation of the Child Labor Act as to justify the payment of double compensation under the Workmen's Compensation Act, § 25-5-34. Willis v. Storey, 268 Ala. 205, 105 So. 2d 128 (1958).

Collateral references. — 56 C.J.S., Master & Servant, § 194.

§ 25-8-14. Employment and age certificates — Application for certificates.

(a) The person authorized to issue employment certificates shall not issue any certificate unless the child personally makes application to him, and until he receives, approves and files the following papers duly executed:

(1) A written statement of the person, firm or corporation into whose service the child is to enter to the effect that he intends to employ the child, which statement shall give the nature of the occupation for which the child is employed;

(2) If the child is to work outside school hours on school days, a school record signed by the principal or teacher of the school attended by the child to the effect that he is a regular attendant at school and is performing satisfactory school work;

(3) One of the following evidences of age, establishing the fact that the minor is of the legal minimum age for the job in which he is to be employed, is required in the order designated:

a. A certified copy of the child's birth certificate;

b. A certified copy of the child's baptismal record showing the date of birth and place of baptism;

c. A bona fide contemporary Bible record of birth;

d. A life insurance policy which has been in force for at least one year;

e. A passport or certificate of arrival in the United States which shows the age of the child; or

f. If, in any instance the officer authorized to issue such certificates is satisfied that none of the above proofs of age can be produced and the parent, guardian or custodian shall make affidavit that none of the above proofs of age can be produced by him, other evidence of age, satisfactory to the person authorized to issue employment certificates, such as a school record of age, if available, and an affidavit of age sworn to by the parent, guardian or custodian of such child, when accompanied by a certificate of physical age of such child, signed by a duly licensed physician, but a school record, or parent's, guardian's or custodian's affidavit, certificate or other written statement of age alone shall not be accepted;

(4) A statement signed and dated by a parent or guardian of the minor stating the minor's age and date of birth and approval of said minor's performing duties described by the prospective employer.

(b) The issuing officer is authorized to administer oaths for affidavits establishing age. (Acts 1919, No. 629, p. 867; Code 1923, § 3506; Acts 1931, No. 356, p. 412; Code 1940, T. 26, § 356; Acts 1947, No. 613, p. 460, § 8; Acts 1980, No. 80-748, p. 1520.)

Cited in Ward v. State Farm Mut. Auto. Ins. Co., 241 F.2d 134 (5th Cir. 1957).

Collateral references. — 43 C.J.S., Infants, § 99. 56 C.J.S., Master & Servant, §§ 14, 194.

48A Am. Jur. 2d, Labor & Labor Relations, §§ 2653-2661.

§ 25-8-15. Employment and age certificates — Issuance.

(a) The superintendent, or if there is no superintendent, the principal, of any school, shall issue employment and age certificates or authorize in writing a person acting in his name to issue such certificates, but no person employed by a person, firm or corporation employing children, other than a teacher in a school, shall be so authorized to issue employment certificates. When there is no superintendent or principal of a school, employment and age certificates shall be issued by the county superintendent of education or he may authorize in writing a person to issue such certificates.

(b) An employment certificate shall permit the employment of a child 14 or 15 years of age only outside school hours and during vacation periods and only in occupations not prohibited for children of these ages by this chapter.

(c) Employment and age certificates shall be issued in triplicate and a copy of each certificate issued during the month preceding shall be transmitted to the Department of Industrial Relations together with the report as provided in this chapter. (Acts 1919, No. 629, p. 867; Code 1923, § 3505; Code 1940, T. 26, § 355; Acts 1947, No. 613, p. 460, § 7.)

Cited in Ward v. State Farm Mut. Auto. Ins. Co., 241 F.2d 134 (5th Cir. 1957).

§ 25-8-16. Employment and age certificates — Issuance of certain age and special employment certificates; revocation or suspension of employment certificate in event of unsatisfactory school performance.

The officer issuing employment certificates is authorized to issue age certificates for children 16 years of age and over in the same manner and upon the same requirements as for issuing employment certificates; except that the school record and parental approval is waived. Such officer is authorized to issue special employment certificates in the same manner and subject to the same requirements as employment certificates, school records being waived for persons who are 12 and under 14 years of age to work in business offices or mercantile establishments during vacation when the public schools are not in session. A certificate issued for the employment of a minor before, or after, school hours on school days or on weekends shall not be valid for the employment of any child under age 16 for more than three hours in any school day, eight hours on any weekend day, and not more than 18 hours in any school week. In the event the school records of any child under age 16 are not satisfactory to the principal of the school, the employment certificate shall be revoked or suspended either by the issuing officer or any person charged with the enforcement of laws regulating the employment of minors. (Acts 1919, No. 629, p. 867; Code 1923, § 3507; Acts 1931, No. 356, p. 412; Code 1940, T. 26, § 357; Acts 1947, No. 613, p. 460, § 9; Acts 1961, Ex. Sess., No. 273, p. 2293, § 6; Acts 1980, No. 80-748, p. 1520; Acts 1987, No. 87-673, p. 1203, § 3.)

§ 25-8-17. Employment and age certificates — Special employment certificates void upon opening of public schools.

Special employment certificates are null and void on and after the date the public schools open for regular session. (Acts 1919, No. 629, p. 867; Code 1923, § 3508; Code 1940, T. 26, § 358; Acts 1947, No. 613, p. 460, § 10.)

§ 25-8-18. Employment and age certificates — Contents.

All employment certificates shall state the full name, place of and date of birth of the child, with the name and address of the parent, guardian or person sustaining the parental relationship to such child, and shall contain a statement dated and signed by the issuing officer that the child has personally appeared before him and that proofs of age and other legal qualifications as required in this chapter have been submitted and filed. The printed form of certificates and other papers required in the issuing of certificates shall be drafted by the Department of Industrial Relations and furnished by it to the local and county superintendents of education. (Acts 1919, No. 629, p. 867; Code 1923, § 3510; Code 1940, T. 26, § 360; Acts 1980, No. 80-748, p. 1520.)

§ 25-8-19. Employment and age certificates — Return and cancellation upon termination of employment.

On the termination of the employment of a child under the age of 16 years, the certificate shall be returned by the employer holding the same to the school authority by whom it was issued within 10 days after the termination of the employment. Every certificate so returned shall be cancelled by the officer who issued the certificate and transmitted to the Department of Industrial Relations with the next succeeding monthly report provided for in Section 25-8-20. (Acts 1919, No. 629, p. 867; Code 1923, § 3511; Code 1940, T. 26, § 361.)

§ 25-8-20. Employment and age certificates — Monthly report of superintendent of schools, etc., to Department of Industrial Relations.

The superintendent or principal of schools in any city, town or district wherever there is one, and where there is none, the county superintendent of education shall, between the first and tenth day of each month, transmit to the office of the Department of Industrial Relations a report, giving the name of each child to whom an employment certificate has been granted or denied during the preceding month, together with the reasons for each such denial. (Acts 1919, No. 629, p. 867; Code 1923, § 3509; Code 1940, T. 26, § 359; Acts 1977, No. 607, p. 812, § 9901.)

§ 25-8-21. Cancellation of illegally or improperly issued employment certificate, age certificate or permit.

Any official charged with the enforcement of this chapter may cancel any employment certificate, age certificate or permit, found to be illegally or improperly issued. When such employment certificate, age certificate or permit is cancelled, the employer of the child for whom the employment certificate, age certificate or permit is issued, shall be notified. It shall be unlawful to employ any child after notice that the employment certificate, age certificate or permit for such child has been cancelled, but such child may be employed after a new employment certificate, age certificate or permit, regularly issued as provided for by law, shall have been granted to him. (Acts 1919, No. 629, p. 867; Code 1923, § 3503; Code 1940, T. 26, § 353; Acts 1961, Ex. Sess., No. 273, p. 2293, § 4.)

§ 25-8-22. Inspection of establishments where minors employed; enforcement of chapter.

The Department of Industrial Relations shall inspect as frequently as possible all establishments wherein minors subject to the provisions of this chapter are or may be employed or permitted to work, and shall enforce the provisions of this chapter. The Department of Industrial Relations shall enforce the provisions of this chapter and shall institute prosecution for the violation of any of the provisions of this chapter. (Acts 1919, No. 629, p. 867; Code 1923, § 3518; Acts 1939, No. 161, p. 232; Code 1940, T. 26, § 368.)

§ 25-8-23. Right of entry, etc., of school attendance officers; reports to Department of Industrial Relations.

Every school attendance officer shall report to the Department of Industrial Relations any and all violations of this chapter coming to his knowledge. Such school attendance officers shall have the same right of access to establishments where minors are or may be employed or detained, and of inspection of such establishments as is given by law to the Department of Industrial Relations; provided, that a report of every such entry and inspection of said establishments shall be made to the Department of Industrial Relations. School attendance officers when authorized by the Department of Industrial Relations shall have the same authority to institute prosecutions as is given by law to the Department of Industrial Relations. (Acts 1919, No. 629, p. 867; Code 1923, § 3519; Code 1940, T. 26, § 369; Acts 1980, No. 80-748, p. 1520.)

§ 25-8-24. Duties of owners of establishments employing minors.

Every person, firm or corporation owning or controlling any establishment wherein minors are employed, subject to the provisions of this chapter, shall keep such establishment in a sanitary condition and properly ventilated, and shall provide suitable and convenient water closets or privies, separate for each sex, and in such number and located in such place or places as may be required by the Department of Industrial Relations. When 20 or more persons are employed, sanitary drinking fountains shall be provided in such number as the department may deem necessary. All water closets shall be maintained inside such establishments, except where, in the opinion of the Department of Industrial Relations, it is impracticable. In all such establishments, there shall be separate water closets or privy compartments for females, to be used by them exclusively, and notice to that effect shall be painted on the outside of such compartments. The entrance to every water closet or privy in such establishments shall be effectively screened by a partition or vestibule. (Acts 1919, No. 629, p. 867; Code 1923, § 3520; Code 1940, T. 26, § 370.)

Collateral references. — 56 C.J.S., Master & Servant, § 282.

§ 25-8-25. Inspection and correction of insanitary or unhealthful conditions.

The Department of Industrial Relations shall inspect thoroughly every establishment wherein minors are employed and shall issue a written order for the correction of insanitary or unhealthful conditions in such establishments, and compel compliance with such orders as provided in this section. (Acts 1919, No. 629, p. 867; Code 1923, § 3521; Code 1940, T. 26, § 371.)

§ 25-8-26. Department of Industrial Relations to have free access to establishments; penalty for obstruction of inspection, etc.
Repealed by Acts 1977, No. 607, p. 812, § 9901, as amended, effective January 1, 1980.

Cross references. — As to refusal to permit inspection, see § 13A-10-3.

§ 25-8-27. Removal of children illegally employed, etc., from establishments.

The Department of Industrial Relations shall remove from any establishment any child found employed, working therein contrary to law, and shall remove therefrom any child who is afflicted with any infectious, contagious or communicable disease, or whose physical condition is such that it makes it hazardous to a child to prosecute such work. (Acts 1919, No. 629, p. 867; Code 1923, § 3523; Code 1940, T. 26, § 373.)

§ 25-8-28. Sale, etc., of article for resale on streets, etc., to person under 16 years of age without permit.

Any person who sells or offers for sale or furnishes any article of any description to a person under 16 years of age to be used for the purpose of sale or barter upon the streets or in any public place, shall first ascertain whether such person has his permit with him as provided in this chapter, and if said person has no permit, no article shall be sold or furnished to him. Any person violating the provisions of this section shall be fined not less than $10.00 nor more than $50.00. Police officers, school attendance officers and other peace officers shall enforce the provisions of this section. (Acts 1919, No. 629, p. 867; Code 1923, § 3517; Code 1940, T. 26, § 367; Acts 1961, Ex. Sess., No. 273, p. 2293, § 11; Acts 1980, No. 80-748, p. 1520.)

§ 25-8-29. False affidavits. Repealed by Acts 1977, No. 607, p. 812, § 9901, as amended, effective January 1, 1980.

§ 25-8-30. Penalty for violations of chapter, etc.

Any person, firm or corporation who violates any of the provisions of this chapter, or who permits any child to be employed, or to work in, or be in or about any establishment contrary to law, or who fails or refuses to obey within a reasonable time any lawful orders or directions given by the state officials charged with the enforcement of this chapter, and any parent, guardian or custodian who suffers or permits a child under his care or control who is under 16 years of age to work in violation of any of the provisions of this chapter, unless a special penalty is otherwise provided in this chapter, shall be deemed guilty of a misdemeanor, and, on conviction, shall be punished by a fine of not less than $100.00 nor more than $500.00 and upon a second or subsequent conviction of any violation of any of the provisions of this chapter, shall be punished by a fine of not less than $500.00 nor more than $1,000.00. (Acts 1919, No. 629, p. 867; Code 1923, § 3524; Code 1940, T. 26, § 374; Acts 1980, No. 80-748, p. 1520.)

§ 25-8-31. Employment of child actors and performers.

The provisions of Sections 25-8-4, 25-8-5, 25-8-13 and 25-8-16 notwithstanding, time and hour restrictions shall not be imposed upon children under age 16 who are employed as actors or performers, and no employment or age certificates shall be required for persons under age 17 in such occupations. Persons under the age of 19 may be employed and appear for the purpose of singing and acting or performing in any studio or movie sets of a motion picture approved and coordinated by the Alabama Film Commission in conjunction with and under the jurisdiction and supervision of the Department of Industrial Relations. No child under 16 years of age shall be so employed except under the following conditions and with the written consent of the Alabama Film Commission, the Department of Industrial Relations and the parent, legal guardian or responsible adult of the child so subject to these provisions:

(1) The activities enumerated must not be detrimental to the life, health, safety, welfare or morals of the child.

(2) The activities enumerated must not interfere with the schooling of the child and provisions shall be made for education equivalent to full-time school attendance in the public schools for children under 16 years of age.

(3) A parent, guardian, or a responsible adult so designated by the parent or guardian, shall accompany each child under 16 years of age at all rehearsals, appearances and performances.

All such work performed by persons under age 19 shall be in compliance with the provisions of Sections 25-8-11(3) and 25-8-12. (Acts 1982, No. 82-548, p. 907, § 1.)

CHAPTER 9.

COAL MINE SAFETY.

ARTICLE 1.
GENERAL PROVISIONS.

Cross references. — As to surface mining reclamation generally, see § 9-16-1 et seq. As to prohibition against working of convicts in coal mines, see § 14-5-3. As to coal severance tax, see § 40-13-1 et seq.

§ 25-9-1. Short title; purpose of chapter.

This chapter shall be known as the "Alabama Coal Mine Safety Law of 1975." The purpose of this chapter is to provide reasonable laws to promote the safety and health of those engaged in the mining of coal and for the protection and preservation of property. (Acts 1949, No. 207, p. 242, § 1; Acts 1975, 4th Ex. Sess., No. 147, p. 2866, § 1.)

Chapter not for benefit of public gener-ally. — This chapter was not enacted (except where expressly stated) for the benefit of the public generally. Coalite, Inc. v. Aldridge, 45 Ala. App. 277, 229 So. 2d 524 (1968), reversed on other grounds, 285 Ala. 137, 229 So. 2d 539 (1969).

§ 25-9-2. Definitions.

Unless the context clearly requires otherwise, as used in this chapter, the following terms have the following meanings:

(1) DIRECTOR. The Director of the Department of Industrial Relations or such other public officer, employee, board, commission or other authority that may by law be assigned the duties and authority of the Director of Industrial Relations under this chapter.

(2) CHIEF. The Chief of the Division of Safety and Inspection of the Department of Industrial Relations or such other public officer, employee, board, commission or other authority that may in emergencies be acting in the stead of the chief or may by law be assigned the duties and authority of the Chief of the Division of Safety and Inspection of the Department of Industrial Relations.

(3) HEAD MINE INSPECTOR. The employee of the Division of Safety and Inspection in charge of mine inspection or such other public officer, employee, board, commission or other authority that may by law be assigned the duties and authority of the head mine inspector.

(4) MINE INSPECTOR. A public employee assigned by the head mine inspector with the approval of the chief to make mine inspections as required by this chapter and other laws from time to time in such cases made and provided.

(5) SUPERINTENDENT. The person placed in overall charge of the operation of a coal mine or mines.

(6) OPERATOR. The owner, part owner, operator or lessee to whom the superintendent reports and is accountable for the operation. The operator may also be the superintendent.

(7) MINE FOREMAN. A person holding a valid certificate of qualification duly issued by action of the board of mine examiners. Such term also includes the person acting in the stead of a mine foreman appointed as provided under this chapter when a certified mine foreman is unavailable.

(8) SUPERVISOR. Such term may be used to designate mine foremen, assistants, section foremen, trafficmen, maintenance foremen, etc., and is restricted in this chapter to mean those persons employed by the operator or superintendent to manage all or a part of the mine operations.

(9) FIRE BOSS. A person holding a valid certificate of qualification duly issued by action of the board of mine examiners and also includes the person acting in the stead of a fire boss appointed as provided under this chapter when a certified fire boss is unavailable.

(10) APPROVED COMPETENT PERSON. A person who has at least nine months of practical experience, has knowledge of mine roof, timbering and ventilation, has good judgment and who has demonstrated knowledge of mine gases and use of permissible flame safety lamps, methane and oxygen detectors, such demonstration to be given and made of record in a manner prescribed by the chief of the division.

(11) APPROVED. A device, process, equipment or method approved by the chief; provided, that if any interested person so requests, the director shall review such approval.

(12) PERMISSIBLE. A device, process, or equipment or method heretofore or hereafter classified by such term by the United States Bureau of Mines when such classification is adopted by the chief and includes, unless otherwise expressly stated in this chapter, all requirements, restrictions, exceptions, limitations and conditions attached to such classification by said bureau. (Acts 1949, No. 207, p. 242, § 2; Acts 1975, 4th Ex. Sess., No. 147, p. 2866, § 1.)

Collateral references. — 58 C.J.S., Mines & Minerals, § 3.

§ 25-9-3. Appointment of mine inspectors and other employees.

There shall be appointed by the Director of Industrial Relations a sufficient number of mine inspectors and other employees, including at least one qualified mining engineer. (Acts 1949, No. 207, p. 242, § 3; Acts 1975, 4th Ex. Sess., No. 147, p. 2866, § 1.)

Collateral references. — 58 C.J.S., Mines & Minerals, § 237.

§ 25-9-4. Certain persons not to have interest in Alabama coal mines.

No person shall be appointed mine inspector, head mine inspector or Chief of the Division of Safety and Inspection who, or the spouse of whom, has any pecuniary interest in any coal mine in Alabama. (Acts 1949, No. 207, p. 242, § 3; Acts 1975, 4th Ex. Sess., No. 147, p. 2866, § 1.)

§ 25-9-5. Qualifications and residence of chief of division.

(a) The Chief of the Division of Safety and Inspection shall:

(1) Be a qualified elector;

(2) Have had 12 or more years' experience in the working, ventilating and drainage of coal mines in this state or eight years of such experience plus four years' experience as a state or federal coal mine inspector;

(3) Have a practical scientific knowledge of all noxious and dangerous gases found in such mines;

(4) Have a mine foreman certificate of competency of the State of Alabama; and

(5) Be not less than 30 years of age.

(b) The chief shall be stationed in a city or town as near the center of the mining industry as is practical. (Acts 1949, No. 207, p. 242, § 3; Acts 1975, 4th Ex. Sess., No. 147, p. 2866, § 1.)

§ 25-9-6. Qualifications and residence of mine inspectors and head mine inspector.

(a) Each mine inspector and head mine inspector shall:

(1) Be a qualified elector;

(2) Possess a mine foreman certificate of competency of the State of Alabama;

(3) Have had eight or more years' practical experience in coal mines; and

(4) Be not less than 28 years of age.

(b) The mine inspectors shall reside at points convenient to their respective districts. (Acts 1949, No. 207, p. 242, § 3; Acts 1975, 4th Ex. Sess., No. 147, p. 2866, § 1.)

§ 25-9-7. Duties of mine inspectors generally; accompanying of inspectors on inspections by representatives of miners; mine examination reports.

The duties of mine inspectors are to make examinations of mines to see that all the requirements of this chapter are strictly observed and carried out. They shall examine the equipment, works and machinery connected with said mines; examine into the state of coal mines as to transportation, ventilation, circulation and conditions of air, electricity, explosives, timbering, drainage, practices and general security and perform such other duties as are required by the director. At the commencement of any inspection of a coal mine as provided herein, the authorized representative of the miners at the mine at the time of such inspection shall be given an opportunity to accompany the mine inspectors on any such inspection. The mine inspectors shall make a record of all examinations of coal mines, showing the date when made, the condition in which the coal mines are found, the extent to which the laws relating to coal mines and mining are observed or violated, the progress made in the improvements and security of life and health sought to be secured by the provisions of this chapter, the number of accidents, injuries received or deaths in or about the coal mines, the number of persons employed in or by each coal mine, together with all such other facts and information of public interest concerning the condition of coal mines, development and progress of coal mining in this state as they may think useful and proper, and so much thereof as may be of public interest to be included in their reports. A comprehensive report of each inspection of each coal mine shall promptly be made by the chief to the operator, superintendent and mine foreman of said coal mine, and said report shall be posted in a conspicuous place at the mine. This report shall be on a form provided for that purpose and compiled by the said chief. The form may be changed by the chief from time to time, as may seem desirable. (Acts 1949, No. 207, p. 242, § 3; Acts 1975, 4th Ex. Sess., No. 147, p. 2866, § 1.)

§ 25-9-8. Certificate of competency for fire bosses and mine foremen — Required.

(a) Except as otherwise provided in this chapter, no person shall act as fire boss in any coal mine in this state unless he is in possession of a certificate of competency.

(b) No person shall be employed as mine foreman in any coal mine in this state unless he is in possession of a certificate of competency as provided for in this article. (Acts 1949, No. 207, p. 242, § 5.)

§ 25-9-9. Certificate of competency for fire bosses and mine foremen — Board of examiners.

There shall be appointed by the Governor a board of examiners, all of whom shall hold Alabama mine foreman's certificates, consisting of the chief or the head mine inspector, as the director may designate, together with three active practical miners, three operators of coal mines and one practicing mining engineer. The members of this board shall be appointed by the Governor and shall hold office for three years and until their successors are appointed and qualified, and, as nearly as possible, two members shall be appointed one year and three the succeeding year. No member of the board shall serve more than two consecutive terms of office. The chief or the head mine inspector shall be ex officio chairman of the board. The chairman shall vote only in the case of a tie vote, and, in the absence of one member of the board, a majority of whom shall act. In the event of the failure to have a quorum, the chairman shall have the authority to select a qualified person or persons. There shall be paid to each member of the board, except the ex officio chairman, who shall serve without extra pay, $10.00 per day. Each board member shall also be entitled to the same per diem and travel allowance as is provided by law for state employees for each day's attendance at meetings of the board. Said board of examiners shall meet every six months at the office of the chief and shall remain in session not longer than eight days, and special meetings may be called by the chairman or a majority of the members of said board. The department shall preserve in its office a record of the meetings and transactions of the board and all certificates issued and revoked. (Acts 1949, No. 207, p. 242, § 4; Acts 1975, 4th Ex. Sess., No. 147, p. 2866, § 1; Acts 1981, No. 81-201, p. 242, § 4; Acts 1984, 2nd Ex. Sess., No. 85-15, p. 17, § 1; Acts 1988, No. 88-135, p. 194, § 3.)

Code commissioner's note. — Acts 1992, No. 92-117, § 2 provides: "The existence and functioning of the Board of Examiners of Mine Personnel, created and functioning pursuant to Section 25-9-9, Code of Alabama 1975, is continued, and that code section is expressly preserved."

§ 25-9-10. Certificate of competency for fire bosses and mine foremen — Examinations; fees.

The board of examiners created by Section 25-9-9 shall examine qualified applicants and give certificates of competency to persons who pass the required examinations to act as mine foremen or fire bosses in any coal mine in this state. A fee to be established by the board, not to exceed $20.00, shall be charged for each examination given by the board, and such fee shall be paid to the treasury of the state before the examination is begun. The examinations shall be conducted under such uniform rules, conditions and regulations as the board shall deem most efficient for carrying into effect the spirit and intent of this chapter. Such rules, when formulated, shall be made a part of the permanent record of the board, and such of them as relate to candidates shall be published for their information and governance prior to each examination. Such rules shall be of uniform application to all candidates. (Acts 1949, No. 207, p. 242, § 4; Acts 1981, No. 81-201, p. 242, § 4.)

§ 25-9-11. Certificate of competency for fire bosses and mine foremen — Qualifications of applicants — Mine foreman.

Each applicant for a mine foreman's certificate of competency shall:
(1) Be a citizen of the United States;
(2) Be at least 23 years old;
(3) Have had four years practical mining experience or have had three years practical experience in or around coal mines and be a graduate of a school accredited by the American Association of Universities or have satisfactorily completed an associate degree program in mine technology at an approved state trade school or university;
(4) Present with his application an affidavit of his meeting the foregoing requirements and of his good moral character and known temperate habits, which affidavit shall be signed by three reputable citizens, at least one of whom shall be the holder of a mine foreman's certificate; and
(5) Present with his application an affidavit that he is not a member of any political party or organization that advocates the overthrow of the government of the United States by force. (Acts 1949, No. 207, p. 242, § 4; Acts 1975, 4th Ex. Sess., No. 147, p. 2866, § 1.)

Collateral references. — 56 C.J.S., Master & Servant, § 222.

§ 25-9-12. Certificate of competency for fire bosses and mine foremen — Qualifications of applicants — Fire boss.

Each applicant for a fire boss's certificate of competency shall meet the same qualifications as those for a mine foreman; except that three years' practical experience in or around coal mines is substituted for the requirements of subdivision (3) of Section 25-9-11, and at least one of the persons signing the affidavit shall be holder of a fire boss's or a mine foreman's certificate. (Acts 1949, No. 207, p. 242, § 4; Acts 1975, 4th Ex. Sess., No. 147, p. 2866, § 1.)

§ 25-9-13. Certificate of competency for fire bosses and mine foremen — Replacement of lost certificates.

In case of the loss or destruction of a certificate of competency, the department may supply a copy thereof to the person losing same upon the payment of $1.00, provided that it shall be shown to the satisfaction of the department that the loss has actually occurred and that the loser was the holder of such certificate. (Acts 1949, No. 207, p. 242, § 4.)

§ 25-9-14. Certificate of competency for fire bosses and mine foremen — Forged or counterfeit certificates; uttering false certificates; false statements or misrepresentations in applications.

Any person who shall forge or counterfeit a certificate or knowingly make or cause to be made any false statement in any certificate of competency provided for in this chapter or in any official copy of the same, or who shall utter or use any false certificate or unofficial copy thereof or shall make, give, utter, produce or make use of any false declaration, representation or statement in any such certificate or copy thereof or any document containing the same or shall make any false statement or misrepresentation in his application before the examining board for any certificate, shall be guilty of a misdemeanor, and his certificate shall be cancelled or annulled by the examining board. (Acts 1949, No. 207, p. 242, § 4.)

§ 25-9-15. Certificate of competency for fire bosses and mine foremen — Suspension, cancellation or revocation.

(a) The board is hereby authorized to issue an official written reprimand of any person certified under this chapter as a disciplinary measure for a first violation of any requirement hereof.

(b) In addition, for any subsequent violation or for any serious first violation, the certificate of any person may be cancelled or revoked by the board of examiners, whenever it shall be established to the satisfaction of said board that the holder thereof has become unworthy of official endorsement by reason of violation of this chapter, intemperate habits, manifest incapacity, abuse of authority or for other causes satisfactory to said board. Any person against whom charges are made shall have an opportunity to be heard in his own behalf. He shall have at least 30 days' notice in writing of such charges by the ex officio chairman, and, if the holder of a certificate is convicted on the hearing of such charge of violating any part of this chapter, his certificate shall be revoked by the board. The director, after a thorough investigation, may suspend such holder pending a meeting of the board of examiners and its final action. (Acts 1949, No. 207, p. 242, § 4; Acts 1988, No. 88-135, p. 194, § 3.)

§ 25-9-16. Failure of fire boss to perform required duties.

Any fire boss in a mine who fails to perform any duty imposed on him by the laws of this state as fire boss shall be guilty of a misdemeanor. (Acts 1949, No. 207, p. 242, § 5; Acts 1975, 4th Ex. Sess., No. 147, p. 2866, § 1.)

§ 25-9-17. Persons authorized to act as fire boss; temporary fire boss or mine foreman.

Except as otherwise provided in this chapter, no person shall act as fire boss in any coal mine in this state unless he is in possession of a certificate of competency. Anyone holding a mine foreman's certificate of competency may serve as fire boss. Whenever any exigency arises by which it is impossible for any operator, owner or lessee to secure the immediate service of a certified mine foreman or fire boss, he may employ a person who has the same qualifications by experience, concurred in by the chief or mine inspector delegated by the chief, to act as temporary mine foreman or fire boss for a period not to exceed 15 days. The requirements for a temporary mine foreman or fire boss shall be no more severe than those contained in federal regulations. (Acts 1949, No. 207, p. 242, § 5; Acts 1975, 4th Ex. Sess., No. 147, p. 2866, § 1.)

Cited in Champion v. Davis, 459 F. Supp. 305 (N.D. Ala. 1978).

§ 25-9-18. Qualifications of mine foremen in underground mines.

No person shall be employed as mine foreman in any underground coal mine in this state unless he is in possession of a certificate of competency as provided for in this chapter. (Acts 1949, No. 207, p. 242, § 5; Acts 1975, 4th Ex. Sess., No. 147, p. 2866, § 1.)

§ 25-9-19. Inspection of working places and abandoned areas of mines by foreman.

The mine foreman or subordinate supervisor shall visit each working place on operating days to assure that proper conditions are maintained in the mine as to timbering, ventilation, supplies and all other conditions pertaining to the safety of the men. He shall further direct and cause to be made a weekly inspection, and more often if necessary, of all accessible abandoned areas in the mine. (Acts 1949, No. 207, p. 242, § 5; Acts 1975, 4th Ex. Sess., No. 147, p. 2866, § 1.)

Cited in Champion v. Davis, 459 F. Supp. 305 (N.D. Ala. 1978).

§ 25-9-20. Schedule of mine inspections.

Mines shall be given one complete inspection every 45 days, and more often if necessary. Special or partial or complete inspections shall be made when deemed necessary by the chief. (Acts 1949, No. 207, p. 242, § 3; Acts 1975, 4th Ex. Sess., No. 147, p. 2866, § 1.)

§ 25-9-21. Instruments for measurement of air and gases in mines.

The department shall be furnished by the state all necessary instruments for measurement of the air and gases in coal mines, mine rescue equipment and whatever other apparatus the said department may need. (Acts 1949, No. 207, p. 242, § 3; Acts 1975, 4th Ex. Sess., No. 147, p. 2866, § 1.)

§ 25-9-22. Witnesses at proceedings under chapter generally.

(a) The chief has the authority to administer oaths and to issue subpoenas requiring the attendance of witnesses to testify under oath in any proceeding and to require witnesses to answer all questions propounded to them. The sheriff or constable in the county in which such witnesses may reside or be found shall execute subpoenas issued as above provided, and they shall each receive for their services in executing such subpoenas the same fees as are allowed them respectively for executing subpoenas in other cases. Any witnesses summoned as above mentioned shall be entitled to the same mileage and per diem as is now allowed by law to such witnesses attending trials in the circuit court.

(b) If any witness subpoenaed as above mentioned shall fail to attend without good excuse, in accordance with the subpoena served on him, or shall fail to testify when attending, the chief before whom said proceedings are being had shall certify to the failure of any witness to attend and testify to a judge of the circuit court in the county where such proceeding is being held. The judge to whom such certificate is made shall cause such witness to appear before him at a time fixed by said judge to show cause why he should not be punished for contempt and shall fine or imprison such witness as such judge may deem proper in case he is found guilty of contempt in the premises. (Acts 1949, No. 207, p. 242, §§ 8, 9.)

Collateral references. — 73 C.J.S., Public Administrative Bodies & Procedures, §§ 76, 90, 128.

§ 25-9-23. Expenses of executing subpoenas, attendance of witnesses and contempt proceedings.

The expenses of executing subpoenas and the attendance of witnesses as well as contempt proceedings under Section 25-9-22 shall be paid out of any funds in the treasury of the state on certificate of the Director of Industrial Relations, approved by the Governor. (Acts 1949, No. 207, p. 242, § 10.)

§ 25-9-24. Reporting and correction of unsafe conditions.

Unsafe conditions, known to any persons underground, that cannot be corrected by them in the course of their normal duties, shall be promptly reported to the mine foreman or direct supervisor. The supervisor to whom unsafe conditions are reported or who detects them in the course of his duties shall be responsible for seeing that they are corrected promptly and that exposure to danger of any person is prevented except as necessary in correcting the condition. (Acts 1949, No. 207, p. 242, § 70.)

Contributory negligence. — It is not contributory negligence on the part of an employee to fail to give notice, within a reasonable time, of a known defective condition. Lockhart v. Sloss-Sheffield Steel & Iron Co., 165 Ala. 516, 51 So. 627 (1910).

§ 25-9-25. Malicious or willful damage or destruction of safety devices or appliances, etc. Repealed by Acts 1977, No. 607, p. 812, § 9901, as amended, effective January 1, 1980.

§ 25-9-26. Persons not employees not to enter mines without consent of operator, etc.

Persons not employees of a coal mine or duly authorized employees of the Department of Industrial Relations shall not enter such mine unless the consent of the operator or his authorized representative has been secured and shall not stand on the tracks or go near the machinery or other place of danger. (Acts 1949, No. 207, p. 242, § 102.)

§ 25-9-27. Entry into mine while intoxicated; transporting intoxicating liquor into mine.

Whoever shall, while under the influence of intoxicating liquor, enter any coal mine or any of the buildings connected with the operation of same within the state, where miners or other workmen are employed, or whoever shall carry intoxicating liquors into the same shall be guilty of a misdemeanor. (Acts 1949, No. 207, p. 242, § 103.)

§ 25-9-28. Solicitation of funds from employees for purposes of retaining or procuring employment, etc.

Any coal mine superintendent, mine foreman or assistant mine foreman, or any other person or persons operating or controlling a coal mine, who shall receive or solicit any sum of money or other valuable consideration from any of his or their employees for the purpose of continuing such employee in his or their employ or for the purpose of procuring employment for such employee or procuring or keeping places for such employee shall be guilty of a misdemeanor and, upon conviction, shall be fined not less than $50.00, nor more than $300.00 and shall be sentenced to hard labor for the county for a term of not less than six months. (Acts 1949, No. 207, p. 242, § 104.)

§ 25-9-29. Giving of orders requiring violation of chapter.

Any person acting as coal mine superintendent, mining engineer, other official or supervisor who gives orders that will require violation of this chapter, shall be guilty of a misdemeanor. (Acts 1949, No. 207, p. 242, § 105.)

§ 25-9-30. Persons under 18 not to work in or about mines.

No person under the age of 18 shall be employed to work or labor in or about any coal mine in this state. (Code 1896, § 2933; Code 1907, § 1035; Acts 1911, No. 493, p. 500; Code 1923, § 1724; Acts 1935, No. 193, p. 241; Code 1940, T. 26, § 158; Acts 1949, No. 207, p. 242, § 106; Acts 1971, No. 2486, p. 3983; Acts 1975, 4th Ex. Sess., No. 147, p. 2866, § 1.)

Cross references. — As to child labor generally, see § 25-8-1 et seq.

Action lies for death of boy employed contrary to this section. — In Sloss-Sheffield Steel & Iron Co. v. Cole, 191 Ala. 626, 68 So. 142 (1915), it was held that an action for the death of a boy under the required age, based solely on the ground that his death resulted proximately from his employment, contrary to this section, could be maintained, and that evidence as to his character and disposition was admissible to determine the measure of damages.

And contributory negligence is no defense. — A boy employed in violation of this section cannot be charged with contributory negligence in respect to any injury received in the mine. De Soto Coal, Mining & Dev. Co. v. Hill, 179 Ala. 186, 60 So. 583 (1912).

Mining company is insurer of age. — A mining company is liable for injuries to a boy under the required age resulting from the employment, and incident to any risks of the master's business, though he or his parents may have misstated his age and led the master to believe that he was above the prohibited age, the effect of this section being that the mining company is an insurer of the age of the boy when it employs him. De Soto Coal, Mining & Dev. Co. v. Hill, 179 Ala. 186, 60 So. 583 (1912).

Evidence of age. — Declarations, both written and oral, are admissible to prove age, under this section, where made by some member of family concerned, since deceased. Sheffield Iron Corp. v. Dennis, 204 Ala. 530, 86 So. 467 (1920).

In an action for injuries to employee under the prohibited age, in violation of this section, it was held that an affidavit of employee's parents furnished employer by employee, at the time he was hired, was not admissible to prove employee's age, but was admissible to impeach employee's testimony that he was under such age. Sheffield Iron Corp. v. Dennis, 304 Ala. 530, 86 So. 467 (1920).

Collateral references. — 48A Am. Jur. 2d, Labor & Labor Relations, § 1866 et seq.

ARTICLE 2.

MISCELLANEOUS SAFETY REQUIREMENTS.

§ 25-9-40. Use of protective clothing, etc.

(a) Welders and helpers shall use proper shields or goggles to protect their eyes.

(b) Employees engaged in haulage operations and other persons employed around moving equipment on the surface and underground shall wear snug-fitting clothing.

(c) Protective gloves shall be worn when material which may injure the hands is handled, but gloves with gauntleted cuffs shall not be worn around moving equipment.

(d) Men exposed for short periods to gas, dust, fume and mist inhalation hazards shall wear permissible respiratory equipment. When the exposure is for prolonged periods, other measures to protect workmen or to reduce the hazard shall be taken. (Acts 1949, No. 207, p. 242, § 67.)

§ 25-9-41. Checking systems.

Each mine shall have a check-in and check-out system that will provide positive identification upon the person of every individual underground. An accurate record of the men in the mine, which shall consist of a written record, a check board or a time clock record, shall be kept on the surface in a place that will not be affected in the event of an explosion. Said record shall bear a number identical to the identification check carried by the person underground. (Acts 1949, No. 207, p. 242, § 68.)

§ 25-9-42. Shafts, mine openings and escapeways.

(a) New shafts and partitions therein, made after August 12, 1949, shall be fireproof.

(b) Mine openings, where there is danger of fire entering the mine, shall have adequate protection against surface fires or dangerous volumes of smoke entering the mine.

(c) There shall be at least two travelable passageways out of each section of each mine, one of which may be the haulage road.

(d) Escapeways shall be equipped with stairways, ladders or cleated walkways when needed, installed in such manner that men using them in emergencies may do so quickly and without undue hazard. Direction signs shall be posted conspicuously to indicate manways and designated escapeways. (Acts 1949, No. 207, p. 242, § 69; Acts 1975, 4th Ex. Sess., No. 147, p. 2866, § 1.)

ARTICLE 3.

ACCIDENTS AND DISASTERS.

§ 25-9-60. Maintenance, etc., of first aid equipment; notice of and treatment of injuries.

(a) Each mine shall have an adequate supply of first aid equipment to be used only in case of injury to employees or on the job sickness. These supplies shall be located at points on the surface, at the bottom of main shafts and main slopes, if over 1,000 feet from the surface, and at other suitable locations convenient to each working section. One stretcher and one broken-back board (or a splint-stretcher combination), 24 triangular bandages (or 15, if a splint-stretcher combination is used), eight four-inch bandage compresses, 12 one-inch adhesive compresses, an adequate approved burn remedy, two cloth blankets, one rubber blanket or equivalent substitute, two tourniquets, one one-ounce bottle of aromatic spirits of ammonia or one dozen ammonia ampules and necessary complements of arm and leg splints or two each inflatable plastic arm and leg splints shall be kept at each location designated and shall be accessible to the miners.

(b) No person shall tamper with or remove any first aid supplies other than for use in caring for injured persons and those who become sick while in the mine.

(c) When an injury occurs, prompt first aid shall be given, and, if immediate medical attention is indicated, a doctor shall be notified and the injured person brought to the surface without delay other than the time needed for rendering first aid. Any person injured sufficiently to deprive him of complete control of his faculties or limbs will be adequately attended by designated persons until he is brought to the surface and turned over to a doctor.

(d) Each employee shall promptly notify his supervisor of all injuries. (Acts 1949, No. 207, p. 242, § 6; Acts 1975, 4th Ex. Sess., No. 147, p. 2866, § 1.)

Failure to comply with section is negligence. — Proof of failure to comply with the requirements of this section is sufficient proof of negligence on the part of a person charged with such failure. Smith v. Wolf, 160 Ala. 644, 49 So. 395 (1909).

And lack of penalty is no bar to recovery. — Although no penalty is provided for the violation of the duty imposed by this section, it presents no obstacle to recovery against the wrongdoer in a proper case, the common law affording a remedy. Wolf v. Smith, 149 Ala. 457, 42 So. 824 (1906).

Pleadings must show employment in mine. — This section is intended for the protection of employees engaged at a mine and not persons not so employed, therefore a plaintiff must aver that his intestate was working in the mine and not merely an employee. Whitmore v. Alabama Consol. Coal & Iron Co., 164 Ala. 125, 51 So. 397 (1909).

§ 25-9-61. Reports and investigations of major accidents.

(a) Each operator shall report promptly to the chief of the division the occurrence at any mine of any fatal accident or accident involving serious personal injury to any person or persons, whether employed or not. The scene of the accident shall not be disturbed pending an investigation except to prevent suspension of use of a slope, entry or facility vital to the operation of a section of a mine. In cases where reasonable doubt exists as to whether to leave the scene unchanged, the operator shall secure prior approval from the chief before any changes are made.

(b) The chief shall go personally or dispatch one or more mine inspectors to the scene of the accident or accidents, investigate causes and issue such orders as may be needed to insure safety of other persons.

(c) Representatives of the operator shall render such assistance as may be needed and shall act in a consulting capacity at the investigation. An employee designated by the employees of the mine shall be notified and as many as three employees designated as representatives of the employees may be present at the investigation in a consulting capacity.

(d) The division shall render a complete report of circumstances and causes of each accident investigated and shall make recommendations for prevention of similar accidents. The division shall furnish one copy of the report to the operator and one copy to the employee representative when he has been present at the investigation. The chief of the division shall maintain a complete file of all accident reports and may give such further publicity as ordered by the director in an effort to prevent coal mine accidents. (Acts 1949, No. 207, p. 242, § 7.)

§ 25-9-62. Removal of large and dangerous accumulations of water in adjoining mines.

In any coal mine or coal mines or parts thereof wherein water may have been allowed to accumulate in large and dangerous quantities, putting in danger the adjoining or adjacent coal mines and the lives of the miners working therein, and when such can be tapped and set free and flow by its own gravity to any point of drainage, any operator or person having a mine so endangered, with the approval of the department, may proceed and remove the said danger by driving a drift or drifts protected by bore holes as provided by this chapter, and, in removing said danger, it shall be lawful to drive across property lines if needful. All coal removed in such driving from adjacent lands shall be paid for on the basis of $.25 per ton of 2,000 pounds. No person shall dam or in any way obstruct the flow of water from said mine or parts thereof when so set on any part of its passage to point of drainage. (Acts 1949, No. 207, p. 242, § 11.)

§ 25-9-63. Mine disasters.

(a) If a disaster occurs in a mine, the chief of the division and the nearest office of the United States Bureau of Mines shall be notified by the quickest available means. All facilities of the mine shall be made available for rescue and recovery operations.

(b) No work other than rescue and recovery work may be attempted or started until and unless authorized by the chief of the division or his designated representatives.

(c) After a disaster, operations may not be resumed until authorized by the chief of the division.

(d) If an explosion occurs in a mine, the fan shall not be reversed except by authority of the official in charge of disaster work and then only after a study of the effect of reversing the fan on survivors who are still underground.

(e) The chief of the division shall make available all the facilities at his disposal in effecting rescue and recovery work, and shall act as a consultant or take personal charge where, in his opinion, the circumstances warrant or where the managerial official's status is either incompetent or inadequate.

(f) The orders of the official in charge of disaster work shall be respected and obeyed by all persons engaged in rescue and recovery work.

(g) The chief of the division shall maintain an up-to-date disaster plan for prompt and adequate employment at any coal mine in the state. All employees of the division shall be kept fully informed and trained in their respective duties in making the disaster plan work effectively. The division's plan shall be published annually and furnished to all operators of coal mines and to representatives of the employees. Changes in the plan shall be published promptly when made and furnished to all operators of coal mines and to representatives of the employees. (Acts 1949, No. 207, p. 242, § 12.)

§ 25-9-64. Establishment of mine rescue stations.

The Chief of the Division of Safety and Inspection of the Department of Industrial Relations shall establish and maintain within the State of Alabama and within said division such mine rescue stations as he may determine necessary to carry out rescue and recovery operations of mine disasters and to comply with federal requirements. The mine rescue stations shall be located as near the center of the mining industry as is practical. The station shall have sufficient room to handle equipment and personnel for at least two teams. (Acts 1982, No. 82-439, p. 689, § 1.)

§ 25-9-65. Rescue crews — Training and employment; wages and workmen's compensation benefits.

Said chief is hereby authorized to have trained and employed at the rescue stations operated by said division within the state, rescue crews as he may determine necessary. Each member of such crews shall devote at least four hours each month, or eight hours bimonthly, for training purposes and shall be available at all times to assist in rescue work. Regular crew members shall receive for such services the highest prevailing hourly wage rate in the industry and shall receive the same per diem and expenses as provided to state employees. Workers' compensation benefits as prescribed by Alabama workers' compensation laws shall be provided for all employees engaged in carrying out the mandates of this section and coal mining laws of the State of Alabama. Sufficient funds shall be appropriated to carry out the provisions of this section, Section 25-9-64 and Sections 25-9-66 through 25-9-70. (Acts 1982, No. 82-439, p. 689, § 2.)

§ 25-9-66. Rescue crews — Training; removal of crew members.

It shall be the duty and responsibility of the chief to see that all crews be properly trained by qualified instructors who have a certificate of training from the Mine Safety and Health Administration. The chief may remove any crew member at any time. (Acts 1982, No. 82-439, p. 689, § 3.)

§ 25-9-67. Rescue crews — Qualifications; record of physical examination.

Members of said crews shall have one year underground experience, be less than 50 years of age and pass a physical examination by a licensed physician annually. A record that such examination was taken shall be kept on file by the operator who employs the crew members and a copy shall be furnished to the chief. (Acts 1982, No. 82-439, p. 689, § 4.)

§ 25-9-68. Jurisdiction of chief in rescue and recovery work; consultation and guidance.

All rescue or recovery work performed by these crews shall be under the jurisdiction of the chief. The division shall consult with company officials, representatives of the Mine Safety and Health Administration and representatives of the miners, and all should be in agreement as far as possible on the proper procedure for rescue and recovery. In all instances, procedures shall be guided by the mine rescue apparatus and auxiliary equipment manuals. (Acts 1982, No. 82-439, p. 689, § 5.)

§ 25-9-69. Compensation for rescue work; workers' compensation benefits.

When engaged in rescue or recovery work during an emergency at a mine, all crew members assigned to the work shall be considered during the period of their work, employees of the mine where the emergency exists and shall be compensated by the operator at the rate established in the area for such work. In no event shall this rate be less than the prevailing wage rate in the industry for the most skilled class of inside mine labor. During the period of their emergency employment, all crew members shall be protected by the workers' compensation benefits of such emergency employer. (Acts 1982, No. 82-439, p. 689, § 6.)

§ 25-9-70. Crews to be informed of existing conditions; applicability of federal regulations; assignments by chief.

(a) During recovery work and prior to entering any mine, all recovery crews shall be properly informed of existing conditions.

(b) Mine rescue and recovery work shall be carried out under provisions of the applicable federal regulations.

(c) The chief may assign rescue and recovery work to inspectors, instructors or other qualified employees of said division as the chief may determine desirable. (Acts 1982, No. 82-439, p. 689, § 7.)

ARTICLE 4.

MINE GASES AND VENTILATION.

§ 25-9-80. Main fans.

(a) All main fans shall be installed on the surface, in fireproof housings, the fan situated not less than 30 feet from its air shaft or air course and on one side of the line of such opening so that the fan will not be in direct line of the force of a blast or explosion. The air duct connecting the fan with the mine opening shall be fireproof and provided with self-closing explosion doors.

(b) In mines ventilated with multiple fans, each main fan shall be equipped with fireproof doors automatically closing in the event of a fan failure to prevent air reversal through the fan.

(c) Every main fan installed after August 12, 1949, ventilating a mine classed as gassy, must have an auxiliary drive mechanism that will operate the fan at not less than 80 percent of its regular volume. Dual fan installations, independently powered so that one is operative at 80 percent of regular volume during electrical failures, meet this requirement.

(d) All main fans are required to be provided with a pressure-recording gauge, or water gauge, and, unless attended constantly, an automatic device to give alarm when the fan slows down or stops. This device shall be placed so that its alarm will be seen or heard by a responsible person.

(e) Each main fan ventilating all or part of a mine shall be on a separate power circuit, independent of the underground circuit.

(f) Main fan installations shall be protected from wood fire, grass fire and rubbish fire for at least 100 feet in all directions from the fan installations, where physical conditions permit.

(g) The main fan shall be inspected daily and a record kept of the inspection. This inspection may be made by any competent person so designated.

(h) In mines, when the main fan fails or stops, immediate action shall be taken to cut off power from the mine or the area of the mine ventilated by that main fan, and the men shall be withdrawn from the face regions. If ventilation is restored in a reasonable time, the face regions and other places where methane is likely to accumulate shall be reexamined by certified persons, and, if found to be free from explosive gas, power may be restored and work resumed. If the interruption continues for an indefinite or extended period, all underground employees shall be required to leave the mine or the part of the mine ventilated by the main fan that is out of operation. Mines ventilated by more than one main fan shall be considered as having only one fan in the application of this section unless all returns to the fans are entirely separated and escapeways to the surface are available from the areas ventilated by other fans without necessity for any person passing through any area not properly ventilated.

(i) Main fans ventilating mines shall be operated continuously, except when the mine is shut down with all power underground cut off and with all men out of the mine. When the fan is started again, the mine shall be examined for gas and other hazards by certified persons and declared safe before underground power may be restored and men other than the examiners permitted to enter the mine. (Acts 1949, No. 207, p. 242, § 13; Acts 1975, 4th Ex. Sess., No. 147, p. 2866, § 1.)

§ 25-9-81. Use of methane detectors.

(a) Methane detectors used for examining in coal mines shall be permissible. When not in use, they shall be in the care of certified officials or other competent designated persons, who shall examine, clean and deliver them in a safe condition to their users before they enter the mine.

(b) Permissible methane detectors shall be entrusted for use only to certified persons or to approved competent persons who have been accredited as users of methane detectors.

(c) An individual knowing his methane detector to be injured or defective shall immediately report its condition to his supervisor, mine foreman or to the designated attendant. (Acts 1975, 4th Ex. Sess., No. 147, p. 2866, § 1.)

§ 25-9-82. Standards and procedures as to gases and air quality.

(a) Air in which men work or travel must promptly be improved if it contains less than 19.5 percent oxygen, more than one percent carbon dioxide or is contaminated with noxious or poisonous gases.

(b) If the air immediately returning from a split that ventilates any active workings contains more than one percent methane or more, the ventilation shall be improved, and, if it contains 1.5 percent or more of methane, the power shall be cut off from the portion of the mine affected, and the employees shall be required to withdraw until ventilation is improved.

(c) Face work must be stopped, power to face equipment cut off and the employees ordered and required to withdraw until ventilation is improved, whenever one percent or more of methane can be detected on an approved type methane detector or whenever gas can be detected on a permissible flame safety lamp at any point not less than 12 inches from the roof, face or rib. This does not apply to other faces in the entry or slope in which work can be safely continued.

(d) When entries or faces are stopped on account of gas for ventilation to be improved, only employees designated to work on improving the ventilation under competent direction may be permitted in the affected area. Power shall not be restored until ventilation is improved. (Acts 1949, No. 207, p. 242, § 14; Acts 1959, No. 347, p. 937; Acts 1975, 4th Ex. Sess., No. 147, p. 2866, § 1.)

§ 25-9-83. Standards as to volume of air.

Sufficient air must be circulated and conducted through all entries, slopes, travelways, working places, air courses and open abandoned areas to dilute, render harmless and carry off noxious and explosive gases emitted in the mine, including smoke from blasting, and shall be not less than 150 cubic feet per man per minute. If mules or horses are used in a mine, 500 cubic feet per animal per minute must be provided in addition to the minimum volume specified for men. (Acts 1949, No. 207, p. 242, § 15; Acts 1975, 4th Ex. Sess., No. 147, p. 2866, § 1.)

Editor's note. — The cases cited below were decided under former statutory provisions.

This section imposes an imperative duty on the operator of a mine to so ventilate the mine as to render it harmless from noxious gases generated therein. Foley v. Pioneer Mining & Mfg. Co., 144 Ala. 178, 40 So. 273 (1906); Walker v. Birmingham Coal & Iron Co., 184 Ala. 425, 63 So. 1012 (1913).

And the duty prescribed by this section is nondelegable. Segrest v. Roden Coal Co., 201 Ala. 382, 78 So. 756 (1917).

No matter from what causes the gases generated arose, the duty of ventilating remains the same. Foley v. Pioneer Mining & Mfg. Co., 144 Ala. 178, 40 So. 273 (1906).

But the section does not make a mine operator an insurer against gases released or entering the mine from their natural habitat by moving layers of coal which form the gas pocket. Walker v. Birmingham Coal & Iron Co., 184 Ala. 425, 63 So. 1012 (1913).

An employee without knowledge to the contrary can assume that the mandate of this section has been obeyed by those upon whom the duty is imposed. Foley v. Pioneer Mining & Mfg. Co., 144 Ala. 178, 40 So. 273 (1906).

But such knowledge may render him guilty of contributory negligence. — Where the employee has knowledge of the existence of gas, for example where he has been warned, he may be guilty of contributory negligence in entering a department. Pratt Consol. Coal Co. v. Davidson, 173 Ala. 667, 55 So. 886 (1911).

Violation of section is not ground for action for wrongful death. — An administrator cannot recover damages for wrongful death of his intestate, caused by the violation of provisions of this section, his exclusive remedy being under the Workmen's Compensation Act. Chapman v. Railway Fuel Co., 212 Ala. 106, 101 So. 879 (1924).

Complaint must aver that noxious gases were generated in mine. — A complaint in an action for injury to a miner, which does not aver that there were noxious gases generated in the mine, fails to show a breach of the statutory duty, since this is the condition upon which is predicated the duty enjoined by this section. Sloss-Sheffield Steel & Iron Co. v. Sharp, 161 Ala. 432, 50 So. 52 (1909).

But need not aver failure of operator to observe duty imposed under this section for such failure is negligence per se. Sloss-Sheffield Steel & Iron Co. v. Sharp, 161 Ala. 432, 50 So. 52 (1909).

Collateral references. — 56 C.J.S., Master & Servant, § 222.

54 Am. Jur. 2d, Mines & Minerals, § 179.

§ 25-9-84. Coursing of air.

(a) Two available openings to the surface are required from each seam or stratum of coal worked. In drift or slope mines, such openings provided after August 12, 1949, must be separated by not less than 40 feet of natural strata, and all crosscuts between them shall be closed with stoppings of fireproof material. In shaft mines, such openings provided after August 12, 1949, must be separated by not less than 200 feet of natural strata. The second opening may be made through an adjoining mine. Until these provisions are met, not over five men in a drift, 10 men in a slope and 20 men in a shaft shall work in the mine at one time, and no additional development shall be permitted until the connection is made to the second opening. In mines wherein final pillar robbing operations necessitate closing the second opening, the above limitations as to the number of men permitted to work will apply until the mine is worked out and abandoned.

(b) Both openings shall be kept in good condition and shall at all times be reasonably safe and convenient for entering and leaving the mine. At all points where the passageway to the escapeway or escapement shaft is intercepted by roadways, entries or other passageways, conspicuous signboards shall be placed indicating the direction to the place of exit.

(c) Not more than 80 persons may be assigned or permitted to work on any split of air.

(d) Stations or rooms containing electrical transformers, rectifiers, motor generator sets, battery chargers, permanent pumps or air compressors, control rooms and such other stationary and semipermanent equipment as would endanger lives of employees in event of equipment fire shall be ventilated by a separate split of air, returning directly to the surface.

(e) Changes in ventilation that may affect the safety of the men shall be made when the mine is idle. Only those men and supervisors engaged in major ventilation changes will be permitted in the mine during the change.

(f) In mines, the doors, other than man doors, used for deflecting and conducting the ventilation shall be installed in pairs in a manner approved by the division. They shall be so spaced as to prevent interruption to the regular coursing of air, and they shall be hung and maintained so that they will be self-closing by gravity or by effective mechanical means. An emergency door, to be used in case of damage to a regular door, shall be provided at all points where doors are in use.

(g) Mine doors in use must not be propped or latched open or by any other means used to be prevented from being self-closing.

(h) Proper breaks-through shall be made in all pillars as necessary to meet ventilation requirements at the working faces. The maximum distance between breaks-through shall be 105 feet and closer when required by the chief of the division. Permission to exceed 105 feet between breaks-through may be granted by the chief of the division only in exceptional conditions and must be in writing. Requests for permission must be initiated by the operator and recommended by the mine inspector.

(i) On entries, stoppings in crosscuts between intakes and returns shall be built solidly, substantially and of incombustible material.

(j) Dead ending of rooms, slopes or entries in mines classed as gassy is prohibited unless it is manifestly impracticable to drive crosscuts at or close to faces.

(k) Workings shall not be turned off slopes or entries in by the last crosscut; except, that the places may be necked during development of slopes and entries and when good mining practice justifies the practice in order to establish a main airway.

(l) Line brattice and ventilation tubing used to conduct air to the faces of working places shall be substantially erected and shall be of flame-resistant materials.

(m) In the event that diffuser or auxiliary fans and tubing are used in lieu of or in conjunction with a line brattice system to provide ventilation of the working face:

(1) The fan shall be of a permissible type, maintained in permissible condition, so located and operated to avoid any recirculation of air at any time and inspected frequently by a certified person when in use.

(2) In places where auxiliary fans are used, accumulations of methane resulting from unscheduled stoppage of the main fan shall be removed after restoration of normal mine ventilation by conducting air current into the place with line brattice or equivalent. Auxiliary fans shall not be operated

in such place during stoppage of normal mine ventilation and until methane accumulations have been removed.

(3) If the auxiliary fan is stopped or fails and the ventilation of the working face is inadequate, the electric equipment in the place shall be stopped and the power disconnected at the power source until adequate ventilation is restored. During such stoppage the ventilation shall be by means of the primary air current conducted into the place in a manner to prevent an accumulation of methane.

(4) In places where auxiliary fans are used, the ventilation during scheduled idle periods such as weekends and idle shifts shall be by means of the primary air current conducted into the place in a manner to prevent accumulation of methane.

(5) If the air passing through the auxiliary fan or tubing contains one percent or more of methane, the provisions of subsection (b) of Section 25-9-82 shall be applied.

(6) To insure that an adequate volume and velocity of air are supplied continuously to the working face where auxiliary fan and tubing are used for face ventilation, a line brattice or other approved device shall be installed before the auxiliary fan is stopped.

(7) All face ventilation systems using auxiliary fans and tubing or machine-mounted diffusers approved by the Mining Enforcement and Safety Administration shall be filed with the chief of the division.

(8) Any variance in the above diffuser and auxiliary fan and tubing use must be approved in writing by the chief of the division.

(n) Overcasts shall be constructed tightly of incombustible materials and of sufficient strength to withstand falls of roof, or protected against falling roof, and shall be of ample area to pass the required volume of air. (Acts 1949, No. 207, p. 242, § 16; Acts 1975, 4th Ex. Sess., No. 147, p. 2866, § 1; Acts 1976, No. 391, p. 496.)

Ground opening held not in compliance with section. — One ground opening divided by a thin wooden partition into two separate and distinct compartments, with no other escape way than through one of these compartments, is not a compliance with this section. Howells Mining Co. v. Gray, 148 Ala. 535, 42 So. 448 (1905), case decided under former Code 1940, Tit. 26, § 84.

§ 25-9-85. Sealing, testing, etc., of abandoned workings.

(a) Abandoned workings that cannot be ventilated adequately with safety to employees must be sealed. The chief of the division will prescribe rules for sealing and periodic testing of air and water behind seals. Failure to comply with rules for sealing and periodic testing will be a violation of this section.

(b) Abandoned workings shall be posted to warn persons against entering, and all accessible abandoned workings shall be examined semimonthly or more often if necessary. When posting is inadequate to warn persons against entering, abandoned workings shall be properly fenced off at all such entrances. (Acts 1949, No. 207, p. 242, § 17.)

§ 25-9-86. Examinations for gases and other dangerous conditions.

(a) Operators of mines are required to employ one or more certified fire bosses and to have a preshift examination made. The duties of the fire boss are to examine for dangerous conditions all manways, slopes and entries used by men in traveling to and from work and to examine for gas and other dangerous conditions all working places, adjoining abandoned places and accessible pillar falls for accumulation of gas. The fire boss will ascertain that the air is traveling in its proper course and that all ventilation appliances are in good condition and working effectively. The fire boss will indicate his examination of working and abandoned places, pillar falls and ventilating appliances by marking his initial and the date conspicuously in or on such places.

(b) Whenever gas is detected or danger exists to men entering any place, the fire boss shall leave at each entrance to the place a conspicuous DANGER sign.

(c) Examination of the first working place in mines shall take place not more than three hours before the men are permitted to enter the mine or to pass a designated station underground.

(d) The fire boss shall meet the oncoming shift at the point or station designated and inform each man as to the condition of his working place or the place in which his machine is parked. Each face boss and direct supervisor shall be informed by the fire boss as to the condition of all places under his direction or control. When man trip schedules or other compelling factors make it impractical for the fire boss to check each man, the fire boss will furnish to responsible supervisors written signed reports of his inspection and these supervisors will be responsible for informing each man as to the condition of his working place.

(e) In multiple shift operations, certified supervisors may be used to make the fire boss examination for the next or succeeding shift. Responsible supervisors of the next or succeeding shift may be used to inform each man as to the condition of his working place and may be held responsible, provided the certified supervisors who made the examination furnish a written, signed report as to condition of each working place.

(f) The fire boss shall record the results of his inspection in ink or indelible pencil in a book kept on the surface for that purpose. Similar records may be kept at designated stations or offices underground. This book shall be countersigned daily by the mine foreman. The mine superintendent or his assistant shall also read and countersign the reports.

(g) Idle and abandoned parts of any mine shall be examined by a certified person immediately before employees are permitted to enter or work in such areas.

(h) Examination for gas and other dangerous conditions shall be made by a certified official or approved competent person before taking loading or cutting machines in by the open breakthrough nearest the face or before applying power to machinery that remains at or near the face at not more than 20-minute intervals during cutting, drilling or mechanical loading, before drilling with electric drills, before blasting, after blasting and before other work is resumed and at such other times as may be necessary or designated by the operator or mine inspector for adequate safety.

(i) All persons underground shall use only permissible electric cap lamps for portable illumination that is worn on the person. This does not preclude the use of other types of permissible electric lamps, permissible flashlights, permissible safety lamps or any other portable illumination classed as permissible.

(j) Open cap lights and smoking and smokers' articles, including matches, are prohibited in underground mines. (Acts 1949, No. 207, p. 242, § 18; Acts 1975, 4th Ex. Sess., No. 147, p. 2866, § 1.)

§ 25-9-87. Use of flame safety lamps.

(a) All flame safety lamps used for examining coal mines or for working therein shall be permissible. When not in use, they shall be in the care of certified officials or other competent designated persons who shall disassemble, examine, clean, fill and deliver them, locked and in safe condition, to their users before they enter the mine. Flame safety lamps shall not be unlocked or disassembled inside any coal mine.

(b) At least two permissible flame safety lamps shall be kept in serviceable condition at each coal mine. Not less than 25 percent of those in use or one, whichever is greater, shall be kept in reserve at each mine for use in emergency.

(c) Permissible flame safety lamps shall be entrusted for use only to certified persons or to approved competent persons who have been accredited as users of flame safety lamps as required in this chapter.

(d) Every person who knows his flame safety lamp to be injured or defective shall immediately extinguish it and promptly report its condition to his supervisor, the mine foreman or to the designated lamp attendant. Defective lamps must be kept separate from others until repaired. (Acts 1949, No. 207, p. 242, § 19; Acts 1975, 4th Ex. Sess., No. 147, p. 2866, § 1.)

Collateral references. — 58 C.J.S., Mines & Minerals, § 233.

§ 25-9-88. Reports as to ventilation, gas content, reopening of mines, etc.

(a) The operator of each coal mine shall send to the division a report monthly, or more often if necessary, showing the amount of ventilation and methane content at the inlet and outlet, the amount of ventilation and the methane content of return air at or near the last crosscut in each working entry, the number of splits and the number of men and animals on each split and the places gas has been detected in old workings. The report shall include a record of the pressure gauge readings at the fan.

(b) A prompt report, by the quickest available means, must be made by the operator to the division upon detection of any dangerous accumulation of methane in any coal mine, whether accompanied by explosion or not. This report shall state precautions taken to safeguard employees and action taken or planned to remove the dangerous accumulation. The division shall issue such supplementary orders as may be indicated and dispatch one or more inspectors promptly to the mine if the circumstances warrant.

(c) A report shall be made by the operator to the division prior to opening any new or reopening any abandoned coal mine or abandoning any coal mine.

(d) A report shall be made by the operator to the division when the workings of any coal mine are approaching an abandoned coal mine, shaft or other underground passages that are known to contain or may contain dangerous accumulations of water or gas.

(e) A report shall be made by the operator to the division upon the accidental closing or prior to the intended abandonment or closing of any passageway to an escapement outlet.

(f) A report shall be made by the operator to the division before breaking through any opening into a coal mine whether from or to the surface or through other mine shafts or other passages. (Acts 1949, No. 207, p. 242, § 20; Acts 1975, 4th Ex. Sess., No. 147, p. 2866, § 1.)

§ 25-9-89. Procedure when workings approaching inaccessible accumulations of gases or water.

When workings are being driven toward any worked out and inaccessible or abandoned area or a shaft, that may contain accumulations of gases or water and cannot be inspected, they shall be narrowed to eight feet or less in width. Persons driving these workings shall constantly keep one bore hole near the center of the working and 20 feet in advance and one bore hole 15 feet deep in each rib at a 45 degree angle and at intervals of six feet as the face is advanced. These test holes shall not be used for blasting. Separate blasting holes, not over four feet deep, must be drilled. These precautions must begin at least 100 feet from the probable source of danger. (Acts 1949, No. 207, p. 242, § 21.)

§ 25-9-90. Duty of employees to report damage or unsafe conditions; correction of damage or unsafe conditions.

Each employee shall promptly inform his supervisor or the mine foreman of damage to or unsafe condition of any ventilation appliance when known by the employee or of any obstruction in air passages or other interference with normal ventilation of which he has knowledge. The supervisor or mine foreman who knows of or to whom such damage or unsafe condition is reported is responsible for prompt correction. (Acts 1949, No. 207, p. 242, § 22.)

§ 25-9-91. Prohibited acts.

It shall be a misdemeanor for any person to enter, without an order from an authoritative official, or go dangerously near any mine or part of a mine of which he has been warned personally or by danger board of the presence of gas in dangerous quantities, or knowingly to destroy, damage or lessen the effectiveness of any ventilation appliance or facility, or to open a ventilating door that is in use without promptly closing the same, or to do any willful act knowing that the consequence of his act might result in accumulation or ignition of gas. (Acts 1949, No. 207, p. 242, § 22.)

ARTICLE 5.

COAL AND ROCK DUST.

§ 25-9-110. Accumulation of coal dust; methods for allaying dust at source.

(a) Coal dust shall not be allowed to accumulate excessively along conveyor lines, roadways, at loading points or at underground tipples, but shall be loaded and sent out of the mines. Coal dust in dangerous quantities in abandoned areas shall, where practicable be rendered inert.

(b) Where mining operations raise an excessive amount of dust into the air currents, water or water with a wetting agent added to it or other effective methods shall be used to allay such dust at its source. (Acts 1949, No. 207, p. 242, § 23.)

§ 25-9-111. Rock dusting.

(a) Rock dust to be used to render coal dust inert shall come within the following specifications:

Combustible matter not more than five percent by volume, quartz or free silica particles not more than five percent by volume, and not unduly absorbent of moisture and preferably light in color. Rock dust shall be pulverized so that 100 percent will pass through a 20 mesh screen and 70 percent or more will pass through a 200 mesh screen.

(b) Rock dust shall be applied and maintained upon the top, floor and sides of all open places, passages and haulageways in such quantities that the incombustible contents of mine dust that could initiate or propagate an explosion will not be less than 65 percent, but the incombustible content in the return air courses shall be no less than 80 percent. Rock dust shall be so applied and maintained to include the last open breakthrough of rooms and entries and to within 40 feet of the faces or closer if necessary.

(c) In back entries and air courses, rock dust barrier protection in lieu of generalized rock dusting may be authorized by the chief of the division upon request by the operator. The chief of the division will prescribe the methods of protection that may be substituted.

(d) Where methane is present in any ventilating current, the percentage of incombustible content shall be increased one percent and four-tenths percent for each one-tenth percent of methane where 65 and 80 percent, respectively, of incombustibles are required.

(e) Mines or locations in mines that are too wet or too high in incombustible content for a coal dust explosion to initiate or propagate are not required to be rock dusted during the time such conditions prevail. (Acts 1949, No. 207, p. 242, § 24; Acts 1975, 4th Ex. Sess., No. 147, p. 2866, § 1.)

ARTICLE 6.

EXPLOSIVES AND BLASTING.

§ 25-9-130. Permissible explosives and blasting methods generally; use of black blasting powder; use of dynamite, etc.

(a) Permissible explosives or permissible blasting methods only shall be used in blasting coal or coal and other material in all mines where on shift.

(b) Black blasting powder shall not be stored or used in underground coal mines.

(c) Prior to use of Cardox or Airdox, both of which are classed as permissible blasting methods, or any other blasting device or method that may later be classed as permissible, the operator must secure written approval from the chief of the division. The chief in granting approval will issue instructions as to storage, transportation, handling, charging, tamping, detonating and handling misfires. These instructions will be made conditions of the approval, and violations of any of them will be considered violations of this section.

(d) Prior to use of dynamite or any other nonpermissible explosive for blasting in rock tunnels, shafts, etc., the operator must secure written approval from the chief of the division. The chief in granting approval shall issue instructions as to storage, transportation, handling, charging, tamping, detonating and handling misfires. These instructions shall be made conditions of the approval, and violations of any of them will be considered violations of this section. (Acts 1949, No. 207, p. 242, § 25; Acts 1951, No. 204, p. 465; Acts 1959, No. 80, p. 488; Acts 1975, 4th Ex. Sess., No. 147, p. 2866, § 1.)

§ 25-9-131. Surface storage of explosives and detonators.

(a) Separate surface magazines shall be provided for the storage of explosives and detonators and shall be kept in good repair.

(b) Magazines shall be constructed of or covered with fire and weather resistant material, shall be reasonably bullet proof and shall have no metal or sparking material exposed inside the magazine. When a magazine is used for more than one type of explosive, each type shall be stored separately.

(c) The only openings shall be doors for entrance, which shall be securely locked when unattended, and properly screened vents.

(d) If artificial light is needed, only an electric flashlight, electric lantern or electric cap lamp shall be used. Smoking, carrying of smokers' articles or open flame are prohibited in or within 25 feet of any magazine. Combustible materials, including rubbish and dry grass, shall be kept clear of any magazine for a distance of 25 feet in all directions.

(e) Other material shall not be stored with explosives or detonators and metallic tools shall not be used for opening containers of explosives.

(f) Distributing magazines, constructed of two inch hardwood, or metal lined with nonsparking material or an equivalent may be used for storage or distribution of not more than 125 pounds of explosives or 5,000 detonators. No magazine shall be placed in a building containing any highly flammable material or waste and shall be at least 20 feet from a stove, furnace, open fire or flame.

(g) All magazines shall be not less than 200 feet from any mine opening, unless effectively barricaded, and suitable danger signs shall be placed near all magazines. (Acts 1949, No. 207, p. 242, § 26.)

Collateral references. — 35 C.J.S., Explosives, § 3.

§ 25-9-132. Underground transportation of explosives and detonators.

(a) Individual containers used to carry permissible explosives or detonators shall be constructed of substantial, nonconductive material, kept closed and maintained in good condition.

(b) When explosives or detonators are transported underground by locomotive, rope or shuttle car they shall be in covered cars or in special containers.

(1) The bodies and covers of special cars and containers shall be constructed of nonconductive material.

(2) If explosives and detonators are hauled in the same explosives car or in the same special containers, they shall be separated by at least a four-inch substantially fastened hardwood partition or the equivalent.

(3) Where quantities of explosives and detonators are transported in special cars or in special containers in cars, they shall be hauled on a special trip not connected to any other trip, and shall not be hauled into or out of a mine within five minutes preceding or following a man-trip or any other trip.

(4) Explosives or detonators shall not be transported on the same trip with workmen other than those required in the transportation of the explosives or detonators.

(c) Explosives and detonators shall be transported underground by belt only under the following conditions:

(1) In the original and unopened case, in special closed cases constructed of nonconductive material or in suitable individual containers.

(2) Clearance requirements shall be the same as those for transporting men on belts.

(3) Suitable loading and unloading stations shall be provided.

(4) There shall be an attendant at loading and unloading points and stop controls at these points.

(d) Explosives or detonators shall not be transported on flight or shaker conveyors or by scraper or mechanical loading machines. (Acts 1949, No. 207, p. 242, § 27.)

Collateral references. — Explosives: liability in connection with fire or explosion of explosives while being stored or transported. 35 ALR3d 1177.

§ 25-9-133. Underground storage of explosives and detonators.

(a) Underground section boxes or magazines shall be constructed of substantial nonsparking material and shall be placed in a crosscut or idle room neck at least 25 feet from roadways, trolley wires or power lines, at least 75 feet from any working face and in a reasonably dry and well rock dusted place, free of oil, grease or other debris.

(b) Explosives and detonators shall be stored separately and at least five feet apart. Not more than a 48-hour supply of explosives and detonators, including any surplus remaining from the previous day, shall be stored underground in section boxes or magazines. This maximum 48-hour supply will include supplies in individual or face boxes where used.

(c) A one day's supply of explosives and detonators may be kept in individual or face boxes. Those boxes shall be wooden with hinged lids and shall be kept not less than 15 feet from roadways, trolley wires or power lines; provided, that 15 feet may be reduced to five feet when the boxes are kept in a niche in the rib at least 75 feet from any working face and in a location out of line of blast where they will not likely be subjected to shock. Separate boxes, kept at least five feet apart, shall be used for explosives and detonators.

(d) Explosives and detonators shall be kept in their containers until removed for use at the working faces.

(e) Care shall be exercised to use the oldest explosives from storage before new supplies are used so that explosives will not remain in underground storage long enough to deteriorate. (Acts 1949, No. 207, p. 242, § 28; Acts 1975, 4th Ex. Sess., No. 147, p. 2866, § 1.)

§ 25-9-134. Blasting practices and procedures generally.

(a) Only competent persons shall be designated or permitted to handle explosives or do blasting. Only electric detonators of proper strength may be used and the use of delay electric detonators is prohibited for blasting coal or coal and other material. Primers shall be made up as needed for blasting and prepared in accordance with the safety standards of the Institute of Makers of Explosives or of the manufacturer of the explosives as approved by the chief; provided, however, that nothing provided in this subsection shall prohibit the use of permissible milli-second blasting in conformity with the requirements, exceptions, limitations, conditions and restrictions on the use thereof established or hereinafter established by the Bureau of Mines of the United States Department of the Interior.

(b) Care shall be used in placement and drilling of holes. Test roof, face, ribs and timbers for dangerous conditions before drilling or preparing holes. Certified official or approved competent persons must test for methane with approved methane detectors before drilling with electric powered drills and before charging bore holes.

(1) Bore holes shall not be drilled beyond the back of the cut or cutting shot nor into the solid ribs, roof or floor.

(2) Where it is impractical to undercut, top cut or shear the coal face and solid shooting is necessary, depending shots are prohibited. The method of placing and firing holes is subject to approval by the chief.

(3) Bore holes shall be cleaned and checked to see that they are placed properly and are of correct depth in relation to the cut before being charged.

(4) To prevent blown-out or windy shots, all portions of the bore holes, where the height of the coal permits, shall have a burden in all directions of at least 18 inches before being fired.

(c) Charges shall not exceed one and one-half pounds in bore holes under six feet in depth. Charges exceeding one and one-half pounds but not exceeding three pounds may be used only if bore holes are six feet or more in depth, have a burden in all directions of at least 18 inches and class A or class B permissible explosives are used.

(d) Bore holes shall be charged with explosives in a continuous train with no cartridges deliberately deformed or crushed, with all cartridges in contact with each other, and with the end cartridges touching the back of the hole and the stemming respectively.

(e) Bore holes shall be tamped with wooden tamping bars, and shall be stemmed with at least 24 inches of incombustible material or at least one half of the length of the hole shall be so stemmed if the hole is less than four feet in depth. Water-filled plastic bags for stemming may be used under the following conditions:

(1) The bags shall be made of polyvinyl chloride not less than six mils in thickness or equivalent in tear resistance and noninflammability.

(2) The bore hole shall be stemmed with at least one water-filled bag not less than 15 inches in length and within one fourth of one inch of the bore hole diameter. Short bore holes may not accommodate the entire bag, but this shall be acceptable.

(3) The bags shall be equipped with self-closing valves or equivalent leakproof protection.

(4) To prevent puncturing, the water-filled bag shall be pushed gently into the bore hole until it touches the charge of explosives and shall not be tamped or forced.

(f) In mines where shooting is done on shift, all shots or series of shots shall be fired promptly after charging and in the following manner:

(1) Remove shunts or untwist ends of leg wires of electric detonators and connect to firing cable.

(2) Move away from face, paying out cable and being sure cable does not contact pipe, pan line or other material that may carry stray currents. Keep leg wires and firing cable up out of water.

(3) Take firing position in protected place around at least one solid corner or in an adequate shelter hole.

(4) Give ample warning before shots are fired and ascertain that all persons are in the clear. See to it that men are removed from adjoining working places when there is possibility of a shot breaking through.

(5) Unshunt ends of firing cable, attach to blasting unit, call "Fire! Fire!" with intervals between each warning and set off charge.

(6) Disconnect firing cable and reshunt ends.

(7) Wait for smoke to clear and immediate roof effect to take place.

(8) Return to face, reeling up firing cable and make tests of face, roof, ribs and timbers for dangerous conditions. In mines classed as gassy, a certified official or approved competent person must make a gas examination on return to the face after blasting.

(9) If gas or other dangerous conditions are found that cannot be made safe in normal course of work, mark place out with DANGER sign and report to mine foreman or supervisor in charge.

(g) Holes shall not be drilled, charged or fired in any place where methane gas can be detected at one percent or more on an approved methane detector.

(h) In mines where shooting is done from the surface with all men out of the mine, a separate blasting circuit must be provided with a switch kept locked when not in use for blasting or written approval of the chief of the division must be secured. Requests to use power or a signal circuit for blasting with all men out of the mine, shaft or slope must state precautions taken to guard against electrocution and premature detonation hazards. Approval by the chief will be conditioned on compliance with these precautions, violations of which will be considered violations of this section of the law.

(i) Mixed charges shall not be charged or fired in any bore hole.

(j) The firing of adobe (mudcap) or other open, unconfined shots is prohibited in any mine. (Acts 1949, No. 207, p. 242, § 29; Acts 1957, No. 197, p. 256; Acts 1965, No. 34, p. 51; Acts 1975, 4th Ex. Sess., No. 147, p. 2866, § 1.)

Collateral references. — 35 C.J.S., Explosives, § 8.

Blasting: liability for property damage by concussion from blasting. 20 ALR2d 1372.

Blasting: liability of strip or other surface mine or quarry operator to person on adjoining premises injured or killed during blasting operations. 84 ALR2d 737.

§ 25-9-135. Blasting cables.

Blasting cables shall be:

(1) Kept well insulated and as long as may be necessary to permit the shot firer to get in a safe place around a corner.

(2) Short circuited at the battery end until ready to attach to the blasting unit.

(3) Staggered as to length or kept well separated when attached to the detonator leg wires.

(4) Kept clear of power wires and all other possible sources of active or stray currents. (Acts 1949, No. 207, p. 242, § 30.)

§ 25-9-136. Misfires.

(a) Where misfires occur with electric detonators, the person firing the shots shall disconnect his firing cable from the source of power and short circuit it by reshunting the ends of the cable. No person shall return to the shot until five minutes has elapsed from the misfire, and the firing cable must not be left behind anyone returning to the face.

(b) If a defect in the firing cable or connections is found, another attempt may be made to fire the shot or shots, exercising such cautions as covered in Section 25-9-134, subsection (f), subdivision (5).

(c) If the misfire is definite, explosives shall be removed by drilling and firing the bore hole for a separate charge at least two feet away from and parallel to the misfired charge, or by washing the stemming and the charge from the bore hole with water or by inserting and firing a new primer after the stemming has been washed out.

(d) A very careful search of the working place, and if necessary, of the coal after it reaches the tipple, shall be made after blasting a misfired hole, to recover any undetonated explosive.

(e) The handling of a misfired shot shall be under the direct supervision of the mine foreman, his assistant or any competent person designated by the mine foreman or his assistant.

(f) If fuses and caps are used for blasting on the surface, misfires may not be approached by anyone until six hours have elapsed, and handling of the misfire must be done with due care and under direction of a supervisor or other competent person. (Acts 1949, No. 207, p. 242, § 31.)

§ 25-9-137. Report of premature explosions.

A prompt report shall be made to the chief of the division in any case of premature detonation or explosion of explosives, whether or not any person is injured. (Acts 1949, No. 207, p. 242, § 32.)

ARTICLE 7.

UNDERGROUND FIRE PREVENTION AND CONTROL.

§ 25-9-150. Building of fires in mines; use of torches; welding and burning.

(a) No person shall build a fire or cause a fire to be built in any coal mine, except as provided hereinafter.

(b) Torches may be used by competent persons in mines for splicing trailing cables, provided suitable precautions are taken against ignition of methane, coal dust or combustible materials. Torches must be maintained at all times in good operating condition and leakproof.

(c) Welding and burning may be done in mines provided all equipment and gauges are maintained in good order and not abused and suitable precautions are taken against ignition of methane, coal dust or combustible materials. Only persons who have demonstrated competence in welding and burning are entrusted to do this work. Adequate eye protection will be used by all persons doing welding or burning, and precautions shall be taken to prevent other persons from exposure that might be harmful to their eyes.

Certified officials or approved competent persons shall examine for gas with approved methane detectors before welding or burning and at 20-minute intervals until work is complete.

When torches are used and welding and burning is done, a minimum of 150 pounds of rock dust and/or a 2A 10-B:C fire extinguisher shall be provided for prompt extinguishing of fires accidentally started.

(d) Approval of the chief of the division will be secured before firing coal seams in connection with gassification or other mining methods that may be practiced experimentally or commercially entailing controlled burning of coal in mines. Before granting approval, the chief will ascertain that the proposal entails no undue hazards to persons and that public property and property of other owners will not be endangered. (Acts 1949, No. 207, p. 242, § 33; Acts 1975, 4th Ex. Sess., No. 147, p. 2866, § 1.)

Collateral references. — Liability for injury or damage resulting from fire started by use of blow torch. 49 ALR2d 368.

§ 25-9-151. Examinations for fire.

In any mine or part of a mine which will be neither fire-bossed nor worked on the following shift, a supervisor or other responsible person shall examine all working places after face work ceases for evidence of fire. (Acts 1949, No. 207, p. 242, § 34.)

§ 25-9-152. Use, storage, etc., of oil, grease and lubricants; fire extinguishing equipment.

(a) Oiling or greasing of mine cars inside coal mines is permitted only when the work and storage areas are kept reasonably clean at all times. Storage of oil or grease for this purpose is limited to three barrels, and must be in a fireproof compartment connecting with return airway direct to the surface and without contacting active workings.

(b) Lubricants for use in underground shops must be kept in approved portable containers, kept securely closed when not in use and are not to exceed a one day's supply; provided, that more than a one day's supply may be stored underground in reasonable quantities if stored in a fireproof compartment connecting with return airway to the surface and without contacting active workings.

(c) Lubricants for use in sections using mechanical equipment must be kept in approved portable containers, kept securely closed when not in use in minimum quantities required for operations, not exceeding 48 hours.

(d) All points at which lubricants are used, kept or stored shall be kept reasonably clean and free of avoidable spillage.

(e) Five hundred pounds of rock dust or sand or a 2A 10-B:C fire extinguisher shall be kept convenient to each oil or grease storage area in mines.

(f) Two hundred pounds of rock dust or sand or a fire extinguisher suitable for use in class A fires will be kept convenient to each set of doors used for ventilation in mines.

(g) Five hundred pounds of rock dust or sand or a 2A 10-B:C fire extinguisher shall be kept convenient to each station or room containing mine transformers, rectifiers, motor generator sets, battery chargers, permanent pump or air compressor control rooms and such other stationary and permanent or semipermanent equipment as may be classed by the chief of the division as a serious hazard in event of fire. (Acts 1949, No. 207, p. 242, § 35; Acts 1975, 4th Ex. Sess., No. 147, p. 2866, § 1.)

§ 25-9-153. Underground stables.

No underground stables shall be constructed or used in coal mines after August 12, 1949, and straw for bedding or hay for feeding animals shall not be sent into coal mines. This does not apply to mines stabling animals underground on August 12, 1949. Rules for preventing fires and for maintenance of such stables and for handling straw and hay shall be prescribed in writing by the chief. Failure to comply with these rules shall constitute a violation of this chapter. (Acts 1949, No. 207, p. 242, § 36.)

§ 25-9-154. Procedure upon discovery of fire.

(a) The first person to discover a fire and any person in the vicinity shall take prompt steps to extinguish the fire.

(b) If the fire cannot be quickly extinguished, word shall be sent immediately to a competent official of the mine, who shall take charge and order all workmen out of the affected area except those designated for fire fighting.

(c) If the fire gets out of control, workmen shall be withdrawn pending action to flood or seal off the affected area. The phase shall be under the direction of the senior mine official available, in consultation with the chief of the division or a designated inspector. (Acts 1949, No. 207, p. 242, § 37.)

§ 25-9-155. Operators to report fires; assistance, etc., of chief in extinguishing fires, etc.

Immediately upon knowledge of serious fire in or about a mine, the operator shall report by the quickest available means to the chief of the division giving all information known to him. Based on the information, the chief shall take prompt action to go in person or dispatch qualified subordinates to the scene of the fire for consultation, and assist in the extinguishing of the fire and the protection of exposed persons. In event of difference of opinion as to measures required, the decision of the chief or his designated subordinate shall be final, but must be given to the operator in writing to have the force of an order. (Acts 1949, No. 207, p. 242, § 38.)

ARTICLE 8.

ELECTRICAL EQUIPMENT.

§ 25-9-170. Transformers, conversion equipment, etc.

(a) All surface transformers, unless of "dead front" construction or if installed at least eight feet above ground, shall be enclosed in a house or surrounded by a fence at least six feet high. If the enclosure is of metal, it shall be grounded effectively. The gate or door to the enclosure shall be kept locked at all times unless authorized persons are present.

(b) Underground transformers installed after August 12, 1949, shall be air-cooled or nonflammable liquid cooled.

(c) Underground stations containing transformers or circuit breakers filled with inflammable oil shall be provided with door sills or their equivalent which will confine the oil if leakage or explosion occurs, and shall be of fireproof construction.

(d) Transformers shall be provided with automatic cutouts.

(e) All underground transformers or conversion equipment, whether permanent or portable, shall be kept in housings of fireproof construction; provided, that equipment designed and constructed to be fireproof is exempted from this requirement.

(f) The operator of every mine where permanent transformers or conversion equipment is installed underground shall designate or cause to be designated on the map provided for by law the locations of transformer and conversion equipment stations.

(g) "Danger — High Voltage" signs shall be posted conspicuously on all transformer enclosures, high-potential switchboards and other high-potential installations. (Acts 1949, No. 207, p. 242, § 39; Acts 1975, 4th Ex. Sess., No. 147, p. 2866, § 1.)

§ 25-9-171. Power wires and circuits; signal and telephone wires; trolley and feeder wires.

(a) All power circuits entering a mine shall be protected against lightning by lightning arrestors at or near the points of entrance to the mine. All power circuits shall be protected against lightning or other surges by adequate circuit breakers, fuses or both.

(b) All power wires, except trailing cables and ground wires, whether bare or insulated, shall be supported on well-installed insulators and shall not touch combustible material, roof or ribs. Power wires or cables installed prior to August 12, 1949, in locations inaccessible without prohibitive expense may be continued in use if approved by the division.

(c) Power wires shall be insulated properly when passing through doors and stoppings and where they cross other power circuits.

(d) Signal wires and telephone wires shall be run at a safe distance and, where possible, shall be placed on the opposite side of the slope or heading from the power wires.

(e) Where track is used as a power conductor:

(1) Tracks shall be bonded and cross-bonded in such manner as to assure adequate return.

(2) Switches on entries shall be well bonded.

(f) Employees called upon to do work on energized electric circuits or energized parts of electrical equipment shall use properly tested lineman's electric gloves and leather protector gloves.

(g) Trolley and feeder wires shall be installed as follows:

(1) Aligned properly and where installed after August 12, 1949, at least six inches outside the track gauge line.

(2) Provided with cutout switches at intervals of not more than 2,000 feet and near the beginning of all branch lines.

(3) Kept taut and not permitted to touch roof, rib or cross bars. Particular care should be taken where they pass through door openings to preclude bare wires coming in contact with combustible material.

(4) Trolley or bare feeder cables shall be guarded adequately where it is necessary for men to pass or work under them regularly unless the wires are more than six and one-half feet above the top of the rail. They shall also be guarded adequately on both sides of doors and regardless of height at all stations designated for loading and unloading of mantrips and at sand boxes. (Acts 1949, No. 207, p. 242, § 40.)

§ 25-9-172. Grounding of frames, casings and other electrical equipment.

Where grounding wires are used to ground metallic sheaths, armors, conduits, frames, casings and other metallic enclosures, such grounding wires must comply with the following conditions:

(1) The cross-sectional area (size) of the grounding wire shall be at least one-half the cross-sectional area (size) of the power conductor where the power conductor used is No. 6 A.W.G. or larger.

(2) Where the power conductor used is less than No. 6 A.W.G., the cross-sectional area (size) of the grounding wire shall be equal to the cross-sectional area (size) of the power conductor. (Acts 1949, No. 207, p. 242, § 41; Acts 1975, 4th Ex. Sess., No. 147, p. 2866, § 1.)

§ 25-9-173. Circuit breakers, etc.; insulating platforms.

(a) Circuit breakers or other overload devices shall be provided to protect power circuits.

(b) Insulating platforms of dry wood, rubber or other suitable nonconductive material shall be kept in place at each switchboard, underground telephone station, power control switches and at stationary machinery where shock hazards exist; provided, that metal plates on which a person normally would stand and which are kept at the same potential as the grounded, metal noncurrent-carrying parts of the power switches to be operated may be used. (Acts 1949, No. 207, p. 242, § 42; Acts 1975, 4th Ex. Sess., No. 147, p. 2866, § 1.)

§ 25-9-174. Telephones.

Telephone service or approved equivalent means of communication shall be provided at the bottom of each main shaft or slope and in all mines from the surface to the working sections of the mine where the mine workers are more than 1,500 feet from the surface. (Acts 1949, No. 207, p. 242, § 43.)

§ 25-9-175. Electric drills, etc.; trailing cables; cables for portable equipment.

(a) Electric drills or other electrically operated rotating tools intended to be held in hands shall have the electric switch constructed so as to break the circuit when the hand releases the switch or shall be equipped with friction or safety clutches.

(b) All new trailing cables installed after November 21, 1975, shall meet the requirements set out by the Secretary of the Interior in Bureau of Mines schedule 2G and in subsequent revisions.

(c) Cables for portable underground electric equipment shall be provided with suitable overload protection and power taps, unless properly connected to permissible junction or distribution boxes. (Acts 1949, No. 207, p. 242, § 44; Acts 1975, 4th Ex. Sess., No. 147, p. 2866, § 1.)

§ 25-9-176. Electric lights.

Electric lights shall be installed so that they cannot come in contact with combustible materials. The wires shall be supported by suitable insulators and fastened securely to the power conductors. (Acts 1949, No. 207, p. 242, § 45.)

ARTICLE 9.

ROOF SUPPORT.

§ 25-9-190. Testing and examination of roof, faces, ribs, etc.; correction of and precautions against unsafe conditions.

(a) It shall be the duty of the mine foreman and his subordinate supervisors to ascertain that all workmen are trained in proper methods of testing the roof, face and ribs. The mine foreman shall designate the tool or tools to be used for testing.

(b) Face workers and other employees whose work exposes them to hazards of falls of rock and coal shall thoroughly test the roof, face and ribs before starting work or before starting a machine and frequently thereafter. The required test may be made by any competent person for a crew. No person shall start work in a place tested by another unless he is satisfied as to the thoroughness of the test, or until after he himself has made a test.

(c) If the roof, face or rib conditions are found to be unsafe, they shall be corrected by taking down loose material or securely supporting the same before work is started.

(d) If roof, face or rib conditions are found to be unsafe and cannot be corrected by normal taking down or supporting practices, the place shall be guarded or danger boarded to prevent unauthorized entrance and the supervisor shall be promptly notified. The supervisor shall take the necessary action to correct the dangerous condition, delegating for this work only men who are capable.

(e) Precautions as outlined in subsections (b), (c) and (d) of this section shall be taken at any time during work that unsafe roof, face or rib conditions are found to exist.

(f) At least once each shift the supervisor shall examine the roof, faces, ribs and timbers or supports of all working places for unsafe conditions. Unsafe conditions found shall be corrected promptly.

(g) The mine foreman or subordinate supervisor shall examine or cause to be examined by a competent person the condition of the roof and ribs of passageways where men travel, at least once each 24 hours of operation. Unsafe conditions found shall be corrected promptly. (Acts 1949, No. 207, p. 242, § 46.)

Collateral references. — Duty of an employer with respect to the timbering of a mine, under the common law and general statutes. 15 ALR 1380.

Duty of an employer with respect to the timbering of a mine, under statutes relating specifically to the subject. 15 ALR 1430.

§ 25-9-191. Installation, etc., of timbering or other roof support systems.

(a) Timbering or other adequate roof support systems suitable to the roof conditions and mining system of each mine or part of a mine shall be adopted, complied with and required. Additional timbering or supporting will be done where necessary.

(b) It shall be the duty of the mine foreman and his subordinate supervisors to ascertain that all workmen are trained in the proper methods of setting timbers or placing supports. (Acts 1949, No. 207, p. 242, § 47.)

§ 25-9-192. Maintenance of supply of timbers or other roof supports.

(a) The operator of each mine shall keep on hand at the mine a sufficient supply of timbers of suitable length and cap pieces to be used as required in timbering underground workings. Timbers and cap pieces in required quantities and lengths as ordered shall be delivered to the working places designated or in cars to the point at which cars are accepted by the miners.

In hand loading mines, the miner shall order timbers and cap pieces at least one day in advance in order to have in his working place a sufficient supply for his needs. He shall place his order with the mine foreman or subordinate supervisor, stating the number and length of timbers needed. In mechanical mining, the mine foreman shall set up a systematic procedure for ordering and supplying of timbers and cap pieces. When timbers are needed in any working place and are not available, no person shall work in that place.

(b) In mines using roof supports other than timber, it shall be the responsibility of the operator to maintain an adequate supply of materials required and to insure their delivery in sufficient quantities to the working places as needed. (Acts 1949, No. 207, p. 242, § 48.)

Editor's note. — The cases cited below were decided under former statutory provisions.

Section imposes imperative duty. — The provisions of this section are mandatory, and impose on operators of mines an imperative duty. Stith Coal Co. v. Sanford, 192 Ala. 601, 68 So. 990 (1915).

Which is performed when sufficient and suitable props are furnished. — A mine operator who furnishes sufficient props of suitable length and sizes, where desired by employee, performs the duty required, and it is not essential that he furnish props of the exact length demanded by the employee. Stith Coal Co. v. Sanford, 192 Ala. 601, 68 So. 990 (1915).

And timber need not be cut and kept to meet every possible emergency. It is suffi-cient when timber is kept which may be cut and delivered at the designation of the miner. Kelly v. Altoona Coal Co., 205 Ala. 78, 87 So. 541 (1920).

Employee must designate props desired. — Under this section it is the duty of the employee to designate the props or timbers desired, or to give notice of their number and kind, and of the place at which they are to be delivered. Altoona Coal Co. v. Kelly, 203 Ala. 338, 83 So. 62 (1919).

But he has no duty to prop entries. — This section does not require miners to prop or look after the safety of entries; the duty rests upon the operator of the mines. Sloss-Sheffield Steel & Iron Co. v. Green, 159 Ala. 178, 49 So.

301 (1909); Lookout Fuel Co. v. Phillips, 11 Ala. App. 657, 66 So. 946 (1914).

Compliance with this section relieves a mine operator from liability for injury received by a contractor caused by a rock falling from the entry roof. Bowen v. Pennsylvania Coal Co., 179 Ala. 410, 60 So. 835 (1913).

It is for the jury to determine from the evidence whether the mine operator furnished suitable props as required by this section, and thereby relieved himself of liability to an employee injured by rock falling on him. Stith Coal Co. v. Sanford, 192 Ala. 601, 68 So. 990 (1915).

Complaint stating cause of action. — A complaint alleging the relation of master and servant, and that the employee requested the delivery of props, that it was the duty of the employer to promptly deliver the same, that the duty was breached, and as a proximate consequence thereof, the employee was injured, states a cause of action under this section. Stith Coal Co. v. Sanford, 192 Ala. 601, 68 So. 990 (1915).

Collateral references. — 56 C.J.S., Master & Servant, § 222.

54 Am. Jur. 2d, Mines & Minerals, § 180.

Duty of an employer with respect to the timbering of a mine under statutes relating specifically to the subject. 15 ALR 1430.

ARTICLE 10.

HOISTING AND HAULAGE.

§ 25-9-210. Hoist engineers; signal codes, etc.; safety features of cages, hoist engines, hoist ropes and hoist shafts; hoisting of tools, timber, animals, etc.

(a) Only competent engineers shall be placed in charge of or permitted to operate any engine used for conveying into and hoisting out of any coal mine. When men are being lowered or hoisted, an additional engineer competent to act in emergencies shall be present at the hoist controls. At all times when men are in the mine, a competent hoist engineer shall be available to receive notice or signals requiring his presence at the hoist engine controls. No engineer shall be required for automatically operated cages, elevators or platforms.

(1) Only authorized persons shall enter the hoist engine room and no person shall interfere with or intimidate the hoist engineer in the discharge of his duties. No person shall speak to the hoist engineer while the engine is in motion, except to give signals to him. This subdivision shall be posted on the door of each hoist engine house.

(2) Assigned and relief hoist engineers shall be given and required to take annual physical examinations to ascertain that no disability or infirmity has arisen that might expose others to hazards. No hoist engineer shall be removed as a result of a physical examination unless it is recommended by the examining doctor and it is established that his physical condition renders continued employment as hoist engineer potentially hazardous to lives and/or property.

(b) There shall be a dependable method of signaling, audible to the hoist engineer, from all landings in shafts and slopes. Signal codes, approved by the division, shall be used and posted prominently in the engine house and at all places where signals are given.

(c) Cages used for lowering and hoisting men shall have the following safety features:

(1) Approved safety catches, which shall at all times be kept in good working condition.

(2) Suitable covers of sheet iron or equivalent covers, at least one fourth of an inch thick, or its equivalent, and hinged to open upward.

(3) Bars or rings in sufficient numbers and so located that every person permitted on the cage will have a secure handhold.

(4) Bridle chains attached to the main hoisting rope above the socket, from the top crosspiece of the carriage or cage, so that no single chain may be used for lowering or hoisting persons.

(5) Automatic self-detaching hooks, unless the hoisting engine be equipped with automatic stopping device, effective to prevent overwinding.

(6) Secure floor or platform that will not tip or dump or effective locking device to prevent tipping or dumping, kept locked whenever men or supplies are being lowered or hoisted.

(7) Floor adequate to carry the load and constructed so that it will be impossible for a person's foot or body to enter any opening in the floor.

(8) Enclosed sides and gates, safety chains or bars across the ends of the cage.

(9) Daily inspection and a written record kept. A test of safety catches and of rope attachments shall be made on each inspection by the division in a manner approved by the chief, and results shall be noted in the report of inspection.

(d) Hoist engines shall have the following safety features:

(1) Adequate brakes capable of stopping and holding the fully loaded unbalanced cage or trip at any point in the shaft, slope or on the incline.

(2) An accurate and reliable indicator showing the position of the cage or trip shall be placed in clear view of the engineer.

(3) When men are being lowered or hoisted, the maximum speed shall not exceed 900 feet per minute.

(4) One round trip shall be made not more than one-half hour before hoisting or lowering men. Chainer may ride this check trip in slope hoisting.

(5) Inspected daily by a designated competent person and a record made of inspections.

(e) Hoist ropes shall have the following safety features:

(1) Adequate size to handle the load and a proper factor of safety as defined in the American Standards Association wire rope standards, and shall be replaced when use becomes dangerous as determined by inspection.

(2) The rope shall have at least three full turns on the drum when extended to its maximum working length and shall make at least one full turn on the drum shaft or around the spoke of the drum (in case of a free drum) and be fastened securely by means of clamps or other means approved by the chief of the division.

(3) The hoisting rope shall be fastened to its load by a zinc-filled socket, thimbles and clamps or other means approved by the chief of the division.

(4) Ropes shall be examined daily by a competent person and replaced when necessary. A record shall be made of all inspections showing condition of ropes and fastenings. Hoist ropes in shafts shall be kept well lubricated.

(f) Hoist shafts shall have the following features:

(1) All landings shall be kept clear and free from loose materials, and shall be securely fenced with automatic or other gates to prevent men or materials from falling into the shaft.

(2) At the bottom of each hoisting shaft and at all intermediate landings, a "run-around" shall be provided for safe passage from one side of the shaft to the other so that men or animals are not required to pass under or across the cage. This passageway shall not be less than five feet in height and three feet in width.

(3) Positive stop blocks or derails shall be placed near all shaft landings.

(4) An attendant shall be on duty at the surface when men are being hoisted or lowered at the beginning and end of each operating shift and when men are working in the shaft. Where automatic elevators or cages are used, no attendants shall be required at the elevator or cage stations.

(5) Persons engaged in deepening a shaft in which hoisting from an upper level is going on shall be protected from the danger of falling material by a suitable covering extending over the whole area of the shaft, sufficient openings being left in the covering for the passage of men or a bucket or other conveyance used in the sinking operations. No hoisting shall be done in any compartment of a shaft while repairs are being made in that compartment, except such hoisting as is necessary in order to make such repairs.

(g) No person shall ride upon a cage, elevator, skip or bucket that is loaded with tools, timber, powder, coal rock or other material except as follows:

(1) When tools and supplies are required for repairs to the shaft, or when a rider is required to assist in passing materials through a shaft or incline. In those cases a special signal must be used and extra care exercised by the hoist engineer.

(2) When hand tools or small amounts of supplies are carried by workmen in one hand, leaving the other free to hold onto the bar or ring provided.

(h) When tools, timber or other materials are loaded so that their ends project above, they shall be securely fastened to the hoisting rope or to the upper part of the cage, skip or bucket.

(i) No coal or rock shall be hoisted in any shaft while men are being lowered.

(j) No person shall ride on a cage containing a loaded car or on a single deck cage with an empty car.

(k) When a bucket is used for hoisting, safety hooks must be used and adequate means must be employed to control the bucket against spinning or excessive swinging.

(l) No driver or other person shall be permitted to descend or ascend a shaft with any horse or mule, unless the said horse or mule is secured in a suitable box or safely penned, and only the driver in charge of said horse or mule and such assistants as he may need shall accompany it in any case.

(m) Workmen repairing shafts or tipples shall use safety belts when they are exposed to hazards of falls. (Acts 1949, No. 207, p. 242, § 49; Acts 1975, 4th Ex. Sess., No. 147, p. 2866, § 1.)

When safety catches not required. — This section does not require that cars operated upon a slope or inclined track, though used for the hoisting and lowering of persons, should be equipped with safety catches. Green v. Bessemer Coal, Iron & Land Co., 162 Ala. 609, 50 So. 289 (1909), decided under former Code 1940, Tit. 26, § 97.

Collateral references. — 56 C.J.S., Master & Servant, § 222.12

Products liability: sufficiency of evidence to support product misuse defense in actions concerning commercial or industrial equipment and machinery. 64 ALR4th 10.

§ 25-9-211. Maintenance, etc., of mine locomotives and other haulage equipment.

(a) Mine locomotives must be maintained so that brakes are adequate and in good order, sand riggings are operative and locomotives are in safe operating condition.

(b) Other rolling stock must be maintained so that its condition does not entail undue hazards to transportation crews or to workmen whose duties require them to work around the haulage.

(c) Cars must be kept reasonably tight to hold coal spillage within practical limits.

(d) Motormen shall inspect locomotives before operating and report conditions found that make operation hazardous. They shall exercise a degree of care of haulage equipment consistent with the type of service and conditions of operation. (Acts 1949, No. 207, p. 242, § 50; Acts 1975, 4th Ex. Sess., No. 147, p. 2866, § 1.)

Collateral references. — Products liability: sufficiency of evidence to support product misuse defense in actions concerning commercial or industrial equipment and machinery. 64 ALR4th 10.

§ 25-9-212. Construction, installation and maintenance of elements of track of haulage roads.

(a) The roadbed, rails, joints, switches, frogs and other elements of the track of all haulage roads shall be constructed, installed and maintained in a manner consistent with speed and the type of haulage operations being conducted to insure safe operation.

(b) Track switches, except room and entry development switches, shall be provided with properly installed throws, bridle bars and guard rails. Switch throws and stands, where possible, shall be placed on the clearance side. (Acts 1949, No. 207, p. 242, § 51.)

§ 25-9-213. Clearances, crossovers and shelter holes on haulage roads.

(a) Haulage roads on entries developed after August 12, 1949, shall have a continuous unobstructed clearance of at least 24 inches from the farthest projection of moving equipment, on the clearance side.

(b) On haulage roads where trolley lines are used, the clearance shall be on the side opposite the trolley lines.

(c) On the trolley wire or "tight" side, there shall be six inches of clearance on track haulages developed prior to March 30, 1970, and 12 inches of clearance on track haulages developed after that date.

(d) After August 12, 1949, all new sidetracks, partings or entries equipped with more than one track shall have a clearance of at least 24 inches between the outermost projection of moving traffic.

(e) The clearance space on all haulage roads on entries driven before or after August 12, 1949, shall be kept free of loose rock, coal, supplies or other materials; provided, that not more than 24 inches need be kept free of such obstructions.

(f) In those exceptional instances where extremely thin seams of coal entail taking more rock than coal, the provisions of subsections (a) and (e) of this section shall be modified for room entries, such modification to be by the chief in writing; provided, that all persons shall be instructed to and required to use shelter holes when trips or cars are passing.

(g) In those exceptional instances where extremely bad roof conditions in thin seams require special timbering, the unobstructed clearance provided for in subsections (a) and (e) of this section may be regarded as measured from the rib or gob line, collar legs notwithstanding.

(h) Ample clearance shall be provided at all points where supplies are loaded or unloaded along haulage roads or conveyors.

(i) Where it is necessary for men to cross conveyors regularly and where the width of conveyors or low roof introduces a hazard, suitable crossover bridges shall be provided.

(j) Shelter holes shall be provided along haulage entries driven after August 12, 1949, where locomotive, rope or animal haulage is used. Such shelter holes shall be spaced not more than 80 feet apart. Except where the trolley wire is six feet six inches or more above the roadbed or guarded effectively at the shelter holes, they shall be on the side of the entry opposite the trolley wire.

(k) Shelter holes made after August 12, 1949, shall be at least five feet in depth, not more than four feet in width and six feet in height or as high as the traveling space if the traveling space is less than six feet high. Room necks and cross cuts may be used as shelter holes even though their width exceeds four feet.

(l) Shelter holes shall be kept clear of refuse and other obstructions.

(m) Shelter holes shall be provided at switch throws, except where more than six feet of clearance is maintained and at room switches.

(n) At each landing of a slope where men are passing and cars are handled, a shelter hole at least 10 feet deep, four feet wide and six feet high shall be provided.

(o) Where the only travelway to or from work is an incline plane, rope or locomotive roads on which men travel on foot while such incline planes, rope or locomotive roads are used for hoisting or haulage, shelter holes as specified in subsection (k) of this section shall be provided at not more than 80 foot intervals. These shelter holes shall be provided even though the travelway was driven prior to August 12, 1949; except, that they will not be required on locomotive roads where six feet or more clearance exists from the outermost projection of moving traffic, nor in those cases where adequate safeguards have been provided to secure men against exposure to danger from wrecks and such safeguards are approved by the division. (Acts 1949, No. 207, p. 242, § 52; Acts 1975, 4th Ex. Sess., No. 147, p. 2866, § 1.)

§ 25-9-214. Certain machinery prohibited underground.

Nonpermissible internal combustion engines or other machinery which gives off noxious fumes shall not be permitted underground in any coal mine. (Acts 1949, No. 207, p. 242, § 53.)

Collateral references. — Products liability: sufficiency of evidence to support product misuse defense in actions concerning commercial or industrial equipment and machinery. 64 ALR4th 10.

§ 25-9-215. Safety devices and practices.

(a) Locomotives shall be equipped with proper devices for the rerailing of locomotives and cars.

(b) An audible warning device and headlights shall be provided on each locomotive.

(c) Approved trip markers shall be used on the rear of trips pulled or pushed and on the front of trips lowered into slopes. Markers are not required to be used during gathering operations at working faces. Permissible trip lights, efficient reflectors or closed nonpermissible trip lights are acceptable as trip markers.

(d) Other than the motorman and trip rider, no person shall ride on a locomotive unless authorized by the mine foreman, and no person shall ride on loaded cars or between cars of any trip; except, that the trip rider may ride on the part of the trip adjudged safest by the mine foreman and concurred in by the mine inspector, preferably the first or the last car. When officials or other persons authorized by the mine foreman, trafficman, haulage boss or dispatcher are transported on loaded trips, an empty car shall be placed between the locomotive and the first loaded car, or when physical conditions of haulage require it as a safety measure, the mine foreman may designate the rear of trips for the empty to be placed.

(e) Motormen and trip riders shall not get on or off the cars, trips or locomotives in motion; except, that a trip rider may get on or off the rear end of a slowly moving trip to throw a switch or perform other necessary haulage duties.

(f) Slides, skids or other adequate means shall be used on descending trips on grades where the locomotive or car tugger hoist is not adequate to control the trip.

(g) On any slope or plane where the grade is against loaded trip, a drag or other suitable device, adequate to derail cars or the trip of cars in case they break loose and run back, shall be used.

(h) Uniform haulage signals shall be adopted for each mine or mines operated, and shall be complied with by all haulage crews.

(i) Flying or running switches are forbidden. Mine rules as to block signals and other haulage practices not covered in these laws shall be complied with by all officials, haulage crews and other workmen. (Acts 1949, No. 207, p. 242, § 54.)

Collateral references. — Products liability: sufficiency of evidence to support product misuse defense in actions concerning commercial or industrial equipment and machinery. 64 ALR4th 10.

§ 25-9-216. Transportation of men.

(a) Man-trips shall be operated at safe speeds consistent with the condition of roads and type of equipment used, but not to exceed 12 miles an hour in mine cars or 15 miles an hour when special, substantially covered man-trip cars are used.

(b) Each man-trip shall be under the charge of a responsible person and it shall be operated independently of any loaded trip of coal or other material.

(c) Cars on the man-trip shall not be overloaded and sufficient cars in good mechanical condition shall be provided.

(d) No person shall ride under the trolley wire unless suitably covered man-cars are used.

(e) No material or tools shall be transported in the same mine car with men and all persons shall ride inside of man-trip cars, except the motorman and brakeman or person in charge of the man-trip. Where compartmented man-cars are used, tools or supplies, other than explosives, secured so that they cannot cause injury to men in other compartments, may be transported in a compartment designated for that purpose.

(f) Men shall not load or unload before the cars in which they are to ride or are riding come to a full stop and men shall proceed in an orderly manner to and from man-trips.

(g) A waiting station shall be provided where men are required to wait for man-trips or man-cages. At places where men enter or leave man-trip conveyances, ample clearance shall be provided and provisions made to prevent persons from coming into contact with energized electric circuits. Adequate seating facilities shall be provided.

(h) Where hoists are used for handling men in underground slopes, in pitching beds or on slopes between two or more beds, the provision as to man-trips applies and special care shall be exercised to insure that cars do not break loose while being hoisted or lowered.

(i) Where belts are used for transporting men, a minimum clearance of 18 inches shall be maintained between the belt and the roof or crossbars, projecting equipment, cap pieces, overhead cables, wiring and other objects, but where the height of the coal bed permits, the clearance shall not be less than 24 inches.

(j) The belt speed shall not exceed 300 feet a minute when vertical clearance is less than 24 inches and shall not exceed 350 feet a minute where clearance is more than 24 inches while men are being transported. Belt conveyors shall be stopped while men are loading or unloading.

(k) The space between men riding on a belt line shall be not less than five feet.

(l) Loading and unloading stations shall be illuminated properly.

(m) An official or some other person designated by the mine foreman shall supervise the man-trip loading and unloading of belts. (Acts 1949, No. 207, p. 242, § 55; Acts 1975, 4th Ex. Sess., No. 147, p. 2866, § 1.)

Cited in Pledger v. Department of Indus. Relations, 40 Ala. App. 127, 108 So. 2d 697 (1959).

ARTICLE 11.

OPERATION AND MAINTENANCE OF MACHINERY.

§ 25-9-230. Face equipment.

(a) The cutter chains of mining machines shall be locked securely at all times except when the machine is cutting, the chain is being oiled or tested after repairs or when the chain is moved to spot bits.

(1) When the chain is being oiled or tested after repairs, an operator must be at the controls ready to stop movement of the chain instantly. When the chain is being oiled, the bar must be free of the kerf and of material that might cause it to deflect, the person oiling must position himself before the chain is started, the chain must run in reverse and slowly and must be stopped and the lock replaced immediately after oiling is completed. Oiling devices or other methods that do not expose a workman to hazard from the moving chain may be used.

(2) When the chain is moved to spot bits, all persons must be in the clear of the bar and the lock must be replaced after the chain is moved and before the bits are spotted.

(3) When the chain is operated to test it after repairs, all persons must be in the clear of the bar and the lock must be replaced immediately after testing is completed.

(b) Care must be exercised at all times in the operation of mining and loading machines. Shields must be kept in place. Timbers removed by a cutting or loading crew must be reset or the roof otherwise secured. Care must be exercised to prevent persons not engaged in operation of machines from exposing themselves dangerously near the machines. Operators of machines that are self-tramming or machines that are loaded for tramming shall be alert to clearances and will observe all applicable laws and rules pertaining to haulage or movement of traffic.

(c) Conveyors and duckbills shall be properly installed and operated with care. Timbers removed in installing, moving or sluicing a conveyor shall be reset promptly or the roof otherwise adequately secured.

(d) Care must be exercised in setting of and working around jack pipes used in operation of mining machines, conveyors and loading machines.

(e) Operators of shuttle cars will satisfy themselves that brakes are adequate before and during operation and will exercise care to prevent knocking out timbers. They will promptly reset or report timbers unavoidably knocked out, will keep cars under control during operations and give warning before making turns or passing through curtains or other points of obstructed vision.

(f) Face equipment must be stopped before being lubricated, wiped or repaired, except as provided in subdivision (a) (1) of this section, and must not be restarted until persons oiling, wiping or repairing have given a clear signal. This does not apply to lubrication of equipment that is designed or modified so that lubrication may be performed without exposure to moving parts.

(g) The mine foreman and his assistants are responsible that operators of face equipment are trained in the requirements of their work before they are entrusted with operation of face equipment, other than while undergoing training by competent operators.

(h) The mine operator and the mine officials are responsible for seeing that face equipment is adequately maintained as to safe operating conditions. Equipment operators are responsible for exercising reasonable care in the operation of the equipment entrusted to them and for reporting defects known to them.

(i) All junction or distribution boxes used for making multiple power connections inby the last open crosscut shall be permissible.

(j) All handheld electric drills, blower and exhaust fans, electric pumps and such other low horsepower electric face equipment which are taken into or used inby the last open crosscut of any coal mine shall be permissible.

(k) All other electric face equipment which is taken into or used inby the last open crosscut of any coal mine shall be permissible.

(l) The operator of each coal mine shall maintain in safe condition all permissible type electric face equipment which is taken into or used inby the last open crosscut of any such mine.

(m) Trailing cables used in coal mines shall meet the requirements established for flame-resistant cables.

(n) Short-circuit protection for trailing cables shall be provided by an automatic circuit breaker or other no less effective device, approved by the chief of the division, of adequate current-interrupting capacity in each underground conductor. Disconnecting devices used to disconnect power from trailing cables shall be plainly marked and identified, and such devices shall be equipped or designed in such a manner that it can be determined from visual observation that the power is disconnected.

(o) When two or more trailing cables junction to the same distribution center, means shall be provided to assure against connecting a trailing cable to the wrong size circuit breaker.

(p) One temporary splice may be made in any trailing cable. Such trailing cable may only be used for the next 24-hour period. No temporary splice shall be made in a trailing cable within 25 feet of the machine, except cable reel equipment. Temporary splices in trailing cables shall be made in a workman-like manner and shall be mechanically strong and well insulated. Trailing cables or hand cables which have exposed wires or which have splices that heat or spark under load shall not be used.

(q) When permanent splices in trailing cables are made, they shall be mechanically strong with adequate electrical conductivity and flexibility, effectively insulated and sealed so as to exclude moisture and vulcanized or otherwise treated with suitable materials to provide flame-resistant qualities and good bonding to the outer jacket.

(r) Trailing cables shall be clamped to machines in a manner to protect the cables from damage and to prevent strain on the electrical connections. Trailing cables shall be adequately protected to prevent damage by mobile equipment.

(s) Trailing cable and power cable connections to junction boxes shall not be made or broken under load.

(t) All electrical equipment shall be frequently examined, tested and properly maintained by a qualified person to assure safe operating conditions. When a potentially dangerous condition is found on electrical equipment, such equipment shall be removed from service until such condition is corrected. A record of such examinations shall be kept and made available to an authorized representative of the chief of the division and to the miners in such mine. (Acts 1949, No. 207, p. 242, §§ 56, 57; Acts 1975, 4th Ex. Sess., No. 147, p. 2866, § 1.)

§ 25-9-231. Shop equipment, etc.

(a) Gears, sprockets, friction devices and couplings with protruding bolts or nuts, shafting and projecting shaft ends that are within seven feet of floor or platform level, belt or rope drives that are within seven feet of floor or platform level, fly wheels and circular and band saws and planers shall be guarded adequately.

(b) Grinders shall be installed and maintained in such manner that wheel speeds will not exceed rated speeds and reasonable protection is afforded against danger of flying particles and wheel disintegration.

(c) Repair pits shall be kept covered or guarded at all times when not in use to prevent falls into them.

(d) Machinery must be stopped before being lubricated, wiped or repaired and reasonable precautions must be taken to prevent other persons from restarting them while such work is in progress. This does not apply as to lubrication of machinery that is designed or modified so that lubrication may be performed without exposure to danger from moving parts. (Acts 1949, No. 207, p. 242, § 58.)

§ 25-9-232. Operation of machinery by repairmen.

Repairmen shall not operate machinery unless they are thoroughly familiar with requirements for safe operation. No person will order or require repairmen to operate machinery for moving or testing without ascertaining that the repairmen are thoroughly familiar with requirements for safe operation. (Acts 1949, No. 207, p. 242, § 59.)

ARTICLE 12.

SURFACE STRUCTURES AND PRACTICES.

§ 25-9-250. Use of electrical equipment; maintenance, etc., in tipples and cleaning plants.

(a) In dangerously dusty locations, electric motors, switches and controls shall be of dust-tight construction or enclosed with reasonably dust-tight housing or enclosures. Open-type motors, switches or controls now in use in tipples and cleaning plants in dusty locations may be continued in use until such dust-tight equipment can be procured or until they can be corrected with reasonably dust-tight housing or enclosures.

(b) Structures shall be kept free of excessive coal dust accumulations.

(c) Where coal is dumped at or near air intake openings, reasonable provisions shall be made to prevent the dust from entering the mine.

(d) Where repairs are being made to the plant, proper scaffolding and proper overhead protection shall be provided for workmen wherever necessary.

(e) Welding shall not be done in dusty atmosphere or dusty locations, and firefighting apparatus shall be readily available during welding. (Acts 1949, No. 207, p. 242, § 60.)

§ 25-9-251. Storage of flammable liquids in lamp houses.

Naphtha or other flammable liquids in lamp houses shall be kept in approved containers or other safe dispensers. (Acts 1949, No. 207, p. 242, § 61.)

§ 25-9-252. Maintenance, etc., of stairways, elevated platforms and runways.

(a) Stairways, elevated platforms and runways shall be equipped with handrails.

(b) Elevated platforms and stairways shall be provided with toeboards where necessary, and they shall be kept clear of refuse and maintained in good repair. (Acts 1949, No. 207, p. 242, § 62; Acts 1975, 4th Ex. Sess., No. 147, p. 2866, § 1.)

§ 25-9-253. Housekeeping practices.

Good housekeeping shall be practiced in and around mine buildings and yards. Such practices include cleanliness, orderly storage of materials and the removal of possible sources of injury, such as stumbling hazards, protruding nails and broken glass. (Acts 1949, No. 207, p. 242, § 63.)

§ 25-9-254. Fire prevention in surface structures.

(a) Oil, grease and similar flammable materials shall be stored in closed containers, separate from other materials so as not to create a fire hazard to nearby buildings or mines. If oil or grease is stored in a building, the building or the room in which it is stored shall be of fire-resistive material and well-ventilated. Tight metal receptacles shall be provided for oily waste.

(b) Smoking in or about surface structures shall be restricted to places where it will not cause fire or an explosion.

(c) Unless existing structures located within 100 feet of any mine opening are of reasonably fireproof construction, fire doors shall be erected at effective points in mine openings to prevent smoke or fire from outside sources endangering men working underground. These doors shall be tested at least monthly to insure effective operation. (Acts 1949, No. 207, p. 242, § 64.)

ARTICLE 13.

SURFACE MINING OPERATIONS.

§ 25-9-270. Applicability of provisions.

All other provisions of this chapter, except those obviously peculiar to underground operations and also those specifically provided for in this article, are applicable to surface mining operations. All provisions contained in this article applicable to surface operations of underground coal mines and not specifically covered elsewhere in this chapter apply to all coal mines. (Acts 1949, No. 207, p. 242, § 72; Acts 1975, 4th Ex. Sess., No. 147, p. 2866, § 1.)

Article not for benefit of public generally. — Whatever might be done or required under this section or § 25-9-284 would not affect the rights and duties between a mining company and the owners of a house allegedly damaged by blasting operations. This is because this article was not enacted (except where expressly stated, e.g., § 25-9-280(c) blasting near roads) for the benefit of the public generally. Coalite, Inc. v. Aldridge, 45 Ala. App. 277, 229 So. 2d 524 (1968), reversed on other grounds, 285 Ala. 137, 229 So. 2d 539 (1969).

§ 25-9-271. Maintenance, etc., of banks; overburden, etc., of open pits.

(a) *Guards.* — Excavations shall be provided with substantial barriers at points where passageways, tracks, roadways or buildings adjoin such excavation.

(b) *Loose material.* — All pit walls shall be kept free of unsafe loose materials. Hazardous areas shall be flagged, and no work shall be permitted in such areas.

(c) *Scaling.* — Safe, acceptable methods shall be used for removing loose materials from the highwalls.

(d) *Slope of material.* — Spoil piles shall be kept safely sloped to prevent loose material from sliding into the work area.

(e) *Overburden.* — The area immediately above the highwall shall be cleared to a safe distance to prevent loose hazardous material from falling into the pit. (Acts 1949, No. 207, p. 242, § 73; Acts 1975, 4th Ex. Sess., No. 147, p. 2866, § 1.)

§ 25-9-272. Maintenance, etc., of means of access to pits.

(a) *Access.* — Safe means of access shall be provided to all working places in any pit.

(b) *Fastening ladders.* — All fixed ladders shall be properly installed, securely fastened and provided with back guards where necessary. At least three inches of toe clearance shall be provided.

(c) *Incline of ladders.* — Under no circumstances shall any ladder inclining backward from the vertical be installed or used.

(d) *Maintenance.* — Ladderways where used shall be maintained in safe condition and shall be inspected regularly.

(e) *Steps.* — Where stairs are used, they shall comply with the requirements set forth in the basic safety manual, State of Alabama.

(f) *Travel.* — Access to pits over railway haulage shall be provided with adequate warning signs.

(g) *Walkway.* — Where access to pits is by walkway, it shall be properly graded, and if travel along the walkway is unsafe by reason of danger of falling into the pit, the walkway shall be protected by handrails. Drain ditches shall be laid out and both walk and drain ditches shall be kept free of broken stone, trash and debris at all times. (Acts 1949, No. 207, p. 242, § 74; Acts 1975, 4th Ex. Sess., No. 147, p. 2866, § 1.)

§ 25-9-273. Operation, inspection and maintenance of shovels and draglines.

(a) *Inspection.* — Shovels and draglines shall be inspected at the beginning of each shift, and such inspection shall include all mechanical equipment. Electrical equipment shall be regularly inspected by a qualified person.

(b) *Maintenance.* — Where mechanical shovels and draglines are used at night, all lights shall be inspected before darkness, defective globes replaced and defective wiring repaired.

(c) *Oiling.* — Mechanical equipment on shovels and draglines shall not be cleaned or oiled while in motion, except where so designed or modified as to make lubrication while in motion safe.

(d) *Steps, etc.* — All steps, handrails, grab irons and floors shall be kept free from grease and extraneous material.

(e) *Unauthorized person.* — No unauthorized person shall be allowed on any power shovel or dragline.

(f) *Passage of persons.* — No person shall pass under the boom or bucket of a shovel or dragline while in operation.

(g) *Warning.* — The operator of a shovel or dragline shall sound a warning prior to placing the machine in operation. (Acts 1949, No. 207, p. 242, § 75; Acts 1975, 4th Ex. Sess., No. 147, p. 2866, § 1.)

§ 25-9-274. Electrical equipment installations and inspections; grounding and insulation of electrical equipment; trailing cables.

(a) *Installations and inspections.* — All electrical equipment installations shall be approved and all electrical inspections made by a qualified person.

(b) *Grounding.*

(1) Where grounding wires are used to ground metallic sheaths, armors, conduits, frames, casings and other metallic enclosures, such grounding wires will be approved if:

a. The cross-sectional area (size) of the grounding wire is at least one-half the cross-sectional area (size) of the power conductor where the power conductor used is No. 6 A.W.G. or larger.

b. Where the power conductor used is less than No. 6 A.W.G., the cross-sectional area (size) of the grounding wire is equal to the cross-sectional area (size) of the power conductor.

(2) The protective grounding of electrical circuits and equipment to water pipe systems, when available, is desired as such grounding offers the most effective protection to life and property. Gas or air pipelines shall not be used for grounding circuits. Metal well casings, metal drain pipes and similar buried metal structures of considerable extent may be used in lieu of extended buried water piping systems.

(3) The ground connection to metallic piping systems shall be made by means of a suitable connection firmly attached to the pipe after all rust and scale have been removed, or by means of a brass plug which has been

tightly screwed into a pipe fitting or, where the pipe is of sufficient thickness, screwed into a hole in the pipe itself or by other equivalent means. The grounding conductor shall be attached to the clamp or to the plug by means of solder or a suitable solderless connector.

(4) If conduit, couplings or fittings having protective coatings of nonconducting material, such as enamel, are used, such coating shall be thoroughly removed from couplings, conduits and such surfaces of fittings where the conduit or ground connection is secured in order to obtain a good connection.

(5) Artificial grounds should be located where practicable below permanent moisture level, or, failing in this, a suitable means of grounding shall be used.

(6) Where copper ground plates are used, they should be at least six hundredths of an inch thick. When driven pipes are used, they should be of galvanized iron and not smaller than three fourths of an inch internal diameter, and when cast iron plates are used they should be at least twenty-five hundredths of an inch thick.

(c) *Insulation.*

(1) All fixed electric light and power lines, regardless of voltage, shall be properly supported on standard insulators.

(2) Drop cord extension light lines shall be flexible with heavy rubber insulation, equipped with a heavy wire light globe shield, hook and heavy rubber handle.

(d) *Trailing cables.*

(1) Where employees are required to handle energized high voltage trailing cables, they shall be required to use cable tongs and wear rubber gloves. Where surroundings are wet, such employees shall also be required to wear rubber boots.

(2) Damage to the insulation of trailing cables shall be promptly reported and repairs made. Splicing shall be done only by a competent electrician or person competent to splice cables, and splices shall be made moisture-proof. Where it is necessary for mechanical equipment to cross a cable, safe cable bridges shall be provided and used. Where armored cables or conduit are used, the armor or metal conduit shall be electrically continuous, and, when necessary to splice armored cable, the broken section of the armor shall be bonded to insure electrical continuity. (Acts 1949, No. 207, p. 242, § 76; Acts 1975, 4th Ex. Sess., No. 147, p. 2866, § 1.)

§ 25-9-275. Guarding of exposed engines, wheels, etc.; safety of tools.

(a) All exposed engines, wheels, screens, shafting, gears, belting or other moving equipment shall be covered or adequately guarded in such a way as to make employees safe from injury through contact with such equipment.

(b) The operator shall be responsible for the safe condition of tools furnished employees by the operator and shall not permit the use of tools which are unsafe or permit the misuse of any tools.

(c) The employee shall be responsible for the safe condition of tools he furnishes and shall not use any such tools which are not in safe condition for use.

(d) The employee shall promptly report to the superintendent or foreman any tool being used by him which is in an unsafe condition, and said tool shall be promptly replaced or made safe by the person furnishing it. (Acts 1949, No. 207, p. 242, § 77.)

Collateral references. — Products liability: sufficiency of evidence to support product misuse defense in actions concerning commercial or industrial equipment and machinery. 64 ALR4th 10.

§ 25-9-276. "Blasting agent" and "explosives" defined; storage and transportation of blasting agents, explosives and detonators generally.

(a)(1) "Blasting agent," as used in this article, means any material consisting of a mixture of fuel and oxidizer which:

a. Is used or intended for use in blasting;

b. Is not classed as an explosive by the department of transportation;

c. Contains no ingredients classed as an explosive by the department of transportation; and

d. Cannot be detonated by a No. 8 blasting cap when tested as recommended in Bureau of Mines information circular 8179.

(2) The term "explosives," as used in this article, includes blasting agents, unless blasting agents are expressly excluded.

(b) Main explosive storage magazines shall be located outside of the pit and shall comply with Section 25-9-131. Blasting agents shall be stored in the manner prescribed by Part 181, Title 26, Code of Federal Regulations, U.S. Department of the Treasury, and administered by the Internal Revenue Service.

(c) Explosives, excluding blasting agents, transported in motor trucks or other conveyances shall be transported in their original containers, and the motor trucks, vehicles and other conveyances shall be so constructed that the explosives will be protected against shock and friction and the containers against contact with any exposed metal. Motor trucks, vehicles or conveyances transporting explosives shall be plainly marked or placarded on both sides and the rear with the words "Explosives — Dangerous" in letters not less than three inches high.

(d) Motor trucks, vehicles or other conveyances transporting explosives shall be handled in a safe and careful manner, and no person while smoking or under the influence of intoxicating liquor shall ride upon, drive, load or unload a vehicle carrying explosives.

(e) No person other than those authorized to transport, load or unload motor trucks, vehicles or other conveyances carrying explosives shall ride with any load of explosives.

(f) No tools, other than for truck repairs, detonators, matches or other flame producing materials shall be carried in any motor truck, vehicle or other conveyance transporting explosives unless adequately protected against sparking.

(g) Explosives, excluding blasting agents, shall not be transported in any form of trailer nor shall any trailer be attached to a motor truck, vehicle or other conveyance hauling explosives.

(h) All detonators shall be transported into the pit in the original containers or in suitable containers provided for the express purpose of transporting detonators or electric detonators.

(i) Persons engaged in transporting explosives, charging drill holes or handling explosives for any purpose shall not be permitted to smoke or to use or carry any open flame.

(j) Where explosives are transported by hand, the explosives shall be carried in the original or a suitable container and capped fuse or electric detonators shall be carried separately in a separate container. (Acts 1949, No. 207, p. 242, § 78; Acts 1975, 4th Ex. Sess., No. 147, p. 2866, § 1.)

Collateral references. — Explosives: liability in connection with fire or explosion of explosives while being stored or transported. 35 ALR3d 1177.

§ 25-9-277. Handling and use of explosives and detonators.

(a) Only designated persons shall cut, cap and issue capped fuses and explosives.

(b) When cutting fuse, it shall be cut square across with a sharp clean instrument and the cap crimper used shall be of a type recommended by explosive manufacturers. A bench type crimper is recommended.

(c) No explosives container shall be opened with any metallic instrument.

(d) No person shall remove any explosives from a pit magazine without permission of the pit superintendent, foreman or a person designated by the operator.

(e) Capped fuse or electric detonators shall not be stored within 50 feet of other explosives, power lines, cables or other electrical conductors.

(f) Oils or other combustible substances shall not be stored within 50 feet of any explosives.

(g) Detonators shall not be removed from containers except as they are used for capping fuses or, in the case of electric detonators, as they are used in preparing primers, except when placed in other containers as recommended by manufacturers.

(h) Fuse shall not be cut and capped nearer than 50 feet to any explosives magazine.

(i) Paper, sawdust, wooden boxes or cartons shall be placed at a safe distance from any magazine, and each day's accumulation shall be removed at the end of the shift.

(j) Fuse shall be cut long enough to extend beyond the collar of a loaded drill hole, and in no case shall it be less than four feet in length.

(k) Small supplies of explosives or detonators stored in a pit shall be stored in magazines constructed in accordance with the specifications set forth in section 25-9-131. In no case shall more than 200 pounds of explosives be stored at one time in such magazine.

(*l*) Magazines located in the pit should not be nearer than those standards set forth in the American Table of Distances for Storage of Explosives, a publication of the Institute of Makers of Explosives.

(m) No fuse shall be used that burns faster than one foot in 30 seconds or slower than one foot in 55 seconds according to the manufacturer's rating.

(n) In capping fuse, at least one inch shall be cut from the end of each coil or roll of fuse used. (Acts 1949, No. 207, p. 242, § 79; Acts 1975, 4th Ex. Sess., No. 147, p. 2866, § 1.)

§ 25-9-278. Blasting practices and procedures generally.

(a) All blasting shall be done in a safe manner after all persons have been removed to a safe place.

(b) All blasting should be done electrically or with detonating fuse.

(c) Primers shall be made up near the working place by competent persons experienced in handling explosives. Competent persons shall also load, assist in loading or supervise the loading or charging of drill holes.

(d) Primers shall be prepared in accordance with safety standards of the Institute of Makers of Explosives or of the manufacturer of the explosives as approved by the chief. Holes made in the primer cartridge for the purpose of inserting the detonator shall be made with a wooden or other nonsparking implement.

(e) In tamping holes, only a wooden tamping bar or other nonsparking tamping bar shall be used. Before charging drill holes, except well holes, they shall be thoroughly cleaned. Explosives shall not be violently tamped in the drill hole but may be firmly charged; except, that undue pressure shall not be used against the primer cartridge when placing it in a drill hole. The primer cartridge shall not be slit.

(f) When a drill hole has been charged with explosives, it shall be filled to the collar with stemming material, as nearly free from rock as practical. The stemming material should be well tamped.

(g) No loading operations shall be carried on in working places where rock falling from the face or rolling rock is likely to endanger the loading operations. Working places shall be made safe for loading operations before loading is begun.

(h) Fuse igniters of the "hot wire" type or punk or their equivalent shall be used for igniting safety fuse.

(i) The number of detonations shall be counted as far as possible. Misfires shall be reported to the authorized person responsible for blasting, and no person shall return to the vicinity of the suspected misfire until 30 minutes have elapsed in the case of fuse blasting and until 15 minutes have elapsed in the case of electrical blasting. No regular pit operations shall be conducted in the area where an unexpected detonation of a misfired hole shall endanger employees. Misfires, except in the case of vertical holes, shall be reblasted by inserting a new primer in the drill hole. In such case, stemming or tamping material may be washed from the drill hole with water before inserting the new primer.

(j) In case of misfire in a vertical hole, if it is not possible or safe to insert a new primer, a new hole may be drilled under the personal supervision of the person responsible for blasting, and such hole shall be started not less than two feet from the original drill hole and shall be drilled at such an angle as to eliminate all danger of meeting or coming closer than two feet of the original drill hole. In the case of sprung holes, the new drill hole shall be placed and carried at such an angle that there will be no possibility of its meeting any part of the misfire charge; provided, that in case of a misfired vertical drilled hole, it shall not be disturbed, nor any attempt made to fire it, without permission of the superintendent or person responsible for blasting.

(k) "Bootlegs" or "guns," if the bottom of the hole cannot be seen, shall be washed out with water or cleaned with a wooden stick whether or not explosives remain in them. If explosives are found in such "bootleg" or "gun," the hole shall be treated as a misfired shot. All persons working in an area where explosives are found in the muck pile shall be alerted, and caution shall be exercised in recovering such explosives. Such recovered explosive shall be removed and later destroyed following procedure recommended by the explosive manufacturers. Any leftover explosive, capped fuse or detonators remaining after loading the drill holes shall be returned to the storage magazine after loading operations have been completed.

(l) Oversize rock material set aside for blasting shall be examined to determine whether or not any unexploded powder remained in such rock or boulder. The person responsible for blasting shall determine whether or not rocks or boulders set aside for blasting are safe to drill.

(m) Boulders which must be broken by blasting shall be block holed. "Adobe," "plaster" or "mud-capped" shots shall be prohibited, except, that such shots may be permitted where no means of drilling such boulders is available; provided, that they shall then be fired under supervision of the person responsible for blasting.

(n) Where drill holes are sprung, the temperature of the chamber shall be determined before placing the final charge, and no hole shall be loaded with the final charge until the chamber has been cooled to 80 degrees Fahrenheit. No drill holes shall be sprung when adjacent to a loaded sprung hole.

(o) Cartridges shall not be forced into drill holes. Cartridges shall be placed in drill holes in the original wrapper.

(p) Where detonators are used, nothing less than No. 6 detonators or electric detonators shall be used to explode charges. Electric detonators from different manufacturers shall not be used in the same shot.

(q) One person shall not be allowed to light more than 10 fuses at one time. (Acts 1949, No. 207, p. 242, § 80; Acts 1975, 4th Ex. Sess., No. 147, p. 2866, § 1.)

Collateral references. — Blasting: liability for property damage by concussion from blasting. 20 ALR2d 1372.

Blasting: liability of strip or other surface mine or quarry operator to person on adjoining premises injured or killed during blasting operations. 84 ALR2d 737.

§ 25-9-279. Electrical blasting practices and procedures.

(a) When loading or charging blast holes with electric detonators, all electric power within an unsafe distance of the place to be blasted shall be deenergized.

(b) Electric blasting with blasting machines or special circuit is permissible. With blasting machines, connections shall be made in series or in a combination connection recommended by the manufacturer. With power currents, connections shall be made in series, parallel or a combination of the two.

(c) When blasting is by means of a special blasting circuit, no one shall enter the place in which the blasting has been done until the permanent blasting wires have been disconnected from the source of electrical energy and the blasting switch has been locked in the open position.

(d) The person responsible for blasting shall be in charge of the blasting machine when it is in the pit. No other person shall connect the blasting machine to the leading wires, and such connection shall not be made until the area has been made safe preparatory to the firing. An audible warning shall be sounded prior to the blasting.

(e) Electric current from power circuits shall not be used for firing shots in a pit except when the electric connections to power circuits are made within the enclosed switch box described in these rules.

(f) Permanent blasting lines shall be kept well in the clear from all power circuits and from all pipes, rails, etc., and shall be run or strung at least 20 feet away from all power circuits.

(g) Grounded circuits or systems shall not be used for electrical blasting.

(h) Permanent blasting lines, safety switches and blasting switches shall be maintained by a competent electrician or other competent and experienced person.

(i) Leading wires from portable generating blasting devices or approved type batteries shall be not less than those recommended by the Institute of Makers of Explosives.

(j) Permanent blasting wires shall be so installed and maintained that they provide the current capacity required by the electrical firing device. All such wires shall be in conduit, shall consist of type "S" cable or equivalent or shall consist of two rubber covered wires strung on glass insulators or porcelain knobs. If rubber covered wires are used, they shall be kept at least five inches apart.

(k) Connecting wires shall be not less than those recommended by the Institute of Makers of Explosives.

(*l*) At the location where the shot firing is to be controlled, there shall be installed a suitable blasting circuit enclosed externally operated pole switch with the handle or lever arranged to be locked in the "off" position only.

(m) Where the blasting lines run to a single face to be blasted, a "safety" switch of the same type as required for the blasting switch shall be installed between the switch and the face. This switch shall be installed in a safe location guarded from flying rock.

(n) Where a single blasting switch is used for several blasting circuits, a safety switch shall be installed in each circuit immediately adjacent to the blasting switch. In addition, a second safety switch shall be installed in the circuit adjacent to the area to be blasted.

(o) A blasting galvanometer or circuit tester especially designed for blasting work shall be used for testing.

(p) Leg wires of electric detonators shall be kept short circuited by means of a short-circuiting device or by twisting the ends of the leg wires together, except that the short-circuiting devices may be removed temporarily for the purpose of testing detonators with the galvanometer.

(q) Before connecting the temporary wires to the leg wires or bus wires, the ends of the temporary wires that are to be connected to the safety switch shall be "shorted" by being twisted together. The man making or supervising the connection at the face must have the "shorted" ends of the temporary wires in his possession, and, after making the connections at the face, he shall run the temporary wires to the safety switch. He shall never attach the temporary wires to the safety switch before attaching them to the leg wires or bus wires.

(r) At the safety switch, said man shall untwist the temporary wires, unlock the safety switch, attach the temporary wires to the safety switch and then place the safety switch in the "on" position. He shall then proceed or signal to a designated person at the blasting switch, and he or such designated person shall unlock the blasting switch, throw it in the "on" position to fire the shot, then immediately return the blasting switch to the "off" position and lock it in that position. After blasting, no one shall go nearer the face that has been blasted than the safety switch until the safety switch has been opened, the temporary wires disconnected and the safety switch locked in the "off" position.

(s) Loading and charging of blasting holes shall cease upon the approach of an electrical storm and shall not resume until conditions are safe. All persons shall be removed a safe distance from the charged area until conditions are safe.

(t) The minimum necessary number of persons shall be at the loading places when making the blasting connections. All other persons shall be a safe distance away from the loading place when blasting connections are made. (Acts 1949, No. 207, p. 242, § 81; Acts 1975, 4th Ex. Sess., No. 147, p. 2866, § 1.)

§ 25-9-280. Handling of explosives during blasting operations; warnings, guards, etc.

(a) Explosives, excluding blasting agents, must be unloaded in a safe manner and at a safe distance from the blasting place.

(b) If several boxes of explosives, except blasting agents, are deposited near the blasting circuit, the boxes shall be stacked in an orderly manner and protected from the sun by means of canvas or similar material so placed as to allow free circulation of air under the canvas and around the stacked boxes.

(c) Where blasting is carried on in dangerous proximity to public thoroughfares, such thoroughfares shall be blocked off previous to blasting or guards shall be stationed at each end of the endangered portion of such thoroughfare and all traffic shall be halted, with no person or vehicle allowed within the danger zone. Guards shall be provided with a metal sign having the words "Stop — Blasting" plainly printed thereon and shall also use a red flag for warning purposes.

(d) Packages containing explosives shall not be handled roughly, shall not be slid across floors, rocks or other packages of explosives and shall not be thrown or dropped. Frozen explosives shall not be thawed or used but must be destroyed. (Acts 1949, No. 207, p. 242, § 82; Acts 1975, 4th Ex. Sess., No. 147, p. 2866, § 1.)

§ 25-9-281. Safety devices and practices for compressed air receivers, etc.

(a) All compressed air receivers, cylinders or other vessels used in or around surface mining operations shall be protected by safety or relief valves to insure safe operation. All oxygen, acetylene or similar compressed gas cylinders shall comply with manufacturer's recommendations.

(b) Safety or relief valves shall be tested once each operating day.

(c) All compressed air receivers, tanks, etc., shall be equipped with a drain valve and a pressure gauge.

(d) Drain valves shall be operated at least once each operating day. (Acts 1949, No. 207, p. 242, § 83; Acts 1975, 4th Ex. Sess., No. 147, p. 2866, § 1.)

§ 25-9-282. First aid equipment; training of personnel in first aid methods.

(a) At or near every pit there shall be adequate approved first aid materials as follows: one stretcher and one broken-back board, or, if a splint stretcher combination is used, it will satisfy both the stretcher and broken-back board requirement; 24 triangular bandages (15, if a splint-stretcher combination is used); eight four-inch bandage compresses; an adequate approved burn remedy; two cloth blankets; one rubber blanket or equivalent substitute; two tourniquets; one one-ounce bottle of aromatic spirits of ammonia and one dozen ammonia ampules; and necessary complements of arm and leg splints or two each inflatable plastic arm and leg splints. All such supplies shall be kept at each location designated and shall be accessible to the miners. First aid materials shall be kept in a sanitary and usable condition. The cloth and waterproof blankets shall be kept in a moisture and dustproof container. A portable first aid kit shall be kept as near the working place as feasible.

(b) Adequate and suitable first aid equipment shall be kept at or near every pit and placed at some convenient location about the pit for use only in caring for persons needing first aid attention.

(c) Selected personnel at each surface mining operation shall be trained in first aid methods. (Acts 1949, No. 207, p. 242, § 84; Acts 1975, 4th Ex. Sess., No. 147, p. 2866, § 1.)

§ 25-9-283. Provision of sanitary toilets, potable drinking water and drinking cups or fountains.

(a) Approved sanitary toilets shall be provided and kept in a clean and sanitary condition. Such toilets should be in a central location for use by employees.

(b) Potable drinking water shall be provided for all employees.

(c) Individual drinking cups or bubbling fountains shall be provided. (Acts 1949, No. 207, p. 242, § 85; Acts 1975, 4th Ex. Sess., No. 147, p. 2866, § 1.)

§ 25-9-284. Increase in hazards of pit operations to be reported.

In case of any occurrence or change of conditions tending materially to increase the hazards of pit operations, whether or not personal injury results, a report thereof shall be promptly sent to the department by the operator. (Acts 1949, No. 207, p. 242, § 86.)

ARTICLE 14.

MAPS AND SURVEYS.

§ 25-9-300. Map of mine — Required; contents; filing; examination, etc.

The owner, operator or lessee of any underground coal mine in this state shall make or cause to be made by a competent engineer an accurate and exact detail map of said mine, showing the exact position of said mine in reference to the section line, which shall be connected with known boundary lines of the section or subdivision of the section. Such map shall show accurately the position of any branches, creeks, rivers, railroads, oil and gas pipelines under which said mine workings extend and, as near as possible, the position of any coal mines nearby. The location of all oil and gas wells shall be shown on said map. Said maps shall show all shafts, slopes, tunnels or other openings to the surface or to the workings of a contiguous coal mine; all excavations, entries, rooms and crosscuts; the location of the fan and the direction of the air currents; the location of pumps, hauling engines, engine planes, abandoned works, fire walls and standing water; and, the boundary line of any surface outcrop of the seam. A separate and similar map, drawn to the same scale in all cases, shall be made of each and every seam which shall be worked in any coal mine and the maps of all such seams shall show all shafts, inclined planes or passageways connecting the same. Each map shall also show by elevation in feet and decimals thereof the rise and dip of the seam from the opening in either direction to the face of the workings. Said map shall be sworn to by the engineer making the same. The map provided for in this section shall be filed with the department during the month of January next after the opening of said mine and shall show its condition on said January 1. All new work inside of the mine must be added to said map or a new map filed each year thereafter, showing the condition of the mine on January 1 of the same year and this provision for additions to maps shall apply to all maps which have heretofore been filed in the office of the department. Said maps shall be filed in the office of the department, which shall provide a suitable and safe place for keeping them. The department shall refuse to accept maps when made by persons known to be incapable of doing such work. The engineer preparing such map shall certify on each map as to the correctness of such map to the best of his knowledge and belief. Said map shall be made on a legible scale. The persons entitled to examine maps, plats and records of a coal mine shall be the owner, operator or lessee or agent of such coal mine, the person financially interested in such mine, the owner or owners of land adjacent to such mine, the owner, operator or lessee or agent of a coal mine adjacent to such mine and the authorized representative of the employees of such or the employees driving any breakthrough liable to break into an adjacent mine. The department shall not permit such maps, plans, records and papers to be removed from its office, and shall not furnish copies thereof to any person except by request of the owner, operator, lessee or agent of the mine to which such maps, plans and records pertain. (Acts 1949, No. 207, p. 242, § 89; Acts 1975, 4th Ex. Sess., No. 147, p. 2866, § 1.)

Collateral references. — 58 C.J.S., Mines & Minerals, § 240.

§ 25-9-301. Map of mine — Failure or refusal to furnish.

Whenever the operator of any coal mine shall neglect or refuse or for any cause not satisfactory to the department fails to furnish to it the map or plan of such mine or a copy thereof or of the extension thereto, as provided for in this article, such operator shall be deemed guilty of a misdemeanor. In addition thereto, the department may make or cause to be made an accurate map or plan of such mine at the expense of the owner thereof, and the cost of the same may be recovered by law from the operator in the same manner as other debts by civil action in the name of the Director of Industrial Relations and for its use. (Acts 1949, No. 207, p. 242, § 90; Acts 1975, 4th Ex. Sess., No. 147, p. 2866, § 1.)

§ 25-9-302. Map of mine — Incomplete, inaccurate or imperfect maps.

If the department shall find that any map or plan of any coal mine made or furnished in pursuance of the provisions of this article is materially incomplete, inaccurate or imperfect, then it may cause a correct survey and map or plan of said mine to be made at the expense of the operator thereof, the cost of which shall be recoverable from said operator as other debts are recoverable by law. When the department shall cause a new survey and map or plan of such coal mine and it is found that the map or plan furnished by the operator was substantially correct, then the cost of the survey, map or plan caused to be made by the department shall be paid by the state. (Acts 1949, No. 207, p. 242, § 91.)

§ 25-9-303. Intermediate surveys.

The department shall order a survey to be made between the regular survey periods of the workings of any coal mines and the results to be extended on the maps of the same and the copies thereof whenever, in its judgment, the safety of the employees, the support of the surface and the conservation of the property or the safety of an adjacent coal mine require it. (Acts 1949, No. 207, p. 242, § 92; Acts 1975, 4th Ex. Sess., No. 147, p. 2866, § 1.)

§ 25-9-304. Final survey.

When any coal mine is worked out or is about to be abandoned or indefinitely closed, the operator of the same shall make or cause to be made a final survey where not already made of all parts of such mine, and the results of the same shall be duly extended on all maps of the mine and copies thereof, so as to show all excavations and the most advanced workings of the mine and their exact relation to the boundary or section lines on the surface, and such openings of abandoned mines shall be properly barricaded. (Acts 1949, No. 207, p. 242, § 93; Acts 1975, 4th Ex. Sess., No. 147, p. 2866, § 1.)

ARTICLE 15.

BOUNDARIES AND ADJACENT LANDOWNERS.

§ 25-9-320. Distance of mine workings from boundary line of mine owner's coal rights.

In no case shall the workings of any coal mine be driven nearer than 15 feet to the boundary line of the coal rights of the owner of said mine, except for the purpose of establishing an underground communication between contiguous mines as provided for elsewhere in this chapter. By mutual consent of adjacent property owners, this distance may be reduced or eliminated entirely, and any operator working up to an abandoned coal mine may be permitted to work to his property line, if approved by the department, but in such cases proper precautions must be taken as provided in this chapter. (Acts 1949, No. 207, p. 242, § 94.)

Collateral references. — 58 C.J.S., Mines & Minerals, § 137.

§ 25-9-321. Survey of mine upon petition of adjacent landowner.

Whenever the owner, operator or lessee of any land adjacent to other land on which any coal mine is being worked shall have reason to believe that such mine is being so worked as to encroach upon his land and has been refused by the owner, operator or manager of the mine permission at reasonable times to enter said mine with a competent engineer for the purpose of inspecting and surveying such mine, he may make appeal under oath to the probate court of the county in which the mine is situated, setting out the facts and praying for an order that such mine shall be surveyed. Upon the hearing, after such notice to the owner, operator or lessee of the mine as the court may prescribe, the court may make an order requiring the department to employ a competent engineer to make a survey of such mine and file such survey in the office of the judge of probate and such survey when filed shall be received in any court as prima facie correct. The court may at any time during the progress of the proceedings require security for costs and may tax the costs in such manner as may be just and equitable. (Acts 1949, No. 207, p. 242, § 95.)

§ 25-9-322. Refusal to permit adjacent landowner or lessee to inspect mine.

Any owner, operator or manager of any mine who refuses to permit an adjacent owner or lessee of land or a competent engineer selected by him to enter and inspect such mine for the purpose of ascertaining whether the same is being so worked as to encroach upon the land of such adjacent owner or lessee must, on conviction, be fined not more than $100.00. (Acts 1949, No. 207, p. 242, § 96.)

ARTICLE 16.

SCALES AND WEIGHING.

Cross references. — As to weights and measures generally, see § 8-16-1 et seq.

§ 25-9-340. Owners to provide scales at mines where miners paid by weight.

The owner or operator of each coal mine at which the miners are paid by weight shall provide such mines with suitable scales of standard make for the weighing of all coal when contracted to be weighed. (Acts 1949, No. 207, p. 242, § 97.)

§ 25-9-341. Coal to be weighed and credited to miner.

All coal mined in this state contracted for payment by the ton or other measure shall be weighed or measured and the full weight or measure thereof shall be credited to the miner of such coal and 2,000 pounds shall constitute a ton of coal. (Acts 1949, No. 207, p. 242, § 98.)

§ 25-9-342. Miners may furnish check weighman to examine scales, etc.

In all coal mines the miners employed and working therein may furnish a check weighman or check measurer who shall at all times have full access to and the right to examine the scales, and to see all measures and weights and accounts kept of same, and shall keep an accurate account of the coal, but not more than the above authorized persons shall have such right of access, examination and inspection of scales, measures and accounts at the same time. (Acts 1949, No. 207, p. 242, § 99.)

Editor's note. — The cases cited below were decided under former statutory provisions.

This section is not unconstitutional as delegating legislative power. Porter Coal Co. v. Davis, 231 Ala. 359, 165 So. 93 (1935).

Miners can pursue own method of selecting weighman. — Under this section, miners can pursue their own method of selection and a coal company has no right in that respect so long as there is no question about weighman's selection, capacity and conduct, as regards liability of company to weighman for preventing performance of his employment by miners. Porter Coal Co. v. Davis, 231 Ala. 359, 165 So. 93 (1935).

Action by weighman against coal company is action in tort. — Action by check weighman against coal company which had prevented check weighman from inspecting or weighing coal is an action in tort, in which punitive damages might be recovered. Porter Coal Co. v. Davis, 231 Ala. 359, 165 So. 93 (1935).

Instructions held proper. — In action by check weighman against coal company which had prevented check weighman from inspecting or weighing coal, a charge that coal company was entitled to reasonable notice that majority of miners had selected check weighman, but that company might "waive" any objection by not raising it, and that jury should decide whether company insisted on proof or waived it, was held proper and not misleading by use of the word "waive." Porter Coal Co. v. Davis, 231 Ala. 359, 165 So. 93 (1935).

In an action by check weighman against coal company which had prevented check weighman from inspecting or weighing coal, refusal to charge that limit of recovery for lost earnings should be wages for days company was operated while plaintiff was prevented from working, so as to exclude time in which strike took place and company did not operate, was held prejudicial error. Porter Coal Co. v. Davis, 231 Ala. 359, 165 So. 93 (1935).

§ 25-9-343. Testing of scales.

The weighman and check weighman shall properly test the scales with U.S. standard test weights before coal is weighed thereon. (Acts 1949, No. 207, p. 242, § 99.)

§ 25-9-344. Access to scales, etc.

The mine inspector, miners employed in the coal mines and the owner of the land or persons interested in the rental and royalty of such mines shall at all times have full right of access to scales used at said mines, including tally sheets or tally books in which the weight of the coal is kept, to examine the amount of coal mined for the purpose of testing the accuracy thereof. (Acts 1949, No. 207, p. 242, § 100.)

§ 25-9-345. Failure of mine operators to weigh coal accurately and correctly.

Any person or corporation operating any coal mine in which miners or other laborers are employed to mine or cut coal for a compensation to be determined by the weight of the coal mined or cut, who fails to weigh or causes to be weighed accurately and correctly any coal so mined or cut by such miners or laborers, must, on conviction, be fined for each offense not less than $10.00 nor more than $100.00. (Acts 1949, No. 207, p. 242, § 101.)

ARTICLE 17.

ENFORCEMENT.

§ 25-9-360. Suspension of compliance with chapter; compliance with and enforcement of chapter generally.

(a) Whenever any equipment or supplies required by this chapter, including rock-dusting machines, flame safety lamps and permissible electric equipment are unobtainable, compliance with the requirements of this chapter with respect thereto is suspended to the extent that such items remain unobtainable until they are obtainable. Due allowance shall also be made for planning, institution of change procedures and installation of new equipment.

(b) Compliance with the requirements of this chapter shall be started promptly and prosecuted diligently until the provisions of the chapter have been fulfilled. (Acts 1949, No. 207, p. 242, § 113.)

§ 25-9-361. Superintendent, mine foremen, etc., to comply with and ensure compliance with chapter.

It shall be the duty of the superintendent, mine foreman, subordinate supervisors, fire bosses or mine examiners and other officials to comply with and to see that others comply with the provisions of this chapter. (Acts 1949, No. 207, p. 242, § 65.)

§ 25-9-362. Employees, etc., to comply with chapter and rules, etc., of operators.

It shall be the duty of all employees and check weighmen to comply with this chapter and to cooperate with management and the division in carrying out the provisions of this chapter. Reasonable rules and regulations of the operators for the protection of employees and preservation of property that are in harmony with the provisions of this chapter or other applicable laws shall be complied with. They shall be printed on cardboard or in book form in the English language and posted at some conspicuous place about the mine or mines or given to each employee. (Acts 1949, No. 207, p. 242, § 66.)

§ 25-9-363. Quarterly reports of mine operators.

The operator of every coal mine shall make to the department a correct report each three months of the calendar year specifying the name of the owner and operator of the mine and the location of the offices of said coal mine or mines and the quantity and kind of coal produced in each such mine for each such calendar quarter. Said report shall be furnished on or before April 15, July 15, October 15 and January 15, covering the previous three months' operation of said mine. Said report shall be prima facie evidence of the information contained therein and shall be in such form and give such additional information regarding said mines as may be, from time to time, required and prescribed by the department. Blank forms for such reports shall be furnished to said owner or operator by the department. (Acts 1949, No. 207, p. 242, § 88; Acts 1975, 4th Ex. Sess., No. 147, p. 2866, § 1.)

§ 25-9-364. Posting of abstract of chapter at mines; defacing, etc., of abstract.

For the purpose of making known the rules and provisions of this chapter to all persons employed in or about coal mines to which this law applies, an abstract of the law and rules shall be furnished by the department and posted up in legible character in some conspicuous place or places at or near the mines where they may be conveniently read by the persons employed and so often as they become obliterated or destroyed, the owner, operator, lessee or superintendent shall cause them to be renewed with all reasonable dispatch. It is unlawful for any person to pull down, injure or deface such abstract of the law or rules when put up in pursuance of the provisions of this chapter. (Acts 1949, No. 207, p. 242, § 88.)

§ 25-9-365. Inspectors may order suspension of mine operations for violations imminently hazardous to workmen.

Any mine inspector shall have the authority to order suspension of operations of a coal mine or pit or any part thereof when violations of this chapter are of such gravity as to be or become imminently hazardous to workmen therein. Upon correction of such hazardous conditions, the mine or part thereof may resume operations. (Acts 1949, No. 207, p. 242, § 107.)

§ 25-9-366. Review by chief of orders of inspectors.

The decisions and orders of an inspector shall take effect as he shall specify in a written notice to the superintendent of said mine and shall not be subject to review unless within 10 days after giving such notice the owner or operator shall have appealed to the chief for such review, who shall render a decision within 10 days of notice of appeal. (Acts 1949, No. 207, p. 242, § 108.)

§ 25-9-367. Judicial review of orders suspending mine operations.

If the chief shall, upon review, continue or modify such order, the owner or operator may apply to the circuit court of the county wherein the mine is located for a trial de novo without jury as to whether or not (1) the order to close the mine was justified and (2) conditions in the mine at the time of trial justify a continuance, modification or withdrawal of such order. Appeals may be taken from the ruling of the circuit court in the manner provided for other appeals. (Acts 1949, No. 207, p. 242, § 109.)

§ 25-9-368. Injunctions.

In addition to any other remedy, the director may, for persistent, continued or imminent violations of this chapter, apply for a permanent injunction. (Acts 1949, No. 207, p. 242, § 110.)

Collateral references. — 58 C.J.S., Mines & Minerals, § 242.

§ 25-9-369. Representation of department.

The department may be represented by its general counsel or other attorneys, district attorneys or the Attorney General. (Acts 1949, No. 207, p. 242, § 111.)

§ 25-9-370. Unlawful acts for which no other penalty provided.

Any unlawful act for which no other penalty is provided in this chapter shall be a misdemeanor punishable by a fine of not less than $10.00 and not more than $500.00 or by imprisonment in jail for not more than one year, or by both such fine and imprisonment. (Acts 1949, No. 207, p. 242, § 112.)

CHAPTER 10.

SMALL BUSINESS ASSISTANCE.

§ 25-10-1. Short title.

This chapter shall be known and may be cited as "The Small Business Assistance Act of 1975." (Acts 1975, No. 1229, p. 2582, § 1.)

§ 25-10-2. Declaration of public policy and legislative intent.

The legislative intent of this chapter is declared to be as follows: The most important element of the American economic system of private enterprise is free and vigorous competition. Only through the existence of free and vigorous competition can free entry into business and opportunities for personal initiative and individual achievement be assured. The preservation and expansion of such competition is essential for our economic well-being. In order to insure such competition, small business concerns must be encouraged and developed, and it is the declared policy of the state to aid, counsel and assist, in every practical manner, the interests of small business concerns in order to preserve free competitive enterprise and to insure that a fair proportion of the total purchases and contracts or subcontracts for property, commodities and services for the state be placed with small businesses. (Acts 1975, No. 1229, p. 2582, § 2.)

§ 25-10-3. Definitions.

For the purposes of this chapter, the following terms shall have the following meanings, respectively, unless the context clearly indicates a different meaning:

(1) SMALL BUSINESS. A business which is independently owned and operated. In addition, such business must have either fewer than 50 employees or less than $1,000,000.00 in gross receipts per year.

(2) DIVISION. The Division of Purchases and Stores of the Department of Finance.

(3) DEPARTMENT. The Department of Industrial Relations. (Acts 1975, No. 1229, p. 2582, § 3.)

§ 25-10-4. Powers and duties of Department of Industrial Relations generally.

The department is authorized and empowered to:

(1) Provide technical and managerial assistance to small business concerns, by advising and counseling on matters in connection with state procurement policies, practices of good management, including, but not limited to, cost accounting, methods of financing, business insurance, accident control, wage incentives, methods engineering and legal questions, by cooperating and advising with voluntary business, professional, educational and other organizations, associations and institutions and with federal and state agencies, by maintaining a clearinghouse for information concerning the managing, financing and operation of small business enterprises, by disseminating such information and by such other activities as are deemed appropriate;

(2) Make a complete inventory of all productive facilities of small business concerns in the state;

(3) Coordinate and ascertain the means by which the productive capacity of small business concerns can be most effectively utilized;

(4) Obtain information as to the methods and practices of prime contractors in letting subcontracts and take action to encourage the letting of subcontracts by prime contractors to small business concerns at prices and on conditions and terms which are fair and equitable;

(5) Determine the concerns, firms, persons, corporations, partnerships, cooperatives or other business enterprises which are to be designated small business concerns for the purposes of effectuating the provisions of this chapter; and to carry out the purposes of this chapter, the office shall designate individual concerns as small business concerns in accordance with the provisions of this chapter. Any such designation shall be subject to revocation when the concern covered thereby ceases to be a small business;

(6) Obtain from any state department or agency engaged in procurement or in the financing of procurement such reports and information concerning the letting of contracts and subcontracts, purchases or procurement of articles, commodities, materials, supplies or services as it may deem pertinent in carrying out its functions under this chapter;

(7) Make studies, conduct workshops and seminars and make recommendations to state agencies or the legislature to insure that a fair proportion of the total purchases and contracts for articles, commodities, supplies and services for the state is placed with small business enterprises;

(8) Promote the mobilization of activities and resources of state and local governments, businesses and trade associations, universities, foundations, professional organizations and volunteer and other groups toward the

growth of small business enterprises and facilitate the coordination of the efforts of these groups with those of federal departments and agencies; and

(9) Promulgate such rules and regulations as are necessary to administer and effectuate the purposes of this chapter. (Acts 1975, No. 1229, p. 2582, § 4.)

§ 25-10-5. Public hearings; powers of department as to witnesses, records, etc.

In the administration of this chapter, the department shall have the power to conduct public hearings for the purposes of determining the law's effectiveness, determining methods and standards of administration and to otherwise assist in carrying out the purposes of this chapter.

The department shall have the authority to administer oaths and affirmations, take depositions, issue subpoenas and compel the attendance of witnesses and production of books, papers, correspondence, memoranda and other records deemed necessary as evidence. (Acts 1975, No. 1229, p. 2582, § 7.)

§ 25-10-6. Advisory council.

There is hereby created an advisory council to the department to be composed of representatives of designated small business enterprises to be named as follows: five by the Governor, two each by the President of the Senate and the Speaker of the House of Representatives and one by the director of the department to serve ex officio as chairman of the council. The members of the council shall serve without compensation but may be reimbursed for travel and other necessary expenses out of any funds appropriated to the department. The council shall meet at least quarterly or more often when necessary at the call of the chairman in consultation with the director of the department, who shall also serve without additional compensation as executive director of the council. (Acts 1975, No. 1229, p. 2582, § 10.)

§ 25-10-7. Reports and recommendations of department.

The department shall make a written report to the Governor, the President of the Senate, the Speaker of the House of Representatives and the chairman of the Senate and House commerce committees at least once each year, such report to be made no later than December 1. The report shall advise the Governor, the speaker, the president and the designated chairmen concerning the administration and operation of this chapter and shall contain such recommendations for amendment of this chapter as the department and the advisory council provided for in Section 25-10-6 deem proper. (Acts 1975, No. 1229, p. 2582, § 9.)

§ 25-10-8. Cooperation of department with federal agencies; adoption of administrative rules, regulations, etc.; cooperation of other state departments or agencies with department.

In the administration of this chapter, the department shall cooperate to the fullest extent consistent with the provisions of this chapter with those agencies of the United States government whose programs are complimentary to the objectives and purposes hereof, and shall take such action, through the adoption of administrative rules, regulations, and standards, as may be necessary to secure to this state and its citizens all advantages available under such federal programs and to otherwise assist the citizens of this state in realizing their full economic potential. Each department or other agency of the state shall cooperate with the department in carrying out the purposes of this chapter and shall, when so requested by the department, submit such reports and information as may be necessary or helpful. (Acts 1975, No. 1229, p. 2582, § 6.)

§ 25-10-9. Meaningful percentage of total purchases of articles, services, etc., of state departments or agencies to be awarded, etc., to small businesses; designation of meaningful percentage; waiver of requirements of section.

Notwithstanding the provisions of the state bid law or other conflicting statutes of this state, it is herewith provided:

(1) It shall be the policy of the state that, whenever practical, a meaningful percentage of each department's or agency's total purchases of articles, equipments, commodities, supplies, materials, services or contracts be procured or otherwise awarded to small businesses.

(2) This meaningful percentage shall not be less than 10 percent of the annual value of any department's or agency's total purchases of articles, materials, commodities, supplies, services or contracts unless that department or agency files with the division a statement explaining the reasons why that agency cannot meet the requirements of this policy. If the division is satisfied that the department's or agency's reasons for its inability to comply with the requirements of this chapter are supported by substantial evidence, it may issue a waiver for that department or agency to the extent it cannot comply. However, such waiver shall be granted for a period not to exceed one year; provided, however, that such waiver may be renewed upon application by the department or agency, review and approval by the division.

(3) The only reasons that shall justify a department or agency being granted a waiver from the provisions of this section are:

a. Impossibility or unreasonable difficulty in procuring such articles, commodities, supplies, materials, services or contracts from small business enterprises;

b. Inability to procure such articles, supplies, materials, services or contracts from such small business enterprises at the lowest bid; or

c. Substantial differences in the quality of such articles, supplies, materials, services or contracts available from small business enterprises as compared to the quality of such items if procured otherwise. (Acts 1975, No. 1229, p. 2582, § 5.)

§ 25-10-10. Liberal construction of chapter.

This chapter shall be liberally construed to carry out its purposes and objectives of assisting small businesses to successfully enter and remain in the economic mainstream and to otherwise achieve the statement of legislative policy contained herein. (Acts 1975, No. 1229, p. 2582, § 8.)